Best PLAYS

of the Modern American Theatre

SECOND SERIES

Edited with an Introduction by

JOHN GASSNER

CROWN PUBLISHERS INC.

New York,

ISBN: 0-517-509482

Twentieth Printing, June, 1978

PRINTED IN THE UNITED STATES OF AMERICA

CONTENTS

Introduction

THE YEARS OF CRISIS

By JOHN GASSNER

Not only is anthologizing a habit from which one seldom recovers, but let the anthologist succeed just once and he is apt to find strong reasons for repeating his performance. The publisher, however, is the real hero or villain of this apology; he converted a slight temptation on my part into a sense of obligation. My previous collection of plays had represented the theatre of the 1929–1939 depression, which was disorderly in all respects but two: It comprised a good round figure for a volume, and the decade's serious drama covered contiguous areas of social awareness. Was it not incumbent upon a conscientious historian to take note of the greater crisis of the war years as well? The investigation would surely have some bearing upon theatre history, and we could probably scrape up a dozen or more plays that did not discredit the American record. A roll call of acceptable playwrights also disclosed a number of additions to the ranks—seven or eight newcomers, including Saroyan, d'Usseau, Gow, Tennessee Williams, and Arthur Laurents—which may be tantamount to the emergence of a new generation into the flickering light of Broadway respectability. Without being exactly in the position of playing Scheherezade to new wonders in the fabulous region of the theatre, one might be able to tell a round, unvarnished tale about the war-time American stage. So reasonable an argument could not be resisted by an editor by now inured to finding some favorite selections unobtainable for an anthology and no longer embarrassed at the conventional "Best" in the title. The result is this volume devoted to the 1939–45 period, with some leeway in either direction to account for trends a little before and a little after the fact of war.

1.

Like Frost's oven bird, anyone who reviews the American theatre of this period frames the question of "what to make of a diminished thing." If he should be disposed to applaud the theatre's freedom from hysteria and chauvinism, or to honor its maintenance of civilized values in the face of everything that militated against civilization, he must restrain enthusiasm and know "in singing not to sing." After all, most playwrights and producers operated at considerable distance from the battlefront, and the American public could afford the luxury of comparative serenity. We were not actually involved in the war until more than two years after the beginning of hostilities abroad, our shores remained inviolate, and our cities were not reduced to rubble. The traumatic shock of Pearl Harbor wore off with remarkable rapidity, and any later anguish we may have felt as a nation was dispelled by exuberant exertions on the home front, congenital self-confidence, and habitual optimism. Our stage enjoyed a freedom from interruption, censorship, or anxiety found nowhere else on the globe, not even in the precariously neutral countries. No other theatre faced a comparable test of its powers. Of no other theatre could more be expected.

It must be conceded at once that, measured by the standard of such expecta-

ix

tions, our stage proved disappointing. Neither the war nor its issues evoked many plays that scaled the heights or plumbed the depths, while the general level of play-making was lamentable. Long intervals each season left us wondering how long the theatre could flounder without collapsing. It seemed as if the remoteness from the battlefront that gave us so many advantages was also depriving us of some catalytic agency.

If we look for fundamental causes of this sorry state of affairs, we shall have no great difficulty in locating them. We were a people dimly threading our way through a maze of uncertainties. Although we sought sure footing in our ingrained respect for human rights, although we held on to an elementary sense of justice, we were ill prepared for negotiating the quicksilver ground. We managed, it is true, to stagger across the terrain, extricating one foot after the other. But, at least so far as the drama is concerned, this was no heroic march.

The younger playwrights, who were most immediately involved in the struggle, and from whom the greatest zeal could have been expected, had no tingling sense of an enemy uncovered or confronted. His shadow had long been familiar to writers who had been vocal in every movement to check his advance while we were generally still hobnobbing with Mussolini, appeasing Hitler, selling scrap-iron to Japan, and maintaining a dubious embargo in the Spanish civil war. The subject of fascism both abroad and at home had been standard in New Theatre League. Theatre Union. and Group Theatre productions. Now that the war was in full swing, others were first discovering what was already a platitude to left-of-center playwrights. These had nothing much to add to what they had said or shouted, and they took hollow pride in calling themselves premature anti-fascists while men of their persuasion were still being penalized with suspicion or discrimination in the government services. Nor could these dramatists derive any solace from the expectation of a millennium to be won when they reflected that it was taking a global war to solve the unemployment problem. The spectre of the business cycle was not exorcized for them by pitched battles in Asia or Europe, and capital and labor would be arrayed against each other again after the patriotic tumult and shouting were over. The war had to be fought and won, of course. Some enthusiasm could be engendered by the thought that at least the issue had been joined at last, that fascism was being fought in the field finally, and that with the resistance movement flaring up everywhere in the occupied countries, this was a "people's war" now, and not an imperialistic holocaust. Nevertheless, the bloom was off the rose of idealistic vision.

The younger playwrights could only choose between a *status quo* they had found inacceptable and a world dominated by Hitler's and Hirohito's master-races. As between a catastrophic "wave of the future" and an unsatisfactory present, they chose the present. Nobody in his right mind could do otherwise. But they could not endorse the alternative without reflecting that they were being forced to make a choice they had not wanted to make, and could not even take exception to the *status quo* without running the risk of abetting the enemy. The drama of social protest had been their forte; they could no longer write it. Panegyrics they had reserved for a brave new world; but there was no such world that they could scan on a horizon clouded by their doubts and fears. For comedy they had no aptitude, nor would they approve fiddling during a conflagration. They were fated, so it seemed, to write plays with only two chambers of the heart.

Our theatre was bound to find itself on *terra incognita,* in any case, being pacifistic and anti-heroic by temperament and conviction. The modern American drama had been cradled in post-war disillusionment. It had taken special delight in deflating military pomp and circumstance, in scorning saber-rattling, and pouring cold water on heroic posturing. *What Price Glory?* was the ultimate expression of our attitude, and was suitably rewarded by critical acclaim and success at the box-office. During the 'thirties, the radical playwrights had been even more violently pacifistic, sounding warnings like *Peace on Earth* and *Ten Million Ghosts* and attributing war to the machinations of imperialists and munitions magnates. Sophistication, in the popular sense, was the rage—a state of mind, as Van Wyck Brooks once defined it, of "knowing too much while at the same time knowing too little," or "a sort of cosmetic equivalent of wisdom." Post-war "sophistication" in the 'twenties had whittled down man's stature. A popular sport was to take a cynical view of his motives and an indifferent attitude toward his aspirations. To be smart and sceptical was the *summum bonum,* and even to be smart-alecky was preferable to being "stuffy," an adjective that covered everything from crass babbittism to simple earnestness. The attitude was carried into the 'thirties by those who had been reared on it. The present writer, who had been conditioned by the 'twenties but had espoused the social drama of the 'thirties, recalls wincing almost by reflex action when a colleague referred to him as an earnest critic. Time passed, and the brilliant and urbane gentleman whose praise had included this abrasive particle was the first drama critic to volunteer for service after Pearl Harbor.

We know of course that the gilded age of the stock-market boom and Prohibition provided sufficient provocation to cynicism. Middle-class materialism, exacerbated into the philosophy of rotarianism and super-salesmanship, invited a viewpoint that did not exactly clothe the race in shining armor. As for the lower classes, they were allegedly losing their individuality in the machine-age, being reduced to the robot state of *The Adding Machine's* unsouled Mr. and Mrs. Zero. (It is tempting to imagine how astonished the playwrights and novelists would have been if they could have had a prevision of their white-collar slaves at Iwo Jima and Anzio. During the 'twenties nearly everybody with a pen in his hand was selling America short while the stockbrokers were selling America high.) Then the stage discovered psychoanalysis, pronounced our Puritan heritage deleterious, found ordeals for every minor Mark Twain, and predicated frustration as a condition of life in America for the artist and the thinker.

While writers of comedy had themselves a Mencken holiday, their more somber *confrères* took a tragic view of the situation. But they missed tragic exaltation as their characters went down to defeat with a whimper. If it is true that the later radical theatre of the 'thirties created a class hero in many a rebel against prevailing conditions, the left-wingers had their own brand of anti-heroism. They either conceived the individual as a socially determined creature in an iron cage of economics or saw him sacrificed on Mammon's altar.

Finally, both generations of dramatists had been accustomed to criticizing our way of life. To affirm it in the face of the decidedly less agreeable "wave of the future" was going to entail breaking an old habit.

War posed, in addition, a special craft-problem. Our modern writers had learned to dispense with the melodramatic and sentimental devices of the older theatre, to scorn adventitiousness, plottiness, and any other trappings of Sardoodle-dom that we may care to recall. But motivation, feeling and action in war-time crises or actual combat tend to make old-fashioned theatre as surely as death is the most commonplace of experiences. War *is* melodrama, and its cruelty is heartrendingly old-fashioned. The minor Elizabethans never imagined anything so melodramatic by way of horror as did the sadists of the concentration camps and the liquidation centers. The death march on Bataan was a more horrible show than anything that has appeared on any stage since Aeschylus materialized the Furies and caused miscarriages in the Theatre of Dionysus. The hair-breadth escapes by grace of which soldiers and civilians are now alive exceeded the invention of the most ingenious play contriver; even Boucicault's imagination could not stretch so far.

The contemporary dramatist found himself in the dilemma that the present writer tried to explain to his magazine readers, and ultimately to foreign readers by courtesy of the O.W.I.'s Overseas Branch. The explanation was by way of apologizing for our failure to produce worthy war-drama as late as the spring of '43, with the uncertain exception of *The Eve of St. Mark*.

"The writer of heroic drama can bog down in any number of morasses. If he gives precedence to ideas, the necessary emotion may suffer diminution; if he favors character drama, an audience, geared to war-time feelings and tired of years of costly inaction, may become sensible of a want of action. But if he dispenses with the drama of ideas or with deeply realized characterization, he runs the risk of melodramatic baldness. Should he maintain that the times *are* violent and melodramatic, he still cannot overcome the opinion of critics and playgoers that melodrama on the grand scale is something to be disdained. They remember it as the old-fashioned theatre of Sardou and William Gillette that Ibsen, Chekhov, and Shaw interred generations ago, and they are acutely conscious of theatrical devices, even though the present struggle is more melodramatic than anything ever seen on the stage.

"The clichés and the stereotypes of heroic theatre have been accumulating for centuries, and they cannot be employed on our stage without great risk. The presence of a traitor, a spy, or a last-minute rescue is immediately suspect behind the proscenium arch, although the present world is full of traitors, spies, and last-minute rescues. If the heroes are valiant, they immediately call to mind the countless *chevaliers sans peur et sans reproche* who peopled the thrillers of the past. If, on the contrary, a dramatist endeavors to avoid so-called heroics, his work may seem tepid by comparison with present reality. He is apt to succumb to the theatre's most recent clichés of understatement; thus the character who is remarkably nonchalant during an air raid and goes about the ordinary business of life has become a stereotype of English war plays, and so has the daring warrior who is secretly terrified. . . . Finally, the dramatist must make a difficult choice between singling out some individual for his hero, in which case his story lacks extension, or dramatizing a group and so saddling himself with simultaneously occurring plots. It would seem that the playwright cannot win, no matter what course he pursues."

The situation remained unchanged during the remainder of the period. Only toward the close of the war did we get war plays of some distinction, *The Hasty Heart, Home of the Brave,* and *Sound of Hunting,* and even these had at best only moderate success with the public.

The sober fact is that the American dramatist found varying degrees of difficulty in adjusting himself to the crisis. And it may as well be added that he received scant encouragement or correction from the audiences that had grown accustomed to his old wares and were, besides, understandably avid for entertainment. If an articulate minority, consisting mostly of irate critics, clamored for substance, the vast majority seemed content with trivia as a release from tension. No form of theatre enjoyed such success and actually experienced such progress as musical comedy. Nor were producers laggard in sailing with the tide of popular taste. In fact, there were no longer at the beginning of the period any producing organizations, with the exception of The Playwrights Company and the Theatre Guild, to demand serious exertions by playwrights. The Theatre Guild found itself in financial straits until the phenomenal success of *Oklahoma* in the spring of 1943, and the Group Theatre, moribund after 1939, collapsed in the autumn of 1940. The left-wing Theatre Union had yielded to financial duress a few years earlier. Orson Welles' Mercury Theatre had disintegrated after two seasons. The depression-born Federal Theatre had been abolished on June 30, 1939 by an anti-New Deal Congress.

The American theatre entered the war period with depleted resources, unhappy memories, and jaded nerves. Considerable time was to elapse before it could recuperate from its neurasthenia. And if at long last the war served as a stimulant, it was not sufficiently energizing to make the American drama surge forward along new paths toward new goals. In the 'twenties, America domesticated modern dramatic art. In the 'thirties, we discovered and developed the insurgent social theatre. It is impossible to discern what the theatre of the 'forties has discovered, if anything; thus far it has certainly produced no distinct style or dominant content. Those of our critics who returned to reportage from the aisles after release from their war duties in 1945 had an uncomfortable feeling of having stepped into a partial vacuum. Their sense of alienation caused them to alternate between mildly depressive deprecation of the current scene and too generous enthusiasms, as if they too were wondering what to make of a diminished thing.

2.

In the theatre, as in all things, there is nevertheless a world of difference between something and nothing, and the composition of obituaries on so favorite a funereal subject as the theatre may be reserved for those who have no stake in the stage and no share in its diurnal churnings. So long as theatre exists at all there will always be two standards, the absolute standard of the litterateurs who can live at a comfortable distance from the stage, and the relative one of those compelled by profession or inclination to live with the stage and come to terms with it. Whatever the compensations reserved for the former, including a reputation for inviolable discrimination, the workaday wit has his rewards too. Sometimes the miracle happens and a performance, a bit of stage business, a scene or an act, even an entire play, materializing before his eyes, compensates arid evenings and weary bones. Perhaps, too, this affords the poor fellow who will never know critical purity (even George Jean Nathan is denied this visitation since he has loved the theatre too well) a clearer glimmer of the truth. There is more error in the blithe assurance that nothing ever lives unless it is snugly placed in the empyrean, and it is also historically incorrect to assume that the great ages of the theatre did not have their substantial share of rubbish. An absolutist critic of our six or seven years of war-time theatre should be whisked back in time like the hero of *Berkeley Square*. He should be forced to do an equal stretch of assiduous play-going in the good old days of the Mermaid Tavern.

The rest of this chronicle will be flagrantly impure and relativistic. It will report that the American stage held much hard-won ground after 1939 so long as it maintained the saving sense of comedy, the humanistic attitude ranging all the way from *Flight to the West* topical liberalism to *Skin of Our Teeth* general affirmativeness, and the sense of wonder that writers like Saroyan and Tennessee Williams managed to dispense. If we make an inventory of the entire period, instead of any single season or fraction of it, we may actually take ourselves by surprise. The experience is not unlike a bird's-eye view of a large stretch of the Pacific—full of islands that would ease the wayfarer if only he could cut down the traveling time between them. It is the time consumed that creates the tedium and the sense of a void. In the theatre, we experienced a similar tedium as we waited from one acceptable play to another. Now that we can look back telescopically and see all the dots of land in the waste some of us may even wonder how it is we were so wearied, although this does not obliterate the fact that we *were* wearied and *were* sometimes driven to distraction.

It is to be noted first of all that in many respects our stage experienced expansion rather than diminution. The number of productions was limited only by available playhouses, since no new theatres could be erected in war time, and plays had longer runs than before the war. New experimental groups, however shortlived and limited owing to high costs or trade-union regulations, arose constantly. In New York, the New School's Studio Theatre established by Erwin Piscator enjoyed three fruitful seasons, reviving classics of liberalism like the Klabund version of *The Circle of Chalk* and Lessing's *Nathan the Wise* in workmanlike fashion and introducing meritorious new plays like Frank Gabrielson's college drama *The Days of Our Youth* and Dan James's *Winter Soldiers*. For two seasons, Broadway producers conducted a rudimentary Experimental Theatre, and the city of New York maintained low-priced productions in its City Center. Pro-New Deal groups devoted to both progressivism and maximum war effort at home organized Stage for Action, which exhibited politically slanted skits and one-acters in many cities, and which promises to remain an active post-war organization. An "American Actors Company" in New York struggled for several seasons and managed to introduce the work of a promising young playwright, Horton Foote. Hollywood actors, many of them formerly connected with the Group Theatre, established an Actor's Laboratory Theatre in the heart of the motion-picture industry, and gave distinguished productions. In Harlem, an American Negro Theatre was active under the leadership of the young Negro playwright Abram Hill; it even unfolded a vivid genre play, *Anna Lucasta,* for Broadway. With John Golden's assistance and the co-operation of Equity, the Equity Library Theatre, led by Sam Jaffe and George Freedley, revived numerous plays in New York's libraries and enabled little known or unknown actors and directors to display their talent and improve their craft. Beyond the metropolis, the National Theatre Conference of university and community theatres exhibited an unusual spurt of activity with nation-wide productions of Saroyan's *Jim Dandy* and Maxwell Anderson's *The Eve of St. Mark.* On Roanoke Island, Paul Green made the production of his historical pageants *The Lost Colony* and *The Highland Call* an annual regional festival. Only the summer and university theatres suffered a sharp reduction, once gas-rationing became the order of the day and enlistments depleted the student register. But against this condition must be set the tremendous expansion of theatre in war-camps and on many sectors of the war front, and it is not too much to say that U.S.O. shows brought more theatre to more Americans than any theatrical enterprise since the demise of the Federal Theatre.

Qualitatively, too, there is something to report. Although no single war-time season could be considered generally rewarding or even satisfactory, it rarely failed to be enlivened by some meritorious efforts, and when the new plays proved distressing there were excellent revivals like Margaret Webster's Shakespeare productions, including the Paul Robeson *Othello,* as well as a few intelligently chosen importations like *The Corn Is Green* and *Blithe Spirit,* to stay us with flagons. This, we may as well remember, is the time-span that included the delights of *Life With ather, The Time of Your Life* and *Oklahoma,* the enchantment of *Harvey* and *The Glass Menagerie,* the trumpeting of *Native Son* and *Deep Are the Roots,* and the recapitulatory chords of *The Skin of Our Teeth, The Patriots,* and *In Time to Come.* (And of *Abe Lincoln in Illinois,* if we extend the period backward a little to allow an important playwright to flex his muscles for the onset of the conflict.)

We left a play here and a play there, a scene here and a scene there, to prove that at least we labored. If we failed to reach new purlieus for mind or spirit because our playwrights, unlike Ibsen or Shaw, had found no new realizations, we tried to hold on to those that had already been discovered. We remembered by our works the heritage of reason and liberalism, of wit and taste, of flexible dramaturgy and imagination. If our memory failed us on many dreadful first-night occasions, it somehow managed to come back just as we were about to conclude that we had lost it. And in the meantime we kept the theatre moving along instead of letting it stagnate altogether in consequence of global disaster and our own temporarily stunned or enfeebled consciousness. A critic can purchase a reputation for discrimination and brilliance at too little cost while his victims are busily making their bricks without straw.

3.

One way to examine the record is to consider what the established playwrights were doing before any new talent emerged. New production methods can be no more than accessories to the dramatist's achievement in a theatre that depends as greatly upon his product as ours does. As a matter of fact, the period revealed no new forms of staging, in the strict sense, except for the full utilization of modern ballet technique in musical plays. Some experimentation in the form of so-called epic theatre in the "learning" play style of Erwin Piscator and Berthold Brecht was attempted, mainly by the Studio Theatre under Piscator's direction. It may be argued that some dramatists would have been able to cope more fully with the multiple aspects of the exploding world if they had been attracted to the epic style's multi-scened plays and cinematic technique. The Sidney Howard prize play, Dan James's *Winter Soldiers,* which came closest to showing the diversity and scope of the struggle, was also closest to this type of theatre. But "epic's" magnetic field reached no further than a production here and there, and the chronicle form of an *Eve of St. Mark, The Patriots* or *In Time to Come* was not actually a departure for American playwrights and directors. Although the United States became the haven of European directors renowned for their inventiveness, they had scant opportunity to experiment here. The burden of dramatic expression rested almost entirely upon the playwrights, except, of course, in the case of musical entertainment, which elicited important contributions from a resourceful director like Mamoulian and from talented choreographers like Agnes de Mille and Jerome Robbins.

By 1939 the writers who had made their mark in the 1920's were middle-aged, caught in the grooves of an established style as a result of plying it for a decade or longer, accustomed to ways of responding and thinking that had reaped ample rewards. Above all, they were conditioned to an urbane rather than a belligerent attitude. The second generation of depression-bred, Marxist-oriented dramatists and critics had already airily dismissed them as jaded and inclined to evade reality. A brilliantly written book by one of the militants, Eleanor Flexner's *American Playwrights 1918–1938,* was in effect an obituary on these worthies; it was suitably subtitled "The Theatre Retreats from Reality."

Nevertheless, the men of the 'twenties continued to account for the greatest number of war-inspired contributions. Since they were too old to serve with the armed forces, they could practice their craft without interruption. If they had been too set in urbane ways or economically too comfortable to become firebrands during the pre-war depression, if they had been disinclined to rest their faith in tidings of a proletarian dawn, they could respond easily enough to the final crass challenge of fascism. Once the dragon was in plain sight and was spewing fire, they did not have to cross "class lines" or violate habits of mind to take a stand. After all, the values he was trying to devastate were their own values.

Simplifications of issues by war led, of course, to oversimplification in play-writing, to clichés, and to stereotypes of characterization and situation. This was evident in such plays as Maxwell Anderson's *Candle in the Wind, The Eve of St. Mark,* and *Storm Operation,* Elmer Rice's *Flight to the West,* Philip Barry's *Liberty Jones* and *Without Love,* Behrman's *The Talley Method,* Frederick Hazlitt Brennan's *The Wookey,* and Kaufman and Ferber's *The Land Is Bright.* And that is perhaps the main reason why the best work was more creditable than inspired. The one colleague who would have completely trans-figured the aspect of the crisis, who would have rejected contentment with routine or journalistic responses, was Eugene O'Neill. But he was far from Broadway, ailing, and brooding in his tent for the duration. Although he was writing new pieces and doggedly struggling with an eleven-play cycle tenta-tively entitled *A Tale of Possessors Self-Dispossessed,* none of his work reached the stage.

It was natural that veteran practitioners of humor should encounter the greatest difficulty in accustoming themselves to a situation that upset the stable ground of social intercourse on which comedy turns its capers. When George S. Kauf-man, collaborating with Moss Hart, gave us *The American Way* in 1939, in order to honor the values that America was being called upon to preserve, he drew an appealing portrait of an assimilated immigrant but produced a some-what perfunctory chronicle of his life on these shores. When the collaboration with Edna Ferber *The Land Is Bright* cast a backward glance at mistakes in our recent past, the well-intended three-generation story abounded in stereo-types and commonplaces. When Moss Hart, moved by patriotic fervor, pro-duced his tribute to the American Air Force, *The Winged Victory,* he stirred large audiences more by the timely appeal to sentiment than by dint of original writing. Ben Hecht earnestly succumbed to strained symbolism in the nobly intended drama of good and evil *Lily of the Valley.* In composing a parable on dictatorship with the intelligently written family play *The Talley Method,* S. N. Behrman fell uncomfortably between the stools of comedy and drama. Philip Barry, whose talent for comedy of manners was confirmed again in the spring of 1939 with his *Philadelphia Story,* felt deeply on the subject of totali-tarianism. He had come close in 1938 to materializing his reflections on the anti-human, Nay-saying spirit which was fascism in his rather distinguished *Here Come the Clowns,* but had been entangled by symbolist complexity in this work of singular imaginativeness but almost equally singular confusion. His next reflective effort early in 1941, *Liberty Jones,* was an allegory devoid of passion; it was a much too genteel musical-comedy danger signal. The ambivalent relations of England and Ireland formed the political counterpoint to a domestic comedy in the same author's *Without Love,* a year later, but the two themes were unsuccessfully matched, and Philip Barry gave up the unequal struggle to dramatize politics. Instead, he gave the season of 1944–45 the Tallulah Bankhead *tour de force* of *Foolish Notion*. Only Paul Osborn managed the comic and the serious styles with equal competence during the period. Although his dramatization of *The Innocent Voyage* was not entirely successful, it combined comedy of adolescence with psychological insight and compassion. He gave the season of 1939–40 the delightfully homespun small-town comedy *Morning's at Seven* and the season of '44–'45 the moving dramatization of John Hersey's novel *A Bell for Adano*, by far the best expression of American idealism in action.

S. N. Behrman spoke prophetically for many of his fellow-playwrights in *No Time for Comedy*, produced on the eve of the world struggle, in the spring of 1939. Behrman's playwright hero, who had written pleasant comedy all his life, considered his comedies irrelevances and anachronisms while Germany and Italy were waging an undeclared war in Spain. But he failed miserably when he tried to write a tragedy relevant to the times, and he reluctantly returned to writing a comedy which might at most refract "the disturbances and the agonies of the times." Behrman's character realized that his serious play "was inadequate to its idea—that I wasn't equipped to do it—indignation without form—passion without authority. I saw exactly what it would be—not tragic, but thin, petulant."

The writers of comedy succeeded most when they continued to serve comedy. A few months after the storm lowered upon the world, James Thurber and Elliott Nugent turned out a delightful satire on academic life *The Male Animal*. It managed to say a great deal more in behalf of liberalism than Mr. Nugent expressed in a sober political preachment several years later. Clare Boothe's farcical melodrama *Margin for Error* engaged the Nazi spectre more effectively than many sombre exhibitions. In *Jason*, Samson Raphaelson purveyed intelligent though restrained comedy through a fastidious intellectual's embroilment with a "natural man" or man of the people. Rose Franken's comedy of an adolescent-minded girl's adjustment to marriage, *Claudia*, was superior to her treatment of the problem of the returning soldier in *A Soldier's Wife*. (Her *Outrageous Fortune*, which engaged the subject of intolerance and contained some remarkable writing, was jettisoned by the unnecessary confusion of racial problems with the theme of sexual inversion.) Ruth Gordon's *Over 21* extracted considerable entertainment from a liberal editor's desire to become an officer in the Air Force and his frantic effort to master the mathematical complexities of flight. Norman Krasna's *Dear Ruth* and F. Hugh Herbert's *Kiss and Tell*—no masterpieces, to be sure—treated adolescence in war time with some freshness and considerable hilarity. Precociousness among the youngsters of the war period was indeed a favorite topic, and Jerome Chodorov did better by it in *Junior Miss* than by the French resistance movement in his play *The French Touch*.

Howard Lindsay and Russel Crouse, who had hitherto excelled in writing and doctoring musical comedies, dramatized an American classic in *Life with Father*, and continued to delight audiences with it throughout the difficult years. As producers, they were also partly responsible for the success of Joseph Kesselring's *Arsenic and Old Lace*, the most entertaining comedy-melodrama of the American stage. George Kelly barely missed writing a masterpiece with his satire on feminine intuition, *The Deep Mrs. Sykes*. S. N. Behrman exhibited customary skill in adapting the Lunt-Fontanne antic *The Pirate*, and in domesticating Franz Werfel's *Jacobowsky and the Colonel*. This play, in its original form, was the one completely successful Broadway contribution of the refugee authors. It may also be set down as a minor miracle, since it managed to transform tragedy into comedy without sacrificing content relevant to the fall of France and the struggle with the reactionary ideologies. Behrman's craftsmanship was largely responsible for turning the trick so neatly.

George S. Kaufman and Moss Hart may have lacked sufficient inspiration when they championed causes, but they added another triumph to their list of collaborations with their barbed and witty character study *The Man Who Came to Dinner*. Mr. Kaufman's dramatization of *The Late George Apley* also had its gleaming points, although, as John Mason Brown has observed, so far as outlook is concerned "only the New York, New Haven and Hartford Railroad connects" the New York wit and the Bostonian Mr. Marquand. Moss Hart, functioning independently, acquitted himself adeptly as the showman of *Lady in the Dark*.

When Richard Rodgers and Oscar Hammerstein II, old hands at musical comedy, created *Oklahoma* out of Lynn Riggs' *Green Grow the Lilacs* they gave America its outstanding musical comedy, although it must be noted that they were in fine fettle, too, when they turned *Liliom* into the darker-colored *Carousel*. Considerable success also attended the musical comedies *Bloomer Girl* and *One Touch of Venus,* and the war directly inspired the best American musical revue in more than a decade, Irving Berlin's *This Is the Army*. Although the stage was glutted with innumerable puerilities masquerading as comedy and certainly discovered no rivals for the laurels of Molière or Shaw, our war-time humor often attained a high level of competence.

The art of comedy, it may be added, was enriched by the English-born John van Druten who had become a naturalized citizen. Among several expertly written comedies like *Old Acquaintance* and *The Damask Cheek,* he gave us the brilliantly executed three-character war-time romance *The Voice of the Turtle* and the affecting chronicle of *I Remember Mama*. The last-mentioned piece even added something to our spiritual armory with its account of an immigrant woman's heartening influence and her terrifying brother's rough-hewn courage and benevolence. And let us also note that Elmer Rice, who had virtually abandoned the gay science long ago and seemed to have lost familiarity with its graces, eased himself back with the comic fantasia of *Dream Girl*.

The adaptation of the serious-minded elder statesmen is another story. They did not, of course, have to renounce cap and bells in order to function responsibly. Some of them did, however, have to reconsider previously achieved attitudes or inclinations, and others had to find new ways of expressing a rooted conviction.

No transition from an older viewpoint was necessary in the case of Elmer Rice, who could be expected to rush into the breach of every liberal outpost. Had he not trumpeted his scorn of a regimented society as long ago as 1923 when he wrote his most original play *The Adding Machine?* That play had concluded with a peroration as prophetic as it was eloquent. It was addressed to Mr. Zero, the slave-minded robot who had long ago cast his shadow across the road to the uninviting future. "True, you move and eat and digest and excrete and reproduce. But any microscopic organism can do as much. . . . Back you go—back to your sunless groove—the raw slums and wars—the ready prey of the first jingo or demagogue or political adventurer who takes the trouble to play upon your ignorance and credulity and provincialism." Rice had also written and produced one of the first indictments of National Socialism in his Reichstag-Fire inspired *Judgment Day*. On the eve of the war, in 1938, the rather inchoate fantasy of *American Landscape* had embodied liberal prescriptions for the healing of class-conflict and an equally liberal admonition against prejudice as something inconsistent with the mixed racial and social ancestry of *homo Americanus*. The war in Europe was barely fifteen months old when Rice's *Flight to the West* read us a sermon from the behavior of passengers conveniently thrown together on a transatlantic clipper. In addition to drawing sharp attention to the canker in Europe and the danger of local infection while we were still non-belligerent, Rice drove home a prophecy, at that time actually a hope rather than a certainty. He set down the conflict between fascism and democracy as an issue of heartless logic warring against humane impulse. Although the point could perhaps be debated on surer grounds since it was the Nazi philosophers who often elevated instinct above reason in their appeal to sadism and their cult of "blood," there was a fine bravura in the American professor's reply to a German emissary: "It's just this: rationality carried to its ruthless logical extreme becomes madness. . . . That's the issue: rational madness against irrational sanity. It sounds paradoxical but it's true. And, in the long run, madness will lose; because madness is disease and sanity is health and, if disease wins, it means the end of the world and no healthy man can believe in that." That this kind of reasoning is circular may be overlooked. That the high-minded author discussed his issue more thoroughly than he dramatized it was more unfortunate, since it is evident that Mr. Rice had something to impart to troubled playgoers. But he proved incapable of quite overcoming an established habit of discourse in this play, as well as in the decidedly less impressive drama *A New Life* which followed it.

Maxwell Anderson's star had declined after the writing of *Winterset* and *High Tor* in 1935 and 1936. He was not only bogged down in rhetoric but trapped in a philosophy of negation with respect to social action. In the third act of *Winterset* he had substituted spiritual consolation for the pursuit of justice, and *High Tor* had ennobled precipitate flight from our materialistic society. All the comfort held out for us was that "Nothing is made by men but makes, in the end, good ruins," to which his hero Van replied "Well, that's something. But I can hardly wait." By the time Mr. Anderson wrote his Rudolph of Hapsburg tragedy *The Masque of Kings* early in 1937, he seemed to regard all action designed to destroy evil as futile because likely to be supplanted only by another, and possibly greater, evil. But the triumphs of totalitarianism and the start of the war in Europe led him to reverse his position. In November 1939, he proclaimed a positive attitude in the rather verbose verse-drama *Key Largo,* and demonstrated that no man could, or should, avoid taking a definite stand in the struggle. His hero, who had deserted the International Brigade and returned to America only to find the shape of the same evil at home, concluded that "A man must die for what he believes . . . and if he won't then he'll end up believing in nothing at all—and that's death, too." In October 1941, the fall of France evoked the still prolix if romantically exalted *Candle in the Wind,* in which an indefatigable American actress rescued her French lover from a concentration camp. Like his colleague Rice, Anderson placed his reliance upon some residue of human feeling which not even years of National Socialist conditioning would eradicate from the soul of Hitler's goose-steppers. It was a consoling philosophy from a distance, even if it was to be of no avail to millions of less securely remote Europeans. But, then, the role of the Paraclete was vastly appealing to our eloquent playwrights.

Finally, America's embroilment in the war gave birth in 1942 to Anderson's best war-time drama, *The Eve of St. Mark*. Although vitiated by the Keatsian dream episode implied in the title, the play moved its audience with its story of an American farm boy's gradual transformation into a heroic figure. Although Anderson's fulsome verse had been for some time the object of legitimate criticism, his prose had always commanded respect, and the dialogue recalled the excellence of his early realistic plays. Unfortunately his return to colloquial speech failed to bring comparable results in his next war drama *Storm Operation,* as well as in his bout with the problems of post-war readjustment in *Truckline Café,* a play evidently dear to the heart of this man of good will since he defended it with more heat than circumspection.

The established American novelists also made forays into the theatre, bringing some vital matter with occasional contributions. Among them were writers of such distinction as Ernest Hemingway, John Steinbeck, and Thornton Wilder. Hemingway's *The Fifth Column,* drawn from his experience of the Spanish Civil War, was the earliest and therefore the least noticed. The crisp and brutal Hemingway method served notice that the struggle with fascism was not going to be a gentleman's war. In retrospect, *The Fifth Column* may be appreciated as a welcome astringent after the gentle reassurances offered by other, more adept, dramatists. Hemingway's picture of the civil war was not pretty, and its realism had a dramatic force conspicuously absent in many later plays.

Thornton Wilder, always a philosophical writer except in his early one-acters, kept his peace until he could make some commentary *sub specie aeternitatis.* This he did in the fall of 1942 with *The Skin of Our Teeth,* which had many of the qualities of *Our Town*—the same unconventionality of play structure and the same respect for human aspiration. Telescoping time present and time past, Wilder contributed a burlesque history of the eternal Adam fighting his way up from the Ice Age while his sensible Eve plods indefatigably beside him. A continuous struggle pervaded this history: struggle with the elements, with his own pardonable folly and understandable despair, and with incarnate evil in his son, the protean Cain who rages from paleolithic to modern times without losing either his anti-social behavior or his sultry conscience. Mr. Antrobus, the all-enduring man, survived the Ice Age by discovering fire, and pulled himself up from primordial slime by inventing the alphabet and arithmetic; he survived, Noah-like, the flood, and he escaped extinction in all the grievous wars. His reason and good will, it was indicated, will probably enable him to save himself once more. If Mr. Wilder resorted to too much theatrical skittishness in avoiding didactic solemnity (too much "High-Brow Ha-Ha," as England's Ivor Brown calls it), if he also succumbed to obscurity in the concluding episode of war and its uncertain aftermath, he nevertheless produced a wise and stirring work. Its originality and universality set *The Skin of Our Teeth* apart from other plays, and may even ensure its escape, "by the skin of its teeth," from the pit that yawns for virtually all war-time drama.

The European resistance movement drew John Steinbeck away from the American scene to which he had brought so much compassion for uprooted humanity. Like Wilder, Steinbeck attempted a universal statement in *The Moon Is Down* by generalizing the locale of the action, although no one could fail to identify it as a town in Norway. The tone of the play was subdued and, toward the end, philosophical as the Norwegian mayor went quietly to his death quoting Socrates. The emphasis was typically Steinbeck in its affirmation of the common man's resilience: At first, the invaders encounter little resistance because free and peaceful people are easily caught off-guard. But before long the invaders find themselves floundering in a hostile land where even the silences are ominous. As a hysterical German officer remarks, the flies (and the conqueror has considered the conquered as mere flies) have conquered the flypaper. The morale of the enemy crumbles, and it becomes plain in Steinbeck's exegesis that whereas "herd men" win all the battles, it is free men who win all the wars. Like his colleagues in the theatre, Steinbeck tried to offer us the bread of comfort. If Broadway was not particularly grateful for it, regarding the play as too lukewarm and colorless, Europeans tended to rate the play higher. No doubt they could fill in the details with personal experience and translate Steinbeck's mild propositions into acute actuality.

Writers like Rice, Anderson, Wilder, and Steinbeck were accustomed to trying to set down articles of faith for Western man, and it is possible that they found them too easily. At least it is certain that a faith worked for, rather than a faith drawn from a copy-book of convictions, is more conducive to dramatic force. For the theatre, therefore, Robert E. Sherwood's war-time record is more engrossing. Being more acutely aware of his own evolution, Sherwood managed to express the evolution of an attitude that his more simply constituted or less self-scrutinizing colleagues seemed to take for granted.

Sherwood, who had been an impulsive volunteer in the Canadian Black Watch during the first World War and had been gassed and wounded, emerged from his experiences a confirmed pacifist. His first successful comedy *The Road to Rome* satirized military glory in the figure of Hannibal, and his first acceptable melodrama, *Waterloo Bridge,* involved a denunciation of the futility of war. He even became a belated "Waste-Lander" when the depression and rising fascism in 1934 disposed him to concede defeat for the human race in *The Petrified Forest,* which concluded that nature was "taking the world away from the intellectuals and giving it back to the apes." The same sense of *Weltuntergang* prevailed several years later in *Acropolis* which showed Pericles and Socrates losing the world to the apes, and in the spring of 1936 Sherwood reached the nadir of his despair with *Idiot's Delight,* which he was later to describe as "completely American in that it represented a compound of blank pessimism and desperate optimism, of chaos and jazz." As the war drew closer, however, and perhaps as this playwright watched his valiant President and favorite political leader, Sherwood began to take heart. His *Abe Lincoln in Illinois,* produced during the dark preludial days of the Munich appeasement, drew sustenance from the example of an American hero who had reluctantly moved into the arena of political action and had saved the world from the apes. The result was a chronicle which, although lethargic for more than an act, managed to be heartening. Sherwood became an active New Dealer, following the credo of his Lincoln, who had told his townspeople to "cultivate the natural world that is about us, and the intellectual world that is within us, so that we may secure an individual, social and political prosperity, whose course shall be forward, and which, while the earth endures, shall not pass away."

In very little time, this American dream seemed doomed forever, as the German octopus arched his tentacles across Europe. But far from losing heart, Sherwood stood by his new-found faith. He became one of the leaders of the Committee to Defend America by Aiding the Allies, he locked horns with Charles Lindbergh and other isolationist leaders, and he uttered battle-cries with noteworthy eloquence. "It was a bitter moment for me," Sherwood admitted, "when I found myself on the same side as the Big Navy enthusiasts."

The invasion of Finland, during the Soviet-Nazi pact, evoked his play, *There Shall Be No Night,* sympathetically performed by Alfred Lunt and Lynn Fontanne. Its purely journalistic elements were soon to be confounded by developments which threw Russia on the side of the Allies and Finland on the side of the enemy, and Sherwood was to acknowledge this by revising the background of his story for a London production. If the ease with which this was accomplished gives the cue to criticism, suggesting as it does that Sherwood was writing from the top of his head, there is one mitigating circumstance. He knew his hero better than may be imagined, since he was writing about himself, too. Dr. Valkonen was, like Sherwood's Lincoln and like Sherwood himself, "a man of peace who had to face the issue of appeasement of war." Through Valkonen, besides, the play was recapitulating the dilemma of all men of reason and good will: Sherwood's pacifistic scientist joins his country's forces at long last. He comes to realize that if war is a disease of the mind, it is even greater madness to hope to insulate oneself against it; that there are times when civilization cannot be preserved without recourse to arms. If Sherwood failed to crystallize a play for the ages in *There Shall Be No Night*, he managed to convey glimpses of a more than merely topical agony peculiar to the liberal mind and spirit. He proved less successful in the season of 1945–46 with *The Rugged Path*, a rather diffuse chronicle of a journalist's struggle against his family's isolationism and social irresponsibility. Sherwood had made playwriting a barometer for the political atmosphere. He had also turned crusader. He saved himself from the customary penalties for this kind of writing only when he found a vital character like Lincoln or Valkonen to sustain the crusade.

4.

Of the young writers who had so often prodded their elders during the depression, the report must be more meager, since many of them were in the services and nearly all of them had their earlier mentioned incubi to live with or to shake off. Robert Ardrey's *Thunder Rock*, which opened on November 14, 1939, came closest to expressing the problem of the younger radical generation, especially its sense of spent effort. Ardrey's journalist hero had become disheartened by the failure of the world to heed his warnings and had found himself a light-house retreat. He emerged from it only after an intense inner struggle and a fantasy in which he saw past generations experiencing but surviving classic tribulations. Although it seemed that the hero's ultimate resolve to fight for peace was a quixotic conclusion once the war had started, the play managed to advertise an imperative recovery of the spirit. Although unsuccessful on Broadway, *Thunder Rock* proved heartening to harassed Britons when it was later produced in blitzed London.

Clifford Odets appeared to have used up his best ammunition in the early plays *Waiting for Lefty, Awake and Sing, Golden Boy,* and the one-act underground drama *Till the Day I Die,* one of the first anti-Nazi pieces. Much was expected of Odets' first war-time contribution *Clash by Night,* produced in December 1941, but its meaning was submerged in a labored domestic triangle concerning an unemployed, continually humiliated worker who goes berserk when his wife betrays him. A better fate should have been reserved for something in which Odets negotiated the "Little Man, What Now?" theme. He had tried to find a private parallel for the public fact that there was an economic base for the desperation that drove the little people into the ways of violence and fascism. A year later, Odets undertook the adaptation of Konstantin Simonov's *The Russian People* for the Theatre Guild with no particular success, and thereafter was heard no more. The question of what had happened to the white hope of the 'thirties became a favorite topic for his regretful admirers.

Loss of revolutionary faith and zeal, growing introspection too deep for dramatic projection, the lure of Hollywood, or simultaneous disillusionment with both theatre and man? The present writer has no answer definitive enough to be put on paper. But if disillusionment is the explanation, it is possible to say that Odets came honorably by it.

The Russian People was one of several plays to represent the heartening news of Russian resistance. Another adaptation, *Counterattack,* by Peggy Phillips and Philip Stevenson, proved more effective by virtue of the intense suspense of its story of a Soviet counterattack. The best drama, *Winter Soldiers,* was written by a young man, Dan James, and was produced in the New School's Studio Theatre. The multi-scened epic traced the resistance movement from the Balkans, Austria and Poland to the very gates of Moscow, where a long gathering momentous German offensive is sent reeling back as the result of the underground's efforts. The play represented the standard radical principle of the unity of all the fronts and all the people—the concept of "a peoples' war."

The embattled writers also turned to history for guidance and sustenance. An understanding of historical forces was, after all, supposed to be their long suit. It was with the stick of history that the radicals had belabored capitalism in the final accounting, pronouncing doom on a once progressive and now decadent social system. It was history, too, that the liberals marshalled against the economic die-hards, maintaining the Parrington thesis that this country had always known a struggle between those who believed in the common man and those who had distrusted him; between those who had put human rights ahead of property rights, and *vice versa.* This was also the theme of *The Patriots,* the recapitulatory drama of the Jefferson-Hamilton imbroglio of our formative years contributed by Sidney Kingsley. Rejecting charges of villainy against Hamilton, and recognizing the selfless sincerity of one who had as yet no reason to believe in the efficacy of a democracy even in a republic, Kingsley demonstrated at the close of his chronicle that Hamilton and Jefferson could compose their differences when the preservation of the country was at stake. It was a point well worth making after Pearl Harbor when a nation divided between interventionists and isolationists closed its ranks to oppose the common enemy. Nevertheless, a partisan view was to be expected from the author of the social study of medicine *Men in White,* the "merchants of death" diatribe *Ten Million Ghosts,* and that tender salute to the plain man's courage and decency *The World We Make,* which had appeared in the fall of 1939. It was the glowing portrait of Jefferson, the pigments for which had been drawn from Kingsley's deepest convictions, that transfigured a chronicle that would have otherwise remained a prosaic history lesson.

Throughout the war another historical figure, Woodrow Wilson, was never far from the thoughts of those who believed that disaster would have been avoided if America had entered the League of Nations, and the young writers Howard Koch and John Huston were quick to express their sentiment in *In Time to Come.* Their play opened on Broadway exactly three weeks after Pearl Harbor. Although the colorless character of their hero and the necessity of recounting political facts militated against the success of *In Time to Come,* it proved to be a generally impressive analysis of past error and a warning against our ever again shirking international responsibilities.

Before, as well as after, December 7, 1941 our most immediate problem, however, was not peace but war, and by far the most effective realization of its coming was written by Lillian Hellman, already the author of such impressive pieces as *The Children's Hour* and *The Little Foxes*. Miss Hellman, who was by then a master of taut drama, saw the finger of fate pointing at America, which was still nominally neutral when *Watch on the Rhine* was produced on April 1, 1941. The play brought the European struggle into an upper-class American home that had been a model of well-bred amiability until a German underground worker and a Nazi tool prefigured our destiny by fighting each other to the death within its walls. Miss Hellman made her *Watch on the Rhine* one of the most forceful plays of the crisis because she let her symbolism and prophecy emanate from vividly realized characters, especially from the underground leader Kurt who is a lovable family man and deprecates violence even when he has to commit it.

Two seasons later, Miss Hellman also recapitulated history—the history of criminal retreat and appeasement while the fascists made hay in the sunlight of our benevolence—in the less successful chronicle *The Searching Wind*. For this theme Miss Hellman strained a parallel between diplomatic spinelessness and the moral frailty of upper-class characters, Miss Hellman having little kindness for upper-class representatives, less for vacillating liberals, and none for people without backbone or conviction. (It has even been charged that this hard-driving playwright has no love for humanity, to which she could possibly reply that it is necessary to be hard in order to be effectively kind, and that it is "love" that is the cause of all her impatience. She could with reason refute the charge by pointing to the good and strong people she has approved, to Kurt and his family, for example. More probably, however, she would disdain apologies and anyone who presumed to make them for her. She would rest her case on the reality of evil and on its highly dramatic nature—a fact recognized by her peers and superiors down the ages. As for the weak, rather than the evil, let who will find them lovable; from her standpoint, their compliance becomes complicity.) The author also employed a somewhat diffuse retrospective—"flashback"—technique in order to enable her searching wind to uncover past error, which was a drastic departure for our most adept writer of "well-made" plays. Its scanty success has probably confirmed her addiction to the technique that worked so well for her in *The Little Foxes* and *Watch on the Rhine*. Miss Hellman returned to it in almost Sardou fashion in the last act of *Another Part of the Forest* in the fall of 1946. And there is possibly something to be regretted in this tightening of the reins, since she draws characters so well that she could afford to let them lead her where they wish; the results might be fascinating to watch.

Since the younger writers were naturally sensible of a large stake in the future, mention is also in order for plays which pointed at problems that would continue to exert their pressure after the war. Although the record was neither large nor impressive until peace was around the corner, note must be taken of Edward Chodorov's *Decision,* which prefigured in 1944 the kind of social melodrama that the future probably holds in store. The play warned against fascist tendencies in conflicts between capital and labor once war-time ideals were forgotten. And plaudits were earned by *Tomorrow the World,* by the young writers Arnold d'Usseau and James Gow who in the spring of 1943 raised the problem of the denazification of German youth. Their effective characterization of a viciously conditioned German child enabled them to avoid most, if not all, the pitfalls of sociological problem drama. The ordinary sociological approach was sufficiently represented by such a demonstration as Elsa Shelley's *Pickup Girl*. Although the play examined the rise of delinquency during war time, it had scant success on Broadway in 1944, but it managed to thrive in reform-conscious England during 1946.

We cannot, however, close the record without acknowledging that not all the younger writers or newcomers were embattled. They contributed the usual crop of psychological melodramas, comedies, farces, and fantasies. Some of these—we might single out Thomas Job's *Uncle Harry* and the Leontovich-Miramova farce *Dark Eyes*—even seemed sufficient unto the day, and the Margaret Curtis fantasy *A Highland Fling* might have presented some luminosity but for a foggy production. Several elevations beyond such efforts, moreover, and reaching for a silvery moon, one could descry the highly individual arabesques of a brisk *bravo* and brashly tender harlequin, William Saroyan, a Yea-sayer and dancer while darkness enveloped us.

Known until 1939 solely as a remarkable story teller, William Saroyan was introduced as a playwright by the Group Theatre with his short piece *My Heart's in the Highlands* in the spring of 1940. Instantly acclaimed as a masterpiece by discerning critics, this indefinable drama, as staged by the Group's Robert Lewis, proved to be a work of elusive beauty. All it said in its vignettes of an impoverished poet, his little son, and an old man with a trumpet, if it is permissible to formulate sensibility, is that there is such a thing as Goethe's *"reine Menschlichkeit"*; that benevolence binds mankind together, and that all kinds of people have the thirst for beauty. It is unlikely that the bloom will fade from *My Heart's in the Highlands*. A few weeks after the play opened, Saroyan wrote his first full-length work, *The Time of Your Life*, a panoramic picture of variously troubled or agitated characters in a honky-tonk which deservedly won both the Drama Critics Prize and the Pulitzer Prize for its bizarre humanity and colloquial lyricism. The same season saw the production of *Love's Old Sweet Song*, the tender fable of the awakening of a spinster, and this was followed by the delicate poetic play *The Beautiful People* in 1942. Saroyan continued to write short and long plays of variable merit, although regrettably all of them, with the exception of the superb one-acter *Hello Out There*, suffered from anarchic fantasy and disorderly sentimentality.

Saroyan came to the theatre as a self-indulgent poet who managed to bring balm to the troubled spirit of his times. He also reflected both the strength and weakness of the period during which he produced his most successful plays. His indiscriminately benevolent attitude amounted to an affirmation of our humanitarian idealism. His buoyant improvisatory humor and his gospel of uncritical love expressed our desire to remain optimistic on a volcano, benign in the midst of evil, and self-assured in the midst of disheartening uncertainties. Saroyan's failure to enjoy any real success after 1942 coincided with the American people's—but not Saroyan's—realization of the immediate seriousness of the struggle against the Axis powers.

5.

As the war approached its conclusion, the American stage experienced a spurt of activity, almost as if the theatre were resolved to recover a reputation that had been jeopardized by several previous seasons. The rising tide of Allied victories and the prospect of a not too distant termination seemed to hearten the playwrights and producers. This may, however, be an illusory deduction, and all that can be said with certainty is that the stage showed some of its earlier resilience during the 1944–45 season and that the evidence continued to trickle in from the productions of 1945–46.

Several of the more distinguished musical comedies of the war period appeared at this time. *Carousel,* in particular, was more than a mere musicalization of *Liliom* and in spite of some obvious deficiencies marked a definite advance in music-drama with its serious theme, its folk quality, and its approach to operatic style without too much loss of informality. Less ambitious but refreshing was the lively production of *On the Town* which captured the wonder and the brash reality of the metropolis with a tale of footloose sailors in pursuit of the subway beauty "Miss Turnstiles." An unusually sharp *Pal Joey* vein of satire distinguished the *Billion Dollar Baby* recapitulation of the heyday of Prohibition and Wall Street speculation just before the Wall Street crash. A brisk native idiom, catapulted by the unfailingly vigorous Ethel Merman who can turn vulgarity into a personal triumph, enlivened *Annie Get Your Gun.* And in the spring of 1946 came the breezy and provocative revue *Call Me Mister* that celebrated the return of the soldier to his wonderful but not immaculate homeland. The seasons of clearing skies enjoyed a well-deserved festival of music.

A steady stream of serious drama added weight to the period. If the psychological drama *One Man Show* by Ruth Goodman and Arthur Goetz somehow missed the mark with its story of an abnormal father-daughter relationship, it nevertheless displayed good taste and sensitiveness. If Irwin Shaw's poorly produced *The Assassin* came within uncomfortable range of fustian melodrama, it managed to present a forceful interpretation of the *affaire* Darlan, as well as an appropriate protest against collaboration with undemocratic forces. It also drew an affecting hypothetical character in Darlan's royalist assassin.

As noted previously, American ideals were well affirmed by the conduct of Major Joppolo in the Paul Osborn dramatization *A Bell for Adano.* The young soldier novelist Harry Brown wrote our most authentic front-line war drama, *A Sound of Hunting,* a story of the common soldier's comradeship and unpretentious heroism; and another soldier-playwright, John Patrick, gave us that meritorious war-play *The Hasty Heart.* It contained a premise not easily discountable in the world to come: If its dying hero rejected pity from his nurse and comrades, he was not being ungratefully cantankerous; by his suspicions and irritability he was expressing a plucky character and reflecting an unhappy life as one of the world's many stepchildren. And it is not too much to say that he was implicitly challenging the world to assure little people some hospitality while they are still alive to enjoy it. Although too static for complete success, *The Hasty Heart* was a tender play and a muted statement concerning the common man's quarrel with society, as well as a quite glowing expression of human comradeship.

The same period witnessed the emergence of a new talent in a third war drama, *Home of the Brave,* by still another ex-soldier, Arthur Laurents. For two acts it proved to be an arresting treatment of the effect of racial intolerance on a Jewish soldier who has retreated into a paralyzing psychoneurosis. Narcosynthesis evoked two vibrant flashback scenes dramatizing the case history; and if the third-act cure had possessed the same dramatic excitement, *Home of the Brave* would have been completely successful. Fortunately avoiding a pedestrian tract on anti-semitism, the young author moved his story into the regions of complex human behavior. Although forthright, he was subtle; although impassioned, fair. First and last, he adhered to a broad concept of human solidarity rather than to any narrow partisanship. Such merits could go far toward cancelling any defects to which one could point.

Another treatment of racial intolerance was contributed by the authors of *Tomorrow the World* when they dynamited the façade of false liberalism in the Negro problem play *Deep Are the Roots*. To this exposé of surface magnanimity and rooted prejudice they added the tragic picture of young lovers renouncing a passion incompatible with the realities of their environment. If the second theme had not overcomplicated the broad social issue, and if some plot devices had not been strained too far, the play would have been as memorable as it was immediately exciting and provocative. The Negro issue was, in fact, a major concern toward the close of our period as dramatists who had noted the crimes of the German nation turned to their own backyard. The theme was variously engaged by Maxine Wood's *On Whitman Avenue,* which for a change pointed the accusing finger at the North, by a dramatization of the sensational novel *Strange Fruit,* by Robert Ardrey's *Jeb,* and by two plays produced by the Catholic Blackfriar's Guild, one inept and the other, Edwin Bronner's *Young American,* intelligent.

It would be a mistake, nevertheless, to assume that these and other plays formed a pattern of post-war disillusionment. No intense disappointment was possible because the theatre of the war years had not indulged in any illusions that victory on the battlefront would bring redemption. The social plays merely continued the theatre of protest that had receded after Pearl Harbor. Now that the fire-spuming dragons were dead, it was opportune to engage the smaller domestic beasts of prey. Far from expressing a philosophy of despair, the younger playwrights, regardless of the disconcerting question of their competence, behaved as if they had never heard of such a thing as negation or defeat. . . . It was appropriate that the theatre should have uncovered a monument to Justice Oliver Wendell Holmes in *The Magnificent Yankee.* Its producer, Arthur Hopkins, rightly called it "a sort of gesture of faith." Although quiet and leisurely, as well as somewhat awkward, Emmet Lavery's play made a deep impression with its portrait of the great man who had been a mainstay of American liberalism for half a century.

There was exuberance, as well as resolve, in the theatre's rededication during this first post-war season. It was evident in a small 1945–46 trend toward political and social comedy in which the liberal viewpoint was driven home entertainingly rather than with the flat seriousness that has capsized so many problem plays. In the course of their sparkling play *The State of the Union,* Howard Lindsay and Russel Crouse managed to combine a shrewd "What Every Woman Knows" exercise with an even shrewder exposé of some of the major malfeasances of American politics. *Born Yesterday* pleasantly strangled a small-time monopolist and power-lust exponent with his own strings when his chorus-girl mistress undid him with the assistance of a *New Republic* reporter. Humor so extravagant and yet so pertinent as Garson Kanin's had appeared so rarely in the preceding years that it looked like a post-war discovery. Although the play had a familiar George S. Kaufman tint, the dye had a good deal more red blood in it. It was supplied by a younger generation of which Kanin was a charter member.

Finally, it is to be noted that the penultimate season of 1944–45 found crowning achievements in Mary Chase's Pulitzer Prize *Harvey* and Tennessee Williams' Drama Critics Prize winner *The Glass Menagerie.* Both plays were sufficiently rooted in American life. *Harvey,* with its charitable attitude toward a confirmed toper, reflected our congenial view of human frailty, and its high-handed treatment of a psychiatrist accorded with our easy irreverence. *The Glass Menagerie* recalled the tenaciousness and impoverishment of Americans during the depression. But both works, like the earlier Saroyan improvisations, revealed an original talent for which there are no easily definable classifications. They indicated that the professional American stage is never closed to experiment in spite of its costliness, and that the American drama is never free from surprises. The hallucinatory six-foot rabbit "Harvey" was by himself warrant for this comforting conclusion. Although all of *Harvey* was not written with the finesse that characterized its hero, and although scattered dramaturgy damaged several scenes, this comedy was recognized as one of our most entrancing plays.

A stronger talent verging on genius was evident in the work of Tennessee Williams, who had already attracted attention with several published one-acters and one unsuccessfully produced full-length play. His lyrical gift and sensitive characterization made *The Glass Menagerie* a minor masterpiece and, what was more remarkable in the case of a fragile play, it became a popular Broadway success in Eddie Dowling's superb production. Structurally, *The Glass Menagerie* was a reminiscence framed by a narrator, and a delicate patina covered the retrospective scenes. What the narrator remembered was, besides, always revealing and always affecting. An ineluctable reality pervaded the characters of the desperately nagging and addled mother, the Marie-Laurencin sister, and the breezy "Gentleman Caller." One and all, they made the slough of their lives luminous with human bravery, past logic and past routine sociology.

After the spring of '46 we found ourselves temporarily depleted of original contributions, and the season of 1946-47 started out as a revival holiday, which is a polite way of denoting a deficiency of fresh playwriting. The revivals themselves were of uncertain quality, although efforts to fill a long-felt need for repertory such as Theatre Incorporated plans and the newly founded American Repertory Company's series of productions were welcome on principle. The one notable new piece of the early autumn was Eugene O'Neill's *The Iceman Cometh*, which had been completed in 1939 and belonged to an earlier period of disillusionment in its author's long career. The despair of *The Iceman Cometh* will be regarded as timely rather than timeless only if the world should quickly repeat some such tragedy as the one from which it has so recently emerged. Toward the close of the year, new plays appeared in quick succession: George Kelly's domestic comedy *The Fatal Weakness*, Maxwell Anderson's retelling of the St. Joan story *Joan of Lorraine*, Moss Hart's divorce drama *Christopher Blake*, Ruth Gordon's reminiscence *Years Ago*, and Lillian Hellman's account of "Little Foxes" origins, *Another Part of the Forest*.

Consideration of these plays, however, would be out of bounds here, and they cannot be used to swell the record of the war period. They may not even serve as suitable coda to this at long last concluded chronicle. The theatre is incalculable, and only a chronic optimist would make himself so vulnerable as to predict that the peace-time stage is about to cover itself with glory. We shall see what we shall see.

———

I conclude with a note on our selections—not without a quaver. The 1939-45 period covered in this collection is represented in its actual variety. If the weight of the evidence is in favor of comedy and plays in which the war appears only incidentally, if at all, the actual record is the excuse.

The Glass Menagerie and *The Time of Your Life* represent the few sports and surprises in the period's harvest. If *Harvey* had been available for this anthology, it would have been added to this group of imaginative and unique creations. At the other extreme, *Arsenic and Old Lace* represents the melodramas, and it is certain that the choice will not be questioned unless the book encounters an unusually rigorous moralist. *Life with Father* and *I Remember Mama* do very well by the retrospective drama, if we reserve historical chronicles for a separate classification. For all the pudder raised by dour anti-"escapists," the remembrance of things past remains justifiable human indulgence, and I have often felt, as who has not, that what matters in escape is less what we escape from than what we escape into. On that score, the two plays acquit themselves honorably.

The Man Who Came to Dinner does justice to the large area of Kaufman and pseudo-Kaufman comedy that has been traditional in these parts for a good long stretch. *The Philadelphia Story,* which might have been but was not anachronistic, does its bit by the comedy of manners, and is included for its pronounced competence and superiority to later products like the same author's *Without Love.* Its taffeta drama would belong here if only to show that Broadway didn't erase accepted patterns any more than did the nation in which even war relief and stage-door canteens involved the wonted social graces, not to mention the social register. *The Voice of the Turtle* makes its bow to wartime romance, and *Dream Girl* heeds anything from nubility to feminine escape mechanisms—in short, a state of grace which even a state of war somehow fails to abolish for the race. (If there should be some irony, to Mr. Rice's mind, in his being represented by a play that contained so much less social content than most of his work, and that was so much more successful, it is nevertheless a tribute to his showmanship. It is this congenial and profitable talent that he has often immolated on the altar of social responsibility, and this too redounds to his honor—at least as a citizen of his country and its theatre.) *The Male Animal* and *Born Yesterday* represent the vein of social satire, which would have been further enriched within these covers if *State of the Union* had been available to us.

As for the heavy artillery, *Abe Lincoln in Illinois* and *The Patriots* represent the recapitulatory historical mood bearing upon the ardors and endurances of the period. (*In Time to Come* might have been added, albeit with some hesitation, if space had allowed.) *Tomorrow the World* takes heed of the immediate future embodied in the immediate present. *Watch on the Rhine* best shows our playwrights heeding the struggle abroad and expecting it to overflow into America. *The Hasty Heart* and *Home of the Brave* exhibit the actual war and the continuous challenge of some of its issues. *Jacobowsky and the Colonel* would have qualified under the category if it could have been set down as a wholly indigenous product. While recognizing the substantial contribution by S. N. Behrman, a Drama Critics Circle ruling voted Franz Werfel's drama into the foreign play classification, and there cannot be any appeal, of course, from the highest court. Not, at least, by one who participated in the verdict! *The Eve of St. Mark* qualified as to nativity; but although quite willing to compliment Maxwell Anderson, I was not convinced that the omission would be serious. I had the same conviction or lack of conviction in the case of *Sound of Hunting.* If *There Shall Be No Night* would have added points to our dramatists' overseas war record, I preferred to represent Robert Sherwood with his earlier *Abe Lincoln in Illinois* as a more potent expression of ideals at the heart of the struggle and as less dehydrated by journalistic exigencies.

I am not aware of any other arguable omissions except *The Skin of Our Teeth.* Unfortunately for both the editor of this book and for those who acquire it, Mr. Wilder did not want his play to appear in any anthology. His decision deprives us of the period's most original contribution. If the present editor goes Mr. Wilder one better and deprives readers of the period's most successful one—namely, *Oklahoma,* the reason lies in my affection for the achievement rather than in any intention to disparage it. It would pain me (as, I daresay, it would pain others) to see *Oklahoma* shorn of its proper glories, its Richard Rodgers music and Agnes de Mille choreography. Although good drama can always be good theatre, it does not follow that good theatre always makes good drama.

The final word on the question of the selections cannot quite evade the skimpiness of war drama. If the entire introduction to this book is, in a sense, an attempted explanation, conscience returns to the problem as surely as a criminal is supposed to return to the scene of his crime, since nothing can completely exculpate us. We can find solace only in the familiar assurance that the best war plays have appeared after, and not during, a war, as a more or less Wordsworthian experience of emotion recollected in tranquility. And even so, there is no warrant for certainty that this will be the case again. There may be more point to the hypothesis that plays about the first World War exhausted the realist's resources, and that any account of the battlefront could have added little to what had already been accomplished by earlier dramatists. May we not, then, raise the further question of what an actual war play should be after all, now that realism is no longer the novelty it was when *What Price Glory?* and *Journey's End* supplanted the romantic tradition of plume-waving? A General Electric scientist said about lightning: "If you heard the thunder, the lightning did not strike you. If you saw the lightning, it missed you; and if it did strike you, you would not have known it." It is perhaps in the totality of drama galvanized by the war situation—here about eight of our sixteen selections—that we have the age impinging on the theatre; in the thunder we *heard* and the lightning we *saw*—that is, in our awareness of what was going on.

THE GLASS MENAGERIE
By TENNESSEE WILLIAMS

THE GLASS MENAGERIE was first produced by Eddie Dowling and Louis J. Singer at the Playhouse Theatre, New York City, on March 31, 1945. The play was staged by Eddie Dowling and Margo Jones; setting by Jo Mielziner; original music by Paul Bowles. The cast was as follows:

THE MOTHER...............Laurette Taylor
HER SON...........................Eddie Dowling
HER DAUGHTER..............Julie Haydon
THE GENTLEMAN CALLER
Anthony Ross

The scene is an Alley in St. Louis.

PART I. Preparation for a Gentleman Caller.

PART II. The Gentleman calls.

Time: Now and the Past.

THE AUTHOR

As a descendant of Indian-fighting Tennessee pioneers Tennessee Williams, who was born in Columbus, Mississippi (in 1914), comes naturally by his restiveness. He has traveled extensively in America and Mexico. In fact, it is always a problem for his agents and producers where to locate him. Broadway is his beat only when he has business to transact or when he cannot roam elsewhere.

After graduation from the University of Iowa, he began serving an indirect apprenticeship to literature and the theatre as a bell hop in New Orleans, a handyman in a shoe-warehouse (like the hero of The Glass Menagerie), *a teletypist with a corps of engineers in Jacksonville, Florida, and a waiter and reciter of verse in a Greenwich Village night club. Throughout all these efforts to hold body and soul together he was writing furiously, mostly for the stage.*

His talents were recognized several years before he received a professional production. The Group Theatre awarded him a cash prize for four one-act pieces appropriately entitled American Blues, *since the young author was one well acquainted with the pre-war depression and memorialized it. Theresa Helburn and John Gassner gave him a scholarship to their advanced playwrights' seminar at the New School for Social Research. It was in this class that he wrote his second full-length play* The Battle of Angels. *It was the first to get a professional production after the instructors, who were both Theatre Guild associates, presented the script officially to the Guild. Lawrence Langner, the other member of the Guild trio that concerned itself with playwrights, took charge of the lyrical play, Margaret Webster was assigned to direct it, and Miriam Hopkins was engaged for the leading role. Unfortunately,* The Battle of Angels *was abandoned in Boston where it caused a minor scandal, and plans to revamp the play for New York failed to materialize. According to report, Mr. Williams considers it his best effort to date, and he is perhaps not far from right. If it is ever given some intelligent revision and a sound production, it is certain to enhance its author's reputation. Mr. Williams also received a Rockefeller Foundation Fellowship in 1940 and was awarded a thousand dollar grant for work in drama by the American Academy and National Institute of Arts and Letters.*

The Glass Menagerie *frightened Broadway producers. Eddie Dowling and Louis Singer tested it in Chicago before bringing it to New York in March, 1945. Mr. Williams was fortunate in having Eddie Dowling as the director of his play, and the production was the occasion for the triumphant return of Laurette Taylor to the New York stage. The mother in* The Glass Menagerie *was also to be Miss Taylor's last role on the stage of this world, and her seasoned performance was the high-water mark of her notable career.*

Mr. Williams' earlier written collaboration, You Touched Me, *a dramatization of a D. H. Lawrence story, was produced in the fall of 1945. Although it fell short of the success of* The Glass Menagerie, *it again revealed an aptitude for sensitive characterization and dialogue.*

THE GLASS MENAGERIE

SCENE I

The Wingfield apartment is in the rear of the building, one of those vast hive-like conglomerations of cellular living-units that flower as warty growths in overcrowded urban centers of lower middle-class population and are symptomatic of the impulse of this largest and fundamentally enslaved section of American society to avoid fluidity and differentiation and to exist and function as one interfused mass of automatism.

The apartment faces an alley and is entered by a fire-escape, a structure whose name is a touch of accidental poetic truth, for all of these huge buildings are always burning with the slow and implacable fires of human desperation. The fire-escape is included in the set—that is, the landing of it and steps descending from it.

The scene is memory and is therefore nonrealistic. Memory takes a lot of poetic license. It omits some details; others are exaggerated, according to the emotional value of the articles it touches, for memory is seated predominantly in the heart. The interior is therefore rather dim and poetic.

At the rise of the curtain, the audience is faced with the dark, grim rear wall of the Wingfield tenement. This building, which runs parallel to the footlights, is flanked on both sides by dark, narrow alleys which run into murky canyons of tangled clotheslines, garbage cans and the sinister lattice-work of neighboring fire-escapes. It is up and down these side alleys that exterior entrances and exits are made, during the play. At the end of Tom's *opening commentary, the dark tenement wall slowly reveals (by means of a transparency) the interior of the ground floor Wingfield apartment.*

Downstage is the living room, which also serves as a sleeping room for Laura, *the sofa unfolding to make her bed. Upstage, center, and divided by a wide arch or second proscenium with transparent faded portieres (or second curtain), is the dining room. In an old-fashioned what-not in the living room are seen scores of transparent glass animals. A blown-up photograph of the father hangs on the wall of the living room, facing the audience, to the left of the archway. It is the face of a very handsome young man in a doughboy's First World War cap. He is gallantly smiling, ineluctably smiling, as if to say, "I will be smiling forever."*

The audience hears and sees the opening scene in the dining room through both the transparent fourth wall of the building and the transparent gauze portieres of the dining-room arch. It is during this revealing scene that the fourth wall slowly ascends, out of sight. This transparent exterior wall is not brought down again until the very end of the play, during Tom's *final speech.*

The narrator is an undisguised convention of the play. He takes whatever license with dramatic convention as is convenient to his purposes.

Tom *enters dressed as a merchant sailor from alley, stage left, and strolls across the front of the stage to the fire-escape. There he stops and lights a cigarette. He addresses the audience.*

TOM. Yes, I have tricks in my pocket, I have things up my sleeve. But I am the opposite of a stage magician. He gives you illusion that has the appearance of truth. I give you truth in the pleasant disguise of illusion.

To begin with, I turn back time. I reverse it to that quaint period, the thirties, when the huge middle class of America was matriculating in a school for the blind. Their eyes had failed them, or they had failed their eyes, and so they were having their fingers pressed forcibly down on the fiery Braille alphabet of a dissolving economy.

In Spain there was revolution. Here there was only shouting and confusion.

In Spain there was Guernica. Here there were disturbances of labor, sometimes pretty violent, in otherwise peaceful cities such as Chicago, Cleveland, Saint Louis . . .

This is the social background of the play.

(MUSIC.)

The play is memory.

Being a memory play, it is dimly lighted, it is sentimental, it is not realistic.

In memory everything seems to happen to music. That explains the fiddle in the wings.

I am the narrator of the play, and also a character in it.

The other characters are my mother, Amanda, my sister, Laura, and a gentleman caller who appears in the final scenes. He is the most realistic character in the play, being an emissary from a world of reality that we were somehow set apart from.

But since I have a poet's weakness for symbols, I am using this character also as a symbol; he is the long delayed but always expected something that we live for.

There is a fifth character in the play who doesn't appear except in this larger-than-life-size photograph over the mantel.

This is our father who left us a long time ago.

He was a telephone man who fell in love with long distances; he gave up his job with the telephone company and skipped the light fantastic out of town . . .

The last we heard of him was a picture post-card from Mazatlan, on the Pacific coast of Mexico, containing a message of two words—

"Hello— Good-bye!" and no address.

I think the rest of the play will explain itself. . . .

(AMANDA's *voice becomes audible through the portieres.*)

(LEGEND ON SCREEN: "OU SONT LES NEIGES.") (*He divides the portieres and enters the upstage area.*)

(AMANDA *and* LAURA *are seated at a drop-leaf table. Eating is indicated by gestures without food or utensils.* AMANDA *faces the audience.* TOM *and* LAURA *are seated in profile.*)

(*The interior has lit up softly and through the scrim we see* AMANDA *and* LAURA *seated at the table in the upstage area.*)

AMANDA (*calling*). Tom?

TOM. Yes, Mother.

AMANDA. We can't say grace until you come to the table!

TOM. Coming, Mother. (*He bows slightly and withdraws, reappearing a few moments later in his place at the table.*)

AMANDA (*to her son*). Honey, don't *push* with your *fingers*. If you have to push with something, the thing to push with is a crust of bread. And chew—chew! Animals have sections in their stomachs which enable them to digest food without mastication, but human beings are supposed to chew their food before they swallow it down. Eat food leisurely, son, and really enjoy it. A well-cooked meal has lots of delicate flavors that have to be held in the mouth for appreciation. So chew your food and give your salivary glands a chance to function!

(TOM *deliberately lays his imaginary fork down and pushes his chair back from the table.*)

TOM. I haven't enjoyed one bite of this dinner because of your constant directions on how to eat it. It's you that makes me rush through meals with your hawk-like attention to every bite I take. Sickening—spoils my appetite—all this discussion of —animals' secretion—salivary glands—mastication!

AMANDA (*lightly*). Temperament like a Metropolitan star! (*He rises and crosses downstage.*) You're not excused from the table.

TOM. I'm getting a cigarette.

AMANDA. You smoke too much.

(LAURA *rises.*)

LAURA. I'll bring in the blanc mange.

(*He remains standing with his cigarette by the portieres during the following.*)

AMANDA (*rising*). No, sister, no, sister—you be the lady this time and I'll be the darky.

LAURA. I'm already up.

AMANDA. Resume your seat, little sister— I want you to stay fresh and pretty—for gentlemen callers!

LAURA. I'm not expecting any gentlemen callers.

AMANDA (crossing out to kitchenette. Airily). Sometimes they come when they are least expected! Why, I remember one Sunday afternoon in Blue Mountain—

(Enters kitchenette.)

TOM. I know what's coming!

LAURA. Yes. But let her tell it.

TOM. Again?

LAURA. She loves to tell it.

(AMANDA returns with bowl of dessert.)

AMANDA. One Sunday afternoon in Blue Mountain—your mother received—seventeen!—gentlemen callers! Why, sometimes there weren't chairs enough to accommodate them all. We had to send the nigger over to bring in folding chairs from the parish house.

TOM (remaining at portieres). How did you entertain those gentlemen callers?

AMANDA. I understood the art of conversation!

TOM. I bet you could talk.

AMANDA. Girls in those days knew how to talk, I can tell you.

TOM. Yes?

(IMAGE: AMANDA AS A GIRL ON A PORCH, GREETING CALLERS.)

AMANDA. They knew how to entertain their gentlemen callers. It wasn't enough for a girl to be possessed of a pretty face and a graceful figure—although I wasn't slighted in either respect. She also needed to have a nimble wit and a tongue to meet all occasions.

TOM. What did you talk about?

AMANDA. Things of importance going on in the world! Never anything coarse or common or vulgar. (She addresses TOM as though he were seated in the vacant chair at the table though he remains by portieres. He plays this scene as though he held the book.) My callers were gentlemen—all! Among my callers were some of the most prominent young planters of the Mississippi Delta—planters and sons of planters!

(TOM motions for music and a spot of light on AMANDA.)

(Her eyes lift, her face glows, her voice becomes rich and elegiac.)

(SCREEN LEGEND: "OU SONT LES NEIGES.")

There was young Champ Laughlin who later became vice-president of the Delta Planters Bank.

Hadley Stevenson who was drowned in Moon Lake and left his widow one hundred and fifty thousand in Government bonds.

There were the Cutrere brothers, Wesley and Bates. Bates was one of my bright particular beaux! He got in a quarrel with that wild Wainwright boy. They shot it out on the floor of Moon Lake Casino. Bates was shot through the stomach. Died in the ambulance on his way to Memphis. His widow was also well-provided for, came into eight or ten thousand acres, that's all. She married him on the rebound —never loved her—carried my picture on him the night he died!

And there was that boy that every girl in the Delta had set her cap for! That beautiful, brilliant young Fitzhugh boy from Greene County!

TOM. What did he leave his widow?

AMANDA. He never married! Gracious, you talk as though all of my old admirers had turned up their toes to the daisies!

TOM. Isn't this the first you've mentioned that still survives?

AMANDA. That Fitzhugh boy went North and made a fortune—came to be known as the Wolf of Wall Street! He had the Midas touch, whatever he touched turned to gold!

And I could have been Mrs. Duncan J. Fitzhugh, mind you! But—I picked your father!

LAURA (rising). Mother, let me clear the table.

AMANDA. No, dear, you go in front and study your typewriter chart. Or practice your shorthand a little. Stay fresh and pretty!—It's almost time for our gentlemen callers to start arriving. (She flounces girlishly toward the kitchenette.) How many do you suppose we're going to entertain this afternoon?

(TOM throws down the paper and jumps up with a groan.)

LAURA *(alone in the dining room)*. I don't believe we're going to receive any, Mother.

AMANDA *(reappearing, airily)*. What? No one—not one? You must be joking! *(LAURA nervously echoes her laugh. She slips in a fugitive manner through the half-open portieres and draws them gently behind her. A shaft of very clear light is thrown on her face against the faded tapestry of the curtains.* MUSIC: "THE GLASS MENAGERIE" UNDER FAINTLY. *Lightly.)* Not one gentleman caller? It can't be true! There must

be a flood, there must have been a tornado!

LAURA. It isn't a flood, it's not a tornado, Mother. I'm just not popular like you were in Blue Mountain. . . . *(TOM utters another groan.* LAURA *glances at him with a faint, apologetic smile, her voice catching a little.)* Mother's afraid I'm going to be an old maid.

THE SCENE DIMS OUT WITH "GLASS MENAGERIE" MUSIC

SCENE II

"Laura, Haven't You Ever Liked Some Boy?"
On the dark stage the screen is lighted with the image of blue roses.
Gradually LAURA's *figure becomes apparent and the screen goes out.*
The music subsides.
LAURA *is seated in the delicate ivory chair at the small claw-foot table.*
She wears a dress of soft violet material for a kimono—her hair tied back from her forehead with a ribbon.
She is washing and polishing her collection of glass.
AMANDA *appears on the fire-escape steps. At the sound of her ascent,* LAURA *catches her breath, thrusts the bowl of ornaments away and seats herself stiffly before the diagram of the typewriter keyboard as though it held her spellbound.*
Something has happened to AMANDA. *It is written in her face as she climbs to the landing: a look that is grim and hopeless and a little absurd.*
She has on one of those cheap or imitation velvety-looking cloth coats with imitation fur collar. Her hat is five or six years old, one of those dreadful cloche hats that were worn in the late twenties and she is clasping an enormous black patent-leather pocketbook with nickel clasps and initials. This is her full-dress outfit, the one she usually wears to the D.A.R.
Before entering she looks through the door.
She purses her lips, opens her eyes very wide, rolls them upward and shakes her head.
Then she slowly lets herself in the door. Seeing her mother's expression LAURA *touches her lips with a nervous gesture.*

LAURA. Hello, Mother, I was— *(She makes a nervous gesture toward the chart on the wall.* AMANDA *leans against the shut door and stares at* LAURA *with a martyred look.)*

AMANDA. Deception? Deception? *(She slowly removes her hat and gloves, continuing the sweet suffering stare. She lets the hat and gloves fall on the floor—a bit of acting.)*

LAURA *(shakily)*. How was the D.A.R. meeting? *(AMANDA slowly opens her purse and removes a dainty white handkerchief which she shakes out delicately and delicately touches to her lips and nostrils.)* Didn't you go to the D.A.R. meeting, Mother?

AMANDA *(faintly, almost inaudibly)*. —No. —No. *(Then more forcibly.)* I did not have the strength—to go to the D.A.R. In fact, I did not have the courage! I wanted to find a hole in the ground and hide myself in it forever! *(She crosses slowly to the wall and removes the diagram of the typewriter keyboard. She holds it in front of her for a second, staring at it sweetly and sorrowfully—then bites her lips and tears it in two pieces.)*

LAURA *(faintly)*. Why did you do that, Mother? *(AMANDA repeats the same procedure with the chart of the Gregg Alphabet.)* Why are you—

AMANDA. Why? Why? How old are you, Laura?

LAURA. Mother, you know my age.

AMANDA. I thought that you were an adult; it seems that I was mistaken. *(She crosses slowly to the sofa and sinks down and stares at LAURA.)*

LAURA. Please don't stare at me, Mother.

(AMANDA closes her eyes and lowers her head. Count ten.)

AMANDA. What are we going to do, what is going to become of us, what is the future? *(Count ten.)*

LAURA. Has something happened, Mother? *(AMANDA draws a long breath and takes out the handkerchief again. Dabbing process.)* Mother, has—something happened?

AMANDA. I'll be all right in a minute, I'm just bewildered— *(Count five.)* —by life. . . .

LAURA. Mother, I wish that you would tell me what's happened!

AMANDA. As you know, I was supposed to be inducted into my office at the D.A.R. this afternoon. *(IMAGE: A SWARM OF TYPEWRITERS.)* But I stopped off at Rubicam's business college to speak to your teachers about your having a cold and ask them what progress they thought you were making down there.

LAURA. Oh. . . .

AMANDA. I went to the typing instructor and introduced myself as your mother. She didn't know who you were. Wingfield, she said. We don't have any such student enrolled at the school!

I assured her she did, that you had been going to classes since early in January.

"I wonder," she said, "if you could be talking about that terribly shy little girl who dropped out of school after only a few days' attendance?"

"No," I said, "Laura, my daughter, has been going to school every day for the past six weeks!"

"Excuse me," she said. She took the attendance book out and there was your name, unmistakably printed, and all the dates you were absent until they decided that you had dropped out of school.

I still said, "No, there must have been

some mistake! There must have been some mix-up in the records!"

And she said, "No—I remember her perfectly now. Her hands shook so that she couldn't hit the right keys! The first time we gave a speed-test, she broke down completely—was sick at the stomach and almost had to be carried into the wash-room! After that morning she never showed up any more. We phoned the house but never got any answer—while I was working at Famous and Barr, I suppose, demonstrating those— Oh!"

I felt so weak I could barely keep on my feet!

I had to sit down while they got me a glass of water!

Fifty dollars' tuition, all of our plans—my hopes and ambitions for you—just gone up the spout, just gone up the spout like that.

(LAURA draws a long breath and gets awkwardly to her feet. She crosses to the victrola and winds it up.)

What are you doing?

LAURA. Oh! *(She releases the handle and returns to her seat.)*

AMANDA. Laura, where have you been going when you've gone out pretending that you were going to business college?

LAURA. I've just been going out walking.

AMANDA. That's not true.

LAURA. It is. I just went walking.

AMANDA. Walking? Walking? In winter? Deliberately courting pneumonia in that light coat? Where did you walk to, Laura?

LAURA. All sorts of places—mostly in the park.

AMANDA. Even after you'd started catching that cold?

LAURA. It was the lesser of two evils, Mother. (IMAGE: WINTER SCENE IN PARK.) I couldn't go back up. I—threw up—on the floor!

AMANDA. From half past seven till after five every day you mean to tell me you walked around in the park, because you wanted to make me think that you were still going to Rubicam's Business College?

LAURA. It wasn't as bad as it sounds. I went inside places to get warmed up.

AMANDA. Inside where?

LAURA. I went in the art museum and the bird-houses at the Zoo. I visited the penguins every day! Sometimes I did without lunch and went to the movies. Lately I've been spending most of my afternoons in the Jewel-box, that big glass house where they raise the tropical flowers.

AMANDA. You did all this to deceive me, just for deception? *(LAURA looks down.)* Why?

LAURA. Mother, when you're disappointed, you get that awful suffering look on your face, like the picture of Jesus' mother in the museum!

AMANDA. Hush!

LAURA. I couldn't face it.

(Pause. A whisper of strings.)

(LEGEND: "THE CRUST OF HUMILITY.")

AMANDA *(hopelessly fingering the huge pocketbook)*. So what are we going to do the rest of our lives? Stay home and watch the parades go by? Amuse ourselves with the glass menagerie, darling? Eternally play those worn-out phonograph records your father left as a painful reminder of him?

We won't have a business career—we've given that up because it gave us nervous indigestion! *(Laughs wearily.)* What is there left but dependency all our lives? I know so well what becomes of unmarried women who aren't prepared to occupy a position. I've seen such pitiful cases in the South—barely tolerated spinsters living upon the grudging patronage of sister's husband or brother's wife!—stuck away in some little mouse-trap of a room—encouraged by one in-law to visit another—little birdlike women without any nest—eating the crust of humility all their life!
Is that the future that we've mapped out for ourselves?

I swear it's the only alternative I can think of!

It isn't a very pleasant alternative, is it?

Of course—some girls *do marry*.

(LAURA twists her hands nervously.)

Haven't you ever liked some boy?

LAURA. Yes. I liked one once. *(Rises.)* I came across his picture a while ago.

AMANDA *(with some interest)*. He gave you his picture?

LAURA. No, it's in the year-book.

AMANDA *(disappointed)*. Oh—a high-school boy.

(SCREEN IMAGE: JIM AS HIGH-SCHOOL HERO BEARING A SILVER CUP.)

LAURA. Yes. His name was Jim. *(LAURA lifts the heavy annual from the claw-foot table.)* Here he is in *The Pirates of Penzance*.

AMANDA *(absently)*. The what?

LAURA. The operetta the senior class put on. He had a wonderful voice and we sat across the aisle from each other Mondays, Wednesdays and Fridays in the Aud. Here he is with the silver cup for debating! See his grin?

AMANDA *(absently)*. He must have had a jolly disposition.

LAURA. He used to call me—Blue Roses.

(IMAGE: BLUE ROSES.)

AMANDA. Why did he call you such a name as that?

LAURA. When I had that attack of pleurosis —he asked me what was the matter when I came back. I said pleurosis—he thought that I said Blue Roses! So that's what he always called me after that. Whenever he saw me, he'd holler, "Hello, Blue Roses!" I didn't care for the girl that he went out with. Emily Meisenbach. Emily was the best-dressed girl at Soldan. She never struck me, though, as being sincere . . . It says in the Personal Section—they're engaged. That's—six years ago! They must be married by now.

AMANDA. Girls that aren't cut out for business careers usually wind up married to some nice man. *(Gets up with a spark of revival.)* Sister, that's what you'll do!

(LAURA utters a startled, doubtful laugh. She reaches quickly for a piece of glass.)

LAURA. But, Mother—

AMANDA. Yes? *(Crossing to photograph.)*

LAURA *(in a tone of frightened apology).* I'm—crippled!

(IMAGE: SCREEN.)

AMANDA. Nonsense! Laura, I've told you never, never to use that word. Why, you're not crippled, you just have a little defect—hardly noticeable, even! When people have some slight disadvantage like that, they cultivate other things to make up for it—develop charm—and vivacity—and—*charm!* That's all you have to do! *(She turns again to the photograph.)* One thing your father had *plenty of*—was *charm!*

(TOM motions to the fiddle in the wings.)

THE SCENE FADES OUT WITH MUSIC

SCENE III

LEGEND ON SCREEN: "AFTER THE FIASCO—"
TOM *speaks from the fire-escape landing.*

TOM. After the fiasco at Rubicam's Business College, the idea of getting a gentleman caller for Laura began to play a more and more important part in Mother's calculations.

It became an obsession. Like some archetype of the universal unconscious, the image of the gentleman caller haunted our small apartment. . . .

(IMAGE: YOUNG MAN AT DOOR WITH FLOWERS.)

An evening at home rarely passed without some allusion to this image, this sceptre, this hope. . . .

Even when he wasn't mentioned, his presence hung in Mother's preoccupied look and in my sister's frightened, apologetic manner—hung like a sentence passed upon the Wingfields!

Mother was a woman of action as well as words.

She began to take logical steps in the planned direction.

Late that winter and in the early spring—realizing that extra money would be needed to properly feather the nest and plume the bird—she conducted a vigorous campaign on the telephone, roping in subscribers to one of those magazines for matrons called *The Home-maker's Companion,* the type of journal that features the serialized sublimations of ladies of letters who think in terms of delicate cup-like breasts, slim, tapering waists, rich, creamy thighs, eyes like wood-smoke in autumn, fingers that soothe and caress like strains of music, bodies as powerful as Etruscan sculpture.

(SCREEN IMAGE: GLAMOR MAGAZINE COVER.)

(AMANDA enters with phone on long extension cord. She is spotted in the dim stage.)

AMANDA. Ida Scott? This is Amanda Wingfield!

We *missed* you at the D.A.R. last Monday! I said to myself: She's probably suffering with that sinus condition! How is that sinus condition?

Horrors! Heaven have mercy!—You're a Christian martyr, yes, that's what you are, a Christian martyr!

Well, I just now happened to notice that your subscription to the *Companion's* about to expire! Yes, it expires with the next issue, honey!—just when that wonderful new serial by Bessie Mae Hopper is getting off to such an exciting start. Oh, honey, it's something that you can't miss! You remember how *Gone With the Wind* took everybody by storm? You simply couldn't go out if you hadn't read it. All everybody *talked* was Scarlett O'Hara. Well, this is a book that critics already compare to *Gone With the Wind.* It's the *Gone With the Wind* of the post-World War generation!—What?—Burning?—Oh, honey, don't let them burn, go take a look in the oven and I'll hold the wire! Heavens—I think she's hung up!

DIM OUT

(LEGEND ON SCREEN: "YOU THINK I'M IN LOVE WITH CONTINENTAL SHOEMAKERS?")

(Before the stage is lighted, the violent voices of TOM and AMANDA are heard.)

(They are quarrelling behind the portieres. In front of them stands LAURA with clenched hands and panicky expression)

(A clear pool of light on her figure throughout this scene.)

TOM. What in Christ's name am I—

AMANDA *(shrilly).* Don't you use that—

TOM. Supposed to do!

AMANDA. Expression! Not in my—

TOM. Ohhh!

AMANDA. Presence! Have you gone out of your senses?

TOM. I have, that's true, *driven* out!

AMANDA. What is the matter with you, you —big—big—IDIOT!

TOM. Look!—I've got *no thing,* no single thing—

AMANDA. Lower your voice!

TOM. In my life here that I can call my OWN! Everything is—

AMANDA. Stop that shouting!

TOM. Yesterday you confiscated my books! You had the nerve to—

AMANDA. I took that horrible novel back to the library—yes! That hideous book by that insane Mr. Lawrence. *(TOM laughs wildly.)* I cannot control the output of diseased minds or people who cater to them— *(TOM laughs still more wildly.)* BUT I WON'T ALLOW SUCH FILTH BROUGHT INTO MY HOUSE! No, no, no, no, no!

TOM. House, house! Who pays rent on it, who makes a slave of himself to—

AMANDA *(fairly screeching).* Don't you DARE to—

TOM. No, no, *I* mustn't say things! *I've* got to just—

AMANDA. Let me tell you—

TOM. I don't want to hear any more! *(He tears the portieres open. The upstage area is lit with a turgid smoky red glow.)*

(AMANDA's hair is in metal curlers and she wears a very old bathrobe, much too large for her slight figure, a relic of the faithless Mr. Wingfield.)

(An upright typewriter and a wild disarray of manuscripts is on the drop-leaf table. The quarrel was probably precipitated by AMANDA's interruption of his creative labor.

A chair is lying overthrown on the floor.)

(Their gesticulating shadows are cast on the ceiling by the fiery glow.)

AMANDA. You *will* hear more, you—

TOM. No, I won't hear more, I'm going out!

AMANDA. You come right back in—

TOM. Out, out, out! Because I'm—

AMANDA. Come back here, Tom Wingfield! I'm not through talking to you!

TOM. Oh, go—

LAURA *(desperately).* —Tom!

AMANDA. You're going to listen, and no more insolence from you! I'm at the end of my patience!

(He comes back toward her.)

TOM. What do you think I'm at? Aren't I supposed to have any patience to reach the end of, Mother? I know, I know. It seems unimportant to you, what I'm *doing*— what I *want* to do—having a little *difference* between them! You don't think that—

AMANDA. I think you've been doing things that you're ashamed of. That's why you act like this. I don't believe that you go every night to the movies. Nobody goes to the movies night after night. Nobody in their right minds goes to the movies as often as you pretend to. People don't go to the movies at nearly midnight, and movies don't let out at two A.M. Come in stumbling. Muttering to yourself like a maniac! You get three hours' sleep and then go to work. Oh, I can picture the way you're doing down there. Moping, doping, because you're in no condition.

TOM *(wildly).* No, I'm in no condition!

AMANDA. What right have you got to jeopardize your job? Jeopardize the security of us all? How do you think we'd manage if you were—

TOM. Listen! You think I'm crazy *about* the *warehouse?* *(He bends fiercely toward her slight figure.)* You think I'm in love with the Continental Shoemakers? You think I want to spend fifty-five *years* down there in that—*celotex interior!* with— *fluorescent—tubes!* Look! I'd rather somebody picked up a crowbar and battered out my brains—than go back mornings! I *go!*

Every time you come in yelling that God damn *"Rise and Shine!" "Rise and Shine!"* I say to myself, "How *lucky dead* people are!" But I get up. I *go!* For sixty-five dollars a month I give up all that I dream of doing and being *ever!* And you say self—*self's* all I ever think of. Why, listen, if self is what I thought of, Mother, I'd be where he is—GONE! *(Pointing to father's picture.)* As far as the system of transportation reaches! *(He starts past her. She grabs his arm.)* Don't grab at me, Mother!

AMANDA. Where are you going?

TOM. I'm going to the *movies!*

AMANDA. I don't believe that lie!

TOM *(crouching toward her, overtowering her tiny figure. She backs away, gasping).* I'm going to opium dens! Yes, opium dens, dens of vice and criminals' hang-outs, Mother. I've joined the Hogan gang, I'm a hired assassin, I carry a tommy-gun in a violin case! I run a string of cat-houses in the Valley! They call me Killer, Killer Wingfield, I'm leading a double-life, a simple, honest warehouse worker by day, by night a dynamic *czar* of the *underworld, Mother.* I go to gambling casinos, I spin away fortunes on the roulette table! I wear a patch over one eye and a false mustache, sometimes I put on green whiskers. On those occasions they call me—*El Diablo!* Oh, I could tell you things to make you sleepless! My enemies plan to dynamite this place. They're going to blow us all sky-high some night! I'll be glad, very happy, and so will you! You'll go up, up on a broomstick, over Blue Mountain with seventeen gentlemen callers! You ugly —babbling old—*witch.* . . . *(He goes through a series of violent, clumsy movements, seizing his overcoat, lunging to the door, pulling it fiercely open. The women watch him, aghast. His arm catches in the sleeve of the coat as he struggles to pull it on. For a moment he is pinioned by the bulky garment. With an outraged groan he tears the coat off again, splitting the shoulder of it, and hurls it across the room. It strikes against the shelf of* LAURA'S *glass collection, there is a tinkle of shattering glass.* LAURA *cries out as if wounded.)*

*(*MUSIC. LEGEND: "THE GLASS MENAGERIE."*)*

LAURA *(shrilly).* My glass!—menagerie. . . . *(She covers her face and turns away.)*

(But AMANDA *is still stunned and stupefied by the "ugly witch" so that she barely notices this occurrence. Now she recovers her speech.)*

AMANDA *(in an awful voice).* I won't speak to you—until you apologize! *(She crosses through portieres and draws them together behind her.* TOM *is left with* LAURA. LAURA *clings weakly to the mantel with her face averted.* TOM *stares at her stupidly for a moment. Then he crosses to shelf. Drops awkwardly on his knees to collect the fallen glass, glancing at* LAURA *as if he would speak but couldn't.)*

("The Glass Menagerie" steals in as)

THE SCENE DIMS OUT

SCENE IV

The interior is dark. Faint light in the alley.

A deep-voiced bell in a church is tolling the hour of five as the scene commences.

TOM appears at the top of the alley. After each solemn boom of the bell in the tower, he shakes a little noise-maker or rattle as if to express the tiny spasm of man in contrast to the sustained power and dignity of the Almighty. This and the unsteadiness of his advance makes it evident that he has been drinking.

As he climbs the few steps to the fire-escape landing light steals up inside. LAURA *appears in night-dress, observing* TOM'S *empty bed in the front room.*

TOM fishes in his pockets for door-key, removing a motley assortment of articles in the search, including a perfect shower of movie-ticket stubs and an empty bottle. At last he finds the key, but just as he is about to insert it, it slips from his fingers. He strikes a match and crouches below the door.

TOM *(bitterly).* One crack—and it falls through!

*(*LAURA *opens the door.)*

LAURA. Tom! Tom, what are you doing?

TOM. Looking for a door-key.

LAURA. Where have you been all this time?

TOM. I have been to the movies.

LAURA. All this time at the movies?

TOM. There was a very long program. There was a Garbo picture and a Mickey Mouse and a travelogue and a newsreel and a preview of coming attractions. And there was an organ solo and a collection for the milk-fund—simultaneously—which ended up in a terrible fight between a fat lady and an usher!

LAURA (innocently). Did you have to stay through everything?

TOM. Of course! And, oh, I forgot! There was a big stage show! The headliner on this stage show was Malvolio the Magician. He performed wonderful tricks, many of them, such as pouring water back and forth between pitchers. First it turned to wine and then it turned to beer and then it turned to whiskey. I know it was whiskey it finally turned into because he needed somebody to come up out of the audience to help him, and I came up—both shows! It was Kentucky Straight Bourbon. A very generous fellow, he gave souvenirs. (He pulls from his back pocket a shimmering rainbow-colored scarf.) He gave me this. This is his magic scarf. You can have it, Laura. You wave it over a canary cage and you get a bowl of gold-fish. You wave it over the gold-fish bowl and they fly away canaries. . . . But the wonderfullest trick of all was the coffin trick. We nailed him into a coffin and he got out of the coffin without removing one nail. (He has come inside.) There is a trick that would come in handy for me—get me out of this 2 by 4 situation! (Flops onto bed and starts removing shoes.)

LAURA. Tom—Shhh!

TOM. What're you shushing me for?

LAURA. You'll wake up Mother.

TOM. Goody, goody! Pay 'er back for all those "Rise an' Shines." (Lies down, groaning.) You know it don't take much intelligence to get yourself into a nailed-up coffin, Laura. But who in hell ever got himself out of one without removing one nail?

(As if in answer, the father's grinning photograph lights up.)

SCENE DIMS OUT

(Immediately following: The church bell is heard striking six. At the sixth stroke the alarm clock goes off in AMANDA's room, and after a few moments we hear her calling: "Rise and Shine! Rise and Shine! Laura, go tell your brother to rise and shine!")

TOM (sitting up slowly). I'll rise—but I won't shine.

(The light increases.)

AMANDA. Laura, tell your brother his coffee is ready.

(LAURA slips into front room.)

LAURA. Tom!—It's nearly seven. Don't make Mother nervous. (He stares at her stupidly. Beseechingly.) Tom, speak to Mother this morning. Make up with her, apologize, speak to her!

TOM. She won't to me. It's her that started not speaking.

LAURA. If you just say you're sorry she'll start speaking.

TOM. Her not speaking—is that such a tragedy?

LAURA. Please—please!

AMANDA (calling from kitchenette). Laura, are you going to do what I asked you to do, or do I have to get dressed and go out myself?

LAURA. Going, going—soon as I get on my coat! (She pulls on a shapless felt hat with nervous, jerky movement, pleadingly glancing at TOM. Rushes awkwardly for coat. The coat is one of AMANDA's, inaccurately made-over, the sleeves too short for LAURA.) Butter and what else?

AMANDA (entering upstage). Just butter. Tell them to charge it.

LAURA. Mother, they make such faces when I do that.

AMANDA. Sticks and stones can break our bones, but the expression on Mr. Garfinkel's face won't harm us! Tell your brother his coffee is getting cold.

LAURA (at door). Do what I asked you, will you, will you, Tom?

(He looks sullenly away.)

AMANDA. Laura, go now or just don't go at all!

LAURA (*rushing out*). Going—going! (*A second later she cries out.* TOM *springs up and crosses to door.* AMANDA *rushes anxiously in.* TOM *opens the door.*)

TOM. Laura?

LAURA. I'm all right. I slipped, but I'm all right.

AMANDA (*peering anxiously after her*). If anyone breaks a leg on those fire-escape steps, the landlord ought to be sued for every cent he possesses! (*She shuts door. Remembers she isn't speaking and returns to other room.*)

(*As* TOM *enters listlessly for his coffee, she turns her back to him and stands rigidly facing the window on the gloomy gray vault of the areaway. Its light on her face with its aged but childish features is cruelly sharp, satirical as a Daumier print.*)

(MUSIC UNDER: "AVE MARIA.")

(TOM *glances sheepishly but sullenly at her averted figure and slumps at the table. The coffee is scalding hot; he sips it and gasps and spits it back in the cup. At his gasp,* AMANDA *catches her breath and half turns. Then catches herself and turns back to window.*)

(TOM *blows on his coffee, glancing sidewise at his mother. She clears her throat.* TOM *clears his. He starts to rise. Sinks back down again, scratches his head, clears his throat again.* AMANDA *coughs.* TOM *raises his cup in both hands to blow on it, his eyes staring over the rim of it at his mother for several moments. Then he slowly sets the cup down and awkwardly and hesitantly rises from the chair.*)

TOM (*hoarsely*). Mother. I—I apologize, Mother. (AMANDA *draws a quick, shuddering breath. Her face works grotesquely. She breaks into childlike tears.*) I'm sorry for what I said, for everything that I said, I didn't mean it.

AMANDA (*sobbingly*). My devotion has made me a witch and so I make myself hateful to my children!

TOM. *No, you don't.*

AMANDA. I worry so much, don't sleep, it makes me nervous!

TOM (*gently*). I understand that.

AMANDA. I've had to put up a solitary battle all these years. But you're my right-

hand bower! Don't fall down, don't fail!

TOM (*gently*). I try, Mother.

AMANDA (*with great enthusiasm*). Try and you will SUCCEED! (*The notion makes her breathless.*) Why, you—you're just *full* of natural endowments! Both of my children —they're *unusual* children! Don't you think I know it? I'm so—*proud!* Happy and—feel I've—so much to be thankful for but— Promise me one thing, Son!

TOM. What, Mother?

AMANDA. Promise, Son, you'll never be a drunkard!

TOM (*turns to her grinning*). I will never be a drunkard, Mother.

AMANDA. That's what frightened me so, that you'd be drinking! Eat a bowl of Purina!

TOM. Just coffee, Mother.

AMANDA. Shredded wheat biscuit?

TOM. No. No, Mother, just coffee.

AMANDA. You can't put in a day's work on an empty stomach. You've got ten minutes—don't gulp! Drinking too-hot liquids makes cancer of the stomach. . . . Put cream in.

TOM. No, thank you.

AMANDA. To cool it.

TOM. No! No, thank you, I want it black.

AMANDA. I know, but it's not good for you. We have to do all that we can to build ourselves up. In these trying times we live in, all that we have to cling to is—each other. . . . That's why it's so important to— Tom, I— I sent out your sister so I could discuss something with you. If you hadn't spoken I would have spoken to you. (*Sits down.*)

TOM (*gently*). What is it, Mother, that you want to discuss?

AMANDA. *Laura!*

(TOM *puts his cup down slowly.*)

(LEGEND ON SCREEN: "LAURA.")

(MUSIC: "THE GLASS MENAGERIE.")

TOM. —Oh.—Laura . . .

AMANDA (*touching his sleeve*). You know how Laura is. So quiet but—still water runs deep! She notices things and I think she—broods about them. (TOM *looks up*.) A few days ago I came in and she was crying.

TOM. What about?

AMANDA. You.

TOM. Me?

AMANDA. She has an idea that you're not happy here.

TOM. What gave her that idea?

AMANDA. What gives her any idea? However, you do act strangely. I—I'm not criticizing, understand *that!* I know your ambitions do not lie in the warehouse, that like everybody in the whole wide world—you've had to—make sacrifices, but—Tom—Tom—life's not easy, it calls for Spartan endurance! There's so many things in my heart that I cannot describe to you! I've never told you but I—*loved* your father. . . .

TOM (*gently*). I know that, Mother.

AMANDA. And you—when I see you taking after his ways! Staying out late—and—well, you *had* been drinking the night you were in that—terrifying condition! Laura says that you hate the apartment and that you go out nights to get away from it! Is that true, Tom?

TOM. No. You say there's so much in your heart that you can't describe to me. That's true of me, too. There's so much in my heart that I can't describe to *you!* So let's respect each other's—

AMANDA. But, why—*why,* Tom—are you always so *restless?* Where do you *go* to, nights?

TOM. I—go to the movies.

AMANDA. Why do you go to the movies so much, Tom?

TOM. I go to the movies because—I like adventure. Adventure is something I don't have much of at work, so I go to the movies.

AMANDA. But, Tom, you go to the movies *entirely* too *much!*

TOM. I like a lot of adventure.

(AMANDA *looks baffled, then hurt. As the familiar inquisition resumes he becomes hard and impatient again.* AMANDA *slips back into her querulous attitude toward him.*)

(IMAGE ON SCREEN: SAILING VESSEL WITH JOLLY ROGER.)

AMANDA. Most young men find adventure in their careers.

TOM. Then most young men are not employed in a warehouse.

AMANDA. The world is full of young men employed in warehouses and offices and factories.

TOM. Do all of them find adventure in their careers?

AMANDA. They do or they do without it! Not everybody has a craze for adventure.

TOM. Man is by instinct a lover, a hunter, a fighter, and none of those instincts are given much play at the warehouse!

AMANDA. Man is by instinct! Don't quote instinct to me! Instinct is something that people have got away from! It belongs to animals! Christian adults don't want it!

TOM. What do Christian adults want, then, Mother?

AMANDA. Superior things! Things of the mind and the spirit! Only animals have to satisfy instincts! Surely your aims are somewhat higher than theirs! Than monkeys—pigs—

TOM. I reckon they're not.

AMANDA. You're joking. However, that isn't what I wanted to discuss.

TOM (*rising*). I haven't much time.

AMANDA (*pushing his shoulders*). Sit down.

TOM. You want me to punch in red at the warehouse, Mother?

AMANDA. You have five minutes. I want to talk about Laura.

(LEGEND: "PLANS AND PROVISIONS.")

TOM. All right! What about Laura?

AMANDA. We have to be making some plans and provisions for her. She's older than you, two years, and nothing has happened. She just drifts along doing nothing. It frightens me terribly how she just drifts along.

TOM. I guess she's the type that people call home girls.

AMANDA. There's no such type, and if there is, it's a pity! That is unless the home is hers, with a husband!

TOM. What?

AMANDA. Oh, I can see the handwriting on the wall as plain as I see the nose in front of my face! It's terrifying!

More and more you remind me of your father! He was out all hours without explanation!—Then *left! Good-bye!*

And me with the bag to hold. I saw that letter you got from the Merchant Marine. I know what you're dreaming of. I'm not standing here blindfolded.

Very well, then. Then *do* it!

But not till there's somebody to take your place.

TOM. What do you mean?

AMANDA. I mean that as soon as Laura has got somebody to take care of her, married, a home of her own, independent—why, then you'll be free to go wherever you please, on land, on sea, whichever way the wind blows you!

But until that time you've got to look out for your sister. I don't say me because I'm old and don't matter! I say for your sister because she's young and dependent.

I put her in business college—a dismal failure! Frightened her so it made her sick at the stomach.

I took her over to the Young People's League at the church. Another fiasco. She spoke to nobody, nobody spoke to her. Now all she does is fool with those pieces of glass and play those worn-out records. What kind of a life is that for a girl to lead?

TOM. What can I do about it?

AMANDA. Overcome selfishness! Self, self, self is all that you ever think of!

(TOM *springs up and crosses to get his coat. It is ugly and bulky. He pulls on a cap with earmuffs.*)

Where is your muffler? Put your wool muffler on!

(*He snatches it angrily from the closet and tosses it around his neck and pulls both ends tight.*)

Tom! I haven't said what I had in mind to ask you.

TOM. I'm too late to—

AMANDA (*catching his arm—very importunately. Then shyly*). Down at the warehouse, aren't there some—nice young men?

TOM. No!

AMANDA. There *must* be—*some*. . . .

TOM. Mother—

(*Gesture.*)

AMANDA. Find out one that's clean-living —doesn't drink and—ask him out for sister!

TOM. What?

AMANDA. For *sister!* To *meet!* Get *acquainted!*

TOM (*stamping to door*). Oh, my *go-osh!*

AMANDA. Will you? (*He opens door. Imploringly.*) Will you? (*He starts down.*) Will you? *Will* you, dear?

TOM (*calling back*). YES!

(AMANDA *closes the door hesitantly and with a troubled but faintly hopeful expression.*)

(SCREEN IMAGE: GLAMOR MAGAZINE COVER.)

(*Spot* AMANDA *at phone.*)

AMANDA. Ella Cartwright? This is Amanda Wingfield!

How are you, honey?

How is that kidney condition?

(*Count five.*)

Horrors!

(*Count five.*)

You're a Christian martyr, yes, honey, that's what you are, a Christian martyr! Well, I just now happened to notice in my little red book that your subscription to the *Companion* has just run out! I knew that you wouldn't want to miss out on the wonderful serial starting in this new issue. It's by Bessie Mae Hopper, the first thing she's written since *Honeymoon for Three.*

Wasn't that a strange and interesting story? Well, this one is even lovelier, I believe. It has a sophisticated, society background. It's all about the horsey set on Long Island!

FADE OUT

SCENE V

LEGEND ON SCREEN: "ANNUNCIATION." *Fade with music.*
It is early dusk of a spring evening. Supper has just been finished in the Wingfield apartment. AMANDA *and* LAURA *in light-colored dresses are removing dishes from the table, in the upstage area, which is shadowy, their movements formalized almost as a dance or ritual, their moving forms as pale and silent as moths.*
TOM, *in white shirt and trousers, rises from the table and crosses toward the fire-escape.*

AMANDA *(as he passes her).* Son, will you do me a favor?

TOM. What?

AMANDA. Comb your hair! You look so pretty when your hair is combed! (TOM *slouches on sofa with evening paper. Enormous caption "Franco Triumphs.")* There is only one respect in which I would like you to emulate your father.

TOM. What respect is that?

AMANDA. The care he always took of his appearance. He never allowed himself to look untidy. *(He throws down the paper and crosses to fire-escape.)* Where are you going?

TOM. I'm going out to smoke.

AMANDA. You smoke too much. A pack a day at fifteen cents a pack. How much would that amount to in a month? Thirty times fifteen is how much, Tom? Figure it out and you will be astounded at what you could save. Enough to give you a night-school course in accounting at Washington U! Just think what a wonderful thing that would be for you, Son!

(TOM is unmoved by the thought.)

TOM. I'd rather smoke. *(He steps out on landing, letting the screen door slam.)*

AMANDA *(sharply).* I know! That's the tragedy of it. . . . *(Alone, she turns to look at her husband's picture.)*

(DANCE MUSIC: "ALL THE WORLD IS WAITING FOR THE SUNSHINE!")

TOM *(to the audience).* Across the alley from us was the Paradise Dance Hall. On evenings in spring the windows and doors were open and the music came outdoors. Sometimes the lights were turned out except for a large glass sphere that hung from the ceiling. It would turn slowly about and filter the dusk with delicate rainbow colors. Then the orchestra played a waltz or a tango, something that had a slow and sensuous rhythm. Couples would come outside, to the relative privacy of the alley. You could see them kissing behind ash-pits and telephone poles.

This was the compensation for lives that passed like mine, without any change or adventure.

Adventure and change were imminent in this year. They were waiting around the corner for all these kids.

Suspended in the mist over Berchtesgaden, caught in the folds of Chamberlain's umbrella—

In Spain there was Guernica!

But here there was only hot swing music and liquor, dance halls, bars, and movies, and sex that hung in the gloom like a chandelier and flooded the world with brief, deceptive rainbows. . . .

All the world was waiting for bombardments!

(AMANDA *turns from the picture and comes outside.)*

AMANDA *(sighing).* A fire-escape landing's a poor excuse for a porch. *(She spreads a newspaper on a step and sits down, gracefully and demurely as if she were settling into a swing on a Mississippi veranda.)* What are you looking at?

TOM. The moon.

AMANDA. Is there a moon this evening?

TOM. It's rising over Garfinkel's Delicatessen.

AMANDA. So it is! A little silver slipper of a moon. Have you made a wish on it yet?

TOM. Um-hum.

AMANDA. What did you wish for?

TOM. That's a secret.

AMANDA. A secret, huh? Well, I won't tell mine either. I will be just as mysterious as you.

TOM. I bet I can guess what yours is.

AMANDA. Is my head so transparent?

TOM. You're not a sphinx.

AMANDA. No, I don't have secrets. I'll tell you what I wished for on the moon. Success and happiness for my precious children! I wish for that whenever there's a moon, and when there isn't a moon, I wish it, too.

TOM. I thought perhaps you wished for a gentleman caller.

AMANDA. Why do you say that?

TOM. Don't you remember asking me to fetch one?

AMANDA. I remember suggesting that it would be nice for your sister if you brought home some nice young man from the warehouse. I think that I've made that suggestion more than once.

TOM. Yes, you have made it repeatedly.

AMANDA. Well?

TOM. We are going to have one.

AMANDA. *What?*

TOM. A gentleman caller!

(THE ANNUNCIATION IS CELEBRATED WITH MUSIC.)

(AMANDA *rises.*)

(IMAGE ON SCREEN: CALLER WITH BOUQUET.)

AMANDA. You mean you have asked some nice young man to come over?

TOM. Yep. I've asked him to dinner.

AMANDA. You really did?

TOM. I did!

AMANDA. You did, and did he—*accept?*

TOM. He did!

AMANDA. Well, well—well, well! That's —lovely!

TOM. I thought that you would be pleased.

AMANDA. It's definite, then?

TOM. Very definite.

AMANDA. Soon?

TOM. Very soon.

AMANDA. For heaven's sake, stop putting on and tell me some things, will you?

TOM. What things do you want me to tell you?

AMANDA. *Naturally* I would like to know when he's *coming!*

TOM. He's coming tomorrow.

AMANDA. *Tomorrow?*

TOM. Yep. Tomorrow.

AMANDA. But, Tom!

TOM. Yes, Mother?

AMANDA. Tomorrow gives me no time!

TOM. Time for what?

AMANDA. Preparations! Why didn't you phone me at once, as soon as you asked him, the minute that he accepted? Then, don't you see, I could have been getting ready!

TOM. You don't have to make any fuss.

AMANDA. Oh, Tom, Tom, Tom, of course I have to make a fuss! I want things nice, not sloppy! Not thrown together. I'll certainly have to do some fast thinking, won't I?

TOM. I don't see why you have to think at all.

AMANDA. You just don't know. We can't have a gentleman caller in a pig-sty! All my wedding silver has to be polished, the monogrammed table linen ought to be laundered! The windows have to be washed and fresh curtains put up. And how about clothes? We have to *wear* something, don't we?

TOM. Mother, this boy is no one to make a fuss over!

AMANDA. Do you realize he's the first young man we've introduced to your sister? It's terrible, dreadful, disgraceful that poor little sister has never received a single gentleman caller! Tom, come inside! *(She opens the screen door.)*

TOM. What for?

AMANDA. I want to ask you some things.

TOM. If you're going to make such a fuss, I'll call it off, I'll tell him not to come!

AMANDA. You certainly won't do anything of the kind. Nothing offends people worse than broken engagements. It simply means I'll have to work like a Turk! We won't be brilliant, but we will pass inspection. Come on inside. *(TOM follows, groaning.)* Sit down.

TOM. Any particular place you would like me to sit?

AMANDA. Thank heavens I've got that new sofa! I'm also making payments on a floor lamp I'll have sent out! And put the chintz covers on, they'll brighten things up! Of course I'd hoped to have these walls repapered. . . . What is the young man's name?

TOM. His name is O'Connor.

AMANDA. That, of course, means fish—tomorrow is Friday! I'll have that salmon loaf—with Durkee's dressing! What does he do? He works at the warehouse?

TOM. Of course! How else would I—

AMANDA. Tom, he—doesn't drink?

TOM. Why do you ask me that?

AMANDA. Your father *did*!

TOM. Don't get started on that!

AMANDA. He *does* drink, then?

TOM. Not that I know of!

AMANDA. Make sure, be certain! The last thing I want for my daughter's a boy who drinks!

TOM. Aren't you being a little bit premature? Mr. O'Connor has not yet appeared or the scene!

AMANDA. But will tomorrow. To meet your sister, and what do I know about his character? Nothing! Old maids are better off than wives of drunkards!

TOM. Oh, my God!

AMANDA. Be still!

TOM *(leaning forward to whisper).* Lots of fellows meet girls whom they don't marry!

AMANDA. Oh, talk sensibly, Tom—and don't be sarcastic! *(She has gotten a hairbrush.)*

TOM. What are you doing?

AMANDA. I'm brushing that cow-lick down! What is this young man's position at the warehouse?

TOM *(submitting grimly to the brush and the interrogation).* This young man's position is that of a shipping clerk, Mother.

AMANDA. Sounds to me like a fairly responsible job, the sort of a job *you* would be in if you just had more *get-up*. What is his salary? Have you any idea?

TOM. I would judge it to be approximately eighty-five dollars a month.

AMANDA. Well—not princely, but—

TOM. Twenty more than I make.

AMANDA. Yes, how well I know! But for a family man, eighty-five dollars a month is not much more than you can just get by on. . . .

TOM. Yes, but Mr. O'Connor is not a family man.

AMANDA. He might be, mightn't he? Some time in the future?

TOM. I see. Plans and provisions.

AMANDA. You are the only young man that I know of who ignores the fact that the future becomes the present, the present the past and the past turns into everlasting regret if you don't plan for it!

TOM. I will think that over and see what I can make of it.

AMANDA. Don't be supercilious with your Mother! Tell me some more about this—what do you call him?

TOM. James D. O'Connor. The D. is for Delaney.

AMANDA. Irish on *both* sides! *Gracious!* And doesn't drink?

TOM. Shall I call him up and ask him right this minute?

AMANDA. The only way to find out about those things is to make discreet inquiries at the proper moment. When I was a girl in Blue Mountain and it was suspected that a young man drank, the girl whose attentions he had been receiving, if any girl *was,* would sometimes speak to the minister of his church, or rather her father would if her father was living, and sort of feel out on the young man's character. That is the way such things are discreetly handled to keep a young woman from making a tragic mistake!

TOM. Then how did you happen to make a tragic mistake?

AMANDA. That innocent look of your father's had everyone fooled!

He *smiled*—the world was *enchanted!*

No girl can do worse than put herself at the mercy of a handsome appearance!

I hope that Mr. O'Connor is not too good-looking.

TOM. No, he's not too good-looking. He's covered with freckles and hasn't too much of a nose.

AMANDA. He's not right-down homely, though?

TOM. Not right-down homely. Just medium homely, I'd say.

AMANDA. Character's what to look for in a man.

TOM. That's what I've always said, Mother.

AMANDA. You never said anything of the kind and I suspect you would never give it a thought.

TOM. Don't be so suspicious of me.

AMANDA. At least I hope he's the type that's up and coming.

TOM. I think he really goes in for self-improvement.

AMANDA. What reason have you to think so?

TOM. He goes to night school.

AMANDA (*beaming*). Splendid! What does he do, I mean study?

TOM. Radio engineering and public speaking!

AMANDA. Then he has visions of being advanced in the world!

Any young man who studies public speaking is aiming to have an executive job some day!

And radio engineering? A thing for the future!

Both of these facts are very illuminating. Those are the sort of things that a mother should know concerning any young man who comes to call on her daughter. Seriously or—not.

TOM. One little warning. He doesn't know about Laura. I didn't let on that we had dark ulterior motives. I just said, why don't you come and have dinner with us? He said okay and that was the whole conversation.

AMANDA. I bet it was! You're eloquent as an oyster.

However, he'll know about Laura when he gets here. When he sees how lovely and sweet and pretty she is, he'll thank his lucky stars he was asked to dinner.

TOM. Mother, you mustn't expect too much of Laura.

AMANDA. What do you mean?

TOM. Laura seems all those things to you and me because she's ours and we love her. We don't even notice she's crippled any more.

AMANDA. Don't say crippled! You know that I never allow that word to be used!

TOM. But face facts, Mother. She is and—that's not all—

AMANDA. What do you mean "not all"?

TOM. Laura is very different from other girls.

AMANDA. I think the difference is all to her advantage.

TOM. Not quite all—in the eyes of others—strangers—she's terribly shy and lives in a world of her own and those things make her seem a little peculiar to people outside the house.

AMANDA. Don't say peculiar.

TOM. Face the facts. She is.

(THE DANCE-HALL MUSIC CHANGES TO A TANGO THAT HAS A MINOR AND SOMEWHAT OMINOUS TONE.)

AMANDA. In what way is she peculiar—may I ask?

TOM (gently). She lives in a world of her own—a world of—little glass ornaments, Mother. . . . (Gets up. AMANDA remains holding brush, looking at him, troubled.) She plays old phonograph records and— that's about all— (He glances at himself in the mirror and crosses to door.)

AMANDA (sharply). Where are you going?

TOM. I'm going to the movies. (Out screen door.)

AMANDA. Not to the movies, every night to the movies! (Follows quickly to screen door.) I don't believe you always go to the movies! (He is gone. AMANDA looks worriedly after him for a moment. Then vitality and optimism return and she turns from the door. Crossing to portieres.) Laura! Laura! (LAURA answers from kitchenette.)

LAURA. Yes, Mother.

AMANDA. Let those dishes go and come in front! (LAURA appears with dish towel. Gaily.) Laura, come here and make a wish on the moon!

(SCREEN IMAGE: MOON.)

LAURA (entering). Moon—moon?

AMANDA. A little silver slipper of a moon. Look over your left shoulder, Laura, and make a wish!

(LAURA looks faintly puzzled as if called out of sleep. AMANDA seizes her shoulders and turns her at an angle by the door.)

Now!

Now, darling, wish!

LAURA. What shall I wish for, Mother?

AMANDA (her voice trembling and her eyes suddenly filling with tears). Happiness! Good fortune!

(The violin rises and the stage dims out.)

CURTAIN

SCENE VI

IMAGE: HIGH SCHOOL HERO.

TOM. And so the following evening I brought Jim home to dinner. I had known Jim slightly in high school. In high school Jim was a hero. He had tremendous Irish good nature and vitality with the scrubbed and polished look of white chinaware. He seemed to move in a continual spotlight. He was a star in basketball, captain of the debating club, president of the senior class and the glee club and he sang the male lead in the annual light operas. He was always running or bounding, never just walking. He seemed always at the point of defeating the law of gravity. He was shooting with such velocity through his adolescence that you would logically expect him to arrive at nothing short of the White House by the time he was thirty. But Jim apparently ran into more interference after his graduation from Soldan. His speed had definitely slowed. Six years after he left high school he was holding a job that wasn't much better than mine.

(IMAGE: CLERK.)

He was the only one at the warehouse with whom I was on friendly terms. I was valuable to him as someone who could remember his former glory, who had seen him win basketball games and the silver cup in debating. He knew of my secret practice of retiring to a cabinet of the wash-room to work on poems when business was slack in the warehouse. He called me Shakespeare. And while the other boys in the warehouse regarded me with suspicious hostility, Jim took a humorous attitude toward me. Gradually his attitude affected the others, their hostility wore off and they also began to smile at me as people smile at an oddly fashioned dog who trots across their path at some distance.

I knew that Jim and Laura had known each other at Soldan, and I had heard Laura speak admiringly of his voice. I didn't know if Jim remembered her or not. In high school Laura had been as unobtrusive as Jim had been astonishing. If he did remember Laura, it was not as my sister, for when I asked him to dinner, he grinned and said, "You know, Shakespeare, I never thought of you as having folks!"

He was about to discover that I did. . . .

(LIGHT *up* STAGE.)

(LEGEND ON SCREEN: "THE ACCENT OF A COMING FOOT.")

(*Friday evening. It is about five o'clock of a late spring evening which comes "scattering poems in the sky."*)

(*A delicate lemony light is in the Wingfield apartment.*)

(AMANDA *has worked like a Turk in preparation for the gentleman caller. The results are astonishing. The new floor lamp with its rose-silk shade is in place, a colored paper lantern conceals the broken light fixture in the ceiling, new billowing white curtains are at the windows, chintz covers are on chairs and sofa, a pair of new sofa pillows make their initial appearance.*)

(*Open boxes and tissue paper are scattered on the floor.*)

(LAURA *stands in the middle with lifted arms while* AMANDA *crouches before her, adjusting the hem of the new dress, devout and ritualistic. The dress is colored and designed by memory. The arrangement of* LAURA's *hair is changed; it is softer and more becoming. A fragile, unearthly prettiness has come out in* LAURA: *she is like a piece of translucent glass touched by light, given a momentary radiance, not actual, not lasting.*)

AMANDA (*impatiently*). Why are you trembling?

LAURA. Mother, you've made me so nervous!

AMANDA. How have I made you nervous?

LAURA. By all this fuss! You make it seem so important!

AMANDA. I don't understand you, Laura. You couldn't be satisfied with just sitting home, and yet whenever I try to arrange something for you, you seem to resist it. (*She gets up.*)

Now take a lock at yourself.

No, wait! Wait just a moment—I have an idea!

LAURA. What is it now?

(AMANDA *produces two powder puffs which she wraps in handkerchiefs and stuffs in* LAURA's *bosom.*)

LAURA. Mother, what are you doing?

AMANDA. They call them "Gay Deceivers"!

LAURA. I won't wear them!

AMANDA. You will!

LAURA. Why should I?

AMANDA. Because, to be painfully honest, your chest is flat.

LAURA. You make it seem like we were setting a trap.

AMANDA. All pretty girls are a trap, a pretty trap, and men expect them to be.

(LEGEND: "A PRETTY TRAP.")

Now look at yourself, young lady. This is the prettiest you will ever be!

I've got to fix myself now! You're going to be surprised by your mother's appearance! (*She crosses through portieres, humming gaily.*)

(LAURA *moves slowly to the long mirror and stares solemnly at herself.*)

(*A wind blows the white curtains inward in a slow, graceful motion and with a faint, sorrowful sighing.*)

AMANDA (*off stage*). It isn't dark enough yet. (*She turns slowly before the mirror with a troubled look.*)

(LEGEND ON SCREEN: "THIS IS MY SISTER: CELEBRATE HER WITH STRINGS!" MUSIC.)

AMANDA (*laughing, off*). I'm going to show you something. I'm going to make a spectacular appearance!

LAURA. What is it, Mother?

AMANDA. Possess your soul in patience—you will see!

Something I've resurrected from that old trunk! Styles haven't changed so terribly much after all. . . .

(*She parts the portieres.*)

Now just look at your mother!

(*She wears a girlish frock of yellowed voile with a blue silk sash. She carries a bunch of jonquils—the legend of her youth is nearly revived. Feverishly.)*

This is the dress in which I led the cotillion. Won the cakewalk twice at Sunset Hill, wore one spring to the Governor's ball in Jackson!

See how I sashayed around the ballroom, Laura?

(She raises her skirt and does a mincing step around the room.)

I wore it on Sundays for my gentlemen callers! I had it on the day I met your father—

I had malaria fever all that spring. The change of climate from East Tennessee to the Delta—weakened resistance—I had a little temperature all the time—not enough to be serious—just enough to make me restless and giddy!—Invitations poured in —parties all over the Delta!—"Stay in bed," said Mother, "you have fever!"—but I just wouldn't.—I took quinine but kept on going, going!—Evenings, dances!— Afternoons, long, long rides! Picnics— lovely!—So lovely, that country in May.— All lacy with dogwood, literally flooded with jonquils!—That was the spring I had the craze for jonquils. Jonquils became an absolute obsession. Mother said, "Honey, there's no more room for jonquils." And still I kept on bringing in more jonquils. Whenever, wherever I saw them, I'd say, "Stop! Stop! I see jonquils!" I made the young men help me gather the jonquils! It was a joke, Amanda and her jonquils! Finally there were no more vases to hold them, every available space was filled with jonquils. No vases to hold them? All right, I'll hold them myself! And then I— *(She stops in front of the picture. MUSIC.)* met your father!

Malaria fever and jonquils and then—this —boy. . . .

(She switches on the rose-colored lamp.)

I hope they get here before it starts to rain.

(She crosses upstage and places the jonquils in bowl on table.)

I gave your brother a little extra change so he and Mr. O'Connor could take the service car home.

LAURA *(with altered look).* What did you say his name was?

AMANDA. O'Connor.

LAURA. What is his first name?

AMANDA. I don't remember. Oh, yes, I do. It was—Jim!

(LAURA sways slightly and catches hold of a chair.)

(LEGEND ON SCREEN: "NOT JIM!")

LAURA *(faintly).* Not—Jim!

AMANDA. Yes, that was it, it was Jim! I've never known a Jim that wasn't nice!

(MUSIC: OMINOUS.)

LAURA. Are you sure his name is Jim O'Connor?

AMANDA. Yes. Why?

LAURA. Is he the one that Tom used to know in high school?

AMANDA. He didn't say so. I think he just got to know him at the warehouse.

LAURA. There was a Jim O'Connor we both knew in high school— *(Then, with effort.)* If that is the one that Tom is bringing to dinner—you'll have to excuse me, I won't come to the table.

AMANDA. What sort of nonsense is this?

LAURA. You asked me once if I'd ever liked a boy. Don't you remember I showed you this boy's picture?

AMANDA. You mean the boy you showed me in the year book?

LAURA. Yes, that boy.

AMANDA. Laura, Laura, were you in love with that boy?

LAURA. I don't know, Mother. All I know is I couldn't sit at the table if it was him!

AMANDA. It won't be him! It isn't the least bit likely. But whether it is or not, you will come to the table. You will not be excused.

LAURA. I'll have to be, Mother.

AMANDA. I don't intend to humor your silliness, Laura. I've had too much from you and your brother, both!

So just sit down and compose yourself till they come. Tom has forgotten his key so you'll have to let them in, when they arrive.

LAURA (*panicky*). Oh, Mother, *you* answer the door!

AMANDA (*lightly*). I'll be in the kitchen—busy!

LAURA. Oh, Mother, please answer the door, don't make me do it!

AMANDA (*crossing into kitchenette*). I've got to fix the dressing for the salmon. Fuss, fuss—silliness!—over a gentleman caller!

(*Door swings shut.* LAURA *is left alone.*)

(LEGEND: "TERROR!")

(*She utters a low moan and turns off the lamp—sits stiffly on the edge of the sofa, knotting her fingers together.*)

(LEGEND ON SCREEN: "THE OPENING OF A DOOR!")

(TOM *and* JIM *appear on the fire-escape steps and climb to landing. Hearing their approach,* LAURA *rises with a panicky gesture. She retreats to the portieres.*)

(*The doorbell.* LAURA *catches her breath and touches her throat. Low drums.*)

AMANDA (*calling*). Laura, sweetheart! The door!

(LAURA *stares at it without moving.*)

JIM. I think we just beat the rain.

TOM. Uh-huh. (*He rings again, nervously.* JIM *whistles and fishes for a cigarette.*)

AMANDA (*very, very gaily*). Laura, that is your brother and Mr. O'Connor! Will you let them in, darling?

(LAURA *crosses toward kitchenette door.*)

LAURA (*breathlessly*). Mother—you go to the door!

(AMANDA *steps out of kitchenette and stares furiously at* LAURA. *She points imperiously at the door.*)

LAURA. Please, please!

AMANDA (*in a fierce whisper*). What is the matter with you, you silly thing?

LAURA (*desperately*). Please, you answer it, *please!*

AMANDA. I told you I wasn't going to humor you, Laura. Why have you chosen this moment to lose your mind?

LAURA. Please, please, please, you go!

AMANDA. You'll have to go to the door because I can't!

LAURA (*despairingly*). I can't either!

AMANDA. *Why?*

LAURA. I'm *sick!*

AMANDA. I'm sick, too—of your nonsense! Why can't you and your brother be normal people? Fantastic whims and behavior!

(TOM *gives a long ring.*)

Preposterous goings on! Can you give me one reason— (*Calls out lyrically.*) COMING! JUST ONE SECOND!—why you should be afraid to open a door? Now you answer it, Laura!

LAURA. Oh, oh, oh . . . (*She returns through the portieres. Darts to the victrola and winds it frantically and turns it on.*)

AMANDA. Laura Wingfield, you march right to that door!

LAURA. Yes—yes, Mother!

(*A faraway, scratchy rendition of "Dardanella" softens the air and gives her strength to move through it. She slips to the door and draws it cautiously open.*)

(TOM *enters with the caller,* JIM O'CONNOR.)

TOM. Laura, this is Jim. Jim, this is my sister, Laura.

JIM (*stepping inside*). I didn't know that Shakespeare had a sister!

LAURA (*retreating stiff and trembling from the door*). How—how do you do?

JIM (*heartily extending his hand*). Okay!

(LAURA *touches it hesitantly with hers.*)

JIM. Your hand's *cold*, Laura!

LAURA. Yes, well—I've been playing the victrola. . . .

TOM (*disinterest*). Yeah? (*Lights cigarette and crosses back to fire-escape door.*)

JIM. Where are *you* going?

TOM. I'm going out on the terrace.

JIM (*goes after him*). You know, Shakespeare—I'm going to sell you a bill of goods!

TOM. What goods?

JIM. A course I'm taking.

TOM. Huh?

JIM. In public speaking! You and me, we're not the warehouse type.

TOM. Thanks—that's good news.
But what has public speaking got to do with it?

JIM. It fits you for—executive positions!

TOM. Awww.

JIM. I tell you it's done a helluva lot for me.

(IMAGE: EXECUTIVE AT DESK.)

TOM. In what respect?

JIM. In every! Ask yourself what is the difference between you an' me and men in the office down front? Brains?—No!—Ability?—No! Then what? Just one little thing—

TOM. What is that one little thing?

JIM. Primarily it amounts to—social poise! Being able to square up to people and hold your own on any social level!

AMANDA (off stage). Tom?

TOM. Yes, Mother?

AMANDA. Is that you and Mr. O'Connor?

TOM. Yes, Mother.

AMANDA. Well, you just make yourselves comfortable in there.

TOM. Yes, Mother.

AMANDA. Ask Mr. O'Connor if he would like to wash his hands.

JIM. Aw, no—no—thank you—I took care of that at the warehouse. Tom—

TOM. Yes?

JIM. Mr. Mendoza was speaking to me about you.

TOM. Favorably?

JIM. What do you think?

TOM. Well—

JIM. You're going to be out of a job if you don't wake up.

TOM. I am waking up—

JIM. You show no signs.

TOM. The signs are interior.

(IMAGE ON SCREEN: THE SAILING VESSEL WITH JOLLY ROGER AGAIN.)

TOM. I'm planning to change. (He leans over the rail speaking with quiet exhilaration. The incandescent marquees and signs of the first-run movie houses light his face from across the alley. He looks like a voyager.) I'm right at the point of committing myself to a future that doesn't include the warehouse and Mr. Mendoza or even a night-school course in public speaking.

JIM. What are you gassing about?

TOM. I'm tired of the movies.

JIM. Movies!

TOM. Yes, movies! Look at them— (A wave toward the marvels of Grand Avenue.) All of those glamorous people—having adventures—hogging it all, gobbling the whole thing up! You know what happens? People go to the movies instead of moving! Hollywood characters are supposed to have all the adventures for everybody in America, while everybody in America sits in a dark room and watches them have them! Yes, until there's a war. That's when adventure becomes available to the masses! Everyone's dish, not only Gable's! Then the people in the dark room come out of the dark room to have some adventures themselves—Goody, goody!—It's our turn now, to go to the South Sea Island—to make a safari—to be exotic, far-off!—But I'm not patient. I don't want to wait till then. I'm tired of the movies and I am about to move!

JIM (incredulously). Move?

TOM. Yes.

JIM. When?

TOM. Soon!

JIM. Where? Where?

(THEME THREE MUSIC SEEMS TO ANSWER THE QUESTION, WHILE TOM THINKS IT OVER. HE SEARCHES AMONG HIS POCKETS.)

TOM. I'm starting to boil inside. I know I seem dreamy, but inside—well, I'm boiling!—Whenever I pick up a shoe, I shudder a little thinking how short life is and what I am doing!—Whatever that means, I know it doesn't mean shoes—except as something to wear on a traveler's feet! (Finds paper.) Look—

JIM. What?

TOM. I'm a member.

JIM *(reading)*. The Union of Merchant Seamen.

TOM. I paid my dues this month, instead of the light bill.

JIM. You will regret it when they turn the lights off.

TOM. I won't be here.

JIM. How about your mother?

TOM. I'm like my father. The bastard son of a bastard! See how he grins? And he's been absent going on sixteen years!

JIM. You're just talking, you drip. How does your mother feel about it?

TOM. Shhh!—Here comes Mother! Mother is not acquainted with my plans!

AMANDA *(enters portieres)*. Where are you all?

TOM. On the terrace, Mother.

(They start inside. She advances to them. TOM is distinctly shocked at her appearance. Even JIM blinks a little. He is making his first contact with girlish Southern vivacity and in spite of the night-school course in public speaking is somewhat thrown off the beam by the unexpected outlay of social charm.)

(Certain responses are attempted by JIM but are swept aside by AMANDA's gay laughter and chatter. TOM is embarrassed but after the first shock JIM reacts very warmly. Grins and chuckles, is altogether won over.)

(IMAGE: AMANDA AS A GIRL.)

AMANDA *(coyly smiling, shaking her girlish ringlets)*. Well, well, well, so this is Mr. O'Connor. Introductions entirely unnecessary. I've heard so much about you from my boy. I finally said to him, Tom—good gracious!—why don't you bring this paragon to supper? I'd like to meet this nice young man at the warehouse!—Instead of just hearing him sing your praises so much!

I don't know why my son is so stand-offish —that's not Southern behavior!

Let's sit down and—I think we could stand a little more air in here! Tom, leave the door open. I felt a nice fresh breeze a moment ago. Where has it gone to?

Mmm, so warm already! And not quite summer, even. We're going to burn up when summer really gets started.

However, we're having—we're having a very light supper. I think light things are better fo' this time of year. The same as light clothes are. Light clothes an' light food are what warm weather calls fo.' You know our blood gets so thick during th' winter—it takes a while fo' us to *adjust* ou'selves!—when the season changes . . .

It's come so quick this year. I wasn't prepared. All of a sudden—heavens! Already summer!—I ran to the trunk an' pulled out this light dress— Terribly old! Historical almost! But feels so good--so good an' co-ol, y' know. . . .

TOM. Mother—

AMANDA. Yes, honey?

TOM. How about—supper?

AMANDA. Honey, you go ask Sister if supper is ready! You know that Sister is in full charge of supper!

Tell her you hungry boys are waiting for it.

(To JIM.)

Have you met Laura?

JIM. She—

AMANDA. Let you in? Oh, good, you've met already! It's rare for a girl as sweet an' pretty as Laura to be domestic! But Laura is, thank heavens, not only pretty but also very domestic. I'm not at all. I never was a bit. I never could make a thing but angel-food cake. Well, in the South we had so many servants. Gone, gone, gone. All vestige of gracious living! Gone completely! I wasn't prepared for what the future brought me. All of my gentlemen callers were sons of planters and so of course I assumed that I would be married to one and raise my family on a large piece of land with plenty of servants. But man proposes—and woman accepts the proposal!—To vary that old, old saying a little bit—I married no planter! I married a man who worked for the telephone company!—That gallantly smiling gentleman over there! *(Points to the picture.)* A telephone man who—fell in love with long-distance!—Now he travels and I don't even know where!—But what am I going on for about my—tribulations?

Tell me yours—I hope you don't have any! Tom?

TOM *(returning).* Yes, Mother?

AMANDA. Is supper nearly ready?

TOM. It looks to me like supper is on the table.

AMANDA. Let me look— *(She rises prettily and looks through portieres.)* Oh, lovely! —But where is Sister?

TOM. Laura is not feeling well and she says that she thinks she'd better not come to the table.

AMANDA. What?—Nonsense!—Laura? Oh, Laura!

LAURA *(off stage, faintly).* Yes, Mother.

AMANDA. You really must come to the table. We won't be seated until you come to the table!

Come in, Mr. O'Connor. You sit over there, and I'll—

Laura? Laura Wingfield!

You're keeping us waiting, honey! We can't say grace until you come to the table!

(The back door is pushed weakly open and LAURA comes in. She is obviously quite faint, her lips trembling, her eyes wide and staring. She moves unsteadily toward the table.)

(LEGEND: "TERROR!")

(Outside a summer storm is coming abruptly. The white curtains billow inward at the windows and there is a sorrowful murmur and deep blue dusk.)

(LAURA suddenly stumbles—she catches at a chair with a faint moan.)

TOM. Laura!

AMANDA. Laura!

(There is a clap of thunder.)

(LEGEND: "AH!")

(Despairingly.)

Why, Laura, you *are* sick, darling! Tom, help your sister into the living room, dear! Sit in the living room, Laura—rest on the sofa.

Well!

(To the gentleman caller.)

Standing over the hot stove made her ill! —I told her that it was just too warm this evening, but—

(TOM comes back in. LAURA is on the sofa.)

Is Laura all right now?

TOM. Yes.

AMANDA. What *is* that? Rain? A nice cool rain has come up!

(She gives the gentleman caller a frightened look.)

I think we may—have grace—now . . .

(TOM looks at her stupidly.)

Tom, honey—you say grace!

TOM. Oh . . .

"For these and all thy mercies—"

(They bow their heads, AMANDA stealing a nervous glance at JIM. In the living room LAURA, stretched on the sofa, clenches her hand to her lips, to hold back a shuddering sob.)

God's Holy Name be praised—

THE SCENE DIMS OUT

SCENE VII

A Souvenir.

Half an hour later. Dinner is just being finished in the upstage area which is concealed by the drawn portieres.

As the curtain rises LAURA is still huddled upon the sofa, her feet drawn under her, her head resting on a pale blue pillow, her eyes wide and mysteriously watchful. The new floor lamp with its shade of rose-colored silk gives a soft, becoming light to her face, bringing out the fragile, unearthly prettiness which usually escapes attention. There is a steady murmur of rain, but it is slackening and stops soon after the scene begins; the air outside becomes pale and luminous as the moon breaks out.

A moment after the curtain rises, the lights in both rooms flicker and go out.

JIM. Hey, there, Mr. Light Bulb!

(AMANDA *laughs nervously*.)

(LEGEND: "SUSPENSION OF A PUBLIC SERV-
ICE.")

AMANDA. Where was Moses when the lights
went out? Ha-ha. Do you know the answer
to that one, Mr. O'Connor?

JIM. No, Ma'am, what's the answer?

AMANDA. In the dark!

(JIM *laughs appreciatively*.)

Everybody sit still. I'll light the candles.
Isn't it lucky we have them on the table?
Where's a match? Which of you gentle-
men can provide a match?

JIM. Here.

AMANDA. Thank you, sir.

JIM. Not at all, Ma'am!

AMANDA. I guess the fuse has burnt out.
Mr. O'Connor, can you tell a burnt-out
fuse? I know I can't and Tom is a total
loss when it comes to mechanics.

(SOUND: GETTING UP: VOICES RECEDE A LIT-
TLE TO KITCHENETTE.)

Oh, be careful you don't bump into something. We don't want our gentleman caller
to break his neck. Now wouldn't that be
a fine howdy-do?

JIM. Ha-ha!

Where is the fuse-box?

AMANDA. Right here next to the stove. Can
you see anything?

JIM. Just a minute.

AMANDA. Isn't electricity a mysterious
thing?

Wasn't it Benjamin Franklin who tied a
key to a kite?

We live in such a mysterious universe,
don't we? Some people say that science
clears up all the mysteries for us. In my
opinion it only creates more!

Have you found it yet?

JIM. No, Ma'am. All these fuses look okay
to me.

AMANDA. Tom!

TOM. Yes, Mother?

AMANDA. That light bill I gave you several days ago. The one I told you we got
the notices about?

(LEGEND: "HA!")

TOM. Oh.—Yeah.

AMANDA. You didn't neglect to pay it by
any chance?

TOM. Why, I—

AMANDA. Didn't! I might have known it!

JIM. Shakespeare probably wrote a poem
on that light bill, Mrs. Wingfield.

AMANDA. I might have known better than
to trust him with it! There's such a high
price for negligence in this world!

JIM. Maybe the poem will win a ten-dollar
prize.

AMANDA. We'll just have to spend the remainder of the evening in the nineteenth
century, before Mr. Edison made the
Mazda lamp!

JIM. Candlelight is my favorite kind of
light.

AMANDA. That shows you're romantic! But
that's no excuse for Tom.

Well, we got through dinner. Very considerate of them to let us get through
dinner before they plunged us into everlasting darkness, wasn't it, Mr. O'Connor?

JIM. Ha-ha!

AMANDA. Tom, as a penalty for your care-
lessness you can help me with the dishes.

JIM. Let me give you a hand.

AMANDA. Indeed you will not!

JIM. I ought to be good for something.

AMANDA. Good for something? (*Her tone
is rhapsodic*.)

You? Why, Mr. O'Connor, nobody, *nobody's* given me this much entertainment
in years—as you have!

JIM. Aw, now, Mrs. Wingfield!

AMANDA. I'm not exaggerating, not one
bit! But Sister is all by her lonesome. You
go keep her company in the parlor!

I'll give you this lovely old candelabrum
that used to be on the altar at the church
of the Heavenly Rest. It was melted a little
out of shape when the church burnt down.
Lightning struck it one spring. Gypsy

Jones was holding a revival at the time and he intimated that the church was destroyed because the Episcopalians gave card parties.

JIM. Ha-ha.

AMANDA. And how about you coaxing Sister to drink a little wine? I think it would be good for her! Can you carry both at once?

JIM. Sure. I'm Superman!

AMANDA. Now, Thomas, get into this apron!

(*The door of kitchenette swings closed on* AMANDA's *gay laughter; the flickering light approaches the portieres.*)

(LAURA *sits up nervously as he enters. Her speech at first is low and breathless from the almost intolerable strain of being alone with a stranger.*)

(THE LEGEND: "I DON'T SUPPOSE YOU REMEMBER ME AT ALL!")

(*In her first speeches in this scene, before* JIM's *warmth overcomes her paralyzing shyness,* LAURA's *voice is thin and breathless as though she has just run up a steep flight of stairs.*)

(JIM's *attitude is gently humorous. In playing this scene it should be stressed that while the incident is apparently unimportant, it is to* LAURA *the climax of her secret life.*)

JIM. Hello, there, Laura.

LAURA (*faintly*). Hello. (*She clears her throat.*)

JIM. How are you feeling now? Better?

LAURA. Yes. Yes, thank you.

JIM. This is for you. A little dandelion wine. (*He extends it toward her with extravagant gallantry.*)

LAURA. Thank you.

JIM. Drink it—but don't get drunk!

(*He laughs heartily.* LAURA *takes the glass uncertainly; laughs shyly.*)

Where shall I set the candles?

LAURA. Oh—oh, anywhere . . .

JIM. How about here on the floor? Any objections?

LAURA. No.

JIM. I'll spread a newspaper under to catch the drippings. I like to sit on the floor. Mind if I do?

LAURA. Oh, no.

JIM. Give me a pillow?

LAURA. What?

JIM. A pillow!

LAURA. Oh . . . (*Hands him one quickly.*)

JIM. How about you? Don't you like to sit on the floor?

LAURA. Oh—yes.

JIM. Why don't you, then?

LAURA. I—will.

JIM. Take a pillow! (LAURA *does. Sits on the other side of the candelabrum.* JIM *crosses his legs and smiles engagingly at her.*) I can't hardly see you sitting way over there.

LAURA. I can—see you.

JIM. I know, but that's not fair, I'm in the limelight. (LAURA *moves her pillow closer.*) Good! Now I can see you! Comfortable?

LAURA. Yes.

JIM. So am I. Comfortable as a cow! Will you have some gum?

LAURA. No, thank you.

JIM. I think that I will indulge, with your permission. (*Musingly unwraps it and holds it up.*) Think of the fortune made by the guy that invented the first piece of chewing gum. Amazing, huh? The Wrigley Building is one of the sights of Chicago.—I saw it summer before last when I went up to the Century of Progress. Did you take in the Century of Progress?

LAURA. No, I didn't.

JIM. Well, it was quite a wonderful exposition. What impressed me most was the Hall of Science. Gives you an idea of what the future will be in America, even more wonderful than the present time is! (*Pause. Smiling at her.*) Your brother tells me you're shy. Is that right, Laura?

LAURA. I—don't know.

JIM. I judge you to be an old-fashioned

type of girl. Well, I think that's a pretty good type to be. Hope you don't think I'm being too personal—do you?

LAURA *(hastily, out of embarrassment).* I believe I *will* take a piece of gum, if you —don't mind. *(Clearing her throat.)* Mr. O'Connor, have you—kept up with your singing?

JIM. Singing? Me?

LAURA. Yes. I remember what a beautiful voice you had.

JIM. When did you hear me sing?

(VOICE OFF STAGE IN THE PAUSE.)

VOICE *(off stage).*

> O blow, ye winds, heigh-ho,
> A-roving I will go!
> I'm off to my love
> With a boxing glove—
> Ten thousand miles away!

JIM. You say you've heard me sing?

LAURA. Oh, yes! Yes, very often . . . I— don't suppose—you remember me—at all?

JIM *(smiling doubtfully).* You know I have an idea I've seen you before. I had that idea soon as you opened the door. It seemed almost like I was about to remember your name. But the name that I started to call you—wasn't a name! And so I stopped myself before I said it.

LAURA. Wasn't it—Blue Roses?

JIM *(springs up. Grinning).* Blue Roses! —My gosh, yes—Blue Roses!

That's what I had on my tongue when you opened the door!

Isn't it funny what tricks your memory plays? I didn't connect you with high school somehow or other.

But that's where it was; it was high school. I didn't even know you were Shakespeare's sister!

Gosh, I'm sorry.

LAURA. I didn't expect you to. You—barely knew me!

JIM. But we did have a speaking acquaintance, huh?

LAURA. Yes, we—spoke to each other.

JIM. When did you recognize me?

LAURA. Oh, right away!

JIM. Soon as I came in the door?

LAURA. When I heard your name I thought it was probably you. I knew that Tom used to know you a little in high school. So when you came in the door—

Well, then I was—sure.

JIM. Why didn't you *say* something, then?

LAURA *(breathlessly).* I didn't know what to say, I was—too surprised!

JIM. For goodness' sakes! You know, this sure is funny!

LAURA. Yes! Yes, isn't it, though . . .

JIM. Didn't we have a class in something together?

LAURA. Yes, we did.

JIM. What class was that?

LAURA. It was—singing—Chorus!

JIM. Aw!

LAURA. I sat across the aisle from you in the Aud.

JIM. Aw.

LAURA. Mondays, Wednesdays and Fridays.

JIM. Now I remember—you always came in late.

LAURA. Yes, it was so hard for me, getting upstairs. I had that brace on my leg—it clumped so loud!

JIM. I never heard any clumping.

LAURA *(wincing at the recollection).* To me it sounded like—thunder!

JIM. Well, well, well, I never even noticed.

LAURA. And everybody was seated before I came in. I had to walk in front of all those people. My seat was in the back row. I had to go clumping all the way up the aisle with everyone watching!

JIM. You shouldn't have been self-conscious.

LAURA. I know, but I was. It was always such a relief when the singing started.

JIM. Aw, yes, I've placed you now! I used to call you Blue Roses. How was it that I got started calling you that?

LAURA. I was out of school a little while with pleurosis. When I came back you asked me what was the matter. I said I had pleurosis—you though* I said Blue Roses. That's what you always called me after that!

JIM. I hope you didn't mind.

LAURA. Oh, no—I liked it. You see, I wasn't acquainted with many—people. . . .

JIM. As I remember you sort of stuck by yourself.

LAURA. I—I—never have had much luck at—making friends.

JIM. I don't see why you wouldn't.

LAURA. Well, I—started out badly.

JIM. You mean being—

LAURA. Yes, it sort of—stood between me—

JIM. You shouldn't have let it!

LAURA. I know, but it did, and—

JIM. You were shy with people!

LAURA. I tried not to be but never could—

JIM. Overcome it?

LAURA. No, I—I never could!

JIM. I guess being shy is something you have to work out of kind of gradually.

LAURA (sorrowfully). Yes—I guess it—

JIM. Takes time!

LAURA. Yes—

JIM. People are not so dreadful when you know them. That's what you have to remember! And everybody has problems, not just you, but practically everybody has got some problems.

You think of yourself as having the only problems, as being the only one who is disappointed. But just look around you and you will see lots of people as disappointed as you are. For instance, I hoped when I was going to high school that I would be further along at this time, six years later, than I am now— You remember that wonderful write-up I had in The Torch?

LAURA. Yes! (She rises and crosses to table.)

JIM. It said I was bound to succeed in anything I went into! (LAURA returns with the annual.) Holy Jeez! The Torch! (He accepts it reverently. They smile across it with mutual wonder. LAURA crouches beside him and they begin to turn through it. LAURA's shyness is dissolving in his warmth.)

LAURA. Here you are in The Pirates of Penzance!

JIM (wistfully). I sang the baritone lead in that operetta.

LAURA (raptly). So—beautifully!

JIM (protesting). Aw—

LAURA. Yes, yes—beautifully—beautifully!

JIM. You heard me?

LAURA. All three times!

JIM. No!

LAURA. Yes!

JIM. All three performances?

LAURA (looking down). Yes.

JIM. Why?

LAURA. I—wanted to ask you to—autograph my program.

JIM. Why didn't you ask me to?

LAURA. You were always surrounded by your own friends so much that I never had a chance to.

JIM. You should have just—

LAURA. Well, I—thought you might think I was—

JIM. Thought I might think you was—what?

LAURA. Oh—

JIM (with reflective relish). I was beleaguered by females in those days.

LAURA. You were terribly popular!

JIM. Yeah—

LAURA. You had such a—friendly way—

JIM. I was spoiled in high school.

LAURA. Everybody—liked you!

JIM. Including you?

LAURA. I—yes, I—I did, too— (She gently closes the book in her lap.)

JIM. Well, well, well!—Give me that program, Laura. (She hands it to him. He signs it with a flourish.) There you are—better late than never!

LAURA. Oh, I—what a—surprise!

JIM. My signature isn't worth very much right now.

But some day—maybe—it will increase in value!

Being disappointed is one thing and being discouraged is something else. I am disappointed but I am not discouraged.

I'm twenty-three years old.

How old are you?

LAURA. I'll be twenty-four in June.

JIM. That's not old age!

LAURA. No, but—

JIM. You finished high school?

LAURA (with difficulty). I didn't go back.

JIM. You mean you dropped out?

LAURA. I made bad grades in my final examinations. (She rises and replaces the book and the program. Her voice strained.) How is—Emily Meisenbach getting along?

JIM. Oh, that kraut-head!

LAURA. Why do you call her that?

JIM. That's what she was.

LAURA. You're not still—going with her?

JIM. I never see her.

LAURA. It said in the Personal Section that you were—engaged!

JIM. I know, but I wasn't impressed by that—propaganda!

LAURA. It wasn't—the truth?

JIM. Only in Emily's optimistic opinion!

LAURA. Oh—

(LEGEND: "WHAT HAVE YOU DONE SINCE HIGH SCHOOL?")

(JIM lights a cigarette and leans indolently back on his elbows smiling at LAURA with a warmth and charm which lights her inwardly with altar candles. She remains by the table and turns in her hands a piece of glass to cover her tumult.)

JIM (after several reflective puffs on a cigarette). What have you done since high school? (She seems not to hear him.)

Huh? (LAURA looks up.) I said what have you done since high school, Laura?

LAURA. Nothing much.

JIM. You must have been doing something these six long years.

LAURA. Yes.

JIM. Well, then, such as what?

LAURA. I took a business course at business college—

JIM. How did that work out?

LAURA. Well, not very—well—I had to drop out, it gave me—indigestion—

(JIM laughs gently.)

JIM. What are you doing now?

LAURA. I don't do anything—much. Oh, please don't think I sit around doing nothing! My glass collection takes up a good deal of time. Glass is something you have to take good care of.

JIM. What did you say—about glass?

LAURA. Collection I said—I have one— (She clears her throat and turns away again, acutely shy.)

JIM (abruptly). You know what I judge to be the trouble with you?

Inferiority complex! Know what that is? That's what they call it when someone low-rates himself!

I understand it because I had it, too. Although my case was not so aggravated as yours seems to be. I had it until I took up public speaking, developed my voice, and learned that I had an aptitude for science. Before that time I never thought of myself as being outstanding in any way whatsoever!

Now I've never made a regular study of it, but I have a friend who says I can analyze people better than doctors that make a profession of it. I don't claim that to be necessarily true, but I can sure guess a person's psychology, Laura! (Takes out his gum.) Excuse me, Laura. I always take it out when the flavor is gone. I'll use this scrap of paper to wrap it in. I know how it is to get it stuck on a shoe.

Yep—that's what I judge to be your principal trouble. A lack of confidence in yourself as a person. You don't have the proper amount of faith in yourself. I'm basing that fact on a number of your remarks and also on certain observations I've made. For instance that clumping you thought was so awful in high school. You say that you even dreaded to walk into class. You see what you did? You dropped out of school, you gave up an education because of a clump, which as far as I know was practically non-existent! A little physical defect is what you have. Hardly noticeable even! Magnified thousands of times by imagination!

You know what my strong advice to you is? Think of yourself as *superior* in some way!

LAURA. In what way would I think?

JIM. Why, man alive, Laura! Just look about you a little. What do you see? A world full of common people! All of 'em born and all of 'em going to die!

Which of them has one-tenth of your good points! Or mine! Or anyone else's, as far as that goes—Gosh!

Everybody excels in some one thing. Some in many!

(Unconsciously glances at himself in the mirror.)

All you've got to do is discover in *what!* Take me, for instance.

(He adjusts his tie at the mirror.)

My interest happens to lie in electro-dynamics. I'm taking a course in radio engineering at night school, Laura, on top of a fairly responsible job at the warehouse. I'm taking that course and studying public speaking.

LAURA. Ohhhh.

JIM. Because I believe in the future of television!

(Turning back to her.)

I wish to be ready to go up right along with it. Therefore I'm planning to get in on the ground floor. In fact I've already made the right connections and all that remains is for the industry itself to get under way! Full steam—

(His eyes are starry.)

Knowledge—Zzzzzp! Money—Zzzzzzp! —Power!

That's the cycle democracy is built on!

(His attitude is convincingly dynamic. LAURA stares at him, even her shyness eclipsed in her absolute wonder. He suddenly grins.)

I guess you think I think a lot of myself!

LAURA. No—o-o-o, I—

JIM. Now how about you? Isn't there something you take more interest in than anything else?

LAURA. Well, I do—as I said—have my—glass collection—

(A peal of girlish laughter from the kitchen.)

JIM. I'm not right sure I know what you're talking about.

What kind of glass is it?

LAURA. Little articles of it, they're ornaments mostly!

Most of them are little animals made out of glass, the tiniest little animals in the world. Mother calls them a glass menagerie!

Here's an example of one, if you'd like to see it!

This one is one of the oldest. It's nearly thirteen.

(MUSIC: "THE GLASS MENAGERIE.")

(He stretches out his hand.)

Oh, be careful—if you breathe, it breaks!

JIM. I'd better not take it. I'm pretty clumsy with things.

LAURA. Go on, I trust you with him!

(Places it in his palm.)

There now—you're holding him gently! Hold him over the light, he loves the light! You see how the light shines through him?

JIM. It sure does shine!

LAURA. I shouldn't be partial, but he is my favorite one.

JIM. What kind of a thing is this one supposed to be?

LAURA. Haven't you noticed the single horn on his forehead?

JIM. A unicorn, huh?

LAURA. Mmm-hmmm!

JIM. Unicorns, aren't they extinct in the modern world?

LAURA. I know!

JIM. Poor little fellow, he must feel sort of lonesome.

LAURA (smiling). Well, if he does he doesn't complain about it. He stays on a shelf with some horses that don't have horns and all of them seem to get along nicely together.

JIM. How do you know?

LAURA (lightly). I haven't heard any arguments among them!

JIM (grinning). No arguments, huh? Well, that's a pretty good sign! Where shall I set him?

LAURA. Put him on the table. They all like a change of scenery once in a while!

JIM (stretching). Well, well, well, well— Look how big my shadow is when I stretch!

LAURA. Oh, oh, yes—it stretches across the ceiling!

JIM (crossing to door). I think it's stopped raining. (Opens fire-escape door.) Where does the music come from?

LAURA. From the Paradise Dance Hall across the alley.

JIM. How about cutting the rug a little, Miss Wingfield?

LAURA. Oh, I—

JIM. Or is your program filled up? Let me have a look at it. (Grasps imaginary card.) Why, every dance is taken! I'll just have to scratch some out. (WALTZ MUSIC: "LA GOLONDRINA.") Ahhh, a waltz! (He executes some sweeping turns by himself then holds his arms toward LAURA.)

LAURA (breathlessly). I—can't dance!

JIM. There you go, that inferiority stuff!

LAURA. I've never danced in my life!

JIM. Come on, try!

LAURA. Oh, but I'd step on you!

JIM. I'm not made out of glass.

LAURA. How—how—how do we start?

JIM. Just leave it to me. You hold your arms out a little.

LAURA. Like this?

JIM. A little bit higher. Right. Now don't tighten up, that's the main thing about it —relax.

LAURA (laughing breathlessly). It's hard not to.

JIM. Okay.

LAURA. I'm afraid you can't budge me.

JIM. What do you bet I can't? (He swings her into motion.)

LAURA. Goodness, yes, you can!

JIM. Let yourself go, now, Laura, just let yourself go.

LAURA. I'm—

JIM. Come on!

LAURA. Trying!

JIM. Not so stiff— Easy does it!

LAURA. I know but I'm—

JIM. Loosen th' backbone! There now, that's a lot better.

LAURA. Am I?

JIM. Lots, lots better! (He moves her about the room in a clumsy waltz.)

LAURA. Oh, my!

JIM. Ha-ha!

LAURA. Oh, my goodness!

JIM. Ha-ha-ha! (They suddenly bump into the table. JIM stops.) What did we hit on?

LAURA. Table.

JIM. Did something fall off it? I think—

LAURA. Yes.

JIM. I hope it wasn't the little glass horse with the horn!

LAURA. Yes.

JIM. Aw, aw, aw. Is it broken?

LAURA. Now it is just like all the other horses.

JIM. It's lost its—

LAURA. Horn! It doesn't matter. Maybe it's a blessing in disguise.

JIM. You'll never forgive me. I bet that that was your favorite piece of glass.

LAURA. I don't have favorites much. It's no tragedy, Freckles. Glass breaks so easily.

No matter how careful you are. The traffic jars the shelves and things fall off them.

JIM. Still I'm awfully sorry that I was the cause.

LAURA *(smiling)*. I'll just imagine he had an operation.

The horn was removed to make him feel less—freakish!

(They both laugh.)

Now he will feel more at home with the other horses, the ones that don't have horns. . . .

JIM. Ha-ha, that's very funny!

(Suddenly serious.)

I'm glad to see that you have a sense of humor.

You know—you're—well—very different! Surprisingly different from anyone else I know!

(His voice becomes soft and hesitant with a genuine feeling.)

Do you mind me telling you that?

(LAURA is abashed beyond speech.)

I mean it in a nice way . . .

(LAURA nods shyly, looking away.)

You make me feel sort of—I don't know how to put it!

I'm usually pretty good at expressing things, but—

This is something that I don't know how to say!

(LAURA touches her throat and clears it— turns the broken unicorn in her hands.) (Even softer.)

Has anyone ever told you that you were pretty?

(PAUSE: MUSIC.)

(LAURA looks up slowly, with wonder, and shakes her head.)

Well, you are! In a different way from anyone else.

And all the nicer because of the difference, too.

(His voice becomes low and husky. LAURA turns away, nearly faint with the novelty of her emotions.)

I wish that you were my sister. I'd teach you to have some confidence in yourself. The different people are not like other people, but being different is nothing to be ashamed of. Because other people are not such wonderful people. They're one hundred times one thousand. You're one times one! They walk all over the earth. You just stay here. They're common as—weeds, but—you—well, you're—*Blue Roses!*

(IMAGE ON SCREEN: BLUE ROSES.)

(MUSIC CHANGES.)

LAURA. But blue is wrong for—roses . . .

JIM. It's right for you!—You're—pretty!

LAURA. In what respect am I pretty?

JIM. In all respects—believe me! Your eyes —your hair—are pretty! Your hands are pretty!

(He catches hold of her hand.)

You think I'm making this up because I'm invited to dinner and have to be nice. Oh, I could do that! I could put on an act for you, Laura, and say lots of things without being very sincere. But this time I am. I'm talking to you sincerely. I happened to notice you had this inferiority complex that keeps you from feeling comfortable with people. Somebody needs to build your confidence up and make you proud instead of shy and turning away and—blushing—

Somebody—ought to—

Ought to—*kiss* you, Laura!

(His hand slips slowly up her arm to her shoulder.)

(MUSIC SWELLS TUMULTUOUSLY.)

(He suddenly turns her about and kisses her on the lips.)

(When he releases her, LAURA sinks on the sofa with a bright, dazed look.)

(JIM backs away and fishes in his pocket for a cigarette.)

(LEGEND ON SCREEN: "SOUVENIR.")

Stumble-john!

(He lights the cigarette, avoiding her look.)

(There is a peal of girlish laughter from AMANDA in the kitchen.)

*(LAURA slowly raises and opens her hand

It still contains the little broken glass animal. She looks at it with a tender, bewildered expression.)

Stumble-john!

I shouldn't have done that— That was way
off the beam.

You don't smoke, do you?

(She looks up, smiling, not hearing the
question.)

(He sits beside her a little gingerly. She
looks at him speechlessly—waiting.)

(He coughs decorously and moves a little
farther aside as he considers the situation
and senses her feelings, dimly, with per-
turbation.)

(Gently.) Would you—care for a—mint?

(She doesn't seem to hear him but her
look grows brighter even.)

Peppermint—Life-Saver?

My pocket's a regular drug store—wherever I go . . .

(He pops a mint in his mouth. Then gulps
and decides to make a clean breast of it.
He speaks slowly and gingerly.)

Laura, you know, if I had a sister like you,
I'd do the same thing as Tom. I'd bring
out fellows and—introduce her to them.
The right type of boys of a type to—
appreciate her.

Only—well—he made a mistake about me.
Maybe I've got no call to be saying this.
That may not have been the idea in having
me over. But what if it was?

There's nothing wrong about that. The
only trouble is that in my case—I'm not in
a situation to—do the right thing.

I can't take down your number and say
I'll phone.

I can't call up next week and—ask for a
date.

I thought I had better explain the situation
in case you—misunderstood it and—hurt
your feelings. . . .

(Pause.)

(Slowly, very slowly, LAURA's look changes,
her eyes returning slowly from his to the
ornament in her palm.)

(AMANDA utters another gay laugh in the
kitchen.)

LAURA (faintly). You—won't call again?

JIM. No, Laura, I can't.

(He rises from the sofa.)

As I was just explaining, I've—got strings
on me.

Laura, I've—been going steady!

I go out all of the time with a girl named
Betty. She's a home-girl like you, and
Catholic, and Irish, and in a great many
ways we—get along fine.

I met her last summer on a moonlight boat
trip up the river to Alton, on the *Majestic*.
Well—right away from the start it was—
love!

(LEGEND: LOVE!)

(LAURA sways slightly forward and grips
the arm of the sofa. He fails to notice, now
enrapt in his own comfortable being.)

Being in love has made a new man of me!

(Leaning stiffly forward, clutching the
arm of the sofa, LAURA struggles visibly
with her storm. But JIM is oblivious, she
is a long way off.)

The power of love is really pretty tremendous!

Love is something that—changes the whole
world, Laura!

(The storm abates a little and LAURA leans
back. He notices her again.)

It happened that Betty's aunt took sick, she
got a wire and had to go to Centralia. So
Tom—when he asked me to dinner—I
naturally just accepted the invitation, not
knowing that you—that he—that I—

(He stops awkwardly.)

Huh—I'm a stumble-john!

(He flops back on the sofa.)

(The holy candles in the altar of LAURA's
face have been snuffed out. There is a look
of almost infinite desolation.)

(JIM glances at her uneasily.)

I wish that you would—say something.

(She bites her lip which was trembling
and then bravely smiles. She opens her
hand again on the broken glass ornament.
Then she gently takes his hand and raises

it level with her own. She carefully places the unicorn in the palm of his hand, then pushes his fingers closed upon it.) What are you—doing that for? You want me to have him?—Laura? *(She nods.)* What for?

LAURA. A—souvenir . . . *(She rises unsteadily and crouches beside the victrola to wind it up.)*

(LEGEND ON SCREEN: "THINGS HAVE A WAY OF TURNING OUT SO BADLY!")

(OR IMAGE: "GENTLEMAN CALLER WAVING GOOD-BYE!—GAILY.")

(At this moment AMANDA rushes brightly back in the front room. She bears a pitcher of fruit punch in an old-fashioned cut-glass pitcher and a plate of macaroons. The plate has a gold border and poppies painted on it.)

AMANDA. Well, well, well! Isn't the air delightful after the shower? I've made you children a little liquid refreshment. *(Turns gaily to the gentleman caller.)*

Jim, do you know that song about lemonade?

"Lemonade, lemonade
  Made in the shade and stirred with a spade—
  Good enough for any old maid!"

JIM *(uneasily)*. Ha-ha! No—I never heard it.

AMANDA. Why, Laura! You look so serious!

JIM. We were having a serious conversation.

AMANDA. Good! Now you're better acquainted!

JIM *(uncertainly)*. Ha-ha! Yes.

AMANDA. You modern young people are much more serious-minded than my generation. I was so gay as a girl!

JIM. You haven't changed, Mrs. Wingfield.

AMANDA. Tonight I'm rejuvenated! The gaiety of the occasion, Mr. O'Connor! *(She tosses her head with a peal of laughter. Spills lemonade.)*

Oooo! I'm baptizing myself!

JIM. Here—let me—

AMANDA *(setting the pitcher down)*. There

now. I discovered we had some maraschino cherries. I dumped them in, juice and all!

JIM. You shouldn't have gone to that trouble, Mrs. Wingfield.

AMANDA. Trouble, trouble? Why, it was loads of fun!

Didn't you hear me cutting up in the kitchen? I bet your ears were burning! I told Tom how outdone with him I was for keeping you to himself so long a time! He should have brought you over much, much sooner! Well, now that you've found your way, I want you to be a frequent caller! Not just occasional but all the time. Oh, we're going to have a lot of gay times together! I see them coming!

Mmm, just breathe that air! So fresh, and the moon's so pretty!

I'll skip back out—I know where my place is when young folks are having a—serious conversation!

JIM. Oh, don't go out, Mrs. Wingfield. The fact of the matter is I've got to be going.

AMANDA. Going, now? You're joking! Why, it's only the shank of the evening, Mr. O'Connor!

JIM. Well, you know how it is.

AMANDA. You mean you're a young workingman and have to keep workingmen's hours. We'll let you off early tonight. But only on the condition that next time you stay later.

What's the best night for you? Isn't Saturday night the best night for you working-men?

JIM. I have a couple of time-clocks to punch, Mrs. Wingfield. One at morning, another one at night!

AMANDA. My, but you *are* ambitious! You work at night, too?

JIM. No, Ma'am, not work but—Betty!

(He crosses deliberately to pick up his hat. The band at the Paradise Dance Hall goes into a tender waltz.)

AMANDA. Betty? Betty? Who's—Betty!

(There is an ominous cracking sound in the sky.)

JIM. Oh, just a girl. The girl I go steady with! (*He smiles charmingly. The sky falls.*)

(LEGEND: "THE SKY FALLS.")

AMANDA (*a long-drawn exhalation*). Ohhhh . . . Is it a serious romance, Mr. O'Connor?

JIM. We're going to be married the second Sunday in June.

AMANDA. Ohhhh—how nice!

Tom didn't mention that you were engaged to be married.

JIM. The cat's not out of the bag at the warehouse yet.

You know how they are. They call you Romeo and stuff like that. (*He stops at the oval mirror to put on his hat. He carefully shapes the brim and the crown to give a discreetly dashing effect.*)

It's been a wonderful evening, Mrs. Wingfield. I guess this is what they mean by Southern hospitality.

AMANDA. It really wasn't anything at all.

JIM. I hope it don't seem like I'm rushing off. But I promised Betty I'd pick her up at the Wabash depot, an' by the time I get my jalopy down there her train'll be in. Some women are pretty upset if you keep 'em waiting.

AMANDA. Yes, I know— The tyranny of women!

(*Extends her hand.*)

Good-bye, Mr. O'Connor.

I wish you luck—and happiness—and success! All three of them, and so does Laura! —Don't you, Laura?

LAURA. Yes!

JIM (*taking her hand*). Good-bye, Laura. I'm certainly going to treasure that souvenir. And don't you forget the good advice I gave you.

(*Raises his voice to a cheery shout.*)

So long, Shakespeare!

Thanks again, ladies— Good night!

(*He grins and ducks jauntily out.*)

(*Still bravely grimacing,* AMANDA *closes the door on the gentleman caller. Then she* turns back to the room with a puzzled expression. She and LAURA don't dare to face each other. LAURA crouches beside the victrola to wind it.*)

AMANDA (*faintly*). Things have a way of turning out so badly.

I don't believe that I would play the victrola.

Well, well—well—

Our gentleman caller was engaged to be married!

Tom!

TOM (*from back*). Yes, Mother?

AMANDA. Come in here a minute. I want to tell you something awfully funny.

TOM (*enters with macaroon and a glass of the lemonade*). Has the gentleman caller gotten away already?

AMANDA. The gentleman caller has made an early departure.

What a wonderful joke you played on us!

TOM. How do you mean?

AMANDA. You didn't mention that he was engaged to be married.

TOM. Jim? Engaged?

AMANDA. That's what he just informed us.

TOM. I'll be jiggered! I didn't know about that.

AMANDA. That seems very peculiar.

TOM. What's peculiar about it?

AMANDA. Didn't you call him your best friend down at the warehouse?

TOM. He is, but how did I know?

AMANDA. It seems extremely peculiar that you wouldn't know your best friend was going to be married!

TOM. The warehouse is where I work, not where I know things about people!

AMANDA. You don't know things anywhere! You live in a dream; you manufacture illusions!

(*He crosses to door.*)

Where are you going?

TOM. I'm going to the movies.

AMANDA. That's right, now that you've had

us make such fools of ourselves. The effort, the preparations, all the expense! The new floor lamp, the rug, the clothes for Laura! All for what? To entertain some other girl's fiancé!

Go to the movies, go! Don't think about us, a mother deserted, an unmarried sister who's crippled and has no job! Don't let anything interfere with your selfish pleasure!

Just go, go, go—to the movies!

TOM. All right, I will! The more you shout about my selfishness to me the quicker I'll go, and I won't go to the movies!

AMANDA. Go, then! Then go to the moon—you selfish dreamer!

(TOM *smashes his glass on the floor. He plunges out on the fire-escape, slamming the door.* LAURA *screams—cut by door.*)

(*Dance-hall music up.* TOM *goes to the rail and grips it desperately, lifting his face in the chill white moonlight penetrating the narrow abyss of the alley.*)

(LEGEND ON SCREEN: "AND SO GOODBYE . . .")

(TOM's *closing speech is timed with the interior pantomime. The interior scene is played as though viewed through sound-proof glass.* AMANDA *appears to be making a comforting speech to* LAURA *who is huddled upon the sofa. Now that we cannot hear the mother's speech, her silliness is gone and she has dignity and tragic beauty.* LAURA's *dark hair hides her face until at the end of the speech she lifts it to smile at her mother.* AMANDA's *gestures are slow and graceful, almost dance-like, as she comforts the daughter. At the end of her speech she glances a moment at the father's picture—then withdraws through the portieres. At close of* TOM's *speech,* LAURA *blows out the candles, ending the play.*)

TOM. I didn't go to the moon, I went much

further—for time is the longest distance between two places—

Not long after that I was fired for writing a poem on the lid of a shoe-box.

I left Saint Louis. I descended the steps of this fire-escape for a last time and followed, from then on, in my father's footsteps, attempting to find in motion what was lost in space—

I traveled around a great deal. The cities swept about me like dead leaves, leaves that were brightly colored but torn away from the branches.

I would have stopped, but I was pursued by something.

It always came upon me unawares, taking me altogether by surprise. Perhaps it was a familiar bit of music. Perhaps it was only a piece of transparent glass—

Perhaps I am walking along a street at night, in some strange city, before I have found companions. I pass the lighted window of a shop where perfume is sold. The window is filled with pieces of colored glass, tiny transparent bottles in delicate colors, like bits of a shattered rainbow.

Then all at once my sister touches my shoulder. I turn around and look into her eyes . . .

Oh, Laura, Laura, I tried to leave you behind me, but I am more faithful than I intended to be!

I reach for a cigarette, I cross the street, I run into the movies or a bar, I buy a drink, I speak to the nearest stranger—anything that can blow your candles out!

(LAURA *bends over the candles.*)

—for nowadays the world is lit by lightning! Blow out your candles, Laura—and so good-bye. . . .

(*She blows the candles out.*)

THE SCENE DISSOLVES

THE TIME OF YOUR LIFE

By WILLIAM SAROYAN

THE TIME OF YOUR LIFE was first presented by the Theatre Guild in association with Eddie Dowling in New York City on October 25, 1939.

THE PEOPLE

JOE..A young loafer with money and a good heart
TOM.....................................His admirer, disciple, errand boy, stooge and friend
KITTY DUVAL...A young woman with memories
NICK.......Owner of Nick's Pacific Street Saloon, Restaurant, and Entertainment Palace
ARAB..An Eastern philosopher and harmonica-player
KIT CARSON..An old Indian-fighter
MC CARTHY........................An intelligent and well-read longshoreman
KRUPP.................His boyhood friend, a waterfront cop who hates his job but doesn't
know what else to do instead
HARRY.....................A natural-born hoofer who wants to make people laugh but can't
WESLEY...........A colored boy who plays a mean and melancholy boogie-woogie piano
DUDLEY...A young man in love
ELSIE..A nurse, the girl he loves
LORENE...An unattractive woman
MARY L.............................An unhappy woman of quality and great beauty
WILLIE...A marble-game maniac

BLICK.............................A heel   A SAILOR
MA...........................Nick's mother   A SOCIETY GENTLEMAN
A KILLER   A SOCIETY LADY
HER SIDE KICK   THE DRUNKARD
A COP   THE NEWSBOY
ANOTHER COP   ANNA.........................Nick's daughter

THE PLACE

Nick's Pacific Street Saloon, Restaurant, and Entertainment Palace at the foot of Embarcadero, in San Francisco. A suggestion of room 21 at The New York Hotel, upstairs, around the corner.

The Time: Afternoon and night of a day in October, 1939.

THE AUTHOR

William Saroyan, the Armenian flame from Fresno, California, already had a reputation as an original short-story writer when the Group Theatre introduced him as an equally original playwright with My Heart's in the Highlands. *This long one-acter, brilliantly staged by Robert Lewis, was produced on April 13, 1939. A portion of the press expressed utter bewilderment, but some of our most prominent critics acclaimed the piece as a remarkable work of artistry; a few of them went so far as to vote it the "best play of the season" at the Drama Critics Circle annual conclave.*

Mr. Saroyan was born in 1908 and knocked about for many years as an itinerant worker, a Western Union messenger, and a laborer in his uncle's vineyard. He forsook his native haunts "for some of the rest of the world" at the age of seventeen. Without any formal education other than the customary exposure to grammar school in his home town, the young man resolved that he had enough experience to write and that he had enough to say for anybody's money. Short Story maga-zine printed his first piece The Daring Young Man on a Flying Trapeze *in its February, 1934 issue. This was all the encouragement Saroyan needed; he began writing with lightning speed, and later in 1934 he had enough substance for a first volume. For these stories he arrived at a number of rules that were to apply not only to all his stories but to his later plays. The first rule, which he claims to have set down at the age of eleven, reads: "Do not pay attention to the rules other people make. . . . They make them for their own protection, and to hell with them." Rule number two, which he discovered somewhat later, reads: "Forget everybody who ever wrote anything." The third rule was: "Learn to typewrite, so you can turn out stories as fast as Zane Grey." He considers this last precept one of his best rules, and the haste with which he has turned out plays, as well as stories, has often been regrettably apparent. Concerning his later fiction we may confine ourselves to noting a delightful collection of fictionized memories* My Name Is Aram *(1940), a charming first novel* The Human Comedy *(1943), and a dubious war-novel* The Adventures of Wesley Jackson *(1946) drawn somewhat from the author's unhappy experiences in the Army. He spent some time in the Signal Corps' Photographic Center in Astoria, Long Island where he wrote film scripts. Subsequently he was transferred to the European theatre of operations. He was discharged some time before the end of the war and returned to California for convalescence.*

Saroyan wrote his first play Subway Circus *in 1935 but never got it to Broadway.* My Heart's in the Highlands *was written in 1938. Encouraged by the interest in this first production, Saroyan wrote his first full-length drama* The Time of Your Life *in record time and received a notable production in the fall of 1939 from Eddie Dowling and the Theatre Guild. Brooks Atkinson defined it aptly as "a prose poem in ragtime." The play provided an occasion for full agreement between the Drama Critics Circle and the Pulitzer Prize Committee, but Saroyan refused to accept the Pulitzer Prize. This chef d'oeuvre was followed in the spring of 1940 by the less successful production of* Love's Old Sweet Song. *A year later he turned producer with his elusively fanciful piece* The Beautiful People. *A good many short and long plays followed:* Sweeney in the Trees, Across the Board of Tomorrow Morning, Jim Dandy *(produced by the National Theatre Conference),* Get Away, Old Man *(produced by George Abbott in 1943),* Afton Water, *and various unproduced pieces. His superb one-acter* Hello Out There *was presented by Eddie Dowling in conjunction with a revival of Chesterton's* Magic *in September, 1942.*

THE TIME OF YOUR LIFE

ACT ONE

In the time of your life, live—so that in that good time there shall be no ugliness or death for yourself or for any life your life touches. Seek goodness everywhere, and when it is found, bring it out of its hiding-place and let it be free and unashamed. Place in matter and in flesh the least of the values, for these are the things that hold death and must pass away. Discover in all things that which shines and is beyond corruption. Encourage virtue in whatever heart it may have been driven into secrecy and sorrow by the shame and terror of the world. Ignore the obvious, for it is unworthy of the clear eye and the kindly heart. Be the inferior of no man, nor of any man be the superior. Remember that every man is a variation of yourself. No man's guilt is not yours, nor is any man's innocence a thing apart. Despise evil and ungodliness, but not men of ungodliness or evil. These, understand. Have no shame in being kindly and gentle, but if the time comes in the time of your life to kill, kill and have no regret. In the time of your life, live—so that in that wondrous time you shall not add to the misery and sorrow of the world, but shall smile to the infinite delight and mystery of it.

Nick's is an American place: a San Francisco waterfront honky-tonk. At a table, JOE: always calm, always quiet, always thinking, always eager, always bored, always superior. His expensive clothes are casually and youthfully worn and give him an almost boyish appearance. He is thinking. Behind the bar, NICK: a big red-headed young Italian-American with an enormous naked woman tattooed in red on the inside of his right arm. He is studying The Racing Form. The ARAB, at his place at the end of the bar. He is a lean old man with a rather ferocious old-country mustache, with the ends twisted up. Between the thumb and forefinger of his left hand is the Mohammedan tattoo indicating that he has been to Mecca. He is sipping a glass of beer. It is about eleven-thirty in the morning. SAM is sweeping out. We see only his back. He disappears into the kitchen. The SAILOR at the bar finishes his drink and leaves, moving thoughtfully, as though he were trying very hard to discover how to live. The NEWSBOY comes in.

NEWSBOY *(cheerfully).* Good-morning, everybody. *(No answer. To NICK.)* Paper, Mister? *(NICK shakes his head, no. The NEWSBOY goes to JOE.)* Paper, Mister?

(JOE shakes his head, no. The NEWSBOY walks away, counting papers.)

JOE *(noticing him).* How many you got?

NEWSBOY. Five.

(JOE gives him a quarter, takes all the papers, glances at the headlines with irritation, throws them away.)

(The NEWSBOY watches carefully, then goes.)

ARAB *(picks up paper, looks at headlines, shakes head as if rejecting everything else a man might say about the world).* No foundation. All the way down the line.

(The DRUNK comes in. Walks to the telephone, looks for a nickel in the chute, sits down at JOE's table.)

(NICK takes the DRUNK out. The DRUNK returns.)

DRUNK *(champion of the Bill of Rights).* This is a free country, ain't it?

(WILLIE, the marble-game maniac, explodes through the swinging doors and

41

*lifts the forefinger of his right hand com-
ically, indicating one beer. He is a very
young man, not more than twenty. He is
wearing heavy shoes, a pair of old and
dirty corduroys, a light green turtle-neck
jersey with a large letter "F" on the chest,
an oversize two-button tweed coat, and a
green hat, with the brim up. NICK sets out
a glass of beer for him, he drinks it,
straightens up vigorously, saying Aaah,
makes a solemn face, gives NICK a one-
finger salute of adieu, and begins to leave,
refreshed and restored in spirit. He walks
by the marble game, halts suddenly, turns,
studies the contraption, gestures as if to
say, Oh, no. Turns to go, stops, returns to
the machine, studies it, takes a handful of
small coins out of his pants pocket, lifts a
nickel, indicates with a gesture, One game,
no more. Puts the nickel in the slot, pushes
in the slide, making an interesting noise.)*

NICK. You can't beat that machine.

WILLIE. Oh, yeah?

*(The marbles fall, roll, and take their
place. He pushes down the lever, placing
one marble in position. Takes a very deep
breath, walks in a small circle, excited at
the beginning of great drama. Stands
straight and pious before the contest. Himself vs. the machine. Willie vs. Destiny.
His skill and daring vs. the cunning and
trickery of the novelty industry of America,
and the whole challenging world. He is
the last of the American pioneers, with
nothing more to fight but the machine,
with no other reward than lights going
on and off, and six nickels for one. Before
him is the last champion, the machine.
He is the last challenger, the young man
with nothing to do in the world. WILLIE
grips the knob delicately, studies the situation carefully, draws the knob back, holds
it a moment, and then releases it. The first
marble rolls out among the hazards, and
the contest is on. At the very beginning
of the play "The Missouri Waltz" is coming from the phonograph. The music ends
here.)*

*(This is the signal for the beginning of
the play.)*

*(JOE suddenly comes out of his reverie.
He whistles the way people do who are
calling a cab that's about a block away,*

*only he does it quietly. WILLIE turns
around, but JOE gestures for him to return to his work. NICK looks up from The
Racing Form.)*

JOE *(calling).* Tom. *(To himself.)* Where
the hell is he, every time I need him?
*(He looks around calmly: the nickel-in-
the-slot phonograph in the corner; the
open public telephone; the stage; the marble-game; the bar; and so on. He calls
again, this time very loud.)* Hey, Tom.

NICK *(with morning irritation).* What
do you want?

JOE *(without thinking).* I want the boy
to get me a watermelon, that's what *I*
want. What do *you* want? Money, or
love, or fame, or what? You won't get
them studying The Racing Form.

NICK. I like to keep abreast of the times.

*(TOM comes hurrying in. He is a great
big man of about thirty or so who appears
to be much younger because of the child-
like expression of his face: handsome,
dumb, innocent, troubled, and a little bewildered by everything. He is obviously
adult in years, but it seems as if by all
rights he should still be a boy. He is de-
fensive as clumsy, self-conscious, overgrown boys are. He is wearing a flashy
cheap suit. JOE leans back and studies him
with casual disapproval. TOM slackens his
pace and becomes clumsy and embarrassed,
waiting for the bawling-out he's pretty
sure he's going to get.)*

JOE *(objectively, severely, but a little
amused).* Who saved your life?

TOM *(sincerely).* You did, Joe. Thanks.

JOE *(interested).* How'd I do it?

TOM *(confused).* What?

JOE *(even more interested).* How'd I do
it?

TOM. Joe, you know how you did it.

JOE *(softly).* I want you to answer me.
How'd I save your life? I've forgotten.

TOM *(remembering, with a big sorrowful
smile).* You made me eat all that chicken
soup three years ago when I was sick and
hungry.

JOE (*fascinated*). Chicken soup?

TOM (*eagerly*). Yeah.

JOE. Three years? Is it that long?

TOM (*delighted to have the information*). Yeah, sure. 1937. 1938. 1939. This is 1939, Joe.

JOE (*amused*). Never mind what year it is. Tell me the whole story.

TOM. You took me to the doctor. You gave me money for food and clothes, and paid my room rent. Aw, Joe, you know all the different things you did.

(JOE *nods, turning away from* TOM *after each question.*)

JOE. You in good health now?

TOM. Yeah, Joe.

JOE. You got clothes?

TOM. Yeah, Joe.

JOE. You eat three times a day. Sometimes four?

TOM. Yeah, Joe. Sometimes five.

JOE. You got a place to sleep?

TOM. Yeah, Joe.

(JOE *nods. Pauses. Studies* TOM *carefully.*)

JOE. Then, where the hell have you been?

TOM (*humbly*). Joe, I was out in the street listening to the boys. They're talking about the trouble down here on the waterfront.

JOE (*sharply*). I want you to be around when I need you.

TOM (*pleased that the bawling-out is over*). I won't do it again. Joe, one guy out there says there's got to be a revolution before anything will ever be all right.

JOE (*impatient*). I know all about it. Now, here. Take this money. Go up to the Emporium. You know where the Emporium is?

TCM. Yeah, sure, Joe.

JOE. All right. Take the elevator and go up to the fourth floor. Walk around to the back, to the toy department. Buy me a couple of dollars' worth of toys and bring them here.

TOM (*amazed*). Toys? What *kind* of toys, Joe?

JOE. Any kind of toys. Little ones that I can put on this table.

TOM. What do you want toys for, Joe?

JOE (*mildly angry*). *What?*

TOM. All right, all right. You don't have to get sore at *everything*. What'll people think, a big guy like me buying toys?

JOE. *What people?*

TOM. Aw, Joe, you're always making me do crazy things for you, and *I'm* the guy that gets embarrassed. You just sit in this place and make me do all the dirty work.

JOE (*looking away*). Do what I tell you.

TOM. O.K., but I wish I knew *why*. (*He makes to go.*)

JOE. Wait a minute. Here's a nickel. Put it in the phonograph. Number seven. I want to hear that waltz again.

TOM. Boy, I'm glad *I* don't have to stay and listen to it. Joe, what do you hear in that song anyway? We listen to that song ten times a day. Why can't we hear number six, or two, or nine? There are a lot of other numbers.

JOE (*emphatically*). Put the nickel in the phonograph. (*Pause.*) Sit down and wait till the music's over. Then go get me some toys.

TOM. O.K. O.K.

JOE (*loudly*). Never mind being a martyr about it either. The cause isn't worth it.

(TOM *puts the nickel into the machine, with a ritual of impatient and efficient movement which plainly shows his lack of sympathy or enthusiasm. His manner also reveals, however, that his lack of sympathy is spurious and exaggerated. Actually, he is fascinated by the music, but is so confused by it that he pretends he dislikes it.*)

*(The music begins. It is another variation
of "The Missouri Waltz," played dreamily
and softly, with perfect orchestral form,
and with a theme of weeping in the horns
repeated a number of times.)*

(At first TOM *listens with something close
to irritation, since he can't understand
what is so attractive in the music to* JOE,
*and what is so painful and confusing in it
to himself. Very soon, however, he is carried away by the melancholy story of grief
and nostalgia of the song.)*

*(He stands, troubled by the poetry and
confusion in himself.)*

*(*JOE, *on the other hand, listens as if he
were not listening, indifferent and unmoved. What he's interested in is* TOM.
He turns and glances at TOM.*)*

*(*KITTY DUVAL, *who lives in a room in The
New York Hotel, around the corner,
comes beyond the swinging doors, quietly,
and walks slowly to the bar, her reality
and rhythm a perfect accompaniment to
the sorrowful American music, which is
her music, as it is Tom's. Which the world
drove out of her, putting in its place
brokenness and all manner of spiritually
crippled forms. She seems to understand
this, and is angry. Angry with herself, full
of hate for the poor world, and full of pity
and contempt for its tragic, unbelievable,
confounded people. She is a small powerful girl, with that kind of delicate and
rugged beauty which no circumstance of
evil or ugly reality can destroy. This beauty
is that element of the immortal which is
in the seed of good and common people,
and which is kept alive in some of the
female of our kind, no matter how acci-
dently or pointlessly they may have entered
the world.* KITTY DUVAL *is somebody.
There is an angry purity, and a fierce
pride, in her.)*

*(In her stance, and way of walking, there
is grace and arrogance.* JOE *recognizes
her as a great person immediately. She goes
to the bar.)*

KITTY. Beer.

*(*NICK *places a glass of beer before her
mechanically.)*

*(She swallows half the drink, and listens
to the music again.)*

*(*TOM *turns and sees her. He becomes dead
to everything in the world but her. He
stands like a lump, fascinated and undone
by his almost religious adoration for her.*
JOE *notices* TOM.*)*

JOE *(gently)*. Tom. *(*TOM *begins to move
toward the bar, where* KITTY *is standing.
Loudly.)* Tom. *(*TOM *halts, then turns,
and* JOE *motions to him to come over to
the table.* TOM *goes over. Quietly.)* Have
you got everything straight?

TOM *(out of the world)*. What?

JOE. What do you mean, what? I just gave
you some instructions.

TOM *(pathetically)*. What do you want,
Joe?

JOE. I want you to come to your senses.

*(He stands up quietly and knocks Tom's
hat off.* TOM *picks up his hat quickly.)*

TOM. I got it, Joe. I got it. The Emporium.
Fourth floor. In the back. The toy department. Two dollars' worth of toys. That
you can put on a table.

KITTY *(to herself)*. Who the hell is he to
push a big man like that around?

JOE. I'll expect you back in a half hour.
Don't get side-tracked anywhere. Just do
what I tell you.

TOM *(pleading)*. Joe? Can't I bet four bits
on a horse race? There's a long shot—
Precious Time—that's going to win by ten
lengths. I got to have money.

*(*JOE *points to the street.* TOM *goes out.*
NICK *is combing his hair, looking in the
mirror.)*

NICK. I thought you wanted him to get you
a watermelon.

JOE. I forgot. *(He watches* KITTY *a moment. To* KITTY, *clearly, slowly, with great
compassion.)* What's the dream?

KITTY *(moving to* JOE, *coming to)*. What?

JOE *(holding the dream for her)*. What's
the dream, *now*?

KITTY *(coming still closer)*. What dream?

JOE. What dream! The dream you're dreaming.

NICK. Suppose ne did bring you a watermelon? What the hell would you do with it?

JOE (*irritated*). I'd put it on this table. I'd look at it. Then I'd eat it. What do you *think* I'd do with it, sell it for a profit?

NICK. How should ι know what *you'd* do with *anything*? What I'd like to know is, where do you get your money from? What work do you do?

JOE (*looking at* KITTY). Bring us a bottle of champagne.

KITTY. Champagne?

JOE (*simply*). Would you rather have something else?

KITTY. What's the big idea?

JOE. I thought you might like some champagne. I myself am very fond of it.

KITTY. Yeah, but what's the big idea? You can't push *me* around.

JOE (*gently but severely*). It's not in my nature to be unkind to another human being. I have only contemp. for wit. Otherwise I might say something obvious. there fore cruel, and perhaps un ue.

KITTY. You be careful what you think about me.

JOE (*slowly, not looking at her*). I have only the noblest thoughts for both your person, and your spirit.

NICK (*having listened carefully and not being able to make it out*). What are you talking about?

KITTY. You shut up. You—

ICE. He owns this place. He's an important man. All kinds of people come to him looking for work. Comedians. Singers. Dancers.

KITTY. I don't care. He can't call me names.

NICK. All right, sister. I know how it is with a two-dollar whore in the morning.

KITTY (*furiously*). Don't you dare call me names. I used to be in burlesque.

NICK. If you were ever in burlesque, I used to be Charlie Chaplin.

KITTY (*angry and a little pathetic*). I *was* in burlesque. I played the burlesque circuit from coast to coast. I've had flowers sent to me by European royalty. I've had dinner with young men of wealth and social position.

NICK. You're dreaming.

KITTY (*to* JOE). I was in burlesque. Kitty Duval. That was my name. Life-size photographs of me in costume in front of burlesque theaters all over the country.

JOE (*gently, coaxingly*). I believe you. Have some champagne.

NICK (*going to table, with champagne bottle and glasses*). There he goes again.

JOE. Miss Duval?

KITTY (*sincerely, going over*). That's not my *real* name. That's my *stage* name.

JOE. I'll call you by your stage name.

NICK (*pouring*). All right, sister, make up your mind. Are you going to have champagne with him, or not?

JOE. Pour the lady some wine.

NICK. O.K., Professor. Why you come to this joint instead of one of the high-class dumps uptown is more than I can understand. Why don't you have champagne at the St. Francis? Why don't you drink with a lady?

KITTY (*furiously*). Don't you call me names—you dentist.

JOE. Dentist?

NICK (*amazed, loudly*). What kind of cussing is that? (*Pause. Looking at* KITTY, *then at* JOE, *bewildered.*) This guy doesn't belong here. The only reason I've got champagne is because *he* keeps ordering it all the time. (*To* KITTY.) Don't think you're the only one he drinks champagne with. He drinks with *all* of them. (*Pause.*) He's crazy. Or something.

JOE (*confidentially*). Nick, I think you're going to be all right in a couple of centuries.

NICK. I'm sorry, I don't understand your English.

(JOE *lifts his glass.*)

(KITTY *slowly lifts hers, not quite sure of what's going on.*)

JOE (*sincerely*). To the spirit, Kitty Duval.

KITTY (*beginning to understand, and very grateful, looking at him*). Thank you.

(*They drink.*)

JOE (*calling*). Nick.

NICK. Yeah?

JOE. Would you mind putting a nickel in the machine again? Number—

NICK. Seven. I know. I know. I don't mind at all, Your Highness, although, personally, I'm not a lover of music. (*Going to the machine.*) As a matter of fact I think Tchaikowsky was a dope

JOE. Tchaikowsky? Where'd you ever hear of Tchaikowsky.

NICK. He was a dope.

JOE. Yeah. Why?

NICK. They talked about him on the radio one Sunday morning. He was a sucker. He let a woman drive him crazy.

JOE. I see.

NICK. I stood behind that bar listening to the God damn stuff and cried like a baby. *None but the lonely heart!* He was a dope.

JOE. What made you cry?

NICK. What?

JOE (*sternly*). What made you cry, Nick?

NICK (*angry with himself*). I don't know.

JOE. I've been underestimating you, Nick. Play number seven.

NICK. They get everybody worked up. They give everybody stuff they shouldn't have.

(NICK *puts the nickel into the machine and the Waltz begins again. He listens to the music. Then studies* The Racing Form.)

KITTY (*to herself, dreaming*). I like champagne, and everything that goes with it. Big houses with big porches, and big rooms with big windows, and big lawns, and big trees, and flowers growing everywhere, and big shepherd dogs sleeping in the shade.

NICK. I'm going next door to Frankie's to make a bet. I'll be right back.

JOE. Make one for me.

NICK (*going to* JOE). Who do you like?

JOE (*giving him money*). Precious Time.

NICK. Ten dollars? Across the board?

JOE. No. On the nose.

NICK. O.K. (*He goes.*)

(DUDLEY R. BOSTWICK, *as he calls himself, breaks through the swinging doors, and practically flings himself upon the open telephone beside the phonograph.*)

(DUDLEY *is a young man of about twenty-four or twenty-five, ordinary and yet extraordinary. He is smallish, as the saying is, neatly dressed in bargain clothes, overworked and irritated by the routine and dullness and monotony of his life, apparently nobody and nothing, but in reality a great personality. The swindled young man. Educated, but without the least real understanding. A brave, dumb, salmon-spirit struggling for life in weary, stupefied flesh, dueling ferociously with a banal mind which has been only irritated by what it has been taught. He is a great personality because, against all these handicaps, what he wants is simple and basic: a woman. This urgent and violent need, common yet miraculous enough in itself, considering the unhappy environment of the animal, is the force which elevates him from nothingness to greatness. A ridiculous greatness, but in the nature of things beautiful to behold. All that he has been taught, and everything he believes, is phony, and yet he himself is real, almost super-real, because of this indestructible force in himself. His face is ridiculous. His personal rhythm is tense and jittery. His speech is shrill and violent. His gestures are wild. His ego is disjointed and epileptic. And yet deeply he possesses the same wholeness of spirit, and directness of energy, that is in all species of animals. There is little innate or cultivated spirit in him, but there is no absence of innocent animal force. He is a young man who has been taught that he has a chance, as a person, and believes it. As a matter of fact, he hasn't a chance in the world, and should have been told by somebody, or should not have had his natural and valuable ignorance spoiled by education, ruining an otherwise perfectly good and charming member of the human race.*)

(At the telephone he immediately begins to dial furiously, hesitates, changes his mind, stops dialing, hangs up furiously, and suddenly begins again.)

(Not more than half a minute after the firecracker arrival of DUDLEY R. BOSTWICK, *occurs the polka-and-waltz arrival of* HARRY.)

*(*HARRY *is another story.)*

(He comes in timidly, turning about uncertainly, awkward, out of place everywhere, embarrassed and encumbered by the contemporary costume, sick at heart, but determined to fit in somewhere. His arrival constitutes a dance.)

(His clothes don't fit. The pants are a little too large. The coat, which doesn't match, is also a little too large, and loose.)

(He is a dumb young fellow, but he has ideas. A philosophy, in fact. His philosophy is simple and beautiful. The world is sorrowful. The world needs laughter. HARRY *is funny. The world needs* HARRY. HARRY *will make the world laugh.)*

(He has probably had a year or two of high school. He has also listened to the boys at the pool room.)

(He's looking for Nick. He goes to the ARAB, *and says, Are you Nick? The* ARAB *shakes his head. He stands at the bar, waiting. He waits very busily.)*

HARRY *(as* NICK *returns).* You Nick?

NICK *(very loudly).* I am Nick.

HARRY *(acting).* Can you use a great comedian?

NICK *(behind the bar).* Who, for instance?

HARRY *(almost angry).* Me.

NICK. You? What's funny about you?

*(*DUDLEY *at the telephone, is dialing. Because of some defect in the apparatus the dialing is very loud.)*

DUDLEY. Hello. Sunset 7349? May I speak to Miss Elsie Mandelspiegel?

(Pause.)

HARRY *(with spirit and noise, dancing).* I dance and do gags and stuff.

NICK. In costume? Or are you wearing your costume?

DUDLEY. All I need is a cigar.

KITTY *(continuing the dream of grace).* I'd walk out of the house, and stand on the porch, and look at the trees, and smell the flowers, and run across the lawn, and lie down under a tree, and read a book. *(Pause.)* A book of poems, maybe.

DUDLEY *(very, very clearly).* Elsie Mandelspiegel. *(Impatiently.)* She has a room on the fourth floor. She's a nurse at the Southern Pacific Hospital. Elsie Mandelspiegel. She works at night. Elsie. Yes. *(He begins waiting again.)*

*(*WESLEY, *a colored boy, comes to the bar and stands near* HARRY, *waiting.)*

NICK. Beer?

WESLEY. No, sir. I'd like to talk to you.

NICK *(to* HARRY). All right. Get funny.

HARRY *(getting funny, an altogether different person, an actor with great energy, both in power of voice, and in force and speed of physical gesture).* Now, I'm standing on the corner of Third and Market. I'm looking around. I'm figuring it out. There it is. Right in front of me. The whole city. The whole world. People going by. They're going somewhere. I don't know where, but they're going. I ain't going *anywhere.* Where the hell can you go? I'm figuring it out. All right, I'm a citizen. A fat guy bumps his stomach into the face of an old lady. They were in a hurry. Fat and old. *They bumped.* Boom. I don't know. It may mean war. *War.* Germany. England. Russia. I don't know for sure. *(Loudly, dramatically, he salutes, about faces, presents arms, aims, and fires.)* WAAAAAR. *(He blows a call to arms.* NICK *gets sick of this, indicates with a gesture that* HARRY *should hold it, and goes to* WESLEY.)*

NICK. What's on *your* mind?

WESLEY *(confused).* Well—

NICK. Come on. Speak up. Are you hungry, or what?

WESLEY. Honest to God, I ain't hungry. All I want is a job. I don't want no charity.

NICK. Well, what can you do, and how good are you?

WESLEY. I can run errands, clean up, wash dishes, anything.

DUDLEY (*on the telephone, very eagerly*). Elsie? Elsie, this is Dudley. Elsie, I'll jump in the bay if you don't marry me. Life isn't worth living without you. I can't sleep. I can't think of anything but you. All the time. Day and night and night and day. Elsie, I love you. I love you. What? (*Burning up.*) Is this Sunset 7-3-4-9? (*Pause.*) 7943? (*Calmly, while* WILLIE *begins making a small racket.*) Well, what's *your* name? *Lorene? Lorene Smith?* I thought you were Elsie Mandelspiegel. What? Dudley. Yeah. Dudley R. Bostwick. Yeah. R. It stands for Raoul, but I never spell it out. I'm pleased to meet *you*, too. What? There's a lot of noise around here. (WILLIE *stops hitting the marble-game.*) Where am I? At Nick's, on Pacific Street. I work at the S. P. I told them I was sick and they gave me the afternoon off. Wait a minute. I'll ask them. I'd like to meet *you*, too. Sure. I'll ask them. (*Turns around to* NICK.) What's this address?

NICK. Number 3 Pacific Street, you cad.

DUDLEY. Cad? You don't know how I've been suffering on acount of Elsie. I take things too ceremoniously. I've got to be more lackadaisical. (*Into telephone.*) Hello, Elenore? I mean, Lorene. It's number 3 Pacific Street. Yeah. Sure. I'll wait for you. How'll you know me? You'll *know* me. I'll recognize you. Good-bye, now. (*He hangs up.*)

HARRY (*continuing his monologue, with gestures, movements, and so on*). I'm standing there. I didn't do anything to anybody. Why should *I* be a soldier? (*Sincerely, insanely.*) BOOOOOOOOOM. *WAR!* O.K. War. *I* retreat. *I* hate war. I move to Sacramento.

NICK (*shouting*). All right, Comedian. Lay off a minute.

HARRY (*broken-hearted, going to* WILLIE). Nobody's got a sense of humor any more. The world's dying for comedy like never before, but nobody knows how to *laugh.*

NICK (*to* WESLEY). Do you belong to the union?

WESLEY. What union?

NICK. For the love of Mike, where've you been? Don't you know you can't come into a place and ask for a job and get one and go to work, just like that. You've got to belong to one of the unions.

WESLEY. I didn't know. I got to have a job. Real soon.

NICK. Well, you've got to belong to a union.

WESLEY. I don't want any favors. All I want is a chance to earn a living.

NICK. Go on into the kitchen and tell Sam to give you some lunch.

WESLEY. Honest, I ain't hungry.

DUDLEY (*shouting*). What I've gone through for Elsie.

HARRY. I've got all kinds of funny ideas in my head to help make the world happy again.

NICK (*holding* WESLEY). No, he isn't hungry.

(WESLEY *almost faints from hunger.* NICK *catches him just in time. The* ARAB *and* NICK *go off with* WESLEY *into the kitchen.*)

HARRY (*to* WILLIE). See if you think this is funny. It's my own idea. I created this dance myself. It comes after the monologue.

(HARRY *begins to dance.* WILLIE *watches a moment, and then goes back to the game. It's a goofy dance, which* HARRY *does with great sorrow, but much energy.*)

DUDLEY. Elsie. Aw, gee, Elsie. What the hell do I want to see Lorene Smith for? Some girl I don't know.

(JOE *and* KITTY *have been drinking in silence. There is no sound now except the soft shoe shuffling of* HARRY, *the Comedian.*)

JOE. What's the dream now, Kitty Duval?

KITTY (*dreaming the words and pictures*). I dream of home. Christ, I always dream of home. I've no *home.* I've no place. But I always dream of all of us together again. We had a farm in Ohio. There was nothing good about it. It was always sad. There was always trouble. But I always dream about it as if I could go back and Papa would be there and Mamma and Louie and my little brother Stephen and my sister Mary. I'm Polish. Duval! My name isn't Duval, it's Koranovsky. Katerina Koranovsky. We lost everything. The house, the farm, the trees, the horses, the cows, the chickens. Papa died. He was old. He was thirteen years older than Mamma. We moved to Chicago. We tried to work. We tried to stay together. Louie got into trouble. The fellows he was with killed him for something. I don't know what. Stephen ran away from home. Seventeen years old. I don't know where he is. Then Mamma died. *(Pause.)* What's the dream? I dream of home.

(NICK comes out of the kitchen with WESLEY.)

NICK. Here. Sit down here and rest. That'll hold you for a *while.* Why didn't you tell me you were hungry? You all right now?

WESLEY *(sitting down in the chair at the piano).* Yes, I am. Thank you. I didn't know I was *that* hungry.

NICK. Fine. *(To HARRY who is dancing.)* Hey. What the hell do you think you're doing?

HARRY *(stopping).* That's my own idea. I'm a natural-born dancer and comedian.

(WESLEY begins slowly, one note, one chord at a time, to play the piano.)

NICK. You're no good. Why don't you try some other kind of work? Why don't you get a job in a store, selling something? What do you want to be a comedian for?

HARRY. I've got something for the world and they haven't got sense enough to let me give it to them. Nobody knows me.

DUDLEY. Elsie. Now I'm waiting for some dame I've never seen before. Lorene Smith. Never saw her in my life. Just happened to get the wrong number. She turns on the personality, and I'm a cooked Indian. Give me a beer, please.

HARRY. Nick, you've got to see my act. It's the greatest thing of its kind in America. All I want is a chance. No salary to begin. Let me try it out tonight. If I don't wow 'em, O.K., I'll go home. If vaudeville wasn't dead, a guy like me would have a chance.

NICK. You're not funny. You're a sad young punk. What the hell do you want to try to be funny for? You'll break every-

body's heart. What's there for you to be funny about? You've been poor all your life, haven't you?

HARRY. I've been poor all right, but don't forget that some things count more than some other things.

NICK. What counts more, for instance, than what else, for instance?

HARRY. Talent, for instance, counts more than money, for instance, that's what, and I've got talent. I get new ideas night and day. Everything comes natural to me. I've got style, but it'll take me a little time to round it out. That's all.

(By now WESLEY is playing something of his own which is very good and out of the world. He plays about half a minute, after which HARRY begins to dance.)

NICK *(watching).* I run the lousiest dive in Frisco, and a guy arrives and makes me stock up with champagne. The whores come in and holler at me that they're ladies. Talent comes in and begs me for a chance to show itself. Even society people come here once in a while. I don't know what for. Maybe it's liquor. Maybe it's the location. Maybe it's my personality. Maybe it's the crazy personality of the joint. The old honky-tonk. *(Pause.)* Maybe they can't feel at home anywhere else.

(By now WESLEY is really playing, and HARRY is going through a new routine. DUDLEY grows sadder and sadder.)

KITTY. Please dance with me.

JOE *(loudly).* I never learned to dance.

KITTY. Anybody can dance. Just hold me in your arms.

JOE. I'm very fond of you. I'm *sorry.* I *can't* dance. I wish to God I could.

KITTY. Oh, please.

JOE. Forgive me. I'd like to very much.

(KITTY dances alone. TOM comes in with a package. He sees KITTY and goes ga-ga again. He comes out of the trance and puts the bundle on the table in front of JOE.)

JOE *(taking the package).* What'd you get?

TOM. Two dollars' worth of toys. That's what you sent me for. The girl asked me what I wanted with toys. I didn't know what to tell her. *(He stares at* KITTY, *then back at* JOE.*)* Joe? I've got to have some money. After all you've done for me, I'll do anything in the world for you, but, Joe, you got to give me some money once in a while.

JOE. What do you want it for?

*(*TOM *turns and stares at* KITTY *dancing.)*

JOE *(noticing).* Sure. Here. Here's five. *(Shouting.)* Can you dance?

TOM *(proudly).* I got second prize at the Palomar in Sacramento five years ago.

JOE *(loudly, opening package).* O.K., dance with her.

TOM. You mean *her?*

JOE *(loudly).* I mean Kitty Duval, the burlesque queen. I mean the queen of the world burlesque. Dance with her. She wants to dance.

TOM *(worshipping the name Kitty Duval, helplessly).* Joe, can I tell you something?

JOE *(he brings out a toy and winds it).* You don't have to. I know. You love her. You *really* love her. I'm not blind. I know. But take care of yourself. Don't get sick that way again.

NICK *(looking at and listening to* WESLEY *with amazement).* Comes in here and wants to be a dish-washer. Faints from hunger. And then sits down and plays better than Heifetz.

JOE. Heifetz plays the violin.

NICK. All right, don't get careful. He's good, ain't he?

TOM *(to* KITTY*).* Kitty.

JOE *(he lets the toy go, loudly).* Don't *talk.* Just *dance.*

*(*TOM *and* KITTY *dance.* NICK *is at the bar, watching everything.* HARRY *is dancing.* DUDLEY *is grieving into his beer.* LORENE SMITH, *about thirty-seven, very overbearing and funny-looking, comes to the bar.)*

NICK. What'll it be, lady?

LORENE *(looking about and scaring all the young men).* I'm looking for the young man I talked to on the telephone. Dudley R. Bostwick.

DUDLEY *(jumping, running to her, stopping, shocked).* Dudley R. *(Slowly.)* Bostwick? Oh, yeah. He left here ten minutes ago. You mean Dudley Bostwick, that poor man on crutches?

LORENE. Crutches?

DUDLEY. Yeah. Dudley Bostwick. That's what he *said* his name was. He said to tell you not to wait.

LORENE. Well. *(She begins to go, turns around.)* Are you sure *you're* not Dudley Bostwick?

DUDLEY. Who—me? *(Grandly.)* My name is Roger Tenefrancia. I'm a French-Canadian. I never saw the poor fellow before.

LORENE. It seems to me your voice is like the voice I heard over the telephone.

DUDLEY. A coincidence. An accident. A quirk of fate. One of those things. Dismiss the thought. That poor cripple hobbled out of here ten minutes ago.

LORENE. He said he was going to commit suicide. I only wanted to be of help. *(She goes.)*

DUDLEY. Be of help? What kind of help could she be, of? *(*DUDLEY *runs to the telephone in the corner.)* Gee whiz, Elsie. Gee whiz. I'll never leave you again. *(He turns the pages of a little address book.)* Why do I always forget the number? I've tried to get her on the phone a hundred times this week and I still forget the number. She won't come to the phone, but I keep trying anyway. She's out. She's not in. She's working. I get the wrong number. Everything goes haywire. I can't sleep. *(Defiantly.)* She'll come to the phone one of these days. If there's anything to true love at all, she'll come to the phone. Sunset 7349.

(He dials the number, as JOE *goes on studying the toys. They are one big mechanical toy, whistles, and a music box.* JOE *blows into the whistles, quickly, by way of getting casually acquainted with them.)*

*(*TOM *and* KITTY *stop dancing.* TOM *stares at her.)*

DUDLEY. Hello. Is this Sunset 7349? May I speak to Elsie? Yes. *(Emphatically, and bitterly.)* No, this is *not* Dudley Bostwick. This is Roger Tenefrancia of Montreal,

THE TIME OF YOUR LIFE

Canada. I'm a childhood friend of Miss Mandelspiegel. We went to kindergarten together. *(Hand over phone.)* God damn it. *(Into phone.)* Yes. I'll wait, thank you.

TOM. I love you.

KITTY. You want to go to my room? *(TOM can't answer.)* Have you got two dollars?

TOM *(shaking his head with confusion).* I've got *five* dollars, but I *love* you.

KITTY *(looking at him).* You want to spend *all* that money?

(TOM embraces her. They go. JOE watches. Goes back to the toy.)

JOE. Where's that longshoreman, McCarthy?

NICK. He'll be around.

JOE. What do you think he'll have to say today?

NICK. Plenty, as usual. I'm going next door to see who won that third race at Laurel.

JOE. Precious Time won it.

NICK. That's what you think. *(He goes).*

JOE *(to himself).* A horse named McCarthy is running in the sixth race today.

DUDLEY *(on the phone).* Hello. Hello, Elsie? Elsie? *(His voice weakens; also his limbs.)* My God. She's come to the phone. Elsie, I'm at Nick's on Pacific Street. You've got to come here and talk to me. Hello. Hello, Elsie? *(Amazed.)* Did she hang up? Or was I disconnected?

(He hangs up and goes to bar.)

(WESLEY is still playing the piano. HARRY is still dancing. JOE has wound up the big mechanical toy and is watching it work.)

(NICK returns.)

NICK *(watching the toy).* Say. That's some gadget.

JOE. How much did I win?

NICK. How do you know you *won*?

JOE. Don't be silly. He said Precious Time was going to win by ten lengths, didn't he? He's in love, isn't he?

NICK. O.K. I don't know why, but Precious Time won. You got eighty for ten. How do you do it?

JOE *(roaring).* Faith. Faith. How'd he win?

NICK. By a nose. Look him up in The Racing Form. The slowest, the cheapest, the worst horse in the race, and the worst jockey. What's the matter with my luck?

JOE. How much did you lose?

NICK. Fifty cents.

JOE. You should never gamble.

NICK. Why not?

JOE. You always bet fifty cents. You've got no more faith than a flea, that's why.

HARRY *(shouting).* How do you like this, Nick? *(He is really busy now, all legs and arms.)*

NICK *(turning and watching).* Not bad. Hang around. You can wait table. *(To WESLEY.)* Hey. Wesley. Can you play that again tonight?

WESLEY *(turning, but still playing the piano).* I don't know for sure, Mr. Nick. I can play *something*.

NICK. Good. *You* hang around, too. *(He goes behind the bar.)*

(The atmosphere is now one of warm, natural, American ease; every man innocent and good; each doing what he believes he should do, or what he must do. There is deep American naïveté and faith in the behavior of each person. No one is competing with anyone else. No one hates anyone else. Every man is living, and letting live. Each man is following his destiny as he feels it should be followed; or is abandoning it as he feels he must, by now, be abandoned; or is forgetting it for the moment as he feels he should forget it. Although everyone is dead serious, there is unmistakable smiling and humor in the scene; a sense of the human body and spirit emerging from the world-imposed state of stress and fretfulness, fear and awkwardness, to the more natural state of casualness and grace. Each person belongs to the environment, in his own person, as himself: WESLEY is playing better than ever. HARRY is hoofing better than ever. NICK is behind the bar shining glasses. JOE is smiling at the toy and studying it. DUDLEY, although still troubled, is at least calm now and full of melancholy poise. WILLIE, at the

marble-game, is happy. The ARAB is deep in his memories, where he wants to be.)

(Into this scene and atmosphere comes BLICK.)

(BLICK is the sort of human being you dislike at sight. He is no different from anybody else physically. His face is an ordinary face. There is nothing obviously wrong with him, and yet you know that it is impossible, even by the most generous expansion of understanding, to accept him as a human being. He is the strong man without strength—strong only among the weak—the weakling who uses force on the weaker.)

(BLICK enters casually, as if he were a customer, and immediately HARRY begins slowing down.)

BLICK (oily, and with mock-friendliness). Hello, Nick.

NICK (stopping his work and leaning across the bar). What do you want to come here for? You're too big a man for a little honky-tonk.

BLICK (flattered). Now, Nick.

NICK. Important people never come here. Here. Have a drink. (Whiskey bottle.)

BLICK. Thanks, I don't drink.

NICK (drinking the drink himself). Well, why don't you?

BLICK. I have responsibilities.

NICK. You're head of the lousy Vice Squad. There's no vice here.

BLICK (sharply). Street-walkers are working out of this place.

NICK (angry). What do you want?

BLICK (loudly). I just want you to know that it's got to stop.

(The music stops. The mechanical toy runs down. There is absolute silence, and a strange fearfulness and disharmony in the atmosphere now. HARRY doesn't know what to do with his hands or feet. WESLEY's arms hang at his sides. JOE quietly pushes the toy to one side of the table eager to study what is happening. WILLIE stops playing the marble-game, turns around and begins to wait. DUDLEY straightens up very, very vigorously, as if to say: "Nothing can scare me. I know love is the only

thing." The ARAB is the same as ever, but watchful. NICK is arrogantly aloof. There is a moment of this silence and tension, as though BLICK were waiting for everybody to acknowledge his presence. He is obviously flattered by the acknowledgment of Harry, Dudley, Wesley, and Willie, but a little irritated by Nick's aloofness and unfriendliness.)

NICK. Don't look at me. I can't tell a street-walker from a lady. You married?

BLICK. You're not asking me questions. I'm telling you.

NICK (interrupting). You're a man of about forty-five or so. You ought to know better.

BLICK (angry). Street-walkers are working out of this place.

NICK (beginning to shout). Now, don't start any trouble with me. People come here to drink and loaf around. I don't care who they are.

BLICK. Well, I do.

NICK. The only way to find out if a lady is a street-walker is to walk the streets with her, go to bed, and make sure. You wouldn't want to do that. You'd like to, of course.

BLICK. Any more of it, and I'll have your joint closed.

NICK (very casually, without ill-will). Listen. I've got no use for you, or anybody like you. You're out to change the world from something bad to something worse. Something like yourself.

BLICK (furious pause, and contempt). I'll be back tonight. (He begins to go.)

NICK (very angry but very calm). Do yourself a big favor and don't come back tonight. Send somebody else. I don't like your personality.

BLICK (casually, but with contempt). Don't break any laws. I don't like yours, either.

(He looks the place over, and goes.)

(There is a moment of silence. Then WILLIE turns and puts a new nickel in the slot and starts a new game. WESLEY turns to the piano and rather falteringly begins to play. His heart really isn't in it. HARRY walks about, unable to dance. DUDLEY lapses *into his customary melancholy, at a table.* NICK *whistles a little: suddenly stops.* JOE *winds the toy.)*

JOE *(comically).* Nick. You going to kill that man?

NICK. I'm disgusted.

JOE. Yeah? Why?

NICK. Why should I get worked up over a guy like that? Why should I hate *him?* He's nothing. He's nobody. He's a mouse. But every time he comes into this place I get burned up. He doesn't want to drink. He doesn't want to sit down. He doesn't want to take things easy. Tell me one thing?

JOE. Do my best.

NICK. What's a punk like *that* want to go out and try to change the world for?

JOE *(amazed).* Does *he* want to change the world, too?

NICK *(irritated).* You know what I mean. What's he want to bother people for? He's *sick.*

JOE *(almost to himself, reflecting on the fact that* BLICK *too wants to change the world).* I guess he wants to change the world at that.

NICK. So I go to work and hate him.

JOE. It's not him, Nick. It's everything.

NICK. Yeah, *I know.* But I've still got no use for him. He's no good. You know what I mean? He hurts little people. *(Confused.)* One of the girls tried to commit suicide on account of him. *(Furiously.)* I'll break his head if he hurts anybody around here. This is *my* joint. *(Afterthought.)* Or anybody's *feelings,* either.

JOE. He may not be so bad, deep down underneath.

NICK. I know all about him. He's no good.

(During this talk WESLEY *has really begun to play the piano, the toy is rattling again, and little by little* HARRY *has begun to dance.* NICK *has come around the bar, and*

now, very much like a child—forgetting all his anger—is watching the toy work. He begins to smile at everything: turns and listens to WESLEY: watches HARRY: nods at the ARAB: shakes his head at DUDLEY: and gestures amiably about WILLIE. It's his joint all right.)*

(It's a good, low-down, honky-tonk American place that lets people alone.)

NICK. I've got a good joint. There's nothing wrong here. Hey. Comedian. Stick to the dancing tonight. I think you're O.K. Wesley? Do some more of that tonight. That's fine!

HARRY. Thanks, Nick. Gosh, I'm on my way at last. *(On telephone.)* Hello, Ma? Is that you, Ma? Harry. I got the job. *(He hangs up and walks around, smiling.)*

NICK *(watching the toy all the time).* Say, that really is something. What is that, anyway?

(MARY L. comes in.)

JOE *(holding it toward NICK, and MARY L.).* Nick, this is a toy. A contraption devised by the cunning of man to drive boredom, or grief, or anger out of children. A noble gadget. A gadget, I might say, infinitely nobler than any other I can think of at the moment.

(Everybody gathers around JOE's *table to look at the toy. The toy stops working.* JOE *winds the music box. Lifts a whistle: blows it, making a very strange, funny and sorrowful sound.)*

Delightful. Tragic, but delightful.

(WESLEY plays the music-box theme on the piano. MARY L. *takes a table.)*

NICK. Joe. That girl, Kitty. What's she mean, calling me a dentist? I wouldn't hurt anybody, let alone a tooth.

(NICK goes to MARY L.'s table. HARRY imitates the toy. Dances. The piano music comes up, the light dims slowly, while the piano solo continues.)

CURTAIN

ACT TWO

An hour later. All the people who were at Nick's when the curtain came down are still there. JOE *at his table, quietly shuffling and turning a deck of cards, and at the same time watching the face of the woman, and looking at the initials on her handbag, as though they were the symbols of the lost glory of the world. The* WOMAN, *in turn, very casually regards* JOE *occasionally. Or rather senses him; has sensed him in fact the whole hour. She is mildly tight on beer, and* JOE *himself is tight, but as always completely under control; simply sharper. The others are about, at tables, and so on.*

JOE. Is it Madge—Laubowitz?

MARY. Is what *what?*

JOE. Is the name Mabel Lepescu?

MARY. What name?

JOE. The name the initials M. L. stand for. The initials on your bag.

MARY. No.

JOE *(after a long pause, thinking deeply what the name might be, turning a card, looking into the beautiful face of the woman).* Margie Longworthy?

MARY *(all this is very natural and sincere, no comedy on the part of the people involved: they are both solemn, being drunk).* No.

JOE *(his voice higher-pitched, as though he were growing alarmed).* Midge Laurie? (MARY *shakes her head.)* My initials are J. T.

MARY *(Pause).* John?

JOE. No. *(Pause.)* Martha Lancaster?

MARY. No. *(Slight pause.)* Joseph?

JOE. Well, not exactly. That's my first name, but everybody calls me Joe. The last name is the tough one. I'll help you a little. I'm Irish. *(Pause.)* Is it just plain Mary?

MARY. Yes, it is. I'm Irish, too. At least on my father's side. English on my mother's side.

JOE. I'm Irish on both sides. Mary's one of my favorite names. I guess that's why I didn't think of it. I met a girl in Mexico City named Mary once. She was an American from Philadelphia. She got married there. In Mexico City, I mean. While I was *there.* We were in love, too. At least *I* was. You never know about anyone else. They were engaged, you see, and her

mother was with her, so they went through with it. Must have been six or seven years ago. She's probably got three or four children by this time.

MARY. Are you still in love with her?

JOE. Well—no. To tell you the truth, I'm not sure. I guess I am. I didn't even knew she was engaged until a couple of days before they got married. I thought *I* was going to marry her. I kept thinking all the time about the kind of kids we would be likely to have. My favorite was the third one. The first two were fine. Handsome and fine and intelligent, but that third one was different. Dumb and goofy-looking. I liked *him* a lot. When she told me she was going to be married, I didn't feel so bad about the first two, it was that dumb one.

MARY *(after a pause of some few seconds).* What do you do?

JOE. Do? To tell you the truth, nothing.

MARY. Do you always drink a great deal?

JOE *(scientifically).* Not *always.* Only when I'm awake. I sleep seven or eight hours every night, you know.

MARY. How nice. I mean to drink when you're awake.

JOE *(thoughtfully).* It's a privilege.

MARY. Do you really *like* to drink?

JOE *(positively).* As much as I like to *breathe.*

MARY *(beautifully).* Why?

JOE *(dramatically).* Why do I like to drink? *(Pause.)* Because I don't like to be gypped. Because I don't like to be dead most of the time and just a little alive every once in a long while. *(Pause.)* If I don't drink, I become fascinated by unimportant things—like everybody else. I get busy. Do things. All kinds of little stupid things, for all kinds of little stupid reasons. Proud, selfish, *ordinary* things. I've done them. Now I don't do anything. *I live all the time.* Then I go to sleep. *(Pause.)*

MARY. Do you sleep well?

JOE *(taking it for granted)*. Of course.

MARY *(quietly, almost with tenderness)*. What are your plans?

JOE *(loudly, but also tenderly)*. Plans? I haven't *got* any. *I just get up.*

MARY *(beginning to understand every-thing)*. Oh, yes. Yes, of course.

(DUDLEY puts a nickel in the phonograph.)

JOE *(thoughtfully)*. Why do I drink? *(Pause, while he thinks about it. The thinking appears to be profound and complex, and has the effect of giving his face a very comical and naïve expression.)* That question calls for a pretty compli-cated answer. *(He smiles abstractly.)*

MARY. Oh, I didn't mean—

JOE *(swiftly, gallantly)*. No. No. I *insist*. I *know* why. It's just a matter of finding words. Little ones.

MARY. It really doesn't matter.

JOE *(seriously)*. Oh, yes, it does. *(Clini-cally.)* Now, why do I drink? *(Scientifi-cally.)* No. Why does *anybody* drink? *(Working it out.)* Every day has twenty-four hours.

MARY *(sadly, but brightly)*. Yes, that's true.

JOE. Twenty-four hours. Out of the twenty-four hours at *least* twenty-three and a half are—my God, I don't know why—dull, dead, boring, empty, and murderous. Minutes on the clock, *not time of living.* It doesn't make any difference who you are or what you do, twenty-three and a half hours of the twenty-four are spent *waiting*.

MARY. Waiting?

JOE *(gesturing, loudly)*. And the more you wait, the less there is to wait for.

MARY *(attentively, beautifully his student)*. Oh?

JOE *(continuing)*. That goes on for days and days, and weeks and months and years, and years, and the first thing you know *all* the years are dead. All the min-utes are dead. You yourself are dead.

There's nothing to wait for any more. Nothing except *minutes* on the *clock*. No time of life. Nothing but minutes, and idiocy. Beautiful, bright, intelligent idiocy. *(Pause.)* Does that answer your question?

MARY *(earnestly)*. I'm afraid it does. Thank you. You shouldn't have gone to all the trouble.

JOE. No trouble at all. *(Pause.)* You have children?

MARY. Yes. Two. A son and a daughter.

JOE *(delighted)*. How swell. Do they look like you?

MARY. Yes.

JOE. Then why are you sad?

MARY. I was always sad. It's just that after I was married I was allowed to drink.

JOE *(eagerly)*. Who are you waiting for?

MARY. No one.

JOE *(smiling)*. I'm not waiting for any-body, either.

MARY. My husband, of course.

JOE. Oh, sure.

MARY. He's a lawyer.

JOE *(standing, leaning on the table)*. He's a great guy. I like him. I'm very fond of him.

MARY *(listening)*. You have responsibili-ties?

JOE *(loudly)*. *One*, and *thousands*. As a matter of fact, I feel responsible to every-body. At least to everybody I met. I've been trying for three years to find out if it's possible to live what I think is a civi-lized life. I mean a life that can't hurt any other life.

MARY. You're famous?

JOE. Very. Utterly unknown, but very fa-mous. Would you like to dance?

MARY. All right.

JOE *(loudly)*. I'm *sorry*. I don't dance. I didn't think you'd like to.

MARY. To tell you the truth, I don't like to dance at all.

JOE *(proudly. Commentator)*. I can hardly walk.

MARY. You mean you're tight?

JOE *(smiling)*. No. I mean *all* the time.

MARY *(looking at him closely)*. Were you ever in Paris?

JOE. In 1929, and again in 1934.

MARY. What month of 1934?

JOE. Most of April, all of May, and a little of June.

MARY. I was there in November and December that year.

JOE. We were there almost at the same time. You were married?

MARY. Engaged. *(They are silent a moment, looking at one another. Quietly and with great charm.)* Are you *really* in love with me?

JOE. Yes.

MARY. Is it the champagne?

JOE. Yes. Partly, at least. *(He sits down.)*

MARY. If you don't see me again will you be very unhappy?

JOE. Very.

MARY *(getting up)*. I'm so pleased. *(JOE is deeply grieved that she is going. In fact, he is almost panic-stricken about it, getting up in a way that is full of furious sorrow and regret.)* I must go now. Please don't get up. *(JOE is up, staring at her with amazement.)* Good-by.

JOE *(simply)*. Good-by.

(The WOMAN *stands looking at him a moment, then turns and goes. JOE stands staring after her for a long time. Just as he is slowly sitting down again, the NEWSBOY enters, and goes to Joe's table.)*

NEWSBOY. Paper, Mister?

JOE. How many you got this time?

NEWSBOY. Eleven.

(JOE buys them all, looks at the lousy headlines, throws them away.)

(The NEWSBOY *looks at* JOE, *amazed. He walks over to* NICK *at the bar.)*

NEWSBOY *(troubled)*. Hey, Mister, do you own this place?

NICK *(casually but emphatically)*. I own this place.

NEWSBOY. Can you use a great lyric tenor?

NICK *(almost to himself)*. Great lyric tenor? *(Loudly.)* Who?

NEWSBOY *(loud and the least bit angry)*. Me. I'm getting too big to sell papers. I don't want to holler headlines all the time. I want to *sing*. You can use a great lyric tenor, can't you?

NICK. What's lyric about you?

NEWSBOY *(voice high-pitched, confused)*. My voice.

NICK. Oh. *(Slight pause, giving in.)* All right, then—sing!

(The NEWSBOY *breaks into swift and beautiful song: "When Irish Eyes Are Smiling."* NICK *and* JOE *listen carefully:* NICK *with wonder,* JOE *with amazement and delight.)*

NEWSBOY *(singing)*.
When Irish eyes are smiling,
Sure 'tis like a morn in Spring.
In the lilt of Irish laughter,
You can hear the angels sing.
When Irish hearts are happy,
All the world seems bright and gay.
But when Irish eyes are smiling—

NICK *(loudly, swiftly)*. Are you Irish?

NEWSBOY *(speaking swiftly, loudly, a little impatient with the irrelevant question)*. No. I'm Greek. *(He finishes the song, singing louder than ever.)*

Sure they steal your heart away.

(He turns to NICK *dramatically, like a vaudeville singer begging his audience for applause.* NICK *studies the boy eagerly.* JOE *gets to his feet and leans toward the* BOY *and* NICK.)*

NICK. Not bad. Let me hear you again about a year from now.

NEWSBOY *(thrilled)*. Honest?

NICK. Yeah. Along about November 7th, 1940.

NEWSBOY *(happier than ever before in his life, running over to* JOE)*. Did you hear it too, Mister?

JOE. Yes, and it's great. What part of Greece?

NEWSBOY. Salonica. Gosh, Mister. Thanks.

JOE. Don't wait a year. Come back with some papers a little later. You're a great singer.

NEWSBOY (*thrilled and excited*). Aw, thanks, Mister. So long. (*Running, to* NICK.) Thanks, Mister.

(*He runs out.* JOE *and* NICK *look at the swinging doors.* JOE *sits down.* NICK *laughs.*)

NICK. Joe, people are so wonderful. Look at that kid.

JOE. Of course they're wonderful. Every one of them is wonderful.

(MC CARTHY *and* KRUPP *come in, talking.*)

(MC CARTHY *is a big man in work clothes, which make him seem very young. He is wearing black jeans, and a blue workman's shirt. No tie. No hat. He has broad shoulders, a lean intelligent face, thick black hair. In his right back pocket is the longshoreman's hook. His arms are long and hairy. His sleeves are rolled up to just below his elbows. He is a casual man, easy-going in movement, sharp in perception, swift in appreciation of charm or innocence or comedy, and gentle in spirit. His speech is clear and full of warmth. His voice is powerful, but modulated. He enjoys the world, in spite of the mess it is, and he is fond of people, in spite of the mess they are.*)

(KRUPP *is not quite as tall or broad-shouldered as* MC CARTHY. *He is physically encumbered by his uniform, club, pistol, belt, and cap. And he is plainly not at home in the role of policeman. His movement is stiff and unintentionally pompous. He is a naïve man, essentially good. His understanding is less than McCarthy's, but he is honest and he doesn't try to bluff.*)

KRUPP. You don't understand what I mean. Hi-ya, Joe.

JOE. Hello, Krupp.

MC CARTHY. Hi-ya, Joe.

JOE. Hello, McCarthy.

KRUPP. Two beers, Nick. (*To* MC CARTHY.) All I do is carry out orders, carry out orders. I don't know what the idea is behind the order. Who it's for, or who it's against, or why. All I do is carry it out.

(NICK *gives them beer.*)

MC CARTHY. You don't read enough.

KRUPP. I do read. I read *The Examiner* every morning. *The Call-Bulletin* every night.

MC CARTHY. And carry out orders. What are the orders now?

KRUPP. To keep the peace down here on the waterfront.

MC CARTHY. Keep it for who? (*To* JOE.) Right?

JOE (*sorrowfully*). Right.

KRUPP. How do I know for who? The peace. Just keep it.

MC CARTHY. It's got to be kept for somebody. Who would you suspect it's kept for?

KRUPP. For citizens!

MC CARTHY. I'm a citizen!

KRUPP. All right, I'm keeping it for you.

MC CARTHY. By hitting me over the head with a club? (*To* JOE.) Right?

JOE (*melancholy, with remembrance*). I don't know.

KRUPP. Mac, you know I never hit you over the head with a club.

MC CARTHY. But you will if you're on duty at the time and happen to stand on the opposite side of myself, on duty.

KRUPP. We went to Mission High together. We were always good friends. The only time we ever fought was that time over Alma Haggerty. Did you marry Alma Haggerty? (*To* JOE.) Right?

JOE. Everything's right.

MC CARTHY. No. Did you? (*To* JOE.) Joe, are you with me or against me?

JOE. I'm with everybody. One at a time.

KRUPP. No. And that's just what I mean.

MC CARTHY. You mean neither one of us is going to marry the thing we're fighting for?

KRUPP. *I don't even know what it is.*

MC CARTHY. You don't read enough, I tell you.

KRUPP. Mac, you don't know what you're fighting for, either.

MC CARTHY. It's so simple, it's fantastic.

KRUPP. All right, what are you fighting for?

MC CARTHY. For the rights of the inferior. Right?

JOE. Something like that.

KRUPP. The who?

MC CARTHY. The inferior. The world is full of Mahoneys who haven't got what it takes to make monkeys out of everybody else, near by. The men who were created equal. Remember?

KRUPP. Mac, you're not inferior.

MC CARTHY. I'm a longshoreman. And an idealist. I'm a man with too much brawn to be an intellectual, exclusively. I married a small, sensitive, cultured woman so that my kids would be sissies instead of suckers. A strong man with any sensibility has no choice in this world but to be a heel, or a *worker*. I haven't the heart to be a heel, so I'm a worker. I've got a son in high school who's already thinking of being a writer.

KRUPP. I wanted to be a writer once.

JOE. Wonderful. (*He puts down the paper, looks at* KRUPP *and* MC CARTHY.)

MC CARTHY. They *all* wanted to be writers. Every maniac in the world that ever brought about the murder of people through war started out in an attic or a basement writing poetry. It stank. So they got even by becoming important heels. And it's still going on.

KRUPP. Is it really, Joe?

JOE. Look at today's paper.

MC CARTHY. Right now on Telegraph Hill is some punk who is trying to be Shakespeare. Ten years from now he'll be a senator. Or a communist.

KRUPP. Somebody ought to do something about it.

MC CARTHY (*mischievously, with laughter in his voice*). The thing to do is to have more magazines. Hundreds of them. *Thousands.* Print everything they write, so they'll believe they're immortal. That way keep them from going haywire.

KRUPP. Mac, you ought to be a writer yourself.

MC CARTHY. I hate the tribe. They're mischief-makers. Right?

JOE (*swiftly*). Everything's right. Right and wrong.

KRUPP. Then why do you read?

MC CARTHY (*laughing*). It's relaxing. It's soothing. (*Pause.*) The lousiest people born into the world are writers. Language is all right. It's the people who use language that are lousy. (*The* ARAB *has moved a little closer, and is listening carefully.*) (*To the* ARAB.) What do you think, Brother?

ARAB (*after making many faces, thinking very deeply*). No foundation. All the way down the line. What. What-not. Nothing. I go walk and look at sky. (*He goes.*)

KRUPP. What? What-not? (*To* JOE.) What's that mean?

JOE (*slowly, thinking, remembering*). What? What-not? That means this side, that side. Inhale, exhale. What: birth. What-not: death. The inevitable, the astounding, the magnificent seed of growth and decay in all things. Beginning, and end. That man, in his own way, is a prophet. He is one who, with the help of *beer,* is able to reach that state of deep understanding in which what and what-not, the reasonable and the unreasonable, are one.

MC CARTHY. Right.

KRUPP. If you can understand that kind of talk, how can you be a longshoreman?

MC CARTHY. I come from a long line of McCarthys who never married or slept with anything but the most powerful and quarrelsome flesh. (*He drinks beer.*)

KRUPP. I could listen to you two guys for hours, but I'll be damned if I know what the hell you're talking about.

MC CARTHY. The consequence is that all the McCarthys are too great and too strong to be heroes. Only the weak and unsure perform the heroic. They've *got* to. The more heroes you have, the worse the history of the world becomes. Right?

JOE. Go outside and look at it.

KRUPP. You sure can philos—philosoph— Boy. you can talk.

MC CARTHY. I wouldn't talk this way to anyone but a man in uniform, and a man who couldn't understand a word of what I was saying. The party I'm speaking of, my friend, is YOU.

(The phone rings.)

(HARRY gets up from his table suddenly and begins a new dance.)

KRUPP *(noticing him, with great authority).* Here, here. What do you think you're doing?

HARRY *(stopping).* I just got an idea for a new dance. I'm trying it out. Nick. Nick, the phone's ringing.

KRUPP *(to MC CARTHY).* Has he got a right to do that?

MC CARTHY. The living have danced from the beginning of time. I might even say, the dance and the life have moved along together, until now we have— *(To HARRY.)* Go into your dance, son, and show us what we have.

HARRY. I haven't got it worked out *completely* yet, but it starts out like this. *(He dances.)*

NICK *(on phone).* Nick's Pacific Street Restaurant, Saloon, and Entertainment Palace. Good afternoon. Nick speaking. *(Listens.)* Who? *(Turns around.)* Is there a Dudley Bostwick in the joint?

(DUDLEY jumps to his feet and goes to phone.)

DUDLEY *(on phone).* Hello. Elsie? *(Listens.)* You're coming down? *(Elated. To the saloon.)* She's coming down. *(Pause.)* No. I won't drink. Aw, gosh, Elsie.

(He hangs up, looks about him strangely, as if he were just born, walks around touching things, putting chairs in place, and so on.)

MC CARTHY *(to HARRY.)* Splendid. Splendid.

HARRY. Then I go into this little routine.

(He demonstrates.)

KRUPP. Is that good, Mac?

MC CARTHY. It's awful, but it's honest and ambitious, like everything else in this great country.

HARRY. Then I work along into this. *(He demonstrates.)* And *this* is where I *really* get going. *(He finishes the dance.)*

MC CARTHY. Excellent. A most satisfying demonstration of the present state of the American body and soul. Son, you're a genius.

HARRY *(delighted, shaking hands with MC-CARTHY).* I go on in front of an audience for the first time in my life tonight.

MC CARTHY. They'll be delighted. Where'd you learn to dance?

HARRY. Never took a lesson in my life. I'm a natural-born dancer. And *comedian,* too.

MC CARTHY *(astounded).* You can make people *laugh?*

HARRY *(dumbly).* I can be funny, but they won't laugh.

MC CARTHY. That's odd. Why not?

HARRY. I don't know. They just won't laugh.

MC CARTHY. Would you care to be funny now?

HARRY. I'd like to try out a new monologue I've been thinking about.

MC CARTHY. Please do. I promise you if it's funny I shall *roar* with laughter.

HARRY. This is it. *(Goes into the act, with much energy.)* I'm up at Sharkey's on Turk Street. It's a quarter to nine, daylight saving. Wednesday, the eleventh. What I've got is a headache and a 1918 nickel. What I *want* is a cup of coffee. If I buy a cup of coffee with the nickel, I've got to walk home. I've got an eight-ball problem. George the Greek is shooting a game of snooker with Pedro the Filipino. *I'm in rags.* They're wearing thirty-five dollar suits, made to order. I haven't got a cigarette. They're smoking Bobby Burns panatelas. I'm thinking it over, like I always do. George the Greek is in a tough spot. If I buy a cup of coffee, I'll want another cup. What happens? My *ear* aches! My ear. George the Greek takes the cue. Chalks it. Studies the table. Touches the cue-ball delicately. Tick. What happens? He makes the three-ball! What do I do. I get confused. *I go out and buy a morning paper.* What the hell do I want with a morning paper? What I *want* is a cup of coffee, and a good used car. I go out and buy a morning paper. Thursday, the twelfth. Maybe the headline's about *me*. I take a quick look. *No. The headline is not about me.* It's about Hitler. Seven thousand miles away. I'm here. Who the hell is Hitler? Who's behind the eight-ball? I turn around. *Everybody's behind the eight-ball!*

(*Pause.* KRUPP *moves toward* HARRY *as if to make an important arrest.* HARRY *moves to the swinging doors.* MC CARTHY *stops* KRUPP.)

MC CARTHY (*to* HARRY). It's the funniest thing I've ever heard. Or *seen*, for that matter.

HARRY (*coming back to* MC CARTHY). Then, why don't you laugh?

MC CARTHY. I don't know, *yet*.

HARRY. I'm always getting funny ideas that nobody will laugh at.

MC CARTHY (*thoughtfully*). It may be that you've stumbled headlong into a new kind of comedy.

HARRY. Well, what good is it if it doesn't make anybody laugh?

MC CARTHY. There are *kinds* of laughter, son. I must say, in all truth, that I *am* laughing, although not *out loud*.

HARRY. I want to *hear* people laugh. *Out loud.* That's why I keep thinking of funny things to say.

MC CARTHY. Well. They may catch on in time. Let's go, Krupp. So long, Joe. (MC CARTHY *and* KRUPP *go*.)

JOE. So long. (*After a moment's pause.*) Hey, Nick.

NICK. Yeah.

JOE. Bet McCarthy in the last race.

NICK. You're crazy. That horse is a double-crossing, no-good—

JOE. Bet everything you've got on McCarthy.

NICK. I'm not betting a nickel on him. *You* bet everything you've got on McCarthy.

JOE. I don't need money.

NICK. What makes you think McCarthy's going to win?

JOE. McCarthy's name's McCarthy, isn't it?

NICK. Yeah. So what?

JOE. The *horse* named McCarthy is going to win, *that's all*. Today.

NICK. Why?

JOE. You do what I tell you, and everything will be all right.

NICK. McCarthy likes to talk, that's all. (*Pause.*) Where's Tom?

JOE. He'll be around. He'll be miserable, but he'll be around. Five or ten minutes more.

NICK. You don't believe that Kitty, do you? About being in burlesque?

JOE (*very clearly*). I believe dreams sooner than statistics.

NICK (*remembering*). She sure is somebody. Called me a dentist.

(TOM, *turning about, confused, troubled, comes in, and hurries to Joe's table.*)

JOE. What's the matter?

TOM. Here's your five, Joe. I'm in trouble again.

JOE. If it's not organic, it'll cure itself. If it is organic, science will cure it. What is it, organic or non-organic?

TOM. Joe, I don't know— (*He seems to be completely broken-down.*)

JOE. What's eating you? I want you to go on an errand for me.

TOM. It's Kitty.

JOE. What about her?

TOM. She's up in her room, crying.

JOE. Crying?

TOM. Yeah, she's been crying for over an hour. I been talking to her all this time, but she won't stop.

JOE. What's she crying about?

TOM. I don't know. I couldn't understand anything. She kept crying and telling me about a big house and collie dogs all around and flowers and one of her brother's dead and the other one lost somewhere. Joe, I can't stand Kitty crying.

JOE. You want to marry the girl?

TOM (*nodding*). Yeah.

JOE (*curious and sincere*). Why?

TOM. I don't know why, exactly, Joe. (*Pause.*) Joe, I don't like to think of Kitty out in the streets. I guess I love her, that's all.

JOE. She's a nice girl.

TOM. She's like an angel. She's not like those other street-walkers.

JOE (*swiftly*). Here. Take all this money and run next door to Frankie's and bet it on the nose of McCarthy.

TOM (*swiftly*). All this money, Joe? McCarthy?

JOE. Yeah. Hurry.

TOM (*going*). Ah, Joe. If McCarthy wins we'll be rich.

JOE. Get going, will you?

(TOM *runs out and nearly knocks over the* ARAB *coming back in.* NICK *fills him a beer without a word.*)

ARAB. No foundation, anywhere. Whole world. No foundation. All the way down the line.

NICK (*angry*). McCarthy! Just because you got a little lucky this morning, you have to go to work and throw away eighty bucks.

JOE. He wants to marry her.

NICK. Suppose she doesn't want to marry *him*?

JOE (*amazed*). Oh, yeah. (*Thinking*). Now, why wouldn't she want to marry a nice guy like Tom?

NICK. She's been in burlesque. She's had flowers sent to her by European royalty. She's dined with young men of quality and social position. She's above Tom.

(TOM *comes running in.*)

TOM (*disgusted*). They were running when I got there. Frankie wouldn't take the bet. McCarthy didn't get a call till the stretch. I thought we were going to save all this money. Then McCarthy won by two lengths.

JOE. What'd he pay, fifteen to one?

TOM. Better, but Frankie wouldn't take the bet.

NICK (*throwing a dish towel across the room*). Well, for the love of Mike.

JOE. Give me the money.

TOM (*giving back the money*). We would have had about a thousand five hundred dollars.

JOE (*bored, casually, inventing*). Go up to Schwabacher-Frey and get me the biggest Rand-McNally map of the nations of Europe they've got. On your way back stop at one of the pawn shops on Third Street, and buy me a good revolver and some cartridges.

TOM. She's up in her room crying, Joe.

JOE. Go get me those things.

NICK. What are you going to do, study the map, and then go out and shoot somebody?

JOE. I want to read the names of some European towns and rivers and valleys and mountains.

NICK. What do you want with the revolver?

JOE. I want to study it. I'm interested in things. Here's twenty dollars, Tom. Now go get them things.

TOM. A big map of Europe. And a revolver.

JOE. Get a good one. Tell the man you don't know anything about firearms and you're trusting him not to fool you. Don't pay more than ten dollars.

TOM. Joe, you got something on your mind. Don't go fool with a revolver.

JOE. Be sure it's a good one.

TOM. Joe.

JOE (*irritated*). What, Tom?

TOM. Joe, what do you send me out for crazy things for all the time?

JOE (*angry*). They're not crazy, Tom. Now, get going.

TOM. What about Kitty, Joe?

JOE. Let her cry. It'll do her good.

TOM. If she comes in here while I'm gone, talk to her, will you, Joe? Tell her about me.

JOE. O.K. Get going. Don't load that gun. Just buy it and bring it here.

TOM (*going*). You won't catch me loading any gun.

JOE. Wait a minute. Take these toys away.

TOM. Where'll I take them?

JOE. Give them to some kid. (*Pause.*) No. Take them up to Kitty. Toys stopped me from crying once. That's the reason I had you buy them. I wanted to see if I could find out *why* they stopped me from crying. I remember they seemed awfully stupid at the time.

TOM. Shall I, Joe? Take them up to Kitty? Do you think they'd stop *her* from crying?

JOE. They might. You get curious about the way they work and you forget whatever it is you're remembering that's making you cry. That's what they're for.

TOM. Yeah. Sure. The girl at the store asked me what I wanted with toys. I'll take them up to Kitty. (*Tragically.*) She's like a little girl. (*He goes.*)

WESLEY. Mr. Nick, can I play the piano again?

NICK. Sure. Practice all you like—until I tell you to stop.

WESLEY. You going to pay me for playing the piano?

NICK. Sure. I'll give you enough to get by on.

WESLEY (*amazed and delighted*). Get money for playing the piano?

(*He goes to the piano and begins to play quietly.* HARRY *goes up on the little stage and listens to the music. After a while he begins a soft shoe dance.*)

NICK. What were you crying about?

JOE. My mother.

NICK. What about her?

JOE. She was dead. I stopped crying when they gave me the toys.

(NICK'S MOTHER, *a little old woman of sixty or so, dressed plainly in black, her face shining, comes in briskly, chattering loudly in Italian, gesturing.* NICK *is delighted to see her.*)

NICK'S MOTHER (*in Italian*). Everything all right, Nickie?

NICK (*in Italian*). Sure, Mamma.

(NICK'S MOTHER *leaves as gaily and as noisily as she came, after half a minute of loud Italian family talk.*)

JOE. Who was that?

NICK (*to* JOE, *proudly and a little sadly*). My mother. (*Still looking at the swinging doors.*)

JOE. What'd she say?

NICK. Nothing. Just wanted to see me. (*Pause.*) What do you want with that gun?

JOE. I study things, Nick.

(*An old man who looks as if he might have been Kit Carson at one time walks in importantly, moves about, and finally stands at Joe's table.*)

KIT CARSON. Murphy's the name. Just an old trapper. Mind if I sit down?

JOE. Be delighted. What'll you drink?

KIT CARSON (*sitting down*). Beer. Same as I've been drinking. And thanks.

JOE (*to* NICK). Glass of beer, Nick.

(NICK *brings the beer to the table,* KIT CARSON *swallows it in one swig, wipes his big white mustache with the back of his right hand.*)

KIT CARSON (*moving in*). I don't suppose you ever fell in love with a midget weighing thirty-nine pounds?

JOE (*studying the man*). Can't say I have, but have another beer.

KIT CARSON (*intimately*). Thanks, thanks. Down in Gallup, twenty years ago. Fellow by the name of Rufus Jenkins came to town with six white horses and two black ones. Said he wanted a man to break the horses for him because his left leg was wood and he couldn't do it. Had a meeting at Parker's Mercantile Store and finally came to blows, me and Henry Walpal. Bashed his head with a brass cuspidor and ran away to Mexico, but he didn't die.

Couldn't speak a word. Took up with a cattle-breeder named Diego, educated in California. Spoke the language better than you and me. Said, Your job, Murph, is to feed them prize bulls. I said, Fine, what'll I feed them? He said, Hay, lettuce, salt, beer, and aspirin.

Came to blows two days 'ater over an

accordion he claimed I stole. I had *borrowed* it. During the fight I busted it over his head; ruined one of the finest accordions I ever saw. Grabbed a horse and rode back across the border. Texas. Got to talking with a fellow who looked honest. Turned out to be a Ranger who was looking for me.

JOE. Yeah. You were saying, a thirty-nine-pound midget.

KIT CARSON. Will I ever forget that lady? Will I ever get over that amazon of small proportions?

JOE. Will you?

KIT CARSON. If I live to be sixty.

JOE. Sixty? You look more than sixty now.

KIT CARSON. That's trouble showing in my face. Trouble and complications. I was fifty-eight three months ago.

JOE. That accounts for it, then. Go ahead, tell me more.

KIT CARSON. Told the Texas Ranger my name was Rothstein, mining engineer from Pennsylvania, looking for something worth while. Mentioned two places in Houston. Nearly lost an eye early one morning, going down the stairs. Ran into a six-footer with an iron-claw where his right hand was supposed to be. Said, You broke up my home. Told him I was a stranger in Houston. The girls gathered at the top of the stairs to see a fight. Seven of them. Six feet and an iron claw. That's bad on the nerves. Kicked him in the mouth when he swung for my head with the claw. Would have lost an eye except for quick thinking. He rolled into the gutter and pulled a gun. Fired seven times. I was back upstairs. Left the place an hour later, dressed in silk and feathers, with a hat swung around over my face. Saw him standing on the corner, waiting. Said, Care for a wiggle? Said he didn't. I went on down the street and left town. I don't suppose you ever had to put a dress on to save your skin, did you?

JOE. No, and I never fell in love with a midget weighing thirty-nine pounds. Have another beer?

KIT CARSON. Thanks. *(Swallows glass of beer.)* Ever try to herd cattle on a bicycle?

JOE. No. I never got around to that.

KIT CARSON. Left Houston with sixty cents in my pocket, gift of a girl named Lucinda. Walked fourteen miles in fourteen hours. Big house with barb-wire all around, and big dogs. One thing I never could get around. Walked past the gate, anyway, from hunger and thirst. Dogs jumped up and came for me. Walked right into them, growing older every second. Went up to the door and knocked. Big negress opened the door, closed it quick. Said, On your way, white trash.

Knocked again. Said, On your way. Again. On your way. Again. This time the old man himself opened the door, ninety, if he was a day. Sawed-off shotgun, too.

Said, I ain't looking for trouble, Father. I'm hungry and thirsty, name's Cavanaugh.

Took me in and made mint juleps for the two of us.

Said, Living here alone, Father?

Said, Drink and ask no questions. Maybe I am and maybe I ain't. You saw the lady. Draw your own conclusions.

I'd heard of that, but didn't wink out of tact. If I told you that old Southern gentleman was my grandfather, you wouldn't believe me, would you?

JOE. I might.

KIT CARSON. Well, it so happens he wasn't. Would have been romantic if he had been, though.

JOE. Where did you herd cattle on a bicycle?

KIT CARSON. Toledo, Ohio, 1918.

JOE. Toledo, Ohio? They don't herd cattle in Toledo.

KIT CARSON. They don't anymore. They did in 1918. One fellow did, leastaways. Bookkeeper named Sam Gold. Straight from the East Side, New York. Sombrero, lariats, Bull Durham, two head of cattle and two bicycles. Called his place The Gold Bar Ranch, two acres, just outside the city limits.

That was the year of the War, you'll remember.

JOE. Yeah, I remember, but how about herding them two cows on a bicycle? How'd you do it?

KIT CARSON. Easiest thing in the world. Rode no hands. Had to, otherwise couldn't lasso the cows. Worked for Sam Gold till the cows ran away. Bicycles scared them. They went into Toledo. Never saw hide nor hair of them again. Advertised in every paper, but never got them back. Broke his heart. Sold both bikes and returned to New York.

Took four aces from a deck of red cards and walked to town. Poker. Fellow in the game named Chuck Collins, liked to gamble. Told him with a smile I didn't suppose he'd care to bet a hundred dollars I wouldn't hold four aces the next hand. Called it. My cards were red on the blank side. The other cards were blue. Plumb forgot all about it. Showed him four aces. Ace of spades, ace of clubs, ace of diamonds, ace of hearts. I'll remember them four cards if I live to be sixty. Would have been killed on the spot except for the hurricane that year.

JOE. Hurricane?

KIT CARSON. You haven't forgotten the Toledo hurricane of 1918, have you?

JOE. No. There was no hurricane in Toledo in 1918, or any other year.

KIT CARSON. For the love of God, then what do you suppose that commotion was? And how come I came to in Chicago, dream-walking down State Street?

JOE. I guess they scared you.

KIT CARSON. No, that wasn't it. You go back to the papers of November 1918, and I think you'll find there was a hurricane in Toledo. I remember sitting on the roof of a two-story house, floating northwest.

JOE (seriously). Northwest?

KIT CARSON. Now, son, don't tell me you don't believe me, either?

JOE (pause. Very seriously, energetically and sharply). Of course I believe you. Living is an art. It's not bookkeeping. It takes a lot of rehearsing for a man to get to be himself.

KIT CARSON (thoughtfully, smiling, and amazed). You're the first man I've ever met who believes me.

JOE (seriously). Have another beer.

(TOM comes in with the Rand-McNally book, the revolver, and the box of cartridges. KIT goes to bar.)

JOE (to TOM). Did you give her the toys?

TOM. Yeah, I gave them to her.

JOE. Did she stop crying?

TOM. No. She started crying harder than ever.

JOE. That's funny. I wonder why.

TOM. Joe, if I was a minute earlier, Frankie would have taken the bet and now we'd have about a thousand five hundred dollars. How much of it would you have given me, Joe?

JOE. If she'd marry you—all of it.

TOM. Would you, Joe?

JOE (opening packages, examining book first, and revolver next). Sure. In this realm there's only one subject, and you're it. It's my duty to see that my subject is happy.

TOM. Joe, do you think we'll ever have eighty dollars for a race sometime again when there's a fifteen-to-one shot that we like, weather good, track fast, they get off to a good start, our horse doesn't get a call till the stretch, we think we're going to lose all that money, and then it wins, by a nose?

JOE. I didn't quite get that.

TOM. You know what I mean.

JOE. You mean the impossible. No, Tom, we won't. We were just a little late, that's all.

TOM. We might, Joe.

JOE. It's not likely.

TOM. Then how am I ever going to make enough money to marry her?

JOE. I don't know, Tom. Maybe you aren't.

TOM. Joe, I got to marry Kitty. (Shaking his head.) You ought to see the crazy room she lives in.

JOE. What kind of a room is it?

TOM. It's little. It crowds you in. It's bad, / Joe. Kitty don't belong in a place like that.

JOE. You want to take her away from there?

TOM. Yeah. I want her to live in a house where there's room enough to live. Kitty ought to have a garden, or something.

JOE. You want to take care of her?

TOM. Yeah, sure, Joe. I ought to take care of somebody good that makes me feel like *I'm* somebody.

JOE. That means you'll have to get a job. What can you do?

TOM. 1 finished high school, but I don't know what I can do.

JOE. Sometimes when you think about it, what do you think you'd like to do?

TOM. Just sit around like you, Joe, and have somebody run errands for me and drink champagne and take things easy and never be broke and never worry about money.

JOE. That's a noble ambition.

NICK (to JOE). How do you do it?

JOE. I really don't know but I think you've got to have the full co-operation of the Good Lord.

NICK. I can't understand the way you talk.

TOM. Joe, shall I go back and see if I can get her to stop crying?

JOE. Give me a hand and I'll go with you.

TOM (amazed). What! You're going to get up already?

JOE. She's crying, isn't she?

TOM. She's crying. Worse than ever now.

JOE. I thought the toys would stop her.

TOM. I've seen you sit in one place from four in the morning till two the next morning.

JOE. At my best, Tom, I don't travel by foot. That's all. Come on. Give me a hand. I'll find some way to stop her from crying.

TOM (helping JOE). Joe, I never did tell you. You're a different kind of guy.

JOE (swiftly, a little angry). Don't be silly. I don't understand things. I'm trying to understand them.

(JOE is a little drunk. They go out together. The lights go down slowly, while WESLEY plays the piano, and come up slowly on:)

ACT THREE

A cheap bed in Nick's to indicate room 21 of The New York Hotel, upstairs, around the corner from Nick's. The bed can be at the center of Nick's or up on the little stage. Everything in Nick's is the same, except that all the people are silent, immobile and in darkness, except WESLEY who is playing the piano softly and sadly. KITTY DUVAL, in a dress she has carried around with her from the early days in Ohio, is seated on the bed, tying a ribbon in her hair. She looks at herself in a hand mirror. She is deeply grieved at the change she sees in herself. She takes off the ribbon, angry and hurt. She lifts a book from the bed and tries to read. She begins to sob again. She picks up an old picture of herself and looks at it. Sobs harder than ever, falling on the bed and burying her face. There is a knock, as if at the door.

KITTY (sobbing). Who is it?

TOM'S VOICE. Kitty, it's me. Tom. Me and Joe.

(JOE, followed by TOM, comes to the bed quietly. JOE is holding a rather large toy carousel. JOE studies KITTY a moment.)

(He sets the toy carousel on the floor, at the foot of Kitty's bed.)

TOM (standing over KITTY and bending down close to her). Don't cry any more, Kitty.

KITTY (not looking, sobbing). I don't like this life.

(JOE starts the carousel which makes a strange, sorrowful, tinkling music. The music begins slowly, becomes swift, gradually slows down, and ends. JOE himself is interested in the toy, watches and listens to it carefully.)

TOM (eagerly). Kitty. Joe got up from his chair at Nick's just to get you a toy and come here. This one makes music. We rode all over town in a cab to get it. Listen.

(KITTY *sits up slowly, listening, while* TOM *watches her. Everything happens slowly and somberly.* KITTY *notices the photograph of herself when she was a little girl. Lifts it, and looks at it again.*)

TOM (*looking*). Who's that little girl, Kitty?

KITTY. That's me. When I was seven.

(KITTY *hands the photo to* TOM.)

TOM (*looking, smiling*). Gee, you're pretty, Kitty.

(JOE *reaches up for the photograph, which* TOM *hands to him.* TOM *returns to* KITTY *whom he finds as pretty now as she was at seven.* JOE *studies the photograph.* KITTY *looks up at* TOM. *There is no doubt that they really love one another.* JOE *looks up at them.*)

KITTY. Tom?

TOM (*eagerly*). Yeah, Kitty.

KITTY. Tom, when you were a little boy what did you want to be?

TOM (*a little bewildered, but eager to please her*). What, Kitty?

KITTY. Do you remember when you were a little boy?

TOM (*thoughtfully*). Yeah, I remember sometimes, Kitty.

KITTY. What did you want to be?

TOM (*looks at* JOE. JOE *holds Tom's eyes a moment. Then* TOM *is able to speak*). Sometimes I wanted to be a locomotive engineer. Sometimes I wanted to be a policeman.

KITTY. I wanted to be a great actress. (*She looks up into Tom's face.*) Tom, didn't you ever want to be a doctor?

TOM (*looks at* JOE. JOE *holds Tom's eyes again, encouraging Tom by his serious expression to go on talking*). Yeah, now I remember. Sure, Kitty. I wanted to be a doctor—*once.*

KITTY (*smiling sadly*). I'm so glad. Because I wanted to be an actress and have a young doctor come to the theater and see me and fall in love with me and send me flowers.

(JOE *pantomimes to* TOM, *demanding that he go on talking.*)

TOM. I would do that, Kitty.

KITTY. I wouldn't know who it was, and then one day I'd see him in the street and fall in love with him. I wouldn't know *he* was the one who was in love with me. I'd think about him all the time. I'd dream about him. I'd dream of being near him the rest of my life. I'd dream of having children that looked like him. I wouldn't be an actress all the time. Only until I found him and fell in love with him. After that we'd take a train and go to beautiful cities and see the wonderful people everywhere and give money to the poor and whenever people were sick he'd go to them and make them well again.

(TOM *looks at* JOE, *bewildered, confused, and full of sorrow.* KITTY *is deep in memory, almost in a trance.*)

JOE (*gently*). Talk to her, Tom. Be the wonderful young doctor she dreamed about and never found. Go ahead. Correct the errors of the world.

TOM. Joe. (*Pathetically.*) I don't know what to say.

(*There is rowdy singing in the hall. A loud young* VOICE *sings: "Sailing, sailing, over the bounding main."*)

VOICE. Kitty. Oh. Kitty! (KITTY *stirs, shocked, coming out of the trance.*) Where the hell are you? Oh, Kitty.

(TOM *jumps up, furiously.*)

WOMAN'S VOICE (*in the hall*). Who you looking for, Sailor Boy?

VOICE. The most beautiful lay in the world.

WOMAN'S VOICE. Don't go any further.

VOICE (*with impersonal contempt*). You? No. Not you. Kitty. You stink.

WOMAN'S VOICE (*rasping, angry*). Don't you dare talk to me that way. You pickpocket.

VOICE (*still impersonal, but louder*). Oh, I see. Want to get tough, hey? Close the door. Go hide.

WOMAN'S VOICE. You pickpocket. All of you.

(The door slams.)

VOICE *(roaring with laughter which is very sad).* Oh—Kitty.

Room 21. Where the hell is that room?

TOM *(to JOE).* Joe, I'll kill him.

KITTY *(fully herself again, terribly frightened).* Who is it?

(She looks long and steadily at TOM and JOE. TOM is standing, excited and angry. JOE is completely at ease, his expression full of pity. KITTY buries her face in the bed.)

JOE *(gently).* Tom Just take him away.

VOICE. Here it is. Number 21. Three naturals. Heaven. My blue heaven. The west, a nest, and you. Just Molly and me. *(Tragically.)* Ah, to hell with everything.

(A young SAILOR, a good-looking boy of no more than twenty or so, who is only drunk and lonely, comes to the bed, singing sadly.)

SAILOR. Hi-ya, Kitty. *(Pause.)* Oh. Visitors. Sorry. A thousand apologies. *(To KITTY.)* I'll come back later.

TOM *(taking him by the shoulders, furiously).* If you do, I'll kill you.

(JOE holds TOM. TOM pushes the frightened boy away.)

JOE *(somberly).* Tom. You stay here with Kitty. I'm going down to Union Square to hire an automobile. I'll be back in a few minutes. We'll ride out to the ocean and watch the sun go down. Then we'll ride down the Great Highway to Half Moon Bay. We'll have supper down there, and you and Kitty can dance.

TOM *(stupefied, unable to express his amazement and gratitude).* Joe, you mean you're going to go on an errand for me? You mean you're not going to send me?

JOE. That's right.

(He gestures toward KITTY, indicating that TOM shall talk to her, protect the innocence in her which is in so much danger when TOM isn't near, which TOM loves so deeply. JOE leaves. TOM studies KITTY, his face becoming child-like and somber. He sets the carousel into motion, listens, watching KITTY, who lifts herself slowly, looking only at TOM. TOM lifts the turning carousel and moves it slowly toward KITTY, as though the toy were his heart. The piano music comes up loudly and the lights go down, while HARRY is heard dancing swiftly.)

BLACKOUT

ACT FOUR

A little later.
WESLEY, *the colored boy, is at the piano.*
HARRY *is on the little stage, dancing.*
NICK *is behind the bar.*
The ARAB is in his place.
KIT CARSON *is asleep on his folded arms.*
The DRUNKARD comes in. Goes to the telephone for the nickel that might be in the return-chute. NICK comes to take him out. He gestures for NICK to hold on a minute. Then produces a half dollar. NICK goes behind the bar to serve the DRUNKARD whiskey.

THE DRUNKARD. To the old, God bless them. *(Another.)* To the new, God love them. *(Another.)* To—children and small animals, like little dogs that don't bite. *(Another. Loudly.)* To reforestation. *(Searches for money. Finds some.)* To—President Taft. *(He goes out.)*

(The telephone rings.)

KIT CARSON *(jumping up, fighting).* Come on, *all* of you, if you're looking for trouble. I never asked for quarter and I always gave it.

NICK *(reproachfully).* Hey, Kit Carson.

DUDLEY *(on the phone).* Hello. Who? Nick? Yes. He's here. *(To NICK.)* It's for you. I think it's important.

NICK *(going to the phone).* Important! *What's* important?

DUDLEY. He sounded like big-shot.

NICK. Big *what*? (*To* WESLEY *and* HARRY.) Hey, you. Quiet. I want to hear this important stuff.

(WESLEY *stops playing the piano.* HARRY *stops dancing.* KIT CARSON *comes close to* NICK.)

KIT CARSON. If there's anything I can do, name it. I'll do it for you. I'm fifty-eight years old; been through three wars; married four times; the father of countless children whose *names* I don't even know. I've got no money. I live from hand to mouth. But if there's anything I can do, name it. I'll do it.

NICK (*patiently*). Listen, Pop. For a moment, please sit down and go back to sleep—*for me.*

KIT CARSON. I can do that, too.

(*He sits down, folds his arms, and puts his head into them. But not for long. As* NICK *begins to talk, he listens carefully, gets to his feet, and then begins to express in pantomime the moods of each of Nick's remarks.*)

NICK (*on phone*). Yeah? (*Pause.*) Who? Oh, I see. (*Listens.*) Why don't you leave them alone? (*Listens.*) The church-people? Well, to hell with the church-people. I'm a Catholic myself. (*Listens.*) All right. I'll send them away. I'll tell them to lay low for a couple of days. Yeah, I know how it is. (*Nick's daughter* ANNA *comes in shyly, looking at her father, and stands unnoticed by the piano.*) What? (*Very angry.*) Listen. I don't like that Blick. He was here this morning, and I told him not to come back. I'll keep the girls out of here. You keep Blick out of here. (*Listens.*) I know his brother-in-law is important, but I don't want him to come down here. He looks for trouble everywhere, and he always finds it. I don't break any laws. I've got a dive in the lousiest part of town. Five years nobody's been robbed, murdered, or gypped. I leave people alone. Your swanky joints uptown make trouble for you every night. (NICK *gestures to* WESLEY—*keeps listening on the phone—puts his hand over the mouthpiece. To* WESLEY *and* HARRY.) Start playing again. My ears have got a headache. Go into your dance, son. (WESLEY *begins to play again.* HARRY *begins to dance.* NICK,

into mouthpiece.) Yeah. I'll keep them out. Just see that Blick doesn't come around and start something. (*Pause.*) O.K. (*He hangs up.*)

KIT CARSON. Trouble coming?

NICK. That lousy Vice Squad again. It's that gorilla Blick.

KIT CARSON. Anybody at all. You can count on me. What kind of a gorilla is this gorilla Blick?

NICK. Very dignified. Toenails on his fingers.

ANNA (*to* KIT CARSON, *with great warm, beautiful pride, pointing at* NICK). That's my father.

KIT CARSON (*leaping with amazement at the beautiful voice, the wondrous face, the magnificent event*). Well, bless your heart, child. Bless your lovely heart. I had a little daughter point me out in a crowd once.

NICK (*surprised*). Anna. What the hell are you doing here? Get back home where you belong and help Grandma cook me some supper.

(ANNA *smiles at her father, understanding him, knowing that his words are words of love. She turns and goes, looking at him all the way out, as much as to say that she would cook for him the rest of her life.* NICK *stares at the swinging doors.* KIT CARSON *moves toward them, two or three steps.* ANNA *pushes open one of the doors and peeks in, to look at her father again. She waves to him. Turns and runs.* NICK *is very sad. He doesn't know what to do. He gets a glass and a bottle. Pours himself a drink. Swallows some. It isn't enough, so he pours more and swallows the whole drink.*)

(*To himself.*) My beautiful, beautiful baby. Anna, she is you again. (*He brings out a handkerchief, touches his eyes, and blows his nose.* KIT CARSON *moves close to* NICK, *watching Nick's face.* NICK *looks at him. Loudly, almost making* KIT *jump.*) You're broke, aren't you?

KIT CARSON. Always. Always.

NICK. All right. Go into the kitchen and give Sam a hand. Eat some food and when you come back you can have a couple of beers.

KIT CARSON (*studying* NICK). Anything at all. I know a good man when I see one.

(*He goes.*)

(ELSIE MANDELSPIEGEL *comes into Nick's. She is a beautiful, dark girl, with a sorrowful, wise, dreaming face, almost on the verge of tears, and full of pity. There is an aura of dream about her. She moves softly and gently, as if everything around her were unreal and pathetic.* DUDLEY *doesn't notice her for a moment or two. When he does finally see her, he is so amazed, he can barely move or speak. Her presence has the effect of changing him completely. He gets up from his chair, as if in a trance, and walks toward her, smiling sadly.*)

ELSIE (*looking at him*). Hello, Dudley.

DUDLEY (*broken-hearted*). Elsie.

ELSIE. I'm sorry. (*Explaining.*) So many people are sick. Last night a little boy died. I love you, but— (*She gestures, trying to indicate how hopeless love is. They sit down.*)

DUDLEY (*staring at her, stunned and quieted*). Elsie. You'll never know how glad I am to see you. Just to *see* you. (*Pathetically.*) I was afraid I'd never see you again. It was driving me crazy. I didn't want to live. Honest. (*He shakes his head mournfully, with dumb and beautiful affection.* TWO STREETWALKERS *come in, and pause near* DUDLEY, *at the bar.*) I know. You told me before, but I can't help it, Elsie. I love you.

ELSIE (*quietly, somberly, gently, with great compassion*). I know you love me, and I love you, but don't you see love is impossible in this world?

DUDLEY. Maybe it isn't, Elsie.

ELSIE. Love is for birds. They have wings to fly away on when it's time for flying. For tigers in the jungle because they don't know their end. We know *our* end. Every night I watch over poor, dying men. I hear them breathing, crying, talking in their sleep. Crying for air and water and love, for mother and field and sunlight. *We* can never know love or greatness. We *should* know both.

DUDLEY (*deeply moved by her words*). Elsie, I love you.

ELSIE. You want to live. *I* want to live, too, but where? Where can we escape our poor world?

DUDLEY. Elsie, we'll find a place.

ELSIE (*smiling at him*). All right. We'll try again. We'll go together to a room in a cheap hotel, and dream that the world is beautiful, and that living is full of love and greatness. But in the morning, can we forget debts, and duties, and the cost of ridiculous things?

DUDLEY (*with blind faith*). Sure, we can, Elsie.

ELSIE. All right, Dudley. Of course. Come on. The time for the new pathetic war has come. Let's hurry, before they dress you, stand you in line, hand you a gun, and have you kill and be killed.

(ELSIE *looks at him gently, and takes his hand.* DUDLEY *embraces her shyly, as if he might hurt her. They go, as if they were a couple of young animals. There is a moment of silence. One of the* STREETWALKERS *bursts out laughing.*)

KILLER. Nick, what the hell kind of a joint are you running?

NICK. Well, it's not out of the world. It's on a street in a city, and people come and go. They bring whatever they've got with them and they say what they must say.

THE OTHER STREETWALKER. It's floozies like her that raise hell with our racket.

NICK (*remembering*). Oh, yeah. Finnegan telephoned.

KILLER. That mouse in elephant's body?

THE OTHER STREETWALKER. What the hell does *he* want?

NICK. Spend your time at the movies for the next couple of days.

KILLER. They're all lousy. (*Mocking.*) All about love.

NICK. Lousy or not lousy, for a couple of days the flat-foots are going to be romancing you, so stay out of here, and lay low.

KILLER. I always was a pushover for a man in uniform, with a badge, a club and a gun.

(KRUPP *comes into the place. The girls put down their drinks.*)

NICK. O.K., get going.

(*The* GIRLS *begin to leave and meet* KRUPP.)

THE OTHER STREETWALKER. We was just going.

KILLER. We was formerly models at Magnin's. (*They go.*)

KRUPP (*at the bar*). The strike isn't enough, so they've got to put us on the tails of the girls, too. I don't know. I wish to God I was back in the Sunset holding the hands of kids going home from school, where I belong. I don't like trouble. Give me a beer.
(NICK *gives him a beer. He drinks some.*) Right now, McCarthy, my best friend, is with sixty strikers who want to stop the finks who are going to try to unload the *Mary Luckenbach* tonight. Why the hell McCarthy ever became a longshoreman instead of a professor of some kind is something I'll never know.

NICK. Cowboys and Indians, cops and robbers, longshoremen and finks.

KRUPP. They're all guys who are trying to be happy; trying to make a living; support a family; bring up children; enjoy sleep. Go to a movie; take a drive on Sunday. They're all good guys, so out of nowhere, comes trouble. All they want is a chance to get out of debt and relax in front of a radio while Amos and Andy go through their act. What the hell do they always want to make trouble for? I been thinking everything over, Nick, and you know what I think?

NICK. No. What?

KRUPP. I think we're all crazy. It came to me while I was on my way to Pier 27. All of a sudden it hit me like a ton of bricks. A thing like that never happened to me before. Here we are in this wonderful world, full of all the wonderful things—here we are—all of us, and look at us. Just look at us. We're crazy. We're nuts. We've got everything, but we always feel lousy and dissatisfied just the same.

NICK. Of course we're crazy. Even so, we've got to go on living together. (*He waves at the people in his joint.*)

KRUPP. There's no hope. I don't suppose it's right for an officer of the law to feel the way I feel, but, by God, right or not right, that's how I feel. Why are we all so lousy? This is a good world. It's wonderful to get up in the morning and go out for a little walk and smell the trees and see the streets and the kids going to school and the clouds in the sky. It's wonderful just to be able to move around and whistle a song if you feel like it, or maybe try to sing one. This is a nice world. So why do they make all the trouble?

NICK. I don't know. Why?

KRUPP. We're crazy, that's why. We're no good any more. All the corruption everywhere. The poor kids selling themselves. A couple of years ago they were in grammar school. Everybody trying to get a lot of money in a hurry. Everybody betting the horses. Nobody going quietly for a little walk to the ocean. Nobody taking things easy and not wanting to make some kind of a killing. Nick, I'm going to quit being a cop. Let somebody else keep law and order. The stuff I hear about at headquarters. I'm thirty-seven years old, and I still can't get used to it. The only trouble is, the wife'll raise hell.

NICK. Ah, the wife.

KRUPP. She's a wonderful woman, Nick. We've got two of the swellest boys in the world. Twelve and seven years old. (*The* ARAB *gets up and moves closer to listen.*)

NICK. I didn't know that.

KRUPP. Sure. But what'll I do? I've wanted to quit for seven years. I wanted to quit the day they began putting me through the school. I didn't quit. What'll I do if I quit? Where's money going to be coming in from?

NICK. That's one of the reasons we're all crazy. We don't know where it's going to be coming in from, except from wherever it happens to be coming in from at the time, which we don't usually like.

KRUPP. Every once in a while I catch myself being mean, hating people just because they're down and out, broke and hungry, sick or drunk. And then when I'm with the stuffed shirts at headquarters, all of a sudden I'm nice to them, trying to make an impression. On who? People I don't like. And I feel disgusted. (*With finality.*) I'm going to quit. That's all. Quit. Out.

I'm going to give them back the uniform and the gadgets that go with it. I don't want any part of it. This is a good world. What do they want to make all the trouble for all the time?

ARAB (*quietly, gently, with great understanding*). No foundation. All the way down the line.

KRUPP. What?

ARAB. No foundation. No foundation.

KRUPP. I'll say there's no foundation.

ARAB. All the way down the line.

KRUPP (*to* NICK). Is that all he ever says?

NICK. That's all he's been saying *this* week.

KRUPP. What is he, anyway?

NICK. He's an Arab, or something like that.

KRUPP. No, I mean what's he do for a living?

NICK (*to* ARAB). What do you do for a living, brother?

ARAB. Work. Work all my life. All my life, work. From small boy to old man, work. In old country, work. In new country, work. In New York. Pittsburgh. Detroit. Chicago. Imperial Valley. San Francisco. Work. No beg. Work. For what? Nothing. Three boys in old country. Twenty years, not see. Lost. Dead. Who knows? What. What-not. No foundation. All the way down the line.

KRUPP. What'd he say last week?

NICK. Didn't say anything. Played the harmonica.

ARAB. Old country song, I play. (*He brings a harmonica from his back pocket.*)

KRUPP. Seems like a nice guy.

NICK. Nicest guy in the world.

KRUPP (*bitterly*). But crazy. Just like all the rest of us. Stark raving mad.

(WESLEY *and* HARRY *long ago stopped*

playing and dancing. They sat at a table together and talked for a while; then began playing casino or rummy. When the ARAB begins his solo on the harmonica, they stop their game to listen.*)

WESLEY. You hear that?

HARRY. That's *something*.

WESLEY. That's crying. That's crying.

HARRY. I want to make people laugh.

WESLEY. That's deep, deep crying. That's crying a long time ago. That's crying a thousand years ago. Some place five thousand miles away.

HARRY. Do you think you can play to that?

WESLEY. I want to *sing* to that, but I can't *sing*.

HARRY. You try and play to that. I'll try to dance.

(WESLEY *goes to the piano, and after closer listening, he begins to accompany the harmonica solo.* HARRY *goes to the little stage and after a few efforts begins to dance to the song. This keeps up quietly for some time.*)

(KRUPP *and* NICK *have been silent, and deeply moved.*)

KRUPP (*softly*). Well, anyhow, Nick.

NICK. Hmmmmmmm?

KRUPP. What I said. Forget it.

NICK. Sure.

KRUPP. It gets me down once in a while.

NICK. No harm in talking.

KRUPP (*the* POLICEMAN *again, loudly*) Keep the girls out of here.

NICK (*loud and friendly*). Take it easy.

(*The music and dancing are now at their height.*)

CURTAIN

ACT FIVE

That evening. Fog-horns are heard throughout the scene. A man in evening clothes and a top hat, and his woman, also in evening clothes, are entering.

WILLIE is still at the marble-game. NICK is behind the bar. JOE is at his table, looking at the book of maps of the countries of Europe. The box containing the revolver and the box containing the cartridges are on the table, beside his glass. He is at peace, his hat tilted back on his head, a calm expression on his face. TOM is leaning against the bar, dreaming of love and Kitty. The ARAB is gone. WESLEY and HARRY are gone. KIT CARSON is watching the boy at the marble-game.

LADY. Oh, come on, please.

(The gentleman follows miserably.)

(The SOCIETY MAN and WIFE take a table. NICK gives them a menu.)

(Outside, in the street, the Salvation Army people are playing a song. Big drum, tambourines, cornet and singing. They are singing "The Blood of the Lamb." The music and words come into the place faintly and comically. This is followed by an old sinner testifying. It is the DRUNKARD. His words are not intelligible, but his message is unmistakable. He is saved. He wants to sin no more. And so on.)

DRUNKARD *(testifying, unmistakably drunk)*. Brothers and sisters. I was a sinner. I chewed tobacco and chased women. Oh, I sinned, brothers and sisters. And then I was saved. Saved by the Salvation Army, God forgive me.

JOE. Let's see now. Here's a city. Pribor. Czecho-slovakia. Little, lovely, lonely Czecho-slovakia. I wonder what kind of a place Pribor was? *(Calling.)* Pribor! Pribor! (TOM *leaps.)*

LADY. What's the matter with him?

MAN *(crossing his legs, as if he ought to go to the men's room)*. Drunk.

TOM. Who you calling, Joe?

JOE. Pribor.

TOM. Who's Pribor?

JOE. He's a Czech. And a Slav. A Czecho-slovakian.

LADY. How interesting.

MAN *(uncrosses legs)*. He's drunk.

JOE. Tom, Pribor's a city in Czecho-slovakia.

TOM. Oh. *(Pause.)* You sure were nice to her, Joe.

JOE. Kitty Duval? She's one of the finest people in the world.

TOM. It sure was nice of you to hire an automobile and take us for a drive along the ocean-front and down to Half Moon Bay.

JOE. Those three hours were the most delightful, the most somber, and the most beautiful I have ever known.

TOM. Why, Joe?

JOE. Why? I'm a student. *(Lifting his voice.)* Tom. *(Quietly.)* I'm a student. I study all things. All. All. And when my study reveals something of beauty in a place or in a person where by all rights only ugliness or death should be revealed, then I know how full of goodness this life is. And that's a good thing to know. That's a truth I shall always seek to verify.

LADY. Are you *sure* he's drunk?

MAN *(crossing his legs)*. He's either drunk, or just naturally crazy.

TOM. Joe?

JOE. Yeah.

TOM. You won't get sore or anything?

JOE *(impatiently)*. What is it, Tom?

TOM. Joe, where do you get all that money? You paid for the automobile. You paid for supper and the two bottles of champagne at the Half Moon Bay Restaurant. You moved Kitty out of the New York Hotel around the corner to the St. Francis Hotel on Powell Street. I saw you pay her rent. I saw you give her money for new clothes. Where do you get all that money, Joe? Three years now and I've never asked.

JOE *(looking at TOM sorrowfully, a little*

irritated, not so much with TOM *as with the world and himself, his own superiority. He speaks clearly, slowly and solemnly).* Now don't be a fool, Tom. Listen carefully. If anybody's got any money—to hoard or to throw away—you can be sure he stole it from other people. Not from rich people who can spare it, but from poor people who can't. From their lives and from their dreams. I'm no exception. I *earned* the money I throw away. I stole it like everybody else does. I hurt people to get it. Loafing around this way, I *still* earn money. The money itself earns *more.* I *still* hurt people. I don't know who they are, or where they are. If I did, I'd feel worse than I do. I've got a Christian conscience in a world that's got no conscience at all. The world's trying to get some sort of a *social* conscience, but it's having a devil of a time trying to do *that.* I've got money. I'll always have money, as long as this world stays the way it is. I don't work. I don't make anything. *(He sips.)* I drink. I worked when I was a kid. I worked *hard.* I mean hard, Tom. People are supposed to enjoy living. I got tired. *(He lifts the gun and looks at it while he talks.)* I decided to get even on the world. Well, you can't enjoy living unless you work. Unless you do something. I don't do anything. I don't *want* to do anything any more. There isn't anything I can do that won't make me feel embarrassed. Because I can't do simple, good things. I haven't the patience. And I'm too smart. Money is the guiltiest thing in the world. It stinks. Now, don't ever bother me about it again.

TOM. I didn't mean to make you feel bad, Joe.

JOE *(slowly).* Here. Take this gun out in the street and give to to some worthy hold-up man.

LADY. What's he saying?

MAN *(uncrosses legs).* You wanted to visit a honky-tonk. Well, *this* is a honky-tonk. *(To the world.)* Married twenty-eight years and she's still looking for adventure.

TOM. How should I know who's a hold-up man?

JOE. Take it away. Give it to somebody.

TOM *(bewildered).* Do I *have* to *give* it to somebody?

JOE. Of course.

TOM. Can't I take it back and get some of our money?

JOE. Don't talk like a business man. Look around and find somebody who appears to be in need of a gun and give it to him. It's a good gun, isn't it?

TOM. The man said it was, but how can I tell who needs a gun?

JOE. Tom, you've seen good people who needed guns, haven't you?

TOM. I don't remember. Joe, I might give it to the wrong kind of guy. He might do something crazy.

JOE. All right. I'll find somebody myself. *(*TOM *rises.)* Here's some money. Go get me this week's *Life, Liberty, Time,* and six or seven packages of chewing gum.

TOM *(swiftly, in order to remember each item). Life, Liberty, Time,* and six or seven packages of chewing gum?

JOE. That's right.

TOM. All that chewing gum? What kind?

JOE. Any kind. Mix 'em up. All kinds.

TOM. Licorice, too?

JOE. Licorice, by all means.

TOM. Juicy Fruit?

JOE. Juicy Fruit.

TOM. Tutti-frutti?

JOE. Is there such a gum?

TOM. I think so.

JOE. All right. Tutti-frutti, too. Get *all* the kinds. Get as many kinds as they're selling.

TOM. *Life, Liberty, Time,* and all the different kinds of gum. *(He begins to go.)*

JOE *(calling after him loudly).* Get some jelly beans too. All the different colors.

TOM. All right, Joe.

JOE. And the longest panatela cigar you can find. Six of them.

TOM. Panatela. I got it.

JOE. Give a news-kid a dollar.

TOM. O.K., Joe.

JOE. Give some old man a dollar.

TOM. O.K., Joe.

JOE. Give them Salvation Army people in the street a couple of dollars and ask them to sing that song that goes— *(He sings loudly.)* Let the lower lights be burning, send a gleam across the wave.

TOM *(swiftly)*. Let the lower lights be burning, send a gleam across the wave.

JOE. That's it. *(He goes on with the song, very loudly and religiously.)* Some poor, dying, struggling seaman, you may rescue, you may save. *(Halts.)*

TOM. O.K., Joe. I got it. *Life, Liberty, Time,* all the kinds of gum they're selling, jelly beans, six panatela cigars, a dollar for a news-kid, a dollar for an old man, two dollars for the Salvation Army. *(Going.)* Let the lower lights be burning, send a gleam across the wave.

JOE. That's it.

LADY. He's absolutely insane.

MAN *(wearily crossing legs)*. You asked me to take you to a honky-tonk, instead of to the Mark Hopkins. You're *here* in a honky-tonk. I can't help it if he's crazy. Do you want to go back to where people *aren't* crazy?

LADY. No, not just yet.

MAN. Well, all right then. Don't be telling me every minute that he's crazy.

LADY. You needn't be huffy about it.

(MAN refuses to answer, uncrosses legs.)

(When JOE began to sing, KIT CARSON turned away from the marble-game and listened. While the man and woman are arguing he comes over to Joe's table.)

KIT CARSON. Presbyterian?

JOE. I attended a Presbyterian Sunday School.

KIT CARSON. Fond of singing?

JOE. On occasion. Have a drink?

KIT CARSON. Thanks.

JOE. Get a glass and sit down.
(KIT CARSON gets a glass from NICK, returns to the table, sits down, JOE pours him

a drink, they touch glasses just as the Salvation Army people begin to fulfill the request. They sip some champagne, and at the proper moment begin to sing the song together, sipping champagne, raising hell with the tune, swinging it, and so on. The SOCIETY LADY *joins them, and is stopped by her* HUSBAND.)
Always was fond of that song. Used to sing it at the top of my voice. Never saved a seaman in my life.

KIT CARSON *(flirting with the* SOCIETY LADY *who loves it)*. I saved a seaman once. Well, he wasn't exactly a seaman. He was a darky named Wellington. Heavy-set sort of a fellow. Nice personality, but no friends to speak of. Not until I came along, at any rate. In New Orleans. In the summer of the year 1899. No. Ninety-eight. I was a lot younger of course, and had no mustache, but was regarded by many people as a man of means.

JOE. Know anything about guns?

KIT CARSON *(flirting)*. All there is to know. Didn't fight the Ojibways for nothing. Up there in the Lake Takalooca Country, in Michigan. *(Remembering.)* Along about in 1881 or two. Fought 'em right up to the shore of the Lake. Made 'em swim for Canada. One fellow in particular, an Indian named Harry Daisy.

JOE *(opening the box containing the revolver)*. What sort of a gun would you say this is? Any good?

KIT CARSON *(at sight of gun, leaping)*. Yep. That looks like a pretty nice hunk of shooting iron. That's a six-shooter. Shot a man with a six-shooter once. Got him through the palm of his right hand. Lifted his arm to wave to a friend. Thought it was a bird. Fellow named, I believe, Carroway. Larrimore Carroway.

JOE. Know how to work one of these things? *(He offers* KIT CARSON *the revolver, which is old and enormous.)*

KIT CARSON *(laughing at the absurd question)*. Know how to work it? Hand me that little gun, son, and I'll show you all about it. *(JOE hands* KIT *the revolver.)* *(Importantly.)* Let's see now. This is probably a new kind of six-shooter. After my time. Haven't nicked an Indian in years. I believe this here place is supposed to move out. (*He fools around and get the barrel out for loading.*) That's it. There it is.

JOE. Look all right?

KIT CARSON. It's a good gun. You've got a good gun there, son. I'll explain it to you. You see these holes? Well, that's where you put the cartridges.

JOE (*taking some cartridges out of the box*). Here. Show me how it's done.

KIT CARSON (*a little impatiently*). Well, son, you take 'em one by one and put 'em in the holes, like this. There's one. Two. Three. Four. Five. Six. Then you get the barrel back in place. Then cock it. Then all you got to do is aim and fire.

(*He points the gun at the* LADY *and* GENTLEMAN *who scream and stand up, scaring* KIT CARSON *into paralysis.*)

(*The gun is loaded, but uncocked.*)

JOE. It's all set?

KIT CARSON. Ready to kill.

JOE. Let me hold it.

(KIT *hands* JOE *the gun. The* LADY *and* GENTLEMAN *watch, in terror.*)

KIT CARSON. Careful, now, son. Don't cock it. Many a man's lost an eye fooling with a loaded gun. Fellow I used to know named Danny Donovan lost a nose. Ruined his whole life. Hold it firm. Squeeze the trigger. Don't snap it. Spoils your aim.

JOE. Thanks. Let's see if I can unload it.

(*He begins to unload it.*)

KIT CARSON. Of course you can.

(JOE *unloads the revolver, looks at it very closely, puts the cartridges back into the box.*)

JOE (*looking at gun*). I'm mighty grateful to you. Always wanted to see one of those things close up. Is it really a good one?

KIT CARSON. It's a beaut, son.

JOE (*aims the empty gun at a bottle on the bar*). Bang!

WILLIE (*at the marble-game, as the machine groans*). Oh, Boy! (*Loudly, triumphantly.*) There you are, Nick. Thought I couldn't do it, hey? *Now*, watch. (*The machine begins to make a special kind of noise. Lights go on and off. Some red, some green. A bell rings loudly six times.*) One. Two. Three. Four. Five. Six. (*An American flag jumps up.* WILLIE *comes to attention. Salutes.*) Oh, boy, what a beautiful country. (*A loud music-box version of the song "America."* JOE, KIT, *and the* LADY *get to their feet.*) (*Singing.*) My country, 'tis of thee, sweet land of liberty, of thee I sing. (*Everything quiets down. The flag goes back into the machine.* WILLIE *is thrilled, amazed, delighted.* EVERYBODY *has watched the performance of the defeated machine from wherever he happened to be when the performance began.* WILLIE, *looking around at everybody, as if they had all been on the side of the machine.*) O.K. How's that? I knew I could do it. (*To* NICK.) Six nickels.

(NICK *hands him six nickels.* WILLIE *goes over to* JOE *and* KIT.) Took me a little while, but I finally did it. It's scientific, really. With a little skill a man can make a modest living beating the marble-games. Not that that's what I want to do. I just don't like the idea of anything getting the best of me. A machine or anything else. Myself, I'm the kind of a guy who makes up his mind to do something, and then goes to work and does it. There's no other way a man can be a success at anything.

(*Indicating the letter "F" on his sweater.*)

See that letter? That don't stand for some little-bitty high school somewhere. That stands for *me*. Faroughli. Willie Faroughli. I'm an Assyrian. We've got a civilization six or seven centuries old, I think. Somewhere along in there. Ever hear of Osman? Harold Osman? He's an Assyrian, too. He's got an orchestra down in Fresno.

(*He goes to the* LADY *and* GENTLEMAN.)

I've never seen you before in my life, but I can tell from the clothes you wear and the company you keep (*Graciously indicating the* LADY.) that you're a man who looks every problem straight in the eye, and then goes to work and *solves* it. I'm that way myself. Well. (*He smiles beautifully, takes* GENTLEMAN's *hand furiously.*) It's been wonderful talking to a nicer type of people for a change. Well. I'll be seeing you. So long. (*He turns, takes two steps, returns to the table. Very politely and seriously.*) Good-bye, lady. You've got a good man there. Take good care of him.

(WILLIE *goes, saluting* JOE *and the world.*)

KIT CARSON *(to* JOE*).* By God, for a while there I didn't think that young Assyrian was going to do it. That fellow's got something.

(TOM *comes back with the magazines and other stuff.*)

JOE. Get it all?

TOM. Yeah. I had a little trouble finding the jelly beans.

JOE. Let's take a look at them.

TOM. These are the jelly beans.

(JOE *puts his hand into the cellophane bag and takes out a handful of the jelly beans, looks at them, smiles, and tosses a couple into his mouth.*)

JOE. Same as ever. Have some. *(He offers the bag to* KIT.*)*

KIT CARSON *(flirting).* Thanks! I remember the first time I ever ate jelly beans. I was six, or at the most seven. Must have been in *(Slowly.)* eighteen—seventy-seven. Seven or eight. Baltimore.

JOE. Have some, Tom. (TOM *takes some.*)

TOM. Thanks, Joe.

JOE. Let's have some of that chewing gum.

(*He dumps all the packages of gum out of the bag onto the table.*)

KIT CARSON *(flirting).* Me and a boy named Clark. Quinton Clark. Became a Senator.

JOE. Yeah. Tutti-frutti, all right. *(He opens a package and folds all five pieces into his mouth.)* Always wanted to see how many I could chew at one time. Tell you what, Tom. I'll bet I can chew more at one time than you can.

TOM *(delighted).* All right. *(They both begin to fold gum into their mouths.)*

KIT CARSON. I'll referee. Now, one at a time. How many you got?

JOE. Six.

KIT CARSON. All right. Let Tom catch up with you.

JOE *(while* TOM's *catching up).* Did you give a dollar to a news-kid?

TOM. Yeah, sure.

JOE. What'd he say?

TOM. Thanks.

JOE. What sort of a kid was he?

TOM. Little, dark kid. I guess he's Italian.

JOE. Did he seem pleased?

TOM. Yeah.

JOE. That's good. Did you give a dollar to an old man?

TOM. Yeah.

JOE. Was he pleased?

TOM. Yeah.

JOE. Good. How many you got in your mouth?

TOM. Six.

JOE. All right. I got six, too. *(Folds one more in his mouth.* TOM *folds one too.)*

KIT CARSON. Seven. Seven each. *(They each fold one more into their mouths, very solemnly, chewing them into the main hunk of gum.)* Eight. Nine. Ten.

JOE *(delighted).* Always wanted to do this. *(He picks up one of the magazines.)* Let's see what's going on in the world. *(He turns the pages and keeps folding gum into his mouth and chewing.)*

KIT CARSON. Eleven. Twelve. (KIT *continues to count while* JOE *and* TOM *continue the contest. In spite of what they are doing, each is very serious.*)

TOM. Joe, what'd you want to move Kitty into the St. Francis Hotel for?

JOE. She's a better woman than any of them tramp society dames that hang around that lobby.

TOM. Yeah, but do you think she'll feel at home up there?

JOE. Maybe not at first, but after a couple of days she'll be all right. A nice big room. A bed for sleeping in. Good clothes. Good food. She'll be all right, Tom.

TOM. I hope so. Don't you think she'll get lonely up there with nobody to talk to?

JOE *(looking at* TOM *sharply, almost with admiration, pleased but severe).* There's nobody *anywhere* for *her* to talk to—except *you.*

TOM *(amazed and delighted).* Me, Joe?

JOE (*while* TOM *and* KIT CARSON *listen carefully,* KIT *with great appreciation*). Yes, you. By the grace of God, you're the other half of that girl. Not the angry woman that swaggers into this waterfront dive and shouts because the world has kicked her around. *Anybody* can have *her*. You belong to the little kid in Ohio who once dreamed of living. Not with her carcass, for *money*, so she can have food and clothes, and pay rent. With *all* of her. I put her in that hotel, so she can have a chance to gather herself together again. She can't do that in the New York Hotel. You saw what happens there. There's nobody anywhere for her to talk to, except you. They all make her talk like a whore. After a while, she'll *believe* them. Then she won't be able to remember. She'll get lonely. Sure. People can get lonely for *misery*, even. I want her to go on being lonely for *you*, so she can come together again the way she was meant to be from the beginning. Loneliness is good for people. Right now it's the only thing for Kitty. Any more licorice?

TOM (*dazed*). What? Licorice? (*Looking around busily.*) I guess we've chewed all the licorice in. We still got Clove, Peppermint, Doublemint, Beechnut, Teaberry, and Juicy Fruit.

JOE. Licorice used to be my favorite. Don't worry about her, Tom, she'll be all right. You really want to marry her, don't you?

TOM (*nodding*). Honest to God, Joe. (*Pathetically.*) Only, I haven't got any money.

JOE. Couldn't you be a prize-fighter or something like that?

TOM. Naaaah. I couldn't hit a man if I wasn't sore at him. He'd have to do something that made me hate him.

JOE. You've got to figure out something to do that you won't mind doing very much.

TOM. I wish I could, Joe.

JOE (*thinking deeply, suddenly*). Tom, would you be embarrassed driving a truck?

TOM (*hit by a thunderbolt*). Joe, I never thought of that. I'd like that. Travel. Highways. Little towns. Coffee and hot cakes. Beautiful valleys and mountains and streams and trees and daybreak and sunset.

JOE. There *is* poetry in it, at that.

TOM. Joe, that's just the kind of work I *should* do. Just sit there and travel, and look, and smile, and bust out laughing. Could Kitty go with me, sometimes?

JOE. I don't know. Get me the phone book. Can you drive a truck?

TOM. Joe, you know I can drive a truck, or any kind of thing with a motor and wheels. (TOM *takes* JOE *the phone book.* JOE *turns the pages.*)

JOE (*looking*). Here! Here it is. Tuxedo 7900. Here's a nickel. Get me that number. (TOM *goes to telephone, dials the number.*)

TOM. Hello.

JOE. Ask for Mr. Keith.

TOM (*mouth and language full of gum*). I'd like to talk to Mr. Keith. (*Pause.*) Mr. Keith.

JOE. Take that gum out of your mouth for a minute. (TOM *removes the gum.*)

TOM. Mr. Keith. Yeah. That's right. Hello, Mr. Keith?

JOE. Tell him to hold the line.

TOM. Hold the line, please.

JOE. Give me a hand, Tom. (TOM *helps* JOE *to the telephone. At phone, wad of gum in fingers delicately.*) Keith? Joe. Yeah. Fine. Forget it. (*Pause.*) Have you got a place for a good driver? (*Pause.*) I don't think so. (*To* TOM.) You haven't got a driver's license, have you?

TOM (*worried*). No. But I can get one, Joe.

JOE (*at phone*). No, but he can get one easy enough. To hell with the union. He'll join later. All right, call him a Vice-President and say he drives for relaxation. Sure. What do you mean? Tonight? I don't know why not. San Diego? All right, let him start driving without a license. What the hell's the difference? Yeah. Sure. Look him over. Yeah. I'll send him right over. Right. (*He hangs up.*) Thanks. (*To telephone.*)

TOM. Am I going to get the job?

JOE. He wants to take a look at you.

TOM. Do I look all right, Joe?

JOE *(looking at him carefully)*. Hold up your head. Stick out your chest. How do you feel? *(TOM does these things.)*

TOM. Fine.

JOE. You *look* fine, too.

(JOE takes his wad of gum out of his mouth and wraps Liberty *magazine around it.)*

JOE. You win, Tom. Now, look. *(He bites off the tip of a very long panatela cigar, lights it, and hands one to* TOM, *and another to* KIT.) Have yourselves a pleasant smoke. Here. *(He hands two more to* TOM.) Give those slummers each one. *(He indicates the* SOCIETY LADY *and* GENTLEMAN.)

(TOM goes over and without a word gives a cigar each to the MAN *and the* LADY.)

(The MAN *is offended; he smells and tosses aside his cigar. The* WOMAN *looks at her cigar a moment, then puts the cigar in her mouth.)*

MAN. What do you think you're doing?

LADY. Really, dear. I'd like to.

MAN. Oh, this is too much.

LADY. I'd *really*, really like to, dear. *(She laughs, puts the cigar in her mouth. Turns to* KIT. *He spits out tip. She does the same.)*

MAN *(loudly)*. The mother of five grown men, and she's still looking for *romance*. *(Shouts as* KIT *lights her cigar.)* No. I forbid it.

JOE *(shouting)*. What's the matter with you? Why don't you leave her alone? What are you always pushing your women around for? *(Almost without a pause.)* Now, look, Tom. *(The* LADY *puts the lighted cigar in her mouth, and begins to smoke, feeling wonderful.)* Here's ten bucks.

TOM. Ten bucks?

JOE. He may want you to get into a truck and begin driving to San Diego tonight.

TOM. Joe, I got to tell Kitty.

JOE. I'll tell her.

TOM. Joe, take care of her.

JOE. She'll be all right. Stop worrying about her. She's at the St. Francis Hotel. Now, look. Take a cab to Townsend and Fourth. You'll see the big sign. Keith Motor Transport Company. He'll be waiting for you.

TOM. O.K., Joe. *(Trying hard.)* Thanks, Joe.

JOE. Don't be silly. Get going.

(TOM goes.)

(LADY starts puffing on cigar.)

(As TOM *goes,* WESLEY *and* HARRY *come in together.)*

NICK. Where the hell have you been? We've got to have some entertainment around here. Can't you see them fine people from uptown? *(He points at the* SOCIETY LADY *and* GENTLEMAN.)

WESLEY. You said to come back at ten for the second show.

NICK. Did I say that?

WESLEY. Yes, sir, Mr. Nick, that's exactly what you said.

HARRY. Was the first show all right?

NICK. That wasn't a show. There was no one here to see it. How can it be a show when no one sees it? People are afraid to come down to the waterfront.

HARRY. Yeah. We were just down to Pier 27. One of the longshoremen and a cop had a fight and the cop hit him over the head with a blackjack. We saw it happen, didn't we?

WESLEY. Yes, sir, we was standing there looking when it happened.

NICK *(a little worried)*. Anything else happen?

WESLEY. They was all talking.

HARRY. A man in a big car came up and said there was going to be a meeting right away and they hoped to satisfy everybody and stop the strike.

WESLEY. Right away. *Tonight.*

NICK. Well, it's about time. Them poor cops are liable to get nervous and—shoot somebody. *(To* HARRY, *suddenly.)* Come back here. I want you to tend bar for a while. I'm going to take a walk over to the pier.

HARRY. Yes, sir.

NICK (*to the* SOCIETY LADY *and* GENTLEMAN). You society people made up your minds yet?

LADY. Have you champagne?

NICK (*indicating* JOE). What do you think he's pouring out of that bottle, water or something?

LADY. Have you a chilled bottle?

NICK. I've got a dozen of them chilled. He's been drinking champagne here all day and all night for a month now.

LADY. May we have a bottle?

NICK. It's six dollars.

LADY. I think we can manage.

MAN. I don't know. I *know* I don't know.

(NICK *takes off his coat and helps* HARRY *into it.* HARRY *takes a bottle of champagne and two glasses to the* LADY *and the* GENTLEMAN, *dancing, collects six dollars, and goes back behind the bar, dancing.* NICK *gets his coat and hat.*)

NICK (*to* WESLEY). Rattle the keys, a little, son. Rattle the keys.

WESLEY. Yes, sir, Mr. Nick. (NICK *is on his way out. The* ARAB *enters.*)

NICK. Hi-ya, *Mahmed.*

ARAB. No foundation.

NICK. All the way down the line. (*He goes.*)

(WESLEY *is at the piano, playing quietly. The* ARAB *swallows a glass of beer, takes out his harmonica, and begins to play.* WESLEY *fits his playing to the Arab's.*)

(KITTY DUVAL, *strangely beautiful, in new clothes, comes in. She walks shyly, as if she were embarrassed by the fine clothes, as if she had no right to wear them. The* LADY *and* GENTLEMAN *are very impressed.* HARRY *looks at her with amazement.* JOE *is reading* Time *magazine.* KITTY *goes to his table.* JOE *looks up from the magazine, without the least amazement.*)

JOE. Hello, Kitty.

KITTY. Hello, Joe.

JOE. It's nice seeing you again.

KITTY. I came in a cab.

JOE. You been crying again? (KITTY *can't answer. To* HARRY.) Bring a glass. (HARRY *comes over with a glass.* JOE *pours* KITTY *a drink.*)

KITTY. I've got to talk to you.

JOE. Have a drink.

KITTY. I've never been in burlesque. We were just poor.

JOE. Sit down, Kitty.

KITTY (*sits down*). I tried other things.

JOE. Here's to you, Katerina Koranovsky. Here's to you. And Tom.

KITTY (*sorrowfully*). Where *is* Tom?

JOE. He's getting a job tonight driving a truck. He'll be back in a couple of days.

KITTY (*sadly*). I told him I'd marry him.

JOE. He wanted to see you and say good-by.

KITTY. He's too good for me. He's like a little boy. (*Wearily.*) I'm— Too many things have happened to me.

JOE. Kitty Duval, you're one of the few truly innocent people I have ever known. He'll be back in a couple of days. Go back to the hotel and wait for him.

KITTY. That's what I mean. I can't stand being alone. I'm no good. I tried very hard. I don't know what it is. I miss— (*She gestures.*)

JOE (*gently*). Do you really want to come back here, Kitty?

KITTY. I don't know. I'm not sure. Everything *smells* different. I don't know how to feel, or what to think. (*Gesturing pathetically.*) I know I don't belong there. It's what I've wanted all my life, but it's too *late.* I try to be happy about it, but all I can do is remember everything and cry.

JOE. I don't know what to tell you, Kitty. I didn't mean to hurt you.

KITTY. You haven't hurt me. You're the only person who's ever been good to me. I've never known anybody like you. I'm not sure about love any more, but I know I love you, and I know I love Tom.

JOE. I love you too, Kitty Duval.

KITTY. He'll want babies. I know he will. I know *I* will, too. Of course I will. I can't— (*She shakes her head.*)

JOE. Tom's a baby himself. You'll be very happy together. He wants you to ride with him in the truck. Tom's good for you. You're good for Tom.

KITTY (*like a child*). Do you want me to go back and wait for him?

JOE. I can't *tell* you what to do. I think it would be a good idea, though.

KITTY. I wish I could tell you how it makes me feel to be alone. It's almost worse.

JOE. It might take a whole week, Kitty. (*He looks at her sharply, at the arrival of an idea.*) Didn't you speak of reading a book? A book of poems?

KITTY. I didn't know what I was saying.

JOE (*trying to get up*). Of course you knew. I think you'll like poetry. Wait here a minute, Kitty. I'll go see if I can find some books.

KITTY. All right, Joe. (*He walks out of the place, trying very hard not to wobble.*)

(*Fog-horn. Music. The* NEWSBOY *comes in. Looks for* JOE. *Is broken-hearted because* JOE *is gone.*)

NEWSBOY (*to* SOCIETY GENTLEMAN). Paper?

MAN (*angry*). No.

(*The* NEWSBOY *goes to the* ARAB.)

NEWSBOY. Paper, Mister?

ARAB (*irritated*). No foundation.

NEWSBOY. What?

ARAB (*very angry*). No foundation. (*The* NEWSBOY *starts out, turns, looks at the* ARAB, *shakes head.*)

NEWSBOY. No foundation? How do you figure?

(BLICK *and* TWO COPS *enter.*)

NEWSBOY (*to* BLICK). Paper, mister?

(BLICK *pushes him aside. The* NEWSBOY *goes.*)

BLICK (*walking authoritatively about the place, to* HARRY). Where's Nick?

HARRY. He went for a walk.

BLICK. Who are you?

HARRY. Harry.

BLICK (*to the* ARAB *and* WESLEY). Hey, you. Shut up. (*The* ARAB *stops playing the harmonica,* WESLEY *the piano.*)

BLICK (*studies* KITTY). What's your name, sister?

KITTY (*looking at him*). Kitty Duval. What's it to you?

(KITTY's *voice is now like it was at the beginning of the play: tough, independent, bitter and hard.*)

BLICK (*angry*). Don't give me any of your gutter lip. Just answer my questions.

KITTY. You go to hell, you.

BLICK (*coming over, enraged*). Where do you live?

KITTY. The New York Hotel. Room 21.

BLICK. Where do you work?

KITTY. I'm not working just now. I'm look-for work.

BLICK. What kind of work? (KITTY *can't answer.*) What kind of work? (KITTY *can't answer.*) (*Furiously.*) WHAT KIND OF WORK? (KIT CARSON *comes over.*)

KIT CARSON. You can't talk to a lady that way in *my* presence. (BLICK *turns and stares at* KIT. *The* COPS *begin to move from the bar.*)

BLICK (*to the* COPS). It's all right, boys. I'll take care of this. (*To* KIT.) *What'd you say?*

KIT CARSON. You got no right to hurt people. Who are *you?*

(BLICK, *without a word, takes* KIT *to the street. Sounds of a blow and a groan.* BLICK *returns, breathing hard.*)

BLICK (*to the* COPS). O.K., boys. You can go now. Take care of him. Put him on his feet and tell him to behave himself from now on. (*To* KITTY *again.*) Now answer my question. What kind of work?

KITTY (*quietly*). I'm a whore, you son of a bitch. You know what kind of work I do. And I know what kind you do.

MAN (*shocked and really hurt*). Excuse me, officer, but it seems to me that your attitude—

BLICK. Shut up.

MAN (*quietly*). —is making the poor child say things that are not true.

BLICK. Shut up, I said.

LADY. Well. (*To the* MAN.) Are you going to stand for such insolence?

BLICK (*to* MAN, *who is standing*). Are you?

MAN (*taking the* WOMAN's *arm*). I'll get a divorce. I'll start life all over again. (*Pushing the* WOMAN). Come on. Get the hell out of here!

(*The* MAN *hurries his* WOMAN *out of the place,* BLICK *watching them go.*)

BLICK (*to* KITTY). Now. Let's begin again, and see that you tell the truth. What's your name?

KITTY. Kitty Duval.

BLICK. Where do you live?

KITTY. Until this evening I lived at the New York Hotel. Room 21. This evening I moved to the St. Francis Hotel.

BLICK. Oh. To the St. Francis Hotel. Nice place. Where do you work?

KITTY. I'm looking for work.

BLICK. What kind of work do you do?

KITTY. I'm an actress.

BLICK. I see. What movies have I seen you in?

KITTY. I've worked in burlesque.

BLICK. You're a liar.

(WESLEY *stands, worried and full of dumb resentment.*)

KITTY (*pathetically, as at the beginning of the play*). It's the truth.

BLICK. What are you doing here?

KITTY. I came to see if I could get a job here.

BLICK. Doing what?

KITTY. Singing—and—dancing.

BLICK. You can't sing or dance. What are you lying for?

KITTY. I can. I sang and danced in burlesque all over the country.

BLICK. You're a liar.

KITTY. I said lines, too.

BLICK. So you danced in burlesque?

KITTY. Yes.

BLICK. All right. Let's see what you did.

KITTY. I can't. There's no music, and I haven't got the right clothes.

BLICK. There's music. (*To* WESLEY). Put a nickel in that phonograph. (WESLEY *can't move.*) Come on. Put a nickel in that phonograph. (WESLEY *does so. To* KITTY). All right. Get up on that stage and do a hot little burlesque number. (KITTY *stands. Walks slowly to the stage, but is unable to move.* JOE *comes in, holding three books.*) Get going, now. Let's see you dance the way you did in burlesque, all over the country. (KITTY *tries to do a burlesque dance. It is beautiful in a tragic way.*)

BLICK. All right, start taking them off!

(KITTY *removes her hat and starts to remove her jacket.* JOE *moves closer to the stage, amazed.*)

JOE (*hurrying to* KITTY). Get down from there. (*He takes* KITTY *into his arms. She is crying. To* BLICK.) What the hell do you think you're doing!

WESLEY (*like a little boy, very angry*). It's that man, Blick. *He* made her take off her clothes. He beat up the old man, too.

(BLICK *pushes* WESLEY *off, as* TOM *enters.* BLICK *begins beating up* WESLEY.)

TOM. What's the matter, Joe? What's happened?

JOE. Is the truck out there?

TOM. Yeah, but what's happened? Kitty's crying again!

JOE. You driving to San Diego?

TOM. Yeah, Joe. But what's he doing to that poor colored boy?

JOE. Get going. Here's some money. Everything's O.K. (*To* KITTY.) Dress in the truck. Take these books.

WESLEY'S VOICE. You can't hurt me. You'll get yours. You wait and see.

TOM. Joe, he's hurting that boy. I'll kill him!

JOE (*pushing* TOM). Get out of here! Get married in San Diego. I'll see you when you get back. *(TOM and KITTY go. NICK enters and stands at the lower end of the bar. JOE takes the revolver out of his pocket. Looks at it.)* I've always wanted to kill somebody, but I never knew who it should be. *(He cocks the revolver, stands real straight, holds it in front of him firmly and walks to the door. He stands a moment watching BLICK, aims very carefully, and pulls trigger. There is no shot.)*

(NICK runs over and grabs the gun, and takes JOE aside.)

NICK. What the hell do you think you're doing?

JOE *(casually, but angry)*. That dumb Tom. Buys a six-shooter that won't even shoot once.

(JOE sits down, dead to the world.)

(BLICK comes out, panting for breath.)

(NICK looks at him. He speaks slowly.)

NICK. Blick! I told you to stay out of here! Now get out of here. *(He takes BLICK by the collar, tightening his grip as he speaks, and pushing him out.)* If you come back again, I'm going to take you in that room where you've been beating up that colored boy, and I'm going to murder you—slowly—with my hands. Beat it! *(He pushes BLICK out. To HARRY.)* Go take care of the colored boy. *(HARRY runs out.)* *(WILLIE returns and doesn't sense that anything is changed. WILLIE puts another nickel into the machine, but he does so very violently. The consequence of this violence is that the flag comes up again. WILLIE, amazed, stands at attention and salutes. The flag goes down. He shakes his head.)*

WILLIE *(thoughtfully)*. As far as I'm concerned, this is the *only* country in the world. If you ask me, *nuts* to Europe! *(He is about to push the slide in again when the flag comes up again. Furiously, to NICK, while he salutes and stands at attention, pleadingly.)* Hey, Nick. This machine is out of order.

NICK *(somberly)*. Give it a whack on the side.

(WILLIE does so. A hell of a whack. The result is the flag comes up and down, and WILLIE keeps saluting.)

WILLIE *(saluting)*. Hey, Nick. Something's wrong.

(The machine quiets down abruptly. WILLIE very stealthily slides a new nickel in, and starts a new game.)

(From a distance two pistol shots are heard, each carefully timed.)

(NICK runs out.)

(The NEWSBOY enters, crosses to Joe's table, senses something is wrong.)

NEWSBOY *(softly)*. Paper, Mister?

(JOE can't hear him.)

(The NEWSBOY backs away, studies JOE, wishes he could cheer JOE up. Notices the phonograph, goes to it, and puts a coin in it, hoping music will make JOE happier.)

(The NEWSBOY sits down. Watches JOE. The music begins. "The Missouri Waltz.")

(The DRUNKARD comes in and walks around. Then sits down. NICK comes back.)

NICK *(delighted)*. Joe, Blick's dead! Somebody just shot him, and none of the cops are trying to find out who. *(JOE doesn't hear. NICK steps back, studying JOE.)*

NICK *(shouting)*. Joe.

JOE *(looking up)*. What?

NICK. Blick's dead.

JOE. Blick? Dead? Good! That God damn gun wouldn't go off. I *told* Tom to get a good one.

NICK *(picking up gun and looking at it)*. Joe, you wanted to kill that guy! *(HARRY returns. JOE puts the gun in his coat pocket.)* I'm going to buy you a bottle of champagne.

(NICK goes to bar. JOE rises, takes hat from rack, puts coat on. The NEWSBOY jumps up, helps JOE with coat.)

NICK. What's the matter, Joe?

JOE. Nothing. Nothing.

NICK. How about the champagne?

JOE. Thanks. *(Going.)*

NICK. It's not eleven yet. Where you going, Joe?

JOE. I don't know. Nowhere.

NICK. Will I see you tomorrow?

JOE. I don't know. I don't think so.

(KIT CARSON enters, walks to JOE. JOE and KIT look at one another knowingly.)

JOE. Somebody just shot a man. How are you feeling?

KIT. Never felt better in my life. *(Loudly, bragging, but somber.)* I shot a man once. In San Francisco. Shot him two times. In 1939, I think it was. In October. Fellow named Blick or Glick or something like that. Couldn't stand the way he talked to ladies. Went up to my room and got my old pearl-handled revolver and waited for him on Pacific Street. Saw him walking, and let him have it, two times. Had to throw the beautiful revolver into the Bay.

(HARRY, NICK, the ARAB and the DRUNKARD close in around him.)

(JOE searches his pockets, brings out the revolver, puts it in Kit's hand, looks at him with great admiration and affection. JOE walks slowly to the stairs leading to the street, turns and waves. KIT, and then one by one everybody else, waves, and the marble-game goes into its beautiful American routine again: flag, lights, and music. The play ends.)

CURTAIN

I REMEMBER MAMA

By JOHN van DRUTEN

Adapted from Kathryn Forbes' book *Mama's Bank Account*

I REMEMBER MAMA was first produced by Messrs. Richard Rodgers and Oscar Hammerstein II at the Shubert Theatre, New Haven, Connecticut, on September 28, 1944, and subsequently at the Music Box Theatre, New York City, on October 19, 1944. The play was staged by Mr. van Druten; settings and lighting by George Jenkins. The cast was as follows:

KATRIN	Joan Tetzel	MR. THORKELSON	Bruno Wick
MAMA	Mady Christians	DR. JOHNSON	William Pringle
PAPA	Richard Bishop	ARNE	Robert Antoine
DAGMAR	Carolyn Hummel	A NURSE	Marie Gale
CHRISTINE	Frances Heflin	ANOTHER NURSE	Dorothy Elder
MR. HYDE	Oswald Marshall	SODA CLERK	Frank Babcock
NELS	Marlon Brando	MADELINE	Cora Smith
AUNT TRINA	Adrienne Gessner	DOROTHY SCHILLER	Ottilie Kruger
AUNT SIGRID	Ellen Mahar	FLORENCE DANA MOORHEAD	
AUNT JENNY	Ruth Gates		Josephine Brown
UNCLE CHRIS	Oscar Homolka	BELL-BOY	Herbert Kenwith
A WOMAN	Louise Lorimer		

The action passes in and around San Francisco some years ago.

THE AUTHOR

When John van Druten adapted Kathryn Forbes' novel Mama's Bank Account *for the firm of Rodgers and Hammerstein, he departed from his well-tested taste for cosmopolitan and literate characters. He wrote, in effect, a folk comedy whose charm and strength lay in its firm delineation of plain backbone people. If Mr. van Druten contributed to our playgoing pleasures, America gave something in return to its benefactor from an ample heritage of democratic vigor and a rich diversity of racial strains.*

Mr. van Druten proved himself as adept at adaptation as at original playwriting. He also exhibited a facility for the horizontal, chronicle type of play construction that writers of comedy, who build their drawing-room plots vertically, rarely practice and rarely manage with facility. The dramatist also performed as director in a production notable for fluency, charm, and feeling. The dramatization opened on Broadway in the fall of 1944 and was instantly acclaimed as a heart-warming American and human document.

(For details on John van Druten's career, see p. 230.)

I REMEMBER MAMA

ACT ONE

The period of the play is around 1910.

On either side of the stage, down front, are two small turntables, left and right, on which the shorter front scenes are played against very simplified backgrounds. As each scene finishes the lights dim and the table revolves out, leaving an unobstructed view of the main stage. The main stage is raised by two steps, above which traveler curtains open and close.

When the curtain rises, KATRIN, *in a spotlight, is seated at a desk on the right turntable, facing the audience. She is writing and smoking a cigarette.* KATRIN *is somewhere in her early twenties. She should be played by an actress who is small in stature, and capable of looking sufficiently a child not to break the illusion in subsequent scenes. She is a blonde. Her hair, when we see her first, is in a modern "up" style, capable of being easily loosened to fall to shoulder length for the childhood scenes. She wears a very short dress, the skirt of which is concealed for the prologue by the desk behind which she is seated.*

KATRIN *writes in silence for a few moments, then puts down her pen, takes up her manuscript, and begins to read aloud what she has written.*

KATRIN (*reading*). "For as long as I could remember, the house on Steiner Street had been home. Papa and Mama had both been born in Norway, but they came to San Francisco because Mama's sisters were here. All of us were born here. Nels, the oldest and the only boy—my sister Christine—and the littlest sister, Dagmar." (*She puts down her manuscript and looks out front.*) It's funny, but when I look back, I always see Nels and Christine and myself looking almost as we do today. I guess that's because the people you see all the time stay the same age in your head. Dagmar's different. She was always the baby—so I see her as a baby. Even Mama—it's funny, but I always see Mama as around forty. She couldn't *always* have been forty. (*She puts out her cigarette, picks up her manuscript and starts to read again.*) "Besides us, there was our boarder, Mr. Hyde. Mr. Hyde was an Englishman who had once been an actor, and Mama was very impressed by his flowery talk and courtly manners. He used to read aloud to us in the evenings. But first and foremost, I remember Mama."

(*The light dims down, leaving* KATRIN *only faintly visible. Lights come up on the main stage, revealing the house on Steiner Street—a kitchen room. It has a back flat, with a dresser C., holding china. On either side of the dresser is a door; the one to the R. leads to the pantry;* the one to the L. to the rest of the house. *The L. wall is a short one. It is the wall of the house, and contains a door upstage leading into the street, being presumably the back door of the house, but the one most commonly used as the entry-door. Beyond it the street is visible, with a single lamp-post L., just outside the house. Behind the room rises the house itself with upper windows lighted, and behind it a painted backdrop of the San Francisco hills, houses, and telegraph posts.*

The furniture of the kitchen is simple. A table C., with two chairs above it, armchairs at either end, and a low bench below it. Against the R. wall upstage, a large stove; below it another armchair. The window is below the door in the L. wall and has a low Norwegian chest under it.)

KATRIN'S VOICE (*continuing in the half-dark, as the scene is revealed*). "I remember that every Saturday night Mama would sit down by the kitchen table and count out the money Papa had brought home in the little envelope."

(*By now the tableau is revealed in full, and the light on* KATRIN *dwindles further. The picture is as she described.* MAMA—*looking around forty—is in the armchair R. of the table, emptying the envelope of its silver dollars and smaller coins.* PAPA —*looking a little older than* MAMA—*stands*

87

above her. His English throughout is better than hers, with less accent.)

MAMA. You call the children, Lars. Is good they should know about money.

(PAPA goes to the door back L., and calls.)

PAPA. Children! Nels—Christine—Katrin!

CHILDREN'S VOICES *(off, answering)*. Coming, Papa!

MAMA. You call loud for Katrin. She is in her study, maybe.

PAPA. She is where?

MAMA. Katrin make the old attic under the roof into a study.

PAPA *(amused)*. So? *(Shouting.)* Katrin! Katrin!

KATRIN *(still at her desk, down front)*. Yes, Papa. I heard.

PAPA *(returning to the room)*. A study now, huh? What does Katrin study?

MAMA. I think Katrin wants to be author.

PAPA. Author?

MAMA. Stories she will write. For the magazines. And books, too, maybe, one day.

PAPA *(taking out his pipe)*. Is good pay to be author?

MAMA. I don't know. For magazines, I think maybe yes. For books, I think no.

PAPA. Then she become writer for magazines.

MAMA. Maybe. But I like she writes books. Like the ones Mr. Hyde reads us. *(DAGMAR enters from the pantry. She is a plump child of about eight and carries an alley cat in her arms.)* Dagmar, you bring that cat in again?

DAGMAR. Sure, she's my Elizabeth—my beautiful Elizabeth! *(She crosses to the chest under the window, and sits, nursing the cat.)*

PAPA. Poor Elizabeth looks as if she had been in fight again.

DAGMAR. Not poor Elizabeth. *Brave* Elizabeth. Elizabeth's a Viking cat. She fights for her honor!

PAPA *(exchanging an amused glance with MAMA)*. And just what is a cat's honor, little one?

DAGMAR. The honor of being the bravest cat in San Francisco. *(CHRISTINE comes in back L. She, like KATRIN, should be played by a small young actress, but not a child. Her hair is to her shoulders—her dress short—her age indeterminate. Actually, she is about 13 at this time. She is the cool, aloof, matter-of-fact one of the family.)* Aren't you, Elizabeth?

CHRISTINE *(sitting above the table)*. That disgusting cat!

DAGMAR. She's not disgusting. She's beautiful. Beautiful as the dawn!

CHRISTINE. And when have *you* ever seen the dawn?

DAGMAR. I haven't seen it, but Mr. Hyde read to us about it. *(MR. HYDE comes in from door back L. He is a slightly seedy, long-haired man in his fifties. Rather of the old-fashioned English "laddie" actor type. He wears a very shabby long overcoat, with a deplorable fur collar, and carries his hat. His accent is English.)* Didn't you, Mr. Hyde? Didn't you read to us about the dawn?

MR. HYDE. I did, my child of joy. The dawn, the rosy-finger-tipped Aurora. . . .

DAGMAR. When can I get to *see* the dawn, Mama?

MAMA. Any morning you get up early.

DAGMAR. Is there a dawn every morning?

MAMA. Sure.

DAGMAR *(incredulous)*. It's all that beautiful, and it happens every *morning?* Why didn't anyone *tell* me?

MR. HYDE. My child, that is what the poets are for. To tell you of *all* the beautiful things that are happening every day, and that no one sees until they tell them.

(He starts for the door L.)

MAMA. You go out, Mr. Hyde?

MR. HYDE. For a few moments only, dear Madam. To buy myself a modicum of that tawny weed, tobacco. that I lust after, as

Ben Jonson says. I shall be back in time for our nightly reading. *(He goes out and disappears down the street, into the wings, off L.)*

MAMA *(who has gone to the door back L., calls with a good deal of sharpness and firmness).* Nels! Katrin! You do not hear Papa call you?

NELS *(from off, upstairs).* Coming, Mama!

KATRIN *(at her desk).* Yes, Mama. I'm coming.

(She rises. In her few moments in the dark, she has loosened her hair to her shoulders, and we see that her skirt is short as she walks from her desk, and up the steps into the set. As soon as she has left it, the turntable revolves out. Immediately after her, NELS comes in back L. He is a tall, strapping young fellow—old enough to look 18 or 19, or 15 or 16, according to his dress, or demeanor. Now, he is about 15.)

PAPA. So now all are here.

MAMA. Come, then. *(CHRISTINE, NELS and KATRIN gather around the table. DAGMAR remains crooning to ELIZABETH. Sorting coins.)* First, for the landlord. *(She makes a pile of silver dollars. It gets pushed down the table from one member of the family to the next, each speaking as he passes it. PAPA comes last.)*

NELS *(passing it on).* For the landlord.

KATRIN *(doing likewise).* For the landlord.

CHRISTINE *(passing it to PAPA).* The landlord.

PAPA. For the landlord. *(He dumps the pile at his end of the table, writing on a piece of paper which he wraps around the pile.)*

MAMA *(who has been sorting).* For the grocer. *(The business is repeated. During this repeat, Dagmar's crooning to the cat becomes audible, contrapuntally to the repetitions of "For the grocer.")*

DAGMAR *(in a crescendo).* In all the United States no cat was as brave as Elizabeth. *(Fortissimo.)* In all the *world* no cat was as brave as Elizabeth!

MAMA *(gently).* Hush, Dagmar. Quietly. You put Elizabeth back into the pantry.

DAGMAR *(in a loud, stage whisper, as she crosses to pantry).* In Heaven or HELL no cat was as brave as Elizabeth! *(She goes out with the cat.)*

MAMA. For Katrin's shoes to be half-soled. *(She passes a half dollar.)*

NELS. Katrin's shoes.

KATRIN *(proudly).* My shoes!

CHRISTINE *(contemptuously).* Katrin's old shoes.

PAPA. Katrin's shoes.

CHRISTINE. Mama, Teacher says this week I'll need a new notebook.

MAMA. How much it will be?

CHRISTINE. A dime.

MAMA *(giving her a dime).* For the notebook. You don't lose it.

CHRISTINE. I won't lose it. *(She wraps it in her handkerchief.)*

MAMA. You take care when you blow your nose.

CHRISTINE. I'll take care.

PAPA. Is all, Mama?

MAMA. Is all for this week. Is good. We do not have to go to the Bank. *(She starts to gather up the few remaining coins. KATRIN leaves the group, comes and sits on steps, front.)*

NELS. Mama. . . . *(She looks up, catching an urgency in his tone. PAPA suspends smoking for a moment.)* Mama, I'll be graduating from grammar school next month. Could I . . . could I go on to High, do you think?

MAMA *(pleased).* You want to go to High School?

NELS. I'd like to . . . if you think I could.

MAMA. Is good. *(PAPA nods approvingly.)*

NELS *(awkwardly).* It . . . it'll cost a little money. I've got it all written down. *(Producing a piece of paper from his pocket.)* Carfare, clothes, notebooks, things I'll really need. I figured it out with Cy Nichols. He went to High last year.

(MAMA and PAPA come close together, to look at the paper he puts before them.)

MAMA. Get the *Little* Bank, Christine. (CHRISTINE *gets a small box from the dresser.*)

KATRIN (*from the steps—herself again, in the present—looking out front*). The Little Bank! That was the most important thing in the whole house. It was a box we used to keep for emergencies—like the time when Dagmar had croup and Papa had to go and get medicine to put in the steam kettle. I can *smell* that medicine now! The things that came out of the Little Bank! Mama was always going to buy herself a warm coat out of it, when there was enough, only there never was. (*Meanwhile,* MAMA *has been counting the contents.*)

NELS (*anxiously*). Is there enough, Mama?

MAMA (*shaking her head*). Is not much in the Little Bank right now. We give to the dentist, you remember? And for your roller-skates?

NELS (*his face falling*). I know. And there's your warm coat you've been saving for.

MAMA. The coat I can get another time. But even so . . .

(*She shakes her head.*)

CHRISTINE. You mean Nels can't go to High?

MAMA. Is not enough here. We do not want to have to go to the Bank, do we?

NELS. No, Mama, no. I'll work in Dillon's grocery after school.

(MAMA *writes a figure on the paper and starts to count on her fingers.* PAPA *looks over, and does the sum in his head.*)

PAPA. Is not enough.

MAMA (*finishing on her fingers against her collarbone*). No, is not enough.

PAPA (*taking his pipe out of his mouth and looking at it a long time*). I give up tobacco.

(MAMA *looks at him, almost speaks, then just touches his sleeve, writes another figure and starts on her fingers again.*)

CHRISTINE. I'll mind the Maxwell children Friday nights. Katrin can help me.

(MAMA *writes another figure.* PAPA *looks over—calculates again, nods with satisfaction.*)

MAMA (*triumphantly*). Is good! Is enough!

NELS. Gee!

MAMA. We do not have to go to the Bank.

(DAGMAR *returns, without the cat.*)

DAGMAR (*hearing the last line*). Where is the Bank?

CHRISTINE. Downtown.

DAGMAR. What's it look like?

CHRISTINE. Just a building.

DAGMAR. Like a prison?

CHRISTINE (*sharply*). No, nothing like a prison.

DAGMAR. Well, then, why does Mama always say "We don't want to go to the Bank"?

CHRISTINE. Because . . . well, because no one ever wants to go to the Bank.

DAGMAR. Why not?

CHRISTINE. Because if we went to the Bank all the time, there'd be no money left there. And then if we couldn't pay our rent, they'd turn us out like Mrs. Jensen down the street.

DAGMAR. You mean, it's like saving some of your candy for tomorrow?

MAMA. Yes, my Dagmar. Is exactly like saving your candy.

DAGMAR. But if . . . if all the other people go to the Bank, then there won't be any money left for us, either.

NELS (*kindly*). It isn't like that, Dagmar. Everyone can only get so much.

DAGMAR. How much?

NELS. However much you've got there . . . put away. You see, it's *our* money that we put there, to keep safe.

DAGMAR. When did we put it there?

NELS. I . . . I don't know when. A long time back, I guess. Wasn't it, Mama?

MAMA. Is enough about the Bank.

DAGMAR. How much money have we got in the Bank?

NELS. I don't know. How much, Mama?

MAMA. Enough.

(During the last speeches AUNT TRINA *appears from the wings down front L. She is a timid, mouselike little woman of about 40, with some prettiness about her. She wears her hat and coat, and a pathetic feather boa. She comes up the street and knocks on the house door.)*

MAMA *(hearing the knock)*. Was the door?

CHRISTINE *(quickly)*. If it's the Aunts, I'm going to my boodwar.

KATRIN *(rising, entering the scene)*. And I'm going to my study.

MAMA *(stopping them)*. You cannot run away. We must be polite to the Aunts. *(*PAPA *has opened the door.)* Why, is Trina!

PAPA. Trina, and all by herself!

MAMA. Say good evening to Aunt Trina, children.

CHILDREN *(together)*. Good evening, Aunt Trina.

TRINA. Good evening, children. How well they all look.

MAMA. You have a feather boa. Is new. *(Inspecting it.)* Beautiful.

TRINA *(simpering a little)*. It was a present.

MAMA *(smiling)*. A present! Look, Lars. Trina has a present.

PAPA *(feeling it)*. Is fine.

(He puts Trina's hat, coat and boa on the chest under the window.)

MAMA. Jenny and Sigrid don't come with you, Trina?

TRINA *(embarrassed)*. No, I . . . I didn't tell them I was coming. I want to talk to you, Marta.

MAMA *(smiling)*. So. Sit then, and we talk.

TRINA *(nervously agitated)*. Could we talk alone?

MAMA. Alone?

TRINA. If you wouldn't mind.

MAMA *(going to the stove)*. Children, you leave us alone a little. I call you. Dagmar, you go with Katrin.

KATRIN *(protesting)*. Oh, but, Mama . . .

MAMA *(firmly)*. Katrin, you take Dagmar!

KATRIN. Yes, Mama. *(Pushing* DAGMAR, *resentfully.)* Come on.

(The CHILDREN *go out back L.)*

MAMA. Now—what is it, Trina?

TRINA *(looking down, embarrassed)*. Marta . . .

MAMA *(helpfully)*. Yes?

TRINA. Oh, no, I can't say it.

MAMA *(anxiously)*. Trina, what is it?

TRINA. It's . . . something very personal.

MAMA. You want Lars should go outside?

TRINA. Would you mind, Lars? Just for a minute?

PAPA *(good-humoredly)*. No, I go. I know what women's secrets are. *(Teasing.)* As your Uncle Chris say—"Vomen! Pff!"

MAMA. You have your pipe, Lars? Is fine night. *(*PAPA *takes out his pipe—then lays it down.)* What is it?

PAPA. I forget. I give up tobacco.

MAMA. Is still some tobacco in your pouch? *(*PAPA *nods.)* Then you do not give up tobacco till you have finish. You give up *more* tobacco—not the tobacco you already have.

PAPA. Is not right, Marta.

(He pats her, takes his pipe, and goes out L., standing outside the house, under the lamp-post, and looking up at the stars, smoking.)

MAMA. So, Trina. Now. What is it?

TRINA. Marta. . . . I want to get married.

MAMA. You mean . . . you want to get married, or there is someone you want to marry?

TRINA. There's someone I want to marry.

MAMA. Does *he* want to marry *you*?

TRINA. He says he does.

MAMA *(delighted)*. Trina! Is wonderful!

TRINA *(crying a little)*. I think it is.

MAMA. Who is?

TRINA. Mr. Thorkelson.

MAMA. From the Funeral Parlor?

(TRINA *nods.* MAMA *nods, speculatively, but with less enthusiasm.*)

TRINA. I know he isn't very handsome or . . . or tall. I know it isn't what most people would think a very nice profession, but . . .

MAMA. You love him, Trina? (TRINA *nods ecstatically.*) Then is good. (*She pats Trina's hand.*)

TRINA. Marta, will you . . . will you help me tell the others?

MAMA. Oh . . . Jenny and Sigrid . . . they do not know?

TRINA. No. I was afraid they'd laugh at me. But if *you* tell them . . .

MAMA. Jenny will not like you tell me first.

TRINA (*desperately*). I can't help that. You've got to tell them not to laugh at me. If they laugh at me, I'll . . . I'll kill myself.

MAMA (*with decision*). Jenny and Sigrid will not laugh. I promise you, Trina.

TRINA. Oh, thank you, Marta. And . . . Uncle Chris?

MAMA (*with some seriousness*). Ah!

TRINA. Will you talk to him?

MAMA. It is Mr. Thorkelson who must talk to Uncle Chris. Always it is the husband who must talk to the head of the family.

TRINA. Yes. I know, but . . . well, Uncle Chris is so very frightening. He's so big and black, and he shouts so. And Mr. Thorkelson is . . . well, kind of timid, really.

MAMA (*gently*). But, Trina, if he is to be your husband, he must learn not to be timid. You do not want husband should be timid. *You* are timid. Is not good when *both* are timid. (*Then firmly.*) No! Jenny and Sigrid I speak to, but Mr. Thorkelson must go to Uncle Chris.

PAPA (*re-enters the house*). Marta, Trina, I do not want to interrupt your talk, but Jenny and Sigrid are coming.

TRINA (*alarmed*). Oh, dear!

PAPA. I see them get off the cable-car. They come up the hill.

TRINA (*in a flurry*). I'd better go to your room for a minute.

(*She starts for the door, turns back, gets her things from the chest, and runs out, carrying them, back L. Meanwhile,* MAMA *has been whispering the news to* PAPA.)

MAMA. The coffee is ready—I get more cups.

(*During the above,* AUNTS JENNY *and* SIGRID *have entered from the wings L., front.* JENNY *is a domineering woman in her fifties;* SIGRID, *whining and complaining.*)

SIGRID (*in the street*). Wait, Jenny, I must get my breath. This hill kills me every time I climb it.

JENNY. You climbed bigger hills than that in the old country.

SIGRID. I was a *girl* in the old country.

(*They march to the door and knock—* SIGRID *following* JENNY.)

MAMA (*opening the door to them.*) Jenny. Sigrid. Is surprise. (*To* SIGRID.) Where's Ole?

SIGRID. Working. He's always working. I never see anything of him at all.

MAMA (*crossing to the stove for coffee-pot*). Is good to work.

SIGRID. It's good to see your husband once in a while, too.

JENNY (*no nonsense about her*). Has Trina been here?

MAMA Trina?

JENNY. She's gone somewhere. And she doesn't know anyone but *you.* . . .

MAMA. That is what *you* think.

JENNY. What do you mean by that?

MAMA. Give Lars your coat. I give you some coffee. Then we talk about Trina.

SIGRID (*as* PAPA *helps with coats*). She *has* been here?

MAMA. Yes, she has been here. (*Pouring coffee and passing cups.*)

JENNY. What did Trina want?

MAMA. She want to talk to me.

JENNY. What about?

MAMA. Marriage.

SIGRID. What?

MAMA (pouring calmly). Marriage. (Passing Sigrid's cup.) Trina wants to get married.

JENNY. That's no news. Of course she wants to get married. Every old maid wants to get married.

MAMA. There is someone who wants to marry Trina.

JENNY. Who'd want to marry Trina?

MAMA. Mr. Thorkelson.

SIGRID. Peter Thorkelson? Little Peter? (She gestures a midget.)

MAMA. He is not so little.

SIGRID. He's hardly bigger than my Arne —and Arne is not ten yet.

MAMA. So he is hardly bigger than your Arne. Does every husband have to be big man?

JENNY. Trina's making it up. That happens with old maids, when they get to Trina's age.

MAMA (firmly). No, Jenny—it is true. Mr. Thorkelson wants to marry Trina.

JENNY (changing her tactics slightly). Mr. Thorkelson. She'd be the laughing stock. (She laughs.)

MAMA (moving to her). Jenny, Trina is here. She will come in in a minute. This is serious for her. You will not laugh at her.

JENNY. I shall do what I please.

MAMA. No, Jenny, you will not.

JENNY. And why won't I?

MAMA. Because I will not let you.

JENNY. And how will you stop me?

MAMA. If you laugh at Trina, I will tell her of the time before your wedding when your husband try to run away.

SIGRID. What is that?

JENNY. Who told you that?

MAMA. I know.

SIGRID (intrigued). Erik . . . tried to run away?

JENNY. It's not true.

MAMA. Then you do not mind if I tell Trina.

JENNY. Uncle Chris told you.

SIGRID (tenaciously). Tried to run away?

MAMA. It does not matter, Sigrid. Jenny will not laugh at Trina now. Nor will you! For if you laugh at her, I will tell of your wedding night with Ole, when you cry all the time, and he bring you home to Mother.

PAPA (with sudden enjoyment). This I do not know!

MAMA (reprovingly). Is no need you should know. I do not tell these stories for spite—only so they do not laugh at Trina. Call her, Lars. You like more coffee, Jenny? Sigrid?

(PAPA goes to the door back L., calls, "Trina." MAMA pours coffee for JENNY. MR. HYDE reappears down front L., and lets himself into the house.)

MR. HYDE (seeing company). Oh, I beg your pardon. I was not aware . . .

MAMA. Mr. Hyde, these are my sisters.

MR. HYDE. Enchanted, ladies. Madame. Madame. The Three Graces. (He bows. SIGRID giggles coyly. He goes to the door back L.) You will excuse me?

MAMA. Sure, Mr. Hyde.

MR. HYDE. I shall be in my room. (He goes out.)

JENNY. So that's your famous boarder. Has he paid you his rent yet? Three months he's been here, hasn't he?

MAMA. Is hard to ask. Surely he will pay soon.

JENNY (with a snort). Surely he won't! If I ran my boarding house the way you run this place . . .

PAPA. Maybe your boarders wouldn't always leave you.

JENNY. If Marta thinks she's going to get the warm coat she's always talking about out of that one . . .

MAMA. Jenny, Mr. Hyde is a gentleman.

He reads to us aloud. Wonderful books . . . Longfellow, and Charles Dickens, and Fenimore Kipling.

(TRINA *steals back.*)

MAMA (*seeing her hesitant in the doorway*). Come in, Trina. The coffee is getting cold. (*She pours a cup. There is a silence.*) I tell them.

JENNY. Why did you come to Marta first?

PAPA. She thought Marta would understand.

JENNY. Aren't Sigrid and I married women, too?

PAPA. You have been married longer than Marta. She think maybe you forget.

JENNY. What sort of a living does Mr. Thorkelson make?

TRINA. I . . . I haven't asked.

SIGRID. Can he keep you?

TRINA. I don't think he would have asked me to marry him if he couldn't.

JENNY. Maybe he thinks you are going to keep *him.*

MAMA (*warningly*). Jenny!

SIGRID. Maybe he thinks Trina will have a dowry like the girls at home.

TRINA. Well, why shouldn't I? You all had dowries. . . .

JENNY. We were married in Norway. And our parents were alive. Where would your dowry come from, I'd like to know?

TRINA. Uncle Chris. He's head of the family.

JENNY. And who will ask him?

TRINA. He won't need asking. When Mr. Thorkelson goes to see him . . .

JENNY. Uncle Chris will eat him!

SIGRID (*giggling maliciously*). Little Peter and Uncle Chris!

MAMA (*with meaning*). Maybe Uncle Chris will tell him some family stories. He knows many, does Uncle Chris.

(*The* AUNTS *put down their cups, discomfited.*)

JENNY (*to change the subject*). Where are the children? Aren't we going to see them before we go?

PAPA. Of course, I'll call them. (*He goes to the door and does so, shouting.*) Children! Your Aunts are *leaving!*

CHILDREN'S VOICES (*eagerly*). Coming, Papa!

JENNY. You come with us, Trina?

MAMA. I think maybe Trina like to stay here and listen to Mr. Hyde read to us. You like, Trina?

TRINA. Well, if I wouldn't be in the way. I asked Mr. Thorkelson to call for me here. He'll see me home. I'll help you with the coffee things. (*She takes the tray of coffee cups and goes into the pantry.*)

(KATRIN *returns, back L. She carries her diary,* DAGMAR *follows her, and behind them,* CHRISTINE.)

KATRIN *and* DAGMAR (*curtseying*). Good evening, Aunt Sigrid. Good evening, Aunt Jenny.

(CHRISTINE *sketches a perfunctory curtsey without speaking.*)

JENNY. Where have *you* all been hiding yourselves?

DAGMAR (*going into the pantry*). We've been in Christine's boodwar.

JENNY. Her *what?*

MAMA. Christine makes the little closet into a boudoir. I give her those bead portieres, Jenny, that you lend us when we come from the old country.

SIGRID. And what does she do there?

CHRISTINE (*impertinently*). What people usually do in boudoirs.

MAMA. Christine, that is rude. It is her little place to herself.

(NELS *enters, back L.*)

NELS. Hello, Aunt Sigrid. Hello, Aunt Jenny.

SIGRID (*shaking hands*). Good evening, Nels. My, how tall he is getting!

MAMA (*proudly*). Yes, is almost as tall as his Papa.

SIGRID. He looks to me as if he was outgrowing his strength. Dagmar was looking pale, too.

(DAGMAR *returns now, carrying the cat again.*)

SIGRID *(jumping).* Goodness, what a horrid-looking cat.

DAGMAR. She's not. She's beautiful.

PAPA. Is her new friend. She goes with Dagmar everywhere.

CHRISTINE. She does. First thing you know, she'll have the cat sleeping with her.

DAGMAR *(eagerly).* Oh, Mama, can I? Can I, Mama?

JENNY. Certainly not. Don't you know a cat draws breath from a sleeping child? You wouldn't want to wake up some morning *smothered,* would you?

DAGMAR. I wouldn't care. Elizabeth can have *all* my breath! *(She blows into the cat's face.)* There!

JENNY *(putting on gloves).* Elizabeth—what a very silly name for a cat.

NELS. It's a very silly name for *that* cat. It's a Tom.

MAMA. Nels, how you know?

NELS. I looked!

DAGMAR. How can you tell?

NELS. You can.

DAGMAR. But how?

MAMA *(quickly warning).* Nels, you do not say how!

NELS *(to DAGMAR).* So you'd better think up another name for him.

DAGMAR. I won't. He's Elizabeth. And he's going to *stay* Elizabeth.

PAPA. We could call him *Uncle* Elizabeth!

DAGMAR *(laughing delightedly).* Uncle Elizabeth! Do you hear, Elizabeth? You're called *Uncle* Elizabeth now!

JENNY. Such foolishness! Well, good-by, all. Marta. Lars.

(Good-bys are exchanged all around, the CHILDREN *curtseying formally.)*

MAMA. Good-by, Jenny. Good-by, Sigrid. Nels, you go tell Mr. Hyde we are ready for the reading.

*(*NELS *goes off, back L. The* AUNTS *leave and walk down L.* MAMA *stands in the doorway, waving good-by.)*

SIGRID *(as they go).* Well, I never thought we'd live to see Trina get married.

JENNY. She's not married yet. She's got Uncle Chris to deal with first.

(They disappear into wings L.)

MAMA *(returning to the room and calling into the pantry).* Trina, they have gone Dagmar, you put Elizabeth out for the night now.

DAGMAR *(correcting her).* Uncle Elizabeth!

MAMA. *Uncle* Elizabeth!! (DAGMAR *goes out into the pantry with the cat.* TRINA *comes in as* MR. HYDE *and* NELS *return back L.)* Mr. Hyde, this is my sister Trina.

MR. HYDE *(bowing).* Enchanted!

MAMA *(seating herself R. of the table).* Mr. Hyde reads to us "The Tales From Two Cities." Is a beautiful story. But sad.

TRINA *(brightly).* I like sad stories. *(She gets out her handkerchief.)*

(The whole family group themselves around the table, DAGMAR *returning and seating herself on the floor below* MAMA. MR. HYDE *takes the armchair L. of table.* KATRIN *is on the steps R. front.)*

MR. HYDE. Tonight, I would like to finish it.

MAMA. Is good.

MR. HYDE. Are you ready?

CHILDREN. Yes, please, Mr. Hyde.

MR. HYDE. I will go on from where we left off. *(He starts to read.)* "In the black prison of the Conciergerie, the doomed of the day awaited their fate. They were in number as the weeks of the year. Fifty-two were to roll that afternoon on the life-tide of the City to the boundless, everlasting sea. . . ."

(The lights dim down slowly, leaving spots on KATRIN *and* MR. HYDE *only.)*

KATRIN. I don't think I shall ever forget that night. It was almost midnight when he came to the end, and none of us had noticed.

MR. HYDE *(reading from the last page).* "It is a far, far better thing that I do than

I have ever done; it is a far, far better rest that I go to than I have ever known." *(He closes the book.)* "The End."

(The R. turntable revolves in again. KATRIN *rises from the step, and crosses to her desk on the turntable.)*

KATRIN. I wrote in my diary that night before I went to bed. *(She reads aloud from it.)* "Tonight Mr. Hyde finished 'The Tale of Two Cities.' The closing chapters are indeed superb. How beautiful a thing is self-sacrifice. I wish there were someone *I* could die for." *(She sits looking out front.)* Mr. Hyde read us all kinds of books. He thrilled us with "Treasure Island," and terrified us with "The Hound of the Baskervilles." I can still remember the horror in his voice as he read. . . .

MR. HYDE *(still on the main stage in his spot, reading).* "Dr. Mortimer looked strangely at us for an instant, and his voice sank almost to a whisper as he answered: 'Mr. Holmes, they were the footprints of a gigantic *hound!*'" *(He closes the book.)* We will continue tomorrow night. If you are interested.

KATRIN *(looking out front).* If we were interested! You couldn't have kept us from it. It meant a lot to Mama, too, because Nels stopped going nights to the street corner to hang about with the neighborhood boys. The night they got into trouble for breaking into Mr. Dillon's store, Nels was home with us. And sometimes Mr. Hyde read us poetry. "The Lady of the Lake" . . . and the "Rime of the Ancient Mariner."

MR. HYDE *(reading).*

"About, about, in reel and rout
The death-fires danced at night.
The water, like a witch's oils,
Burnt green and blue and white."

(His spot goes out, and the traveler curtains close on the kitchen scene.)

KATRIN. There were many nights I couldn't sleep for the way he had set my imagination dancing. *(Reading from her diary again.)* "What a wonderful thing is literature, transporting us to realms unknown." *(To herself.)* And all the time my school teacher kept telling me that I ought to write about things I knew. I did write a piece for her once about Uncle Chris, and

she said it wasn't nice to write like that about a member of one's own family. Papa called Mama's Uncle Chris a black Norwegian, because of his dark hair and fierce mustache, but there were others in the family who claimed that he was black in a different way. The Aunts, for example.

(Spot goes up on L. front turntable, representing Jenny's kitchen. JENNY *and* TRINA *are discovered.* JENNY *is rolling pastry.* TRINA *is crocheting.)*

JENNY. Black! I'll say he's black. Black in his heart. Cursing and swearing . . .

TRINA. Marta says that's only because it hurts him to walk.

JENNY. Rubbish. I know all about his limp and the accident back in the old country—but has anyone ever heard him complain? Marta's always making excuses for him.

TRINA. I know . . . but he *is* good to the children. All those oranges he's always sending them . . .

JENNY. Oranges! What good is oranges? Turn 'em yellow. They're the only things he's ever been known to give away, anyway. He's got other uses for his money.

TRINA. What you mean?

JENNY. Bottles! And that woman he lives with!

TRINA. He *says* she's his housekeeper.

JENNY. Well, he couldn't very well come right out and call her what she is, could he? Though *I* will one of these days. And to his face, too.

(SIGRID comes through the curtains C. She crosses to JENNY and TRINA.)

SIGRID. Jenny. Trina. What do you think? What do you think Uncle Chris has done now?

TRINA. What?

JENNY. Tell us.

SIGRID. You know my little Arne's knee —that fall he had two months ago? The man at the drugstore said it was only a bruise, but today it was hurting him again, so I left him home when I went to do the marketing. I asked Mrs. Schultz next door to keep an eye on him, and who should turn up, not ten minutes after I'd gone, but Uncle Chris. And what do you think?

JENNY. Well, tell us, if you're going to. Don't keep *asking* us.

SIGRID. He took one look at Arne's knee, bundled him into that rattletrap old automobile of his, and rushed him straight off to the hospital. I've just come from there . . . and what do you think? They've operated! They've got him in Plaster of Paris!

JENNY. Without consulting you?

SIGRID. It seems the doctor is a friend of his . . . that's why he did it. No, this time he's gone too far. To put a child of Arne's age through all that pain! They wouldn't even let me *see* Arne. I'm going to tell Uncle Chris exactly what I think of him. . . .

JENNY. That's right.

SIGRID. I'm going to tell him right now. (*Weakening a little.*) Come with me, Jenny.

JENNY. Well, I . . . No, I can't leave my baking.

SIGRID. You must, Jenny. We must stand together. You come, too, Trina, and ask about your dowry. *Make* him give it to you.

TRINA. Oh, but . . . Marta said Mr. Thorkelson should do that. . . .

JENNY. Well, then, go and get Mr. Thorkelson. Go down to the mortuary and get him now. Sigrid's quite right. We girls have got to stand together!

(*Blackout. Turntable revolves out.*)

KATRIN (*at her desk*). Nobody knew where Uncle Chris lived. That was part of the mystery about him. He used to roam up and down the state buying up farms and ranches that had gone to pieces, and bullying them back into prosperity. Then he'd sell at a profit and move on again. Two or three times a year he'd descend on the city in his automobile and come roaring and stamping into our house.

(*Her light dims.*)

(*The sound of a very old and noisy Ford car changing gears is heard off L. A grinding and screaming as it comes to a* standstill. *Then* UNCLE CHRIS' VOICE, *shouting.*)

UNCLE CHRIS' VOICE. Marta! Lars! Children—vere are you?

(*The curtains part on the kitchen again. Outside in the street is Uncle Chris' car —an antique model. A woman is seated beside the empty driver's seat.* UNCLE CHRIS *is knocking on the house door. He is an elderly, powerful, swarthy man with a limp. In the kitchen,* NELS *and* CHRISTINE *are cowering.*)

UNCLE CHRIS. Marta! Lars!

CHRISTINE (*scared*). It's Uncle Chris.

NELS (*equally so*). I know.

CHRISTINE. What'll we do?

UNCLE CHRIS. Is nobody home? Hey, there —is nobody home? (*Banging on the door.*) Hey—someone—answer the door. (*He tries the door handle; it opens and he strides, limpingly, in. He has a strong accent, and uses the Norwegian pronunciation of the children's names.*) So, vat is—you do not answer the door? You do not hear me calling? (*The* CHILDREN *cower silently.*) I say, you do not hear me calling? I do not call loud enough?

CHRISTINE. Y-yes, Uncle Chris.

UNCLE CHRIS. Which yes? Yes, you do not hear me—or yes I do not call loud enough?

NELS. We heard you, Uncle Chris.

UNCLE CHRIS. Then why you do not come?

NELS. We . . . we were just going to.

(KATRIN *has left her desk and come up the steps.*)

UNCLE CHRIS. Let me look at you. You too, Katrinë, do not stand there—come and let me look at you. (*They line up as though for inspection. He thumps* NELS *between the shoulder blades.*) Stand tall! (*They all straighten up.*) Um-hum. By the dresser, where the marks are. (NELS *goes to the wall by the dresser.* UNCLE CHRIS *compares his mark with the previous one—and makes a new one on the wall, writing by it.*) Two inches. Two inches in . . . (*Examining the date.*) Six months. Is good. Christinë. (CHRISTINE *replaces* NELS.) Show me your teeth. (*She does so.*) You brush them goot?

(She nods.) Nils, there is a box of oranges in the automobile. You fetch them in. *(NELS goes out L. UNCLE CHRIS measures CHRISTINE.)* Where is the little von? Dagmar?

KATRIN. She's sick, Uncle Chris.

UNCLE CHRIS *(arrested)*. Sick? What is the matter with her?

KATRIN. It's her ear. She's had an earache for two days. Bad earache. Mama sent for the doctor.

UNCLE CHRIS. Goot doctor? What he say?

KATRIN. He's in there now.

(She points off, back L. Meanwhile CHRISTINE has remained standing by the wall, afraid to move.)

UNCLE CHRIS. I go in.

(He starts to the door back L., but MAMA and DR. JOHNSON come into the room as he does so. During this NELS has gone to the car, and with nervous smiles at the woman seated by the driver's seat, has heaved out a huge box of oranges. He returns with the oranges during the ensuing scene.)

MAMA *(greeting him)*. Uncle Chris.

UNCLE CHRIS. How is with Dagmar?

MAMA. Is bad. Doctor, this is my Uncle, Mr. Halvorsen.

DOCTOR. How do you do, sir?

UNCLE CHRIS. What is with the child?

DOCTOR. We must get her to a hospital. At once. We'll have to operate.

MAMA. Operate?

DOCTOR. I'm afraid so.

MAMA. Can wait? Until my husband comes home from work?

DOCTOR. I'm afraid not. Her best chance is for us to operate immediately.

MAMA *(after a second)*. We go. *(She goes to the dresser for the Little Bank.)*

UNCLE CHRIS *(who has watched her decision with approval, turns to the doctor)*. What is with the child?

DOCTOR. I'm afraid it's a mastoid.

UNCLE CHRIS. Ah . . . then you operate immediately.

DOCTOR *(resenting this)*. That's what I said.

UNCLE CHRIS. Immediately!

MAMA *(who has poured the contents of the Little Bank onto the table)*. Doctor . . . is enough?

DOCTOR. I was thinking of the County Hospital.

MAMA. No. No. We pay. Is enough?

KATRIN. If there isn't, we can go to the Bank.

CHRISTINE. We've got a Bank Account.

MAMA. Is enough without we go to the Bank, Doctor? My husband is carpenter. Make good money.

UNCLE CHRIS. If there is need of money, I pay.

DOCTOR *(mainly in dislike of Uncle Chris)*. It'll be all right. We'll take her to the Clinic. You pay what you can afford.

UNCLE CHRIS. Goot. Goot. I have a patient there already. My nephew, Arne. They operate this morning on his knee.

DOCTOR. Are you a physician, sir?

UNCLE CHRIS. I am better physician than most doctors. Nils, there, my other nephew, he become doctor when he grow up.

(NELS looks up, surprised.)

DOCTOR *(chillily)*. Oh, indeed . . . very interesting. Well, now, if you will have the child at the Clinic in . . . shall we say an hour's time. . . .

UNCLE CHRIS. The child will be at the Clinic in *ten minutes'* time. I haf my automobile.

DOCTOR. I can hardly make arrangements in ten minutes.

UNCLE CHRIS. *I* make arrangements. I know doctors.

MAMA. Uncle Chris, Dr. Johnson arrange. He is good doctor.

DOCTOR *(ironically)*. Thank you, Madam.

MAMA. You go, Doctor. We come.

DOCTOR. Very well, in an hour, then. And Dagmar will be well taken care of, I promise you. I will do the operation myself.

UNCLE CHRIS. I watch.

DOCTOR. You will do no such thing, sir.

UNCLE CHRIS. Always I watch operations. I am head of family.

DOCTOR. I allow no one to attend my operations.

UNCLE CHRIS. Are so bad?

DOCTOR (to MAMA). Mrs. Hanson, if I am to undertake this operation and the care of your child, it must be on the strict understanding that this gentleman does not come near either me or my patient.

MAMA. Yes, Doctor, I talk to him. . . . You go to hospital now, please.

DOCTOR. Very well. But you understand . . . nowhere near me, or I withdraw from the case. (He goes.)

UNCLE CHRIS. I go see Dagmar.

MAMA. Wait. Uncle Chris, is kind of you, but Dagmar is sick. You frighten her.

UNCLE CHRIS. I frighten her?

MAMA. Yes, Uncle Chris. You frighten everyone. . . .

UNCLE CHRIS (amazed). I??

MAMA. Everyone but me. Even the girls. . . . Jenny, Sigrid, Trina . . . they are frightened of you.

UNCLE CHRIS. The girls! Vomen! Pff!

MAMA. And the children, too. So Nels and I get Dagmar. You drive us to hospital in your automobile, but you do not frighten Dagmar. And you leave Doctor alone. Dr. Johnson is *fine* doctor. You come with me, Nels. You carry Dagmar.

(NELS and MAMA go out back L. UNCLE CHRIS stands in amazement and puzzlement. The TWO GIRLS watch him, hardly daring to move.)

UNCLE CHRIS. Is true? I frighten you? Christinë . . . Katrinë . . . you are frightened of me? Come, I ask you. Tell me the truth. You are frightened of me?

KATRIN (tremulously). A . . . a little, Uncle Chris.

UNCLE CHRIS. No? And you, Christinë?

CHRISTINE. Y . . . yes, Uncle Chris.

UNCLE CHRIS. But Nils . . . Nils is a boy . . . he is not frightened?

CHRISTINE Not . . . not as much as we are. . . .

UNCLE CHRIS. But he is frightened?

CHRISTINE. Yes, Uncle Chris.

UNCLE CHRIS. But, why? What is there to be frightened of? I am your Uncle Chris . . . why do I frighten you?

CHRISTINE. I don't know.

UNCLE CHRIS. But that is bad. Very bad. The Aunts, yes, I like to frighten them. (THE GIRLS giggle.) That makes you laugh. You do not like the Aunts? Come, tell me. You do not like the Aunts? Say!

KATRIN. Not . . . very much, Uncle Chris.

UNCLE CHRIS. And which do you not like the most? Jenny . . . Sigrid . . . Trina. . . . Tell me—huh?

KATRIN. I think I like Aunt Jenny least. She's so . . . so bossy.

CHRISTINE. I can't stand Aunt Sigrid. Always whining and complaining.

UNCLE CHRIS (with a great roar of laughter). Is good. Jenny, bossy. Sigrid, whining. Is true! But your Mama, she is different. And she cook goot. The Aunts, they cannot cook at all. Only you do not tell your Mama we have talked of them so. It is a secret, for us. Then you cannot be frightened of me any more . . . when we have secret. I tell you my secret, too. *I* do not like the Aunts. And so that they do not bother me, I frighten them and shout at them. You I do not shout at if you are goot children, and clean your teeth goot, and eat your oranges.

(He takes out a snuff-box and partakes of its contents.)

(On the cue "You I do not shout at" the posse of AUNTS appears, in outdoor clothes, accompanied by MR. THORKELSON, a terrified little man. They come in down L. and start up to the house.)

SIGRID (stopping in the street). Jenny. Do you see what I see? A woman, in his automobile.

JENNY. How shameful!

SIGRID. Ought we to bow?

JENNY. Bow? To a woman like that? We cut her. That's what we do. I'll show you.

(She strides to the front door, ignoring the woman in the car, and enters the house. The others follow.)

JENNY *(entering)*. Uncle Chris, Sigrid has something to say to you.

SIGRID *(with false bravery)*. Uncle Chris, you took Arne to the hospital. . . .

UNCLE CHRIS. Yes, I take Arne to the hospital. And now we take Dagmar to the hospital, so you do not clutter up the place.

JENNY. What's the matter with Dagmar?

CHRISTINE. It's her ear. Dr. Johnson's going to operate.

SIGRID *(catching her favorite word)*. Operate? This is some more of Uncle Chris' doings. Did you hear what he did to Arne?

UNCLE CHRIS *(turning on her)*. Sigrid, you are a whining old fool, and you get out of here. . . .

SIGRID *(deflating)*. We'd better go, Jenny. . . .

JENNY *(stoutly)*. No . . . there has been enough of these high-handed goings on. . . .

UNCLE CHRIS. And you, Jenny . . . you are a bossy old fool, and you get out of here, too, and we take Dagmar to hospital. *(NELS enters, carrying DAGMAR in his arms, wrapped in a blanket.)* You got her goot, Nils?

NELS. Sure, Uncle Chris.

UNCLE CHRIS. We go.

JENNY *(getting between them and the door)*. No! You are going to hear me out. *(Weakening.)* That is, you are going to hear *Sigrid* out. . . .

UNCLE CHRIS. If you do not get out of the way of the door before I count three, I trow you out. And Sigrid, too, as big as she is. Von. . . . *(SIGRID moves.)* Two. . . . *(JENNY moves. He looks back at the children with a wink and a smile.)* Is

goot! You put her in back of the car, Nils. *(NELS goes out, carrying DAGMAR, and lifts her into the car. UNCLE CHRIS follows and starts cranking.)*

TRINA *(running to the door after him, with MR. THORKELSON)*. But, Uncle Chris, I want to introduce Mr. Thorkelson. . . .

(But UNCLE CHRIS ignores her, continuing to crank. She returns crestfallen into the room with MR. THORKELSON. MAMA re-enters back L., wearing hat and coat and carrying a cheap little overnight case.)

MAMA. Jenny . . . Trina, we go to hospital. *(She goes to KATRIN and CHRISTINE.)* You will be good children until Mama comes home?

THE GIRLS. Sure, Mama.

UNCLE CHRIS *(calling from the car.)* Marta, we go!

MAMA *(calling back)*. I come! *(She turns to the children again.)* There is milk in the cooler, and fruit and cookies for your lunch.

CHRISTINE. We'll be all right, Mama. Don't worry.

MAMA. I go now. *(She starts for the door.)*

SIGRID *(stopping her)*. Marta!

MAMA. What is it?

SIGRID. You *can't* go in his automobile.

MAMA. Why not?

UNCLE CHRIS *(calling again)*. Marta, we go!

MAMA. I come!

SIGRID. Because . . . because *she's* in it. The . . . the woman!

MAMA. So it will kill me, or Dagmar, if we sit in the automobile with her? I have see her. She looks nice woman. *(Calling off, as she goes.)* I come!

UNCLE CHRIS. We go!

(She climbs into the rear of the car, which backs noisily off during the next speeches.)

MR. THORKELSON *(in a low whisper to TRINA)*. Is that woman his wife?

TRINA *(nervously)*. Yes. . . .

MR. THORKELSON. Yes?

TRINA (*whispering back, loudly*). No!

JENNY (*to* THE GIRLS). Don't stand there gaping like that, girls. (*She shoos them into the pantry.*) Go away! Go away! (THE GIRLS *go.* JENNY *turns and sees the disappearing car through the open door.*) Oh! They've gone! We go after them! Sigrid, you lead the way! (*She gives* SIGRID *a push and the four go out, with* JENNY *dragging* MR. THORKELSON, *and* TRINA *following. Blackout. The travelers close.*)

(*Spot on R. turntable, representing a kind of closet-room. Roller-skates hanging on the wall.* KATRIN *and* CHRISTINE *are seated on a small kitchen stepladder with glasses of milk, and cookies on plates.*)

KATRIN. How long have they been gone now?

CHRISTINE. About three hours. And I wish you wouldn't keep asking that.

KATRIN. How long do operations take? I heard Aunt Sigrid telling about Mrs. Bergman who was five hours on the table.

CHRISTINE. Aunt Sigrid's friends always have everything worse than anyone else. And it gets worse each time she tells it, too.

(KATRIN *smiles—drinks some milk and eats a cookie.*)

KATRIN (*with a certain melancholy enjoyment*). The house feels lonesome, doesn't it—without Mama? It's like in a book. "The sisters sat huddled in the empty house, waiting for the verdict that was to spell life or death to the little family."

CHRISTINE. Oh, don't talk such nonsense.

KATRIN. It's not nonsense.

CHRISTINE. It is, too. In the first place, we're not a little family. We're a big one. And who said anything about life or death, anyway? Always trying to make everything so dramatic!

KATRIN. Well, it *is* dramatic.

CHRISTINE. It's not. It's just . . . well, worrying. But you don't have to make a tragedy out of it.

(*Pause.*)

KATRIN. You're not eating anything.

CHRISTINE. I know that.

KATRIN. You're not drinking your milk, either. Aren't you hungry?

CHRISTINE. No. And you wouldn't be, either, if you'd any feeling for Mama and Dagmar, instead of just heartlessly sitting there eating and enjoying making a story out of it.

KATRIN. Oh, Chris, I'm not heartless. I do have feeling for them. I can't help it if it goes into words like that. Everything always does with me. But it doesn't mean I don't feel it. And I think we *ought* to eat. I think Mama would want us to.

(*Pause.* CHRISTINE *hesitates a moment, then takes a bite of a cookie. They both eat in silence. The light dims on them, and the turntable revolves out.*)

(*The travelers part on the hospital corridor. A main back flat representing the wall, running diagonally up from the front of the main stage L. toward the back. Down front L. is a bench, on which* MAMA *and* NELS *are sitting, holding hands, looking off. Below the bench is the elevator, and above the bench, set back a little, is a closet for brooms and mops, etc. The reception desk, at which a nurse is sitting, is R.C., toward the front. The wall goes up into darkness, and behind the nurse's desk is darkness.*)

(*As the curtains open, there is a hubbub down front by the nurse's desk, where the* AUNTS *are haranguing* UNCLE CHRIS. MR. THORKELSON *stands slightly in back of them.*)

SIGRID. But, Uncle Chris, I tell you I must see him.

UNCLE CHRIS (*storming*). You don't understand English? No visitors for twenty-four hours.

SIGRID. But *you've* seen him.

UNCLE CHRIS. I am not visitor. I am exception.

SIGRID. Well, then, his mother should be an exception, too. I'll see the doctor.

UNCLE CHRIS. *I* have seen doctor. I have told him you are not good for Arne.

SIGRID. Not good for my own son . . .

UNCLE CHRIS. Not goot at all. You cry over him. I go now. (*He starts to do so, but* JENNY *pushes* TRINA *forward.*)

TRINA *(with desperate courage)*. Uncle Chris . . . Uncle Chris . . . I *must* speak to you.

UNCLE CHRIS. I have business.

TRINA. But, Uncle Chris. . . . I want to get married.

UNCLE CHRIS. Well, then, *get* married. *(He starts off again.)*

TRINA. No, wait, I . . . I want to marry Mr. Thorkelson. Here. *(She produces him from behind her.)* Peter, this is Uncle Chris. Uncle Chris, this is Mr. Thorkelson.

UNCLE CHRIS *(staring at him)*. So?

MR. THORKELSON. How are you, sir?

UNCLE CHRIS. Busy. *(He turns again.)*

TRINA. Please, Uncle Chris. . . .

UNCLE CHRIS. What is? You want to marry him? All right, marry him. I have other things to think about.

TRINA *(eagerly)*. Then . . . then you give your permission?

UNCLE CHRIS. Yes, I give my permission. If you want to be a fool, I cannot stop you.

TRINA *(gratefully)*. Oh, thank you, Uncle Chris.

UNCLE CHRIS. So. Is all?

TRINA *(anxious to escape)*. Yes, I think is all.

JENNY *(firmly)*. No!!

UNCLE CHRIS. No?

(MR. THORKELSON is pushed forward again.)

MR. THORKELSON. Well, there . . . there was a little something else. You see, Trina mentioned . . . well, in the old country it was always usual . . . and after all, we do all come from the old country. . . .

UNCLE CHRIS. What is it? What do you want?

MR. THORKELSON. Well, it's a question of Trina's . . . well, not to mince matters . . . her dowry.

UNCLE CHRIS *(shouting)*. Her what?

MR. THORKELSON *(very faintly.)* Her dowry . . .

UNCLE CHRIS. Ah. Her dowry. Trina wants a dowry. She is forty-two years old. . . .

TRINA *(interrupting)*. No, Uncle Chris. . . .

UNCLE CHRIS *(without pausing)*. And it is not enough she gets husband. She must have dowry.

NURSE *(who has been trying to interrupt, now bangs on her desk)*. PLEASE! Would you mind going and discussing your family matters somewhere else? This is a hospital, not a marriage bureau!

UNCLE CHRIS *(after glaring at the NURSE, turns to MR. THORKELSON)*. You come into waiting room. I talk to you about dowry. *(He strides off into the darkness behind the nurse's desk. MR. THORKELSON, with an appealing look back at TRINA, follows him. The AUNTS now remember MAMA, sitting on the bench, and cross to her.)*

JENNY. Did you hear that, Marta?

MAMA *(out of a trance)*. What?

JENNY. Uncle Chris.

MAMA. No, I do not hear. I wait for doctor. Is two hours since they take Dagmar to operating room. More.

SIGRID. Two hours? That's nothing! When Mrs. Bergman had her gall bladder removed she was *six* hours on the table.

MAMA. Sigrid, I do not want to hear about Mrs. Bergman. I do not want to hear about anything. I wait for doctor. Please, you go away now. You come this evening.

TRINA. But, Marta, you can't stay here all by yourself.

MAMA. I have Nels. Please, Trina . . . I wait for doctor . . . you go now.

JENNY. We go.

TRINA. Oh, but I must wait for Peter and Uncle Chris. . . .

JENNY. We'll go next door and have some coffee. Sigrid, do you have money?

SIGRID. Yes, I . . . I have a little.

JENNY. Good. Then I treat you. We'll be next door if you want us, Marta.

(MAMA nods without looking at them, her eyes still fixed on the elevator door. The AUNTS leave going down the steps from

the stage as though they were the hospital steps, and off L.)

(For a moment, the stage is quiet. Then a SCRUBWOMAN *enters from down R., carrying a mop and pail which she puts into the closet, and then leaves. The elevator door opens and a doctor in white coat comes out, followed by an orderly, carrying a tray of dressings. They disappear up R. behind the desk.* MAMA *rises, agitatedly, looking after them. Then* DR. JOHNSON *returns from R. front, carrying his hat and bag. He sees* MAMA *and crosses to her, C.)*

DOCTOR. Oh, Mrs. Hanson. . . .

MAMA. Doctor. . . .

DOCTOR. Well, Dagmar's fine. She came through it beautifully. She's back in bed now, sleeping off the anesthetic.

MAMA. Thank you, Doctor. *(She shakes hands with him.)*

DOCTOR. You're very welcome.

MAMA. Is good of you, Doctor. *(She shakes hands with him again.)* Where is she? I go to her now.

DOCTOR. Oh, I'm sorry, but I'm afraid that's against the rules. You shall see her tomorrow.

MAMA. Tomorrow? But, Doctor, she is so little. When she wakes she will be frightened.

DOCTOR. The nurses will take care of her. Excellent care. You needn't worry. You see, for the first twenty-four hours, clinic patients aren't allowed to see visitors. The wards must be kept quiet.

MAMA. I will not make a sound.

DOCTOR. I'm very sorry. Tomorrow. And now . . . *(He glances at his watch.)* Good afternoon. *(He puts on his hat and goes out L., down the steps and off.)*

*(*MAMA *stands still a moment, looking after him.)*

MAMA. Come, Nels. We go find Dagmar.

NELS. But, Mama, the doctor said . . .

MAMA. We find Dagmar. *(She looks vaguely around her. Then goes to the nurse's desk.)* You tell me, please, where I can find my daughter?

NURSE. What name?

MAMA. Dagmar.

NELS. Dagmar Hanson.

NURSE *(looking at her record book).* Hanson, Ward A. Along there. *(She points upstage.* MAMA *starts to go up.)* Oh, just a moment. *(*MAMA *returns.)* When did she come in?

MAMA. This morning. They just finish operation.

NURSE. Oh, well, then I'm afraid you can't see her today. No visitors for the first twenty-four hours.

MAMA. Am not visitor. I am her Mama.

NURSE. I'm sorry, but it's against the rules.

MAMA. Just for one minute. Please.

NURSE. I'm sorry. It's against the rules.

*(*MAMA *stands staring.* NELS *touches her arm. She looks at him, nods, trying to smile, then turns and walks with him to L. and down the steps.)*

MAMA. We must think of some way.

NELS. Mama, they'll let you see her tomorrow. They said so.

MAMA. If I don't see her today how will I know that all is well with her? What can I tell Papa when he comes home from work?

NELS. The nurses will look after her, Mama. Would you like to come next door for some coffee?

MAMA *(shaking her head).* We go home. We have coffee at home. But I must see Dagmar today. *(She plods off L. with* NELS. *The travelers close.)*

(Spot goes up on R. turntable. UNCLE CHRIS *and* MR. THORKELSON *are seated on a bench and chair, as in a waiting-room. A table with a potted plant is between them. A clock on the wall points to 2:30.)*

UNCLE CHRIS. Well, it comes then to this. You love my niece, Trina? *(*MR. THORKELSON, *very scared, gulps and nods.)* You want to marry her? *(*MR. THORKELSON *nods again.)* You are in a position to support her? *(*MR. THORKELSON *nods again.)* Why, then, you want dowry? *(No answer. He shouts.)* What for you want dowry?

MR. THORKELSON. Well . . . well, it would be a nice help. And it is customary.

UNCLE CHRIS. Is not customary. Who give dowries? Parents. Why? Because they are so glad they will not have to support their daughters any more, they pay money. I do not support Trina. I do not care if Trina gets married. Why then should I pay to have her married?

MR. THORKELSON. I never thought of it like that.

UNCLE CHRIS. Is insult to girl to pay dowry. If I do not give dowry, will you still marry Trina?

MR. THORKELSON. I . . . I don't know.

UNCLE CHRIS. You don't know? You don't know?? You think I let Trina marry a man who will not take her without dowry?

MR. THORKELSON. No, I suppose you wouldn't.

UNCLE CHRIS. What kind of man would that be? I ask you, what kind of man would that be?

MR. THORKELSON (fascinated—helpless). Well, not a very nice kind of man.

UNCLE CHRIS. And are you that kind of man?

MR. THORKELSON. I . . . I don't think so.

UNCLE CHRIS (conclusively). Then you don't want dowry!!

MR. THORKELSON (giving up). No, I . . . guess I don't.

UNCLE CHRIS (slapping his back). Goot. Goot. You are goot man. I like you. I give you my blessing. And I send you vedding present. I send you box of oranges! (While he is boisterously shaking Mr. Thorkelson's hand, blackout. Turntable revolves out.)

(The curtains open on the kitchen. It is empty. MAMA and NELS come up the hill from the L. and let themselves into the house. There is silence as they take off their hats and coats).

MAMA (after a moment). Where are the girls?

NELS. I guess they're upstairs. (Goes to door back L. and calls.) Chris! Katrin!

GIRLS' VOICES. Coming!

NELS. Shall I make you some coffee? (MAMA shakes her head.) You said you'd have coffee when you got home.

MAMA. Later. First I must think.

NELS. Mama, please don't worry like that. Dagmar's all right. You know she's all right.

(THE GIRLS come in back L.)

CHRISTINE (trying to be casual). Well, Mama, everything all right?

MAMA (nodding). Is all right. You have eaten?

KATRIN. Yes, Mama.

MAMA. You drink your milk?

CHRISTINE. Yes, Mama.

MAMA. Is good.

CHRISTINE (seeing her face). Mama, something's the matter.

KATRIN (over-dramatically). Mama, Dagmar's not—? She isn't—? Mama!

MAMA. No, Dagmar is fine. The doctor say she is fine. (She rises.) What is time?

NELS. It's three o'clock.

MAMA. Three hours till Papa come. (She looks around and then goes slowly into the pantry, back R.)

KATRIN. Nels, what is it? There is something the matter.

NELS. They wouldn't let Mama see Dagmar. It's a rule of the hospital.

CHRISTINE. But Dagmar's all right?

NELS. Oh, yes, she's all right?

CHRISTINE (impatiently). Well, then . . . !

NELS. But Mama's very upset. She started talking to me in Norwegian in the streetcar.

KATRIN (emotionally). What can we do?

CHRISTINE (coldly). You can't do anything. When will they let her see Dagmar?

NELS. Tomorrow.

CHRISTINE. Well, then, we'll just have to wait till tomorrow.

KATRIN. Chris, how can you be so callous? Can't you see that Mama's heart is breaking?

CHRISTINE. No, I can't. And you can't, either. People's hearts don't break.

KATRIN. They do, too.

CHRISTINE. Only in books. (MAMA *comes back; she wears an apron, and carries a scrub brush and a bucket of hot water.*) Why, Mama, what are you going to do?

MAMA. I scrub the floor. (*She gets down on her knees.*)

CHRISTINE. But you scrubbed it yesterday.

MAMA. I scrub it again. (*She starts to do so.*)

KATRIN. But, Mama . . .

MAMA (*bending low*). Comes a time when you've got to get down on your knees.

KATRIN (*to* CHRISTINE). Now do you believe me?

(CHRISTINE, *suddenly unendurably moved, turns and rushes from the room.*)

NELS. Mama, don't. Please don't. You must be tired.

KATRIN (*strangely*). Let her alone, Nels.

(*They stand in silence watching* MAMA *scrub. Suddenly she stops.*)

MAMA (*sitting back on her haunches*). I think of something! (*Slowly.*) I think I think of something!

(*The lights dim and the curtains close on the kitchen.*)

(*From down front L.* UNCLE CHRIS' VOICE *singing. The lights slowly come up on the L. turntable, showing* ARNE (*a child of about eight*) *in a hospital bed, with* UNCLE CHRIS *beside him.*)

UNCLE CHRIS (*singing*).
"Ten t'ousand Svedes vent t'rough de veeds
   At de battle of Coppen-hagen.
Ten t'ousand Svedes vent t'rough de veeds
   Chasing vun Nor-ve-gan!"

ARNE. Uncle Chris!

UNCLE CHRIS. Yes, Arne?

ARNE. Uncle Chris, does it *have* to hurt like this?

UNCLE CHRIS. If you vant it to be vell, and not to valk always like Uncle Chris, it does . . . for a little. Is very bad?

ARNE. It is . . . kinda. . . . Oo—oo . . . !

UNCLE CHRIS. Arne, don't you know any svear vords?

ARNE. W-what?

UNCLE CHRIS. Don't you know any svear vords?

ARNE. N-no, Uncle Chris. Not real ones.

UNCLE CHRIS. Then I tell you two fine vons to use when pain is bad. Are "Damn" and "Damittohell." You say them?

ARNE. N-now?

UNCLE CHRIS. No, not now. When pain comes again. You say them then. They help plenty. I know. I haf pain, too. I say them all the time. And if pain is *very* bad, you say, "*God*damittohell." But only if is *very* bad. Is bad now?

ARNE. No, it's . . . it's a little better.

UNCLE CHRIS. You sleep some now, maybe?

ARNE. I'll try. Will . . . will you stay here, Uncle Chris?

UNCLE CHRIS. Sure. Sure. I stay here. You are not frightened of Uncle Chris?

ARNE. No. Not any more.

UNCLE CHRIS. Goot. Goot. You like I sing some more?

ARNE. If you wouldn't mind. But maybe something a little . . . well, quieter.

UNCLE CHRIS (*tenderly*). Sure. Sure. (*He begins quietly to sing a Norwegian lullaby; in the midst,* ARNE *cries out.*)

ARNE. Oo—oo. . . . Oh, *damn*. Damn. Damittohell!

UNCLE CHRIS (*delighted*). Goot! It helps —eh?

ARNE (*with pleased surprise*). Yes—yes.

UNCLE CHRIS. Then you sleep some! (*He fixes Arne's pillows for him, and resumes the lullaby, seated on his chair beside the bed. After another verse, he leans over, assuring himself that the child is asleep, and then very quietly, without interrupting his singing, takes a flask from his pocket and lifts it to his lips, as the light dims. The table revolves out.*)

(*The curtains part on the hospital corridor again. There is a different* NURSE *now at the reception desk, talking on the tele-*

phone as MAMA *and* KATRIN *come in from L. and up the steps.)*

MAMA *(as they come up, in an undertone).* Is not the same nurse. Katrin, you take my hat and coat. *(She takes them off, revealing that she still wears her apron.)*

KATRIN. But, Mama, won't they . . .

MAMA *(interrupting, finger to lips).* Ssh! You let me go ahead. You wait on bench for me. *(She goes to the closet door above the bench and opens it.* KATRIN *stares after her in trepidation.* MAMA *takes out a damp mop and pail, and gets down on her knees in front of the nurse's desk, starting to clean the floor. The* NURSE *looks up.* MAMA *catches her eye.)*

MAMA *(brightly).* Very dirty floors.

NURSE. Yes, I'm glad they've finally decided to clean them. Aren't you working late?

MAMA *(quickly, lowering her head).* Floors need cleaning. *(She pushes her way, crawling on hands and knees, up behind the desk, and disappears up the corridor, still scrubbing.* KATRIN *steals to the bench, where she sits, still clutching Mama's hat and coat, looking interestedly around her. The light dims, leaving her in a single spot, as she starts to talk to herself.)*

KATRIN *(to herself).* "The Hospital" . . . A poem by Katrin Hanson. *(She starts to improvise.)*
"She waited, fearful, in the hall, And held her bated breath."

Breath—yes, that'll rhyme with death. *(She repeats the first two lines.)*

"She waited fearful in the hall
And held her bated breath.
She trembled at the least footfall,
And kept her mind on death."

(She gets a piece of paper and pencil from her pocket and begins to scribble, as a NURSE *comes out of the elevator, carrying some charts, which she takes to the desk, and then goes out down R.* KATRIN *goes on with her poem.)*

"Ah, God, 'twas agony to wait.
To wait and watch and wonder. . . ."

Wonder—under—bunder—funder—sunder. Sunder! *(Nods to herself and goes on again.)*

"To wait and watch and wonder,
About her infant sister's fate,
If Death's life's bonds would sunder."

(Then to herself again, looking front.)

That's beautiful. Yes, but it isn't true. Dagmar isn't dying. It's funny—I don't want her to die—and yet when Mama said she was all right, I was almost—well, almost disappointed. It wasn't exciting any more. Maybe Christine's right, and I haven't any heart. How awful! "The girl without a heart." That'd be a nice title for a story. "The girl without a heart sat in the hospital corridor. . . ."

(The lights come up again as UNCLE CHRIS *appears, up R. behind the desk. He wears his hat and is more than a little drunk. He sees* KATRIN.*)*

UNCLE CHRIS. Katrinë! What you do here? *(He sits on the bench beside her.)*

KATRIN *(nervously).* I'm waiting for Mama.

UNCLE CHRIS. Where is she?

KATRIN *(scared).* I . . . I don't know.

UNCLE CHRIS. What you mean . . . you don't know?

KATRIN *(whispering).* I think . . . I think she's seeing Dagmar.

UNCLE CHRIS *(shaking his head).* Is first day. They do not allow visitors first day.

KATRIN *(trying to make him aware of the* NURSE*).* I know. But I think that's where she is.

UNCLE CHRIS. Where *is* Dagmar?

KATRIN. I don't know.

(UNCLE CHRIS *rises and goes to the* NURSE *at the desk.)*

UNCLE CHRIS. In what room is my greatniece, Dagmar Hanson?

NURSE *(looking at her book).* Hanson . . . Hanson . . . when did she come in?

UNCLE CHRIS. This morning.

NURSE. Oh, yes. Were you wanting to see her?

UNCLE CHRIS. What room is she in?

NURSE. I asked were you wanting to see her.

UNCLE CHRIS. And *I* ask what room she is in.

NURSE. We don't allow visitors the first day.

UNCLE CHRIS. Have I said I vant to visit her? I ask what room she is in.

NURSE. Are you by any chance, Mr. . . . *(Looking at her book.)* Halvorsen?

UNCLE CHRIS *(proudly, and correcting her pronunciation)*. Christopher Halvorsen.

NURSE. Did you say you were her uncle?

UNCLE CHRIS. Her great-uncle.

NURSE. Well, then, I'm afraid I can't tell you anything about her.

UNCLE CHRIS. Why not?

NURSE. Orders.

UNCLE CHRIS. Whose orders?

NURSE. Dr. Johnson's. There's a special note here. Patient's uncle, Mr. Halvorsen, not to be admitted or given information under any circumstances.

UNCLE CHRIS *(after a moment's angry stupefaction)*. Goddamittohell! *(He strides away down L., taking out his flask, and shaking it, only to find it empty.* MAMA *returns from up R., carrying the mop and pail, walking now and smiling triumphantly.)*

MAMA *(to the* NURSE*)*. Thank you. *(She replaces the mop and pail in the closet, and then sees* UNCLE CHRIS*.)* Uncle Chris, Dagmar is fine!

UNCLE CHRIS *(coming back to her, amazed)*. You see her?

MAMA. Sure, Uncle Chris, I see her.

UNCLE CHRIS *(reiterating, incredulous)*. You see Dagmar?!

MAMA. Sure. *(She takes her hat from* KATRIN *and starts to put it on.)* Is fine hospital. But such floors! A mop is never good. Floors should be scrubbed with a brush. We go home. Uncle Chris, you come with us? I make coffee.

UNCLE CHRIS. Pah! Vot good is coffee? I go get drink.

MAMA *(reprovingly)*. Uncle Chris!

UNCLE CHRIS. Marta, you are fine voman. Fine. But I go get drink. I get drunk.

MAMA *(quickly aside to* KATRIN*)*. His leg hurts him.

UNCLE CHRIS. And you do not make excuses for me! I get drunk because I like it.

MAMA *(conciliating him)*. Sure, Uncle Chris.

UNCLE CHRIS *(shouting)*. I like it! *(Then, with a change.)* No, is not true. You know is not true. I do not like to get drunk at all. But I do not like to come home with you, either. *(Growing slightly maudlin.)* You have family. Is fine thing. You do not know how fine. Katrinë, one day when you grow up, maybe you know what a fine thing family is. I haf no family.

KATRIN. But, Uncle Chris, Mama's always said you were the *head* of the family.

UNCLE CHRIS. Sure. Sure. I am head of the family, but I haf no family. So I go get drunk. You understand, Marta?

MAMA. Sure, Uncle Chris. You go get drunk. *(Sharply.)* But don't you feel sorry for yourself! (UNCLE CHRIS *glares at her o moment, then strides off R., boisterously singing his song of "Ten Thousand Swedes."* MAMA *watches him go, then takes her coat from* KATRIN*.)* Is fine man. Has fine ideas about family. (KATRIN *helps her on with her coat)*. I can tell Papa now that Dagmar is fine. She wake while I am with her. I explain rules to her. She will not expect us now until tomorrow afternoon.

KATRIN. You won't try and see her again before that?

MAMA *(gravely)*. No. That would be against the rules! Come. We go home.

(They go off L.)

CURTAIN

ACT TWO

Scene: *Opening, exactly as in Act One.* Katrin *at her desk.*

KATRIN *(reading)*. "It wasn't very often that I could get Mama to talk—about herself, or her life in the old country, or what she felt about things. You had to catch her unawares, or when she had nothing to do, which was very, very seldom. I don't think I can ever remember seeing Mama unoccupied." *(Laying down the manuscript and looking out front.)* I do remember one occasion, though. It was the day before Dagmar came home from the hospital. And as we left, Mama suggested treating me to an ice-cream soda. *(She rises, gets her hat from beside her—a school girl hat—puts it on and crosses C. while she speaks the next lines.)* She had never done such a thing before, and I remember how proud it made me feel—just to sit and talk to her quietly like a grown-up person. It was a kind of special *treat*-moment in my life that I'll always remember—quite apart from the soda, which was *wonderful. (She has reached C. stage now.* MAMA *has come from between the curtains, and starts down the steps.)*

MAMA. Katrin, you like we go next door, and I treat you to an ice-cream soda?

KATRIN *(young now, and overcome)*. Mama—do you mean it?

MAMA. Sure. We celebrate. We celebrate that Dagmar is well, and coming home again. *(They cross to the L., where the turntable represents a drugstore, with a table and two chairs at which they seat themselves.)* What you like to have, Katrin?

KATRIN. I think a chocolate . . . no a strawberry . . . no, a chocolate soda.

MAMA *(smiling)*. You are sure?

KATRIN *(gravely)*. I think so. But, Mama, can we *afford* it?

MAMA. I think this once we can afford it.

(The SODA CLERK *appears from L.)*

SODA CLERK. What's it going to be, ladies?

MAMA. A chocolate ice-cream soda, please —and a cup of coffee.

(The SODA CLERK *goes.)*

KATRIN. Mama, he called us "ladies"! *(*MAMA *smiles.)* Why aren't you having a soda, too?

MAMA. Better I like coffee.

KATRIN. When can I drink coffee?

MAMA. When you are grown up.

KATRIN. When I'm eighteen?

MAMA. Maybe before that.

KATRIN. When I graduate?

MAMA. Maybe. I don't know. Comes the day you are grown up, Papa and I will know.

KATRIN. Is coffee really nicer than a soda?

MAMA. When you are grown up, it is.

KATRIN. Did you used to like sodas better . . . before you were grown up?

MAMA. We didn't have sodas before I was grown up. It was in the old country.

KATRIN *(incredulous)*. You mean they don't have sodas in Norway?

MAMA. Now, maybe. Now I think they have many things from America. But not when I was little girl.

(The SODA CLERK *brings the soda and the coffee.)*

SODA CLERK. There you are, folks. *(He sets them and departs.)*

KATRIN *(after a good pull at the soda)*. Mama, do you ever want to go back to the old country?

MAMA. I like to go back once to look, maybe. To see the mountains and the fjords. I like to show them once to you all. When Dagmar is big, maybe we all go back once . . . one summer . . . like tourists. But that is how it would be. I would be tourist there now. There is no one I would know any more. And maybe we see the little house where Papa and I live when we first marry. And . . . *(Her eyes grow misty and reminiscent.)* something else I would look at.

KATRIN. What is chat? (MAMA *does not answer.*) What would you look at, Mama?

MAMA. Katrin, you do not know you have brother? Besides Nels?

KATRIN. No! A brother? In Norway? Mama . . .

MAMA. He is my first baby. I am eighteen when he is born.

KATRIN. Is he there now?

MAMA (*simply*). He is dead.

KATRIN (*disappointed*). Oh. I thought you meant . . . I thought you meant a real brother. A long-lost one, like in stories. When did he die?

MAMA. When he is two years old. It is his grave I would like to see. (*She is suddenly near tears, biting her lip and stirring her coffee violently, spilling a few drops on her suit. She gets her handkerchief from her pocketbook, dabs at her skirt, then briefly at her nose, then she returns the handkerchief and turns to* KATRIN *again. Matter-of-factly.*) Is good, your ice-cream soda?

KATRIN (*more interested now in* MAMA *than in it*). Yes. Mama . . . have you had a very *hard* life?

MAMA (*surprised*). Hard? No. No life is easy all the time. It is not meant to be.

KATRIN. But . . . rich people . . . aren't *their* lives easy?

MAMA. I don't know, Katrin. I have never known rich people. But I see them sometimes in stores and in the streets, and they do not *look* as if they were easy.

KATRIN. Wouldn't you like to be rich?

MAMA. I would like to be rich the way I would like to be ten feet high. Would be good for some things—bad for others.

KATRIN. But didn't you come to America to *get* rich?

MAMA (*shocked*). No. We come to America because they are all here—all the others. Is good for families to be together.

KATRIN. And did you like it right away?

MAMA. Right away. When we get off the ferry boat and I see San Francisco and all the family, I say: "Is like Norway," only it is better than Norway. And then you are all born here, and I become American citizen. But not to get rich.

KATRIN. *I* want to be rich. Rich and famous. I'd buy you your warm coat. When are you going to get that coat, Mama?

MAMA. Soon now, maybe—when we pay doctor, and Mr. Hyde pay his rent. I think now I *must* ask him. I ask him tomorrow, after Dagmar comes home.

KATRIN. When I'm rich and famous, I'll buy you lovely clothes. White satin gowns with long trains to them. And jewelry. I'll buy you a pearl necklace.

MAMA. We talk too much! (*She signs to the* SODA CLERK.) Come, finish your soda. We must go home. (*The* SODA CLERK *comes.*) How much it is, please?

SODA CLERK. Fifteen cents.

MAMA. Here are two dimes. You keep the nickel. And thank you. Was good coffee. (*They start out and up the steps toward the curtains C.*) Tomorrow Dagmar will be home again. And, Katrin, you see Uncle Elizabeth is there. This afternoon again she was asking for him. You keep Uncle Elizabeth in the house all day until she comes home.

(*They disappear behind the curtains.*)

(*After a second, the howls of a cat in pain are heard from behind the curtains— low at first, then rising to a heart-rending volume, and then diminishing again as the curtains part on the kitchen once more.* MAMA, PAPA, *and* DAGMAR *are entering the house.*)

DAGMAR (*standing on threshold, transfixed*). It's Uncle Elizabeth, welcoming me home! That's his song of welcome. Where is he, Mama? (*She looks around for the source of the howls.*)

MAMA. He is in the pantry. . . . (*As* DAGMAR *starts to rush thither*). But wait . . . wait a minute, Dagmar. I must tell you. Uncle Elizabeth is . . . sick.

DAGMAR. Sick? What's the matter with him?

PAPA. He has been in fight. Last night He come home this morning very sick indeed.

(DAGMAR *starts for the pantry door, back R., as* NELS *comes out.*)

MAMA. Nels, how is Uncle Elizabeth? Nels has been doctoring him.

NELS. He's pretty bad, Mama. I've dressed all his wounds again with boric acid, but . . . (*As* DAGMAR *tries to get past him.*) I wouldn't go and see him now, baby.

DAGMAR. I've got to. He's *my* cat. I haven't seen him in a whole month. More. (*She runs into the pantry and disappears.*)

MAMA. Nels, what you think?

NELS. I think we ought to have had him put away before she came home.

MAMA. But she would have been so unhappy if he was not here *at all*.

NELS. She'll be unhappier still if he dies.

(*Another howl is heard from the pantry, and then* DAGMAR *comes rushing back.*)

DAGMAR. Mama, what happened to him? What happened to him? Oh, Mama . . . when I tried to pick him up, his bandage slipped over his eye. It was bleeding. Oh, Mama, it looked awful. Oh . . . (*She starts to cry.*)

MAMA (*fondling her.*) He look like that all over. Nels, you go see to his eye again. (*Wearily,* NELS *returns to the pantry.*) Listen, Dagmar . . . *Lille Ven* . . . would it not be better for the poor thing to go quietly to sleep?

DAGMAR. You mean—go to sleep and never wake up again? (MAMA *nods gently.*) No.

PAPA. I think he die, anyway. Nels try to make him well. But I do not think he can.

DAGMAR. Mama can. Mama can do everything. (*Another howl from offstage. She clutches* MAMA *agonizedly.*) Make him live, Mama. Make him well again. *Please!*

MAMA. We see. Let us see how he gets through the night. And now, Dagmar, you must go to bed. I bring you your supper.

DAGMAR. But you will fix Uncle Elizabeth? You promise, Mama?

MAMA. I promise I try. Go now. (DAGMAR *goes out, back L.*) I must fix her supper. (*She starts for the pantry. Howls again. She and* PAPA *stand and look at each other.* NELS *comes out.*)

NELS. Mama, it's just cruelty, keeping that cat alive.

MAMA. I know.

PAPA (*as another howl, the loudest yet, emerges*). You say we see how the cat get through the night. I ask you how do *we* get through the night? Is no use, Marta. We must put the cat to sleep. Nels, you go to the drugstore, and get something. Some chloroform, maybe. (*He gives him a coin.*)

NELS. How much shall I get?

PAPA. You ask the man. You tell him it is for a cat. He knows. (NELS *goes out L. and down the street into the wings. Looking at Mama's face.*) Is best. Is the only thing.

MAMA. I know. But poor Dagmar. It is sad homecoming for her. And she has been so good in hospital. Never once she cry. (*She pulls herself together.*) I get her supper. (*Another howl from offstage.*) And I take the cat outside. Right outside, where we . . . where *Dagmar* cannot hear him. (*She goes into the pantry.* PAPA *takes a folded newspaper from his pocket, puts on his glasses and starts to read. The door, back L., opens gently and* MR. *Hyde peeps out. He wears his hat and coat and carries his suitcase and a letter.* PAPA *has his back to him.* MR. HYDE *lays the letter on the dresser and then starts to tiptoe across to the door. Then* PAPA *sees him.*)

PAPA. You go out, Mr. Hyde?

MR. HYDE (*pretending surprise*). Oh. . . . Oh, I did not see you, Mr. Hanson. (*He puts down the suitcase.*) I did not know you were back. As a matter of fact, I . . . was about to leave this letter for you. (*He fetches it.*) The fact is . . . I . . . I have been called away.

PAPA. So?

MR. HYDE. A letter I received this morning necessitates my departure. My immediate departure.

PAPA. I am sorry. (MAMA *returns with a tray, on which are milk, bread, butter, and jelly.*) Mama, Mr. Hyde says he goes away.

MAMA (*coming to the table with the tray*). Is true?

MR. HYDE. Alas, dear Madam, yes. 'Tis true, 'tis pity. And pity 'tis, 'tis true. You will find here . . . (*He presents the letter.*) my check for all I owe you, and a note expressing my profoundest thanks for all your most kind hospitality. You will say good-by to the children for me? (*He bows, as* MAMA *takes the letter.*)

MAMA (*distressed*). Sure. Sure.

MR. HYDE (*bowing again*). Madam, my deepest gratitude. (*He kisses her hand.* MAMA *looks astonished. He bows to* PAPA.) Sir—my sincerest admiration! (*He opens the street door.*) It has been a privilege. Ave Atque Vale! Hail and farewell! (*He makes a gesture and goes.*)

MAMA. Was wonderful man! Is too bad. (*She opens the letter, takes out the check.*)

PAPA. How much is the check for?

MAMA. Hundred ten dollar! Is four months.

PAPA. Good. Good.

MAMA. Is wonderful. Now we pay doctor everything.

PAPA. And you buy your warm coat. With fur now, maybe.

MAMA (*sadly*). But there will be no more reading. You take the check, Lars. You get the money?

PAPA (*taking it*). Sure, I get it. What does he say in his letter?

MAMA. You read it while I fix supper for Dagmar. (*She starts to butter the bread, and spread jelly, while* PAPA *reads.*)

PAPA (*reading*). "Dear Friends, I find myself compelled to take a somewhat hasty departure from this house of happiness. . . ."

MAMA. Is beautiful letter.

PAPA (*continuing*). "I am leaving you my library for the children. . . ."

MAMA. He leaves his books?

PAPA. He says so.

MAMA. But is wonderful. Go see, Lars. See if they are in his room.

(PAPA *lays down the letter and goes out back* L. NELS *and* CHRISTINE *appear down* L., *coming up to the house.* CHRISTINE *carries school books.*)

CHRISTINE. I'm sure it was him, Nels. Carrying his suitcase, and getting on the cable-car. I'm sure he's going away.

NELS. Well, I hope he's paid Mama. (*They open the street door.*)

CHRISTINE (*bursting in*). Mama, I saw Mr. Hyde getting on the cable-car.

MAMA. I know. He leave.

CHRISTINE. Did he pay you?

MAMA. Sure, he pay me. Hundred ten dollar. . . .

NELS. Gee. . . .

MAMA (*smiling*). Is good.

CHRISTINE. Are you going to put it in the Bank?

MAMA. We need it right away. (PAPA *returns, staggering under an armload of books.*) Mr. Hyde leaves his books, too. For you.

NELS. Say! (PAPA *stacks them on the table.* NELS *and* CHRISTINE *rush to them, reading the titles.*) The Pickwick Papers, The Complete Shakespeare . . .

CHRISTINE. Alice in Wonderland, The Oxford Book of Verse . . .

NELS. The Last of the Mohicans, Ivanhoe . . .

CHRISTINE. We were right in the middle of that.

MAMA. Nels can finish it. He can read to us now in the evenings. He has fine voice, too, like Mr. Hyde. (NELS *flushes with pleasure.*) Is wonderful. So much we can learn. (*She finishes the supper-making.*) Christine, you take the butter back to the cooler for me, and the yelly, too. (CHRISTINE *does so*). I go up to Dagmar now. (*She lifts the tray, then pauses.*) You get it, Nels?

NELS. What? . . . Oh. . . . (*Taking a druggist's small bottle from his pocket.*) Here.

MAMA. You put it down. After I come back, we do it. You know how?

NELS. Why, no, Mama, I . . .

MAMA. You do not ask?

NELS. No, I . . . I thought Papa . . .

MAMA. You know, Lars?

PAPA. No, I don't *know* . . . but it cannot be difficult. If you *hold* the cat . . .

MAMA. And watch him die? No! I think better you get rags . . . and a big sponge, to soak up the chloroform. You put it in the box with him, and cover him over. You get them ready out there.

NELS. Sure, Mama.

MAMA. I bring some blankets.

(NELS *goes off to the pantry, as* CHRISTINE *comes back. Again* MAMA *lifts the tray and starts for the door back L. But there is a knock on the street door from* AUNT JENNY, *who has come to the house from down L. in a state of some excitement.*)

MAMA (*agitated.*) So much goes on! See who it is, Christine.

CHRISTINE (*peeping*). It's Aunt Jenny. (*She opens the door.*)

MAMA. Jenny. . . .

JENNY (*breathless*). Marta . . . has he gone?

MAMA. Who?

JENNY. Your boarder . . . Mr. Hyde. . . .

MAMA. Yes. he has gone. Why?

JENNY. Did he pay you?

MAMA. Sure he pay me.

JENNY. How?

MAMA. He give me a check. Lars has it right there.

JENNY (*with meaning*). A check!

MAMA. Jenny, what is it? Christine, you give Dagmar her supper. I come soon. (CHRISTINE *takes the tray from her and goes out back L.*) What is it, Jenny? How do you know that Mr. Hyde has gone?

JENNY. I was at Mr. Kruper's down the street . . . you know, the restaurant and bakery . . . and he told me Mr. Hyde was there today having his lunch, and when he left he asked if he would cash a check for him. For fifty dollars. (*She pauses.*)

PAPA. Well, go on.

JENNY. Your fine Mr. Hyde didn't expect Mr. Kruper to take it to the bank until tomorrow, but he did. And what do you think? Mr. Hyde hasn't even an *account* at that bank!

(NELS *returns and stands in the pantry doorway.*)

MAMA. I don't understand.

PAPA (*taking the check from his pocket*). You mean the check is no good?

JENNY. No good at all. (*Triumphantly.*) Your Mr. Hyde was a crook, just as I always thought he was, for all his reading and fine ways. Mr. Kruper said he'd been cashing them all over the neighborhood. (MAMA *stands quite still, without answering.*) How much did he owe you? Plenty, I'll bet. (*Still no answer.*) Eh, Marta, I said I bet he owed you plenty. Didn't he?

MAMA (*looks around, first at* NELS *and then down at the books on the table. She touches them.*) No. No, he owed us nothing. (*She takes the check from* PAPA, *tearing it.*) Nothing.

JENNY (*persistently*). How much was that check for? (*She reaches her hand for it.*)

MAMA (*evading her*). It does not matter. He pay with better things than money. (*She goes to the stove, where she throws the check, watching it burn.*)

JENNY. I told you right in the beginning that you shouldn't trust him. But you were so sure . . . just like you always are. Mr. Hyde was a gentleman. A gentleman! I bet it must have been a hundred dollars that he rooked you of. Wasn't it?

MAMA (*returning*). Jenny, I cannot talk now. Maybe you don't have things to do. I have.

JENNY (*sneeringly*). What? What have *you* got to do that's so important?

MAMA (*taking up the medicine bottle*). I have to chloroform a cat!

(JENNY *steps back in momentary alarm, almost as though* MAMA *were referring to her, as she goes out into the pantry with the medicine bottle, not so very unlike Lady Macbeth with the daggers.*)

(*Blackout and curtains close.*)

(*After a moment, the curtains part again on the kitchen, the next morning. The books have been taken off the table, and*

MAMA *is setting the breakfast dishes, with* PAPA *helping her.* DAGMAR *comes bursting into the room, back L.)*

DAGMAR. Good morning, Mama. 'Morning, Papa. Is Uncle Elizabeth all better?

MAMA. Dagmar, there is something I must tell you.

DAGMAR. I want to see Uncle Elizabeth first. *(She runs into the pantry.* MAMA *turns helplessly to* PAPA.*)*

MAMA. Do something! Tell her!

PAPA. If we just let her think the cat die . . . by itself. . . .

MAMA. No. We cannot tell her lies. *(*PAPA *goes to the pantry door, opening it.)*

DAGMAR *(heard in pantry, off).* What a funny, funny smell. Good morning, my darling, my darling Elizabeth. *(*MAMA *and* PAPA *stand stricken.* DAGMAR *comes in, carrying the cat, wrapped in an old shirt, with its head covered.)* My goodness, you put enough blankets on him! Did you think he'd catch cold?

MAMA *(horror-stricken).* Dagmar, you must not. . . . *(She stops at the sight of the cat, whose tail is twitching, quite obviously alive.)* Dagmar, let me see . . . Let me see the cat! *(She goes over to her, and uncovers its head.)*

DAGMAR *(overjoyed).* He's well. Oh, Mama, I *knew* you'd fix him.

MAMA *(appalled).* But, Dagmar, I didn't. I . . .

DAGMAR *(ignoring her).* I'm going to take him right up and show him to Nels. *(She runs off back L., calling.)* Nels! Nels! Uncle Elizabeth's well again!

MAMA *(turning to* PAPA). Is a miracle!

PAPA *(shrugging).* You cannot have used enough chloroform. You just give him good sleep, and that cures him. We rechristen the cat, Lazarus!

MAMA. But, Lars, we must tell her. Is not *good* to let her grow up believing I can fix *everything!*

PAPA. Is best thing in the world for her to believe. *(He chuckles.)* Besides, I know *exactly* how she feels. *(He lays his hand on hers.)*

MAMA *(turning with embarrassment from his demonstrativeness).* We finish getting breakfast. *(She turns back to the table. The curtains close.)*

(Lights up down front R. KATRIN *and* CHRISTINE *enter from the wings, in school clothes, wearing hats.* CHRISTINE *carries schoolbooks in a strap.* KATRIN *is reciting.)*

KATRIN.
"The quality of mercy is not strained,
　It droppeth as the gentle rain from heaven
　Upon the place beneath: it is twice blest;
　It blesseth him that gives, and him that
　　takes. . . ."

(She dries up.)

". . . him that takes. It blesseth him that gives and him that takes. . . ." *(She turns to* CHRISTINE.*)* What comes after that?

CHRISTINE. I don't know. And I don't care.

KATRIN. Why, Chris!

CHRISTINE. I don't. It's all I've heard for weeks. The school play, and your graduation, and going on to High. And never a thought of what's happening at home.

KATRIN. What do you mean?

CHRISTINE. You see—you don't even know!

KATRIN. Oh, you mean the strike?

CHRISTINE. Yes, I mean the strike. Papa hasn't worked for four whole weeks, and a lot you care. Why, I don't believe you even know what they're striking *for.* Do you? All you and your friends can talk about is the presents you're going to get. You make me ashamed of being a girl.

(Two girls, MADELINE *and* DOROTHY, *come through the curtains, C., talking.)*

MADELINE *(to* DOROTHY*).* Thyra Walsh's family's going to add seven pearls to the necklace they started for her when she was a baby. Oh, hello, Katrin! Did you hear about Thyra's graduation present?

KATRIN *(not very happily).* Yes, I heard.

MADELINE. I'm getting an onyx ring, with a diamond in it.

KATRIN. A real diamond?

MADELINE. Yes, of course. A *small* diamond.

DOROTHY. What are *you* getting?

KATRIN. Well . . . well, they haven't actually told me, but I think . . . I think I'm going to get that pink celluloid dresser set in your father's drugstore.

DOROTHY. You mean that one in the window?

KATRIN (*to* MADELINE). It's got a brush and comb and mirror . . . and a hair-receiver. It's genuine celluloid!

DOROTHY. I wanted Father to give it to me, out of stock, but he said it was too expensive. Father's an awful tightwad. They're giving me a bangle.

MADELINE. Oh, there's the street-car. We've got to fly. 'By, Katrin. 'By, Christine. See you tomorrow. Come on, Dorothy.

(*The* TWO GIRLS *rush off L.*)

CHRISTINE. Who said you were going to get the dresser set?

KATRIN. Nobody's said so . . . for certain. But I've sort of hinted, and . . .

CHRISTINE. Well, you're not going to get it.

KATRIN. How do you know?

CHRISTINE. Because I know what you *are* getting. I heard Mama tell Aunt Jenny. Aunt Jenny said you were too young to appreciate it.

KATRIN. What is it?

CHRISTINE. Mama's giving you her brooch. Her *solje.*

KATRIN. You mean that old silver thing she wears that belonged to Grandmother? What would I want an old thing like that for?

CHRISTINE. It's an heirloom. Mama thinks a lot of it.

KATRIN. Well, then, she ought to keep it. You don't really mean that's *all* they're going to give me?

CHRISTINE. What more do you want?

KATRIN. I want the dresser set. My goodness, if Mama doesn't realize what's a suitable present . . . why, it's practically the most important time in a girl's life, when she graduates.

CHRISTINE. And you say you're not selfish!

KATRIN. It's not selfishness.

CHRISTINE. Well, I don't know what else you'd call it. With Papa not working, we need every penny we can lay our hands on. Even the Little Bank's empty. But you'll devil Mama into giving you the dresser set somehow. So why talk about it? I'm going home. (*She turns and goes up the steps and through the curtains.*)

(KATRIN *stands alone with a set and stubborn mouth, and then sits on the steps.*)

KATRIN. Christine was right. I got the dresser set. They gave it to me just before supper on graduation night. Papa could not attend the exercises because there was a strike meeting to decide about going back to work. I was so excited that night, I could hardly eat, and the present took the last remnants of my appetite clean away.

(*The curtains part on the kitchen.* PAPA, MAMA, *and* DAGMAR *at table, with coffee.* CHRISTINE *is clearing dishes.*)

CHRISTINE. I'll just stack the dishes now, Mama. We'll wash them when we come home. (*She carries them into the pantry.*)

PAPA (*holding up a cube of sugar*). Who wants coffee-sugar? (*He dips it in his coffee.*) Dagmar? (*He hands it to her.*) Katrin? (*She rises from the step, coming into the scene for the sugar.*)

MAMA. You get your coat, Katrin; you need it.

(KATRIN *goes out back L.*)

DAGMAR. Aunt Jenny says if we drank black coffee like you do at our age, it would turn our complexions dark. I'd like to be a black Norwegian. Like Uncle Chris. Can I. Papa?

PAPA. I like you better blonde. Like Mama.

DAGMAR. When do you get old enough for your complexion *not* to turn dark? When can we drink coffee?

PAPA. One day, when you are grown up. (JENNY *and* TRINA *have come to the street door L.* JENNY *knocks.*)

MAMA. There are Jenny and Trina. (*She goes to the door.*) Is good. We can start now. (*She opens the door.* JENNY *and* TRINA *come in.*)

JENNY. Well, are you all ready? Is Katrin very excited?

PAPA (*nodding*). She ate no supper.

(MAMA *has started to put on her hat, and to put on Dagmar's hat and coat for her.* CHRISTINE *comes back from the pantry.* PAPA *gives her a dipped cube of sugar.*)

JENNY. Is that *black* coffee you dipped that sugar in? Lars, you shouldn't. It's not good for them. It'll . . .

PAPA (*finishing for her*). Turn their complexions black. I know. Well, maybe it is all right if we have *one* colored daughter.

JENNY. Lars, really!

(KATRIN *returns with her coat.*)

KATRIN. Aunt Jenny, did you see my graduation present? (*She gets it from a chair.* CHRISTINE *gives her a disgusted look, and goes out back L.* KATRIN *displays the dresser set.*) Look! It's got a hair-receiver.

JENNY. But I thought . . . Marta, I thought you were going to give her . . .

MAMA. No, you were right, Jenny. She is too young to appreciate that. She like something more gay . . . more modern.

JENNY. H'm. Well it's very pretty, I suppose, but . . . (*She looks up as* MAMA *puts on her coat.*) You're not wearing your *solje!*

MAMA (*quickly*). No. I do not wear it tonight. Come, Trina, we shall be late.

TRINA. Oh, but Peter isn't here yet.

MAMA. Katrin has her costume to put on. He can follow. Or do you like to wait for Peter?

TRINA. I think . . . if you don't mind . . .

MAMA. You can stay with Lars. He does not have to go yet.

JENNY. I hope Katrin knows her part.

PAPA. Sure she knows it. *I* know it, too.

TRINA. It's too bad he can't see Katrin's debut as an actress.

MAMA. You will be back before us, Lars?

PAPA (*nodding*). I think the meeting will not last long

MAMA. Is good. We go now. (*She goes out with* JENNY *and* DAGMAR. CHRISTINE *and* NELS *return from back L., and follow, waiting outside for* KATRIN, *while the others go ahead.* KATRIN *puts on her hat and coat and picks up the dresser set.*)

PAPA (*to* TRINA). You like we play a game of checkers while we wait?

TRINA. Oh, I haven't played checkers in years.

PAPA. Then I beat you. (*He rises to get the checker set.* KATRIN *kisses him.*)

KATRIN. Good-by, Papa.

PAPA. Good-by, daughter. I think of you.

KATRIN. I'll see you there, Aunt Trina.

TRINA. Good luck!

PAPA. I get the checkers.

(KATRIN *goes out L.,* PAPA *gets the checker set from a cupboard under the dresser, brings it to the table and sets it up during the ensuing scene, which is played outside in the street.*)

CHRISTINE (*contemptuously*). Oh, bringing your cheap trash with you to show off?

KATRIN. It's not trash. It's beautiful. You're just jealous.

CHRISTINE. I told you you'd devil Mama into giving it to you.

KATRIN. I didn't. I didn't devil her at all. I just showed it to her in Mr. Schiller's window. . . .

CHRISTINE. And made her go and sell her brooch that her very own mother gave her.

KATRIN. What?

NELS. Chris . . . you weren't supposed to tell that!

CHRISTINE. I don't care. I think she ought to know.

KATRIN. Is that true? Did Mama—Nels—?

NELS. Well, yes, as a matter of fact, she did. Now, come on.

KATRIN. No, no, I don't believe it. I'm going to ask Papa.

NELS. You haven't time.

KATRIN. I don't care. (*She rushes back to the house and dashes into the kitchen.* CHRISTINE *goes off down L.,* NELS *follows her.)* Papa—Papa—Christine says— Papa, did Mama sell her brooch to give me this?

PAPA. Christine should not have told you that.

KATRIN. It's true, then?

PAPA. She did not sell it. She traded it to Mr. Schiller for your present.

KATRIN *(near tears)*. Oh, but she shouldn't. ... I never meant ...

PAPA. Look, Katrin. You wanted the present. Mama wanted your happiness; she wanted it more than she wanted the brooch.

KATRIN. But I never meant her to do *that*. *(Crying.)* She *loved* it so. It was all she had of Grandmother's.

PAPA. She always meant it for you, Katrin. And you must not cry. You have your play to act.

KATRIN *(sobbing)*. I don't want to act in it now.

PAPA. But you must. Your audience is waiting.

KATRIN *(as before)*. I don't care.

PAPA. But you must care. Tonight you are not Katrin any longer. You are an actress. And an actress must act, whatever she is feeling. There is a saying—what is it—

TRINA *(brightly)*. The mails must go through!

PAPA. No, no. The show must go on. So you stop crying, and go and act your play. We talk of this later. Afterwards.

KATRIN *(pulling herself together)*. All right. I'll go. *(Sniffing a good deal, she picks up the dresser set and goes back to the street and off down L. PAPA and TRINA exchange glances, and then settle down to their checkers.)*

PAPA. Now we play.

(The lights fade and the curtains close.)

(Spot up on stage R. turntable. The two girls from the earlier scene are dressing in costumes for "The Merchant of Venice" before a plank dressing table.)

DOROTHY. I'm getting worried about Katrin. If anything's happened to *her* ...

MADELINE *(pulling up her tights)*. I'll forget my lines. I know I will. I'll look out and see Miss Forrester sitting there, and forget every single line. *(KATRIN rushes in from the L. She carries the dresser set, places it on the dressing table.)* We thought you'd had an accident, or something. ...

KATRIN. Dorothy, is your father here tonight?

DOROTHY. He's going to be. Why?

KATRIN. I want to speak to him. *(As she pulls off her hat and coat.)* Will you tell him ... please ... not to go away without speaking to me? After. After the exercises.

DOROTHY. What on earth do you want to speak to Father for?

KATRIN. I've got something to say to him. Something to ask him. It's important. *Very* important.

MADELINE. Is that the dresser set? *(Picking it up.)* Can I look at it a minute?

KATRIN *(snatching it from her, violently)*. No!

MADELINE. Why, what's the matter? I only wanted to look at it.

KATRIN *(emotionally)*. You can't. You're not to touch it. Dorothy, you take it and put it where I can't see it. *(She thrusts it at her.)* Go on. ... Take it! Take it! Take it!!

(Blackout.)

(Curtains part on the kitchen. MAMA and PAPA in conclave at the table with cups of coffee.)

MAMA. I am worried about her, Lars. When it was over, I see her talking with Mr. Schiller—and then she goes to take off her costume and Nels tells me that he will bring her home. But it is long time, and is late for her to be out. And in the play, Lars, she was not good. I have heard her practice it here, and she was good, but tonight, no. It was as if ... as if she was thinking of something else all the time.

PAPA. I think maybe she was.

MAMA. But what? What can be worrying her?

PAPA. Marta . . . tonight, after you leave, Katrin found out about your brooch.

MAMA. My brooch? But how? Who told her?

PAPA. Christine.

MAMA *(angry)*. Why?

PAPA. I do not know.

MAMA *(rising with a sternness we have not seen before, and calling)*. Christine! Christine!

CHRISTINE *(emerging from the pantry, wiping a dish)*. Were you calling me, Mama?

MAMA. Yes. Christine, did you tell Katrin tonight about my brooch?

CHRISTINE *(frightened, but firm)*. Yes.

MAMA. Why did you?

CHRISTINE. Because I hated the smug way she was acting over that dresser set.

MAMA. Is no excuse. You make her unhappy. You make her not good in the play.

CHRISTINE. Well, she made *you* unhappy, giving up your brooch for her selfishness.

MAMA. Is not your business. I choose to give my brooch. Is not for you to judge. And you know I do not want you to tell. I am angry with you, Christine.

CHRISTINE. I'm sorry. But I'm not sorry I told. *(She goes back to the pantry with a set, obstinate face.)*

PAPA. Christine is the stubborn one.

(NELS and KATRIN have approached the house outside L. They stop and look at each other in the lamplight. KATRIN looks scared. Then NELS pats her, and she goes in, NELS following. MAMA looks up inquiringly and searchingly into KATRIN's face. KATRIN turns away, taking off her hat and coat, and taking something from her pocket.)

NELS. What happened at the meeting Papa?

PAPA. We go back to work tomorrow.

NELS. Gee, that's bully. Isn't it, Mama?

MAMA *(absently)*. Yes, is good.

KATRIN *(coming to MAMA)*. Mama . . . here's your brooch. *(She gives it to her.)* I'm sorry I was so bad in the play. I'll go and help Christine with the dishes. *(She turns and goes into the pantry.)*

MAMA *(unwrapping the brooch from tissue paper)*. Mr. Schiller give it back to her?

NELS. We went to his house to get it. He didn't want to. He was planning to give it to his wife for her birthday. But Katrin begged and begged him. She even offered to go and work in his store during her vacation if he'd give it back.

PAPA *(impressed)*. So? So!

MAMA. And what did Mr. Schiller say?

NELS. He said that wasn't necessary. But he gave her a job all the same. She's going to work for him, afternoons, for three dollars a week.

MAMA. And the dresser set—she gave that back?

NELS. Yes. She was awful upset, Mama. It was kinda hard for her to do. She's a good kid. Well, I'll say good night. I've got to be up early.

PAPA. Good night, Nels.

NELS. Good night, Papa. *(He goes out back L.)*

MAMA. Good night, Nels.

PAPA. Nels is the kind one. *(He starts to refill Mama's coffee cup. She stops him, putting her hand over her cup.)* No?

MAMA *(rising, crossing R. and calling)*. Katrin! Katrin!

KATRIN *(coming to the pantry door)*. Yes, Mama?

MAMA. Come here. *(KATRIN comes to her. MAMA holds out the brooch.)* You put this on.

KATRIN. No . . . it's yours.

MAMA. It is your graduation present. I put it on for you. *(She pins the brooch on Katrin's dress.)*

KATRIN *(near tears)*. I'll wear it always. I'll keep it forever.

MAMA. Christine should not have told you.

KATRIN. I'm glad she did. Now.

PAPA. And I am glad, too. (*He dips a lump of sugar and holds it out to her.*) Katrin?

KATRIN (*tearful again, shakes her head*). I'm sorry, Papa. I . . . I don't feel like it. (*She moves away and sits on the chest under the window, with her back to the room.*)

PAPA. So? So? (*He goes to the dresser.*)

MAMA. What you want, Lars?

(*He does not answer, but takes a cup and saucer, comes to the table and pours a cup of coffee, indicating* KATRIN *with his head.* MAMA *nods, pleased, then checks his pouring and fills up the cup from the cream pitcher which she empties in so doing.* PAPA *puts in sugar, and moves to* KATRIN.)

PAPA. Katrin.

(*She turns. He holds out the cup.*)

KATRIN (*incredulous*). For me?

PAPA. For our grown-up daughter.

(MAMA *nods.* KATRIN *takes the cup, lifts it—then her emotion overcomes her. She thrusts it at* PAPA *and rushes from the room.*)

PAPA. Katrin is the dramatic one! Is too bad. Her first cup of coffee, and she does not drink it.

MAMA. It would not have been good for her, so late at night.

PAPA (*smiling*). And you, Marta, you are the practical one.

MAMA. You drink the coffee, Lars. We do not want to waste it. (*She pushes it across to him.*)

(*Lights dim. Curtains close.*)

(*Lights up on L. turntable, representing the parlor of Jenny's house. A telephone on a table, at which* TRINA *is discovered, talking.*)

TRINA (*into phone*). Yes, Peter. Yes, Peter. I know, Peter, but we don't know where he is. It's so long since we heard from him. He's sure to turn up soon. Yes, I know, Peter. I know, but . . . (*Subsiding obediently.*) Yes, Peter. Yes, Peter. (*Sentimentally.*) Oh, Peter, you know I do. Good-by, Peter. (*She hangs up, and turns, to see* JENNY, *who has come in behind her, eating a piece of toast and jam.*)

JENNY. What was all that about?

TRINA. Peter says we shouldn't wait any longer to hear from Uncle Chris. He says we should send the wedding invitations out right away. He was quite insistent about it. Peter can be very masterful, sometimes . . . when he's alone with *me!*

(*The telephone rings again.* JENNY *answers it, putting down the toast, which* TRINA *takes up and nibbles at during the scene.*)

JENNY. This is Mrs. Stenborg's boarding house. Mrs. Stenborg speaking. Oh, yes, Marta . . . what is it? (*She listens.*)

(*Spot up on R. turntable, disclosing* MAMA *standing at a wall telephone booth. She wears hat and coat, and has an opened telegram in her hand.*)

MAMA. Jenny, is Uncle Chris. I have a telegram. It says if we want to see him again we should come without delay.

JENNY. Where is he?

MAMA (*consulting the telegram*). It comes from a place called Ukiah. Nels says it is up north from San Francisco.

JENNY. Who is the telegram from?

MAMA. It does not say.

JENNY. That . . . woman?

MAMA. I don't know, Jenny. I think maybe.

JENNY. I won't go. (SIGRID *comes in through the curtains C., dressed in hat and coat, carrying string marketing bags, full of vegetables.* JENNY *speaks to her, whisperingly, aside.*) It's Uncle Chris. Marta says he's dying. (*Then, back into phone.*) Why was the telegram sent to *you?* I'm the eldest.

MAMA. Jenny, is not the time to think of who is eldest. Uncle Chris is dying.

JENNY. I don't believe it. He's too mean to die. Ever. (NELS *comes to booth from wings, R., and hands* MAMA *a slip of paper.*) I'm not going.

MAMA. Jenny, I cannot stop to argue. There is a train at eleven o'clock. It takes four hours. You call Sigrid.

JENNY. Sigrid is here now.

MAMA. Good. Then you tell her.

JENNY. What do you say the name of the place is?

MAMA. Ukiah. (*Spelling in Norwegian.*) U.K.I.A.H.

JENNY. I won't go.

MAMA. That *you* decide. (*She hangs up. Her spot goes out.*)

SIGRID. Uncle Chris dying!

JENNY. The wages of sin.

TRINA. Oh, he's old. Maybe it is time for him to go.

JENNY. Four hours by train, and maybe have to stay all night. All that expense to watch a wicked old man die of the D.T.'s.

SIGRID. I know, but . . . there is his will. . . .

JENNY. Huh, even supposing he's anything to leave—you know who he'd leave it *to*, don't you?

SIGRID. Yes. But all the same, he's dying now, and blood is thicker than water. Especially when it's Norwegian. I'm going. I shall take Arne with me. Uncle Chris was always fond of children.

TRINA. I agree with Sigrid. I think we *should* go.

JENNY. Well, *you* can't go, anyway.

TRINA. Why not?

JENNY. Because of that woman. You can't meet a woman like that.

TRINA. Why not? If you two can . . .

SIGRID. We're married women.

TRINA. I'm engaged!

JENNY. That's not the same thing.

SIGRID. Not the same thing at all!

TRINA. Nonsense. I've never met a woman like that. Maybe I'll never get another chance. Besides, if he's going to change his will, there's still my dowry, remember. Do you think we should take Peter?

JENNY. Peter Thorkelson? Whatever for?

TRINA. Well, after all, I mean . . . I mean, his profession . . .

JENNY. Trina, you always were a fool. Anyone would know the last person a dying man wants to see is an undertaker!

(*Blackout. Turntable revolves out.*)

(*Spot up on* KATRIN, *standing down front, R.C. She wears her school-girl hat.*)

KATRIN. When Mama said I was to go with her, I was excited and I was frightened. It was exciting to take sandwiches for the train, almost as though we were going on a picnic. But I was scared at the idea of seeing death, though I told myself that if I was going to be a writer, I had to experience everything. But all the same, I hoped it would be all over when we got there. (*She starts to walk toward C. and up the steps.*) It was afternoon when we arrived. We asked at the station for the Halvorsen ranch, and it seemed to me that the man looked at us strangely. Uncle Chris was obviously considered an odd character. The ranch was about three miles from the town; a derelict, rambling old place. There was long grass, and tall trees, and a smell of honeysuckle. We made quite a cavalcade, walking up from the gate. (*The procession comes in from the R., behind* KATRIN. MAMA, JENNY, TRINA, SIGRID, *and* ARNE.) The woman came out on the steps to meet us.

(*The procession starts toward the C., moving upwards. The* WOMAN *comes through the curtains, down one step. The* AUNTS *freeze in their tracks.* MAMA *goes forward to her.*)

MAMA. How is he? Is he—?

WOMAN (*with grave self-possession*). Come in, won't you?

(*She holds the curtains slightly aside.* MAMA *goes in.* KATRIN *follows, looking curiously at the* WOMAN. *The* AUNTS *walk stiffly past her,* SIGRID *clutching* ARNE *and shielding him from contact with the* WOMAN. *They disappear behind the curtains. The* WOMAN *stands a moment, looking off into the distance. Then she goes in behind the curtains, too.*)

(*The curtains draw apart, revealing Uncle Chris' bedroom. It is simple, and shabby. The door to the room is at the back, L. In the L. wall is a window, with curtains, drawn aside now. In front of it, a washstand. The afternoon sunlight comes through the window, falling onto the big double bed, in which* UNCLE CHRIS *is propped up on pillows. Beside him, R., on a small table is a pitcher of water. He has a glass in his hand.* MAMA *stands to the R. of him:* JENNY *to the L. The others are ranged below the window. The* WOMAN *is not present.)*

UNCLE CHRIS *(handing* MAMA *the empty glass)*. I want more. You give me more. Is still some in the bottle.

MAMA. Uncle Chris, that will not help now.

UNCLE CHRIS. It always help. *(With a glance at* JENNY.*)* Now especially.

JENNY *(firmly)*. Uncle Chris, I don't think you realize . . .

UNCLE CHRIS. What I don't realize? That I am dying? Why else do I think you come here? Why else do I think you stand there, watching me? *(He sits upright.)* Get out. Get out. I don't want you here. Get out!

JENNY. Oh, very well. Very well. We'll be outside on the porch, if you want us. *(She starts toward the door.)*

UNCLE CHRIS. That is where I want you ·–on the porch! *(*JENNY *goes out.* TRINA *follows.* SIGRID *is about to go, too, when* UNCLE CHRIS *stops her.)* Wait. That is Arne. Come here, Arne. *(*ARNE, *propelled by* SIGRID, *advances toward the bed.)* How is your knee?

ARNE. It's fine, Uncle Chris.

UNCLE CHRIS. Not hurt any more? You don't use svear vords any more?

ARNE. N-no, Uncle Chris.

UNCLE CHRIS. You walk goot? Quite goot? Let me see you walk. Walk around the room. *(*ARNE *does so.)* Fast. Fast. Run! Run! *(*ARNE *does so.)* Is goot.

SIGRID *(encouraged and advancing)*. Uncle Chris, Arne has always been so fond of you. . . .

UNCLE CHRIS *(shouting)*. I tell you all to get out. Except Marta. *(As* KATRIN *edges with the* AUNTS *to the door.)* And Katrinë. Katrinë and I haf secret. You remember, Katrinë?

KATRIN. Yes, Uncle Chris.

MAMA. Uncle Chris, you must lie down again.

UNCLE CHRIS. Then you give me drink.

MAMA. No, Uncle Chris.

UNCLE CHRIS. We cannot waste what is left in the bottle. You do not drink it . . . who will drink it when I am gone? What harm can it do . . . now? I die, anyway. . . . You give it to me. *(*MAMA *goes to the wash-stand, pours him a drink of whiskey and water, and takes it to him, sitting on the bed beside him. He drinks, then turns to her, leaning back against her arm and the pillows.)* Marta, I haf never made a will. Was never enough money. But you sell this ranch. It will not bring moch. I have not had it long enough. And there is mortgage. Big mortgage. But it leave a little. Maybe two, tree hundred dollars. You give to Yessie.

MAMA. Yessie?

UNCLE CHRIS. Yessie Brown. My housekeeper. No, why I call her that to you? You understand. She is my voman. Twelve years she has been my voman. My wife, only I cannot marry her. She has husband alive somewhere. She was trained nurse, but she get sick and I bring her to the country to get well again. There will be no money for *you*, Marta. Always I wanted there should be money to make Nils doctor. But there were other things . . . quick things. And now there is no time to make more. There is no money, but you make Nils doctor, all the same. You like?

MAMA. Sure, Uncle Chris. It is what Lars and I have always wanted for him. To help people who suffer. . . .

UNCLE CHRIS. Is the greatest thing in the world. It is to have a little of God in you. Always I wanted to be doctor myself. Is the only thing I have ever wanted. Nils must do it for me.

MAMA. He will, Uncle Chris.

UNCLE CHRIS. Is goot. *(He strokes her hand.)* You are the goot one. I am glad you come, *Lille Ven*. *(He moves his head restlessly.)* Where is Yessie?

MAMA. I think she wait outside.

UNCLE CHRIS. You do not mind if she is here?

MAMA. Of course not, Uncle Chris.

UNCLE CHRIS. You call her. I like you both be here. (MAMA *goes, with a quick glance at* KATRIN. UNCLE CHRIS *signs to* KATRIN *to come closer. She sits on the chair beside the bed.*) Katrinë, your Mama write me you drink coffee now? (*She nods. He looks at her affectionately.*) Katrinë, who will be writer. . . . You are not frightened of me now?

KATRIN. No, Uncle Chris.

UNCLE CHRIS. One day maybe you write story about Uncle Chris. If you remember.

KATRIN (*whispering*). I'll remember.

(MAMA *returns with the* WOMAN. *They come to the side of his bed.*)

UNCLE CHRIS (*obviously exhausted and in pain*). I like you both stay with me . . . now. I think best now maybe Katrinë go away. Good-by, Katrinë. (*Then he repeats it in Norwegian.*) Farvell, Katrinë.

KATRIN. Good-by, Uncle Chris.

UNCLE CHRIS. You say it in Norwegian, like I do.

KATRIN (*in Norwegian*). Farvell, Onkel Chris. (*She slips out, in tears*).

UNCLE CHRIS. Yessie! Maybe I should introduce you to each other. Yessie, this is my niece, Marta. The only von of my nieces I can stand. Marta, this is Yessie, who have give me much happiness. . . .

(*The* TWO WOMEN *shake hands.*)

MAMA. I am very glad to meet you.

JESSIE. I am, too.

UNCLE CHRIS (*as they shake*). Is goot. And now you give me von more drink. You have drink with me . . . both of you. That way we finish the bottle. Yes?

(JESSIE *and* MAMA *look at each other.*)

MAMA. Sure, Uncle Chris.

UNCLE CHRIS. Goot. Yessie, you get best glasses. (*With a chuckle to* MAMA.) Yessie does not like to drink, but this is special occasion. (JESSIE *gets three glasses from a wall shelf.*) What is the time?

MAMA. It is about half past four, Uncle Chris.

UNCLE CHRIS. The sun come around this side the house in afternoon. You draw the curtain a little maybe. Is strong for my eyes. (MAMA *goes over and draws the curtain over the window. The stage darkens.* JESSIE *pours three drinks, filling two of the glasses with water. She is about to put water in the third when* UNCLE CHRIS *stops her.*) No, no, I take it now without water. Always the last drink without water. Is Norwegian custom. (*To* MAMA, *with a smile.*) True? (JESSIE *sits on the bed beside him, about to feed his drink to him, but he pushes her aside.*) No. No, I do not need you feed it to me. I can drink myself. (*He takes the glass from her.*) Give Marta her glass. (JESSIE *hands a glass to* MAMA. *The two women stand on either side of the bed, holding their glasses.*) So. . . . Skoal!

JESSIE (*clinking glasses with him*). Skoal.

MAMA (*doing likewise*). Skoal.

(*They all three drink. Slow dim to blackout. Curtains close.*)

(*Spot up on R. turntable. A porch with a bench, and a chair, on which the three* AUNTS *are sitting.* JENNY *is dozing.*)

SIGRID (*flicking her handkerchief*). These gnats are awful. I'm being simply eaten alive.

TRINA. Gnats are always worse around sunset. (*She catches one.*)

JENNY (*rousing herself*). I should never have let you talk me into coming. To be insulted like that . . . turned out of his room . . . and then expected to sit here hour after hour without as much as a cup of coffee. . . .

SIGRID. I'd make coffee if I knew where the kitchen was.

JENNY. *Her* kitchen? It would poison me. (*Rising.*) No, I'm going home. Are you coming, Trina?

TRINA. Oh, I think we ought to wait a little longer. After all, you can't hurry these things. . . . I mean . . . (*She breaks off in confusion at what she has said.*)

JENNY (*to* SIGRID). And all your talk about his will. A lot of chance we got to say a word!

TRINA. Maybe Marta's been talking to him. (MAMA *comes from between the curtains C.*)

JENNY. Well?

MAMA. Uncle Chris has . . . gone.

(There is a silence.)

JENNY *(more gently than is her wont).* Did he . . . say anything about a will?

MAMA. There is no will.

JENNY. Well, then, that means . . . we're his nearest relatives. . . .

MAMA. There is no money, either.

SIGRID. How do you know?

MAMA. He told me. *(She brings out a small notebook that she is carrying.)*

JENNY. What's that?

MAMA. Is an account of how he spent the money.

JENNY. Bills from a liquor store.

MAMA. No, Jenny. No. I read it to you. *(JENNY sits again.)* You know how Uncle Chris was lame . . . how he walked always with limp. It was his one thought . . . lame people. He would have liked to be doctor and help them. Instead, he help them other ways. I read you the last page. . . . *(She reads from the notebook.)* "Joseph Spinelli. Four years old. Tubercular left leg. Three hundred thirty-seven dollars, eighteen cents." *(Pause.)* "Walks now. Esta Jensen. Nine years. Club-foot. Two hundred seventeen dollars, fifty cents. Walks now." *(Then, reading very slowly.)* "Arne Solfeldt. . . ."

SIGRID *(startled).* My Arne?

MAMA *(reading on).* "Nine years. Fractured kneecap. Four hundred forty-two dollars, sixteen cents."

(KATRIN and ARNE come running in from the L. across the stage.)

ARNE *(calling as he comes running across).* Mother . . . Mother . . . Are we going to eat soon? *(He stops, awed by the solemnity of the group, and by MAMA, who puts out her hand gently, to silence him.)* What is it? Is Uncle Chris . . .?

MAMA *(to the AUNTS).* It does not tell the end about Arne. I like to write "Walks now." Yes?

SIGRID *(very subdued).* Yes.

MAMA *(taking a pencil from the book).* Maybe even . . . "runs"? *(SIGRID nods, moist-eyed. TRINA is crying. MAMA writes in the book, and then closes it.)* So. Is finished. Is all. *(She touches JENNY on the shoulder.)* It was good.

JENNY *(after a gulping moment).* I go and make some coffee.

(The woman, JESSIE, appears from between the curtains on the steps.)

JESSIE. You can go in and see him now if you want. *(JENNY looks back, half-hesitant at the others. Then she nods and goes in. TRINA follows her, mopping her eyes. SIGRID puts her arm suddenly around ARNE in a spasm of maternal affection, and they, too, go in. MAMA, KATRIN, and JESSIE are left alone.)* I'm moving down to the hotel for tonight . . . so that you can all stay. *(She is about to go back, when MAMA stops her.)*

MAMA. Wait. What will you do now . . . after he is buried? You have money? *(JESSIE shakes her head.)* Where you live?

JESSIE. I'll find a room somewhere. I'll probably go back to nursing.

MAMA. You like to come to San Francisco for a little? To our house? We have room. Plenty room.

JESSIE *(touched, moving to MAMA).* That's very kind of you, but . . .

MAMA. I like to have you. You come for a little as our guest. When you get work you can be our boarder.

JESSIE *(awkwardly grateful).* I don't know why you should bother. . . .

MAMA *(touching her).* You were good to Uncle Chris. *(JESSIE grasps her hand, deeply moved, then turns and goes quickly back through the curtains. MAMA turns to KATRIN.)* Katrin, you come and see him?

KATRIN *(scared).* See him? You mean . . .

MAMA. I like you see him. You need not be frightened. He looks . . . happy and at peace. I like you to know what death looks like. Then you are not frightened of it, ever.

KATRIN. Will you come with me?

MAMA. Sure. (*She stretches out her hand, puts her arm around her, and then leads her gently in through the curtains.*)

(*Spot up on L. turntable, representing a park bench against a hedge.* TRINA, *and* MR. THORKELSON, *in outdoor clothes, are seated together.* TRINA *is cooing over a baby-carriage.*)

TRINA. Who's the most beautiful Norwegian baby in San Francisco? Who's going to be three months old tomorrow? Little Christopher Thorkelson! (*To* MR. THORKELSON.) Do you know, Peter, I think he's even beginning to *look* a little like Uncle Chris! Quite apart from his black curls—and those, of course, he gets from *you*. (*To baby again.*) He's going to grow up to be a black Norwegian, isn't he, just like his daddy and his Uncle Chris? (*Settling down beside* MR. THORKELSON.) I think there's something about his mouth . . . a sort of . . . well . . . firmness. Of course, it's *your* mouth, too. But then I've always thought you had quite a lot of Uncle Chris about you. (*She looks back at the baby.*) Look—he's asleep!

MR. THORKELSON. Trina, do you know what next Thursday is?

TRINA (*nodding, smiling*). Our anniversary.

MR. THORKELSON. What would you think of our giving a little party?

TRINA. A party?

MR. THORKELSON. Oh, quite a modest one. Nothing showy or ostentatious—but, after all, we have been married a year, and with your having been in mourning and the baby coming so soon and everything, we've not been able to entertain. I think it's time you . . . took your place in society.

TRINA (*scared*). What . . . sort of a party?

MR. THORKELSON. An evening party. (*Proudly.*) A soirée! I should say about ten people . . . some of the Norwegian colony . . . and Lars and Marta, of course. . . .

TRINA (*beginning to count on her fingers*). And Jenny and Sigrid . . .

MR. THORKELSON. Oh . . . I . . . I hadn't thought of asking Jenny and Sigrid.

TRINA. Oh, we'd have to. We couldn't leave them out.

MR. THORKELSON. Trina, I hope you won't be offended if I say that I have never really felt . . . well, altogether comfortable with Jenny and Sigrid. They have always made me feel that they didn't think I was . . . well . . . *worthy* of you. Of course, I know I'm not, but . . . well . . . one doesn't like to be reminded of it . . . *all* the time.

TRINA (*taking his hand*). Oh, Peter.

MR. THORKELSON. But you're quite right. We must ask them. Now, as to the matter of refreshments . . . what would you suggest?

TRINA (*flustered*). Oh, I don't know. I . . . what would you say to . . . ice cream and cookies for the ladies . . . and coffee, of course . . . and . . . perhaps port wine for the gentlemen?

MR. THORKELSON (*anxiously*). Port wine?

TRINA. Just a little. You could bring it in already poured out, in *little* glasses. Jenny and Sigrid can help me serve the ice cream.

MR. THORKELSON (*firmly*). No. if Jenny and Sigrid come, they come as guests, like everyone else. You shall have someone in to help you in the kitchen.

TRINA. You mean a waitress? (MR. THORKELSON *nods, beaming.*) Oh, but none of us have *ever* . . . do you really think . . . I mean . . . you did say we shouldn't be ostentatious. . . .

MR. THORKELSON (*nervously*). Trina, there's something I would like to say. I've never been very good at expressing myself or my . . . well . . . *deeper* feelings—but I want you to know that I'm not only very fond of you, but very . . . well . . . very *proud* of you as well, and I want you to have the best of everything, as far as it's in my power to give it to you. (*As a climax.*) I want you to have a waitress!

TRINA (*overcome*). Yes, Peter. (*They hold hands.*)

(*The lights fade and the turntable revolves out.*)

(*Curtains part on kitchen, slightly changed, smartened and refurnished now.*

MAMA *and* PAPA *seated as usual.* DAGMAR, *looking a little older, is seated on the chest, reading a solid-looking book.* NELS *enters from back L. door, carrying a newspaper. He wears long trousers now, and looks about seventeen.*)

NELS. Hello! Here's your evening paper, Papa.

(PAPA *puts down the morning paper he is reading, and takes the evening one from* NELS.)

PAPA. Is there any news?

NELS. No. (*He takes out a package of cigarettes with elaborate unconcern.* MAMA *watches with disapproval. Then, as he is about to light his cigarette, he stops, remembering something.*) Oh, I forgot. There's a letter for Katrin. I picked it up on the mat as I came in. (*Going to door back L., and calling.*) Katrin! Katrin! There's a letter for you.

KATRIN (*answering from off stage*). Coming!

MAMA. Nels, you know who the letter is from?

NELS. Why, no, Mama. (*Hands it to her.*) It looks like her own handwriting.

MAMA (*gravely inspecting it*). Is bad.

PAPA. Why is bad?

MAMA. She get too many like that. I think they are stories she send to the magazines.

DAGMAR (*closing her book loudly, rising*). Well, I'll go and see if I have any puppies yet. Mama, I've just decided something.

MAMA. What have you decided?

DAGMAR. If Nels is going to be a doctor, when I grow up, I'm going to be a— (*Looking at the book-title, and stumbling over the word.*) vet-vet-veterinarian.

MAMA. And what is that?

DAGMAR. A doctor for animals.

MAMA. Is good. Is good.

DAGMAR. There are far more animals in the world than there are human beings, and far more human doctors than animal ones. It isn't fair. (*She goes to the pantry door.*) I suppose we couldn't have a horse, could we? (*This only produces a concerted laugh from the family. She turns, sadly.*) No. . . . I was afraid we couldn't. (*She goes into the pantry.* KATRIN *comes in, back L. She wears a slightly more adult dress than before. Her hair is up and she looks about eighteen.*)

KATRIN. Where's the letter?

MAMA (*handing it to her*). Here.

(KATRIN *takes it, nervously. She looks at the envelope, and her face falls. She opens it, pulls out a manuscript and a rejection slip, looks at it a moment, and then replaces both in the envelope. The others watch her covertly. Then she looks up, with determination.*)

KATRIN. Mama . . . Papa . . . I want to say something.

PAPA. What is it?

KATRIN. I'm not going to go to college.

PAPA. Why not?

KATRIN. Because it would be a waste of time and money. The only point in my going to college was to be a writer. Well, I'm not going to be one, so . . .

MAMA. Katrin, is it your letter that makes you say this? It is a story come back again?

KATRIN. Again is right. This is the tenth time. I made this one a test. It's the best I've ever written, or ever shall write. I know that. Well, it's no good.

NELS. What kind of a story is it?

KATRIN. Oh . . . it's a story about a painter, who's a genius, and he goes blind.

NELS. Sounds like "The Light That Failed."

KATRIN. Well, what's wrong with that?

NELS (*quickly*). Nothing. Nothing!

KATRIN. Besides, it's not like that. My painter gets better. He has an operation and recovers his sight, and paints better than ever before.

MAMA. Is good.

KATRIN (*bitterly unhappy*). No, it isn't. It's rotten. But it's the best I can do.

MAMA. You have asked your teachers about this?

KATRIN. Teachers don't know anything

about writing. They just know about literature.

MAMA. If there was someone we could ask . . . for advice . . . to tell us . . . tell us if your stories are good.

KATRIN. Yes. Well, there isn't. And they're *not.*

PAPA *(looking at the evening paper).* There is something here in the paper about a lady writer. I just noticed the headline. Wait. *(He looks back for it and reads.)* "Woman writer tells key to literary success."

KATRIN. Who?

PAPA. A lady called Florence Dana Moorhead. It gives her picture. A fat lady. You have heard of her?

KATRIN. Yes, of course. Everyone has. She's terribly successful. She's here on a lecture tour.

MAMA. What does she say is the secret?

PAPA. You read it, Katrin. *(He hands her the paper.)*

KATRIN *(gabbling the first part).* "Florence Dana Moorhead, celebrated novelist and short story writer . . . blah-blah-blah . . . interviewed today in her suite at the Fairmont . . . blah-blah-blah . . . pronounced sincerity the one essential quality for success as a writer." *(Throwing aside the paper.)* A lot of help that is.

MAMA. Katrin, this lady . . . maybe if you sent her your stories, *she* could tell you what is wrong with them?

KATRIN *(wearily).* Oh, Mama, don't be silly.

MAMA. Why is silly?

KATRIN. Well, in the first place because she's a very important person . . . a celebrity . . . and she'd never read them. And in the second, because . . . you seem to think writing's like . . . well, like cooking, or something. That all you have to have is the recipe. It takes a lot more than that. You have to have a gift for it.

MAMA. You have to have a gift for cooking, too. But there are things you can learn, if you have the gift.

KATRIN. Well, that's the whole point. I haven't. I *know* . . . now. So, if you've

finished with the morning paper, Papa, I'll take the want ad. section, and see if I can find myself a job. *(She takes the morning paper and goes out R.)*

MAMA. Is bad. Nels, what you think?

NELS. I don't know, Mama. Her stories seem all right to me, but I don't know.

MAMA. It would be good to know. Nels, this lady in the paper . . . what else does she say?

NELS *(taking up the paper).* Not much. The rest seems to be about *her* and her home. Let's see. . . . *(He reads.)* "Apart from literature, Mrs. Moorhead's main interest in life is gastronomy."

MAMA. The stars?

NELS. No—eating. "A brilliant cook herself, she says that she would as soon turn out a good soufflé as a short story, or find a new recipe as she would a first edition."

MAMA *(reaching for the paper).* I see her picture? *(She looks at it.)* Is kind face. *(Pause while she reads a moment. Then she looks up and asks.)* What is first edition?

(Blackout.)

(Lights up on L. turntable, representing the lobby of the Fairmont hotel. A couch against a column with a palm behind it. An orchestra plays softly in the background. MAMA *is discovered seated on the couch, waiting patiently. She wears a hat and a suit, and clutches a newspaper and a bundle of manuscripts. A couple of guests come through the curtains and cross, disappearing into the wings L.* MAMA *watches them. Then* FLORENCE DANA MOORHEAD *enters through the curtains. She is a stout, dressy, good-natured, middle-aged woman. A* BELL-BOY *comes from the R., paging her.)*

BELL-BOY. Miss Moorhead?

F. D. MOORHEAD. Yes?

BELL-BOY. Telegram.

F. D. MOORHEAD. Oh. . . . Thank you. *(She tips him, and he goes.* MAMA *rises and moves towards her.)*

MAMA. Please . . . Please . . . Miss Moorhead . . . Miss Moorhead.

F. D. MOORHEAD *(looking up from her*

telegram, on the steps). Were you calling me?

MAMA. Yes. You are . . . Miss Florence Dana Moorhead?

F. D. MOORHEAD. Yes.

MAMA. Please . . . might I speak to you for a moment?

F. D. MOORHEAD. Yes—what's it about?

MAMA. I read in the paper what you say about writing.

F. D. MOORHEAD *(with a vague social smile).* Oh, yes?

MAMA. My daughter, Katrin, wants to be writer.

F. D. MOORHEAD *(who has heard that one before).* Oh, really? *(She glances at her watch on her bosom.)*

MAMA. I bring her stories.

F. D. MOORHEAD. Look, I'm afraid I'm in rather a hurry. I'm leaving San Francisco this evening. . . .

MAMA. I wait two hours here for you to come in. Please, if I may talk to you for one, two minutes. That is all.

F. D. MOORHEAD *(kindly).* Of course, but I think I'd better tell you that if you want me to read your daughter's stories, it's no use. I'm very sorry, but I've had to make it a rule never to read anyone's unpublished material.

MAMA *(nods—then after a pause).* It said in the paper you like to collect recipes . . . for eating.

F. D. MOORHEAD. Yes, I do. I've written several books on cooking.

MAMA. I, too, am interested in gastronomy. I am good cook. Norwegian. I make good Norwegian dishes. Lutefisk. And Kjöd-boller. That is meat-balls with sauce.

F. D. MOORHEAD. Yes, I know, I've eaten them in Christiania.

MAMA. I have a special recipe for Kjöd-boller . . . my mother give me. She was best cook I ever knew. Never have I told this recipe, not even to my own sisters, because they are not good cooks.

F. D. MOORHEAD *(amused).* Oh?

MAMA. But . . . if you let me talk to you

. . . I give it to you. I promise it is good recipe.

F. D. MOORHEAD *(vastly tickled now).* Well, that seems fair enough. Let's sit down. *(They move to the couch and sit.)* Now, your daughter wants to write, you say? How old is she?

MAMA. She is eighteen. Just.

F. D. MOORHEAD. *Does* she write, or does she just . . . *want* to write?

MAMA. Oh, she writes all the time. Maybe she should not be author, but it is hard to give up something that has meant so much.

F. D. MOORHEAD. I agree, but . . .

MAMA. I bring her stories. I bring twelve.

F. D. MOORHEAD *(aghast).* Twelve!

MAMA. But if you could read maybe just one . . . To know if someone is good cook, you do not need to eat a whole dinner.

F. D. MOORHEAD. You're very persuasive. How is it your daughter did not come herself?

MAMA. She was too unhappy. And too scared . . . of you. Because you are celebrity. But I see your picture in the paper. . . .

F. D. MOORHEAD. That frightful picture!

MAMA. Is the picture of woman who like to eat good. . . .

F. D. MOORHEAD *(with a rueful smile).* It certainly is. Now, tell me about the Kjödboller.

MAMA. When you make the meat-balls you drop them in boiling stock. Not water. That is one of the secrets.

F. D. MOORHEAD. Ah!

MAMA. And the cream sauce. That is another secret. It is half *sour* cream, added at the last.

F. D. MOORHEAD. That sounds marvelous.

MAMA. You must grind the meat six times. I could write it out for you. And . . . *(Tentatively.)* while I write, you could read?

F. D. MOORHEAD *(with a laugh).* All right. You win. Come upstairs to my apartment. *(She rises.)*

MAMA. Is kind of you. (*They start out L.*) Maybe if you would read *two* stories, I could write the recipe for Lutefisk as well. You know Lutefisk . . . ?

(*They have disappeared into the wings, and the turntable revolves out.*)

(*Spot up, R. turntable.* KATRIN *at her desk.*)

KATRIN. When Mama came back, I was sitting with my diary, which I called my Journal now, writing a Tragic Farewell to my Art. It was very seldom that Mama came to the attic, thinking that a writer needed privacy, and I was surprised to see her standing in the doorway. (*She looks up.* MAMA *is standing on the steps, C.*) Mama!

MAMA. You are busy, Katrin?

KATRIN (*jumping up*). No, of course not. Come in.

MAMA (*coming down*). I like to talk to you.

KATRIN. Yes, of course.

MAMA (*seating herself at the desk*). You are writing?

NATRIN. No. I told you, that's all over.

MAMA. That is what I want to talk to you about.

KATRIN. It's all right, Mama. Really, it's all right. I was planning to tear up all my stories this afternoon, only I couldn't find half of them.

MAMA. They are here.

KATRIN. Did *you* take them? What for?

MAMA. Katrin, I have been to see Miss Moorhead.

KATRIN. Who's Miss . . . ? You don't mean Florence Dana Moorhead? (MAMA *nods.*) You don't mean . . . Mama, you don't mean you took her my stories?

MAMA. She read five of them. I was two hours with her. We have glass of sherry. Two glass of sherry.

KATRIN. What . . . what did she say about them?

MAMA (*quietly*). She say they are not good.

KATRIN (*turning away*). Well, I knew

that. It was hardly worth your going to all that trouble just to be told that.

MAMA. She say more. Will you listen, Katrin?

KATRIN (*trying to be gracious*). Sure. Sure. I'll listen.

MAMA. I will try and remember. She say you write now only because of what you have read in other books, and that no one can write good until they have felt what they write about. That for years she write bad stories about people in the olden times, until one day she remember something that happen in her own town . . . something that only she could know and understand . . . and she feels she must tell it . . . and that is how she write her first good story. She say you must write more of things you know. . . .

KATRIN. That's what my teacher always told me at school.

MAMA. Maybe your teacher was right. I do not know if I explain good what Miss Moorhead means, but while she talks I think I understand. Your story about the painter who is blind . . . that is because . . . forgive me if I speak plain, my Katrin, but it is important to you . . . because you are the dramatic one, as Papa has said . . . and you think it would feel good to be a painter and be blind and not complain. But never have you imagined how it would really be. Is true?

KATRIN (*subdued*). Yes, I . . . I guess it's true.

MAMA. But she say you are to go on writing. That you have the gift. (KATRIN *turns back to her, suddenly aglow.*) And that when you have written story that is real and true . . . then you send it to someone whose name she give me. (*She fumbles for a piece of paper.*) It is her . . . agent . . . and say she recommend you. Here. No, that is recipe she give me for goulash as her grandmother make it . . . here . . . (*She hands over the paper.*) It helps, Katrin, what I have told you?

KATRIN (*subdued again*). Yes, I . . . I guess it helps. Some. But what have *I* got to write about? I haven't seen anything, or been anywhere.

MAMA. Could you write about San Francisco, maybe? Is fine city. Miss Moorhead write about her home town.

KATRIN. Yes, I know. But you've got to have a central character or something. She writes about her grandfather . . . he was a wonderful old man.

MAMA. Could you maybe write about Papa?

KATRIN. Papa?

MAMA. Papa is fine man. Is wonderful man.

KATRIN. Yes, I know, but . . .

MAMA (rising). I must go fix supper. Is late. Papa will be home. (She goes up the steps to the curtains, and then turns back.) I like you should write about Papa. (She goes inside.)

KATRIN (going back to her seat behind the desk). Papa. Yes, but what's he ever done? What's ever happened to him? What's ever happened to any of us? Except always being poor and having illnesses, like the time when Dagmar went to the hospital and Mama . . . (The idea hits her like a flash.) Oh. . . . Oh. . . . (Pause —then she becomes the KATRIN of today.) And that was how it was born . . . suddenly in a flash . . . the story of "Mama and the Hospital" . . . the first of all the stories. I wrote it . . . oh, quite soon after that. I didn't tell Mama or any of them. But I sent it to Miss Moorhead's agent. It was a long time before I heard anything . . . and then one evening the letter came. (She takes an envelope from the desk in front of her.) For a moment I couldn't believe it. Then I went rushing into the kitchen, shouting. . . . (She rises from the desk, taking some papers with her, and rushes upstage, crying, "Mama, Mama." The curtains have parted on the kitchen—and the family tableau—MAMA, PAPA, CHRISTINE, and NELS. DAGMAR is not present. KATRIN comes rushing in, up the steps. The R. turntable revolves out as soon as she has left it.) Mama . . . Mama . . . I've sold a story!

MAMA. A story?

KATRIN. Yes, I've got a letter from the agent . . . with a check for . . . (Gasping.) five hundred dollars!

NELS. No kidding?

MAMA. Katrin . . . is true?

KATRIN. Here it is. Here's the letter. Maybe I haven't read it right. (She hands the letter. PAPA and MAMA huddle and gloat over it.)

CHRISTINE. What will you do with five hundred dollars?

KATRIN. I don't know. I'll buy Mama her warm coat, I know that.

CHRISTINE. Coats don't cost five hundred dollars.

KATRIN. I know. We'll put the rest in the Bank.

NELS (kidding). Quick. Before they change their mind, and stop the check.

KATRIN. Will you, Mama? Will you take it to the Bank downtown tomorrow? (MAMA looks vague.) What is it?

MAMA. I do not know how.

NELS. Just give it to the man and tell him to put it in your account, like you always do. (MAMA looks up at PAPA.)

PAPA. You tell them . . . now.

CHRISTINE. Tell us what?

MAMA (desperately). Is no Bank Account! Never in my life have I been inside a bank.

CHRISTINE. But you always told us . . .

KATRIN. Mama, you've always said . . .

MAMA. I know. But was not true. I tell a lie.

KATRIN. But why, Mama? Why did you pretend?

MAMA. Is not good for little ones to be afraid . . . to not feel secure. But now . . . with five hundred dollar . . . I think I can tell.

KATRIN (going to her, emotionally). Mama!

MAMA (stopping her, quickly). You read us the story. You have it there?

KATRIN. Yes.

MAMA. Then read.

KATRIN. Now?

MAMA. Yes. No— Wait. Dagmar must hear. (She opens pantry door and calls.) Dagmar.

DAGMAR (off). Yes, Mama?

MAMA (calling). Come here, I want you.

DAGMAR (off). What is it?

MAMA. I want you. No, you leave the rabbits! (She comes back.) What is it called . . . the story?

KATRIN (seating herself in the chair that Mr. Hyde took in the opening scene). It's called "Mama and the Hospital."

PAPA (delighted). You write about Mama?

KATRIN. Yes.

MAMA. But I thought . . . I thought you say . . . I tell you . . . (She gestures at PAPA, behind his back.)

KATRIN. I know, Mama, but . . . well, that's how it came out.

(DAGMAR comes in.)

DAGMAR. What is it? What do you want?

MAMA. Katrin write story for magazine. They pay her five hundred dollar to print it.

DAGMAR (completely uninterested). Oh. (She starts back for the pantry.)

MAMA (stopping her). She read it to us. I want you should listen. You are ready, Katrin?

KATRIN. Sure.

MAMA. Then read.

(The group around the table is now a duplicate of the grouping around MR. HYDE in the first scene, with KATRIN in his place.)

KATRIN (reading). "For as long as I could remember, the house on Steiner Street had been home. All of us were born there. Nels, the oldest and the only boy . . ." (NELS looks up, astonished to be in a story.) "my sister, Christine . . ." (CHRISTINE does likewise.) "and the littlest sister, Dagmar. . . ."

DAGMAR. Am I in the story?

MAMA. Hush, Dagmar. We are all in the story.

KATRIN. "But first and foremost, I remember Mama." (The lights begin to dim and the curtain slowly to fall. As it descends, we hear her voice continuing.) "I remember that every Saturday night Mama would sit down by the kitchen table and count out the money Papa had brought home in the little envelope. . . ."

(By now, the curtain is down.)

THE END

CLARENCE DAY'S

LIFE WITH FATHER

MADE INTO A PLAY

By HOWARD LINDSAY and RUSSEL CROUSE

LIFE WITH FATHER was produced by Oscar Serlin at the Empire Theatre, New York City, on the night of November 8, 1939. The play was staged by Bretaigne Windust; setting and costumes by Stewart Chaney. The cast was as follows:

ANNIE	Katherine Bard	MARY	Teresa Wright
VINNIE	Dorothy Stickney	THE REVEREND DR. LLOYD	
CLARENCE	John Drew Devereaux		Richard Sterling
JOHN	Richard Simon	DELIA	Portia Morrow
WHITNEY	Raymond Roe	NORA	Nellie Burt
HARLAN	Larry Robinson	DR. HUMPHREYS	A. H. Van Buren
FATHER	Howard Lindsay	DR. SOMERS	John C. King
MARGARET	Dorothy Bernard	MAGGIE	Timothy Kearse
CORA	Ruth Hammond		

SCENES

The time: late in the 1880's. The entire action takes place in the Morning Room of the Day home on Madison Avenue.

ACT I: Scene 1. Breakfast time. An early summer morning.

Scene 2. Tea time. The same day.

ACT II: Scene 1. Sunday, after church. A week later.

Scene 2. Breakfast time. Two days later. (During Scene 2 the curtain is lowered to denote a lapse of three hours.)

ACT III: Scene 1. Mid-afternoon. A month later.

Scene 2. Breakfast time. The next morning.

THE AUTHORS

*The Lindsay and Crouse partnership was a good twelve years old when it won
the Pulitzer Prize for* State of the Union *in 1946. By then this team, heralded in*
Life *magazine as the most successful one since Gilbert and Sullivan, had eight
plays to its credit, and seven of these were successes.*

*Mr. Lindsay, who was born in Waterford, New York, in 1889, became an
elocutionist at the tender age of ten in Atlantic City, and his unprofessional
success led him to cast an eye on the stage until the close of his freshman year
at Harvard. Although he then entertained notions of preparing himself for the
ministry (he would have filled a pulpit quite impressively), he soon found himself
examining a catalogue of the American Academy of Dramatic Arts. He abandoned
Harvard for the Academy and, after a year's preparation, started his stage career
in 1909 in* Polly of the Circus. *He spent four years with road companies, worked
as an extra in Hollywood, played in vaudeville, and joined Margaret Anglin's
repertory as an actor and assistant stage manager. He regards his five years with
Miss Anglin as his university education. The first World War found him in the
infantry sporting a corporal's stripes. When he reappeared on Broadway it was
to play in Kaufman and Connelly's* Dulcy. *He also began to write plays, in
collaboration with Bertrand Robinson:* Tommy, Your Uncle Dudley *(1929), and*
Oh Promise Me *(1930). After another term in Hollywood, he directed* Gay
Divorce, *starring Fred Astaire on Broadway, and both wrote and directed the
successful college play* She Loves Me Not *(1933), which introduced the talent
of Burgess Meredith. The year 1935 saw a collaboration with Damon Runyon*
A Slight Case of Murder. *Lindsay and Crouse were introduced to each other
in the summer of 1934 by Vinton Freedley who was then trying to launch the
musical comedy* Anything Goes *for which he needed a new story. Mr. Lindsay
was then recuperating from the "flu" and needed sustenance from Mr. Crouse,
who is a generous dispenser of sunshine, humor, and wit.*

*Mr. Crouse hailed from Findlay, Ohio, where he had been born in 1893 to an
editor and owner of various Midwestern newspapers. Mathematics was Mr.
Crouse's weak point and it cost him an appointment to Annapolis. Journalism
and the theatre gained thereby. Mr. Crouse did a two years' stint as reporter on
the* Cincinnati Commercial-Tribune, *moved to the* Kansas City Star, *and after
seeing service with the Navy during the first World War worked on New York
newspapers and graduated into the ranks of columnists on the* Post. *He published
books (one of them was on Currier and Ives) and wrote two musical comedies;
one of them was the successful Joe Cook show* Hold Your Horses.

*The first Lindsay-Crouse collaboration was a striking success. The next, some-
what less successful, one was the musical* Red, Hot and Blue *(1936), which introduced Bob Hope to the public. Then the friends served Ed Wynn with the
clever musical satire on "merchants of death" and international espionage,*
Hooray for What. *This was in 1937, and in that year they began speculating on a
dramatization of Clarence Day's books of reminiscence which eventuated in the
memorable* Life With Father *opening on November 8, 1939. Next, Lindsay and
Crouse branched out as the producers of* Arsenic and Old Lace *and* The Hasty
Heart, *and put a portion of their fabulous earnings into the purchase of the
Hudson Theatre. They did not lay down their pens, however. They tried to
contribute to war-time morale with* Strip for Action, *which fell short of success,
and they retrieved their laurels with* State of the Union *in the season of 1945–46.
No one will be surprised if their next play will be* Life With Mother.

LIFE WITH FATHER

ACT ONE

SCENE I

The Morning Room of the Day home at 420 Madison Avenue. In the custom of the Victorian period, this was the room where the family gathered for breakfast, and because it was often the most comfortable room in the house, it served also as a living-room for the family and their intimates.

There is a large arch in the center of the upstage wall of the room, through which we can see the hall and the stairs leading to the second floor, and below them the rail of the stairwell leading to the basement. The room can be closed off from the hall by sliding doors in the archway. The front door of the house, which is stage right, can't be seen, but frequently is heard to slam.

In the Morning Room the sunshine streams through the large window at the right which looks out on Madison Avenue. The room itself is furnished with the somewhat less than comfortable furniture of the period, which is the late 1880's. The general color scheme in drapes and upholstery is green. Below the window is a large comfortable chair where Father generally sits to read his paper. Right of center is the table which serves as a living-room table, with its proper table cover and fruit bowl; but now, expanded by extra leaves, it is doing service as a breakfast table. Against the back wall, either side of the arch, are two console tables which are used by the maid as serving tables. Left of center is a sofa, with a table just above its right end holding a lamp, framed photographs, and other ornaments. In the left wall is a fireplace, its mantel draped with a lambrequin. On the mantel are a clock and other ornaments, and above the mantel is a large mirror in a Victorian frame. The room is cluttered with the minutiæ of the period, including the inevitable rubber plant, and looking down from the walls are the Day ancestors in painted portraits. The room has the warm quality that comes only from having been lived in by a family which enjoys each other's company—a family of considerable means.

As the curtain rises, ANNIE, *the new maid, a young Irish girl, is finishing setting the table for breakfast. After an uncertain look at the result she crosses over to her tray on the console table.* VINNIE *comes down the stairs and into the room.* VINNIE *is a charming, lovable, and spirited woman of forty. She has a lively mind which darts quickly away from any practical matter. She has red hair.*

ANNIE. Good morning, ma'am.

VINNIE. Good morning, Annie. How are you getting along?

ANNIE. All right, ma'am, I hope.

VINNIE. Now, don't be worried just because this is your first day. Everything's going to be all right—but I do hope nothing goes wrong. *(Goes to the table.)* Now, let's see, is the table all set? *(AN-NIE follows her.)* The cream and the sugar go down at this end.

ANNIE *(placing them where VINNIE has indicated)*. I thought in the center, ma'am; everyone could reach them easier.

VINNIE. Mr. Day sits here.

ANNIE *(gets a tray of napkins, neatly rolled and in their rings, from the console table)*. I didn't know where to place the napkins, ma'am.

VINNIE. You can tell which go where by the rings. *(Takes them from the tray and puts them down as she goes around the table.* ANNIE *follows her.)* This one belongs to Whitney—it has his initial on it, "W"; that one with the little dog on it is Harlan's, of course. He's the baby. This "J" is for John and the "C" is for Clarence. This narrow plain one is mine. And this is Mr. Day's. It's just like mine

133

—except that it got bent one morning. And that reminds me—always be sure Mr. Day's coffee is piping hot.

ANNIE. Ah, your man has coffee instead of tea of a morning?

VINNIE. We all have coffee except the two youngest boys. They have their milk. And, Annie, always speak of my husband as Mr. Day.

ANNIE. I will that.

VINNIE (correcting her). "Yes, ma'am," Annie.

ANNIE. Yes, ma'am.

VINNIE. And if Mr. Day speaks to you, just say: "Yes, sir." Don't be nervous— you'll get used to him.

(CLARENCE, the eldest son, about seventeen, comes down the stairs and into the room. He is a manly, serious, good-looking boy. Because he is starting at Yale next year, he thinks he is grown-up. He is red-headed.)

CLARENCE. Good morning, Mother. (He kisses her.)

VINNIE. Good morning, Clarence.

CLARENCE. Did you sleep well, Mother?

VINNIE. Yes, thank you, dear. (CLARENCE goes to FATHER's chair and picks up the morning paper.) (To ANNIE.) We always start with fruit, except the two young boys, who have porridge. (ANNIE brings the fruit and porridge to the table. CLARENCE, looking at the paper, makes a whistling sound.)

CLARENCE. Jiminy! Another wreck on the New Haven. That always disturbs the market. Father won't like that.

VINNIE. I do wish that New Haven would stop having wrecks. If they knew how it upset your father— (Sees that CLARENCE's coat has been torn and mended.) My soul and body, Clarence, what's happened to your coat?

CLARENCE. I tore it. Margaret mended it for me.

VINNIE. It looks terrible. Why don't you wear your blue suit?

CLARENCE. That looks worse than this one. You know, I burnt that hole in it.

VINNIE. Oh, yes—well, you can't go around looking like that. I'll have to speak to your father. Oh, dear!

(JOHN, who is about fifteen, comes down the stairs and into the room. JOHN is gangly and a little overgrown. He is red-headed.)

JOHN. Good morning, Mother. (He kisses her.)

VINNIE. Good morning, John.

JOHN (to CLARENCE). Who won?

CLARENCE. I haven't looked yet.

JOHN. Let me see. (He tries to take the paper away from CLARENCE.)

CLARENCE. Be careful!

VINNIE. Boys, don't wrinkle that paper before your father's looked at it.

CLARENCE (to JOHN). Yes!

(VINNIE turns to ANNIE.)

VINNIE. You'd better get things started. We want everything ready when Mr. Day comes down. (ANNIE exits.) Clarence, right after breakfast I want you and John to move the small bureau from my room into yours.

CLARENCE. What for? Is somebody coming to visit us?

JOHN. Who's coming?

VINNIE. I haven't said anyone was coming. And don't you say anything about it. I want it to be a surprise.

CLARENCE. Oh! Father doesn't know yet?

VINNIE. No. And I'd better speak to him about a new suit for you before he finds out he's being surprised by visitors.

(ANNIE enters with a tray on which are two glasses of milk, which she puts at HARLAN's and WHITNEY's places at the table.)

(WHITNEY comes down the stairs and rushes into the room. He is about thirteen. Suiting his age, he is a lively active boy. He is red-headed.)

WHITNEY. Morning. (He kisses his mother quickly, then runs to CLARENCE and JOHN.) Who won?

JOHN. The Giants, 7 to 3. Buck Ewing hit a home run.

WHITNEY. Let me see!

(HARLAN *comes sliding down the banister. He enters the room, runs to his mother, and kisses her.* HARLAN *is a roly-poly, lovable, good-natured youngster of six. He is red-headed.*)

VINNIE. How's your finger, darling?

HARLAN. It itches.

VINNIE (*kissing the finger*). That's a sign it's getting better. Now don't scratch it. Sit down, boys. Get in your chair, darling. (*The boys move to the table and take their places.* CLARENCE *puts the newspaper beside his father's plate.* JOHN *stands waiting to place* VINNIE's *chair when she sits.*) Now, Annie, watch Mr. Day, and as soon as he finishes his fruit— (*Leaves the admonition hanging in mid-air as the sound of* FATHER's *voice booms from upstairs.*)

FATHER'S VOICE. Vinnie! Vinnie!

(*All eyes turn toward the staircase.* VINNIE *rushes to the foot of the stairs, speaking as she goes.*)

VINNIE. What's the matter, Clare?

FATHER'S VOICE. Where's my necktie?

VINNIE. Which necktie?

FATHER'S VOICE. The one I gave you yesterday.

VINNIE. It isn't pressed yet. I forgot to give it to Margaret.

FATHER'S VOICE. I told you distinctly I wanted to wear that necktie today.

VINNIE. You've got plenty of neckties. Put on another one right away and come down to breakfast.

FATHER'S VOICE. Oh, damn! Damnation!

(VINNIE *goes to her place at the table.* JOHN *places her chair for her, then sits.* WHITNEY *has started eating.*)

CLARENCE. Whitney!

VINNIE. Wait for your father, Whitney.

WHITNEY. Oh, and I'm in a hurry! John, can I borrow your glove today? I'm going to pitch.

JOHN. If I don't play myself.

WHITNEY. Look, if you need it, we're playing in that big field at the corner of Fifty-seventh and Madison.

VINNIE. 'Way up there!

WHITNEY. They're building a house on that vacant lot on Fiftieth Street.

VINNIE. My! My! My! Here we move to Forty-eighth Street just to get out of the city!

WHITNEY. Can't I start breakfast, Mother? I promised to be there by eight o'clock.

VINNIE. After breakfast, Whitney, you have to study your catechism.

WHITNEY. Mother, can't I do that this afternoon?

VINNIE. Whitney, you have to learn five questions every morning before you leave the house.

WHITNEY. Aw, Mother—

VINNIE. You weren't very sure of yourself when I heard you last night.

WHITNEY. I know them now.

VINNIE. Let's see. (WHITNEY *rises and faces his mother.*) "What is your name?"

WHITNEY. Whitney Benjamin.

VINNIE. "Who gave you this name?"

WHITNEY. "My sponsors in baptism, wherein I was made a member of Christ, the child of God and an inheritor of the Kingdom of Heaven." Mother, if I hadn't been baptized wouldn't I have a name?

VINNIE. Not in the sight of the Church. "What did your sponsors then for you?"

WHITNEY. "They did promise and vow three things in my name—"

(FATHER *makes his appearance on the stairway and comes down into the room.* FATHER *is in his forties, distinguished in appearance, with great charm and vitality, extremely well dressed in a conservative way. He is red-headed.*)

FATHER (*heartily*). Good morning, boys. (*They rise and answer him.*) Good morning, Vinnie. (*He goes to her and kisses her.*) Have a good night?

VINNIE. Yes, thank you, Clare.

FATHER. Good! Sit down, boys.

(The doorbell rings and a postman's whistle is heard.)

VINNIE. That's the doorbell, Annie. *(*ANNIE *exits.)* Clare, that new suit looks very nice.

FATHER. Too damn tight! *(He sits in his place at the head of the table.)* What's the matter with those fellows over in London? I wrote them a year ago they were making my clothes too tight!

VINNIE. You've put on a little weight, Clare.

FATHER. I weigh just the same as I always have. *(Attacks his orange. The boys dive into their breakfasts.* ANNIE *enters with the mail, starts to take it to* VINNIE. FATHER *sees her.)* What's that? The mail? That goes to me.

*(*ANNIE *gives the mail to* FATHER *and exits with her tray.)*

VINNIE. Well, Clarence has just managed to tear the only decent suit of clothes he has.

FATHER *(looking through the mail)*. Here's one for you, Vinnie. John, hand that to your mother. *(He passes the letter on.)*

VINNIE. Clare dear, I'm sorry, but I'm afraid Clarence is going to have to have a new suit of clothes.

FATHER. Vinnie, Clarence has to learn not to be so hard on his clothes.

CLARENCE. Father, I thought—

FATHER. Clarence, when you start in Yale in the fall, I'm going to set aside a thousand dollars just to outfit you, but you'll get no new clothes this summer.

CLARENCE. Can't I have one of your old suits cut down for me?

FATHER. Every suit I own still has plenty of wear in it. I wear my clothes until they're worn out.

VINNIE. Well, if you want your clothes worn out, Clarence can wear them out much faster than you can.

CLARENCE. Yes, and, Father, you don't get a chance to wear them out. Every time you get a new batch of clothes, Mother sends the old ones to the missionary barrel.

I guess I'm just as good as any old missionary.

*(*ANNIE *returns with a platter of bacon and eggs and a pot of coffee.)*

VINNIE. Clarence, before you compare yourself to a missionary, remember the sacrifices they make.

FATHER *(chuckling)*. I don't know, Vinnie, I think my clothes would look better on Clarence than on some Hottentot. *(To* CLARENCE.*)* Have that black suit of mine cut down to fit you before your mother gets her hands on it.

*(*ANNIE *clears the fruit.)*

CLARENCE. Thank you, Father. *(To John.)* One of Father's suits! Thank you, sir!

FATHER. Whitney, don't eat so fast.

WHITNEY. Well, Father, I'm going to pitch today and I promised to get there early, but before I go I have to study my catechism.

FATHER. What do you bother with that for?

VINNIE *(with spirit)*. Because if he doesn't know his catechism he can't be confirmed!

WHITNEY *(pleading)*. But I'm going to pitch today.

FATHER. Vinnie, Whitney's going to pitch today and he can be confirmed any old time.

VINNIE. Clare, sometimes it seems to me that you don't care whether your children get to Heaven or not.

FATHER. Oh, Whitney'll get to Heaven all right. *(To* WHITNEY.*)* I'll be there before you are, Whitney; I'll see that you get in.

VINNIE. What makes you so sure they'll let you in?

FATHER. Well, if they don't I'll certainly raise a devil of a row.

*(*ANNIE *is at* FATHER's *side with the platter of bacon and eggs, ready to serve him, and draws back at this astounding declaration, raising the platter.)*

VINNIE *(with shocked awe)*. Clare, I do hope you'll behave when you get to Heaven.

(FATHER *has turned to serve himself from the platter, but* ANNIE, *not yet recovered from the picture of* FATHER *raising a row at the gates of Heaven, is holding it too high for him.*)

FATHER (*storming*). Vinnie, how many times have I asked you not to engage a maid who doesn't even know how to serve properly?

VINNIE. Clare, can't you see she's new and doing her best?

FATHER. How can I serve myself when she's holding that platter over my head?

VINNIE. Annie, why don't you hold it lower?

(ANNIE *lowers the platter.* FATHER *serves himself, but goes on talking.*)

FATHER. Where's she come from anyway? What became of the one we had yesterday? I don't see why you can't keep a maid.

VINNIE. Oh, you don't!

FATHER. All I want is service. (ANNIE *serves the others nervously. So far as* FATHER *is concerned, however, the storm has passed, and he turns genially to* WHITNEY.) Whitney, when we get to Heaven we'll organize a baseball team of our own.

(*The boys laugh.*)

VINNIE. It would be just like you to try to run things up there.

FATHER. Well, from all I've heard about Heaven, it seems to be a pretty unbusiness-like place. They could probably use a good man like me. (*Stamps on the floor three times. It is his traditional signal to summon* MARGARET, *the cook, from the kitchen below.*)

VINNIE. What do you want Margaret for? What's wrong?

(ANNIE *has reached the sideboard and is sniffling audibly.*)

FATHER (*distracted*). What's that damn noise?

VINNIE. Shhh—it's Annie.

FATHER. Annie? Who's Annie?

VINNIE. The maid. (ANNIE, *seeing that she has attracted attention, hurries out into the hall where she can't be seen or heard.*) Clare, aren't you ashamed of yourself?

FATHER (*surprised*). What have I done now?

VINNIE. You made her cry—speaking to her the way you did.

FATHER. I never said a word to her—I was addressing myself to you.

VINNIE. I do wish you'd be more careful. It's hard enough to keep a maid—and the uniforms just fit this one.

(MARGARET, *the cook, a small Irishwoman of about fifty, hurries into the room.*)

MARGARET. What's wanting?

FATHER. Margaret, this bacon is *good.* (MARGARET *beams and gestures deprecatingly.*) It's good. It's done just right!

MARGARET. Yes, sir!

(*She smiles and exits.* ANNIE *returns, recovered, and starts serving the coffee.* VINNIE *has opened her letter and glanced through it.*)

VINNIE. Clare, this letter gives me a good idea. I've decided that next winter I won't give a series of dinners.

FATHER. I should hope not.

VINNIE. I'll give a big musicale instead.

FATHER. You'll give a what?

VINNIE. A musicale.

FATHER (*peremptorily*). Vinnie, I won't have my peaceful home turned into a Roman arena with a lot of hairy fiddlers prancing about.

VINNIE. I didn't say a word about hairy fiddlers. Mrs. Spiller has written me about this lovely young girl who will come for very little.

FATHER. What instrument does this inexpensive paragon play?

VINNIE. She doesn't play, Clare, she whistles.

FATHER. Whistles? Good God!

VINNIE. She whistles sixteen different pieces. All for twenty-five dollars.

FATHER (*stormily*). I won't pay twenty-five dollars to any human peanut stand.

(He tastes his coffee, grimaces, and again stamps three times on the floor.)

VINNIE. Clare, I can arrange this so it won't cost you a penny. If I invite fifty people and charge them fifty cents apiece, there's the twenty-five dollars right there!

FATHER. You can't invite people to your own house and charge them admission.

VINNIE. I can if the money's for the missionary fund.

FATHER. Then where will you get the twenty-five dollars to pay that poor girl for her whistling?

VINNIE. Now, Clare, let's not cross that bridge until we come to it.

FATHER. And if we do cross it, it will cost me twenty-five dollars. Vinnie, I'm putting my foot down about this musicale, just as I've had to put my foot down about your keeping this house full of visiting relatives. Why can't we live here by ourselves in peace and comfort?

(MARGARET comes dashing into the room.)

MARGARET. What's wanting?

FATHER *(sternly)*. Margaret, what is this? *(He holds up his coffee cup and points at it.)*

MARGARET. It's coffee, sir.

FATHER. It is not coffee! You couldn't possibly take water and coffee beans and arrive at that! It's slops, that's what it is —slops! Take it away! Take it away, I tell you!

(MARGARET takes FATHER's cup and dashes out. ANNIE starts to take VINNIE's cup.)

VINNIE. Leave my coffee there, Annie! It's perfectly all right!

(ANNIE leaves the room.)

FATHER *(angrily)*. It is not! I swear I can't imagine how she concocts such an atrocity. I come down to this table every morning hungry—

VINNIE. Well, if you're hungry, Clare, why aren't you eating your breakfast?

FATHER. What?

VINNIE. If you're hungry, why aren't you eating your breakfast?

FATHER *(thrown out of bounds)*. I am. *(He takes a mouthful of bacon and munches it happily, his eyes falling on HARLAN.)* Harlan, how's that finger? Come over here and let me see it. *(HARLAN goes to his father's side. He shows his finger.)* Well, that's healing nicely. Now don't pick that scab or it will leave a scar, and we don't want scars on our fingers, do we? *(He chuckles.)* I guess you'll remember after this that cats don't like to be hugged. It's all right to stroke them, but don't squeeze them. Now go back and finish your oatmeal.

HARLAN. I don't like oatmeal.

FATHER *(kindly)*. It's good for you. Go back and eat it.

HARLAN. But I don't like it.

FATHER *(quietly, but firmly)*. I'll tell you what you like and what you don't like. You're not old enough to know about such things. You've no business not to like oatmeal. It's good.

HARLAN. I hate it.

FATHER *(firmly, but not quietly)*. That's enough! We won't discuss it! Eat that oatmeal at once!

(In contrast to HARLAN, WHITNEY has been eating his oatmeal at a terrific rate of speed. He pauses and puts down his spoon.)

WHITNEY. I've finished *my* oatmeal. May I be excused?

FATHER. Yes, Whitney, you may go. *(WHITNEY slides off his chair and hurries to the stairs.)* Pitch a good game.

VINNIE. Whitney!

WHITNEY. I'm going upstairs to study my catechism.

VINNIE. Oh, that's all right. Run along.

WHITNEY *(on the way up)*. Harlan, you'd better hurry up and finish your oatmeal if you want to go with me.

(Throughout breakfast FATHER has been opening and glancing through his mail. He has just reached one letter, however, that bewilders him.)

FATHER. I don't understand why I'm always getting damn fool letters like this!

VINNIE. What is it, Clare?

FATHER. "Dear Friend Day: We are assigning you the exclusive rights for Staten Island for selling the Gem Home Popper for popcorn—"

CLARENCE. I think that's for me, Father.

FATHER. Then why isn't it addressed to Clarence Day, Jr.? *(He looks at the envelope.)* Oh, it is. Well, I'm sorry. I didn't mean to open your mail.

(MARGARET returns and slips a cup of coffee to the table beside FATHER.)

VINNIE. I wouldn't get mixed up in that, Clarence. People like popcorn, but they won't go all the way to Staten Island to buy it.

(FATHER has picked up the paper and is reading it. He drinks his coffee absentmindedly.)

FATHER. Chauncey Depew's having another birthday.

VINNIE. How nice.

FATHER. He's always having birthdays. Two or three a year. Damn! Another wreck on the New Haven!

VINNIE. Yes. Oh, that reminds me. Mrs. Bailey dropped in yesterday.

FATHER. Was she in the wreck?

VINNIE. No. But she was born in New Haven. Clarence, you're having tea with Edith Bailey Thursday afternoon.

CLARENCE. Oh, Mother, do I have to?

JOHN *(singing)*. "I like coffee, I like tea. I like the girls and the girls like me."

CLARENCE. Well, the girls don't like me and I don't like them.

VINNIE. Edith Bailey's a very nice girl, isn't she, Clare?

FATHER. Edith Bailey? Don't like her. Don't blame Clarence.

(FATHER goes to his chair by the window and sits down with his newspaper and a cigar. The others rise. HARLAN runs upstairs. ANNIE starts clearing the table and exits with the tray of dishes a little later. VINNIE speaks in a guarded tone to the two boys.)

VINNIE. Clarence, you and John go upstairs and do—what I asked you to.

JOHN. You said the small bureau, Mother?

VINNIE. Shh! Run along.

(The boys go upstairs, somewhat unwillingly. MARGARET enters.)

MARGARET. If you please, ma'am, there's a package been delivered with a dollar due on it. Some kitchen knives.

VINNIE. Oh, yes, those knives from Lewis & Conger's. *(She gets her purse from the drawer in the console table and gives MARGARET a dollar.)* Here, give this dollar to the man, Margaret.

FATHER. Make a memorandum of that, Vinnie. One dollar and whatever it was for.

VINNIE *(looking into purse)*. Clare, dear, I'm afraid I'm going to need some more money.

FATHER. What for?

VINNIE. You were complaining of the coffee this morning. Well, that nice French drip coffee pot is broken—and you know how it got broken.

FATHER *(taking out his wallet)*. Never mind that, Vinnie. As I remember, that coffee pot cost five dollars and something. Here's six dollars. *(He gives her six dollars.)* And when you get it, enter the exact amount in the ledger downstairs.

VINNIE. Thank you, Clare.

FATHER. We can't go on month after month having the household accounts in such a mess.

VINNIE *(she sits on the arm of FATHER's chair)*. No, and I've thought of a system that will make my bookkeeping perfect.

FATHER. I'm certainly relieved to hear that. What is it?

VINNIE. Well, Clare dear, you never make half the fuss over how much I've spent as you do over my not being able to remember what I've spent it for.

FATHER. Exactly. This house must be run on a business basis. That's why I insist on your keeping books.

VINNIE. That's the whole point, Clare. All we have to do is open charge accounts everywhere and the stores will do my bookkeeping for me.

FATHER. Wait a minute, Vinnie—

VINNIE. Then when the bills come in you'd know exactly where your money had gone.

FATHER. I certainly would. Vinnie, I get enough bills as it is.

VINNIE. Yes, and those bills always help. They show you just where I spent the money. Now if we had charge accounts everywhere—

FATHER. Now, Vinnie, I don't know about that.

VINNIE. Clare dear, don't you hate those arguments we have every month? I certainly do. Not to have those I should think would be worth something to you.

FATHER. Well, I'll open an account at Lewis & Conger's—and one at McCreery's to start with—we'll see how it works out. (He shakes his head doubtfully. Her victory gained, VINNIE moves away.)

VINNIE. Thank you, Clare. Oh—the rector's coming to tea today.

FATHER. The rector? I'm glad you warned me. I'll go to the club. Don't expect me home until dinner time.

VINNIE. I do wish you'd take a little more interest in the church. (Goes behind FATHER's chair and looks down at him with concern.)

FATHER. Vinnie, getting me into Heaven's your job. If there's anything wrong with my ticket when I get there, you can fix it up. Everybody loves you so much—I'm sure God must, too.

VINNIE. I'll do my best, Clare. It wouldn't be Heaven without you.

FATHER. If you're there, Vinnie, I'll manage to get in some way, even if I have to climb the fence.

JOHN (from upstairs). Mother, we've moved it. Is there anything else?

FATHER. What's being moved?

VINNIE. Never mind, Clare. I'll come right up, John. (She goes to the arch, stops. Looks back at FATHER.) Oh, Clare, it's eight-thirty. You don't want to be late at the office.

FATHER. Plenty of time. (VINNIE looks nervously toward the door, then goes upstairs. FATHER returns to his newspaper. VINNIE has barely disappeared when something in the paper arouses FATHER's indignation.) Oh, God!

(VINNIE comes running downstairs.)

VINNIE. What's the matter, Clare? What's wrong?

FATHER. Why did God make so many damn fools and Democrats?

VINNIE (relieved). Oh, politics. (She goes upstairs again.)

FATHER (shouting after her). Yes, but it's taking the bread out of our mouths. It's robbery, that's what it is, highway robbery! Honest Hugh Grant! Honest! Bah! A fine mayor you've turned out to be. (FATHER launches into a vigorous denunciation of Mayor Hugh Grant, addressing that gentleman as though he were present in the room, called upon the Day carpet to listen to FATHER's opinion of Tammany's latest attack on his pocketbook.) If you can't run this city without raising taxes every five minutes, you'd better get out and let someone who can. Let me tell you, sir, that the real-estate owners of New York City are not going to tolerate these conditions any longer. Tell me this—are these increased taxes going into public improvements or are they going into graft—answer me that, honestly, if you can, Mr. Honest Hugh Grant. You can't! I thought so. Bah! (ANNIE enters with her tray. Hearing FATHER talking, she curtsies and backs into the hall, as if uncertain whether to intrude on FATHER and the Mayor. VINNIE comes downstairs.) If you don't stop your plundering of the pocketbooks of the good citizens of New York, we're going to throw you and your boodle Board of Aldermen out of office.

VINNIE. Annie, why aren't you clearing the table?

ANNIE. Mr. Day's got a visitor.

FATHER. I'm warning you for the last time.

VINNIE. Oh, nonsense, he's just reading his paper, Annie. Clear the table.

(VINNIE goes off through the arch. ANNIE

comes in timidly and starts to clear the table.)

FATHER *(still lecturing Mayor Grant)*. We pay you a good round sum to watch after our interests, and all we get is inefficiency! *(ANNIE looks around trying to see the Mayor and, finding the room empty, assumes FATHER's remarks are directed at her.)* I know you're a nincompoop and I strongly suspect you of being a scalawag. *(ANNIE stands petrified. WHITNEY comes downstairs.)* It's graft—that's what it is —Tammany graft—and if you're not getting it, somebody else is.

WHITNEY *(to FATHER)*. Where's John? Do you know where John is?

FATHER. Dick Croker's running this town and you're just his cat's-paw.

(VINNIE comes in from downstairs, and HARLAN comes down from upstairs. FATHER goes on talking. The others carry on their conversation simultaneously, ignoring FATHER and his imaginary visitor.)

HARLAN. Mother, where's John?

VINNIE. He's upstairs, dear.

FATHER. And as for you, Richard Croker —don't think, just because you're hiding behind these minions you've put in public office, that you're going to escape your legal responsibilities.

WHITNEY *(calling upstairs)*. John, I'm going to take your glove!

JOHN *(from upstairs)*. Don't you lose it! And don't let anybody else have it either!

VINNIE. Annie, you should have cleared the table long ago.

(ANNIE loads her tray feverishly, eager to escape.)

FATHER *(rising and slamming down the paper in his chair)*. *Legal* responsibilities —by gad, sir, I mean *criminal* responsibilities.

(The boys start toward the front door.)

VINNIE *(starting upstairs)*. Now you watch Harlan, Whitney. Don't let him be anywhere the ball can hit him. Do what Whitney says, Harlan. And don't be late for lunch.

(FATHER has reached the arch on his way out of the room, where he pauses for a final shot at Mayor Grant.)

FATHER. Don't forget what happened to William Marcy Tweed—and if you put our taxes up once more, we'll put you in jail!

(He goes out of the archway to the left. A few seconds later he is seen passing the arch toward the outer door wearing his square derby and carrying his stick and gloves. The door is heard to slam loudly.)

(ANNIE seizes her tray of dishes and runs out of the arch to the left toward the basement stairs. A second later there is a scream from ANNIE and a tremendous crash.)

(JOHN and CLARENCE come rushing down and look over the rail of the stairs below. VINNIE follows them almost immediately.)

VINNIE. What is it? What happened?

CLARENCE. The maid fell downstairs.

VINNIE. I don't wonder, with your Father getting her so upset. Why couldn't she have finished with the table before she fell downstairs?

JOHN. I don't think she hurt herself.

VINNIE. And today of all days! Boys, will you finish the table? And, Clarence, don't leave the house until I talk to you. *(She goes downstairs.)*

(During the following scene CLARENCE and JOHN remove VINNIE's best breakfast tablecloth and cram it carelessly into the drawer of the console table, then take out the extra leaves from the table, push it together, and replace the living-room table cover and the bowl of fruit.)

JOHN. What do you suppose Mother wants to talk to you about?

CLARENCE. Oh, probably about Edith Bailey.

JOHN. What do you talk about when you have tea alone with a girl?

CLARENCE. We don't talk about anything. I say: 'Isn't it a nice day?' and she says: 'Yes,' and I say: 'I think it's a little warmer than yesterday,' and she says: 'Yes, I like warm weather, don't you?' and I say: 'Yes,' and then we wait for the tea to come in. And then she says: 'How many lumps?' and I say: 'Two, thank you,' and she says 'You must have a sweet tooth,' and I can't say: 'Yes' and I can't say: 'No,' so we just sit there and look at each other for half an hour. Then I say: 'Well, it's time I was going,' and she says: 'Must you?' and I say: 'I've enjoyed seeing you very much,' and she says: 'You must come again,' and I say 'I will,' and get out.

JOHN (shaking his head). Some fellows like girls.

CLARENCE. I don't.

JOHN. And did you ever notice fellows, when they get sweet on a girl—the silly things a girl can make them do? And they don't even seem to know they're acting silly.

CLARENCE. Well, not for Yours Truly!

(VINNIE returns from downstairs.)

VINNIE. I declare I don't see how anyone could be so clumsy.

CLARENCE. Did she hurt herself?

VINNIE. No, she's not hurt—she's just hysterical! She doesn't make sense. Your father may have raised his voice; and if she doesn't know how to hold a platter properly, she deserved it—but I know he didn't threaten to put her in jail. Oh, well! Clarence, I want you to move your things into the front room. You'll have to sleep with the other boys for a night or two.

CLARENCE. You haven't told us who's coming.

VINNIE (happily). Cousin Cora. Isn't that nice?

CLARENCE. It's not nice for me. I can't get any sleep in there with those children.

JOHN. Wait'll Father finds out she's here! There'll be a rumpus.

VINNIE. John, don't criticize your father. He's very hospitable after he gets used to the idea.

(The doorbell rings. JOHN and VINNIE go to the window.)

JOHN. Yes, it's Cousin Cora. Look, there's somebody with her.

VINNIE (looking out). She wrote me she was bringing a friend of hers. They're both going to stay here. (A limping AN-NIE passes through the hall.) Finish with the room, boys.

CLARENCE. Do I have to sleep with the other boys and have tea with Edith Bailey all in the same week?

VINNIE. Yes, and you'd better take your father's suit to the tailor's right away, so it will be ready by Thursday.

(VINNIE goes down the hall to greet CORA and MARY. CLARENCE hurries off, carrying the table leaves.)

VINNIE'S VOICE (in the hall). Cora dear—

CORA'S VOICE. Cousin Vinnie, I'm so glad to see you! This is Mary Skinner.

VINNIE'S VOICE. Ed Skinner's daughter! I'm so glad to see you. Leave your bags in the hall and come right upstairs.

(VINNIE enters, going toward the stairs. CORA follows her, but, seeing JOHN, enters the room and goes to him. MARY follows CORA in timidly. CORA is an attractive country cousin of about thirty. MARY is a refreshingly pretty small-town girl of sixteen.)

CORA (seeing John). Well, Clarence, it's so good to see you!

VINNIE (coming into the room). Oh, no, that's John.

CORA. John! Why, how you've grown! You'll be a man before your mother! (She laughs herself at this time-worn quip.) John, this is Mary Skinner. (They exchange greetings.) Vinnie, I have so much to tell you. We wrote you Aunt Carrie broke her hip. That was the night Robert Ingersoll lectured. Of course she couldn't get there; and it was a good thing for Mr. Ingersoll she didn't. (CLAR-ENCE enters.) And Grandpa Ebbetts hasn't been at all well.

CLARENCE. How do you do, Cousin Cora? I'm glad to see you.

CORA. This can't be Clarence!

VINNIE. Yes, it is.

CORA. My goodness, every time I see you boys you've grown another foot. Let's see—you're going to St. Paul's now, aren't you?

CLARENCE (*with pained dignity*). St. Paul's! I was through with St. Paul's long ago. I'm starting in Yale this fall.

MARY. Yale!

CORA. Oh, Mary, this is Clarence—Mary Skinner. (MARY *smiles, and* CLARENCE, *the woman-hater, nods politely and walks away*). This is Mary's first trip to New York. She was so excited when she saw a horse car.

VINNIE. We'll have to show Mary around. I'll tell you—I'll have Mr. Day take us all to Delmonico's for dinner tonight.

MARY. Delmonico's!

CORA. Oh, that's marvelous! Think of that, Mary—Delmonico's! And Cousin Clare's such a wonderful host.

VINNIE. I know you girls want to freshen up. So come upstairs. Clarence, I'll let the girls use your room now, and when they've finished you can move, and bring up their bags. They're out in the hall. (*Starts upstairs with* CORA.) I've given you girls Clarence's room, but he didn't know about it until this morning and he hasn't moved out yet.

(VINNIE *and* CORA *disappear upstairs.*)

(MARY *follows more slowly and on the second step stops and looks back.* CLARENCE *has gone into the hall with his back toward* MARY *and stares morosely in the direction of their luggage.*)

CLARENCE. John, get their old bags.

(JOHN *disappears toward the front door. The voices of* VINNIE *and* CORA *have trailed off into the upper reaches of the house.* CLARENCE *turns to scowl in their direction and finds himself looking full into the face of* MARY.)

MARY. Cora didn't tell me about you. I never met a Yale man before.

(*She gives him a devastating smile and with an audible whinny of girlish excitement she runs upstairs.* CLARENCE *stares after her a few seconds, then turns toward the audience with a look of "What happened to me just then?" Suddenly, however, his face breaks into a smile which indicates that, whatever has happened, he likes it.*)

CURTAIN

SCENE II

The same day. Tea time.

VINNIE *and the* RECTOR *are having tea.* THE REVEREND DR. LLOYD *is a plump, bustling man, very good-hearted and pleasant.* VINNIE *and* DR. LLOYD *have one strong point in common: their devotion to the Church and its rituals.* VINNIE's *devotion comes from her natural piety;* DR. LLOYD's *is a little more professional.*

At rise, DR. LLOYD *is seated with a cup of tea.* VINNIE *is also seated and* WHITNEY *is standing next to her, stiffly erect in the manner of a boy reciting.* HARLAN *is seated next to his mother, watching* WHITNEY's *performance.*

WHITNEY (*reciting*). "—to worship Him, to give Him thanks; to put my whole trust in Him, to call upon Him—" (*He hesitates.*)

VINNIE (*prompting*). "—to honor—"

WHITNEY. "—to honor His Holy Name and His word and to serve Him truly all the days of my life."

DR. LLOYD. "What is thy duty toward thy neighbor?"

WHITNEY. Whew! (*He pulls himself together and makes a brave start.*) "My duty toward my neighbor is to love him as myself, and to do to all men as I

would they should do unto me; to love, honor, and succor my father and my mother; to honor and obey—"

VINNIE. "—civil authorities."

WHITNEY. "—civil authorities. To—to—to—"

VINNIE (*to* DR. LLOYD). He really knows it.

WHITNEY. I know most of the others.

DR. LLOYD. Well, he's done very well for so young a boy. I'm sure if he applies himself between now and Sunday I could hear him again—with the others.

VINNIE. There, Whitney, you'll have to study very hard if you want Dr. Lloyd to send your name in to Bishop Potter next Sunday. I must confess to you, Dr. Lloyd, it's really my fault. Instead of hearing Whitney say his catechism this morning I let him play baseball.

WHITNEY. We won, too; 35 to 27.

DR. LLOYD. That's splendid, my child. I'm glad your side won. But winning over your catechism is a richer and fuller victory.

WHITNEY. Can I go now?

VINNIE. Yes, darling. Thank Dr. Lloyd for hearing you and run along.

WHITNEY. Thank you, Dr. Lloyd.

DR. LLOYD. Not at all, my little man.

(WHITNEY *starts out, turns back, takes a piece of cake and runs out.*)

VINNIE. Little Harlan is very apt at learning things by heart.

HARLAN (*scrambling to his feet*). I can spell Constantinople. Want to hear me? (DR. LLOYD *smiles his assent.*) C-o-enna-conny—annaconny—sissaconny—tan-tan-tee—and a nople and a pople and a Constantinople!

DR. LLOYD. Very well done, my child.

VINNIE (*handing him a cake from the tea-tray*). That's nice, darling. This is what you get for saying it so well.

(HARLAN *quickly looks at the cake and back to* DR. LLOYD.)

HARLAN. Want me to say it again for you?

VINNIE. No, darling. One cake is enough. You run along and play with Whitney.

HARLAN. I can spell "huckleberry pie."

VINNIE. Run along, dear.

(HARLAN *goes out, skipping in rhythm to his recitation.*)

HARLAN. H-a-huckle—b-a-buckle—h-a-huckle-high. H-a-huckle—b-a-buckle—huckleberry pie!

DR. LLOYD (*amused*). You and Mr. Day must be very proud of your children. (VINNIE *beams.*) I was hoping I'd find Mr. Day at home this afternoon.

VINNIE (*evasively*). Well, he's usually home from the office by this time.

DR. LLOYD. Perhaps he's gone for a gallop in the park—it's such a fine day. He's very fond of horseback riding, I believe.

VINNIE. Oh, yes.

DR. LLOYD. Tell me—has he ever been thrown from a horse?

VINNIE. Oh, no! No horse would throw Mr. Day.

DR. LLOYD. I've wondered. I thought he might have had an accident. I notice he never kneels in church.

VINNIE. Oh, that's no accident! But I don't want you to think he doesn't pray. He does. Why, sometimes you can hear him pray all over the house. But he never kneels.

DR. LLOYD. Never kneels! Dear me! I was hoping to have the opportunity to tell you and Mr. Day about our plans for the new edifice.

VINNIE. I'm so glad we're going to have a new church.

DR. LLOYD. I'm happy to announce that we're now ready to proceed. The only thing left to do is raise the money.

VINNIE. No one should hesitate about contributing to that.

(*The front door slams.*)

DR. LLOYD. Perhaps that's Mr. Day now.

VINNIE. Oh, no, I hardly think so. (FATHER *appears in the archway.*) Why, it is!

FATHER. Oh, damn! I forgot.

VINNIE. Clare, you're just in time. Dr. Lloyd's here for tea.

FATHER. I'll be right in. (*He disappears the other side of the archway.*)

VINNIE. I'll send for some fresh tea. (*She goes to the bell-pull and rings for the maid.*)

DR. LLOYD. Now we can tell Mr. Day about our plans for the new edifice.

VINNIE (*knowing her man*). After he's had his tea.

(FATHER *comes back into the room.* DR. LLOYD *rises.*)

FATHER. How are you, Dr. Lloyd?

(CLARENCE *comes down the stairs and eagerly looks around for* MARY.)

CLARENCE. Oh, it was Father.

DR. LLOYD. Very well, thank you. *(They shake hands.)*

CLARENCE *(to* VINNIE*).* They're not back yet?

VINNIE. No! Clarence, no!

(CLARENCE *turns, disappointed, and goes back upstairs.)*

DR. LLOYD. It's a great pleasure to have a visit with you, Mr. Day. Except for a fleeting glimpse on the Sabbath, I don't see much of you.

(FATHER *grunts and sits down.* DELIA, *a new maid, enters.)*

DELIA. Yes, ma'am.

VINNIE. Some fresh tea and a cup for Mr. Day. (DELIA *exits and* VINNIE *hurries down to the tea table to start the conversation.)* Well, Clare, did you have a busy day at the office?

FATHER. Damn busy.

VINNIE. Clare!

FATHER. Very busy day. Tired out.

VINNIE. I've ordered some fresh tea. *(To* DR. LLOYD.*)* Poor Clare, he must work very hard. He always comes home tired. Although how a man can get tired just sitting at his desk all day, I don't know. I suppose Wall Street is just as much a mystery to you as it is to me, Dr. Lloyd.

DR. LLOYD. No, no, it's all very clear to me. My mind often goes to the business man. The picture I'm most fond of is when I envision him at the close of the day's work. There he sits—this hard-headed man of affairs—surrounded by the ledgers that he has been studying closely and harshly for hours. I see him pausing in his toil—and by chance he raises his eyes and looks out of the window at the light in God's sky and it comes over him that money and ledgers are dross. (FATHER *stares at* DR. LLOYD *with some amazement.)* He realizes that all those figures of profit and loss are without importance or consequence—vanity and dust. And I see this troubled man bow his head and with streaming eyes resolve to devote his life to far higher things.

FATHER. Well, I'll be damned!

(At this moment DELIA *returns with the fresh tea for* FATHER.*)*

VINNIE. Here's your tea, Clare.

(FATHER *notices the new maid.)*

FATHER. Who's this?

VINNIE *(quietly).* The new maid.

FATHER. Where's the one we had this morning?

VINNIE. Never mind, Clare.

FATHER. The one we had this morning was prettier. (DELIA, *with a slight resentment, exits.* FATHER *attacks the tea and cakes with relish.)* Vinnie, these cakes are good.

DR. LLOYD. Delicious!

VINNIE. Dr. Lloyd wants to tell us about the plans for the new edifice.

FATHER. The new what?

VINNIE. The new church—Clare, you knew we were planning to build a new church.

DR. LLOYD. Of course, we're going to have to raise a large sum of money.

FATHER *(alive to the danger).* Well, personally I'm against the church hop-skipping-and-jumping all over the town. And it so happens that during the last year I've suffered heavy losses in the market —damned heavy losses—

VINNIE. Clare!

FATHER. —so any contribution I make will have to be a small one.

VINNIE. But, Clare, for so worthy a cause!

FATHER. —and if your Finance Committee thinks it's too small they can blame the rascals that are running the New Haven Railroad!

DR. LLOYD. The amount everyone is to subscribe has already been decided.

FATHER *(bristling).* Who decided it?

DR. LLOYD. After considerable thought we've found a formula which we believe is fair and equitable. It apportions the burden lightly on those least able to carry it and justly on those whose shoulders we know are stronger. We've voted that our supporting members should each contribute a sum equal to the cost of their pews.

(FATHER's *jaw drops.*)

FATHER. I paid five thousand dollars for my pew!

VINNIE. Yes, Clare. That makes our contribution five thousand dollars.

FATHER. That's robbery! Do you know what that pew is worth today? Three thousand dollars. That's what the last one sold for. I've taken a dead loss of two thousand dollars on that pew already. Frank Baggs sold me that pew when the market was at its peak. He knew when to get out. (*He turns to* VINNIE.) And I'm warning you now that if the market ever goes up I'm going to unload that pew.

VINNIE. Clarence Day! How can you speak of the Lord's temple as though it were something to be bought and sold on Wall Street!

FATHER. Vinnie, this is a matter of dollars and cents, and that's something you don't know anything about!

VINNIE. Your talking of religion in the terms of dollars and cents seems to me pretty close to blasphemy.

DR. LLOYD (*soothingly*). Now, Mrs. Day, your husband is a business man and he has a practical approach toward this problem. We've had to be practical about it too—we have all the facts and figures.

FATHER. Oh, really! What's the new piece of property going to cost you?

DR. LLOYD. I think the figure I've heard mentioned is eighty-five thousand dollars —or was it a hundred and eighty-five thousand dollars?

FATHER. What's the property worth where we are now?

DR. LLOYD. Well, there's quite a difference of opinion about that.

FATHER. How much do you have to raise to build the new church?

DR. LLOYD. Now, I've seen those figures— let me see—I know it depends somewhat upon the amount of the mortgage.

FATHER. Mortgage, eh? What are the terms of the amortization?

DR. LLOYD. Amortization? That's not a word I'm familiar with.

FATHER. It all seems pretty vague and unsound to me. I certainly wouldn't let any customer of mine invest on what I've heard.

(*The doorbell rings.*)

DR. LLOYD. We've given it a great deal of thought. I don't see how you can call it vague.

(DELIA *passes along the hall toward the front door.*)

FATHER. Dr. Lloyd, you preach that some day we'll all have to answer to God.

DR. LLOYD. We shall indeed!

FATHER. Well, I hope God doesn't ask you any questions with figures in them.

(CORA's *voice is heard in the hall, thanking* DELIA. VINNIE *goes to the arch just in time to meet* CORA *and* MARY *as they enter, heavily laden with packages, which they put down.* FATHER *and* DR. LLOYD *rise.*)

CORA. Oh, Vinnie, what a day! We've been to every shop in town and— (*She sees* FATHER.) Cousin Clare!

FATHER (*cordially*). Cora, what are you doing in New York?

CORA. We're just passing through on our way to Springfield.

FATHER. We?

(CLARENCE *comes downstairs into the room with eyes only for* MARY.)

VINNIE. Oh, Dr. Lloyd, this is my favorite cousin, Miss Cartwright, and her friend, Mary Skinner. (*They exchange mutual how-do-you-do's.*)

DR. LLOYD. This seems to be a family reunion. I'll just run along.

FATHER (*promptly*). Goodbye, Dr. Lloyd.

DR. LLOYD. Goodbye, Miss Cartwright. Goodbye, Miss—er—

VINNIE. Clarence, you haven't said how-do-you-do to Dr. Lloyd.

CLARENCE. Goodbye, Dr. Lloyd.

VINNIE (to DR. LLOYD). I'll go to the door with you. (DR. LLOYD and VINNIE go out, talking.)

FATHER. Cora, you're as welcome as the flowers in May! Have some tea with us. (To DELIA.) Bring some fresh tea—and some more of those cakes.

CORA. Oh, we've had tea! We were so tired shopping we had tea downtown. (With a gesture FATHER countermands his order to DELIA, who removes the tea table and exits.)

MARY. At the Fifth Avenue Hotel.

FATHER. At the Fifth Avenue Hotel, eh? Who'd you say this pretty little girl was?

CORA. She's Ed Skinner's daughter. Well, Mary, at last you've met Mr. Day. I've told Mary so much about you, Cousin Clare, that she's just been dying to meet you.

FATHER. Well, sit down! Sit down! Even if you have had tea you can stop and visit for a while. As a matter of fact, why don't you both stay to dinner?

(VINNIE enters just in time to hear this and cuts in quickly.)

VINNIE. That's all arranged, Clare. Cora and Mary are going to have dinner with us.

FATHER. That's fine! That's fine!

CORA. Cousin Clare, I don't know how to thank you and Vinnie for your hospitality.

MARY. Yes, Mr. Day.

FATHER. Well, you'll just have to take pot luck.

CORA. No, I mean—

(VINNIE speaks quickly to postpone the revelation that FATHER has house guests.)

VINNIE. Clare, did you know the girls are going to visit Aunt Judith in Springfield for a whole month?

FATHER. That's fine. How long are you going to be in New York, Cora?

CORA. All week.

FATHER. Splendid. We'll hope to see something of you, eh, Vinnie?

(CORA looks bewildered and is about to speak.)

VINNIE. Did you find anything you wanted in the shops?

CORA. Just everything.

VINNIE. I want to see what you got.

CORA. I just can't wait to show you. (She goes coyly to FATHER.) But I'm afraid some of the packages can't be opened in front of Cousin Clare.

FATHER. Shall I leave the room? (Laughs at his own joke.)

CORA. Clarence, do you mind taking the packages up to our room—or should I say your room? (To FATHER.) Wasn't it nice of Clarence to give up his room to us for a whole week?

FATHER (with a sudden drop in temperature). Vinnie!

VINNIE. Come on, Cora, I just can't wait to see what's in those packages.

(CORA, MARY, and VINNIE start out. CLARENCE is gathering up the packages.)

FATHER (ominously). Vinnie, I wish to speak to you before you go upstairs.

VINNIE. I'll be down in just a minute, Clare.

FATHER. I wish to speak to you now! (The girls have disappeared upstairs.)

VINNIE. I'll be up in just a minute, Cora. (We hear a faint "All right" from upstairs.)

FATHER (his voice is low but stern). Are those two women encamped in this house?

VINNIE. Now, Clare!

FATHER (much louder). Answer me, Vinnie!

VINNIE. Just a minute—control yourself, Clare. (VINNIE, sensing the coming storm, hurries to the sliding doors. CLARENCE has reached the hall with his packages and he, too, has recognized the danger signal and as VINNIE closes one door he closes the other, leaving himself out in the hall and FATHER and VINNIE facing each other in the room.) (Persuasively.) Now, Clare, you know you've always liked Cora.

FATHER (*exploding*). What has that got to do with her planking herself down in my house and bringing hordes of strangers with her?

VINNIE (*reproachfully*). How can you call that sweet little girl a horde of strangers?

FATHER. Why don't they go to a hotel? New York is full of hotels built for the express purpose of housing such nuisances.

VINNIE. Clare! Two girls alone in a hotel! Who knows what might happen to them?

FATHER. All right. Then put 'em on the next train. If they want to roam—the damned gypsies—lend 'em a hand! Keep 'em roaming!

VINNIE. What have we got a home for if we can't show a little hospitality?

FATHER. I didn't buy this home to show hospitality—I bought it for my own comfort!

VINNIE. Well, how much are they going to interfere with your comfort living in that little room of Clarence's?

FATHER. The trouble is, damn it, they don't live there. They live in the bathroom! Every time I want to take my bath it's full of giggling females—washing their hair. From the time they take, you'd think it was the Seven Sutherland Sisters. I tell you, I won't have it! Send 'em to a hotel. I'll pay the bill gladly, but get them out of here!

(CLARENCE *puts his head through the sliding door.*)

CLARENCE. Father, I'm afraid they can hear you upstairs.

FATHER. Then keep those doors closed!

VINNIE (*with decision*). Clarence, you open those doors—open them all the way! (CLARENCE *does so.*)

VINNIE (*to* FATHER, *lowering her voice, but maintaining her spirit*). Now, Clare, you behave yourself! (FATHER *glares at her angrily.*) They're here and they're going to stay here.

FATHER. That's enough, Vinnie! I want no more of this argument. (*He goes to his chair by the window, muttering.*) Damnation!

CLARENCE (*to* VINNIE). Mother, Cousin Cora's waiting for you.

FATHER. What I don't understand is why this swarm of locusts always descends on us without any warning. (*He sits down.* VINNIE *looks at him; then, convinced of her victory, she goes upstairs.*) Damn! Damnation! Damn! (*He follows her upstairs with his eyes; he remembers he is very fond of her.*) Vinnie! Dear Vinnie! (*He remembers he is very angry at her.*) Damn!

CLARENCE. Father, can't I go along with the rest of you to Delmonico's tonight?

FATHER. What's that? Delmonico's?

CLARENCE. You're taking Mother, Cora, and Mary to Delmonico's for dinner.

FATHER (*exploding*). Oh, God! (*At this sound from* FATHER, VINNIE *comes flying downstairs again.*) I won't have it. I won't have it. (FATHER *stamps angrily across the room.*)

VINNIE (*on the way down*). Clarence, the doors!

FATHER. I won't stand it, by God! I won't stand it! (VINNIE *and* CLARENCE *hurriedly close the sliding doors again.*)

VINNIE. Clare! What's the matter now?

FATHER (*with the calm of anger that has turned to ice*). Do I understand that I can't have dinner in my own home?

VINNIE. It'll do us both good to get out of this house. You need a little change. It'll make you feel better.

FATHER. I have a home to have dinner in. Any time I can't have dinner at home this house is for sale!

VINNIE. Well, you can't have dinner here tonight because it isn't ordered.

FATHER. Let me tell you I'm ready to sell this place this very minute if I can't live here in peace. And we can all go and sit under a palm tree and live on breadfruit and pickles.

VINNIE. But, Clare, Cora and Mary want to see something of New York.

FATHER. Oh, that's it! Well, that's no affair of mine! I am not a guide to Chinatown and the Bowery. (*Drawing himself*

*up, he stalks out, throwing open the slid-
ing doors. As he reaches the foot of the
stairs,* MARY *comes tripping down.)*

MARY. I love your house, Mr. Day. I
could just live here forever. (FATHER *utters
a bark of disgust and continues on upstairs.* MARY *comes into the room a little
wide-eyed.)* Cora's waiting for you, Mrs.
Day.

VINNIE. Oh, yes, I'll run right up. *(She
goes upstairs.)*

CLARENCE. I'm glad you like our house.

MARY. Oh, yes, I like it very much. I like
green.

CLARENCE. I like green myself. *(She looks
up at his red hair.)*

MARY. Red's my favorite color.

(Embarrassed, CLARENCE *suddenly hears
himself talking about something he has
never thought about.)*

CLARENCE. It's an interesting thing about
colors. Red's a nice color in a house, too;
but outside, too much red would be bad.
I mean, for instance, if all the trees and
the grass were red. Outside, green is the
best color.

MARY *(impressed)*. That's right! I've never
thought of it that way—but when you do
think of it, it's quite a thought! I'll bet
you'll make your mark at Yale.

CLARENCE *(pleased, but modest)*. Oh!

(The outer door is heard to slam.)

MARY. My mother wants me to go to college. Do you believe in girls going to
college?

CLARENCE. I guess it's all right if they want
to waste that much time—before they get
married, I mean.

*(*JOHN *comes in, bringing* The Youth's
Companion.*)*

JOHN. Oh, hello! Look! A new *Youth's
Companion!*

(They say "Hello" to him.)

CLARENCE *(from a mature height)*. John
enjoys *The Youth's Companion.* (JOHN
sits right down and starts to read. CLARENCE
is worried by this.) John! (JOHN *looks at
him non-plussed.* CLARENCE *glances toward*

MARY. JOHN *remembers his manners and
stands.* CLARENCE *speaks formally to
MARY.)* Won't you sit down?

MARY. Oh, thank you!

(She sits. JOHN *sits down again quickly
and dives back into* The Youth's Companion. CLARENCE *sits beside* MARY.*)*

CLARENCE. As I was saying—I think it's
all right for a girl to go to college if she
goes to a girls' college.

MARY. Well, Mother wants me to go to
Ohio Wesleyan—because it's Methodist.
(Then almost as a confession.) You see,
we're Methodists.

CLARENCE. Oh, that's too bad! I don't
mean it's too bad that you're a Methodist.
Anybody's got a right to be anything they
want. But what I mean is—we're Episcopalians.

MARY. Yes, I know. I've known ever since
I saw your minister—and his collar. *(She
looks pretty sad for a minute and then
her face brightens.)* Oh, I just remembered—my father was an Episcopalian. He
was baptized an Episcopalian. He was
an Episcopalian right up to the time he
married my mother. *She* was the Methodist.

*(*MARY'S *tone would have surprised her
mother—and even* MARY, *if she had been
listening.)*

CLARENCE. I'll bet your father's a nice
man.

MARY. Yes, he is. He owns the livery stable.

CLARENCE. He does? Well, then you must
like horses.

MARY. Oh, I love horses! *(They are happily united again in their common love
of horses.)*

CLARENCE. They're my favorite animal.
Father and I both think there's nothing
like a horse!

*(*FATHER *comes down the stairs and into
the room. The children all stand.)*

MARY. Oh, Mr. Day, I'm having such a
lovely time here!

FATHER. Clarence is keeping you entertained, eh?

MARY. Oh, yes, sir. We've been talking about everything—colors and horses and religion.

FATHER. Oh! (*To* JOHN.) Has the evening paper come yet?

JOHN. No, sir.

FATHER. What are you reading?

JOHN. *The Youth's Companion,* sir.

(WHITNEY *and* HARLAN *enter from the hall,* WHITNEY *carrying a small box.*)

WHITNEY. Look what we've got!

FATHER. What is it?

WHITNEY. Tiddle-dy-winks. We put our money together and bought it.

FATHER. That's a nice game. Do you know how to play it?

WHITNEY. I've played it lots of times.

HARLAN. Show me how to play it.

FATHER. Here, I'll show you. (*Opens the box and arranges the glass and disks.*)

MARY (*hopefully to* CLARENCE). Are you going out to dinner with us tonight?

CLARENCE (*looking at* FATHER). I don't know yet—but it's beginning to look as though I might.

FATHER. It's easy, Harlan. You press down like this and snap the little fellow into the glass. Now watch me— (*He snaps it and it goes off the table.*) The table isn't quite large enough. You boys better play it on the floor.

WHITNEY. Come on, Harlan, I'll take the reds, and you take the yellows.

FATHER. John, have you practiced your piano today?

JOHN. I was going to practice this evening.

FATHER. Better do it now. Music is a delight in the home.

(JOHN *exits, passing* CORA *and* VINNIE *as they enter, coming downstairs.*)

VINNIE. Clare, what do you think Cora just told me? She and Clyde are going to be married this fall!

FATHER. Oh, you finally landed him, eh? (*Everybody laughs.*) Well, he's a very lucky man. Cora, being married is the only way to live.

CORA. If we can be half as happy as you and Cousin Vinnie—

VINNIE (*who has gone to the children*). Boys, shouldn't you be playing that on the table?

WHITNEY. The table isn't big enough. Father told us to play on the floor.

VINNIE. My soul and body! Look at your hands! Delia will have your supper ready in a few minutes. Go wash your hands right away and come back and show Mother they're clean.

(*The boys pick up the tiddle-dy-winks and depart reluctantly. From the next room we hear* JOHN *playing "The Happy Farmer."*)

FATHER (*sitting down on the sofa with* MARY). Vinnie, this young lady looks about the same age you were when I came out to Pleasantville to rescue you.

VINNIE. Rescue me! You came out there to talk me into marrying you.

FATHER. It worked out just the same. I saved you from spending the rest of your life in that one-horse town.

VINNIE. Cora, the other day I came across a tin-type of Clare taken in Pleasantville. I want to show it to you. You'll see who needed rescuing. (*She goes to the table and starts to rummage around in its drawer.*)

FATHER. There isn't time for that, Vinnie. If we're going to Delmonico's for dinner hadn't we all better be getting ready? It's after six now.

CORA. Gracious! I'll have to start. If I'm going to dine in public with a prominent citizen like you, Cousin Clare—I'll have to look my best. (*She goes to the arch.*)

MARY. I've changed already.

CORA. Yes, I know, but I'm afraid I'll have to ask you to come along and hook me up, Mary.

MARY. Of course.

CORA. It won't take a minute and then you can come right back.

(FATHER *rises.* MARY *crosses in front of* FATHER *and starts toward the hall, then turns and looks back at him.*)

MARY. Mr. Day, were you always an Episcopalian?

FATHER. What?

MARY. Were you always an Episcopalian?

FATHER. I've always gone to the Episcopal church, yes.

MARY. But you weren't baptized a Methodist or anything, were you? You were baptized an Episcopalian?

FATHER. Come to think of it, I don't believe I was ever baptized at all.

MARY. Oh!

VINNIE. Clare, that's not very funny, joking about a subject like that.

FATHER. I'm not joking—I remember now —I never was baptized.

VINNIE. Clare, that's ridiculous, everyone's baptized.

FATHER (sitting down complacently). Well, I'm not.

VINNIE. Why, no one would keep a little baby from being baptized.

FATHER. You know Father and Mother— free-thinkers, both of them—believed their children should decide those things for themselves.

VINNIE. But, Clare—

FATHER. I remember when I was ten or twelve years old, Mother said I ought to give some thought to it. I suppose I thought about it, but I never got around to having it done to me.

(The shock to VINNIE is as great as if FATHER had calmly announced himself guilty of murder. She walks to FATHER staring at him in horror. CORA and MARY, sensing the coming battle, withdraw to the neutral shelter of the hall.)

VINNIE. Clare, do you know what you're saying?

FATHER. I'm saying I've never been baptized.

VINNIE (in a sudden panic). Then something has to be done about it right away.

FATHER (not the least concerned). Now, Vinnie, don't get excited over nothing.

VINNIE. Nothing! (Then as only a woman can ask such a question.) Clare, why haven't you ever told me?

FATHER. What difference does it make?

VINNIE (the panic returning). I've never heard of anyone who wasn't baptized. Even the savages in darkest Africa—

FATHER. It's all right for savages and children. But if an oversight was made in my case it's too late to correct it now.

VINNIE. But if you're not baptized you're not a Christian!

FATHER (rising in wrath). Why, confound it, of course I'm a Christian! A damn good Christian, too! (FATHER's voice tells CLARENCE a major engagement has begun. He hurriedly springs to the sliding doors and closes them, removing himself, MARY, and CORA from the scene of action.) A lot better Christian than those psalm-singing donkeys in church!

VINNIE. You can't be if you won't be baptized.

FATHER. I won't be baptized and I will be a Christian! I beg to inform you I'll be a Christian in my own way.

VINNIE. Clare, don't you want to meet us all in Heaven?

FATHER. Of course! And I'm going to!

VINNIE. But you can't go to Heaven if you're not baptized!

FATHER. That's a lot of folderol!

VINNIE. Clarence Day, don't you blaspheme like that! You're coming to church with me before you go to the office in the morning and be baptized then and there!

FATHER. Vinnie, don't be ridiculous! If you think I'm going to stand there and have some minister splash water on me at my age, you're mistaken!

VINNIE. But, Clare—

FATHER. That's enough of this, Vinnie. I'm hungry. (Draws himself up and starts for the door. He does not realize that he and VINNIE are now engaged in a battle to the death.) I'm dressing for dinner. (Throws open the doors, revealing WHITNEY and HARLAN, who obviously have been eavesdropping and have heard the awful revelation of FATHER's paganism. FATHER *stalks past them upstairs. The two boys come down into the room staring at their mother, who has been standing, too shocked at* FATHER'S *callous impiety to speak or move.)*

WHITNEY. Mother, if Father hasn't been baptized he hasn't any name. In the sight of the Church he hasn't any name.

VINNIE. That's right! *(To herself.)* Maybe we're not even married!

(This awful thought takes possession of VINNIE. *Her eyes turn slowly toward the children and she suddenly realizes their doubtful status. Her hand goes to her mouth to cover a quick gasp of horror as the curtain falls.)*

CURTAIN

ACT TWO

SCENE I

The same.
The following Sunday. After church.
The stage is empty as the curtain rises. VINNIE *comes into the archway from the street door, dressed in her Sunday best, carrying her prayer book, hymnal, and a cold indignation. As soon as she is in the room,* FATHER *passes across the hall in his Sunday cutaway and silk hat, carrying gloves and cane.* VINNIE *looks over her shoulder at him as he disappears.* CORA, WHITNEY, *and* HARLAN *come into the room,* CORA *glancing after* FATHER *and then toward* VINNIE. *All three walk as though the sound of a footfall might cause an explosion, and speak in subdued tones.*

HARLAN. Cousin Cora, will you play a game of tiddle-dy-winks with me before you go?

CORA. I'm going to be busy packing until it's time to leave.

WHITNEY. We can't play games on Sunday. *(We hear the door close and* JOHN *enters and looks into the room apprehensively.)*

CORA. John, where are Clarence and Mary?

JOHN. They dropped behind—'way behind! *(He goes upstairs.* WHITNEY *takes* HARLAN'S *hat from him and starts toward the arch.)*

VINNIE. Whitney, don't hang up your hat. I want you to go over to Sherry's for the ice-cream for dinner. Tell Mr. Sherry strawberry—if he has it. And take Harlan with you.

WHITNEY. All right, Mother. *(He and* HARLAN, *trained in the good manners of the period, bow and exit.)*

CORA. Oh, Vinnie, I hate to leave. We've had such a lovely week.

VINNIE *(voice quivers in a tone of scandalized apology).* Cora, what must you think of Clare, making such a scene on his way out of church today?

CORA. Cousin Clare probably thinks that you put the rector up to preaching that sermon.

VINNIE *(tone changes from apology to self-defense with overtones of guilt).* Well, I had to go to see Dr. Lloyd to find out whether we were really married. The sermon on baptism was his own idea. If Clare just hadn't *shouted* so—now the whole congregation knows he's never been baptized! But he's going to be, Cora— you mark my words—he's going to be! I just couldn't go to Heaven without Clare. Why, I get lonesome for him when I go to Ohio.

(FATHER enters holding his watch. He's also holding his temper. He speaks quietly.)

FATHER. Vinnie, I went to the dining-room and the table isn't set for dinner yet.

VINNIE. We're having dinner late today.

FATHER. Why can't I have my meals on time?

VINNIE. The girls' train leaves at one-thirty. Their cab's coming at one o'clock.

FATHER. Cab? The horse cars go right past our door.

VINNIE. They have those heavy bags.

FATHER. Clarence and John could have gone along to carry their bags. Cabs are just a waste of money. Why didn't we have an early dinner?

VINNIE. There wasn't time for an early dinner and church, too.

FATHER. As far as I'm concerned this would have been a good day to miss church.

VINNIE (spiritedly). I wish we had!

FATHER (flaring). I'll bet you put him up to preaching that sermon!

VINNIE. I've never been so mortified in all my life! You stamping up the aisle roaring your head off at the top of your voice!

FATHER. That Lloyd needn't preach at me as though I were some damn criminal! I wanted him to know it, and as far as I'm concerned the whole congregation can know it, too!

VINNIE. They certainly know it now!

FATHER. That suits me!

VINNIE (pleading). Clare, you don't seem to understand what the church is for.

FATHER (laying down a new Commandment). Vinnie, if there's one place the church should leave alone, it's a man's soul!

VINNIE. Clare, dear, don't you believe what it says in the Bible?

FATHER. A man has to use his common sense about the Bible, Vinnie, if he has any. For instance, you'd be in a pretty fix if I gave all my money to the poor.

VINNIE. Well, that's just silly!

FATHER. Speaking of money—where are this month's bills?

VINNIE. Clare, it isn't fair to go over the household accounts while you're hungry.

FATHER. Where are those bills, Vinnie?

VINNIE. They're downstairs on your desk. FATHER exits almost eagerly. Figures are

something he understands better than he does women.) Of all times! (To CORA.) It's awfully hard on a woman to love a man like Clare so much.

CORA. Yes, men can be aggravating. Clyde gets me so provoked! We kept company for six years, but the minute he proposed —the moment I said "Yes"—he began to take me for granted.

VINNIE. You have to expect that, Cora. I don't believe Clare has come right out and told me he loves me since we've been married. Of course I know he does, because I keep reminding him of it. You have to keep reminding them, Cora.

(The door slams.)

CORA. That must be Mary and Clarence.

(There's a moment's pause. The two women look toward the hall—then at each other with a knowing sort of smile. CORA rises, goes up to the arch, peeks out —then faces front and innocently asks:) Is that you, Mary?

MARY (dashing in). Yes!

(CLARENCE crosses the arch to hang up his hat.)

CORA. We have to change our clothes and finish our packing. (Goes upstairs.)

(CLARENCE returns as MARY starts up the stairs.)

MARY (to CLARENCE). It won't take me long.

CLARENCE. Can I help you pack?

VINNIE (shocked). Clarence! (MARY runs upstairs. CLARENCE drifts into the living-room, somewhat abashed. VINNIE collects her hat and gloves, starts out, stops to look at CLARENCE, then comes down to him.) Clarence, why didn't you kneel in church today?

CLARENCE. What, Mother?

VINNIE. Why didn't you kneel in church today?

CLARENCE (troubled). I just couldn't.

VINNIE. Has it anything to do with Mary? I know she's a Methodist.

CLARENCE. Oh, no, Mother! Methodists kneel. Mary told me. They don't get up and down so much, but they stay down longer.

VINNIE. If it's because your father doesn't kneel—you must remember he wasn't brought up to kneel in church. But you were—you always have—and, Clarence, you want to, don't you?

CLARENCE. Oh, yes! I wanted to today! I started to—you saw me start—but I just couldn't.

VINNIE. Is that suit of your father's too tight for you?

CLARENCE. No, it's not too *tight*. It fits fine. But it *is* the suit. Very peculiar things have happened to me since I started to wear it. I haven't been myself since I put it on.

VINNIE. In what way, Clarence? How do you mean?

(CLARENCE *pauses, then blurts out his problem.*)

CLARENCE. Mother, I can't seem to make these clothes do anything Father wouldn't do!

VINNIE. That's nonsense, Clarence—and not to kneel in church is a sacrilege.

CLARENCE. But making Father's trousers kneel seemed more of a sacrilege.

VINNIE. Clarence!

CLARENCE. No! Remember the first time I wore this? It was at Dora Wakefield's party for Mary. Do you know what happened? We were playing musical chairs and Dora Wakefield sat down suddenly right in my lap. I jumped up so fast she almost got hurt.

VINNIE. But it was all perfectly innocent.

CLARENCE. It wasn't that Dora was sitting on my lap—she was sitting on Father's trousers. Mother, I've got to have a suit of my own. (CLARENCE's *metaphysical problem is one that* VINNIE *can't cope with at this particular minute.*)

VINNIE. My soul and body! Clarence, you have a talk with your father about it. I'm sure if you approach him the right way—you know—tactfully—he'll see—

(MARY *comes downstairs and hesitates at the arch.*)

MARY. Oh, excuse me.

VINNIE. Gracious! Have you finished your packing?

MARY. Practically. I never put my comb and brush in until I'm ready to close my bag.

VINNIE. I must see Margaret about your box lunch for the train. I'll leave you two together. Remember, it's Sunday. (*She goes downstairs.*)

CLARENCE. I was hoping we could have a few minutes together before you left.

MARY (*not to admit her eagerness*). Cora had so much to do I wanted to get out of her way.

CLARENCE. Well, didn't you want to see me?

MARY (*self-consciously*). I did want to tell you how much I've enjoyed our friendship.

CLARENCE. You're going to write me when you get to Springfield, aren't you?

MARY. Of course, if you write me first.

CLARENCE. But you'll have something to write about—your trip—and Aunt Judith —and how things are in Springfield. You write me as soon as you get there.

MARY. Maybe I'll be too busy. Maybe I won't have time. (*She sits on the sofa.*)

CLARENCE (*with the authority of* FATHER'S *trousers*). You find the time! Let's not have any nonsense about that! You'll write me first—and you'll do it right away, the first day! (*Sits beside her.*)

MARY. How do you know I'll take orders from you?

CLARENCE. I'll show you. (*He takes a quick glance toward the hall.*) Give me your hand!

MARY. Why should I?

CLARENCE. Give me your hand, confound it!

(MARY *gives it to him.*)

MARY. What do you want with my hand?

CLARENCE. I just wanted it. (*Holding her hand, he melts a little and smiles at her. She melts, too. Their hands, clasped together, are resting on* CLARENCE's *knee nd they relax happily.)* What are you *h*inking about?

MARY. I was just thinking.

*C*LARENCE. About what?

*M*ARY. Well, when we were talking about *w*riting each other I was hoping you'd *w*rite me first because that would mean *y*ou liked me.

*C*LARENCE *(with the logic of the male).* *W*hat's writing first got to do with my *l*iking you?

MARY. Oh, you *do* like me?

*C*LARENCE. Of course I do. I like you *b*etter than any girl I ever met.

MARY *(with the logic of the female).* But *y*ou don't like me well enough to write *f*irst?

*C*LARENCE. I don't see how one thing's got *a*nything to do with the other.

MARY. But a girl can't write first—because *s*he's a *girl.*

*C*LARENCE. That doesn't make sense. If a *g*irl has something to write about and a *f*ellow hasn't, there's no reason why she *s*houldn't write first.

MARY *(starting a flanking movement).* You know, the first few days I was here *y*ou'd do anything for me and then you *c*hanged. You used to be a lot of fun— *a*nd then all of a sudden you turned into *a*n old sober-sides.

*C*LARENCE. When did I?

MARY. The first time I noticed it was *w*hen we walked home from Dora Wake-*f*ield's party. My, you were on your dig-*n*ity! You've been that way ever since. You even dress like an old sober-sides. *(*CLARENCE's *face changes as* FATHER's *pants rise to haunt him. Then he notices that their clasped hands are resting on these very pants, and he lifts them off. Agony obviously is setting in.* MARY *sees the expression on his face.)* What's the matter?

CLARENCE. I just happened to remember *s*omething.

MARY. What? *(*CLARENCE *doesn't answer, but his face does.)* Oh, I know. This is *t*he last time we'll be together. *(She puts her hand on his shoulder. He draws away.)*

CLARENCE. Mary, please!

MARY. But, Clarence! We'll see each other in a month. And we'll be writing each other, too. I hope we will. *(She gets up.)* Oh, Clarence, please write me first, be-cause it will show me how much you like me. Please! I'll show you how much I like you! *(She throws herself on his lap and buries her head on his shoulder.* CLARENCE *stiffens in agony.)*

CLARENCE *(hoarsely).* Get up! Get up! *(She pulls back her head and looks at him, then springs from his lap and runs away, covering her face and sobbing.* CLARENCE *goes to her.)* Don't do that, Mary! Please don't do that!

MARY. Now you'll think I'm just a bold and forward girl.

CLARENCE. Oh, no!

MARY. Yes, you will—you'll think I'm bold,

CLARENCE. Oh, no—it's not that.

MARY *(hopefully).* Was it because it's Sunday?

CLARENCE *(in despair).* No, it would be the same any day— *(He is about to ex-plain, but* MARY *flares.)*

MARY. Oh, it's just because you didn't want me sitting on your lap.

CLARENCE. It was nice of you to do it.

MARY. It was nice of me! So you told me to get up! You just couldn't bear to have me sit there. Well, you needn't write me first. You needn't write me any letters at all, because I'll tear them up without opening them! *(*FATHER *enters the arch-way, a sheath of bills in his hand and his account book under his arm.)* I guess I know now you don't like me! I never want to see you again. I—I—

(She breaks and starts to run toward the stairs. At the sight of FATHER *she stops, but only for a gasp, then continues on up-stairs, unable to control her sobs.* CLARENCE, *who has been standing in unhappy indeci-sion, turns to follow her, but stops short at the sight of* FATHER, *who is standing in the arch looking at him with some amaze-ment.* FATHER *looks from* CLARENCE *toward*

the vanished MARY, *then back to* CLAR-
ENCE.)

FATHER. Clarence, that young girl is crying—she's in tears. What's the meaning
of this?

CLARENCE. I'm sorry, Father, it's all my
fault.

FATHER. Nonsense! What's that girl trying to do to you?

CLARENCE. What? No, she wasn't—it was
—I—how long have you been here?

FATHER. Well, whatever the quarrel was
about, Clarence, I'm glad you held your
own. Where's your mother?

CLARENCE *(desperately)*. I have to have a
new suit of clothes—you've *got* to give
me the money for it.

*(*FATHER's *account book reaches the table
with a sharp bang as he stares at* CLARENCE
in astonishment.)

FATHER. Young man, do you realize you're
addressing your father?

*(*CLARENCE *wilts miserably and sinks into
a chair.)*

CLARENCE. I'm sorry, Father—I apologize
—but you don't know how important this
is to me. (CLARENCE's *tone of misery gives*
FATHER *pause.)*

FATHER. A suit of clothes is so—? Now,
why should a—? *(Something dawns on*
FATHER *and he looks up in the direction
in which* MARY *has disappeared, then
looks back at* CLARENCE.) Has your need
for a suit of clothes anything to do with
that young lady?

CLARENCE. Yes, Father.

FATHER. Why, Clarence! *(Suddenly realizes
that women have come into* CLARENCE's
*emotional life and there comes a yearn-
ing to protect this inexperienced and de-
fenseless member of his own sex.)* This
comes as quite a shock to me.

CLARENCE. What does, Father?

FATHER. Your being so grown up! Still,
I might have known that if you're going
to college this fall—yes, you're at an age
when you'll be meeting girls. Clarence,
there are things about women that I think
you ought to know! *(He goes up and
closes the doors, then comes down and sits*

beside CLARENCE, *hesitating for a momen*
before he speaks.) Yes, I think it's bette
for you to hear this from me than to hav
to learn it for yourself. Clarence, wome
aren't the angels that you think they are
Well, now—first, let me explain this t
you. You see, Clarence, we men have t
run this world and it's not an easy jol
It takes work, and it takes thinking. *A*
man has to be sure of his facts an
figures. He has to reason things out. Nov
you take a woman—a woman thinks—n
I'm wrong right there—a woman doesn'
think at all! She gets stirred up! And sh
gets stirred up over the damnedest things
Now, I love my wife just as much as an
man, but that doesn't mean I should stanc
for a lot of folderol! By God! I won'
stand for it! *(Looks around toward th
spot where he had his last clash with*
VINNIE.)

CLARENCE. Stand for what, Father?

FATHER *(to himself)*. That's the one thing
I will not submit myself to. *(Has cease
explaining women to* CLARENCE *and is now
explaining himself.)* Clarence, if a mar
thinks a certain thing is the wrong thing
to do he shouldn't do it. If he thinks a
thing is right he should do it. Now tha
has nothing to do with whether he love
his wife or not.

CLARENCE. Who says it has, Father?

FATHER. They do!

CLARENCE. Who, sir?

FATHER. Women! They get stirred up anc
then they try to get you stirred up, too
If you can keep reason and logic in the
argument, a man can hold his own, of
course. But if they can *switch* you—pretty
soon the argument's about whether you
love them or not. I swear I don't know
how they do it! Don't you let 'em, Clarence! Don't you let 'em!

CLARENCE. I see what you mean so far
Father. If you don't watch yourself, love
can make you do a lot of things you don't
want to do.

FATHER. Exactly!

CLARENCE. But if you do watch out and
know just how to handle women—

FATHER. Then you'll be all right. All a
man has to do is be firm. You know how
sometimes I have to be firm with your

nother. Just now about this month's household accounts—

CLARENCE. Yes, but what can you do when they cry?

FATHER (he gives this a moment's thought). Well, that's quite a question. You just have to make them understand that what you're doing is for their good.

CLARENCE. I see.

FATHER (rising). Now, Clarence, you know all about women. (Goes to the table and sits down in front of his account book, opening it. CLARENCE rises and looks at him.)

CLARENCE. But, Father—

FATHER. Yes, Clarence.

CLARENCE. I thought you were going to tell me about—

FATHER. About what?

CLARENCE. About women.

FATHER realizes with some shock that CLARENCE expected him to be more specific.)

FATHER. Clarence, there are some things gentlemen don't discuss! I've told you all you need to know. The thing for you to remember is—be firm. (CLARENCE turns away. There is a knock at the sliding doors.) Yes, come in.

(MARY opens the doors.)

MARY. Excuse me!

(MARY enters. FATHER turns his attention to the household accounts. MARY goes to the couch and picks up her hankerchief and continues around the couch. CLARENCE crosses to meet her above the couch, determined to be firm. MARY passes him without a glance. CLARENCE wilts, then again assuming firmness, turns up into the arch in an attempt to quail MARY with a look. MARY marches upstairs ignoring him. CLARENCE turns back into the room defeated. He looks down at his clothes unhappily, then decides to be firm with his father. He straightens up and steps toward him. At this moment FATHER, staring at a bill, emits his cry of rage.)

FATHER. Oh, God!

(CLARENCE retreats. FATHER rises and holds the bill in question between thumb and forefinger as though it were too repulsive to touch. VINNIE comes rushing down the stairs.)

VINNIE. What's the matter, Clare? What's wrong?

FATHER. I will not send this person a check!

(VINNIE looks at it.)

VINNIE. Why, Clare, that's the only hat I've bought since March and it was reduced from forty dollars.

FATHER. I don't question your buying the hat or what you paid for it, but the person from whom you bought it—this Mademoiselle Mimi—isn't fit to be in the hat business or any other.

VINNIE. I never went there before, but it's a very nice place and I don't see why you object to it.

FATHER (exasperated). I object to it because this confounded person doesn't put her name on her bills! Mimi what? Mimi O'Brien? Mimi Jones? Mimi Weinstein?

VINNIE. How do I know? It's just Mimi.

FATHER. It isn't just Mimi. She must have some other name, damn it! Now, I wouldn't make out a check payable to Charley or to Jimmy, and I won't make out a check payable to Mimi. Find out what her last name is, and I'll pay her the money.

VINNIE. All right. All right. (She starts out.)

FATHER. Just a minute, Vinnie, that isn't all.

VINNIE. But Cora will be leaving any minute, Clare, and it isn't polite for me—

FATHER. Never mind Cora. Sit down. (CLARENCE goes into the hall, looks upstairs, wanders up and down the hall restlessly. VINNIE reluctantly sits down opposite FATHER at the table.) Vinnie, you know I like to live well, and I want my family to live well. But this house must be run on a business basis. I must know how much money I'm spending and what for. For instance, if you recall, two weeks ago I gave you six dollars to buy a new coffee pot—

VINNIE. Yes, because you broke the old one. You threw it right on the floor.

FATHER. I'm not talking about that. I'm simply endeavoring—

VINNIE. But it was so silly to break that nice coffee pot, Clare, and there was nothing the matter with the coffee that morning. It was made just the same as always.

FATHER. It was not! It was made in a damned barbaric manner!

VINNIE. I couldn't get another imported one. That little shop has stopped selling them. They said the tariff wouldn't let them. And that's your fault, Clare, because you're always voting to raise the tariff.

FATHER. The tariff protects America against cheap foreign labor. (*He sounds as though he is quoting.*) Now I find that—

VINNIE. The tariff does nothing but put up the prices and that's hard on everybody, especially the farmer. (*She sounds as though she is quoting back.*)

FATHER (*annoyed*). I wish to God you wouldn't talk about matters you don't know a damn thing about!

VINNIE. I do too know about them. Miss Gulick says every intelligent woman should have some opinion—

FATHER. Who, may I ask, is Miss Gulick?

VINNIE. Why, she's that current-events woman I told you about and the tickets are a dollar every Tuesday.

FATHER. Do you mean to tell me that a pack of idle-minded females pay a dollar apiece to hear another female gabble about the events of the day? Listen to me if you want to know anything about the events of the day!

VINNIE. But you get so excited, Clare, and besides, Miss Gulick says that our President, whom you're always belittling, prays to God for guidance and—

FATHER (*having had enough of Miss Gulick*). Vinnie, what happened to that six dollars?

VINNIE. What six dollars?

FATHER. I gave you six dollars to buy a new coffee pot and now I find that you apparently got one at Lewis & Conger's and charged it. Here's their bill: "One coffee pot—five dollars."

VINNIE. So you owe me a dollar and you can hand it right over. (*She holds out her hand for it.*)

FATHER. I'll do nothing of the kind! What did you do with that six dollars?

VINNIE. Why, Clare, I can't tell you now, dear. Why didn't you ask me at the time?

FATHER. Oh, my God!

VINNIE. Wait a moment! I spent four dollars and a half for that new umbrella I told you I wanted and you said I didn't need, but I did, very much.

(FATHER *takes his pencil and writes in the account book.*)

FATHER. Now we're getting somewhere. One umbrella—four dollars and a half.

VINNIE. And that must have been the week I paid Mrs. Tobin for two extra days' washing.

FATHER (*entering the item*). Mrs. Tobin.

VINNIE. So that was two dollars more.

FATHER. Two dollars.

VINNIE. That makes six dollars and fifty cents. And that's another fifty cents you owe me.

FATHER. I don't owe you anything. (*Stung by* VINNIE's *tactics into a determination to pin her butterfly mind down.*) What you owe me is an explanation of where my money's gone! We're going over this account book item by item. (*Starts to sort the bills for the purposes of cross-examination, but the butterfly takes wing again.*)

VINNIE. I do the very best I can to keep down expenses. And you know yourself that Cousin Phoebe spends twice as much as we do.

FATHER. Damn Cousin Phoebe!—I don't wish to be told how she throws her money around.

VINNIE. Oh, Clare, how can you? And I thought you were so fond of Cousin Phoebe.

FATHER. All right, I am fond of Cousin Phoebe, but I can get along without hearing so much about her.

VINNIE. You talk about your own relatives enough.

FATHER (hurt). That's not fair, Vinnie. When I talk about my relatives I criticize them.

VINNIE. If I can't even speak of Cousin Phoebe—

FATHER. You can speak of her all you want to—but I won't have Cousin Phoebe or anyone else dictating to me how to run my house. Now this month's total—

VINNIE (righteously). I didn't say a word about her dictating, Clare—she isn't that kind!

FATHER (dazed). I don't know what you said, now. You never stick to the point. I endeavor to show you how to run this house on a business basis and you wind up by jibbering and jabbering about everything under the sun. If you'll just explain to me—

(Finally cornered, VINNIE realizes the time has come for tears. Quietly she turns them on.)

VINNIE. I don't know what you expect of me. I tire myself out chasing up and down those stairs all day long—trying to look after your comfort—to bring up our children—I do the mending and the marketing and as if that isn't enough, you want me to be an expert bookkeeper, too.

FATHER (touched where VINNIE has hoped to touch him). Vinnie, I want to be reasonable; but can't you understand?—I'm doing all this for your own good. (VINNIE rises with a moan. FATHER sighs with resignation.) I suppose I'll have to go ahead just paying the bills and hoping I've got enough money in the bank to meet them. But it's all very discouraging.

VINNIE. I'll try to do better, Clare.

(FATHER looks up into her tearful face and melts.)

FATHER. That's all I'm asking. (She goes to him and puts her arm around his shoulder.) I'll go down and make out the checks and sign them. (VINNIE doesn't seem entirely consoled, so he attempts a lighter note to cheer her up.) Oh, Vinnie, maybe I haven't any right to sign those checks, since in the sight of the Lord I haven't any name at all. Do you suppose the bank will feel that way about it too —or do you think they'll take a chance?

(He should not have said this.)

VINNIE. That's right! Clare, to make those checks good you'll have to be baptized right away.

FATHER (retreating angrily). Vinnie, the bank doesn't care whether I've been baptized or not!

VINNIE. Well, I care! And no matter what Dr. Lloyd says, I'm not sure we're really married.

FATHER. Damn it, Vinnie, we have four children! If we're not married now we never will be!

VINNIE. Oh, Clare, don't you see how serious this is? You've got to do something about it.

FATHER. Well, just now I've got to do something about these damn bills you've run up. (Sternly.) I'm going downstairs.

VINNIE. Not before you give me that dollar and a half!

FATHER. What dollar and a half?

VINNIE. The dollar and a half you owe me!

FATHER (thoroughly enraged). I don't owe you any dollar and a half! I gave you money to buy a coffee pot for me and somehow it turned into an umbrella for you.

VINNIE. Clarence Day, what kind of a man are you? Quibbling about a dollar and a half when your immortal soul is in danger! And what's more—

FATHER. All right. All right. All right. (He takes the dollar and a half from his change purse and gives it to her.)

VINNIE (smiling). Thank you, Clare.

(VINNIE turns and leaves the room. Her progress upstairs is a one-woman march of triumph.)

(FATHER puts his purse back, gathers up his papers and his dignity, and starts out. CLARENCE waylays him in the arch.)

CLARENCE. Father—you never did tell me—can I have a new suit of clothes?

FATHER. No, Clarence! I'm sorry, but I have to be firm with you, too!

(He stalks off. JOHN *comes down the stairs carrying a traveling bag, which he takes out toward the front door. He returns empty-handed and starts up the stairs again.)*

CLARENCE. John, come here a minute.

JOHN *(coming into the room).* What do you want?

CLARENCE. John, have you got any money you could lend me?

JOHN. With this week's allowance, I'll have about three dollars.

CLARENCE. That's no good. I've got to have enough to buy a new suit of clothes.

JOHN. Why don't you earn some money? That's what I'm going to do. I'm going to buy a bicycle—one of those new low kind, with both wheels the same size—you know, a safety.

CLARENCE. How are you going to earn that much money?

JOHN. I've got a job practically. Look, I found this ad in the paper. *(He hands* CLARENCE *a clipping from his pocket.)*

CLARENCE *(reading).* "Wanted, an energetic young man to handle household necessity that sells on sight. Liberal commissions. Apply 312 West Fourteenth Street, Tuesday from eight to twelve." Listen, John, let me have that job.

JOHN. Why should I give you my job? They're hard to get.

CLARENCE. But I've got to have a new suit of clothes.

JOHN. Maybe I could get a job for both of us. *(The doorbell rings.)* I'll tell you what I'll do, I'll ask the man.

FATHER *(hurrying to the foot of the stairs).* Vinnie! Cora! The cab's here. Hurry up! *(Goes through the arch toward the front door.)*

CLARENCE. We've both got to get down there early Tuesday—the first thing.

JOHN. Oh, no you don't—I'm going alone But I'll put in a good word with the bos about you.

FATHER *(off).* They'll be right out. Vinnie Cora! *(He comes back to the foot of the stairs and calls up.)* Are you coming? The cab's waiting!

VINNIE *(from upstairs).* We heard you Clare. We'll be down in a minute.

*(*FATHER *comes into the room.)*

FATHER. John, go upstairs and hurry then down.

*(*JOHN *goes upstairs.* FATHER *crosses to the window and looks out, then consults his watch.)*

FATHER. What's the matter with those women? Don't they know cabs cost money? Clarence, go see what's causing this infernal delay!

*(*CLARENCE *goes out to the hall.)*

CLARENCE. Here they come, Father.

*(*MARY *comes sedately downstairs. She passes* CLARENCE *without a glance and goes to* FATHER.*)*

MARY. Goodbye, Mr. Day. I can't tell you how much I appreciate your hospitality

FATHER. Not at all! Not at all!

*(*VINNIE *and* CORA *appear at top of stairs and come down.* JOHN *follows with the bags and takes them out.)*

CORA. Goodbye, Clarence. *(She starts into the room.)*

FATHER. Cora, we can say goodbye to you on the sidewalk.

VINNIE. There's no hurry. Their train doesn't go until one-thirty.

FATHER. Cabs cost money. If they have any waiting to do they ought to do it at the Grand Central Depot. They've got a waiting-room there just for that.

VINNIE *(to* MARY*).* If there's one thing Mr. Day can't stand it's to keep a cab waiting.

CORA. It's been so nice seeing you again, Clarence. *(She kisses him.)*

*(*MARGARET *enters with a box of lunch.)*

MARGARET. Here's the lunch.

FATHER. All right. All right. Give it to me. Let's get started.

(MARGARET *gives it to him and exits.*)

CORA. Where's John?

FATHER. He's outside. Come on. *(Leads the way.* CORA *and* VINNIE *follow.* MARY *starts.)*

CLARENCE. Mary, aren't you going even to shake hands with me?

MARY. I don't think I'd better. You may remember that when I get too close to you you feel contaminated. *(Starts out.* CLARENCE *follows her.)*

CLARENCE. Mary! *(She stops in the arch. He goes to her.)* You're going to write me, aren't you?

MARY. Are you going to write first?

CLARENCE *(resolutely).* No, Mary. There are times when a man has to be firm.

(John enters.)

JOHN. Mary, Mother says you'd better hurry out before Father starts yelling. It's Sunday.

MARY. Goodbye, John. I'm very happy to have made *your* acquaintance.

(She walks out. We hear the door close. JOHN *goes out.* CLARENCE *takes a step toward the door, stops, suffers a moment, then turns to the writing desk, takes paper and pen and ink to the table, and sits down to write a letter.)*

CLARENCE *(writing).* Dear Mary—

CURTAIN

SCENE II

The same.
Two days later. The breakfast table.
HARLAN *and* WHITNEY *are at the table, ready to start breakfast.* CLARENCE *is near the window reading the paper. The places of* JOHN *and* VINNIE *and* FATHER *are empty.* NORA, *a new maid, is serving the fruit and cereal.* NORA *is heavily built and along toward middle age. The doorbell rings and we hear the postman's whistle.* CLARENCE *drops the paper and looks out the window toward the door.* NORA *starts toward the arch.*

CLARENCE. Never mind, Nora. It's the postman. I'll go. *(He runs out through the arch.)*

WHITNEY *(to* NORA*).* You forgot the sugar. It goes here between me and Father.

*(*CLARENCE *comes back with three or four letters which he sorts eagerly. Then his face falls in utter dejection.* FATHER *comes down the stairs.)*

FATHER. Good morning, boys! John late? *(He shouts).* John! John! Hurry down to your breakfast.

CLARENCE. John had his breakfast early, Father, and went out to see about something.

FATHER. See about what?

CLARENCE. John and I thought we'd work this summer and earn some money.

FATHER. Good! Sit down boys. *(Goes to his chair.)*

CLARENCE. We saw an ad in the paper and John went down to see about it.

FATHER. Why didn't you go, too?

CLARENCE. I was expecting an answer to a letter I wrote, but it didn't come. Here's the mail. *(He seems depressed.)*

FATHER *(sitting).* What kind of work is this you're planning to do?

CLARENCE. Sort of salesman, the ad said.

FATHER. Um-hum. Well, work never hurt anybody. It's good for them. But if you're going to work, work hard. King Solomon had the right idea about work. "Whatever thy hand findeth to do," Solomon said, "do thy damnedest!" Where's your mother?

NORA. If you please, sir, Mrs. Day doesn't want any breakfast. She isn't feeling well, so she went back upstairs to lie down again.

FATHER (*uneasily*). Now, why does your mother do that to me? She knows it just upsets my day when she doesn't come down to breakfast. Clarence, go tell your mother I'll be up to see her before I start for the office.

CLARENCE. Yes, sir. (*He goes upstairs.*)

HARLAN. What's the matter with Mother?

FATHER. There's nothing the matter with your mother. Perfectly healthy woman. She gets an ache or a twinge and instead of being firm about it, she just gives in to it. (*The postman whistles. Then the doorbell rings.* NORA *answers it.*) Boys, after breakfast you find out what your mother wants you to do today. Whitney, you take care of Harlan.

(NORA *comes back with a special-delivery letter.*)

NORA. It's a special delivery.

(*She hands it to* FATHER, *who tears it open at once.* CLARENCE *comes rushing down the stairs.*)

CLARENCE. Was that the postman again?

WHITNEY. It was a special delivery.

CLARENCE. Yes? Where is it?

WHITNEY. It was for Father.

CLARENCE (*again disappointed*). Oh— (*He sits at the table.*)

(FATHER *has opened the letter and is reading it. Bewildered, he turns it over and looks at the signature.*)

FATHER. I don't understand this at all. Here's a letter from some woman I never even heard of.

(FATHER *tackles the letter again.* CLARENCE *sees the envelope, picks it up, looks at the postmark, worried.*)

CLARENCE. Father!

FATHER. Oh, God!

CLARENCE. What is it, Father?

FATHER. This is the damnedest nonsense I ever read! As far as I can make out this woman claims that she sat on my lap and I didn't like it. (CLARENCE *begins to turn red.* FATHER *goes on reading a little further and then holds the letter over in front of* CLARENCE.) Can you make out what that word is? (CLARENCE *begins* *feverishly to read as much as possible, but* FATHER *cuts in.*) No, that word right there. (*He points.*)

CLARENCE. It looks like—"curiosity."

(FATHER *withdraws the letter,* CLARENCE'S *eyes following it hungrily.*)

FATHER (*reads*). "I only opened your letter as a matter of curiosity." (*Breaks off reading aloud as he turns the page.*)

CLARENCE. Yes? Go on.

FATHER. Why, this gets worse and worse! It just turns into a lot of sentimental lovey-dovey mush. (*Crushes the letter, stalks across the room, and throws it into the fireplace,* CLARENCE *watching him with dismay.*) Is this someone's idea of a practical joke? Why must I be the butt—

(VINNIE *comes hurrying down the stairs. Her hair is down in two braids over her shoulder. She is wearing a lacy combing jacket over her corset cover, and a striped petticoat.*)

VINNIE. What's the matter, Clare? What's wrong?

FATHER (*going to her*). Nothing wrong— just a damn fool letter. How are you, Vinnie?

VINNIE (*weakly*). I don't feel well. I thought you needed me, but if you don't I'll go back to bed.

FATHER. No, now that you're here, sit down with us. (*He moves out her chair.*) Get some food in your stomach. Do you good.

VINNIE (*protesting*). I don't feel like eating anything, Clare.

(NORA *enters with a tray of bacon and eggs, stops at the serving table.*)

FATHER (*heartily*). That's all the more reason why you should eat. Build up your strength! (*He forces* VINNIE *into her chair and turns to speak to* NORA, *who has her back to him.*) Here— (*Then to* CLARENCE.) What's this one's name?

CLARENCE. Nora.

FATHER. Nora! Give Mrs. Day some of the bacon and eggs.

VINNIE. No, Clare! (NORA, *however, has gone to* VINNIE'S *side with the platter.*)

No, take it away, Nora. I don't even want to smell it.

(The maid retreats, and serves FATHER; *then* CLARENCE; *then serves coffee and exits.)*

FATHER. Vinnie, it's just weak to give in to an ailment. Any disease can be cured by firmness. What you need is strength of character.

VINNIE. I don't know why you object to my complaining a little. I notice when you have a headache you yell and groan and swear enough.

FATHER. Of course I yell! That's to prove to the headache that I'm stronger than it is. I can usually swear it right out of my system.

VINNIE. This isn't a headache. I think I've caught some kind of a germ. There's a lot of sickness around. Several of my friends have had to send for the doctor. I may have the same thing.

FATHER. I'll bet this is all your imagination, Vinnie. You hear of a lot of other people having some disease and then you get scared and think you have it yourself. So you go to bed and send for the doctor. The doctor—all poppycock!

VINNIE. I didn't say anything about my sending for the doctor.

FATHER. I should hope not. Doctors think they know a damn lot, but they don't.

VINNIE. But Clare, dear, when people are seriously ill you have to do something.

FATHER. Certainly you have to do something! Cheer 'em up—that's the way to cure 'em!

VINNIE *(with slight irony).* How would you go about cheering them up?

FATHER. I? I'd tell 'em—bah! *(VINNIE, out of exasperation and weakness, begins to cry.* FATHER *looks at her amazed.)* What have I done now?

VINNIE. Oh, Clare—hush up! *(She moves from the table to the sofa, where she tries to control her crying.* HARLAN *slides out of his chair and runs over to her.)* Harlan dear, keep away from Mother. You might catch what she's got. Whitney, if you've finished your breakfast—

WHITNEY *(rising).* Yes, Mother.

VINNIE. I promised Mrs. Whitehead to send over Margaret's recipe for floating-island pudding. Margaret has it all written out. And take Harlan with you.

WHITNEY. All right, Mother. I hope you feel better.

(WHITNEY and HARLAN exit. FATHER *goes over and sits beside* VINNIE *on the sofa.)*

FATHER. Vinnie. *(Contritely.)* I didn't mean to upset you. I was just trying to help. *(He pats her hand.)* When you take to your bed I have a damned lonely time around here. So when I see you getting it into your head that you're sick, I want to do something about it. *(He continues to pat her hand vigorously with what he thinks is reassurance.)* Just because some of your friends have given in to this is no reason why you should imagine you're sick, Vinnie.

VINNIE *(snatching her hand away).* Oh, stop, Clare!—get out of this house and go to your office!

*(FATHER *is a little bewildered and somewhat indignant at this rebuff to his tenderness. He gets up and goes out into the hall, comes back with his hat and stick, and marches out of the house, slamming the door.* VINNIE *rises and starts toward the stairs.)*

CLARENCE. I'm sorry you're not feeling well, Mother.

VINNIE. Oh, I'll be all right, Clarence. Remember last fall I had a touch of this and I was all right the next morning.

CLARENCE. Are you sure you don't want the doctor?

VINNIE. Oh, no. I really don't need him—and besides doctors worry your father. I don't want him to be upset.

CLARENCE. Is there anything I can do for you?

VINNIE. Ask Margaret to send me up a cup of tea. I'll try to drink it. I'm going back to bed.

CLARENCE. Do you mind if John and I go out today or will you need us?

VINNIE. You run right along. I just want to be left alone.

(She exits up the stairs. CLARENCE *starts for the fireplace eager to retrieve Mary's letter.* NORA *enters. He stops.)*

CLARENCE. Oh!—Nora—will you take a cup of tea up to Mrs. Day in her room?

NORA. Yes, sir. *(Exits.)*

*(*CLARENCE *hurries around the table, gets the crumpled letter, and starts to read it feverishly. He reads quickly to the end, then draws a deep, happy breath. The door slams. He puts the letter in his pocket.* JOHN *enters, carrying two heavy packages.)*

CLARENCE. Did you get the job?

JOHN. Yes, for both of us. Look, I've got it with me.

CLARENCE. What is it?

JOHN. Medicine.

CLARENCE *(dismayed)*. Medicine! You took a job for us to go out and sell medicine!

JOHN. But it's wonderful medicine. *(Gets a bottle out of the package and reads from the label.)* "Bartlett's Beneficent Balm—A Boon to Mankind." Look what it cures! *(He hands the bottle to* CLARENCE.*)*

CLARENCE *(reading)*. "A sovereign cure for colds, coughs, catarrh, asthma, quincy, and sore throat; poor digestion, summer complaint, colic, dyspepsia, heartburn, and shortness of breath; lumbago, rheumatism, heart disease, giddiness, and women's complaints; nervous prostration, St. Vitus' dance, jaundice, and la grippe; proud flesh, pink eye, seasickness, and pimples."

(As CLARENCE *has read off the list he has become more and more impressed.)*

JOHN. See?

CLARENCE. Say, that sounds all right!

JOHN. It's made "from a secret formula known only to Dr. Bartlett."

CLARENCE. He must be quite a doctor!

JOHN *(enthusiastically)*. It sells for a dollar a bottle and we get twenty-five cents commission on every bottle.

CLARENCE. Well, where does he want us to sell it?

JOHN. He's given us the territory of all Manhattan Island.

CLARENCE. That's bully! Anybody that's

sick at all ought to need a bottle of thi Let's start by calling on friends of Fathe and Mother.

JOHN. That's a good idea. But wait minute. Suppose they ask us if we us it at our house?

CLARENCE *(a little worried)*. Oh, yes. would be better if we could say we did.

JOHN. But we can't because we haven' had it here long enough.

*(*NORA *enters with a tray with a cup o tea. She goes to the table and puts th sugar bowl and cream pitcher on it.)*

CLARENCE. Is that the tea for Mrs. Day?

NORA. Yes.

(The suspicion of a good idea dawns o CLARENCE*).*

CLARENCE. I'll take it up to her. Yo needn't bother.

NORA. Thank you. Take it up right awa while it's hot. *(She exits.* CLARENCE *watche her out.)*

CLARENCE *(eyeing* JOHN*)*. Mother wasn' feeling well this morning.

JOHN. What was the matter with her?

CLARENCE. I don't know—she was jus complaining.

JOHN *(getting the idea immediately an consulting the bottle)*. Well, it says her it's good for women's complaints.

(They look at each other. CLARENCE *open the bottle and smells its contents.* JOH leans over and takes a sniff, too. Then h nods to* CLARENCE, *who quickly reache for a spoon and measures out a teaspoon ful, which he puts into the tea.* JOHN, *want ing to be sure* MOTHER *has enough to cur her, pours still more into the tea fron the bottle as the curtain falls.)*

*(*THE CURTAIN *remains down for a few seconds to denote a lapse of three hours.*

(When the curtain rises again, the break fast things have been cleared and the room is in order. HARLAN *is kneeling on* FATHER' *chair looking out the window as if watch ing for someone.* MARGARET *comes dow from upstairs.)*

MARGARET. Has your father come yet?

HARLAN. Not yet.

(NORA *enters from downstairs with a steaming tea-kettle and a towel and meets* MARGARET *in the hall.*)

MARGARET. Hurry that upstairs. The doctor's waiting for it. I've got to go out.

NORA. Where are you going?

MARGARET. I have to go and get the minister. (NORA *goes upstairs.*)

HARLAN. There's a cab coming up the street.

MARGARET. Well, I hope it's him, poor man—but a cab doesn't sound like your father. (*She hurries downstairs.*)

(HARLAN *sees something through the window, then rushes to the stairwell and shouts down to* MARGARET.)

HARLAN. Yes, it's Father. Whitney got him all right. (*Runs back to the window. The front door slams and* FATHER *crosses the arch and hurries upstairs.* WHITNEY *comes into the room.*) What took you so long?

WHITNEY. Long? I wasn't long. I went right down on the elevated and got Father right away and we came all the way back in a cab.

HARLAN. I thought you were never coming.

WHITNEY. Well, the horse didn't go very fast at first. The cabby whipped him and swore at him and still he wouldn't gallop. Then Father spoke to the horse personally— How is Mother?

HARLAN. I don't know. The doctor's up there now.

WHITNEY. Well, she'd better be good and sick or Father may be mad at me for getting him up here—'specially in a cab.

(FATHER *comes down the stairs muttering to himself.*)

FATHER (*indignantly*). Well, huh!—It seems to me I ought to be shown a little consideration. I guess I've got some feelings, too!

WHITNEY (*hopefully*). Mother's awfully sick, isn't she?

FATHER. How do I know? I wasn't allowed to stay in the same room with her.

WHITNEY. Did the doctor put you out?

FATHER. No, it was your mother, damn it! (*He goes out and hangs up his hat and stick, then returns.* FATHER *may be annoyed, but he is also worried.*) You boys keep quiet around here today.

WHITNEY. She must be pretty sick.

FATHER. She must be, Whitney! I don't know! Nobody ever tells me anything in this house. Not a damn thing!

(DR. HUMPHREYS *comes down the stairs. He's the family-doctor type of the period, with just enough whiskers to make him impressive. He carries his satchel.*)

DR. HUMPHREYS. Mrs. Day is quieter now.

FATHER. How sick is she? What's the matter with her?

DR. HUMPHREYS. She's a pretty sick woman, Mr. Day. I had given her a sedative just before you came—and after you left the room I had to give her another. Have you a telephone?

FATHER. A telephone! No—I don't believe in them. Why?

DR. HUMPHREYS. Well, it would only have saved me a few steps. I'll be back in ten minutes. (*He turns to go.*)

FATHER. Wait a minute—I think I'm entitled to know what's the matter with my wife.

(DR. HUMPHREYS *turns back.*)

DR. HUMPHREYS. What did Mrs. Day have for breakfast this morning?

FATHER. She didn't eat anything—not a thing.

DR. HUMPHREYS. Are you sure?

FATHER. I tried to get her to eat something, but she wouldn't.

DR. HUMPHREYS (*almost to himself*). I can't understand it.

FATHER. Understand what?

DR. HUMPHREYS. These violent attacks of nausea. It's almost as though she were poisoned.

FATHER. Poisoned!

DR. HUMPHREYS. I'll try not to be gone more than ten or fifteen minutes. (*He exits.*)

FATHER *(trying to reassure himself.)* Damn doctors! They never know what's the matter with anybody. Well, he'd better get your mother well, and damn soon or he'll hear from me.

WHITNEY. Mother's going to get well, isn't she?

(FATHER looks at WHITNEY sharply as though he is a little angry at anyone even raising the question.)

FATHER. Of course she's going to get well!

HARLAN *(running to FATHER)*. I hope she gets well soon. When Mamma stays in bed it's lonesome.

FATHER. Yes, it is, Harlan. It's lonesome. *(He looks around the room and finds it pretty empty.)* What were you boys supposed to do today?

WHITNEY. I was to learn the rest of my catechism.

FATHER. Well, if that's what your mother wanted you to do, you'd better do it.

WHITNEY. I know it—I think.

FATHER. You'd better be sure.

WHITNEY. I can't be sure unless somebody hears me. Will you hear me?

FATHER *(with sudden willingness to be useful)*. All right. I'll hear you, Whitney.

(WHITNEY goes to the mantel and gets VINNIE's prayer book. FATHER sits on the sofa. HARLAN climbs up beside him.)

HARLAN. If Mamma's still sick will you read to me tonight?

FATHER. Of course I'll read to you.

(WHITNEY opens the prayer book and hands it to FATHER.)

WHITNEY. Here it is, Father. Just the end of it. Mother knows I know the rest. Look, start here. *(He points.)*

FATHER. All right. *(Reading.)* "How many parts are there in a Sacrament?"

WHITNEY *(reciting)*. "Two; the outward visible sign, and the inward spiritual grace."

(FATHER nods in approval.)

FATHER. "What is the outward visible sign or form in Baptism?"

WHITNEY. "Water; wherein the person is baptized, in the name of the Father, and of the Son, and of the Holy Ghost." You haven't been baptized, Father, have you?

FATHER *(ignoring it)*. "What is the inward and spiritual grace?"

WHITNEY. If you don't have to be baptized, why do I have to be confirmed?

FATHER *(ignoring this even more)*. "What is the inward and spiritual grace?"

WHITNEY. "A death unto sin, and a new birth unto righteousness; for being by nature born in sin, and the children of wrath, we are hereby made the children of grace." Is that why you get mad so much, Father—because you're a child of wrath?

FATHER. Whitney, mind your manners! You're not supposed to ask questions of your elders! "What is required of persons to be baptized?"

WHITNEY. "Repentance, whereby—whereby—" *(He pauses.)*

FATHER *(quickly shutting the book and handing it to WHITNEY)*. You don't know it well enough, Whitney. You'd better study it some more.

WHITNEY. Now?

FATHER *(softening)*. No, you don't have to do it now. Let's see, now, what can we do?

WHITNEY. Well, I was working with my tool chest out in the back yard. *(Edges toward the arch.)*

FATHER. Better not do any hammering with your mother sick upstairs. You'd better stay here.

WHITNEY. I wasn't hammering—I was doing wood-carving.

FATHER. Well, Harlan—how about you? Shall we play some tiddle-dy-winks?

HARLAN *(edging toward WHITNEY)*. I was helping Whitney.

FATHER. Oh—all right. *(The boys go out. FATHER goes to the stairwell.)* Boys, don't do any shouting. We all have to be very quiet around here. *(He stands in the hall and looks up toward VINNIE, worried. Then he tiptoes across the room and stares gloomily out of the window. Then he tip-*

toes back into the hall and goes to the rail of the basement stairs, and calls quietly.) Margaret! *(There is no answer and he raises his voice a little.)* Margaret! *(There is still no answer and he lets loose.)* Margaret! Why don't you answer when you hear me calling?

(At this moment MARGARET, *hat on, appears in the arch from the right, having come through the front door.)*

MARGARET. Sh—sh—

*(*FATHER *turns quickly and sees* MARGARET.*)*

FATHER. Oh, there you are!

MARGARET *(reprovingly)*. We must all be quiet, Mr. Day—Mrs. Day is very sick.

FATHER *(testily)*. I know she's sick. That's what I wanted you for. You go up and wait outside her door in case she needs anything. *(*MARGARET *starts upstairs.)* And what were you doing out of the house, anyway?

MARGARET. I was sent for the minister.

FATHER *(startled)*. The minister!

MARGARET. Yes, he'll be right in. He's paying off the cab.

*(*MARGARET *continues upstairs. The door slams.* THE REVEREND DR. LLOYD *appears in the archway and meets* FATHER *in the hall.)*

DR. LLOYD. I was deeply shocked to hear of Mrs. Day's illness. I hope I can be of some service. Will you take me up to her?

FATHER *(with a trace of hostility)*. She's resting now. She can't be disturbed.

DR. LLOYD. But I've been summoned.

FATHER. The doctor will be back in a few minutes and we'll see what he has to say about it. You'd better come in and wait.

DR. LLOYD. Thank you. *(Comes into the room.* FATHER *follows him reluctantly.)* Mrs. Day has been a tower of strength in the parish. Everyone liked her so much. Yes, she was a fine woman.

FATHER. I wish to God you wouldn't talk about Mrs. Day as if she were dead.

*(*NORA *comes down the stairs and looks into the room.)*

NORA. Is the doctor back yet?

FATHER. No. Does she need him?

NORA. She's kinda' restless. She's talking in her sleep and twisting and turning.

(She goes downstairs. FATHER *looks up toward* VINNIE's *room, worried, then looks angrily toward the front door.)*

FATHER. That doctor said he'd be right back. *(He goes to the window.)*

MARGARET *(coming downstairs)*. Here comes the doctor. I was watching for him out the window. *(She goes to the front door. A moment later* DR. HUMPHREYS *enters.)*

FATHER. Well, doctor—seems to me that was a pretty long ten minutes.

DR. HUMPHREYS *(indignantly)*. See here, Mr. Day, if I'm to be responsible for Mrs. Day's health, I must be allowed to handle this case in my own way.

FATHER. Well, you can't handle it if you're out of the house.

DR. HUMPHREYS *(flaring)*. I left this house because— *(*DR. SOMERS, *an imposing medical figure, enters and stops at* DR. HUMPHREYS's *side.)* This is Dr. Somers.

DR. SOMERS. How do you do?

DR. HUMPHREYS. I felt that Mrs. Day's condition warranted my getting Dr. Somers here as soon as possible for consultation. I hope that meets with your approval.

FATHER *(a little awed)*. Why, yes, of course. Anything that can be done.

DR. HUMPHREYS. Upstairs, doctor! *(The two doctors go upstairs.* FATHER *turns back into the room, obviously shaken.)*

DR. LLOYD. Mrs. Day is in good hands now, Mr. Day. There's nothing you and I can do at the moment to help.

(After a moment's consideration FATHER *decides there is something that can be done to help. He goes to* DR. LLOYD. FATHER *indicates the seat in front of the table to* DR. LLOYD *and they both sit.)*

FATHER. Dr. Lloyd, there's something that's troubling Mrs. Day's mind. I think you know what I refer to.

DR. LLOYD. Yes, you mean the fact that you've never been baptized.

FATHER. I gathered you knew about it from your sermon last Sunday. (*Looks at him a second with indignant memory.*) But let's not get angry. I think something had better be done about it.

DR. LLOYD. Yes, Mr. Day.

FATHER. When the doctors get through up there I want you to talk to Mrs. Day. I want you to tell her something.

DR. LLOYD (*eagerly*). Yes, I'll be glad to.

FATHER. You're just the man to do it! She shouldn't be upset about this—I want you to tell her that my being baptized would just be a lot of damn nonsense.

(*This isn't what* DR. LLOYD *has expected and it is hardly his idea of how to help* MRS. DAY.)

DR. LLOYD. But, Mr. Day!

FATHER. No, she'd take your word on a thing like that—and we've got to do everything we can to help her now.

DR. LLOYD (*rising*). But baptism is one of the sacraments of the Church—

FATHER (*rising*). You're her minister and you're supposed to bring her comfort and peace of mind.

DR. LLOYD. But the solution is so simple. It would take only your consent to be baptized.

FATHER. That's out of the question! And I'm surprised that a grown man like you should suggest such a thing.

DR. LLOYD. If you're really concerned about Mrs. Day's peace of mind, don't you think—

FATHER. Now see here—if you're just going to keep her stirred up about this, I'm not going to let you see her at all. (*He turns away.* DR. LLOYD *follows him.*)

DR. LLOYD. Now, Mr. Day, as you said, we must do everything we can— (*The doctors come downstairs.* FATHER *sees them.*)

FATHER. Well, doctor, how is she? What have you decided?

DR. HUMPHREYS. We've just left Mrs. Day. Is there a room we could use for our consultation?

FATHER. Of course. (MARGARET *starts downstairs.*) Margaret, you go back upstairs! I don't want Mrs. Day left alone!

MARGARET. I have to do something for the doctor. I'll go back up as soon as I get it started.

FATHER. Well, hurry. And, Margaret, show these gentlemen downstairs to the billiard room.

MARGARET. Yes, sir. This way, doctor—downstairs. (*Exits, followed by* DR. SOMERS. FATHER *delays* DR. HUMPHREYS.)

FATHER. Dr. Humphreys, you know now, don't you—this isn't serious, is it?

DR. HUMPHREYS. After we've had our consultation we'll talk to you, Mr. Day.

FATHER. But surely you must—

DR. HUMPHREYS. Just rest assured that Dr. Somers will do everything that is humanly possible.

FATHER. Why, you don't mean—

DR. HUMPHREYS. We'll try not to be long. (*Exits.* FATHER *turns and looks at* DR. LLOYD. *He is obviously frightened.*)

FATHER. This Dr. Somers—I've heard his name often—he's very well thought of, isn't he?

DR. LLOYD. Oh, yes indeed.

FATHER. If Vinnie's really—if anyone could help her, he could—don't you think?

DR. LLOYD. A very fine physician. But there's a greater Help, ever present in the hour of need. Let us turn to Him in prayer. Let us kneel and pray. (FATHER *looks at him, straightens, then walks to the other side of the room.*) Let us kneel and pray. (FATHER *finally bows his head.* DR. LLOYD *looks at him and, not kneeling himself, raises his head and speaks simply in prayer.*) Oh, Lord, look down from Heaven—behold, visit, and relieve this Thy servant who is grieved with sickness, and extend to her Thy accustomed goodness. We know she has sinned against Thee in thought, word, and deed. Have mercy on her, O Lord, have mercy on this miserable sinner. Forgive her—

FATHER. She's not a miserable sinner and you know it! (*Then* FATHER *speaks directly to the Deity.*) O God! You know

'innie's not a miserable sinner. She's a
amn fine woman! She shouldn't be made
o suffer. It's got to stop, I tell You, it's
ot to stop!

VINNIE *appears on the stairway in her
ightgown.)*

INNIE. What's the matter, Clare? What's
rong?

ATHER *(not hearing her).* Have mercy, I
iy, have mercy, damn it!

INNIE. What's the matter Clare? What's
rong?

FATHER *turns, sees* VINNIE, *and rushes
o her.)*

ATHER. Vinnie, what are you doing down
ere? You shouldn't be out of bed. You
et right back upstairs. *(He now has his
rms around her.)*

INNIE. Oh, Clare, I heard you call. Do
ou need me?

FATHER *(deeply moved).* Vinnie—I know
now how much I need you. Get well,
Vinnie. I'll be baptized. I promise. I'll be
baptized.

VINNIE. You will? Oh, Clare!

FATHER. I'll do anything. We'll go to
Europe, just we two—you won't have to
worry about the children or the household
accounts— (VINNIE *faints against* FATHER's
shoulder.) Vinnie! *(He stoops to lift her.)*

DR. LLOYD. I'll get the doctor. But don't
worry, Mr. Day—she'll be all right now.
*(*FATHER *lifts* VINNIE *up in his arms.)* Bless
you for what you've done, Mr. Day.

FATHER. What did I do?

DR. LLOYD. You promised to be baptized!

FATHER *(aghast).* I did? *(With horror*
FATHER *realizes he has been betrayed—
and by himself.)* OH, GOD!

CURTAIN

ACT THREE

SCENE I

*The same.
A month later. Mid-afternoon.*
VINNIE *is seated on the sofa embroidering petit point.* MARGARET *enters, as usual
ncomfortable at being upstairs.*

MARGARET. You wanted to speak to me,
na'am?

INNIE. Yes, Margaret, about tomorrow
norning's breakfast—we must plan it very
arefully.

MARGARET *(puzzled).* Mr. Day hasn't com-
lained to me about his breakfasts lately.
As a matter of fact, I've been blessing my
ick!

INNIE. Oh, no, it's not that. But tomor-
ow morning I'd like something for his
reakfast that would surprise him.

MARGARET *(doubtfully).* Surprising Mr.
)ay is always a bit of a risk, ma'am. My
notto with him has always been "Let
ell enough alone."

INNIE. But if we think of something he
specially likes, Margaret—what would
ou say to kippers?

MARGARET. Well, I've served him kippers,
but I don't recall his ever saying he liked
them.

VINNIE. He's never said he didn't like
them, has he?

MARGARET. They've never got a stamp on
the floor out of him one way or the other.

VINNIE. If Mr. Day doesn't say he doesn't
like a thing you can assume that he does.
Let's take a chance on kippers, Margaret.

MARGARET. Very well, ma'am. *(She starts
out.)*

VINNIE *(innocently).* And, Margaret, you'd
better have enough breakfast for two extra places.

MARGARET *(knowingly).* Oh—so that's it!
We're going to have company again.

VINNIE. Yes, my cousin, Miss Cartwright,

and her friend are coming back from Springfield. I'm afraid they'll get here just about breakfast time.

MARGARET. Well, in that case I'd better make some of my Sunday morning hot biscuits, too.

VINNIE. Yes. We *know* Mr. Day likes those.

MARGARET. I've been getting him to church with them for the last fifteen years. *(The door slams.* MARGARET *goes to the arch and looks.)* Oh, it's Mr. Clarence, ma'am. *(Goes off downstairs and* CLARENCE *enters with a large package.)*

CLARENCE. Here it is, Mother. *(He puts it on the table.)*

VINNIE. Oh, it was still in the store! They hadn't sold it! I'm so thrilled. Didn't you admire it, Clarence? *(She hurries over to the table.)*

CLARENCE. Well, it's unusual.

VINNIE *(unwrapping the package).* You know, I saw this down there the day before I got sick. I was walking through the bric-a-brac section and it caught my eye. I was so tempted to buy it! And all the time I lay ill I just couldn't get it out of my head. I can't understand how it could stay in the store all this time without somebody snatching it up. *(She takes it out of the box. It is a large china pug dog.)* Isn't that the darlingest thing you ever saw! It does need a ribbon, though. I've got the very thing somewhere. Oh, yes, I know. *(Goes to the side table and gets a red ribbon out of the drawer.)*

CLARENCE. Isn't John home yet?

VINNIE. I haven't seen him. Why?

CLARENCE. Well, you know we've been working, and John went down to collect our money.

VINNIE. That's fine. *(She ties the ribbon around the dog's neck.)* Oh, Clarence, I have a secret for just the two of us; who do you think is coming to visit us tomorrow?—Cousin Cora and Mary.

CLARENCE. Yes, I know.

VINNIE. How did you know?

CLARENCE. I happened to get a letter.

*(*JOHN *enters, carrying two packages of medicine.)*

VINNIE. John, did you ever see anything so sweet?

JOHN. What is it?

VINNIE. It's a pug dog. Your father would never let me have a real one, but he can't object to one made of china. This ribbon needs pressing. I'll take it down and have Margaret do it right away. *(Exits with the beribboned pug dog.)*

CLARENCE. What did you bring home more medicine for? *(Then, with sudden fright.)* Dr. Bartlett paid us off, didn't he?

JOHN. Oh, yes!

CLARENCE *(heaving a great sigh of relief).* You had me scared for a minute. When I went down to McCreery's to get that pug dog for Mother, I ordered the daisiest suit you ever saw. Dr. Bartlett owed us sixteen dollars apiece, and the suit was only fifteen. Wasn't that lucky? Come on, give me my money.

JOHN. Clarence, Dr. Bartlett paid us off in medicine.

CLARENCE. You let him pay us off with that old Beneficent Balm!

JOHN. Well, he thanked us, too, for our services to mankind.

CLARENCE *(in agony).* But my suit!

JOHN. You'll just have to wait for your suit.

CLARENCE. I can't wait! I've got to have it tomorrow—and besides they're making the alterations. I've got to pay for it this afternoon! Fifteen dollars!

JOHN *(helpfully).* Why don't you offer them fifteen bottles of medicine?

*(*CLARENCE *gives it a little desperate thought.)*

CLARENCE. They wouldn't take it. Mc Creery's don't sell medicine.

*(*JOHN *is by the window and looks out.)*

JOHN. That's too bad. Here comes Father

CLARENCE. I'll have to brace him for that fifteen dollars. I hate to do it, but I've got to—that's all—I've got to.

JOHN. I'm not going to be here when you do. I'd better hide this somewhere anyway. (*Takes the packages and hurries upstairs. The door slams.* FATHER *enters and looks into the room.*)

CLARENCE. Good afternoon, sir.

FATHER. How's your mother, Clarence? Where is she?

CLARENCE. She's all right. She's downstairs with Margaret. Oh, Father—

(FATHER *goes off down the hall and we hear him calling downstairs.*)

FATHER. Vinnie! Vinnie! I'm home. (*Comes back into the room, carrying his newspaper.*)

CLARENCE. Father, Mother will be well enough to go to church with us next Sunday.

FATHER. That's fine, Clarence. That's fine.

CLARENCE. Father, have you noticed that I haven't been kneeling down in church lately?

FATHER. Clarence, don't let your mother catch you at it.

CLARENCE. Then I've got to have a new suit of clothes right away!

FATHER (*after a puzzled look*). Clarence, you're not even making sense!

CLARENCE. But a fellow doesn't feel right in cut-down clothes—especially your clothes. That's why I can't kneel down in church—I can't do anything in them you wouldn't do.

FATHER. Well, that's a damn good thing! If my old clothes make you behave yourself I don't think you ought to wear anything else.

CLARENCE (*desperately*). Oh, no! You're you and I'm me! I want to be myself! Besides, you're older and there are things I've got to do that I wouldn't do at your age.

FATHER. Clarence, you should never do anything I wouldn't do.

CLARENCE. Oh, yes,—look, for instance: Suppose I should want to kneel down in front of a girl?

FATHER. Why in Heaven's name should you want to do a thing like that?

CLARENCE. Well, I've got to get married sometime. I've got to propose to a girl sometime.

FATHER (*exasperated*). Before you're married, you'll be earning your own clothes, I hope. Don't get the idea into your head I'm going to support you and a wife, too. Besides, at your age, Clarence—

CLARENCE (*hastily*). Oh, I'm not going to be married right away, but for fifteen dollars I can get a good suit of clothes.

FATHER (*bewildered and irritated*). Clarence! (*He stares at him. At this second,* VINNIE *comes through the arch.*) Why, you're beginning to talk as crazy as your mother. (*He sees her.*) Oh, hello, Vinnie. How're you feeling today?

VINNIE. I'm fine, Clare. (*They kiss.*) You don't have to hurry home from the office every day like this.

(CLARENCE *throws himself in the chair by the window, sick with disappointment.*)

FATHER. Business the way it is, no use going to the office at all.

VINNIE. But you haven't been to your club for weeks.

FATHER. Can't stand the damn place. You do look better, Vinnie. What did you do today? (*Drops on the sofa.* VINNIE *stands behind the sofa. Her chatter does not succeed in diverting* FATHER *from his newspaper.*)

VINNIE. I took a long walk and dropped in to call on old Mrs. Whitehead.

FATHER. Well, that's fine.

VINNIE. And, Clare, it was the most fortunate thing that ever happened. I've got wonderful news for you! Who do you think was there? Mr. Morley!

FATHER (*not placing him*). Morley?

VINNIE. You remember—that nice young minister who substituted for Dr. Lloyd one Sunday?

FATHER. Oh, yes! Bright young fellow preached a good sensible sermon.

VINNIE. It was the only time I ever saw you put five dollars in the plate!

FATHER. Ought to be more ministers like him. I could get along with that young man without any trouble at all.

VINNIE. Well, Clare, his parish is in Audubon—you know, 'way up above Harlem.

FATHER. Is that so?

VINNIE. Isn't that wonderful? Nobody knows you up there. You'll be perfectly safe!

FATHER. Safe? Vinnie, what the devil are you talking about?

VINNIE. I've been all over everything with Mr. Morley and he's agreed to baptize you.

FATHER. Oh, he has—the young whippersnapper! Damn nice of him!

VINNIE. We can go up there any morning, Clare—we don't even have to make an appointment.

FATHER. Vinnie, you're just making a lot of plans for nothing. Who said I was going to be baptized at all?

VINNIE (aghast). Why, Clare! You did!

FATHER. Now, Vinnie!—

VINNIE. You gave me your promise—your Sacred Promise. You stood right on that spot and said: "I'll be baptized. I promise—I'll be baptized."

FATHER. What if I did?

VINNIE (amazed, she comes down and faces him). Aren't you a man of your word?

FATHER (rising). Vinnie, that was under entirely different circumstances. We all thought you were dying, so naturally I said that to make you feel better. As a matter of fact, the doctor told me that's what cured you. So it seems to me pretty ungrateful of you to press this matter any further.

VINNIE. Clarence Day, you gave me your Sacred Promise!

FATHER (getting annoyed). Vinnie, you were sick when I said that. Now you're well again.

(MARGARET enters with the pug dog, which now has the freshly pressed ribbon tied around its neck. She puts it on the table.)

MARGARET. Is that all right, Mrs. Day?

VINNIE (dismissingly). That's fine, Margaret, thank you. (MARGARET exits.) My being well has nothing to do with it. You gave me your word! You gave the Lord your word. If you had seen how eager Mr. Morley was to bring you into the fold. (FATHER, trying to escape, has been moving toward the arch when suddenly the pug dog catches his eye and he stares at it fascinated.) And you're going to march yourself up to his church some morning before you go to the office and be christened. If you think for one minute that I'm going to—

FATHER. What in the name of Heaven is that?

VINNIE. If you think I'm going to let you add the sin of breaking your Solemn and Sacred Promise—

FATHER. I demand to know what that repulsive object is!

VINNIE (exasperated in her turn). It's perfectly plain what it is—it's a pug dog!

FATHER. What's it doing in this house?

VINNIE (defiantly). I wanted it and I bought it.

FATHER. You spent good money for that?

VINNIE. Clare, we're not talking about that! We're talking about you. Don't try to change the subject!

FATHER. How much did you pay for that atrocity?

VINNIE. I don't know. I sent Clarence down for it. Listen to me, Clare—

FATHER. Clarence, what did you pay for that?

CLARENCE. I didn't pay anything. I charged it.

FATHER (looking at VINNIE). Charged it! I might have known. (To CLARENCE.) How much was it?

CLARENCE. Fifteen dollars.

FATHER. Fifteen dollars for that eyesore?

VINNIE (to the rescue of the pug dog). Don't you call that lovely work of art an eyesore! That will look beautiful sitting on a red cushion by the fireplace in the parlor.

FATHER. If that sits in the parlor, I won't! Furthermore, I don't even want it in the same house with me. Get it out of here!

(He starts for the stairs.)

VINNIE. You're just using that for an excuse. You're not going to get out of this room until you set a date for your baptism.

(FATHER turns at the foot of the stairs.)

FATHER. I'll tell you one thing! I'll never be baptized while that hideous monstrosity is in this house. *(He stalks upstairs.)*

VINNIE *(calling after him)*. All right! *(She goes to the pug dog.)* All right! It goes back this afternoon and he's christened first thing in the morning.

CLARENCE. But, Mother—

VINNIE. Clarence, you heard him say that he'd be baptized as soon as I got this pug dog out of the house. You hurry right back to McCreery's with it—and be sure they credit us with fifteen dollars.

(The fifteen dollars rings a bell in CLARENCE'S mind.)

CLARENCE. Oh, say, Mother, while I was at McCreery's, I happened to see a suit I would like very much and the suit was only fifteen dollars.

VINNIE *(regretfully)*. Well, Clarence, I think your suit will have to wait until after I get your father christened.

CLARENCE *(hopefully)*. No. I meant that since the suit cost just the same as the pug dog, if I exchange the pug dog for the suit—

VINNIE. Why, yes! Then your suit wouldn't cost Father anything! Why, how bright of you, Clarence, to think of that!

CLARENCE *(quickly)*. I'd better start right away before McCreery's closes. *(They have collected the box, wrapper, and tissue paper.)*

VINNIE. Yes. Let's see. If we're going to take your father all the way up to Audubon—Clarence, you stop at Ryerson & Brown's on your way back and tell them to have a cab here at eight o'clock tomorrow morning.

CLARENCE. Mother, a cab! Do you think you ought to do that?

VINNIE. Well, we can't walk to Audubon.

CLARENCE *(warningly)*. But you know what a cab does to Father!

VINNIE. This is an important occasion.

CLARENCE *(with a shrug)*. All right! A brougham or a Victoria?

VINNIE. Get one of their best cabs—the kind they use at funerals.

CLARENCE. Those cost two dollars an hour! And if Father gets mad—

VINNIE. Well, if your father starts to argue in the morning, you remember—

CLARENCE *(remembering his suit)*. Oh, he agreed to it! We both heard him!

(VINNIE has removed the ribbon and is about to put the pug dog back in the box.)

VINNIE *(regretfully)*. I did have my heart set on this. *(An idea comes to her.)* Still —if they didn't sell him in all that time, he might be safe there for a few more weeks. *(She gives the dog a reassuring pat and puts him in the box. She begins to sing "Sweet Marie" happily. FATHER comes down the stairs. CLARENCE takes his hat and the box and goes happily and quickly out. FATHER watches him.)* I hope you notice that Clarence is returning the pug dog.

FATHER. That's a sign you're getting your faculties back. *(VINNIE is singing quietly to herself in a satisfied way.)* Good to hear you singing again, Vinnie. *(Suddenly remembering something.)* Oh!—on my way uptown I stopped in at Tiffany's and bought you a little something. Thought you might like it. *(He takes out of his pocket a small ring-box and holds it out to her. She takes it.)*

VINNIE. Oh, Clare. *(She opens it eagerly.)* What a beautiful ring! *(She takes the ring out, puts it on her finger, and admires it.)*

FATHER. Glad if it pleases you. *(He settles down to his newspaper on the sofa.)*

VINNIE. I don't know how to thank you. *(She kisses him.)*

FATHER. It's thanks enough for me to have you up and around again. When you're sick, Vinnie, this house is like a tomb. There's no excitement.

VINNIE (*sitting beside him*). Clare, this is the loveliest ring you ever bought me. Now that I have this, you needn't buy me any more rings.

FATHER. Well, if you don't want any more.

VINNIE. What I'd really like now is a nice diamond necklace.

FATHER (*alarmed*). Vinnie, do you know how much a diamond necklace costs?

VINNIE. I know, Clare, but don't you see? —your giving me this ring shows that I mean a little something to you. Now, a diamond necklace—

FATHER. Good God, if you don't know by this time how I feel about you! We've been married for twenty years and I've loved you every minute of it.

VINNIE. What did you say? (*Her eyes well with tears at* FATHER's *definite statement of his love.*)

FATHER. I said we'd been married twenty years and I've loved you every minute of it. But if I have to buy out jewelry stores to prove it—if I haven't shown it to you in my words and actions, I might as well— (*He turns and sees* VINNIE *dabbing her eyes and speaks with resignation.*) What have I done now?

VINNIE. It's all right, Clare—I'm just so happy.

FATHER. Happy!

VINNIE. You said you loved me! And this beautiful ring—that's something else I didn't expect. Oh, Clare, I love surprises.

(*She nestles against him.*)

FATHER. That's another thing I can't understand about you, Vinnie. Now, *I* like to know what to expect. Then I'm prepared to meet it.

VINNIE (*putting her head on his shoulder*). Yes, I know. But, Clare, life would be pretty dull if we always knew what was coming.

FATHER. Well, it's certainly not dull around here. In this house you never know what's going to hit you tomorrow.

VINNIE (*to herself*). Tomorrow! (*She starts to sing,* FATHER *listening to her happily.*)

> "Every daisy in the dell,
>   Knows my secret, knows it well,
>   And yet I dare not tell,
>   Sweet Marie!"

CURTAIN

SCENE II

The same.
The next morning. Breakfast. All the family except JOHN *and* VINNIE *are at the table and in good spirits.*

JOHN (*entering*). Mother says she'll be right down. (*He sits at the table.*)

(MAGGIE, *the new maid, enters with a plate of hot biscuits and serves* FATHER. *As* FATHER *takes a biscuit, he glances up at her and shows some little surprise.*)

FATHER. Who are you? What's your name?

MAGGIE. Margaret, sir.

FATHER. Can't be Margaret. We've got one Margaret in the house.

MAGGIE. At home they call me Maggie, sir.

FATHER (*genially*). All right, Maggie. (MAGGIE *continues serving the biscuits.*)

Boys, if her name's Margaret, that's a good sign. Maybe she'll stay awhile. You know, boys, your mother used to be just the same about cooks as she is about maids. Never could keep them for some reason. Well, one day about fifteen years ago—yes, it was right after you were born, John—my, you were a homely baby. (*They all laugh at* JOHN's *expense.*) I came home that night all tired out and what did I find—no dinner, because the cook had left. Well, I decided I'd had just about enough of that, so I just marched over to the employment agency on Sixth Avenue and said to the woman in charge: "Where do you keep the cooks?" She tried to hold me up with a lot of red-tape folderol, but I just walked into the room where the girls were waiting, looked 'em over, saw Margaret, pointed at her, and said: "I'll take that one." I walked her home, she cooked dinner that night, and she's been cooking for us ever since. Damn good cook, too. (*He stamps on the floor three times.*)

(VINNIE *comes down the stairs dressed in white. Somehow she almost has the appearance of a bride going to her wedding.*)

VINNIE. Good morning, Clare. Good morning, boys.

(*The boys and* FATHER *rise.* VINNIE *takes her bonnet and gloves and lays them on the chair below the fireplace.* FATHER *goes to* VINNIE'S *chair and holds it out for her, glancing at her holiday appearance.* VINNIE *sits.*)

FATHER. Sit down, boys. (*As* FATHER *returns to his own chair, he notices that all of the boys are dressed in their Sunday best.*) Everyone's dressed up this morning. What's on the program for this fine day? (VINNIE, *who always postpones crises in the hope some miracle will aid her, postpones this one.*)

VINNIE. Well, this afternoon May Lewis's mother is giving a party for everyone in May's dancing class. Harlan's going to that.

HARLAN. I don't want to go, Mamma.

VINNIE. Why, Harlan, don't you want to go to a party and get ice cream and cake?

HARLAN. May Lewis always tries to kiss me.

(*This is greeted with family laughter.*)

FATHER (*genially*). When you get a little older, you won't object to girls' wanting to kiss you, will he, Clarence?

(MARGARET *comes hurrying in.*)

MARGARET. What's wanting?

FATHER. Margaret, these kippers are good. (MARGARET *makes her usual deprecatory gesture toward him.*) Haven't had kippers for a long time. I'm glad you remembered I like them.

MARGARET. Yes, sir.

(MARGARET *and* VINNIE *exchange knowing looks.* MARGARET *goes out happy.*)

FATHER. What's got into Margaret this morning? Hot biscuits, too!

VINNIE. She knows you're fond of them. (*The doorbell rings.* MAGGIE *goes to answer it.* VINNIE *stirs nervously in her chair.*) Who can that be? It can't be the mail man because he's been here.

FATHER (*with sly humor*). Clarence has been getting a good many special deliveries lately. Is that business deal going through, Clarence?

(*The family has a laugh at* CLARENCE. MAGGIE *comes back into the arch with a suit box.*)

MAGGIE. This is for you, Mr. Day. Where shall I put it?

CLARENCE (*hastily*). Oh, that's for me, I think. Take it upstairs, Maggie.

FATHER. Wait a minute, Maggie, bring it here. Let's see it.

(CLARENCE *takes the box from* MAGGIE, *who exits. He holds it toward his father.*)

CLARENCE. See, it's for me, Father—Clarence Day, Jr.

FATHER. Let me look. Why, that's from McCreery's and it's marked "Charge." What is it?

VINNIE. It's all right, Clare. It's nothing for you to worry about.

FATHER. Well, at least I think I should know what's being charged to me. What is it?

VINNIE. Now, Clare, stop your fussing. It's a new suit of clothes for Clarence and it's not costing you a penny.

FATHER. It's marked "Charge fifteen dollars"—it's costing me fifteen dollars. And I told Clarence—

VINNIE. Clare, can't you take my word it isn't costing you a penny?

FATHER. I'd like to have you explain why it isn't.

VINNIE (*triumphantly*). Because Clarence took the pug dog back and got the suit instead.

FATHER. Of course, and they'll charge me fifteen dollars for the suit.

VINNIE. Nonsense, Clare. We gave them the pug dog for the suit. Don't you see?

FATHER. Then they'll charge me fifteen dollars for the pug dog.

VINNIE. But, Clare, they can't! We haven't got the pug dog. We sent that back.

FATHER (*bewildered, but not convinced*). Now wait a minute, Vinnie. There's something wrong with your reasoning.

VINNIE. I'm surprised, Clare, and you're supposed to be so good at figures. Why, it's perfectly clear to me.

FATHER. Vinnie! They're going to charge me for one thing or the other.

VINNIE. Don't you let them!

(FATHER *gets up and throws his napkin on the table.*)

FATHER. Well, McCreery's aren't giving away suits and they aren't giving away pug dogs. (*He walks over to the window in his irritation.*) Can't you get it through your— (*Looking out the window.*) Oh, God!

VINNIE. What is it, Clare? What's wrong?

FATHER. Don't anybody answer the door.

VINNIE. Who is it? Who's coming?

FATHER. Those damn women are back!

WHITNEY. What women?

FATHER. Cora and that little idiot. (CLARENCE *dashes madly up the stairs clutching the box containing his new suit.*) They're moving in on us again, bag and baggage! (*The doorbell rings.*) Don't let them in!

VINNIE. Clarence Day, as if we could turn our own relatives away!

FATHER. Tell them to get back in that cab and drive right on to Ohio. If they're extravagant enough to take cabs when horse cars run right by our door—

(MAGGIE *crosses the hall to answer the doorbell.*)

VINNIE. Now, Clare—you be quiet and behave yourself. They're here and there's nothing you can do about it. (*She starts toward the hall.*)

FATHER (*shouting after her*). Well, why do they always pounce on us without warning?—the damn gypsies!

VINNIE (*from the arch*). Shhh!—Clare!

(*Then in her best welcoming tone.*) Cora! Mary! It's so nice to have you back again.

CORA. How are you, Vinnie? We've been so worried about you.

VINNIE. Oh, I'm fine now!

(CORA *and* MARY *and* VINNIE *enter and* CORA *sweeps right down into the room.*)

CORA. Hello, Harlan! Whitney! Well, Cousin Clare. Here we are again! (*Kisses* FATHER *on the cheek. He draws back sternly.* MARY *looks quickly around the room for* CLARENCE, *then greets and is greeted by the other boys.*) And John! Where's Clarence?

MARY. Yes, where is Clarence?

VINNIE. John, go find Clarence and tell him that Cora and Mary are here.

JOHN. Yes, Mother. (*Goes upstairs.*)

VINNIE. You got here just in time to have breakfast with us.

CORA. We had breakfast at the depot.

VINNIE. Well, as a matter of fact, we'd just finished.

FATHER (*with cold dignity*). *I* haven't finished my breakfast!

VINNIE. Well, then sit down, Clare. (*To* CORA *and* MARY.) Margaret gave us kippers this morning and Clare's so fond of kippers. Why don't we all sit down? (*Indicates the empty places and the girls sit.* FATHER *resumes his chair and breakfast in stony silence.* MAGGIE *has come into the room to await orders.*) Maggie, clear those things away. (*She indicates the dishes in front of the girls, and* MAGGIE *removes them.* FATHER *takes a letter from his stack of morning mail and opens it.*) Clare, don't let your kippers get cold. (*To* CORA.) Now—tell us all about Springfield.

CORA. We had a wonderful month—but tell us about you, Cousin Vinnie. You must have had a terrible time.

VINNIE. Yes, I was pretty sick, but I'm all right again now.

CORA. What was it?

VINNIE. Well, the doctors don't know exactly, but they did say this—that they'd never seen anything like it before, whatever it was.

CORA. You certainly look well enough now. Doesn't she, Clare?

(Whatever is in the letter FATHER *has been reading comes to him as a shock.)*

FATHER. Oh, God!

VINNIE. What's the matter, Clare? What's wrong?

FATHER. John! John!

(JOHN is seen halfway up the stairs with the girls' bags. He comes running down the stairs, going to FATHER.)

JOHN. Yes, Father?

FATHER. Have you been going around this town selling medicine?

JOHN *(a little frightened).* Yes, Father.

FATHER. Dog medicine?

JOHN *(indignantly).* No, Father, not dog medicine!

FATHER. It must have been dog medicine!

JOHN. It wasn't dog medicine, Father—

FATHER. This letter from Mrs. Sprague says you sold her a bottle of this medicine and that her little boy gave some of it to their dog and it killed him! Now she wants ten dollars from me for a new dog.

JOHN. Well, he shouldn't have given it to a dog. It's for humans! Why, it's Bartlett's Beneficent Balm—"Made from a secret formula"!

FATHER. Have you been going around among our friends and neighbors selling some damned Dr. Munyon patent nostrum?

JOHN. But it's good medicine, Father. I can prove it by Mother.

FATHER. Vinnie, what do you know about this?

VINNIE. Nothing, Clare, but I'm sure that John—

JOHN. No, I mean that day Mother—

FATHER. That's enough! You're going to every house where you sold a bottle of that concoction and buy it all back.

JOHN *(dismayed).* But it's a dollar a bottle!

FATHER. I don't care how much it is. How many bottles did you sell?

JOHN. A hundred and twenty-eight.

FATHER *(roaring).* A hundred and twenty-eight!

VINNIE. Clare, I always told you John would make a good business man.

FATHER *(calmly).* Young man, I'll give you the money to buy it back—a hundred and twenty-eight dollars. And ten more for Mrs. Sprague. That's a hundred and thirty-eight dollars. But it's coming out of your allowance! That means you'll not get another penny until that hundred and thirty-eight dollars is all paid up.

(JOHN starts toward the hall, counting on his fingers, then turns and addresses his father in dismay.)

JOHN. I'll be twenty-one years old!

(FATHER glares at him. JOHN turns and goes on up the stairs, with the bags.)

VINNIE *(persuasively).* Clare, you know you've always encouraged the boys to earn their own money.

FATHER. Vinnie, I'll handle this. *(There is a pause. He buries himself in his newspaper.)*

CORA *(breaking through the constraint).* Of course, Aunt Judith sent her love to all of you—

VINNIE. I haven't seen Judith for years. You'd think living so close to Springfield —maybe I could run up there before the summer's over.

CORA. Oh, she'll be leaving for Pleasantville any day now. Grandpa Ebbetts has been failing very fast and that's why I have to hurry back.

VINNIE. Hurry back? Well, you and Mary can stay with us a few days at least.

CORA. No, I hate to break the news to you, Vinnie, but we can't even stay overnight. We're leaving on the five o'clock train this afternoon.

VINNIE *(disappointed).* Oh, what a pity!

(FATHER lowers the paper.)

FATHER *(heartily).* Well, Cora, it certainly is good to see you again. *(To Mary.)*

Young lady, I think you've been enjoying yourself—you look prettier than ever.

(MARY *laughs and blushes.*)

WHITNEY. I'll bet Clarence will think so.

(*The doorbell rings.* MAGGIE *crosses to answer it.*)

FATHER. That can't be another special delivery for Clarence. (*To* MARY, *slyly.*) While you were in Springfield our postman was kept pretty busy. Sure you girls don't want any breakfast?

MARY. No, thank you. (*Rises and goes to the arch and stands looking upstairs, watching for* CLARENCE.)

CORA. Oh, no, thank you, Cousin Clare, we've had our breakfast.

FATHER. At least you ought to have a cup of coffee with us. Vinnie, you might have thought to order some coffee for the girls.

CORA. No, no, thank you, Cousin Clare.

(MAGGIE *appears again in the arch.*)

MAGGIE. It's the cab, ma'am. (*Exits.*)

FATHER. The cab! What cab?

VINNIE. The cab that's to take us to Audubon.

FATHER. Who's going to Audubon?

VINNIE. We all are. Cora, the most wonderful thing has happened!

CORA. What, Cousin Vinnie?

VINNIE (*happily*). Clare's going to be baptized this morning.

FATHER (*not believing his ears*). Vinnie—what are you saying?

VINNIE (*with determination*). I'm saying you're going to be baptized this morning!

FATHER. I am not going to be baptized this morning or any other morning!

VINNIE. You promised yesterday that as soon as I sent that pug dog back you'd be baptized.

FATHER. I promised no such thing!

VINNIE. You certainly did!

FATHER. I never said anything remotely like that!

VINNIE. Clarence was right here and heard it. You ask him!

FATHER. Clarence be damned! I know what I said! I don't remember exactly, but it wasn't that!

VINNIE. Well, I remember. That's why I ordered the cab!

FATHER (*suddenly remembering*). The cab! Oh, my God, that cab! (*He rises and glares out the window at the cab, then turns back and speaks peremptorily.*) Vinnie! You send that right back!

VINNIE. I'll do nothing of the kind. I'm going to see that you get to Heaven.

FATHER. I can't go to Heaven in a cab!

VINNIE. Well, you can start in a cab! I'm not sure whether they'll ever let you into Heaven or not, but I know they won't unless you're baptized.

FATHER. They can't keep me out of Heaven on a technicality.

VINNIE. Clare, stop quibbling! You might as well face it—you've got to make your peace with God.

FATHER. I never had any trouble with God until you stirred Him up!

(MARY *is tired of waiting for* CLARENCE *and chooses this moment to interrupt.*)

MARY. Mrs. Day?

(VINNIE *answers her quickly, as if expecting* MARY *to supply her with an added argument.*)

VINNIE. Yes, Mary?

MARY. Where do you suppose Clarence is?

FATHER. You keep out of this, young lady! If it hadn't been for you, no one would have known whether I was baptized or not. (MARY *breaks into tears.*) Damn! Damnation!

VINNIE. Harlan! Whitney! Get your Sunday hats. (*Calls upstairs.*) John! Clarence!

(HARLAN *and* WHITNEY *start out, but stop as* FATHER *speaks.*)

FATHER (*blazing with new fire*). Vinnie, are you mad? Was it your plan that my own children should witness this indignity?

VINNIE. Why, Clare, they'll be proud of you!

FATHER. I suppose Harlan is to be my godfather! (*With determination.*) Vinnie, it's no use. I can't go through with this thing and I won't. That's final.

VINNIE. Why, Clare dear, if you feel that way about it—

FATHER. I do!

VINNIE. —the children don't have to go.

(JOHN *enters.*)

JOHN. Yes, Mother?

(FATHER *sees* JOHN *and an avenue of escape opens up.*)

FATHER. Oh, John! Vinnie, I can't do anything like that this morning. I've got to take John down to the office and give him the money to buy back that medicine. (*To* JOHN.) When I think of you going around this town selling dog medicine!—

JOHN (*insistently*). It wasn't dog medicine, Father.

FATHER. John, we're starting downtown this minute!

VINNIE. You're doing no such thing! You gave me your Sacred Promise that day I almost died—

JOHN. Yes, and she would have died if we hadn't given her some of that medicine. That proves it's good medicine!

FATHER (*aghast*). You gave your mother some of that dog medicine!

VINNIE. Oh, no, John, you didn't! (*Sinks weakly into the chair below the fireplace.*)

JOHN. Yes, we did, Mother. We put some in your tea that morning.

FATHER. You did what? Without her knowing it? Do you realize you might have killed your mother? You did kill Mrs. Sprague's dog. (*After a solemn pause.*) John, you've done a very serious thing. I'll have to give considerable thought as to how you're going to be punished for this.

VINNIE. But, Clare—

FATHER. No, Vinnie. When I think of that day—with the house full of doctors—why, Cora, we even sent for the minister. Why, we might have lost you! (*He goes to* VINNIE, *really moved, and puts his hand on her shoulder.*) It's all right now, Vinnie, thank God. You're well again. But what I went through that afternoon—the way I felt—I'll never forget it.

VINNIE. Don't talk that way, Clare. You've forgotten it already.

FATHER. What do you mean?

VINNIE. That was the day you gave me your Sacred Promise.

FATHER. But I wouldn't have promised if I hadn't thought you were dying—and you wouldn't have almost died if John hadn't given you that medicine. Don't you see? The whole thing's illegal!

VINNIE. Suppose I had died! It wouldn't make any difference to you. You don't care whether we meet in Heaven or not —you don't care whether you ever see me and the children again.

(*She almost succeeds in crying.* HARLAN *and* WHITNEY *go to her in sympathy, putting their arms around her.*)

FATHER (*distressed*). Now, Vinnie, you're not being fair to me.

VINNIE. It's all right, Clare. If you don't love us enough there's nothing we can do about it.

(*Hurt,* FATHER *walks away to the other side of the room.*)

FATHER. That's got nothing to do with it! I love my family as much as any man. There's nothing within reason I wouldn't do for you, and you know it! All these years I've struggled and worked just to prove— (*He has reached the window and looks out.*) There's that damn cab! Vinnie, you're not well enough to go all the way up to Audubon.

VINNIE (*perkily*). I'm well enough if we ride.

FATHER. But that trip would take all morning. And those cabs cost a dollar an hour.

VINNIE (*with smug complacence*). That's one of their best cabs. That costs two dollars an hour.

(FATHER *stares at her a second, horrified —then explodes.*)

FATHER. Then why aren't you ready? Get your hat on! Damn! Damnation! Amen!

(*Exits for his hat and stick.* VINNIE *is stunned for a moment by this sudden surrender, then hastily puts on her bonnet.*)

WHITNEY. Let's watch them start! Come on, Cousin Cora, let's watch them start!

CORA. I wouldn't miss it!

(WHITNEY, HARLAN, *and* CORA *hurry out.* VINNIE *starts, but* JOHN *stops her in the arch.*)

JOHN (*contritely*). Mother, I didn't mean to almost kill you.

VINNIE. Now, don't you worry about what your father said. (*Tenderly.*) It's all right, dear. (*She kisses him.*) It worked out fine! (*She exits.* JOHN *looks upstairs, then at* MARY, *who has gone to the window.*)

JOHN. Mary! Here comes Clarence!

(JOHN *exits.* MARY *sits in* FATHER'S *chair.*

CLARENCE *comes down the stairs in his new suit. He goes into the room and right to* MARY. *Without saying a word he kneels in front of her. They both are starry-eyed.*)

(FATHER, *with hat and stick, comes into the arch on his way out. He sees* CLARENCE *kneeling at* MARY'S *feet.*)

FATHER. *Oh, God!*

(CLARENCE *springs up in embarrassment.* VINNIE *re-enters hurriedly.*)

VINNIE. What's the matter? What's wrong?

CLARENCE. Nothing's wrong, Mother— (*Then, for want of something to say.*) Going to the office, Father?

FATHER. No! I'm going to be baptized, damn it!

(*He slams his hat on angrily and stalks out.* VINNIE *gives a triumphant nod and follows him. The curtain starts down, and as it falls,* CLARENCE *again kneels at* MARY'S *feet.*)

CURTAIN

BORN YESTERDAY

By GARSON KANIN

———

BORN YESTERDAY was presented by Max Gordon at the Lyceum Theatre, New York City, on February 4, 1946. It was staged by the author. Donald Oenslager designed the setting. The cast was as follows:

BILLIE DAWN	Judy Holliday	THE ASSISTANT MANAGER	
HARRY BROCK	Paul Douglas		Carroll Ashburn
PAUL VERRALL	Gary Merrill	HELEN, A MAID	Ellen Hall
ED DEVERY	Otto Hulett	A BELLHOP	William Harmon
SENATOR NORVAL HEDGES		ANOTHER BELLHOP	Rex King
	Larry Oliver	A BARBER	Ted Mayer
MRS. HEDGES	Mona Bruns	A MANICURIST	Mary Laslo
EDDIE BROCK	Frank Otto	A BOOTBLACK	Parris Morgan
		A WAITER	C. L. Burke

———

The scene is Washington, D. C.

ACT I: September, 1945.

ACT II: Two months later.

ACT III: Late that night.

———

THE AUTHOR

After a slow start as Western Union messenger, Macy's clerk, vaudevillian, saxophonist, and bit player, following some study at the American Academy of Dramatic Arts, Garson Kanin developed meteoric qualities. He did not achieve any singularity as an actor, but he came to the attention of George Abbott as a willing young man with a flair for staging. Mr. Kanin could not have had a better mentor in the field of directing than Mr. Abbott, with whom he was associated in the profitable ventures of Three Men on a Horse, Boy Meets Girl, Room Service, *and* Brother Rat. *An alert acolyte could learn a good deal from the famous Abbott aptitude for fast and telling timing. Mr. Kanin, in turn, gave good value for the instruction by helping to discover Betty Field, Sam Levene, Allyn Joslyn and other capable players for the productions.*

Sam Goldwyn, who has a keen eye for talent and backs his judgment with conspicuous action, brought the young man to Hollywood in 1937 when Kanin was only twenty-five and gave him an opportunity to familiarize himself with motion picture technique. R.K.O. allowed him to direct A Man to Remember, *and Kanin became "the boy wonder" of the Barbary Coast. Subsequently, he directed the Ginger Rogers picture* Bachelor Mother, My Favorite Wife, They Knew What They Wanted, *and* Tom, Dick and Harry. *When the war came he enlisted as a private and emerged a captain. The army was astute enough to keep him to his last, and in consequence Kanin was able to direct numerous and valuable documentary films. He climaxed this phase of his career with* The True Glory.

Released from military service, Captain Kanin turned to the challenging task of directing Robert Sherwood's The Rugged Path *and took his first public fling at writing a play. The result was the extraordinarily successful* Born Yesterday, *which he also directed. The play opened in New York on February 4, 1946. He had hardly settled down to enjoying his literary success than the distaff side of his household represented by Ruth Gordon called upon his services. He staged Miss Gordon's autobiographical reminiscence* Years Ago *out of town and then restaged it in the fall of 1946 with conspicuous success. Whether Mr. Kanin will enliven the stage by writing more plays of the calibre of* Born Yesterday *remains to be seen. Broadway will be in his debt if he does. His is the freshest new talent for Broadway comedy to appear on the stage in many years.*

BORN YESTERDAY

ACT ONE

SCENE: This happens in the sitting room of Suite 67D, a large part of the best hotel in Washington, D. C. 67D is so called because it is a duplex apartment on the sixth and seventh floors of the hotel. It is a masterpiece of offensive good taste, colorful and lush and rich. There are mops and brooms in the doorway when the curtain rises and in the room a chambermaid's cleaning unit. The main door is open and the telephone bell is ringing. A maid comes down the staircase which leads from the bedrooms, carrying a large vase of yellow roses. She sets them down, and goes off to the service wing, paying the phone no mind. It rings some more. In a moment, the maid returns and tends to a few more chores in the room. The phone stops. A man walks by the open door. He looks in, but passes. A moment later he returns and stands in the doorway. This is PAUL VERRALL, *of the* New Republic's Washington *staff.* VERRALL *is in his middle thirties, handsome, alert, and energetic. There is nothing wrong with him at all, in fact, with the possible exception of a tendency to take things, and himself, too seriously. He knows this. He is carrying several books, magazines, and newspapers. He wears eyeglasses. He lights a cigarette and leans in the doorway.*

PAUL. Who's coming in here, Helen, do you know?

HELEN. Hello, Mr. Verrall. No, I don't.

PAUL. A Harry Brock, by any chance?

HELEN. I'm not the room clerk, please.

PAUL. I'm supposed to meet this guy, that's all. I wondered if maybe he was coming in here.

(HELEN *looks at the card stuck in among the roses.*)

HELEN. Brock. (*She goes about her work.*)

PAUL (*looking around*). I figured. (*He steps into the room.*)

HELEN. Who's Brock?

PAUL. *Harry* Brock.

HELEN. Never heard of him.

PAUL. You will, Helen. Big man. Ran a little junk yard into fifty million bucks, with no help from anyone or anything—except maybe World War II.

HELEN. Anybody checks into 67D I got no desire to meet. Believe me.

PAUL. Why not?

HELEN. Listen, you know what they charge for this layout? (*She is about to continue, impressively, when* PAUL *interrupts.*)

PAUL. Two hundred and thirty-five a day.

HELEN. Who told you?

PAUL. Frank.

HELEN. Oh.

PAUL. What about it?

HELEN. Listen, anybody's got two hundred and thirty-five dollars a day to spend on a hotel room there ought to be a law.

PAUL. Too many laws already.

HELEN. While I'm getting eighteen a week I don't see why anybody should spend two hundred and thirty-five a day.

PAUL. For a hotel room.

HELEN. That's what I say.

PAUL (*smiling*). I know some people who'd call you a communist.

HELEN (*darkly*). Tell them I'm thinking about it. Seriously.

(PAUL *is at the window, looking out over the city.*)

HELEN. Changed much, do you think?

PAUL. What?

HELEN. Washington?

PAUL. Not enough. I could stand a little more change. The idea of the war wasn't to leave everything the same, you know.

HELEN. The trouble with you, Mr. Verrall, you think too much. Most fellows your age get more—

(*She breaks off as a bellhop enters, carrying a large leather box and several brief cases. He is followed by* EDDIE BROCK, *who is* HARRY BROCK'S *cousin—and servant.*)

EDDIE. This stays down. The rest goes up.

THE BELLHOP. Yes, sir.

(HELEN *picks up her paraphernalia and goes.* PAUL *is on his way out. So is the* BELLHOP. *As they reach the door, however, they step aside.* HARRY BROCK *stamps in, followed by the* ASSISTANT MANAGER. *Then* BILLIE DAWN *appears wearing a mink coat and carrying another.* BROCK *is a huge man in his late thirties. Gross is the word for him.* BILLIE *is breathtakingly beautiful and breathtakingly stupid. The* BELLHOP *leaves.*)

THE ASSISTANT MANAGER (*a Rotarian*). Here we are.

(BROCK *and* BILLIE *are looking around.* BROCK *is impressed by the room, but tries not to show it. As he looks around he sees* PAUL, *but doesn't particularly notice him.*)

BROCK (*without enthusiasm*). It's all right.

THE ASSISTANT MANAGER (*pointing*). Service wing. Terrace. (*Going toward the staircase.*) And the bedchambers are right this way.

(*He goes up.* BILLIE *follows.* EDDIE *is unpacking bottles of liquor from the leather box and putting them on a side table.* BROCK *sits on a large modern sofa, the principal piece of furniture in the room, and removes his shoes.* PAUL *comes down to him.*)

PAUL (*extending his hand*). Hello, Mr. Brock.

BROCK (*brusquely, ignoring* PAUL's *hand*). How are you? (*He turns away.* PAUL *thinks a moment, then leaves.*)

BROCK. Who the hell was that?

EDDIE. Search me.

BROCK. What kind of a joint is this—people in and out of your place all the time?

(*The* ASSISTANT MANAGER *returns.*)

THE ASSISTANT MANAGER. Mrs. Brock seems delighted with the bedchambers.

BROCK. It's not Mrs. Brock.

THE ASSISTANT MANAGER (*gulping*). I see.

BROCK. All right. Just don't get nosey.

THE ASSISTANT MANAGER. Not at all.

BROCK. There ain't no Mrs. Brock, except my mother. And she's dead.

THE ASSISTANT MANAGER. I see.

BROCK (*snapping his fingers*). Eddie! Take care of him. (EDDIE *comes over, reaches into his pocket, and takes out a roll of bills. He looks at* BROCK. *They reach a swift, silent, understanding as to how much.* EDDIE *hands the* ASSISTANT MANAGER *two ten-dollar bills.*)

THE ASSISTANT MANAGER (*to Eddie*). Thank you. (*Then, to* BROCK.) That is, thank *you.* So much.

BROCK. All right, all right. Just listen. Anybody works in this room just tell 'em to do it good and do it quick and nobody'll get hurt. I'm a big tipper, tell 'em, and I don't like a lot of people around all the time and I don't like to wait for nothin'. I ain't used to it.

THE ASSISTANT MANAGER. I'm sure everything will be just that, Mr. Brock.

BROCK (*with a wave*). Okay. Knock off.

THE ASSISTANT MANAGER. Thank you *very* much, Mr. Brock. (*He leaves.*)

BROCK (*rising and shouting*). Billie!!

BILLIE (*appearing on the balcony*). What?

BROCK (*indicating the room*). Not bad, huh?

BILLIE (*without enthusiasm*). It's all right.

(*The door buzzer sounds.* EDDIE *goes to answer it.*)

BROCK (*sore*). All right, she says. You know what this place costs a day?

BILLIE. Two hundred and thirty-five. You told me.

(*She leaves, with a bored wave of her hips.* EDDIE *opens the door.* ED DEVERY *comes in, slightly drunk.*)

DEVERY. Hello, Eddie.

EDDIE. Hello.

(*About* ED DEVERY. *Thirty years ago, when he was secretary to a great Supreme Court Justice, he was known as a young man destined for greatness. The white star shone clearly on his forehead. Fifteen years later, he was still so known—except to himself. He knew then that he had lost his way. Now everyone knows. They speak of his past brilliance in law and charitably forget that he now has but one client,* HARRY BROCK, *who might have difficulty in finding a reputable lawyer to serve him. But* ED DEVERY *is past caring.* BROCK *represents over $100,000 a year, which buys plenty of the best available Scotch.)*

DEVERY. Welcome to our city.

BROCK. Yeah.

EDDIE. Say I got this ticket to be fixed.

(He reaches into his pocket, searching for it.)

DEVERY *(annoyed)*. What's it about?

EDDIE. Ah, some louse just as we blew into town. Here. *(He hands over a pink traffic summons.)*

DEVERY *(loud and mean)*. I should like to impress one thing on your nonexistent intellect . . . the fact that I am a lawyer does not mean that I own the law.

EDDIE. What'd *I* do? What'd I *do?*

DEVERY. All right. I'll see what I can manage. *(He takes a deep, weary breath.)*

BROCK. You plastered again?

DEVERY. Still.

BROCK. I told you I got a couple things can't wait.

DEVERY. Don't worry about me, massa, I can see a loophole at twenty paces.

BROCK. How'd we make out?

DEVERY. It's going to be all right. May cost slightly more than we estimated, but there is no cause for alarm.

BROCK. How much more?

DEVERY. It's negligible.

BROCK. Why more?

DEVERY. Supply and demand, Harry. A crook is becoming a rare item in these parts. Therefore, he comes high. Don't worry.

BROCK. What do you mean, "don't worry"? This kind of stuff ain't deductible, you know.

DEVERY. I'm not sure. Perhaps we should make a trial issue of it. *(Dictating.)* To the Collector of Internal Revenue. Herewith additional deduction for Tax Return now on file, one bribe, $80,000.

BROCK *(outraged)*. Eighty?

(The phone rings.)

DEVERY. What's the matter?

BROCK. You said—uh—negligible.

DEVERY. We figured fifty, didn't we?

EDDIE *(answering phone)*. Yeah?

BROCK *(to DEVERY)*. You're very handy with *my* dough, you know it?

EDDIE *(on the phone)*. . . . Yes, he is. Who wants him? Wait a second. *(To* DEVERY*)*. Some guy for *you.* Verrall.

DEVERY *(going to phone)*. Thanks. *(Into phone.)* How are you, Paul? . . . Good. . . . How's the crusade business? . . . Sure, any time now. Sooner the better. Fine. . . . See you. . . . *(He hangs up).*

BROCK. What's all that?

DEVERY. Paul Verrall. I told you about him.

BROCK. I don't remember no Verrall.

DEVERY. He's a writer. *New Republic.* Wants an interview. Smart boy. He's just back from a long time in the service with lots of ideas and lots of energy.

BROCK. I don't want to talk to no writers. I got to get shaved.

DEVERY. I think you'd better talk to this one.

BROCK. What's so important?

DEVERY. Just do it.

BROCK. Why?

DEVERY. This is one of the few fellows in Washington to look out for. Thing to do is take him in. Then he doesn't go poking.

BROCK *(loudly)*. Eddie!

DEVERY. How's Billie?

BROCK. She's all right. Upstairs. *(*EDDIE *comes in.)* Get me a shave up here.

EDDIE. Right.

DEVERY. Harry—

BROCK. What?

EDDIE (on the phone). Barber shop.

DEVERY. Tell Billie to wear something nice and plain for the Senator. He may be bringing his wife.

BROCK. Tell her yourself. You ain't pregnant.

EDDIE (on the phone). This is Harry Brock's apartment. Send up a barber and a manicure. Right away. . . . Harry Brock. . . . That's right. . . . Okay, make it snappy.

BROCK (yelling). And a shine!

EDDIE (echoing him). And a shine! (He hangs up.) Be right up.

DEVERY. Eddie, how would you like to save my life?

EDDIE. Soda or plain water?

DEVERY. Neat.

EDDIE. Right! (He goes to work with the liquor.)

BROCK (removing his jacket and tie). Don't worry about Billie. One thing, she knows how to dress. You know what it costs me for clothes for her?

DEVERY. That's not all I'm worried about, Harry.

BROCK. What?

DEVERY. Well, did you have to bring Billie?

BROCK. I may be here God knows how long.

DEVERY. Trouble is, this is a city of few secrets and much chat.

BROCK. Anybody chats me I'll bust 'em in half.

DEVERY. Fine. That'll get you right where you want to go. Up with the dress-for-dinner bunch.

BROCK. What do I care?

DEVERY. I don't know. What do you care? (EDDIE hands him a drink.) Thanks. (Sitting down beside BROCK.) Listen, Harry, you've got a chance to be one of the men who runs this country. Better than that. You can run the men who run

it. It takes power. You've got some. It takes money. You've got plenty. Above all, it takes judgment and intelligence. (A pause.) That's why you pay me a hundred thousand a year.

BROCK. What's all the excitement?

DEVERY. Nothing. I'm just trying to make it clear where I fit in.

BROCK. You don't have to holler.

DEVERY. All right.

BROCK. Honest to God, I thought I done somethin' wrong. (He rises and moves away.)

DEVERY. When Verrall gets here, be friendly. Treat him nicely. Don't bull him. Just be yourself. Treat him like a woman you're trying to make.

BROCK. Wait a minute!

(The buzzer sounds.)

DEVERY. I'll leave you alone with him. Better that way. I want to see Billie, anyway. (DEVERY opens the door and admits VERRALL.) Hello, Paul.

PAUL. Ed. (They shake hands.)

DEVERY. Harry Brock, Paul Verrall.

PAUL. How do you do, sir? (He bows, slightly and sharply. A habit.)

BROCK. How are you? (He looks at Paul, quizzically.) Ain't I seen you some place before? (PAUL just smiles at him.) Excuse me for my coat off. I have to get shaved and so forth. I hope you don't mind.

PAUL (to DEVERY). What have you been telling this guy about me?

DEVERY. If you gentlemen will excuse me—

(He goes upstairs.)

BROCK. Sit down. What'll you drink?

(PAUL sits.)

PAUL. Scotch, please—if you've got it.

BROCK (with a short laugh). If I've got it. (He calls out, loudly.) Eddie!! (To PAUL.) I got everything. Where do you think you are? (EDDIE appears.) Stick around, willya, for Christ's sake, and give the man a Scotch and— (To PAUL.) soda?

PAUL. Plain water.

BROCK (to EDDIE). Plain water.

EDDIE. Right. Rye ginger ale for you?

BROCK. Right. (To PAUL, happily.) He always knows what I feel to drink. Yeah. He's worked for me I don't know how many years. Also, he's my cousin. He knows me insides out. (To EDDIE.) Right?

EDDIE. That's right.

PAUL. Maybe I should be interviewing Eddie. (A great howl of laughter from BROCK.)

BROCK. Hey, you maybe got somethin' there. That's pretty good. What's it gonna be, pal? A plug or a pan?

PAUL. Why—

BROCK. I like to know these things. Then I know how to talk, if I know your angle.

PAUL. No angle. Just, well—just the facts.

BROCK. Oh, a pan! (He laughs, confident of his boorish charm. EDDIE brings their drinks.)

PAUL. Not exactly. (Taking the drink.) Thanks.

(EDDIE pads around the room, placing cigarettes, matches, and cigars in the right places.)

BROCK. It's okay! Don't worry. Write what you want. See, the way I look at it is like this. You can't hurt me and you can't help me. Nobody can. (They drink.) I'm only talkin' with you because Ed Devery asked me. What the hell, I pay a guy a hundred grand a year for advice so I'm a sucker if I don't take it. Right?

EDDIE (from a remote part of the room, answers automatically). That's right.

BROCK (screaming at him). Butt out, willya? (EDDIE looks up, confused and hurt, then goes on with his activity.) Devery likes it when I get wrote about.

(He goes to a newly placed humidor.)

PAUL. Well, of course, in Washington, Mr. Brock, there's a certain amount of value in the right kind of—

BROCK (getting out a magnificently boxed cigar and bringing it to PAUL). Cut it out, willya? You're breakin' my heart. Washington! I licked every town I ever decided, so what's different? Have a cigar!

PAUL (taking it). Thanks. (He looks at it carefully.) I'll give it to a Congressman.

BROCK. Five bucks apiece they cost me. From Cuba someplace.

PAUL. Well, in that case, I'll give it to a Senator. (He puts it in his pocket.)

BROCK (thoughtfully). Senators are pretty big stuff around here, huh?

PAUL (hardly knowing how to answer this). Yes.

BROCK (in disgust). Christ!

PAUL. Why? Shouldn't they be?

BROCK. Listen, you know what a Senator is to me? A guy who makes a hundred and fifty bucks a week.

(PAUL smiles, then takes a few sheets of folded note paper from his breast pocket, a pencil from another pocket, and makes a note.)

BROCK. What are you puttin' in?

PAUL (writing). Your little joke.

BROCK (delighted). You like it, huh?

PAUL. First class.

BROCK. Maybe I oughta be on the radio.

PAUL. Maybe.

BROCK. How much you wanna bet I make more money than Amos and Andy?

PAUL. No bet.

(EDDIE carries a bottle of Poland Water upstairs. BROCK lights a cigarette and stretches out on the sofa, happily. He feels he is doing well. He puts his feet up.)

BROCK (expansively). Well, fella, what do you wanna know?

PAUL (suddenly). How much money have you got?

BROCK (startled). What?

PAUL. How much money have you got?

BROCK. How should I know? What am I, an accountant?

PAUL (moving to him). You don't know?

BROCK. Not exactly.

PAUL. Fifty million?

BROCK. I'll tell you the truth. I don't know.

PAUL. Ten million?

BROCK. Maybe.

PAUL. One million?

BROCK. More.

PAUL (*pressing*). How much?

BROCK. Plenty.

(PAUL *gives up, turns away, and crosses back to his chair.*)

PAUL. Okay.

BROCK. And listen. I made every nickel. Nobody ever give me nothin'.

PAUL. Nice work. (*He sits.*)

BROCK (*putting out his cigarette and rising*). I can tell already. You're gonna give me the business.

PAUL (*trying to charm him*). Wait a minute—

BROCK. Go ahead! I like it.

PAUL. —you've got me wrong.

BROCK. Go ahead. Work for me. I got more people workin' for me than knows it. (*He moves away.*)

PAUL (*after a pause*). What do you think about—?

BROCK (*turning violently*). Go ahead! Pan me. Tell how I'm a mugg and a roughneck. You'll do me good.

PAUL. Listen, Mr. Brock—

BROCK. Lemme tell you about Cleveland. In 1937 there's a big dump there, see? And the city wants to get rid of it. High class scrap. So I go out there to look it over myself. There's a lot of other guys there, too. From Bethlehem even and like that. I didn't have a chance and I knew it. I figure I'm out of my class on the deal and I'm ready to pull out when all of a sudden the God-damnedest thing comes out there in one of the papers. About me. A big write-up. It says my name and about how come the city is gonna do business with hoodlums. Mind you, I was out of my class. I didn't have the kind of buttons a guy needs for a deal like that. So the next day—again. This time they got a picture of me. Next thing you know, a guy calls me up. A guy from the Municipal Commission. He comes up

to see me and he says they don't want no trouble. So I naturally string him along and I get busy on the phone and I raise some dough with a couple of boys from *De*troit. Then comes the big pan. On the front page. Next day I close the deal and in a week, I'm cartin'.

(EDDIE *comes downstairs.*)

PAUL (*after a pause*). What's your point?

BROCK. My point is you can't do me no harm if you make me out to be a mugg. Maybe you'll help me. Everybody gets scared, and for me that's good. Everybody scares easy.

PAUL. Well, not everybody.

BROCK. Well, enough. You can't hurt me. All you can do is build me up or shut up. Have a drink. (*He snaps his fingers at* EDDIE.)

(EDDIE *picks up* PAUL's *glass.*)

PAUL (*to* EDDIE). No, thanks. Really.

(EDDIE *puts the glass down and starts to turn away.*)

BROCK (*to* EDDIE). Do what I'm tellin' you! Who the hell pays you around here? (EDDIE *picks up the glass again, quickly, and does as he is told.*) When I'm home, he shaves me in the mornin'. I've got my own barber chair. (*To* EDDIE.) Right?

EDDIE. That's right.

BROCK (*moving back to the sofa*). Well, go ahead, pal. I thought you wanted to interview me.

(*There is a pause.*)

PAUL. Where were you born?

BROCK (*settling back again*). Jersey. Plainfield, New Jersey. 1907. I went to work when I was twelve years old and I been workin' ever since. I'll tell you my first job. A paper route. I bought a kid out with a swift kick in the keester.

PAUL (*writing*). And you've been working ever since.

BROCK (*missing the point*). Right. I'll tell you how I'm the top man in my racket. I been in it over twenty-five years. In the same racket.

PAUL. Steel.

BROCK. Junk. Not steel. *Junk*.

PAUL. Oh.

BROCK. Look, don't butter me up. I'm a junk man. I ain't ashamed to say it.

PAUL. All right.

BROCK. Lemme give you some advice, sonny boy. Never crap a crapper. I can sling it with the best of 'em.

(EDDIE *goes upstairs.*)

PAUL. Twenty-five years, you say?

BROCK. I'll tell you. I'm a kid with a paper route. I've got this little wagon. So on my way home nights, I come through the alleys pickin' up stuff. I'm not the only one. All the kids are doin' it. The only difference is, they keep it. Not me. I sell it. First thing you know, I'm makin' seven, eight bucks a week from that. Three bucks from papers. So I figure out right off which is the right racket. I'm just a kid, mind you, but I could see that. Pretty soon, the guy I'm sellin' to is handin' me anywheres from fifteen to twenty a week. So he offers me a job for ten. Dumb jerk. I'd be sellin' this guy his own stuff back half the time and he never knew.

PAUL. How do you mean?

BROCK (*relishing the memory*). Well, in the night, see, I'm under the fence and I drag it out and load up. In the mornin', I bring it in the front way and collect.

PAUL. Twelve years old, you were?

BROCK. Somethin' like that.

PAUL. So pretty soon you owned the whole yard.

BROCK. Damn right! This guy, the jerk? He works for me now. And you know who else works for me? The kid whose paper route I swiped. I figure I owe him. That's how I am.

PAUL. Pretty good years for the—junk business, these last few.

BROCK (*with a mysterious grin*). I ain't kickin'.

PAUL. Do you anticipate a decline now?

BROCK (*frowning suddenly*). Talk plain, pal.

(*The buzzer sounds.*)

PAUL. Is it still going to be good, do you think?

BROCK (*darkly*). We'll make it good.

PAUL (*quickly*). Who's we?

(*A pause.* BROCK *senses he is being cornered.*)

BROCK. We is me, that's who.

PAUL. I see.

BROCK. Fancy talk don't go with me.

(EDDIE *opens the door for the barber, the manicurist, and the bootblack.*)

THE BARBER. Good evening. In here, sir?

BROCK. Yeah. (*He removes his shirt and hands it to* EDDIE.)

PAUL (*rising*). Well, I'll get out of your—

BROCK. Don't go. Sit down. Sit down.

(*The* BARBER *and* MANICURIST *go about their work.* PAUL *sits down.* BROCK *looks at him and smiles.*)

BROCK. Sit down—I like you. You play your cards right, I'll put you on the payroll. You know what I mean?

PAUL. Sure.

BROCK (*to the barber*). Once over easy and no talkin'. (*To the* MANICURIST.) Just brush 'em up. I get a manicure every day.

THE MANICURIST. Yes, sir.

(*The* BOOTBLACK *gets into position, then notices that* BROCK *is not wearing shoes. He looks up, confused.*)

BROCK. Over there someplace.

(*The* BOOTBLACK *moves his equipment, finds the shoes, and works on them.*)

BROCK (*to* PAUL). Keep goin'. It's okay.

PAUL. I've been wondering what you're doing in Washington.

BROCK (*genially*). None of your God damn business.

PAUL. Sure it is.

BROCK. How come?

PAUL. You're a big man, Mr. Brock.

(*The* BARBER *is putting a towel around* BROCK's *neck.*)

BROCK *(for no reason)*. Not so tight!

THE BARBER. Sorry, sir.

BROCK *(to Paul)*. Sightseein'. That's what I'm in Washington for. Sightseein'.

PAUL. All right.

BROCK. Put that in the write-up, then nobody'll be scared.

PAUL. How long do you think you'll be around?

BROCK. Depends on how many sights I got to see.

PAUL. There's some talk you may be around for a long, long time.

BROCK. Where'd you get that?

PAUL. Around.

BROCK. Bull. What the hell do I care about politics? I got trouble enough in my own racket. I don't know nothin' about the politics racket.

PAUL. I hear you've come to find out.

BROCK. Listen, pal, so far I been nice to you. Don't pump me.

PAUL. My life's work.

BROCK. Well, don't work on me. I like to be friends with you.

(DEVERY appears on the balcony and starts downstairs.)

DEVERY *(to PAUL)*. How are you getting on with the monarch of all he surveys?

PAUL. Great. I found out he was born in Plainfield, New Jersey. He sure is a tough man to dig.

(A grunt from BROCK, as the BARBER works on his face. A BELLHOP knocks and enters, carrying a freshly pressed suit. He gives it to EDDIE, who takes it upstairs.)

DEVERY. I can't believe that. He loves to talk.

PAUL. Not to me.

BROCK. Why, I told you the story of my life, practically.

(BILLIE comes down.)

PAUL *(to DEVERY)*. He wouldn't even tell me how much money he's got.

BROCK. I don't know, I'm tellin' you.

(BILLIE goes to the liquor table and selects a bottle.)

PAUL *(to DEVERY)*. And he wouldn't tell me what he was doing in Washington.

BROCK. Because it's none of your business.

DEVERY. No secret. Just a little tax stuff. I told you.

PAUL. Yes, I know, but I didn't believe you.

(BILLIE starts back upstairs carrying the bottle.)

DEVERY. Oh, Billie, this is my friend Paul Verrall. *(To PAUL.)* Billie Dawn.

PAUL *(making his bow)*. How do you do?

(BILLIE nods and continues to move.)

BROCK. Wait a minute.

BILLIE *(slightly scared)*. What's the matter?

BROCK. Where do you think you're goin' with that?

BILLIE. Upstairs.

BROCK. Put it back.

BILLIE. I just wanted—

BROCK. I know what you wanted. Put it back.

BILLIE. Why can't I—?

BROCK *(mean)*. Because I say you can't, that's why. We got somebody comin'. Somebody important. I don't want you stinkin'.

BILLIE. Well, can't I just have—?

BROCK. No! Now put it back and go upstairs and change your clothes and don't give me no trouble.

(BILLIE stands motionless, humiliated.)

BROCK *(too loud)*. Do what I'm tellin' you!!

(BILLIE obeys. PAUL and DEVERY have half turned away in embarrassment. BROCK settles back in his chair to let the BARBER continue. BILLIE goes back upstairs. There is silence in the room. Nobody watches her go. About halfway up, she turns and regards PAUL with strange interest, but continues her move. If you were close enough, you might even recognize the

faint beginnings of a smile. She goes into her room. EDDIE *returns.*)

DEVERY. Barber, what'll you take to cut his throat?

(BROCK *sits up so suddenly that the barber almost does so.*)

BROCK *(in a fury).* There's some kind of jokes I don't like, Ed.

DEVERY. Don't get excited.

BROCK. Don't tell me what to do!

(*He strides over to* DEVERY *and pushes his face, hard.* DEVERY *is thrown off balance, but* PAUL *keeps him from falling.*)

DEVERY *(weakly).* Jesus, Harry. It was just a joke.

BROCK *(to the barber).* That's all.

BARBER. Not quite finished, sir.

BROCK. That's all, I told you. Beat it.

BARBER. Very good, sir.

BROCK *(to the* MANICURIST*).* You too. (*To* EDDIE, *indicating the help.*) Eddie, take care of 'em.

(*The* BARBER, *the* MANICURIST, *and the* BOOTBLACK *prepare to leave.*)

PAUL. I guess I'd better be—

(EDDIE *is attending to the tips.*)

BROCK. Don't go.

PAUL. I really should. I've got some work.

BROCK. Stick around, can't you? Looks like you're about the only friend I got left around here.

PAUL. Well, I'm not far. If anyone starts beating you, just scream and I'll come running.

(BROCK *laughs. The* BARBER, *the* MANICURIST, *and the* BOOTBLACK *leave.* EDDIE *picks up the shoes and takes them upstairs.*)

BROCK. You live in the hotel here?

PAUL. Right down the hall.

BROCK. Fine.

(*They shake hands.*)

PAUL. Other side of the tracks, of course.

BROCK. Say, don't kid me. I hear you do fine.

PAUL *(to* DEVERY*).* Good night, Ed.

DEVERY *(quietly).* Night.

(*He walks to the liquor table and pours himself a stiff drink.*)

BROCK *(to* PAUL*).* See you soon.

PAUL *(as he leaves).* Good night. Thanks for everything.

BROCK. Don't mention it.

DEVERY *(getting his brief case).* I need Billie's signature on a few things. Eddie, too.

BROCK. Sure. *(Yells.)* Billie!

BILLIE'S VOICE. What?

BROCK. Come on down here. Right away. *(To* DEVERY.) What are you sore about?

DEVERY. Not sore, Harry.

BROCK. You look funny.

DEVERY. I know.

BROCK. Don't you feel good? You want an aspirin?

DEVERY. No, no. I'm fine. In fact, considering that I have been dead for sixteen years, I am in remarkable health.

(BILLIE *comes down, wearing her most dignified dress.*)

BROCK *(to* DEVERY*).* Swear to God, sometimes I don't understand you at all.

DEVERY *(smiling).* Sometimes?

BILLIE. What do you want?

BROCK. Ed.

DEVERY. A few things I want you to sign, honey.

BILLIE. That's all I do around here is sign.

BROCK. Too bad about you. *(To* DEVERY.) When is he comin'? This Senator guy?

DEVERY. Any time now.

BROCK. I better get fixed up, huh?

(*Still in his undershirt, and shoeless, he picks up his jacket and tie and starts up. He glances at* BILLIE, *stops, and moves to examine every detail of her get-up.*)

BROCK. She look all right to you?

BILLIE. Look who's talkin'!

DEVERY. Perfect.

BROCK. You *sure* now?

BILLIE (*in a prideful whine*). What's the matter with me?

(BROCK *pays no attention to her.*)

BROCK. Tell me if somethin's wrong. I don't want to start off on no left foot.

DEVERY. Don't worry.

(BROCK *leaves.* DEVERY *brings out a sheaf of legal papers and spreads them out for* BILLIE *to sign. He hands her his fountain pen.*)

BILLIE. What's got into *him?*

DEVERY. Nothing. He just wants to make a good impression.

BILLIE. So let him.

DEVERY (*pointing out a line*). Two places on this one, please.

(EDDIE *enters and goes upstairs.*)

BILLIE (*signing, her head quite close to the paper*). What happened to all that stuff I signed last week?

DEVERY (*smiling*). All used up.

BILLIE. I bet I've signed about a million of these.

DEVERY. What you get for being a multiple corporate officer.

BILLIE. I *am?* (DEVERY *nods.*) What do you know?

DEVERY. You've come a long way from the chorus all right.

BILLIE. I wasn't only in the chorus. In *Anything Goes* I spoke lines.

DEVERY. Really?

BILLIE. Of course.

DEVERY. How many?

BILLIE. How many what?

DEVERY (*blotting*). Lines did you speak?

BILLIE. Five.

DEVERY. I never knew that.

BILLIE. Ask anybody.

DEVERY. I believe you.

BILLIE (*signing*). I could of been a star probably. If I'd of stuck to it.

DEVERY. Why didn't you?

BILLIE (*signing*). Harry didn't want me being in the show. He likes to get to bed early.

DEVERY. I see.

BILLIE. He's changed, Harry. Don't you think so?

DEVERY. How?

BILLIE. I don't know. He used to be like more satisfied. Now he's always runnin' around. Like this. What did he have to come to Washington, D. C., for?

DEVERY (*blotting*). Long story.

BILLIE. Well, don't tell it to me, I don't care where he goes. I just wish he'd settle down.

DEVERY. Ambitious.

BILLIE (*signing*). I know. He *talks* all the time now. He never used to. Now he's got me up half the night tellin' me what a big man he is. And how he's gonna be bigger. Run everything.

DEVERY. He may, at that.

BILLIE. Personally, I don't care one way or the other.

DEVERY. Very few people do, that's why he may get to do it. The curse of civilization. Don't-care-ism. Satan's key to success.

BILLIE. What kind of talk is that? You drunk or sump'n?

DEVERY (*blotting*). I'm drunk *and* "sump'n."

BILLIE. All right. I give up. (*She goes to the liquor table.*)

DEVERY (*without looking at her*). Take it easy.

BILLIE. Look now, don't *you* start.

DEVERY. Better if you drink later, Billie, after they've gone.

BILLIE. What's the deal, anyway?

DEVERY. No deal. Just important people, that's all.

BILLIE. Who? This Senator guy?

DEVERY. And *Mrs.* Hedges.

BILLIE. Harry told me this fellow works for him.

DEVERY. In a way.

BILLIE. So what's he puttin' it on for?

DEVERY. I suppose he wants him to *keep* working for him.

BILLIE. Too deep for me.

(The buzzer sounds. EDDIE comes downstairs and goes to the door.)

DEVERY *(dropping his voice).* All you have to do is be nice and no rough language.

BILLIE. I won't open my mush.

DEVERY. I didn't mean that.

BILLIE. I don't have to be down here, at all, you know. I *could* go upstairs. *(She starts out.)* In fact, I think I will.

(DEVERY moves to her.)

DEVERY. I'm telling you, Billie. Harry wouldn't like it.

BILLIE *(making a violent about-face).* All right all right all right! *(She moves to the sofa and sits.)*

(EDDIE opens the door to admit SENATOR NORVAL HEDGES and MRS. HEDGES. DEVERY moves to greet them.)

DEVERY. How are you, Norval?

HEDGES. Can't complain.

DEVERY *(to MRS. HEDGES).* Haven't seen you for a long time, Anna.

MRS. HEDGES. No, you haven't.

DEVERY. Come on in.

(SENATOR HEDGES is a worried man of sixty—thin, pale, and worn. MRS. HEDGES bears out Fanny Dixwell Holmes's comment that Washington is a city filled with great men and the women they married when they were very young. Except that the Senator is not a great man. He just looks like a great man.)

HEDGES *(to BILLIE).* Good evening.

BILLIE. Good evening.

DEVERY. Senator, you ought to remember this little lady. A great first-nighter like you. She used to be Billie Dawn?

HEDGES *(vaguely).* Oh yes . . . Yes, indeed.

DEVERY. Billie, this is Senator Norval Hedges I've told you so much about.

(HEDGE offers his hand. BILLIE takes it.)

HEDGES. How do you do?

BILLIE. How do you do?

DEVERY. And this is Mrs. Hedges, Billie.

MRS. HEDGES. Glad to meet you.

BILLIE. Glad to meet you.

(MRS. HEDGES seats herself beside BILLIE. There is an awkward pause. MRS. HEDGES suddenly extends her hand. BILLIE takes it.)

DEVERY. What do you say to a drink?

MRS. HEDGES. Love one.

HEDGES. Sounds all right to me.

DEVERY. Whiskey?

HEDGES. Be fine.

DEVERY *(to EDDIE).* Whiskey all around, Eddie.

EDDIE. Right. *(He goes to work on the drinks.)*

HEDGES. That's going to hit the spot just fine. *(He sits down.)*

MRS. HEDGES *(to BILLIE).* He's awfully tired.

DEVERY *(to HEDGES).* What have you been doing? Standing over a hot resolution all day?

HEDGES. Just about.

MRS. HEDGES. How do you like Washington, Mrs. Brock?

(There is a tiny pause. BILLIE, turned slightly away, does not realize for an instant that she is being addressed. DEVERY, having taken such pains to avoid identifying her too exactly during the course of the introductions, is afraid BILLIE may now correct MRS. HEDGES and ruin his careful diplomacy. BILLIE catches his eye.)

BILLIE. I haven't seen it yet.

MRS. HEDGES. You mean to say this is the very first time you've been here?

BILLIE. That's what I mean. I never went on the road.

HEDGES. Well, we must show you around. Beautiful city.

MRS. HEDGES. Too bad the Supreme Court isn't in session. You'd love that.

(*A pause.*)

BILLIE. What is it?

(MRS. HEDGES *doesn't know what to make of this. She looks over at the* SENATOR *to see if he has any ideas.* DEVERY *saves the moment by bursting into laughter.*)

DEVERY. Lots of people would like to know the answer to that one, Billie.

(*The* SENATOR *and* MRS. HEDGES *now settle for* BILLIE's *remark as a brand of metropolitan humor which they have never been able to get, quite. They join in the laughter.* EDDIE *serves the drinks.*)

DEVERY. What's this jam Wallace has gotten himself into?

HEDGES. Give him enough rope. I've said so from the start.

DEVERY. I know.

HEDGES. Trouble with these professional do-gooders is they never seem to— (*He stops as* BROCK *enters from above, carefully brushed and dressed.*)

BROCK. Hello, everybody!

DEVERY. Here we are.

(*The* SENATOR *rises. For some reason,* MRS. HEDGES *rises, too.*)

DEVERY. Senator Hedges, Harry Brock.

BROCK (*very hearty*). Say, it's about time us two got together, Senator. (*He shakes hands with* HEDGES *using both hands.*)

HEDGES. About time.

BROCK (*moving across the room*). And I suppose this is Mrs. Hedges.

MRS. HEDGES. That's right.

(*They shake hands, and* BROCK *nearly knocks her down with cordiality.*)

BROCK. I certainly am happy to make your acquaintance. Sit down. (*To* HEDGES.) Senator, sit down.

(SENATOR *and* MRS. HEDGES *sit.*)

HEDGES. Have a good trip down?

BROCK. Oh, sure. I come down in my own car. I came. Had to stop in Baltimore on the way down. I got a yard there, you know. A junk yard.

HEDGES. Is that so?

BROCK. Yeah. Just a *little* racket. Tell you the truth, it ain't worth the trouble it takes to run it, but I like it. It was the second yard I picked up. Before that I only had one yard.

MRS. HEDGES. How many do you have now?

BROCK. Hell, I don't know.

(*He stops abruptly, then addresses a blushing apology to* MRS. HEDGES.)

BROCK. *Excuse me.*

MRS. HEDGES (*being big about it*). Oh, that's all right.

BROCK (*to* HEDGES). I don't know why I like that little Baltimore outfit. I just always get kind of a feelin' from it. You know what I mean?

HEDGES. Sentimental.

BROCK. That's it! I'm sentimental. Like you say.

MRS. HEDGES. I think we're *all* a bit sentimental.

(*There is a pause. It seems* BILLIE's *turn to speak.*)

BILLIE. Well— (*They all look at her.*) It's a free country.

BROCK (*covering quickly*). How's things with you, Senator?

HEDGES. Same old grind.

BROCK. Lemme tell you something, Senator. You got one job I don't never wanna be. Everybody pesterin' you all the time, probably.

HEDGES. Part of the job.

MRS. HEDGES. Do you play bridge, Mrs. Brock?

BILLIE. No. Only gin.

MRS. HEDGES. I beg your pardon?

BILLIE. Gin rummy.

MRS. HEDGES. Oh, yes, of course. I was going to ask you to join us. A few of the girls? We meet now and then.

BILLIE. Yuh. Well, I don't play bridge.

BROCK *(to* BILLIE*).* You could learn to if you wanted.

BILLIE. I don't think so.

BROCK. Sure you could. *(To* MRS. HEDGES.*)* She couldn't play gin till I learned her. Now she beats my brains out.

DEVERY. How are you fixed for time tomorrow, Norval?

HEDGES. Pretty tight, I'm afraid.

DEVERY. Oh. I wanted to bring Harry over on a few things.

HEDGES. Ten o'clock all right?

DEVERY. How's that for you, Harry?

BROCK. In the mornin'?

HEDGES. Yes.

BROCK. Pretty early for me.

BILLIE. I'll say.

*(*BROCK *throws her a look.)*

HEDGES. Eleven?

BROCK. Okay.

DEVERY. Where'll you be?

HEDGES *(awkwardly).* Well, I can drop by here if that's all right.

DEVERY. Sure.

HEDGES *(lamely).* It's right on my way.

(There is a pause. BILLIE *rises and speaks to* MRS. HEDGES.*)*

BILLIE. You wanna wash your hands or anything, honey?

MRS. HEDGES *(so shocked that her reply is inaudible).* No, thank you.

*(*BILLIE *moves upstairs, through an atmosphere of tense embarrassment.)*

DEVERY *(to* HEDGES*).* I hope you're free on Friday night.

HEDGES. I think so. Are we, dear?

MRS. HEDGES. Well, we *can* be.

BROCK. Atta girl! *(He moves to sit beside her and puts his arm on the back of the sofa just behind her.)*

DEVERY. Fine. I'm doing a little dinner. Few people I want Harry to meet.

HEDGES. And who want to meet *him,* I'm sure.

BROCK *(coyly).* Say, listen, Senator. I'm just a junk man.

HEDGES. That's no disgrace in America.

DEVERY *(almost sardonic).* No—not if you're a *big* junk man.

(A pause. SENATOR HEDGES *rises and moves to* BROCK.*)*

HEDGES *(softly).* I want to thank you, Mr. Brock. For everything.

BROCK. Call me Harry, Senator, willya?

HEDGES. I haven't written you about it. Harry. Not considered good form. But I want you to know that I'm grateful for all you've done. For your support.

BROCK. Don't mention it. Just tit for tat. *(He stops, confused, then turns to* MRS. HEDGES.*)* Excuse *me!*

MRS. HEDGES *(at sea).* Quite all right.

BROCK. You see, Senator, what I think is —there's a certain kind of people ought to stick together.

HEDGES. My feeling.

BROCK. You know what I'm interested in. Scrap iron. I wanna buy it—I wanna move it—and I wanna sell it. And I don't want a lot of buttin' in with rules and regulations at no stage of the game.

HEDGES. Obviously.

BROCK *(rising).* I ain't talkin' about peanuts, mind you. All this junk I been sellin' for the last fifteen years—well, it's junk again. And I can sell it again once I lay my hands on it. Do you know how much scrap iron is layin' around all over Europe? Where the war's been?

HEDGES. No, I don't.

BROCK. Well, I don't either. Nobody knows. Nobody ever *will* know. It's more than you can think of. Well, I want to pick it up and bring it back where it belongs. Where it came from. Where I can use it. Who does it belong to anyway?

MRS. HEDGES. Why—isn't that interesting?

HEDGES. I have a copy for you of the preliminary survey made by—

BROCK (*sitting opposite* HEDGES). Boil it down and give it to me fast. I didn't come down here to have to do a lot of paper work. See, the way I work is like this. It's every man for himself—like dog eat dog. Like you gotta get the other guy before he gets you.

HEDGES. Exactly.

BROCK. What I got in mind is an operatin' combo—all over the world. There's enough in it for everybody—if they're *in,* that is. Up to now, I'm doin' fine. Everybody's lined up, everybody understands everybody. I want to get movin', see?—that's all. Only thing is, Ed here comes up with some new trouble every day. *This* law, *that* law, tariffs, taxes, State Department, *this* department, *that* department—

DEVERY. I'm sure you understand, Norval, that in an operation of this kind—

BROCK. Listen, all that stuff is just a lot of hot air to me. There's a way to do anything. That's all I know. It's up to you guys to find out how.

DEVERY. Norval's been working along those lines.

HEDGES. Yes. The Hedges-Keller Amendment, for example, guarantees no interference with free enterprise—foreign or domestic. We're doing everything we can to get it through quickly.

BROCK. Well, see that you do, 'cause that's why I'm here, to see that I get what I paid for.

DEVERY (*picking up the* SENATOR's *glass*). One more?

HEDGES. I think not.

BROCK. One for the road.

HEDGES. All right.

(DEVERY *hands the glass to* EDDIE.)

BROCK. How do things look to you, Senator?

HEDGES. Generally?

BROCK. Yeah, generally.

HEDGES. Well, not too bad. Just a question of staying on the alert. Too many crackpots around with their foot in the White House door.

BROCK. Tellin' me.

HEDGES (*confidentially*). He listens to everything, you know.

BROCK. Sure.

HEDGES. I said to Sam only last week, "This country will soon have to decide if the people are going to run the government or the government is going to run the people."

BROCK. You said it. (EDDIE *distributes fresh drinks.*) You know where I'd be if I had to start my business today? Up the creek. (*He looks at* MRS. HEDGES.) Excuse me.

(*This time she simply nods.*)

DEVERY. That's good sound thinking, Norval.

HEDGES. Thank you.

DEVERY. Worthy of Holmes.

HEDGES. Great man, Holmes.

DEVERY. My personal god.

BROCK. Who?

DEVERY. Oliver Wendell Holmes, Junior.

HEDGES. A wonderful man.

BROCK. Is he comin' Friday night?

(*An awkward pause.*)

DEVERY (*quietly*). I don't think so.

BROCK. Oh.

HEDGES. Well, we mustn't keep you.

MRS. HEDGES. No, we mustn't.

(*They rise and prepare to leave.*)

BROCK. Don't go. We stay up all the time.

HEDGES. Well, don't think of this as a proper visit. We just wanted to say hello. We'll be seeing a lot of each other, I'm sure.

BROCK. Right. Wait a second! (*He moves quickly to the cigar box and takes out a handful.*) Brought these down special.

(*He hands them to* HEDGES.)

HEDGES (*taking them.*) Very kind of you.

BROCK. Don't mention it.

HEDGES. Good night, Harry.

(They shake hands. BILLIE *returns.)*

BROCK. Senator, it's a pleasure.

MRS. HEDGES. Good night, Mrs. Brock.

BILLIE. Good night.

MRS. HEDGES *(to* BROCK*).* Good night and thank you so much.

BROCK. For what? Wait till I get settled down here. I'll show you somethin' to thank me for.

MRS. HEDGES. Good night. Good night, Ed.

DEVERY. See you tomorrow, Norval.

HEDGES. That's right. Good night.

BILLIE. Good night, all.

(The HEDGES *leave.* EDDIE *picks up the empty glasses.)*

BROCK. Okay, Eddie. Knock off.

EDDIE. Right.

*(*EDDIE *starts out.)*

DEVERY. Wait a minute.

*(*EDDIE *stops.* DEVERY *goes to his brief case and gets out some papers which* EDDIE *signs during the following.)*

BILLIE. Drips.

BROCK. What?

BILLIE. I said they're drips.

BROCK. Who the hell are you to say?

BILLIE *(stretching out on the sofa).* I'm myself, that's who.

BROCK. Well, shut up. Nobody asked you.

(He sits down and removes his shoes.)

BILLIE. Pardon me for living.

BROCK. Get upstairs.

BILLIE. Not yet.

BROCK *(rising).* Get upstairs, I told you.

*(*BILLIE *goes, quietly, attempting to retain her little dignity by giving him a look of contempt.)*

EDDIE *(signing).* Here too?

DEVERY. Yes.

EDDIE. Since when I'm only Vice-President?

DEVERY. You're slipping.

BROCK *(worried).* She's gonna be in the way, that dame.

DEVERY. What are you going to do about it?

BROCK *(sitting).* I don't know. Right now I feel like to give her the brush.

DEVERY. Pretty complicated.

BROCK. I know.

DEVERY. At the moment, she owns more of you than *you* do. On paper.

BROCK. Your idea.

DEVERY. Yes, and a damned good one, too. Keeps you in the clear and you know what it saves you?

BROCK. I know, I know. You told me a million times.

DEVERY. Sorry.

BROCK. You better think somethin' up. She's gonna louse me up all the way down the line. God-damn dumb broad.

DEVERY. Send her home.

BROCK. No.

DEVERY. Why not?

BROCK *(softly).* I'm nuts about her.

*(*DEVERY *looks at him quickly, in surprise.)*

DEVERY *(turning away).* Can't have your cake and eat it.

BROCK. What?

DEVERY. Just a saying?

BROCK. It don't make sense.

DEVERY. All right.

(There is a long, long pause.)

BROCK. What's cakes got to do with it?

DEVERY. Nothing, Harry.

*(*EDDIE *finishes signing.)*

EDDIE. Okay?

*(*DEVERY *picks up the papers and looks them over.)*

DEVERY. Okay.

*(*EDDIE *leaves.)*

BROCK. Must be a way to smarten her up a little. Ain't there?

DEVERY. I suppose so.

BROCK. Some kinda school we could send her to, maybe?

DEVERY. I doubt that.

BROCK. Then what?

DEVERY. Well, we might be able to find someone who could smooth the rough edges off.

BROCK. How?

DEVERY. Let me think about it. And while I'm thinking about that, Harry, there's something you might be turning over in *your* mind.

BROCK. Yeah, what?

DEVERY. Well, if you've got to have her around you--the possibility of getting married.

BROCK. Not me.

DEVERY. Why not?

BROCK. I *been* married. I don't like it.

DEVERY. How long have you—you know —been with Billie?

BROCK. I don't know. Eight, nine years. Why?

DEVERY. Well, what the hell?

BROCK. It gets different when you get married.

DEVERY. Why should it?

BROCK. How do I know why should it? It just does, that's all.

DEVERY. All right.

BROCK. This way, I give her somethin', I'm a hell of a fella. We get married, she's got it comin', she thinks.

DEVERY. Billie's not like that.

BROCK. A broad's a broad.

DEVERY. Time may come you'll be sorry.

BROCK (*rising*). Listen, don't shove me.

DEVERY. All right. (*He gives* BROCK *a patronizing look, and pours a drink.*)

BROCK (*irritated*). Don't make out like I'm some kind of a dope. I know what I'm doin'.

DEVERY. Sure you do.

BROCK. All right. So don't make them Harvard College expressions on your face. So far you still work for me.

DEVERY. That's right, Harry.

BROCK. Okay. Just tell me what you think. If I feel like it, I'll do it. If not, no. And don't give me them looks down your nose.

(DEVERY *nods, quietly.* BROCK *slumps into a chair and sulks for a moment.*)

BROCK. What's so important I should get married all of a sudden?

DEVERY. You're moving up, Harry. Bigger places. Bigger people. No matter what goes on underneath, these people make sure of their respectable fronts.

BROCK. The hell with 'em.

DEVERY. That's just talk. You're in the Big League now, and there are certain rules.

BROCK. Like what? Like you got to be married?

DEVERY. No. Like you can't expect to just pass off a setup like this. There's such a thing as being *too* colorful.

BROCK. All right. I'll let you know. But if I do or if I don't we got to do somethin' with her. She just don't fit in. Do you think so?

DEVERY. You're right.

BROCK. Every time she opened her kisser tonight, somethin' wrong come out.

DEVERY. The hell of it is she doesn't realize.

BROCK (*desperately*). Ed, couldn't you have a talk with her?

DEVERY. Take more than a talk, I'm afraid.

BROCK. Then what?

DEVERY. It's a big job, Harry. It's not easy to make a person over. Maybe impossible. She has to have a great many things explained to her. I won't be around enough, and even if I were, I couldn't do it. No patience, too old, and I don't know enough myself. Not the kind of things she—

(BROCK *has been thinking hard. Now he cuts in, suddenly.*)

BROCK. Wait a minute!

DEVERY. What?

(BROCK *doesn't get ideas often. When he does, he thrills to the sensation.*)

BROCK (*very quietly*). The guy from down the hall?

DEVERY. Who?

BROCK. The interview guy. There's a smart little cookie.

DEVERY. Well—

BROCK (*selling it*). Knows the town. Knows the angles. Very classy, with that bowing. (*He illustrates, in an imitation of Paul's mannerism.*)

DEVERY. He could do it, probably, but he won't.

BROCK. Why not?

DEVERY. Well, he's not—

BROCK. I'll pay him whatever he wants.

DEVERY. I don't think so.

BROCK. Make you a bet. (*He goes to the phone.*) What's his name again?

DEVERY. Wait a minute, Harry.

BROCK. What?

DEVERY. Verrall. Paul Verrall. Harry, I'm not sure—

BROCK. I like it. (*Into the phone.*) Give me Verrall. . . . Yeah . . . Mr. Verrall.

DEVERY (*losing his temper*). I wish you wouldn't sail into things.

BROCK. Shut up. (*Into phone.*) Hello, pal. . . . Harry Brock. . . . You got a minute? I wanna have a little talk. . . . Got a proposition to make you. . . . What? No, no. Nothin' like that. This is all right. . . . Absolutely legitimate. . . . Do that, will you? . . . Fine. . . . I'll be right here. (*He hangs up.*) I like that guy.

DEVERY. Well enough to have him around with Billie all the time?

BROCK. Are you kiddin'? With them glasses? Listen, this is all right. I can feel it. I might even tap him for a little dope myself once in a while.

DEVERY. What about Billie? She may not care for the idea.

BROCK. She'll do what I tell her.

DEVERY. That's not the point, Harry. People don't learn anything unless they want to.

BROCK. She knows what's good for her, she'll want to.

DEVERY. You know best.

BROCK. Damn right. Listen, what do you think I ought to give him?

DEVERY. Seems to me you ought to try just putting it on a friendly basis.

BROCK. I don't believe in nothin' on no friendly basis.

(*The buzzer sounds.*)

DEVERY. I know this fellow.

BROCK. I know lots of fellas. Money talks. I don't want nobody doing me no favors.

DEVERY. Why not talk it over with him and see what—?

(BROCK *goes to the door and opens it.* PAUL *comes in.*)

BROCK (*heartily*). Come on in, pal. Come on in.

PAUL. Thanks.

BROCK. Have a drink.

PAUL. No, thanks. I'm just in the middle of something.

BROCK. Sit down, I want to ask you somethin'.

(PAUL *sits.*)

PAUL. Sure.

BROCK. How much do you make a week?

PAUL. How should I know? What am I, an acountant?

(BROCK *is delighted to hear himself quoted. He laughs.*)

BROCK (*to* DEVERY). I love this guy. (*To* PAUL, *as he sits down beside him.*) What's your name again?

PAUL. Verrall.

BROCK. No, I mean your regular name.

PAUL. Paul.

BROCK. Listen, Paul. Here's the layout. I got a friend. Nice kid. I think you probably seen her in here before. Billie?

PAUL. Oh, yes.

BROCK. Well, she's a good kid, see? Only to tell you the truth, a little on the stupid side. Not her fault, you understand. I got her out of the chorus. For the chorus she was smart enough, but I'm scared she's gonna be unhappy in this town. She's never been around with such kind of people, you know what I mean?

PAUL. No.

BROCK. Well, I figure a guy like you could help her out. And me, too.

PAUL. How?

BROCK. Show her the ropes, sort of. Explain her what goes on and all like that. In your spare time. What do you say?

PAUL. No, I don't think I could handle it, Mr. Brock.

BROCK. Means a lot to me. I'll give you two hundred bucks a week.

PAUL. All right, I'll do it.

(BROCK looks at DEVERY and laughs again.)

BROCK. I'm tellin' you. I love this guy.

PAUL. When do I start?

BROCK. Right now. Why not right now?

PAUL. Fine.

BROCK. Let me introduce you like and you take it from there.

PAUL. Good.

BROCK (getting up and calling loudly). Billie!

BILLIE'S VOICE. What?

BROCK. Come on down here a minute. (To PAUL.) She's a hell of a good kid. You'll like her.

(BILLIE comes out onto the landing, brushing her hair. She is wearing a negligee that does all the proper things. PAUL rises.)

BILLIE (as she sees PAUL). I'm not dressed.

BROCK. It's all right. It's all right. He's a friend of the family. (BILLIE hesitates). Come on, I'm tellin' you! (BILLIE comes down into the room.) Honey, this is Paul Verrall!

BILLIE. Yes, I know.

BROCK. He wants to talk to you.

BILLIE. What about?

BROCK. You'll find out. Sit down. (BILLIE sits.) Come on up a minute, willya, Ed?

DEVERY. Sure.

BROCK. Bring the stuff.

(DEVERY picks up his brief case and follows BROCK out of the room. There is a pause when they have gone. Finally, Paul smiles at BILLIE. No response. He stops smiling.)

PAUL. Your—friend, Mr. Brock, has an idea he'd like us to spend a little time together. You and me, that is.

BILLIE. You don't say.

PAUL. Yes.

BILLIE. What are you? Some kind of gigolo?

PAUL. Not exactly.

BILLIE. What's the idea?

PAUL. Nothing special. (He sits on the sofa, some distance from BILLIE.) He just wants me to put you wise to a few things. Show you the ropes. Answer any questions.

BILLIE. I got no questions.

PAUL. I'll give you some.

BILLIE. Thanks.

PAUL. Might be fun for you, in a way. There's a lot to see down here. I'd be glad to show you around.

BILLIE. You know this Supreme Court?

PAUL. Yes.

BILLIE. I'd like to take that in.

PAUL. Sure. We're on, then?

BILLIE. How do you mean?

PAUL. The arrangement.

BILLIE. I don't mind. I got nothin' much to do.

PAUL. Good.

BILLIE. What's he payin' you?

PAUL. Two hundred.

BILLIE. You're a sucker. You could of got more. He's got plenty.

PAUL. I'd have done it for nothing. (BILLIE looks at him with rare disbelief and gives a mirthless little laugh.) I would.

BILLIE. Why?

PAUL. This isn't work. I like it.

(BILLIE *smiles*.)

BILLIE. He thinks I'm too stupid, huh?

PAUL. Why, no—

BILLIE. He's right. I'm stupid and I like it.

PAUL. You do?

BILLIE. Sure. I'm happy. I got everything I want. Two mink coats. Everything. If there's somethin' I want, I ask. And if he don't come across—I don't come across. (*This candor has* PAUL *off balance*.) If you know what I mean.

PAUL (*with a gulp*). Yes, I do.

BILLIE. So as long as I know how to get what I want, that's all I want to know.

PAUL. As long as you know what you want.

BILLIE. Sure. What?

PAUL. As long as you know what you want.

BILLIE. You tryin' to mix me up?

PAUL. No.

(*A pause*.)

BILLIE. I'll tell you what I *would* like.

PAUL. Yes?

BILLIE. I'd like to learn how to talk good.

PAUL. All right.

BILLIE. Is it hard to learn?

PAUL. I don't think so.

BILLIE. What do I have to do?

PAUL. Well, I might give you a few books to start with. Then, if you don't mind, I'll correct you now and then.

BILLIE. Go ahead.

PAUL. When *I* know, that is. I don't—talk so good myself.

BILLIE. You'll do.

PAUL. Fine.

BILLIE. I never say "ain't." Did you notice that? Never.

PAUL. I do.

BILLIE. Well, I'll correct *you* then.

PAUL. Do that.

BILLIE. Since I was very small, I never say it. We had this teacher. She used to slug you if you did it.

PAUL. Did what?

BILLIE. Said ain't.

PAUL. Oh.

BILLIE. So I got out of the habit.

PAUL. I wonder if it was worth the slugging.

BILLIE. Well, not hard.

PAUL. It's the principle of the thing. There's too much slugging. I don't believe in it.

BILLIE. All right, I don't believe in it either.

PAUL. Good.

BILLIE. I learn pretty fast, don't I?

PAUL (*smiling*). You're great, Miss Dawn.

BILLIE. Billie.

PAUL. Billie. (*A tiny pause*.) Sort of an odd name, isn't it?

BILLIE. What are you talkin'? Half the kids I know are named it. Anyway, it's not my real name.

PAUL. What is?

(*She has to think a moment before she can answer*.)

BILLIE. My God! Emma.

PAUL. What's the matter?

BILLIE. Do I look to you like an Emma?

PAUL. No. You don't look like a Billie, either.

BILLIE. So what do I look like?

PAUL. To me?

BILLIE. Yuh, to you.

PAUL. You look like a little angel.

(*A pause*.)

BILLIE. Lemme ask you. Are you one these talkers, or would you be interes in a little action?

PAUL (*stunned*). Huh?

BILLIE. I got a yen for you right off.

PAUL. Do you get many?

BILLIE. Now and then.

PAUL. What do you do about them?

BILLIE. Stick around. You'll find out.

PAUL. All right, I will.

BILLIE. And if you want a tip, I'll tell you. Sweet-talk me. I like it. Like that angel line. (PAUL *looks upstairs with a frown.*) Don't worry about him. He don't see a thing. He's too dizzy from being a big man.

PAUL (*rising and moving away*). This is going to be a little different than I thought.

BILLIE. You mind?

PAUL. No.

BILLIE. It's only fair. We'll educate each other.

PAUL (*in a weak attempt to get on safer ground*). Now, about those books.

BILLIE. Yes?

PAUL. I'll get them for you tomorrow. I'll look around my place, too. If there's anything interesting, I'll drop it by later.

BILLIE. All right.

PAUL. We can figure out time every day the day before.

(BILLIE *beckons.* PAUL *comes to her. She reaches up, takes his lapel, and brings his ear close.*)

BILLIE. Or the night.

PAUL (*straightening*). Sure.

(BROCK *and* DEVERY *come down.* BROCK *now wears a silk lounging jacket.*)

BROCK. Well! You two gonna get together?

PAUL. I think we're all set.

BROCK. Great, great!

(DEVERY *picks up his hat.*)

PAUL. Well, if you'll excuse me—

BROCK. Have a drink.

PAUL. No, thanks.

DEVERY. See you tomorrow, Harry.

BROCK. Right.

DEVERY. Good night, Billie.

BILLIE. So long.

(DEVERY *leaves.*)

PAUL (*to* BILLIE). Good night.

BILLIE. Good night.

BROCK (*taking* PAUL *to the door*). So long, kid. Appreciate it.

PAUL (*with a look at* BILLIE). So do I.

(*He leaves.* BROCK, *beaming satisfaction, comes back into the room. He stops, looks at* BILLIE, *and takes a deck of cards out of his pocket. He moves over to the table and starts to shuffle the cards.* BILLIE *falls automatically into this nightly routine. She brings a box of cigarettes to the table. They cut the cards. He wins. He sits down and begins to deal.* BILLIE *mixes two drinks and brings them to the table. She sits down, takes up her hand, and arranges her cards with flourish. The game begins. They play swiftly, professionally, with no sense of enjoyment. She takes three of his discards in quick succession. He grows tenser and tenser.*)

BILLIE (*laying down her hand*). Gin.

BROCK. Forty-one.

(BILLIE *shoves the cards to him and picks up the score pad.*)

BILLIE. Forty-one?

BROCK. Forty-one.

(*She marks the score, after computing it by drumming her fingers on her temple. He shuffles, cuts, and hands her the pack. She deals. They pick up their cards and play again.*)

BROCK. If you pay attention, that Verrall guy can do you some good.

BILLIE. All right.

BROCK. You're in the Big League now. I want you to watch your step.

BILLIE. All right.

BROCK. You got to learn to fit in. If not, I can't have you around, and that's no bull. (*A pause, as they play.*) You got to be careful what you do. (*He draws a card, looks at it, discards it.*) And—what you say. (*She picks it up and lays down her hand.*)

BILLIE. Three!

BROCK. Twenty-eight.

BILLIE. Twenty-eight?

BROCK. Twenty-eight.

(*She scores. He shuffles, cuts. She deals. They play again.*)

BILLIE. You could use a little education yourself, if you ask me.

BROCK. Who asked you?

BILLIE. Nobody.

BROCK. So shut up.

BILLIE. Can't I talk?

BROCK. Play your cards.

(*A pause.*)

BILLIE (*mumbling*). It's a free country.

BROCK. That's what *you* think. (*They play.* BILLIE *starts to hum "Anything Goes."* BROCK's *nerves are further shaken.*) Do you mind?!!

BILLIE (*laying down her hand*). Gin.

BROCK. Thirty-four.

BILLIE. Thirty-four?

BROCK. Thirty-four.

(*He shuffles the cards as she scores.*)

BILLIE. Schneider.

BROCK. Where do you get the schneid?

(BILLIE *hands him the score.*)

BILLIE. Fifty-five dollars. And sixty cents.

BROCK. All right, that's all!

(BROCK *throws down the cards and rises. He crosses and pours a drink.*)

BILLIE. Pay me now.

BROCK (*yelling*). What the hell's the matter? Don't you trust me?

BILLIE. What are you hollerin' for? You always make *me* pay.

BROCK. Christ's sake!

BILLIE (*taunting him*). Sore loser.

BROCK. Shut up!

BILLIE. Fifty-five dollars. And sixty cents.

(*He brings a large roll of bills from his pocket, peels off a few, and puts them on the table.* BILLIE *looks at him, hard, until he provides the sixty cents.*)

BILLIE. Thanks.

(BROCK *starts for the staircase.*)

BROCK. Come on up.

BILLIE. In a minute.

BROCK. Now.

BILLIE. In a minute, I told you.

(*This is the one moment of the day of which* BILLIE *is boss.* BROCK *goes up quietly and shuts the door.* BILLIE *lays out a hand of solitaire. As she plays, she sings, softly, and interpolates little orchestral figures.*)

"In olden days a glimpse of stocking
Was looked on as something shocking,
But now Lord knows (tyah dah)
Anything goes. (tata tata—tata tata—tzing!)

Good authors, too, who once—"

(*The door buzzer. She stops singing, throws a look up the stairs, makes a few personal adjustments, and goes to the door.* PAUL *enters, carrying a few books and two newspapers.*)

PAUL. Hello.

BILLIE. Hello.

PAUL. Morning papers.

(BILLIE *takes them.*)

BILLIE. You could of saved yourself the trouble. I don't read papers.

PAUL. Never?

BILLIE. Once in a while the back part.

PAUL. I think you should. The front part.

BILLIE. Why?

PAUL. It's interesting.

BILLIE. Not to me.

PAUL. How do you know if you never read it?

BILLIE. Look, if you're gonna turn out to be a pest, we could call the whole thing off right now.

PAUL. Sorry.

BILLIE. I look at the papers sometimes. I just never understand it. So what's the sense?

PAUL. Tell you what you do. You look through these. Anything you don't understand, make a mark. (*He hands her a red editing pencil.*) Then tomorrow, I'll explain whatever I can. All right?

BILLIE. All right.

PAUL (*handing her the books*). And I thought you might like these.

BILLIE. I'll try. (*She puts the books and papers on a near-by table.*)

PAUL. No, don't do that. Just start reading. If you don't like it, stop. Start something else.

BILLIE. There's only one thing. My eyesight isn't so hot.

PAUL. Well, why don't you wear glasses?

BILLIE. Glasses!

PAUL. Why not?

BILLIE. Because it's terrible.

(*They look at each other for a time. She notices his glasses, but can't think of anything to say that will soften her remark. She moves in closer to him. Then closer still. It looks as though they are about to dance. She leans toward him. Now they are touching.* PAUL *responds. He puts his arms about her and kisses her. A long, expert kiss. They come out of it.*)

BILLIE. Of course, they're not so bad **on** men.

PAUL (*softly*). Good night, Billie.

BILLIE. Good night.

(PAUL *leaves.* BILLIE *looks around for the light switch, finds it, and turns out the lights in the sitting room. The balcony, however, is still illuminated. She starts up the stairs, slowly, and begins singing again.*)

BILLIE. "Good authors, too, who once knew better words
Now only use four-letter words
Writing prose (tyah dah)—"

(*She stops, turns, and looks back at the books and papers, her new key to something or other. She moves back into the room, picks them up, and, clutching them tightly, starts up again, continuing the song.*)

"Writing prose (tyah dah)—"

(*She turns out the balcony light, sings the "tyah dah" at the door to* BROCK's *room as two notes of derision, then goes into her room and slams the door as we hear her last triumphant.*)

"Anything goes—!"

CURTAIN

ACT TWO

SCENE: *Two months or so have passed. The room looks lived in. A new piece of furniture has been added—a desk, which stands to one side. It is loaded with books, papers, magazines, and clippings. On the walls are some lovely framed reproductions of French and American moderns, and one or two small originals. In another part of the room stands a large globe-map. There is also a library dictionary on a stand near the desk. At the other side of the room, a Capehart. On the floor beside the instrument are stacks of record albums. In every part of the room, more books, magazines, pictures, and books. It is early evening and* BILLIE, *wearing lounging pajamas and eyeglasses, is sitting on the sofa, her legs stretched out before her, reading a newspaper. She makes a mark on the paper, then lifts it high to continue her reading. The front page of the paper is covered with red marks. It looks like a newspaper with the measles. She puts the paper down with a sign of fatigue and moves to the Capehart, stretching. She selects a few records, puts them on the machine, starts it, and goes back to the sofa. The room is soon filled with the soothing sounds of the Sibelius "Concerto in D Minor for Violin and Orchestra, op. 47." The door buzzer sounds.* EDDIE *comes through, still wearing his hat, and opens the door to admit* PAUL. BILLIE *looks around and smiles. She takes off her glasses, quickly.*

PAUL. How are you, Eddie?

EDDIE. Great.

BILLIE. Hello.

(EDDIE *goes.*)

PAUL. Hello, smarty-pants. *(He moves to her.)* How you coming?

BILLIE. Not so bad?

PAUL. Hm?

BILLIE. *-ly,* bad*ly.* Would you like some tea?

PAUL *(sitting down).* No, thanks. *(He indicates the music.)* Nice, that.

BILLIE. Sibelius, opp forty-seven. *(They listen for a moment.)* Guess who I just had for tea? *To* tea?

PAUL. Who?

BILLIE. Mrs. Hedges.

PAUL. Really? How was it?

BILLIE. Don't ask! You know, she's pretty stupid, too, but in a refined sort of way. Of course, we didn't have very much to talk about—so then she happened to notice my book laying there—

PAUL. Lying.

BILLIE. —my book lying there, and she said, "Oh, I've been meaning to read that again for years!"

PAUL. What was it?

BILLIE. *David Copperfield.*

PAUL. Oh, yes.

BILLIE. So then we got to talking about it and you want to know something?

PAUL. What?

BILLIE. She's never read it at all.

PAUL. How do you know?

BILLIE. I could tell from the way we were talking.

PAUL. Does that surprise you?

BILLIE. What, that she'd never read it?

PAUL. Yes.

BILLIE. No.

PAUL. Then what?

BILLIE. Well, why should she make out like she did? It's no crime if she didn't.

PAUL. Everybody does that, more or less.

BILLIE. Do you?

PAUL. Sometimes.

BILLIE. I don't.

PAUL. I know, Billie. You have the supreme virtue of honesty.

BILLIE. Thanks.

(A WAITER *comes in from the service wing, crosses to the coffee table, and picks up the tray. A letter lies under it.)*

BILLIE. I'm glad I got something after two months of this.

(The WAITER *starts out.)*

PAUL. You didn't get that from me, I'm afraid.

BILLIE. I'm not so sure.

PAUL *(prompting).* Thank you.

BILLIE. You're welcome.

PAUL *(indicating the waiter).* No.

BILLIE. Oh . . . *(She calls out to the* WAITER.*)* Thank you! *(The* WAITER *nods and leaves. She picks up the letter.)* I got this letter today. From my father.

PAUL. New York?

BILLIE. Yes. I can't get over it.

PAUL. Why?

BILLIE. Well, it's the first time he ever wrote me in about eight years. We had a fight, sort of. He didn't want me to go with Harry.

PAUL. What does he do?

BILLIE. My father?

PAUL. Yes.

BILLIE. Gas Company. He used to read meters, but in this letter he says how he can't get around so good any more so they gave him a different job. Elevator man. *(A pause, as she remembers back. The music is still playing.)* Goofy old guy. He used to take a little frying pan to work every morning, and a can of Sterno, and cook his own lunch. He said everybody should have a hot lunch. *(Another pause.)* I swear I don't know how he did it. There were four of us. Me and my three brothers, and he had to do everything. My mother died. I never knew her. He used to feed us and give us a bath and buy our clothes. Everything. That's why all my life I used to think how some day I'd like to pay him back. Funny how it worked out. One night, I brought home a hundred dollars and I gave it to him. You know what he did? He threw it in the toilet and pulled the chain. I thought he was going to hit me, sure, but he didn't. In his whole life, he never hit me once.

PAUL (carefully). How'd he happen to write you? I mean, after all this time.

BILLIE. Because I wrote him.

PAUL (smiling). Oh.

BILLIE. He says he's thought about me every day. God. I haven't thought about him, I bet, once even, in five years. That's nothing against him. I haven't thought of anything.

PAUL. Be nice to see him, maybe.

BILLIE. I guess so—but he said I should write him again and I should have a hot lunch every day and I should let him know how I am but that he didn't want to see me if I was still living the life of a concubine. I looked it up. . . . He always used to say: "Don't ever do nothin' you wouldn't want printed on the front page of the New York Times." (A pause.) Hey— I just realized. I've practically told you the whole story of my life by now, practically.

PAUL. I've enjoyed it very much.

BILLIE. How about the story of your life?

PAUL. Oh, no. It's too long—and mostly untrue. (BILLIE takes the letter over to the desk and puts it in a drawer.) What'd you do this morning?

BILLIE (brightening). Oh, I went to the newsreel and then over to the National Gallery like you said.

PAUL. How was it?

BILLIE. Wonderful. Quiet and peaceful and so interesting and did you ever notice? It smells nice. (PAUL smiles.) It does.

PAUL. How long did you stay?

BILLIE. Oh—a couple hours. I'm going again.

PAUL. Good.

BILLIE. Only the next time I wish you could come along.

PAUL. All right.

BILLIE. Boy, there's sure some things there that could use some explaining. (She moves toward PAUL.) Oh, and you know what else I did today? I went down to Brentano's and I just walked around, like you said I should, and looked at all the different kinds of books, and then the ones I thought maybe I'd like to read I took.

PAUL. That's right.

BILLIE. Well, pretty soon I had a whole big pile, too big to carry even. So I stopped. And I thought, my God, it'll take me about a year to read this many. Then I looked around, and compared to all the books there, my little pile was like nothing. So then I realized that even if I read my eyes out till the day I die I couldn't even make a little dent in that one store. Next thing you know I bust out crying.

(She sits down, dejected.)

PAUL. Nobody reads everything.

BILLIE. They don't?

PAUL. Of course not.

BILLIE. I've sure been trying to.

PAUL (rising and going to the desk). I don't suppose you got a chance to read my piece? (He holds up a copy of the New Republic.)

BILLIE. What are you talking? Of course I read it. Twice. (A pause.)

PAUL. What'd you think?

BILLIE (slowly). Well, I think it's the best thing I ever read. I didn't understand one word.

PAUL. What didn't you understand?

BILLIE. None of it.

PAUL. Here. Show me what.

(BILLIE puts on her eyeglasses and moves to join him at the desk. PAUL laughs.)

BILLIE. What's so funny? That I'm blind, practically?

PAUL. Practically blind.

BILLIE. —practically blind?

PAUL. You're wonderful.

BILLIE. I'm sorry I look funny to you.

PAUL. You don't. They make you look lovelier than ever.

BILLIE. You sound like one of those ads for eyeglasses. (She sits down at the desk and puts her attention on the article. PAUL points to it.)

PAUL. What?

BILLIE. Well, like the name of it. "The Yellowing Democratic Manifesto."

PAUL. Simple.

BILLIE. To who? Whom.—Whom? Well, anyway, not to me.

PAUL. Well, look. You know what "yellowing" means?

BILLIE. Not this time.

PAUL. When a piece of paper gets old, what happens to it?

(BILLIE thinks.)

BILLIE. You throw it away.

PAUL. No, it turns yellow.

BILLIE. It does?

PAUL. Of course.

BILLIE. What do you know?

PAUL. Now, "democratic." You know what that means, don't you?

BILLIE (nodding). Not Republican.

PAUL. Well, not exactly. It just means pertaining to our form of government, which is a democracy.

(There is a pause.)

BILLIE (understanding). Oh. (A sudden frown.) What's "pertaining"?

PAUL (with a gesture). Has to do with.

BILLIE (musing). Pertaining. Nice word.

(She makes a note of it.)

PAUL. All right, now—"manifesto."

BILLIE. I don't know.

PAUL. Why didn't you look it up?

BILLIE. I did look it up. I still don't know.

PAUL. Well, look—when I say "manifesto," I mean the set of rules and ideals and—principles and hopes on which the United States is based.

BILLIE. And you think it's turning yellow.

PAUL. Well, yes. I think the original inspiration has been neglected, and forgotten.

BILLIE. And that's bad.

PAUL. And that's bad.

(She thinks it over for a moment, hard. We seem to see it soaking in. She picks up the magazine.)

BILLIE (reading). "Even a— (She looks at PAUL.) —cursory? (He nods.) —examination of contemporary society in terms of the Greek philosophy which defines the whole as a representation of its parts, sends one immediately to a consideration of the individual as a citizen and the citizen as an individual."

PAUL. Well—

BILLIE. I looked up every word!

PAUL. Well, listen—thousands of years ago, a Greek philosopher— (He pauses to make sure she is following.) —once said that the world could only be as good as the people who lived in it.

(There is a pause as BILLIE thinks this over.)

BILLIE. Makes sense.

PAUL. All right. So I said, you take one look at America today and right away you figure you better take a look at the people in it. One by one, sort of.

BILLIE. Yuh.

PAUL. That's all.

BILLIE (pointing to the article). That's this?

PAUL. Sure.

BILLIE. Well, why didn't you say so?

PAUL. Too fancy, huh? (He moves to the other side of the room.) You know, I think I'm going to do that piece again Plainer.

BILLIE. Oh, and you know that little thing you gave me about Napoleon?

PAUL. No, what?

BILLIE. By Robert G. Ingersoll?

PAUL. Oh, yes.

BILLIE. Well, I'm not sure if I get that either.

PAUL. No deep meaning there.

BILLIE. There must be. He says about how he goes and looks in Napoleon's tomb.

PAUL. Yuh.

BILLIE. And he thinks of Napoleon's whole sad life.

PAUL. Yuh.

BILLIE. And then in the end he says he himself would have rather been a happy farmer.

PAUL (quoting). "—and I said I would rather have been a French peasant and worn wooden shoes. I would rather have lived in a hut with a vine growing over the door, and the grapes growing purple in the kisses of the autumn sun. I would rather have been that poor peasant, with my loving wife by my side, knitting as the day died out of the sky—with my children upon my knees and their arms about me—I would rather have been that man and gone down to the tongueless silence of the dreamless dust, than to have been that imperial impersonation of force and murder, known as 'Napoleon the Great.'"

BILLIE (impressed). How can you remember all that stuff?

(The music, which has by now become part of the background, suddenly changes. A Debussy record comes to a close and a wild Benny Goodman side replaces it. PAUL is startled, so is BILLIE. Then BILLIE rushes over and turns it off.)

BILLIE. Once in a while. Just for a change.

(PAUL laughs.)

PAUL. Don't try so hard, Billie. Please. You miss the whole point.

BILLIE. Well, I like to like what's better to like.

PAUL. There's room for all sorts of things in you. The idea of learning is to be bigger, not smaller.

BILLIE. You think I'm getting bigger?

PAUL. Yes.

BILLIE. Glad to hear it. (She sits at the desk again.) So he would rather be a happy peasant than be Napoleon. So who wouldn't?

PAUL. So Harry wouldn't, for one.

BILLIE. What makes you think not?

PAUL. Ask him.

BILLIE. He probably never heard of Napoleon.

PAUL. What's worse, he probably never heard of a peasant.

BILLIE. Do you hate him like poison?

PAUL. Who, Harry?

BILLIE. Yuh.

PAUL. No.

BILLIE. But you don't like him.

PAUL (moving away). No.

BILLIE. On account of me and him?

PAUL. One reason. There are lots more.

BILLIE. What?

PAUL. Well, if you think about it, you'll see that Harry is a menace.

BILLIE. He's not so bad. I've seen worse.

PAUL. Has he ever done anything for anyone, except himself?

BILLIE. Me.

PAUL. What?

BILLIE. Well, I got two mink coats.

PAUL. That was a trade. You gave him something, too.

(There is an awkward pause before BILLIE replies, very quietly.)

BILLIE. Don't get dirty. You're supposed to be so wonderful, so don't get dirty.

PAUL. Has he ever thought about anybody but himself?

BILLIE. Who does?

PAUL (with increasing fervor and volume). Millions of people, Billie. The whole damned history of the world is the story of a struggle between the selfish and the unselfish!

BILLIE. I can hear you.

PAUL *(patiently)*. All the bad things in the world are bred by selfishness. Sometimes selfishness even gets to be a cause, an organized force, even a government. Then it's called Fascism. Can you understand that?

BILLIE. Sort of.

PAUL *(loudly)*. Well, think about it, Billie.

BILLIE *(softly)*. You're crazy about me, aren't you.

PAUL. Yes.

BILLIE. That's why you get so mad at Harry.

PAUL. Billie, listen, I hate his life, what he does, what he stands for. Not him. He just doesn't know any better.

BILLIE. I go for you, too.

PAUL. I'm glad, Billie.

BILLIE. That's why I started doing all this. I guess you know.

PAUL. No, I didn't.

BILLIE. A lot of good it did me. I never had this kind of trouble before, I can tell you.

PAUL. Trouble?

BILLIE. After that first night when I met you—I figured it was all going to work dandy. Then, when you wouldn't step across the line—I figured maybe the way to *you* was through your head.

PAUL *(very slowly)*. Well—no.

BILLIE. Anyway, it doesn't matter now—but I like you anyway. Too late for the rest.

PAUL. Why?

BILLIE. Why? Look, Paul, there's a certain time between a fellow and a girl when it either comes off or not and if it doesn't then, then it never does.

PAUL. Maybe we haven't got to our time yet.

BILLIE. I think we did. And you dropped the ball.

PAUL. Don't be so sure.

BILLIE. I know. I've had lots of fellas and I *haven't* had lots of fellas. If you know what I mean.

PAUL. Yes.

BILLIE *(moving away)*. But I sure never thought I'd go through a thing like this for anybody.

PAUL. Like what?

BILLIE. Like getting all mixed up in my head. Wondering and worrying and *thinking*—and stuff like that. And, I don't know if it's good to find out so much so quick. *(She sits on the sofa.)*

PAUL. What the hell, Billie. Nobody's *born* smart. You know what's the stupidest thing on earth? An infant.

BILLIE. What've you got against babies all of a sudden?

PAUL. Nothing. I've got nothing against a brain three weeks old and empty. But when it hangs around for thirty years without absorbing anything, I begin to think something's the matter with it.

BILLIE *(rising in fury)*. What makes you think I'm thirty?

PAUL. I didn't mean you, especially.

BILLIE. Yes, you did.

PAUL. I swear.

BILLIE. You certainly know how to get me sore.

PAUL. I'm sorry.

BILLIE. Thirty! Do I look thirty to you?

PAUL. No.

BILLIE. Then what'd you say it for?

PAUL. I don't know. *(A short pause.)* How old *are* you?

BILLIE. Twenty-nine.

(They look at each other. PAUL smiles. She responds. He comes over and kisses her, softly.)

PAUL. Don't stop. *(She kisses him.)* I meant don't stop studying.

BILLIE. Oh.

PAUL. Will you?

BILLIE. I don't know why it's so important to you.

PAUL. It's sort of a cause. I want everybody to be smart. As smart as they can be. A world full of ignorant people is too dangerous to live in.

BILLIE (*sitting again*). I know. That's why I wish I was doing better.

PAUL. You're doing wonderfully.

BILLIE. Yeah, but it's just no use. I bet most people would laugh at me if they knew what I was trying to do.

PAUL. I'm not laughing.

BILLIE. I am. I'm sort of laughing at myself. Who do I think I am anyway?

PAUL. What's the matter?

BILLIE. All them books!

PAUL (*coming to her*). It isn't only books, Billie. I've told you a hundred times.

BILLIE. It's mostly.

PAUL (*sitting beside her*). Not at all. Listen, who said this? "The proper study of Mankind is Man."

BILLIE. I don't know.

PAUL. You should.

BILLIE. Why?

PAUL. I've told you.

BILLIE. I forgot.

PAUL. Pope.

BILLIE. The Pope?

PAUL. No, not the Pope. Alexander Pope.

BILLIE. "The proper study of—

PAUL. —Mankind is Man."

BILLIE. —Mankind is Man." Of course, that means women, too.

PAUL. Yes.

BILLIE. Yes, I know.

PAUL. Don't worry about books so much.

BILLIE. I *been* studying different mankind lately. The ones you told me. Jane Addams last week, and this week Tom Paine. And then all by myself I got to thinking about Harry. He works so hard to get what he

wants, for instance, but he doesn't know what he wants.

PAUL. More of what he's got, probably.

BILLIE. Money.

PAUL. Money, more people to push around, money.

BILLIE. He's not so bad as you think he is.

PAUL. I know. He's got a brain of gold.

(*There is the sound of a key in the door. Brock comes in.*)

BROCK. Hello.

PAUL. Hello, Harry. We were just talking about you.

BROCK (*removing his hat and coat and putting them on a chair*). Yeah? Well, that ain't what I pay you for. She knows enough about me. Too much, in fact. Ed here?

BILLIE. No.

BROCK. God damn it! He's supposed to meet me. (*He sits down and removes his shoes.*)

PAUL (*to* BILLIE). What did you find out about Tom Paine?

BILLIE. Well, he was quite a fella.

PAUL. Where was he born? Do you remember?

BILLIE. London. Or England. Some place like that.

BROCK. What do you mean London or England? It's the same thing.

BILLIE. It is?

BROCK. London is *in* England. It's a city, London. England is a whole country.

BILLIE. I forgot.

BROCK (*to* PAUL). Honest to God, boy. You got some patience.

PAUL. Take it easy.

BROCK. How can anybody get so dumb?

PAUL. We can't all know everything, Harry.

BILLIE (*to* BROCK). Who's Tom Paine, for instance?

BROCK. What?

BILLIE. You heard me. Tom Paine.

BROCK. What the hell do I care who he is?

BILLIE. *I* know.

BROCK. So what? If I wanted to know who he is I'd know who he is. I just don't care. *(To* PAUL.*)* Go ahead. Don't let me butt in.

PAUL *(to* BILLIE*).* Which of his books did you like best?

BILLIE. Well, I didn't read *by* him yet— only about him.

PAUL. Oh.

BILLIE. But I made a list of—

BROCK *(suddenly).* Who's Rabbit Maranville?

BILLIE. Who?

BROCK. Rabbit Maranville.

BILLIE. I don't know any rabbits.

BROCK. Think you're so smart.

PAUL. Used to play shortstop for the Braves, didn't he?

BROCK *(to* PAUL*).* What are you? Some kind of genius?

PAUL. No.

BROCK. I hire and fire geniuses every day.

PAUL. I'm sure you do. *(He turns to* BILLIE.*)* Where's that list?

BILLIE *(handing it over).* Here.

PAUL *(studying it).* Well, suppose you start with *The Age of Reason.*

BILLIE *(writing it down).* The—Age—of —Reason.

PAUL. Then, next, you might—

BROCK. Who's Willie Hop?

PAUL *(turning slightly).* National billiard champion. And I think it's pronounced —Hoppe.

BROCK. That's what I said. Anyway, I didn't ask you, I asked her.

PAUL. Sorry. *(He turns back to* BILLIE.*)* Where were we?

BILLIE. *Age of Reason.*

PAUL. All right, then try *The Rights of Man.*

BILLIE *(writing).* The—Rights—of—Man.

PAUL. I think that'll give you a rough idea of what—

BROCK *(coming over to them).* What's a peninsula?

BILLIE. Sshhh!!

BROCK. Don't give me that shush—! You think you know so much—what's a peninsula?

PAUL. It's a—

BROCK. Not you.

BILLIE *(with condescending superiority).* It's that new medicine!

BROCK. It is not.

BILLIE. What then?

BROCK. It's a body of land surrounded on three sides by water.

BILLIE. So what's that to know?

BROCK. So what's this Sam Paine to know?

BILLIE. Some difference! Tom Paine—not Sam Paine—*Tom* Paine practically started this whole country.

BROCK. You mean he's dead?

BILLIE. Of course.

BROCK *(to* PAUL*).* What the hell are you learnin' her about dead people? I just want her to know how to act with live people.

PAUL. Education is a difficult thing to control or to channel, Harry. One thing leads to another. It's a matter of awaken ing curiosity—stimulating imagination— developing a sense of independence.

BROCK *(cutting in).* Work on her, not me.

PAUL. No extra charge.

BROCK. I don't need nothin' you can tell me.

PAUL. Oh, I'm sure we could tell each other lots of interesting things, Harry.

BROCK *(a warning tone).* What the hell does that mean?

PAUL. Just trying to be friendly.

BROCK. Who asked you? You know, every time I see you I don't like you as much. For a chump who's got no place, you're pretty fresh. You better watch out—I got an eye on you.

PAUL. All right. Let's both watch out.

BROCK. You know, I could knock your block off, if I wanted.

PAUL. Yes, I know.

BROCK. All right, then—just go ahead and do what you're supposed to—and that's all.

PAUL. It's all right—we'll stop for now.

BROCK. No, go ahead. I want to see how you do it.

PAUL. Not just now, if you don't mind— I've got to go lie down. You don't realize how hard I work.

BILLIE. Ha ha. Some joke.

BROCK (petulant). Two hundred bucks a week and I can't even watch!

PAUL (to BILLIE). See you later.

BILLIE. Goodbye, Paul. Thanks.

PAUL. Not a bit.

(He leaves.)

BROCK. London or England. Honest to God.

(He opens an envelope on the desk and studies its contents throughout the following, without once looking at BILLIE.)

BILLIE. Harry.

BROCK. Yeah?

BILLIE. What's this business we're in down here? Could you tell me?

BROCK. What do you mean—we?

BILLIE. Well, I figure I'm sort of a partner, in a way.

BROCK. A silent partner.

BILLIE. So?

BROCK. So shut up.

BILLIE. I got a right to know.

BROCK. You got a right to get the hell out of my hair. Just put your nose in your book and keep it.

BILLIE. I don't want to do anything if it's against the law. That's one sure thing.

LROCK. You'll do what I tell you.

BILLIE. I think I know what it is—only I'm not sure.

BROCK. You should worry. You're doin' all right. Somethin' you want you ain't got maybe?

BILLIE. Yuh.

BROCK. What?

BILLIE. I want to be like the happy peasant.

BROCK. I'll buy it for you.

(HELEN enters from the service wing, carrying a book.)

BROCK. Now will you stop crabbing?

(Helen puts the book on one of the shelves.)

HELEN. Well, I finished finally. Thanks loads for the loan of it.

BILLIE. How'd you like it?

HELEN. Pretty punk.

BILLIE. Really, Helen? I enjoyed it.

HELEN. Not me. I don't go for these stories where it shows how miserable it is to be rich.

BILLIE. Well, it can be.

BROCK. All—right—can the coffee klotch. (To HELEN.) Knock off.

HELEN. Sorry, Mr. Brock. (She leaves, quickly, with a little see-you-later wave to BILLIE.)

BROCK. Don't get so pally with everybody.

BILLIE. Paul says it's all right.

BROCK. Never mind Paul says. I don't like it.

BILLIE. You know what you are?

BROCK. What?

BILLIE. Uh—

(She can't think of it, so she goes to the large dictionary and starts looking for the word. The door buzzer sounds. EDDIE comes in to open the front door. BILLIE finds what she has been looking for. She looks up from the dictionary.)

BILLIE. Antisocial!

BROCK. You're God damn right I am!

(EDDIE opens the door to admit DEVERY and SENATOR HEDGES.)

DEVERY. Good evening.

BROCK. Where the hell have you guys been? You know what time it is?

DEVERY. Sorry.

BROCK. You're always sorry.

HEDGES. My fault. *(To* BILLIE). Good evening.

BILLIE. Good evening. Won't you sit down?

HEDGES. Thank you.

DEVERY. How are you, Billie?

BILLIE. Superb. New word.

BROCK. All right—all right. What happened?

(An awkward pause. DEVERY *and* HEDGES *exchange a look and silently gird their loins.)*

HEDGES *(softly).* It's just this, Harry. I'm afraid it's going to take a little more time and— *(He pauses.)*

DEVERY *(picking it up).* —and a little more money.

BROCK *(angry).* Why?

DEVERY. Well, for one thing, the whole amendment has to be re-drafted.

BROCK. I don't want no re-drafted and I don't want to wait.

HEDGES. I'm afraid you'll have to.

BROCK. Don't tell me what I have to!

HEDGES. If you'd let me—

BROCK. Listen, I don't like you. You're makin' me feel like some sucker.

DEVERY. I'm sure Norval's doing his best.

BROCK. Well, his best ain't good enough.

DEVERY. Don't be unreasonable, Harry. There are ninety-six votes up there. Norval's just one guy.

BROCK. He's the wrong guy. What the hell? We've handled it before.

HEDGES. Things aren't the same.

BROCK. We'll make 'em the same. That's your job, ain't it?

DEVERY. Pretty tough assignment.

BROCK. What do I care? *(To* HEDGES.) And you. You better get movin' or I'll butcher you—you'll wind up a God damn YMCA secretary again before you know it

DEVERY. Harry—

BROCK. I'm gonna get it fixed so I can do business where I want and how I want and as big as I want. If you ain't with me, you're against me.

HEDGES. I'm with you.

BROCK *(starting up the stairs).* All right, then, you'll have to pull your weight in the God damn boat or I'll get somebody who can. You understand me?

(He slams out. There is an awkward pause.)

HEDGES. He has quite a temper, hasn't he?

DEVERY. Don't mind him, he's always lived at the top of his voice. *(Pouring a drink.)* Anybody with me? Norval?

HEDGES. No, thank you.

BILLIE *(to* HEDGES). I don't think Harry should talk to you like that. After all, you're a Senator.

HEDGES. Oh, well.

BILLIE. I don't think anybody should talk to a Senator like that or be able to. A Senator is a wonderful thing.

HEDGES. Thank you.

BILLIE. The way it looks to me—if he pushes you around, it's like he's pushing a few million people around.

HEDGES. How do you mean?

BILLIE. The people who picked you.

HEDGES. Well, not quite that many.

BILLIE. How many then?

HEDGES. Eight hundred and six thousand, four hundred and thirty-four.

BILLIE. Well, *that's* quite a few to push around.

HEDGES. *You're* not one of my constituents by any chance, are you?

BILLIE *(after thinking a moment).* I don't think I know that one.

DEVERY. The Senator means are you one of the people who voted for him?

BILLIE. I never voted for anybody.

HEDGES *(smiling).* Why not?

BILLIE. I don't know. I guess I wouldn't know how.

DEVERY. Very simple. You just press a button.

BILLIE. Yuh, but which one? Like suppose it's between different people?

DEVERY (smiling). Well, you listen to the speeches—you read the papers—you make up your own mind. You take a look and see who's for who—that's *very* important. Once you take a stand on something—take a look and see who's on the other side and who's on your side.

HEDGES (lightly). That's all there is to it.

BILLIE (to HEDGES). Well, why do you take it from Harry? That's what I want to know. You're more important than him. You're a Senator.

HEDGES. Yes, and as such, you see—I have a great many duties and responsibilities—

BILLIE. Yuh?

HEDGES (stalling). The operation of government is very complex.

BILLIE. Why should it be? I understand it pretty good in the books and when Paul tells me—but then when I see a thing like this—it's like different.

HEDGES. How?

BILLIE. Well, when it comes down to what should be the laws and what shouldn't—is Harry more important than anybody else?

HEDGES (meaning yes). No.

BILLIE. Then how come he's got so much to say? After all, nobody ever voted for *him.*

HEDGES (rising and starting out). Well, we'll have a nice long talk about it sometime.

BILLIE. All right.

HEDGES. Goodbye.

BILLIE. Goodbye.

(DEVERY takes HEDGES up to the door.)

HEDGES. Quite a little girl.

DEVERY. Oh, yes.

HEDGES. Goodbye.

DEVERY. Goodbye.

(HEDGES leaves. DEVERY goes quietly to his brief case and takes out a sheaf of papers.)

DEVERY (to BILLIE). Few things here for you.

(He spreads the papers out for signing. BILLIE comes over. She picks up her glasses. He hands her his fountain pen, then goes over and pours another drink. BILLIE puts on her glasses and stands looking at the papers. She starts to read the top one. A moment later, DEVERY turns back into the room. He looks at BILLIE in amazement, then takes a step or two into the room.)

BILLIE. What is this?

DEVERY. Same old stuff.

BILLIE. What?

DEVERY. Take too long to explain.

BILLIE. No it wouldn't. I like having things explained to me. I found that out.

DEVERY. Some other time.

BILLIE. Now.

DEVERY. You want me to tell Harry?

BILLIE. Tell him what?

DEVERY. That you won't sign this stuff?

BILLIE. Who said anything about that? I just want to know what it is.

DEVERY. A merger.

BILLIE. What's that?

DEVERY. Several companies being formed into one.

BILLIE. All Harry's?

DEVERY. No.

BILLIE. Whose then?

DEVERY. A few of Harry's and some others. French, Italian, and so on.

BILLIE (with the shock of recognition). A cartel!

DEVERY. What are you talking about?

BILLIE. About cartels. If that's what this is, then I'm against it. Paul explained me the whole thing.

(DEVERY is dumbfounded.)

DEVERY. It's perfectly all right. Don't worry.

BILLIE. You sure?

DEVERY. Ask Harry.

BILLIE. All right.

DEVERY. He won't like it.

BILLIE. Why not?

DEVERY. He just won't, that's all. He doesn't like people butting in.

BILLIE. I'm not people.

DEVERY. Listen to me, Billie. Be smart.

BILLIE. How can I be smart if nobody ever tells me anything?

DEVERY. I'm telling you something.

BILLIE. What?

DEVERY. Sign the stuff and don't start up with him.

BILLIE. Tomorrow.

DEVERY. Why tomorrow?

BILLIE. I want to look them over, so I'll know what I'm doing.

DEVERY *(losing his temper)*. It's all right!

BILLIE. Must be something fishy. If not, you'd tell me.

DEVERY. Take my word for it.

BILLIE. No.

(DEVERY tries hard to think of another approach.)

BILLIE. I know what you feel bad about. You don't like to be doing all his dirty work—because you know you're better than him.

DEVERY *(white)*. That's enough.

BILLIE. But I'm not so sure—maybe you're worse!

(DEVERY looks at her for a moment, then rushes up the stairs in angry determination. BILLIE picks up the papers, also a small dictionary, brings them to the sofa, and sits down to read. Now BROCK appears on the balcony. He comes down into the room, slowly. Too slowly. BILLIE looks up, once, and continues what she is doing. BROCK crosses the room. She senses his silent fury as he passes behind her. He goes to where the liquor is, directly behind BILLIE, and takes a drink. Then he moves into the room and sits down, facing her. He watches her, quietly. BILLIE looks up at him for a moment, but says nothing. She is frightened. BROCK gives no sign of anger or violence. He just looks at her. Finally, he breaks the silence.)

BROCK. Interesting?

BILLIE *(without looking up)*. Not very.

BROCK. I suppose you're used to reading more high-toned stuff.

BILLIE. Yes, I am.

(There is another long pause.)

BROCK. What's the matter, kid?

BILLIE. Nothing.

BROCK. All of a sudden.

BILLIE. I don't like that Ed.

BROCK. Why, what'd he do to you?

BILLIE. He didn't do nothing, *anything,* to me. It's what he's done to himself.

BROCK. Done what?

BILLIE. He used to be Assistant Attorney General of the United States.

BROCK. Who?

BILLIE. Ed.

BROCK. So what's wrong with that?

BILLIE. Nothing's wrong. Just look at him now.

(BROCK frowns, trying hard to follow.)

BILLIE. Did you know he once wrote a book? *The Roots of Freedom.* That was the name of it. I read it. It was wonderful.

BROCK. Where'd you get all this?

BILLIE. I looked it up.

BROCK. Why?

BILLIE. No reason. I was just in the library. And look at him now. He hangs around and helps you promote and lets you walk all over him just because you pay for it.

BROCK. Oh, so we finally got around to me.

BILLIE. Yuh. I'm not so sure I like you either. You're selfish, that's your trouble.

BROCK. Since when is all this?

BILLIE. Since now.

BROCK. You don't say.

BILLIE. I used to think you were a big man, Harry. Now I'm beginning to see you're not. All through history there's been bigger men than you and better. Now, too.

BROCK. Who, for instance?

BILLIE. Thousands.

BROCK. Name one.

BILLIE. My father.

BROCK (*contemptuously*). Twenty-five a week.

BILLIE. "—a brain of gold."

BROCK (*confused*). What?

BILLIE. Never mind.

(BROCK *rises, moves across the room, and sits beside her.*)

BROCK. Listen, cutie, don't get nervous just because you read a book. You're as dumb as you ever were.

BILLIE. You think so?

BROCK. Sure, but I don't mind. You know why? (*He makes a rude pass.*) Because you've got the best little—

BILLIE (*rising and moving away swiftly*). Leave me alone, Harry.

BROCK. Come here.

BILLIE. No.

BROCK. I never seen you like this.

BILLIE. I never been like this. I feel like I want to go away someplace.

BROCK. Where?

BILLIE. I don't know.

BROCK. I may wind up here in a few weeks. We'll go to Florida maybe.

BILLIE. I mean alone.

BROCK. You know what I think? I think you've gone nuts.

BILLIE. Maybe.

BROCK. Calm down.

BILLIE. I can't.

BROCK. Why not?

BILLIE. I don't know. I just know I hate my life. There's a better kind, I know it. If you read some of these books, you'd know it, too. Maybe it's right what you say, I'm still dumb, but I know one thing I never knew before. There's a better kind of life than the one I got. Or you.

BROCK (*as he gets up and moves to her*). I suppose you figure you'da been better off with that lousy saxophone player.

BILLIE. At least he was honest.

BROCK. He was a dime-a-dozen chump.

BILLIE. He worked for a living, that's one thing—

BROCK. I work. I been workin' since I was twelve years old—nobody ever give me nothin'.

BILLIE. If a man goes and robs a house— that's work, too.

BROCK. In my whole life—

(HELEN, *carrying towels, enters from the service wing and goes upstairs.* BROCK *holds it until she is out of sight.*)

BROCK. —in my whole life I never robbed a house. What the hell are you talkin' about?

BILLIE. You can hardly understand anything, can you?

BROCK. Get off that high horse—you dumb little pot!

BILLIE. You— (*She tries hard to think of something worse.*) —menace!

BROCK. I picked you up out of the gutter and I can throw you back there, too. Why, you never had a decent meal before you met me.

BILLIE. Yeah, but I had to have 'em with you. You eat terrible. You got no manners. Takin' your shoes off all the time—that's another thing . . . and pickin' your teeth. You're just not couth!

(HELEN *comes down the stairs and goes out through the service entrance.*)

BROCK (*shouting*). I'm as couth as you are!

BILLIE (*with considerable disgust*). And that cheap perfume you put on yourself.

BROCK. Cheap? I don't own nothin' cheap. Except you.

BILLIE (*very quietly*). You don't own me. Nobody can own anybody. There's a law says.

BROCK. Don't tell me about the law. If I was scared of the law, I wouldn't be where I am.

BILLIE. Where are you?

BROCK. All right, you've talked enough. If you don't like it here, beat it. You'll be back.

(BILLIE *starts out of the room.*)

BROCK. Wait a minute. (*He gets the documents from the coffee table.*) First this.

BILLIE. Not now.

BROCK. Right now.

BILLIE. No. (*She starts up the stairs.*)

BROCK (*loudly*). Come here!

BILLIE. I'm not going to sign anything any more till I know what I'm signing. From now on.

BROCK. Do what I'm telling you!

(BILLIE *stands rigid and frightened.* BROCK *is suddenly in front of her. He raises his arm to strike her.*)

BILLIE (*cringing*). Harry, please! Don't!

(*Her last word is cut in two by a stinging slap. Then another. The seed of her rebellion is suddenly uprooted. She sags and sobs, defeated.* BROCK *propels her to the desk in a series of rough shoves. Still sobbing, she follows his directions and signs the documents, one by one. When she has finished,* BROCK *takes them up, folds them, and puts them into his pocket.* BILLIE's *head goes to her folded arms on the desk.* BROCK *crosses to the liquor and gets a drink.*)

BROCK. All right, now get the hell out of here.

BILLIE. What?

BROCK. Don't be bawlin' around here, that's what. I don't like it. I been treatin' you too good, that's the trouble. You don't appreciate it. Nothin'. I ain't gonna have nobody around here who don't know their place. So get the hell out of here. Go sit on a park bench someplace till you're ready to behave yourself. (BILLIE *is rigid with fright.*) Go on! (*She starts for the stairs.* BROCK *points to the front door.*) This way out.

BILLIE (*in a small voice*). I've got to put something on.

BROCK. Well, hurry up—I don't want you around here like this. You bother me.

(BILLIE *starts up the stairs. Halfway up, she stops and turns to* BROCK.)

BILLIE. Big Fascist!

BROCK. What?

(*She goes into her room quickly.* BROCK *turns and sees a pile of books before him. Instantly, he identifies them as the reason for his present despair. He pushes them to the floor, violently—he kicks them out of his way—he finds a strange release in this, so he picks up one of the books, and begins tearing out the pages. There is mingled fury, excitement, and satisfaction in his heart as he completes the destruction of the book. He starts on a second as* DEVERY *comes down.* BROCK *stops, as though discovered in an indecent act.*)

DEVERY. All set?

BROCK. Certainly all set. What'd you think —I'm gonna let a broad talk back?

DEVERY. Where is she?

BROCK. I told her to take a walk. If there's one thing I can't stand it's a crier.

DEVERY. What's she crying about?

BROCK. What do I know?

DEVERY. She's becoming a strange girl.

BROCK. She's all right. All this book stuff's got her nervous, that's all.

DEVERY (*softly*). "A little learning is a dangerous thing."

BROCK. What?

DEVERY (*sitting*). Nothing, Harry. Looks like your passion for educating her was a mistake.

BROCK. I didn't know it would turn out like this, did I?—Remind me to fire that four-eyed Verrall skunk.

DEVERY. Why blame him?

BROCK. He must have told her *too* much. (*A pause.*) You know what she called me before? A Fach-ist.

DEVERY (*almost smiling*). She did?

BROCK. What the hell's that? Some kinda European, ain't it? It don't make sense. I was born in Plainfield, New Jersey. She knows that.

(He stares at the door of BILLIE's *room moodily.)*

DEVERY. What's the matter, Harry?

BROCK. I love that broad. *(There is a pause.* BROCK *appears to be thinking. He looks up, in despair.)* Ed. You think we could maybe find somebody to make her dumb again?

*(*BILLIE *comes down, dressed for the street, and moves toward the front door.)*

BROCK *(without turning).* And don't be late if you don't want a bloody nose.

*(*BILLIE *stops and moves a step into the room.)*

BILLIE *(very, very gently).* Would you do me a favor, Harry?

BROCK *(mean).* What?

BILLIE. Drop dead?

(She leaves quickly, before BROCK *recovers.)*

CURTAIN

ACT THREE

SCENE: *Later that evening.* DEVERY, *coatless, is on the sofa working over a pile of documents. He is somewhat drunker than before.* BROCK, *in pajamas and dressing gown, is pacing the floor.*

BROCK. What time is it already?

DEVERY. One-thirty.

BROCK. I'll slug her senseless when she comes back.

DEVERY. *If.*

BROCK. Listen, I've had this with her before. She always winds up where I want her.

DEVERY. I hope so.

(There is a pause.)

BROCK. What time is it?

DEVERY. One-thirty.

BROCK. You said that before.

DEVERY. One-thirty-one.

BROCK. What time she go out?

DEVERY. I don't know. Five, six o'clock.

BROCK. Eight hours.

DEVERY. What?

BROCK. She's been gone eight hours.

DEVERY. Maybe she's seeing a double feature.

BROCK. Yeah. . . . *That* don't take eight hours! *(A pause.)* She coulda got into an accident.

DEVERY. You'd hear.

BROCK. She coulda got raped! *(*DEVERY *looks at him.)* It happens all the time.

DEVERY. Not to Billie. Maybe the other way around, but not to Billie.

BROCK. You'd think Eddie'd call up at least.

(A pause.)

DEVERY. Be damned inconvenient if he doesn't find her. I've got some more for her to sign. It can't wait.

*(*EDDIE *comes in.)*

EDDIE. She here?

BROCK. What do you mean, "she here"? *No!*

EDDIE. The guy downstairs said he seen her go out and then he seen her come in.

BROCK. He's blind. Go out and look some more.

EDDIE. I been all over town.

BROCK. Well, go over it again. *(There is the slightest possible hesitation from* ED-DIE.*)* Do what I'm tellin' you!

EDDIE. Sure. *(He starts for his room.)* Just change my shoes. *(He goes out.)*

DEVERY. If I thought I could make those stairs I'd go lie down.

(There is a tiny pause.)

BROCK. I sure never thought she was gonna turn out like this.

DEVERY. Have you thought any more about that matter we discussed in connection with her?

BROCK. What connection?

DEVERY. Marrying her.

BROCK. Still harpin', huh?

DEVERY. Seems to have gone beyond the reasons of appearance, Harry. If she's going to be truculent, I'm thinking of your legal safety. On paper, she owns—

BROCK. I know what she owns.

DEVERY. You've got to do it, Harry.

(A long pause.)

BROCK *(softly)*. They always hook you in the end, them broads. *(He pours a drink.)* It's crazy, you know it?

DEVERY. How?

BROCK. A whole trouble because a dame reads a book.

DEVERY. Just goes to show you.

BROCK. Yuh.

DEVERY. It's the new world, Harry—force and reason change places. Knowledge is power. You can lead a horse to water.

BROCK. What?

DEVERY. Honesty is the best policy. A stitch in time saves nine. *(He starts up the stairs and trips.)*

BROCK. I don't like the way things are going around here. You stewed all the time—the broad outa line—and that's some fine Senator you bought me.

DEVERY. I think he's cute.

BROCK. I could get me a better Senator out of Lindy's.

DEVERY. Best I could do.

BROCK. I'd like to trade him in, no kiddin'.

DEVERY. They're not all for sale, Harry. That's the trouble with this town—too many honest men in it.

(DEVERY goes off into BROCK's room. BROCK paces, lights a cigarette—then stops and stares at the books. He selects a particu-

larly slender one and moves to the sofa. He reads. EDDIE comes through.)

EDDIE. I'll take a look downstairs and see if she's—

(He stops abruptly at the unbelievable sight before his eyes. BROCK turns to see him gaping.)

BROCK. What's the matter?

EDDIE. Nuthin'.

BROCK. Didn't you ever see a person readin' a book, for Christ's sake?

EDDIE. Sure.

BROCK. All right then. Get the hell out of here!

EDDIE. Sure.

(He goes quietly. BROCK reads. Behind him the door opens noiselessly and BILLIE looks in. She closes the door. BROCK reads a bit longer, then gives up. He tears the book in two and throws it away. He goes upstairs and into his room, turning off the main light on his way. A moment later BILLIE comes in and looks around.

She goes up the stairs, stops at BROCK's door, and listens. Then she comes down to the door again and whispers to someone just outside.

PAUL joins her and closes the door. BILLIE moves to the desk and starts looking through the papers on it. She holds one out to PAUL. He examines it carefully, and nods. Quietly, systematically, they go through the desk. PAUL makes a pile of documents, letters, checkbooks, and papers. BILLIE crosses and picks up the material left by DEVERY. PAUL follows her and adds this to his.)

BILLIE *(in a whisper)*. Okay?

PAUL. This ought to do it fine.

BILLIE. I probably won't see you again, Paul—

PAUL. What!

BILLIE. Ssshh!

PAUL *(whispering)*. What?!

BILLIE. So I want to say goodbye and thank you for everything.

PAUL. Where are you going?

BILLIE. Just away from here, that's all I know.

PAUL. Where? You can tell *me*.

BILLIE. I don't know. I thought I might go see my father for a while.

PAUL. And have a hot lunch every day?

BILLIE. Yeah.

PAUL. I've got a better idea.

BILLIE. What?

PAUL. Let's get married.

BILLIE. You must be daffy.

PAUL. I love you, Billie.

BILLIE. You don't love me. You just love my brain.

PAUL. That, too.

BILLIE. What would the boss of the *New Republic* say?

PAUL. I don't know. Probably—congratulations.

BILLIE. I'll think it over, but I can tell you now the answer is no. And I wish you'd hurry up out of here. (PAUL *kisses her.*) What are you doing?

PAUL. Well, if you don't know, I must be doing it wrong. (*He kisses her again.*)

BILLIE (*sitting on the sofa*). What's more important right now—crabbing Harry's act—or romancing?

PAUL (*sitting next to her*). They're one and the same thing to me.

BILLIE. Honest, Paul—I wish you'd—

(*The door opens and* EDDIE *comes in. He switches on the lights. He stops on the landing, surprised.* PAUL *and* BILLIE *rise.*)

EDDIE. What's this? Night school? (*To* BILLIE.) Where were you anyway? I looked all over town.

BILLIE. I walked over to the White House and back.

EDDIE. How's everybody over there? (*To* PAUL.) You better knock off, brother.

PAUL. Why?

EDDIE. I'm supposed to tell him she's back. I don't think he'll like you horsin' around

with his girl in the middle of the night. He's funny that way.

PAUL. I'll take a chance.

BILLIE. You better go.

EDDIE. She's right. Take my advice.

PAUL. What's it to you?

EDDIE. Listen—noise I can stand, but blood makes me nervous. (*He goes upstairs and into* BROCK's *room.*)

BILLIE. Please, Paul.

PAUL. Sure you'll be all right?

BILLIE. Don't worry.

PAUL. Goodbye, Billie.

BILLIE. Goodbye.

(PAUL *goes.* BILLIE *picks up the phone.*)

BILLIE. Porter, please. (*She sorts out a few things on the desk.*) Hello, porter? This is 67D. Could you send somebody up for my bags? . . . No, right now . . . thank you.

(EDDIE *appears on the balcony, rubbing his stomach, and gasping softly.*)

BILLIE. What's the matter?

EDDIE. Right in the stomach he hit me.

BILLIE. Why didn't you hit him back?

EDDIE. What?

BILLIE. Why didn't you hit him back?

EDDIE. He's been sayin' you've gone nuts. I could believe it, you know it?

BILLIE. Would you do me a favor?

EDDIE. What?

BILLIE. Pack my things up there?

EDDIE. You scrammin' again?

BILLIE. For good.

EDDIE. I'll tell you the truth, I'm sorry. I think he's gonna be sorry, too.

BILLIE. He's going to be worse than sorry.

EDDIE. Where you goin'?

BILLIE. Never mind.

EDDIE. You sore at me, too?

BILLIE. In a way.

EDDIE. What'd *I* do? What'd I *do?*

BILLIE. It's a new thing with me, Eddie. I'm going to be sore at anybody who just takes it. From now on.

EDDIE. Listen, don't get me thinkin'. I got enough trouble now.

(He goes into BILLIE's *room.* BILLIE *begins to sort out her belongings, as* BROCK *appears.)*

BROCK. Fine time.

BILLIE *(gay)*. Hello, Harry.

BROCK *(coming down)*. Where you been?

BILLIE. I took a walk like you told me.

BROCK. That took you till now?

BILLIE. What's the matter, Harry? You miss me?

BROCK. I decided somethin' to tell you. Somethin' good. I don't like to wait when I get an idea.

BILLIE. Yuh, I know.

BROCK. Now I see you, I don't know if I should tell you it.

BILLIE. Why not?

BROCK. Runnin' out, talkin' fresh, slammin' doors. I knew you'd be back, though.

BILLIE. You did, huh?

BROCK. I told Ed, even. He was worried. Not me.

BILLIE. Not yet.

BROCK. What took you so long?

BILLIE. I had a lot to think.

BROCK. For instance?

BILLIE. Just where I stand around here.

BROCK. That's what I'm tryin' to tell you.

BILLIE. What?

BROCK. Where you stand.

BILLIE. Yuh.

BROCK. Well—first thing, that Verrall stuff is through. It gets in my way—and I don't like you upset so much. It's bad for you. And the next thing—we're gonna get married.

BILLIE. No.

BROCK. Only you got to behave yourself . . . No?! What do you mean, no?

BILLIE. I don't want to, that's what I mean. No. In fact, I've never been so insulted.

BROCK *(in a whisper)*. Well, that's the God damndest thing I ever heard.

BILLIE. Why?

BROCK. Who the hell are you to say no, if I tell you?

BILLIE. Don't knock yourself out, you've got a lot of surprises coming.

BROCK. Just tell me first.

BILLIE. What?

BROCK. How can *you* not want to marry *me?*

BILLIE. Well, you're too dumb—for one thing. I've got a different kind of life in mind, Harry. Entirely. I'm sorry, but you just wouldn't fit in.

BROCK. Listen, Billie, I don't understand what the hell's happenin'!

BILLIE. I do.

BROCK. What'd I do? What did I? All right, I talked rough to you once in a while. Maybe I hit you a couple of times. Easy. Is that a reason to treat me like this? I done good for you, too. Couldn't we straighten it out?

BILLIE. No.

BROCK. Why not?

BILLIE *(very simply)*. Well, all this stuff I've been reading—all that Paul's been telling me—it just mixed me up. But when you hit me before, it was like everything knocked itself together in my head—and made sense. All of a sudden I realized what it means. How some people are always giving it and some taking. And it's not fair. So I'm not going to let you any more. *Or anybody else.*

(She goes back to the desk.)

BROCK. Listen, kid. I got an idea. Come on upstairs and I'll calm you down. (BILLIE *continues her work.*) We used to have a pretty good time, remember? (BILLIE *slams a drawer.*) You want to come to Florida? I think you ought to marry me, don't you? *(He is suddenly off the handle.)* Listen, Billie, I want you to marry me. I don't want to argue about it. I've heard enough. Now you do what I'm tellin' you or you'll be damn good and sorry.

BILLIE. I'm not scared of you any more, Harry, that's another thing.

BROCK. You're not, huh?

(He starts moving toward her, ominously, but stops as the door buzzer sounds. The door opens and two bellhops appear.)

BILLIE. Come on in! Right up there.

BROCK. What the hell's this?

BILLIE. Oh, didn't I tell you? I'm leaving.

BROCK. What?

BILLIE. Yuh, for good.

BROCK *(to the bellhops)*. Wait a second. *(They stop.)* Beat it. *(The bellhops hesitate.)* Hurry up! *(They hurry down and out.)*

BELLHOP *(at the door)*. Thank you, sir.

BROCK *(to BILLIE)*. Let's get organized around here! You can't just walk out, cutie. You're in too deep with me. I'm right in the middle of the biggest thing I ever done. Maybe I made a mistake hookin' you in with it—but you're in.

BILLIE. Well, I'm not going to be. I decided.

BROCK. All right, fine. You want to wash it up, we'll wash it up. I'm too important to monkey around with what you think. *(He shouts up.)* Ed! *(He looks through the papers on the desk.)* I'll fix it so you can be out of here in no time. You're spoiled. I spoiled you. You're no good to me no more. I was ready to make you a real partner. So you don't want it? So fine. See how you'll do without me. You don't look like you looked nine years ago. In fact, you look lousy, if you want the truth. I'm glad to get rid of you.

BILLIE. And as far as I'm concerned . . .

BROCK. Yeah?

BILLIE. *Visa versa!*

(DEVERY comes down.)

DEVERY *(to BILLIE)*. You're back. *(To BROCK.)* All set?

BROCK. Shut up!

DEVERY. What's the matter?

BROCK *(rummaging through the desk)*. She's off her nut. We're gonna settle everything up and get her the hell outa here.

DEVERY *(to BILLIE)*. You sure you know what you're doing?

BILLIE. First time in my life I *do* know.

BROCK. What'd you do with that stuff you wanted her to . . . ?

DEVERY *(pointing to the sofa)*. Right there.

BROCK. Where right there?

(DEVERY moves to the desk. They begin looking, feverishly.)

BILLIE *(nonchalantly)*. With blue covers?

DEVERY. Yeah.

(A pause.)

BILLIE. Three copies?

BROCK. That's right.

(Another pause.)

BILLIE. I gave 'em to Paul.

(BROCK and DEVERY freeze at the desk in odd positions.)

BROCK. When?

BILLIE. Just now.

DEVERY. What for?

BILLIE. What do you think for? To put in the paper. I guess.

BROCK. There's some kinda jokes I don't like.

BILLIE. It's no joke. Paul says it's the worst swindle since—uh—the teapot. Something like that.

(DEVERY and BROCK exchange a horrified look.)

BILLIE. What are you getting so white about? You told me yourself it was perfectly all right.

BROCK. You double-crossing little—

BILLIE. I don't see it like that. If there's a fire and I call the engines—so who am I double-crossing—the fire?

DEVERY. I'd better get Norval.

BROCK. I know who to get. Eddie!!

DEVERY *(on the phone)*. Decatur 9124.

(EDDIE appears.)

BROCK. You know where Verrall's room is?

EDDIE. Sure.

BROCK. Tell him to get in here right away.

EDDIE. Right. *(He starts out.)*

BROCK. Wait a minute—tell him Billie wants him.

(EDDIE goes.)

DEVERY *(on the phone.)* Hello, Norval? Ed. Wake you? . . . Oh, good. I'm over here at Harry's. Can you drop by? Important. . . . No, it can't. . . . All right.

(He hangs up.)

BILLIE. Paul's got nothing to do with this. It was my own idea.

BROCK. I'll show you ideas.

BILLIE. If you think you can strong-arm him—you're wasting your time. For a fellow with eyeglasses, he's very stubborn.

DEVERY *(pouring a drink)*. Oh, dear.

BROCK *(to DEVERY)*. If you don't stop belly-achin', get the hell out of here!

DEVERY. We're in trouble, Harry.

BROCK. Is that gonna help?

DEVERY. No. *(He downs his drink.)*

BROCK. I'll trim this guy. Watch me.

DEVERY. All right.

BROCK. You get in a spot, you fold up. Remind me to have a heart-to-heart talk with you.

DEVERY. Be that as it may—if this stuff breaks—nobody'll play with us.

BROCK. So what's to do?

DEVERY. Might be best—under the circumstances—to forget the whole deal. Let him publish. If nothing happens, he looks silly.

BROCK. What do you mean if nothin' happens? I've spent two months down here and I don't know how much dough. I'm supposed to let all that ride?

DEVERY. If you want to play it safe.

BROCK. Well, I don't. I want what I'm after.

DEVERY. Going to be tough to get.

BROCK. Why? Because some little weasel with eyeglasses wants to get noisy? I'll cut his tongue out!

DEVERY. Listen, Harry!

BROCK. You're chicken!

DEVERY. You think so?

BROCK. I think so.

DEVERY. You're off the handle because it looks like I've been right and you've been wrong.

BROCK. Talk.

DEVERY. I've told you again and again. Get too big and you become a target. It's easier to steal diamonds than elephants.

BROCK. Shut up! I'll handle this.

DEVERY. All right.

BROCK. You brought this guy around in the first place. Remember that. *(DEVERY sighs.)* You're about as much help to me as a boil on the—

(EDDIE comes back with PAUL, who immediately senses the trap. BROCK crosses to him and speaks with quiet menace.)

BROCK. I think you got somethin' by mistake that belongs to me.

PAUL. That so?

BROCK. How about it?

(There is no answer. BROCK signals EDDIE, who grabs PAUL's arms. BROCK frisks him.)

BROCK. Sit down.

(PAUL sits beside BILLIE.)

PAUL. Hello.

BILLIE. How've you been?

PAUL. Fine, and you?

BILLIE. Fine.

BROCK *(to DEVERY)*. Get the stuff out of his room.

(DEVERY starts out.)

PAUL. Not there, Ed.

(DEVERY stops.)

BROCK. Where, then? (PAUL *looks at him and smiles.*) All right, if you want to play it rough. I know how to do that, too.

(BROCK *walks to the service wing and bolts the door. Then* EDDIE *moves to the front door and does the same.* BROCK's *determination and purpose strike a kind of terror in the room. He moves back to the sofa.*)

BROCK. Now you listen, you two heels. I mean business. I got too much at stake down here. You got somethin' that belongs to me. And if you wanna get out of here alive—you're gonna give it back. I'm no blowhard. (*To* BILLIE.) Tell him.

BILLIE. He's no blowhard. He's had people killed before. Like once, about six years ago, there was a strike at one of his—

BROCK. Shut up! You ain't gonna be tellin' nobody nothin' pretty soon.

BILLIE (*derisively*). Double negative. (*To* PAUL.) Right?

PAUL. Right.

BROCK. You don't seem to be gettin' the idea. You never been in trouble like you're gonna be if you don't do what I'm tellin' you.

DEVERY. Wait a minute, Harry. There's another way to handle this. (*To* PAUL.) I really think you've pulled a boner, Paul. My advice to you is to lay off.

PAUL. And my advice to you is to stop sticking your noses into my business.

BILLIE. Yuh!

BROCK. Look who's talkin' about stickin' noses. You're the God-damndest buttinski I ever run into!

PAUL. I think I told you once before, Harry, that's my job.

BROCK. What? Gettin' in my way?

PAUL. Not exactly.

BROCK. What then? I'd like to know. No kiddin'.

PAUL. To find out what goes on and get it to the people.

BROCK. What people?

PAUL. The people.

BROCK. Never heard of them.

BILLIE. You will, Harry, some day. They're getting to be more well-known all the time. (EDDIE *brings* BROCK *a drink.*)

DEVERY. What if I told you this whole operation is strictly according to law?

PAUL. Then I'd say the law needs revision.

BROCK. Who are you? The government?

PAUL. Of course.

BROCK. Since when?

BILLIE. Since—uh—1779! (*To* PAUL.) Right?

BROCK. What?

PAUL. Of course I'm the government. What do you think the government is, Harry? A man, a monster, a machine? It's you and me and a few million more. We've got to learn to look after each other.

BROCK. Thanks, I can look after myself.

BILLIE (*to* PAUL). He doesn't get it. I think it's because you still talk too fancy. (*To* BROCK.) Look, Harry, the idea is that you can only get away with your kind of shenanigans if nobody cares about it.

BROCK. I know what I'm doin'. I got my rights the same as anybody else.

BILLIE. More! You keep buying more and more rights for yourself.

BROCK. You got nothin' to say to me.

(*The door buzzer.* EDDIE *goes to the door, unlocks and opens it, and* SENATOR HEDGES *comes in. Then he locks it again.*)

HEDGES. Good evening, Eddie! (*Gay.*) Well, this is a late little party, isn't it?

BROCK. Shut up!

HEDGES. What?

BROCK. Don't be so happy!

HEDGES. What's the trouble?

DEVERY. Well, Verrall here has—uh—stumbled on a whole pocketful of information. I don't know what he thinks it means.

PAUL. I'll tell you. Just that the connection between Harry's combine and the Senator's amendment is more than coincidence.

HEDGES. Now, just a moment, son. I've got nothing against you young radicals—used to be one myself—but you simply won't be practical. Now, what we're doing is common practice. Done every day. I don't know why you single us out to make a fuss about.

BROCK. Yeah, why?

PAUL. It's done every day, sir, right. I have no doubt that an undiscovered murder is committed every day. What does that prove? All this under-cover pressure—this bribery—and corruption—this government between friends—sure it goes on all the time and it's tough to crack. Ask me. I've tried for years. You need more than the knowing about it. You've got to have the facts and the figures and, most important —the names.

BILLIE. And he's got 'em.

HEDGES (angry). You be careful, young man, when you use the word bribery in my presence.

BILLIE. Eighty thousand dollars you got. What word would you like him to use?

(HEDGES *pales and looks helplessly over to* BROCK.)

HEDGES. Harry, I honestly feel—

BROCK. What the hell do I care what you feel? I feel, too.

HEDGES. I can't take any smearing now. It's a bad time.

BROCK. Knock off. (To PAUL.) All right, now we've all had our little beat around the bush, let's get down to it. What can we work out?

PAUL. You just heard your lawyer say it was all according to law.

BROCK. Yeah.

PAUL. If that's the case, what's bothering you?

BROCK. I don't like a lot of noise, that's all.

PAUL. I'll be very quiet.

DEVERY. It just starts a lot of snooping, you know that. Gets to be uncomfortable.

BILLIE. Maybe if it gets to be uncomfortable enough, you'll cut it out.

(HEDGES *sits down, miserable.*)

BROCK. What'll you take, Paul?

PAUL. I'll take a drink, please, if I may.

BROCK. Don't be fancy with me. I never met a guy yet who didn't have his price.

PAUL (*pouring drink*). I have.

BROCK (to PAUL). I'm talkin' about big numbers.

BILLIE. You and your big numbers. If you don't watch out you'll be wearing one across your chest.

BROCK. I'll get to you later. (To PAUL.) Make up your mind. There's just two ways we can do business. One—you play ball— make it worth your while. Two—you better start watchin' your step. There'll be no place you can walk—no place you can live, if you monkey-wrench me! What do you say?

PAUL. I'd like to think it over!

BROCK. All right. You got two minutes.

(PAUL *sits down and thinks. He looks at* BILLIE. *He smiles. She smiles. He looks at* DEVERY. *She looks at* HEDGES. *They both look at* BROCK. *Suddenly,* PAUL *rises.*)

PAUL. Come on, Billie.

(BILLIE *rises.* PAUL *is moving to the door.* EDDIE *seems about to intercept him.* BROCK *is moving toward him.*)

DEVERY. Wait a minute, Harry!

HEDGES. Now, let's not lose our tempers.

(BROCK, *in a sudden inhuman burst, swings* PAUL *around, grabs him by the throat, and begins to choke him.* PAUL *goes to his knees.* BROCK *hangs on.*)

DEVERY (*in a panic*). Stop it!

BILLIE. Harry!

HEDGES. Oh, my God!

(HEDGES, DEVERY, *and* EDDIE *are desperately attempting to prevent murder.* BILLIE *rushes to the phone and screams.*)

BILLIE. Operator! *Operator!!!*

(*A signal from* DEVERY, *and* EDDIE *goes to* BILLIE, *removes the phone from her hands, and seats her. The combined forces of* DEVERY *and* HEDGES *now tear* BROCK *loose. They throw him on the sofa, where he sits, spent, and subdued.* BILLIE *is helping* PAUL, *who sits on the stairs, groggy.*)

DEVERY (*to* BROCK). You God-damned fool! Where the hell do you think you are?

Can't you see all this muscle stuff is a thing of the past? You cut it out, or you'll be a thing of the past, too.

BROCK. I got mad.

PAUL *(coming down to* BROCK*).* Who are *you* to get mad? You big baboon! You ought to be grateful you're allowed to walk around free.

BROCK *(in a warning tone).* You don't know me good enough for that kind of talk.

PAUL. I know you. I've seen your kind down here for years—with red hair and white hair and no hair—but you're always the same—you're usually right here in this room. What the hell do you guys want, anyway? You've *got* damn near all the oil and the lumber and the steel and coal and aluminum—what do you want now —all the people? All the laws?

BROCK *(rising).* Don't blow your top. I'm still ready to do business. How's a hundred grand?

PAUL. A hundred grand is beautiful—but I can't do it.

BROCK. Why not?

(A pause.)

PAUL. My wife wouldn't like it.

BILLIE *(softly).* She certainly wouldn't.

BROCK. All right, then, what's your idea?

PAUL. To try and stop you from buying and selling legislation as though it were junk.

BILLIE. "This country with its institutions belongs to the people who inhibit it."

PAUL. "Inhabit."

BILLIE. "Inhabit."

BROCK. What the hell are you two battin' about? I don't see what I'm doin' so wrong. This is America, ain't it? Where's all this free enterprise they're always talkin' about?

DEVERY *(toasting).* To free enterprise.

BROCK. You're just sore because I made good and you ain't. Everybody had the same chance as me—all them kids I used to know—so where are they now?

BILLIE. No place. Because you beat them out, like you said. You always want to hold everybody down so you can get it all for yourself. That's why there's people like my father—and like me. He couldn't give me what he wanted—so I wind up with an empty head and with you.

BROCK. I always did what I want and I'm always gonna.

BILLIE. Try it.

BROCK. Who's gonna stop me?

BILLIE. Us two.

BROCK. Youse two? Don't make me split a gut. Be some fine country where a hundred-and-a-quarter-a-week hick and a broad that ain't been off her end for ten years can stop *me*. *(He turns and crosses to* DEVERY, *in a fury.)* What the hell are you standin' around like a deaf-and-dumby? What do I pay you for? Go on, say somethin'!

DEVERY. All right. I'll say something.

BROCK. Well?

DEVERY. They're right.

BROCK. You think they can stop me? Stop a Senator? What the hell kind of a world is it if your money's no good? How can they lick me? *I* got all the money.

DEVERY. The Republicans had all the money, too. Remember?

*(*EDDIE *puts another drink into* BROCK'S *hand.)*

BROCK *(to* EDDIE*).* What the hell do *you* want?

EDDIE. Rye ginger ale.

BROCK. Who asked you? Knock off!

*(*EDDIE *retreats.)*

PAUL. Maybe another time, Harry, not now. And if you're going to try again—do it fast. It gets harder all the time—people get wiser—they hear more—they read more—they talk more. When enough of them know enough—that'll be the end of you.

BROCK. Don't worry about me.

PAUL. I do, though. I worry like hell. I stay up nights. When you live in Washington, it's enough to break your heart. You see a perfect piece of machinery—the democratic structure—and somebody's always tampering with it and trying to make it hit the jackpot.

DEVERY *(toasting)*. To the jackpot.

BROCK. I'm no gambler. I'm a business man.

PAUL. You certainly are, but you're in the wrong business now.

BILLIE. When you steal from the government, you're stealing from yourself, you dumb ox.

PAUL. Sure, you nearsighted empire-builders have managed to *buy* little pieces of it once in a while—but you can't have it all —if you do, it won't be this country any more.

BROCK *(to DEVERY, softly)*. Of all the guys in this town—why the hell did you have to pick *him* out? *(To PAUL).* Do what you want. I'm goin' ahead.

BILLIE. Wait a minute! I'll tell you where you're going.

BROCK. You?!

BILLIE. Sure. In this whole thing—I guess you forgot about me—about how I'm a partner? Ed once told me—a hundred and twenty-six different yards I own.

DEVERY. Control.

BILLIE *(to DEVERY)*. Same thing. *(To BROCK.)* So here's how it's going to be. I don't want them. I don't want anything of yours—or to do with you. So I'm going to sign them all back.

BROCK. All right!

BILLIE. Only not all at once—just one at a time—*one a year!* (BROCK *is stunned.)* Only you've got to behave yourself—because if you don't, I'm going to let go on everything. For what you've done—even since I've known you only—I bet you could be put in jail for about nine hundred years. You'd be a pretty old man when you got out.

BROCK *(to DEVERY)*. What's goin' on around here?

DEVERY. A revolution.

BROCK. You got me into this—*get me out!*

DEVERY. Somehow, I don't feel as clever as I used to.

BILLIE. Come on, Paul. *(To BROCK.)* I'll send for my things.

BROCK. You little crumb—you'll be sorry for this day—wait and see. Go on—go with him—you ain't got a chance. If I ever seen anybody outsmart themself, it's you.

BILLIE *(starts to go)*. Goodbye, all.

BROCK *(to PAUL)*. And you!

PAUL. Me?

BROCK. Yeah—you're fired!

PAUL. I'm sorry, Harry. I've enjoyed working for you very much indeed.

(BILLIE *is at the door).*

BILLIE *(to EDDIE)*. Open up!

EDDIE. All right, Harry?

BILLIE *(to EDDIE, in imitation of BROCK)*. Do what I'm tellin' you!

(EDDIE *opens the door quickly.* BILLIE *and* PAUL *go out, smiling.* DEVERY *pours himself a drink.)*

BROCK *(trying hard to laugh off his disaster)*. How do you like that? He coulda had a hundred grand—and she coulda had me. So they both wind up with nothin'. *(A pause.)* Dumb chump.

HEDGES. Yes.

BROCK. Crazy broad.

HEDGES. Quite right.

DEVERY *(toasting, his glass held high)*. To all the dumb chumps and all the crazy broads, past, present, and future—who thirst for knowledge—and search for truth—who fight for justice—and civilize each other—and make it so tough for sons-of-bitches like you— *(To HEDGES.)* —and you— *(To BROCK.)* —and me. *(He drinks.)*

CURTAIN

THE VOICE OF THE TURTLE

By JOHN van DRUTEN

THE VOICE OF THE TURTLE was first presented by Alfred de Liagre, Jr., at the Shubert Theatre, New Haven, Conn., on November 4, 1943, and at the Morosco Theatre, New York City, on December 8, 1943. The play was staged by the author; setting by Stewart Chaney. The cast was as follows:

SALLY MIDDLETON..............................Margaret Sullavan
OLIVE LASHBROOKE..............................Audrey Christie
BILL PAGE..Elliott Nugent

SCENES

ACT I: Scene 1. Friday afternoon.

Scene 2. Friday evening.

ACT II: Scene 1. Saturday morning.

Scene 2. Late Saturday night.

ACT III: Scene 1. Sunday morning.

Scene 2. Late Sunday afternoon.

The action, throughout, takes place over a week-end in early April in an apartment in the East Sixties, near Third Avenue, New York City.

THE AUTHOR

John van Druten was born in London in 1901 of a Dutch father and an English mother. He was educated at the University College School of the metropolis and subsequently studied law, qualifying as solicitor of the Supreme Court of Judicature and receiving a Bachelor of Laws degree from London University. Evidently his interest ranged further than is customary with barristers, since he became lecturer in English Law and English Legal History at University College in Wales. He held that post for three years and enlivened them with articles, stories, and poems for Punch, The London Mercury, *and other periodicals. He also began writing plays while enjoying academic immunity.*

His second play Young Woodley *was a sensitive adolescent study and a criticism of the English public school system. It was evidently too critical of the status quo in the opinion of the Lord Chamberlain, who forbade production in London. New York saw the play first, in 1925, and acclaimed it; London first saw* Young Woodley *three years later. Mr. van Druten, who was eager to give his story to England in spite of the Lord Chamberlain's licensing power over stage productions, also novelized his matter, drawing high praise from reviewers. Arnold Bennett declared that a good play had become a better book.*

Mr. van Druten first came here in 1926 for a lecture tour and returned for a longer tour the following year. He was quite a successful lecturer but once Young Woodley *proved its stageworthiness there was to be a steady flow of stage pieces from his pen. He had nineteen productions, mostly comedies of manners and character, between 1928 and 1942, including that charming adult study of feminine friendship* Old Acquaintance *and the sensitive collaboration with Lloyd Morris* Damask Cheek, *with which Mr. van Druten also proved a talent for directing plays. He also directed* The Voice of the Turtle *for Alfred de Liagre in 1943.*

Mr. van Druten had previously practiced much economy in his use of casts. Back in the season of 1931–32 his successful piece There's Always Juliet *had coasted along with only four characters. He got along even better with three actors in* The Voice of the Turtle, *which survived the season of 1943–44 and several additional seasons. The New York premiere fell on December 8, 1943. By then, owing to long association with the American theater and predilection for these shores, he was sufficiently domesticated to be added to the roster of American playwrights. He completed his naturalization in Los Angeles on August 11, 1944.*

Mr. van Druten happens to be one of those playwrights who do not evoke lengthy critical ponderings. This is the case because instead of heaving with the world's problems and proffering political or philosophical comment, he has been content to study people and mores, *and to set them down for what they are rather than for what they may be worth as symbols. If he has rarely been a robust writer, he has always been an acute observer and a master of civilized dialogue. Since there is never a superabundance of these qualities in the American theatre, America has welcomed him.*

THE VOICE OF THE TURTLE

ACT ONE

THE SCENE *throughout is a smallish apartment in New York, in the East Sixties, near Third Avenue. The set comprises the entire apartment, with the exception of the bathroom. We see the bedroom, with double bed, to the right of the stage; living room center; kitchen, through a swing-door, left. The kitchen has an icebox, stove and sink in a combined unit in the left wall. The front door to the apartment is in the back wall, center, opening into the living room, which is down two steps. The windows are in the right wall of the bedroom, back wall of living room, and back wall of kitchen. Under the living-room window is a day-bed, disguised as a couch. The telephone is below the bed in the bedroom. The bathroom and dressing room are off right of the back wall of the bedroom.*

SCENE I

The apartment, late in the afternoon of a Friday at the beginning of April.

When the curtain rises, SALLY MIDDLETON *is discovered in the kitchen, fixing a tray of drinks which she carries into the living room through the swing-door. She sets the tray down on a table, muttering to herself as she does so. Actually, she is running over the words of the Potion Scene from* Romeo and Juliet, *but only becomes audible as she reaches the end.* SALLY *is twenty-two, small, direct, naive and very pretty.*

SALLY *(finishing the speech aloud)*. Stay, Tybalt, stay! Romeo, I come!

(She pushes open the swing-door again, returning to the kitchen.)

This do I drink to thee!

(Then in her own voice.)

There, I know it!

(She opens the icebox and gets out the tray of ice cubes. During the ensuing business, she starts the Potion Scene again, acting it to herself, and not overdoing it; the only thing that makes it ridiculous is the business that punctuates it.)

Farewell!

(Slams icebox door.)

God knows when we shall meet again!
I have a faint, cold fear thrills through my veins—

(Turns on the hot faucet to run over the ice tray.)

That almost freezes up the heat of life.
I'll call them back again to comfort me.

(Ice breaks into sink. She turns off tap.)

Nurse! What should she do here?
My dismal scene I needs must act alone.
Come. vial.

(Takes up ice-bucket, and starts to pick up ice.)

What if this mixture do not work at all?
Shall I be married then tomorrow morning?

No, no, this shall forbid it.

(Looks around for a prop, sees mixing spoon and uses it.)

Lie thou there!

(She places the spoon on the drain-board, then takes the ice-bucket into the living room, where she puts it on the drink-table, still reciting.)

What if it be a poison which the friar
Subtly have ministered to have me dead . . .

(She dries up.)

Have me dead . . . have me dead . . .

(She crosses to the couch where a Temple Shakespeare is lying open, and refreshes her memory.)

Lest in this marriage he should be dishonor'd,
Because he married me before to Romeo.

(Front-door buzzer rings. She goes to answer it, gabbling the next lines.)

231

I fear it is, and yet methinks it should not,
For he hath still been tried a holy . . .

(She opens the door. OLIVE LASHBROOKE
*is standing outside. She is about twenty-
eight, smart and attractive, without being
good-looking, and rather gay.)*

Olive!

OLIVE. Sally! Darling! *(They kiss.)*

SALLY. Come in. How are you?

OLIVE. Couldn't be better. *(Looks around.)*
So this is it! It's very grand.

SALLY *(pleased).* Do you think so?

OLIVE. Very. How long have you had it?

SALLY. Six weeks.

OLIVE *(inspecting; impressed).* Um!

SALLY *(naively excited).* Do you want to
see it all?

OLIVE. Sure.

SALLY. Well, this is the living room. It's
sunken. Kitchen's in here. *(Opens door.
They go through.)*

OLIVE. Darling, it's enormous! You could
feed the whole army. Do you have a maid?

SALLY. Colored. Daily. *When* she comes.
Which isn't very often. I think she's got
a complicated love life.

OLIVE. Don't we all? *(They return to living room.)* How did you find this?

SALLY. It's Claire Henley's. Claire's on the
road with the Lunts.

OLIVE *(as they re-cross living room).* I
don't know how that girl gets the break
she does. I was sick about *your* show. Did
you get my message, opening night?

SALLY. Yes, I didn't know where to thank
you. You were jumping around so.

OLIVE. Darling, I *know.* Split weeks and
one-night stands. It's heaven to be through.
How long did you run, actually?

SALLY. Five days.

OLIVE. Did you get any notices?

SALLY. A couple of mentions. *(Opening
bedroom door.)* Here's the bedroom.

OLIVE *(going in).* Very saucy. *(Flippantly.)*
Luxe.

SALLY. What?

OLIVE *(as before).* Luxe. French, darling.
One of those untranslatable expressions.
It means luxury. And beds like that!

SALLY *(pointing off).* Bathroom and dressing room in there.

OLIVE *(impressed).* Dressing room! *(She
peeps in.)*

SALLY *(excusing it).* Well . . .

OLIVE. Darling, it's the cutest place I ever
saw in all my life. *(Going to the window).*
Where do you look out?

SALLY. Onto the summer garden of the
"Bonne Chanson." That French restaurant
next door.

OLIVE. What's that like?

SALLY. Lovely. But terribly expensive. You
know, no menu. The man just comes and
suggests.

OLIVE. Put yourself right next door to
temptation, eh? Or is it for the boy-friends
when they come to take you out? *(Acting.)* "Where shall we eat?" "Wherever
you say." "How about the place next
door?" "Okay." *(Back to her own voice.)*
I know. I once thought of taking an apartment over the Colony, myself. What are
you paying Claire for this?

SALLY *(slightly embarrassed).* A hundred
and a quarter.

OLIVE. Have you got another job?

SALLY. No.

OLIVE. No! And there's nothing in the of-
fing, this late in the season, for any of us.

SALLY. I know. But I still have a little
money left over from that radio serial I
did. And it's when you're out of work you
need a nice place to live. When you're *in*
work . . .

OLIVE. You live at Sardi's—if you can get
in. Yes, but all the same! What did you
want to move for, anyway?

SALLY. I was tired of a hotel-room. And
there were reasons.

OLIVE *(eagerly).* What?

SALLY (*evasively*). Not now. Come and have a drink.

OLIVE. Lovely.

(*They return to the living room.*)

SALLY (*as they go*). What'll you have?

OLIVE. What have you got?

SALLY. Whatever you want. Gin . . . rum . . . Scotch . . .

OLIVE. Scotch? You *have* been on a bust. (*Flippantly.*) Or is all this . . . guilty splendor?

SALLY. Don't be silly. Scotch?

OLIVE. Sure. (SALLY *pours two Scotches. A large one for* OLIVE, *and a smaller one for herself.* OLIVE *picks up the Shakespeare.*) What on earth are you studying Juliet for?

SALLY (*pouring*). Practice.

OLIVE. Darling, you're out of your mind. You know, you take the theatre too seriously. You'll be going to Madame Pushkin's school next, studying "de free body," and learning how to act *milk!* (*Breaking off.*) I had the greatest success telling about Madame Pushkin in the company, by the way. Henry Atherton adored her. I gave you credit for inventing her.

SALLY (*bringing her the drink*). Was it wonderful playing with Henry Atherton? I've always had the most terrific thing about him. You used to have, too.

OLIVE. Did I? Well, it's gone now, if I did. He isn't interested in anything a day over twenty. There was a little ingenue in the company—she couldn't have been more than eighteen. You've never seen such carryings-on . . . holding hands and giggling in the wings, all through my one decent scene.

SALLY (*disappointed*). Oh!

OLIVE (*drinking*). It's good to be back in New York. By the way, I've asked someone to call for me here. Is that all right?

SALLY. Of course. Who is it?

OLIVE. A man called Bill Page.

SALLY. An actor?

OLIVE. No, just a man. At least, he used to be. He's a soldier now. He's at Camp Something-or-Other up the Hudson. Got a week-end pass, starting this afternoon. I left a message at my hotel telling him to come on here and pick me up.

SALLY. What's he like?

OLIVE. He's sweet. And he's mine!

SALLY. I didn't mean . . .

OLIVE. I know, darling, but I thought I'd tell you. I've known him for ages. He used to live in Pittsburgh, and whenever I played there we always had a "gay little something." Though when I say "whenever," I think actually it was only twice. I'd lost sight of him for years, and then when we were in Detroit about six weeks ago, he turned up again. He was stationed somewhere near, and came to see the show. Now, he's moved up here.

SALLY (*smiling*). And are you still having a "gay little something"?

OLIVE. Well, we did in Detroit.

SALLY. Are you in love with him?

OLIVE. No, darling, not a bit. But he's attractive. Only he's sort of the . . . reserved kind. You never know what he's thinking, or get any further with him.

SALLY. It doesn't sound as though there was much further left for you to get. (*Rises.*) By the way, what's happened to the Commander?

OLIVE. Ned Burling? Ah, darling, now you're talking! He's at sea somewhere . . . I guess. What makes you ask about him?

SALLY. I was just remembering *that* "gay little something" of yours.

OLIVE. And it *was* something!

SALLY. Do you ever hear from him?

OLIVE. No, he's not the writing kind. He was . . . you know . . . just "Butch." Besides, that was one of those . . . (*Mocking.*) "lovely things that isn't meant to last. A little Intermezzo, or a wild, brief gypsy Czardas." Ah, me! Quel goings-on!

SALLY (*moving away, repeating the phrase, reflectively*). "One of those lovely things that isn't meant to last."

OLIVE (*catching her tone, crosses to her*). Sally, what's the matter? You're unhappy about something. What is it? Is it . . . love?

SALLY. I guess so. If you can call it that.

OLIVE. You can always call it that. Come on. Tell Auntie Olive all about it. Well?

SALLY. Well, you've heard of Kenneth Bartlett—the producer?

OLIVE. Yes. Darling, it isn't *him*? (SALLY nods.) Sally, how simply sensational! And he's putting on *Romeo and Juliet* for you!

SALLY. Don't be silly. You know he only does musicals.

OLIVE. Yes, the new one opened last night. It's a smash, from the notices. Where did you meet him?

SALLY. At a cocktail party. (*She stops.*)

OLIVE (*eagerly*). Well, go on. Tell.

SALLY (*slowly*). Well, he's terribly nice. And young, and attractive. At least, I guess he's around forty, but he seemed young. And we talked . . . about the theatre, of course . . . and then he took me on to dinner. We went next door. That was the first time I'd been there.

OLIVE. But not the last.

SALLY (*shyly*). No. It sort of became . . . "our" place.

OLIVE. How long ago was all this?

SALLY. Two months. His show was in rehearsal, then. He told me all about it . . . sang me some of the songs. He made me feel wonderful . . . like being starred, and getting the star dressing room. Do you know?

OLIVE. I know.

SALLY. Well, then I found that Claire was going away, and had this place right next door to . . .

OLIVE. "Your" place . . .

SALLY. So I took it. You know, it was funny . . . when I came to see it, Claire had the radio on, and it was playing the Londonderry Air. That's always been my lucky tune. I thought it meant the apartment would be lucky.

OLIVE. So you let her soak you a hundred and a quarter.

SALLY. Well, it was nice to have. And . . . (*Timidly.*) just occasionally he stayed all night . . . and I got breakfast, and . . . oh, I don't know . . . but it was nice. I love having someone to do for. Even in that tiny hotel room . . . that time *you* stayed with me, because of the snow, do you remember? . . . It was sort of exciting, like having "Cousin Olive" to stay overnight when one was little. (*Pointing below window.*) By the way, if you ever want it, that's a day-bed.

OLIVE. Lovely. But what happened with "Cousin Bartlett"? What went wrong?

SALLY (*grimly*). I did.

OLIVE. Yes, I know, dear. But what went wrong?

SALLY. Well, he talked a lot about keeping it *gay* . . . not bringing love into it . . . or getting serious about each other . . .

OLIVE. And *you* did, and he didn't like that?

SALLY. He said I made scenes.

OLIVE. Did you?

SALLY. I guess I did. At least, they wouldn't be scenes if they were in a play, but . . . yes, I guess I made scenes. Little ones. You see, he's married.

OLIVE. Did you know that?

SALLY. Yes, he told me that the first evening. But they don't get on, and she's a lot older than he is. Oh, *he* didn't tell me that. He didn't say anything about her, except to let me know he *had* a wife. And they've two children, so you see, it couldn't be anything serious for *him*. Oh, he was very sweet about it . . . really he was. Only he said that it couldn't go on like that . . . for *my* sake. So, it's all over. We said good-bye a month ago. (*Rising and starting to pace.*) I've been so miserable ever since. We've had the most awful weather. I don't think spring's *ever* coming, this year. I've just stayed home, and studied *Juliet* and read Dorothy Parker's poems. I never used to mind being by myself, but now . . . since Ken . . . Well, it's the first time I've had an apartment of my own, and it seems such waste.

OLIVE. I know. I feel the same way whenever I go to a hotel, and they give me a big double room all to myself.

SALLY. Oh, what did I have to go and fall in love for? Or, if I did, why did I have to go and show it? Or, worse still, talk about it? I believe there's nothing men hate so much as talking about it.

OLIVE. There's nothing they hate so much as *your* talking about it.

SALLY. Well, it's not going to happen again. Sex, I mean. Not for a long, long time. Not till I'm thirty. It should never have started in the first place. Father was quite right about the theatre.

OLIVE. Oh, darling, you're not going to start blaming it on the theatre?

SALLY. If I'd stayed home in Joplin, none of this would have happened.

OLIVE. Don't they . . . in Joplin?

SALLY. Olive, tell me something. Something I want to know.

OLIVE. What?

SALLY. Well, *do* ordinary girls? I was raised to think they didn't. Didn't even want to. And what I want to know is—don't they? They don't in movies. Oh, I know that's censorship . . . but . . . the people who go and *see* the movies . . . are they like that too? Or else don't they notice that it's all false?

OLIVE. I've wondered about that, myself.

SALLY. Even in Shakespeare, his heroines don't. Ever. Juliet carries on like crazy about not. I don't know whether what Mother and Father taught me was right, or true, or anything. Were you raised like that?

OLIVE. Oh, sure. And I wasn't even legitimate. But Mama raised me just as strict as if I was.

SALLY. Did you have qualms when you started?

OLIVE. Never.

SALLY. What did you feel?

OLIVE. I just felt—"So, this is it! I like it!" (*Then, kindly.*) Oh, Sally, darling, you're not starting a conscience, or thinking you're promiscuous, because you've had one affair, are you?

SALLY (*unhappily*). I've had two. There was that boy in the company at Skowhegan last summer that I was so unhappy about. I told you.

OLIVE. Well, two, then.

SALLY. No, I . . . don't think I'm promiscuous . . . yet. Though I don't imagine anyone ever does think that about themselves. Do . . . (*She stops.*)

OLIVE. Do *I* . . . were you going to say?

SALLY. Well, I was, only I suddenly realized how awful it sounded.

OLIVE. No, I don't. Maybe you're right, and no one does, but I just think for a gal with a funny face, I've really done rather well. *You're* pretty. You can afford to be choosey. (*Walking away.*) I wonder what's happened to Bill. I hope they gave him the message. Would you mind if I called up the hotel to ask?

SALLY. No, do. It's in the bedroom. Can I fix you another drink?

OLIVE (*nodding*). A tiny one. (*She goes into bedroom, where she dials a number on the telephone.*)

SALLY. I'll just get a glass for *him*. (*She goes into kitchen, and gets a third glass, then comes back and fixes a drink for OLIVE.*)

OLIVE (*in bedroom, on phone*). Give me the desk, please. Hello, desk? This is Miss Lashbrooke. Has a Sergeant Page called for me? I left a note . . . Oh, he did? How long ago? Oh, thank you. By the way, you might just see if there are any messages for me. I'll hold on. (SALLY *comes into the bedroom. To* SALLY.) He's on his way here.

SALLY. Good. (*Hands* OLIVE *her glass.*)

OLIVE. Thanks. (*Drinks. Then, into phone.*) Hello . . . yes . . . yes . . . I see . . . all right, just leave it in my box. Anything else? Who called? (*Her voice rising in excitement.*) Lieutenant Comm . . . *what* number? Wait a minute, I'll get a pencil. (*She gets one from the telephone table, scribbling on a pad.*) Give me that number again. Eldorado . . . yes

. . . What time was that? Thanks. *(She hangs up, and sits staring.)*

SALLY. Was that *the* Commander?

OLIVE *(a little dazed and excited. Nods).* He's in town. He called at five o'clock. I must call him. *(SALLY starts to leave.)* Don't go. *(Lifts receiver and dials.)* Wouldn't you know it would happen like this? Well, at least he called me. That's something.

SALLY *(sits on bed, staring at her).* You're still crazy about him, aren't you?

OLIVE. Yes, damn it. In the worst way.

SALLY. Well, don't let him know it.

OLIVE *(laughing with slight bitterness).* You—giving *me* advice now! *(Into phone.)* Hello . . . is Commander Burling there? Ned? This is Olive. Yes, I just called the hotel and they told me. When did you get into town? You did? You are? When? You mean, you're just here till . . . Well, I never got it. I've been on the road with a play, and I guess the mail got . . . Oh, I can't. I'm terribly sorry, but I can't. How about lunch tomorrow? *(Disappointed.)* Oh. No, I'm tied up the whole week-end. I've got someone to look after. Yes, I know. Darling, I know. I know, but . . . *(She is growing agonized.)* Oh, hell, I will! Yes, yes, I will. I don't know how I . . . but I will. What's the time now? Oh, my God, no, no, make it eight, will you? Eight at my hotel. Yes . . . lovely to talk to *you.* Good-bye now. *(She hangs up, and looks at SALLY.)* There. There's an object lesson in how not to act with a man.

SALLY. You're seeing him tonight?

OLIVE. It's his last leave. He's got till Sunday afternoon. And he called *me* right away. He wrote to me! I'm going to dinner with him. *(She rises.)*

SALLY. But . . . What about . . . *this* one? *(Pointing to front door.)*

OLIVE. I don't know. I must think. What am I going to do? Bill's on his way here. Sally, what am I going to say?

SALLY *(unhelpfully).* I don't know.

OLIVE. No, but be some help.

SALLY. I can't. Why did you have to have dinner with him? You could have met him later . . . say, for supper.

OLIVE. And let Bill spend the whole evening . . . "expecting"? That's the kind of thing men never forgive. No, this way, he'll at least have a chance to fix up something else for himself. Could I say that my family . . . ? No, he knows I haven't any. Besides, one can always ditch one's family after midnight. Who *can't* one ditch? That's what it comes down to. Who can't one ditch? Mother . . . father . . . brother . . . grandmother. *(Suddenly.)* I've got it. Husband!

SALLY. Whose husband?

OLIVE. Mine!

SALLY. Doesn't he know you haven't a husband?

OLIVE. He hasn't seen me for about two years. Except that flash in Detroit . . . and that wasn't the kind of occasion when one would mention being married. And now my husband's turned up on his last leave. . . .

SALLY *(slightly shocked).* Olive, you can't!

OLIVE. I've got to tell him *something.* Oh, darling, I know it's awful of me, but you've not seen Ned. It's nearly a year since I have, and he's so divine. *(Front-door buzzer sounds.)* There *is* Bill. Listen, you'll help me?

SALLY. How?

OLIVE. With the husband story.

SALLY. I'll slip out, and let you talk to him.

OLIVE. No, don't do that. Stay and back me up.

SALLY. I couldn't.

OLIVE. *I* would . . . for you.

(Buzzer again.)

SALLY. I *must* answer the door.

OLIVE *(as they go into living room).* What's the time?

SALLY. A quarter of seven.

OLIVE. Oh, my God, and I've got to be dressed by eight. Why do things like this always have to happen to me?

SALLY. Shall I let him in?

OLIVE. I guess you'll have to.

(SALLY *goes to the front door, and admits* BILL PAGE. *He is about thirty-two, adult, quiet and attractive. He wears a Sergeant's stripes, and carries an evening paper and a tiny week-end-toilet-case.*)

BILL. Miss Sally Middleton?

SALLY. Yes, won't you come in? Olive's here.

OLIVE (*coming into view—brightly*). Bill —darling!

BILL (*coming in*). Hello. (*They kiss.*)

OLIVE. Sally, this is Bill Page. Sally Middleton.

SALLY. How do you do?

BILL. How do you do?

SALLY. May I take your things? (*She takes his cap and bag and puts them on desk.*) Let me give you a drink.

BILL. Thanks.

SALLY. Scotch?

BILL. Swell. (*Looking around.*) This is very pleasant. I haven't been in an apartment like this for quite a time. It's two years since I was in New York.

OLIVE. How does it look to you?

BILL. Like every other place these days . . . a lot too full of soldiers. But it's still good. *You're* looking blooming.

OLIVE (*uncomfortably bright*). Oh, yes, I'm fine.

BILL. I don't know whether you've made any plans for this week-end, but I've got a lot.

OLIVE (*miserably*). You have?

BILL. I thought tonight, we'd just have a quiet dinner . . . not go anywhere afterwards . . . just concentrate on good food, good drink and good . . . (SALLY *hands him his glass.*) Thank you so much. (*Then, turning back to* OLIVE.) Then I thought tomorrow we might take in a theatre. There was a notice in the evening paper of a new musical that opened last night. I imagine it will be all sold out, but I thought that, being in the theatre, you might know some way of getting tickets. (*Pause.*) How about it? Have you got any strings you can pull?

OLIVE (*nerving herself*). Bill . . . I've got something to tell you. (SALLY *edges to the bedroom door.*) Don't go, Sally.

SALLY. You left your glass in the bedroom.

OLIVE. I don't want another drink.

SALLY. I'll just get it. (*She goes into the bedroom, closing the door behind her.* BILL *notices this with slight surprise, as he turns back to* OLIVE. *In the bedroom,* SALLY *goes over to the window, looks out, draws the curtains and then sits, doing nothing, unwilling to return to the living room.*)

BILL. Well, what is it?

OLIVE. Bill, darling, I don't know how to tell you, but . . . I'm afraid our week-end's off.

BILL. How do you mean?

OLIVE. Darling, I can't come out with you. I . . . Listen, you didn't know I was married, did you?

(OLIVE *plays this scene with all the conviction possible. There must be no sense that she is lying, or doing it badly. Whether or not* BILL *is deceived is another question.*)

BILL. No—when?

OLIVE. About eighteen months ago. It didn't take. That's why I didn't tell you in Detroit.

BILL. Well?

OLIVE. Well, just this afternoon, he called me up. He's in the Navy. It's his last leave, and . . . he wanted to see me.

BILL. Yes?

OLIVE. I've got to have dinner with him.

BILL. Oh, that's tough for you. And for me.

OLIVE. I know.

BILL. Well, we'll meet later.

OLIVE (*quickly*). Oh, darling, I can't. I . . .

BILL. What?

OLIVE (*very uncomfortable*). Well, he . . . he *is* my husband. I mean, we're not divorced, or anything.

BILL. You mean—you're going back to him?

OLIVE *(not altogether liking this)*. Well, I . . . I don't know about permanently, but . . . it's his last leave, and . . .

BILL *(sparing her more)*. I see.

OLIVE. You're not mad at me?

BILL. No. But you can't expect me not to be a little disappointed. It's all right, though. These things happen. Not often, I guess, but . . .

OLIVE. I'll see you next time you get leave.

BILL *(smiling)*. Okay.

OLIVE. You do understand?

BILL *(smiling and patting her hand)*. Sure. Everything.

OLIVE *(not liking this, either)*. Bill, you're sweet. You always were. And, look, I've got to go. It's so late.

BILL *(rising)*. Right now?

OLIVE. I'm meeting Ned at eight.

BILL. What's his other name?

OLIVE *(after a slight pause)*. Burling.

BILL *(looking at her)*. Mrs. Ned Burling! Who'd have thought it?

OLIVE *(very uncomfortable now)*. He's a Commander. I *must* go. *(Calls.)* Sally! Sally!

BILL. Do you want me to take you anywhere?

OLIVE *(hurriedly)*. No . . . no . . . you stay here, and have your drink in peace. *(*SALLY *returns.)* I've broken it to him, Sally, and he's been sweet.

SALLY *(smiling politely)*. Oh?

OLIVE. And now I've got to fly.

SALLY. It's started to rain.

OLIVE. Oh, hell, can you get a taxi anywhere around here?

SALLY. Sometimes on Third Avenue. But not when it's raining.

OLIVE. I'll find one. Good-bye, Bill, and do forgive me. I'll call you. Where are you staying?

BILL. I don't know yet. I went straight from the station to your hotel. I asked if they'd a room there, but they were all full up. So I just came on here.

OLIVE *(abashed)*. Oh, Bill . . . I should have gotten you a room. New York's so full, only . . .

BILL. Don't worry. I'll find something.

OLIVE. I'll call you too, Sally. Bless you, and . . . *(She breaks off, floundering, kisses her and goes to the door.)* Good-bye, Bill.

BILL. Good-bye. Have fun.

OLIVE *(turning, reproachfully)*. Oh, Bill, that's not kind.

BILL. I'm sorry.

OLIVE *(as before)*. No, it's not kind at all!

(She goes.)

BILL *(turning to* SALLY, *with a slightly rueful grin)*. Well . . .

SALLY *(smiling)*. Well?

BILL. Give her a minute to get clear, and then I'll go along.

SALLY. There's no hurry.

BILL. Aren't you going out?

SALLY. No.

BILL. Well, all the same . . . I wonder if I might use your telephone.

SALLY *(going to the bedroom door)*. Yes, of course. It's in there.

BILL. Thank you so much.

(He goes into the bedroom. SALLY *closes the door on him, to give him privacy, and then draws the curtains, lights the lamps and settles down with the evening paper on the couch. In the bedroom,* BILL *takes out a small notebook from his pocket, looks up a number, dials it, sitting on the bed.)*

BILL. Hello? Can I speak to Miss Westbury, please? Miss Joan Westbury. Isn't that . . . *(Referring to his book again.)* Butterfield 8-1747? Don't Mr. and Mrs. Arthur Westbury live there? Oh, I see. Can you tell me where they're living now? I see. Thank you. *(Hangs up, gets notebook out again, and looks up another number, dialing it.)* Hello . . . Is Miss

Van Huysen there, please? Oh, are you expecting her in? Oh, I see. Well, will you tell her, Monday, that Mr. Page called, Friday? Mr. Bill Page, of Pittsburgh. No, no number. *(Hangs up again, and then dials another number after a moment's reflection and search.)* Hello, is Mr. Frank Archer there? Frank? This is Bill Page. Yes. Oh, I'm in town for the week-end. Say, you don't happen to know Joan's number, do you? Joan Westbury. I called her old number, but . . . no kidding? I hadn't heard. How does she look in her uniform? Say, whatever happened to Alice . . . what was her other name? That's right . . . Alice Hopewell. She *is*? When did she *get* married? What—Phyllis, too? Well, that's about all the old gang, isn't it? Frank, could *we* have some dinner tonight? Oh, you are? That's all right. It was just that I got stood up, that's all. Oh, I don't know. I'll probably go to the Stage Door Canteen, or something. I'm not stopping *anywhere* at the moment. I'll call *you*. Sure. Good-bye. *(Hangs up again. Looks in book again, thumbing leaves . . . is about to dial another number, then mutters, "Oh, the hell with it. She's probably dead." Rises, looks out of window, says, "Oh, damn the rain!" and returns to the other room.)*

SALLY *(looking up with a polite smile)*. Did you get your number?

BILL. Yes, thanks. Well . . .

SALLY. Won't you have another drink?

BILL. You're sure you're in no hurry?

SALLY. None at all.

BILL. Well, then, thanks. I'd like to.

SALLY. Help yourself, won't you?

BILL *(going to drink-table)*. Will *you*?

SALLY. I don't think so, thanks. *(She watches him commiseratingly, but unable to think of anything to talk about.)*

BILL *(making conversation)*. Are you and Olive old friends?

SALLY. We are, rather. She was in the first play I was ever in.

BILL. Oh. I ought to know, of course, but I haven't been around. Are you a well-known actress?

SALLY *(laughing)*. Me? I've never been in anything but flops. My longest run was three weeks.

BILL. You're not in anything now?

SALLY. No, nor likely to be, for months.

BILL *(coming back with his drink)*. What do actresses do between jobs?

SALLY. Well, *I* just sit and think about how I'm going to act all the parts I'll never get a chance to act. Like Juliet, or Nina in *The Sea Gull*. That's a Russian play.

BILL. I know.

SALLY. Oh, I'm sorry. I didn't mean to be patronizing. Only not a lot of people do know, and I didn't know if you knew anything about the theatre. *I* don't know anything about real life.

BILL *(amused)*. Real life?

SALLY. I always think of it like that. I mean, all of us . . . actors, and authors, too . . . we aren't really living in the real world at all. We're giving our whole lives to . . . make-believe.

BILL *(sitting)*. Why do you do it, then?

SALLY. I guess because I'm made that way. And in the hope of . . .

BILL. Of some day seeing your name in lights?

SALLY. Oh, I hope it isn't that. Of course, it's part of it. It would be silly to pretend it wasn't. But the hope . . . of one day being able to express . . . well, that thing one feels one's got to express . . .

BILL. "That one Talent which is death to hide?"

SALLY *(struck)*. Oh . . . what's that?

BILL. Milton. The sonnet on his blindness.

SALLY. Oh . . . it's lovely. Say it again. Say it all.

BILL. I don't think I can remember it all. It's years since I've looked at it. But . *(Quietly.)*

"When I consider how my light is spent Ere half my days in this dark world and wide, And that one Talent which is death to hide, Lodged with me useless . . ."

I don't remember any more.

SALLY *(savoring it)*. Oh . . . yes.

BILL. Well, that's wonderful . . . if you *have* the talent.

SALLY. Have *you?* I mean . . . do you do anything creative?

BILL. No, I'm afraid the only talent *I've* ever had is a talent for appreciation.

SALLY. What *did* you do before the war?

BILL. I didn't do anything at all till I was twenty-five, except have a very good time.

SALLY. Were you a . . . playboy?

BILL. Well, that's not a thing one would ever think of oneself as being . . . but, I suppose—by present-day standards, any-way—that's what I was. My family had a lot of money . . . and I went to Princeton, and Europe and . . . appreciated things. Very much indeed.

SALLY. And then?

BILL. Well, then things went wrong with the family, and the business went smash, and I had to come back and buckle down to . . . "real life."

SALLY. Was that awful for you?

BILL. A little. I told myself it was good for me. I guess maybe it was.

SALLY. And then the Army?

BILL. Yes.

SALLY. And . . . afterwards?

BILL. I haven't any plans for afterwards. I just hope there'll still be things left to appreciate.

SALLY. There'll always be. So long as there are people. Free people. That's what it's all about, isn't it? The war, I mean?

BILL. You mustn't ask a soldier what the war's about.

SALLY *(after a pause, tasting the phrase again)*. "That one Talent which is death to hide . . ."

BILL *(smiling at her)*. That sums you up, does it?

SALLY. Oh, no. Milton could say that. I'm not that conceited. But it's what it *feels* like, when you're out of work, or doing something second-rate. It's like having something *entrusted* to you . . . for the benefit of others . . . that you're wasting. *(Breaking off.)* Oh, no . . . that sounds awful! Phony and arty, like Madame Pushkin.

BILL. Who's she?

SALLY. Madame Pushkin? Oh, she's an imaginary character that Olive and I invented. An old Russian actress who runs a school where she teaches the Pushkin method. Her husband, Dr. Pushkin, is a very great director, and every morning he chases her around the bedroom for one hour in her nightgown to "giff her de free body." Didn't Olive ever tell you about her?

BILL. Olive and I have never talked like this.

SALLY *(abashed)*. I'm sorry.

BILL. What for?

SALLY. Going on about myself.

BILL. I've liked it. And *I've* gone about myself, too . . . which is something I haven't done for years. Will you have dinner with me?

SALLY *(after a second)*. Oh . . . no, thanks.

BILL. Why not?

SALLY. You don't have to ask me.

BILL. I know I don't. But will you?

SALLY. Well . . . we go Dutch.

BILL. No, I asked you.

SALLY. Only because Olive let you down.

BILL. Only because if she hadn't, I wouldn't have had the chance.

SALLY *(embarrassed by the compliment)*. Well, thank you very much, then.

BILL. Where shall we go?

SALLY. Wherever you say.

BILL. What's the place next door like?

SALLY *(after a half-second's pause, with an echo in her ears)*. Very expensive.

BILL. But good?

SALLY. Yes, but . . .

BILL. Let's go there. *(He notices a hesitation about her.)* Have you anything against it?

SALLY. N-no . . . But it's . . . *very* expensive.

BILL. All the same. Besides, it's raining quite hard now, so *let's* go next door. There was a restaurant of the same name in Paris that I used to go to quite a lot, once upon a time. Did you know Paris?

SALLY. No. I never went to Europe. I was only eighteen when the war broke out.

BILL. My God. That hurts.

SALLY. What?

BILL. That that's possible, already. *(He looks at her.)*

SALLY *(after an embarrassed pause).* I'll just get my coat. *(She starts into the bedroom.* BILL *stands looking after her.)*

CURTAIN

SCENE II

SCENE: *The same. About 10:30 the same night.*
The stage is as we left it. Then the sound of a key is heard in the front door. BILL *and* SALLY *come in.*

BILL. What a night! *(Closes the door behind him.)* Did you get wet?

SALLY. Running from next door? No. Come in and sit down, won't you?

(BILL shakes out his cap, and puts it down. He helps SALLY *off with her coat. She switches on the lamps.)*

SALLY. Would you like a drink?

BILL. Not after all that brandy. I must have had five, waiting for the rain to stop.

SALLY *(after a moment's pause, going to the radio).* Would you like the news?

BILL. I don't think so. Unless *you* would.

SALLY. I don't think . . . really. *(She starts to wander purposely.)* Have a candy? *(Offers box.)*

BILL. No, thanks. You don't have to entertain me, you know. Relax. What are you fussing about?

SALLY. Was I fussing? I didn't mean to. *(Pause.)* That was a lovely dinner. Thank you.

BILL. You were right. It's a good place.

SALLY. It was better even than usual tonight. That was your remembering the proprietor from Paris. And he you. You must have gone there a lot.

BILL. I did. I used to go with . . . a girl I used to go with. Almost every evening, at one time, for weeks on end.

SALLY. Was it a famous place?

BILL. No, just tiny. But we used to think of it as "our" place. We were very young.

SALLY. Were you in love with her?

BILL. I used to think I was.

SALLY. What happened to her?

BILL. She got married. Women do, you know.

SALLY. Yes. This isn't being a very amusing evening for you. Going to that restaurant . . . sort of upset you, didn't it?

BILL. Did that show?

SALLY. I *thought* . . .

BILL. I'm sorry. But "upset" is too strong a word. It was just . . . seeing it all done up exactly like the place in Paris, the same pictures on the walls, the same lamps on the tables, the same tablecloths . . . Well, it brought things back.

SALLY. The girl, you mean? Was she a French girl?

BILL. No, she was an American. I wasn't having an affair with Mimi, the little Midinette. But I didn't only mean the girl. I meant everything. Those were happy years. I was very happy then.

SALLY. And you're not now?

BILL. Is anyone?

SALLY. It's awful, but *I* am. Quite often.

BILL. It's not at all awful. It's wonderful. But I'm afraid I infected you at dinner. You were a bit low, too, I thought.

SALLY (moving away). Well, strangely, that place has memories for me, too. More recent ones than yours, but . . .

BILL. Why didn't you tell me?

SALLY (vaguely). Oh . . .

BILL. I'm afraid it wasn't a very good choice, for either of us.

SALLY. I am sorry. You're having a miserable time.

BILL. No, I'm having a grand time. (Yawns.) Oh, I'm sorry.

SALLY. You see!

BILL. That wasn't misery . . . or boredom. It was too much dinner, and not enough sleep.

SALLY. Don't you get enough?

BILL. I haven't had enough for months. Tomorrow morning, I shall stay in bed till lunchtime. Sunday, I probably shan't get up at all . . . till it's time to go back.

SALLY. Is that how you want to spend your leave?

BILL. Well, there are worse ways.

SALLY. But it wasn't what you'd planned.

BILL (putting out his cigarette). No! (Then, after a second.) Did you know Olive was going to tell me all that story?

SALLY (startled). What do you mean?

BILL. You don't think I believed it, do you? You didn't think I would believe it? (SALLY stares at him.) Olive's far too . . . well, too frank and free a person, not to have mentioned a husband if she had one.

SALLY. But you haven't seen each other.

BILL. We saw each other in Detroit, six weeks ago.

SALLY. Yes, but then you . . .

BILL. What?

SALLY (unable to go on, without giving away too much). Nothing.

BILL. Oh, she told you about it, did she? I guess girls always do.

SALLY (after just too long a pause). I don't know what you're talking about.

BILL (smiling). Okay.

SALLY (rising). Are you in love with Olive?

BILL. Is that your favorite question?

SALLY (blushing and subsiding). I'm sorry.

BILL. I'm not in the least in love with her. So don't worry. I guess I'm a little sore at her for letting me down. But I'll get over that, by tomorrow.

SALLY (slightly shocked). As quickly as that?

BILL. Oh, I think so. (He yawns again.) Oh, I am sorry. I should be going.

SALLY (rising). Well, if you're sleepy. Has the rain stopped?

BILL. I don't know. (Goes to window and looks out.) No, I think it's worse.

SALLY (following him to window). You can't go out in that.

BILL. If it doesn't let up soon, I'll have to.

SALLY. Well, don't go yet. It's sure to stop.

BILL (returning to the couch). Tell me some more about Madame Pushkin.

SALLY (laughing). Oh, it's silly.

BILL. No, I like the sound of her. What is the Pushkin Method?

SALLY. Well, to begin with, she believes that you must never play a part the way it's written. That's too easy. (Assuming a mock-Russian accent and personality.) Always you must look for de odder side of a character. Ven I play Lady Macbess, I concentrate on her . . . her child-like qvalities. Ven ve com to de scene from de sleep-valkings, I skip! (And does so.)

BILL (laughing). You're a fool!

SALLY (laughing, too). I know. There's heaps more. Her parents were on the stage. too, you know. She was conceived during an intermission of The Cherry Orchard.

BILL. Are you making all this up as you go along?

SALLY. Certainly. Olive and I do it for hours on end. We call it "How to be ham though high-brow." Olive . . . (She stops *a little self-consciously on the mention of* OLIVE's *name.)*

BILL. Look, you needn't get self-conscious about mentioning Olive's name to me. She hasn't broken my heart.

SALLY. Has anyone, ever? Did the girl in Paris?

BILL. At it again?

SALLY. Oh, dear, it's an obsession.

BILL. Why's it an obsession?

SALLY. I don't know. Because I'm a fool, I guess. I always think that everyone ought to be in love with *someone.*

BILL. Are *you?*

SALLY. I . . . I think I am.

BILL. Not sure? Have you been in love often?

SALLY *(seriously, considering it).* No . . . not often.

BILL *(kidding her a little).* I suppose actresses need to fall in love a lot . . . to be good actresses?

SALLY *(becoming Madame Pushkin instantly).* Oh, *yes,* Meester Payche! Alvays ven I play a rôle I must be in lof. Sometimes I valk de streets for hours, to find someone to fall in lof viz! *(Telephone rings. She continues in the accent.)* De telephone. Excuse please. I go. *(She goes into the bedroom, and turns on the light, answering the telephone very gaily, in Pushkin accents.* BILL *sits alone, amused, for a moment, then returns to the window, looks out again, then throws himself on the divan, below it, playing with the radio. He turns it on very softly to some gentle instrumental music, lights a cigarette, and stretches out full length on his back, listening to it.)*

SALLY *(on the telephone).* Hillo . . . *(Then, remembering, in her own voice.)* I mean—hello. *(Then, recognizing* OLIVE's *voice, she resumes the accent.)* Is Madame Pushkin speakink, Miss Lashbrooke. *(Then, back to her own voice again.)* I was just telling about her . . . To Bill . . . Yes, he's still here . . . No, we went out to dinner. . . . No, I've had a very *nice* evening. He wasn't a bit miserable. Where are you? . . . Well, it was a good thing you didn't, because that *was* where

we went. . . . Oh, we had the most wonderful Vichysoisse, and duck with oranges, salad with a lot of garlic. . . . What? Yes, I guess we do . . . and Crêpes Suzettes . . . Olive, you don't *mind* our having gone to dinner, do you? It was just that he asked me, and he hadn't any other place to go. . . No, I don't think he has. I don't think he's tried. . . . Well, it's raining. Hard . . . Are *you* having fun? What did *you* have to eat? . . . Oh, lovely. Yes, of course he's all right. Why not? . . . Well, I won't tell him if you don't want me to. Good-bye, Olive. *(She hangs up, a little bothered and puzzled. Then she returns to the other room, where she stops at the sight of* BILL, *who has fallen asleep, with the cigarette burning between his fingers. She takes it gently from his hand, and he wakes.)*

BILL *(sitting up).* What . . . ? Oh, I'm sorry. I've been asleep.

SALLY. I'm sorry I woke you, but you might have set yourself on fire. *(She gives him the cigarette back.)*

BILL *(rising).* I might have set the place on fire. I'd better get along and look for a hotel room.

SALLY. Yes, you'll have awful trouble, finding one. The hotels are all full up.

BILL. Are they?

SALLY. Ol . . . *(She checks herself).* The friend who just called up said they were.

BILL *(registering her change of phrase).* Well, I'll dig up something. This is liable to keep up all night. So . . . *(He crosses to* SALLY, *extending his hand.)*

SALLY *(as they shake hands, with a sudden thought).* Would you want to stay here? That's a day-bed. It's quite comfortable.

BILL. I know it is. But . . . I don't think I should do that.

SALLY. I can give you a toothbrush.

BILL. I've got that with me.

SALLY. It seems silly to go out in all that rain. You'll get so wet looking for a taxi. You haven't any change of clothes. You're tired. I'll give you breakfast in the morning.

BILL. Oh, you needn't do that.

SALLY. I'd like to.

BILL. Well, it's very good of you . . .

SALLY. Then you will?

BILL. Yes, thank you. (*Yawns again*). Oh
. . .

SALLY (*commiseratingly*). Ah, look at
you! Why don't you go to bed, right away?
It's all made up. I've only got to take the
cover off.

BILL. Let me help you.

SALLY. Oh, thank you. (*She takes the cush-
ions from the day-bed, while* BILL *strips
off the cover.*)

SALLY (*after a moment*). Would you like
some pajamas?

BILL. I couldn't wear your pajamas.

SALLY. They aren't mine. They're men's
pajamas. My . . . brother stays here sometimes.

BILL. Oh . . . well, then, thank you very
much. That would be a luxury.

SALLY. I'll get them for you. (*She goes to
the bedroom, taking her coat with her,
and gets a pair of men's pajamas and bedroom slippers from a drawer. Meanwhile,
BILL takes off his coat, hanging it over the
back of a chair in the living room. SALLY
returns.*)

SALLY (*handing him the pajamas*). Here
. . .

BILL (*after the tiniest pause—taking
them*). Thanks. These are very resplendent.

SALLY. I brought you some slippers, too.

BILL. All the comforts of home. (*There is a
tiny movement of embarrassment. Then
he slumps onto the bed.*) Gee, I'm tired.
(*He starts to unlace his shoes.*)

SALLY. I'll just empty the ashtrays. (*She
starts emptying them into the largest,
while he continues to unlace his shoes. The
radio starts playing the Londonderry Air,
and she pauses, raising her head to listen
to it.*)

BILL (*noticing*). What is it?

(*She crosses to the radio, and turns it
louder, to hear better. She smiles.*)

SALLY. That's my lucky tune.

BILL. The Londonderry Air?

SALLY. It's silly, but whenever I hear that,
nice things always seem to happen to me.
(*Collecting herself.*) I'll just take these
out. The bathroom's through there. (*She
goes into the kitchen. BILL takes his toilet
case and the pajamas and goes into the
bathroom. In the kitchen, SALLY empties
the ashtrays and washes them. Then she
gets a tray with a Thermos set from the
shelves, and fills the jug with ice-water
from the icebox, taking the tray into the
living room and setting it on the desk. She
clears the drink-table of its tray, which she
takes to the kitchen. Back in the living
room again, she tidies the room, turning
down the day-bed, and arranging the ottoman footrest of the armchair as a night-
table, with the Thermos tray, cigarettes,
matches, and ashtray, beside the bed.
Throughout this business, the radio continues. Then she goes into the bedroom.*)

SALLY (*calling to the closed bathroom
door*). Have you everything you want?

BILL (*putting his head around the door,
toothbrush in hand*). Did you call?

SALLY. I said, have you everything you
want?

BILL. Oh, sure, thanks. Everything.

(*She smiles at him, and he shuts the door
again. She strips the cover from her own
bed, folds it and lays it on top of the chest
of drawers. Then she goes back to the
living room, switching off lights. BILL
returns in pajamas, carrying his folded
clothes. He looks around.*)

BILL (*indicating a chair*). This all right?

SALLY. Sure. (*He lays his clothes neatly
across the chair.*)

BILL (*coming to the bed*). You don't know
how good that looks. (*Sits on it*). And
feels. (*He kicks off the slippers, and gets
into bed.*) And is. (*He sits up, smiling.*)

SALLY. What are you smiling at?

BILL. I was just remembering a novel I
once read about life in 1910 . . . where the
heroine was compromised because she was
seen coming out a man's apartment, after
dark.

SALLY. I guess things *have* changed.

BILL. You're not kidding.

SALLY *(dubiously).* Although I don't know that my mother would . . . *quite* understand this. It's silly, because it couldn't be more sensible. But there are a lot of people still who wouldn't believe in it.

BILL. Well, don't tell 'em.

SALLY. I don't intend to. *(Pause.)* Well . . . good night.

BILL. Good night, Sally.
(He switches out the bed light.)

SALLY. Good night, Cousin Bill.

BILL. Huh?

SALLY. Nothing. Oh, I left the kitchen light on. *(She goes back to the kitchen, talking from there, over her shoulder.)*

I'll just leave a note for Verona, to tell her not to disturb you. *If* she comes. *(She starts to scribble a note on a pad hanging on a nail.)* Verona's the colored maid. I don't expect she'll show up, but I'll be on the safe side. *(She finishes the note, tears off the sheet and places it prominently. Then she switches off the kitchen light. The only remaining light is now in the bedroom. She returns to the dark living room.)*

SALLY. Are you all right?

(There is no answer. BILL *is asleep.* SALLY *tiptoes on into the bedroom, closing the door behind her. She sits on the bed, takes off her shoes, and is starting on her stockings as*

THE CURTAIN FALLS

ACT TWO

SCENE I

SCENE: *The same. Around noon, the next day.*
When the curtain rises, BILL *is in the kitchen, squeezing orange juice at the sink. A coffee percolator is bubbling on the stove. A tray is set with cup and saucer and cream pitcher. The day-bed in the living room has been made, and in the bedroom* SALLY's *bed has also been made, and the room tidied.*
After a moment, SALLY *lets herself in at the front door. She is in outdoor things, and carries some marketing bags, and a manuscript. Her manner is gay, and ever so lightly "high."* BILL *hears the door, and comes into the living room.*

BILL. Good morning.

SALLY *(dumping her packages on the couch).* Good morning.

BILL *(smiling).* How are you this morning?

SALLY. I'm fine. *(She looks around.)* Is Verona here?

BILL. I haven't seen her.

SALLY. Did *you* make your bed?

BILL. Sure.

SALLY. You shouldn't have.

BILL. Why not?

SALLY. Because . . . it's not a man's thing to do.

BILL. You'd be surprised what a lot of men are doing it, nowadays.

SALLY. Yes, but this is your vacation. Have you had breakfast?

BILL I've just put on some coffee, as you said in your note I might.

SALLY. I was *afraid* Verona wasn't going to show up. I meant to get your breakfast myself, but I had to go out.

BILL. Did *you* have breakfast?

SALLY. No. I had a cocktail.

BILL. A what?

SALLY. A cocktail.

BILL. When?

SALLY. Oh, about half an hour ago. It's made me a little heady.

BILL. Didn't you have any breakfast *before* the cocktail?

SALLY. No, there wasn't time. I thought if you were still here, and hadn't a date, we might have lunch. I did some marketing.

BILL. You seem to have done a lot.

SALLY. I can never resist a delicatessen. I hate eating alone, except things you can sort of cuddle up on the couch with . . . like potato salad. *(She pats the package, indicating it.)*

BILL. I should never have thought of cuddling up with potato salad.

SALLY. I'd better take these in the kitchen. *(She starts to do so, talking as she goes.)* I wish I'd started housekeeping before rationing. It must have been so easy, then. I always do everything too late. *(She returns to the living room.)* It's the loveliest spring morning out. The weather's changed at last. In more ways than one, I think.

BILL. What do you mean by that?

SALLY. I think *my* weather's changed, too. I've got a job.

BILL. You have?

SALLY. That's what I went out about. That's what I had the cocktail about, too. They called me at half-past nine. I didn't disturb you, did I? I tried not to.

BILL. I didn't know a thing till half-past eleven.

SALLY. I was afraid the telephone might have woken you. *(Correcting herself.)* Wakened you. But you were still sleeping when I left.

BILL. Not snoring, I hope?

SALLY. No, you were very peaceful. *(Turning to him with her characteristic sudden directness.)* Don't you think there's something rather . . . frightening about people asleep? They look so unlike themselves, and sort of . . . vulnerable. I always feel one oughtn't to look.

BILL. When you have to sleep with fifty other men every night, you get over feeling like that.

SALLY. Do you hate it all?

BILL *(briefly)*. No.

SALLY. Like it?

BILL. That would be going a little far. I don't think you're expected to *like* it.

SALLY. A job to be done?

BILL. You do like to talk about things, don't you?

SALLY. Yes, it's my besetting sin. I always hope if I talk about things, it will help me know what I feel about them. But it never does. It only muddles me more. *(Looking at him.)* You're depressed this morning.

BILL. No, I just haven't had my coffee yet. It should be ready by now. You'd better have some, too.

SALLY. *I'm* not depressed.

BILL *(with meaning)*. No, I know . . .

SALLY. You think I'm tight.

BILL *(unconvincingly)*. No, I don't.

SALLY. I am. A little. And I'm happy, too.

BILL *(as they go into kitchen)*. Tell me about the job.

SALLY. Oh, it's a lovely job. Only . . . may I tell you when we sit down? I hate telling a story in bits . . . if it's a good story.

BILL. All right. *(He gets another cup and saucer from the shelves, and puts it on the tray.* SALLY *starts putting her packages in the icebox.)* By the way, your telephone rang while you were out. It rang twice.

SALLY. Oh, who was it?

BILL. I don't know.

SALLY. Didn't you answer?

BILL. No.

SALLY. Why not?

BILL. I didn't think it would sound very well to have a man's voice answering your telephone.

SALLY. I wouldn't have thought of that.

BILL. Suppose it had been your Aunt Minnie from Duluth? Or . . . your brother, for that matter?

SALLY. My . . . ?

BILL *(quickly)*. Whose very handsome pajamas I wore last night.

SALLY. Oh . . . yes. *(He takes the tray and goes into the living room.* SALLY *follows with the percolator.)* You mean you just let it ring? I don't think I could do that, even in someone else's house. It always sounds to me as if it was going crazy when I don't answer. Besides, it might be something lovely.

BILL *(setting the tray down and sitting down to it with her).* For instance?

SALLY *(pouring coffee).* Well . . . a long-lost uncle with a lot of money, or a lovely party, or a job.

BILL. How often has it been one of those?

SALLY. It was a job this morning.

BILL. Yes, you win on that. *(Takes his cup.)* Now do you feel settled enough to tell about it?

SALLY *(taking hers).* Yes, I think so. Well, as I say, it's really a lovely job. It's a play that's in rehearsal already. I knew about it from a friend of mine who was going to be in it. Well, yesterday was the fifth day. Oh, I don't guess you know about that. You can fire actors up to the fifth day, if they're no good.

BILL. No, I didn't know. What happens *after* the fifth day?

SALLY. You have to keep them, or pay them two weeks' salary. It's a rule of Equity. Well, it seems they fired her yesterday.

BILL. Your friend?

SALLY. Yes. I feel sort of badly about that . . . getting her part, I mean . . . though, actually, she couldn't have been in it very long, if it had run, because she's going to have a baby, only she didn't tell them that. And I don't think it was quite honorable. I mean, it may be an act of God, but not if it's already started, I should think.

BILL *(bewildered).* What *are* you talking about? What may be an act of God?

SALLY. Having a baby. It is, in the theatre.

BILL. I never knew the theatre was that different. I see now what you mean about real life! Well, go on . . . They fired her, and sent for you?

SALLY. Yes. I'm starting rehearsals Monday. The author took me next door for a cocktail, and I didn't like to tell him I hadn't had any breakfast. It sounded too pathetic. And then he told me something really thrilling.

BILL. What was that?

SALLY. Well, I'm not supposed to tell. But . . . well, you don't know anyone in the theatre, do you?

BILL. Only Olive.

SALLY. Well, I don't guess you'll be seeing her.

BILL. I guess not.

SALLY. I think I can tell you. You see, the leading man isn't very good, but he was all they could get, because of the draft.

BILL. You mean—he's 4-F?

SALLY. I guess so. Anyway, his acting's 4-F. Well, now, with Olive's tour closing, there's a chance they might get Henry Atherton. And that'd be wonderful. I've always had the most terrific crush on him.

BILL *(surprised).* That wizened, whimsy little man with dyed gold hair?

SALLY. Oh, he's sweet. And it's not dyed. Is it?

BILL. Olive said it was. And she said he used to make passes at all the kids in the company.

SALLY. Yes, she told me. But he's a great star, and it would be a big chance for me. I told you last night that was my lucky tune.

BILL. What kind of a part have you got in this play?

SALLY. Oh, a lovely part. I have to go mad in one act. Do you know anything about insanity?

BILL. Not a thing. Why?

SALLY. I thought you might give me some pointers. Although, as a matter of fact, I know just how I want to do it, if I can.

BILL. How is that?

SALLY. I want to play it very quietly, and as if I thought I were quite sane, myself. I mean, I don't imagine mad people ever *think* they're mad. They probably think everyone else is.

BILL *(in Pushkin accents)*. You are qvite right. Dat is how I teach my vife, Madame Pushkin, to play Ophelia.

SALLY. I don't go *very* mad. I mean, not straws and things.

BILL. I'm glad of that. I don't like plays where people go *very* mad.

SALLY. Nor do I. Though they're fun to do. What other kinds of plays don't you like?

BILL. Plays about men who are paralyzed from the waist down. Plays where a lot of people all get caught together in a catastrophe—a flood, or an earthquake, or an air raid—and all face death in a lump. There's always a prostitute in those plays, have you noticed? Usually a clergyman, too. That's what's called "taking a cross-section of humanity." I don't like plays about prostitutes.

SALLY. They're lovely to act. Olive's played lots. I haven't been one since I was in high school. And then they called it a courtesan.

BILL *(laughing)*. I bet you were immense.

(He rises to get cigarettes from the pocket of his coat which is hanging over a chair. SALLY rises, too, taking the percolator back to the kitchen.)

BILL. Well, things *are* looking up for you. I guess you're right, and the weather *has* changed. The rain is over, the winter is past, and the voice of the turtle is heard in our land.

SALLY *(arrested in the doorway)*. What did you say?

BILL. I was quoting from the Bible.

SALLY. Oh. *(She comes back for the tray, and then stops again, worriedly.)* But turtles don't *have* voices . . . do they?

BILL. Turtle *dove.*

SALLY. Oh. *(As she goes back to the kitchen with the tray.)* I never could understand the Bible. I don't see why they give it to children to read. *(She returns to the living room.)*

BILL. You know, we ought to do something to celebrate this job of yours. Will you have dinner with me?

SALLY. You took me to dinner last night.

BILL. So what?

SALLY. So you shouldn't do it again.

BILL. But I want to do it again. Very much. And what do you say we go to a theatre? That new musical. Do you like musicals?

SALLY. I adore them. If they're good.

BILL. Well, this is supposed to be very good.

SALLY. Yes, it is. I've heard some of the songs.

BILL. Well, let's go, then.

SALLY. We'd never get seats.

BILL. Not even through a broker?

SALLY. I don't think so. After those no-tices . . . and the first Saturday.

BILL. I wondered whether Olive mightn't have some pull. I started to ask her yesterday.

SALLY. I know. But I don't think she has. And I wouldn't want to ask her now, anyway.

BILL. Why not?

SALLY. Well, you're *her* friend, and Olive's rather hot against that kind of thing. Beau-snatching. I don't know that I really ought to come at all.

BILL. Now you listen to me. In the first place, you haven't snatched me. Any snatching that's been going on, *I've* been doing. And in the second, I'm not her beau . . . any more. She gave me the good, old-fashioned gate last night, even though I did suspect she was trying to leave it on the latch. The point is, we're going to that musical. How *does* one get tickets for a show like that, at the last moment? People do.

SALLY. Well, there are things called house seats.

BILL. What are they?

SALLY. They're tickets that the management keeps up its sleeve for friends, and influential people.

BILL. Who is the management?

SALLY. Kenneth Bartlett's putting it on.

BILL. Do you know him?

SALLY (*remotely*). Yes, I . . . know him.

BILL. Well, then call him up. Tell him a friend of yours . . . a service man . . . is in town . . . you can say it's his last furlough . . .

SALLY (*faintly alarmed*). Is it?

BILL. No, but it makes a better story. And can he please buy two of the house seats for tonight? (SALLY *sits dumbly.*) What's the matter?

SALLY. I can't ask him.

BILL. Don't you know him well enough?

SALLY. It isn't that.

BILL. What then?

SALLY. It's just that . . . I can't. There are reasons. Really, there are. I can't.

BILL. Well, then, I'll go foraging this afternoon when I look for a hotel room, and you can stay here and study how to go slightly mad.

SALLY. I'm afraid you won't get anything.

BILL. Well, don't be so worried about it.

SALLY. But you wanted to see it. You're having an awful leave. You're not doing any of the things you planned to do.

BILL. I'm enjoying the things I'm doing, instead.

SALLY (*suddenly, as always*). Do you believe in pride?

BILL. Now what do you mean by that?

SALLY. Suppose someone had . . . not treated you badly, it's not that . . . suppose you'd behaved badly to someone . . . do you think you ought to ask them for a favor?

BILL. I should hardly think so. What's this about? The theatre tickets?

SALLY (*quickly*). No. Oh, no. Just general principles.

BILL. Have *you* behaved badly to someone?

SALLY. Well, not badly in the ordinary sense. But . . . well . . . What's the difference between true pride and false?

BILL. I really wouldn't know.

SALLY. I'm sure you oughtn't to.

BILL. Oughtn't to what?

SALLY. Ask the favor.

BILL (*after a moment*). Well, let's stop this abstract speculation and get lunch.

SALLY (*coming out of her reverie*). Oh . . . yes. (*She rises.*)

BILL. Sally.

SALLY. What?

BILL. You're very sweet. (*She looks up at him with surprise. He takes her hands.*) I haven't the faintest idea what goes on in that funny little head of yours, but you're very sweet. (*He leans forward and kisses her, gently. They hold the kiss for a moment, then he releases her.*)

SALLY. Oh . . . that was a surprise.

BILL. Do you mind?

SALLY. No, it was nice.

BILL. I thought so, too. Come and show me where things are. (*He goes into the kitchen. She follows him, more disturbed than ever.*) What are we going to have? Not potato salad, I hope?

SALLY (*still in a slight trance*). No, I thought maybe . . . scrambled eggs.

BILL. Good.

SALLY (*reaching down below stove*). I'll get the frying pan.

BILL. Do you have a double boiler? I think they're better in a double boiler.

SALLY (*bringing one out, abstractedly*). Are they? I've never used one.

BILL. Do you like them wet or dry?

SALLY. What?

BILL. Your eggs.

SALLY. Oh . . . wet, I think.

BILL. Good. So do I. And how about coming out of that trance?

SALLY. I'm sorry. (*Then, suddenly*). Will you excuse me a minute? (*She leaves quickly and goes to the bedroom, closing the door firmly behind her. She looks at the telephone hesitantly for a moment, then sits, grasps it with determination, and dials. Meanwhile BILL is collecting things for the meal in the kitchen—eggs, milk, pepper, salt, etc., filling the base of the double boiler and putting it on the* stove. *Into phone.*) Hello? Is Mr. Bartlett there? Miss Middleton. Miss Sally Middleton. Thanks. *(She holds on nervously.)* Hello . . . Ken? Yes. I'm fine. Ken, I wonder if I can ask you a favor? . . . Well, a friend of mine . . . a soldier . . . is in town on leave, and he wanted terribly to go to your show tonight. I wondered if you had any seats left he could buy . . . Well, two . . . yes, yes, I was going with him . . . You could? Oh, that's wonderful. It was the only thing he wanted to see and . . . it's terribly nice of you . . . Oh, are you going to be there? Good. Yes, yes, of course, we'd like to . . . Page. Sergeant Page . . . Oh, that's sweet of you. I do appreciate it. . . . Ken, I read the notices. I'm so glad it's such a hit. Well, thank you again . . . so much. Good-bye, Ken. *(She hangs up with a little exhausted "Phew" from the strain, then returns to the kitchen.)*

BILL *(breaking eggs into a bowl).* Now come and learn how to make scrambled eggs properly.

SALLY. All right.

BILL. First you break the eggs.

SALLY. Yes, I do know that.

BILL. Oh . . . do you have an egg-beater?

SALLY *(getting it).* Yes. It's always scared me to death.

BILL. They're better if you beat them.

SALLY *(as* BILL *breaks the last egg).* Bill . . .

BILL *(pausing).* What?

SALLY. It's all right about tonight. I've got the tickets.

BILL. You have? How?

SALLY. I called up Kenneth Bartlett. They're at the theatre, in your name. You're to pick them up by seven o'clock. He wants us to have a drink with him in the intermission.

BILL. Good. What's he like?

SALLY. He's nice. Very nice.

BILL. What made you suddenly change your mind?

SALLY. I don't know. Yes, I do.

BILL. What was it?

SALLY. Your kissing me.

BILL. I don't quite see the connection.

SALLY. I don't think I could explain.

BILL. May I kiss you again for getting them?

SALLY. If you want to.

BILL. I do. *(He kisses her again.)* Thank you.

SALLY *(smiling).* Thank *you.*

BILL. We're going to have a nice evening. Now then . . . *(He starts beating the eggs.)*

CURTAIN

SCENE II

SCENE: *The same. Two* A.M.
When the curtain rises, the stage is in darkness. The radio is playing. The announcer's voice is heard.

ANNOUNCER. W.O.T.C. New York. Two A.M., Saturn Watch time. We bring you now an electrically transcribed program of the latest dance rhythms.

(Music starts. After it has been playing a moment the telephone begins to ring. After three or four rings, the front door opens. BILL *and* SALLY *come in. She wears a dinner dress under a day coat.)*

SALLY. It is! I told you it was! *(She starts for the bedroom.)*

BILL. Wait a minute. You don't want to answer that.

SALLY *(arrested).* Why not?

BILL. Because you know perfectly well who it is.

SALLY *(whispering).* Olive?

BILL. Sure. And I don't know what you're whispering for. She can't possibly hear you. *(SALLY stands irresolute, looking at him pleadingly. The bell continues.)* Do you want to talk to her . . . now?

SALLY. Not really.

BILL *(takes her hand and pulls her toward sofa).* Well, then this is your chance for a first lesson in self-control with the telephone. Sit down, and let it ring.

(SALLY sits down. The telephone continues. It is obviously an effort to her to stay where she is. BILL *switches on the lamps and stands watching her with amusement. Silence for a moment. Then she leaps up.)*

SALLY. It's no good. I can't stand it.

(The telephone stops.)

BILL. There. It's all over. It's stopped.

SALLY. I feel as if it had died. And *I'd* killed it. *(She now notices the radio.)* Did you turn the radio on?

BILL. No.

SALLY. Then it must have *been* on. We must have left it on. *(She goes to radio and turns it off.)* It must have been playing all evening . . . all by itself.

BILL *(amused).* Does that bother you, too?

SALLY. Yes, it does. Sort of hurting its feelings . . . no one listening.

BILL. You're crazy.

SALLY *(taking off her coat).* It's sort of spooky, too. The telephone and the radio, both going, and no one paying any attention. It's like . . . like a world where everyone's dead, and *they're* still going on.

BILL *(taking the coat from her).* You have pretty fancies, don't you? I hate to spoil it, but if everyone *were* dead, there wouldn't be any telephone and radio to go on.

SALLY. Why not?

BILL. Because they don't work without human agency . . . yet.

SALLY. I don't think of things like that. Isn't it funny, to think that all those things, like electricity, were there all the time . . . just waiting to be discovered?

BILL. I bet they got awfully impatient. Thought Benjamin Franklin and Marconi were just *never* coming along.

SALLY *(looking worried).* Oh . . .

BILL. Stop it.

SALLY. What?

BILL. Getting sorry for electricity.

SALLY *(laughing).* Oh . . . I was, too. *(She rises.)* Do you want a drink?

BILL. I could do with a nightcap. Are you going to have one?

SALLY. I think I'll have a glass of milk . . . if you don't mind.

BILL. Why should I mind?

SALLY. Men do . . . sometimes.

BILL. I wish you'd stop thinking that *I'm* "men." As a matter of fact, I'll have a glass of milk, too.

SALLY *(as they go through to the kitchen).* Good. Would you like some cookies? My mother made them. She sent them to me.

BILL *(taking the cookie jar).* Where does your mother live?

SALLY *(getting the milk from the icebox).* At home. Joplin, Missouri.

BILL. I've never been to Joplin.

SALLY *(pouring two glasses).* Why should you?

BILL. Have you a large family?

SALLY. Um. Rather.

BILL. Are you fond of them?

SALLY. Yes, very. Only I can't stand them for more than two weeks at a time, any more. That's sad, don't you think?

BILL. I think it's natural.

SALLY. I hate myself for it. But it's no good, trying. That's another reason why I'm so happy about this job coming now. I was afraid I'd have to go back home for the summer.

(They return to the living room, settling on the couch, with the milk and cookies.)

SALLY *(as they go).* I guess a family's really only good when you're sick . . . once you're grown up. And I'm never sick. So . . . *(Sitting and taking up her milk.)* I wonder if that *was* Olive on the telephone?

BILL. She's probably been calling ever since we left the theatre.

SALLY. It was too bad we had to run into her. We should have seen her in the intermission. Or afterwards. She'll think we were avoiding her.

BILL. Sure. That's why she's calling.

SALLY. But we weren't. We couldn't help it.

BILL (eating, calmly). I know.

SALLY. Doesn't that worry you?

BILL (as before). Not a bit. I didn't think the guy looked so hot, did you? Of course, I may be prejudiced, but I don't think I'd have turned down me for him.

SALLY. I was a little disappointed.

BILL (after a pause, watching her). I liked your friend, Kenneth Bartlett.

SALLY (eagerly). He is nice, isn't he?

BILL. I thought he was grand. He likes you, too.

SALLY. How do you know?

BILL. He said so. Told me what a grand kid you were, and a good little actress . . . and generally tops.

SALLY (wondering a little). Did he? When?

BILL. In the men's room at the Plaza. That's where men always tell each other things like that.

SALLY. You didn't mind our going on with his party, did you?

BILL. No, it was a good party. I've had a grand evening. And a grand day. Except that I've not seen much of you.

SALLY (laughing). You've seen me steadily for the last thirty hours!

BILL. I haven't. I slept ten of them, damn it. Spent three alone this afternoon getting a hotel room . . . sat beside you in a crowded theatre all evening, and shared you with a party of ten ever since. Will you spend tomorrow with me, to make up?

SALLY. I'd love to.

BILL. Good. (There is a small pause. He rises, walking away and looking into his milk.) Did you notice the girl at the Persian Room that I went over to talk to?

SALLY. Yes.

BILL. Do you know who that was?

SALLY. No. Not . . . ?

BILL (nodding). That was the girl from Paris.

SALLY. It's been that kind of an evening! How . . . how long since you'd seen her?

BILL. Seven years.

SALLY. Not since Paris?

BILL. We said good-bye at the Gare du Nord, on May the second, 1936.

SALLY. Were you engaged, or anything?

BILL. We were engaged, and everything. We were going to be married that summer. But that was the summer that things busted up for me. She couldn't see herself living in Pittsburgh, with no money.

SALLY. She married someone else, you said. Was that her husband with her tonight?

BILL. Yes. This is my evening for running into my successors, isn't it?

SALLY. What was he like?

BILL. Well, there again I guess I'm prejudiced.

SALLY. Was it awful . . . seeing her again?

BILL. No. Not after the first moment. And that was funny, because . . . last night at the restaurant it did get me down, remembering it all. And then the minute we'd said hello, the corner of my mouth suddenly stopped twitching, and I found myself looking at her and wondering what the hell it had all been about. I don't know when I stopped loving her—I just stopped thinking of her, I guess, and didn't realize I had . . . until tonight. Last night must have been just a . . . sort of reflex action.

SALLY. Haven't you been in love since?

BILL (briefly). No. Nor wanted to. That was quite enough.

SALLY. You don't believe in love?

BILL. I don't believe in being unhappily in love, and I'm not taking chances.

SALLY. I know what you mean. Does it feel . . . good, to be over it?

BILL. Good, but a little shocking, if you've been cherishing the illusion that you weren't.

SALLY. Yes. *(Then looking away from him, after a pause.)* I was in love with Kenneth Bartlett. At least, I thought I was.

BILL *(quietly)*. I know.

SALLY. How do you know?

BILL *(quickly)*. Oh, he didn't tell me. I guessed. *(Gently.)* Did *you* find you were over it tonight?

SALLY *(nodding)*. I was dreading seeing him at the theatre. And then he came up to us, and it was all right. I just thought how nice he was.

BILL. That's wonderful. I wish *I'd* been able to think that . . . about *her.*

SALLY. I'm sorry you couldn't. It's a good feeling. But you're right. It *is* a little shocking.

BILL. I think it's only one's vanity that's shocked. One likes to think one's the kind that *doesn't* get over things.

SALLY. But you do think one *ought* to . . . get over them, I mean?

BILL. Good God, yes. *(He sits beside her on the couch.)*

SALLY *(after a pause)*. It's funny our being in the same boat.

BILL. It's a good boat. *(Taking her hand.)* Sally . . .

SALLY. What?

BILL. You don't think . . . *my* coming along had anything to do with helping to set you free, do you?

SALLY. I . . . don't know.

BILL. I'd like to think it did.

SALLY. I think it did.

BILL. I'm glad.

SALLY. So am I . . . Did . . . *(She stops.)* No, I won't ask that.

BILL. Why not?

SALLY. No, I won't.

BILL. Were you going to ask whether *your* coming along helped to set *me* free?

SALLY. You don't have to answer that. And I *didn't* ask it.

BILL. If I say I think I was free already . . . let me say, too, that I think it was your coming along that helped me *know* I was, and that I'm very grateful.

SALLY. I'm glad.

BILL. So am I. *(He draws her to him and kisses her.)* You're very sweet.

SALLY. You're very nice.

BILL. I couldn't have imagined . . . possibly . . . having so nice a time as this.

SALLY. Me, too. I've had such miserable week-ends here alone.

(Silence for a moment. He continues to fondle her, his lips against her hair and cheek, moving toward her lips again. Again they kiss. Then, suddenly, she thrusts him aside, and rises abruptly and agitatedly.)

BILL. What's the matter?

SALLY. We mustn't go on like this.

BILL. Why not?

SALLY. Because I've given it up!

BILL. What?

SALLY. That sort of thing.

BILL. For Lent?

SALLY. No . . . permanently.

BILL *(protesting, laughing)*. Oh, Sally . . . darling . . .

SALLY. I have. I'm sorry, but I have.

BILL. Why have you?

SALLY. I *can't* go on doing it with every man I meet.

BILL *(amused)*. Do you?

SALLY. I *did.* No, I didn't, *really,* but . . . I've got to draw the line somewhere.

BILL. So you draw it at me?

SALLY. There's nothing personal about it. I do *like* you, but . . . we mustn't go on like that.

BILL. I'm sorry. Do you want me to go?

SALLY. No, but, well, maybe you'd rather.

BILL. Because you won't let me make love to you?

SALLY. Yes.

BILL. Is this another of your theories about "men"?

SALLY. It's a true one. If you start something like that . . . well you've no right to start it, if you don't mean to go through with it. And I *don't* mean to . . . and I *shouldn't* have started it. And you've every right to be mad at me.

BILL. I'm not mad at you.

SALLY. Aren't you?

BILL. No, I think you're absurd, but sweet.

SALLY. I'm terribly sorry.

BILL. It's all right . . . so long as you like me.

SALLY. I do.

BILL. And you'll see me tomorrow?

SALLY. If you still want to.

BILL. Sure, I want to. I want to see you *all* tomorrow.

SALLY. I thought you were going to sleep all day.

BILL. That was in another life. What shall we do?

SALLY. Do you want to come to breakfast?

BILL. Yes, please. What time?

SALLY. What time would you like it?

BILL. Any time. Nine o'clock?

SALLY. Certainly.

BILL. And then?

SALLY. Well, if it's fine, and it really looked tonight as if it might be . . . we can . . . walk in the Park . . . go to the Zoo . . . take a bus some place. Up to the Cloisters, maybe.

BILL. That sounds swell. Well, if we're breakfasting at nine . . . (*He makes a move.*)

SALLY. We don't have to. Why don't you call me when you wake up?

BILL. I might not wake up. And I don't want to waste any of tomorrow with you. I'll leave a call for eight o'clock.

SALLY. Oh, but that's awful for you. Eight o'clock on Sunday morning when you're on leave.

BILL. I don't mind. Would *you* like to call me when *you* wake up?

SALLY. No, I don't mind waking at eight.

BILL. You won't have to. You can sleep till half-past.

SALLY. I don't see that *either* of us has to. Why don't you stay here again?

BILL. Do you mean that?

SALLY. If you weren't too uncomfortable.

BILL. What sort of places do you think I've *been* sleeping in this last year?

SALLY. Well, then, please do. Then you can sleep as late as you want in the morning, and we'll just do whatever we feel like. I like days like that.

BILL. So do I.

SALLY (*worried again*). Of course, it does waste your hotel room.

BILL. And disappoints the Hotel Taft. But I think it can take that.

SALLY. Well, then, will you?

BILL (*after a tiny pause*). Sure. Thanks.

SALLY. Do you want to turn in now?

BILL. Well, it's almost three. I should think I might. (*Goes to divan, and strips cover.*) This is where I came in!

SALLY. You haven't got your bag this time. You'll want a toothbrush. I'll get it for you.

BILL. Why don't you go ahead, and get yourself to bed first? You were up hours earlier than I was.

SALLY. I'm all right.

BILL. No, do. You don't have to play hostess to me tonight. (*He gives her her coat.*) I'll tidy up, and empty the ashtrays . . . Go on.

SALLY. All right, then. I won't be long. (*She goes into the bedroom, taking her coat, strips her bed cover, and takes off her shoes.* BILL *performs the night ritual with the ashtrays, drinks the last of his milk and takes the glasses, cookie jar and ash trays into the kitchen. Meanwhile* SALLY *tries to get out of her dress, but the zipper catches. She tugs at it for quite a while, despairingly. Then she calls.)* Bill! Bill! *(But* BILL *is in the kitchen and does not hear. She comes into the living room and calls again.)* Bill! Where are you, Bill!

*(*BILL *emerges from the kitchen.)*

BILL. Were you calling?

SALLY. Yes, my zipper's stuck.

BILL. Oh. Let me see. *(He examines it.)*

SALLY. I've pulled and pulled. *(He fidgets with it.)* It's never done this, before.

BILL. Yes, it's good and stuck. It's a good thing I'm here, or you'd have had to sleep in it. You still may, of course. Have you a pair of pliers?

SALLY. There are some tools in the kitchen in a box under the sink. *(*BILL *goes for them.)* I don't really know what's there. I'm the kind who's no use with tools. Even keys won't work for me, and then someone else comes along, and it turns as easily as anything. *(She fidgets again with her zipper.)* You know, this is one of my nightmares, having this happen to me in the theatre . . . during a quick change.

BILL *(in kitchen).* Here we are.

SALLY *(calling).* Find it?

BILL *(returning).* Found it. Now then, hold still, take a deep breath, and I'll try not to hurt. *(He applies the pliers, missing the first time.)* Damn. That's better . . . now it's coming . . . there! *(The zipper unzips, and her dress falls to the floor, leaving her in her slip.)* Oh, I'm sorry. I'm afraid that was rather overdoing it.

SALLY *(stooping and picking up her dress).* Thank you so much.

BILL *(embarrassed).* Girls who wear zippers shouldn't live alone. Modern proverb.

SALLY. Well . . . thank you. *(She is about to go. He catches her.)*

BILL. Sally . . . *(He kisses her, and she responds. As the kiss threatens to grow more passionate, she pulls herself away.)*

SALLY *(releasing herself, as he tries to hold her).* Don't, Bill . . . please don't. *(He lets her go. She goes back to the bedroom, where she stands a moment, fighting tears. Then she hangs her dress in the closet,* with her coat, and goes through to the bathroom.)*

(Bill stands looking after her. Then he shrugs, turns down the day-bed, removes his coat, sits and unlaces one shoe and takes it off. He is about to start the second shoe, when he stops, looking first at his bed and then at the bedroom door.)

BILL *(to himself).* No, this is all too god-damned silly! *(He puts his shoe on again, and also his coat. Then he goes to the desk, takes paper and pencil and starts to write a note.)*

*(*SALLY *comes back into the bedroom, wearing pajamas, and looking very small and young. Her mood is still melancholy, and she is near tears. She switches out the lights, except for the bed lamp, and gets into bed.)*

(During the above BILL *has finished his note. He lays it on the day-bed, switches off the lamps and takes his cap, going to the door, as* SALLY *calls:)*

SALLY *(in a muffled voice).* Bathroom's all clear. *(He hears her, and stands with his hand on the knob of the front door.)* Bill! I said the bathroom's all clear. *(He goes over, cap in hand, and opens the bedroom door.)*

BILL. Sally, I'm not staying. *(He comes into the room.)*

SALLY. Why not?

BILL. Because it's silly.

SALLY. Why?

BILL. Well, because . . . as they'd say in one of those plays we both hate . . . because I'm a man, and you're a woman.

SALLY *(after a tiny pause—gravely, but with quote marks).* And I . . . rouse the beast in you?

BILL. Exactly . . . So . . . I'll see you tomorrow. *(He starts to go.)*

SALLY. Bill . . . there's a beast in me, too! *(He stands looking at her, and then comes slowly to the bed).* I'm sorry, Bill, for being such a fool.

BILL *(tenderly).* Sally . . . *(He sits on the bed and takes her in his arms. She melts into them. In the kiss).* Oh, Sally, sweet . . .

SALLY. Oh, Bill . . . (*The telephone rings. She starts, disengages herself, stretching out her hand, automatically, to answer it.*)

BILL (*slapping her hand*). Uh huh. No, no!

SALLY (*looking stricken*). Oh . . . (*He draws her into his arms again. She remains pressed against him, her cheek against his, looking at the telephone with scared eyes. Whispering.*) You shouldn't be here.

BILL. Ssh.

SALLY. She'll come around in the morning.

BILL. Let the morning look after itself. (*He kisses her again and, without breaking the embrace, switches out the bed light. The telephone goes on ringing. In the dark.*) I love you, Sally.

SALLY. No. No, don't say that. You mustn't. We must keep this gay!

(*The telephone goes on ringing.*)

CURTAIN

ACT THREE

SCENE I

SCENE: *The same. Noon. Sunday.*
When the curtain rises, a card-table has been set up and laid for breakfast for two. SALLY's bed has been made; the day-bed is still turned down and unslept in, as it was left. In the bedroom, BILL's coat and cap are on the back of a chair.

In the kitchen, breakfast is cooking—coffee on the stove, and water boiling in a sauce-pan. SALLY comes through into the living room with two glasses of orange juice, which she puts on the table, attending to the toaster and starting to pour the coffee which she also fetches from the kitchen. BILL comes into the bedroom from the bathroom, fully dressed, except for his coat.

BILL (*calling*). How's everything coming?

SALLY (*calling back*). Everything's ready!

(BILL *puts on his coat, tossing his cap onto the bed, and goes into the living room.*)

BILL. Oh, boy, sump'n smells good!

SALLY. It's the coffee. I wish coffee tasted as good as it smells.

BILL. I think if I were a woman, I'd *wear* coffee as a perfume. (*He kisses her and then, feeling thoroughly at home, removes his coat and throws it across the back of the couch.*)

SALLY (*rising*). I'll just see if the water's boiling for the eggs.

BILL. No, don't. Sit down. Be still. There's lots of time for the eggs.

SALLY. But the water will boil over.

BILL. No, it won't. Unless you've over-filled the saucepan. It'll just boil away. And I suppose that'll worry you. Mustn't leave the water alone. It'll get hurt.

SALLY (*smiling*). I'd better turn it off. (*Goes into kitchen.*) Don't you *want* eggs? I can just as easily put them on.

BILL. And then keep hopping up and down, watching the time? No, let's have our coffee in peace.

SALLY. All right. (*She turns off the stove and comes back to living room, where she takes the toast from the toaster, bringing it to the table.*)

BILL (*rising*). One thing I'll do before we really settle.

SALLY. What's that?

BILL. Cover up the day-bed. Don't you think it looks kind of deserted and re-proachful . . . all unslept in?

SALLY (*helping him with the cover*). Yes, I do. I always think a bed that hasn't been slept in looks sort of forlorn in the morning. If ever I come in very late at night, and my bed's been turned down, I always want to say to it, "It's all right. Here I am."

BILL (*straightening the cover*). Do you have a Sunday paper?

SALLY (*returning to the table*). No, we'll have to go out for one. We should have thought of it last night.

BILL. I'll go and get it, later. I must have my funnies.

SALLY. Me, too. It wouldn't be Sunday to me, without Dick Tracy.

BILL. Let's get *all* the Sunday papers, and really mess up the apartment. (*Comes back to the table and sits.*) This is so pleasant, Sally *dear*. Our second breakfast together. Quite an old married couple. You're nice to have breakfast with.

SALLY. So are you. Have you . . . have you had breakfast with a lot of girls?

BILL (*putting down his cup*). Sally, that is not a question to ask *now*. If ever.

SALLY. I wasn't being curious . . . about your life, I mean. I was just wondering whether there was a lot of difference between girls at breakfast.

BILL. Yes. Quite a lot.

SALLY. Do some of them . . . bother you . . . *talking* about things?

BILL. Sally, stop it.

SALLY. I'm asking quite impersonally.

BILL. You can't. It's an extremely personal question.

SALLY. I'm sorry. There ought to be a book of rules for conversation on occasions like this.

BILL. There oughtn't to be a book at all. Just be natural, and yourself.

SALLY. I *was* being myself.

BILL. Well, then, *don't* be yourself. Think of the other fellow for a change.

SALLY. I didn't mean . . .

BILL. Sally, I said "stop."

SALLY. I'm sorry. Shall I start some more toast?

BILL. Yes, please, unless it means fetching it from the kitchen.

SALLY. No, I've got it right here.

BILL. Then, yes, please.

(*She rises. The front-door buzzer goes. They both start.*)

SALLY (*in a stricken whisper*). Olive!

BILL (*also whispering*). Don't answer it.

SALLY (*whispering*). Oh, but I must!

BILL (*whispering*). Let her think you've gone out. She'll go away.

SALLY (*still whispering*). She'll ask the elevator man, and he'll tell her I haven't. She'll come back.

BILL. Let her.

SALLY. I can't. I'll get rid of her. You go into the bathroom. (*She starts him toward the bathroom.*)

BILL. And suppose *she* wants to go to the bathroom?

SALLY. Then go into the kitchen. Take all that with you. (*Indicating table.*)

BILL. Really!

(*The buzzer sounds again.*)

SALLY (*whispering feverishly*). Please!

(BILL *unwillingly takes the table and carries it through to the kitchen.* SALLY *follows with the toaster. Then she looks around, straightening the chairs. The buzzer goes again.*)

SALLY (*calling*). I'm just coming! (*She starts for the door, and then remembers* BILL's *coat, lying over the back of the couch. She gets that, too, and thrusts it at him in the kitchen. Then, in a wild scramble, she opens the door.* OLIVE *is outside.*)

SALLY (*with creditable surprise*). Olive!

OLIVE. I've been ringing and ringing.

SALLY. I'm sorry. I was in the bathroom. I *thought* I heard the buzzer.

(*Throughout the ensuing scene,* BILL *is in the kitchen, listening and pantomiming reactions to what goes on, while he puts on his coat and drinks the remainder of his coffee.*)

OLIVE. Well, how are you this morning?

SALLY (*wandering around, looking for traces of* BILL *to cover*). I'm fine.

OLIVE. You were out very late last night.

SALLY. I know. (*Then, quickly.*) How do *you* know?

OLIVE. I called you until three o'clock. What time did you get in?

SALLY. Oh, about . . . a quarter past, I think.

OLIVE. Where did you go?

SALLY (*still wandering*). To the Persian Room with Ken.

OLIVE. Ken? Bartlett? Are you and he on again?

SALLY. Oh, no. We met at the theatre. What did you call up for?

OLIVE. I wanted to talk to you. Why did you and Bill cut me last night?

SALLY (*indignant and stopping her walk*). We didn't. We waved and waved. You saw us. You waved back.

OLIVE. I mean in the intermission. I looked for you everywhere.

SALLY. We went next door for a drink with Ken. (*She starts to prowl again, tidying things.*)

OLIVE. How did you get tickets? Ned had to pay $17.60 each for the twenty-seventh row or something. You were way down front.

SALLY (*straightening the cover on the day-bed*). Ken gave us the house seats.

OLIVE. What *are* you fidgeting around like that for? Come and sit down, for goodness' sake.

SALLY. I'm sorry. (*She picks up the evening paper lying on the desk, and suddenly remembers that this is where BILL's cap has formerly been. She wonders where it is and then, with a glance at the bedroom, remembers with a gasp.*)

OLIVE (*noticing the gasp*). What's the matter?

SALLY. Nothing. Why?

OLIVE. The way you jumped.

SALLY (*innocently*). I just remembered something.

OLIVE. What?

SALLY. Something I've got to do. Listen, is that the telephone?

OLIVE. I don't hear anything.

SALLY. I think it is. I'll just go see. (*She goes into the bedroom, picks the cap up quickly, goes to the night table, stuffs it into the drawer, looks around again and then picks up the telephone.*) Hello? Hello? No, I guess it wasn't. (*She returns to the living room.*)

OLIVE. Well, then, now will you sit down and relax?

SALLY. Yes, now I'll sit down and relax. (*She does so.*)

OLIVE. You and Bill have certainly been seeing a lot of each other!

SALLY. Well, I don't think he knows many people in New York.

OLIVE (*sarcastically*). So you thought you'd be kind to him.

SALLY (*sharply*). It wasn't a question of being kind to him. He's very nice. Very nice indeed. (*She turns her head slightly toward kitchen, where BILL pantomimes his reaction to this.*)

OLIVE. I know he is. I introduced him to you. Where did he finally end up staying?

SALLY. He got a room at the Hotel Taft.

OLIVE. Is he there now, do you know?

SALLY. How should I know?

OLIVE. Would you mind if I called him up?

SALLY. No, of course not.

OLIVE (*starting across to bedroom. Stops in doorway*). Come and talk to me.

(SALLY, *who has made a small start toward kitchen, follows her.* BILL *applies his eye to the door crack and sees them go. He waits a moment, and then takes the opportunity to slip out. He makes for the front door, looks around for his cap, remembers where it is, gives a panic-stricken look at the bedroom, and then shrugs his shoulders and slips out. In the meantime, in the bedroom, the following scene takes place.*)

OLIVE. Where's the book? (*She puts her hand to the night-table drawer.*)

SALLY (*hastily*). It's underneath . . . on the floor.

OLIVE. Oh, yes. You are nervous this morning.

SALLY (*sitting on bed*). I'm sorry.

OLIVE (*hunting for the number*). What did you think of the show last night?

SALLY. I thought it was lovely.

OLIVE. I thought it stank.

SALLY. Oh . . . why?

OLIVE. What do you mean—why?

SALLY. I mean—why?

OLIVE (crossly). I don't know why. I thought it did. If I tell you a piece of fish stinks, you don't ask me why, do you?

(Dials number.)

SALLY. It's a big hit.

OLIVE. Anything's a hit in war time.

SALLY. Not the plays I'm in. Oh . . .

OLIVE (into phone). I want to speak to Sergeant Page, please. Oh, all right. (To SALLY.) What were you going to say?

SALLY. I've got a job.

OLIVE. You haven't! What? (Into phone.) I want to speak to Sergeant Page, please. Sergeant William Page. Yes, he's registered there. (To SALLY.) What's the job?

SALLY. They've let Myra Foley out of The Dark Dreamer. They sent for me yesterday.

OLIVE. Darling, how exciting! I hear it's a wonderful part. (Flatly.) I had an offer yesterday, too.

SALLY. Oh, what was it?

OLIVE (grimly). They want me to go out with Tobacco Road!

SALLY. Are you going?

OLIVE. Darling . . . all those turnips? (Into phone.) Oh . . . well, will you say Miss Lashbrooke called? Lashbrooke. L-A-S—No, S as in . . . Oh, hell, say Olive. Yes, Olive. (Hangs up). Not there.

SALLY. He's probably gone out.

OLIVE. Aren't you smart?

SALLY. Olive, don't be that way. What's the matter?

OLIVE (turning on her). The matter is that I don't like the way you've acted over Bill. He was my beau, and . . .

SALLY. And you left him on my hands.

OLIVE. Not for you to take over.

SALLY. I haven't "taken him over."

OLIVE. I thought I was safe with you.

SALLY. Well, I like that. Why?

OLIVE. I thought you were all broken up about Kenneth Bartlett. I should have known that was just the dangerous time.

(She goes into the living room.)

SALLY (following her). What was I to do? Leave him alone all week-end?

OLIVE. That wasn't your business.

SALLY. You turned him down for your Commander friend. What's happened to him, by the way?

OLIVE. He had to go call on his grandmother in Gramercy Park. We're meeting for lunch at the Brevoort.

SALLY. You've been having fun this week-end. Why shouldn't I?

OLIVE. Did you say fun?

SALLY. Hasn't it been?

OLIVE. You went to the Persian Room last night. What do you thing we did?

SALLY. What?

OLIVE. Played gin rummy at the 1-2-3 until four o'clock, when he practically passed out from Cubre Libres. He's only just discovered gin rummy. That's the kind of a guy he is. I think the real reason I hated the show so much last night was that he worshipped it. And so noisily.

SALLY. Yes, I heard his laugh.

OLIVE. It stopped the show in one place. The whole audience turned around. Of course, I know he's good-looking. . . .

SALLY (involuntarily). Oh . . . (She stops).

OLIVE. What were you going to say?

SALLY. I was sort of . . . disappointed in his looks.

OLIVE. Oh, no, he's terribly good-looking. Although the hairline did seem to me to have receded a little since last year. And to think I passed up Bill for that! What time's Bill going back tonight—do you know?

SALLY. No, I don't.

OLIVE. Maybe we could dine together. If not, let's you and me. Dutch.

SALLY. I . . . I don't think I can.

OLIVE. Why? What are you doing?

SALLY. I've got to work on the part.

OLIVE. Just an early dinner. I'd like to get to bed early, anyway.

SALLY *(rising)*. We'll see, but I don't think so. Thank you very much.

OLIVE. Now *you're* mad at *me!*

SALLY. Well, I don't think you've any right . . .

OLIVE *(rising)*. I have a perfect right. Bill was *my* gink.

SALLY *(courageously for a second)*. Well, he isn't any more!

OLIVE. You know, I'm a fool. That's what's the matter with me. Trusting everyone! Gullible Gertie! You . . . who were so worried about yourself the other afternoon . . . who were going to "give it all up" . . .

SALLY. Well, I meant that . . .

OLIVE *(rising)*. Only Bill came along, and you couldn't keep your hands off him.

SALLY *(angry, and also agonized, imagining that* BILL *can hear)*. Olive . . . I think you'd better go!

OLIVE. Oh, I'll go fast enough, only . . . *(The telephone rings. They both start.)* There's your telephone.

*(*SALLY *goes into the bedroom and answers it.)*

SALLY. Hello . . . yes . . . Who's that? *(Her mouth opens in astonishment. She looks involuntarily toward the kitchen.)* Where are you? How did you . . . ? *(She smiles.)* Yes . . . yes, of course you can come around. Olive's here. She's just been calling you at the Taft.

OLIVE *(coming into the room)*. Let me talk to him.

SALLY. She wants to talk to you. . . . Yes, as soon as you like. Yes, I know. I've got it. *No!* All right. Here. Here's Olive. *(She hands the phone to* OLIVE.*)*

OLIVE *(cooing a little)*. Bill? How are you? I've been calling and calling you. What are you doing? How soon? *(Looks at her watch.)* Well, don't make it any more. I've got to run. I'll see you. *(She hangs up.)* Where was he?

SALLY. At a drug store.

OLIVE. Where—did he say?

SALLY. He said quite near.

OLIVE. I'll just wait and say hello to him.

SALLY. What time is your lunch?

OLIVE. One.

SALLY. It must be almost that now.

OLIVE. He can wait. *(Honeyedly.)* What were we talking about?

SALLY *(primly)*. I think I'd asked you to go, and you said you would.

OLIVE. Oh, darling, you didn't mean that. Nor did I. *(She kisses her.)*

SALLY *(with distaste)*. Let's go in the other room. Oh . . . *(She pauses.)*

OLIVE. What is it?

SALLY. Just . . . the thing I remembered before. Something I have to give the elevator man. You go on. I'll be right after you. *(She moves toward the dressing room, as though she were going in, to deceive* OLIVE. OLIVE *goes on into the living room, where she sees the manuscript on a table, and picks it up to read.* SALLY *takes* BILL's *cap from the drawer of the night table and looks around for something to wrap it in. All there is is a copy of* Vogue. *She thrusts it between the pages, and goes out to the front door.)*

OLIVE. What have you got there?

SALLY. Just a copy of *Vogue.*

OLIVE. What does the elevator man want a copy of *Vogue* for?

SALLY *(opening the door)*. For his wife.

OLIVE. Really! You don't mind my looking at your script?

SALLY *(as she goes)*. No, of course not. *(She goes out, leaving the door open.* OLIVE *sits puzzledly with the script, not looking at it.* SALLY *returns from the elevator, smiling contentedly.)*

OLIVE *(suspiciously)*. You're very pleased with yourself about something.

SALLY *(airily)*. No, no. I'm just happy.

OLIVE. What about?

SALLY (*vaguely*). Oh . . . everything.

OLIVE (*after a moment's scrutiny of her*). Sally . . . you wouldn't be going and getting silly and sentimental over Bill, would you? Because, if you do, you'll lose him even quicker than you lost Kenneth Bartlett.

SALLY. I've no intention of getting sentimental.

OLIVE (*sweetly*). No, darling, no intention —but you're the kind who can't sew a button on for a man without thinking it's for life. And Bill's told me, over and over again, that he's no place for sentiment in his scheme of things.

SALLY (*after a silence, rising*). Well, I've told you before, neither have I . . . any more. So that's all right. (*Doorbell rings.*) There he is.

OLIVE. He's got here quick.

(SALLY *opens door. Enter* BILL. *He wears his cap, carries the Sunday newspaper, and some flowers in paper.*)

BILL (*gesturing with his cap*). Hello.

SALLY (*smiling broadly*). Hello.

OLIVE. Hello, Bill.

BILL (*pleasantly, but perfunctorily*). Hello. (*To* SALLY.) I was afraid I might be calling too early for you, but I had to go out to get my Sunday paper, so I brought you these. (*He hands her the flowers.*)

SALLY. Oh . . . how lovely! (*She looks at them.*) "Daffodils . . . that come before the swallow dares . . ."

BILL (*finishing the quotation*). "And take the winds of March with beauty."

OLIVE. What a cute saying!

BILL. He was a cute sayer.

OLIVE. Who?

BILL. Shakespeare.

SALLY. I love spring flowers. Thank you so much. I'll just put them in water. (*She takes them to the kitchen.*)

BILL. Well, what sort of a time have *you* been having?

OLIVE. Not a lot of fun. What time do you have to go back tonight?

BILL. Around ten.

OLIVE. Well, Ned's train goes at four. I wonder . . . could we dine together?

BILL. I'm afraid I have a dinner date.

OLIVE. Oh, that's too bad. Well, maybe a cocktail?

BILL. I'm afraid that's gone, too.

OLIVE (*defeated*). Oh. Oh, well, I'm sorry. (*Telephone rings.*) There's the telephone. Sally! Sally! Telephone!

SALLY (*coming from kitchen*). I know. I heard it. (*She goes through to the bedroom, leaving the door open.*)

OLIVE. I have to go. I'll just wait until Sally's through. (*She starts to put on her gloves.*)

SALLY (*into telephone*). Hello? Yes . . . Well, I . . . You have? Oh, how wonderful! Where? Yes . . . yes, of course. Right away. (*She hangs up, stands a moment, bothered, and then returns to the living room.*)

SALLY. I've got to go out.

BILL (*disappointed*). Oh . . . where?

SALLY. That was the producer calling. They've made another change in the cast. The leading man's out, and they've got Henry Atherton! (OLIVE *pulls a face.*) He was the star of Olive's show that just closed.

BILL. Yes, I know. He was the one with the . . . (*He indicates his hair.*) Yes, I remember.

SALLY. They want me to go and work with him this afternoon.

BILL. Could you lunch with me first?

SALLY. I'm afraid I can't. I've got to go right away. *They've* all had big breakfasts.

BILL. Well, can I take you there?

SALLY (*nodding*). I'll just go and change. (*She runs back to the bedroom, closing the door behind her, and disappears into the dressing-room.*)

OLIVE (*sugaredly*). Sally's sweet, isn't she?

BILL. She certainly is.

OLIVE. But, you know, playing with Henry Atherton, I'm afraid she's headed for trouble. She's just about the age he likes them.

BILL. Oh, I should think Sally could take care of herself.

OLIVE. Oh, yes, she can . . . if she wants to. But a star's a star, and she's always had a crush on him. (*Collecting herself to go.*) Can you still not manage cocktails, by the way?

BILL. I'm afraid I can't.

OLIVE. Well, you'll let me know next time you're coming, won't you? And . . . (*Seductively.*) I won't let *anything* interfere.

BILL. Olive, I'm afraid I don't play around with married women.

OLIVE (*after a defeated second*). Oh, but that's all over. We talked it out thoroughly. I'm not seeing him again.

BILL. You mean—you're divorcing?

OLIVE. Yes.

BILL. Do you think that looks well—to divorce a service man?

OLIVE. Just what are you trying to say?

BILL. Just . . . very tactfully, and with no hard feelings . . . that I think we'd better . . . leave things as they are.

OLIVE (*rallying after a moment*). I guess I bought that all right! Well, I've got to lunch with my ex. Good-bye, Bill.

BILL. Good-bye, Olive.

(*They shake hands.*)

OLIVE. Say good-bye to Sally for me. (*She turns at the door.*) By the way, did Sally *tell* you anything about Ned?

BILL. No. But I saw him with you last night. And, Olive, you'd never have married that—not in a million years.

OLIVE (*looking at him*). I never knew men could be such bitches! (*She goes.*)

(BILL *laughs, takes a cigarette.* SALLY *returns in a hurry, having changed her dress and carrying her hat, bag, gloves and shoes.*)

SALLY. Has she gone?

BILL. She's gone. I'm afraid that's the end of a beautiful friendship.

SALLY (*putting on her shoes*). I'm afraid . . . for *me*, too.

BILL. Well, it can't be helped. Where are you rehearsing?

SALLY. At Henry Atherton's apartment. It's on 90th Street.

BILL. Is that usual?

SALLY. What?

BILL. Rehearsing in actors' apartments?

SALLY. Oh . . . yes . . . quite. If they're stars.

BILL. Is anyone else going to be there?

SALLY. I guess so. Why—what's the matter?

BILL (*briefly*). Nothing. (*Changing his mood.*) How long will it go on?

SALLY. All afternoon, I'm afraid.

BILL (*lightly*). What am *I* going to do?

SALLY. Would you like to come back here? I'll give you the key, and you can . . . use the apartment as if it were your own.

BILL. I thought that's what I *had* been doing. You'll have dinner with me?

SALLY. Yes.

BILL. Promise?

SALLY. I promise. Now I must go.

BILL (*stopping her and holding her*). Sally, I don't see anything of you . . . at all! I want to talk to you . . . about so many things.

SALLY (*shying*). No—why? We don't need to talk. There's nothing to talk about. We've had a lovely time, and . . . well, we don't want to get . . . sentimental about it. Do we?

BILL (*quietly—disappointed*). I guess not.

SALLY. Well, then. Come along. I'm late. (*She goes to the door. He stands still. She looks back at him.*) Aren't you coming?

BILL (*after a second*). Sure.

SALLY. I'll just ring for the elevator.

(*She goes out. He looks after her a moment, putting out his cigarette, his face puzzled and unhappy. Then he picks up his cap, shrugs, and follows her out.*)

CURTAIN

SCENE II

SCENE: *The same. About six-thirty.*

The card-table is set up again, laid now for supper. The whole room has been made to look as attractive as possible. The daffodils are in a vase, and there are a number of other vases of spring flowers, including some sprays of white lilac.

BILL *is kneeling on the day-bed, a book in his hand, dividing his attention between it and the window from which he is watching for* SALLY's *return. After a moment, he sees her coming, goes into the kitchen, opens the icebox and takes out a bottle of champagne, which he brings to the living room, setting it on a side-table, where two champagne glasses are waiting. Then the buzzer sounds, and he goes to the door and opens it.* SALLY *is outside.*

SALLY *(subduedly)*. Hi!

BILL. Hi!

SALLY *(seeing the table)*. Why, what's all this?

BILL. I thought we'd have dinner home tonight.

SALLY. It'll be rather a picnic one.

BILL. Well . . .

SALLY. Lunch sausage and marinated herring, I'm afraid.

BILL. That's all right.

SALLY. Where did these flowers come from? *(She turns, looking around.)* Oh, but all these . . . Bill, you shouldn't!

BILL. You said you liked spring flowers, and the streets were full of them.

SALLY. Oh, but they're beautiful. *(She goes from vase to vase.)* The whole room smells of them. I've never had so many. Bill, you darling . . . *(She goes to him impulsively and kisses him. Then she retreats, subduedly.)* Thank you *so* much.

BILL *(slightly constrained, too)*. How about a drink?

SALLY *(seeing the tray)*. Champagne? Where did you find that?

BILL *(opening the bottle)*. I found it.

SALLY. Not in *my* wine cellar!

BILL. Like some?

SALLY. Yes, please! Oh, Bill, this is very nice.

BILL. I'm glad you're pleased.

SALLY *(sitting on the couch)*. It's the loveliest spring evening out.

BILL. I know. I've been looking at it, watching for you to come back.

SALLY. You know, two days ago . . . the day you got here . . . it was still all grim and wintry . . . and suddenly since then it's come with a rush. Sometimes I feel that I can't bear the spring, it's so exciting!

BILL *(handing her a glass)*. I know. I walked in the Park after I left you, and it's bursting all over it. All the trees and shrubs in a kind of young green haze, and all the flowers on the corner stands looked as if they were growing there, and you wanted to buy great armfuls . . .

SALLY. You *did* buy great armfuls.

BILL. I bought all I could carry. *(Lifting his glass.)* Well . . . to the spring.

SALLY. The spring.

(They drink.)

BILL *(affecting casualness)*. How was the rehearsal?

SALLY. That was exciting, too.

BILL. And Henry Atherton?

SALLY. He was good. You're right, though. It *is* dyed. But he's going to be wonderful in it. I don't know . . . I daren't say it yet . . . but I really think that this may be what I've been waiting for all these years.

BILL *(with slight double meaning)*. This . . . play, you mean?

SALLY *(not getting it)*. Yes. Perhaps that's part of the spring, too.

BILL *(in a new voice)*. Sally . . .

SALLY. What?

BILL *(sitting beside her)*. This is . . . *our* spring, isn't it? We'll have it together?

SALLY (*a little evasive*). Of course . . . if you're going to be here.

BILL. I think I am. I think I can count on the spring and summer . . . if I'm lucky. I've been thinking of it all afternoon. Things that we can do together.

SALLY (*smiling nervously and taking a cigarette*). Give me a light.

BILL (*taking the cigarette from her*). Sally, don't do that.

SALLY. What?

BILL. Hold out on me.

SALLY. I don't know what you mean.

BILL. I wanted us to have dinner here tonight, because . . . well, partly because I wanted to talk to you . . .

SALLY. I wish you wouldn't.

BILL. Sally . . . if I told you that . . . given the least possible encouragement from you . . . I think I could be . . . very much in love with you . . . what would you say?

SALLY (*after a second*). I wouldn't give it to you.

BILL. Why not?

SALLY. Because I don't want you to be in love with me . . . or think you are.

BILL. Why don't you?

SALLY. Because . . . that isn't how we started this.

BILL. Sally, you don't go into a love affair *deliberately* . . .

SALLY. I know, but . . . I don't want it to *be* like that. This way it's . . . fun.

BILL. Will it be any less fun if I'm in love with you?

SALLY (*positively*). Oh . . . *yes!* Bill, we don't have to talk about it. It *has* been fun . . . it *is* fun . . . it can go on being fun, if you won't spoil it.

BILL. That is a remark I seem to have heard before . . . but not from anyone like you.

SALLY. What do you mean?

BILL. It's the kind of thing old-fashioned women used to say . . . the older, married women . . . when they wanted to keep you hanging around.

SALLY. But I do want to keep you . . . well, not *hanging* around . . . but *around* if you want to be.

BILL. I do.

SALLY. Well, then . . . (*She moves away.*)

BILL (*after a moment*). I can't be so crazy as to have got you *all* wrong, but . . . you baffle me, Sally.

SALLY. I don't see why.

BILL. I guess it's the times.

SALLY (*puzzled*). The *Times?*

BILL. I don't mean the newspaper. I mean . . . the times . . . the war, or something. Or perhaps it's the theatre.

SALLY. I still don't know what you're talking about.

BILL (*rising and going to her*). Sally, you're not the kind of girl who has affairs . . . promiscuously . . . Or are you?

SALLY. I don't know.

BILL. What do you mean?

SALLY. I mean, I don't know what constitutes "promiscuously." I have affairs. I mean, I've *had* affairs.

BILL (*quietly*). Many affairs?

SALLY. You told me that was a question that one shouldn't ask.

BILL. I was quite right. One shouldn't. But, Sally, if I said that rather than keep this . . . just an affair . . . I'd sooner . . . call the whole thing off—what would you say?

SALLY (*after a long pause*). I think I'd say . . . we'd better call it off.

BILL. Are you afraid of getting hurt?

SALLY. Maybe.

BILL. Sally, I wouldn't hurt you.

SALLY. That's something that I don't see how anyone can promise anyone . . . ever. And I wish you wouldn't talk about it.

BILL. There was a book of poems by your bed . . . (*Fetching it from the day-bed.*) Poems by Dorothy Parker. You had a whole lot of them marked. Why did you have them marked?

SALLY. I guess . . . because I liked them.

BILL. This one . . . *(He finds it and reads.)*

"I will not make you songs of hearts denied,
And you, being man, would have no tears of me,
And should I offer you fidelity
You'd be, I think, a little terrified."

(He closes the book.) That one's *double*-marked. You must have liked it a lot.

SALLY. I do.

BILL. Was that, by any chance, your experience with Kenneth Bartlett?

SALLY. Perhaps . . . a little.

BILL. And you're afraid of it happening again?

SALLY. It always happens . . . doesn't it?

BILL. I don't think so.

SALLY. Well, it always does to me.

BILL. Always?

SALLY. Yes, always.

BILL *(gently)*. How *often* has it happened to you?

SALLY. Twice. So far.

BILL *(smiling, relieved)*. Is that all?

SALLY. What do you mean?

BILL. Is that all the affairs you've had? Two?

SALLY *(turning to him—with naive pleasure)*. You don't think that a lot?

BILL. No. Though I think it's two too many . . . for *you*.

SALLY. How many have *you* had?

BILL. I've never counted. And if I had, I wouldn't tell you.

SALLY. I told *you*.

BILL. I know.

SALLY *(with tiny sarcasm)*. You think it's different for a man?

BILL. I think the permissible *number* is different for a man.

SALLY. You knew about me, didn't you? You didn't believe that story about the pajamas?

BILL. No.

SALLY. Well, then . . .

BILL. Yes . . . but, Sally, I want this to have *meant* something to you.

SALLY. It did. It was terribly sweet . . .

BILL. But that's all? You won't let it mean more? Not even if I tell you that . . . if you offered me fidelity, I'd be . . . I think . . . a little *gratified*? In fact, that if you *don't* offer it to me, I'd feel as if I'd had a door slammed right bang in my face.

SALLY *(moved, protesting)*. Oh, Bill!

BILL. As if the spring had suddenly turned around and said, "That's all there is. Now you can go back to winter."

SALLY. Not winter. We can keep it spring.

BILL. Nothing *stays* spring. And I wouldn't want it. There'd be something stultified and horrible about the spring, if it always stayed like that. It's *got* to become summer, and fall, and . . .

SALLY *(bitterly)*. Winter.

BILL. Yes, one day. But for both of us . . . at the same time. Sally, I *am* in love with you. There's still time to turn back . . . for me to turn back, I mean . . . without its hurting too much. I told you I didn't believe in being unhappily in love. I don't. And I'm not going to be. I'm not having an awfully happy time right now. None of us are. That's not a bid for pity. It's just telling you why I feel this way. I gave up looking forward to anything seven years ago, and I've got along all right that way. With . . . Olive . . . and taking what came. That's how I wanted it. And I can go on like that. But I can't begin again . . . hoping . . . and wanting . . . and planning . . . unless there is *some* chance of those plans working out. *You're* scared of getting hurt again. Well, so am I. *Bitterly* scared.

SALLY *(almost in tears)*. What do you want?

BILL *(beside her now)*. I want you to let yourself love me . . . if you *can*. Because I think you can. I think you've a great talent for love, Sally, and that you're trying to fritter it and dissipate it . . . because it's been trodden on before. And if you go on like that, you'll kill it. And . . . *(Slowly.)* I think that's one talent that *is* death to hide. *(SALLY bursts into tears.)* Yes, cry, if you want to. Please, please cry. Only . . . don't shut me out . . . and don't shut yourself out.

SALLY *(sobbing).* Oh, Bill . . .

BILL. I'm not asking such a great deal. I think I'd like to marry you, but we won't talk of *that,* yet. I want you to love me . . . *terribly,* but I'm not even asking *that* of you, yet.

SALLY *(between tears).* I do love you! I love you terribly! That's the hell of it! *(Scrambling to her knees on the couch beside him.)* I won't make scenes, Bill. I won't be troublesome. . . .

BILL *(taking her face in his hands).* Ssh. You've said all I wanted you to say now. *(He kisses her gently.)* Drink up your drink. It's getting warm.

SALLY *(gulping it and tears at the same time).* I shall be tight again. I haven't had any food.

BILL. What—not all day? Well, then, you must have dinner right away. Come and sit down.

SALLY. It'll take a little while to fix.

BILL. It's all fixed. They're sending it up from next door. From . . . "our" place. It's coming up at seven. The first course is in the icebox. Vichysoisse. I'll get it right now. *(He starts to the kitchen.)*

SALLY. Bill . . . *(She moves toward him.)*

BILL *(at kitchen door).* You pour yourself another drink and sit down. Pour me one, too. *(He goes into the kitchen and takes two cups of soup from the icebox. SALLY, moving a little as if in a dream, refills the glasses and bring them to the table, where she sits. BILL returns and places the soup.)* There. *(He bends and kisses her lightly on the top of her head. Then, standing waiter-like, with his napkin over his arm.)* Madame est servie. *(He sits. SALLY is still blinking away tears. She dips a spoon, and tastes.)*

SALLY. Oh, Bill, this is heaven.

BILL *(who hasn't touched his—looking at her).* Isn't it? *(He puts out his hand, and holds hers. They look at each other and smile, and then, still holding hands, dip their spoons and begin to eat.)*

CURTAIN

THE MALE ANIMAL

By JAMES THURBER and ELLIOTT NUGENT

THE MALE ANIMAL was first presented by Herman Shumlin at the Cort Theatre, New York City. The play was staged by Mr. Shumlin; setting by Aline Bernstein. The cast was as follows:

CLEOTA......................Amanda Randolph
ELLEN TURNER...........Ruth Matteson
TOMMY TURNER...........Elliott Nugent
PATRICIA STANLEY.....Gene Tierney
WALLY MYERS.................Don De Fore
DEAN FREDERICK DAMON
                   Ivan Simpson
MICHAEL BARNES..............Robert Scott

JOE FERGUSON...................Leon Ames
MRS. BLANCHE DAMON
                  Minna Phillips
ED KELLER..........................Matt Briggs
MYRTLE KELLER.........Regina Wallace
"NUTSY" MILLER.....Richard Beckhard
NEWSPAPER REPORTER
                  John Boruff

SCENES

Time: The present. Scene: The living room in the house of Professor Thomas Turner, in a mid-western university town.

        ACT I: Late Fall. A Friday evening.

        ACT II: Scene 1. The following day, after lunch.

                   Scene 2. Three hours later.

        ACT III: Two days later, noon.

THE AUTHORS

James Thurber needs no introduction to the reading public. His one public venture in the theatre found him collaborating with his Phi Psi fraternity brother at Ohio State, Elliott Nugent, who gravitated into the theatre at an early age while Mr. Thurber worked for the State Department in Washington and Paris and then became a newspaperman in his home town, Columbus, Ohio. *Working together on* The Male Animal *was a kind of class reunion for the boys from Ohio. Their only previous collaboration had been as editors on Ohio State's campus paper* The Lantern.

Elliott Nugent was born in 1899 in Dover, Ohio. Since his father is the old-time popular actor J. C. Nugent, *the son appeared in perhaps a hundred productions in stock and on Broadway with his parent. He also collaborated on about fifteen plays, mostly with the elder Nugent.* A Clean Town, The Dumb-Bell, The Poor Nut, The Trouper, The Breaks *and* Fast Service *are some of them. Mr. Nugent acted in a number of films and directed sixteen motion pictures. He proved himself a potent stage director, too, when he undertook the direction of* Tomorrow the World.

Mr. Nugent has done some tall thinking about the state of the world, and a play of his, A Place of Our Own, *trumpeted his views in the season of 1945. But his long suit as playwright is light and fast comedy; and if* The Male Animal, *in which the liberal attitude was leavened by laughter, is any indication, he has no reason to slight his talent in favor of sober evangelism. The Nugents have been "show folk" for several generations, and this means a congenital aptitude for entertainment. The youngest member of the dynasty has been no exception to the family tradition.*

THE MALE ANIMAL

ACT ONE

SCENE: *The living room of a pleasant, inexpensive little house. There is no distinction of architectural design, but someone with natural good taste has managed to make it look attractive and liveable on a very modest budget. There are some good prints on the walls. The hangings are cheerful, and the furniture, picked up through various bargains and inheritances, goes together to make a pleasing, informal atmosphere.*

The front door, opening onto a porch, is upstage Left, the outer wall jogging into the room for a few feet. The inside of this outer wall is lined with book-shelves which continue around the corner to the fireplace in the Left wall. Below this fireplace is a stand with a radio-phonograph. In the Center of the rear wall, a bay window with window seat. This corner is used by the Turner family as a casual depository for visitors' hats and coats, although they have also a coat-rail just inside the front door. In front of the bay window, a long table backs a comfortable sofa facing front. To the Right of the bay window are more book-shelves, a small landing, and a stairway running up and off Right. In the corner below the stair near the dining room door, a table up Right against stairs has been prepared today to serve as a temporary bar, with a tray, cocktail shaker, and two or three bottles and glasses. In the Right wall, two doors, the upper one leading to the dining room, the lower one to another porch and back yard. There are two small settees, one down Right, the other down Left near the fireplace. An arm-chair Right Center, a couple of small end or coffee tables, and one or two straight chairs complete the furnishings of the room. There are two or three vases of flowers, and the books and magazines which frequently litter this room have been put tidily away.

At the rise of the Curtain, the phone on table Right Center behind sofa is ringing. CLEOTA, *a colored maid, enters from the dining room Right and answers it.*

CLEOTA. Professah Turner's res-i-dence— Who?—You got de wrong numbah— Who?— What you say?— Oh, Mistah Turner! No, he ain't heah. He jus' went out to buy some likkah— Who is dis callin'? Yessuh. Yessuh. Ah doan' get dat, but Ah'll tell him Doctah Damon. Ah say Ah'll tell him. *(Hangs up; starts for dining room.)*

ELLEN'S VOICE *(off upstairs)*. Who was it, Cleota?

CLEOTA. It was Doctah Damon. *(Crossing to stair landing and looking upstairs.)* He say he comin' ovah to see Mistah Turner or Mistah Turner come over to see him, or sumpin'. *(Turns on lights from wall switch Left of dining room door.)*

ELLEN *(appearing on stairs)*. What was that again, Cleota? *(She crosses down Left toward coffee table. She is an extremely pretty young woman about twenty-nine or thirty. Quick of speech and movement she has a ready smile and a sweetness of personality that warms the room. She is*

completely feminine and acts always from an emotional, not an intellectual stimulus.)

CLEOTA *(from above down Right settee)*. Doctah Damon doan talk up. He kinda muffles.

ELLEN *(picks up magazines on down Left table. Crossing up Left to bookcase with them)*. I'm afraid it's you that kind of muffles.

CLEOTA. Yessum. Miz Turner, Ah'm fixin' them hor doves for the pahty. Did you say put dem black seed ones in de oven?

ELLEN *(at bookcase)*. Black seed ones? Oh, heavens, Cleota, you're not heating the caviar?

CLEOTA. No'm, ah ain't heatin' it, but taste lak' sumpin' oughtta be done to it.

ELLEN *(crossing up Right)*. It's to be served cold. Here, you pick up the rest of the magazines. I'll take a look at the canapés. *(Exits to dining room.)*

CLEOTA. Yessum. Ah ain't no hand at 'em. People where Ah worked last jus' drank without eatin' anything. *(She comes down Right to magazines, settee down Right. Sound of whistling;* TOMMY TURNER *enters Left. He is a young associate professor, thirty-three years old. He wears glasses, is rather more charming than handsome. His clothes are a little baggy. He has a way of disarranging his hair with his hands, so that he looks like a puzzled spaniel at times. He is carrying chrysanthemums and two bottles of liquor, wrapped in paper and tied with string.)* Oh, hello, Mr. Turner!

TOMMY *(putting flowers and bottles on sofa).* Hello, Cleota! *(Removes and hangs up coat and hat.)*

CLEOTA *(taking magazines upstage to bookcase up Right Center).* You bettah not mess up dis room, 'cause dey is guess comin'.

TOMMY. All right, Cleota. I'll be good.

*(*CLEOTA *exits to dining room up Right.* TOMMY *picks up bundles, comes Right Center—looks for place to put down bottles—puts them on chair Right Center—unwraps flowers, throwing paper on floor—throws string down Center—sticks flowers in vase in middle of other flowers; sees book, picks it up, looks at it disapprovingly, looks upstairs and makes a gesture of disgust, throws it in waste-basket—crosses to pick up liquor.)*

ELLEN *(enters from dining room up Right. Crossing to* TOMMY). Hello, dear!

TOMMY. Hello, Ellen! Those are for you. *(Indicates his flowers.)*

ELLEN. Oh, thank you, Tommy. They're lovely. *(Surveys the flowers.)*

TOMMY. The ones in the middle.

ELLEN. Yes—

TOMMY. I got the liquor, too.

ELLEN *(taking* TOMMY'S *flowers out of vase Right).* Did you get the right kind? *(Picks up paper.)*

TOMMY. I got both kinds.

*(*ELLEN *puts paper in waste-basket—crosses above* TOMMY *to Right Center—picks up string Center.)*

ELLEN. Tommy, you're a house-wrecker, but you're nice. *(Kisses him—then crosses up Center to sofa. Puts flowers on sofa.)*

TOMMY. Did I do something right?

ELLEN. Cleota— *(Takes vase from table up Center—starts across for dining room door up Right.)* Cleota, will you fill this vase with water, please? *(Hands it to* CLEOTA *in doorway—comes to table Right behind sofa.)* What became of the book that was on this table?

TOMMY. That? Oh, I threw it in the wastebasket. It's trash.

ELLEN *(rescuing book).* But you can't throw it away. Wally gave it to Patricia.

TOMMY. Oh, he did?

ELLEN. Besides, it's just the right color for this room. *(*VOICES *off-scene up Left.* ELLEN *crosses Left to up Center sofa—picks up flowers.)*

PAT'S VOICE *(off—up Left).* Oh, Wally, quit arguing! *(Door is opened, and* PAT *backs into room.)* I'm going to dinner with Mike, and then to the rally with you. You can't feed me at the training table. *(Hangs coat up on wall hooks. She is a pretty, lively girl of 19 or 20.)*

WALLY *(appears in doorway. He is six-feet-one, and weighs 190 pounds, mostly muscle. He is full of energy and health, and not without a good deal of naive charm.)* Aw, that guy Barnes! I don't see why you have to— Oh, how do you do, Mrs. Turner—Professor Turner?

TOMMY. Hello, Butch!

ELLEN *(carries flowers to Center of upstage table).* That's Wally Myers.

TOMMY. Oh, hello!

WALLY *(crossing into room a step).* Oh, has Butch been coming here, too?

*(*TOMMY *crosses down Right.)*

PATRICIA *(pushing* WALLY). Go on, get out of here, half-back. I have to get dressed. *(Crosses into room—crosses to Right Center chair.)* Hey, Ellen, excited about seeing the great Ferguson, again? He just drove up to the Beta House in a Deusenberg! *(Sits chair Right Center.)*

(CLEOTA *re-enters with vase;* ELLEN *takes it;* CLEOTA *exits.*)

ELLEN. Did you see him?

PATRICIA. No, the kids were telling me. Has he still got his hair?

ELLEN (*arranging flowers up Center table*). I haven't seen him in ten years. We'll soon find out. (TOMMY *crosses to down Right.*)

WALLY (*crosses to Left end up Center sofa*). Say, is he coming here?

ELLEN. Yes. Why don't you come back and meet him, Wally? You can tell him all about the game tomorrow.

WALLY. Gee, thanks! But nobody could tell Joe Ferguson anything about a football game. He's all-time All-American, you know. (*Crosses to door up Left.*) Well, thanks, Mrs. Turner. I'll be back. See you later, Pat. (*Exits up Left.*)

PATRICIA (*closes door; then opens it and sticks head into room*). So long! (*Sits chair Right Center. Takes bottle of nail-polish from her pocket book and starts to fix run in stocking.*)

TOMMY (*from down Right*). Does he mean that now Joe belongs to the ages, like Lincoln? (*Lights cigarette.*)

ELLEN. Um-hum, in a way.

TOMMY (*has picked several magazines from bookcase up Right Center and is looking through them. Crossing Left to bookcase*). Well, I suppose he has passed into legend. I used to admire him myself —almost.

ELLEN (*from up Center*). Pat, why don't you and Michael stay here for dinner? Supper, rather. It's just a bite. We're all going out to eat after the rally.

PATRICIA. No, thanks. You know how Mike feels about Mr. Keller. He'd spit in his eye.

TOMMY (*crossing to down Left settee*). Why do we have to have Ed Keller to this party?

ELLEN. Oh, Joe has to have someone to talk football with. Ed's his closest friend here. He practically paid Joe's way through college. You can stand the Kellers one night. (*Puts books from up Center table in up Right Center bookcase.*)

TOMMY. Just barely. I don't know how to entertain trustees. (*Sits settee Left.*)

PATRICIA. Well, you'd better be entertaining tonight with the great Ferguson coming. (*Rises; crossing up Right to stair landing.*) Weren't you engaged to him once, Ellen?

ELLEN. Not officially. Just for fun.

PATRICIA (*starting up stairs*). Baby, that can be dangerous, too! (*Exits.*) (TOMMY *has found an article in "Harper's" and is reading.*)

ELLEN (*arranging flowers up Center*). Oh, Dean Damon phoned, Tommy.

TOMMY. What'd he want?

ELLEN. I don't know. Cleota answered the phone.

TOMMY. Oh—I see— Oh, I'll bet I know. I saw the Dean this morning. What do you think?

ELLEN. Oh, I don't know— Oh, Tommy, you don't mean—?

TOMMY. Yes, I do.

ELLLEN (*crossing down Left to* TOMMY *and kissing his forehead*). Oh Tommy, that's wonderful! It's three hundred and fifty more a year, isn't it?

TOMMY. Five hundred! I'm no piker.

ELLEN. Well, you certainly deserve it.

TOMMY. Now I can get you that fur coat next February. People must think I let you freeze in the winter.

ELLEN (*crossing up Center to table*). No, they don't. And, don't worry about me— (*At flowers.*) You need some new things, yourself.—I love the flowers, Tommy. And this promotion couldn't have come on a better day for me. Do you know what day it is? (*Crossing Right.*)

TOMMY. Friday, isn't it? Why?

ELLEN. Oh, nothing—never mind. (*Down Right. Glances around room. Throws string from flowers in waste-basket.*) What became of all the match-boxes? (*Crossing Left to* TOMMY.) I had one in each ash tray.

TOMMY (*she is digging in his pockets*). I haven't seen any match-boxes. (*She finds two. He smiles guiltily.*) Say, you look very pretty tonight. That's a new dress, isn't it?

ELLEN (*right of Left settee*). No—- It's my hair that's bothering you. It's done a new way—

TOMMY. Doesn't bother me. I like it.

ELLEN (*looking around*). One more.

TOMMY. Oh, you exaggerate this match-box thing. Oh! (*Hands her one.* ELLEN *crosses and puts it on table up Center.*) I ought to take you out to dinner more and show you off.

ELLEN (*up Center table*). Well, we're going out tonight after the rally.

TOMMY. I mean just the two of us. Tonight will be like old times. Remember how Joe was always horning in on our dinner dates? I don't believe we ever had one that he didn't come over and diagram the Washington Monument play or something on the tablecloth with a pencil.

ELLEN (*crossing Right to Right end of table*). Statue of Liberty play, darling.

TOMMY. He was always coming. I never saw him going.

ELLEN. There's still one missing. (*Crossing Left to* TOMMY.)

TOMMY. I haven't got it— (*Finds match-box.*) I'll bet Joe does something to get his wife down. Probably cleans his guns with doilies. (ELLEN *crossing Right puts box on down Right table.*) Clumsy guy. Always knocking knives and forks on the floor.

ELLEN. He wasn't clumsy. He was very graceful. (*Crossing to up Right Center bookcase, fixes books.*) He was a swell dancer.

TOMMY. I remember he got the first and the last dance with you, the last time we all went to a dance together.

ELLEN. Phi Psi Christmas dance, wasn't it?

TOMMY. No, the May Dance. Out at the Trowbridge Farm. Remember how it rained?

ELLEN (*crosses down to Right table*). I remember I had the last dance with Joe because you disappeared somewhere.

TOMMY. No, I was watching—from behind some ferns.

ELLEN (*fixes flowers*). They played "Three O'Clock in the Morning" and "Who"? It was a lovely night, wasn't it?

TOMMY. No, it poured down. (*Rises; crossing up Left to bookcase.*) You and Joe were dancing out on the terrace when it started. You both got soaked, but you kept right on dancing.

ELLEN (*down Left to coffee table—straightens it. Picks up magazine*). Oh, yes, I remember. My dress was ruined.

TOMMY (*crossing to Left Center*). You were shining wet—like Venus and Triton.

ELLEN. Why didn't you cut in? (*Crossing up Left to bookcase with magazines from down Left table; puts them in bookcase.*)

TOMMY. I had a cold. Besides, my feet hurt. (*Crossing to up Right platform.*) I'll dress. (*Doorbell rings.*) I hope he isn't here already.

(ELLEN *admits* DAMON *and* MICHAEL. DAMON, *the head of the English Department, is a tall, thin, distinguished-looking man of some 65 years. He has gray hair, eyes capable of twinkling through glasses whose rims he has a habit of peering over. He talks slowly, selecting his words, in a voice at once compelling and humorous. He often hesitates, peers over his glasses before saying the last word of a phrase or a sentence.* MICHAEL BARNES *is a Senior in the Arts College, an intensely serious young man and a fine literary student. The older people who surround him find his youthful grimness about life's problems sometimes amusing, but more frequently alarming.*)

ELLEN. Oh, come in, Doctor Damon.

MICHAEL. How do you do, sir? (*Crosses down Left to radio cabinet.*)

DAMON (*crossing to* TOMMY). Hello, Thomas!

ELLEN (*crossing door*). Where's Mrs. Damon?

DAMON (*crossing down to Center*). I shall pick her up and bring her along shortly for the festivities. This is in the nature of an unofficial call.

TOMMY (*crossing down Left to* MICHAEL). Hello, Michael! You both look a little grim. Has anything happened?

DAMON *(showing paper)*. Michael has written another of his fiery editorials.

PATRICIA *(runs down the stairs)*. Ellen, did you see my—oh! How do you do, Doctor Damon? Hi, Michael!

MICHAEL. H'lo! *(Crosses upstage.)*

DAMON. Sit down, my dear. *(PATRICIA sits Left end of settee Right.* MICHAEL *crosses down Left.)* I have here an editorial written by Michael for *The Lit,* which comes out tomorrow. Perhaps, to save time, one of us should read it aloud— *(Reading.)* "When this so-called University forces such men out of its faculty as Professor Kennedy, *(ELLEN sits down Left.* TOMMY *crosses to up Left Center.)* Professor Sykes, and Professor Chapman, because they have been ignorantly called Reds, it surrenders its right to be called a seat of learning. It admits that it is nothing more nor less than a training school—you will recognize the voice of our good friend, Hutchins, of Chicago—a training school for bond salesmen, farmers, real-estate dealers, and ambulance chasers. It announces to the world that its faculty is subservient—" *(DAMON peers over glasses at MICHAEL.)*

MICHAEL *(is pacing up and down Left. Crossing Right to DAMON)*. Oh, I didn't mean you, of course, Doctor Damon.

DAMON. "—that its faculty is subservient to its trustees, and that its trustees represent a political viewpoint which must finally emerge under its proper name, which is—Fascism." *(TOMMY sits up Center sofa.)*

PATRICIA *(from down Right. Rising)*. Oh, Michael! There you go again!

DAMON *(a step to her)*. Wait till you hear where he has actually gone. *(MICHAEL crosses to bookcase up Right Center.)*

PATRICIA. Isn't that all?

DAMON. Unhappily, there is more. *(TOMMY lights cigarette.)*

PATRICIA *(sits)*. Oh, Lord!

DAMON *(crosses Center)*. "These professors were not Reds. They were distinguished liberals. Let us thank God that we still have one man left who is going ahead teaching what he believes should be taught."

TOMMY *(lights cigarette)*. Who's that?

(MICHAEL crosses down.)

DAMON. "He is not afraid to bring up even the Sacco-Vanzetti case. He has read to his classes on the same day Vanzetti's last statement and Lincoln's letter to Mrs. Bixby." I hope we are not alienating the many friends of Abraham Lincoln. "The hounds of bigotry and *(TOMMY rises, crosses Right to DAMON.* MICHAEL *crosses up.)* reaction will, of course, be set upon the trail of this courageous teacher, but, if they think they are merely on the spoor of a lamb they are destined to the same disappointment as the hunters who in chasing the wild boar, came accidentally upon a tigress and her cubs. *(ELLEN looks at MICHAEL.)* Our hats are off to Professor Thomas Turner of the English Department." That's all.

ELLEN. Tommy?

TOMMY. Michael, I think you might have consulted me about this. *(Crosses to MICHAEL at up Left Center.)*

PATRICIA *(rises)*. Michael, you fool! They'll kick you out of school for this—and Tommy too!

ELLEN. You never told me you had brought up the Sacco-Vanzetti case in your classes, Tommy.

DAMON *(crossing to TOMMY)*. Yes, just what is this Vanzetti letter you have read?

TOMMY. I haven't read it yet.

MICHAEL. When you told me the other day you were going to read it, I thought you meant that day.

TOMMY. No, Michael. I just meant some day. But I was talking to you as a friend, I was not giving an interview to an editor.

ELLEN. But why were you going to read this letter, Tommy? *(MICHAEL crosses Left to bookcase; then down Left.)*

TOMMY. Because it's a fine piece of English composition, and I'm teaching a class in English composition. An obscure little class. I don't want any publicity, Michael. I just want to be left alone.

ELLEN. But nobody thinks of Vanzetti as a writer, Tommy.

TOMMY. It happens that he developed into an extraordinary writer. *(Crossing to DAMON.)* I don't think you could help being interested in the letter yourself, Doctor Damon.

DAMON. You would be surprised at my strength of will in these matters, Thomas. What I am interested in is preserving some air of academic calm here at Midwestern—

PATRICIA (*crossing to Right Center*). You don't want to get Tommy kicked out of school, do you, Michael?

MICHAEL. No. I didn't think of that. (*Crossing to Left Center.*) I thought Mr. Turner was about the only man we had left who would read whatever he wanted to to his classes. (*Up to* TOMMY.) I thought he was the one man who would stand up to these stadium builders. (DAMON *crosses to up Center.*)

TOMMY (*at Left Center*). I'm not standing up to anyone, Michael. I'm not challenging anyone. This is just an innocent little piece I wanted to read. (MICHAEL *crosses up Left to bookcase, then downstage.*)

ELLEN (*rises. Crossing to* TOMMY). I'm sure this piece must be fine, Tommy, but you can't read it now. Keller and the other trustees kicked Don Chapman out last month for doing things just as harmless as this. (*Turning to* MICHAEL.) You'll have to change that editorial, Michael. (TOMMY *crosses Right.*)

MICHAEL. I can't. The magazines were run off the presses last night. They've already been delivered to the news stands.

DAMON. They go on sale in the morning. (*Crossing Left to* ELLEN.) I think that our —er—tigress here may have to issue a denial tomorrow. After all, he hasn't read it yet.

ELLEN (*crossing to* TOMMY). Yes, and you mustn't read it now.

PATRICIA (*crossing Left to* DAMON). Will Michael be kicked out of school, Doctor Damon? (TOMMY *sits Right settee.*)

DAMON. Sufficient unto the day is the evil thereof, my dear. (*Crosses up. Gets hat.*)

PATRICIA (*crossing down Left to* MICHAEL). There! You see—

DAMON (*crossing down to* TOMMY). Of course I quite understand how you meant to present this letter, Thomas; but our good friend Mr. Keller would rot. (TOMMY *starts to speak.* DAMON *stops him.*) Do not underestimate Mr. Edward K. Keller. He rolls like the juggernaut over the careers of young professors.

TOMMY. I know.

DAMON (*crossing up Left to door*). Since he must be with us tonight let us confine our conversation to the—woeful inadequacies of the Illinois team.

TOMMY (*rising*). It isn't Illinois we're playing—it's Michigan.

DAMON. Oh, I must remember that. (*Exits up Left.*)

PATRICIA (*down Left*). There, you see! You will be kicked out.

MICHAEL. He didn't say that.

PATRICIA. Yes, he did. You needn't bother to come back for me, Michael. (*Crossing towards stairs.*) I'm staying here for supper. (*Runs up stairs.*)

MICHAEL (*crossing to Left Center*). I see. I'm sorry, Mr. Turner. I guess I got—well —carried away.

TOMMY (*crossing Left to* MICHAEL). I know, Michael. Sometimes, when I see that light in your eye I wish I could be carried away too.

MICHAEL. Yes, sir. (*Exits up Left. Slight pause.*)

TOMMY (*crossing up Left a few steps after him*). Well—

ELLEN (*crossing to* TOMMY *Left Center*). I'm sorry, Tommy.

TOMMY. Oh it's all right. Maybe I can read this thing later on, after all the fuss quiets down—say next spring.

ELLEN. It would still be dangerous.

TOMMY (*crossing up Right*). Yes, I guess it would. (*Turns back to* ELLEN.) I know I'm not a tiger, but I don't like to be thought of as a pussy-cat either.

ELLEN. It's getting late. (*Crossing Right to* TOMMY.) You'd better go and put on that gray suit I laid out for you. (*Crossing Left Center.*) And be sure your socks are right side out, and Tommy—don't try to be a tiger in front of Ed Keller.

TOMMY (*at stair landing*). I won't. I'm scared of those Neanderthal men. I'll talk about football.

ELLEN. Thank you, darling. (*Crossing Left to mantel.*) That's swell. You know how Joe is—always cheerful. And we do want it to be a good party. (*Straightens mantel.*)

TOMMY. I'll be cheerful. I'll be merry and bright. I'll be the most cheerful son-of-a-gun in this part of the country. (*He sings as he exits up the stairs.*)

"Who's afraid of the Big Bad Wolf?
The Big Bad Wolf?
The Big Bad Wolf?
Who's afraid tum-tee-ump—"

(ELLEN *looks after him doubtfully. Door-bell rings.*)

ELLEN (*calling upstairs*). Hurry, Tommy! They're here! (*Crosses to Left door; admits* JOE FERGUSON, *followed by* WALLY MYERS.) Hello, Joe!

JOE. Ellen, darling! How are you? Gosh, you look great! Why, you're younger and prettier than ever! If I were a braver man, I'd kiss you. Doggone it, I *will* kiss you! (*Kisses her on cheek, hugs her, lifts her off the floor—whirls her down to Center.* JOE *is big, handsome, successful, and pleasing, about 35.*)

(WALLY *closes door—stands up Left Center.*)

ELLEN. It's terribly nice to see you again, Joe. If I were a younger woman, I'd say it's been all of ten years.

JOE (*crossing up to sofa; puts box of flowers down*). Gosh, this is swell! Where's the great Thomas?

ELLEN. Tommy will be right down. I see Wally found you—so you've met? (JOE *crosses to* WALLY, *who helps him take off coat and hangs it on hook.*)

JOE. Yeh. We joined forces outside. (*Thanks* WALLY.)

ELLEN. Come on over here and sit down. (*Crossing to down Left settee and sitting Left end.*)

JOE. I forgot to ask you Wally, who's going in at the other half tomorrow? Stalenkiwiecz?

WALLY. No, sir. Wierasocka.

JOE. Oh, is he?

WALLY. Yeh. He's a Beta. From Oregon.

JOE. Oh, yeh—yeh, I know him.

WALLY (*crossing and sitting Center down Left settee*). Stalenkiwiecz is laid up. They think he's got whooping cough.

JOE. That's bad! (*Crossing down Left.—To* ELLEN. *Looking for room on settee.*) I've got a thousand fish on that game. (*Sits Right end settee. It is very crowded.*)

WALLY. I think it's safe, all right, Mr. Ferguson, but I wish we had you. Stalenkiwiecz, Wierasocka, Myers and Whirling Joe Ferguson.

ELLEN. Do they still call you that, Joe?

JOE. Oh, sure, remember how—

WALLY. Say, he was the greatest open-field runner there ever was.

ELLEN. Yes, Joe. How does it happen you've never even—

WALLY. Why, you made Red Grange look like a cripple.

JOE. Aw, they say you're not so bad yourself. Say, Ellen, how's—

WALLY. Aw, I'm just fair, that's all. (*Produces a clipping from coat pocket.*) This is what Grantland Rice said about me. (*Hands it to* JOE.)

JOE. Yeh.—Too bad this is Wally's last year. We're going to miss him—eh, Ellen?

ELLEN. Have you got anything to do, Wally?

WALLY. Well—the Coach wants me to help him with the back-field next season. Not much money in it, of course.

JOE (*hands clipping back to* WALLY). Well, if you want my advice, don't go in for coaching. I had a sweet offer from Cincinnati in 'Twenty-nine. Remember that, Ellen?

ELLEN. I remember very well. Do you remember when—

WALLY. Nineteen twenty-nine! (*Leaning forward meditatively.*) —I was only twelve years old then—

TOMMY (*comes downstairs. Crossing to* JOE). Hello, Joe! It's nice to see you again!

JOE (*rises. Crossing to him.* WALLY *rises*). Tommy, old man, how are you? Ten years! Teaching must be good for you. And Ellen, here, looks like a million bucks! That reminds me—I came laden with gifts. *(Turns and almost runs into* WALLY. *He goes and gets flowers up Center sofa.)* These are a few flowering weeds— *(Crosses to* ELLEN.*)* (WALLY *still behind* JOE.*)*

ELLEN *(from Left settee).* Thank you, Joe. They're lovely. Tommy, will you call Cleota? (WALLY *leans over back of settee Left.)*

TOMMY. Sure! *(Goes into dining room, calls.)* Cleota!

ELLEN. It's fun to get flowers. Very festive.

JOE. Oh, it's nothing much, but I wanted you to know I remembered the great day. Think I'd forget it was your birthday?

ELLEN. You never used to. (TOMMY *re-enters.* ELLEN *crosses to Center and meets* TOMMY*).* Tommy gave me some flowering weeds, too—for my birthday.

TOMMY. For your—oh—yes— Not such nice ones, I'm afraid. *(To* ELLEN.*)* I'm a lucky man. *(Turns back. She pats his hand.)* (CLEOTA *enters to* ELLEN *from dining room.)*

ELLEN. Will you find something to put these in, Cleota?

CLEOTA *(sighs).* Yassum. Ah guess Ah'll hafta put 'em in de sink wit dat ice. *(Exits to dining room.)*

JOE. Boy, it's sure great to be here! *(Crossing down Left.)*

(WALLY *crosses around down Left to fireplace bench.)*

TOMMY. It's nice to have you.—Staying long?

JOE. Got to be in Washington next week. *(Noticing bookcases).* Well, Tommy, I see you've still got a lot of books.

TOMMY. Oh, yes.

JOE. You know I never get a chance to read books. *(Sits Left settee.)*

WALLY. Say, you must have a swell job! *(Sits on bench front of fireplace.)* (ELLEN *crosses to Left Center.)*

JOE. By the time I get through at night, I'm lucky if I can keep up with what's going on in the world. Way things are changing, you gotta do that. I take fifteen magazines. That keeps me busy.

ELLEN *(crosses Left to* TOMMY. *Takes his arm).* Tommy's had several articles in *Harper's* and the *Atlantic.*

JOE. No! Say, that's fine! But you'll have to boil them down to *The Reader's Digest* to reach me, Tommy. (JOE *and* WALLY *laugh.)* You know, that's a great little magazine.

TOMMY. Do you like bouillon cubes?

ELLEN *(hurrying him out).* Tommy, you'd better make a drink.

TOMMY *(crossing below her to up Right door).* Yes. We have a lot of celebrating to do. *(Crosses into dining room calling "Cleota.")*

ELLEN. How've you been, Joe? *(Sits next to* JOE.*)*

JOE. Fine, except for a little sinus trouble.

WALLY. You know, Mrs. Turner, I recognized him right away from that big picture in the gym. (TOMMY *re-enters with bowl of ice. Crosses to up Right table; mixes drinks.)*

ELLEN. That's fine. How's Brenda? I meant to ask before.

JOE. Fine! Great! Little heavier, maybe. We're being divorced, you know.

ELLEN. But I didn't know. Oh, Joe, I'm sorry.

JOE. Nothing to be sorry about. It's just one of those things. (JOE *and* WALLY *laugh.)*

TOMMY *(from up Right).* What's the matter?

ELLEN. Joe and his wife are breaking up.

TOMMY. Oh, that's too bad.

JOE. No, it's all fine. We're both taking it in our stride. Took her out to dinner last week—along with her new boy friend. (WALLY *takes this big—very funny.)*

TOMMY. Wasn't that rather complicated?

ELLEN. Oh, you're not up to date, Tommy. That's the modern way of doing things.

JOE. Sure! Take it in your stride. Gosh, Ellen, I can't take my eyes off you. *(This is cute so* WALLY *laughs again.* JOE *notices* TOMMY *watching.)* Nice little place you got here. *(Rises.)* Need any help, Tommy?

I'm a demon on Manhattans. *(Crosses above Left settee to* TOMMY *up Right.)* *(Doorbell rings.)*

TOMMY. I'm all right, thanks.

JOE *(crossing down Right).* I hope that's Ed, the old scoundrel.

ELLEN *(goes to the door Left and admits the* DAMONS*).* I'm so glad— Hello, Mrs. Damon!

BLANCHE *(entering).* Hello, Ellen dear! How do you do, Mr. Turner? *(*WALLY *rises.)*

ELLEN *(coming down with* BLANCHE*).* You must know Joe Ferguson.

BLANCHE. Oh, of course!

ELLEN. This is Mrs. Damon, Joe. You remember Dean Damon?

JOE. Yes indeed! Nice to see you again, sir.

DAMON *(crossing to him and shaking hands).* Back for the slaughter of the— uh—Michigan innocents, eh?

JOE. That's right.

*(*ELLEN *and* BLANCHE *have crossed down Left to* WALLY. DAMON *crosses up; puts coat on up Left chair; hat on up Center table.)*

ELLEN. Mrs. Damon, may I present Mr. Myers?

BLANCHE. Oh, yes of course we all know about our great fullback.

*(*TOMMY *gives away cocktails.* JOE *gets cocktail from* TOMMY*.)*

WALLY. How do you do?

ELLEN. Let me help you with your coat.

BLANCHE. Thank you, dear. *(To* WALLY*.)* Tell me, are you nervous about the game?

WALLY. No, ma'am.

BLANCHE. Not the least little bit?

*(*ELLEN *takes* BLANCHE's *coat up to window seat; stands* DAMON's *umbrella above sofa.)*

WALLY. No, ma'am.

BLANCHE. That's nice. *(Sits down Left.)*

DAMON *(crossing Right to* JOE*).* I remember you not only from the gridiron

but from my Shakespeare class. You slept very quietly.

JOE. You know, I never did finish reading *Hamlet.* I always wondered how that came out. *(He laughs heartily.)* *(*DAMON *laughs politely.)*

TOMMY *(crossing Left with two cocktails).* Does anybody mind a Manhattan.

BLANCHE. Oh, Ellen! Could we have sherry?

ELLEN. Certainly. Tommy—

TOMMY. Sherry coming right up. *(Crossing down Left to* WALLY*.)* Here, Wally. *(Gives him cocktail.)*

WALLY. No, thanks. I'm in training.

TOMMY *(crossing to* DAMON*).* Well, just hold it. *(*WALLY *puts glass down on down Left table.)* Sherry for you too, Doctor Damon?

DAMON. When Mrs. Damon says we, she means me. Sherry, thanks. *(*TOMMY *crosses up Right.* DAMON *crosses down Left to* BLANCHE, *then up to bookcase Left.)*

BLANCHE *(drinking other cocktail).* A little sherry is such fun. *(*WALLY *offers her cigarette from box on coffee table.)* No thanks, I'll smoke my "Spuds"! *(She does.)* *(*WALLY *lights* BLANCHE's *cigarette.)*

PATRICIA *(coming downstairs).* Hello, everybody! *(General "hellos!")*

ELLEN *(brings her down to* JOE*).* This is my sister Patricia.

PATRICIA. How do you do?

JOE *(admiring her).* How do you *do?* My goodness! Why, you're as big and pretty as your sister. How about a drink?

PATRICIA. No, thanks. *(To* ELLEN, *crosses Center.)* Still has his hair. *(*TOMMY *looks up at this.* PATRICIA, *crossing to* WALLY.*)* Hello, Wally! *(*TOMMY *pours sherry for* DAMONS.*)*

WALLY. Hi, Pat! Look, can I pick you up at Hennick's a little earlier?

PATRICIA. I'm not going to Hennick's. I'm eating here. That date's off.

WALLY *(crossing to* PATRICIA*).* With Barnes? Say, that's swell. *(Smacks* PATRICIA *on the back, almost knocking her* *down. Crosses to* ELLEN.*)* I got to run along, Mrs. Turner. Nice party. *(Shakes* ELLEN's *hand heartily. Crosses to* JOE.*)* Glad I met you, Joe—I mean, Mr. Ferguson. *(They shake hands.)* I'll be seeing you. Goodbye, everybody! I'll go out the back way. *(Exits down Right.)*

JOE. Take it easy, old man. Don't break a leg on me. Remember, I've got a thousand fish on that game. *(Follows* WALLY *out.)*

WALLY *(off)*. I won't.

BLANCHE. He's a handsome boy, Patricia. *(Doorbell rings.)* And seems very healthy.

PATRICIA. I have to keep in training for him. *(Crosses to fireplace. Sits down stage end of bench.)* *(*TOMMY *crosses up Left to door.* DAMON *sits upper end fireplace bench.)*

TOMMY. I'll get it.

(The KELLERS *come into the room.* ED KELLER *is a big, loud, slightly bald man of about thirty-eight, heavy around the middle. He is a prosperous real-estate man, owns the Keller Building, is a trustee and as such, the biggest voice and strongest hand on the Board.* MYRTLE KELLER, *also in her late thirties, dresses well and is not bad-looking, was once pretty, but is now a slightly faded blonde.)*

ED. Hello, Ellen! Hi, Turner! Where is he? *(Passes* TOMMY *fast, without handshake:* JOE *reappears;* ED *comes down and meets* JOE *Right Center. This is a typical meeting between two old friends of the hale-and-hearty, back-slapping variety who haven't met for years.)* Hiya, you old rascal! Hahya, boy?

JOE *(running to meet him, so that they clinch in the middle of the room, hugging, slapping backs, etc.* ELLEN *is helping* MYRTLE *take off her coat up Left.)* Hello, you old son-of-a-gun! How are you, Ed? *(Crosses to* MYRTLE.*)* Hello, Myrtle! Gosh, I'm glad to see you! *(Hugs her.)*

MYRTLE *(screams)*. I'm glad to see you, too! Ellen—

JOE *(back to* ED*)*. Gee, you're looking swell, Ed, old boy, old boy!

ED. Judas Priest, this is swell! How are you anyway, Joe? *(Resumes back-slap-*

ping.) *(The* MEN's *voices predominate during the following.)*

JOE. Fine! Swell! Never better. You've put on a little weight, eh, Eddie? And what's happened to the crowning glory?

ED. Worry: real-estate, Roosevelt. Wonder I got any left.

*(*ED *takes off coat and hat.* TOMMY *puts them on window seat.)*

MYRTLE. How do you do, Doctor Damon? How do you do, Mrs. Damon? Haven't seen you in a long, long time. Hello, Patricia—Oh, quiet down! Ed! *(Sits down Left.)* Are we late, Ellen?

ELLEN. Not at all. Just in time for the canapés. *(Puts* MYRTLE's *coat up Left chair.)*

JOE. How long's it been, Ed? Seven, eight years, isn't it?

ED. Eight, anyway. *(*TOMMY *crosses down Right.)*

ELLEN *(crosses to* ED*)*. Look, you two, will you break it up and say hello to people?

ED. All right, Ellen, but it sure is fine to see The Whirler again. *(Crossing Left to* DAMON.*)* How do you do, Doctor Damon? Not drinking straight Scotch, I hope? *(*JOE *moves down Right.* ELLEN *goes up Right for drinks.)*

DAMON *(rising)*. If I did that, my stomach —and Mrs. Damon—would punish me severely.

ELLEN *(crossing Left to* ED*)*. Won't you have a cocktail, Ed? *(Crosses to* ED *with drink.)*

ED *(moves to up Right Center)*. Thanks.

JOE *(down Right)*. Say, this is Ellen's birthday. How about a little toast? *(*DAMON *crosses to Left bookcase.)*

TOMMY. Well, fill 'em up. *(Pours drinks, one for himself. Sits down Right.)*

ED *(crossing Center)*. Well, happy birthday, Ellen!

(They drink; ED *starts the "Happy Birthday To You" song, and they* ALL *sing. It is obvious* TOMMY *is bored; he takes a drink —then noticing everybody standing, he rises, sings the last line very off key.* CLEOTA *enters up Right, comes up behind* DAMON *up Left with plate of canapés.)*

CLEOTA *(after song dies)*. Hor doves?

DAMON. I beg your pardon—oh! Thank you. *(Takes one.)*

JOE *(as TOMMY pours another round)*. Let's drink one toast to The Big Red Team. What do you say? *(TOMMY starts humming "The Big Bad Wolf." CLEOTA is passing canapés to LADIES on settee down Left.)*

ED. The Big Red Team. *(MYRTLE gets deep in conversation with BLANCHE.)*

TOMMY *(singing softly; crossing around Right above JOE and ED to Center.)*

"The Big Red Team—
Big Red Team.
Who's afraid of The Big Red Team—"

ED. What's that?

TOMMY. Huh? *(ED glares at him. To ELLEN.)* What did I do? *(ED crosses to JOE at down Right settee.)*

ELLEN *(meets him Center)*. Tommy! You'd better eat something. Those cocktails are strong.

TOMMY *(crossing Right to JOE)*. I'm doing all right, honey. *(ED sits Left end down Right settee.)* How's everything in Detroit, Joe?

JOE *(taking a canapé ELLEN is serving)*. I don't know. All right, I guess. *(Sits Right end down Right settee.)*

ELLEN. Tommy means Pittsburgh. The Bryson Steel Company is in Pittsburgh, Tommy. *(Crosses to CLEOTA up Center.)*

(CLEOTA gives ELLEN tray and exits dining room.)

TOMMY *(stands back of chair Right Center)*. Oh, yes, sure. Well, how's everything in Pittsburgh? *(DAMON sits fireplace bench.)*

JOE. Well, it might be worse.

ED *(stuffing caviar into his mouth)*. Couldn't be much worse out here.

TOMMY. Have a drink.

ELLEN *(crossing down Left to MYRTLE—serving canapés)*. How are the kids, Myrtle?

MYRTLE. They're all right. The baby has some kind of rash on her little hips, but it's nothing, really. Makes her cross, though.

ED *(to JOE)*. Time sure does fly. Now Buster wants to go to Princeton. No matter how you watch 'em, they get in with the wrong kids. *(TOMMY crosses up Left.)*

(The WOMEN's voices predominate. ELLEN serves canapés down Left.)

BLANCHE. How's your sister?

MYRTLE. They took a stone out of her as big as a walnut. She can't weigh more than ninety pounds.

JOE *(spreading this)*. I remember when I actually got along with only one car, and thought it was plenty. Now I've got three, and the bills are terrific —Do you know what my gas bill was last month?

(DAMON rises, bored and crosses up Left to bookcase—picks out book and glances through it.)

BLANCHE. They cut old Mrs. Wilmot open for the same trouble, and didn't find a thing!

(Ad lib from MEN down Right.)

MYRTLE *(turns to ED who is talking to JOE down Right)*. Ed, when was it I had that impacted tooth out?

ED *(hastily stopping conversation with JOE)*. Seven years ago. Year the banks closed. 'Thirty-three. *(Right back to JOE.)*

TOMMY *(center)*. Fill 'em up. *(Pours himself another.)*

ELLEN *(crossing Right to TOMMY)*. Tommy! *(She takes shaker away from him. Returns to LADIES.)* Dividend for the women folks. Give me your glass, Myrtle. *(Crosses to MYRTLE down Left.)*

MYRTLE *(offers her glass)*. Thanks.

BLANCHE. No more for us. Mercy, we'll be light-headed.

TOMMY *(follows ELLEN over, takes shaker, pours himself another)*. But we're celebrating the homecoming game. Banks closing and everything.

JOE. How's building out here now, Ed?

TOMMY *(crossing Right to ED)*. Yeh, how's building?

ED. Lousy. Whatta ya expect with that man in the White House? You know what *I* think? I think he's crazy.

JOE. You know what I heard? *(The* WOMEN *stop their talk to listen, but* JOE *whispers in* ED's *ear.* TOMMY *crosses up Right Center, puts shaker on bookcase.)*

ED. I wouldn't be a damn bit surprised. (ED's *voice predominates in the following.)*

ED. Only hope for business I see is some big new industry. And he'll probably do something to ruin that.

BLANCHE (*sotto voce*). Patricia, may I see the little girl's room?

MYRTLE. Me, too.

PATRICIA. Yes, I'll show you. *(They start toward stairs.)*

MYRTLE *(as they start upstairs)*. Is it serious?

BLANCHE *(disappearing upstairs)*. They took a pint of pus out of her! *(*DAMON *slams book shut and looks after them: crosses down.* TOMMY *and* ELLEN *cross up Center to sofa and sit.)*

ED. Well, Doctor Damon, we men on the Board of Trustees are certainly glad that this Red scare is over.

DAMON *(crosses toward Center with book under his arm)*. No doubt you are.

ED. Now maybe the new stadium project will get somewhere.

DAMON *(crossing to down Left Center)*. And the Endowment Fund?

ED. Yeh, sure—that's important too. I'm working to convince the substantial alumni that we've got all this Parlor Pink business over and done with. Got 'em all weeded out. *(*DAMON *crosses up to* ELLEN.*)*

JOE. Yeah—all that newspaper stuff was pretty bad.

ED. Sure! Nobody felt like coming through for anything when they read about men like Kennedy and Sykes and Chapman being in the faculty. That Chapman was nothing but a damn Red.

TOMMY. No, he wasn't, Mr. Keller. Don Chapman was a humanist.

ELLEN. We knew him very well.

JOE. How do you know he wasn't a Red, Tommy?

ED. He went to Soviet Russia for his vacation once, didn't he?

TOMMY *(crossing down Right to* ED). He just went to see the Drama Festival.

ED *(suspiciously)*. Well, it's a mighty long way to go to see a show.

CLEOTA *(who has just entered up Right)*. Suppah is se'ved. *(Exits.)*

ELLEN *(quickly)*. Shall we go into the dining room? It's only a salad. We're going out to eat afterwards. Come along, Ed, we don't want to miss that rally. *(She links her arm through* ED's *and they exit up Right.)*

ED *(off)*. Say, that's right. I haven't missed a Michigan rally in seventeen years.

ELLEN *(re-enters; goes to stairs; calls up)*. Supper's ready. *(*PATRICIA, BLANCHE, *and* MYRTLE *come downstairs.)*

BLANCHE. Come, Frederick. *(Takes* DAMON's *arm and follows into dining room.)*

ELLEN. Patricia, you get a plate for Mr. Ferguson. He's the guest of honor you know.

JOE. And I'll get a plate for you, Ellen. Come on. *(*JOE *and* PATRICIA *exit up Right.)*

MYRTLE *(as she goes into dining room)*. Oh, what a lovely table, Ellen!

(During the following scene until ED's *re-entrance, there is the general conversation in the dining room, as* EVERYBODY *is finding his supper and beginning to eat.)*

ELLEN *(crossing to* TOMMY *Center)*. Tommy, don't say any more about Don Chapman tonight, please.

TOMMY. All right, I won't. Let's get something to eat. *(*ELLEN *takes his arm. They start for dining room.)* Joe looks better, doesn't he?

ELLEN. Better?

TOMMY. Well, bigger anyway. *(They exit.)*

*(*CLEOTA *has entered with cleanup tray. She clears drinks and tray on down Right table; crosses to down Left table, puts dirty glasses on her tray. She is singing "I Can't Give You Anything But Love" during all this. She finds one glass with*

some liquor in it. After a long scrutiny she raises it to her lips, is just about to drink when she hears.)

ED *(off).* Come on, Myrtle! Hurry up! Joe's got to speak at this rally.

(CLEOTA drinks and quickly puts glass on tray and resumes song as ED enters and sits down Right settee. BLANCHE and MYRTLE enter with DAMON following them and carrying two plates.)

BLANCHE. Frederick, put it down there on the table. *(Gestures down Left table.)*

MYRTLE *(as they're crossing down Left).* What makes you think there was something suspicious about it?

BLANCHE *(sitting down Left on Right end settee).* Well, his family won't allow a post mortem. *(DAMON puts her plate on table, crosses up to Left bookcase with his own plate. MYRTLE sits Left end of down Left settee.)* Thank you, Frederick, that's fine. *(CLEOTA has gone out. ELLEN enters with JOE to Center. JOE sits sofa up Center.)*

ELLEN. I hope you can all find a place to sit.

JOE. What's the matter with this? Come on, Ellen.

ELLEN *(smiles and sits beside him, speaking to PATRICIA, who appears in dining room door).* Pat, is Tommy getting some food?

PATRICIA. Yeh, he's all right. *(Crosses down and sits on fireplace bench.)*

TOMMY *(entering up Right).* Sure, I'm fine. *(Crosses Center, looking around for a place to settle.)*

ELLEN. Bring in the coffee, please, Cleota.

ED *(making room on the settee).* There's room here for somebody.

TOMMY. I'll sit— *(Looks around for a place away from ED—only vacant space is Right Center chair.)* here.

MYRTLE. Eat your vegetables, Ed.

ED. Aw, this is a party. *(Eating like a horse from his heaped plate.)*

BLANCHE. Where's Michael Barnes this evening, Patricia? Frederick tells me he's written a remarkable editorial. *(DAMON*

drops his fork on plate.) Be careful, Frederick!

ED *(his mouth is full).* Barnes—Barnes—? I haven't read a decent editorial since Brisbane died.

PATRICIA. Michael couldn't come. He doesn't like Mr.—er— *(ELLEN gives PATRICIA a "shush" signal.)*

MYRTLE. Doesn't like what?

PATRICIA. Doesn't like parties.

BLANCHE. I'm always so interested in *The Literary Magazine.* What was the editorial, Patricia?

DAMON *(coming around to her Right upstage of settee).* Eat your dinner, my dear. Remember, Mr. Keller—wants to get to the rally.

ED. Huh?

BLANCHE. What's the matter with you? *(To PATRICIA.)* I hope I haven't said anything, dear. *(PATRICIA shakes her head. DAMON moves back to bookcase.)*

ED. What's going on over there? Who is this Barnes?

TOMMY. One of Patricia's beaux.

ED. Some writer!

TOMMY. He's a student. Editor on *The Literary Magazine.*

ED. Oh, yeah, I've heard of him. What's he done now?

ELLEN. Oh, it's nothing really.

TOMMY. Well, since it's come up, Ellen, we might as well tell Mr. Keller. He'll read about it tomorrow— *(ELLEN rises; crosses to TOMMY.)* I told Michael I was going to read something to one of my English classes and he got a mistaken idea about it and wrote a sort of— *(CLEOTA serving coffee.)*

ELLEN *(coming down, breaking in quickly).* Just a silly little editorial—that's all.

ED. I see.

PATRICIA *(from fireplace bench).* Because Tommy isn't really going to read it at all.

(MYRTLE rises. Exits up Right carrying plate of food.)

ED. What was it this kid said, you were going to read? Anything important?

TOMMY (*after a moment*). It's a short, but beautifully written piece of English by Bartolomeo Vanzetti.

ED. Never heard of him. (*Takes coffee from* CLEOTA. *Pause.*) Hey, you don't mean Vanzetti of Sacco and Vanzetti!

TOMMY. Yes, the same man.

ED. You mean you're going to read something *he* wrote?

TOMMY. Yes, I was going to.

ELLEN (*quickly*). But now he's not—Michael didn't understand.

ED. Why would you ever think of such a dumb thing in the first place?

TOMMY. It's part of a series. I read many such letters to my class. (*Rises; crosses up. Puts dish table above Right settee.*) (ELLEN *crosses to up Left Center.*)

ED. You mean letters by anarchists?

TOMMY (*restrains himself*). No, letters by men who were not professional writers—like Lincoln, General Sherman—

ED. Well, it's a good thing you changed your mind. Putting Lincoln and General Sherman in a class with Vanzetti! Wouldn't look very good.

JOE (*from Center*). What's this?

ED (*to* JOE). Wait a minute. (*To* TOMMY.) Is this thing going to be printed? This editorial?

DAMON (*crossing down a step*). We discovered it too late to stop it.

ED. And this kid didn't submit it to the Publications Committee?

DAMON. Unfortunately, he did not. (*Moves up Center to* ELLEN.) Ellen dear, Mrs. Damon and I must be running along.

ELLEN. Oh, I'm sorry.

DAMON. I have a committee meeting.

BLANCHE. What committee?

DAMON (*crossing up*). Come, Blanche.

BLANCHE (*rising*). Oh, yes, that little committee. (*They move up to get their hats and coats,* ELLEN *goes up to help them.*)

ED. Well, I hope this thing's not too bad.

You better deny it quick, Turner. I tell you. I'll call the papers in the morning.

TOMMY. No, I'll take care of it. (*He moves upstage as* MYRTLE *enters from dining room with two dishes of sherbet.*)

JOE. What's going on here? (*Rises; crosses downstage.*)

MYRTLE (*enters from dining room; crossing down Right*). Here's some sherbet, Ed.

ED (*indicates down Right table*). Put it down there. (*She puts it on table and sits Right end of Right settee.*) I'm just telling Turner here we've had enough of this Red business among the students and the faculty. Don't want any more.

TOMMY (*sits sofa Center*). This isn't Red, Mr. Keller.

ED. Maybe not, but it looks bad. We don't want anything Red—or even Pink—taught here. (DAMON *puts on coat.*)

TOMMY. But who's to decide what is Red or what is Pink?

ED. We are! Somebody's got to decide what's fit to teach. If we don't, who would.

(ELLEN *crosses Center.* DAMON *and* BLANCHE *move downstage.*)

DAMON. I thought the faculty had—

ED. No sir. You fellows are too wishy-washy. We saw that in the Chapman case. Americanism is what we want taught here.

(DAMONS *move up;* DAMON *gets hat.*)

JOE. Americanism is a fine thing.

TOMMY. Fine! But how would you define Americanism?

ED. Why—er—everybody knows what Americanism is. What do you believe in?

TOMMY. I believe that a college should be concerned with ideas. Not just your ideas or my ideas, but all ideas.

ED (*drowning him out*). No, sir! That's the *trouble*—too many ideas floating around—You put ideas of any kind into young people's heads, and the first thing you know, they start believing them.

DAMON (*coming down, at* JOE). On the contrary. I have been putting ideas into young people's heads for forty-two years with no (*Twinkles slyly at* JOE.) —visible

—results whatever. (*There is a dubious laugh from* ED *and* JOE *until* JOE *gets* DAMON's *meaning.*)

BLANCHE. Come, Frederick. Good night, Ellen! Lovely party! (*She bustles* DAMON *out up Left.*)

ED (*rises. Crossing to* TOMMY). Turner, you better think twice before you read anything. I can promise you the trustees will clamp down on any professor who tries anything funny. I'm telling you that for your own good.

JOE. Say, I thought we were going to have some fun. Let's break this up. How about some music? (*Crosses down Left to Victrola. He puts on a record which starts to play Wayne King's recording of "Corn-silk."*)

ED. That's right. We're celebrating tonight. Just wanted to get that out of my system. (*Crosses Right, sits on settee. He picks up the dish of ice.*) Oh, I didn't want this —I wanted some of that ice cream. (*Rises. He starts for the dining room.*)

MYRTLE. He means he wants both. Here, I'll show you. (*She follows him into the dining room.*)

PATRICIA (*at a sign from* ELLEN). I'll bet you'd like some ice cream, too, Mr. Ferguson.

JOE. No, I— (PATRICIA *winks at him; he glances at* TOMMY.) Oh, sure! Sure, I would. (*He follows* PATRICIA *into dining room.*)

PATRICIA (*as they exit*). Can you still skip?

JOE. No—not at my age. (TOMMY *crosses up Right.*)

ELLEN. Tommy, have you had too much to drink?

TOMMY. No. Not enough.

ELLEN. Your eyes have that funny look.

TOMMY (*crossing down Center*). Did you hear what Mr. Keller said to me? I don't like to be talked to like that.

ELLEN (*crossing to him*). Just because he was nasty and you've had a few drinks. Tommy, you're not going to go ahead and read that letter.

TOMMY. Yes, Ellen, I think I have to.

ELLEN. Tommy, try to be practical for once. At least wait until you're not so mad. Try to think of this the way any other man would think of it.

TOMMY. I'm not any other man.

ELLEN. Well, try to be. Do you think Joe would do something that would get him into trouble just because somebody irritated him?

TOMMY. *Joe!* I don't see why you don't try to understand how *I* feel about this.

ELLEN. I'm simply trying to keep you out of a lot of trouble. I don't see why—

TOMMY. But you see how Joe would feel. That's very plain to you, isn't it?

ELLEN. Yes, it is. Joe wouldn't get all mixed up.

TOMMY. I'm not mixed up. I'm trying to understand what goes on in your mind. It *can't* be like Joe Ferguson's mind!

ELLEN. Oh, you and your mind! I have to go through such a lot with your mind! (*Crossing down Right.*)

TOMMY. Maybe you wouldn't if you understood it better.

ELLEN (*turns; crosses back to him*). Oh, I know, I know! I'm too dumb for you!

TOMMY (*crossing Right to Center*). Now, Ellen, I didn't say that.

ELLEN (*crossing Left to Center*). You said Joe and I were stupid.

TOMMY. I said he was.

ELLEN. But he isn't. He's a big man. In some ways he's smarter than you.

TOMMY (*crossing below* ELLEN *to down Right*). Well, you ought to know.

ELLEN. Oh, look, Tommy—what are we fighting about?

TOMMY (*turns*). You said I was dumb.

ELLEN. Tommy, you've had too many drinks or you wouldn't say that.

TOMMY. No, I haven't, but I don't feel very well. I feel very unhappy and slightly sick.

ELLEN. I'll get you some bicarbonate of soda. (*Starts up.*)

TOMMY. No, you won't. I'll go upstairs and

lie down for a few minutes myself. I can do that much. Let's not bring this down to the level of bicarbonate of soda. (*Crosses to stairway—starts up slowly. Suddenly can contain himself no longer—makes a mad dash for it.*)

ELLEN (*hesitates for a minute at the foot of the stairs—calls after him*). Tommy! Tommy, I didn't—

JOE (*enters from up Right*). Anything the matter? (CLEOTA *enters up Right. Crosses down Right, straightening up the room.*)

ELLEN. Oh—no. Tommy's not feeling well. He got sick once before at a party. He's not used to drinking, and he's very sensitive about it. Cleota. Will you get Mr. Turner some bicarbonate of soda from the kitchen? (CLEOTA *nods—exits up Right.* JOE *crosses down Left to Victrola.*) Cleota will get him some bicarbonate of soda from the kitchen. He'd never find it upstairs.

JOE (*turns off the music and takes off the record*). Why wouldn't he? Where do you keep it?

ELLEN. In the medicine chest.

JOE (*smiles*). What was that stuff between him and Ed?

ELLEN. Oh, it's nothing, really. I'll tell you about it tomorrow.

JOE (*finds another record*). Fine— Say, look what I found! "Who?" Remember that, Ellen? (*He puts the record on, starts it.*) (ELLEN *moves closer to the Victrola and listens as it plays:*)

"Who-o-o stole my heart away?
Who-o-o makes me dream all day?
Dreams I know can never come true.
Seems as though I'd ever be blue
Who-o-o means my happiness—"

(*As naturally as if they were always dancing to this song, they* BOTH *begin to dance.*)

Gee, this takes me back— The May Dance. Remember? (*They are dancing Center.*)

ELLEN. Um-huh—it rained.

JOE. You said you didn't know it was raining. I know I didn't. (*Holds her closer.*)

ELLEN (*breaks away*). I'm a little rusty,

Joe. I haven't danced in—oh, I don't remember when. Makes me feel young.

JOE. Then what are we stopping for? Come on.

ELLEN (*Center*). Well—all right. (*They go back into the dance.* JOE *gets her Center and stops, so that they stand looking at each other, he ardently, she caught up in the music.*)

JOE. I can answer all those questions— (*As the music goes into the instrumental reprise,* JOE *kisses her, and she kisses back for a long moment, then tries to pull away.*) No one but you—

ELLEN (*as he tries to kiss her again*). Oh, no, Joe, please, I—Say, how many cocktails did I have? (*They stand for an instant, looking at each other. Offstage we hear:*)

MYRTLE. Ed, get away from that ice cream. You've had enough. (JOE *and* ELLEN *quietly start dancing again.*)

ED. Oh—all right. (TOMMY *has come down the stairs—sees them dancing there as* MYRTLE *and* ED *enter up Right.*)

MYRTLE (*nudging* ED. JOE *and* ELLEN *dance up Left* JOE *facing stage*). Look, Ed! Just like the old days, isn't it? Seeing them dancing together?

ED. I'll say. (*Then, loudly.*) They make a darn handsome couple, don't they?

(TOMMY, *although he has not seen the kiss, has sensed the whole intimacy of the scene and the meaning of* ED's *remark.*)

JOE. She dances like a dream.

ED (*chuckling, crossing Right*). Like a "dream can never come true," eh, Joe? You look mighty sweet in there, boy.

(ELLEN *sees* TOMMY. *Following her glance,* ED *and* MYRTLE *and* JOE *turn and look at* TOMMY.)

ELLEN (*breaking away*). Oh—Tommy— are you all right?

TOMMY (*coming down*). Yes, thanks.— Don't—let me spoil the party.

ED. Party's breaking up anyway, Tommy

(JOE *crosses down Left, turns off Victrola.*

TOMMY. I just thought I'd get some more air— (*Crosses to door down Right.*)

ED (*crossing up Left*). I don't want to miss any of that rally. (*A band is heard in the distance, approaching. Holds out* MYRTLE's *coat*.) Myrtle! (MYRTLE *goes up Left to him.*)

PATRICIA (*enters from dining room with bicarbonate of soda in glass*). Who's this for, Ellen? (ED *and* JOE *are getting their hats,* JOE *getting* ELLEN's *coat for her.*)

ELLEN. Tommy! (*To* TOMMY, *as he stands with his back turned, breathing the fresh air.*) Tommy, will you take this bicarbonate?

TOMMY. Just—put it by for a moment. You go to the rally, Ellen— I'm going to walk around out here—and cool off. Good night, everybody— You're coming to lunch tomorrow, aren't you, Joe?

JOE. Yes, sir!

TOMMY. That's what I thought. (*He goes out, down Right, closing the screen door.*)

(ELLEN *puts soda on table.*)

PATRICIA (*looks out the window; the band is heard louder, coming down*). Ellen! It's the team and the band and a lot of the kids! They must be going in the Neil Avenue gate! (*Runs back to window.*)

ED. Come on, let's step on it! (*Opens door up Left.*)

(*Band noise louder.*)

JOE. Yeh. (*Listens to music coming closer.*) Boy, that sounds good! Gosh, doesn't that take you back? (*Gets coat.*)

MYRTLE (*up Left getting coat*). Where'll we go after the rally? (*Crosses down Left Center.*)

JOE. I'll take you all to the Dixie Club! Whatta ya say, Ellen?

ELLEN. Oh, I haven't been there in years! It would be fun— But, no, I'm not going. (*Calls to off down Right.*) I'm going to stay here and get you to bed, Tommy.

TOMMY's VOICE (*off*). No, I'd rather you didn't—really.

PATRICIA (*as music gets much louder*). Hey! They're stopping in front of the house!

WALLY (*enters up Left. Crosses down Right Center*). Ready, Pat?

PATRICIA. Sure!

WALLY (*crossing to* JOE. *He is breathless and excited*). Look, Mr. Ferguson, we brought the band over to escort you to the chapel. You're going to ride in the Axline Buggy! We hauled it out of the trophy rooms !

(*Music stops at end of piece.*)

ED. The Axline Buggy! Wow!

WALLY. Yes! We got two horses—not the old black ones, but we got two horses! Whatta ya say?

ED. Fine! Fine!

NUTSY (*runs in, dressed in band-leader's uniform and carrying his glistening stick. From up Left, by door*). Hey come on! Let's get going! The carriage waits, Mr. Ferguson! (*Does drum major's salute and clicks heels.*)

WALLY (*pointing to* NUTSY). This is Nutsy Miller, the leader of the band.

JOE (*walks to* NUTSY). Hiya, Nutsy?

NUTSY (*waves a salute*). Hiya, Joe?

JOE. Okay, fellas! Whatta ya say, Ellen— you ride with me.—Some fun, huh?

ELLEN (*in the spirit of it*). Oh—all right. Hurray!

JOE (*puts coat around her*). Hit her, Ed!

ED, JOE, WALLY, ELLEN, PATRICIA, NUTSY (*sing*).

"And if we win the game,
We'll buy a keg of booze,
And we'll drink to old Midwestern
Till we wobble in our shoes."

(*They* ALL *go out,* JOE *and* ELLEN *the center of the gay, excited group, arm in arm. A shout goes up as* JOE *appears outside.*)

VOICES (*outside*).

Oh, we don't give a damn
For the whole state of Michigan
The whole state of Michigan
The whole state of Michigan
Oh, we don't give a damn
For the whole state of Michigan
Now or ever more.

Rah-rah-rah-rah.   Ferguson—Ferguson—
Ferguson.

(The band starts another march. TOMMY
*has reappeared in the lower Right door a
moment after the general exit. He crosses
slowly, absently picking up soda on the
way, looks out after them, then closes the
door. The cheers for Ferguson and the
band music slowly die away as* TOMMY
*comes down, muttering: "Rah. Rah. Rah."
He looks at the soda in distaste; distaste
for himself. Glances at Victrola, switches it
on, dropping needle about twelve bars
from the end of the chorus. Victrola plays:)*

"Dreams I know can never come true.
Seems as though I'll always be blue.
Who-o-o means my happiness?
Who-o-o? Shall I answer yes?
Who-o-o? Well, you ought to guess.
Who? Who? No one but you."

*(*TOMMY *listens for a moment, then makes
awkwardly, solemnly, a couple of dance
steps, frowns, shakes his head, and drops
into settee Left giving it up. He drinks
the bitter cup of soda as the music ends
and)*

THE CURTAIN FALLS

ACT TWO

SCENE I

Same as Act One. About 1:00 P. M., the following day.
AT RISE: JOE, *with coat off, is Center, arranging plates, knives, forks, etc., on the
floor in the form of a football team's backfield. The end table has been moved below
the down Right settee and has evidently been used for serving luncheon as there are still
a plate, cup, etc.* ELLEN *is seated Center, finishing her coffee and watching* JOE.
PATRICIA *is down on her knees on the floor, Left Center, studying the array of dishes,
napkins, salt cellars and glasses which are ankle-deep around* JOE *in football formation.*
CLEOTA *enters from the dining room, carrying an empty tray. She crosses to the end
table down Right, begins clearing away the dishes.*

JOE. Now here—it's a balanced line. Move
those two men out a little more. *(*PATRICIA
moves men out.) This is a wonderful play.
*(Jumps downstage facing up. Puts down-
stage "backfield" in position.)*

ELLEN. Cleota, did you phone Mr. Turner's
office again?

CLEOTA *(at end table clearing away dishes).*
Yessum. Dey ain' no answeh.

PATRICIA. I saw Tommy, Ellen—about an
hour ago.

ELLEN. Where?

PATRICIA. He was walking out on the little
road back of the Ag buildings. Just moping
along. I yelled at him, but he didn't hear
me. *(*JOE *is counting men on the floor.)*

ELLEN. I'm getting worried.

JOE *(intent on his own activity).* Everything's going to be okay. Nothing to worry
about— Now, study this play, girls, or you
won't know it when you see it this afternoon. *(Points to downstage team.)* This
is Michigan. *(Points to upstage team,*

then jumps up.) And this is Midwestern.
—Now! From the balanced line, we shift.
Hup! *(He executes a Notre Dame shift.)*
Wally takes the left end's place, but he
plays out a little.

PATRICIA *(exchanges cup and cream
pitcher.* CLEOTA *moves to above table
Right.)* Isn't Wally going to carry the ball?

JOE. Shh! Michigan spreads out. They're
watching that wide end, but it's too obvious. They're watching the other side
of the line, too.

CLEOTA *(who has moved up Right, comes
down).* What's goin' on heah?

ELLEN. Shh! It's a football game.

JOE. The ball is snapped back. Now look,
here we go! Both of us. *(Carrying a plate
and a napkin up Left.)* Close together.
Fading back but threatening a left end
run as well as a pass.

PATRICIA. But who are you?

JOE. I'm both of them—Lindstrom and
Wierasocka.— *(Comes forward.)* Skolsky
cuts down the left side line deep and take

out Wupperman—that's the jam pot. (*Indicates down Left. Picks up "Wally."*) Wally is running wide around right end. (*Runs around down Right.*) faking as though he had the ball but hasn't really got it—apparently! (*At down Right.*) Now, then, just as Michigan is charging in on Lindstrom and Wierasocka, (*Crosses up Center.*) trying to decide which one has the ball, Wally lets himself out! *He's really got it!*

PATRICIA. Hooray!

JOE. It's a fake fake. It's an old play, so corny only a football genius like Coach Sprague would use it. With no interference at all, Wally cuts over and goes straight down the right side of the field! He stiff-arms the safety man— (*Running with the cream pitcher, around Right, he ends up down Center back to audience.*) Touchdown!

PATRICIA. Whoopee! (*She knocks over the jam pot.*) Oh, Lord, there goes Wupperman!

(*During* JOE's "*touchdown,*" TOMMY *has appeared quietly in door down Right. He watches* JOE *with distaste. No one notices him in the confusion.*)

CLEOTA. Um-hm. You through playin' now? (*PAT and* JOE *help her pick up dishes, working with backs to* TOMMY.)

PATRICIA. I'm sorry, Ellen.

ELLEN. It's all right. You can take the teams to the showers now, Cleota. Can't she, Joe?

JOE. Sure! How do you like it? (*PATRICIA and* CLEOTA *carry dishes up to sofa and pile them on tray.*)

ELLEN. I think it's nice. (*Puts cup on up Center table; crosses up to window.*)

JOE. Nice?! It's marvelous! That play is going to put us in the Rose Bowl. (*He puts dishes on down Right table. To* PATRICIA.) Did I ever tell you about how we used the Statue of Liberty play? (*Assumes attitude down Right.*) I would go back for a pass, and Jonesy would take it out of my hand and cut around to the left. (*CLEOTA picks up tray of dishes and exits up Right. Suddenly* JOE *realizes that, not the imaginary ball but the cup, has been taken out of his hand and that there is no Jonesy. He looks around slowly, puzzled, too late to have seen* TOMMY *quietly returning to the outdoors with the cup. Doorbell rings.*)

ELLEN (*crosses to door Left*). I'll answer it. (*Admits* DAMON *and they ad lib. in doorway.*) (*JOE looks to see where he might have dropped the cup; he is still puzzled.*)

PATRICIA (*starting for the stairs*). It's a wonderful play, Mr. Ferguson. If it works. (*Exits up stairs.*)

JOE. The coach gave it to me in strictest confidence. (*Gives another look for cup—repeats gesture with right arm drawn back and lifted, trying to re-live the scene.*)

(*ELLEN and* DAMON *have been ad libbing up Left.*)

ELLEN. Can you come in and wait, Doctor Damon? Tommy is out somewhere, but I'm expecting him back. (*CLEOTA exits with tray and dishes, leaving coffee things on Right table.*)

DAMON (*crossing down to Left*). I can't wait very long. (*Indicates magazine in pocket.*)

ELLEN (*following him*). Is that *The Literary Magazine?*

DAMON. It's a powder magazine. (*Coming down Center.*) Bombs are bursting all around. (*Sees* JOE, *who has been putting on coat and looking in drapes for cup.*) Oh—good afternoon.

JOE. Good afternoon, Doctor Damon.

(*Phone rings.*)

ELLEN. Excuse me, I'll— (*She goes to phone—picks up receiver.* DAMON *moves down Left Center.* JOE *is still looking for the vanished cup, moving drapes slightly.*) Hello— Yes, thank you. (*Hangs up.*) That was Ed Keller's office, Joe. He's on his way over here.

JOE. Oh, yeah. He called me this morning. He's fit to be tied about this *Literary Magazine* thing. Have you seen it?

DAMON (*from down Left Center*). Yes. This is it.

JOE (*crossing to* DAMON). May I take a look at it? Gosh, I didn't realize what this thing was— (*He takes magazine and scans editorial.*) Calls the trustees Fascists! This kid's dangerous—un-American.

DAMON. Oh, no!

ELLEN (*crossing to* JOE. *At same time*). Oh, no, not really. He's from an old Chillicothe family.

JOE. This is bad stuff for the university. I'm afraid all hell's going to break loose. Of course, it's none of my business, but—

DAMON (*taking the magazine out of* JOE's *hand*). You take the words right out of my mouth. I haven't had such a day since poor Doctor Prendergast shot his secretary. (*Crosses and sits down Left settee.*)

JOE. Well, I'm not a trustee, but I know how they feel.

ELLEN. I know. (*Crosses to down Right Center.*)

JOE. Tommy'd better deny this, pretty fast, and get himself out in the clear. I'm telling you. (*Crosses to* ELLEN.) I'm sorry about this, Ellen— Where is Tommy?

ELLEN. I don't know.

JOE. You don't think— (*Lowers voice to whisper.*) You don't think he may be a little sore about your going out with me last night?

ELLEN. I don't know. Oh, Joe, I'm all upset.

(*Doorbell rings.*)

JOE. Shall I answer it?

ELLEN. Would you?

JOE (*he opens door*). Hi, Ed!

ED (*in doorway*). Turner here?

ELLEN. No, he isn't.

ED. Well, I want to see him before the game. Tell him to call my office. Coming, Joe?

ELLEN (*quickly*). I don't know just when he'll— Won't you come in? Dean Damon is here.

ED. Oh! (*He comes into the room a few steps.* JOE *closes the door.* ED *crosses down to* DAMON.) Well, I'm glad somebody's here. How do you do, sir? Do you know where I could find President Cartwright?

DAMON. His secretary informed me that he is at the barber shop, having his beard trimmed.

ED. That'll be a big help! (*To* ELLEN, *then* JOE.) I thought Turner was going to deny this story. Papers keep calling *me*—they say he hasn't. Here I am, bearing the brunt of this damn disgraceful attack. "Fascists!" You oughta heard Si McMillan! And do you know Kressinger's in town from Detroit? (*Crosses down Left Center.*)

ELLEN. Is he a trustee, too?

DAMON. Oh, yes, young Michael certainly exploded his dynamite at a moment when the concentration of trustees is at its thickest.

ED (*crossing Center*). Yeh. There goes the new stadium. There goes your Endowment Fund! Unless something is done, and done quick! (*Crossing to* ELLEN.) Ellen, you tell your husband what I said!

JOE (*moving in*). Look, Ed, it isn't Ellen's fault.

ED (*crossing to* JOE). It isn't my fault, either. Here, I kept this whole week-end free. I've got my office full of eighteen-year-old Bourbon so we fellows could cut loose a little. And look what happens! All we need now is for Wierasocka to fumble a punt! (*Stomps out up Left.*)

JOE. I'll—see you later. (*Takes overcoat and hat up Left; follows* ED *out.*)

DAMON. I didn't like the way Mr. Keller said "There goes your Endowment Fund." (*Phone rings.*) If that's the newspapers I'm not here.

ELLEN (*rises—going toward phone*). Oh, I don't want to talk to them either. (*Goes to dining-room door. Calls.*) Cleota—

(*Phone rings again.*)

PATRICIA (*runs down the stairs*). I'm going out to talk to Michael. (*Runs into* ELLEN.) I got him on the phone but he hung up on me! (*Phone rings. Crossing Left.*) Good afternoon, Doctor Damon. (*Gets coat up Left.*) I'll knock his ears off. (*Slams out the Left door.*)

(*Phone rings.*)

DAMON (*calling after her*). Good afternoon, Patricia. (CLEOTA *enters from the dining room.*)

ELLEN. Answer the phone, Cleota.

CLEOTA (*crosses to phone*). Hello— Say what?—Says he is?—Ah didn' say yo—

said he was, I say what is it?—No, he ain' heah— No, dis ain' Miz Turner.

ELLEN (*prompting her*). Who is calling, please.

CLEOTA. Who's dis?—Wait a minute— (*Puts hand over mouthpiece—to* ELLEN.) It's de *Daily* sump'n.

ELLEN. Hang up, Cleota.

CLEOTA. G'bye. (*Hangs up and exits up Right.*)

ELLEN (*crossing to* DAMON). Oh, Lord, see what's happened already! Doctor Damon, suppose Tommy didn't read this letter?

DAMON. Let us not take refuge in conditional clauses, my dear.

ELLEN. Would you read it if you were Tommy?

DAMON. Now we go into the subjunctive. My dear, for forty-two years I have read nothing to my classes which was written later than the first half of the seventeenth century.

ELLEN (*turns up Left Center*). There must be some way—some compromise—that wouldn't be too humiliating.

DAMON. The policy of appeasement? Yes, it has its merits, and I'm afraid it's all I have to offer. (*Rises. Crossing to* ELLEN.) I can't wait any longer for Thomas. Tell him that if he decides not to read the letter, I shall feel easier in my mind. Much easier. (*Picks up hat. Comes back.*) And —slightly disappointed— Good afternoon, my dear— (*He opens the door, and in flies* PATRICIA. *They collide.* ELLEN *moves Right Center.*) Wup, wup, *wup!*

PATRICIA. Don't let Michael in! I don't want to talk to him any more! (*Crossing Right a few steps.*)

DAMON. Did you—uh—knock his ears off?

PATRICIA (*turns to* DAMON). I got him told. But he wants to tell me his side of it. He thinks *he* has a side.

DAMON. A common failing, my dear— Good afternoon. (*He goes out up Left.*)

PATRICIA (*bolts the door after him*). There, I've bolted that young genius out! (*Crossing to* ELLEN.) Oh, Ellen! Give me a football player any time. (*Crossing down Left*

Center.) Give me a guy without so much intellect or whatever it is. Somebody that doesn't want to be bawling the world out all the time—always doing something brave or fine or something. (*Turns as* MICHAEL *comes in down Right slamming door.*) Go away!

ELLEN. Quiet down, Patricia— Come in, Michael.

MICHAEL (*down Right. To* PATRICIA). You're being very silly.

ELLEN (*noticing* MICHAEL's *distraught look*). Can I give you a glass of milk?

MICHAEL. No, thank you. She won't listen to me, Mrs. Turner. I'm not trying to ruin your husband's life or my life or anybody's life. It's the principle of the thing she won't see.

PATRICIA. Oh, the principle! (*Crossing to Right Center.*) I'll bet nobody else would make a fool of himself and his friends and —my brother-in-law—over a principle.

(ELLEN, *taking the dishes with her, quietly slips out toward the kitchen, unnoticed by* MICHAEL.)

MICHAEL (*with the enormous gravity of the young man in love. Crossing Left to* PATRICIA). All right, Pat. I'm glad to know the qualities you admire in a man. They are certainly noble virtues, and I'm sure Wally is lousy with them.

PATRICIA. Oh, make up your mind who you're imitating, Ralph Waldo Emerson or Hemingway! You—you *writer!* (*Crosses below* MICHAEL *to down Right.*)

MICHAEL (*turns*). Now who's imitating Hemingway?

PATRICIA (*turns to him*). I wish you'd go away! (*Starts for door down Right.*)

MICHAEL (*crossing to up Left door*). I'm going! (*Goes to door, places hand on knob, turns.* PATRICIA *stops, turns, watches him.*) I'm going for good! I'm going out of your life! (*On the last word he jerks at door to make a dramatic exit, but it won't open, since* PAT *bolted it. Doorknob comes off in his hand.*)

PATRICIA (*with a smile of complete victory*). It's bolted, you dope! (*Exits down Right.*)

(MICHAEL *inserts knob and gets the door open finally. In walks* TOMMY *with the other doorknob in his hand. The two stand and look at each other. The knob has again come out in* MICHAEL'S *hand.*)

MICHAEL (*a little guiltily*). Sorry, Mr. Turner!

TOMMY. What's going on here? (MICHAEL *puts the knob in.* TOMMY *screws the other knob on.*)

MICHAEL. I was just going.

TOMMY. That's all right. Come in if you want to.

MICHAEL. Say, you look terrible.

TOMMY. Me? Why, what's the matter?

MICHAEL. I've got to get out of here.

TOMMY (*shuts door*). Oh, it's all right, Michael. Come in. Did somebody do something to you? (*Crossing Center.*)

MICHAEL. Patricia. She did plenty. I suppose it's just as well I've found out what she wants in life: a handsome, half-witted half-back.

TOMMY (*crossing to foot of stairs and looking up*). Yes, I know how that feels.

MICHAEL. Yes, sir. Well, you can't get anywhere with a woman who doesn't understand what you have to do.

TOMMY (*crosses to* MICHAEL). No. No, you can't, Michael. You'd like to, but you can't— Well— Good-bye, Michael— Come back in about an hour, will you? I want to give you a piece of my mind.

MICHAEL (*puzzled*). Yes, sir. (*Exits up Left.*) (TOMMY *looks around—takes cup out of pocket and puts it on table up Center; hangs up coat and hat up Left, then crosses to settee Left and sits thinking.*)

ELLEN (*enters up Right*). Oh, hello, darling!

TOMMY. Hello.

ELLEN (*crossing to him*). Well, I'm glad you remembered where you live. I was beginning to be worried. We phoned your office three times, but nobody knew where you were.

TOMMY (*looking up slowly*). Huh?

ELLEN. I say nobody knew where you were —since early this morning.

TOMMY. I was walking.

ELLEN. Without any breakfast? All this time?

TOMMY (*rises. Crosses down Left*). Well, I—came around to the back door a while ago, but Joe was doing the Statue of Liberty or something again, so I went away.

ELLEN. You were right here and you went away?

TOMMY (*crosses down Right*). Yes, I couldn't face that right now. Not the Statue of Liberty.

ELLEN. Oh! Well, Doctor Damon's been here—and Ed Keller, and the newspapers have been calling up. There's going to be a lot of trouble if you don't hurry up and deny that story of Michael's—or have you done it?

TOMMY. No—I haven't denied it.

ELLEN (*center. Troubled*). You mean you've made up your mind to read it? Is that what you've been—walking around for? Tommy, I don't know what to say to you.

TOMMY (*turns. Crosses to her*). I think maybe you've said enough already.

ELLEN. That isn't very kind.

TOMMY. None of this is going to sound very kind but I've figured out exactly what I want to say, and I have to get it out before I get all mixed up.

ELLEN. I don't see why you are being so mean.

TOMMY. It's just that last night I began to see you, and myself, clearly for the first time. (*Crosses above* ELLEN *up Left.*)

ELLEN (*turns downstage*). If this is a story you're writing, and you're trying it out on me, it isn't very good.

TOMMY. Oh, I saw you and Joe clearly, too.

ELLEN (*relieved. Crossing to* TOMMY *a little*). Oh, you saw him kiss me— I thought that was it—

TOMMY (*covering*). No— No, I didn't— Did he kiss you? Well, that's fine—I've been meaning to ask you, what became of Housman's "Last Poems"? (*Turns to Left bookcase.*)

ELLEN *(crossing up to* TOMMY*)*. Tommy, *(Puts her hand on his shoulder.)* listen to me—I wanted to have a good time last night, and you spoiled it—

TOMMY *(turns to her)*. Didn't you enjoy it at all?

ELLEN *(piqued)*. Yes, I did. *(Crossing Right two steps.)* I'm not a hundred years old—yet. I just decided to quit worrying about you, and have a little fun. For about an hour I felt like a girl again—wearing flowers at a Spring Dance—when I was young and silly—

TOMMY. Young and happy.

ELLEN *(turns to* TOMMY*)*. All right, he—kissed me. I kissed him, too. *(Crossing to* TOMMY.*)* We didn't go out in the dark to do it.

TOMMY *(piling books he is taking from book shelves on down Left settee)*. I hope you didn't lend that book to anybody; it was a first edition.

ELLEN. Did *you* hear what *I* said?

TOMMY. Sure, I heard you. I'm listening—You said you went out in the dark and kissed Joe.

ELLEN *(turns. Crossing to down Right Center)*. I said no such thing, and you know it.

TOMMY *(still at bookcase)*. I wish we had had separate book-plates.

ELLEN *(turns to him)*. So that when you really make me mad and I get out of here, I can find my own books quickly?

TOMMY *(at bookcase)*. I hate sentimental pawing over things by a couple breaking up. We're not living in the days of Henry James Meredith. Look at Joe and his wife.

ELLEN. Tommy, *(Crossing Left to up Left Center.)* I want you to stop this. If you're going to be jealous *be* jealous, rave or throw things, but don't act like the lead in a Senior Class play! *(This thrust gets home.)*

TOMMY *(up Left)*. I'm trying to tell you that I don't care what you and Joe do. I'm trying to tell you that it's fine. It's very lucky that he came back just now.

ELLEN. What do you mean?

TOMMY. I mean on the money *I* make, I can go on fine alone, reading whatever I want to to my classes. That's what I want. And that's what I'm going to do.

ELLEN. Oh, that's what you want! Suddenly that's what you want. More than me?

TOMMY. It isn't so sudden. *(Crossing Right.)* Not any more sudden than your feeling for Joe. It's logical. We get in each other's way. You wear yourself out picking up after me. Taking matches out of my pockets. *(Finds matches in pockets and throws them on table Right.)* Disarranging my whole way of life. *(Sits on down Right settee.)*

ELLEN *(follows him to chair Right Center)*. Why haven't you said all this before?

TOMMY. I couldn't very well.

ELLEN. Why couldn't you? If you felt this way?

TOMMY. Well, we hadn't split up on this letter issue, for one thing—and then there was no place for you to go. I didn't want you to have to go back to Cleveland, or to work in some tea shoppe.

ELLEN. Oh, I see. Some tea shoppe! That's what you think I'd have to do! *(Crosses up Right.)* Well, you needn't have spared my feelings. I can make as much money as you.

TOMMY. You don't have to, now.

ELLEN *(turns)*. Oh, you mean you waited to tell me this till Joe came along! I thought you were jealous of Joe. I could understand that. You aren't the least bit aroused at the idea of his kissing me— *(Crosses downstage, drives this at him.)* out in the dark—for hours!

TOMMY. No, I'm not.

ELLEN. So that's why you've been wandering around! That's what you've been figuring out! How nice it would be if he would take me off your hands, so you could be left alone with your books and match-boxes and *litter!* *(Crosses to Left Center.)* I suppose any man would do as well as Joe. *(Crosses back to* TOMMY *two steps.)*

TOMMY *(crossing to her)*. He's not just any man, and you know that. He's always been in love with you, and you've always been in love with him! *(He is angry and jealous now.)*

ELLEN *(crossing Left)*. That's ridiculous!

TOMMY *(moving toward her)*. I felt it when I saw you dancing together. It was unmistakable. You've just admitted it.

ELLEN *(turns. Crossing to him)*. Oh, you can't do that now! You can't be jealous now just because you think I want you to be!

TOMMY. I saw you dancing together—like angels! *(ELLEN turns away.)* I saw you go out in that carriage together! I saw you together years ago, when I was young enough and dumb enough to believe that I really took you away from him. *(Ellen turns back.)* There's something that happens when you two dance together that doesn't happen when we dance together!

ELLEN. All right—have it your way. If you want to be free, then I want to be free— and I've gone around for ten years mooning about Joe— Well, maybe I have— maybe I have, because I'm certainly sick of you right now! *(Whirls away from him.)*

TOMMY *(shaking her)*. Ellen—Ellen, listen—

ELLEN. Never mind—all right—*all right*— *ALL RIGHT!* *(She breaks away up Center—suddenly stops short as* JOE *enters Left brightly.)*

JOE. Oh, I'm sorry—if I— *(He stops in embarrassment. There is a pause. He has caught only the tone; but he sees and feels the tension. He is carrying a wrapped bottle and a newspaper. He removes overcoat, lays it on chair up Left.)*

TOMMY *(crossing down right)*. Hello, Joe!

JOE. Hello! *(Pause.)* I brought the rum. *(Holds up bottle, sees only their backs. Crosses down to coffee table Left. Puts bottle on table; holds up newspaper.)* Big picture of Wally all over the front page. *(Silence.)* Good picture, isn't it?

TOMMY. You and Ellen have some rum.

JOE. The rum's for the punch—later.

ELLEN. Could I have some—now? *(Sits on sofa up Center.)* *(Tommy exits up Right.)*

JOE *(surprised)*. Right now?—Sure. *(U[n]wraps bottle; throws paper in waste-bask[et] up Left.)*

TOMMY *(from dining room)*. I'll get yo[u] some glasses. *(Re-enters—crosses Left [.]* JOE *with two glasses, then goes above se[t]tee Left, glancing at* ELLEN.*)*

JOE *(unscrewing the top)*. Tommy, o[ld] man, I just left Ed Keller and Si McMilla[n.] This thing your young friend wrote in th[e] magazine. *(Pours drink.)* I read the pie[ce] over again. He's got you on a spo[t,] Tommy. *(Crosses to* ELLEN—*gives h[er] drink.)*

ELLEN. Want to drink a toast, Joe?—T[o] Tommy's happiness?

JOE *(looks at both of them—then cross[es] down Left.)* Sure— *(Pours himself drin[k] —crosses up—offers toast.)* Your happ[i]ness, Tommy. *(They drink amid a lon[g] silence,* JOE *nervously finishing his;* ELLE[N] *taking a long drink, grimacing as the drin[k] burns her throat.)* What's the matter[?] What's it about? Maybe I could talk [to] Ed—

TOMMY. No. I don't want that. I'll run m[y] own life my own way.

ELLEN. That's what it's about. Tomm[y] wants to—live alone.

JOE. What?

ELLEN. He wants to be left alone—

JOE. I beg your pardon?

ELLEN. Us! Tommy and me! We're breal[k]ing up!

JOE *(awed, puzzled)*. Just before th[e] game—? *(*TOMMY *puts books from sette[e] down Left on fireplace bench.)* You'[re] both crazy! Maybe I better go.

TOMMY. Not at all! You're not exactly [a] stranger around here. You knew Ellen [as] long ago as I did.

JOE. I knew her a long time before yo[u] did—and this is a fine way to be treatin[g] her.

TOMMY *(baiting a hook)*. Yes, I know. [I] was just saying I barged in and took h[er] away from you.

JOE. Oh, no, you didn't. You had nothin[g] to do with it. She got sor[e] at me on ac[c]count of another girl.

TOMMY. Oh, that's where I came in?

JOE. Sure! If you think you took her away from me, you're crazy. Here, you better have some rum.

ELLEN. He can't drink this early.

TOMMY (sits settee down Left). I don't need any rum. Go on, Joe.

JOE (sits Right end of sofa). Well, Ellen and I had a fight. You weren't in on it. You came in later—

ELLEN. Joe, do we have to—

TOMMY. It's all right. It's his turn.

JOE. She said she hated me and never wanted to see me again. She threw something at me. She thought I went away with this girl—I mean—

TOMMY. Never mind—I know what you mean—

ELLEN. I never said you went. I never said that.

JOE. Oh, yes, you did—you intimated it.

ELLEN. No, that was your idea. I thought you were bragging about it.

JOE. Well, you got awfully mad. I thought you never did want to see me again. I guess I was dumb. Brenda says it shows you liked me. (From ELLEN's expression, JOE is reminded of TOMMY's presence; he turns.) Oh—sorry!

TOMMY. Oh, don't mind me. Who's Brenda? Another girl?

JOE. My wife.

TOMMY. Oh, sorry!

JOE. Ellen knows her. She's from Cleveland. Brenda's always been jealous of Ellen. She found a picture of you.

TOMMY. What picture?

ELLEN. I gave him a picture. He wouldn't give it back.

JOE. It's a swell picture. You were wearing that floppy hat. Red.

ELLEN. Blue.

JOE. It had ribbons. Made you look like you were sixteen.

TOMMY. I've never seen it.

ELLEN. It was a silly hat. This was ages ago.

TOMMY. I mean, I've never seen the picture.

ELLEN (angrily). I threw them all away.

JOE (remembering). It kind of went down over one eye.

TOMMY. She looks nice in hats like that.

(ELLEN suddenly begins to cry; collapses on sofa.)

JOE (rising). Now look what you've done!

TOMMY (rising). Look what you've done! Bringing up old floppy blue hats! (JOE moves to ELLEN.) Don't touch her! She doesn't like to be touched when she's crying. (Crosses to Left Center.)

JOE. I've seen her cry. I know what to do.

TOMMY. Oh, you do?

JOE. She cried when we had that fight about the girl. She was lying on the floor and kicking and crying—on her stomach.

ELLEN. I was not!

TOMMY. Be careful what you say!

JOE. Well, I mean I knew what to do. (Crosses to other end of sofa.) I picked her up then.

TOMMY. Well, you're not going to pick her up now. (Crosses below JOE.)

ELLEN. Will you both please let me alone?! Will you please go away!

JOE. There! She wants you to go away. And I don't blame her, if this is the way you treat her. I wouldn't have stood for it ten years ago, and I'm not going to stand for it now.

TOMMY (crossing to JOE a step). But what are you going to do?

JOE. I'm going to get her away from all this! It isn't nice!

TOMMY. It isn't exactly to my taste, either. (Crossing to up Left end of sofa.) I didn't want it to turn out this way, but it did: me feeling like a cad, Ellen crying, and you acting like a fool.

JOE. Me acting like a fool?

ELLEN. Everybody's acting like a fool. (Puts glass up Center table.)

JOE *(crossing down Right Center)*. You've certainly messed things up, brother.

TOMMY. Don't call me brother! *(From up Left Center.)* I can't stand that, now! *(In one step.)*

JOE. If Ellen weren't here, I'd call you worse than brother.

ELLEN *(sitting up)*. Well, I'm not going to be here! Please, please, stop—both of you! Nobody has said a word about what *I* want to do. You're going to settle that between yourselves. Bandying me back and forth!

TOMMY *(crossing to her)*. Nobody's bandying you, Ellen.

ELLEN *(sniffling)*. I know when I'm being bandied! *(Rises—looks at them.)* I don't want either of you! You can both go to hell! *(Runs upstairs, crying.)*

TOMMY *(up to stairs. JOE also crosses to stairs. BOTH look up, then each looks away)*. She means me.

JOE. She said both of us.

TOMMY. She was looking at me.

JOE. How did we get into this anyway?

TOMMY. You two-stepped into it. You kissed your way into it.

JOE *(crossing down to below Right Center chair)*. I'm sorry about that. Sorry it happened.

TOMMY. You're not sorry it happened. You're sorry I found it out. *(Crossing to Left of up Center sofa.)* Do you know anything about women? *(Crossing to JOE.)* Didn't you know what she was thinking about when she was dancing with you?

JOE. No. I don't think when I'm dancing.

TOMMY. I know. You think in your office. Well, you'll have to think in your home after this. She likes to be thought about.

JOE. I thought about her. I remembered her birthday. I brought her flowers.

TOMMY. Well, you'll have to keep on bringing her things—fur coats and things— She's still young and pretty.

JOE. I don't get you.

TOMMY. I'm being broadminded. *(Crossing Left.)* I'm taking things in my stride. It's the modern way of doing things. You ought to know that.

JOE *(shrewdly)*. What makes me think you're still crazy about her and are up to some damn something or other?

TOMMY. Don't be acute. I couldn't stand you being acute. *(Crossing down Left.)*

JOE. I'm not dumb.

TOMMY *(turning back to him)*. Yes, you are. *(Crossing Right to JOE.)* It isn't what I feel that counts. It's what she feels. I think she's always been in love with you. Why, I don't know. It's supposed to be beyond reason. I guess it is.

JOE. You just think that because of last night?

TOMMY. No. Because of what lay behind last night. That wasn't just a kiss. That's nothing. *(Crosses up Center, and turns.)* This thing is too deep for jealousy or for anything but honesty. A woman must not go on living with a man when she dances better with another man.

JOE. That's silly. *(Crossing down Right.)* That's the silliest— *(Crossing up Left to TOMMY up Center.)* Dancing doesn't mean everything.

TOMMY. The way you *do* it does. The things that happen to you. The light you give off.

JOE. *Light?!*

TOMMY. Oh, these things are too subtle for you, Joe. I've made some study of them. *(Turns away.)*

JOE. Maybe all this studying's bad for you.

TOMMY. All I want to know is whether you felt the same thing she felt last night.

JOE. I felt fine. *(Crossing Right.)* This is embarrassing! *(Crossing Left to TOMMY.)* A man makes love to a woman. He doesn't talk it over with her husband!

TOMMY. I'm just trying to be honest.

JOE *(crossing below TOMMY to down Left)*. You're a funny guy. Conscientious. What does it get you? Like this letter you're going to read— Say, is that what started the trouble?

TOMMY. Yes, it's an integral part of the trouble—things like that.

JOE (*sits Right end down Left settee*). Well, what are we going to do? I mean now? I mean from now on?

TOMMY. From now on will work itself out. Right now you'd better go upstairs and comfort her. She'll be expecting you.

JOE. Oh, no. Not me! You ought to know more what to do right now. It's your house. She's still your wife.

TOMMY (*crossing to* JOE). She doesn't want to talk to me. She's just done that. But she oughtn't to be left alone right now. (JOE *hesitates.*) Well, don't be a big baby!!

JOE (*crossing Right to stairs, turns*). It doesn't seem right somehow for me to go upstairs.

TOMMY. This is not a moment for cheap moralizing!

JOE. Well—good God Almighty! (*Goes upstairs.*) (TOMMY *looks after* JOE *then sits on sofa up Center.*)

MICHAEL (*comes in up Left door as* TOMMY *sighs deeply*). What's the matter?

TOMMY (*sees him*). Oh! Why don't you knock? Never mind— (*Rises. Crosses down and paces; he glares upstairs, still has his glare when he turns back to* MICHAEL.)

MICHAEL. Well, I came back like you said.

TOMMY. *As* you said. Oh—never mind! (*The two* MEN *pace, meeting down Right Center.*)

MICHAEL. Before you start in on me, Mr. Turner, please remember that I've been through a lot today. I can't stand much more.

TOMMY (*pats him on shoulder*). Thanks.

MICHAEL (*at Center. Gloomily*). They'll probably do something to you—especially if we lose to Michigan. You know what Keller did the last time they beat us in a Homecoming Game? He ran the flag on his office building down to half mast.

TOMMY (*looking upstairs—distracted. Crossing around to up Right Center; then to landing.*) Don't worry about me.

MICHAEL. Well, I'm feeling better. I've put her out of my mind. It's ended as simply as that. (*Drops into chair Right Center.*)

There's a girl who could sit with you and talk about Shelley. Well, I'm glad I found out about women. (*Crash upstairs.*) What was that?

TOMMY. I'm sure I don't know. What were you saying? (*Crosses up Center.*)

MICHAEL. I say Patricia knew things. She knew odd things like, "A Sonnet on Political Greatness": (TOMMY *paces up Left Center.*) she quoted that one night. Wouldn't you think a girl like that had some social consciousness?

TOMMY (*sits sofa up Center*). That's the sonnet that ends: "Quelling the anarchy of hopes and fears,
Being himself alone."

MICHAEL. Yes, but when an issue comes up and a man has to be himself alone, she reveals the true stature of her character and goes off to Hennick's with that football player. I saw them—right in the front window—drinking Seven-Up—he uses a straw.

TOMMY (*crossing down to* MICHAEL). Yes, but he's handsome. (*Paces.*) What is more, he whirls. He's a hunter. He comes home at night with meat slung over his shoulders, and you sit there drawing pictures on the wall of your cave. (*Crosses around Left to down Left; then up Center.*)

MICHAEL. I see. Maybe I ought to sock him with a ball bat.

TOMMY (*crossing Center*). No. You are a civilized man, Michael. If the male animal in you doesn't like the full implications of that, he must nevertheless be swayed by Reason. You are not living in the days of King Arthur when you fought for your woman. (*Crossing down Left.*) Nowadays, the man and his wife and the other man talk it over. Quietly and calmly. They all go out to dinner together. (*Sits Right end settee down Left.*)

MICHAEL. Intellectually, Patricia is sleeping with that guy. I feel like going out to-night with the Hot Cha-cha.

TOMMY. With the what?

MICHAEL. It's a girl. They call her that. What if she was kicked out of the Pi Phi House? She's honest! She does what she believes in! And—well, Hot Cha-cha doesn't argue all the time anyway.

TOMMY. Look, Michael, hasn't she got a name? You don't call her *that,* do you?

MICHAEL. Marcia Gardner. They just call her—

TOMMY. Yes, you told me what they call her. *(Slight pause.)*

MICHAEL *(transformed).* Patricia's not coming to class when you read that letter. She's gone over to the Philistines— Oh, Mr. Turner, I wish I were like you! Middle-aged, settled down, happily marrried— *(TOMMY takes off his glasses and peers across at MICHAEL.)* and through with all this hell you feel when you're young and in love.

TOMMY *(nettled).* Middle-aged?

MICHAEL. Yes, you know what Rupert Brooke says:

"That time when all is over, *(TOMMY writhes, turns his back.)*
And love has turned to kindliness."

Is kindliness peaceful?

TOMMY. Don't ask me. *(Two quick crashes from upstairs bring TOMMY to his feet as JOE enters down the stairs, looking worn and worried, his hair slightly disarranged. TOMMY crosses to JOE. Sharply.)* You look ruffled!

JOE *(just as sharply, but a bit absently).* What? *(The two MEN look each other over.)*

TOMMY. I say—what ruffled you?

JOE. Do we have to discuss these things in front of this boy?

MICHAEL *(rising. Crossing to JOE).* I am not a boy.

TOMMY. This is Michael Barnes. *(Goes up Left Center, looking upstairs.)*

JOE *(turning to MICHAEL).* Oh, so you're the little boy that started all this! I want to tell you that you write too much, you have too much to say, you get too many people into too much trouble. You've not only got Tommy and Ellen involved, but me. *(Gesturing to TOMMY—upstairs—to himself.)*

MICHAEL. I don't see how this concerns you, do you, Mr. Turner?

TOMMY. Yes. *(Crosses down to Right end of settee Left.)*

MICHAEL. What?

JOE *(waving MICHAEL out).* Goodbye!

MICHAEL *(in wordless wrath at being treated like a child).* Oh! *(Exits down Right to garden.)*

JOE. Oh, God, I wish I was in Pittsburgh: *(Sits Right Center chair.)*

TOMMY *(eagerly).* What happened?

JOE. Well, old man, I guess you're right. She was pretty bitter—about you. She picked up something you'd given her and threw it against the wall and broke it into a thousand pieces.

TOMMY. What was it?

JOE. I didn't see it till after she threw it.

TOMMY *(sits sofa up Center).* Oh!

JOE. Every time she mentioned your name, she threw something. Kept me ducking.

TOMMY *(sadly).* I see. You want to marry Ellen, don't you?

JOE. Well, I always liked her, but I don't like to go through so much. *(Pause.)* Are you sure you understand women?

TOMMY. Yes.

JOE. Well, when Ellen and I had that fight about the girl, she threw things on account of me, and Brenda thinks that meant she was in love with me. Now she throws things on account of *you.*

TOMMY *(after an instant of hope).* In both instances, she threw them at *you,* didn't she?

JOE *(glumly).* Yeh, I guess so.

TOMMY. Well, there you are. What did she say when you left? What was she doing?

JOE. She was in a terrible state. I don't think she'll be able to go to the game. She may have a sick headache for days. What do you do then?

TOMMY. Get her a hot water bottle. *(Rises. Crossing up Right to dining room.)* Cleota!—Cleota!

CLEOTA *(off).* Yes, suh?

TOMMY. There's a hot water bottle out there in the—somewhere. *(Returning.)* Fill it and bring it in, please.

CLEOTA (off). Yes, suh.

(TOMMY crosses and sits on sofa up Center.)

JOE (rises. Glances at wrist-watch. Crossing down Left). I don't want to miss this game. I sort of wish Stalenkiwiecz wasn't laid up, don't you? (Crossing to Center.)

TOMMY. I haven't given it much thought one way or another.

JOE (crossing down Right). Of course, Wierasocka's all right, but Stalenkiwiecz is a better pass-receiver.

TOMMY. Is he? Why?

JOE (turning to TOMMY). I don't know why. He just is. "Why!" (His pacing has carried him to lower door, Right. He remembers the vanishing cup and takes one more look.) 'Course they may not give Brenda a divorce. (Crossing Left.)

TOMMY. I think they will.

JOE. I don't know.

CLEOTA (enters up Right with hot water bottle and folded towel. She hands them to TOMMY on up Center sofa). Is you gotta pain?

TOMMY. No.—Oh, thank you.

(CLEOTA exits up Right.)

JOE (pacing Left). I don't suppose we ought to go and leave her.

TOMMY (rises. Going to him with bottle). Oh, I'm not going. Here. (Hands him bottle and towel.)

JOE (taking it. It burns his hand). Ow!

TOMMY. Hold it by the end.

JOE. Won't this thing burn her?

TOMMY (impatiently). You wrap the towel around it. (Places towel around shoulders of bottle. Crosses up Center, then down around Right Center chair to down Right.)

JOE. You shouldn't stay here in the house alone with her, things being the way they are, should you?

TOMMY. Please don't worry about that!

JOE (looking at the bottle). I thought these things were different now than they used to be.

TOMMY. What do you mean, different?

JOE. I mean better looking—somehow. (There is a pause during which JOE tries to wrap the towel around the hot water bottle but various parts of it insist on remaining exposed. Finally TOMMY, who has moved upstage, crosses down to JOE angrily.)

TOMMY. Well, why don't you take it up to her?

ELLEN (coming down the stairs). It's time to get started, isn't it? (The two MEN turn and stare at her, JOE still holding the hot water bottle. ELLEN is utterly serene, with no sign of tears or hysterics. Washed and powdered, with her hat on, she stands at the foot of the stairs, putting on her gloves.) Do you realize what time it is? The Kellers will be waiting for us at Esther Baker's. We'll leave the car there and walk to the stadium. It's only a block. (The MEN are still staring. She crosses to JOE.) What are you doing with that thing, Joe?

TOMMY. He was going to lie down with it for a while.

JOE. I was not! Here! (Tries to hand it to TOMMY.)

TOMMY. I don't want it.

ELLEN. We've got to hurry, Joe. (Takes the bottle from JOE and puts it on sofa up Center.) Have you got the tickets?

JOE. Yeh, I've got them. (Down Left to radio.) Say, what number is the game on?

ELLEN. It's around 1210 on the dial. (As JOE turns on radio and fiddles with dial—to TOMMY.) Sure you won't go to the game?

TOMMY. Oh, no— (With shy politeness.) How are you?

(Dance music is heard on the radio. JOE keeps fiddling with dials trying to find the right station.)

ELLEN. Me? I'm fine.

(Band music is heard on the radio.)

TOMMY. That's good.

JOE (after listening to music). Well, it hasn't started yet—just music. Let's go. (Gets ELLEN's coat from hook.) This yours?

ELLEN (as he helps her into coat). Yes.

JOE. Well, is it warm enough?

ELLEN. Yes. Oh, it's very warm.

TOMMY. No, it isn't.

CLEOTA (*enters with thermos. Gives it to* TOMMY *at Center*). Here's your thermos bottle, Mr. Turner.

TOMMY. Thank you. (*Takes it.*) (CLEOTA *exits up right.*)

ELLEN. It's a very warm day, anyway, and we'll have the laprobe from the car.

TOMMY. Ellen. (*She crosses to him eagerly.*) You forgot your thermos bottle— You'd better make a note of this, Joe. It gets cold in stadiums late in the afternoon. Ellen gets chilly sometimes, so she likes hot coffee. (JOE *nods, goes to the Left door and opens it.* ELLEN, *who has been staring at* TOMMY, *suddenly throws the thermos bottle on the floor, then rushes out, passing* JOE. JOE *looks after her, then comes back to face* TOMMY *threateningly.*)

JOE. Did you slap her?

TOMMY. No, I kicked her.

JOE. Well, you must have done something! (*The radio, which has been playing band music changes to an* ANNOUNCER'S VOICE.)

JOE (*picks thermos bottle up from floor, puts it on down Left table, listens to* radio *for a moment.*) Here I get her all calmed down and you make her cry again. I see now what kind of a life she has here. I'm going to take her away from this and keep her away!

TOMMY (*shouting*). All right! Why don't you get started?

ANNOUNCER'S VOICE (*over band*). Well, here we are on Midwestern field on a mighty fine afternoon for a football game. (*Voice quieter.*) It looks like the Big Day of the year, folks. Neither one of these great teams has lost a game. The Michigan squad is out on the field, warming up. They look even bigger than last year.—

JOE (*topping him*). Because I've got a few more things to say to you. First! (*As he takes a breath, the* ANNOUNCER'S VOICE *comes through clearly.*)

ANNOUNCER'S VOICE. Here comes the Scarlet Stampede now! (*There is a roar of cheering and the Band's music swells.*)

JOE (*turns to radio, then in an agonized voice to* TOMMY). My God, they're coming out on the field! We'll miss the kick-off! (*Turns and dashes out the Left door.*)

(TOMMY *stands looking after them as*

THE CURTAIN FALLS

SCENE II

The Turner living room, two hours later. It is growing dark outside.

TOMMY *on settee down Right and* MICHAEL *in chair Right Center, wide apart, facing the audience, so that they have to turn their heads to see each other. Each has a glass in his hand, and they are sprawled in their seats, silent, brooding. The room shows indications of quite a bout: a bottle here, a few magazines flung there, a cushion on the floor.* TOMMY *gets the Scotch bottle, pours a little into* MICHAEL's *glass, emptying the bottle. He starts to pour some into his own glass, finds the bottle empty so pours some from* MICHAEL's *glass into his own. Throws the bottle into waste-basket. There is a pause.*

MICHAEL. He is probably still running with that ball—

TOMMY (*pause*). Quiet—quiet!— What time it it?

MICHAEL (*looks at wrist-watch, has trouble seeing it*). It's getting dark.

TOMMY (*pause*). Do you know the first law of human nature?

MICHAEL. Yes. Self-propagation.

TOMMY. Not any more. That's gone with last year's nightingale.

MICHAEL. Gone with last year's rose.

TOMMY (*slight pause*). Yes— Defense of the home—against prowlers and predatory —prowlers— Do you know what the tiger does when the sanctity of his home is jeopardized?

MICHAEL. I know. You told me. He talks it over with the other man, quietly and calmly.

TOMMY. He does not. I'm ashamed of you.

MICHAEL. I think we must have another drink—possibly.

TOMMY. All right. Hey! *Hey!* (*He is pleased with this shouting.*) That's the way to talk to 'em. *(He puts back his head and yells.)* Heyyy!!

(CLEOTA enters: she turns on the lights up Right.)

CLEOTA *(hurrying down to* TOMMY, *worried)*. Mistah Turner, what is it?

TOMMY. What do you want?—Oh, we should like to have something more to drink.

CLEOTA *(disgusted)*. Dey ain' no more to drink. I'll make you all some black coffee. *(Exits up Right.)*

TOMMY *(pause)*. What'd she say?

MICHAEL. Nothing.

TOMMY. Where was I?

MICHAEL. Let's see—you were talking about tigers.

TOMMY. Oh, yes. But let us take the wolf. What does he do? I mean, when they come for his mate. He tears 'em to pieces. *(Illustrates.)*

MICHAEL. But we are civilized men. Aren't we?

TOMMY. And so does the leopard, and the lion, and the hawk. They tear 'em to pieces. Without a word.

MICHAEL. You had it figured out the other way around a while ago. You said we should give up our women. *(*TOMMY *stands, falters.)* It's better sitting down. *(*TOMMY *sits.)*

TOMMY. Let us say that the tiger wakes up one morning and finds that the wolf has come down on the fold. What does he—? Before I tell you what he does, I will tell you what he does not do.

MICHAEL. Yes, sir.

TOMMY. He does not expose everyone to a humiliating intellectual analysis. He comes out of his corner like this— *(Assumes awkward fighting pose, fists up—rises—sits quickly.)* The bull elephant in him is aroused.

MICHAEL *(holds up forefinger)*. Can't you stick to one animal?

TOMMY. No, that's my point. All animals are the same, including the human being. We are male animals, too.

MICHAEL *(stares at him, bewildered)*. You said—

TOMMY *(with emotion)*. Even the penguin. He stands for no monkey-business where his mate is concerned. Swans have been known to drown Scotties who threatened their nests.

MICHAEL *(after some thought)*. I don't think so.

TOMMY. There it is, in us always, though it may be asleep. The male animal. The mate. When you are married long enough, you become a mate— Think of the sea lion for a minute.

MICHAEL. All right.

TOMMY. His mate is lying there in a corner of the cave on a bed of tender boughs or something. *(Turns to* MICHAEL *for confirmation.)* Is that all right, "tender boughs"?

MICHAEL. Yeah!

TOMMY *(imitating fish swimming with hand gestures)*. Now, who comes swimming quietly in through the early morning mist, sleek and powerful, dancing and whirling and throwing kisses?

MICHAEL. Joe Ferguson.

TOMMY. And what do I do?

MICHAEL. You say, "Hello."

TOMMY. The sea lion knows better. He snarls. He gores. He roars with his antlers. He knows that love is a thing you do something about. He knows it is a thing that words can kill. You do something. You don't just sit there. *(*MICHAEL *rises.)* I don't mean you. *(*MICHAEL *sits.)* A woman likes a man who does something. All the male animals fight for the female, from the land crab to the bird of paradise. They don't just sit and talk. *(*MICHAEL *is almost asleep.)* They act. *(He has run-down, now stops, almost asleep. His head jerks and wakens him. He removes glasses and blinks owlishly around.)* I hope I have made all this clear to you. Are there any questions?

MICHAEL *(rousing)*. No, sir.

(ELLEN and JOE enter up Left. ELLEN goes down Center, sees the disordered room, bottles on the floor, TOMMY's *and* MI-

CHAEL's *condition.* MICHAEL *and* TOMMY *rise.*)

ELLEN. Tommy! What in the world have you been doing. (MICHAEL *holds out glass to illustrate.*)

TOMMY. Drinking.

ELLEN. What for?

TOMMY (*crossing to* ELLEN). I was celebrating. Ellen, I have found myself. (*Sways for a second. Surveys* JOE.) I know now what I have to do.

ELLEN. Yes, I know. We've been through all that.

TOMMY. I think perhaps you had better go away for a little while. (*Waves toward upstairs.*)

ELLEN. I'm going. I'll be down in a minute, Joe. (*She slams upstairs.*)

JOE. Boy, wasn't that some football game? I'm running Wally Myers for President.

TOMMY (*beckoning to* MICHAEL, *who follows him to settee down Left*). Come on. (*He and* MICHAEL *begin moving furniture to the sides of the room. Moves settee Left to against Left wall.*)

JOE (*crosses up Right end of sofa. Watches, slightly puzzled, making talk*). Yes, sir, some game, wasn't it? What did you think of Michigan going into the lead like that? If Wally hadn't snared that pass—

MICHAEL. We didn't listen to the game. (*Moving coffee table to Left wall.*)

JOE. You didn't listen to the game? (*Crosses slowly to Left end of sofa.*)

MICHAEL. No, we turned it off. (*Gesture of turning off radio.*)

TOMMY (*crossing to chair Right Center.* MICHAEL *follows*). The game didn't last all this time. Where have you been?

JOE. Well, we stopped in at President Cartwright's house.

TOMMY (*they swing Right Center chair, moving it upstage a little*). What for?

JOE. 'Cause Ellen and I were making one last effort to get you out of this mess.

TOMMY. Ellen and you. (TOMMY *and* MICHAEL *get down Right end table,*

MICHAEL *on Left end,* TOMMY *Right end.*) You would know exactly what to do, wouldn't you?

JOE. You guys are pie-eyed!

TOMMY. Did you hear that? (*As* MICHAEL *swings his end of table all the way around up Right,* TOMMY *looks for him—then finds him upstage. They put end table down.*)

MICHAEL. Yes.

JOE. What's the idea of moving all the furniture around like this?

TOMMY (*crossing Center*). I don't want you to break anything when you fall. (MICHAEL *picks up seltzer bottles down Right Center and puts them on end table Right.*)

JOE. I'm not going to fall.

TOMMY. Yes, you are. (*Crosses to down Right table and puts down glasses; crosses Left to* JOE, *rolling up his sleeves.*) I am going to knock you cold. (MICHAEL *sits Left arm down Right settee—faces Left.*)

JOE (*kindly*). Now, Tommy—let's sit down and talk this over.

TOMMY (*turning to* MICHAEL). "Talk," he says, to a man of action. (*Crossing to* MICHAEL.) "Sit down," he says, (*Crossing back to* JOE.) to a tigress and her cubs!

JOE. How in the—? How did you guys get so cock-eyed? (*Crossing to stairs.*) I wish Ellen'd hurry up. (*Crossing to up Right door.*) Cleota!

TOMMY (*at up Left Center*). Don't call for help. I could take Cleota and you in the same ring!

JOE (*crossing to* TOMMY). Well, what's this all about?

TOMMY. You crept into this house to take Ellen away, didn't you? You thought it was the house of a professor who would talk and talk and talk—

JOE. And so you have! (*Crossing below* TOMMY *to Left Center, turns back.*) I came here to see a football game—

MICHAEL. That's a lie.

JOE. Why don't you go home?

MICHAEL. 'Cause I want to watch.

JOE. Well, there isn't going to be anything to watch.

TOMMY (*assuming fighter's pose*). Come on, put up your fists. (MICHAEL *rises, crosses to stand behind* TOMMY.)

JOE. Get away from me, Tommy. (*Pushes* TOMMY'S *arm which pivots* TOMMY *around so he faces* MICHAEL.) I'd break you in two, and I don't want to do that.

TOMMY (*at first to* MICHAEL, *then realizing he is facing the wrong way he turns to* JOE). Why don't you want to do that?

JOE. 'Cause how would it look if I came here and took Ellen and knocked you down on the way out?

MICHAEL. Maybe he's right. That's a point of honor, Mr. Turner.

TOMMY. Is it?

MICHAEL. But we could fight him about something else.

TOMMY. About what?

MICHAEL. He doesn't want you to read that letter.

TOMMY (*to* MICHAEL). That has nothing to do with this (*Realizes it has.*) —oh, yes! (MICHAEL *crosses above* TOMMY *and* JOE *to Left until he is in back of* JOE *and facing* TOMMY *who is Right Center.*) Going to President Cartwright's house. Trying to make me lose my job.

JOE. Why would I?

TOMMY. So you could get Ellen.

JOE. Now, Tommy, listen—

TOMMY. Oh, yes! Now I see I'm going to have to knock you further than I had previously decided upon. Come out in the back yard. (*Pulls* JOE *who breaks away from* TOMMY.)

(MICHAEL *pushes* JOE.)

JOE (*turns and strides back to* MICHAEL). Don't push me!

TOMMY. Hey!! (*He lunges at* JOE *with a badly aimed "haymaker."*)

JOE (*ducks and catches* TOMMY *to keep him from falling*). Now look, if you do ever get in a fight, Tommy, don't lead with your right. It leaves you wide open.

TOMMY. Oh, does it?

ELLEN (*enters from stairs with suitcase, which she drops when she sees odd positions of belligerents*). Tommy! What's happened? What are you doing now?

TOMMY. Fighting.

(*The music of the band is heard in the distance. Through the following scene it grows louder to* ELLEN'S *exit, then dies away as the band goes around the corner and comes up again to medium for the end of the Scene.*)

ELLEN. Fighting! What about? (*As she comes into room.*)

MICHAEL (*crosses Center*). Penguins.

ELLEN. What!

JOE (*down Left Center. Trying to explain*). Oh, it was all mixed up—about a lot of tigers and a cub. Tommy doesn't care what you and I are trying to do! He wants us to stay out of it!

ELLEN (*to* TOMMY). Oh, I see. That's what you were fighting about.

TOMMY. It wasn't about you.—Point of honor.

(*Band grows louder.*)

ELLEN. Oh yes, I see. You don't want me mixed up with anything. All right. You can pull the house down on top of you with your birds and letters and whiskey. Just let me get out of—what is all that racket?

JOE (*opens the door Left a crack—then closes it and crosses down Center*). Oh, they're having a victory parade and they want me to ride in that carriage with Wally Myers and the band. (*Crosses down Right.*)

TOMMY (*following* JOE). You attract bands like flies, don't you!

(*Band softer.*)

ELLEN (*as she starts for Left door*). Goodbye, Tommy! I'll be out in the car, Joe. Bring my bag, please! (*She slams out.*)

(*The* MEN *look after her.* JOE *goes up to stair landing and gets bag and crosses to* TOMMY *who sits down Right.*)

JOE. You're getting me in deeper and deeper. I should'a taken a poke at you when I had the chance!

TOMMY (*rising. Mad*). Fine! Come out in the back yard! (*Walks to door down Right and opens it.*)

(MICHAEL *crosses to stand behind* JOE.)

JOE. I'm not coming out in the back yard! (MICHAEL *pushes him. Very mad, he turns on* MICHAEL.) "Don't push me!" I said, I don't like to be pushed!

TOMMY (*turns* JOE *around facing him*). You said, "Don't lead with your right." (*He hits* JOE *on the nose with his left fist.*)

JOE (*pinching bridge of nose and dropping suitcase on settee*). Ow-w-w! Now you've started my sinus trouble! All right, if you want a fight, you've got a fight! (*He pushes* TOMMY *outside.*)

MICHAEL (*pulls a chair up in front of the door and sits watching the fight off stage. He applauds its progress of blows*). Hit him! Hit him! (*Quotes softly.*)

"And all the summer afternoon
They hunted us and slew!
But tomorrow—by the living God!"

Don't forget to lead with your right, Mr. Turner!—
That's right! Right in the eye!

(CLEOTA *enters to dining room door.* WALLY *and* PATRICIA *come in up Left laughing—see what's happening.*)

PATRICIA. Michael!! (*Rushes over down Right.*)

WALLY. What's going on here? (*Runs downstage.*)

CLEOTA (*up stage of down Right settee*). Godamighty!

PATRICIA. Oh—Michael, stop them! Wally, stop them!

MICHAEL (*spreading arms wide across door*). No, don't stop them! Let Mr. Turner alone and he'll tear him to pieces!

(*Crash outside.*)

WALLY. Get away from that door! (*He hurls* MICHAEL *aside, tipping him over, goes out down Right.*)

PATRICIA (*runs and kneels beside* MICHAEL). Michael! Michael!

(CLEOTA *grabs chair in which* MICHAEL *has been sitting and moves it upstage out of doorway.*)

ELLEN (*re-enters Left door, calling*). Joe, are you coming? (*She sees* MICHAEL *and* PATRICIA, *and looks around the room for* TOMMY *and* JOE.)

MICHAEL (*sitting on the floor with* PATRICIA's *arm around him, continues to quote poetry dramatically, declaiming toward the open door Right. With rapid fervor*).

"And many-a broken heart is here,"

ELLEN. What is it?

MICHAEL.

"And many-a broken head,
But tomorrow—by the living God!—
We'll try the game again!"

(*He tries to rise but collapses.*)

(JOE *and* WALLY *enter down Right carrying the unconscious* TOMMY. *They carry him to sofa up Center.*)

PATRICIA (*drops* MICHAEL *in disgust*). Oh, Michael!

ELLEN (*screaming as she sees* TOMMY *being carried in, out cold*). Tommy!!

(*The phone rings insistently.*)

CLEOTA (*goes to the phone, picks up the receiver and in her usual way says*). Pro-fessah Turner's res-i-dence!

THE CURTAIN FALLS SWIFTLY

ACT THREE

SCENE: *The Turner living room. Same as Acts One and Two.*
About noon, Monday.
The room is neat and orderly, but the flowers and other signs of festivity have been removed.
   The stage is empty, but the phone bell is ringing. A moment later, the doorbell also begins to sound insistently. CLECTA *enters from the dining room, wiping her hands on her apron, scuttles for an instant between the bells, picks up phone.*

CLEOTA (*into phone*). Stop ringin' dis thing both at once—Who?—Ah cain' heah you foh de ringin'. Hol' on— (*Putting down the receiver, she hurries to the Left door and opens it cautiously, bracing herself to prevent a forced entrance. She speaks through the crack of the door.*) Ah tol' you stop ringin' eve'ything. Ah'm heah, ain' I?

REPORTER'S VOICE (*off*). I'd like to see Mr. Turner.

CLEOTA. Is you a newspapah?

REPORTER'S VOICE (*enters, pushing her back*). Yeh, I'm from the *Daily Journal*.

CLEOTA (*interrupting*). He cain' see no-body—he's sick.

REPORTER. I know—but will he be up to-day? Is he going to his class?

CLEOTA. He ain' goin' nowheah. His haid huhts him. He's sick. Go 'way. (*Starts to push him out. He resists, so she shoves him away out with a "Go, 'way!" She forces the door shut, bolts it, returns to the telephone.*) Professah Turner's res-i-dence— *Daily* what?—You jus' *was* heah —No, Professah Turner ain' talkin' to nobody. He's sick in bed with his haid— No, he ain't goin' an' you ain' comin'. He ain't not talkin' 'cause he don' wanta talk. He jus' ain't talkin' cause he cain' talk. Goodbye. (*The bolted Left door is rattled from outside, then the door-bell begins to ring insistently.* CLEOTA *looks at the door angrily and starts for it. Looks back at the phone and mutters.*) What's the matter with dis house? Will you please stop ringin' dat bell? (*As she opens door—sees* PATRICIA *and laughs, em-barrassed.*) Oh! It's YOU!

PATRICIA (*entering*). What's the matter? (*Puts books and purse on coffee-table down Left.*)

CLEOTA. I thought it was that newspapah again. He just left.

PATRICIA. He didn't go—he's outside picket-ing. (*Takes off coat—hangs it up Left.*) Where's my sister, Cleota?

CLEOTA (*has crossed Right, turns back to* PATRICIA). Upstairs. Miss Patricia, Ah wish Ah knew bettah what's goin' on heah.

PATRICIA (*coming down*). Never mind.

CLEOTA. Mr. Michael jus' left.

PATRICIA (*crosses Right to* CLEOTA). Oh. Well, if Mr. Michael Barnes comes here again, *don't let him in!*

CLEOTA. No, ma'am. (*Exits up Right.*)

(ELLEN *comes from upstairs; she looks depressed.*)

PATRICIA. Hello, Ellen! How's Tommy? Is he still asleep?

ELLEN. Yes, but he tosses around and mutters. The doctor says he can get up this afternoon.

PATRICIA. No concussion, then?

ELLEN. Yes, a little.

PATRICIA (*crossing down Right, sits set-tee*). I guess when anybody's as crazy as Tommy or Michael, a little concussion doesn't make any difference.

ELLEN. Did you get the butter?

PATRICIA. Oh, Lord, no—I'll go back (*Jumps up. Starts Left.*)

ELLEN. Never mind. I need a little air. (*Crosses Left to clothes hooks.*)

PATRICIA (*from Right Center*). How's your head?

ELLEN (*getting coat*). Oh, all right.

PATRICIA. Is it? *(Sits sofa Right.)* Say, what is this second springtime you're all going through, anyway?

ELLEN *(putting on coat).* Tommy won't let me in on what he's really thinking about. He thinks I'm not smart enough to understand it—that's what it comes down to.

PATRICIA. Oh, a mental problem! I haven't been exactly listening at key-holes, but isn't there a Joe Something-or-other mixed up in this?

ELLEN. Oh, there's more to it than a fight about Joe.

PATRICIA. Pretty good one round here Saturday about Joe. You know Tommy was fighting for you in his mid-Victorian way, don't you?

ELLEN. Oh, but he was drunk. When he's sober he despises me. *(Crossing to Center.)* He thinks I'm a dimwit.

PATRICIA. But he wouldn't want you any other way than you are.

ELLEN. Thanks.

PATRICIA *(laughing).* I mean you're smart enough for Tommy and you know it, and he knows it.

ELLEN. I'm all mixed up. *(Crossing Left up Left Center.)* I want to go away some place where I can think.

PATRICIA. Look, this is a new century. You're not Diana of the Crossways or somebody.

ELLEN *(turns back to PATRICIA).* Well, what do you want me to do—stay here when he doesn't want me?

PATRICIA. No, but if you're going away, go away with Joe. Tommy's certainly been throwing you at him. Why don't you take him up on it? See what happens.

ELLEN *(crossing in a few steps).* Is this advice to the lovelorn? Do you think he would come running after me?

PATRICIA. Well, you've got to quit moping around and do something. I thought we Stanley women were supposed to have some resources. *(Rises; crossing Left to ELLEN.)* Look, your great-grandmother chased her man all the way to Nebraska in a covered wagon.

ELLEN. Well, I'm not going to chase anybody anywhere! I'm going to talk this over with Tommy, fairly and squarely, face to face. *(Crosses up Left to door and opens it.)*

PATRICIA. "Fairly and squarely!" How did your generation ever get through the 1920's?

ELLEN *(sadly).* We didn't. *(She exits.)*

(PATRICIA sits on sofa up Center; sighs.)

TOMMY *(comes slowly down stairs. He wears terrycloth bathrobe, and has a wet turkish towel twisted about his head).* Hello, Pat!

PATRICIA *(rises. Worried).* Tommy—you shouldn't be up!

TOMMY. I'm all right. What day is this?

PATRICIA. Monday.

TOMMY *(calls off up Right).* Cleota—Cleota! *(To PATRICIA.)* Can I take this thing off? *(Moves down.)*

PATRICIA. You're not supposed to. You ought to lie down.

TOMMY *(sits chair Right Center).* I'll just lean back. *(Does so. Winces.)* No—I guess I won't.

CLEOTA *(appears in Right door. Sees TOMMY).* Mistah Turner—is you up?

TOMMY. Yes, I'm up. Cleota, don't let anyone in this house except Mr. Michael Barnes.

(PATRICIA shakes her head violently "No" to CLEOTA from above TOMMY.)

CLEOTA. Yessuh—Ah do de best Ah can. *(Exits up Right.)*

TOMMY. Where's Ellen?

PATRICIA *(saunters down Right to settee. Sits).* She went out to *(Teasing.)*—to get the transfer man—for her trunk.

TOMMY. She's going away?

PATRICIA. Oh, no. She just likes to call on transfer men. Didn't you know that?

TOMMY. I can't stand irony so early in the day, Patricia.

PATRICIA. You're all right now, you see. She wouldn't go before. I don't know why.

TOMMY. You ought to know why. Your sister wouldn't walk out on anybody when he's down—even when he's down with delirium tremens.

PATRICIA. You didn't have D.T.'s. You had concussion.

TOMMY. Seemed more like D.T.'s.

PATRICIA. You don't know very much about my little sister, do you?

TOMMY. I know a lot more than I did last Friday. (Rises. Crossing up to sofa Center.) I think I will lie down.

PATRICIA. Why do you have to make everything as hard as you can? (TOMMY winces with pain. She rises. Crossing to him.) Do you want another cold towel?

TOMMY (patting her arm). No, thanks. (Phone rings. Lies back on sofa.) Oh, those bells!!

PATRICIA (crosses. Answering phone). Yes?—Who? No, Michael Barnes isn't here.

TOMMY. He was here and he's coming back.

PATRICIA. This is Patricia Stanley— Yes— Yes— I'll be very glad to tell him to call you—if I see him. Goodbye! (Slams receiver down.) That was Hot Cha-cha Gardner.

TOMMY. Oh-oh! Why did she call here?

PATRICIA (turns up Right Center). She said they told her Michael was on his way here, but obviously she just called for my benefit— So that's where he went Saturday night! (Turning to TOMMY.) You had that Hot—that Miss Gardner in some of your classes; do you remember her?

TOMMY (reflectively. Sitting up). I don't know. What does she look like?

PATRICIA. Well, she—doesn't wear any— (Gestures.)

TOMMY (lying back). I only had her in Wordsworth.

PATRICIA (turns right). Calling up here! (There is a knock at the door up Left; PATRICIA smiles grimly. She goes up and opens the door. MICHAEL steps in; he is taken aback at seeing PATRICIA.) Good-morning, Michael! Come in.

TOMMY (sits up. Peering over his shoulder). Yes, come in, Michael. (Pantomimes "telephone" for MICHAEL's benefit.)

MICHAEL (comes down a little nervously and stands near TOMMY). I got the car for you—(PATRICIA crosses to below settee down Right)—Feel better now that you're up? (Doesn't get the pantomime.)

TOMMY (pantomiming). Yes, much better. How do you feel?

MICHAEL. I feel all right.

TOMMY. That's good. (Mimics PATRICIA's gesture.)

(MICHAEL doesn't get it. Looks inside his coat to see what's wrong. PATRICIA turns and catches pantomime.)

PATRICIA (crosses up Left; gets coat, then crosses to down Left table for purse). If you'll excuse me—

MICHAEL (coming down Left to her). Oh, Pat, wait!—I—could I talk to you for a minute? Couldn't we go outside there and—

PATRICIA (proud and angry). No, we couldn't go outside there. Is it anything you're ashamed to say in front of Tommy?

MICHAEL (stiffening). No. No, I'm not. Only— Well, I don't want to get off on the wrong foot again. I'm sorry I got so mad Saturday. I said things and did things that—

PATRICIA. You certainly did.

MICHAEL (shouting). Well, I'm sorry, and— (Then, reasonably.) Oh, Pat, you ought to be able to see this my way. We just lost our tempers and—well—Mr. Turner and I are in a jam. I think you ought to—well—make an effort to understand what we're trying to do and stand by us—that is, if you care anything about me at all.

PATRICIA (with false sweetness). Oh, I certainly do. I've been standing by— taking messages for you—phone calls. I'm so glad we had this nice talk. (Shakes his hand.) And before you go, be sure to call (Dropping her sweetness, she yells:) Maple 4307. (Patricia flounces out door up Left.)

MICHAEL (looking after her). Maple 430—. (Crossing up to TOMMY.) Did The Cha-cha call here?

TOMMY. That's what I was trying to tell you. Patricia answered the phone. The—Chow-chow—snapped right in her face.

MICHAEL. And I didn't even do anything. (Sits on sofa.) I hope. (Looks up miserably.)

TOMMY. Michael, you're making me nervous. (Moves further Right on sofa.)

MICHAEL. Will you be able to go to the faculty meeting tonight?

TOMMY. I'll be there.

MICHAEL. They'll be out to get you—I know this is all my fault, Mr. Turner.

TOMMY. Yes, you're certainly the man that lighted the match.

MICHAEL. I just came from the President's office; he flayed me alive.

TOMMY. Are you kicked out?

MICHAEL. Suspended.

TOMMY. Michael, tell me— Are you really a Communist?

MICHAEL. Me?—No—I only know one guy who is. I'm—well, I guess I'm an unconfused liberal. I think I'll go to Stringfellow Barr's school in Annapolis and read the classics.

TOMMY. I wonder where I'll go?

(ELLEN enters Left with parcel.)

ELLEN. Good morning, Michael.

MICHAEL (rises). Hello, Mrs. Turner!

ELLEN (sees TOMMY). Good morning, Tommy— (Crossing to up Right door. Calls.) Cleota—

TOMMY. Good morning.

(CLEOTA enters up Right.)

ELLEN. Here's the butter, Cleota. Will you make Mr. Turner a cup of tea? (Turns back to him.) Would you like a hard-boiled egg?

TOMMY. No, thanks. Nothing hard. My teeth hurt.

(CLEOTA exits.)

ELLEN (crossing up Left takes off coat, hangs it up). Are you waiting for Patricia, Michael?

MICHAEL. I saw her. I'm leaving town, Mrs. Turner.

ELLEN. I'm awfully sorry, Michael.

WALLY'S VOICE (off Right). Pat! Oh, Pat!

ELLEN. Come in, Wally. (Crossing downstage. WALLY comes in down Right.) Patricia's gone out somewhere.

WALLY. Oh, I see. (To MICHAEL.) You waiting for her?

MICHAEL (crossing down Right to him). That's none of your business. Why?

WALLY (crossing in to MICHAEL. Lowers his voice). I know what you did Saturday night, that's why. (Crossing below MICHAEL to ELLEN.) Well, thanks, Mrs. Turner. I just cut across the back way. I'll walk on down to the house. (Starts out down Right.)

MICHAEL (stops him). I think I'll walk along. I want to talk to you.

WALLY. You don't have to. (Pushes MICHAEL.)

MICHAEL. If I didn't have to, I wouldn't do it. I'm no masochist. (Starts out down Right and punches WALLY in stomach.)

WALLY (stares after him blankly, then follows, furious). You don't have to use words like that in front of ladies.

MICHAEL. I'll be back in time to drive you to class, Mr. Turner. (Turns and WALLY bumps into him. MICHAEL pushes WALLY out down Right.)

TOMMY. Thanks.

ELLEN (takes tea from CLEOTA who has entered up Right with cup on tray). Here's your tea.

(CLEOTA goes out.)

TOMMY. Thanks.

ELLEN (with some constraint). How do you feel?

TOMMY. Very strange.

ELLEN. Is everything clear to you now?

TOMMY (stirs tea). Clear in the center. It's kind of fuzzy around the edges.

ELLEN (*crossing down Right; sits on settee*). I hope it's clear enough to give me a chance to say something without your going off on one of your literary tangents.

TOMMY. I don't do that.

ELLEN. I know you think I'm not very bright or something, (TOMMY *tries to demur, but she continues.*) but you must realize that you got me all mixed up Friday and that you were even less helpful Saturday.

TOMMY. That wasn't me, Saturday. That was a drunken sea lion.

ELLEN. I rather liked you as a sea lion.

TOMMY. Yes, I must have been very funny. Did you ever read Hodgson's poem, "The Bull"?

ELLEN (*turns to him*). Oh, Tommy!

TOMMY. It's the story of the defeated male. There is no defeat that can be quite so complete.

ELLEN. You wouldn't admit that this defeat was on account of— No, it has to be something out of a book.

TOMMY. When the bull's head is in the dust, life goes on and leaves him there; it's a psychological fact. The poets understand these things.

ELLEN. And all the cows react the same way? As if they were reading instructions from a blackboard? Oh, Tommy, listen to me— (*Rises. Crosses to* TOMMY.)

(*Doorbell rings.*)

TOMMY. The point is, I don't want any pity.

CLEOTA (*entering from dining room*). Miz Turner; Miz Turner! It's dat prizefightah. I seen him from de windah.

(ELLEN *admits* JOE *Left, who comes in without his old bounce; he is worried and restless.* CLEOTA *stands in up Right doorway, hanging onto every word.*)

ELLEN. Hello, Joe!

JOE. Hello. (*Awkwardly to* TOMMY.) Hello.

TOMMY. Hello!

JOE. I'm sorry, Tommy. I didn't hit you hard. You slipped and hit your head on a bench.

(*Ellen sits Right arm down Left settee.*)

TOMMY. Yeh, I know. What's the matter with your hand?

JOE. You kinda bit me. Ed's out in the car. We just chased a reporter away hanging around out there.

ELLEN. Well, don't let any reporters in, Cleota.

TOMMY. And don't let Keller in.

(CLEOTA *nods and exits up Right.*)

JOE (*indicating wet towel*). Do you have to keep that thing on?

TOMMY. No, I just do it because I like it.

(*Throws down towel.*)

JOE. Could I have a little slug of something? I—

ELLEN (*rises*). Certainly! Scotch?

JOE. Yeh, fine. (ELLEN *exits up Right.* JOE *crosses down Right. There is a pause.* JOE *still wonders about the vanished cup.*) I got the galloping jumps. I can use a little drink. Haven't slept for two nights.

TOMMY. Worrying about something?

JOE (*turns to* TOMMY). Yeh, worrying about something— And my cold's worse.

TOMMY. Want some Kleenex?

JOE (*irritated*). No, I don't want some Kleenex. (*Crossing Left.*) Darn reporters been bothering me, too.

TOMMY. What do they want with you?

JOE. Oh, they wanted me to pick an All-American team.

TOMMY (*incredulously--almost*). Did you?

JOE. Yeh. Kinda took my mind off things.

TOMMY (*sarcastically*). Who'd you pick for right guard?

JOE. Shulig—Kansas State Teachers'. (*Crossing to* TOMMY.) Look, Tommy, where the hell do we all stand now? (TOMMY *picks up towel, presses it to his head again.*) Does that kinda throb?

TOMMY. No.

JOE. Well, I wanta know where we all stand.

TOMMY. Oh, let it alone, Joe. It'll work out. You and I can handle this. I don't want Ellen worried about details now. She's got enough trouble with me—sitting around the house looking like a hot-oil shampoo—

ELLEN (*enters with bottle of Scotch. She pours a drink of straight Scotch at table up Right*). There's been more drinking in this house in the last two days than we've done in ten years.

(JOE *takes off coat, puts it up Left chair; crosses and sits down Left.*)

TOMMY (*after a pause*). Ellen, Joe picked Shulig of Kansas State Teachers' for right guard, on his All-American. Isn't that nice?

JOE (*reminiscently*). It was kinda hard choosing between him and Feldkamp of Western Reserve. Both big and fast.

ELLEN (*crossing with drink*). Here you are, dear— (*She is coolly oblivious of* TOMMY's *hand which he puts out for drink; goes on to* JOE, *who doesn't realize she means him.*) Dear. (*He looks up at her with a start—looks at* TOMMY—*takes drink.*)

TOMMY. I don't want any.

JOE. Say, have you got a Pennsylvania time-table around?

ELLEN (*crossing up, gets* TOMMY's *cup and saucer.*) Where are you going, Joe?

JOE. Well, I've got to be in Washington tomorrow.

ELLEN. That's going to rush me.

JOE. What do you mean?

ELLEN (*crossing above settee down Left*). Well, Joe, I thought you and I might start out late this afternoon and go as far as that little Inn at Granville tonight. Just for a start. (*Puts teacup and saucer on down Left table, sits close to* JOE.)

TOMMY (*rises*). What did you say?

ELLEN (*to* JOE). I think it's the nicest place around here. Don't you?

JOE. I—I—eh— Could I have a little more Scotch? (*Rises; crosses up Right; gets another drink.*)

ELLEN. I don't want you to get drunk, Joe.

JOE. I'll be all right—I'll be all right. What time is it?

TOMMY. Never mind what time it is. (*Crossing to* ELLEN.) Would you mind explaining this a little better.

ELLEN. I'll try to make it as clear as I can for both of you. I simply have to make a fresh start now, Tommy. You understand women; you must see that. I can't stay here now. You've made your plans, and now I have to make mine.

TOMMY. Yes—but not like this—not running off to Granville!

ELLEN. All right, if you're afraid of a scandal, we'll go farther away. Put Granville out of your mind, then. We'll go directly to Pittsburgh.

JOE (*coming down*). Huh?

ELLEN. It's a very big town. Nobody need know anything about it.

JOE (*coming down a step*). About what?

ELLEN. About us. About our eloping together.

(*Both* MEN *stop cold.*)

TOMMY. Ellen!

JOE (*desperately crossing Center*). But you see—I don't live in Pittsburgh. (*He makes a large circular gesture.*) I live in Sewickly. (*Gesture—small.*) And my boss lives there too. (*Starts down Right.*) And my mother. My mother's not very well. My mother—

TOMMY. Oh, you and your mother!

JOE (*crossing Left a little*). Besides, it's a Presbyterian town.

ELLEN. You're not being very gallant, Joe.

TOMMY (*crossing to* JOE). No. Are you trying to get out of this?

JOE. No, but I come from a long line of married people! (TOMMY *crosses below* JOE *to down Right.*) And besides, I'm not going to Pittsburgh directly. I've got to go to Washington, (*Crossing to* ELLEN.) and that's one place I couldn't take you, Ellen!

TOMMY. You'll take her any place she wants to go, but she's not going any place!

ELLEN. Oh, yes, I am!

ED (*there is a loud knock, and* ED KELLER *enters Left*). I can't sit out in that car all day, you know.

JOE (*takes* ED's *hat off, puts it on up Center table*). Oh, I'm sorry, Ed, but—jees, I forgot all about you. (JOE *turns to* TOMMY.) I persuaded Ed to come over and talk to you before this thing gets too bad. (*Leads* ED *down Right Center to* TOMMY.)

TOMMY. It couldn't get any worse!

JOE. I mean about the trustees.

TOMMY. Let the trustees take care of themselves. We have troubles of our own. (*Sits down Right settee.*)

ED. You'll find out this is your trouble. (JOE *goes up Left, closes door. To* JOE.) Is he able to talk?

JOE. Lord, yes!

ED (*crossing to* TOMMY). Well, then, listen. We just had a trustees' meeting in the President's office. Michael Barnes is out, and you're on your way out. You'll be asked to resign tonight.

ELLEN (*rising*). Oh, Tommy!

JOE. Ed's trying to help him while there's still time. After tonight, it will be too late. (*Goes above settee Left.*)

TOMMY (*rises; crossing up Left*). What do you care what happens tonight? You won't be here. You'll be in Granville or somewhere.

(JOE *turns away to fireplace Left.*)

ED. What're you going to be doing in Granville?

TOMMY. Please don't ask personal questions.

ELLEN. Do you mind if I stay a little while, Tommy?

TOMMY (*angrily*). Why shouldn't you stay? It's your house.

ED. Sit down, Ellen. (*She sits down Left.* ED *crossing to* TOMMY *at Left Center.*) There's just one thing you can do: come out with a statement to the papers quick. Say you were sick. Say you didn't know

anything about Barnes' editorial. You think it's an outrage. You're not going to read this Vanzetti thing, and you think Barnes is getting what he deserves. That's the only thing that'll save your neck.

ELLEN (*rises*). Tommy wouldn't say that about Michael, Ed, and you shouldn't ask him to.

TOMMY. Thank you. (*Crosses down Right to settee; sits.*)

ED. All right, then! That's all I had to say. (*Starts for door up Left.*) Goodbye! This is on your own head.

ELLEN. Ed! Just a minute, please. (*Crossing to* TOMMY.) I know that reading this letter must mean something to you, Tommy. Something none of us can quite understand. I wish I could. It might help me to understand a lot of other things, when I can get away where I can think.

TOMMY. Such as what?

ELLEN. Such as what is important to you. What you've been fighting for. Whether it's something you really believe in and love, or just your own selfish pride. I think you got into this just because you were mad at me. And that's ridiculous, because now you don't care what I do or say about it. You're out of that.

ED (*coming down Center*). I don't see what she's talking about.

(JOE *motions him to be quiet.*)

TOMMY. All right, I'll try to explain what it means to me. Perhaps originally pride had something to do with this. And jealousy.

ELLEN. And stubbornness—

TOMMY. And—please. (*Rises.*) I am trying to say that—now—I am not fighting about you and me at all. This is bigger than you and me or any of us.

ELLEN. Is it?

ED (*ironically*). It must be a masterpiece. That letter must be quite a nice piece of propaganda.

TOMMY (*crossing Center to him*). Why don't you read it and find out?

ED. I don't read things like that.

TOMMY. You don't even know what you're objecting to.

JOE (at fireplace). Well, Tommy, why don't you read the letter to us, and let us see what it is?

TOMMY. I'll be glad to read it to you, but I'll read it to my class too. (Crosses up Right Center to bookcase.)

ED (crossing down). You don't have to read it to me. I know what kind of stuff it is.

(The Left door bursts open, and PATRICIA backs in, leaving the door open. WALLY is outside. They talk in excited undertones. TOMMY looks through up Right Center bookcase. ED removes coat, puts it on up Center sofa.)

PATRICIA. But I can't go with you now! I told you I've got to wait here and see what Tommy's going to do.

WALLY (off Left). But you're not going to the class! You said you're not going!

PATRICIA. I'm not! I just want to know!

WALLY (off). I'll bet you are going! You're waiting here for Michael to go with you!

PATRICIA. Oh, go away! (Sees OTHERS.) Oh—I'm sorry. (Crosses down Right.)

(WALLY enters and crosses down to above settee Left.)

ED. What's this now?

JOE (grinning). Hey, Pat, you better think twice before you scrap with Wally here. (TOMMY goes upstairs for book.) He's coming in with me at Pittsburgh next year.

WALLY (crossing to JOE Left). A lot she cares about Pittsburgh! I run sixty-two yards through Michigan and all she wants is to listen to Mike Barnes talk about his love life. (Crosses down Right.)

ED. She does?

ELLEN (trying to stop him, at chair Right Center). Wally, how's Stalenkiwiecz?

WALLY. He's much better. (Crossing to PATRICIA down Right.) If you knew what I know about that guy Barnes—

PATRICIA. I know what you're hinting at! And what if he did? It only shows what an intense person Michael is. I know that no matter what he did, he was thinking of me.

WALLY. That's disgusting!

PATRICIA. And aren't you a little bit disgusting to mention it? I though men had some loyalty! (She goes out down Right.)

WALLY (following her out). Now, listen here— Do you know what he did?—I'll tell you what he did.

ED. What kind of a house is this?

(As they go out the lower door, DAMON, carrying an umbrella, walks quietly in the open front door and looks around, as TOMMY comes downstairs with an open book in his hand.)

TOMMY (coming Center). All right, here it is. Now sit down—or stand up—but listen!—(JOE sits on fireplace bench Left; ED sits up Center sofa.) Oh, come in, Doctor Damon. You're just in time.

DAMON (closes the front door, comes downstage). In time for what? (Sees them.) Has the Inquisition moved its headquarters?

TOMMY. I'm just going to read the Inquisition a letter from one of its victims.

ED. That's about enough of that.

DAMON (crossing down Left). Gentlemen, gentlemen— This may not be wise, Thomas.

TOMMY. It may not be wise, but it's necessary. I think you'll have to take a stand, too. Doctor Damon.

DAMON. I hope not. (Sits down Left settee.)

(ELLEN sits end of down Right settee.)

TOMMY. So did I hope not. I didn't start out to lead a crusade. I simply mentioned one day that I meant to read to my class three letters by men whose profession was not literature, but who had something sincere to say. (Crossing Right.) Once I had declared that very harmless intention, the world began to shake, great institutions trembled, and football players descended upon me and my wife. I realized then that I was doing something important.

ED (sarcastically). You make it sound mighty innocent. Reading Lincoln and

General Sherman—and Vanzetti. What was the reason you gave for picking out Vanzetti?

TOMMY (*crosses to* ED). Originally I chose him to show that broken English can sometimes be very moving and eloquent, but now—

ED. We wouldn't object if this was just a case of broken English—it's more than that.

TOMMY. Yes, you've made it more than that.

ED. Vanzetti was an anarchist! He was executed for murder.

TOMMY. He was accused of murder, but thousands of people believe he was executed simply because of the ideas he believed in.

ED. That's a dangerous thing to bring up.

TOMMY (*getting really mad*). No, it's a dangerous thing to keep down. I'm fighting for a teacher's rights. But if you want to make it political, all right! You can't suppress ideas because you don't like them —not in this country—not yet. (*Crossing to* DAMON.) This is a university! It's our business to bring what light we can into this muddled world—to try to follow truth!

DAMON. You may be right, Thomas, but I wish you would make an effort not to— uh—uh—intone.

TOMMY. I'm not intoning—I'm yelling! Don't you see this isn't about Vanzetti. This is about us! If I can't read this letter today, tomorrow none of us will be able to teach anything except what Mr. Keller here and the Legislature permit us to teach. Can't you see what that leads to —what it has led to in other places? We're holding the last fortress of free thought, and if we surrender to prejudice and dictation, we're cowards. (*Crossing Right.*)

ELLEN (*from Right settee*). Tommy, no matter how deeply you feel about this, what can you *do*? What can any one man do? Except to lose everything—

TOMMY (*crossing to* ELLEN). I have very little more to lose. And I can't tell you what I hope to gain. I can't answer that. I only know that I have to do it.

(PATRICIA *appears in doorway, down Right, stops and listens.*)

DAMON. May we hear the letter—in a slightly calmer mood, perhaps?

TOMMY. Yes, sir— (*Crossing up to* ED.) This may disappoint you a little, Mr. Keller. It isn't inflammatory, so it may make you feel a little silly. At least, I hope so— (*He holds up the book, pauses.* ED *and* JOE *get set in their seats.*) Vanzetti wrote this in April, 1927, after he was sentenced to die. It has been printed in many newspapers. It appears in this book. You could destroy every printed copy of it, but it would not die out of the language, because a great many people know it by heart. (*He reads, hardly referring to the book, watching them.*) "If it had not been for these thing, I might have live out my life talking at street corners to scorning men. I might have die, unmarked, unknown, a failure. Now we are not a failure. Never in our full life could we hope to do so much work for tolerance, for Justice, for man's understanding of man, as now we do by accident. Our words—our lives—our pain—nothing! The taking of our lives—the lives of a good shoemaker and a poor fish-peddler —all! That last moment belongs to us— that agony is our triumph!" (*He closes the book. There is silence for a moment.*) Well, that's it— (*Crosses up Right; puts book up Right table.*)

(KELLER *is puzzled;* ELLEN, *who has been moved by the letter, looks up in surprise, meets* TOMMY's *eyes, then drops hers.*)

JOE (*uncomfortably*). Well, that isn't so bad! That isn't a bad letter.

(DAMON *is delighted at this reaction.*)

ED. Is that all of it?

TOMMY. Yes, that's all.

JOE (*rises. Crossing to* ED). Maybe Tommy's right. I don't see that it would do so much harm.

ED (*slowly*). Yes, it will. If he reads this letter to his class he'll get a lot of those kids worried about that man. Make socialists out of 'em.

JOE (*crosses down Left*). It's got me worried already.

ED (*rises*). No— I won't have it— You fellows are trying to defy the authority of the trustees. You say you're going to take a stand. Well, we've *taken* a stand. I wouldn't care if that letter were by Alexander Hamilton.

TOMMY (*crossing to* ED). Neither would I. The principle is exactly the same.

JOE (*speaking hopefully*). Well, then, read something else. Why can't you read Hoover?

ED. Yeah.

JOE. He writes a lot of stuff—a lot of good stuff in his book.

TOMMY. Hoover can't write as well as Vanzetti.

ED (*winces*). That's a terrible thing to say. You'll get in trouble saying things like that.

TOMMY (*crossing down Right*). Very likely.

JOE (*crossing to* ED). Ed, look—can't we compromise somehow? Seems a shame that a little thing like this should—

ELLEN (*rises*). It isn't little! Joe, you have some influence around here.

TOMMY. I can fight my own battles, Ellen.

ELLEN. Can't I say anything any more— not even on your side?

ED (*crossing to* TOMMY; *stopped by* TOMMY's *line*). All right, Turner, I've heard the letter and—

TOMMY (*answering* ELLEN). Not out of a sense of self-sacrifice or something.

ED. What?

ELLEN. Oh, yes, you always know—

ED (*to* JOE). Do we always have to have women butting into this?

JOE. Ellen isn't women. She's Tommy's wife.

ELLEN. No, I'm not—

ED (*crossing to* TOMMY). No, Turner, it comes to this— (*Turns to* ELLEN.) You're not what? Do you mean to stand there and tell me you two are not—

TOMMY. Will you please not ask personal questions?

ED (*turns to* TOMMY). No. *We can't have that in this school!*

ELLEN. It's Joe and I who are going away together.

ED (*to* TOMMY). Yeh, will you let me— (*Turns to* ELLEN.) You and Joe are going to what! (*Crosses to* JOE *Left Center.*) What the—what is going on here anyway?

JOE. Now don't look at me!

ED. You can't go away with Ellen!

JOE. I didn't say—

ELLEN (*sits down Right settee*). We might as well tell him now. I'm going to Pittsburgh with Joe.

ED (*crossing back to* ELLEN). Why, you can't do that! Why, the newspapers would make Midwestern University look like some kind of a honky-tonk or something. This is worse than that damn letter!

(PATRICIA *crosses up; sits stair landing.*)

TOMMY. Aren't you getting off the subject? (*Crosses around Left toward* ED.)

ED. No! What kind of a woman are you?

TOMMY (*crossing above* ELLEN *to* ED). You come out in the back yard! Right out in the back yard!

JOE (*in a step*). Be careful, Ed!

(TOMMY *crosses down Left.*)

ELLEN. No more fights please!

DAMON (*rises*). I think I shall get a breath of fresh air. (*Goes to door up Left, opens it.*)

ELLEN. Well, I can't stay *here* now.

JOE. Look, Ed, you don't understand. You got things all mixed up.

ED (*crossing to down Left Center*). Well, I've got this much straight—if we can keep sex out of this for a minute. I came here to say to you that if you read this letter today you're out of this university tomorrow! You take this stand and you stand alone!

DAMON (*crossing down to* ED). Mr. Keller, for forty-two years I have followed a policy of appeasement. I might say I have been kicked around in this institution by one Edward K. Keller after another—

ED. There is only one Edward K. Keller.

DAMON. There has always been at least one. But there is an increasing element in the faculty which resents your attitude toward any teacher who raises his voice or so much as clears his throat. I warn you that if you persist in persecuting Thomas Turner, you will have a fight on your hands, my friend.

ED. Do you think that Bryson and Kressinger and I are afraid of a few dissatisfied book-worms who work for twenty-five hundred a year?

DAMON (furious). These men are not malcontents! Some of them are distinguished scholars who have made this University what it is!

ED. They've made it what it is! What about me? Who's getting this new stadium? Who brought Coach Sprague here from Southern Methodist?

JOE (crossing to ED). He means that this thing is bigger than stadiums and coaches.

ED (crossing up to JOE). Nothing's bigger than the new stadium.

(DAMON crosses Left to TOMMY.)

JOE. Now we've all had a bad week-end around here, and you're not helping any.

ED. Do you think I've had a good weekend! (Crosses Left Center.)

(MICHAEL and NUTSY enter up Left with petition.)

MICHAEL (crossing down Left). Come in, Nutsy.

(DAMON crosses to down Left settee; sits.)

ED. Now what!

MICHAEL. We're circulating petitions for Mr. Turner. Show 'em, Nutsy.

NUTSY (crossing below ED to JOE at Center). This one's just from 14th Avenue and the Athletic house. (Turns to TOMMY.) We've got three hundred and fifty-seven names.

DAMON. We want no student insurrections!

JOE. Let me see that thing. (Takes petition from NUTSY; crosses up Right—NUTSY follows.)

ED (crossing down Right Center). You're wasting your time with that handful of names. Turner will be out tomorrow and Barnes is on his way home now.

MICHAEL (crossing to ED). I'm not on my way home yet, sir.

ED (turns to MICHAEL). Ohhh! So you're Barnes! So you're the little puppy that called me a Fascist!

PATRICIA (rises; crossing down between ED and MICHAEL. To ED). Well, the way you're treating everybody, I think you are a Fascist!

ELLEN. Patricia!

TOMMY (up Left). Let her alone.

ELLEN. Oh, she can stand up for Michael, but I can't stand up for you! Is that it?

TOMMY. This is—ah—different.

ED. Do I have to stand here and be insulted by every sixteen-year-old child that comes into this room?

PATRICIA. I'm not sixteen, I'm nineteen!

MICHAEL. She'll soon be twenty.

ED (to MICHAEL). Why don't you get packing?

MICHAEL. You don't need to worry about me. I'll be far away from here by tomorrow. Come on, Nutsy!

(Crosses up Left. NUTSY exits Left.)

PATRICIA (starts after him). If you throw him out, I'm going with him! Wait, Michael! (Crosses to door Left.)

ED. Are you married to this little radical?

PATRICIA. You don't have to be married to somebody to go away with him—do you, Ellen? (Exits.)

(MICHAEL follows her out.)

DAMON (rises. Crossing up Left). I think I shall go home, have my Ovaltine and lie down. (Exit Left, closing door.)

ED. He'll need his Ovaltine. (Crosses upstage.)

JOE (crossing to ED). Say, Ed, look! This thing has been signed by Stalenkiwiecz and Wierasocka.

ED *(crossing to* JOE*).* What! I don't believe it. *(Takes petition, looks at it.)*

JOE. Ed, you ought to have some respect for men like Dean Damon and Stalenkiwiecz and Wierasocka.

ED. They can't do this to me! Two of the biggest men in the university signing the Red petition! You, the greatest half-back we ever had, running away with a woman! Why—they'll never ask us to the Rose Bowl now!

TOMMY *(crossing up Left).* What is the Rose Bowl?

ED *(thrusts petition into* JOE's *hand).* I'm getting out of this house! Coming Joe?

JOE. No.

ED *(putting on coat).* You can't depend on anybody! I've a damn good notion to resign from the board of trustees. *(To* TOMMY*.)* But I'll kick you out if it's the last thing I do.

TOMMY *(crossing up Left).* Just to make things even—I'll kick you out. Here's your hat. *(Opens door, gives him* JOE's *derby from up Center table.)*

ED. We'll see! *(Puts on hat and stomps out.)*

JOE. Hey, that's my hat!

TOMMY. Well, get another one. *(Closes door.)* Well, that's that.

(They look at each other.)

JOE. Yeh, that's that. *(Pause. Crossing down Left.)* Well, I s'pose Ed will never speak to me again.

TOMMY *(takes his own coat and hat from hook, puts them on end of sofa).* I have to go to class. I'll be late. *(Starts for stairs.)*

ELLEN *(appealingly. Crossing to* TOMMY*).* Tommy--I—

TOMMY. I know. I know.

ELLEN. You know what?

TOMMY. I know what you're going to say —but I don't want substitutes. I don't want *loyalty.*

*(*ELLEN *turns away.)*

JOE *(down Left Center).* What's the matter with that?

TOMMY. I just don't want Ellen standing by like a Red Cross nurse because she knows I'm in trouble.

JOE. I don't know whether you need a nurse or a psychoanalyst!

ELLEN. I think he's analyzed it very well himself. It isn't because you think I don't care, it's because you don't.

TOMMY *(crossing down Left to coffee table, almost bursting).* I thought we could settle this *quietly* and *calmly.*

ELLEN. Quietly and calmly! Oh, Lord! *(Picks up large ashtray Right table—smashes it on floor.)*

TOMMY. Now, don't do that! I can throw things, too! *(Picks up cup down Left table.)*

ELLEN *(crossing Right Center).* No, you can't—you haven't got enough blood in you!

*(*TOMMY *glares at her, puts cup down coldly—suddenly snatches it and crashes it into fireplace—reaches for saucer.)*

JOE *(leaps for* TOMMY—*grabs saucer from him).* Now wait—let me handle this. I don't throw things— I just want to say that I came to this city to see a football game.

ELLEN *(crossing to* JOE *Left Center).* Oh, no, you didn't! You came for me. You haven't been here for a ball-game in ten years. You wait till Brenda and you are separated, then you come for me!

JOE. Oh, hell! *(Throws saucer in fireplace then wilts as he realizes this household has affected him, too.)*

TOMMY *(crossing above* JOE *to between them down Left Center, desperately insisting upon his own doom).* That's very smart, Ellen. That's very penetrating. That's all I wanted to know. *(To* JOE*.)* Subconsciously, you came here for Ellen, so don't try to deny it.

JOE *(sits settee down Left).* I don't do things subconsciously! You're full of childish explanations of everything that comes up!

TOMMY. And you're full of psychological evasions!

ELLEN (*screaming*). Oh, shut up! Both of you! I am not going to listen to any more of this! (*Runs upstairs.*)

(TOMMY *sits sofa up Center—there is a long pause.*)

JOE. Well I'll tell you one thing! I'm not going upstairs this time! (*Turns to* TOMMY.) If you'd explained what you were standing for on Saturday, things would have cleared up around here and I'd be in Washington now, talking to Ickes.

TOMMY. Are you still in love with Norma?

JOE. Norma who?

TOMMY. Your wife.

JOE. My wife's name is Brenda. And you're not going to talk her over with me. I can't be alone with you two minutes and have any private life left!

ELLEN's VOICE (*off upstairs*). Tommy! *What did you do with my nail file???!*

JOE. Oh, Lord—she sounds worse than last Saturday.

TOMMY. I haven't got it. (*He absently goes through a pocket, finds it, brings it out.*) Oh! Yeh, I've got it. (*He starts filing a nail.*)

JOE. I've gone through more hell here in three days than I've had with Phyllis in three years.

TOMMY. Yeh! (*Then he gets it; rising.*) Phyllis? Who is Phyllis? (*Crossing down to* JOE.) Are you carrying on with some other woman in Pittsburgh? You can't do this.

JOE (*springing to his feet*). I'm not carrying on with anybody. Phyllis is my secretary and there's nothing between us!

TOMMY. Then why did you say you've been going through hell for three years?

JOE (*yelling*). 'Cause you get me all balled up.

(ELLEN *comes downstairs with bag—sets it down Right.*)

TOMMY (*crossing to* ELLEN). Here— (*Hands her nail file.*) You didn't pack anything!

ELLEN (*puts file in purse*). I've been packed for three days! (*Crosses up Left; gets coat, puts it on; crosses Right to bag.*)

TOMMY. Well, you can't go with just one suitcase— There isn't much here, but— there're the books. They're yours. Most of them I gave to you. (*Turns away.*)

ELLEN (*putting on hat*). Can I have "The Shropshire Lad"? (TOMMY *goes to Right bookcase; looks for book.*) Isn't that the one that has: (*Quotes.*)

"And now the fancy passes by—"

TOMMY (*finds book; brings it to her*).

"And nothing will remain—"

MICHAEL (*sticks his head in door Left*). You've just five minutes to get to your class, Mr. Turner. We'll wait for you in the car.

TOMMY. Thanks! (MICHAEL *exits, closing door. Crossing to* JOE.) Well, so long, Joe. I know you'll get Ellen a place of her own for a while anyway. (*Crossing to* ELLEN.) Ellen, you can take that four-poster money with you. I'll have one more check coming, too. (*Starts upstairs.*)

JOE. What's "four-poster money"?

ELLEN. We were saving up to buy a new bed. (*Cries. Sits on Right settee.*)

JOE. Oh, my Lord, here we go again!

TOMMY (*crossing to* JOE). Why did you have to ask what four-poster money is? (*Crossing to* ELLEN.) Ellen, please.

ELLEN. Oh, go on! Go on! Put on your coat and comb your hair! If you're going to be kicked out of school, you can't go over there looking like a tramp.

TOMMY. All right. (*Goes upstairs.*)

JOE (*pause*). Look, Ellen, everything's gonna be all right. (*Crosses Center.*)

ELLEN. Is it?

JOE (*crossing up Left Center and looking upstairs*). I wouldn't worry about that guy.

ELLEN. I don't.

JOE. I mean he's sure to get another job. He's had more publicity than Wally Myers.

ELLEN. I don't care what becomes of him.

JOE (*crosses to Center. Watches her for a moment*). Come here. (*Crossing to her pulls her to her feet.*) You're still crazy about that guy, aren't you?

ELLEN. I'm kind of scared of him. He used to be just—nice, but now he's wonderful!

(TOMMY *appears on stairs in time to catch the end of this. Very slowly a light begins to dawn upon him.* JOE *sees him but* ELLEN *doesn't.*)

JOE (*looks around, sees Victrola, gets idea, pulls* ELLEN *across stage down Left to it*). I don't think he's so wonderful!

ELLEN. Yes, he is! That letter's wonderful. What he's trying to do is wonderful. He wouldn't let me or you or anyone stop him. Even Ed.

JOE. He's a scrapper all right, but he can't dance. (*Puts needle on.*)

(TOMMY *comes downstairs.* JOE *turns on Victrola which plays "Who."*)

ELLEN. Oh, who wants to dance now?

JOE (*they are dancing*). This is important. It's all in the light you give off.

ELLEN (*he dances her Center*). Light? What are you talking about?

JOE. The important thing about dancing is that the man has got to lead. (*Beckons to* TOMMY *who comes on into room from stairs.*)

TOMMY (*crossing to them*). May I cut in? (*Takes* ELLEN *and dances with her.*)

ELLEN. Tommy! Let me go!

TOMMY (*shouting*). No, I think you're wonderful too!

ELLEN. You think I'm dumb! Were you listening?

TOMMY. No.

JOE (*near door; out-yelling them*). Hey —don't start that again!

TOMMY (*dancing upstage, gets his hat from table up Center and jams it on his head*). Joe—why don't you go back to your wife? We can send her a wire.

JOE. Don't worry about me, brother. I sent her a wire this morning. (*Goes out Left.*)

TOMMY (*dances with* ELLEN). Quit leading!

ELLEN. I'm not leading. You *were* listening!

TOMMY. You were yelling. Well, turn!

ELLEN (*at Center*). Make me turn. (*He does and they turn, which brings them down Center. She finally breaks it.*) Don't be so rough—and put your hat on straight. (*She straightens his hat.*) You look terrible. (*She throws her arms around* TOMMY *and they kiss as—*

THE CURTAIN FALLS

THE MAN WHO CAME
TO DINNER

By GEORGE S. KAUFMAN and MOSS HART

THE MAN WHO CAME TO DINNER was produced by Sam H. Harris at the Music Box Theatre, New York on October 16, 1939. The setting was designed by Donald Oenslager; music and lyrics by Cole Porter. The cast was as follows:

MRS. ERNEST W. STANLEY
.................................Virginia Hammond
MISS PREEN......................Mary Wickes
RICHARD STANLEY
.................................Gordon Merrick
JUNE STANLEY........Barbara Wooddell
JOHN..................................George Probert
SARAH................Mrs. Priestley Morrison
MRS. DEXTER.................Barbara Adams
MRS. McCUTCHEON
.................................Edmonia Nolley
MR. STANLEY.................George Lessey
MAGGIE CUTLER.........Edith Atwater
DR. BRADLEY.............Dudley Clements
SHERIDAN WHITESIDE
.................................Monty Woolley
HARRIET STANLEY.........Ruth Vivian
BERT JEFFERSON.....Theodore Newton
PROFESSOR METZ...........LeRoi Operti
THE LUNCHEON GUESTS:
.................................Phil Sheridan
.................................Charles Washington
.................................William Postance

MR. BAKER.........................Carl Johnson
EXPRESSMAN...................Harold Woolf
LORRAINE SHELDON....Carol Goodner
SANDY...........................Michael Harvey
BEVERLY CARLTON.....John Hoysradt
WESTCOTT.......................Edward Fisher
RADIO TECHNICIANS:
.................................Rodney Stewart
.................................Carl Johnson

SIX YOUNG BOYS........
Daniel Leone
Jack Whitman
Daniel Landon
Donald Landon
DeWitt Purdue
Robert Rea

BANJO...................................David Burns

TWO DEPUTIES...............
Curtis Karpe
Phil Sheridan

A PLAINCLOTHES MAN
.................................William Postance

SCENES

The scene is the home of Mr. and Mrs. Stanley, in a small town in Ohio.

ACT I: Scene 1. A December morning.
Scene 2. About a week later.

ACT II: Another week has passed. Christmas Eve.

ACT III: Christmas morning.

THE AUTHORS

Mr. Kaufman, born in 1889, came to Broadway from Pittsburgh after some desultory study of the law, some clerking, stenography, and travelling salesmanship. He became a columnist and reached his pinnacle in journalism as drama editor of the New York Times. *He graduated from the job into playwriting with an ease rarely granted to drama editors on the* Times *or any other paper.*

The years 1921 to 1924 were his Connelly period. Collaborating with Marc Connelly, Mr. Kaufman produced seven plays, and among them were Dulcy *(1921), the farce which gave the language an employable term for feminine witlessness; the rather warm-hearted comedy* To the Ladies; Merton of the Movies *(1922) which started Hollywood on its least questionable career as a butt for humorists; and* Beggar on Horseback *(1924), a delightful expressionistic satire on the shoddy aspects of our business civilization. Next Mr. Kaufman embarked upon a comic exploration of show business in his solo effort* The Butter and Egg Man *(1925),* The Royal Family *(with Edna Ferber in 1928),* June Moon *(with Ring Lardner in 1929),* Once in a Lifetime *(with Moss Hart in 1930),* Stage Door *(with Edna Ferber in 1936), and in less noteworthy contributions like* The Hollywood Pinafore. *Musical comedy attracted him as early as 1923; his efforts in this direction have been many, and he attained distinction with at least one of them, the delightful political farce* Of Thee I Sing, *written with Morrie Ryskind in 1931. A more philosophical brand of humor in* You Can't Take It With You *(with Moss Hart in 1936) was rewarded with the Pulitzer Prize, and* The Man Who Came to Dinner *in 1939 marked a further advance in the regions of character comedy. Moss Hart again collaborated and Alexander Woolcott contributed himself as the subject. Mr. Kaufman's other plays are too many to be given here, and his prowess as a director requires no comment.*

Moss Hart, the ablest of recent Kaufman collaborators and a playwright of note in his own right, was born in New York in 1904. He appears to have chosen writing as a vacation at an early age. He studied the short story at Columbia University, but it was the theatre that attracted him most. He became secretary to Fiske O'Hara, and using the pseudonym of Robert Conrad, wrote a first piece, The Hold-Up Man, *which ran several weeks in Chicago. His first script to achieve really professional attention was* Once in a Lifetime *and it had the good fortune of attracting Kaufman as collaborator and director. This enterprise was followed by two collaborations on musicals with Irving Berlin,* Face the Music *in 1932 and the extremely popular* As Thousands Cheer *in 1933. After a considerably less commendable adaptation of* The Great Waltz, *Mr. Hart joined forces with Kaufman in the writing of the retrospective drama* Merrily We Roll Along *(1934), wrote the book for the Cole Porter musical* Jubilee *(1935), and returned to the Kaufman orbit with* You Can't Take It With You, I'd Rather Be Right, *(1937),* The Fabulous Invalid *(1938),* The American Way *(1939), and* The Man Who Came to Dinner, *and* George Washington Slept Here *(1940). Mr. Hart's solo efforts, the ingenious Gertrude Lawrence psychoanalytic extravaganza* Lady in the Dark *(1941),* The Winged Victory *written in 1943 for the Air Force, and the semi-expressionist divorce drama* Christopher Blake *(1946) proved variously successful, so that his reputation can stand without buttressing by Messrs. Kaufman, Berlin, and Porter. Like his favorite collaborator, moreover, Mr. Hart has proved himself an able director of his own and other people's plays. He is a showman first and last, and is particularly adept at dealing with children.*

THE MAN WHO CAME TO DINNER

ACT ONE

SCENE I

SCENE: *The curtain rises on the attractive living-room of* MR. *and* MRS. ERNEST W. STANLEY, *in a small town in Ohio. The* STANLEYS *are obviously people of means: the room is large, comfortable, tastefully furnished. Double doors lead into a library* R. *There is a glimpse through an arch* U.R. *of a dining-room at the rear, and we see the steps of a handsome curved staircase,* U.C. *At the left side of the room, a bay window. Another arch,* U.L. *leading into the hallway. Upstage of the hallway is a swinging door leading into the pantry. The outer door to the street is off* U.L. *The library doors are closed.*

MRS. STANLEY *enters from upstairs. As she reaches the lower third step the door-bell rings. She pauses a moment, then continues on her way towards the library. A nurse* (MISS PREEN) *in full uniform emerges—scurries rather—out of the room* R., *as the bell rings. An angry voice from within speeds her on her way: "Great dribbling cow!"*

MRS. STANLEY (*eagerly*). How is he? Is he coming out?

(*But* MISS PREEN *has already disappeared into the dining-room up* R.)

(*Simultaneously the door-bell rings—at the same time a young lad of twenty-one,* RICHARD STANLEY, *is descending the stairs* C.)

RICHARD (*crosses to door* L.). I'll go, Mother.

(JOHN, *a white-coated servant, comes hurrying in from the library and starts up the stairs, two at a time.*)

MRS. STANLEY. What's the matter? What is it, John?

JOHN. They want pillows. (*And he is out of sight.*)

(*Meanwhile* MISS PREEN *is returning to the sick-room. She enters as soon as she picks up a tray with a bowl of cornflakes, off* U.R.)

MRS. STANLEY (*to her*). Anything I can do, Miss Preen?

MISS PREEN (*exit to library*). No, thank you.

(*The* VOICE *is heard again as she opens the doors. "Don't call yourself a Doctor in my presence! You're a quack if I ever saw one!"*)

(RICHARD *returns from the hall* L., *carrying two huge packages and a sheaf of cablegrams.*)

RICHARD (*crosses to sofa, puts packages on floor* R. *of sofa, telegrams on table back of sofa.*) Four more cablegrams and more packages . . . Dad is going crazy upstairs, with that bell ringing all the time.

(*Meanwhile* JUNE, *the daughter of the house, has come down the stairs* C. *An attractive girl of twenty.*)

(*At the same time the telephone is ringing.* JUNE *crosses* D.R. *to phone.*)

MRS. STANLEY. Oh, dear! . . . June, will you go? . . . What did you say, Richard?

RICHARD (*examining the packages*). One's from New York and one from San Francisco.

MRS. STANLEY. There was something from Alaska early this morning.

RICHARD. Really?

JUNE (*at the telephone*). Yes? . . . Yes, that's right.

MRS. STANLEY. Who is it?

(*Before* JUNE *can answer, the double doors are opened again.* MISS PREEN *appears* D.R. *The* VOICE *calls after her: "Doesn't that bird-brain of yours ever function?"*)

MISS PREEN (*enters* D.R. *Crosses* L.). I—I'll get them right away. . . . He wants some Players' Club cigarettes.

MRS. STANLEY. Players' Club?

(JOHN *enters from stairs* C. *with pillows. Gives pillows to* MISS PREEN D.R., *exits up* R.)

RICHARD. They have 'em at Kitchener's. I'll run down and get 'em. (*He is off* L.)

JUNE (*still at the phone*). Hello . . . Yes, I'm waiting.

319

MRS. STANLEY. Tell me, Miss Preen, is he—are they bringing him out soon?

MISS PREEN (wearily). We're getting him out of bed now. He'll be out very soon . . . Oh, thank you. (This last is to JOHN who has descended the stairs with three or four pillows. MISS PREEN starts off R.)

MRS. STANLEY. Oh, I'm so glad. He must be very happy.

(And again we hear the invalid's VOICE as MISS PREEN passes into the room, R. "Trapped like a rat in this hell-hole! Take your fish-hooks off me!")

JUNE (at the phone). Hello . . . Yes, he's here, but he can't come to the phone right now . . . London? (She covers the transmitter with her hand.) It's London calling Mr. Whiteside.

MRS. STANLEY. My, my!

JUNE (at phone). Two o'clock? Yes, I think he could talk then. All right. (She hangs up.) Well, who do you think that was? Mr. H. G. Wells from London.

MRS. STANLEY (wild-eyed). H. G. Wells? On our telephone?

(The door-bell again.)

JUNE (crosses L. to door L. Exit). I'll go. This is certainly a busy house.

(Meantime SARAH, the cook, has come from the dining-room up R. with a pitcher of orange juice.)

SARAH. I got his orange juice.

MRS. STANLEY (as SARAH knocks on double doors D.R.). Oh, that's fine, Sarah. Is it fresh?

SARAH. Yes, ma'am. (She knocks on the door.)

(The doors are opened; SARAH hands the orange juice to the nurse. The VOICE roars once more: "You have the touch of a sex-starved cobra!")

SARAH (beaming). His voice is just the same as on the radio. (She disappears into the dining-room as JUNE returns from the entrance hall, L., ushering in two friends of her mother's, MRS. DEXTER and MRS. MCCUTCHEON. One is carrying a flowering plant, partially wrapped; the other is holding, with some care, what turns out to be a jar of calf's-foot jelly.)

THE LADIES (enter L. Cross to C.). Good morning.

MRS. STANLEY (to them). Girls, what do you think? He's getting up and coming out this morning!

MRS MCCUTCHEON. You don't mean it!

MRS. DEXTER. Can we stay and see him?

MRS. STANLEY. Why, of course—he'd love it. (JUNE enters L. Crosses to stairs.) Girls, do you know what just happened?

JUNE (departing upstairs). I'll be upstairs, Mother, if you want me.

MRS. STANLEY. What? . . . Oh, yes. June, tell your father he'd better come down, will you? Mr. Whiteside is coming out.

JUNE. Yes, Mother. (She exits upstairs.)

MRS. DEXTER. Is he really coming out this morning? I brought him a plant—do you think it's all right if I give it to him?

MRS. STANLEY. Why, I think that would be lovely.

MRS. MCCUTCHEON. And some calf's-foot jelly.

MRS. STANLEY. Why, how nice! Who do you think was on the phone just now? H. G. Wells, from London. And look at those cablegrams. (The LADIES cross L.) He's had calls and messages from all over this country and Europe. The New York Times—and Felix Frankfurter, and Dr. Dafoe, the Mount Wilson Observatory—I just can't tell you what's been going on, I'm simply exhausted. (Crosses R., sits chair R.C.)

MRS. DEXTER (crossing to MRS. STANLEY R.). There's a big piece about it in this week's Time. Did you see it?

MRS. STANLEY. No—really?

MRS. MCCUTCHEON (crosses R., gives MRS. DEXTER calf's-foot jelly, reads from Time.) Your name's in it too, Daisy. Listen: "Portly Sheridan Whiteside, critic, lecturer, wit, radio orator, intimate friend of the great and near great, last week found his celebrated wit no weapon with which to combat an injured hip. The Falstaffian Mr. Whiteside, trekking across the country on one of his annual lecture tours, met his Waterloo in the shape of a small piece of ice on the doorstep of Mr. and Mrs. Ernest

W. Stanley, of Mesalia, Ohio. Result: Cancelled lectures and disappointment to thousands of adoring clubwomen in Omaha, Denver, and points West. Further result: The idol of the air waves rests until further notice in home of surprised Mr. and Mrs. Stanley. Possibility: Christmas may be postponed this year." What's *that* mean?

MRS. STANLEY. Why, what do you think of that? *(She takes magazine: reads.)* "A small piece of ice on the doorstep of Mr. and Mrs. . . ." Think of it!

MRS. MCCUTCHEON *(crosses L. to sofa D.L., sits).* Of course if it were *my* house, Daisy, I'd have a bronze plate put on the step, right where he fell. *(MRS. DEXTER eases back of couch.)*

MRS. STANLEY. Well, of course, I felt terrible about it. He just never goes to dinner anywhere, and he finally agreed to come here, and then *this* had to happen. Poor Mr. Whiteside! But it's going to be so wonderful having him with us, even for a little while. Just think of it! We'll sit around in the evening, and discuss books and plays, all the great people he's known. And he'll talk in that wonderful way of his. He may even read "Good-bye, Mr. Chips" to us.

(MR. STANLEY, solid, substantial—the American business man—is descending the stairs C.)

STANLEY *(coming down C.).* Daisy, I can't wait any longer. If Mr. Whiteside—ah, good morning, ladies.

LADIES. Good morning.

MRS. STANLEY *(rises, crosses C.).* Ernest, he's coming out any minute, and H. G. Wells telephoned from London, and we're in *Time.* Look. *(She hands* Time *to STANLEY.)*

STANLEY *(as he hands the magazine back to her).* I don't like this kind of publicity at all, Daisy. When do you suppose he's going to leave?

MRS. STANLEY. Well, he's only getting up this morning—after all, he's had quite a shock, and he's been in bed for two full weeks. He'll certainly have to rest a few days, Ernest.

STANLEY. Well, I'm sure it's a great honor his being in the house, but it *is* a little upsetting—phone going all the time, bells ringing, messenger boys running in and out— *(Out of the sick-room comes a business-like-looking young woman about thirty, with letters and notebook. Her name is MARGARET CUTLER—MAGGIE to her friends.)*

MAGGIE *(closing library doors).* Pardon me, Mrs. Stanley—have the cigarettes come yet? *(STANLEY eases U.L.)*

MRS. STANLEY *(crosses R.).* They're on the way, Miss Cutler. My son went for them.

MAGGIE *(crosses L. to chair R.).* Thank you.

MRS. STANLEY. Ah—this is Miss Cutler, Mr. Whiteside's secretary.

MAGGIE. How do you do. May I move this chair?

MRS. STANLEY *(all eagerness).* You mean he's coming out now?

(JOHN appears in doorway up R.C.)

MAGGIE *(moves chair up C. of desk). (Quietly.)* He is indeed.

MRS. MCCUTCHEON *(rises, crosses D.L.).* He's coming out!

MRS. DEXTER *(crossing to MRS. MCCUTCHEON D.L.).* I can hardly wait!

MRS. STANLEY. Ernest, call June. June! June! Mr. Whiteside is coming out!

JOHN *(beckoning to SARAH off U.R.).* Sarah! Sarah! Mr. Whiteside is coming out!

MRS. STANLEY. I'm so excited I just don't know what to do!

MRS. DEXTER. Me too! I know that I'll simply—

(SARAH and JOHN appear in dining-room entrance, JUNE on the stairs. MRS. STANLEY and the two other ladies are keenly expectant; even STANLEY is on the qui vive. The double doors are opened once more and DR. BRADLEY appears, bag in hand, D.R. He has taken a good deal of punishment, and speaks with a rather false heartiness.)

MRS. STANLEY. Good morning, Dr. Bradley.

DR. BRADLEY. Good morning, good morning. Well, here we are, merry and bright. Bring our little patient out, Miss Preen.

(A moment's pause, and then a wheelchair is rolled through the door by the nurse. It is full of pillows, blankets, and SHERIDAN WHITESIDE. SHERIDAN WHITESIDE *is indeed portly and Falstaffian. He is wearing an elaborate velvet smoking-jacket and a very loud tie, and he looks like every caricature ever drawn of him. There is a hush as the wheelchair rolls into the room* D.R. *Welcoming smiles break over every face. The chair comes to a halt;* WHITESIDE *looks slowly around, into each and every beaming face. His fingers drum for a moment on the arm of the chair. He looks slowly around once more.* MAGGIE *comes* D.R. DR. BRADLEY *crosses to the wheelchair, then* MRS. STANLEY. *She laughs nervously. And then* HE *speaks.)*

WHITESIDE (R.C., *quietly to* MAGGIE). I may vomit.

MRS. STANLEY (*with a nervous little laugh*). Good morning, Mr. Whiteside. I'm Mrs. Ernest Stanley—remember? And this is Mr. Stanley.

STANLEY (*coming to* D.C.). How do you do, Mr. Whiteside? I hope that you are better.

WHITESIDE. Thank you. I am suing you for a hundred and fifty thousand dollars.

STANLEY. How's that? What?

WHITESIDE. I said I am suing you for a hundred and fifty thousand dollars.

MRS. STANLEY. You mean—because you fell on our steps, Mr. Whiteside?

WHITESIDE. Samuel J. Liebowitz will explain it to you in court. Who are those two harpies standing there like the kiss of death? (MRS. MCCUTCHEON, *with a little gasp, drops the calf's-foot jelly. It smashes to the floor.)*

MRS. MCCUTCHEON. Oh, dear! My calf's-foot jelly.

WHITESIDE. Made from your own foot, I have no doubt. And now, Mrs. Stanley, I have a few small matters to take up with you. Since this corner druggist at my elbow tells me that I shall be confined to this mouldy mortuary for at least another ten days, due entirely to your stupidity and negligence, I shall have to carry on my activities as best I can. I shall require the exclusive use of this room, as well as that drafty sewer which you call the library.

I want no one to come in or out while I am in this room.

STANLEY. What do you mean, sir?

MRS. STANLEY (*stunned*). We have to go up the stairs to get to our rooms, Mr. Whiteside.

WHITESIDE. Isn't there a back entrance?

MRS. STANLEY. Why—yes.

WHITESIDE. Then use that. I shall also require a room for my secretary, Miss Cutler. Let me see. I will have a great many incoming and outgoing calls, so please do not use the telephone. I sleep until noon and must have quiet through the house until that hour. There will be five for lunch today. Where is the cook?

STANLEY. Mr. Whiteside, if I may interrupt for a moment—

WHITESIDE. You may not, sir. Will you take your clammy hand off my chair? (*This last to* MISS PREEN *as she arranges his pillow.)* . . . And now will you all leave quietly, or must I ask my secretary to pass among you with a baseball bat?

(MRS. DEXTER *and* MRS. MCCUTCHEON *are beating a hasty retreat,* MRS. DEXTER's *gift still in her hand.)*

MRS. MCCUTCHEON. Well—good-bye, Daisy. We'll call you—Oh, no, we mustn't use the phone. Well—we'll see you.

MRS. DEXTER. Good-bye. (*Both exit up* L.)

STANLEY (*boldly*). Now look here, Mr. Whiteside—

WHITESIDE. There is nothing to discuss, sir. Considering the damage I have suffered at your hands, I am asking very little. Good day.

STANLEY (*controlling himself, crosses* L., *exit* L.). I'll call you from the office later, Daisy.

WHITESIDE. Not on this phone, please.

(STANLEY *gives him a look, but goes.)*

WHITESIDE. Here is the menu for lunch. (*He extends a slip of paper to* MRS. STANLEY.)

MRS. STANLEY. But—I've already ordered lunch.

WHITESIDE. It will be sent up to you on a tray. I am using the dining-room for my guests . . . Where are those cigarettes?

MRS. STANLEY (*eases up*). Why—my son went for them. I don't know why he— here, Sarah. Here is the menu for lunch. (*She hands* SARAH *the luncheon slip, when she has crossed to* MRS. STANLEY.) I'll— have mine upstairs on a tray. (SARAH *and* JOHN *depart up* R.)

WHITESIDE (*to* JUNE, *who has been posed on the landing during all this.*) Young lady, I cannot stand indecision. Will you either go up those stairs or come down them?

(JUNE *is about to speak, decides against it and ascends the stairs with a good deal of spirit.*)

(MRS. STANLEY *is hovering uncertainly on the steps as* RICHARD *returns with the cigarettes.*)

RICHARD (*crosses to* R.C.). Oh, good morning, Mr. Whiteside. Here are the cigarettes. --I'm sorry I was so long—I had to go to three different stores.

WHITESIDE. How did you travel? By ox-cart? You were gone long enough to have a baby. (RICHARD *is considerably taken aback. His eyes go to his mother, who motions to him to come up the stairs. They disappear together, their eyes unsteadily on* WHITESIDE.) Is there a man in the world who suffers as I do from the gross inadequacies of the human race! (*To* MISS PREEN *who is fussing around the chair again tucking blanket about him.*) Take those canal boats away from me! (*She obeys hastily.*) Go in and read the life of Florence Nightingale and learn how unfitted you are for your chosen profession.

(MISS PREEN *glares at him, but goes* D.R., *leaves doors open.*)

BRADLEY (*heartily—coming down to* L. *of chair*). Well, I think I can safely leave you in Miss Cutler's capable hands. Shall I look in again this afternoon?

WHITESIDE. If you do, I shall spit right in your eye.

BRADLEY. Ah! What a sense of humor you writers have! By the way, it isn't really worth mentioning, but—I've been doing a little writing myself. About my medical experiences.

WHITESIDE (*quietly*). Am I to be spared nothing?

BRADLEY. Would it be too much to ask you to—glance over it while you're here?

WHITESIDE (*eyes half closed, as though the pain were too exquisite to bear*). Trapped.

BRADLEY (*delving into his bag*). Well! I just happen to have a copy with me. (*He brings out a tremendous manuscript, places it on* WHITESIDE's *lap.*) "The Story of an Humble Practitioner, or Forty Years an Ohio Doctor."

WHITESIDE. I shall drop everything.

BRADLEY (*crossing* L.). Thank you, and I hope you like it. Well, see you on the morrow. Keep that hip quiet and don't forget those little pills. Good-bye. (*He goes up* L.)

WHITESIDE (*annoyed at* BRADLEY). Oh-h! (*Handing the manuscript to* MAGGIE *who places it on chest* D.R.) Maggie, will you take "Forty Years Below the Navel" or whatever it's called?

MAGGIE (*crossing* L. *to* C., *surveying him*). Well, I must say you have certainly behaved with all your accustomed grace and charm.

WHITESIDE. Look here, Puss—I am in no mood to discuss my behavior, good or bad.

MAGGIE. These people have done everything in their power to make you comfortable. And they happen, God knows why, to look upon you with certain wonder and admiration.

WHITESIDE. If they had looked a little more carefully at their doorstep I would not be troubling them now. I did not wish to cross their cheerless threshold. I was hounded and badgered into it. I now find myself, after two weeks of racking pain, accused of behaving without charm. What would you have me do? Kiss them?

MAGGIE (*giving up, crossing to* WHITESIDE). Very well, Sherry. After ten years I should have known better than to try to do anything about your manners. But when I finally give up this job I may write a book about it all. "Cavalcade of Insult" or

"Through the Years With Prince Charming." (*Tosses him letters.*)

WHITESIDE. Listen, Repulsive, you are tied to me with an umbilical cord made of piano-wire. And now if we may dismiss the subject of my charm, for which, incidentally, I receive fifteen hundred dollars per appearance, (*Enter* HARRIET L.) possibly we can go to work . . . Oh, no, we can't. Yes? (MAGGIE *crosses* R. *to* D.R.)

(*This last is addressed to a wraith-like lady of uncertain years, who has more or less floated into the room. She is carrying a large spray of holly, and her whole manner suggests something not quite of this world.*)

HARRIET (*crosses to him. Her voice seems to float, too*). My name is Harriet Stanley. I know you are Sheridan Whiteside. I saw this holly, framed green against the pine trees. I remembered what you had written about "Tess" and "Jude the Obscure." It was the nicest present I could bring you. (*She places the holly in his lap, and exits upstairs* C.)

WHITESIDE (*his eyes following her*). For God's sake, what was that?

MAGGIE (*crosses* L. *to packages by sofa, takes them to chair up* R.). That was Mr. Stanley's sister, Harriet. I've talked to her a few times—she's quite strange.

WHITESIDE. Strange? She's right out of "The Hound of the Baskervilles" . . . You know, I've seen that face before somewhere.

MAGGIE (*as she puts packages on chair* U.C.). Nonsense. You couldn't have.

WHITESIDE (*dismissing it*). Oh, well! Let's get down to work. (*He hands her the armful of holly.*) Here! Press this in the Doctor's book. (MAGGIE *places holly on sofa. He picks up the first of a pile of letters.*) I see no reason why I should endorse Maiden Form Brassieres. (*He crumples up letter and drops it.*) If young men keep asking me how to become dramatic critics— (*He tears up letter and drops it on the floor.*)

MAGGIE (*who has picked up the little sheaf of messages from the table back of sofa*). Here are some telegrams.

WHITESIDE (*a letter in his hand*). What date is this?

MAGGIE. December tenth. (MAGGIE *sits sofa.*)

WHITESIDE. Send a wire to Columbia Broadcasting: "You can schedule my Christmas Eve broadcast from the New York studio, as I shall return East instead of proceeding to Hollywood. Stop. For special New Year's Eve broadcast will have as my guests Jascha Heifetz, Katharine Cornell, Schiaparelli, the Lunts, and Dr. Alexis Carrel, with Anthony Eden on short wave from England. Whiteside."

MAGGIE. Are you sure you'll be all right by Christmas, Sherry?

WHITESIDE. Of course I will. Send a cable to Sacha Guitry: "Will be in Paris June ninth. Dinner seven-thirty. Whiteside." . . . Wire to *Harper's Magazine:* "Do not worry, Stinky. Copy will arrive. Whiteside." . . . Send a cable to the Maharajah of Jehraput, Bombay: "Dear Boo-Boo: Schedule changed. Can you meet me Calcutta July twelfth? Dinner eight-thirty. Whiteside." . . . Arturo Toscanini. Where *is he?*

MAGGIE. I'll find him.

WHITESIDE. "Counting on you January 4th Metropolitan Opera House my annual benefit Home for Paroled Convicts. As you know this is a very worthy cause and close to my heart. Tibbett, Rethberg, Martinelli, and Flagstad have promised me personally to appear. Will you have quiet supper with me and Ethel Barrymore afterwards? Whiteside." (*Telephone rings.*) (MAGGIE *crosses back of* WHITESIDE *to phone* D.R.) If that's for Mrs. Stanley, tell them she's too drunk to talk.

MAGGIE (*at phone* D.R.). Hello . . . what? . . . Hollywood?

WHITESIDE. If it's Goldwyn, hang up.

MAGGIE. Hello, Banjo! (*Her face lights up.*)

WHITESIDE. Banjo! Give me that phone!

MAGGIE. Banjo, you old so-and-so! How are you, darling?

WHITESIDE. Come on—give me that!

MAGGIE. Shut up, Sherry! . . . Are you coming East, Banjo? I miss you . . . Oh, he's going to live.

WHITESIDE. Stop driveling and give me the phone.

MAGGIE *(hands him phone—stands back of wheelchair).* In fact, he's screaming at me now. Here he is.

WHITESIDE *(taking the phone).* How are you, you fawn's behind? And what are you giving me for Christmas? *(He roars with laughter at* BANJO's *answer.)* What news, Banjo, my boy? How's the picture coming? . . . How are Wacko and Sloppo? . . . No, no, I'm all right . . . Yes, I'm in very good hands. I've got the best horse doctor in town . . . What about you? Having any fun? . . . Playing any cribbage? . . . What? *(Again he laughs loudly.)* . . . Well, don't take all his money—leave a little bit for me. . . . You're what? . . . Having your portrait painted? By whom? Milt Gross? . . . Not really? . . . No, I'm going back to New York from here. I'll be there for twelve days, and then I go to Dartmouth for the Drama Festival. You wouldn't understand . . . Well, I can't waste my time talking to Hollywood riff-raff. Kiss Louella Parsons for me. Good-bye. *(He hangs up and turns to* MAGGIE. MAGGIE *puts phone on table* D.R.*)* He took fourteen hundred dollars from Sam Goldwyn at cribbage last night, and Sam said "Banjo, I will never play garbage with you again."

MAGGIE *(crossing* L. *to* L.C.*).* What's all this about his having his portrait painted?

WHITESIDE. M-m, Salvador Dali. *(MISS PREEN enters* D.R.*)* That's all that face of his needs—a Surrealist to paint it. . . . What do *you* want now, Miss Bed Pan?

(MAGGIE crosses to table back of couch L.*)*

(This is addressed to MISS PREEN *who has returned somewhat apprehensively to the room.)*

MISS PREEN. It's—it's your pills. One every forty-five minutes. *(She drops them into his lap and hurries out of the room—Exit* D.R.*)*

(MAGGIE, back of couch L., *opens cable.)*

WHITESIDE *(looking after her).* . . . Now where were we?

MAGGIE *(the messages in her hand, crosses to* C.*).* Here's a cable from that dear friend of yours, Lorraine Sheldon.

WHITESIDE. Let me see it.

MAGGIE *(reading message, in a tone that gives* MISS SHELDON *none the better of it. Crosses to* C.*).* "Sherry, my poor sweet lamb, have been in Scotland on a shooting party with Lord and Lady Cunard and only just heard of your poor sweet hip." *(MAGGIE gives a faint raspberry, then reads on.)* "Am down here in Surrey with Lord Bottomley. Sailing Wednesday on the *Normandie* and cannot wait to see my poor sweet Sherry. Your blossom girl, Lorraine." . . . In the words of the master, I may vomit.

WHITESIDE. Don't be bitter, Puss, just because Lorraine is more beautiful than you are.

MAGGIE. Lorraine Sheldon is a very fair example of that small but vicious circle you move in.

WHITESIDE. Pure sex jealousy if I ever saw it . . . Give me the rest of those.

MAGGIE *(mumbling to herself, crossing* R. *and handing him cables).* Lorraine Sheldon . . . Lord Bottomley . . . My Aunt Fanny. *(Crossing* U.C.*)*

WHITESIDE *(who has opened the next message).* Ah! It's from Destiny's Tot.

MAGGIE *(crossing to* WHITESIDE*). (Peering over his shoulder.)* Oh, England's little Rover Boy?

WHITESIDE. Um-hm. *(He reads.)* "Treacle face, what is this I hear about a hip fractured in some bordello brawl? Does this mean our Hollywood Christmas Party is off? Finished the new play in Pago-Pago and it's superb. Myself and a ukelele leave Honolulu tomorrow in that order. By the way, the Sultan of Zanzibar wants to meet Ginger Rogers. Let's face it. Oscar Wilde."

MAGGIE *(crossing* L. *to couch, sits).* He does travel, doesn't he. You know, it would be nice if the world went around Beverly Carlton for a change.

WHITESIDE. Hollywood next week—why couldn't he stop over on his way to New York? Send him a cable. "Beverly Carlton. Royal Hawaiian Hotel, Honolulu." *(The door-bell rings.* WHITESIDE *is properly annoyed.)* If these people intend to have their friends using the front door . . . *(JOHN enters up* L.*)*

MAGGIE. What do you want them to do—use a rope ladder? (JOHN *at* L.C., *crosses to exit* L.)

WHITESIDE. I will not have a lot of mildewed pus-bags rushing in and out of this house while I am— (*He stops as the voice of* JOHN *is heard at the front door.* "Oh, good morning, Mr. Jefferson." *The answering voice of* MR. JEFFERSON: "Good morning, John.") (*Roaring—*MAGGIE *rises, crosses to up* L.) There's nobody home! The Stanleys have been arrested for white-slavery! Go away! (*But the visitor, meanwhile, has already appeared in the archway.* JEFFERSON *is an interesting-looking young man in his early thirties.*)

JEFFERSON (*crossing to her, back of couch*). Good morning, Mr. Whiteside. I'm Jefferson, of the Mesalia *Journal*.

WHITESIDE (*sotto voce, to* MAGGIE). Get rid of him.

MAGGIE (*brusquely*). I'm sorry—Mr. Whiteside is seeing no one.

JEFFERSON. Really?

MAGGIE. So will you please excuse us? Good day.

JEFFERSON (*not giving up*). Mr. Whiteside seems to be sitting up and taking notice.

MAGGIE. I'm afraid he's not taking notice of the Mesalia *Journal*. Do you mind?

JEFFERSON (*sizing up* MAGGIE). You know, if I'm going to be insulted I'd like it to be by Mr. Whiteside himself. I never did like carbon copies.

WHITESIDE (*looking around; interested*). M-m, touché, if I ever heard one. And in Mesalia too, Maggie, dear.

MAGGIE (*still on the job*). Will you please leave?

JEFFERSON (*ignoring her. Crosses to* C. MAGGIE *crosses to* R.C.). How about an interview, Mr. Whiteside?

WHITESIDE. I never give them. Go away.

JEFFERSON. Mr. Whiteside, if I don't get this interview, I lose my job.

WHITESIDE. That would be quite all right with me.

JEFFERSON. Now you don't mean that, Mr. Whiteside. You used to be a newspaper man yourself. You know what editors are like. Well, mine's the toughest one that ever lived.

WHITESIDE. You won't get around me that way. If you don't like him, get off the paper.

JEFFERSON. Yes, but I happen to think it's a good paper. William Allen White could have got out of Emporia, but he didn't.

WHITESIDE. You have the effrontery, in my presence, to compare yourself with William Allen White?

JEFFERSON. Only in the sense that White stayed in Emporia, and I want to stay here and say what I want to say.

WHITESIDE. Such as what?

JEFFERSON (*crossing to below couch* L.). Well, I can't put it into words, Mr. Whiteside—it'd sound like an awful lot of hooey. But the *Journal* was my father's paper. It's kind of a sentimental point with me, the paper. I'd like to carry on where he left off.

WHITESIDE. Ah—ahh. So you own the paper, eh?

JEFFERSON. That's right.

WHITESIDE. Then this terrifying editor, this dread journalistic Apocalypse is—you yourself?

JEFFERSON. In a word, yes.

WHITESIDE (*chuckles with appreciation*). I see.

MAGGIE (*annoyed, starts off* R.). In the future, Sherry, let me know when you don't want to talk to people, I'll usher them right in. (*She goes into the library* D.R.)

WHITESIDE. Young man, that kind of journalistic trick went out with Richard Harding Davis . . . Come over here. I suppose you've written that novel?

JEFFERSON (*eases* R.). No. I've written that play.

WHITESIDE. Well, I don't want to read it. But you can send me your paper—I'll take a year's subscription. Do you write the editorials, too?

JEFFERSON. Every one of them.

WHITESIDE. I know just what they're like.

Ah, me! I'm afraid you're that noble young newspaper man—crusading, idealistic, dull. *(He looks up and down.)* Very good casting, too.

JEFFERSON. You're not bad casting yourself, Mr. Whiteside.

WHITESIDE. We won't discuss it. . . . Ah, do these old eyes see a box of goodies over there? Hand them to me on your way out.

JEFFERSON *(crossing D.R. to small desk table).* The trouble is, Mr. Whiteside, that your being in this town comes under the heading of news. Practically the biggest news since the depression. So I just got to get a story. *(Crossing to L. of* WHITESIDE.*) (As he passes candy.)*

WHITESIDE *(examining the candy).* M-m, pecan butternut fudge.

*(*MISS PREEN, *on her way to the kitchen with empty plate on tray, from the library* R. *stops short as she sees* WHITESIDE *with a piece of candy in his hand. She leaves doors open.)*

MISS PREEN *(crossing D.R.).* Oh, my! You mustn't eat candy, Mr. Whiteside. It's very bad for you.

WHITESIDE *(turning).* My Great-aunt Jennifer ate a whole box of candy every day of her life. She lived to be a hundred and two, and when she had been dead three days she looked better than you do now. *(He swings blandly back to his visitor as he eats a candy.)* What were you saying, old fellow? You were about to say?

JEFFERSON *(as* MISS PREEN *makes a hasty exit up* R.*).* I can at least report to my readers that chivalry is not yet dead.

WHITESIDE. We won't discuss it. . . . Well, now that you have won me with your pretty ways, what would you like to know?

JEFFERSON *(crossing in a step to* WHITESIDE*).* Well, how about a brief talk on famous murders? You're an authority on murder as a fine art.

WHITESIDE. My dear boy, when I talk about murder I get paid for it. I have made more money out of the Snyder-Gray case than the lawyers did, so don't expect to get it for nothing.

JEFFERSON. Well, then, what do you think of Mesalia, how long are you going to be here, where are you going, things like that.

WHITESIDE. Very well. (A) Mesalia is a town of irresistible charm; (B) I cannot wait to get out of it, and (C) I am going from here to Crockfield, for my semiannual visit to the Crockfield Home for Paroled Convicts, for which I have raised over half a million dollars in the last five years. From there I go to New York. Have you ever been to Crockfield, Jefferson?

JEFFERSON. No, I haven't. I always meant to.

WHITESIDE. As a newspaper man you ought to go, instead of wasting your time with me. It's only about seventy-five miles from here. Did you ever hear how Crockfield started? *(Candy box in basket on arm of his wheelchair.)*

JEFFERSON *(crossing L.).* No, I didn't.

WHITESIDE. Sit down, Jefferson . . . make yourself comfortable. *(*JEFFERSON *sits on arm of couch.)* It is one of the most endearing and touching stories of our generation. One misty St. Valentine's Eve—the year was 1901—a little old lady who had given her name to an era, Victoria, lay dying in Windsor Castle. Maude Adams had not yet caused every young heart to swell as she tripped across the stage as Peter Pan; Irving Berlin had not yet written the first note of a ragtime rigadoon that was to set the nation's feet a-tapping, and Elias P. Crockfield was just emerging from the State penitentiary. Destitute, embittered, cruel of heart, he wandered, on this St. Valentine's Eve, into a little church. But there was no godliness in his heart that night, no prayer upon his lips. In the faltering twilight, Elias P. Crockfield made his way toward the poorbox. With callous fingers he ripped open this poignant testimony of a simple people's faith. Greedily he clutched at the few pitiful coins within. And then a child's wavering treble broke the twilight stillness. "Please, Mr. Man," said a little girl's voice, "won't you be my Valentine?" Elias P. Crockfield turned. There stood before him a bewitching little creature of five, her yellow curls cascading over her shoulders like a golden Niagara, in her tiny outstretched hand a humble valentine. In that one crystal moment a sealed door opened in the heart of Elias P. Crockfield, and in his mind was born an idea. Twenty-five years later three thousand ruddy-cheeked convicts were gamboling on the broad lawns of Crockfield Home, frolicking in the cool depths of its swimming pool, broadcasting with their own symphony orchestra from their own radio station. Elias P. Crockfield has long since gone to his Maker, but the little girl of the golden curls, now grown to lovely womanhood, is known as the Angel of Crockfield, for she is the wife of the warden. *(Enter* MAGGIE, *stands* D.R.*)* And in the main hall of Crockfield, between a Rembrandt and an El Greco, there hangs, in a simple little frame, a humble valentine.

MAGGIE *(who has emerged from the library in time to hear the finish of this).* And in the men's washroom, every Christmas Eve, the ghost of Elias P. Crockfield appears in one of the booths. . . . Will you sign this, please! *(Hands him a letter— the door-bell is heard.)*

WHITESIDE *(*JEFFERSON *rises, crosses to* C.*).* This ageing ingénue, Mr. Jefferson, I retain in my employ only because she is the sole support of her two-headed brother. *(Signs letter and hands it back to* MAGGIE.*)*

JEFFERSON *(crossing to couch for hat and starting for arch* L.*).* I understand . . . Well, thank you very much, Mr. Whiteside—you've been very kind. By the way, I'm a cribbage player, if you need one while you're here. *(*JOHN *enters up* L.C. *crosses to hall* L.*)*

WHITESIDE. Fine. How much can you afford to lose?

JEFFERSON. I usually win.

WHITESIDE. We won't discuss that. Come back at eight-thirty. We'll play three-handed with Elsie Dinsmore . . . Metz!

METZ. Sherry!

WHITESIDE. Metz! *(*JEFFERSON *eases up stage* L.*)* *(*JOHN, *who has answered the door-bell, has ushered in a strange-looking little man in his fifties. His hair runs all over his head and his clothes are too big for him.* JOHN *carries in a package which he places on table* D.L.*)* Metz, you incredible beetle-hound! What are you doing here?

METZ *(crossing to* C. *With a mild Teutonic accent).* I explain, Sherry. First I kiss my little Maggie.

MAGGIE *(crosses to* C. *Embracing him).* Metz darling, what a wonderful surprise!

WHITESIDE. The enchanted Metz! Why aren't you at the university? . . . Jefferson, you are standing in the presence of one of the great men of our time. When you write that inevitable autobiography, be sure to record the day that you met Professor Metz, the world's greatest authority on insect life.

JEFFERSON. How do you do.

METZ. How do you do. Well, Sherry?

WHITESIDE. Metz, stop looking at me adoringly and tell me why you are here.

METZ *(crosses* R. *to* WHITESIDE. MAGGIE *crosses down to the* R. *of couch).* You are sick, Sherry, so I come to cheer you.

MAGGIE. Metz, you tore yourself away from your little insects and came here? Sherry, you don't deserve it.

WHITESIDE. How are all your little darlings, Metz? Jefferson, would you believe that eight volumes could be written on the mating instinct of the female white ant? He did it.

METZ. Seven on the female, Sherry. One on the male.

WHITESIDE. Jefferson, he lived for two years in a cave with nothing but plant lice. He rates three pages in the Encyclopedia Britannica. Don't you, my little hookworm?

METZ. Please, Sherry, you embarrass me. Look—I have brought you a present to while away the hours. Please— *(Bringing stool at staircase to wheel-chair. He motions to* JOHN, *who carries the package to stool* L. *of wheel-chair. Package is in brown canvas cover.)* I said to my students: "Boys and girls, I want to give a present to my sick friend, Sheridan Whiteside." So you know what we did? We made for you a community of Periplaneta Americana, commonly known as the American cockroach. Behold, Sherry! Roach City! *(He strips off the cover.)* Inside here are ten thousand cockroaches.

JOHN. Ten thousand— *(Headed for the kitchen* U.R. *in great excitement.)* Sarah! Sarah! What do you think! *(Exits up* R.*)*

METZ. And in one week, Sherry, if all goes well, there will be *fifty* thousand.

MAGGIE. If all goes well—? What can go wrong? They're in there, aren't they?

WHITESIDE (*glaring at her*). Quiet, please.

METZ. Here in Roach City they play, they make love, they mate, they die. See—here is the graveyard. They even bury their own dead.

MAGGIE. I'm glad of that, or I'd have to do it.

WHITESIDE. Ssh!

METZ. You can watch them, Sherry, while they live out their whole lives. Look! (*JEFFERSON crosses* C.) Here is where they store their grain, here is the commissary of the aristocracy, here is their maternity hospital. It is fascinating. They do everything that human beings do.

WHITESIDE. Magnificent! This is my next piece for the London *Mercury*.

MAGGIE. Well!

WHITESIDE. Please, Maggie, these are *my* cockroaches.

MAGGIE. Sorry. (*She crosses to back of* WHITESIDE's *chair*.)

WHITESIDE. Go ahead, Metz.

METZ. With these earphones, Sherry, you listen to the mating calls. There are microphones down inside. (*JEFFERSON crosses to the back of* WHITESIDE's *chair*.) Listen!

(*METZ has put the earphones over* WHITESIDE's *ears; he listens rapt*.)

WHITESIDE. Hmmm. How long has this been going on?

(*MRS. STANLEY starts timorously to descend the stairs. She tiptoes as far as the landing, then pauses as she sees the group below*.)

(*Meanwhile, Professor Metz, his mind ever on his work, has moved in the direction of the dining room*.)

METZ (*sniffing, he crosses to* R. *and then* C. *Suddenly his face lights up*). Aha! Periplaneta Americana! There are cockroaches in this house! (*The last addressed to* MRS. STANLEY.)

MRS. STANLEY (*shocked into speech*). I beg your pardon! (*WHITESIDE hands the earphones to* METZ.) (*JEFFERSON crosses* D.R.) (*The door-bell rings*.) Mr. Whiteside, I don't know who this man is, but I will not stand here and—

WHITESIDE. Then go upstairs. (*JOHN enters up* L. *crosses to exit* L.) These are probably my luncheon guests. Metz, you're staying for the day, of course.

METZ. Certainly.

WHITESIDE. Jefferson, stay for lunch?

JEFFERSON. Glad to.

(*CONVICTS and* PRISON GUARD *enter from* U.L.)

WHITESIDE. Maggie, tell 'em there'll be two more. (*MAGGIE exits up* R.) Ah, come right in, Baker. Good morning, gentlemen. (*METZ crosses* D.R.) (*The gentlemen addressed are three in number—two white, one black. They are convicts, and they look the part. Prison gray, hand-cuffed together.* BAKER, *in uniform, is a prison guard. He carries a rifle*.) (*BAKER* D.L. *of couch,* CONVICTS *back of couch*.) Jefferson, here are the fruits of that humble valentine. These men, now serving the final months of their prison terms, have chosen to enter the ivy-covered walls of Crockfield. They have come here today to learn from me a little of its tradition. . . . Gentlemen, I envy you your great adventure. (*To one of the convicts*.) You're Michaelson, aren't you? Butcher shop murders? (*Convicts crossing* R. *to* C.)

MICHAELSON. Yes, sir.

WHITESIDE. Thought I recognized you. . . . The last fellow, Jefferson— (*He lowers his tone*.) is Henderson, the hatchet fiend. Always chopped them up in a salad bowl—remember?

JEFFERSON. Oh, yes.

JOHN (*enter up* R.). Lunch is ready, Mr. Whiteside.

WHITESIDE. Good. Let's go right in, gentlemen. (*The* CONVICTS *and* GUARD *head for dining-room* U.R.)

JEFFERSON (*crossing to* WHITESIDE's *chair*). Can I help you?

WHITESIDE. Thank you. (*His voice rises as he is wheeled by* JEFFERSON *into the dining-room, preceded by* METZ.) We're having chicken livers Tettrazini, and Cherries

Jubilee for dessert. I hope every little tummy is a-flutter with gastric *juices*. *(The curtain starts down.)* John, close the doors. I don't want a lot of people prying on their betters.

(The doors close. Only MRS. STANLEY *is left outside. She collapses quietly against the newel post.)*

CURTAIN

SCENE II

Dining-room door open. Library door open.
Late afternoon, a week later. Only a single lamp is lit.
The room, in the week that has passed, has taken on something of the character of its occupant. Books and papers everywhere. Stacks of books on the tables, some of them just half out of their cardboard boxes. Half a dozen or so volumes, which apparently have not appealed to the Master, have been thrown onto the floor. A litter of crumpled papers around the WHITESIDE *wheelchair; an empty candy box has slid off his lap. An old pair of pants have been tossed over one chair, a seedy bathrobe over another. A handsome Chinese vase has been moved out of its accustomed spot and is doing duty as an ash receiver.*
WHITESIDE *is in his wheelchair, asleep. Roach City is beside him, the earphones over his head. He has apparently dozed off while listening to the mating calls of Periplaneta Americana.*
For a moment only his rhythmic breathing is heard. Then MISS PREEN *enters from the library. She brings some medicine—a glass filled with a murky mixture. She pauses when she sees that he is asleep, then, after a good deal of hesitation, gently touches him on the shoulder.* HE *stirs a little;* SHE *musters up her courage and touches him again.*

WHITESIDE *(slowly opening his eyes).* I was dreaming of Lillian Russell, and I awake to find *you*. *(Takes off earphones.)*

MISS PREEN. Your—your medicine, Mr. Whiteside.

WHITESIDE *(taking glass).* What time is it?

MISS PREEN. About half-past six.

WHITESIDE. Where is Miss Cutler?

MISS PREEN. She went out. *(Enter* JOHN *up* R.*)*

WHITESIDE. Out?

MISS PREEN. With Mr. Jefferson. *(She goes into library, leaves doors open.)* *(*JOHN, *meanwhile, has entered from dining-room.)* *(Switch on* R. *bracket lights.)*

JOHN. All right if I turn the lights up, Mr. Whiteside?

WHITESIDE. Yes. Go right ahead, John.

JOHN *(crosses* L. *to switch on chandelier lights).* And Sarah has something for you, Mr. Whiteside. Made it special.

WHITESIDE. She has? Where is she? My Soufflé Queen! *(*JOHN *crosses to* C.*)*

SARAH *(proudly entering with a tray on which reposes her latest delicacy, crosses down to* WHITESIDE*).* Here I am, Mr. Whiteside.

WHITESIDE. She walks in beauty like the night, and in those deft hands there is the art of Michelangelo. Let me taste the new goody. *(With one hand he pours the medicine into the Chinese vase, then swallows at a gulp one of Sarah's not-so-little cakes. An ecstatic expression comes over his face.)* Poetry! Sheer poetry!

SARAH *(beaming).* I put a touch of absinthe in the dough. Do you like it?

WHITESIDE *(rapturously).* Ambrosia!

SARAH. And I got you your Terrapin Maryland for dinner.

WHITESIDE. I have known but three great cooks in my time. The Khedive of Egypt has one. My Great-aunt Jennifer another, and the third, Sarah, is you.

SARAH. Oh, Mr. Whiteside! . . .

WHITESIDE *(lowering his voice and beckoning to them to come closer).* Tell me? How would you like to come to New York and work for me? You and Johnny?

*(*JOHN *crosses* R.*)*

SARAH. Why, Mr. Whiteside!

JOHN. Sarah!

SARAH. Why, it kind of takes my breath away.

JOHN. It would be wonderful, Mr. White-side, but what would we say to Mr. and Mrs. Stanley?

WHITESIDE. Just "Good-bye."

SARAH. But—but they'd be awfully mad, wouldn't they? They've been very kind to us.

WHITESIDE (lightly). Well, if they ever come to New York we can have them for dinner, if I'm not in town. Now run along and think it over. This is our little secret —just between us. And put plenty of sherry in that terrapin . . . Miss Preen! (SARAH and JOHN withdraw, in consider-able excitement.) (Up R. WHITESIDE raises his voice to a roar.) Miss Preen!

MISS PREEN (appearing, breathless, drying her hands). Yes, sir? Yes, sir?

WHITESIDE. What have you got in there, anyway? A sailor?

MISS PREEN. I was—just washing my hands.

WHITESIDE. What time did Miss Cutler go out?

MISS PREEN. Oh, couple hours ago.

WHITESIDE. Mr. Jefferson called for her?

MISS PREEN. Yes, sir.

WHITESIDE (impatiently). All right, all right. Go back to your sex-life.

(MISS PREEN goes. WHITESIDE tries to settle down to his book, but his mind is plainly troubled. He shifts a little; looks anxiously toward the outer door. HARRIET STANLEY comes softly down the steps. She seems delighted to find WHITESIDE alone.)

HARRIET (opening a cardboard portfolio she has brought with her—crossing down c.). Dear Mr. Whiteside, may I show you a few mementoes of the past? I somehow feel that you would love them as I do.

WHITESIDE. I'd be delighted. (Observing her.) Miss Stanley, haven't we met some-where before?

HARRIET. Oh, no. I would have remem-bered. It would have been one of my cher-ished memories—like these. (She spreads the portfolio before him.) Look! Here I

am with my first sweetheart, under our lovely beechwood trees. I was eight and he was ten. I have never forgotten him. What happy times we had! What— (She stops short as she hears footsteps on the stairway.)

STANLEY (from upstairs). But I tell you I'm going to.

HARRIET. There's someone coming! I'll come back! . . . (She gathers up her port-folio and vanishes into the dining-room U.R.) (WHITESIDE looks after her, puzzled.) (It is STANLEY who comes down the stairs. He is plainly coming into the room for a purpose—this is no haphazard descent. He is carrying a slip of paper in his hand, and he is obviously at the boiling-point. A few steps behind comes MRS. STANLEY, appre-hensive and nervous.)

MRS. STANLEY (from stairs). Now, Ernest, please—

STANLEY (to c.). Be quiet, Daisy . . . Mr. Whiteside, I want to talk to you. I don't care whether you're busy or not. I have stood all that I'm going to stand.

WHITESIDE. Indeed?

STANLEY. This is the last straw. I have just received a bill from the telephone com-pany for seven hundred and eighty-four dollars. (He reads from the slip in his hand.) Oklahoma City, Calcutta, Holly-wood, Australia, Rome, New York, New York, New York, New York.— (His voice trails off in an endless succession of New Yorks.) Now I realize, Mr. Whiteside, that you are a distinguished man of let-ters—

MRS. STANLEY (C.). Yes, of course, we both do.

STANLEY. Please . . . But in the past week we have not been able to call our souls our own. We have not had a meal in the dining-room once. I have to tiptoe out of the house in the mornings.

MRS. STANLEY. Now, Ernest—

STANLEY (waving her away). Oh, I come home to find convicts sitting at my dinner-table—butcher-shop murderers. A man putting cockroaches in the kitchen.

MRS. STANLEY. They just escaped, Ernest.

STANLEY. That's not the point. I go into my bathroom and bump into twenty-two Chinese students that you invited here. I tell you I won't stand for it, no matter *who* you are.

WHITESIDE. Have you quite finished?

STANLEY. No, I have not. I go down into the cellar this morning and trip over that octopus that William Beebe sent you. I tell you I won't stand it. Mr. Whiteside, I want you to leave this house— (MRS. STANLEY *starts to tap* STANLEY's *shoulder.*) as soon as you can, and go to a hotel. . . . Stop pawing me, Daisy . . . That's all I've got to say, Mr. Whiteside.

WHITESIDE. And quite enough, I should think. May I remind you again, Mr. Stanley, that I am not a willing guest in this house. I am informed by my doctor that I must remain quiet for another ten days, at which time I shall get out of here so fast that the wind will knock you over, I hope. If, however, you insist on my leaving before that, thereby causing me to suffer a relapse, I shall sue you for every additional day that I am held inactive, which will amount I assure you, to a tidy sum.

STANLEY (*to* MRS. STANLEY). This is outrageous. Outrageous!—

WHITESIDE. As for the details of your petty complaints, those twenty-two Chinese students came straight from the White House, where I assure you they used the bathroom, too!

MRS. STANLEY. Mr. Whiteside, my husband didn't mean—

STANLEY. Yes, I did. I meant every word of it.

WHITESIDE. There is only one point that you make in which I see some slight justice. I do not expect you to pay for my telephone calls, and I shall see to it that restitution is made. Can you provide me with the exact amount?

STANLEY. I certainly can, and I certainly will.

WHITESIDE. Good. I shall instruct my lawyers to deduct it from the hundred and fifty thousand dollars that I am suing you for.

(STANLEY *starts to speak, but simply chokes*

with rage. Furious, he storms up the steps again.)

MRS. STANLEY (*following*). Now, Ernest—

WHITESIDE (*calling after him*). And I'll thank you not to trip over that octopus, which is very sensitive, and which once belonged to Chauncy Depew.

MRS. STANLEY. You—you mustn't get excited. Remember Mr. Whiteside is a guest here. (*Exit upstairs.*)

(*Left alone,* WHITESIDE *enjoys his triumph for a moment, then his mind jumps to more important matters. He looks at his watch, considers a second, then wheels himself over to the telephone.*)

WHITESIDE. Give me the Mesalia *Journal*, please. (*He peers at Roach City while waiting, then taps peremptorily on the glass.*) Hello, *Journal*? . . . Is Mr. Jefferson there? . . . When do you expect him? (RICHARD *and* JUNE *enter* U.L.) No. No message. (*He hangs up; drums impatiently on the arm of his chair. Then he turns sharply at the sound of the outer door opening. But it is the younger* STANLEYS, RICHARD *and* JUNE, *who enter. They are in winter togs, with ice-skates under their arms. In addition,* RICHARD *has a camera slung over his shoulder. Their attitudes change as they see that* WHITESIDE *is in the room.* THEY *slide toward the stairs, obviously trying to be as unobtrusive as possible. Enter* L., *crossing up, then down* C.) Come here, you two. . . . Come on, come on. I'm not going to bite you . . . Now look here. I am by nature a gracious and charming person. If I veer at it, it is on the side of kindness and amiability—I have been observing you two for this past week, and you seem to me to be extremely likable young people. I am afraid that when we first met I was definitely unpleasant to you. For that I am sorry, and I wish that in the future you would not treat me like something out of Edgar Allen Poe. How do you like my new tie?

JUNE (C.). Thank you, Mr. Whiteside. This makes things much pleasanter. And I think the tie is very pretty.

RICHARD. Well, now that we're on speaking terms, Mr. Whiteside, I don't mind telling you that I have been admiring all your ties.

WHITESIDE. Do you like this one?

RICHARD. I certainly do.

WHITESIDE. It's yours. (*He takes it off and tosses it to him.*)

RICHARD (*crosses* R). Oh, thank you.

WHITESIDE. Really, this curious legend that I am a difficult person is pure fabrication. . . . Ice-skating, eh? Ah, me! I used to cut figure eights myself, arm in arm with Betsy Ross, waving the flag behind us.

JUNE. It was wonderful on the ice today. Miss Cutler and Mr. Jefferson were there.

WHITESIDE. Maggie? Ice-skating?

RICHARD. Yes, and she's good, too. I got a marvelous picture of her.

WHITESIDE. Were they still there when you left?

RICHARD. I think so.

JUNE. Yes, they were.

RICHARD. Mr. Whiteside, mind if I take a picture of you? I'd love to have one.

WHITESIDE. Very well. Do you want my profile? (*He indicates his stomach.*)

JUNE (*starting up the stairs*). I'm afraid you're done for, Mr. Whiteside. My brother is a camera fiend.

(WHITESIDE, *slightly startled, turns his head sharply, and in that instant* RICHARD *clicks the camera.*)

RICHARD. Thank you, Mr. Whiteside. I got a great one. (HE *and* JUNE *go up the stairs as* MAGGIE *enters from the hallway. They call a "Hello, Miss Cutler!" as they disappear upstairs.*)

MAGGIE (*enters* L., *puts bag and gloves on table back of couch*). Hello there . . . Good evening, Sherry. Really, Sherry, you've got this room looking like an old parrot-cage . . . Did you nap while I was out? (*Crossing* R. *to* C.) (WHITESIDE *merely glowers at her.*) What's the matter, dear? Cat run away with your tongue?

WHITESIDE (*furious*). Don't look at me with those great cow-eyes, you sex-ridden hag. Where have you been all afternoon? Alley-catting around with Bert Jefferson?

MAGGIE (*her face aglow, crossing to him*). Sherry, Bert read his play to me this after-

noon. It's superb. It isn't just that play written by a newspaperman. It's superb. (*To him.*) I want you to read it *tonight.* (*She puts it in his lap.*) It just cries out for Cornell. Will you send it to her, Sherry? And will you read it tonight?

WHITESIDE. No, I will not read it tonight or any other time. And while we're on the subject of Mr. Jefferson, you might ask him if he wouldn't like to pay your salary, since he takes up all your time.

MAGGIE (*she is on her knees, gathering up debris* L. *of wheelchair*). Oh, come now, Sherry. It isn't as bad as that.

WHITESIDE. I have not even been able to reach you, not knowing what haylofts you frequent.

MAGGIE (*crossing to back of sofa with box of debris*). Oh, stop behaving like a spoiled child, Sherry.

WHITESIDE. Don't take that patronizing tone with me, you flea-bitten Cleopatra. I am sick and tired of your sneaking out like some love-sick high-school girl every time my back is turned.

MAGGIE. Well, Sherry—I'm afraid you've hit the nail on the head. (*Taking off hat and putting it on table back of couch.*)

WHITESIDE. Stop acting like Zazu Pitts and explain yourself.

MAGGIE (*to* C.). I'll make it quick, Sherry. I'm in love.

WHITESIDE. Nonsense. This is merely delayed puberty.

MAGGIE. No, Sherry, I'm afraid this is it. You're going to lose a very excellent secretary.

WHITESIDE. You are out of your mind.

MAGGIE. Yes, I think I am, a little. But I'm a girl who's waited a long time for this to happen, and now it has. Mr. Jefferson doesn't know it yet, but I'm going to try my darndest to marry him. (*Ease* L.)

WHITESIDE (*as she pauses*). Is that all?

MAGGIE. Yes, except that—well—I suppose this is what might be called my resignation, as soon as you've got someone else.

WHITESIDE (*a slight pause*). Now listen to me, Maggie. We have been together for a long time. You are indispensable to me, but I think I am unselfish enough not to let that stand in the way where your happiness is concerned. Because whether you know it or not, I have a deep affection for you.

MAGGIE *(ease R.).* I know that, Sherry.

WHITESIDE. That being the case, I will not stand by and allow you to make a fool of yourself.

MAGGIE. I'm not, Sherry.

WHITESIDE. You are, my dear. You are behaving like a Booth Tarkington heroine. It's—it's incredible. I cannot believe that a girl who for the past ten years has had the great of the world served up on a platter before her, I cannot believe that it is anything but a kind of temporary insanity when you are swept off your feet in seven days by a second-rate, small-town newspaper man.

MAGGIE. Sherry, I can't explain what's happened. I can only tell you that it's so. It's hard for me to believe, too, Sherry. Here I am, a hard-bitten old cynic, behaving like True Story Magazine, and liking it. Discovering the moon, and ice-skating—I keep laughing to myself all the time, but there it is. What can I do about it, Sherry? I'm in love.

WHITESIDE *(with sudden decision).* We're leaving tomorrow. Hip or no hip, we're leaving here tomorrow. I don't care if I fracture the other one. Get me a train schedule and start packing. I'll pull you out of this, Miss Stardust. I'll get the ants out of those moonlit pants.

MAGGIE *(crosses L.).* It's no good, Sherry. It's no good. I'd be back on the next streamlined train.

WHITESIDE. It's completely unbelievable. Can you see yourself, the wife of the editor of the Mesalia *Journal,* having an evening at home for Mr. and Mrs. Stanley, Mr. and Mrs. Poop-Face, and the members of the Book-of-the-Month Club?

MAGGIE *(crosses R.).* Sherry, I've had ten years of the great figures of our time, and don't think I'm not grateful to you for it. I've loved every minute of it. They've been wonderful years, Sherry. Gay, and stimulating—I don't think anyone has ever had the fun we've had. But a girl can't laugh all the time, Sherry. There comes a time

when she wants—Bert Jefferson. You don't know Bert, Sherry. He's gentle and he's unassuming, and—well, I love him, that's all. *(Ease L.)*

WHITESIDE. I see. Well, I remain completely unconvinced. You are drugging yourself into this Joan Crawford fantasy, and before you become completely anesthetized I shall do everything in my power to bring you to your senses.

MAGGIE *(wheeling on him).* Now listen to me, Whiteside. I know you. Lay off. I know what a devil you can be. I've seen you do it to other people, but don't you dare do it to me. Don't drug *yourself* with the idea that all you're thinking of is my happiness. You're thinking of yourself a little bit, too, and all those months of breaking in somebody new. I've seen you in a passion before when your life has been disrupted, and you couldn't dine in Calcutta on July twelfth with Boo-Boo. Well, that's too bad, but there it is. *(Crosses to stairs.)* I'm going to marry Bert if he'll have me, and don't you dare try any of your tricks. I'm on to every one of them. So lay off. That's my message to you, Big Lord Fauntleroy. *(And she is up the stairs.)*

(Left stewing in his own juice, WHITESIDE *is in a perfect fury. He bangs the arm of his chair, then slaps at the manuscript in his lap. As he does so, the dawn of an idea comes into his mind. He sits perfectly still for a moment, thinking it over. Then, with a slow smile, he takes the manuscript out of its envelope. He looks at the title-page, ruffles through the script, then stops and thinks again. His face breaks out into one great smile. He reaches for the telephone receiver.)*

WHITESIDE *(in a lowered voice, in the meanwhile discarding cables from basket until he finds right one).* Long distance, please. I want to put in a Transatlantic call. *(He looks at cablegram again for confirmation.)* Hello. Transatlantic operator? . . . This is Mesalia one-four-two. I want to talk to Miss Lorraine Sheldon—S-h-e-l-d-o-n. She's on the *Normandie.* It sailed from Southampton day before yesterday. *(Door-bell.)* Will it take long? . . . All right. My name is Whiteside . . . thank you. *(He hangs up. He goes back to the*

manuscript again and looks through it.
JOHN *then ushers in* DR. BRADLEY.)

BRADLEY *(offstage)*. Good evening, John.

JOHN. Good evening, Doctor. *(Exits swing-ing-door* U.L.*)*

BRADLEY *(crosses to* R.*)* *(Heartily, as usual)*. Well, well! Good evening, Mr. Whiteside!

WHITESIDE. Come back tomorrow—I'm busy.

BRADLEY *(turning cute)*. Now what would be the best news that I could possibly bring you?

WHITESIDE. You have hydrophobia.

BRADLEY *(laughing it off)*. No, no . . . Mr. Whiteside, you are a well man. You can get up and walk *now*. You can leave here tomorrow.

WHITESIDE. What do you mean?

BRADLEY *(ease* R.*)*. Well, sir! I looked at those X-rays again this afternoon, and do you know what? I had been looking at the wrong X-rays. I had been looking at old Mrs. Moffat's X-rays. You are per-fectly, absolutely well!

WHITESIDE. Lower your voice, will you?

BRADLEY. What's the matter? Aren't you pleased?

WHITESIDE. Delighted . . . Naturally . . . Ah—this is a very unexpected bit of news, however. It comes at a very curious mo-ment. *(He is thinking fast; suddenly he gets an idea. He clears his throat and looks around apprehensively.)* Dr. Bradley, I—ah—I have some good news for you, too. I have been reading your book—ah—"Forty Years"—what is it?

BRADLEY *(eagerly crossing to* WHITESIDE*)*. "An Ohio Doctor"—Yes.

WHITESIDE. I consider it extremely close to being one of the great literary contribu-tions of our time.

BRADLEY. Mr. Whiteside!

WHITESIDE. So strongly do I feel about it, Dr. Bradley, that I have a proposition to make to you. Just here and there the book is a little uneven, a little rough, and what I would like to do is to stay here in Mesalia and work with you on it.

BRADLEY *(all choked up)*. Mr. Whiteside I would be so terribly honored—

WHITESIDE. Yes. But there is just one diffi-culty. You see, if my lecture bureau and my radio sponsors were to learn that I am well, they would insist on my fulfilling my contracts, and I would be forced to leave Mesalia. Therefore we must not tell any-one—not anyone at all—that I am well.

BRADLEY. I see. I see.

WHITESIDE. Not even Miss Cutler, you un-derstand.

BRADLEY. No, I won't. Not a soul. Not even my wife.

WHITESIDE. That's fine.

BRADLEY. Mr. Whiteside. When do we start work—tonight? I've got just one patient that's dying and then I'll be *perfectly free.* *(Phone rings.)*

WHITESIDE *(waving him away—Doctor starts to go)*. Ah—tomorrow morning. This is a private call—would you forgive me? . . . Hello . . . Yes, I'm on. *(He turns again to the Doctor.)* Tomorrow morning.

BRADLEY. Tomorrow morning it is. Good-night. I'll be so proud to work with you. You've made me very proud, Mr. White-side. *(He exits up* L.*)*

WHITESIDE. Yes, yes, I know—very proud. *(Again on the phone.)* Yes, yes, this is Mr. Whiteside on the phone. Put them through . . . Hello. Is this my Blossom Girl? How are you, my lovely? . . . No, no, I'm all right . . . Yes, still out here . . . Lorraine dear, when do you land in New York? . . . Tuesday? That's fine. . . . Now listen closely, my pet. I've great news for you. I've discovered a wonderful play with an enchanting part in it for you. Cornell would give her eye-teeth to play it, but I think I can get it for you. . . . Now wait, wait. Let me tell you. The author is a young newspaper man in this town. Of course he wants Cornell, but if you jump on a train and get out here, I think you could swing it, if you play your cards right. . . . No, he's young, and very attractive, and just your dish, my dear. It just takes a little doing, and you're the girl that can do it. Isn't that exciting, my pet? . . . Yes . . . Yes, that's right . . . And look. Don't send me any messages. Just get **on** the train and arrive. . . . Oh, no, don't thank me, my darling, It's perfectly all right. Have a nice trip and hurry out here. Good-bye, my blossom. *(He hangs up and looks guiltily around. Then he straightens up and gleefully rubs his hands together.* MISS PREEN *enters* D.R., *medicine in hand, and frightened, as usual.)* (WHITESIDE, *jovial as hell.)* Hello, Miss Preen. God, you're looking radiant this evening!

MISS PREEN *(staggered).* What?

(He takes the medicine from her and swallows it at one gulp. MISS PREEN, *still staggered, retreats into the library* D.R., *just as* MAGGIE *comes down the stairs. She is dressed for the street.)*

MAGGIE *(pausing on landing, crossing to* C.). Sherry, I'm sorry for what I said before. I'm afraid I was a little unjust.

WHITESIDE *(all nobility).* That's all right,

Maggie dear. We all lose our tempers now and then.

MAGGIE. I promised to have dinner with Bert and go to a movie, but we'll come back and play cribbage with you instead,

WHITESIDE. Fine.

MAGGIE. See you soon, Sherry dear. *(She kisses him lightly on the forehead and goes on her way. Exit* L.) Good-bye.

WHITESIDE. Good-bye. (WHITESIDE *looks after her until he hears the doors close. Then his face lights up again and he bursts happily into song as he wheels himself into the library.)* "I'se des' a 'ittle wabbit in the sunshine, *(Curtain starts down.)* I'se des' a 'ittle wabbit in the rain. I nibble on my lettuce-leaf all morning—"

CURTAIN

ACT TWO

Scene is the same.
A week later, late afternoon.
The room is now dominated by a large Christmas tree, set in the curve of the staircase, and hung with the customary Christmas ornaments. JOHN *is standing at* L. *of tree.* SARAH *and* JOHN *are passing in and out of the library, bringing forth huge packages which they are placing under the tree.* MAGGIE *sits at a little table* D.R., *going through a pile of correspondence.*

JOHN *(to tree, then* D.R.*).* Well, I guess that's all there are, Miss Cutler. They're all under the tree.

MAGGIE. Thank you, John.

SARAH. My, I never saw anyone get so many presents. I can hardly wait to see what's in 'em.

JOHN. When'll Mr. Whiteside open them, Miss Cutler?

MAGGIE *(rises, crosses to table back of sofa with papers—first switching on lights).* Well, John, you see Christmas is Mr. Whiteside's personal property. He invented it and it belongs to *him.* First thing to-morrow morning Mr. Whiteside will open each and every present, and there will be the God-damnedest fuss you ever saw.

SARAH *(turns on center lamp and crossing to* R. *of tree.* JOHN *crosses to* L. *of tree. Then bending over the packages).* My, look who he's got presents from! Shirley

Temple, William Lyon Phelps, Billy Rose, Ethel Waters, Somerset Maugham—my, I can hardly wait for *tomorrow.* (MAGGIE *crosses* R. *to* D.R. *desk. Sits.) (The doorbell rings.* JOHN *departs for the door* L., *switching on lights on his way.* SARAH *comes downstage.)* My, it certainly is wonderful. And Mr. Whiteside's tree is so beautiful, too. Mr. and Mrs. Stanley had to put theirs in their bedroom, you know. They can hardly *undress at night. (It is* BERT JEFFERSON *who enters* L.)

BERT. Good evening, John.

JOHN. Good evening, Mr. Jefferson, Merry Christmas.

BERT. Hello, Maggie. Merry Christmas, Sarah.

SARAH. Merry Christmas, Mr. Jefferson. (SARAH *disappears into dining-room.* JOHN *exits up* L.)

BERT *(crossing to* C.). *(Observing the pile of packages under tree.)* Say, business is good, isn't it? My, what a little quiet blackmail and a weekly radio hour can get you. What did his sponsors give him?

MAGGIE. They gave him a full year's supply of their product—Cream of Mush.

BERT. Well, he'll give it right back to them, over the air.

MAGGIE (*rises, crosses to couch with papers*). Wait until you hear tonight's broadcast, old fellow. It's so sticky I haven't been able to get it off my fingers since I copied it.

BERT (*to c.*). I'll bet. . . . Look, I'll come clean. Under the influence of God knows what I have just bought you a Christmas present.

MAGGIE (*surprised, crossing to him*). Why, Mr. Jefferson, sir.

BERT. Only I'd like you to see it before I throw away my hard-earned money. Can you run downtown with me and take a look at it?

MAGGIE (*to him*). Bert, this is very sweet of you. I'm quite touched. What is it? I can't wait.

BERT. A two years' subscription to *Pic, Click, Look* and *Listen*. Say, do you think I'm going to tell you? Come down and see.

MAGGIE (*crosses R., then to L. to get coat*). All right. (*She calls into library.*) Sherry! I'm going out for a few minutes. With Horace Greeley. I won't be long. (*She goes into hallway for her coat and hat.*)

BERT (*raising his voice*). Noel, Noel, Mr. W.! How about some cribbage after your broadcast tonight? (*Crossing to WHITESIDE. The Whiteside wheelchair is rolled in by MISS PREEN, D.R. She then exits D.R., closing doors.*)

WHITESIDE (R.C.). No, I will not play cribbage with you, Klondike Harry . . . You have been swindling the be-jesus out of me for two weeks. . . . Where are you off to now, Madam Butterfly?

MAGGIE (*to c.*). I'm being given a Christmas present. Anything you want done downtown?

WHITESIDE. 'Es. Bring baby a lollipop . . . What are *you* giving me for Christmas,

Jefferson? I have enriched your feeble life beyond your capacity to repay me.

BERT. Yes, that's what I figured, so I'm not giving you anything.

WHITESIDE. I see. Well, I was giving you my old truss, but now I shan't . . . (BERT *eases upstage.*) Maggie, what time are those radio men coming?

MAGGIE (*crosses D.R., places phone on stool beside WHITESIDE*). About six-thirty—I'll be here. You've got to cut, Sherry. You're four minutes over. Oh, by the way, there's a wire here from Beverly Carlton. He doesn't know what train he can get out of Chicago, but he'll be here some time this evening.

WHITESIDE. Good! Is he staying overnight?

MAGGIE (*at desk*). No, he has to get right out again. He's sailing Friday on the *Queen Mary*.

BERT (*crossing to WHITESIDE*). Think I could peek in at the window and get a look at him? Beverly Carlton used to be one of my heroes. (MAGGIE *puts letters and book on stool too.*)

WHITESIDE. Used to be, you ink-stained hack? Beverly Carlton is the greatest single talent in the English theatre today.—Take this illiterate numbskull out of my sight, Maggie, and don't bring him back.

BERT. Yes, Mr. Whiteside, sir. I won't come back until Beverly Carlton gets here.

MAGGIE (*crossing L. to exit L. As they go on their way, arm-in-arm*). Where are we going, Bert? I want to know what you've bought me—I'm like a ten-year-old kid.

BERT (*laughing a little*). You know, you look like a ten-year-old kid right now, Maggie, at that. (*They are out of earshot by this time.*)

(WHITESIDE *looks after them intently; listens until the door closes. He considers for a second, then wheels himself over to the phone.*)

WHITESIDE (*on the phone*). Will you give me the Mansion House, please—No, I don't know the number . . . Hello? Mansion House? . . . Tell me, has a Miss Lorraine Sheldon arrived yet? . . . Yes, that's right—Miss Lorraine Sheldon. From New York . . . She hasn't, eh? (*He hangs up; drums with his fingers on the chair arm;*

looks at his watch. He slaps his knees impatiently, stretches. Then, vexed at his self-imposed imprisonment, he looks cautiously around the room, peers up the stairs. Then, slowly, he gets out of his chair, crosses L. and indulges in a few mild dance-steps, looking cautiously around all the while.) (Then the sound of the library doors being opened sends him scurrying back to his chair. It is MISS PREEN *who emerges* D.R., *carrying basin with hot-water bag, inhalator.) (*WHITESIDE, *annoyed.*) What do you want, coming in like that? Why don't you knock before you come into a room?

MISS PREEN *(crossing down to* R. *of wheelchair*). But—I wasn't coming in. I was coming out.

WHITESIDE. Miss Preen, you are obviously *in* this room. That is true, isn't it?

MISS PREEN. Yes, it is, but—

WHITESIDE. Therefore you *came in. (Before* MISS PREEN *can reply, however,* JOHN *enters from dining-room up* R. *crosses* L. *to exit* L.) Hereafter, please knock.

JOHN *(en route to front door up* L.). There're some expressmen here with a crate, Mr. Whiteside. I told them to come around the front.

WHITESIDE. Thank you, John . . . Don't stand there, Miss Preen. You look like a frozen custard. Go away.

MISS PREEN *(controlling herself as best she can*). Yes, sir. *(She goes. Exits up* R.)

(At the same time an EXPRESSMAN *carrying a crate enters from front door.)*

JOHN *(up* L.). Bring it right in here. Careful there—don't scrape the wall. Why, it's some kind of animals. *(Enter* EXPRESSMAN *to up* L.)

EXPRESSMAN *(crossing* R. *to up* C.). I'll say it's animals. We had to feed 'em at seven o'clock this morning.

WHITESIDE. Who's it from, John?

JOHN *(crossing* R.). *(Reading from the top of the crate as they set it down.)* Admiral Richard E. Byrd. Say!

WHITESIDE. Bring it over here. *(*EXPRESSMAN *carries it to chair.* JOHN *crosses to chair.) (Peering through the slats.)* Why, they're penguins. Two—three—four penguins. Hello, my pretties.

EXPRESSMAN *(crossing* L.). Directions for feeding are right on top. Two of those slats are loose.

JOHN *(reading).* "To be fed only whale blubber, eels and cracked lobster."

EXPRESSMAN. They got Coca-Cola this morning. And liked it. *(He goes* L.)

WHITESIDE *(peering through slats again).* Hello, hello, hello. You know, they make the most entrancing companions, John. Admiral Byrd has one that goes on all his lecture tours. I want these put right in the library with me. Take 'em right in.

JOHN *(crossing* R., *exits* D.R.). *(Picking up crate.)* Yes, sir.

WHITESIDE. Better tell Sarah to order a couple of dozen lobsters.

JOHN. Yes, sir.

WHITESIDE. I don't suppose there's any whale blubber in this town . . .

BRADLEY *(enters* L). Good evening.

WHITESIDE. Oh, yes, there is. *(This last is addressed to* BRADLEY, *who has entered from the hall as* JOHN *and the crate disappear into the library.)*

BRADLEY. The door was open, so I—Merry Christmas. *(Crosses to* C.)

WHITESIDE. Merry Christmas, Merry Christmas. Do you happen to know if eels are in season, Doctor?

BRADLEY. How's that?

WHITESIDE. Never mind. I was a fool to ask you. *(*JOHN *returns from library, carefully closing the doors.)*

JOHN *(crossing upstairs).* I opened those two slats a little, Mr. Whiteside—they seemed so crowded in there.

WHITESIDE. Thank you, John.

BRADLEY. Mr. Whiteside— *(*JOHN *goes on his way, he is carrying pillow-cases.)*

WHITESIDE. On your way downtown, Doctor, will you send these air mail? Miss Cutler forgot them. *(He hands him a few letters.)* Good-bye, Doctor. I'm sorry you happened to drop in now. I have to do my Yogi exercises. *(He folds his arms, leans back and closes his eyes.)*

BRADLEY. But, Mr. Whiteside, it's been a

week now. My book—you know—when are we going to start work on my book? (WHITESIDE *places his fingers to his lips.*) I was hoping that today, maybe— (*He stops as* MISS PREEN *enters from* U.R.) Good evening, Miss Preen.

MISS PREEN. Good evening, Doctor Bradley. (*She opens the door into library, then freezes in her tracks. She closes the doors again and turns to* BRADLEY, *glassy-eyed. She raises a trembling hand to her forehead, and goes to* R. *of chair.*) Doctor, perhaps I'm not well—but—when I opened the doors just now I though. I saw a penguin with a thermometer in his mouth.

WHITESIDE. What's this? Have those penguins gotten out of their crate?

MISS PREEN. Oh, thank God. I thought perhaps the strain had been too much.

DOCTOR. Penguins? Did you say penguins?

WHITESIDE. Yes. Doctor, will you go in and capture them, please, and put them back in the crate. There're four of them,

BRADLEY (*crosses* R.). Capture the penguins, yes! Do you suppose that later on, Mr. Whiteside, we might—

WHITESIDE. We'll see, we'll see. First catch the penguins. And, Miss Preen, will you entertain them, please, until I come in? (*She crosses to door* R.)

MISS PREEN (*swallowing hard*). Yes, sir.

JOHN (*descending the stairs*). The Christmas tree in the bedroom just fell on Mr. Stanley. He's got a big bump on his forehead. (JOHN *exits* U.R.)

WHITESIDE (*brightly*). Why, isn't that too bad? (RICHARD *enters from the hall* L. *as* MISS PREEN *goes through library door.*) . . . Go ahead, Doctor. Go on, Miss Preen.

RICHARD (*coming* C.). Hello, Mr. Whiteside.

WHITESIDE. Hello, Dickie, my boy.

BRADLEY (*still lingering*). Well, Mr. Whiteside, will you have some time later?

WHITESIDE (*impatient*). I don't know, Doctor. I'm busy now.

BRADLEY. Well, suppose I wait a little while? I'll—I'll wait a little while. (*Exit* BRADLEY *into library.*)

WHITESIDE. Dr. Bradley is the greatest living argument for mercy killings. Well, Dickie, would you like a candid camera shot of my left nostril this evening?

RICHARD. I'm all stocked up on those. Have you got a minute to look at some new ones I've taken? (*He hands him snapshots.* RICHARD *crosses* U. *to ottoman, places ottoman* L. *of wheelchair.*)

WHITESIDE. I certainly have . . . why, these are splendid, Richard. There's real artistry in them—they're as good as anything by Margaret Bourke White. (RICHARD *sits.*) I like all the things you've shown me. This is the essence of photographic journalism.

RICHARD. Say, I didn't know they were as good as that. I just like to take pictures, that's all.

WHITESIDE. Richard, I've been meaning to talk to you about this. You're not just a kid fooling with a camera any more. These are good. This is what you ought to do. (*Handing back pictures.*) You ought to get out of here and do some of the things you were telling me about. Just get on a boat and get off wherever it stops. Galveston, Mexico, Singapore—work your way through and just take pictures—millions of them, terrible pictures, wonderful pictures—everything.

RICHARD. Say, wouldn't I like to, though! It's what I've been dreaming of for years. If I could do that I'd be the happiest guy in the world.

WHITESIDE. Well, why can't you do it? If I were your age, I'd do it like a shot.

RICHARD (*rises, crosses* L.). Well, you know why, Dad.

WHITESIDE. Richard, do you really want to do this more than anything else in the world?

RICHARD. I certainly do.

WHITESIDE. Then do it. (JUNE *enters up* R. *to* C.)

JUNE. Hello, Dick. Good afternoon, Mr. Whiteside.

WHITESIDE. Hello, my lovely . . . So I'm afraid it's up to you, Richard.

RICHARD (*crossing to stairs*). I guess it is.

Well, thank you, Mr. Whiteside. You've been swell and I'll never forget it.

WHITESIDE. Righto, Richard.

RICHARD (WHITESIDE takes book from ottoman). June, are you coming upstairs?

JUNE. Ah—in a few minutes, Richard.

RICHARD. Well—knock on my door, will you? I want to talk to you. (Exit upstairs.)

JUNE. Yes, I will. (Turning back to WHITESIDE.) Mr. Whiteside . . .

WHITESIDE. June, my lamb, you were too young to know about the Elwell murder, weren't you? Completely fascinating. I have about five favorite murders and the Elwell case is one of them. Would you like to hear about it?

JUNE. Well, Mr. Whiteside, I wanted to talk to you. Would you mind, for a few minutes? It's important.

WHITESIDE. Why, certainly, my dear. I take it this is all about your young Lothario at the factory?

JUNE (nodding). Yes. I just can't seem to make Father understand. It's like talking to a blank wall. He won't meet him—he won't even talk about it. What are we going to do, Mr. Whiteside? Sandy and I love each other. I don't know where to turn.

WHITESIDE. My dear, I'd like to meet this young man. I'd like to see him for myself.

JUNE. Would you, Mr. Whiteside? Would you meet him? He's—he's outside now. He's in the kitchen. (Crosses up a little.)

WHITESIDE. Good! Bring him in.

JUNE (then down to WHITESIDE again). Mr. Whiteside, he's—he's a very sensitive boy. You will be nice to him, won't you?

WHITESIDE. God damn it, June, when will you learn that I am always kind and courteous! Bring this idiot in!

JUNE (up to door U.R. Calling through the dining-room, in a low voice). Sandy. Sandy. (She stands aside as a YOUNG MAN enters. Twenty-three or four, keen-looking, neatly but simply dressed.) Here he is, Mr. Whiteside. This is Sandy. (Coming down with SANDY.)

SANDY. How do you do, sir?

WHITESIDE. How do you do? Young man, I've been hearing a good deal about you from June this past week. It seems, if I have been correctly informed, that you two babes in the woods have quietly gone out of your minds.

JUNE. There's another name for it. It's called love.

WHITESIDE. Well, you've come to the right place. Dr. Sheridan Whiteside, Broken Hearts Mended, Brakes Relined, Hamburgers. Go right ahead.

SANDY. Well, if June has told you anything at all, Mr. Whiteside, you know the jam we're in. You see, I work for the labor union, Mr. Whiteside. I'm an organizer. I've been organizing the men in Mr. Stanley's factory, and Mr. Stanley's pretty sore about it.

WHITESIDE. I'll bet!

SANDY. Did June tell you that?

WHITESIDE. Yes, she did.

SANDY. Well, that being the case, Mr. Whiteside, I don't think I have the right to try to influence June. If she marries me it means a definite break with her family, and I don't like to bring that about. But the trouble is Mr. Stanley's so stubborn about it, so arbitrary. You know, this is not something I've done just to spite him. We fell in love with each other. But Mr. Stanley behaves as though it were all a big plot—John L. Lewis sent me here just to marry his daughter.

JUNE. He's tried to fire Sandy twice, out at the factory, but he couldn't on account of the Wagner Act, thank God!

SANDY. Yes, he thinks I wrote that, too.

JUNE. If he'd only let me talk to him. If he'd let Sandy talk to him.

SANDY. Well, we've gone over all that, June. Anyway, this morning I got word I'm needed in Chicago. I may have to go on to Frisco from there. So you see the jam we're in.

JUNE. Sandy's leaving tonight, Mr. Whiteside. He'll probably be gone a year. We've simply got to decide. Now.

WHITESIDE. My dear, this is absurdly simple. It's no problem at all. Now to my jaundiced eye— (As the telephone rings.

Nods.) Ohh! Hello . . . Yes . . . This is Whiteside. (*To* JUNE *and* SANDY.) Excuse me—it's a Trans-Atlantic call . . . (*Back to the phone.*) (SANDY *crosses to* L. *of* JUNE.) Yes? . . . Yes, I'm on. Who's calling? . . . Oh! Put him on. (*Again an aside.*) It's Walt Disney in Hollywood. (*Into phone.*) Hello . . . Hello . . ., Walt. How's my little dash of genius? . . . Yes, I hoped you would. How'd you know I was here? . . . I see . . . Yes. Yes, I'm listening. Now? Ten seconds more? (*To* SANDY *and* JUNE.) Mr. Disney calls me every Christmas— (*Into phone again.*) Yes, Walt . . . Yes I hear it. It sounds just like static. . . . June! (*He extends the receiver to her; she listens for a second, then crosses back to* SANDY C.) Hello . . . Thanks, old man, and a very Merry Christmas to *you* . . . Tell me, is there any news in Hollywood? Who's in Lana Turner's sweater these days? . . . I see . . . Well, good-bye, and don't worry about "Fantasia." It wasn't your fault— Beethoven hasn't written a hit in years . . . Good-bye. (*He hangs up and turns to* JUNE.) Do you know what that was you listened to? The voice of Donald Duck.

JUNE. Not really?

WHITESIDE. Mr. Disney calls me every Christmas, no matter where I am, so that I can hear it. Two years ago I was walking on the bottom of the ocean in a diving-suit, with William Beebe, but he got me . . . Now, where were we? Oh, yes . . . June, I like your young man. I have an unerring instinct about people—I've never been wrong. That's why I wanted to meet him. My feeling is that you two will be very happy together. Whatever his beliefs are, he's entitled to them, and you shouldn't let anything stand in your way. As I see it, it's no problem at all. Stripped of its externals, what does it come down to? Your father. The possibility of making him unhappy. Is that right?

JUNE. *Very* unhappy.

WHITESIDE. That isn't the point. Suppose your parents *are* unhappy—it's good for them. Develops their characters. Look at *me.* I left home at the age of four and haven't been back since. They hear me on the radio and that's enough for them.

SANDY. Then—your advice is to go ahead, Mr. Whiteside?

WHITESIDE It is. Marry him tonight, June.

JUNE (*almost afraid to make the leap*). You—you mean that, Mr. Whiteside?

WHITESIDE. No, I mean you should marry Hamilton Fish. If I didn't mean it I wouldn't say it. What do you want me to do—say it all over again? My own opinion is you're not worthy of this young man.

STANLEY (*upstairs*). Come along, Daisy— stop dawdling.

JUNE (*Pushing* SANDY *up* R. *and returning to room.* SANDY *exits*). There's Dad.

STANLEY (*descending the stairs, and crossing* L. *to coat-rack*). Forgive us for trespassing, Mr. Whiteside.

WHITESIDE. Not at all, old fellow—not at all. It's Christmas, you know. Merry Christmas, Merry Christmas.

MRS. STANLEY (*nervously*). Ah—yes. Merry Christmas . . . Would you like to come along with us, June? We're taking some presents over to the Dexters'.

JUNE. No--no, thank you, Mother. I—I have to write some letters. (*She goes up the stairs.*)

STANLEY. Come along, Daisy.

WHITESIDE (*entirely too sweetly*). Why, Mr. Stanley, what happened to your forehead? Did you have an accident?

STANLEY. No, Mr. Whiteside. I'm taking boxing lessons. . . . Go ahead, Daisy. (*They go* L.)

(HARRIET, *who has been hovering at the head of the stairs, hurries down as the* STANLEYS *depart. She is carrying a little Christmas package.*)

HARRIET (*crosses* R.). Dear Mr. Whiteside, I've been trying all day to see you. To give you—*this.*

WHITESIDE. Why, Miss Stanley. A Christmas gift, for me?

HARRIET. It's only a trifle, but I wanted you to have it. It's a picture of me as I used to be. It was taken on another Christmas Eve, many years ago. Don't open it until the stroke of midnight, *will you?* (*The doorbell rings.* HARRIET *looks apprehensively over her shoulder.*) Merry Christmas, dear Mr. Whiteside. Merry Christmas. (JOHN *enters up* L. *to exit* L.)

WHITESIDE. Merry Christmas to you, Miss Stanley, and thank you. *(She glides out of the room, up* R.*)* *(In the hallway, as* JOHN *opens the door, we hear a woman's voice, liquid and melting: "This is the Stanley residence, isn't it?" "Yes, it is." "I've come to see* MR. WHITESIDE. *Will you tell him* MISS SHELDON *is here?")* Lorraine! My Blossom Girl!

LORRAINE *(coming into view. Enter* L. *to up* L.*).* Sherry, my sweet. *(And quite a view it is.* LORRAINE SHELDON *is known as the most chic actress on the New York or London stage, and justly so. She glitters as she walks. She is beautiful, and even, God save the word, glamorous. . . . Her rank as one of the Ten Best Dressed Women of the World is richly reserved. She is, in short, a siren of no mean talents, and knows it.)* *(crossing* R. *to him—wasting no time.)* Oh, darling, look at that poor sweet tortured face! Let me kiss it! *(She does.)* You poor darling, your eyes have a kind of gallant compassion. How drawn you are. Sherry, my sweet, I want to cry.

WHITESIDE. All right. You've made a very nice entrance, dear. Now relax.

LORRAINE. But, Sherry, darling, I've been so worried. And now seeing you in that chair . . .

WHITESIDE. This chair fits my fanny as nothing else ever has. I feel better than I have in years, and my only concern is news of the outside world. So take off that skunk and tell me everything. How are you, my dear?

LORRAINE *(crossing* L. *to sofa).* *(Removing a cascade of silver fox from her shoulders.)* Darling, I'm so relieved. You look perfectly wonderful—I never saw you look better. My dear, do I look a wreck? I just dashed through New York. Didn't do a thing about Christmas. Hattie Carnegie and had my hair done, and got right on the train. *(Sits arm of couch. Uses her compact.)* And the *Normandie* coming back was simply hectic. Fun, you know, but simply exhausting. Jock Whitney, and Cary Grant, and Dorothy di Frasso—it was *too* exhausting. And of course London before that was so magnificent, my dear—well, I simply never got to bed at all. *(Rises. Crosses to* C.*)* Darling, I've so much to tell you I don't know where to start.

WHITESIDE. Well, start with the dirt first, dear—that's what I want to hear.

LORRAINE *(sits on stool).* Let me see. Sybil Cartwright was thrown right out of Ciro's —it was the night before I left. She was wearing one of those new cellophane dresses, and you could absolutely see Trafalgar Square. And Sir Harry Montrose —the painter, you know—is suing his mother for disorderly conduct. It's just shocked *everyone.* And oh! before I forget: Anthony Eden told me he's going to be on your New Year's broadcast, Sherry. He said for God's sake not to introduce him as the English Grover Whalen. And Beatrice Lillie gave me a message for you. She says for you to take off twenty-five pounds right away and send them to her by parcel post. She needs them.

WHITESIDE. I'll pack 'em in ice . . . Now come, dear, what about you? What about your love life? I don't believe for one moment you never got to bed at all, if you'll pardon the expression.

LORRAINE. Sherry dear, you're dreadful.

WHITESIDE. What about that splendid bit of English mutton, Lord Bottomley? Haven't you hooked him yet?

LORRAINE. Sherry, please. Cedric is a very dear friend of mine.

WHITESIDE. Now, Blossom Girl, this is Sherry. Don't try to pull the bedclothes over my eyes. Don't tell *me* you wouldn't like to be Lady Bottomley, with a hundred thousand pounds a year and twelve castles. By the way, has he had his teeth fixed yet? Every time I order Roquefort cheese I think of those teeth.

LORRAINE. Sherry, really! . . . Cedric may not be brilliant, but he's rather sweet, poor lamb, and he's very fond of me, and he does represent a kind of English way of living that I like. Surrey, and London for the season—shooting-box in Scotland— that lovely old castle in Wales. You were there, Sherry—you know what I mean.

WHITESIDE. Mm. I do indeed.

LORRAINE. Well, really, Sherry, why not? If I can marry Cedric, I don't know why I shouldn't. Shall I tell you something, Sherry? I think, from something he said just before I sailed, that he's finally coming around to it. It wasn't definite, mind you, but—don't be surprised if I *am* Lady Bottomley before very long.

WHITESIDE. Lady Bottomley! Won't Kansas City be surprised! However, I shall be a flower-girl and give the groom an iron toothpick as a wedding present. Come ahead, my blossom,—let's hear some more of your skulduggery.

LORRAINE. Well . . . *(The library doors are quietly opened at this point and the* DOCTOR's *head appears* D.R.)

BRADLEY *(in a heavy whisper)*. Mr. Whiteside.

WHITESIDE. What? No, no—not now. I'm busy. *(The* DOCTOR *disappears* D.R., *closes doors.)*

LORRAINE. Who's that?

WHITESIDE. He's fixing the plumbing . . . Now come on, come on—I want some news.

LORRAINE. But, Sherry, what about this play? After all, I've come all the way from New York—even on Christmas Eve —I've been so excited ever since your phone call. Where is it? When can I read it?

WHITESIDE. Well, here's the situation. This young author—his name is Bert Jefferson —brought me the play with the understanding that I send it to Kit Cornell. It's a magnificent part, and God knows I feel disloyal to Kit.

LORRAINE. Sherry.

WHITESIDE. Anyhow, there you are. Now *I*'ve done *this* much—the rest is up to you. He's young and attractive—now, just how you'll go about persuading him, I'm sure you know more about than I do.

LORRAINE *(rises, to* c.). Darling, how can I ever thank you? Does he know I'm coming—Mr. Jefferson, I mean?

WHITESIDE. No, no. You're just out here visiting me. You'll meet him, and that's that. Get him to take you to dinner, and work around to the play. Good God, I don't have to tell you how to do these things. How did you get all those other parts?

LORRAINE *(crossing* L. *to sofa for furs and then back)*. Sherry! . . . Well, I'll go back to the hotel and get into something more

attractive. I just dumped my bags and rushed right over here. Darling, you're wonderful. *(Lightly kissing him. Crosses to* c.)

WHITESIDE. All right—now run along and get into your working clothes. Then come right back here and spend Christmas Eve with Sherry and I'll have Mr. Jefferson on tap . . . By the way, I've got a little surprise for you. Who do you think's paying me a flying visit tonight? None other than your old friend and co-star, Beverly Carlton.

LORRAINE *(crosses to* R. *of couch)*. *(Not too delighted.)* Really? Beverly? I thought he was being glamorous again, on a tramp steamer.

WHITESIDE. Come, come, dear—mustn't be bitter because he got better notices than you did.

LORRAINE. Don't be silly, Sherry. I never read notices. I simply wouldn't care to act with him again, that's all. He's not staying here, is he? I hope not.

WHITESIDE. Temper, temper, temper. No, he's not . . . Where'd you get that diamond clip, dear? That's a new bit of loot, isn't it?

LORRAINE. Haven't you seen this before? Cedric gave it to me for his mother's birthday. She was simply furious. Look, darling, I've got a taxi outside. *If* I'm *going* to get back here— *(crossing* L. *to* c.) *(At this point the voice of* MAGGIE *is heard in the hallway.)*

MAGGIE *(entering* L.). Sherry, what do you think I've just been given the most beautiful . *(She stops short and comes to a dead halt as she sees* LORRAINE.)

LORRAINE. Oh, hello, Maggie. I knew you must be around somewhere. How are you, my dear?

WHITESIDE *(*MAGGIE *eases down)*. Santa's been at work, my pet. Blossom Girl just dropped in out of the blue and surprised us.

MAGGIE *(up* L., *quietly)*. Hello, Lorraine.

WHITESIDE *(as* JEFFERSON *appears* L.*)*. Who's that—Bert? Come in, Bert. This is Mr. Bert Jefferson, Lorraine. Young newspaper man. Miss Lorraine Sheldon.

BERT. How do you do, Miss Sheldon?

LORRAINE. How do you do? I didn't quite catch the name—Jefferson?

WHITESIDE (*sweetly*). That's right, Pet.

LORRAINE (*crossing up* L.). (MAGGIE *puts coat off and lays it on stool up* L.) (*Full steam ahead.*) Why, Mr. Jefferson, you don't look like a newspaper man. You don't look like a newspaper man at all.

BERT. Really? I thought it was written all over me in Neon lights.

LORRAINE. Oh, no, not at all. I should have said you were—oh, I don't know—an aviator or an explorer or something. They have that same kind of dash about them. I'm simply enchanted with your town, Mr. Jefferson. It gives one such a warm, gracious feeling. Tell me—have you lived here all your life? (*Crosses to* BERT, *up* L.) (MAGGIE *crossing* R. *to up* C.)

BERT. Practically.

WHITESIDE. If you wish to hear the story of his life, Lorraine, kindly do so on your own time. Maggie and I have work to do. Get out of here, Jefferson. On your way, Blossom. On your way.

LORRAINE. He's the world's rudest man, isn't he? Can I drop you, Mr. Jefferson? I'm going down to the—Mansion House, I think it's called.

BERT. Thank you, but I've got my car. Suppose I drop you?

LORRAINE. Oh, would you? That'd be lovely—we'll send the taxi off. See you in a little while, Sherry. 'Bye, Maggie. (*Eases up* L.)

BERT. Good-bye, Maggie. (*He turns to* WHITESIDE.) I'm invited back for dinner, am I not?

WHITESIDE. Yes—yes, you are. At Christmas I always feed the needy. Now please stop oozing out—*get* out.

LORRAINE. Come on, Mr. Jefferson. I want to hear more about this charming little town. (*Starts to go.*) And I want to know a good deal about *you*, too. (*And they are gone. Exit* L.)

(*There is a slight but pregnant pause after they go.* MAGGIE *simply stands looking at him, waiting for what may come forth.*)

WHITESIDE (*as though nothing had happened*). Now let's see, is there a copy of that broadcast here? How much did you say they wanted out—four minutes?

MAGGIE (*eases down* C.). That's right. Four minutes—She's looking very well, isn't she?

WHITESIDE. What's that? Who?

MAGGIE. The Countess di Pushover. Quite a surprise, wasn't it—her dropping in?

WHITESIDE. Yes—yes, it was. Now come on, Maggie, come on. Get to work. Get to work.

MAGGIE. Why, she must have gone through New York like a dose of salts. How long's she going to stay?

WHITESIDE (*completely absorbed*). What? Oh, I don't know—a few days . . . (*He reads from his manuscript.*) "At this joyous season of the year, when in the hearts of men—" I can't cut that.

MAGGIE. Isn't it curious? There was Lorraine, snug as a bug in somebody's bed on the *Normandie*—

WHITESIDE (*so busy with his manuscript*). "Ere the Yuletide season pass—"

MAGGIE (*quietly taking manuscript out of his hands*). (*Crossing* R. *to him, then back to* C.) Now, Sherry dear, we will talk a bit.

WHITESIDE. Now look here, Maggie. Just because a friend of mine happens to come out to spend Christmas with me— (*The door-bell rings.*) I have a hunch that's Beverly. Maggie, see if it is. Go ahead—run! run! (JOHN *enters up* L. *to exit off* L.) (MAGGIE *looks at him—right through him, in fact. Then she goes slowly toward the door* L. "Magpie"—*from* BEVERLY. *We hear her voice at the door:* "Beverly!" *Then, in clipped English tones:* "A large, moist, incestuous kiss for my Magpie!") (WHITESIDE, *roaring.*) Come in here, you Piccadilly pen-pusher, and gaze upon a soul in agony.

(JOHN *exit up* L.)

(BEVERLY CARLTON *enters* L., *crosses to* C. *arm in arm with* MAGGIE. *Very confident, very British, very Beverly Carlton. He throws his coat over the newel-post,* MAGGIE *puts his hat on table back of couch.*)

BEVERLY. Don't tell me how you are, Sherry dear. I want none of the tiresome details.

I have only a little time, so the conversation will be entirely about *me,* and I shall love it. Shall— *(Eases R.)* I tell you how I glittered through the South Seas like a silver scimitar, or would you rather hear how I frolicked through Zambesia, raping the Major-General's daughter and finishing a three-act play at the same time? *(Crosses to MAGGIE L.)* Magpie dear, you are the moonflower of my middle age, and I love you very much. Say something tender to me.

MAGGIE. Beverly, darling.

BEVERLY. That's my girl. *(Turning to WHITESIDE.)* Now then. Sherry dear, without going into mountainous waves of self-pity, how are you? *(A quick nod of the head.)*

WHITESIDE. I'm fine, you presumptuous Cockney . . . Now, how was the trip, wonderful? *(MAGGIE sits arm of sofa.)*

BEVERLY *(crosses R., then U.L.).* Fabulous. I did a fantastic amount of work. By the way, did I glimpse that little boudoir butterfly, La Sheldon, in a motor-car as I came up the driveway?

MAGGIE. You did indeed. She's paying us a Christmas visit.

BEVERLY. Dear girl! They do say she set fire to her mother, but I don't believe it . . . Sherry, *(Sits on stool R.C.)* my evil one, not only have I written the finest comedy since Molière, but also the best revue since my last one, and an operetta that frightens me it's so good. I shall play it for eight weeks in London and six in New York—that's all. No matinees. Then I am off to the Grecian Islands . . . Magpie, why don't you come along? Why don't you desert this cannon-ball of fluff and come with me?

MAGGIE. Beverly dear, be careful. You're catching me at a good moment.

WHITESIDE *(changing the subject).* Tell me, Beverly, did you have a good time in Hollywood? How long were you there?

BEVERLY *(rises, crosses to C.).* Three unbelievable days. I saw everyone from Adrian to Zanuck. They came, poor dears, as to a shrine. I was insufferably charming and ruthlessly firm in refusing seven million dollars for two minutes' work.

WHITESIDE. What about Banjo? Did you see my wonderful Banjo in Hollywood?

BEVERLY. I did. He gave a dinner for me. I arrived, in white tie and tails to be met at the door by two bewigged butlers, who quietly proceeded to take my trousers off. I was then ushered, in my lemon silk drawers, into a room full of Norma Shearer, Claudette Colbert, and Aldous Huxley, among others. Dear, sweet, incomparable Banjo. *(Crossing to couch, he puts his arm about MAGGIE's shoulder.)*

WHITESIDE. I'll never forget that summer at Antibes, when Banjo put a microphone in Lorraine's mattress, and then played the record the next day at lunch.

BEVERLY *(crossing C.).* I remember it indeed. Lorraine left Antibes by the next boat.

MAGGIE *(half to herself).* I wish Banjo were here now.

BEVERLY *(back to MAGGIE).* What's the matter, Magpie? Is Lorraine being her own sweet sick-making self?

MAGGIE. You wouldn't take her to the Grecian Islands with you, would you, Beverly? Just for me?

WHITESIDE. Now, now. Lorraine is a charming person who has gallantly given up her own Christmas to spend it with me.

BEVERLY *(crosses to C.).* Oh, I knew I had a bit of dirt for us all to nibble on. *(He draws a letter out of his pocket).*

(Again the library doors are opened and the DOCTOR's head comes through, D.R.)

BRADLEY. Mr. Whiteside.

WHITESIDE. No, no, not now. Go away.

(The DOCTOR withdraws D.R., closing the doors.)

BEVERLY. Have you kidnapped someone, Sherry?

WHITESIDE. Yes, that was Charley Ross . . . Go ahead. Is this something juicy?

BEVERLY *(to stool L. of wheelchair—sits).* Juicy as a pomegranate. It is the latest report from London on the winter manoeuvres of Miss Lorraine Sheldon against the left flank—in fact, all flanks—of Lord Cedric Bottomley. Listen: "Lorraine has just left us in a cloud of Chanel Number

Five. Since September, in her relentless pursuit of His Lordship, she has paused only to change girdles and check her oil. She has chased him, panting, from castle to castle, till he finally took refuge, for several week-ends, in the gentlemen's lavatory of the House of Lords. Practically no one is betting on the Derby this year; we are all making book on Lorraine. She is sailing tomorrow on the *Normandie,* but would return on the *Atlantic Clipper* if Bottomley so much as belches in her direction." Have you ever met Lord Bottomley, Magpie dear? *(Rise to* c.)

MAGGIE. No, I haven't.

(HE goes immediately into an impersonation of His Lordship. Very British, very full of teeth, stuttering.)

"Not v-v-very good shooting today, blast it. Only s-s-six partridges, f-f-four grouse, and the D-D-Duke of Sutherland. Haw, haw."

WHITESIDE *(chuckling).* My God, that's Bottomley to his very bottom.

BEVERLY *(still in character).* "R-r-ripping debate in the House today. Old Basil spoke for th-th-three hours. D-d-dropped dead at the end of it. Ripping. Haw!" *(Eases* L.)

MAGGIE. You're making it up, Beverly. No one sounds like that.

WHITESIDE. It's so good it's uncanny . . . Damn it, Beverly, why must you race right out of here? I never see enough of you, you ungrateful moppet.

BEVERLY *(crosses* R. *to* WHITESIDE). Sherry darling, I can only tell you that my love for you is so great that I changed trains at Chicago to spend ten minutes with you and wish you a Merry Christmas. Merry Christmas, my lad. My little Magpie.

*(*MAGGIE *rises to* c.)

MAGGIE. Beverly!

BEVERLY *(a look at his watch, crosses* L. *to piano* D.L.). And now I have just time for one magnificent number, to give you a taste of how brilliant the whole thing is. It's the second number from my new revue. *(He strikes a chord on the piano, but before he can go further the telephone rings.)*

WHITESIDE. Oh, damn! Get rid of them, Maggie.

*(*MAGGIE *crosses to phone* D.R. *on large ottoman* R. *of wheelchair.* MAGGIE, *whose mind is on other things, abstractedly reaches for the phone.)*

MAGGIE. Hello . . . Oh, hello, Bert. Oh! Well, just a minute. Beverly, would you talk to a newspaper man for just two minutes? I kind of promised him.

BEVERLY *(during phone conversation, softly playing a few bars of a "former" hit).* Won't have time, Magpie, unless he's under the piano.

MAGGIE. Oh! *(Into phone.)* Wait a minute. *(To* BEVERLY *again.)* Would you see him at the station, just for a minute before the train goes? *(*BEVERLY *nods.)* Bert, go to the station and wait for him. He'll be there in a few minutes . . . 'Bye.

WHITESIDE. The stalls are impatient, Beverly. Let's have this second-rate masterpiece. *(*MAGGIE *at stool* R.C.)

BEVERLY *(his fingers rippling over the keys).* It's called: "What Am I To Do?"

"Oft in the nightfall
  I think I might fall
   Down from my perilous height;
Deep in the heart of me,
Always a part of me,
   Quivering, shivering light.
Run, little lady,
Ere the shady
   Shafts of time,
Barb you with their winged desire,
Singe you with their sultry fire.
   Softly a fluid
      Druid
        Meets me,
"Olden
   and golden
     the dawn that greets me;
Cherishing,
   So perishing,
Up to the stars
   I climb.

"What am I to do toward
Ending this madness,
This sadness
That's rending me through?
The flowers of yesteryear are haunting me
Taunting me,
Darling, for wanting you.

"What am I to say
To warnings of sorrow,
When morning's tomorrow drinks the
   dew?
Will I see the cosmic Ritz
Shattered and scattered to bits.
What not am I to do?"

MAGGIE (*rising and crossing* L.). Wonderful, Beverly. (BEVERLY *starts to play the second chorus.*)

WHITESIDE. Beverly, it's *superb*. The best thing you've *ever written*. It'll be played by every rag tag orchestra from Salem to Singapore.

(*The doorbell rings and* JOHN *is glimpsed* U.L. *as he goes through the door. It is a trio of* RADIO MEN *who appear in the doorway, their arms filled with equipment for* WHITESIDE'S *broadcast.*)

BEVERLY. Please, let *me* say that.

WHITESIDE. Ah. Come in, Westcott.

BEVERLY (*rises to* D.L. *of piano*). Ah. The airwaves, eh! Well, I shan't have to hear you, thank God. I shall be on a train.

(WESTCOTT *goes to library* D.R., *first handing a microphone to a second* RADIO MAN, *also carrying a mike. A third man carries a portable control board.*)

MAGGIE (*crossing* D.R.). Mr. Westcott, will you go in that room? John, will you show them where to plug in? Come on, Whiteside, say good-bye.

JOHN. Right this way, gentlemen. (THEY *follow him off to dining-room* U.R.)

WHITESIDE (*as* MAGGIE *starts to wheel him into library*). Stop this nonsense.

BEVERLY (*calling after the fast disappearing* WHITESIDE). Au revoir, Sherry, Merry Christmas.

WHITESIDE. Beverly, my lamb—Maggie, what the hell are you—I want to talk to Beverly.

MAGGIE. You can kiss Beverly in London on July twelfth.

WHITESIDE (*as he is pushed through the library door in his wheelchair*). I won't be rushed out of this room like a baby that has to have his diapers changed. (*He is gone.*)

BEVERLY (*gathering up his hat and coat*). Magpie, come get a kiss.

MAGGIE (*crossing up* L.). (*Emerging from library and closing doors behind her.*) Beverly, I want one minute. I must have it. You'll make the train. The station's a minute and a half from here. (BRADLEY *enters* D.R.)

BEVERLY. Why, what's the matter, Magpie?

(*At which the library doors are opened and the* DOCTOR *emerges rather apologetically.*)

WHITESIDE (*offstage*). Go away!

DOCTOR. I'm—I'm just waiting in the kitchen until Mr.—excuse me. (*He darts out through the dining-room. Exits up* R.)

BEVERLY (*back of sofa*). Who *is* that man?

MAGGIE. Never mind . . . Beverly, I'm in great trouble.

BEVERLY. Magpie, dear, what is it?

MAGGIE. I've fallen in love.

BEVERLY. No! (*Taking her hands.*)

MAGGIE. Yes. For the first time in my life. Beverly, I'm in love. I can't tell you about it—there isn't time. But Sherry is trying to break it up. In his own fiendish way he's doing everything he can to break it up.

BEVERLY. Why, the old flounder! What's he doing?

MAGGIE. Lorraine. He's brought Lorraine here to smash it up.

BEVERLY. Oh, it's somebody *here*? In this town?

MAGGIE (*nodding*). He's a newspaper man —the one you're going to see at the station —and he's written a play, and I know Sherry must be using that as bait. You *know* Lorraine—she'll eat him up alive. You've got to help me, Beverly.

BEVERLY. Of course I will, Magpie. What do you want me to do?

MAGGIE. I've got to get Lorraine out of here—the further away the better—and you can do it for me. (WESTCOTT *opens library doors.*)

BEVERLY. But how? How can I? I'm leaving. (*The library doors are opened, and* WESTCOTT *emerges.*)

WESTCOTT. Have you a carbon of the broadcast, Miss Cutler?

MAGGIE. There's one on that table.

WESTCOTT. Thank you. One of those penguins *ate* the original. (*Exit* D.R., *closing doors.*)

WHITESIDE (*calling from his room*). Beverly, are you still there?

MAGGIE (*crossing* L. *of* BEVERLY). No, he's gone, Sherry. (*She lowers her voice.*) Here's what I want you to do. (*Manoeuvring him into the hall up* L. *We see her whisper to him; his head bobs up and down quickly in assent. Then he lets out a shriek of laughter.*) I want you to telephone Lorraine here and pretend you're Lord Bottomley.

BEVERLY. I'd love it. I'd absolutely love it. (MAGGIE *puts a quick finger to his lips; peers toward the* WHITESIDE *room. But* WESTCOTT *has gone in; the doors are closed.*) It's simply enchanting, and bitches Sherry and Lorraine at the same time. It's pure heaven! I adore it, and I shall do it up brown. (*He embraces her.*)

MAGGIE. Darling, the first baby will be named Beverly. You're wonderful.

BEVERLY. Of course I am. Come to Chislewick for your honeymoon and I'll put you up. Goodbye, my lovely. I adore you. (*Sees the time on his wrist-watch.*) Mercy! Let me out of here! (*He is gone,* L.) (MAGGIE *comes back into the room, highly pleased with herself. She even sings a fragment of* BEVERLY'S *song, "What Am I To Do?" "Tra-la-la-la-la-la."*)

(JOHN *entering from dining-room, up* R., *breaks the song.*)

JOHN (*crosses down, puts stool up* R. *of tree*). Shall I straighten up the room for the broadcast, Miss Cutler?

MAGGIE (*crosses to* C.). No, John, it isn't television, thank God, they only hear the liquid voice.

JOHN. He's really wonderful, isn't he? The things he finds time to do.

MAGGIE (*crossing* R.). Yes, he certainly sticks his nose into everything, John.

WESTCOTT (*enters from library* D.R.). Are the boys out there, Miss Cutler?

MAGGIE (*as she exits into library, closing doors*). Yes, they are, Mr. Westcott.

WESTCOTT (*as he goes into dining-room up* R.). Thank you.

(JOHN *crosses to table* L., *putting room in order as he closes a cigarette box on piano* D.L. *Suddenly* JUNE *comes quietly down the stairs. She is dressed for the street and is carrying a suitcase.*)

JOHN (*at down-stage side piano*). Why, Miss June, are you going away?

JUNE (R. *of staircase*). Why—no, John. No—Mr. Whiteside is in there, I suppose?

JOHN. Yes, he's getting ready to go on the radio.

JUNE. Oh! Would you—no, never mind. Look, John— (*Just then* RICHARD *comes downstairs carrying a light bag and a couple of cameras.*)

RICHARD. Where is he? In the library?

JUNE. Yes, he's busy.

RICHARD. Oh! Well, maybe we ought to— (*The door-bell rings again.*) Come on. (RICHARD *immediately scoots out, also via the dining-room up* R., *shooing* JUNE *before him.* JOHN *meanwhile has gone to front door off* L.)

LORRAINE. Thank you, John. (*It is* LORRAINE *who comes in, resplendent now in evening dress and wrap, straight from Paris. At the same time* MAGGIE *emerges from library* D.R. *and* JOHN *goes on his way up* L. MAGGIE *puts the phone back on console* D.R.) (LORRAINE, *to* C.) Hello, dear. Where's Sherry?

MAGGIE. Inside working—he's broadcasting very soon. (MAGGIE *puts presents from the ottoman under tree* U.C.)

LORRAINE (*surveying the room*). Oh, of course—Christmas Eve. What a wonderful man Sheridan Whiteside is. You know, my dear, it must be such an utter joy to be secretary to somebody like Sherry.

MAGGIE. Yes, you meet such interesting people . . . (LORRAINE *crosses to couch.*) That's quite a gown, Lorraine. Going anywhere? (*Chair* D.R.)

LORRAINE. This? Oh, I just threw on anything at all. (*Sits on sofa.*) Aren't you dressing for dinner?

MAGGIE (*crosses to back of sofa*). No, just what meets the eye. (*She has occasion to carry a few papers across the room at this point.* LORRAINE's *eyes watch her narrowly. As* MAGGIE *reaches* C. *she gives* LORRAINE *a polite social smile, then continues to* D.R.)

LORRAINE. Who does your hair, Maggie?

MAGGIE. A little Frenchwoman named Maggie Cutler comes in every morning.

LORRAINE. You know, every time I see you I keep thinking your hair could be so lovely. I always want to get my hands on it.

MAGGIE (*sits; quietly*). I've always wanted to get mine on yours, Lorraine.

LORRAINE (*absently*). What, dear? (*One of the* RADIO MEN *drifts into the room with a table for the control board, puts it* L. *of tree, drifts out again. As he reaches arch* U.R. *he grins broadly.* LORRAINE's *eyes follow him idly. Then she turns to* MAGGIE *again.*) By the way, what time does Beverly get here? I'm not over-anxious to meet him.

MAGGIE. He's been and gone, Lorraine.

LORRAINE. Really? Well, I'm very glad . . . Of course, you're great friends, aren't you—you and Beverly?

MAGGIE. Yes, we are. I think he's a wonderful person.

LORRAINE. Oh, I suppose he is. But really, when I finished acting with him, I was a perfect wreck. All during that tender love scene that the critics thought was so magnificent, he kept dropping peanut shells down my dress. I wouldn't act with him again if I were starving.

MAGGIE (*rises, crosses to* C.). Tell me, Lorraine, have you found a new play yet?

LORRAINE (*at once on guard*). No—no, I haven't. There was a pile of manuscripts waiting in New York for me, but I hurried right out here to Sherry.

MAGGIE. Yes, it was wonderful of you, Lorraine—to drop everything that way and rush to Sherry's wheel-chair.

LORRAINE. Well, after all, Maggie, dear, what else has one in this world but friends?

MAGGIE (*crosses* R. *to* D.R.). That's what I always say . . . (RADIO MAN *enters up* R. *with the control board, puts it on table.*) Everything O.K.?

RADIO MAN. Yes, thank you. (Starting off, *never taking his eyes off* LORRAINE. *He reaches library doors, realizes his mistake, exits into dining-room* U.R.)

LORRAINE. How long will Sherry be in there?

MAGGIE (*crosses to* C.). Not long . . . Did you know that Mr. Jefferson has written quite a good play? The young man that drove you to the hotel.

LORRAINE. Really? No, I didn't. Isn't that interesting?

MAGGIE (*sits*). Yes, isn't it? (*There is a considerable pause. The ladies smile at each other.*)

LORRAINE (*evading* MAGGIE's *eyes*). They've put a polish on my nails I simply loathe. I don't suppose Elizabeth Arden has a branch in this town.

MAGGIE (*busy with her papers*). Not if she has any sense.

LORRAINE (*rises, to back of sofa, then to piano*). Oh, well, I'll just bear it, but it does depress me. (*She wanders aimlessly for a moment. Picks up a book from the table.*) Have you read this, Maggie, everybody was reading it on the boat. I hear you simply can't put it down.

MAGGIE. *I* put it down—*right there*. (LORRAINE *casually strikes a note or two on the piano.*) (*The phone rings.*) (*Taking up the receiver a little too casually.*) Hello . . . yes . . . Yes . . . Miss Lorraine Sheldon? Yes, she's here . . . There's a Trans-Atlantic call coming (*Rises.*) through for you, Lorraine.

LORRAINE (*crossing* R. *to phone*). Trans-Atlantic—for me? Here? Why, what in the world—

MAGGIE (*as she hands over the receiver— eases up* C.). It's London.

LORRAINE. London? . . . Hello. (*Then in a louder tone.*) Hello . . . Cedric! Cedric, is this you? . . . Why, Cedric, you darling! Why, what a surprise! How'd you know I was here? What . . . ? Darling, don't talk so fast and you won't stutter so . . . That's better . . . Yes, now I can hear you . . . Yes, very clearly. It's as though you were just around the corner . . . I see . . . What? . . . Darling! *(Realizing* MAGGIE *is listening.)* Cedric, dearest, would you wait just one moment? *(She turns to* MAGGIE.*)* Maggie, would you mind? It's Lord Bottomley—a *very* personal call. Would you mind?

MAGGIE. Oh, not at all. *(She goes into the dining-room, up* R.*, almost does a little waltz step as she goes.)*

LORRAINE. Yes, my dearest—now tell me . . . Cedric, please don't stutter so. Don't be nervous. *(She listens for a moment again.)* Oh, my darling. Oh, my sweet. You don't know how I've prayed for this, every night on the boat . . . Darling, yes! YES, a thousand times Yes! . . . I'll take a plane right out of here and catch the next boat . . . What? Cedric, don't stutter so . . . Yes, and I love *you,* my darling —oh, so much! . . . Oh, my dear sweet. My darlingest darling. Yes, yes! I will, I will, darling! I'll be thinking of you every moment . . . You've made me the happiest girl in the world . . . Good-bye, good-bye, darling. Good-bye. *(Puts phone on ottoman* D.R.*)* *(Bursting with her news, she turns to library to call* WHITESIDE, *opens the doors, crosses to* C.*)* Sherry! Sherry! Do you know what happened? Cedric just called from London—he's asked me to marry him.

WHITESIDE *(wheeling himself on. He is smoking a cigarette in a long holder).* What!

LORRAINE. Sherry, think of it! At last! I've got to get right out of here and catch the next boat.

MAGGIE *(emerging, mouse-like, from the dining-room, up* R.*).* May I come in?

LORRAINE *(crossing* L.*).* Maggie dear, can I get a plane out of here right away? I've simply got to get the next boat to England. When is it—do you know? Is there a newspaper here?

MAGGIE *(eases down).* The *Queen Mary* sails Friday. What's happened?

LORRAINE *(crossing up* R., *embraces* MAGGIE*).* Maggie, the most wonderful thing in the world has happened. Lord Bottomley has asked me to marry him. Oh, Maggie! *(A gesture toward phone.)*

MAGGIE. Really? Well, what do you know?

LORRAINE. Isn't it wonderful? I'm so excited I can hardly think. Maggie dear, you must help me to get right out of here.

MAGGIE *(crossing to desk* D.R.*).* I'd be delighted to, Lorraine.

LORRAINE. Oh, thank you, thank you. Will you look things up right away?

MAGGIE. Yes, I've a time-table right here. And don't worry, because if there's no train I'll drive you to Cleveland and you can catch the plane from there.

LORRAINE. Maggie darling, you're wonderful. *(She sees* WHITESIDE *puffing furiously on his cigarette.)* Sherry, what's the matter with you? You haven't said a word. You haven't even congratulated me.

WHITESIDE *(rolls down* R.*).* *(He has been sitting through this like a thunder-cloud.)* Let me understand this, Lorraine. Am I to gather from your girlish squeals that you are about to toss your career into the ashcan?

LORRAINE *(to sofa for furs).* Oh, not at all. Of course I may not be able to play this season, but there'll be other seasons, Sherry.

WHITESIDE. I see. And everything goes into the ashcan with it—is that right?

LORRAINE. But Sherry, you couldn't expect me to—

WHITESIDE *(icily).* Don't explain, Lorraine. I understand only too well. And I also understand why Cornell remains the First Actress of our theatre.

MAGGIE *(busy with her time-tables, crossing to* C.*).* Oh, this is wonderful! We're in luck, Lorraine. There's a plane out of Cleveland at ten-three. It takes about an hour to get there.—Why, it all works out wonderfully, doesn't it, Sherry?

WHITESIDE *(through his teeth).* Peachy.

LORRAINE *(heading for the phone, crossing* R. *below phone stool* D.R.*).* Maggie, what's the number of that hotel I'm at? I've got to get my maid started packing.

MAGGIE. Mesalia three-two.

LORRAINE *(into phone).* Mesalia three-two, please . . . Let's see—I sail Friday, five-day boat, that means I ought to be in London Wednesday night . . . *(*MAGGIE *crosses up* L.*)* Hello, this is Miss Sheldon

. . . That's right. Put me through to my maid, will you?

MAGGIE (*at window*). Oh, look, Sherry, it's starting to snow. Isn't that wonderful, Sherry? Oh, I never felt more like Christmas in my life. Don't you, Sherry dear?

WHITESIDE. Shut your nasty little face! (MAGGIE *drifts down* L. *and leans against piano.*)

LORRAINE (*on phone. She sits on ottoman* D.R.). Cosette? . . . Now listen carefully, Cosette. We're leaving here tonight by plane and sailing Friday on the *Queen Mary.* I want you to start packing immediately and I'll call for you in about an hour . . . Yes, that's right . . . Now I want you to send these cables for me. Have you got a pencil? Right? The first one goes to Lord and Lady Cunard—you'll find all these addresses in my little book. It's in my dressing case. "Lord and Lady Cunard. My darlings. Returning Friday *Queen Mary.* Cedric and I being married immediately on arrival. Wanted you to be the first to know. Love—Lorraine." Now send—what? Oh, thank you, Cosette. Thank you very much. (*This last "thank you" followed by a pointed smile at Sherry.*) Now send the same message to Lady Astor, Lord Beaverbrook, and my mother in Kansas City . . . Got that? And send a telegram to Hattie Carnegie, New York. "Please meet me Sherry Netherlands noon tomorrow with sketches of bridal gown and trousseau.— Lorraine Sheldon." And then send one to Monsieur Pierre Cartier, Cartier's, London: "Will you hold in reserve for me the triple string of pearls I picked out in October? Cable me *Queen Mary.*—Lorraine Sheldon." Have you got all that straight, Cosette? . . . That's fine. Now you'll have to rush, my dear—I'll be at the hotel in about an hour, so be ready. Good-bye. (*She hangs up, putting phone on the ottoman. She crosses back of Sherry's chair to* C.) Thank goodness for Cosette—I'd die without her, she's the most wonderful maid in the world . . . Well! Life is really just full of surprises, isn't it? Who'd have thought an hour ago that I'd be on my way to London?

MAGGIE. An *hour* ago? No, I certainly wouldn't have thought it an hour ago.

WHITESIDE (*beside himself with temper*).

Will you both stop this female drooling? I have a violent headache.

MAGGIE (*all solicitude. Crossing* R. *front sofa*). Oh, Sherry! Can I get you something?

LORRAINE (*crossing to Sherry*). Look here, Sherry, I'm sorry if I've offended you, but after all my life is my own and— (*She stops as* BERT *comes in from the outside.*)

BERT (*to* C.). Hello, everybody. Say, do you know it's snowing out? Going to have a real old-fashioned Christmas.

WHITESIDE. Why don't you telephone your scoop to the *New York Times?*

MAGGIE (*crosses to him*). Bert, Miss Sheldon has to catch a plane tonight, from Cleveland. Can we drive her over, you and I?

BERT. Why, certainly. Sorry you have to go, Miss Sheldon. No bad news, I hope.

LORRAINE. Oh, on the contrary—very good news. Wonderful news.

MAGGIE. Yes, indeed—calls for a drink, I think. You're not being a very good host, Sherry. How about a bottle of champagne? (*Crossing* R.)

BERT. Oh, I can do better than that—let me mix you a Jefferson Special. Okay, Mr. Whiteside?

WHITESIDE. Yes, yes, yes, yes, yes. Mix anything. Only stop drivelling.

BERT. Anybody admired my Christmas present yet, Maggie?

MAGGIE. Oh, dear, I forgot. (*She raises her arm, revealing a bracelet.*) Look, everybody! From Mr. Jefferson to me.

LORRAINE. Oh, it's charming. Let me see it. Oh! Why, it's inscribed, too. "To Maggie. Long may she wave. Bert." Maggie, it's a lovely Christmas present. Isn't that sweet, Sherry?

WHITESIDE. Ducky.

MAGGIE (*crosses to* L.C.). I told you it was beautiful, Bert. See?

BERT. Well, shows what you get if you save your coupons.

LORRAINE (*looking from* BERT *to* MAGGIE). Well, what's going on between you two, anyhow? Maggie, are you hiding something from us?

WHITESIDE (*a hand to his head*). Great God, will this drivel never stop? My head is bursting.

BERT (*crosses up R., then back to* WHITESIDE). A Jefferson Special will cure anything . . . By the way, I got a two-minute interview with Beverly Carlton at the station. You were right, Mr. Whiteside—he's quite something. (LORRAINE *crosses up L. and drifts down to piano.*)

MAGGIE (*uneasily*). Go ahead, Bert—mix the drinks.

BERT. On the fire. I was lucky to get even two minutes. He was in a telephone booth most of the time. (*Light slowly starts to dawn on* WHITESIDE.)

MAGGIE. Bert, mix those drinks, will you?

BERT. Okay, couldn't hear what he was saying, but from the faces he was making, it looked like a scene from one of his plays.

MAGGIE. Bert, for goodness' sake, will you—

WHITESIDE (*suddenly galvanized*). Ah—just a minute, if you please, Jefferson. Mr. Carlton was in a telephone booth at the station?

BERT (*coming D.R.*). Certainly was—I thought he'd never come out. Kept talking and making the damnedest faces for about five minutes.

WHITESIDE (*ever so sweetly*). Bert, my boy, I have an idea I shall love the Jefferson Special. Make me a double one, will you? My headache has gone with the wind.

BERT. Okay. (*He goes up R.*)

WHITESIDE (*his eyes gleaming, immediately grabs phone*). Philo Vance is now at work. Hello. (MAGGIE *eases L. to piano front.*) (*On phone—his voice is absolutely musical.*) Operator dear, has there been a call from England over this telephone within the past half hour . . . ? (LORRAINE *eases R.*) Yes, I'll wait.

LORRAINE (*eases R.*). Sherry, what *is* all this?

WHITESIDE. Sssh!—What's that? There have been no calls from England for the past three days? Thank you . . . Blossom Girl. (*She crosses to him.*) Now, will you repeat that, please? (*He beckons to* LORRAINE, *then puts the receiver to her ear.*) Hear it, dear? (*Then again to the opera-*

tor.*) Thank you, operator, and a Merry Christmas. (*He hangs up.*)

LORRAINE (*stunned*). Sherry, what is all this? What does this mean?

WHITESIDE. My dear, you have just played the greatest love-scene of your career with your old friend Beverly Carlton.

LORRAINE. Why—why, that's not true. I was talking to Cedric. What do you mean?

WHITESIDE. I mean, my blossom, that that was Beverly you poured out your girlish heart to, not Lord Bottomley. Ah, me, who'd have thought five minutes ago that you would not be going to London!

LORRAINE. Sherry, I want this explained.

WHITESIDE. Explained? You heard the operator, my dear. All I can tell you is that Beverly was indulging in one of his famous bits of mimicry, that's all. You've heard him do Lord Bottomley before, haven't you?

LORRAINE. Yes . . . Yes, of course . . . But —but why would he want to do such a thing? This is one of the most dreadful— oh, my God! Those cables! Those cables! (*In one bound she crosses back of wheelchair, to phone.*) Give me the hotel— whatever it's called—I want the hotel . . . I'll pay him off for this if it's the last thing that I—why, the skunk!—the louse! The dirty rotten—Mansion House? Connect me with the maid . . . What? . . . Who the hell do you *think* it is? Miss Sheldon, of course . . . Oh, God! Those cables. If only Cosette hasn't—Cosette! Cosette! Did you send those cables? . . . Oh, God! Oh, God! . . . Now listen, Cosette, I want you to send another cable to every one of those people, and tell them somebody has been using my name, and to disregard anything and everything they hear from me— except this, of course . . . Don't ask questions—do as you're told . . . Don't argue with me, you French bitch—God damn it, do as you're told . . . And unpack, we're not going! (*She hangs up and crosses U.L.*)

WHITESIDE. Now steady, my blossom. Take it easy.

LORRAINE (*crossing back to c.*). What do you mean take it easy? Do you realize I'll be the laughing stock of England? Why, I won't dare show my face! I always knew

Beverly Carlton was low, but not this low. Why? WHY? It isn't even funny. Why would he do it, that's what I'd like to know. Why would he do it! Why would anyone in the world want to play a silly trick like this? I can't understand it. Do you, Sherry? Do you, Maggie? You both saw him this afternoon. Why would he walk out of here, *(Crosses to* MAGGIE, *then back to* C.) go right to a phone booth, and try to ship me over to England on a fool's errand! There must have been some reason—there must have. It doesn't make sense otherwise. Why should Beverly Carlton, or anybody else for that matter, want me to? *(She stops as a dim light begins to dawn.)* (MAGGIE *hand to hair.*) Oh! Oh! *(Her eye, which has been on* MAGGIE, *goes momentarily to the dining-room, where* BERT *has disappeared. Then her gaze returns to* MAGGIE *again.*) I—I think I begin to—of course! Of course! That's it. Of course that's it. Yes, and that's a very charming bracelet that Mr. Jefferson gave you—isn't it, Maggie, dear? Of course. It makes complete sense now. And to think that I nearly—well! Wild horses couldn't get me out of here *now,* (*Crossing to* MAGGIE L.) Maggie, and if I were you I'd hang onto that bracelet, dear. It'll be something to remember him by. *(Crosses to front of sofa.)*

(Out of the dining-room comes WESTCOTT, *his hands full of papers. At the same time the two* TECHNICIANS *emerge, first man goes to the control board, the other sets two standing mikes* D.C. *and* L.C. *of wheelchair.)*

WESTCOTT *(his eyes on his watch. Crosses to* R. *of wheelchair*). All right, Mr. Whiteside. Almost time. Hook her up, boys, start testing. Here's your new copy, Mr. Whiteside. *(Hands typed copy to him.)*

WHITESIDE. How much time?

WESTCOTT. Couple of minutes.

(The FIRST RADIO MAN *is talking into his control board apparatus, testing:* "One, two, three, four, one, two, three, four. How are we coming in, New York? . . . A, B, C, D, A, B, C, D. Mary had a little lamb, Mary had a little lamb."*)*

*(*MR. *and* MRS. STANLEY, *having delivered their Christmas presents, enter from hallway* L. STANLEY *stops to take his coat off.* MRS. STANLEY *looks hungrily at the radio goings-on. The voice of the* SECOND RADIO

MAN *drones on:* "Testing." *But* STANLEY *delivers a stern* "Please, Daisy," *and she follows him up the stairs.* "O.K. New York. Mary had a little lamb. Waiting." WESTCOTT *stands with watch in hand. From the dining-room comes* BERT, *tray of four drinks in hand.*)

BERT *(crosses to* C.). Here comes the Jefferson Special . . . Oh! Have we time?

LORRAINE *(below couch* L.). Oh, I'm sure we have. Mr. Jefferson, I'm not leaving after all. My plans are changed.

BERT *(crosses* L.). Really? Oh, that's good.

LORRAINE. And I hear you've written a simply marvelous play, Mr. Jefferson. I want you to read it to me—tonight. Will you? We'll go back to the Mansion House right after dinner. And you'll read me your play. *(She takes a cocktail.)* (MAGGIE *steps downstage.*)

BERT. Why—why, I should say so. I'd be delighted . . . Maggie, did you hear that? *(Crosses* L. *to* D.L.) Say! I'll bet *you* did this. You arranged the whole thing. Well, it's the finest Christmas present you could have given me. (MAGGIE *looks at him for one anguished moment. Then, without a word, she dashes into the hall,* L., *grabs her coat and flings herself out of the house.*) Maggie! Maggie! (BERT *puts tray of drinks on piano and starts after her, but stops when he hears the door slam.* LORRAINE, *in the meanwhile, sits on sofa.*)

FIRST RADIO MAN. Thirty seconds. Waiting.

*(*MR. *and* MRS. STANLEY *come pell-mell down the stairs. Each clutches a letter and they are wild-eyed.*)

STANLEY *(*C.*).* Mr. Whiteside!

WESTCOTT. Quiet, please!

STANLEY. My son has run off on a freighter, and my daughter is marrying an Anarchist.

WESTCOTT. Quiet!

STANLEY. They say you told them to do it.

MRS. STANLEY. My poor June! My poor Richard! This is the most awful—

WESTCOTT. Quiet! Quiet, please! We're going on the air. *(Enter* CHOIR BOYS L., *cross to* C.) (STANLEY *chokes and looks bewilderedly at the letter in his hand.* MRS. STANLEY *is softly crying.*) (DR. BRADLEY *emerges from dining-room.*)

BRADLEY. Oh! I see you're still busy.

STANLEY. Don't tell me to be quiet!

WESTCOTT (*yelling, he pushes the* STANLEYS *upstage*). Quiet! For God's sake, quiet! Step out of the way. Please! All right, boys, right this way. Down here to this mike. (*Crosses* L. *to usher* BOYS *to* C. *mike.*) (*From the hallway come six* CHOIR BOYS *dressed in their robes. They take their places by the microphone. The moment they are set, one of the boys blows the pitch-pipe for key.*)

FIRST RADIO MAN (*completing hookup*). O.K. New York.

(SECOND RADIO MAN *raises his arm when* CHOIR BOYS *are set.* WESTCOTT *is watching him. A dead pause of about five seconds.* JOHN *and* SARAH *are on tip-toe in the dining-room. Then the arm drops.* WESTCOTT *gestures to* CHOIR BOYS *to sing. They raise their lovely voices in* "*Silent Night.*")

WESTCOTT (*into the microphone* C.). Good evening, everybody. Cream of Mush brings you Sheridan Whiteside. (WESTCOTT, *lowering mike, gestures to* CHOIR BOYS *to step forward to mike. Another gesture from* WESTCOTT, *who has crossed to* R. *of chair, and* WHITESIDE *begins to speak, with the* BOYS *singing as a background.*)

CHOIR BOYS (*singing,* "*Silent Night*").
Silent night, holy night,
All is calm, all is bright
Round yon Virgin Mother and Child.
Holy infant so tender and mild,
Sleep in heavenly peace,
Sleep in heavenly peace.

(WESTCOTT *crosses* D.R.)

WHITESIDE (*simultaneously*). This is Whiteside speaking. On this eve of eves, when my own heart is overflowing with peace and kindness, I think it most fitting to tell once again the story of that still and lustrous night, nigh onto two thousand years ago— (*At this point a piercing scream from the library* D.R. *Everybody turns at the interruption as* MISS PREEN *rushes on, holding her hand. The choir continues to sing during all of this.*)

MISS PREEN. A penguin bit me. (BRADLEY *crosses to her.*)

WHITESIDE (*raising his voice to top the sobbing* MISS PREEN, *continues*). When first the star of Bethlehem— (*The curtain starts down.*) was glimpsed in a wondrous sky . . .

THE CURTAIN IS DOWN

ACT THREE

Scene is the same.

Christmas morning. The bright December sunlight streams in through the window. From the library comes the roaring voice of WHITESIDE *again:* "*Miss Preen! Miss Preen!*"

MISS PREEN, *who is just coming through the dining-room, rushes to open the library doors.*

MISS PREEN. Yes, sir. Yes, sir.

WHITESIDE (*as he, plainly in a mood, rolls himself into the room to* D.R.). Where do you disappear to all the time, My Lady Nausea?

MISS PREEN. Mr. Whiteside, I can only be in one place at a time.

WHITESIDE. That's very fortunate for this community.

(MISS PREEN *goes indignantly into the library and slams the doors after her.* JOHN *enters from upstairs, carrying a tray of used dishes.*)

JOHN. Good morning, Mr. Whiteside. Merry Christmas.

WHITESIDE. Merry Christmas, John. Merry Christmas.

JOHN. Are you ready for your breakfast, Mr. Whiteside?

WHITESIDE. No, I don't think I want any breakfast . . . Has Miss Cutler come down yet?

JOHN. No, sir, not yet.

WHITESIDE. Is she in her room, do you know?

JOHN. Yes, sir, she is. Shall I call her?

WHITESIDE. No, no. That's all, John.

JOHN (*going through dining-room* U.R.). Yes, sir.

(WHITESIDE, *left alone, heaves a huge sigh. Then* MAGGIE *comes down the stairs. She wears a traveling suit and carries a bag.* WHITESIDE *waits for her to speak.*)

MAGGIE (*putting bag down* R. *of staircase*). I'm taking the one o'clock train, Sherry. I'm leaving.

WHITESIDE. You're doing nothing of the kind!

MAGGIE. Here are your keys—your driving license. (*Hands them to him.*) The key to the safe-deposit vault is in the apartment in New York. I'll go in here now and clear things up. (*She opens library door.*)

WHITESIDE (*puts keys etc. in pocket*). Just a moment, Mrs. Siddons. Where *were* you until three o'clock this morning? I sat up half the night in this station-wagon, worrying about you. You heard me calling to you when you came in. Why didn't you answer me? (MAGGIE *crosses to* R. *of him.*)

MAGGIE. Look, Sherry, it's over, and you've won. I don't want to talk about it.

WHITESIDE. Oh, come, come, come, come, come. What are you trying to do—make me feel like a naughty, naughty boy? Honestly, Maggie, sometimes you can be very annoying.

MAGGIE (*looking at him in wonder, crossing to* L. *of him*). You know, you're quite wonderful, Sherry, in a way. *You're* annoyed! I wish there was a laugh left in me. Shall I tell you something, Sherry? I think you are a selfish, petty egomaniac who would see his mother burned . . . at the stake . . . if that was the only way he could light his cigarette. I think you'd sacrifice your best friend without a moment's hesitation if he disturbed the sacred routine of your self-centered, paltry little life. I think you are incapable of any human emotion that goes higher up than your stomach, and I was the fool of the world for ever thinking I could trust you.

WHITESIDE. Well, as long as I live, I will never do anyone a good turn again. I won't ask you to apologize, Maggie, because in

six months from now you will be thanking me instead of berating me.

MAGGIE. In six months, Sherry, I expect to be *so far away* from you— (*She is halted by a loud voice from the hallway, as the door bangs.* "Hello—hello—hello!" *It is* BERT JEFFERSON *who enters* L., *a little high.* MAGGIE *crosses* U. *to* R.)

BERT (C.). Merry Christmas, everybody! Merry Christmas! I'm a little high, but I can explain everything. Hi, Maggie. Hi, Mr. Whiteside. Shake hands with a successful playwright. Maggie, why'd you run away last night? Where were you? Miss Sheldon thinks the play is wonderful. I read her the play and she thinks it's wonderful. Isn't that wonderful?

MAGGIE. Yes, that's fine, Bert.

BERT. Isn't that wonderful, Mr. Whiteside?

WHITESIDE. Jefferson, I think you ought to go home, don't you?

BERT. What? No—biggest day of my life. I know I'm a little drunk, but this is a big day. We've been sitting over in Billy's Tavern all night. Never realized it was daylight until it was daylight— (*Crosses to* MAGGIE R.) Listen, Maggie—Miss Sheldon says the play needs just a little bit of fixing—do it in three weeks. She's going to take me to a little place she's got in Lake Placid—just for three weeks. Going to work on the play together. Isn't it wonderful? (*A pause.*) Why don't you say something, Maggie? (*She turns away.*)

WHITESIDE. Look, Bert, I suggest you tell us all about this later. Now, why don't you— (*He stops as* DR. BRADLEY *enters from hallway.*)

BRADLEY (C.). Oh, excuse me! Merry Christmas, everybody. Merry Christmas.

BERT. God bless us all, and Tiny Tim.

BRADLEY. Yes . . . Mr. Whiteside, I thought perhaps if I came very early . . .

BERT (*crosses back of* WHITESIDE *to* BRADLEY). You know what, Doc? I'm going to Lake Placid for three weeks—isn't that wonderful? Ever hear of Lorraine Sheldon, the famous actress? Well, we're going to Lake Placid for three weeks.

WHITESIDE. Dr. Bradley, would you do me a favor? I think Mr. Jefferson would like some black coffee and a little breakfast. Would you take care of him, please?

BRADLEY. Yes, yes, of course . . .

BERT. Dr. Bradley, I'm going to buy breakfast for *you*—biggest breakfast you ever had.

BRADLEY. Yes, yes, Jefferson.

BERT (*putting arm about* BRADLEY, *he starts him off*). You know what, Doctor? Let's climb down a couple of chimneys. I got a friend that doesn't believe in Santa Claus —let's climb down his chimney and frighten the hell out of him. (*He exits with* BRADLEY, L.)

WHITESIDE (*in a burst of magnanimity*). Now listen to me, Maggie. I am willing to forgive your tawdry outburst and talk about this calmly.

MAGGIE. I love him so terribly. Oh, Sherry, Sherry, why did you do it? Why did you do it? (*She goes stumbling into the library—closes doors after her.*) (WHITESIDE, *left alone, looks at his watch; heaves a long sigh. Then* HARRIET *comes down the steps, dressed for the street.*)

HARRIET (*to* C.). Merry Christmas, Mr. Whiteside.

WHITESIDE. Oh! . . . Merry Christmas, Miss Stanley.

HARRIET (*nervously*). I'm afraid I shouldn't be seen talking to you, Mr. Whiteside—my brother is terribly angry. I just couldn't resist asking—did you like my Christmas present?

WHITESIDE. I'm very sorry, Miss Stanley— I haven't opened it. I haven't opened any of my presents yet.

HARRIET. Oh, dear, I was so anxious to— it's right here, Mr. Whiteside. (*She goes to tree.*) Won't you open it now?

WHITESIDE (*as he undoes the string*). I appreciate your thinking of me, Miss Stanley. This is very thoughtful of you. (*He takes out the gift—an old photograph.*) Why, it's lovely. I'm very fond of these old photographs. Thank you very much.

HARRIET. I was twenty-two when that was taken. That was my favorite dress . . . Do you really like it?

WHITESIDE. I do indeed. When I get back to town I shall send you a little gift.

HARRIET. Will you? Oh, thank you, Mr. Whiteside. I shall treasure it— (*She starts to go*). Well, I shall be late for church. Good-bye. Good-bye.

WHITESIDE. Good-bye, Miss Stanley. (*As she goes out the front door* WHITESIDE's *eyes return to the gift. He puzzles over it for a second, shakes his head. Mumbles to himself—"What is there about that woman?" Shakes his head again in perplexity.*)

(JOHN *comes from dining-room, carrying a breakfast tray.*)

JOHN. Sarah's got a little surprise for you, Mr. Whiteside. She's just taking it out of the oven. (*Crossing from* U.R. *to upstairs.*)

WHITESIDE. Thank you, John. (JOHN *disappears up the stairs.*) (*Then suddenly there is a great ringing of the doorbell. It stops for a second, then picks up violently again.*) Miss Preen! Miss Preen! (MISS PREEN *comes hurrying from library.*)

MISS PREEN. Yes, sir. Yes, sir.

WHITESIDE. Answer the door, will you? John is upstairs. (MISS PREEN, *obviously annoyed, hurries to the door.*) (WHITESIDE *puts package in chair basket.*) (*We hear her voice from the hallway "Who is it?" An answering male voice: "Polly Adler's!" Then a little shriek from* MISS PREEN, *and in a moment we see the reason why. She is carried into the room in the arms of a pixie-like gentleman, who is kissing her over and over.*)

THE GENTLEMAN (*carrying* MISS PREEN). (*Coming* D.C.) I love you madly—madly. Did you hear what I said—madly! Kiss me. Again! Don't be afraid of my passion. Kiss me! I can feel the hot blood pounding through your varicose veins.

MISS PREEN (*through all this*). Put me down! Put me down! Do you hear? Don't you dare kiss me! Who are you? Put me down or I'll scream. Mr. Whiteside! Mr. Whiteside!

WHITESIDE. Banjo, for God's sake! Banjo!

BANJO. Hello, Whiteside. Will you sign for this package, please?

MISS PREEN. Mr. Whiteside!

WHITESIDE. Banjo, put that woman down. That is my nurse, you mental delinquent.

BANJO (*putting* MISS PREEN *on her feet*). Come to my room in half an hour and bring some rye bread. (*Slaps* MISS PREEN'S *fanny*.)

MISS PREEN (*outraged*). Really, Mr. Whiteside! (*She adjusts her clothes with a quick jerk or two and marches into the library—closes doors.*) (JOHN, *at the same time, comes hurrying down the stairs;* BANJO *beckons to him. Bending his leg and raising it,* BANJO *puts it in* JOHN'S *hand. Amazed,* JOHN *rushes off* U.R.)

BANJO (*crosses to* C.). Whiteside, I'm here to spend Christmas with you. Give me a kiss.

WHITESIDE. Get away from me, you reform school fugitive. How did you get here anyway?

BANJO (C.). Darryl Zanuck loaned me his reindeer. Whiteside, we finished shooting the picture yesterday and I'm on my way to Nova Scotia. Flew here in twelve hours —borrowed an airplane from Howard Hughes. Whiteside, I brought you a wonderful Christmas present. (*He produces a little tissue-wrapped package. Crosses to* WHITESIDE.) This brassiere was once worn by Hedy Lamarr. (*Dropping it in* WHITESIDE'S *lap*.)

WHITESIDE. Listen, you idiot, how long can you stay?

BANJO. Just long enough to take a bath. I'm on my way to Nova Scotia. Where's Maggie?

WHITESIDE. Nova Scotia? What are you going to Nova Scotia for?

BANJO. I'm sick of Hollywood and there's a dame in New York I don't want to see. So I figured I'd go to Nova Scotia and get some smoked salmon . . . Where the hell's Maggie? I want to see her . . . What's the matter with you? Where is she?

WHITESIDE. Banjo, I'm glad you're here. I'm very annoyed at Maggie. Very!

BANJO. What's the matter? (WHITESIDE *rises, crosses to* L.) Say, what is this? I thought you couldn't walk. (*Crossing to* C.)

WHITESIDE. Oh, I've been all right for weeks. That isn't the point. I'm furious at Maggie. She's turned on me like a viper.

You know how fond I am of her. Well, after all these years she's repaying my affection by behaving like a fishwife.

BANJO. What are you talking about?

WHITESIDE (*a step* L.). But I never believed for a moment she was really in love with him.

BANJO. In love with who? I just got here —remember? (BUSINESS *of pointing to himself*.)

WHITESIDE (*pace* L.). Great God, I'm telling you, you Hollywood nitwit. A young newspaper man here in town.

BANJO. Maggie finally fell—well, what do you know? What kind of a guy is he?

WHITESIDE (*crosses to him*). Oh, shut up and listen, will you?

BANJO. Well, go on. What happened?

WHITESIDE (*pacing* L.). Well, Lorraine Sheldon happened to come out here and visit me.

BANJO. Old hot-pants—here?

WHITESIDE (*back to* BANJO). Now listen! This young fellow, he'd written a play. You can guess the rest. He's going away with Lorraine this afternoon. To "rewrite." So there you are. Maggie's in there now, crying her eyes out. (*Crosses to sofa —sits*.)

BANJO (*crosses* L.). Gee! . . . Say, wait a minute. What do you mean Lorraine Sheldon happened to come out here? I smell a rat, Sherry—a rat with a beard.

(*And it might be well to add, at this point, that Mr. Sheridan Whiteside wears a beard*.)

WHITESIDE. Well, all right, all right. But I did it for Maggie—because I thought it was the right thing for *her*.

BANJO (*crosses* R.). Oh, sure. You haven't thought of yourself in years . . . Gee, poor kid. Can I go in and talk to her?

WHITESIDE. No—no. Leave her alone.

BANJO (*crosses* L.). Any way I could help, Sherry? Where's this guy live—this guy she likes? Can we get hold of him?

WHITESIDE (*rises—crosses to* BANJO). Now wait a minute, Banjo. We don't want any phony warrants, or you pretending to be

J. Edgar Hoover. I've been through all that with you before. *(He paces again* L.*)* I got Lorraine out here and I've got to get her away.

BANJO. It's got to be good, Sherry. Lorraine's no dope. *(Crosses* U.R.*)* . . . Now, there must be *some*thing that would get her out of here like a bat out of hell. *(Crosses to* L.*)* Say! I thing I've got it! That fellow she's so crazy about over in England—what's his name again?—Lord Fanny or whatever it is. Bottomley—that's it! Bottomley!

WHITESIDE *(with a pained expression).* No, Banjo. No.

BANJO. Wait a minute—you don't catch on. We send Lorraine a cablegram from Lord Bottomley—

WHITESIDE. I catch on, Banjo. Lorraine caught on too. It's been tried.

BANJO *(crosses* R.*).* Oh! . . . I told you she was no dope . . . *(He sits in wheelchair.)* Well, we've got a tough proposition on your hands.

WHITESIDE. The trouble is there's so damned little time. Get out of my chair! *(*WHITESIDE *sits in chair as* BANJO *gets out of it and crosses to* C.*)* Lorraine's taking him away with her this afternoon. Oh, damn, damn, damn. There must be some way out. The trouble is I've done this job too well. Hell and damnation!

BANJO *(*C.*,*. Stuck, huh?

WHITESIDE. In the words of one of our greatest lyric poets, you said it.

BANJO. Yeh. Gee, I'm hungry. We'll think of something, Sherry—you watch. We'll get Lorraine out of here if I have to do it one piece at a time. *(*SARAH *enters from dining-room, bearing a tray on which reposes the culinary surprise which* JOHN *has mentioned which she is hiding behind her back.)*

SARAH *(to* L. *of chair).* Merry Christmas, Mr. Whiteside . . . Excuse me. *(This last is to* BANJO.*)* I've got something for you . . . *(*BANJO *lifts the latest delicacy and proceeds to eat it as she presents the empty plate to* WHITESIDE.*)*

SARAH. But, Mr. Whiteside, it was for you.

WHITESIDE. Never mind, Sarah. He's quite mad.

BANJO. Come, Petrushka, we shall dance. We shall dance in the snow! *(He clutches* SARAH *and waltzes her toward the kitchen* U.R.*, loudly humming the Merry Widow Waltz.)*

SARAH *(as she is borne away).* Mr. Whiteside! Mr. Whiteside!

WHITESIDE. Just give him some breakfast, Sarah. He's harmless. *(*WHITESIDE *barely has a moment in which to collect his thoughts before the library doors are opened and* MISS PREEN *emerges. She is dressed for the street and carries a bag.) (She plants herself to the* L. *of* WHITESIDE, *puts down her bag and starts drawing on a pair of gloves.)* And just what does this mean?

MISS PREEN *(*C.*).* It means, Mr. Whiteside, that I am leaving. My address is on the desk inside, you can send me a check.

WHITESIDE. You realize, Miss Preen, that this is completely unprofessional?

MISS PREEN. I do indeed. I am not only walking out on this case, Mr. Whiteside, but I am leaving the nursing profession. I became a nurse because all my life, ever since I was a little girl, I was filled with the idea of serving a suffering humanity. After one month with you, Mr. Whiteside, I am going to work in a munitions factory. From now on anything that I can do to help exterminate the human race will fill me with the greatest of pleasure. If Florence Nightingale had ever nursed you, Mr. Whiteside, she would have married Jack the Ripper instead of founding the Red Cross. Good day. *(She goes* U.L.*)*

*(*MRS. STANLEY, *in a state of great fluttery excitement, rushes down the stairs.)*

MRS. STANLEY *(headed for front door* L.*).* Mr. Stanley is here with June. He's brought June back. Thank goodness, *thank goodness. (We hear her at the door.)* June, June, thank God you're back! You're not married, are you?

JUNE *(from the hallway).* No, Mother, I'm not. And please don't be hysterical. *(Then* MRS. STANLEY *comes into view, her arms around a rebellious* JUNE. *Behind them looms* STANLEY, *every inch the stern father.)*

MRS. STANLEY *(*L.*).* Oh, June, if it had been anyone but that awful boy. Thank goodness you stopped it, Ernest; how did you do it?

STANLEY (D.L.). Never mind that, Daisy. Just take June upstairs. I have something to say to Mr. Whiteside.

MRS. STANLEY. What about Richard? Is there any news?

STANLEY. It's all right, Daisy—all under control. Just take June upstairs.

JUNE. Father, haven't we had enough melodrama? I don't have to be taken upstairs—I'll go upstairs . . . Merry Christmas, Mr. Whiteside. It looks bad for John L. Lewis. Come on, Mother—lock me in my room.

MRS. STANLEY. Now, June, you'll feel much better after you've had a hot bath, I know. Have you had anything to eat? (She follows her daughter up the stairs.) (STANLEY turns to WHITESIDE.)

STANLEY (crosses to C.). I am pleased to inform you, sir, that your plans for my daughter seem to have gone a trifle awry. She is not, nor will she ever be, married to that Labor agitator that you so kindly picked out for her. As for my son, he has been apprehended in Toledo, and will be brought home within the hour. Not having your gift for invective, sir, I cannot tell you what I think of your obnoxious interference in my affairs, but I have now arranged that you will interfere no longer. (He turns toward hallway.) Come in, gentlemen. (Two burly MEN come into view and stand in the archway L.) Mr. Whiteside, these gentlemen are deputy sheriffs. They have a warrant by which I am enabled to put you out of this house, and I need hardly add that it will be the greatest moment of my life, Mr. Whiteside— (He looks at his watch.) I am giving you fifteen minutes in which to pack up and get out. If you are not gone in fifteen minutes, Mr. Whiteside, these gentlemen will forcibly eject you. (He turns to DEPUTIES.) Thank you, gentlemen. Will you wait outside, please? (The MEN file out.) Fifteen minutes, Mr. Whiteside— and that means bag, baggage, wheelchair, penguins, octopus and cockroaches. (Crossing up to stairs.) I am now going upstairs to smash our radio, so that not even accidentally will I ever hear your voice again.

WHITESIDE. Sure you don't want my autograph, old fellow?

STANLEY. Fifteen minutes, Mr. Whiteside. (And he goes upstairs.)

BANJO (enter U.R., hanging hat on tree branch, he crosses to C.). Say, can she cook. Well, Whiteside, I didn't get an idea. Any news from the front?

WHITESIDE. Yes. The enemy is at my rear, and nibbling.

BANJO (crossing toward WHITESIDE). Where'd you say Maggie was? In there?

WHITESIDE. It's no use, Banjo. She's taking the one o'clock train out.

BANJO. No kidding? You didn't tell me that. You mean she's quitting you, after all these years? She's really leaving?

WHITESIDE. She is!

BANJO. That means you've only got till one o'clock to do something?

WHITESIDE. No, dear. I have exactly fifteen minutes— (He looks at his watch.) ah— fourteen minutes—in which to pull out of my hat the God-damnedest rabbit you have ever seen.

BANJO. What do you mean fifteen minutes?

WHITESIDE. In exactly fifteen minutes Baby's rosy little body is being tossed into the snow. Mine host has sworn out a warrant. I am being kicked out.

BANJO. What? I never heard of such a thing. What would he do a thing like that for?

WHITESIDE. Never mind, never mind. The point is, I have only fifteen minutes. Banjo dear, the master is growing a little desperate.

BANJO (paces a moment). What about laying your cards on the table with Lorraine?

WHITESIDE. Now, Banjo. You know Dream Girl as well as I do. What do you think?

BANJO. You're right.

WHITESIDE (wearily). Banjo, go in and talk to Maggie for a minute—right in there. I want to think.

BANJO (crossing R.). Say! If I knew where Lorraine was, I could get a car and run her over. It wouldn't hurt her much.

WHITESIDE. Please, Banjo. I've got to think.

BANJO (*opening library doors*). Pardon me, Miss, is this the Y.M.C.A.?

(*The doors close.*)

(WHITESIDE *is alone again. He leans back, concentrating intensely. He shakes his head as, one after another, he discards a couple of ideas.*) (*We hear the outer door open and close, and from the hallway comes* RICHARD. *Immediately behind him is a stalwart looking* MAN *with an air of authority. They cross to below staircase.*)

THE MAN (*to* RICHARD, *as he indicates* WHITESIDE). Is this your father?

RICHARD (C). No, you idiot . . . Hello, Mr. Whiteside. I didn't get very far. Any suggestions?

WHITESIDE. I'm very sorry, Richard—very sorry indeed. I wish I were in position—

STANLEY (*descending stairs*). Well, you're *not* in position . . . Thank you very much, officer. Here's a little something for your trouble.

THE MAN. Thank you, sir. Good-day. (*He goes out* L.)

STANLEY. Will you go upstairs, please, Richard? (RICHARD *hesitates a second. Looks at his father, then at* WHITESIDE; *silently goes up the steps.*) (STANLEY *follows him, but pauses on the landing.*) Ten minutes, Mr. Whiteside. (*And he goes.*) (*Immediately* JOHN *enters from the dining-room, bringing a glass of orange-juice on a tray.*)

JOHN (*down to* L. *of* WHITESIDE). I brought you some orange-juice, Mr. Whiteside. Feeling any better?

WHITESIDE. Superb, John. Any cyanide in this orange-juice? (*The door-bell rings.*) Open the door, John.

JOHN. Yes, sir.

WHITESIDE. It's probably some mustard gas from an old friend.

JOHN (*en route to door* L.). Say, that crazy fellow made a great hit with Sarah. He wants to give her a *screen test*.

(*At the outer door we hear* LORRAINE's *voice: "Good morning— Is* MR. WHITESIDE *up yet?"* JOHN's *answer: "Yes, he is, Miss Sheldon—he's right here."*)

WHITESIDE. Uhh—

LORRAINE (*entering, in a very smart Christmas morning costume.*) Merry Christmas, darling! Merry Christmas! I've come to have Christmas breakfast with you, my dear. May I? (*She kisses him.* JOHN *coming to* R. *of chair, takes empty glass from* WHITESIDE.)

WHITESIDE (*nothing matters any more*). Of course, my Sprite. John, a tray for Miss Sheldon—better make it one-minute eggs. (JOHN *en route to dining-room and exit.*)

LORRAINE (*crossing to* C.). Sherry, it's the most perfect Christmas morning—the snow is absolutely glistening. Too bad you can't get out.

WHITESIDE. Oh, I'll probably see a bit of it . . . I hear you're off for Lake Placid, my Blossom. What time are you going?

LORRAINE. Oh, Sherry, how did you know? Is Bert here?

WHITESIDE. No, he rolled in a little while ago. Worked rather fast, didn't you, dear?

LORRAINE (*a step to* L.). Darling, I was just swept off my feet by the play—it's fantastically good. Sherry, it's the kind of part that only comes along once in ten years. I'm so grateful to you, darling. Really, Sherry, sometimes I think that you're the only friend I have in the world.

(*Crossing to* WHITESIDE.)

WHITESIDE. Thank you, dear. What time did you say you were leaving—you and Jefferson?

LORRAINE (*crosses to sofa*). Oh, I don't know—I think it's four o'clock. You know, quite apart from anything else, Sherry, Bert is really a very attractive man. It makes it rather a pleasure, squaring accounts with little Miss Vitriol. (*Sits on sofa.*) In fact, it's all worked out beautifully . . . Sherry lamb, I want to give you the most beautiful Christmas present you've ever had in your life. Now, what do you want? Anything! I'm so deliriously happy that— (*A laugh comes from the library. She stops.*) That sounds like Banjo. Is he here?

WHITESIDE. He is, my dear. Just the family circle gathering at Christmas. (*A look at his watch.*) My, how time flies when you're having fun. (BANJO *emerges from library, closes doors.*)

BANJO (*crosses to* c.). Why, hello, Sweetie Pants. How are you?

LORRAINE (*not over-cordial*). Very well, thank you. And you, Banjo?

BANJO. I'm fine, fine. How's the mattress business, Lorraine?

LORRAINE. *Very* funny. It's too bad, Banjo, that your pictures aren't as funny as you seem to think *you* are.

BANJO (c). You've got me there, Mama. Say, you look in the pink, Lorraine . . . Anything in the wind, Whiteside?

WHITESIDE. Not a glimmer.

BANJO. What time does the boat sail?

WHITESIDE. Ten minutes.

LORRAINE. What boat is this?

BANJO. The good ship *Up the Creek.*

(MAGGIE *emerges from library, a sheaf of papers in her hand. She stops.*)

MAGGIE. I've listed everything except the New Year's Eve broadcast. Wasn't there a schedule on that?

WHITESIDE (*uneasily*). I think it's on the table there, some place.

MAGGIE. Thank you. (*She turns to the papers on table.*)

LORRAINE (*obviously for* MAGGIE's *ears*). New Year's Eve? Oh, Bert and I'll hear it in Lake Placid. You were at my cottage up there once, weren't you, Sherry? It's lovely, isn't it? Away from everything. Just snow and clear, cold nights.

(*The door-bell rings.*)

LORRAINE. Oh, that's probably Bert now. I told him to meet me here. (MAGGIE, *as though she had not heard a word, goes quietly into the library, closing the doors after her.* JOHN *enters swing-door* U.L.) You know, I'm looking forward to Lake Placid. Bert's the kind of man who will do all winter sports beautifully.

BANJO (*crosses* D.L.). Will he get time?

(LORRAINE *rises, crosses to* U.R.) (*Loud voices are heard from the hallway, and* JOHN *backs into the room, obviously directing a major operation.*)

EXPRESSMAN. Whiteside?

JOHN Yes, sir.

EXPRESSMAN. American Express!

JOHN. All right—come ahead. Care now —careful—right in here.

LORRAINE. Why, Sherry, what's this?

(*Into view come two* EXPRESSMEN, *groaning and grunting under the weight of nothing more or less than a huge mummy-case.*)

EXPRESSMAN. Careful there. Now swing your end. Where do you want this put?

(LORRAINE *crosses to* R. *of wheelchair.*)

JOHN. Right there. (EXPRESSMEN *put mummy-case* U.C. *below* R. *newel post.*) It's for you, Mr. Whiteside.

WHITESIDE. Dear God, if there was one thing I needed right now it was an Egyptian mummy. (EXPRESSMEN *go* L. JOHN *exits up* L.)

BANJO (*crossing to mummy, reads tag on case*). "Merry Christmas from the Khedive of Egypt." What did you send *him?* Grant's tomb? (STANLEY *has descended the stairs in time to witness this newest hue and cry.*)

STANLEY. Five minutes, Mr. Whiteside. (*He indicates mummy-case.*) Including that. (*And up the stairs again.*)

LORRAINE. Why, what was all that about? Who is that man?

WHITESIDE. He announces the time every few minutes. (BANJO *sits on sofa.*) I pay him a small sum.

LORRAINE. But what on earth *for,* Sherry?

WHITESIDE (*violently*). I lost my watch. (*From the hallway a familiar figure peeps in.*)

BRADLEY (*crossing* R.). Oh, excuse me, Mr. Whiteside, I see you're busy.

WHITESIDE (*closing his eyes*). Good God!

BRADLEY (*coming into the room—tips his hat to the mummy, realizes his mistake*). Pardon me, I'll wait in here. I've written a new chapter on the left kidney. (*He smiles apologetically at* LORRAINE *and* BANJO, *goes into the library* D.R.)

LORRAINE. Is that the plumber again, Sherry? (*Crosses to* L.C.) Oh, dear, I wonder where Bert is . . . Darling, you're not very Christmasy—you're usually bubbling over on Christmas morning. Who sent this to you, Sherry—the Khedive of Egypt? You know, I think it's rather beautiful. I must go to Egypt some day—I really must. I know I'd love it. The first time I went to Pompeii I cried all night. All those people—all those lives. Where are they now? (BANJO *doesn't know. He shrugs his shoulders.*) Sherry! Don't you ever think about that? I do. Here was a woman—like myself—a woman who once lived and loved, full of the same passions, fears, jealousies, hates. And what remains of any of it now? Just this, and nothing more. (*She opens the case, then, with a sudden impulse, steps into it and folds her arms, mummy-fashion.*) A span of four thousand years—a mere atom in the eternity of time—and here am I, another woman living out her life. I want to cry. (*She closes her eyes, and as she stands there, immobilized, the eyes of BANJO and WHITESIDE meet. The same idea has leaped into their minds. BANJO, rising slowly from the couch, starts to approach the mummy-case, casually whistling "Dixie." But just before he reaches it LORRAINE steps blandly out. BANJO circles below couch to back of it.*) Oh, I mustn't talk this way today. It's Christmas! It's Christmas! (BANJO *back of sofa.*)

WHITESIDE (*pure charm*). Lorraine dear, have you ever played St. Joan?

LORRAINE. No, I haven't, Sherry. What makes you ask that?

WHITESIDE. There was something about your expression as you stood in that case—there was an absolute halo about you.

LORRAINE. Why, Sherry, how sweet!

WHITESIDE (BANJO *eases* R.). It transcended any mortal expression I've ever seen. Step into it again, dear.

LORRAINE. Sherry, you're joshing me—aren't you?

WHITESIDE. My dear, I don't make light of these things. I was deeply moved. There was a strange beauty about you, Lorraine—pure da Vinci. Please do it again.

LORRAINE (*as she approaches the case, BANJO takes three steps toward it*). Well, I don't know exactly what it was that I did, but I'll— (*She starts to step into the case again, then turns.*) Oh, I feel too silly, Sherry. (*Crosses down to WHITESIDE.*)

WHITESIDE. Lorraine, dear, in that single moment you approached the epitome of your art, and you should not be ashamed of it. You asked me a little while ago what I wanted for a Christmas present. All that I want, Lorraine, is the memory of you in that mummy-case.

LORRAINE. Why, darling, I'm—all choked up. (*Crossing her arms, she takes a moment to throw herself in the mood, circles slowly* U.C., *then steps reverently into the case.*) "Dust thou art, and dust to dust—" Banjo! (*Bang!* BANJO *has closed the case and fastened it.* WHITESIDE *leaps out of the chair.*)

WHITESIDE. Eureka!

BANJO (*they shake hands*). There's service for you!

WHITESIDE. Will she be all right in there?

BANJO. Sure—she can breathe easy. I'll let her out as soon as we get on the plane . . . What are we going to do now? Say, how do we get this out of here?

WHITESIDE. One thing at a time—that's the next step.

BANJO. Think fast, Captain. Think fast.

(*And* MAGGIE *enters from the library, papers in hand.* WHITESIDE *leaps back to his chair,* BANJO *sits on arm of couch.*)

MAGGIE (L.C.). This is everything, Sherry—I'm leaving three carbons. Is there anything out here? What's in this basket?

WHITESIDE (*eager to be rid of her*). Nothing at all. Thank you, thank you.

MAGGIE (*delving into the basket*). Shall I file these letters? Do you want this picture?

WHITESIDE. No—throw everything away. Wait—give me the picture. I want the picture.

MAGGIE (*handing him picture*). The only thing I haven't done is to put all your broadcasts in order. Do you want me to do that?

WHITESIDE (*a flash of recollection has come to him as he takes* HARRIET's *photograph in his hand, but he contrives to smother his excitement*). What? . . . Ah—do that, will you? Do it right away—it's very important. Right away, Maggie.

MAGGIE. I'll see you before I go, Banjo. *(She goes into library again, closing the doors.)*

WHITESIDE *(watching her out, then rising)*. I've got it.

BANJO *(rising)*. What?

WHITESIDE. I knew I'd seen this face before. Now I know how to get this out of here.

BANJO. What face? How? *(And, at that instant, STANLEY comes down the stairs, watch in hand.)*

STANLEY *(coming D.C.)*. The time is up, Mr. Whiteside. Fifteen minutes. *(BANJO crosses R.)*

WHITESIDE *(crosses to C.)*. Ah, yes, Mr. Stanley. Fifteen minutes. But just one favor before I go. I would like you to summon those two officers and ask them to help this gentleman down to the airport with this mummy-case. Would you be good enough to do that, Mr. Stanley?

STANLEY. I will do nothing of the kind.

WHITESIDE. Oh, I think you will, Mr. Stanley. Or I shall inform my radio audience, on my next broadcast, that your sister, Harriet Stanley, is none other than the famous Harriet Sedley, who murdered her mother and father with an axe twenty-five years ago in Gloucester, Massachusetts . . . *(STANLEY sinks into the sofa.)* Come, Mr. Stanley, it's a very small favor. Or would you rather have the good folk of Mesalia repeating at your very doorstep that once popular little jingle:
"Harriet Sedley took an axe
And gave her mother forty whacks,
And when the job was nicely done,
She gave her father forty-one."
Remember, Mr. Stanley, I too am giving up something. It would make a hell of a broadcast . . . Well?

STANLEY *(rises, crosses to piano D.L.)*. Mr. Whiteside, you are the damnedest person I have ever met.

WHITESIDE. You're a little late in finding that out. Officers, will you come in here, please?

BANJO *(to case)*. Whiteside, you're a *great* man. *(And he kisses his hand and pats the case.)* *(Takes hat from Christmas tree.)*

WHITESIDE *(as DEPUTIES enter L.)*. Come right in, officers. Mr. Stanley would like you to help this gentleman down to the airport with this mummy-case . . . He is sending it to a friend in Nova Scotia.

BANJO. Collect.

(DEPUTIES cross to case and pick it up.)

WHITESIDE. Right, Mr. Stanley?

STANLEY. Yes . . . Yes.

WHITESIDE. Thank you, gentlemen—handle it carefully . . . Banjo, my love, you're wonderful and I may write a book about you.

BANJO. Don't bother—I can't read. *(To MAGGIE, as she enters from library.)* Good-bye, Maggie—love conquers all . . . Don't drop that case, boys—it contains an *antique*. *(And he goes, following the DEPUTIES and the mummy-case off L.)*

MAGGIE *(to C.)*. Sherry! Sherry, was that—?

WHITESIDE. It was indeed. *(Sees fur muff LORRAINE has left on couch back. Presents it to MAGGIE.)* Oh—a little Christmas present for you.

MAGGIE. Sherry! Sherry, you old reprobate!

WHITESIDE. Just send me a necktie some time. My hat and coat, Maggie, I am leaving for New York.

MAGGIE. You're leaving, Sherry?

WHITESIDE. Don't argue, Rat Girl—do as you're told.

MAGGIE. Yes, Mr. Whiteside. *(She goes into library as BERT comes running in from the hallway, breathless.)*

BERT *(to C.)*. Mr. Whiteside, I want to apologize— *(His eyes encounter the very healthy WHITESIDE.)* Say!

WHITESIDE. Don't give it a thought, Bert. There's been a slight change of plan. Miss Sheldon is off on a world cruise—I am taking your play to Katherine Cornell. *(MAGGIE enters from library with WHITESIDE's coat and hat and cane.)* Miss Cutler will explain everything.

BERT. Maggie!

WHITESIDE. Thank you, Maggie, my darling. *(As she assists WHITESIDE with his coat.)* *(The DOCTOR comes hurrying out of the library.)*

BRADLEY (*to below wheelchair*). Mr. Whiteside, are you very busy?

WHITESIDE. Ah, yes, Doctor, yes. Very busy. But if you ever get to New York, Doctor, try and find me . . . Good-bye, my lamb. I love you very much.

MAGGIE. Sherry, you're wonderful.

WHITESIDE (*shakes hands*). Nonsense . . . Good-bye, Jefferson. You'll never know the trouble you've caused.

BERT. Good-bye, Mr. Whiteside. (*Crosses to* MAGGIE.)

WHITESIDE (*crosses* L.). Good-bye, Mr. Stanley. I would like to hear, in the near future, that your daughter has married her young man and that your son has been permitted to follow his own bent. OR ELSE . . . Merry Christmas, *everybody*! (*He exits* L.)

BERT. Maggie, for God's sake, what *is* all this? Where's he going? I didn't know he could walk even.

MAGGIE. It's all right, Bert. You're too young to know. Just don't ask questions.

MRS. STANLEY (*descending the stairs*). Ernest, Richard's being very difficult. You'll have to talk to him. (*There is a loud crash on the porch, followed by an anguished yell.*)

WHITESIDE. Owww—God damn it!

MAGGIE. Bert! Doctor!

BERT (*as he and* DOCTOR *run off* L.). Something's happened! (*Enter down the stairs* RICHARD *and* JUNE.)

RICHARD. What's the matter? What's wrong?

JUNE. Has something happened? What is it?

MRS. STANLEY. Oh, dear! Oh, dear!

WHITESIDE (*off stage*). Miss Preen! . . . (*Into view come* BERT *and* BRADLEY, *carrying* WHITESIDE.) Miss Preen! I want Miss Preen back! (*As* WHITESIDE *is carried past* L. *newel post, the Curtain Starts Down.*)

MAGGIE. Sherry, Sherry, oh my poor Sherry!

MRS. STANLEY (*she faints*). Ohhhh!

SARAH (*entering from* U.R. *with* JOHN). What's the matter? What is it? Oh, dear!

DR. BRADLEY. Bring that chair right over! Bring that chair!

JUNE. Mother! Mother!

BERT. That's all right, Mr. Whiteside. Just relax!

MR. STANLEY. Oh! Oh!

RICHARD. What's the matter, Mother?

(STANLEY *is beating his hands on the piano and tearing his hair.* MRS. STANLEY *has fainted on the stairway.* WHITESIDE *is about to be put in the wheelchair again by* BERT *and* DOCTOR BRADLEY *as*

THE CURTAIN IS DOWN

DREAM GIRL

By ELMER RICE

DREAM GIRL was originally presented by The Playwrights' Company at the Coronet Theatre, New York City, on December 14, 1945. The play was staged by the author; settings by Jo Mielziner. The cast was as follows:

GEORGINA ALLERTON.....Betty Field
LUCY ALLERTON.........Evelyn Varden
A RADIO ANNOUNCER
     Keene Crockett
DR. J. GILMORE PERCIVAL
     William A. Lee
GEORGE ALLERTON
     William A. Lee
MIRIAM ALLERTON LUCAS
     Sonya Stokowski
THE OBSTETRICIAN
     William A. Lee
THE NURSE.................Evelyn Varden
JIM LUCAS........................Kevin O'Shea
CLAIRE BLAKELEY.........Helen Marcy
A STOUT WOMAN.....Philippa Bevans
A DOCTOR..........................Don Stevens
CLARK REDFIELD.......Wendell Corey
A POLICEMAN.................James Gregory
THE JUDGE..................William A. Lee
THE DISTRICT ATTORNEY
     Keene Crockett

GEORGE HAND................Edmon Ryan
BERT..Don Stevens
A MEXICAN.....................Wendell Corey
TWO OTHER MEXICANS:
     David Pressman
     James Gregory
A WAITER............................Stuart Nedd
ARABELLA....................Sonya Stokowski
LUIGI...............................David Pressman
AN USHER.......................Gaynelle Nixon
MISS DELEHANTY.........Helen Bennett
ANTONIO...........................Don Stevens
SALARINO......................Robert Fletcher
A THEATRE MANAGER
     William A. Lee
A HEADWAITER..........Keene Crockett
A WAITER......................Robert Fletcher
JUSTICE OF THE PEACE
   BILLINGS...................William A. Lee
A CHAUFFEUR.................Stuart Nedd

THE AUTHOR

Elmer Rice has been one of the standard-bearers of the progressively minded theatre for over three decades. Mr. Rice, who was born in New York in 1892, endured a bout with business and law for some six years before turning playwright with On Trial *in 1914. The play was produced by the firm of George M. Cohan and Sam Harris and became a sensation owing to a fairly exciting story and an original use of the flashback technique. Since the first World War atmosphere was not congenial to the author's brand of thinking, and Mr. Rice was out of sympathy with what he regarded as an imperialistic imbroglio, his next plays* The Iron Cross *and* The Home of the Free *failed to attract the public. He wooed Broadway after the war with* For the Defense *(1919),* Wake Up Jonathan *(1921), a collaboration with Hatcher Hughes in which Mrs. Fiske did the honors, and* It Is the Law *(1922). These post-war contributions, however, added nothing to his stature and to the modern theatre until he wrote his satire on the industrial age* The Adding Machine, *to which the* Theatre Guild *gave an estimable production in 1923. Its stylization was derived from post-war European expressionism, but Mr. Rice employed it with verve and the play remains his most original piece of writing.*

Mr. Rice made theatre history again with Street Scene *after unsuccessful collaborations with Dorothy Parker,* Close Harmony *(1924), and Philip Barry,* Cock Robin *(1928).* Street Scene, *which was produced in 1929 by William Brady, proved a powerful realistic panorama, as well as an extraordinarily successful enterprise, and earned the Pulitzer Prize for its author. Two years later, after some indifferent efforts, Mr. Rice opened two successful plays* The Left Bank *and* Counsellor-at-Law *within one month of each other. The former took a realistic view of expatriation, which had been a popular pastime of the pre-depression intelligentsia, and* Counsellor-at-Law, *which provided Paul Muni with one of his best stage roles, was well anchored in character comedy.*

The depression evoked Mr. Rice's protest in the hard-driving multi-scened We the People *(1933), Hitler's rise provoked* Judgment Day *(1934), and the conflict between American and Russian ideologies inspired the conversation piece* Between Two Worlds *(1934). Mr. Rice also produced and directed these plays, and their failure on Broadway aroused the embattled author against the New York critics. He retired from the theatre after writing an ingenious satire on the theatre* Not for Children *(1935), which had no Broadway production (it was produced by the London Stage Society and the Pasadena Theatre), and wrote a novel.*

Mr. Rice returned to the theatre to organize The Playwrights Producing Company *with Robert Sherwood, S. N. Behrman, Maxwell Anderson, and Sidney Howard, to write plays for the company, and to direct his own and his colleagues' pieces.* American Landscape *(1938) fared poorly in spite of its timeliness and its ingenious construction.* Two on an Island *presented an appealing tale of young adventure in Manhattan.* Flight to the West *(1940) stayed for some time on Broadway and won the interest of alert playgoers, but had a hard struggle at the box-office.* A New Life *lacked luster.* Dream Girl, *in which Betty Field scored a personal triumph, became an instant success for Mr. Rice both as playwright and director.*

Perhaps it should be added that no truly liberal cause ever failed to win Mr. Rice's intelligent support, and that the Authors' League found in him one of its most sagacious leaders. Strenuous citizenship and generally strenuous playwriting have been this playwright's twin interests. They have made him a highly regarded man of the American theatre. He is reaping another harvest at this writing with a distinguished Kurt Weill musical version of Street Scene.

DREAM GIRL

ACT ONE

As the curtain rises on a dark stage, a deep-toned, distant bell is striking the hour of eight. On the eighth stroke, an alarm clock begins its incessant clamor and, as the lights go up, slowly and dimly at center, a bed glides into view. Beside it is a night table on which are the alarm clock and a small radio. In the bed, a girl, struggling against the rude awakening, turns and twists, then sits bolt upright. She is GEORGINA ALLERTON, young, slender, and pretty. She shakes her head and rubs her closed eyes with her fists. The alarm clock is still ringing.

GEORGINA *(yawning heavily).* Ohhhh! *(Then, angrily, to the alarm clock.)* For heaven's sake, will you please shut up? *(She shuts off the alarm clock; then leans over and pulls up an imaginary window shade. The bed is flooded with morning sunlight.* GEORGINA *moans, shakes her head, and stretches her arms.)* Oh, dear! Another day! How awful! Who was it that said: "Must we have another day?" Dorothy Parker, I suppose. I wonder if she really says all those things. *(With a sigh.)* Well, time to get up, I guess. *(She plumps herself down again and snuggles her head in the pillow.)*

MRS. ALLERTON *(off right).* Georgina! It's time to get up!

GEORGINA *(calling).* Yes, I know. I've been up for hours! *(Indignantly.)* Goodness, you'd think sleep was some sort of a crime. *(Gloomily, as she looks toward the window.)* Yes, another day. And what a day! Beautiful sunshine. Not a cloud in the sky. How wonderful it must be to be able to enjoy it. *(She sighs, then says firmly.)* Well, come on, Georgina, snap out of it, and get yourself up out of bed! *(She switches on the radio and an orchestra is heard softly playing "Paris in the Spring.")* I wonder how long a person can go on like this without developing a psychosis or something. For all I know, I may have a psychosis already. Good grief, what a thought! I wish I could remember that awful nightmare I had last night. Still, they say it's awfully hard to make anything out of your own dreams. That damned little psychic censor gets in your way. And besides, I really don't know very much about dream symbols. Just the obvious ones, like Maypoles and church steeples—and I never seem to dream about them. Oh, well, to hell with it! *(She throws back the covers, swings her legs out of*

bed, and gets into her slippers and negligee. The music stops, and the voice of a radio announcer is heard.)

ANNOUNCER'S VOICE. And so we bring to a close our half hour of recorded music. And friends, don't forget your date tonight at eight-thirty, with your counselor on human relations, Dr. J. Gilmore Percival, brought to you through the courtesy of Kellogg's Kidney Capsules. If you are maladjusted, if you are worried about some emotional problem, come and tell your troubles to Dr. Percival, whose wise and kindly counsel has helped hundreds to solve—

GEORGINA *(switching off the radio indignantly).* How ridiculous! As though that little quack could really solve people's emotional problems for them! Still, I suppose the poor deluded people who go to him get a kind of relief just from spilling their troubles to somebody. After all, that's what psychiatry is—only on a scientific basis of course. *(She sits musing on the bed, her chin in her palm.)* Maybe I should try psychiatry. Only what's the use when I know so well what's the matter with me? Except that the right psychiatrist might help me to forget Jim. But do I want to forget Jim? And suppose it isn't just Jim that's the matter with me! What if it all goes back to something that's lurking deep in my unconscious, quietly festering away? *(Sharply.)* How absurd! In the first place, it costs a fortune. And besides, what do I need a psychiatrist for? I'm a perfectly healthy, normal person. All that's the matter with me is that I'm in love with the wrong man. But that's plenty! Anyhow, how do I know I'm really normal? Is anybody? *(Angrily.)* Honestly, it's disgraceful that they allow charlatans like that Dr. Percival on the air! Imagine standing up in front of a microphone and revealing the things that— *(As she sits musing, the radio lights up again and the voice of the* ANNOUNCER *is heard.)*

ANNOUNCER'S VOICE. And remember, folks, it's the kidneys that are the key to your health. And now here is Dr. Percival.

PERCIVAL'S VOICE. Good evening, friends. Tonight we begin with the problem of Miss G. A. Now, Miss, just step right up to the microphone and tell me what is troubling you.

*(*GEORGINA *picks up the bedside lamp and speaks into it, as though it were a microphone.)*

GEORGINA *(low)*. Well, I—

PERCIVAL'S VOICE. A little louder, please, so that we can all hear you. There's nothing to be nervous about.

GEORGINA. I'm not nervous. It's just—well, it's just that it's a little hard to discuss your personal problems with several million people listening in.

PERCIVAL'S VOICE. I can't help you, unless you—

GEORGINA. I know. Well, you see, I'm in love with a man named Jim—

PERCIVAL'S VOICE. No names, please! No one's identity is ever revealed on this program.

GEORGINA. Oh, I'm sorry! I—

PERCIVAL'S VOICE. Go on, please. You are in love with a man named J. And he does not reciprocate your feeling for him, is that it?

GEORGINA. Oh, that's not the point! It's that he—he—

PERCIVAL'S VOICE. Well, what?

GEORGINA. Well, he happens to be my brother-in-law.

PERCIVAL'S VOICE. One moment, please! Do I understand you to say that you are in love with your brother-in-law?

GEORGINA. Yes. Yes, I am. I have been, for years and years.

PERCIVAL'S VOICE. This is really quite an extraordinary case. And, if I understand you correctly, he is not in love with you.

GEORGINA. Well, I used to think he was. And then suddenly he married Miriam and—

PERCIVAL'S VOICE. No names, please!

GEORGINA. Sorry! He married my sister, two years ago, and that was just about the end of everything for me.

PERCIVAL'S VOICE. And is he aware of your feeling for him?

GEORGINA *(indignantly)*. Certainly not! What kind of a girl do you think I am? Why, I'd die rather than let him know. Nobody knows or even suspects. *(Weepily.)* But I just can't keep it bottled up any longer. That's why I thought I'd—

PERCIVAL'S VOICE. Yes. You have a feeling of guilt about it, haven't you?

GEORGINA. In a way, I suppose. Being in love with your own brother-in-law—well, it seems just a little—a little incestuous.

PERCIVAL'S VOICE *(hastily)*. One moment, Miss A. That is not a word that is acceptable on the air.

GEORGINA. I'm terribly sorry, I—

PERCIVAL'S VOICE. Well, young woman, if you want my advice, you'll put this brother-in-law completely out of your mind and—

GEORGINA. Yes, that's easy to say. I've tried and tried. In fact, there's a man I'm having lunch with, a Mr.—

PERCIVAL'S VOICE. Careful!

GEORGINA. Well. I've been careful, up to now. Oh, you mean about his name. Well, he's a Mr. H.

PERCIVAL'S VOICE. And this Mr. H. is interested in you?

GEORGINA. Well, when a man keeps asking a girl out all the time—especially a married man—

PERCIVAL'S VOICE. Your involvements seem to be exclusively with married men.

GEORGINA. I know.

PERCIVAL'S VOICE. Miss A., I think your situation is a very serious one, indeed. It is hard for me—

MRS. ALLERTON *(off right)*. Georgina! Are you daydreaming again in there? It's almost nine!

GEORGINA (*leaping up*). All right, Mother. I'm practically dressed. (*The lights fade on the scene and come up, at left, on* GEORGINA's *bathroom, which she enters, talking all the while.*) Maybe your mother is right, Georgina. Maybe it's time you cut out the daydreaming—time you stopped mooning around and imagining yourself to be this extraordinary creature with a strange and fascinating psychological life. (*She has removed her negligee and donned a bathing cap; and she now goes around behind the bathroom, invisible but still audible. The sound of a shower is heard.*) Oh, damn it! Cold as ice. There, that's better! (*She sings "Night and Day" lustily. Then the shower is turned off and she reappears wrapped in a large bath towel and stands, her back to the audience, rubbing herself vigorously.*) Still, to be honest, I must admit that, compared to the average girl you meet, I'm really quite complex. Intelligent and well informed too; and a good conversationalist. (*Indignantly, as over her shoulder, she sees someone looking in at her.*) Well, for heaven's sake! Honestly, some people! (*She pulls down an imaginary window shade and the scene is blacked out, her voice coming out of the darkness.*) And my looks are nothing to be ashamed of, either. I have a neat little figure and my legs are really very nice. Of course, my nose is sort of funny, but my face definitely has character—not just one of those magazine-cover deadpans. (*With a yawn.*) Oh, I never seem to get enough sleep! (*The lights come up, as she raises the imaginary shade. She is dressed now in her shoes, stockings, and slip. She seats herself at her dressing table, facing the audience, and brushes her hair.*) If I could only stop lying awake for hours, dreaming up all the exciting things that could happen but never do. Well, maybe this is the day when things really will begin to happen to me. Maybe Wentworth and Jones will accept my novel. They've had it over a month now, and all the other publishers turned it down in less than two weeks. It certainly looks promising. And especially with Jim's recommendation. Wouldn't that be wonderful! With a published novel, I'd really be somebody. Reviews in all the book sections; royalty checks coming in; women nudging each other at Schrafft's and whispering: "Don't look now, but that girl over there—the one with the smart hat —that's Georgina Allerton, the novelist." (*Going to the washbasin.*) Gee, that would be thrilling! To feel that I'd accomplished something. To feel that I had a purpose in life. To feel that— (*She busies herself with a toothbrush, becoming momentarily unintelligible.*) Ubble-ba-glug-ab-lub-mum. Only it wouldn't make up for Jim. (*Going back to the dressing table.*) Fifty novels wouldn't make up for Jim. If Miriam only appreciated him. But she doesn't. She doesn't understand him. All his fine sensitive qualities—they're completely lost on her. It's really ironic. (*Baring her teeth.*) Gosh, my teeth could certainly stand a good cleaning. It's awful the way I put off going to the dentist. Maybe that's psychopathic too. What to do? What to do? Here I am twenty-three years old—no, let's face it, twenty-four next month! And that's practically thirty. Thirty years old—and nothing to show for it. Suppose nothing ever does happen to me. That's a frightening thought! Just to go on and on like this, on through middle age, on to senility, never experiencing anything—what a prospect! (*Putting on her make-up.*) Of course I suppose that up to a certain point there's nothing abnormal about virginity. But the question is, how can you ever be sure you haven't passed that point? Heavens, is that a gray hair? No, thank goodness. What a scare! Still, there must be a lot of women who go right on being virgins until the very day they die. It can be done, I guess. Doesn't sound like much fun though. (*She rises and gets into her dress.*) Well, that brings me right smack back to George Hand. Maybe I shouldn't have accepted his invitation for today. He really is rushing me. Of course, he may not have any intentions at all. No, he's too busy a man to keep on dating up a girl, without having something on his mind. So that puts it squarely up to me. Well, anyhow, if I'm going to play with fire, I may as well look my best. So here goes.

MRS. ALLERTON (*off right*). Georgina, I'm getting tired of keeping the coffee hot.

GEORGINA. Coming! Coming! (*As she quickly crosses the stage, the light fades out on the bathroom and comes up at right on a breakfast table, at which her parents are seated.* MRS. ALLERTON *is a stoutish, good-looking woman in a negligee;* MR. ALLERTON, *a pleasant round-faced man in a business suit. He is busy with the morning's mail.)*

GEORGINA *(briskly, as she takes her place at the table).* Morning, Mother. Morning, Dad.

ALLERTON *(looking up from the letter he is reading).* Oh, good morning, Georgie.

MRS. ALLERTON. Don't tell me you're wearing that new dress to work.

GEORGINA. I have a lunch date.

MRS. ALLERTON *(with lively interest).* Oh?

GEORGINA. No, Mother, he is *not* a matrimonial prospect. We just happen to be going to a swanky place so—

MRS. ALLERTON. I didn't say—I didn't say— *(Suppressing a sneeze.)* a single—solitary —word. *(The sneeze bursts forth.)* Excuse me!

GEORGINA. Goodness, Mother, have you got a cold?

MRS. ALLERTON. Well, what does it sound like—appendicitis?

GEORGINA. I told you not to put your fur coat in storage yet.

MRS. ALLERTON *(sharply).* That has nothing —nothing whatever—nothing whatever to do with it. *(Another sneeze.)* Oh, damn it! I hate colds.

GEORGINA. Some aspirin might do it good.

MRS. ALLERTON. Nothing does a cold any good. And if you want to know how I got it, I got it from sleeping next to an open window. Your father, after consulting the calendar, decided that spring is here, so of course up went the window all the way.

ALLERTON *(mildly).* I offered to change beds with you, Lucy.

MRS. ALLERTON. That would have only meant your getting a cold and I'd have not only had to nurse you, but would have caught it myself. It was much simpler to catch my own cold in the first place.

GEORGINA *(pouring herself some coffee).* But why didn't you close the window?

MRS. ALLERTON. Well, we discussed the pros and cons of that at some length,

but, in the middle of your father's second rebuttal, I fell asleep, with the result that— *(A sneeze.)*

ALLERTON. Some butter, Georgie?

GEORGINA. Dad, aren't you ever going to learn that I don't take butter?

MRS. ALLERTON. How can you swallow that dry toast?

GEORGINA. You get used to it.

MRS. ALLERTON. I would never get used to it. Has it ever occurred to you that if nature had intended our skeletons to be visible it would have put them—on the outside—on the outside of our bodies? *(A sneeze.)*

ALLERTON. Oh, there's a letter for you, Georgie. *(He hands it to her.)*

GEORGINA. From Wentworth and Jones! *(She tears it open, eagerly, then registers deep disappointment.)* Oh, damn! They've turned down my novel.

ALLERTON. Too bad! But you mustn't be discouraged.

GEORGINA. Well, I am! I was sure they were going to accept it. Especially after Jim recommended it for publication.

MRS. ALLERTON. Sounds to me like an excellent reason for turning it down.

GEORGINA. I don't see why you're always picking on poor Jim.

MRS. ALLERTON. Well, I'm fed up with poor Jim. I think a fellow his age shouldn't just be sitting around reading manuscripts at thirty-five dollars a week.

ALLERTON. Oh, give the boy a chance, my dear. He hasn't found himself yet.

GEORGINA. That's exactly it!

MRS. ALLERTON. Well, I'm sick and tired of financing the search. First, I had to see him through law school. Then—

GEORGINA. Don't go all over that again, Mother. Just because he's too sensitive to bring himself—

ALLERTON. Yes. Law, as it's practiced today, is hardly the profession for an idealist.

MRS. ALLERTON. Well, *you* should know! What *is* this case you're going to Washington on?

ALLERTON. It's the Sons of Solomon case.

GEORGINA. Who are they, Dad?

ALLERTON. A religious sect in Montana that's being prosecuted for advocating polygamy. We've lost all along the line, but I'm very hopeful of winning in the Supreme Court.

MRS. ALLERTON. And that will mean a whopping fee, I'm sure.

ALLERTON (rising). No fee at all, win or lose. I'm handling the case as a matter of principle. Free speech, freedom of religion.

GEORGINA. But, Dad, do you believe in polygamy?

ALLERTON. Personally speaking, no.

MRS. ALLERTON. And a lot of good it would do him if he did!

ALLERTON. But I can say with Voltaire: I disapprove of what you say, but I will defend to the death your right to say it.

GEORGINA. Oh, did Voltaire say that?

MRS. ALLERTON (interrupting). George, doesn't anybody ever walk into your office who's been run over by a millionaire's limousine or who's robbed a bank and is willing to give you—to give you half—to get him—get him out of it? (A sneeze.)

GEORGINA. Why, Mother, aren't there enough ambulance-chasers and police-court shysters without Dad becoming one?

ALLERTON. Thank you, Georgie. (He kisses her.) Good-by, dear. (About to kiss MRS. ALLERTON.) Good-by, Lucy.

MRS. ALLERTON (drawing back). Don't kiss me, or you'll have the entire Supreme Court sneezing their heads off.

ALLERTON (solicitously). I'm worried about you. Maybe a little aspirin—

MRS. ALLERTON. If aspirin is mentioned again—I'll—I'll—I'll— (A sneeze.) Sometimes I think that even monogamy is going too far.

ALLERTON. I'll be back late tonight. Don't be downcast about the novel, Georgie. These things take time.

GEORGINA. Yes, it certainly looks that way.

(ALLERTON exits.)

MRS. ALLERTON. Do you have to encourage him?

GEORGINA. Well, I admire him for sticking unselfishly to his principles, instead of just practicing law on a sordid, commercial basis.

MRS. ALLERTON. Yes, there is certainly no taint of commercialism upon this family, including the connections by marriage. And it's a fortunate coincidence that I am able to foot the bills on the income from Grandpa's sordid commercial estate.

GEORGINA. Well, I have every intention of contributing my share, just as soon as—

(MRS. ALLERTON sneezes.)

MRS. ALLERTON. Excuse me. How much did the bookshop lose last month.

GEORGINA. Only a hundred and eighteen dollars. Claire says it's the best month we've had yet.

MRS. ALLERTON (rising). Why, you're right on the highroad to success. (She sneezes.) Well, I'm going to go and suffer in solitude.

GEORGINA. Good-by, Mother. I do hope—

(MRS. ALLERTON has gone off right. GEORGINA sighs as MIRIAM LUCAS, a young attractive woman, enters at left.)

MIRIAM. 'Lo, Sis.

GEORGINA. Why, Miriam!

MIRIAM. Why, look at you, all dressed up to kill.

GEORGINA. Well, I'm lunching at the Canard Rouge, so I thought I'd—

MIRIAM. Oh-oh!

GEORGINA. Nothing like that. Just somebody who's in the book trade. Since when do you get up at daybreak?

MIRIAM. I had a date with a doctor. Where are Mother and Dad?

GEORGINA. Dad's gone to Washington, and Mother's got an awful cold.

MIRIAM. That's good. I mean I'd rather not spring this on the whole family at once. I hate collective reactions.

GEORGINA. Is anything wrong?

MIRIAM. That's a matter of opinion. It seems that the old medico went into a huddle with some mouse or rabbit that he keeps around and they've decided that you're about to become an aunt.

GEORGINA. But Miriam, how exciting! When's it going to be?

MIRIAM. Oh, not for a hell of a while— a good five or six months. All those engineers, with their blueprints, knocking hours off the transcontinental flying time, but not one day do they save us mothers. Well, I guess I'll go break the news to Mother.

GEORGINA. I'll bet Jim is happy about it.

MIRIAM. He doesn't know it yet. I saw no point in getting him into an interesting condition until I was really sure myself. (*Vehemently.*) And to come right out with it, I don't care a hoot whether he's happy about it or not.

GEORGINA (*greatly embarrassed*). Well, I know it's going to make all the difference in the world for you both. Gee, I certainly envy you.

MIRIAM. And may I say that I certainly envy you. Here am I, a seething mass of unpleasant symptoms, and there are you, fit as a fiddle, and positively suffused with the soft glow of vicarious maternity.

GEORGINA. I just wish I could change places with you, that's all.

MIRIAM. It's a deal. I'll send my agent around after lunch. And I hope you have a boy.

GEORGINA. Maybe it'll be twins.

MIRIAM. Don't say things like that! You never know who's listening. (*She exits at right.*)

(GEORGINA *sits looking dreamily after* MIRIAM. *Then, as the light fades on the scene, a chorus of female voices sings "Sleep, Baby, Sleep." The stage is in darkness for a few moments, then the singing dies out and merges into a chorus of wailing infants. The lights come up slowly at the center, revealing a hospital bed, completely surrounded by flowers, in which* GEORGINA *sits propped up. She wears a silk bed jacket and holds a large doll*

in each arm, one wrapped in a blue blanket, the other in pink. At one side of the bed stands an OBSTETRICIAN, *who looks like* ALLERTON; *at the other side, a* NURSE *who looks like* MRS. ALLERTON.)

THE OBSTETRICIAN. Well, my dear, you've come through wonderfully.

GEORGINA. All thanks to you, Doctor. You've been like a father to me.

THE OBSTETRICIAN. In all my years, I've never known a harder confinement or a braver patient. Yes, you're a plucky little woman.

GEORGINA. A lucky one, you mean! (*Smiling down at the babies.*) Just look at my little darlings!

THE OBSTETRICIAN. I've never seen two finer ones.

THE NURSE. You're the envy of every mother in the hospital.

GEORGINA (*beaming*). Well, what's a little suffering compared to that? Besides, pain is a part of life, and to live fully, we must taste every form of human experience.

THE NURSE. Oh, that's beautifully expressed!

GEORGINA. And, Doctor, I definitely *don't* want them to go on the bottle. It's such a joy!

THE OBSTETRICIAN (*patting her head*). Good girl! (*As the* OBSTETRICIAN *exits,* JIM LUCAS *enters. He is an attractive young man, with a face and manner that are almost too sensitive.*)

JIM. Georgina, darling!

GEORGINA. Oh, Jim!

THE NURSE. Not too long, Mr. Lucas. We mustn't tire her.

JIM. No, no. I understand. (*As the* NURSE *exits, he goes to* GEORGINA.)

GEORGINA. Oh, Jim, isn't it wonderful?

JIM. Yes, wonderful! Birth, the most universal experience, and yet the greatest of all miracles. Are you happy, darling?

GEORGINA. Just look at me! I've waited so long for this, afraid it was never going to happen. I'm a new woman, Jim.

JIM. And I'm a new man—with someone to understand me, someone to have faith in me.

GEORGINA. And a new world to build for ourselves—and for them: Gerald and Geraldine.

MIRIAM (*entering at right, smoking a cigarette*). Hand them over quick, Georgina. I'm parked in front of a fire plug.

GEORGINA (*clinging to the babies*). No, you shan't have them! They're mine.

MIRIAM (*coming to the bed*). Yours? Look, darling, it wasn't my idea to have a baby! But having produced a couple of brats, in the customary, antiquated manner, I don't think I'm unreasonable in contending that they're mine.

JIM. Only in the crudest physiological sense.

MIRIAM. Oh, forgive me! Is there some other sense?

GEORGINA. There is indeed!

JIM. You wouldn't have to be told that, Miriam, if you had any feeling for the deeper values of life. There's no real marriage between you and me—no love, no understanding, no spiritual communion. The children of my body may be yours, but the children of my spirit will always be Georgina's.

MIRIAM. All right. I'll settle for that. (*Calling.*) Nurse!

THE NURSE. Coming!

MIRIAM (*snatching one baby and pointing to the other*). Here, you take that one. And hurry up before I get a ticket. (*The* NURSE *takes the other baby from* GEORGINA *and follows* MIRIAM *off, sneezing into the baby's face.*)

MIRIAM (*as she exits*). And watch that sneezing!

JIM (*taking a step after her*). Miriam, I—

GEORGINA (*as the scene fades out*). Jim! Jim! Don't leave me! Don't leave me!

JIM (*stretching his arms toward the disappearing* GEORGINA). I'm sorry, Georgina! I know it isn't right! I know it shouldn't be this way! Georgina! Georgina! Georgina! (*He exits.*)

MRS. ALLERTON (*off right*). Georgina! Georgina, are you still there? (*The lights come up right on* GEORGINA *as she sits at the breakfast table, as before.*)

GEORGINA (*startled*). What? Yes. Yes, I am. (*She hastily wipes her eyes, as* MRS. ALLERTON *enters.*)

MRS. ALLERTON. You'll be late again at the shop. What on earth are you moping about now?

GEORGINA. Just happy about Miriam. And a little wistful at the prospect of being a maiden aunt. Don't you feel sort of—

MRS. ALLERTON. I'm much too furious to feel sort of anything.

GEORGINA. Why? What's the matter?

MRS. ALLERTON. Didn't Miriam tell you about Jim?

GEORGINA (*anxiously*). No, what about him?

MRS. ALLERTON. He's out of a job again.

GEORGINA. He's left Wentworth and Jones?

MRS. ALLERTON. Well, that's one way of putting it. In less diplomatic language, they fired him.

GEORGINA. So that's why she was so upset. Poor Jim!

MRS. ALLERTON. What do you mean, poor Jim! What about poor Miriam?

GEORGINA. It's much worse for him. He's just had nothing but hard luck.

MRS. ALLERTON. Why, the way you stand up for him, anybody would think you were madly in love with him.

GEORGINA (*angrily*). Don't talk such nonsense! Just because I happen to feel some sympathy for a boy who—

MRS. ALLERTON. All right, you can feel all the sympathy you like for him. But, in my opinion, the sooner Miriam gets herself unattached from that balmy dreamer, the better off she'll be.

GEORGINA. Well, I hope you don't tell her anything like that.

MRS. ALLERTON. I just this minute—just this minute—finished telling her! (*A sneeze.*)

GEORGINA. How *could* you, just when she's going to have a baby?

MRS. ALLERTON. That's just exactly it. She'd be a fool to hang on to him, now that he's accomplished what will probably be the only affirmative act of his life.

GEORGINA. But it's just the time when a woman needs her husband most!

MRS. ALLERTON. You read too many serious books. What on earth does she need him for now?

GEORGINA. I don't see how you can be so cynical about your daughter's happiness.

MRS. ALLERTON. I'm not the least bit cynical. If she gets rid of that piece of excess baggage, she has a chance to make a fresh start. Otherwise, she's just stuck with him. Everybody else seems to fire him. Why shouldn't she?

GEORGINA. Well, I trust and pray that Miriam won't pay any attention to you. In fact, I'm going to call her up and tell her so.

MRS. ALLERTON. You keep out of this. If Miriam had wanted your advice, she'd have asked for it. And if that unemployed Galahad comes crying to you, I wish you'd tell him for me that—that—that— *(She sneezes.)* For goodness' sake, will you run along to work now, before I use language unbecoming a grandmother?

GEORGINA. All right, good-by, then. And for heaven's sake, take care of yourself.

MRS. ALLERTON *(as GEORGINA exits).* If you—if I—if anybody—

(The lights fade on the scene and come up, at left, on a corner of a small bookshop. The telephone is ringing. On the third ring, CLAIRE BLAKELY, a brisk young woman about GEORGINA's age, enters and answers it.)

CLAIRE. Mermaid Bookshop. No, madam, I'm terribly sorry. This is not the Bide-a-wee Home. You must have the wrong number. *(A STOUT WOMAN enters and CLAIRE turns to her.)* Good morning. Can I help you?

THE WOMAN. I was just wondering if you happen to have a copy of *Always Opal?*

CLAIRE. No. I'm afraid not at the moment.

THE WOMAN. Oh, dear. This is about the fifth shop I've been to.

CLAIRE. We have a dozen copies but they're all out. And a waiting list of at least fifty. But here's something you might like. Mary Myrtle Miven's latest, *My Heart Is Like a Trumpet.* It's a sort of idyllic love story about two horses. Very tender and poetic.

THE WOMAN. No, I really don't think—

CLAIRE. Well, how about *The Dnieper Goes Rolling Along?* It's that new Soviet novel about the electrification of collective farms. Very stark and powerful.

THE WOMAN. No, what I really want is *Always Opal.* You see, all my friends are reading it, and I feel so out of it. I understand it's very—very—

CLAIRE. Well, it certainly doesn't leave much to the imagination in the way of—

THE WOMAN. Yes, so I understand. *(As she starts to go.)* Oh, I wonder if you happen to have a three-cent stamp.

CLAIRE. Yes, I think so. *(She opens a tin cashbox on the desk.)*

THE WOMAN *(fumbling in her handbag).* Oh, dear, I'm afraid the smallest I have is a five-dollar bill. Could you possibly—?

CLAIRE. I guess I can make it. One, and four is five.

THE WOMAN. Oh, thank you so much.

CLAIRE. Not a bit. Stop in again.

THE WOMAN. Indeed I will! *(She goes out at the right, as GEORGINA enters.)*

GEORGINA. Hello, Claire. Sorry I'm late again. Have you had a busy morning?

CLAIRE. You betcha. I directed two people to Oppenheim Collins, one gal wanted to look at the phone book, another had to go to the john, and I just made a cash sale of a three-cent stamp.

GEORGINA. It's discouraging.

CLAIRE. Oh, I knew there was something else. Frank McClellan called up to say that that asthma of his has got completely out of hand and the doctor has ordered him to Arizona, pronto.

GEORGINA. Oh, the poor guy! But what about his bookshop?

CLAIRE. Well, he thought we might like to take it over.

GEORGINA (*excitedly*). But Claire, how wonderful! Why, compared to this dinky little—

CLAIRE. You can spare me the comparison. He says he clears five or six hundred a month.

GEORGINA. Why, we lost nearly that much one month.

CLAIRE. Yes, dear.

GEORGINA. Well, let's tell him yes, before he changes his mind.

CLAIRE. He wants ten thousand dollars for the business.

GEORGINA. Ten thousand dollars! For heaven's sake!

CLAIRE. Did you think he wanted to make us a present of it? You don't happen to know where we could dig up ten thousand, do you?

GEORGINA. Who, me?

CLAIRE. No, I guess not. Well, it's too bad. (*With firmness.*) Georgie, I don't think you and I are cut out for business. I think the best thing for us to do is board up this hole in the wall and call it a day.

GEORGINA. What, give up the business, when we've put so much into it?

CLAIRE. We could have had sables on what we've put into it.

GEORGINA. But we're not interested in sables.

CLAIRE. We're not?

GEORGINA. Well, what I mean is, we're not the frivolous type, that's willing just to gad around and fritter our time away.

CLAIRE. But what type are we? and what are we good for? What can we do?

GEORGINA. Well, we could go to secretarial school.

CLAIRE. Back to school at twenty-four? Listen, darling, beginning with play school at three, I went to school—let me see, now—sixteen, seventeen, eighteen, nineteen . . . ! My God, nineteen consecutive years! Nineteen years, thousands of dollars, and the efforts of hundreds of specially trained people have been spent in making us not want to do all the useful things we don't know how to do.

GEORGINA. And I'm getting terribly discouraged about my novel, too. Wentworth and Jones have just turned it down. And after Jim Lucas recommended it. I'm beginning to think that maybe I'm not a novelist.

CLAIRE. Oh, don't take that attitude. William DeMorgan had his first novel published at sixty-six.

GEORGINA. But he must have had something to keep him occupied in the meantime. I still have one teeny hope. Jim Lucas said he'd give the manuscript to Clark Redfield. You know—the book reviewer.

CLAIRE. Oh, yes.

GEORGINA. If he turns thumbs down, I'll just—! Oh, well, no use brooding over it. By the way, speaking of Jim Lucas, Miriam is going to have a baby.

CLAIRE. Congratulations! Well, that's something that even we would be capable of, I suppose.

GEORGINA. They say it takes two.

CLAIRE. Yes, that's the hell of it. We're choosy too. Well, let's not be defeatist about things. Can't you think of some way we could raise that ten thousand? How about your grandfather's estate? It's a perfectly safe investment—

GEORGINA. Not a chance of that. It's all tied up in a trust fund with some bank, as long as my mother lives.

CLAIRE. And I suppose she's good for another twenty-five years.

GEORGINA. Why, what a thing to say!

CLAIRE. Oh, I didn't mean it that way. It's just that—oh, you know—always some dead hand, holding us back. Oh, well, I've got to get out this month's bills. (*She starts to go.*) Don't take any more reservations for *Always Opal*. Our lease will be up by the time we fill all we have now. (*She exits behind the book shelves.* GEORGINA *sighs, lights a cigarette, gets up and walks about the shop, lost in thought. Suddenly the telephone rings.*)

GEORGINA (*without going near the telephone*). Hello? Yes, this is she. What? Oh, no, I can't believe it! Yes! Yes! I'll be right there. (*As she hurries center, the lights come up, revealing a* MAN *in a surgeon's uniform with a stethoscope about his neck.*) Oh, Doctor, Doctor, it can't be true about my mother!

THE DOCTOR. Yes, my dear, I'm afraid it is.

GEORGINA. What was it—her heart?

THE DOCTOR. That—and other things. It happens that way, sometimes. We tried to save her, but it was hopeless.

GEORGINA. Did you try sodium pentathol?

THE DOCTOR. Yes, my dear. Everything was done that medical science can do. But there are still some things we haven't mastered. And now, I shall leave you with your father. He needs you, my dear. (*He recedes into the darkness as* ALLERTON *comes forward.*)

GEORGINA (*in his arms*). Dad!

ALLERTON. I'm all alone now, Georgie—except for you!

GEORGINA. You have Miriam, too, Dad.

ALLERTON (*shaking his head*). She has Jim to look out for. And a baby coming soon. So there's only you.

GEORGINA. You can depend on me, Dad. I'll never leave you. You're all I have in the world, too.

ALLERTON. You're a rich girl now, Georgie. Anything that your heart desires—

GEORGINA. Oh, I don't care about the money, Dad. If I do use any of it, it will only be so that Claire and I—

(CLARK REDFIELD, *a young man of twenty-eight, enters at left. He staggers under the load of a double armful of books. He goes to the desk, plumps down the books, looks toward the center, and coughs tentatively. As* GEORGINA *turns and sees him, the lights fade quickly on* ALLERTON.)

CLARK. Good morning, Miss Allerton.

GEORGINA (*approaching* REDFIELD). Oh! Good morning, Mr. Redfield.

CLARK. You seemed preoccupied. I hope I haven't derailed some train of cosmic thought.

GEORGINA (*somewhat flustered*). Of course not. I was just— (*Seeing the books.*) Goodness! More review copies?

CLARK. You betcha! I've got—

GEORGINA (*preoccupied*). Do you mind waiting a minute while I call my mother? She wasn't feeling well this morning and—

CLARK. Nothing serious, I hope!

GEORGINA. Well, I think it's only a cold, but you know how these respiratory disorders flare up sometimes. (*She dials a number. A telephone rings at the right and the lights go up on* MRS. ALLERTON. *She is seated on a chaise longue, dressed as before, and reading a book. The telephone is beside her and she answers it.*)

MRS. ALLERTON. Hello!

GEORGINA. This is me, Mother. How are you feeling?

MRS. ALLERTON. What do you mean, how am I feeling? I'm feeling—feeling fine. (*She sneezes.*)

GEORGINA. You sound awful.

MRS. ALLERTON. I've got a cold in the head and every now and then—I—I—I—have to sneeze. What are you calling up for?

GEORGINA. To find out how you are, of course. I've been worried about you.

MRS. ALLERTON. You mean to say you called up just to ask about my sneezes? You certainly must have very little on your mind.

GEORGINA. Well, you might at least appreciate my—

MRS. ALLERTON. I was appreciating Opal's hot affair with Monseigneur de Montrouget and you interrupted me just as they were about to—to— (*She sneezes and hangs up.*)

GEORGINA (*as the lights fade on* MRS. ALLERTON). All right. I'm just glad you— (*She hangs up.*)

CLARK. Is she all right?

GEORGINA. She seems all right. Just sneezing and very cranky.

CLARK. The typical American mother. (*Rubbing his hands.*) Well, are you ready to do business now?

GEORGINA. What have you there?

CLARK. A fine mixed bag. Three whodunits, a couple of epics of the soil, a survey of the natural resources of Bolivia, and a volume called *Fun with a Chafing Dish.* And here is the prize of the lot: Professor Oglethorpe's two-volume *Life of Napoleon,* with the pages still uncut.

GEORGINA. You mean you haven't read it.

CLARK. Do I look like a boy who, six years out of college, would wade through eleven hundred pages on Napoleon?

GEORGINA. But I read your review of it in the *Globe.*

CLARK. I didn't say I didn't review it. I said I didn't read it.

GEORGINA. How could you review it without reading it?

CLARK. Easy. First I quoted liberally from the introduction and quarreled with the author's approach. Next, I leafed quickly through and called attention to three typographical errors. Then I praised the illustrations, grumbled about the footnotes, and intimated that the book added little to what had already been written. Result, a scholarly column and all done in exactly fifty-seven minutes.

GEORGINA. Is that your idea of literary criticism?

CLARK. Look! I'm a working newspaperman and a member of the Newspaper Guild, whose contract guarantees me a minimum wage for a maximum working week. There's nothing in it that requires me to ruin my eyesight and addle my brain in the interests of a Corsican upstart.

GEORGINA. Well, I've often heard that newspapermen are cynical, but I wouldn't have believed that a man who is entrusted with reviewing books could have so little sense of responsibility.

CLARK. You make me feel like a great big brute.

GEORGINA. I don't see anything funny about it. I think it's disgraceful.

CLARK. Don't twist the sword, Miss Allerton. Just give me the price of my shame and let me go in peace. Well, what do you say? How much am I bid for the lot?

GEORGINA *(examining the books).* Most of these aren't much use to us. How about five dollars?

CLARK. Like all idealists, you drive a hard bargain. But I'm not going to lug these damned things any further, so they're yours.

GEORGINA. Well, I don't want you to feel I'm taking advantage of you. I'll make it six dollars.

CLARK *(holding up his hand).* No, no! Even a cynical newspaperman has his pride. Give!

GEORGINA *(handing him a bill).* You don't have to be so sarcastic about it. We really don't need your secondhand books. Maybe, hereafter, you'd better take them somewhere else.

CLARK. Unfortunately, I'm a creature of habit, Miss Allerton. Let me but tuck a review copy under my arm and immediately there is set in motion a whole series of muscular reflexes that takes me straight to your door.

GEORGINA. If reviewing books is so distasteful to you, why do you do it?

CLARK. Well, you see, I have a periodic rendezvous with my stomach. And I find that reviewing books requires less leg work than covering the police courts. And, not to withhold anything from you, I'm sitting in a very pretty spot for the first opening on the sports page.

GEORGINA *(in amazement).* You mean you'd rather be a sports writer than a literary critic?

CLARK. I'm afraid you don't grasp the practical realities of journalism. What you euphemistically call a literary critic is only a miserable penny-a-liner, whereas a sports writer nestles snugly in the upper brackets.

GEORGINA. I wasn't thinking about the money—

CLARK. Pardon the indelicacy. So you think that writing about books is on a higher level than writing about sports?

GEORGINA. I just think there's no comparison.

CLARK. You're right; there isn't. Any young squirt, fresh out of college, can write book reviews. Just as any beginner in the theater can play Polonius. In fact, the technique is much the same. You put on false whiskers and spout platitudes in a high, squeaky voice. But to go in there and play Hamlet and follow all the sinuous twists and turnings of that tortured soul; or, on the other hand, to analyze the strategy of an intricate football formation or judge a fast ten-round bout on points—that's something else again. To do that, you really have to know your stuff.

GEORGINA. Oh, yes, you're very clever and paradoxical, aren't you?

CLARK. Thank you for the compliment, tinged though it is with a certain asperity. But you see, getting on the sports page is only what might be called a primary objective. For to a really good sports writer, every door is open: literature, movies, radio, politics, anything. Look at Ring Lardner. Look at Heywood Broun. Look at John Kieran. Look—if you can bear it—at Westbrook Pegler. In my daydreams, I write a story about the deciding game of the World Series that stampedes the Democratic Convention, and lands me in the White House. And on my tentative cabinet slate, you're down for Secretary of Labor. Ta-ta, Madam Allerton, I'll see you in Washington.

GEORGINA (as he is about to go). Oh, just a minute. Did Jim Lucas ever give you—

CLARK. Did I hear you aright? Did you mention the name of Jim Lucas?

GEORGINA. Have you got something sarcastic to say about him, too?

CLARK. Not sarcastic, my dear young woman. Sarcasm would be a wholly inadequate instrument for a commentary on that epic character. But perhaps you haven't heard the news about Jim?

GEORGINA. I've heard that he's parted company with Wentworth and Jones, if that's what you mean.

CLARK. Parted company, did you say? Really, Miss Allerton, you have a gift for hyperbolic understatement. The impact of Jim's violent expulsion has rocked Publishers' Row to its foundations. Would you mind telling an inquiring reporter, Miss Allerton, how it feels to be the sister-in-law of the man who sent back the manuscript of *Always Opal,* without even turning in a report on it?

GEORGINA. Is that really true? Did Jim do that?

CLARK. Oh, so you haven't heard. An enterprising book peddler like you should get around more. This Lucas is a celebrity, the greatest bonehead player since Fred Merkle forgot to touch second base.

GEORGINA. Well, that book deserved to be turned down. It's nothing but a lot of dressed-up smut, atrociously written, and all in very bad taste, if you ask me.

CLARK. Wait a minute, Carrie Nation. The verdict of history is already in. Don't try to alibi Jim, or folks will get the impression that you take more than a sisterly-in-law interest in him.

GEORGINA (flaring up). That's an uncalled-for and highly impertinent remark.

CLARK. Or is it just a case of one hand washing the other?

GEORGINA. And what is that supposed to mean?

CLARK. Well, I got the impression that Jim thinks rather highly of that novel of yours that he asked me to read.

GEORGINA (eager for his verdict). Oh, then he did give it to you?

CLARK. Yes, he did.

GEORGINA. And I suppose, following your usual practice, you haven't read it.

CLARK. No, you're wrong. I have read it. All of it—well, almost all.

GEORGINA (after a pause). Well?

CLARK. You mean you want my opinion of it?

GEORGINA. Well, why do you suppose I let Jim give it to you?

CLARK. I wasn't sure. Well, to put the thing as delicately as possible, I think it stinks.

GEORGINA (enraged). Oh, you do, do you?

CLARK. Yes, I do. (Contemplatively.) Yes, that really is a malodorous morsel. In the first place—

GEORGINA (*almost in tears*). Never mind! I'm not interested in what you have to say.

CLARK. Oh, then you really *didn't* want my opinion. That's what I thought.

GEORGINA. I don't call that an opinion. Just a nasty, insulting—

CLARK. I see! You only wanted a favorable opinion.

GEORGINA. Nobody wants criticism that's just destructive. I say if a critic can't be constructive—

CLARK. You mean you want the critic to do the creative job that you failed to do? If that's his function, we might as well dispense with the writer in the first place. Now, if you'll let me give a piece of friendly advice—

GEORGINA. I don't want your advice. I'd never have let Jim give you the manuscript if I had known that you're just a hockey fan.

CLARK. There's a good hockey match at the Garden Saturday night. Want to go?

GEORGINA. No, I don't! And if you'll excuse me now, I have a lot of work to do.

CLARK. You haven't a damn thing to do. You just sit around this shop all day to give yourself the illusion that you're doing something.

GEORGINA. Will you please get out of here?

CLARK. Sore as a boil, aren't you?

GEORGINA. Not in the least. It just happens that I find you very unpleasant. I think you're not only lazy and dishonest, but sadistic and vulgar.

CLARK. Well, I'm glad you're not sore. And I think that novel of yours is just about the most terrific thing I've read since *War and Peace*.

GEORGINA. And another thing, I wish you would not ever come here again.

CLARK. I'll try to remember that. By, now. And thanks for the five bucks. (CLARK *exits right.*)

GEORGINA (*with tears of anger*). You great big ape! (*She stands looking after him for a moment, trembling with rage and humiliation. Then she begins threshing* about, *in uncontrollable fury. She strides to the desk and violently pushes* CLARK's *books to the floor. Then she stands with clenched fists glaring in the direction that* CLARK *has gone and with sudden resolution strides center into the darkness. There is a flash of lightning and a peal of thunder. The lights fade on the bookshop and come up at the right, as the pitiful meowing of a cat is heard.* CLARK, *in his shirt sleeves and wearing a green eyeshade, is seated before a typewriter at an untidy table, piled high with books. Beside him on the floor is a stuffed cat whose tail he is twisting. The meowing is heard again.* CLARK *laughs fiendishly, pours himself a stiff drink of whisky, gulps it down, and begins pecking at the typewriter. Again lightning and thunder, followed by a sharp knocking.*)

CLARK. Who the hell is that? (*He leans over and twists the cat's tail again. There is a wail of pain, as* GEORGINA *enters, wearing a hooded cloak.*)

CLARK (*sneeringly*). Oh, it's you, is it?

GEORGINA. Yes, it's me. I mean it's I.

CLARK. I'm just having a little fun with kitty.

GEORGINA (*grimly*). And I'm going to have a little fun with you! (*She takes a revolver from beneath her cloak and levels it at him.*)

CLARK (*cowering in terror.*) No! No! Not that!

(GEORGINA *fires two shots.* CLARK *shrieks and slumps to the floor. A* POLICEMAN *rushes on at the right and seizes* GEORGINA *roughly.*)

THE POLICEMAN. Come along, you!

GEORGINA (*with quiet dignity*). All right. You needn't be rough about it. I did it and I'm willing to take the consequences.

(*As the* POLICEMAN *takes her off, the lights fade. A tumult of voices and the thumping of a gavel is heard. The lights come up at center. A* JUDGE, *who resembles* ALLERTON, *is seated at the bench, beside which, in the witness chair,* GEORGINA *sits. The* DISTRICT ATTORNEY *and* JIM LUCAS *are seated at the counsel table.*)

THE JUDGE (*banging his gavel*). Order! Order! If there are any more demonstrations, I'll have the courtroom cleared. (*As quiet is restored.*) Proceed with your examination, Mr. District Attorney.

THE DISTRICT ATTORNEY (*pointing an accusing finger*). Then you admit that you went there with the deliberate intention of killing Clark Redfield?

GEORGINA. Yes, I admit it. But I had every justification. He was a savage brute, a man without—

THE DISTRICT ATTORNEY. I object!

THE JUDGE (*banging his gavel*). Objection sustained!

JIM (*jumping up*). Your Honor, I protest. This young woman is on trial for her life. Is she to be railroaded to the chair without even an opportunity to speak in her own defense?

THE JUDGE. The point is well taken. Proceed, Miss Allerton.

GEORGINA. Well, let me just ask you this. If he had attacked me, wouldn't you all agree that I had a right—?

THE JUDGE. One moment! Are we to understand that Clark Redfield attempted to—?

GEORGINA. No, he didn't. But compared to what he did to me, it would have been easy to submit to—to— Well, not easy, but almost preferable. He struck at my dignity, humiliated me, trampled my pride in the dust. And if you men think that an injury to a woman's body is a greater provocation to murder than an injury to her spirit, then you know nothing about feminine nature. That's all! That's my case! (*She glares about defiantly.*)

THE DISTRICT ATTORNEY. Your Honor, the people of the State of New York demand the death penalty!

THE JUDGE. Counsel for the defense will now address the jury. Proceed, Mr. Lucas.

JIM (*rising and addressing the unseen jury*). Ladies and gentlemen of the jury. I speak to you not merely as counsel for Georgina Allerton, but as her brother. And by that I do not refer to my accidental marital relationship to her sister, but to the deep, spiritual, fraternal bond that has long existed between the defendant and myself. I can say, in all honesty, that no one understands her as I do: no

other living being has plumbed so profoundly the depths of that tender, sensitive soul. And, in the light of my knowledge and understanding, I say to you that when she struck down Clark Redfield it was no act of murder, but a simple, human gesture of self-defense. (*A murmur from the unseen* JURORS.) Yes, ladies and gentlemen, self-defense! For what was this novel of hers, that Clark Redfield sought to annihilate with the cruel strokes of his sharp-edged tongue and stabbing wit? It was her baby, ladies and gentlemen, the child of her spirit, as real to her and as dear to her as though it had been, indeed, the flesh-and-blood creation of her body. For it was conceived in the beautiful ecstasy of spiritual passion, nurtured for long months in the dark, secret recesses of her soul, brought forth in an agony of travail. And as it lay nestling in her bosom, so to speak, Clark Redfield struck at it, with his lethal weapons! And with the noble, unerring instinct of outraged maternity, she struck back, struck back at the would-be assassin of her baby. Could any mother, could any woman do less? I leave the answer to you. (*He sits down amid cheers and applause.*)

THE JUDGE (*pounding for order*). What is your verdict, ladies and gentlemen of the jury?

CHORUS OF UNSEEN JURORS. Not guilty!

(*The* DISTRICT ATTORNEY *leaves in a huff.*)

THE JUDGE. The defendant is dismissed.

GEORGINA (*shaking hands with him*). Thank you, Your Honor.

THE JUDGE (*as he leaves the bench*). Not at all. But just a word of fatherly advice, Miss Allerton. In the future, try to avoid the use of firearms.

GEORGINA (*earnestly*). I will, Your Honor. (*Turning to Jim, as the judge exits.*) Oh, Jim, darling, I knew I could depend on you! (*She walks toward* JIM, *but as the telephone rings in the bookshop, she ignores his outstretched arms and hurries to answer it. The lights fade on the courtroom and come up, at left, on the bookshop.*)

GEORGINA. Mermaid Bookshop. No madam, I'm sorry; we're all out of *Always Opal*. You're welcome.

CLAIRE *(who has entered)*. Why, what's the matter with you? You look as though you were ready to commit murder.

GEORGINA. Oh, it's nothing. I'm just mad at myself for losing my temper.

CLAIRE. Who did what to you?

GEORGINA. It's too trivial to talk about. It's just that that Clark Redfield was in and began shooting off his face about a lot of— Honestly, of all the brash, egotistical fools I ever met—!

CLAIRE. Well, I've only met him once or twice, but I had an idea he was kind of nice. How did he like your novel?

GEORGINA. Oh, I really don't know. I didn't even bother to ask him.

CLAIRE. Sorry. Excuse it, please. *(She exits. As* GEORGINA *picks up the scattered books,* JIM LUCAS *enters at right.)*

JIM. Hello, Georgina.

GEORGINA. Oh, hello, Jim.

JIM. Are you busy?

GEORGINA. Well, I have a lunch date at one-thirty and—

JIM. Oh, you've got lots of time.

GEORGINA. I was going to stop at Collette's first, to pick up a new hat she's making for me. But it doesn't matter. Sit down.

JIM *(complying)*. I have something to tell you. But maybe you heard it already from Miriam.

GEORGINA. You mean about your leaving Wentworth and Jones?

JIM. Oh, that, yes! Trust Miriam to waste no time in spreading it around.

GEORGINA. It wasn't from Miriam I heard it. Clark Redfield was just in—

JIM. Good old Clark! Always the reporter. I suppose he told you why they fired me.

GEORGINA. Well, he did mention something about *Always Opal*—

JIM. You don't have to be tactful. I'm not in the least bit sensitive about it. If I had it to do over again, I'd still turn that book down. It's just a piece of trash.

GEORGINA. Well, that's exactly what I said to Redfield!

JIM. Good for you! But what I came in to tell you is that Miriam and I are splitting up.

GEORGINA. Oh, no, Jim. You mustn't do that! Just because you've had some silly quarrel about losing your job—

JIM. It goes much deeper than that. We never were right for each other. She's much too down to earth for me, and I'm much too undependable for her.

GEORGINA. It just doesn't seem right to me. And when you get to thinking it over—

JIM. There's nothing more to think over. It's all settled, and Miriam is just as relieved about it as I am. I haven't felt so free and so hopeful in years. Well, you'd better run along to your lunch date. I just wanted to give you my version of the situation, before you heard about it from the other side of the family.

GEORGINA. Well, I'm glad you did.

JIM *(going to her)*. So am I! It's wonderful to be able to talk to somebody who has some idea of what you're getting at. One of the things I want most, Georgina, is for you and me to get back on our old footing again. I've felt a kind of restraint in you these past two years and I—

GEORGINA *(greatly troubled)*. Well, I—

JIM. Yes, it was natural enough, I suppose. But it doesn't have to be that way any more. Now we can be friends as we used to be. *(Taking her hand.)* Good-by, Georgina. I'll see you soon.

GEORGINA. Yes, Jim.

*(*JIM *exits quickly.* GEORGINA, *on the verge of tears, stands looking after him.)*

CLAIRE *(entering)*. Didn't you say something about a lunch date?

GEORGINA *(startled)*. What? Oh, yes! *(Looking at her watch.)* Heavens, I'm going to keep him waiting again!

CLAIRE. Somebody interesting?

GEORGINA *(with attempted nonchalance)*. Just George Hand.

CLAIRE. George Hand is taking you to lunch again?

GEORGINA. Well, what's wrong about that? He's a book jobber and we run a book-shop—

CLAIRE. Where do you get that "we"? Am I in on this lunch date?

GEORGINA. What a mind you have! Just because Mr. Hand and I happen to discover that we have a few things in common—

CLAIRE. Which he hopes will eventually include a bed.

GEORGINA. Claire, will you please stop! You'll make me so self-conscious that I won't know what to say to him.

CLAIRE. Well, if you can't think of anything else, you can always say no.

GEORGINA. Maybe I should phone the Canard Rouge and tell him I'm not coming. I'm terribly upset and in no mood for one of those fencing matches.

CLAIRE. Goodness, does a little tiff with Clark Redfield make you—

GEORGINA. Certainly not! I've even forgotten Clark Redfield's existence. Jim Lucas was just in to tell me that he and Miriam are divorcing. Isn't that dreadful?

CLAIRE. People do it every day, with the greatest of ease. And from where I sit, Miriam is well rid of that Jim.

GEORGINA. That seems to be a general opinion with which I disagree. Oh, well, I may as well have lunch with George Hand and get it over with. I'll be back as soon as I can.

CLAIRE (as GEORGINA exits at right). Don't hurry! And don't say no, until after the liqueurs. (The telephone rings.) Mermaid Bookshop. No, madam, I'm sorry, we're all out of Always Opal. Well, we're expecting— (Her voice and scene fade out. The lights come up at right on a semicircular upholstered booth in a corner of the Canard Rouge, a chi-chi midtown restaurant. GEORGINA and GEORGE HAND are seated over their coffee and brandy. HAND is a brisk, good-looking man, getting on to forty. GEORGINA is wearing a gay, plumed hat.)

HAND. Think you could manage another brandy?

GEORGINA. I definitely could not manage one other thing. Except maybe a cigarette.

HAND (giving her one and lighting it for her). Oh, sure! What made you go on the wagon?

GEORGINA. Two cocktails and two brandies for lunch! Is that your idea of being on the wagon?

HAND. I used to know a girl who took three Cuba libres with breakfast.

GEORGINA. What interesting people you know! Did she work?

HAND. Well, not in the daytime, I guess. She was a night telephone operator. Is that bookshop keeping you busy?

GEORGINA. Afraid not. In fact, we've about decided to close it.

HAND. That's a good idea. What astrologer advised you to pick that grim location?

GEORGINA. I guess we didn't use very good judgment, did we?

HAND. I don't think you're cut out for a business career.

GEORGINA. That's what my partner says. But what career am I cut out for?

HAND. Have you tried love?

GEORGINA. You won't take me seriously, will you?

HAND. Sure, if I can't have you any other way.

GEORGINA. No, I mean it!

HAND. Well, what would be the point of both of us taking you seriously? No sense in overdoing the thing.

GEORGINA. You think I take myself too seriously?

HAND. Well, let's say seriously enough.

GEORGINA. I suppose I do. And that's bad, isn't it?

HAND. Terrible.

GEORGINA. Why?

HAND. Think of all the fun you miss.

GEORGINA. Yes, maybe I do. I've often wished that I could be just—well, just completely reckless and irresponsible, like —like—oh, I don't know who

HAND. Like Opal?

GEORGINA. Well, yes, now that you mention it! Is that why everybody is so mad to read that silly book?

HAND. What are you being so snooty about? Why, that book is positively a boon to womankind! For two-fifty flat or three cents a day any *Hausfrau* in the land can identify herself with the most luscious yes-woman in all literature.

GEORGINA. Is that really what every woman wants?

HAND. All I can go by is the sales figures.

GEORGINA. So you think we're all harlots at heart?

HAND. Well, I wouldn't want to run for Congress on that platform.

GEORGINA. Still, even if you're right, there seem to be an awful lot of women who manage not to—

HAND. I know. That's what makes life so difficult for a man.

GEORGINA. Oh, poor Mr. Hand! Do we make things difficult for you?

HAND. Very. But I don't complain. No victory without labor, my Sunday-school teacher used to say. And, by the way, my name is George.

GEORGINA. Yes, George.

HAND. That's better. George and Georgina. We sound like a team of adagio dancers. I consider that very auspicious.

GEORGINA. I was named after my father. He's George, too.

HAND. Now, don't tell me you're attracted to me because I remind you of your father.

GEORGINA. You don't remind me in the least of my father. And who told you that I'm attracted to you?

HAND. You know, I am really beginning to go for you in a big way. (*Shaking his head.*) I can't figure this out.

GEORGINA. You mean there's really something you can't figure out?

HAND. Uh-huh. Just one thing. You!

GEORGINA. Oh, so I'm an enigma! What fun!

HAND. No fooling, how does a girl who has all that you have happen to be so unattached?

GEORGINA. Maybe my virtues—no, that isn't the word! Maybe my charms aren't as apparent to everyone as they are to you.

HAND. I don't believe that! Or are you one of those girls who think they're only interested in marriage?

GEORGINA. I'm not in the least interested in marriage.

HAND. You're not? Why?

GEORGINA. Because from what I've seen of it, I think the odds are all against you.

HAND. You're so right! Well, that makes everything much simpler.

GEORGINA. For whom?

HAND. For you, of course. It doesn't cramp your style, doesn't limit the range of your experiences.

GEORGINA. Why, that's true, isn't it? You have a wonderful gift for clarifying things.

HAND. Don't be coy, Georgina. You'll never get me to believe that a sophisticated girl like you has never had any experiences.

GEORGINA. Well, it would be hard to believe that a sophisticated girl could get to be twenty-two without having had *some* experiences.

HAND. Then what the hell? Or does your aversion to marriage extend to men who are already married?

GEORGINA. I often wonder how I'd feel if I were the man's wife. Or is that very unsophisticated?

HAND. Not a bit. Does credit to your upbringing. Only Mollie isn't a bit like that. We get along fine together except when she has a drink too many and then we really go to town. Otherwise, I don't interfere with her and she doesn't interfere with me.

GEORGINA. That's what I mean about marriage.

HAND. I agreed with you, didn't I? But you'll admit I'm not one of the lads who comes crying for sympathy because he's so misunderstood.

GEORGINA. No, that's true. I knew there was *something* about you that was different.

HAND. No flattery, please! Tell me, have you ever been to Mexico?

GEORGINA. Thanks for changing the subject. No, I haven't been to Mexico. But I've always wanted to go.

HAND. Wonderful! But I haven't changed the subject. I have to go down next month and I've been thinking what fun it would be if you and I could sort of meet up there.

GEORGINA. Oh, have you?

HAND. It's a great country. I've been there before and I know my way around. We'd take in jai-alai matches and bullfights—

GEORGINA. I should say not!

HAND. All right, we'll stay away from bullfights. Anyhow, we'd find some village fiestas, look at the Rivera frescoes, and drift along on the flower boats at Xochimilco. And talk about food! Have you ever eaten mole?

GEORGINA. No, I don't think I have.

HAND. It's turkey with a sauce made of chocolate and about fifteen different kinds of pepper. Sounds revolting, doesn't it?

GEORGINA. It certainly does!

HAND. I'm telling you it's tops. Especially when washed down with a bottle of tequila. You've heard of Taxco, haven't you?

GEORGINA. Yes, of course.

HAND. Well, a friend of mine has a house there that he hardly ever uses. Up on a terraced hill, looking down onto the little village plaza. We'd have dinner in the patio and the local folks would come up and serenade us. Why, I can just see you, done up in a rebozo and—

GEORGINA. You *are* a salesman, aren't you?

(Before HAND *can reply, a* MAN *enters at the left and goes right.)*

THE MAN *(as he passes the table).* Hi, George! How are you doing? *(He waves and goes out at right.)*

HAND. Why, hello, Bert! *(Excitedly to* GEORGINA.*)* This is really from the gods!

You know who that is? Bert Glover, the fellow who owns the house in Taxco. *(Jumping up.)* Excuse me! I'll be right back!

GEORGINA. No, wait, please!

HAND. I won't be a minute! *(He exits quickly at right.* GEORGINA *looks after him for a moment, considerably agitated, then sits back, dreamily, lost in her imaginings. As the lights fade slowly on the scene, the sound of singing is heard, center. The lights come up on a corner of an exotic patio bathed in moonlight. A trio of musical-comedy Mexicans is strumming guitars and singing a sentimental Spanish love song. The leader of the trio, a tall, good-looking young man, has the face of* CLARK REDFIELD. *After a moment,* GEORGINA *and* HAND *stroll on at the right,* GEORGINA *wearing a mantilla and bright shawl and carrying a fan. He has his arm about her. They stand listening to the music. The song ends and the* SERENADERS *cover their hearts with their sombreros and bow low.)*

GEORGINA *(clapping her hands).* Oh, lovely, lovely! Buena! Buena! Muchas gracias!

HAND. That was great! *(Reaching into his pocket.)* Here's something for you, boys. *(The* LEADER *comes forward, holding out his sombrero.* HAND *drops a fistful of coins into it.)*

THE SINGER. Gracias, señor! Muchas gracias! Buenas noches, señor! Buenas noches, señorita! *(He bends over* GEORGINA's *hand and kisses it.)*

GEORGINA. Buenas noches! Hasta la vista, caballero!

THE SINGER. Hasta la vista, señorita! Viva los Americanos! *(Bowing and smiling, the* SERENADERS *exit.)*

GEORGINA. Viva Mé-hi-co! Oh, this is really heavenly. That wonderful moon, this clear cool air, filled with the scent of flowers, and that charming song—

HAND. What about that charming singer? Good thing I'm broad-minded. That young man seemed to take quite a fancy to you.

GEORGINA. It's strange. There's something so familiar about him. And yet I can't think of whom he reminds me. (*She fans herself throughout.*)

HAND. Well, don't bother. You're supposed to be concentrating on me, you know. By the way, where did you pick up all that Spanish? Why, you talk it like a native.

GEORGINA (*modestly*). Oh, don't be silly. But I was always good at languages, and Señor Gonzales at Berlitz did tell me I have a good accent.

HAND. Next time you see him, you can tell him I said you're an all-around good girl.

GEORGINA. Well, I'm glad you think so. Oh, that exquisite food! Who would have believed that turkey with chocolate sauce could taste like that!

HAND. I was right about it, wasn't I?

GEORGINA. Indeed you were! You were right about lots of things. Only—well, I can't help thinking that tomorrow all this will end.

HAND. Georgina, there's something I want to say to you. I knew darned well that when you finally agreed to this, it was only because you thought maybe I could help you forget somebody it made you unhappy to think about. It's true, isn't it?

GEORGINA. Yes, it's true. I was trying to escape, desperately running away from a situation I didn't know how to cope with.

HAND. Then tell me something else. Have I helped you forget?

GEORGINA. Yes, George, you have. That's why it's so hard— No, I won't say it!

HAND. You've said all you need to say, all I wanted to know. Georgina, I thought I had nothing more to learn about women, but I was wrong. I don't want this to be the end, but just the beginning.

GEORGINA. Why do you say such things, when you know it's impossible?

HAND. No, it's not impossible. In fact it's all arranged. While you were at the market this afternoon, I called up my wife. I told her I want a divorce and—

GEORGINA. No, I won't hear of it! I'm not one of those girls that breaks up marriages.

That's one reason I've said no to every married man who—

HAND. Wait a minute! You're not breaking up any marriage. My wife jumped at the suggestion. It seems she's interested in some band leader and she had just about made up her mind to ask me for a divorce.

GEORGINA. Are you telling me the truth?

HAND. I couldn't lie to you. I respect you too much, and anyhow I know you're too smart for me to get away with it. Georgina, this is really from the gods! You *can't* say no!

GEORGINA. I—I don't know, George. You've got to give me time to think— (*As they move right and the lights fade on the scene.*) I must have time to think!

(*The lights come up slowly at the right. GEORGINA is seated at the table, as before, lost in her dreams and fanning herself with the luncheon check. She does not see HAND as he hurries on at the right.*)

HAND (*coming up to the table*). Well, we're in great luck. Everything is—

GEORGINA (*almost jumping out of her seat*). Oh! Goodness, you nearly frightened me out of my wits!

HAND. Sorry! You look as though you'd been a million miles away. (*Sitting beside her.*) Listen, Georgina, I've fixed it all up with Bert.

GEORGINA. Bert?

HAND. Yes, about the house in Taxco. He just was down there and won't be going again for months. It's just sitting there waiting for us. Well, what do you say?

GEORGINA. Well, goodness, I can't give you an answer just like that!

HAND. Yes, you can! Never fight your impulses. Take it from me, the things we really regret in life are not those we do, but those we don't do.

GEORGINA. I've got to have time to make up my mind.

HAND. All right. How much time do you want—two days, a week?

GEORGINA. Do you have to pin me down like that?

HAND. Sure I do! Because when a gay time is lost, it's lost forever.

GEORGINA. Well, I'll—I'll think it over. (*Looking at her watch.*) Goodness, it's nearly three o'clock. I've got to get back to the shop. (*She rises.*)

HAND (*signing the check*). And I've got a deskful of work. Can I drop you?

GEORGINA. No, you run along. I want to powder my nose. (*Extending her hand.*) Thanks for a marvelous lunch.

HAND (*holding her hand*). Remember what the voice of experience is saying to you: Don't resist your impulses. Goodby! I won't leave you in peace for long!

GEORGINA (*as he goes off*). Well—! (*She stands looking after him, greatly flustered. A* WAITER *enters, picks up the check, and starts to clear the table.*) Oh, do you think I could have another brandy?

THE WAITER. Certainly, madam. The imported?

GEORGINA. What? Oh, yes, the imported, by all means.

THE WAITER. Yes, madam. (*He goes.* GEORGINA *sits at the table.*)

GEORGINA (*gloomily*). So now you're taking to drink, are you? Just like all the other misfits who can't face their problems and try to make alcohol a substitute for character. Oh, Georgina, Georgina, my girl, you're really in a bad way! (*She shakes her head dolefully, as the lights fade and the curtain falls.*)

CURTAIN

ACT TWO

As the curtain rises, the lights come up on the bookshop, at stage left, as in Act I. CLAIRE *is straightening books on the shelves. A moment later,* GEORGINA *enters, considerably exhilarated.*

GEORGINA. I'm back.

CLAIRE. I was just about to call the Juvenile Delinquents' Court. (*Seeing Georgina's new hat.*) Well, for heaven's sake! (*She examines it at close range.*) Colette has really outdone herself.

GEORGINA. Like it?

CLAIRE. I'm green with envy. How did Mr. Hand react to it?

GEORGINA. He was very polite about it.

CLAIRE. Now, don't hold out on me. Come on, tell Auntie Claire everything that happened.

GEORGINA. Well, we ate and ate, and drank and drank, and talked and talked.

CLAIRE. What did you talk about?

GEORGINA. Oh, all sorts of things. You were right about his intentions. He wants me to go to Mexico with him.

CLAIRE. Just like that? Well, he's obviously not a man who lets the grass grow under his feet.

GEORGINA. No, he isn't. He's been to Mexico and knows all the places to go. Besides that, a friend of his has a house in Taxco and we could have the use of it.

CLAIRE. But how romantic!

GEORGINA. It is sort of. And I've always wanted to go to Mexico.

CLAIRE. Yes, they say that travel broadens the mind. And *he* certainly sounds like a broad-minded boy.

GEORGINA. Well, I must say he was nice and frank about the whole thing. He didn't try to give me any line or pretend a lot of things. He just frankly put it up to me.

CLAIRE. Uh-huh! The direct frontal attack or appeal to the intelligence. After all, we're living in the twentieth century. Let's be modern about this thing. Very flattering.

GEORGINA (*removing her hat*). I suppose so. But I prefer it to the usual line of flattery. If I'm going into something like this, I'd rather go in with my eyes open.

CLAIRE. And are you going into it?

GEORGINA. I promised him I'd think it over.

CLAIRE. Why, Georgina Allerton!

GEORGINA. Does that shock you?

CLAIRE. Well, it just doesn't sound like you. Tell me, are you in love with him?

GEORGINA. Well, he's a clever, successful, good-looking man. And I am attracted to him. He's not making any demand of me, or pretending he's in love with me. If it's all right for him, why isn't it for me?

CLAIRE. You're desperately logical about it.

GEORGINA. Why do men have to have a monopoly on logic?

CLAIRE. I don't know. But somehow, when a woman falls back on logic—

GEORGINA. That's just a hangover from the days when women led sheltered lives. It's time we stopped being a lot of fluttery, scatterbrained little ninnies, who have to rely on something called intuition. Why can't we work out our own problems, just as men do, by using our intelligence?

CLAIRE. It really looks as though Mr. Hand *has* been using the right technique!

GEORGINA. He's not fooling me with any technique. I'm thinking very clearly about the whole thing, and entirely from my own point of view. After all, what would be the harm in it? It's not so unusual these days for a girl to—

CLAIRE. Oh, I don't think it's likely that you'd be put in the stocks and branded with a large, scarlet capital A.

GEORGINA. You mean I might be hurt emotionally? All right, suppose I did get hurt a little! It might be the best thing in the world for me—just what I need, maybe. If I don't begin to have some experiences soon, when will I begin?

CLAIRE. And yet I never met a girl who seemed less eager to go off on a toot with George Hand.

GEORGINA. He thinks I'm puritanical, and I'm afraid he may be right.

CLAIRE. Afraid?

GEORGINA. Well, after all, what is a puritan? Just somebody with such strong desires that she doesn't dare let herself cut loose.

CLAIRE. Oh, so that's what you're afraid of! You think if you say yes to him it will just be your first step on the road to hell?

GEORGINA. That *would* be pretty awful, wouldn't it?

CLAIRE. It would indeed! Well, darling, I think I'll pop out and do some shopping. Think you can look after the trade by yourself?

GEORGINA. Oh, damn it! I wish you'd be a little helpful.

CLAIRE. No, my pet! This is between you and your guardian angel—and I can't wait to see who wins!

GEORGINA (*as* CLAIRE *exits*). Neither can I! (*She sits lost in thought as the lights fade slowly on the scene. To the music of "Poor Butterfly," the lights come up at center on a red fire-alarm lamppost. In the background is an illuminated sign bearing the legend "Joyland."* GEORGINA *enters and swaggers to the lamppost. She wears a cheap red coat with a ratty fur collar and a gaudy hat perched on a tousled blonde wig.* GEORGE HAND, *accompanied by a girl who resembles* MIRIAM, *emerges from the darkness, at the right.*)

HAND (*as they cross*). Well, Arabella, if you've never eaten at Antoine's in New Orleans, you really don't know what food is.

ARABELLA. Yes, so I've heard.

HAND (*glancing at* GEORGINA *as he passes her*). We'd start with oysters Rockefeller, which Ford Madox Ford, who was a great epicure, describes as swimming in a kind of green scum. (*Stopping at left.*) Excuse me a moment! (*He turns and goes back to* GEORGINA, *who starts to go, as she sees him approaching.*)

HAND (*detaining her*). Just a minute, please!

GEORGINA (*in a rough voice*). Hands off, you!

HAND (*turning her about*). Why, I was right! It's Georgina Allerton.

GEORGINA. Well, what's it *to* you?

HAND. What are you doing here, hanging around a street corner?

GEORGINA. Looking after my trade, that's what!

HAND. But—a girl like you! What's brought you to this?

GEORGINA. It would give you a kick, wouldn't it, to hear all about it? You're all like that!

HAND. But in Mexico, you were such a gay, proud girl, full of the joy of living; and dreaming of all the things you were going to do.

GEORGINA (*harshly*). I didn't know how easy it would be to say yes, the next time someone asked me. And the next time after that, it was easier still. Then they stopped asking me—and I began asking them. Now you know all about it. So, go ahead and scram.

HAND. Georgina, if there's anything I can—

GEORGINA. To hell with that! I don't want your pity.

HAND. Well, let me, at least— (*He takes a bill from his pocket and offers it to her.* GEORGINA *snatches it and tears it up.*)

GEORGINA. Go on, now! Beat it! Your girl friend is waiting for you!

(HAND *sighs, shakes his head, and goes left.*)

ARABELLA (*as he rejoins her*). For heaven's sake, what was that all about?

HAND (*as they exit*). It's tragic. I used to know that girl, years ago. And, believe it or not, she was a sweet, modest little—

(*His voice trails off. The tune changes to "Broadway Rose."* GEORGINA *buries her face in her hands and sobs, then as she hears a* MAN *whistling off right, she straightens up and resumes her place at the lamppost.* CLARK REDFIELD *strides on, whistling merrily. He glances quickly at* GEORGINA *as he passes her*).

GEORGINA. Got a date for tonight, dearie?

CLARK. Sorry, baby, but I've got a little wife waiting for me. (*He is about to exit, then stops and turns.*) Say, haven't I seen you somewhere before?

GEORGINA (*brazenly*). Have you?

CLARK. Why, sure enough! You're that girl who used to run that crummy little bookshop on East—! Well, I'll be damned!

GEORGINA (*savagely*). What the hell's so funny about it?

CLARK. Why, who'd have thought it? Little Miss—whatever your name is! The budding literary genius, the highly cultivated young college grad, who lectured me about my manners and thought sports writing was vulgar. Well, it looks like you're doing a little in the sporting line yourself.

GEORGINA. Shut up, you great big ape! (*She slaps his face.*)

CLARK (*in a rage*). Oh, that's how you feel about it, is it? Well, I'll show you! There's a place for tramps like you. (*He goes left.*) Officer! Officer! (*He disappears in the darkness.* GEORGINA *looks about, in terror, then opens her handbag, takes out a small bottle, and drains it. The tune changes to "Hearts and Flowers."*)

JIM (*off right*). Georgina! Stop! For God's sake, stop! (*He rushes on.*)

GEORGINA (*with a wan smile, as she throws the bottle away*). You're too late, Jim. Nothing can save me, now.

JIM. Why have you done this, Georgina? Why? Why didn't you come to me? I would have—

GEORGINA. No, Jim, I couldn't do that. You have Miriam and those three lovely children. Once I brought you two together again, there was no place for me in your life. There's no place for me anywhere. (*She totters.*) Hold me, Jim, hold me! I'm— (*She collapses into his arms.*)

JIM. Georgina, I—

GEORGINA (*faintly*). Don't say anything, Jim. Just hold me. I wanted to live in your arms, but it wasn't meant to be. So let me die in them. It's the only happiness I'll ever know now. Good-by, Jim. Kiss Mother and Dad for me. And ask them to forgive me. And try not to forget me, Jim. There was never anybody for me but you—

JIM. I'll never forget you—never!

GEORGINA. Thank you, Jim. Good-by, darling. (*Standing erect, for a moment.*) It is a far, far better thing that I do than I have ever done. It is a far, far better rest I go to than I have ever known

(She clasps her abdomen in agony, pivots on her heels, and falls inert.)

JIM *(kneeling beside her)*. Georgina! Georgina, my darling! *(CLARK reappears at left, accompanied by a POLICEMAN.)*

THE POLICEMAN. Is that her?

CLARK. Yes, she accosted me! She's nothing but a common—! My God, what's happened to her?

JIM *(looking up)*. She's gone where no one can harm her, now.

CLARK *(removing his hat)*. You mean she's—?

JIM. Yes, Clark Redfield, she is.

CLARK *(with an agonized cry)*. Oh, no! Oh, why did I do it? If only I'd been a little human to her—! *(Turning to the policeman.)* Officer, arrest me! Take me away!

THE POLICEMAN. What for?

CLARK. I'm a murderer. I killed that girl as surely as though I had stabbed her to the heart.

THE POLICEMAN. Then, come along! *(He snaps handcuffs onto CLARK as the light fades on the scene and the clanging of a patrol-wagon bell is heard. The sound merges into that of a ringing telephone. The lights come up left on the bookshop. GEORGINA, seated moodily, is startled by the ringing of the telephone. She hurries to it and answers it.)*

GEORGINA *(greatly flustered)*. Hello! Mermaid Bookshop! *(As she speaks, the lights come up, stage right, on a telephone booth in which CLARK REDFIELD is standing.)*

CLARK. Is Miss Allerton there?

GEORGINA. This is she.

CLARK. Oh, I didn't recognize your voice. You sound scared to death.

GEORGINA *(sharply)*. Who is this, please?

CLARK. Clark Redfield.

GEORGINA *(who knew it all along)*. Oh, it's you, is it? Well, what is it?

CLARK. I want to ask you to—

GEORGINA. I don't care to hear any apologies. The whole thing is of no consequence whatever. I was foolish to let my temper get the better of me. And, as far as I'm concerned, the whole incident is closed.

CLARK. Yes, you have got a temper, haven't you? But are you under the impression that I called up to apologize for something?

GEORGINA. Well, I guess that's foolish too—to expect you to have that much graciousness. Look, I'm quite busy and if you don't mind—

CLARK. I'll bet you haven't done a thing all afternoon.

GEORGINA. If you'll excuse me, Mr. Redfield—

CLARK. Whoa! Wait a minute! Don't hang up on me! I'm calling to ask you—

GEORGINA. Well, what? Please get to the point, will you?

CLARK. I've got a pair of tickets for a show tonight and I thought you might like to—

GEORGINA. Well, of all the unmitigated—! You really *have* got the hide of an elephant. What makes you think I'd consider—

CLARK. Well, it's the opening of *The Merchant of Venice*, with James Zerney as Shylock. And I thought that might appeal to a lover of the classics.

GEORGINA. Well, under ordinary circumstances, it certainly would. Especially with Hilda Vincent playing Portia; but I'm afraid—

CLARK. Is she a favorite of yours?

GEORGINA. It just happens that we went to college together and—

CLARK. Good! Then it's a date!

GEORGINA *(indignantly)*. It certainly is *not* a date! But thank you all the same, though I can't imagine why you—

CLARK. I can't, either. It was just an impulse and I—

GEORGINA. You don't strike me as the impulsive type. I should rather think of you as decidedly calculating.

CLARK. All right. What do you say we settle for a calculated impulse? *(As the operator cuts in.)* All right, just a minute!

GEORGINA. What's that?

CLARK (*fishing in his pockets*). The operator wants another nickel.

GEORGINA. Well, there's no necessity for prolonging—

CLARK. No, wait a minute, Georgina! No, I'm not talking to you, operator. Listen, I haven't got a nickel, operator. (*Flourishing a bill.*) Can you change five dollars for me? Well, where's all that service you people do so much advertising about? Just a second! Look, Georgina, call me back, will you?

GEORGINA. I have nothing further to—

CLARK. No, call me back! The number is Circle 5-7933. Hello! Hello! Oh, damn it! (*He bangs down the receiver, leans back in the booth, and lights a cigarette.*)

GEORGINA. I tell you I—hello! (*She hangs up, and slowly jots down the number on a pad. Then she sits staring at the telephone. She raises her forefinger as though to dial, then lowers it again. The phone rings and she jumps. Picking up the phone.*) I thought you didn't have another—

(*The lights come up quickly at center on* GEORGE HAND *seated at his desk, and talking into the telephone. Throughout,* CLARK *keeps looking at his telephone, waiting for it to ring.*)

HAND. Hello? Is that you, Georgina?

GEORGINA. Yes. Who is this? (*Knowing full well.*)

HAND. This is George. Anything wrong? You sound jumpy.

GEORGINA. It must be all those brandies. I'm not used to—

HAND. Why, I'll have to put you back in training. Look, honey, a business dinner date just blew up on me, so I thought maybe you'd take pity on a poor guy with an evening on his hands and—

GEORGINA (*nervously*). Oh, I really don't think I can tonight, George— (CLARK *is beginning to get impatient.*)

HAND. We can take our time over a nice dinner somewhere and then go dancing —or to a show, if you'd rather.

GEORGINA. I only wish I could. If you'd only called up a half hour sooner! I just promised somebody I'd go to the theater.

HAND. Tough luck! But I called the minute I knew I'd be free. Why don't you get out of it?

GEORGINA. I don't see how, after just saying yes, ten minutes ago.

HAND. Well, then, how about cocktails and dinner? Or a drink after the show?

GEORGINA. I'm afraid that's all included.

HAND. Say, who is this monopolist? I'll sick the Attorney General on him!

GEORGINA. It's nothing like that. Just one of those things that you get into and can't get out of.

HAND. Well, try to get out of at least some part of it. I do want to see you.

GEORGINA. All right, I'll try my best.

HAND. Shall I call you back?

GEORGINA. No, I'm just leaving. If I can fix it, I'll call you.

(CLARK *leaves the booth, and starts to exit, then changes his mind and comes back.*)

HAND. Well, I'll keep my fingers crossed. Because I've got you very much on my mind. And if I do lose tonight, I'll owe you lunch tomorrow—yes?

GEORGINA. All right! Good-by, George. And thanks.

HAND. Good-by, dear.

(*He hangs up and the lights fade out quickly on him.* GEORGINA *hangs up and leans back with a deep sigh. Then she stares at the telephone number, hesitates a moment, then starts slowly to dial.*)

CLARK (*with sudden anger*). Oh, to hell with it! (*He leaves the booth and strides off, right. The phone in the booth rings, then again and once again.* GEORGINA, *very much annoyed, is about to hang up, but* CLARK *comes tearing back and picks up the phone in the booth just in time.*) Hello! Is that you?

GEORGINA. Well, you certainly took your time about answering.

CLARK. I fell asleep waiting for you to call. What's the matter, have you got telephone operator's cramp or something?

GEORGINA. I happened to have another call. You seem to forget I'm running a business.

CLARK. Running conveys an idea of activity.

GEORGINA. The only reason I called back is that I don't want you to have the false impression that I'm sufficiently interested in anything you may have said, this morning or at any other time, to make me feel the slightest bit of resentment.

CLARK (whistling). Phew! I was afraid you were never going to get to the end of that one! Now, to get back to *The Merchant of Venice*—

GEORGINA. Yes, exactly. In the first place, I have no interest whatever in being taken to the theater by you. But I *would* like to see Hilda Vincent play Portia, so—

CLARK. Right! So you'll go.

GEORGINA. Will you please let me finish?

CLARK. If you think you can by eight-forty.

GEORGINA. What I started to say is that I'll consider it only on a strictly business basis.

CLARK. I have a feeling that neither of us knows what you're talking about.

GEORGINA. What I mean is that if you have an extra ticket on your hands, I'll be glad to buy it from you.

CLARK. Can't be done. These are press seats.

GEORGINA (interestedly). Oh, are you going to review the play?

CLARK. I am not. I got them from our movie critic. His mother is getting married tonight and he has to give her away.

GEORGINA. Do the movie critics get tickets for plays, too?

CLARK. Look, Georgina, this is one of those phones where you have to stand up. How about meeting me at—

GEORGINA. Are you dressing?

CLARK. Certainly not! Nobody dresses for Shakespeare, unless Bea Lillie happens to be in it.

GEORGINA. Then I'll meet you in the lobby at eight-thirty. Unless you want to leave the ticket with the ticket-taker.

CLARK. No, I don't! How about dinner?

GEORGINA. I'll have dinner somewhere.

CLARK. You're a resourceful girl. I think I'll do likewise. Maybe we could have it at the same place—purely by coincidence, of course.

GEORGINA. Thank you, but I don't care to—

CLARK. Look, one of the things I don't like to do is eat alone. It makes me feel so unwanted. You don't have to say a word. I'll do all the talking. And you can read a book or sulk in your beer or whatever you like.

GEORGINA. Well—only if it's clearly understood that we go Dutch.

CLARK. I was thinking of going Italian. Do you know Emilio's?

GEORGINA. No, I don't.

CLARK. Well, it's just a spaghetti and red ink joint, but what would be called, in France, a serious house. They have—

GEORGINA. There's no reason why you should take me to dinner and I—

CLARK. There are two reasons—both valid from my point of view. The first is that that five bucks I got from you is burning a hole in my pocket. And the second is that I have something to celebrate.

GEORGINA. Well, I'm afraid I haven't.

CLARK. All right, then, you can watch *me* celebrate. Listen, I'm getting acute claustrophobia. Emilio's at seven.

GEORGINA. I don't know why I'm doing this.

CLARK. Good! That will give you something to brood over at dinner while I talk. I'm hanging up now.

GEORGINA. Just a minute! Where is this Emilio's?

CLARK. Oh, yes, you may as well know *that*. Forty-seventh, just west of Eighth. Good-by!

GEORGINA. Oh, just one other thing— (Then, hastily, as JIM enters.) All right,

Emilio's at seven. *(She hangs up. The light fades quickly on* CLARK.*)*

GEORGINA *(flustered).* Oh, hello, Jim!

JIM. Yes, here I am, back again. But only to ask you if you can have dinner with me.

GEORGINA. Oh, I'm sorry, Jim! I just this minute made a date. Maybe I can break it—only I'm not sure that I know where to—

JIM. That's too bad. I was hoping we could—

GEORGINA. How about lunch tomorrow? I have a sort of tentative date, but I guess I can get out of it.

JIM. I won't be here tomorrow. I'm leaving for Reno tonight.

GEORGINA. You're going to Reno? But I thought you said Miriam—

JIM. Yes, I've had another session with Miriam. She made a great to-do about being separated from her obstetrician, so I said I'd go. Georgina, I've got something very important to say to you, and since I have only these few minutes, you'll forgive me if I seem blunt about it.

GEORGINA. Well, what is it?

JIM. Well, I came here this morning, without knowing why; it was just sheer impulse. But now I do know why. It was because it's you I've always wanted, because unconsciously I've always been reaching out for you.

GEORGINA *(greatly agitated).* You're just imagining all that. It's the way people always behave when they're going through an emotional crisis.

JIM. Yes, I knew you'd say that. You think I'm just turning to you on the bounce. But it isn't so, and I know now that you're the answer to everything I want and need. Does that make you unhappy?

GEORGINA. Oh, no, Jim. Not unhappy. It's just that this is the last thing in the world I was expecting.

JIM. Well, if it disturbs you so, it must mean that you have some deep feeling for me, too. Does it, Georgina? Please be honest with me.

GEORGINA. All right! I will be honest! Yes, I do care for you. I always have, ever since I've known you.

JIM. Then why are you so troubled about it?

GEORGINA. Because I'm afraid you may feel quite differently about it, sitting out there in Reno for six weeks with plenty of time to think it over. Why don't we wait and see if you still feel the same way when you come back to New York?

JIM. I'm not coming back to New York. I've had enough of cities and the treadmill life you have to lead in them. I want to be able to breathe for once. I'm going to find myself a place where I can see the stars and smell the earth.

GEORGINA. Yes, I've often dreamed of that. Just running off somewhere, anywhere— and with you, too!

JIM. Then why don't you get on that plane with me tonight?

GEORGINA. It's not as simple as all that, Jim. People daydream about all sorts of things. But when you're faced with actuality, you have to stop and think. If a man and woman are going to spend their lives together, they must have some plan, some way of living.

JIM. Of course they do. But why can't it be a simple one? Why can't we get ourselves a little farm, or a ranch? We'll work the land together, and work at other things too. I've always wanted to paint, and you have your writing—

GEORGINA. No, I don't think I want to go on with that. Clark Redfield says my novel is a piece of tripe.

JIM. Why do you pay any attention to him? I'll back my judgment of that book to the limit. It expresses all the things that you and I believe in, and beautifully too. Georgina, if you feel that you'd rather not go with me now, promise me at least that you'll come out and join me when I've got my decree.

GEORGINA. It all means too much to me, Jim, to be able to say yes, just like that. First, I want to be absolutely sure that this is right for both of us.

JIM. Well, I'm completely confident about your decision, because I know that this is meant to be. Well, I've got to run along now and pick up my ticket. I wish I could see you again, before I leave, if only for a moment.

GEORGINA. So do I. But I'm afraid I won't be free until after the theater.

JIM. Well, my plane doesn't leave until one. Why don't you meet me at the air terminal about twelve and ride out to the airport with me?

(The telephone rings.)

GEORGINA *(going to the telephone)*. Excuse me, Jim. Mermaid Bookshop.

(As she answers the telephone, the lights go up at right on MRS. ALLERTON, *seated at the telephone in her negligee, as in Act I. A book is beside her.)*

MRS. ALLERTON. I have some news for you, Georgina.

GEORGINA. Oh, just a minute, please. *(Covering the transmitter.)* All right, Jim. I'll be at the air terminal at twelve.

JIM. Thank you, Georgina. *(He presses her free hand, and exits.)*

GEORGINA. I'm sorry, Mother. I had to get rid of a customer.

MRS. ALLERTON. That's right. Don't encourage them. Tell me, have you heard from Miriam?

GEORGINA. No, I haven't.

MRS. ALLERTON. Jim, either?

GEORGINA. No, why? Is anything wrong?

MRS. ALLERTON. On the contrary. They're divorcing. Jim is leaving for Reno tonight. Miriam didn't want to go and since Jim is at leisure again, we decided to ship him out. Of course, I'm footing the bills; but this is one expenditure poor old Grandpa would certainly have approved of.

GEORGINA. Well, I don't approve. I think it's awful.

MRS. ALLERTON. I expected you would. That's why I'm calling you—to warn you not to try to upset things, in case Jim comes crying to you.

GEORGINA. What makes you think he has any intention of doing that?

MRS. ALLERTON. Just a hunch. I suspect that it's you he's always been in love with. *(She sneezes.)*

GEORGINA. Why, Mother, how can you say things like that!

MRS. ALLERTON. Well, maybe it's just this irritation of my mucous membrane that makes me think so. But, if he does turn up, be careful not to say anything that will keep him off that plane. I only hope and pray that he's subject to airsickness. *(A sneeze.)* Well, now that everything is settled I can get back to Opal. I certainly do envy that girl.

GEORGINA. Really, Mother!

MRS. ALLERTON. I just don't understand how she can spend so much time without any clothes on and not catch her death of cold. Well, good-by.

GEORGINA. Oh, I won't be home till late. I'm having dinner out and going to the opening of *The Merchant of Venice*—and somewhere else afterwards.

MRS. ALLERTON. Oh, I hope there's a promising male involved.

GEORGINA. No, there isn't. It's just a boorish, conceited newspaperman in whom nobody could have the slightest interest.

MRS. ALLERTON. Sounds like a charming evening.

GEORGINA. Well, I haven't been to a first night in years. Besides, Hilda Vincent is playing Portia and I want to see her.

MRS. ALLERTON. What is there in it for the young man?

GEORGINA. I don't know. I haven't any idea why he asked me, except that he's sadistic and is planning to spend the evening making me feel uncomfortable.

MRS. ALLERTON. Well, it certainly looks as though Mr. Right had come along at last. Well, have fun. *(As she hangs up, the lights fade on her.* GEORGINA *hangs up. She sits for a moment, steeped in gloom, then rises, and picks up her hat.)*

GEORGINA *(looking at the hat)*. No, not for that uncouth person. *(She replaces the hat on the desk and exits. The lights fade on the scene and come up center, on* CLARK, *seated at a table in Emilio's, a modest*

Italian restaurant. He is munching a bread stick and listening to a Caruso record.)

GEORGINA *(entering as the record comes to an end).* Sorry to be late.

CLARK *(half rising).* O.K. I was just listening to Caruso and wondering if you'd decided to stand me up.

GEORGINA *(sitting at the table).* That doesn't happen to be my way of doing things.

CLARK. All right. Let's not start fighting right away. We have the whole evening ahead of us. *(Calling.)* Oh, Luigi!

LUIGI *(entering).* Yes, Meester Redfield.

CLARK. I think we'll order now. *(To GEORGINA.)* How about a drink first?

GEORGINA. I'd like a Martini.

CLARK. Not with good Italian food. Look, do you mind if I do the ordering?

GEORGINA. Of course not! You know what I want much better than I do.

CLARK. Now you're talking sense! All right, Luigi, we'll have a mixed Vermouth to start with—two parts dry and one part sweet, frappéed and with a slice of lemon peel.

LUIGI. O.K., Meester Redfield. And some antipasto?

CLARK. No, not all that miscellaneous stuff. Just those little bitter olives and some prosciutto.

LUIGI. Then a little minestrone?

GEORGINA. Not for me, thanks. I'm on a diet and I had a huge lunch.

CLARK *(to LUIGI).* Yes, let's have minestrone. Then some spaghetti.

LUIGI. Marinara?

CLARK. No, Bolognese. And then how about a nice scallopini à la Parmigiana?

LUIGI. Ees very good!

CLARK. No, wait a minute! Let's have the scallopini à la Marsala. And eggplant Parmigiana with it.

LUIGI. O.K.

GEORGINA. I hope you're not ordering all this for me, because I really—

CLARK *(ignoring her).* And a mixed green salad. Any zuppe Inglese tonight?

LUIGI. I think so.

CLARK. Well, save a couple portions for us.

GEORGINA *(tartly.)* You already ordered soup!

CLARK. Soup? Oh, you mean zuppe Inglese. Yes, literally English soup, but actually a kind of rum cake. What they call trifle in England. Depend on the English to make any kind of food sound unappetizing.

LUIGI. And about the wine. Some Chianti? Or maybe Lacrime Cristi?

CLARK. Have you got any of that Falerno left?

LUIGI. I guess we got a few bottles.

CLARK. Let's have that. All right, I think that's all for the present.

LUIGI. O.K., Meester Redfield. *(He exits.)*

GEORGINA. What are we going to do with all that when it comes?

CLARK. Eat it. I'm not sure that the Falerno is better than the Lacrime Cristi, but it gives me a kick to drink a wine that is a lineal descendant of the Falernian of ancient Rome. Attica nectareum turbatis mella Falernum. Honey of Attica make thick the nectar-like Falernian. I forget who said it. Do you know?

GEORGINA. No, I don't. I went in for modern languages. Spanish and—

CLARK. I tried that once, thickening the wine with honey. But maybe I had the wrong formula. Or maybe the Romans had different tastes. So you're a friend of Hilda Vincent's?

GEORGINA. Well, not a friend, exactly. We just happened to be at college together. So, naturally, I've always been interested in her work.

CLARK. I know, the old school tie.

GEORGINA. Besides, I once played Portia.

CLARK. You what?

GEORGINA. It was our high school graduation play. Of course, it was only an amateur production, but I don't think I did too badly. I still know the whole thing by heart. At that time, I wanted very much to become an actress.

CLARK. Well, why didn't you?

GEORGINA. Oh, I don't know. My father wanted me to be a lawyer, so I just went along with that, for a while. I even tried one semester at law school. (Sighing.) And now, of course, it's too late to do anything about acting.

CLARK. So you turned to literature?

GEORGINA. Let's keep off that subject, if you don't mind.

CLARK. Which reminds me that I've brought back your novel. (He produces a large envelope from under the table.)

GEORGINA (tartly). That's very thoughtful of you, I'm sure. But it might have been a little more practical to have brought it back tomorrow, instead of lugging it all through dinner and theater.

CLARK. Aren't you forgetting that you told me never to enter your shop again?

GEORGINA (tight-lipped). You could have mailed it.

CLARK (weighing the envelope in his hand). A heck of a lot of postage. And suppose some little postal inspector had peeped into it? Those poor devils have a hard enough life as it is.

GEORGINA. You said you were celebrating something tonight. Did some friend of yours die?

CLARK. Well, it's almost as good as that. Oliver Quinn is leaving the paper.

GEORGINA. I suppose I *should* know who Oliver Quinn is.

CLARK. Yes, you certainly should. He writes one of the three best sports columns in the country.

GEORGINA. Excuse my ignorance. But I never read the sports page—

CLARK. Yes, so you told me. But several million other people do. Of course, most of them are not important people, but still, as you'll hear Portia say, later in the evening, God made them, so therefore let them pass for men. Well, anyhow, Oliver is leaving the paper to take the chair of Icelandic literature at the University of Michigan. That means promotions all

along the line and an opening at the bottom, which the chief says is for me. (As LUIGI enters.) And here, opportunely, is Luigi, so we'll drink to my good luck. (He picks up the glass which Luigi has set before him. LUIGI exits.)

GEORGINA (picking up her glass.) Well, if you consider it good luck—

CLARK. I do indeed, and thanks for the toast.

GEORGINA (savoring the drink). This is quite good.

CLARK. Careful! Don't commit yourself. These olives go well with it.

GEORGINA (taking one). Thank you.

CLARK. And try a little of this raw ham. (He helps her to some.)

GEORGINA. I hope it doesn't give us trichinosis.

CLARK. What in hell is that?

GEORGINA. It's a horrible intestinal disorder you get from eating undercooked pork.

CLARK. Really? Well, if we do get it, it will probably be the only thing we'll ever have in common, so let's go to it. (He takes a large mouthful.)

GEORGINA. I didn't believe that you were serious, this morning, about wanting to be a sports writer.

CLARK. If I have a fault, Georgina, it's that I incline to the serious side.

GEORGINA. I can't understand it. People getting all excited about which team scores the most runs or who knocks out who.

CLARK. Nothing hard about that. Every time the champ comes up with a haymaker, forty thousand customers are taking a swing at the boss or the traffic cop. And when the King of Swat whams it into the bleachers, a million flat-chested runts are right in there, whizzing around the bases.

GEORGINA. That's nothing but escapism.

CLARK. That's right. Like the girls out of college who slam the door with Nora, take a nose dive into the brook with Ophelia, or tumble into a lot of Louis Quartorze beds with Opal.

GEORGINA. We'll just pass over the personal implications and confine ourselves to the abstract question whether an interest in sports and an interest in literature—

CLARK. There is no such thing as an abstract discussion between a man and a woman.

GEORGINA. Well, *that* certainly reveals a narrow and conventional mind.

CLARK. Who's getting personal now? You see, every road we take leads right back to that novel of yours.

GEORGINA. Will you stop harping on that? What's my novel got to do—! I was certainly an idiot ever to show it to you.

CLARK. But you did! And the reason you did was that you thought you'd produced something creative and wanted to show it off.

GEORGINA. Nothing of the kind! I mistook you for a literary critic and I wanted—

CLARK. Baloney! You were just a fond mamma, showing off her baby and blindly oblivious to the fact that it was just an old rag doll with the straw stuffing coming through. Talk about escapism! Why, there isn't a genuine moment in it—just a rehash of all the lady writers from Jane Austen to Virginia Woolf.

GEORGINA. All right, I've heard enough about that!

CLARK. That's what you think! My God, can't a girl who's been around for twenty-three or -four years find—

GEORGINA. Twenty-two, if you don't mind.

CLARK. I don't mind a bit. If you want to write, can't you produce something better than a lot of moony daydreaming about an idiotic young couple who can't bear escalators and modern plumbing and who go off to the great open spaces to live in simple, unwashed happiness among the mosquitoes and shad flies? There's a tasty dish for you—*Love among the Heifers:* a pastoral in nine cantos, with costumes by Abercrombie and Fitch.

GEORGINA. Anything can be made to sound silly, if you're stupid and literal about it. I happened to be writing a fantasy, about two sensitive people who find themselves hemmed in by the steel and stone of the city and who can find freedom only in—

CLARK. Skip it! Can you imagine any girl in her right mind behaving the way that heroine of yours does?

GEORGINA. Yes, I can. If she cared enough about the man, why wouldn't she be willing to give up a lot of meaningless things for him?

CLARK. What! And go tooting off to some nebulous never-never land with that balmy Jim Lucas of a character.

GEORGINA. What's Jim Lucas got to do with it?

CLARK. That just slipped out. But it's not so far off, at that. No wonder he thinks the story is a world-beater. Why, I'm beginning to think that maybe he sat for that portrait.

GEORGINA. I hope I'm not so literal-minded that I have to write about—

CLARK. I know! I know! Why bother to step outside and look at life, when it's so cozy indoors and there's always a shelfful of books handy? For God's sake, hasn't anything ever happened to you? Have you never been drunk? Or socked a guy for making a pass at you? Or lost your panties on Fifth Avenue?

GEORGINA. You think you're going to make me lose my temper, don't you? Well, I'm sorry to disappoint you, but you're not. However, I do find you even more offensive than I had expected, so, if you'll excuse me, I think I'll just leave you to your splendid repast, while I— (*She starts to rise.*)

CLARK (*pushing her back into her seat*). You'll certainly do nothing of the kind! I told you I don't like eating alone. And what's more, I'm going to protect these friends of mine here. They're artists: the preparation and serving of food is a serious business to them. (*As* LUIGI *enters.*) Here's Luigi now, with the minestrone and a dusty bottle of Falerno. Do you think I'm going to have his feelings lacerated by having you walk out on the soup course? No! It's time you learned some manners.

GEORGINA (*aghast*). I beg your pardon! And to think that I turned down two other invitations to—!

CLARK. Well, that was your mistake. Just as it was my mistake to pass up the Wilinski-O'Connell fight at the Garden. But since we are here, you'll just have to see it through. You can say or do whatever you like to me, but I will not allow Emilio's minestrone to be slighted.

LUIGI (smiling, as he starts to serve the soup). Ees nice and hot.

GEORGINA (with great self-restraint). Very well, I shall eat the minestrone.

LUIGI. A leetle cheese, mees?

GEORGINA. No, thank you.

LUIGI (distressed). Oh, ees no good weed-out cheese.

GEORGINA. Well, just a little then. (As he serves her.) Thank you, that's very nice.

CLARK. A lot for me, Luigi.

LUIGI (beaming). Sure ting, Meester Redfield! (He serves CLARK and goes for the wine.)

CLARK. They really do a beautiful minestrone here, don't they? (GEORGINA eats her soup without replying.) You'd think I owned the joint, wouldn't you, the way I go on? You ought to eat here three or four times a week and build yourself up. You're too damned skinny. (She throws him a look but does not reply.) Personally, I find the natural curves of the female body quite appealing. (As LUIGI approaches with the wine bottle.) Ah, here we are! Luigi, did you know that the ancient Romans drank this wine?

LUIGI. No, I didn' know. I come from Napoli. (He fills the glasses and goes.)

CLARK (sniffing the wine). I want you to taste this. But finish your soup first. I'm glad to see you concentrating on your dinner. I can't stand girls who are so busy gabbing that they just pick at their food.

(GEORGINA throws him a withering look. Apparently oblivious of it, he tears off a morsel of bread and pops it into his mouth. As they go on eating their soup, the lights fade slowly on the scene. To the sound of a string quartet playing Elizabethan music, the lights come up dimly at the left on a section of a theater, consisting of eight or ten seats arranged in three rows. The seats face right and the stage of the theater is presumably off right, beyond the proscenium arch. The aisle of the theater runs right and left, downstage of the seats. All the seats are occupied, except the aisle pair in the first and third rows. After a moment, an USHER enters at left, followed by CLARK and GEORGINA. CLARK has GEORGINA's script tucked under his arm.)

THE USHER (stopping at the third row). First two on the aisle. (She hands CLARK the stubs and programs and exits left. GEORGINA takes the second seat and CLARK the one on the aisle.)

GEORGINA. Well, I'm glad we're not late. I hate to come in after the curtain is up.

CLARK. I knew a girl who was dropped from the social register for admitting that she had seen the first act of a play. She finally put an end to herself, by taking an overdose of caviar.

GEORGINA. Why do you come to the theater at all?

CLARK. It fills that awkward gap between liqueurs and highballs.

GEORGINA. Please don't mention food or drink again!

CLARK. Good dinner, wasn't it?

GEORGINA. Oh, yes, the dinner was fine.

CLARK. There's some reservation there.

GEORGINA (looking at her program). That's lovely music. I wonder what it is.

CLARK. Sounds like Purcell.

GEORGINA (finding it in the program). Why, it is Purcell!

CLARK. Sorry! I always seem to be saying the wrong thing.

GEORGINA. It's certainly a mystery to me— (She breaks off.)

CLARK. Oh, come on! Say it!

GEORGINA. Well, it's just that I don't understand why a person who knows as much as you do has so little knowledge of human nature.

CLARK. You mean I have no knowledge of your nature?

GEORGINA. I mean anybody's nature! Either that or what's even worse, you take pleasure in making people feel uncomfortable.

CLARK. What are you uncomfortable about?

GEORGINA. How would you like it if I had spent the whole evening harping on your shortcomings?

CLARK. I might have found it very instructive.

GEORGINA. There you go again—implying that I am afraid to hear about my deficiencies. That's not what I meant at all.

CLARK. Then what did you mean?

GEORGINA. I mean that there are ways of saying things. No sensible person objects to having things pointed out in a—

CLARK. I see! We're back again on destructive versus constructive criticism.

GEORGINA. Yes, we are. It's one thing to be told, in a friendly spirit, how you might improve yourself in certain respects—

CLARK. In other words, you like to hear about your faults in a way that high-lights your virtues.

GEORGINA. If I listened to you, I'd soon believe that I didn't have any virtues. I don't know anything. I can't do anything. I'm just a total loss. Luckily, I don't attach any importance to your opinion of me.

CLARK. Is that why you keep bringing it up?

GEORGINA *(indignantly)*. Well, what do you think I am, some kind of a jellyfish that's just going to sit and let you—

CLARK. If you'd ever tangled with a jellyfish you'd know they're anything but submissive creatures.

(She buries her nose in the program. The USHER *comes down the aisle, followed by* GEORGE HAND *and a* YOUNG WOMAN *in a spectacular evening gown. The* USHER *stops beside the unoccupied row.)*

USHER. These two.

HAND *(as the* USHER *exits)*. Thank you! *(Seeing* GEORGINA *and going up to her.)* Why, hello, Georgina! Fancy meeting you here!

GEORGINA. Why, hello, George! *(CLARK rises.)*

HAND. This is Miss Delehanty. Tessie, Miss Allerton.

MISS DELEHANTY. Hi!

GEORGINA. How do you do? And this is Mr. Redfield. Miss Delehanty, Mr. Hand.

MISS DELEHANTY *(to* CLARK*)*. Hi!

HAND *(shaking hands with* CLARK*)*. Are you the Redfield who writes those book reviews?

CLARK *(eying* MISS DELEHANTY*)*. Afraid so.

GEORGINA. But he doesn't read the books.

HAND *(laughing)*. Well, thank God for that! Think of what he'd say if he did read them. Well, I guess we'd better settle down, Tessie.

MISS DELEHANTY. Yeah! *(She and* HAND *sit in the first row.)*

CLARK *(sotto voce)*. What's his name—Hand?

GEORGINA. George Hand. He's one of the biggest book jobbers in—

CLARK. Oh, yes! I thought it rang a bell somewhere.

GEORGINA. Something wrong about it?

CLARK. No. Not a thing. If books must be sold, there must be people to sell them. I'll bet he catches hell from Tessie, when she finds out this isn't a musical. Well, I guess that accounts for *one* of the dinner dates you turned down.

GEORGINA. Yes, it does. And I almost wish I hadn't.

CLARK. Why did you?

GEORGINA. Because I already had accepted your invitation.

CLARK. You could have called me off.

GEORGINA. Well, that is certainly a gracious remark! As a matter of fact, I would have, if I'd known where to reach you.

CLARK. Always call the paper. If I'm not there, somebody's likely to know where I am.

GEORGINA. I'll remember that—but I doubt that I'll ever have any need for the information.

CLARK. They say this Hand is quite a chaser.

GEORGINA. Do they? Well, I wouldn't know about that.

CLARK. I thought you might.

GEORGINA. What made you think that?

CLARK. I don't know. I get hunches like that sometimes. I have Indian blood in me.

GEORGINA. Well, in the future I wish you would please—

(*The music comes to an end, amid scattered applause.*)

CLARK (*applauding*). Sh! Curtain going up!

(*The lights dim, except that* GEORGINA's *and* CLARK's *faces remain brightly lighted. They look off right, where a glow is now visible, as the curtain presumably rises. There is scattered applause followed by c flourish of trumpets, and then the voices of the unseen actors of "The Merchant of Venice" are heard off right.*)

ANTONIO.
In sooth, I know not why I am so sad:
It wearies me; you say it wearies you;
But how I caught it, found it, or came by it,
What stuff 'tis made of, whereof it is born,
I am to learn;
And such a want-wit sadness makes of me,
That I have much ado to know myself.

SALARINO.
Your mind is tossing on the ocean;
There, where your argosies with portly sail,
Like signiors and rich burghers on the flood,
    Or, as it were, the pageants of the sea,
Do overpeer the petty traffickers
That curtsy to them, do them reverence,
As they fly by them with their woven wings.

(*During the latter part of* SALARINO's *speech, his words grow fainter, as* GEORGINA's *attention wanders from the stage. She sits staring into space, and only a distant murmur of voices is now heard. After a moment, the* THEATER MANAGER, *wearing a dinner jacket and looking for all the world like* MR. ALLERTON, *hurries on at left, downstage of the seats. He makes straight for* GEORGINA *and leans across* CLARK *to speak to her.*)

THE MANAGER (*tensely*). Excuse me, are you Miss Georgina Allerton?

GEORGINA (*in surprise*). Why, yes, I am.

THE MANAGER. I'm the manager of the theater. Miss Hilda Vincent, who was to play Portia tonight, has just collapsed in her dressing room and—

GEORGINA. Oh, how perfectly awful! Is she seriously—?

THE MANAGER. Well, I hope not. But she won't be able to go on. And we have no understudy.

GEORGINA. But what will you do?

THE MANAGER. That's what I've come to see you about.

GEORGINA. Me?

THE MANAGER. Yes, Miss Vincent is under the impression that you are familiar with the role of Portia—

GEORGINA. Well, I did play it once. But that was in high school, years ago.

THE MANAGER. Are you up in the part?

GEORGINA. Oh, I remember every word of it. But I couldn't possibly go on and—

THE MANAGER. Well, won't you please help us out and try it?

GEORGINA (*hesitantly*). Well, I don't know. (*Turning to* CLARK.) Do you think I should, Clark?

CLARK (*laughing*). Are you being funny? You couldn't get up there and act that part for a first-night audience.

GEORGINA (*to the* MANAGER). I guess he's right. I couldn't do it.

THE MANAGER. Please try! It's that or refunding thousands of dollars and sending away all these people disappointed. Miss Vincent told me to beg you in the name of your alma mater to—

GEORGINA. All right! I will! I'll try it!

CLARK (*trying to detain her*). You'll make a fool of yourself!

GEORGINA (*pushing past him*). I'd rather be a fool than a coward.

THE MANAGER. That's the spirit, Miss Allerton! I know you'll come through. This way, please. (*Her head high, she follows him across the stage into the darkness at the right. The light fades out at the left, then there is scattered applause, followed*

by the voice of the MANAGER, *off right.)*
Ladies and gentlemen, I regret to inform
you that Miss Hilda Vincent, who was to
be seen as Portia tonight, will be unable
to appear. *(Murmurs and exclamations
from the unseen audience.)* However,
there happens to be in the audience a
young lady, Miss Georgina Allerton, who,
though not a professional actress, is familiar with the role, and has graciously
consented to replace Miss Vincent.

(Scattered applause and murmurs.)

CLARK *(loudly).* Boo!

THE MANAGER. I am sure you will show
Miss Allerton every indulgence, in view
of the fact that she is going on at a
moment's notice, and without even a rehearsal. I thank you.

*(Applause, followed by a flourish of
music. Then the lights come up at right,
on a small section of an elevated stage.*
GEORGINA, *in the dress of a Venetian doctor of laws, stands on the stage, facing
the spectators at left, among whom only*
CLARK *can be seen, as a spotlight focuses
on his face. He grins sardonically, as*
GEORGINA *begins to speak.)*

GEORGINA.
The quality of mercy is not strain'd,
It droppeth as the gentle rain from heaven
Upon the place beneath: it is twice blest;
It blesseth him that gives and him that
    takes:
'Tis mightiest in the mightiest: it becomes
The throned monarch better than his
    crown;
His sceptre shows the force of temporal
    power,
The attribute to awe and majesty,
Wherein doth sit the dread and fear of
    kings;
But mercy is above this sceptred sway;
It is enthroned in the hearts of kings,
It is an attribute to God himself;
And earthly power doth then show likest
    God's
When mercy seasons justice. Therefore,
    Jew,
Though justice be thy plea, consider this,
That, in the course of justice, none of us
Should see salvation: we do pray for
    mercy;
And that same prayer doth teach us all
    to render
The deeds of mercy.

(As the speech goes on, CLARK'S *expression begins to soften until at the end he
is moved almost to tears. When the speech
is finished, there is an outburst of applause,
cheers, and cries of "Bravo!"* CLARK *sniffles, then takes out a handkerchief and
blows his nose.* GEORGINA *bows, smiles, and
blows kisses to the unseen audience. Two
ushers cross quickly from left to right,
carrying huge bouquets which they hand
up to* GEORGINA. *Her arms filled with flowers, she bows again. Then she disappears.
There is another upsurge of applause, as
the lights fade out at right. Then* CLARK
springs to his feet as he sees GEORGINA
*approaching from the right and meets
her stage center.)*

CLARK. Georgina! You were magnificent!

GEORGINA *(as they go toward their seats).*
Don't try to flatter me. I know you don't
mean it.

CLARK. But I do! I swear to you I do! You
were superb: sincere, moving, eloquent,
forceful, charming.

GEORGINA. That's a lot, isn't it, for a girl
who doesn't know anything, a girl who
can't do anything?

CLARK. I take it all back, Georgina—every
word of it. I've done you an injustice,
completely misunderstood you—

GEORGINA. Next time, maybe you'll be a
little more careful. Only I'm afraid there'll
be no next time for you, as far as I'm
concerned.

(They are seated by now.)

CLARK. Georgina, you mean you want to
be rid of me?

GEORGINA. Yes, and a good riddance too.

PORTIA *(off right).*
A gentle riddance. Draw the curtains, go.
Let all of his complexion choose me so.

*(There is applause as the unseen curtain
falls. As the lights come up again at left,*
GEORGINA, *startled, begins to applaud. The
Elizabethan music is resumed and continues throughout.)*

CLARK *(to* GEORGINA*).* Well, I'm glad you're
back with us.

(The other SPECTATORS *begin to rise and
file out.)*

GEORGINA. It's good, isn't it?

CLARK. Why, I don't believe you heard a word of it.

GEORGINA (*indignantly*). Why, I heard every syllable. What do you mean—?

CLARK. Go on! You were off in some Cloud-Cuckoo-Land.

GEORGINA. I was nothing of the kind!

CLARK (*looking toward* HAND *and* MISS DELEHANTY). Sh! We mustn't give them the impression that we're not en rapport. Besides, I'm dying to know how Tessie interprets the casket plot.

HAND (*as he and* MISS DELEHANTY *join* CLARK *and* GEORGINA). Say, that Vincent girl is a good Portia, isn't she? Why, to meet her at a cocktail party, you'd never think she had it in her.

CLARK. The world is full of girls like that. You have to live with them to know them. Miss Delehanty, how about a cigarette?

MISS DELEHANTY. Yeah, why not?

CLARK (*as they go left*). Well, there might be a number of reasons. Let's look at it, first, from the purely esthetic angle— (*He and* MISS DELEHANTY *exit.*)

HAND. So you turned me down for a book reviewer!

GEORGINA. I had already said yes to him when you—

HAND. Never mind, I can take it. But remember, we're playing a return engagement tomorrow at the Canard Rouge. I've dug up a lot more dope about Mexico. It seems that—

GEORGINA. Save it until tomorrow. We really should join the others.

HAND (*as they go left*). Yes, I guess so. Kind of brash, this Redfield, isn't he?

GEORGINA. Oh, yes—very!

(*As they exit, the lights fade on the scene and the music changes to a jazz rhythm. The lights come up, center, on a table in a night club. A* HEADWAITER *appears, at left, followed by* GEORGINA *and* CLARK, *who still carries the script.*)

THE HEADWAITER. How about this?

CLARK. Yes, this'll do. (*He and* GEORGINA *seat themselves at the table.*)

THE HEADWAITER. Can I take your order?

GEORGINA. Nothing for me. I've only got about a half hour—

CLARK. That's time enough for a drink. Scotch and soda?

GEORGINA. Now, don't spoil things by beginning to ask me what *I* want.

CLARK (*to the* HEADWAITER). Two Scotches and soda. And two smoked whitefish sandwiches on rye toast.

GEORGINA. Do you really think you can eat two sandwiches?

CLARK (*to the* HEADWAITER). Well, just bring one to start with.

THE HEADWAITER. Yes, sir. (*He exits. The band selection comes to an end.*)

CLARK. Now we can really relax and talk things over.

GEORGINA. I couldn't relax even if we had anything to talk over. I don't know why I let you drag me here, when I have to—

CLARK. I know! I got my eye glued on the time. Where is that you have to be at midnight, Cinderella?

GEORGINA. My, but you ask a lot of questions, don't you?

CLARK. Newspaperman. Get the story or get another job.

GEORGINA. Well, if you must know, I'm going to the airport to see somebody off.

CLARK. Good! I'll go with you!

GEORGINA. You'll do nothing of the sort.

CLARK. Well, that's settled! (*He suddenly laughs aloud.*)

GEORGINA (*vexed*). Am I missing something again?

CLARK. I'm thinking of George Hand.

GEORGINA. What's so funny about that?

CLARK. On the way out of the theater, he asked me where we were bound for, and I said we were going to the Blue Grotto and why didn't he join us there. I can just see him turning that gloomy joint upside down in search of us, while Miss

Delehanty sits wrapped in her thoughts —the naked creature!

GEORGINA. Well, of all the adolescent—! (*She laughs in spite of herself.*) I'm only laughing at the picture of Miss Delehanty—

CLARK. It's all right. Don't apologize. Is this George Hand trying to seduce you?

GEORGINA. Heavens, who's talking book language now?

CLARK. Well, I've learned that I mustn't always use the first word that springs to my lips. Of course, if you'd rather I asked you if he's trying to—

GEORGINA (*hastily*). No, I wouldn't! He's asked me to go to Mexico with him. You can put your own interpretation on that.

CLARK. I have. It doesn't worry me.

GEORGINA. Why should it worry *you*?

CLARK. I've just told you it doesn't. I mean it's not what's worrying you, either.

GEORGINA. Who said anything was worrying me?

CLARK (*preoccupied*). Nobody. Tell me something, Georgina. Are you a virgin?

GEORGINA. Didn't you say that the Newspaper Guild limits your working hours?

CLARK (*thoughtfully*). It really doesn't matter much. Well, I'm glad we went to that play. Because suddenly everything clicked. Do you remember my telling you that you were off in a trance?

GEORGINA. I was off in some Cloud-Cuckoo-Land, you said.

CLARK. Yes. I happened to look at you and I saw that you were no longer Georgina Allerton, that college grad who plays at running a bookshop. You were suddenly being somebody up there on the stage, who was pretending to be Portia of Belmont who was pretending to be a doctor of laws in an imaginary Venetian court of justice.

GEORGINA. Well, that's what art is supposed to do for us, isn't it? Make us identify ourselves with—

CLARK. No! Art should reveal reality to us. It shouldn't be something that we use to screen ourselves from reality.

GEORGINA. Is that what you're trying to tell me—that I hide from reality?

CLARK. Yes. Sitting there beside you in the theater and looking at you—

GEORGINA. Weren't you interested in the play?

CLARK. What's that got to do with it?

GEORGINA. I was wondering what made you look at *me*.

CLARK. Let's stick to the point, please.

GEORGINA. I'm sorry!

CLARK. The point is that you're a daydreamer. You live in a world of fantasy, instead of the world of reality.

GEORGINA. What is this reality you keep talking about?

CLARK. I was hoping you wouldn't ask me that because I'm not sure that I know the answer. But I'm pretty sure it means living your life out and not dreaming it away.

GEORGINA. If a dream is real to you, why isn't it as real as something you do?

CLARK. Because dreaming is easy and life is hard. Because when you dream, you make your own rules, but when you try to *do* something, the rules are made for you by the limitations of your own nature and the shape of the world you live in. Because no matter how much you win in your dreams, your gains are illusory, and you always come away empty-handed. But in life, whether you win or lose, you've always got something to show for it—even if it's only a scar or a painful memory.

GEORGINA. Scars are ugly and pain hurts.

CLARK. Without ugliness, there would be no beauty. And if you're afraid to know pain, you'll never know the value of pleasure.

GEORGINA. You're a tough guy, aren't you?

CLARK. Well, I've had to fight my own way through life, ever since I can remember. You either get tough, or else you go under.

GEORGINA. It's not the way I was brought up. I always had people to protect me.

CLARK. If you bandage a muscle long enough, it withers. And that goes for your emotions, too. If you keep smothering them with dreams, they'll die after a while.

GEORGINA. Don't say it. It's what I'm afraid of.

CLARK. Then it's time somebody said it.

GEORGINA. I know. Push her off the dock and she'll learn to swim. But suppose I'm not the one that gets tough. Suppose I'm the one that goes under.

CLARK. All right then. If that's the way you feel about it, go on sitting on the end of the dock for the rest of your life and let the moonbeams turn your blood to water.

GEORGINA. No, I mustn't do that, must I? Keep on telling me. I mustn't do that. Only what do you do, if the thing you always dreamed suddenly faces you? Suppose—well, suppose you cared very much for someone. Couldn't get him out of your thoughts, day or night. And all the while you knew it was hopeless, knew you could never have him. But still you went on, weeping and longing and dreaming. And then, just like that, what you thought could never be, suddenly became possible. What you had prayed for was yours for the asking. Only it was all different—not a bit the way you dreamed it. And he was different, too. But it was reality; it was no longer a dream. And that's your recipe —reality. So that's what I go for, according to you.

CLARK. Not according to me, at all.

GEORGINA. But you said—

CLARK. I said live your life. Lots of people have a beautiful time, yearning unhappily for the pot of gold at the end of the rainbow. But when the rainbow fades, and the pot turns out to be full of ashes, they don't have to hug it to their bosoms. They can leave it be, and say: "Well, looks like I staked out the wrong claim." That is, if they have any guts and any sense of humor they can. If you can make a dream come to life, grab hold of it. But if it dies on you, roll up your sleeves and give it a decent burial, instead of trying to haul the corpse around with you.

(The band begins to play another dance tune.)

GEORGINA (rising). Thank you, teacher.

CLARK (also rising). Do you have to go already?

GEORGINA. Well, the bus to the airport won't wait.

CLARK. Why is it so important that you go?

GEORGINA. I told you I'd promised somebody I'd see them off.

CLARK. What would happen if you didn't?

GEORGINA. Nothing would happen, I guess. Except that they might be disappointed.

CLARK (as the waiter appears with the drinks and sandwich). Well, if you do go, I'll have to eat and drink alone, and I've told you I don't like that.

GEORGINA (hesitantly). Well, if I don't go, I should at least phone the air terminal and say I'm not coming.

(The waiter exits.)

CLARK. Why? If you don't show up, they'll figure out that you're not there.

GEORGINA. Yes, I suppose that's true.

CLARK. Of course, if you enjoy unnecessary telephone conversations—

GEORGINA. No, I really don't.

CLARK (resuming his seat). Then let's sit down.

GEORGINA (complying). I wonder why I listen to you.

CLARK. I have a magnetic personality. (Raising his glass.) God, I've talked my throat dry. Here's to you.

GEORGINA (raising her glass). And here's to you. I'm sorry your throat is dry, but I'm glad you talked to me. Do you mind telling me why?

CLARK (with a shrug). I don't know. I guess I hate to see anybody with such pretty legs walking around in a trance. (Taking a bite of the sandwich.) Say, this is damned good!

GEORGINA. Could I have a bite?

CLARK (pushing the plate over). Why, sure! Maybe I'd better order another one.

GEORGINA. No, let's finish this one, first.

(Taking a bite.) It *is* good. You're always right, aren't you?

CLARK. About ninety per cent of the time. Well—say ninety-five. I hope I'm right about that Wilinski-O'Connell fight. I'm backing Wilinski on the short end of a two-to-one bet.

GEORGINA *(her mouth full)*. It's too bad you didn't go.

CLARK. Oh, that's all right. This is fun, for a change.

GEORGINA. Gee, thanks.

CLARK. You should eat more. You're too skinny.

GEORGINA. You told me that before.

CLARK *(looking at her)*. Jim Lucas?

GEORGINA *(startled)*. What?

CLARK. You heard me. I said Jim Lucas.

GEORGINA. How did you guess?

CLARK. I have a knack for putting one and one together.

GEORGINA. He's going to Reno to get a divorce.

CLARK. Well, what the hell else would anybody go to Reno for?

GEORGINA. He wants me to join him there.

CLARK. And are you going to?

GEORGINA. Maybe.

CLARK. Say, I'd like to have a piece of the agency that handles your travel arrangements. And if you do get there, what then?

GEORGINA. We'd get married and get ourselves a ranch.

CLARK. A ranch. *(Suddenly.)* My God, it's right straight out of that novel of yours.

GEORGINA. Just pushing the girl off the dock isn't enough for you. You have to kick her off. *(Rising.)* Get up!

CLARK. Why?

GEORGINA. I feel like dancing.

CLARK. With me?

GEORGINA. Well, I'm a shy girl. I'd feel funny about accosting some stranger. Don't you like to dance?

CLARK *(rising)*. It depends upon with whom.

GEORGINA. You have a charming way of saying things. Years of experience, I suppose.

(They dance back and forth, across the stage, a spotlight following them.)

CLARK. Well, working on a newspaper, you get around.

GEORGINA. That's what I mean.

CLARK. Your eyes aren't too bad, either.

GEORGINA. Now, don't feel that you have to overdo it.

CLARK. That's a sound criticism. Overstatement is one of my worst faults.

GEORGINA. I'm sure you have plenty of bad ones.

CLARK. Well—enough.

GEORGINA. Is that why no girl has ever married you?

CLARK. I've never asked one to.

GEORGINA. Never met anyone worthy, I suppose.

CLARK. That's partly it. But it's also because I think I'd make a lousy husband.

GEORGINA. Would you? Why?

CLARK. Well, in the first place— *(Breaking off.)* Do you really want to know?

GEORGINA. Well, it gives us something to talk about.

CLARK. We wouldn't have to talk.

GEORGINA. That's true. Only you don't seem very happy when you're not talking.

CLARK. Well, that's the first thing. I'm gabby.

GEORGINA. Maybe that's because you really have a lot of things to say.

CLARK. That doesn't follow. The world is full of windbags. Then again I'm blunt and caustic. I come right out with things.

GEORGINA. That might be honesty.

CLARK. As for egotism—that's my middle name.

GEORGINA. It's a quality that a lot of creative people seem to have.

CLARK. I'm a hard guy to know.

GEORGINA. Complex people usually are.

CLARK. I'm lacking in reverence.

GEORGINA. It could be that you're too penetrating to be taken in by sham.

CLARK. It bores me to listen to other people's troubles.

GEORGINA. Perhaps you think they should stand on their own feet and solve their own problems. .

CLARK. The idea of supporting a wife irks me.

GEORGINA. A man who is independent himself might not respect an able-bodied woman who was willing to be a dependent.

CLARK. I'm an unpredictable bastard. If I have a strong impulse, I'm as likely as not to follow it.

GEORGINA. That could denote imagination and courage.

(The music comes to an end. They stop dancing and applaud, mechanically, both transfused with new-found emotion.)

CLARK. You dance all right.

GEORGINA. Thank you. So do you.

CLARK (as they go back to the table). Why don't we order another drink?

GEORGINA (seating herself). That's a wonderful idea.

CLARK. You order it. I want to make some phone calls. (Fishing in his pockets.) Have you got any nickels? You know how I always get stuck in phone booths without nickels.

GEORGINA (opening her handbag). I think I have. How many do you want?

CLARK. Oh, three or four. (She hands him some nickels.) Thanks. And don't forget to order the drinks.

GEORGINA. I won't.

CLARK. Oh, better order another sandwich, too.

GEORGINA. All right, I will.

CLARK (picking up the remains of his sandwich.) I may as well finish this, while I'm phoning.

(He takes a bite, as he exits. As GEORGINA sits gazing after him, the lights fade out on the scene. A persistent knocking is heard off stage right. The lights come up center on the empty stage. A MAN in slippers and an old-fashioned flannel nightshirt comes on at left, carrying a lighted kerosene lamp. He looks like MR. ALLERTON.)

THE MAN (peering off right, as the knocking continues). Consarn it all, who's there?

CLARK (off). Is Justice of the Peace Billings in?

BILLINGS. Where in tarnation do you think I'd be this time of night?

CLARK (off). Well, open up and let us in.

BILLING. What in thunder for?

CLARK (off). We want to get married.

BILLINGS. Well, jiminy crickets, can't you wait till mornin'?

CLARK (off). No, we can't. It's an emergency.

BILLINGS (as he goes off right). Some folks ain't got the sense they was born with. (A sound of bolts opening and a door creaking. Then BILLINGS reappears, followed by CLARK and GEORGINA.)

CLARK (producing a paper). Here's the license, Judge. Now give us the works.

(BILLINGS peers at the license, as a cuckoo clock sounds two.)

BILLINGS. Well, I'll be danged! Two o'clock. Time you young folks was in bed, 'stead of gallivantin' around.

CLARK. We know it. But we thought we ought to get married first.

BILLINGS (reading the license). Do you, Georgina Allerton, aim to take this bachelor, Clark Redfield, to be your lawful wedded husband?

GEORGINA. I do.

BILLINGS. And do you, Clark Redfield, hanker to take this spinster, Georgina Allerton, to be your lawful wedded wife?

CLARK. That's what I'm here for.

BILLINGS. To love and to cherish. To honor and to obey.

CLARK. No!

GEORGINA (simultaneously). No!

BILLINGS. What's that?

CLARK. Cut out that "obey."

BILLINGS (grumpily). It's part o' the ceremony. Folks ain't expected to take it serious.

GEORGINA. We're very serious people—very serious and very honest.

BILLINGS. When I do the marryin', I don't want no back talk. In sickness and in health. In joy and in sorrow. Until death do you part.

CLARK. I do.

GEORGINA. I— (She stops, as a clatter of horse's hoofs is heard off left.)

JIM (off). Whoa! (The hoofbeats stop and JIM rushes on, dressed as a cowboy.)

JIM. No! No! Stop!

GEORGINA. Jim!

CLARK. Oh, so you're here, are you?

JIM. Yes, I am! And just in the nick of time, it seems.

CLARK. What do you want?

JIM (ignoring him). Georgina, do you realize what you're doing?

GEORGINA. Well, not altogether, Jim. But it gives me such a wonderful feeling, as though I were really alive for the first time.

JIM. You're just yielding to a romantic impulse, just throwing yourself away.

CLARK (to JIM). You keep out of this, Lucas. You're all washed up, as far as this girl is concerned; and I'm taking over now.

JIM. Answer him, Georgina!

GEORGINA. I don't know what to say. I never met anyone like him before. He's a tough guy—he really is. He scares the daylights out of me.

JIM. All right. I'll answer him then. (To CLARK.) She's mine—mine! Do you understand?

CLARK. How do you figure that?

JIM. Because she loves me—she's always loved me. For years she's built her whole secret life around me—yearning, dreaming, hoping against hope. And now I'm free and I want her and I'm going to make her mine.

GEORGINA (to CLARK). It's true what he's saying. He wants me, and I've always loved him and—

CLARK. Scuttlebutt! He doesn't know what he wants and never will. And you don't love him and never did. You've just been in love with some Romeo of your imagination, that never was on land or sea.

GEORGINA. Do you think so? Do you think that's the way it is?

JIM. Don't listen to him, Georgina.

GEORGINA. I have to listen to him, Jim. He may be right. He is—ninety-five per cent of the time.

BILLINGS (impatiently). Well, young lady, I'm goin' back to bed. The law don't require me to stay up all night, waitin' for folks to make up their minds.

GEORGINA. No, wait! It's true. I've got to make up my mind. If I don't now, I never will. All right, Judge, proceed with the ceremony.

BILLINGS. Well, that's better. Do you, Georgina Allerton—

JIM. No, Georgina. You mustn't do this.

BILLINGS. You keep out of this, young feller, unless you want to spend the night in the lockup.

CLARK. Go on, cowboy. Beat it.

(JIM looks appealingly at Georgina, but she averts her head and he exits, dolefully.)

GEORGINA. All right. I'm ready. In sickness and in health. In joy and in sorrow. Until death— (She breaks off as the jazz music from the night club blares forth.) No, no! Stop it, Georgina! You mustn't go on like this! You mustn't! (CLARK and BILLINGS have gone and as the night-club scene appears again, she goes back to her place at the table.) I'm at it again—drugging myself with dreams. And when I come to, all I'll get from him is a slap in the face. He doesn't care a damn for me. He's just having fun with me—just giving me the run-around, that's all. He's calling up to find out if he won his bet on Wilinski—that means more to him than I do. *(Springing to her feet.)* No, I can't take it! I'll never see him again. I'll go before he gets back. I'll—I'll—oh, I don't know. Anything—anything not to hear the bitter truth from him. *(She starts to exit.)*

CLARK *(entering).* I won! Wilinski knocked him out in the— *(Looking at her.)* You look as though you think you're going somewhere.

GEORGINA. Yes, I am. Good-by and congratulate Wilinski for me.

CLARK. We'll send him a joint wire. Where are you going?

GEORGINA. I'm going to take a taxi to the airport and get on that plane with Jim.

CLARK. Why?

GEORGINA. Because you've convinced me that doing something is better than doing nothing. And if I don't go away with Jim, I haven't anything.

CLARK. Well, of course, if that's what you want to do! Only I wish you'd told me just a few minutes sooner.

GEORGINA. What do you mean by that?

CLARK. Well, you know those impulses I get. I suddenly decided to round off the evening by blowing in that dough I won on Wilinski. So I ordered one of those rented limousines to come around and pick us up. The guy wears a peaked cap and gauntlets. It's pretty damned impressive.

GEORGINA. Where were you planning to go?

CLARK. Oh, I thought we could decide that as we went along. We could whirl around Central Park a couple of times, and then maybe work our way up to Bronx Park—or even beyond. It's a nice night for a ride, and sitting back in a car, you get a chance to talk. I haven't been able to get in a word edgewise, all evening. *(He pays the check.)* Oh, didn't you order that sandwich?

GEORGINA. Oh, I'm sorry! I forgot all about it.

CLARK. Daydreaming again?

GEORGINA. Afraid so. About you and me.

CLARK. Why, you're improving. I think this one may really pay off.

(A liveried chauffeur enters.)

THE CHAUFFEUR. Excuse me, are you Mr. Redfield?

CLARK. Yes. Keep your motor racing. We'll be right with you.

THE CHAUFFEUR. Yes, sir. *(He exits.)*

CLARK *(looking after him).* What did I tell you? Well, are you ready?

GEORGINA. Clark—Clark, I'm a serious girl. I wouldn't know how to take any more jokes.

CLARK. Well, I have my serious moments, too. Look, if you don't want to ride around with me, I'll drop you at the airport and take a spin by myself. Only let's get going. You have to pay these birds whether they're moving or standing still.

(He takes her arm, and, as they exit at right, the lights fade quickly on the scene. A telephone rings at left and the lights come up, revealing MRS. ALLERTON in bed, as she turns on the lamp on the night table beside her. In a twin bed, on the other side of the night table, MR. ALLERTON groans and turns over.)

MRS. ALLERTON *(picking up the telephone, sleepily).* Hello!

(She sneezes and gropes under her pillow for cleansing tissue as the lights come up quickly at right, on a double bed. GEORGINA, telephone in hand, is seated on the bed with CLARK close beside her.)

GEORGINA. Hello, Mother! Goodness, you sound worse.

MRS. ALLERTON *(irritably).* What's that? What number are you calling?

(MR. ALLERTON groans again.)

GEORGINA. It's Georgina, Mother.

MRS. ALLERTON. Well, for goodness' sakes! What time is it?

GEORGINA. About three-thirty, I guess. Listen Mother, I'm—

MRS. ALLERTON. What are you calling up at this hour for? Are you in jail?

GEORGINA. No, I'm in Greenwich.

MRS. ALLERTON. What are you doing there?

GEORGINA. I just got married.

MRS. ALLERTON (sneezing). You just got what? Talk a little louder. This damned cold seems to have gone to my ears.

GEORGINA. I said I just got married.

MRS. ALLERTON. Well, for God's sake! George, did you hear that? She's married.

(ALLERTON mumbles unintelligibly.)

GEORGINA. I thought you'd—

MRS. ALLERTON (angrily). Wait a minute, will you? I can't talk to two people at once. (Poking MR. ALLERTON.) George, will you please wake up? She's married.

GEORGINA (to CLARK). She's furious at me for waking her up.

CLARK. I don't blame her.

ALLERTON (raising himself to a sitting position). Who's married?

MRS. ALLERTON. Georgina, of course. Who do you suppose?

ALLERTON. To whom is she married?

MRS. ALLERTON. How the devil should I know?

ALLERTON. Well, ask her.

MRS. ALLERTON (at the telephone). Georgina, your father wants to know to whom you're married.

GEORGINA. Oh, to a man I know.

MRS. ALLERTON. Well, I should hope so. (To ALLERTON.) I can't get a thing out of her.

ALLERTON. Let me talk to her. (Taking the telephone.) Hello, Georgie.

GEORGINA. Hello, Dad! I'm married!

ALLERTON. Can you tell us who your husband is?

GEORGINA. His name is Clark Redfield. He took me to dinner and the theater and then—

MRS. ALLERTON (to ALLERTON). Well, who is it?

ALLERTON (to MRS. ALLERTON). I didn't get the name. Someone who took her to dinner and the theater and—

MRS. ALLERTON. Good grief! (Snatching the telephone.) Don't tell me it's that boorish, conceited newspaperman!

GEORGINA (happily). Yes, that's the one. Wait, I'll let you talk to him. (Handing CLARK the telephone.)

CLARK. Hello, Mrs. Allerton. This is your new son-in-law, Clark Redfield.

MRS. ALLERTON. Clark who? Talk a little louder, can't you? (She sneezes.)

CLARK. Redfield. Red as in Russia, field as in football. Have you got a cold?

MRS. ALLERTON. Only a newspaperman could ask such a foolish question. (She sneezes.)

CLARK. Have you ever tried a little—

MRS. ALLERTON. Look, young man, don't give me any of your advice. You're going to need all you've got for that girl you've married. (To ALLERTON.) I think she's going to have her hands full with him.

CLARK. What's that?

ALLERTON. Let me talk to him. (Taking the telephone.) Hello. This is Georgina's father.

CLARK. Oh, yes. This is her husband.

ALLERTON. Yes, so I understand. I just wondered whether you have any plans.

CLARK. Do you mean future plans or immediate plans?

GEORGINA. Let me talk to him. (Taking the telephone.) Good night, Dad. Tell Mother—

ALLERTON. You'd better tell her. (He hands the telephone to MRS. ALLERTON.)

GEORGINA. I just wanted to say good night, Mother.

MRS. ALLERTON. Have you got everything you need?

GEORGINA. Yes, we bought toothbrushes and popcorn in Mamaroneck!

MRS. ALLERTON. Well, if it's chilly up there, don't let him talk you into leaving the window open. (She sneezes.)

GEORGINA. I won't. Good night. (She hangs up.)

MRS. ALLERTON *(hanging up)*. I hope I didn't sound too damned mushy.

(ALLERTON sneezes loudly, as the lights fade quickly.)

CLARK *(looking at his watch)*. It's three-thirty. I'm not used to being up so late. *(He puts out the lamp beside the bed, leaving the scene in semidarkness.)*

GEORGINA. Wait! There's just one thing I'd like to know. Do I have to give up dreaming altogether? Couldn't I just sort of taper off?

CLARK. Well, I'll be reasonable about it, as long as you run your dreams, instead of letting them run you.

GEORGINA. I know! If you can dream and not make dreams your master—! Do you think Kipling will live?

CLARK *(as he pulls down an imaginary shade)*. Look, I didn't come all the way up here to discuss literature!

(The stage is plunged into darkness. The curtain falls.)

CURTAIN

THE PHILADELPHIA STORY

By PHILIP BARRY

THE PHILADELPHIA STORY was first presented by The Theatre Guild, Inc. at the Shubert Theatre, New York City, on March 28, 1939, with the following cast:

TRACY LORD..........Katherine Hepburn
DINAH LORD.............Lenore Lonergan
MARGARET LORD..............Vera Allen
ALEXANDER (SANDY) LORD
                    Dan Tobin
THOMAS.................Owen Coll
WILLIAM (UNCLE WILLIE)
  TRACY.................Forrest Orr
ELIZABETH (LIZ) IMBRIE
             Shirley Booth

MACAULAY (MIKE) CONNOR
                  Van Heflin
GEORGE KITTREDGE...Frank Fenton
C. K. DEXTER HAVEN
                Joseph Cotton
SETH LORD........................Nicholas Joy
ELSIE.................Lorraine Bate
MAC.................Hayden Rorke
MAY.................Myrtle Tannehill
EDWARD.................Philip Foster

SCENES

The action of the play takes place in the course of twenty-four hours at the Seth Lords' house in the country near Philadelphia. The time is late June.

      ACT I: The sitting room. Late morning, Friday.

      ACT II: Scene 1. The porch. Late evening, Friday.

              Scene 2. The porch. Early morning, Saturday.

      ACT III: The sitting room. Late morning, Saturday.

THE AUTHOR

The Great Ironist has had his way with Philip Barry by giving him an enviable talent for the capers of comedy and a great desire to write serious drama but reserving all the success for the light fantastic toe. Nevertheless, Mr. Barry manages to permeate even his lightest efforts with the sensitiveness and the reflectiveness that have thus far failed to reap rewards when bulked large instead of scattered discreetly through his comedy of manners. For a minority (and the present editor belongs to it), moreover, the serious plays Hotel Universe *and* Here Come the Clowns *are almost as valuable as they are to their author. Perhaps if Mr. Barry possessed some savagery in addition to his unfailing good taste and abundant wit, the minority would become a majority. But to expect savagery from Mr. Barry would be as far-fetched as hoping that Boris Karloff will some day play "De Lawd."*

Philip Barry was born in Rochester, which he abandoned for greener pastures in 1913. After an early education at Catholic schools he went to Yale, took his degree in 1919, and entrained for George Pierce Baker's Workshop 47 at Harvard. Subsequently he clerked and gained poise, if he ever needed any, at the State Department in Washington and in the U. S. Embassy in London.

His apprentice days as playwright ended when Richard Herndon produced the comedy You and I *at the Belmont Theatre in 1923. This well-received production was followed by the unremarkable Benjamin Franklin play* The Youngest *(1924), the clever piece* In a Garden *(1925), the satirical extravaganza* White Wings *(1926) which nearly everybody hopes to musicalize some day, and the biblical story* John *(1927). A month after* John *came the successful comedy of manners* Paris Bound, *an intelligent treatment of adultery and divorce, and its author soon found a second pot of gold in the charming family comedy* Holiday *during the 1928–29 season. Mr. Barry diverged into the psychoanalytic field with the probing* Hotel Universe, *which the Theatre Guild did not quite succeed in promoting on Broadway during the depression year of 1930, but he recovered his public in 1931 and 1932 with the engaging comedies* Tomorrow and Tomorrow *and* The Animal Kingdom.

An evil spell falling on the successful author for reasons we cannot investigate here, Mr. Barry saw his next three plays speeding to Cain's. (Among them was The Joyous Season *which had a warm partisan in Arthur Hopkins, who tried to revive it during the war period). But when Mr. Barry returned to the Broadway battleground he made a deep impression on a minority with* Here Come the Clowns *in 1938 and scored the enormous success of* The Philadelphia Story *in the spring of 1939. His luck and craftsmanship declined in the nobly intended, occasionally beautiful, but somewhat tepid* Liberty Jones *in 1941; his craftsmanship was uncertain but his luck held with the politico-domestic comedy* Without Love *(1942), and he throve exceedingly in the ingeniously constructed Tallulah Bankhead fantastic comedy* The Foolish Notion, *which opened in March 1945.*

The fluctuations in this Broadway fever chart have been many. But being a wise gentleman, Mr. Barry has remained unruffled; besides, the total record shows him well ahead in the race for fortune and reputation. He has a place in American theatre history as both an experimentalist and a cultivated writer of high comedy.

THE PHILADELPHIA STORY

ACT ONE

The sitting room of the Lords' house in the country near Philadelphia is a large, comfortably furnished room of a somewhat faded elegance containing a number of very good Victorian pieces. The entrance from the hall is at Right, upstage, down two broad, shallow steps. The entrance into what the family still call "the parlor" is through double doors downstage Right. At Left are two glass doors leading to the porch. A writing desk stands between them. There is a large marble fireplace in the back wall and a grand piano in the corner at Left. Chairs and a table are at downstage Right and at downstage Left another table, an easy chair and a sofa. There is a large and fine portrait over the fireplace and other paintings here and there. A wall cabinet contains a quantity of bric-a-brac and there is more of it, together with a number of signed photographs in silver frames, upon the tables and piano. There are also several cardboard boxes strewn about.

It is late on a Friday morning in June, an overcast day. DINAH, who is all of thirteen years old, is stretched out on the sofa reading a set of printers' galley proofs. TRACY, a strikingly lovely girl of twenty-four, sits in the chair at Left, a leather writing set between her knees, scribbling notes. She wears slacks and a blouse. MARGARET LORD, their mother, a young and smart forty-seven, comes in from the hall with three more boxes in her arms. She places them upon the table near TRACY.

MARGARET. I'm so terribly afraid that some of the cards for these last-minute presents must have got mixed. Look at them, Tracy —perhaps you can tell.

TRACY. In a minute, Mother. I'm up to my neck in these blank thank-you notes.

(DINAH folds one of the proof sheets she is reading under another.)

DINAH. This stinks!

MARGARET. Not "stinks," darling. If absolutely necessary, "smells"—but only if absolutely necessary. What is it?

DINAH. I found it in Sandy's room. It's something that's going to be in a magazine. It certainly stinks, all right.

MARGARET. Keep out of your brother's things, dear—and his house. *(She studies a list of names.)* Ninety-four for the ceremony, five hundred and six for the reception—I don't know where we'll put them all, if it should rain.

DINAH. It won't rain.

MARGARET. Uncle Willie wanted to insure against it with Lloyd's but I wouldn't let him. If I was God and someone bet I wouldn't let it rain, I'd show him fast enough. This second page is solid Cadwalader. Twenty-six.

DINAH. That's a lot of Cadwalader.

MARGARET. One, my child, is a lot of Cadwalader.

TRACY. How do you spell omelet?

MARGARET. O-m-m-e-l-e-t.

TRACY. I thought there was another "l."

MARGARET. The omelet dish from the—?

TRACY. You said it was an omelet dish.

MARGARET. It might be for fish.

TRACY. Fish dish? That sounds idiotic.

MARGARET. I should simply say "Thank you so much for your lovely silver dish."

TRACY. Here's the tag, "Old Dutch Muffin Ear, Circa 1810"— What the—? *(She drops the card.)* I am simply enchanted with your old Dutch Muffin Ear—with which my husband and I will certainly hear any muffin coming a mile away.

DINAH. Lookit, Tracy: don't you think you've done enough notes for one day?

TRACY. Don't disturb me. *(She examines another card.)* From Cousin Horace Macomber, one pair of game shears, looking like hell. *(Picks up shears.)*

DINAH. He's so awful. What did he send the other time?

TRACY. No one to speak of sent anything the other time.

MARGARET. It's such a pity your brother Junius can't be here for your wedding. London's so far away.

DINAH. I miss old Junius: you did a good job when you had him, Mother.

MARGARET. The first is always the best. They deteriorate as you go on.

TRACY. There was no occasion to send anything the other time.

DINAH *(reading the proof sheets).* This is certainly pretty rooty-tooty all right.

TRACY. It would scarcely be considered a wedding at all, the other time. When you run off to Maryland on a sudden impulse —as Dexter and I did—

DINAH. Ten months is quite long to be married, though. You can have a baby in nine, can't you?

TRACY. I guess, if you put your mind to it.

DINAH. Why didn't you?

TRACY. Mother, don't you think it's time for her nap?

DINAH. I imagine you and George'll have slews of 'em.

TRACY. I hope so, all like you, dear, with the same wild grace.

(She rises from her chair with a box of envelopes, which she places upon the desk.)

DINAH. Lookit: "the other time" —he's back from wherever he's been.

MARGARET. What do you mean?

DINAH. Dexter, of course. I saw his car in front of his house: the roadster. It must be him.

MARGARET. When? When did you?

DINAH. This morning, early, when I was out exercising The Hoofer.

MARGARET. Why didn't you tell us?

(TRACY moves to her unconcernedly.)

TRACY. I'm not worried, Mother. The only trouble Mr. C. K. Dexter Haven ever gave me was when he married me.—*You* might

say the same for one Seth Lord. If you'd just face it squarely as I did—

MARGARET. That will do! I will allow none of you to criticize your father.

TRACY. What are we expected to do when he treats you—

MARGARET. Did you hear me, Tracy?

TRACY. All right, I give up.

MARGARET. —And in view of this second attempt of yours, it might pay you to remind yourself that neither of us has proved to be a very great success as a wife.

TRACY. We just picked the wrong first husbands, that's all.

MARGARET. That's an extremely vulgar remark.

TRACY. Oh, who cares about either of them any more— *(She leans over the back of* MARGARET'S *chair and hugs her.)* Golly Moses, I'm going to be happy now.

MARGARET. Darling.

TRACY. Isn't George an angel?

MARGARET. George is an angel.

TRACY. Is he handsome, or is he not?

MARGARET. George is handsome.

TRACY. Suds. I'm a lucky girl. *(She gathers up her boxes and writing case.)*

DINAH. I like Dexter.

(TRACY moves toward the Hall doorway.)

TRACY. Really? Why don't you ask him to lunch, or something? *(And goes out.)*

DINAH *(looking after her).* She's awfully mean about him, isn't she?

MARGARET. He was rather mean to her, my dear.

DINAH. Did he really sock her?

MARGARET. Don't say "sock," darling. "Strike" is quite an ugly enough word.

DINAH. But did he really?

MARGARET. I'm afraid I don't know the details.

DINAH. Cruelty and drunkenness, it said.

MARGARET. Dinah!

DINAH. It was right in the papers.

MARGARET. You read too much. You'll spoil your eyes.

DINAH. I think it's an awful thing to say about a man. I don't think they like things like that said about them.

MARGARET. I'm sure they don't.

(DINAH *picks up the proof sheets again.*)

DINAH. Father's going to be hopping when he reads all this about himself in that magazine, *Destiny,* when it comes out.

MARGARET. All what? *About whom?*

DINAH. Father—that they're going to publish.

MARGARET. Dinah, what *are* you talking about?

DINAH. It's what they call proof sheets for some article they're going to call, "Broadway and Finance," and Father's in it, and so they just sent it on to Sandy—sort of—you know, on approval. It was just there on the table in his room, and so I—

MARGARET. But the article! What does the article say? *(She takes the proof sheets and examines them.)*

DINAH. Oh, it's partly about Father backing three shows for that dancer—what's her name—Tina Mara—and his early history—and about the stables—and why he's living in New York, instead of with us, any more, and—

MARGARET. Great heaven—what on earth can we do?

DINAH. Couldn't Father sue them for—for liable?

MARGARET. But it's true—it's all— *(She glances at* DINAH.) That is, I mean to say—

DINAH. I don't think the part about Tina Mara is, the way they put it. It's simply full of innundo.

MARGARET. Of what?

DINAH. Of innundo. *(She rests her chin on her hand and stares into space.)* Oh, I do wish something would happen here. Nothing ever possibly in the least ever happens. *(Then suddenly hops up and goes to her mother.)* Next year can I go to the Conservatory in New York? They teach you to sing and dance and act and everything at once. *Can* I, Mother?

MARGARET. Save your dramatics, Dinah. *(She folds the proof sheets and puts them down.)* Oh, why didn't Sandy *tell* me!

DINAH. Mother, why won't Tracy *ask* her own *father* to her *wedding?*

MARGARET. Your sister has very definite opinions about certain things. *(She moves toward the desk at Left.)*

DINAH *(following her).* She's sort of—you know—hard, isn't she?

MARGARET. Not hard—none of my children is that, I hope. Tracy sets exceptionally high standards for herself, that's all, and although she lives up to them, other people aren't always quite able to. If your Uncle Willie Tracy comes in, tell him to wait. I want to see him. *(Having put the desk in order, she moves toward the Porch door.)*

DINAH. Tell me one thing: don't you think it's stinking not at least to *want* Father?

*(*MARGARET *stops in the doorway and turns to her.)*

MARGARET. Yes, darling, between ourselves I think it's good and stinking. *(And goes out.)*

DINAH. And I bet if Dexter knew what she— *(She waits a moment, then goes to the telephone and dials four numbers.)* Hello. May I please speak to Mr. Dexter Haven—what?—Dexter! It's you! *(Then affectedly.)* A very great pleasure to have you back. Dinah, you goat, Dinah Lord. What?—You bet!—Lookit, Dexter, Tracy says why don't you come right over for lunch? What? But she told me to ask you. —Listen, though, maybe it would be better if you'd— Hello!—Hello! *(She replaces the telephone as* TRACY *comes in from the Hall with a large roll of paper.)*

TRACY. Who was that?

DINAH. Wrong number.

TRACY *(spreads the roll of paper out on the table).* Listen, darling, give me a hand with this cockeyed seating arrangement, will you? At least hold it down.—George doesn't want the Grants at the bridal table. *(*SANDY LORD, *twenty-six, comes in from the Hall.)* He says they're fast. He—

SANDY. Hello, kids.

TRACY. Sandy! *(She reaches up to him, hugs him.)*

SANDY. Where's Mother?

TRACY. She's around. How's New York? —How's Sue?—How's the baby?

SANDY. Blooming. They sent their love, sorry they can't make the wedding. Is there a party tonight, of course?

TRACY. Aunt Geneva's throwing a monster.

SANDY. Boy, am I going to get plastered. *(To* DINAH.*)* Hello, little fellah.

DINAH. Hello, yourself.

(He gives her a small flat box.)

SANDY. This is for you, Mug. Get the three race horses into the paddock. It's tough. Work it out.

DINAH. Oh, thanks. *(She begins to work at the puzzle.)*

SANDY *(to* TRACY*)*. Sue's and my wedding present comes by registered mail, Tracy—and a pretty penny it set me back.

TRACY. You're a bonny boy, Sandy. I love you.

SANDY. Mutual—

*(*MARGARET *re-enters from the Porch.)*

MARGARET. I was wondering about you.

*(*SANDY *goes to her and embraces her.)*

SANDY. Give us a kiss.—You look fine.— Imagine this, a *grand*mother. How's everything?

MARGARET. Absolute chaos.

SANDY. Just how you like it, eh? Just when you function best!

MARGARET. How's my precious grandchild?

SANDY. Couldn't be better; Sue too. Ten more days in the hospital, and back home they'll be.

MARGARET. I broke into your house and did up the nursery.

SANDY. Good girl. Where's George, Tracy?

TRACY. He's staying in the Gatehouse. He still nad business things to clear up and I thought he'd be quieter there.

SANDY. Did he see his picture in *Dime?* Was he sore at the "Former Coal Miner" caption?

*(*MARGARET *picks up the proof sheets once more.)*

MARGARET. What about this absurd article about your father and—er—Tina Mara in *Destiny,* Sandy? Can't it be stopped?

TRACY. About Father and—let me see! *(She takes the proof sheets.)*

SANDY. Where'd you get hold of that? *(He tries unsuccessfully to recover them.)*

MARGARET. Get ready for lunch, Dinah.

DINAH. In a minute. I'm busy. *(She flops down on the Hall step and continues to work at her puzzle.)*

TRACY *(reading)*. Oh! The absolute devils— Who publishes *Destiny?*

SANDY. Sidney Kidd.—Also *Dime,* also *Spy,* the picture sheet. I worked on *Dime,* for two summers, you know that.

TRACY. Stopped? It's got to be! I'll go to him myself.

SANDY. A fat lot of good that would do. You're too much alike. God save us from the strong. *(He seats himself.)* I saw Kidd the day before yesterday. It took about three hours, but I finally got through to him.

TRACY. What happened?

SANDY. I think I fixed things.

TRACY. How?

SANDY. That would be telling.

MARGARET. Just so long as your father never hears of it.

SANDY. I had a copy of the piece made, and sent it around to his flat, with a little note saying, "How do you like it?"

*(*TRACY *laughs shortly.)*

TRACY. You are a fellah.

MARGARET. Sandy!

SANDY. Why not? Let him worry a little.

TRACY. Let him worry a lot!

*(*THOMAS *enters from Hall.)*

SANDY. Yes, Thomas?

THOMAS. Mr. Connor and the lady say they will be down directly, sir.

SANDY. Thanks, that's fine. Tell May or Elsie to look after Miss Imbrie, will you?

THOMAS. Very good, sir. *(He goes out.)*

MARGARET. What's all this?

TRACY. "Mr. Connor and—?"

SANDY. Mike Connor—Macaulay Connor, his name is.—And—er—Elizabeth Imbrie. I'm putting them up for over the wedding. They're quite nice. You'll like them.

TRACY. You asked people to stay in this house without even asking us?

MARGARET. I think it's very queer indeed.

TRACY. I think it's queerer than that—*I* think it's paranoiac!

SANDY. Keep your shirt on.—I just sort of drifted into them and we sort of got to talking about what riots weddings are as a rule, and they'd never been to a Philadelphia one, and—

TRACY. You're lying, Sandy.—I can always tell.

SANDY. Now look here, Tracy—

TRACY. Look where? "Elizabeth Imbrie" —I know that name! She's a—wait—damn your eyes, Sandy, she's a photographer!

SANDY. For a fact?

TRACY. For a couple of facts—and a famous one!

SANDY. Well, it might be nice to have some good shots of the wedding.

TRACY. What are they doing here?

SANDY. Just now I suppose they're brushing up and going to the bathroom. They're very interesting people. *(He moves uneasily about the room.)* She's practically an artist, and he's written a couple of books—and—and I thought you liked interesting people.

(Dinah rises from her step.)

DINAH. *I* do.

TRACY *(suddenly)*. I know—now I know! They're from *Destiny*—*Destiny* sent them!

MARGARET. *Destiny?*

SANDY. You're just a mass of intuition, Tracy.

TRACY. Well, they can go right back again.

SANDY. No, they can't. Not till they get their story.

TRACY. Story? What story?

SANDY. The Philadelphia story.

MARGARET. And what on earth's that?

SANDY. Well, it seems Kidd has had Connor and Imbrie and a couple of others down here for two months doing the town: I mean writing it up. It's to come out in three parts in the Autumn. "Industrial Philadelphia," "Historical Philadelphia"—and then the third—

TRACY. I'm going to be sick.

SANDY. Yes, dear, "Fashionable Philadelphia."

TRACY. I *am* sick.

MARGARET. But why us? Surely there are other families who—

TRACY. Yes—why not the Drexels or Biddles or the *qu'est-ce-que-c'est* Cassats?

SANDY. We go even further back: It's those Quakers.—And of course there's your former marriage and your looks and your general prowess in golf and foxhunting, with a little big game on the side, and your impending second marriage into the coal fields—

TRACY. Never mind that!

SANDY. I don't, but they do. It's news, darling, news.

MARGARET. Is there no such thing as privacy any more?

TRACY. Only in bed, Mother, and not always there.

SANDY. Anyhow I thought I was licked—and what else could I do?

TRACY. A trade, eh? So we're to let them publish the inside story of my wedding in order to keep Father's wretched little affair quiet!

MARGARET. It's utterly and completely disgusting.

SANDY. It was my suggestion, not Kidd's. I may have been put in the way of making it. I don't know. It's hard to tell with the future President of the United States.

TRACY. What's the writer's name again?

SANDY. Connor, Macaulay Connor. I don't think he likes the assignment any more than we do—the gal either. They were handling the Industrial end.

(TRACY *goes to the telephone, and dials.*)

TRACY. My heart's breaking for them.

MARGARET. I don't know what the world is coming to. It's an absolute invasion; two strange people tramping through the house, prying and investigating—

TRACY. Maybe we're going through a revolution without knowing it. (*To the telephone.*) Hello, is Mr. Briggs there?—This is Tracy Lord, Mr. Briggs.—Look, I wonder if you happen to have on hand any books by Macaulay Connor? (SANDY *rises.*) You have!—Could you surely send them out this afternoon?— Thanks, Mr. Briggs, you're sweet. (*She replaces the telephone, raging.*) —If they've got to have a story, I'll give them a story— I'll give them one they can't get through the mails!

SANDY. Oh—oh—I was afraid of this—

TRACY. Who the hell do they think they are, barging in on peaceful people—watching every little mannerism—jotting down notes on how we sit, and stand, and talk, and eat and move—

DINAH (*eagerly*). Will they do that?

TRACY. —And all in the horrible snide corkscrew English!—Well, if we have to submit to it to save Father's face—which incidentally doesn't deserve it—I'm for giving them a picture of home life that will stand their hair on end.

MARGARET. You will do nothing of the sort, Tracy.

SANDY. She thinks she'll be the outrageous Miss Lord. The fact is, she'll probably be Sweetness and Light to the neck.

TRACY. Oh, will I?

SANDY. You don't know yet what being under the microscope does to people. I felt it a little coming out in the car. It's a funny feeling.

MARGARET. It's odd how self-conscious we've all become over the worldly possessions that once made us so confident.

SANDY. I know; you catch yourself explaining away your dough, the way you would a black eye: you've just run into it in the dark or something.

MARGARET. We shall be ourselves with them; very much ourselves.

DINAH. But Mother, you want us to create a good impression, don't you?

MARGARET (*to* SANDY). They don't know that *we* know what they're here for, I hope?

SANDY. No; that was understood.

DINAH. I should think it would look awfully funny to them, Father's not being here for his own daughter's wedding.

TRACY. Would you now?

SANDY. That's all right; I fixed that, too.

TRACY. How do you mean you did?

SANDY. I told Sue to send a telegram before dinner. "Confined to bed with a cold, unable to attend nuptials, oceans of love, Father."

MARGARET. Not just in those words!

SANDY. Not exactly.—It'll come on the telephone and Thomas will take it and you won't have your glasses and he'll read it aloud to you.

MARGARET. Tracy, will you promise to behave like a lady, if only for my sake?

TRACY. I'll do my best, Mrs. Lord. I don't know how good that is.

MARGARET. Go put a dress on.

TRACY. Yes, Mother.

MARGARET. There are too many legs around here.

TRACY. Suds! I'll be pure Victorian, all frills and ruffles, conversationally chaste as an egg. (UNCLE WILLIE TRACY, *sixty-two, enters from the Parlor.*) Hello, Uncle Willie. Where did you come from?

UNCLE WILLIE. Your Great-aunt Geneva has requested my absence from the house until dinner time. Can you give me lunch, Margaret?

MARGARET. But of course! With pleasure—

DINAH. Hello, Uncle Willie—

SANDY. How are you, Uncle Willie?

WILLIE. Alexander and Dinah, good morning. *(To Tracy.)* My esteemed wife, the old war-horse, is certainly spreading herself for your party. *I* seriously question the propriety of any such display in such times. But she— Why aren't you being married in church, Tracy?

TRACY. I like the parlor here so much better. Didn't you think it looked pretty as you came through?

UNCLE WILLIE. That is not the point. The point is that I've sunk thousands in that church, and I'd like to get some use of it. —Give me a glass of sherry, Margaret.

MARGARET. Not until lunch time, my dear.

UNCLE WILLIE. These women.

DINAH. You're really a wicked old man, aren't you?

UNCLE WILLIE *(points beyond her to the Porch).* What's that out there?

(DINAH turns to look. He vigorously pinches her behind.)

DINAH. Ouch!

UNCLE WILLIE. Never play with fire, child. *(He looks at the others.)* What's a-lack here? What's a-stirrin'? What's amiss?

SANDY. Uncle Willie, do you know anything about the laws of libel?

UNCLE WILLIE *(seats himself).* Certainly I know about the laws of libel. Why shouldn't I? I know all about them. In 1916, I, Willie Q. Tracy, successfully defended the *Post,* and George Lorimer personally, against one of the cleverest, one of the subtlest—why? What do you want to say?

SANDY. It isn't what *I* want to say—

TRACY. Is it enough if they can simply prove that it is true?

UNCLE WILLIE. Certainly not! Take me; if I was totally bald and wore a toupee, if I had flat feet, with these damnable metal arches, false teeth, and a case of double—

DINAH. Poor Uncle Willie.

UNCLE WILLIE. I said *"If* I had." —And if such facts were presented in the public prints in such a manner as to hold me up to public ridicule, I could collect substantial damages,—and would, if it took me all winter.

TRACY. Suppose the other way around; suppose they printed things that weren't true.

UNCLE WILLIE. Suppose they did? Suppose it was erroneously stated, that during my travels as a young man I was married in a native ceremony to a dusky maiden in British Guinea, I doubt if I could collect a cent. *(He looks past her, toward the Hall door.)* Who are these two strange people coming down the hall?

(The entire family rises.)

MARGARET. Oh, good gracious!

(TRACY takes UNCLE WILLIE by the arm.)

TRACY. Come on—out. *(She leads him toward the Parlor at Right.)* What was she like, Uncle Willie?

WILLIE. Who?

TRACY. British Guinea?

WILLIE. So very unlike your Aunt Geneva, my dear. *(They go out.)*

MARGARET. Dinah—

DINAH. But, Mother, oughtn't we—

MARGARET. Sandy can entertain them until we—until we collect ourselves. *(She directs DINAH into the Parlor.)*

SANDY. What'll I say?

MARGARET. I wish I could tell you—in a few very well-chosen words. *(She goes out.)*

(SANDY is alone for a moment. He hunches his shoulders uncomfortably and clears his throat. MIKE CONNOR, thirty, and LIZ IMBRIE, twenty-eight, come in from the Hall. LIZ has a small and important camera hanging from a leather strap around her neck.)

LIZ. —In here?

MIKE. He said the sitting room. I suppose that's contrasted to the living room, the ballroom—the drawing room—the morning room—the— *(He sees SANDY.)* Oh, hello again. Here you are.

SANDY. Here I am.

MIKE. It's quite a place.

SANDY. It is, isn't it?—I couldn't help overhearing you as you came in. Do you mind if I say something?

MIKE. Not at all. What?

SANDY. Your approach to your job seems definitely antagonistic. I don't think it's fair. I think you ought to give us a break.

MIKE. It's not a job I asked for.

SANDY. I know it's not. But in spite of it, and in spite of certain of our regrettable inherited characteristics, we just might be fairly decent. Why not wait and see?

(MIKE *and* LIZ *seat themselves.*)

MIKE. You have quite a style yourself.— You're on the *Saturday Evening Post,* did you say?

(SANDY *seats himself facing* MIKE *and* LIZ.)

SANDY. I work for it.

MIKE. Which end?

SANDY. Editorial.

MIKE. I have to tell you, in all honesty, that I'm opposed to everything you represent.

SANDY. *Destiny* is hardly a radical sheet: what is it you're doing—boring from within?

MIKE. —And I'm not a Communist, not by a long shot.

LIZ. Just a small pin-feather in the Left Wing. (MIKE *looks at her*). —Sorry.

SANDY. Jeffersonian Democrat?

MIKE. That's more like it.

SANDY. Have you ever seen his house at Monticello? *It's* quite a place too.

LIZ. Home Team One; Visitors Nothing— (*She rises and looks about her.*) Is this house very old, Mr. Lord?

SANDY. No, there are a very few old ones on the Main Line— The Gatehouse is, of course. Father's grandfather built that for a summer place when they all lived on Rittenhouse Square. Father and Mother did this about 1910—the spring before my brother Junius was born. He's the oldest. You won't meet him, he's in the diplomatic service in London.

MIKE (*to* LIZ). Wouldn't you know?

SANDY. *I* worked for Sidney Kidd once. What do you make of him?

MIKE (*after a moment*). A brilliant editor, and a very wonderful man.

LIZ. Also, our bread and butter.

SANDY. Sorry to have been rude.

(MIKE *takes a sheaf of typewritten cards from his pocket and begins to glance through them.*)

MIKE. I suppose you're all of you opposed to the Administration?

SANDY. The present one? No—as a matter of fact we're Loyalists.

MIKE. Surprise, surprise.—The Research Department didn't give us much data.— Your sister's fiancé—George Kittredge— aged thirty-two.—Since last year General Manager Quaker State Coal, in charge of operation.—Is that right?

SANDY. That's right.—And brilliant at it.

MIKE. So I've heard tell. I seem to have read about him first back in '35 or '36.— Up from the bottom, wasn't he?

SANDY. Just exactly—and of the mines.

MIKE. Reorganized the entire works?

SANDY. He did.

MIKE. National hero, new model: makes drooping family incomes to revive again. Anthracite, sweet anthracite.—How did your sister happen to meet him?

SANDY. She and I went up a month ago to look things over.

MIKE. I see. And was it instant?

SANDY. Immediate.

MIKE. Good for her.—He must be quite a guy.—Which side of this—er—fine, aboriginal family does she resemble most, would you say?

SANDY (*looks at him; rises*). The histories of both are in the library; I'll get them out for you. I'll also see if I can round up some of the Living Members.

LIZ. They don't know about *us,* do they? (*Goes above table.*)

SANDY (*in the doorway stops and turns*). —Pleasanter not, don't you think?

LIZ. Much.

SANDY. That's what *I* thought—also what Kidd thought.

MIKE *(rising suddenly)*. Look here, Lord—

SANDY. Yes—?

MIKE. Why don't you throw us out?

SANDY *(laughs shortly, then goes out)*. I hope you'll never know.

LIZ. Meaning what?

MIKE. Search me.

LIZ. Maybe Der Kidder has been up to his little tricks.

MIKE. If only I could get away from his damned paper—

LIZ. It's Sidney himself you can't get away from, dear.

(She begins to tour the room with her camera.)

MIKE. I tried to resign again on the phone this morning.

LIZ. —Knick-knacks—gimcracks—signed photographs! Wouldn't you know you'd have to be rich as the Lords to live in a dump like this? *(Sees the portrait over the mantel.)* Save me—it's a Gilbert Stuart.

MIKE. A what?

LIZ. Catch me, Mike!

MIKE. Faint to the left, will you? *(He returns to the typewritten cards)*. "First husband, C. K.—" Can you imagine what a guy named "C. K. Dexter Haven" must be like?

LIZ. "Macaulay Connor" is not such a homespun tag, my pet.

MIKE. I've been called Mike ever since I can remember.

LIZ. Well, maybe Dexter is "Ducky" to his friends.

MIKE. I wouldn't doubt it.—But I wonder what the "C. K." is for—

LIZ. Maybe it's Pennsylvania Dutch for "William Penn."

MIKE. "C. K. Dexter Haven." God!

LIZ. I knew a plain Joe Smith once. He was only a clerk in a hardware store, but he was an absolute louse.

MIKE. —Also he plays polo. Also designs and races sailboats. "Class" boats, I think they call them. Very upper class, of course.

LIZ. Don't despair. He's out, and Kittredge, man of the people, is in.

MIKE. From all reports, quite a comer too. Political timber.—Poor fellow, I wonder how he fell for it.

LIZ. I imagine she's a young lady who knows what she wants when she wants it.

MIKE. The young, rich, rapacious American female—there's no other country where she exists.

LIZ. I'll admit the idea of *her* scares even me.—Would I change places with her, for all her wealth and beauty? Boy! Just ask me.

MIKE. I know how I'm going to begin. *(He leans back on the sofa, closes his eyes, and declines:)* "—So much for Historical Philadelphia, so much for Industrial. Now, Gentle Reader, consider an entire section of American Society which, closely following the English tradition, lives on the land, but in a new sense. It is not the land that provides the living, it is—"

LIZ. You're ahead of yourself. Wait till you do your documentation.

MIKE. I'm tired. Kidd is a slave-driver. I wish I was home in bed. Also I'm hungry. Tell four footmen to call me in time for lunch.

(DINAH re-enters from the Porch, her manner now very much that of a woman of the world. She rises on her toes like a ballet dancer and advances toward them.)

DINAH. Oh—how do you do?—Friends of Alexander's, are you not?

MIKE *(rises)*. How do you do?—Why, yes, we—

DINAH. I am Dinah Lord. My real name is Diana, but my sister changed it.

LIZ. I'm Elizabeth Imbrie—and this is Macauley Connor. It's awfully nice of—

DINAH *(extends an arched hand to each)* Enchantée de vous voir. Enchantée te faire votre connaisance. —I spoke French before I spoke English. My early childhood was spent in Paris, where my father worked in a bank—the House of Morgan.

LIZ. Really?

DINAH. *C'est vrai—absolument! (She runs up to the piano—leaping a low stool as she goes.)* Can you play the piano? I can. And sing at the same time. Listen—*(She plays and sings.)* "Pepper Sauce Woman; Pepper Sauce Woman—"

LIZ *(speaks lowly to* MIKE*)*. What is this?

MIKE. An idiot, probably. They happen in the best of families, especially in the best.

DINAH. —"Oh, what a shame; she has lost her name. Don't know who to blame, walkin' along to Shango Batcheloor." *(DINAH stops singing and continues in a dreamy voice.)* The Bahamas—how well I remember them.—Those perfumed nights—the flowers—the native wines. I was there, once, on a little trip with Leopold Stowkowski.

(TRACY comes in from the Porch. She has changed into a rather demure dress, high in neck and ample in skirt.)

TRACY. You were there with your governess, after the whooping cough.

(DINAH gestures airily.)

DINAH. —My sister Tracy. Greetings, Sister.

TRACY. Mother wants to see you at once. At once!

(DINAH rises from the piano.)

DINAH. You've got on my hair ribbon.

TRACY. Your face is still dirty. *(As* DINAH *passes her,* TRACY *gives her one, deft, smart spank, then, as* DINAH *goes out into the Hall, comes up to* MIKE *and* LIZ, *cool, collected and charming, all Sweetness and Light.)* It's awfully nice having you here. *(She shakes hands with them.)* I do hope you'll stay for my wedding.

LIZ. We'd like to very much.

MIKE. In fact, that was our idea.

TRACY. I'm so pleased that it occurred to you. *(She indicates the sofa. They seat themselves there and* TRACY *takes a chair facing them.)* The house is rather a mess, of course. We all have to huddle here, and overflow onto the porch.—I hope your rooms are comfortable.

(MIKE takes out a pack of cigarettes.)

LIZ. Oh, very, thanks.

TRACY. Anything you want, ask Mary or Elsie. *(She holds a cigarette box out to them. Each takes one.* LIZ's *camera catches her eye.)* They're magic. What a cunning little camera.

(MIKE has struck a match—sees TRACY *still holds a lighter toward him as she talks to* LIZ—*he slowly bends forward to accept a light for his cigarette—then blows his match out—she graciously smiles at him.)*

LIZ. It's a Contax. I'm afraid I'm rather a nuisance with it. *(She accepts a light from the lighter.)*

TRACY. But you couldn't be: I hope you'll take loads. Dear Papá and Mamá aren't allowing any reporters in—that is, except for little Mr. Grace, who does the social news. *(To* MIKE.*)* Can you imagine a grown-up man having to sink so low?

MIKE. It does seem pretty bad.

TRACY. People have always been so kind about letting us live our simple and uneventful little life here unmolested. Of course, after my divorce last year—but I expect that always happens, and is more or less deserved. Dear Papá was quite angry, though, and swore he'd never let another reporter inside the gate. He thought some of their methods were a trifle underhanded.—You're a writer, aren't you, Mr. Connor?

MIKE. In a manner of speaking.

TRACY. Sandy told me. I've sent for your books. "Macaulay Connor"— What's the "Macaulay" for?

MIKE. My father taught English History. I'm "Mike" to my friends.

TRACY. —Of whom you have many, I'm sure. English history has always fascinated me. Cromwell—Bloody Mary, John the Bastard— Where did he teach? I mean your father—

MIKE. In the high school in South Bend, Indiana.

TRACY. "South Bend"! It sounds like dancing, doesn't it? You must have had a most happy childhood there.

MIKE. It was terrific.

TRACY. I'm so glad.

MIKE. I don't mean it that way.

TRACY. I'm so sorry. Why?

MIKE. Largely due to the lack of the wherewithal, I guess.

TRACY. But that doesn't always cause unhappiness, does it?—not if you're the right kind of man. George Kittredge, my fiancé, never had anything either, but he— Are either of you married?

MIKE. No.

LIZ. I—er—that is, no.

TRACY. You mean *you* were, but now you're divorced?

LIZ. Well, the fact is—

TRACY. Suds—you can't mean you're ashamed of it!

LIZ. Of course I'm not ashamed of it.

MIKE (is staring at her). Wha-at?

LIZ. It was ages ago, when I was a mere kid, in Duluth.

MIKE. Good Lord, Liz—you never told me you were—

LIZ. You never asked.

MIKE. I know, but—

LIZ. Joe Smith, Hardware.

MIKE. Liz, you're the damnedest girl. (Rises.)

LIZ. *I* think I'm sweet.

(MIKE rises, turns once around the sofa and seats himself again.)

TRACY. Duluth—that must be a lovely spot. It's west of here, isn't it?

LIZ. Sort of.—But occasionally we get the breezes.

TRACY. Is this your first visit in Philadelphia?

LIZ. Just about.

TRACY. It's a quaint old place, don't you think? I suppose it's affected somewhat by being the only really big city that's near New York.

LIZ. I think that's a very good point to make about it.

TRACY. —Though I suppose you consider us somewhat provincial?

LIZ. Not at all, I assure you.

TRACY. Odd customs, and such. Where the scrapples eat Biddle on Sunday. Of course it *is* very old—Philadelphia, I mean, the scrapple is fresh weekly. How old are *you*, Mr. Connor?

MIKE. I was thirty last month.

TRACY. Two books isn't much for a man of thirty. I don't mean to criticize. You probably have other interests outside your work.

MIKE. None.—Unless—(He looks at LIZ and smiles.)

TRACY. How sweet! Are you living together?

MIKE. Why—er—that is—

LIZ. That's an odd question, I must say!

TRACY. Why?

LIZ. Well—it just is.

TRACY. I don't see why. I think it's very interesting. (She leans forward seriously, elbow on knee and chin on hand.) Miss Imbrie—don't you agree that all this marrying and giving in marriage is the damndest gyp that's ever been put over on an unsuspecting public?

MIKE (to LIZ). Can she be human!

TRACY. Please, Mr. Connor!—I asked Miss Imbrie a question.

LIZ. No. As a matter of fact, I don't.

TRACY. Good. Nor do I. That's why I'm putting my chin out for the second time tomorrow. (GEORGE off stage, Left, calls "Tracy." She rises and moves toward the Porch.) Here's the lucky man now. I'll bring him right in and put him on view— a one-man exhibition. In here, George! —In here, my dear!

(She goes out, LIZ rises and turns to MIKE.)

LIZ. My God—who's doing the interviewing here?

MIKE. She's a lot more than I counted on.

LIZ. Do you suppose she caught on somehow?

MIKE. No. She's just a hellion.

LIZ. I'm beginning to feel the size of a pin-head.

MIKE. Don't let her throw you.

LIZ. Do you want to take over?

MIKE. I want to go home.

(TRACY *re-enters with* GEORGE KITTREDGE, *aged thirty-two; and brings him up to them.*)

TRACY. Miss Imbrie—Mr. Connor—Mr. Kittredge, my beau.—Friends of Sandy's, George.

GEORGE. Any friend of Sandy's—

(*He shakes hands with them.*)

LIZ. How do you do?

MIKE. How are you?

GEORGE. Fine as silk, thanks.

LIZ. You certainly look it.

GEORGE. Thanks, I've shaken quite a lot of coal-dust from my feet in the last day or two.

TRACY. Isn't he beautiful? Isn't it wonderful what a little soap and water will do?

MIKE. Didn't I read a piece about you in *The Nation* a while ago?

GEORGE. Quite a while ago: I've been resting on my laurels since that—and a couple of others.

MIKE. Quite a neat piece of work— anticipating the Guffey Coal Act the way you did.—Or do I remember straight?

GEORGE. Anyone should have foreseen that —I was just lucky.

LIZ. A becoming modesty.

GEORGE. That's nothing to what's yet to be done with Labor relations.

TRACY. You ought to see him with the men —they simply adore him.

GEORGE. Oh—come on, Tracy!

TRACY. Oh, but they do! Never in my life will I forget that first night I saw you, all those wonderful faces, and the torch-lights, and the way his voice boomed—

GEORGE. You see, I'm really a spellbinder. —That's the way I got her.

TRACY. Except it was me who got you!— I'm going to put these two at the bridal table, in place of the Grants.

GEORGE. That's a good idea.

TRACY. George, it won't rain, will it?— Promise me it won't rain.

GEORGE. Tracy, I'll see to that personally.

TRACY. I almost believe you could.

MIKE. I guess this must be love.

GEORGE. Your guess is correct, Mr. Connor.

TRACY. I'm just his faithful Old Dog Tray.

GEORGE. Give me your paw?

(*She presents her hand.*)

TRACY. You've got it.

(GEORGE *takes her hand and kisses it.* MARGARET *enters from the Parlor, followed by* DINAH. DINAH *remains in the doorway.* MARGARET *goes directly to* LIZ *and* MIKE.)

MARGARET. How do you do? We're so happy to have you. Forgive me for not coming in sooner, but things are in such a state. I'd no idea that a simple country wedding could involve so much. (*She crosses to* TRACY *and* TRACY *to her. They beam fatuously upon one another.*) My little girl— (*She pats her face, then turns back to* LIZ.) —I do hope you'll be comfortable. Those rooms are inclined to be hot in this weather.—Aren't you pretty, my dear! (SANDY *comes in from the Hall.*) Look at the way she wears her hair, Tracy. Isn't it pretty?

TRACY. Mighty fine.

MARGARET. I do wish my husband might be here to greet you, but we expect him presently. He's been detained in New York on business for that lovely Tina Mara. You know her work?

LIZ. Only vaguely!

MARGARET. So talented—and such a lovely person! But like so many artists—no business head, none whatever. (*She gives* TRACY *a knowing smile.* TRACY *and* SANDY *smile.* SANDY *then smirks for* TRACY's *sole benefit.* EDWARD *enters from the Hall, carrying a tray with a sherry decanter and eight glasses.* THOMAS *follows him.* EDWARD *pours.* THOMAS *serves.* MARGARET *beams upon* GEORGE.) Good morning, George!

GEORGE. Good morning, Mrs. Lord!

MARGARET. And this is my youngest daughter, Diana—

(DINAH *curtseys*.)

MIKE. I think we've met.

(THOMAS *gives* MARGARET *a glass of sherry*.)

MARGARET. Thank you, Thomas.

(SANDY *stretches himself out in an easy chair*.)

SANDY. Now let's all relax, and throw ourselves into things. Hi, George!

GEORGE. Hello, Sandy— Welcome home!

(*All take sherry, with the exception of* TRACY *and* DINAH.)

MARGARET. After lunch Sandy must show you some of the sights—the model dairy, and the stables, and the chicken farm— and perhaps there'll be time to run you out to some other places on the Main Line —Devins, Saint Davids. Bryn Mawr, where my daughter Tracy went to college—

DINAH. 'Til she got bounced out on her—

MARGARET. —Dinah!

(UNCLE WILLIE *re-enters from the Parlor*.)

UNCLE WILLIE. It's a pretty kettle of fish when a man has to wait two mortal hours—

(*Suddenly* TRACY *runs to him with her arms out*.)

TRACY. Papá—Dear Papá— (*She embraces him warmly*.) Didn't the car meet you? (UNCLE WILLIE *is completely bewildered*.)

WILLIE. The car?

TRACY. You angel—to drop everything and get here in time for lunch—Isn't he, Mamá?

MARGARET. In—indeed he is.

(UNCLE WILLIE *stares at them*.)

UNCLE WILLIE. I'm not one to jump to conclusions, but—

TRACY. These are our friends, Mr. Connor and Miss Imbrie. Father.—They're here for the wedding.

MIKE. How are you, Mr. Lord?

LIZ. How do you do, Mr. Lord?

UNCLE WILLIE. Dashed fine. How are you?

SANDY. Hi, Pops!

UNCLE WILLIE. —Alexander.

DINAH. Welcome back, Daddy!

UNCLE WILLIE. Dinah— Kittredge— (*He turns to* MARGARET *and bows*.) Margaret, my sweet.

(THOMAS *comes down to his Left with a sherry*. UNCLE WILLIE *tosses it off and returns the glass*.)

TRACY. Mother, don't you think you ought to explain the new arrangement to Father before lunch?

MARGARET (*taking* WILLIE *by the arm*). Why—yes—I think I'd best. (*She slips her arm through* UNCLE WILLIE'*s and leads him to the desk which stands between the Porch doors*.) See here—here is the list now— Seth.

(*In from the Porch comes* DEXTER HAVEN, *twenty-eight*. SANDY *sees him and exclaims*:)

SANDY. Holy cats!

MARGARET (*turns quickly*). Dexter Haven!

DEXTER. Hello, friends and enemies. I came the short way, across the fields.

MARGARET. Well, this *is* a surprise.

GEORGE. I should think it is.

(DEXTER *kisses* MARGARET *lightly upon the cheek*.)

DEXTER. Hello, you sweet thing.

MARGARET. Now you go right home at once!

UNCLE WILLIE. Remove yourself, young man!

DEXTER. But I've been invited. (*He shakes* UNCLE WILLIE'*s hand*.) How are you, sir?

UNCLE WILLIE. No better, no worse. Get along.

DEXTER. Hello, Sandy. (*They shake hands*.)

SANDY. How are you, boy?

DEXTER. Never better. In fact, it's immoral how good I feel.

DINAH. What—what brings you here, Mr Haven?

DEXTER. Dinah, my angel! *(He kisses her cheek.)* Why, she's turned into a raving beauty! *(He turns to* TRACY.) Awfully sweet and thoughtful of you to ask me to lunch, Tray.

TRACY. Not at all.—Extra place, Thomas.

THOMAS. Yes, Miss Tracy. *(He and* EDWARD *go out, into the Hall.* UNCLE WILLIE *and* MARGARET *talk inaudibly at the desk.* TRACY *gestures toward* MIKE *and* LIZ.)

TRACY. Miss Imbrie—Mr. Connor— my former husband, whose name for the moment escapes me.

DEXTER. How do you do?

MIKE. How do you do?

LIZ. How do you do?

DEXTER. —Of course I intended to come anyway, but it did make it pleasanter.— Hello, Kittredge.

GEORGE. How are you, Haven?

DEXTER *(peers at him).* What's the matter? You don't look as well as when I last saw you. *(He pats his arm sympathetically.)* Poor fellow—I know just how you feel. *(He turns to* TRACY; *gazes at her fondly.)* Red head—isn't *she* in the pink, though! —*You* don't look old enough to marry anyone, even for the first time—you never did! She needs trouble to mature her, Kittredge. Give her lots of it.

GEORGE. I'm afraid she can't count on me for that.

DEXTER. No? Too bad.—Sometimes, for your own sake, I think you should have stuck to me longer, Red.

*(*TRACY *goes to* GEORGE *and takes his arm.)*

TRACY. I thought it was for life, but the nice Judge gave me a full pardon.

DEXTER. That's the kind of talk I like to hear; no bitterness, no recrimination—just a good quick left to the jaw.

GEORGE. Very funny.

THOMAS *(reappears in the Hall doorway).* Luncheon is served, Madam.

MARGARET. Thank you, Thomas.

(He goes out. UNCLE WILLIE *advances from the desk.)*

UNCLE WILLIE. I don't suppose a man ever

had a better or finer family. *(He turns and takes* MARGARET's *arm.)* I wake in the night and say to myself—"Seth, you lucky dog. What have you done to deserve it?"

MARGARET. And what *have* you?

(Arm in arm they go out into the Hall.)

TRACY. Do you mind if I go in with Mr. Connor, Miss Imbrie?

LIZ. Why, not in the least.

*(*SANDY *offers* LIZ *his arm.)*

SANDY. Sandy's your boy.

TRACY *(takes* MIKE's *arm).* —Because I think he's such an interesting man.

GEORGE. Come on, Dinah, I draw you, I guess.

DINAH. Dexter—

DEXTER *(to* GEORGE). Isn't snatching one of my girls enough, you cad?

GEORGE. You're a very bright fellow, Haven, I'll hire you.

MIKE *(to* TRACY). No wonder you want to get away from all this.

TRACY. That's very insulting—but consistently interesting. We must talk more.

(They are all approaching the Hall when SETH LORD, *fifty, appears in the Porch doorway, hat in hand, a light topcoat over his arm.)*

SETH. I don't know how welcome I am, but after Sandy's note, I thought the least I could do was to—

*(*DINAH *starts down the Hall steps to him but is stopped by* TRACY *who suddenly cries out to* SETH:)*

TRACY. Uncle Willie! *(She turns to others.)* Please go on in, everyone, I want a word with Uncle Willie.

(They go out. TRACY *crosses the room and faces her father.)*

SETH. Well, daughter?

TRACY. Well?

SETH. Still Justice, with her shining sword —eh? Who's on the spot?

TRACY. We are; thanks to you—Uncle Willie.

CURTAIN

ACT TWO

SCENE I

The Porch, which is more like a room than a Porch. Entrance from the Sitting Room is through the glass doors at back and to the Library, through glass doors at Stage Left; to the Garden, down broad stone steps from the Porch and along a gravel path past shrubbery to the Left and Right. The open side of the Porch is shielded with lattice-work, and there are pots of geraniums on the steps.

Early evening, Friday. The sky has cleared. MIKE *is in a chair on the Porch, making additional notes.* LIZ *is seated on the steps, reloading her camera.*

LIZ. I may need more film.

MIKE. I may need more paper.

LIZ. There's a cousin Joanna, who's definitely crazy.

MIKE. Who told you?

LIZ. Dinah.

MIKE. Dinah should know.

LIZ. Where is she now? I want some more shots of her, while it's still light.

MIKE. She's out schooling a horse somewhere. It's the horses that get the schooling hereabouts. Did you shoot the old Tycoon milking his cows?

LIZ. Several times. He shot one at me, but he missed.

MIKE. Caption: "Seventy Times Seven Fat Kine Has He." (*He consults his notes.*) "George Kittredge, Important Official, Important Company. Controlling interest owned by Seth Lord."

LIZ. What a coincidence and will wonders never cease.

MIKE. I'm inclined to like Kittredge—I can see how she fell for him. I think he's in a tough spot, with Haven prowling around, though.

LIZ. Is a sinister fellow, Dexter.

MIKE. Is very.—But George is interesting. Get him on coal some time.

LIZ. I'd rather have him on toast.

MIKE. Answer me honestly, Liz; what right has a girl like Tracy Lord to exist?

LIZ. Politically, socially, or economically?

MIKE. But what place has she got in the world today? Comes the Revolution she'll be the first to go.

LIZ. Sure; right out under the Red General's arm.

MIKE. She's a new one on me. Maybe Philadelphia produces a different brand of monkey.

LIZ (*looks at him keenly*). You're a funny one, Mike.

MIKE. Why?

LIZ. Use the name "Wanamaker" in a sentence.

MIKE. I bite.

LIZ. I met a girl this morning. I hate her, but I—

MIKE. I get you, but you're wrong. You couldn't be wronger. Women like that bore the pants off me.

LIZ. For a writer, you use your figures of speech most ineptly. You know, I wish they knew why we were here. They're all such sweet innocents, it makes me feel like—

(UNCLE WILLIE *and* SETH *enter from the Garden down Right.*)

UNCLE WILLIE. Would you accept this perfect rose, Miss Imbrie?

LIZ. Why, thank you, Mr. Lord. It's a beauty.

SETH. Miss Imbrie is amused at something.

LIZ. I'm sorry, Mr. Tracy, but it's so funny, you being uncle and nephew. Could I have a picture of you together?

UNCLE WILLIE. Certainly! (*He slips his arm through* SETH'S.) Now stand up straight, Willie. He *is* younger than I. It was a matter of half sisters marrying step-brothers.

LIZ. I see. That is, I think I do. (*She snaps a picture.*)

UNCLE WILLIE. No incest, however.

LIZ. Of course not. (*And snaps another.*)

UNCLE WILLIE. There have been other things, however. (*He looks at* SETH.) Uncle Willie—I'm thinking of asking that little dancer, Tina Mara, to come down and dance for the wedding guests tomorrow. Do you think it's a good idea?

SETH. Excellent. It might put an end to the ridiculous gossip about you and her.

UNCLE WILLIE. Is there gossip?

SETH. There seems to be.

UNCLE WILLIE. Is it ridiculous?

SETH. All gossip is ridiculous.

(SANDY *comes from the Library at Left and crosses the Porch to the Sitting-Room door.*)

SANDY. Look alive, men! Time to dress!

SETH. Right you are. Thanks, Sandy— (*He goes up the steps and over the Porch into the Sitting Room.* SANDY *follows him.*)

UNCLE WILLIE. Miss Imbrie, as a camera-fiend, I think I have another interesting subject for you.

LIZ. Will I have time?

UNCLE WILLIE. Time is an illusion. Come with me, please. (*He offers his arm, which she takes gingerly.*) It's part of the old house, a little removed from it.

LIZ. But what?

UNCLE WILLIE. An ancient granite privy, of superb design—a dream of loveliness.

LIZ. —At sunset—idyllic!

(LIZ *and* UNCLE WILLIE *go out into the Garden.* MIKE *pockets his notebook and moves toward the Sitting Room. Suddenly* TRACY *appears in the Library doorway. She wears a bright-colored dressing gown over the foundation for a white evening dress and has a book in her hand, her finger marking a place toward the end of it.*)

TRACY. Please wait a minute.

MIKE. With pleasure. (*He stops where he is. She goes to him, turns him about and looks at him wonderingly.*) What's the matter?

TRACY. I've been reading these stories. They're so damned beautiful.

MIKE. You like? Thanks—

TRACY. Why Connor, they're almost poetry.

MIKE (*laughs shortly*). Don't fool yourself; they *are!*

TRACY. I can't make you out at all, now.

MIKE. Really? I thought I was easy.

TRACY. So did I, but you're not. You talk so big and tough—and then you write like this. Which is which?

MIKE. I guess I'm both.

TRACY. No—I believe you put the toughness on, to save your skin.

MIKE. You think?

TRACY. Yes. *I* know a little about that—

MIKE. Do you?

TRACY. Quite a lot. (*They look at each other for a moment. Then* TRACY *laughs a little embarressedly and glances away.*) It—the book—it was just such a complete —hell of a surprise, that's all.

MIKE. Yes—it seems you do.

TRACY. What?

MIKE. Know about it.

TRACY. The one called "With the Rich and Mighty"—I think I liked *it* best.

MIKE. I got that from a Spanish peasant's proverb—"With the Rich and Mighty always a little Patience." (TRACY *laughs.*)

TRACY. Good! (*She seats herself, gazes again at the book.*) Tell me something, will you? When you can do a thing like this how can you possibly do anything else?

MIKE. Such as what?

TRACY. You said after lunch—what was it you said?—"Cheap stuff for expensive magazines."

MIKE. Did I?

TRACY. Yes. You did. You said you spent most of your time that way.

(MIKE *seats himself, facing her.*)

MIKE. Practically all. Why? What about it?

TRACY. I can't understand it. And I like to understand things.

MIKE. You'll never believe it, but there are people in this world who have to earn their living.

TRACY. Of course! But people buy books, don't they?

MIKE. Sure they do! They even read them.

TRACY. Well, then?

MIKE. That one represents two solid years' work. It netted Connor something under six hundred dollars.

TRACY. But that shouldn't *be!*

MIKE. —Only unhappily it is.

(*There is a pause.*)

TRACY. And what about your Miss Imbrie?

MIKE. Miss Imbrie is in somewhat the same fix. She is a born painter, and might be an important one. But Miss Imbrie must eat. Also, she prefers a roof over her head to being constantly out in the rain and snow.

(TRACY *ponders this.*)

TRACY. Food and a roof—food and a roof—

MIKE. Those charming essentials.

TRACY. Listen: I've got an idea! (*She rises, goes to him, stands over him.*) Listen: I've got the most marvelous little house in Unionville. It's up on a hill, with a view that would knock you silly. I'm never there except in the hunting season, and not much then, and I'd be so happy to know it was of some use to someone. (*She moves swiftly across the Porch and back again.*) There's a brook and a small lake, no size really, and a patch of woods, and in any kind of weather, it's the— (*She is down the steps now, looking up at the sky.*)—And look at that sky now, will you! Suddenly it's clear as clear! It's going to be fine tomorrow! It's going to be fair! Good for you, God! (*She glances down the Path.*) Hell! (*And quickly re-*

turns *to the Porch.*) Someone's coming—someone I don't want to be alone with. Stand by for a couple of minutes. Will you?

MIKE. Certainly—if you like.

TRACY. You *will* think about the house, won't you?

MIKE. Why, it's terribly nice of you, but—

TRACY. Don't think I'd come trouping in every minute because I wouldn't. I'd never come, except when expressly asked to.

MIKE. It isn't that.

TRACY. What is it?

MIKE. Well, you see—er—you see the idea of artists having a patron has more or less gone out, and—

TRACY (*looks at him steadily*). I see. (*Then waits a moment.*) That wasn't especially kind of you, Mr. Connor. There's no need to rub our general uselessness in.

MIKE. I'm afraid I don't get you.

TRACY. Don't bother. I'm sorry to have seemed—patronizing.

MIKE. I didn't quite mean—

TRACY. Please don't bother, really.

(DEXTER *comes in down the Garden path. He carries a small picture, wrapped in tissue paper.*)

DEXTER. Hello.

TRACY. Hello, fancy seeing you here.

DEXTER (*mounts the porch and goes to the table*). Orange juice? Certainly!

TRACY. You're sure you don't want something stronger? I'll ring if you like. (*He pours himself a glass of orange juice from a pitcher.*)

DEXTER. Not now, thanks. This is fine.

TRACY. Don't tell me you've forsaken your beloved whiskey-and-whiskies—

DEXTER. No, indeed. I've just changed their color, that's all. I go in for the pale pastel shades now. I find they're more becoming. (*He looks at* MIKE *over his glass.*) We met at lunch, didn't we?

MIKE. Yes, I seem to remember. Connor's my name.

DEXTER. —The writer—of course! Do you drink, Mr. Connor?

MIKE. A little. Why?

DEXTER. Not to excess?

MIKE. Not often.

DEXTER. —And a writer! It's extraordinary. I thought all writers drank to excess, and beat their wives. I expect that at one time I secretly wanted to be a writer.

TRACY. Dexter, would you mind doing something for me?

(He replaces the glass upon the table and puts the picture beside it.)

DEXTER. Anything, what?

TRACY. Get the hell out of here.

DEXTER. Oh, no, I couldn't do that. That wouldn't be fair to you. You need me too much.

TRACY. Would you mind telling me just what it is you're hanging around for? *(MIKE moves toward the Library door.)* No—please don't go! I'd honestly much prefer it if you wouldn't.

(Reluctantly MIKE seats himself near the door.)

DEXTER. So should I. Do stay, Mr. Connor. As a writer this ought to be right up your street.

TRACY *(to MIKE)*. Miss not a word!

DEXTER. Honestly, you never looked better in your life; you're getting a fine tawny look—

TRACY. Oh, we're going to talk about me, are we? Goody.

DEXTER. —It's astonishing what money can do for people, don't you agree, Mr. Connor? Not too much, you know,— just more than enough. Particularly for girls. Look at Tracy. There's never been a blow that hasn't been softened for her. There'll never be one that won't be softened—why, it even changed her shape— she was a dumpy little thing originally.

TRACY. —Only as it happens, I'm not interested in myself, for the moment. What interests me now is what, if any, your real point is, in—

DEXTER. Not interested in yourself! My dear, you're fascinated! You're far and away your favorite person in the world.

TRACY. Dexter, in case you don't know it —I—!

DEXTER. Shall I go on—?

TRACY. Oh, yes, please do, by all means— *(She seats herself.)*

DEXTER. Of course, she is kindness itself, Mr. Connor—

TRACY. —Itself, Mr. Connor.

DEXTER. She is generous to a fault —that is, except to other people's faults. For instance, she never had the slightest sympathy toward nor understanding of what used to be known as my deep and gorgeous thirst.

TRACY. That was your problem!

DEXTER. It was the problem of a young man in exceptionally high spirits, who drank to slow down that damned engine he'd found nothing yet to do with—I refer to my mind. You took on that problem with me, when you took me— You were no helpmate there, Tracy—you were a scold.

TRACY. It was disgusting. It made you so unattractive.

DEXTER. A weakness—sure. And strength is her religion, Mr. Connor. She is a goddess, without patience for any kind of human imperfection. And when I gradually discovered that my relation to her was expected to be not that of a loving husband and a good companion, but— *(He turns away from her.)* Oh—never mind—

TRACY. Say it!

DEXTER. —But that of a kind of high priest to a virgin goddess, then my drinks grew more frequent and deeper in hue, that's all.

TRACY. I never considered you as that, nor myself!

DEXTER. You did without knowing it. And the night that *you* got drunk on champagne, and climbed out on the roof and stood there naked, with your arms out to the moon, wailing like a banshee—

(MIKE, with a startled expression, moves sideways out into the Library.)

TRACY. I told you I never had the slightest recollection of doing any such thing!

DEXTER. I know; you drew a blank. You wanted to— Mr. Connor, what would you say in the case of— (*He turns and sees that* MIKE *has gone.*)

TRACY. He's a reporter, incidentally. He's doing us for *Destiny.*

DEXTER. Sandy told me. A pity we can't supply photographs of you on the roof.

TRACY. Honestly, the fuss you made over that silly, childish—

DEXTER. It was enormously important, and most revealing. The moon is also a goddess, chaste and virginal.

TRACY. Stop using those foul words! We were married nearly a year, weren't we?

DEXTER. Marriage doesn't change a true case like yours, my dear. It's an affair of the spirit—not of the flesh.

TRACY. Dexter, what are you trying to make me out as?

DEXTER. Tracy, what do you fancy yourself as?

TRACY. I don't know that I fancy myself as anything.

DEXTER. When I read you were going to marry Kittredge, I couldn't believe it. How in the world can you even think of it?

TRACY (*turns on him*). I love him, that's why! As I never even began to love you.

DEXTER. It may be true, but I doubt it. *I* think it's just a swing from me, and what I represent—but I think it's too violent a swing. That's why I came on. Kittredge is no great tower of strength, you know, Tracy. He's just a tower.

TRACY. You've known him how long?— Half a day.

DEXTER. I knew him for two days two years ago, the time I went up to the fields with your father, but half a day would've done, I think.

TRACY. It's just personal, then—

DEXTER. Purely and completely.

TRACY. You couldn't possibly understand him or his qualities. I shouldn't expect you to.

DEXTER. I suppose when you come right down to it, Tray, it just offends my vanity to have anyone who was ever remotely my wife, remarry so obviously beneath her.

TRACY. "Beneath" me! How dare you— any of you—in this day and age use such a—?

DEXTER. I'm talking about difference in mind and imagination. You could marry Mac, the nightwatchman, and I'd cheer for you.

TRACY. And what's wrong with George?

DEXTER. Nothing—utterly nothing. He's a wizard at his job, and I'm sure he is honest, sober and industrious. He's just not for you.

TRACY. He *is* for me—he's a great man and a good man; already he's of national importance.

DEXTER. Good Lord—you sound like *Destiny* talking. Well, whatever he is, you'll have to stick, Tray. He'll give you no out as I did.

TRACY. I won't require one.

DEXTER. I suppose you'd still be attractive to any man of spirit, though. There's something engaging about it, this virgin goddess business, something more challenging to the male than the more obvious charms.

TRACY. Really?

DEXTER. Oh, yes! We're very vain, you know—"This citadel can and shall be taken—and I'm just the boy to do it."

TRACY. You seem quite contemptuous of me, all of a sudden.

DEXTER. Not of you, Red, never of you. You could be the damnedest, finest woman on this earth. If I'm contemptuous of anything, it's of something in you you either can't help, or make no attempt to; your so-called "strength"—your prejudice against weakness—your blank intolerance—

TRACY. It that all?

DEXTER. That's the gist of it; because you'll never be a first class woman or a first class human being, till you have learned to have some regard for human frailty. It's a pity your own foot can't slip a little sometime—but no, your sense of inner divinity won't allow it. The goddess must and shall remain intact.—You know, I think there are more of you around than people realize. You're a special class of American female now—the Married Maidens.—And of Type Philadelphiaensis, you're the absolute tops, my dear.

TRACY. Damn your soul, Dext, if you say another—!

(He sees George coming in from the Library at Left.)

DEXTER. I'm through, Tracy—for the moment I've said my say.

(GEORGE smiles at them with a great attempt at good humor.)

GEORGE. I suppose I ought to object to this twosome.

DEXTER. That would be most objectionable. Well, anytime either of you want more advice from me— *(He moves toward the steps.)*

GEORGE. When we do, we'll give you a ring, Haven.

DEXTER. Do that, will you? You'll find that I have a most sympathetic and understanding ear— *(He turns to TRACY.)* I left you a little wedding present there on the table, Red—I'm sorry I hadn't any ribbon to tie it up with. *(Then goes out down the path.)*

GEORGE. You see—it's no use even attempting to be friendly.

TRACY. Certainly not. You were a dear to try. Please don't mind him.

(DINAH comes in from the Garden, down the opposite path. She mounts the Porch and crosses to the Sitting Room door.)

DINAH *(to TRACY)*. You got taken when you bought that roan. She's parrot-jawed.

TRACY. Get into a tub. You're revolting.

DINAH. What's more, she swallows wind by the bucket.

TRACY. Where's Miss Imbrie? Wasn't she with you?

DINAH. No. She's gone to the privy with Uncle Willie. *(She goes out, into the Sitting Room.* TRACY *picks up the package left by* DEXTER, *scrutinizes it, shakes it.)*

TRACY. It's anyone's guess what this might be. *(She unwraps it.)* It's, why—it's a photograph of the "True Love."

GEORGE. —The?—What's that?

TRACY. A boat he designed—and built, practically. We sailed her up the coast of Maine and back, the summer we were married. My, she was yare.

GEORGE. "Yare"? What does that mean?

TRACY. It means— Oh, what does it mean? —Easy to handle—quick to the helm— fast—bright—everything a boat should be. *(She gazes at the photograph for a moment without speaking, then drops it upon the table.)* —And the hell with it.

GEORGE. Rather bad taste, I'd say, giving you that.

TRACY. Dexter never concerns himself much with taste.

GEORGE. How'd you ever happen to marry a fellow like that, Tracy?

TRACY. Oh, I don't know—I expect it was kind of a hangover from childhood days. We grew up together, you know.

GEORGE. I see—propinquity.

TRACY. Oh, George—to get away—to get away—! Somehow to feel useful in the world—

GEORGE. Useful?—I'm going to build you an ivory tower with my own two hands.

TRACY. Like fun you are.

GEORGE. You mean you've been in one too long?

TRACY. I mean that, and a lot of things.

GEORGE. I'm going to make a grand life, dear—and you can help, all right.

TRACY. I hope I can.

GEORGE. From now on we'll both stop wasting time on unimportant people.

TRACY. That's all right with me.

GEORGE. Our little house on the river up there. I'd like people to consider it an honor to be asked there.

TRACY. Why an honor, especially?

GEORGE. We're going to represent something, Tracy—something straight and sound and fine.— And then perhaps young Mr. Haven may be somewhat less condescending.

TRACY (*looks at him*). George,—you don't really mind him, do you? I mean the fact of him—

GEORGE. The—? I don't see what you mean, Tracy.

TRACY. I mean that—you know—that he ever was—was my lord and master—that we ever were—

GEORGE. I don't believe he ever was—not really. I don't believe anyone ever was, or ever will be. That's the wonderful thing about you, Tracy.

TRACY (*looks at him, startled*). What? How—?

GEORGE. You're like some marvelous, distant—oh, queen, I guess. You're so cool and fine and—and always so much your own. That's the wonderful *you* in you—that no one can ever really possess—that no one can touch, hardly. It's—it's a kind of beautiful purity, Tracy, that's the only word for it.

TRACY (*now really frightened*). George—

GEORGE. Oh, it's grand, Tracy—it's just grand! Everyone feels it about you. It's what I first worshipped you for, Tracy, from afar.

TRACY. George, listen—

GEORGE. First, now, and always! (*He leans toward her.*) Only from a little nearer, now—eh, darling?

TRACY. I don't want to be worshipped! I want to be loved!

GEORGE. You're that, too. You're that, all right.

TRACY. I mean really loved.

GEORGE. But that goes without saying, Tracy.

TRACY. And now it's you—who doesn't see what *I* mean. (EDWARD, *carrying a tray with cocktail things and a bottle of champagne enters from the Sitting Room, followed by* ELSIE. ELSIE *picks up the orange juice tray from the table.*) You can just leave them, Edward. (EDWARD *places tray.* ELSIE *looks down at* DEXTER'S *present.*)

ELSIE. Shall I put this picture with the other presents, Miss Tracy?

TRACY. No—just leave it there, please.

ELSIE. Yes, Miss. (*They go out, into the Sitting Room.*)

GEORGE (*to* TRACY). Don't let Miss Imbrie get hold of it.

TRACY. I should say not. (*She rewraps the picture.*)

GEORGE. I hope they'll soft pedal the first marriage angle.

TRACY. I wish they'd pedal themselves right out of here.

GEORGE (*after a moment*). They've got a job to do, and it's an honor, you know, Tracy.

TRACY. What is?

GEORGE. Why—to be done by *Destiny*.

(TRACY *frowns at him.*)

TRACY. Are you joking?

GEORGE. Joking—?

TRACY. But you can't seriously mean that you think—!

GEORGE. I think *Destiny* fills a very definite place, Tracy.

(TRACY *stares at him uncomprehendingly.* MARGARET *comes in from the Library, followed by* SETH. *Both are in evening clothes.*)

MARGARET. George, you aren't dressed!—And Tracy, you're the guest of honor—you mustn't be late.

(GEORGE *moves swiftly to the steps.*)

GEORGE. Right on my way, Ma'am! (*He stops and turns to* TRACY.) Wait for me, Tracy. I make the Gatehouse in nothing flat, now. (*He is away, down the path practically at a run.*)

SETH. Does he by any chance ever walk anywhere?

TRACY. When he likes, I expect.

SETH. I have a feeling he's going to take the ring tomorrow and go through center with it.

(MARGARET *laughs and seats herself.*)

MARGARET. Seth, you idiot.

TRACY. That's very amusing, I'm sure.

SETH. Oh, don't take things to heart so, Tracy. You'll wear yourself out.

(LIZ *hurries in from the Garden.*)

LIZ. I won't be a minute.

MARGARET. There's no hurry, Miss Imbrie.

(LIZ *smiles, and goes out, into the Sitting Room.* SETH *is preparing cocktails.*)

SETH. What bothers me at the moment is the spectacle we're all making of ourselves for the benefit of the young man and woman from *Destiny*.

TRACY. Whose fault is it?

SETH. That's beside the point.

MARGARET. Never in my life have I felt so self-conscious. It's all simply dreadful.

SETH. It's worse; it's stupid and childish and completely undignified.

TRACY. So are other things.

SETH. They can publish what they like about me, but—

TRACY. —My idea is, they'll publish nothing about any of us.

SETH. How do you propose to stop them?

TRACY. I don't quite know yet.

SETH. Well, at present the least we can do is to inform Connor and the camera-lady that we are all quite aware of their purpose here. I insist on that.

TRACY. All right! I'll tell them myself.

SETH. I think it will come better from me, don't you—as, at least, titular head of the family? (*He gives* MARGARET *a cocktail. A moment, then* TRACY *speaks deliberately harshly.*)

TRACY. Of course—inasmuch as you let us in for it in the first place.

SETH. Do keep that note out of your voice, Tracy. It's most unattractive.

TRACY. Oh? How does Miss Mara talk? Or does she purr?

MARGARET. Tracy!

SETH. It's all right, Margaret.

TRACY. Sweet and low, I suppose. Dulcet. Very ladylike.—You've got a fine right, you have—after the way you've treated Mother—after the way you've treated us all—a magnificent right you've got to come back here in your best country manner and strike attitudes and make stands and criticize my fiancé and give orders and mess things up generally, just as if you'd done—

MARGARET. Stop it instantly, Tracy!

TRACY (*rises abruptly*). I can't help it. It's sickening. —As if he'd done nothing at all!

MARGARET. It is no concern of yours. If it concerns anyone, it concerns—well, actually, I don't know whom it concerns, except your father.

SETH. That's very wise of you, Margaret. What most wives won't seem to realize is that their husbands' philandering—particularly the middle-aged kind—has nothing whatever to do with them.

TRACY. Oh? Then what has it to do with?

SETH (*reseats himself*). A reluctance to grow old, I think. I suppose the best mainstay a man can have as he gets along in years is a daughter—the right kind of daughter.

TRACY. That's interesting, to say the least.

SETH. —One who loves him blindly—as no good wife ever should, of course.—One for whom he can do no wrong—

TRACY. How sweet.

SETH. I'm talking seriously about something I've thought out thoroughly. I've had to. I think a devoted young daughter gives a man the illusion that youth is still his.

TRACY. Very important, I suppose.

SETH. Very—and without her, he's inclined to go in search of it again, because it's as precious to him as it is to any woman.—But with a girl of his own full of warmth for him, full of foolish, unquestioning, uncritical affection—

TRACY. None of which I've got.

SETH. None. You have a good mind, a pretty face and a disciplined body that does what you tell it. You have more wealth than any of us, thanks to one grandfather's name, and another's red hair, and a shameless play for both of them since about age three. In fact—

TRACY. I never! I loved them!

SETH. —In fact, you have everything it takes to make a lovely woman except the one essential—an understanding heart. Without it, you might just as well be made of bronze.

TRACY (*after a moment*). That's an awful thing to say to anyone.

SETH. Indeed it is.

TRACY. So I'm to blame for Tina Mara, am I?

SETH. If any blame attaches, to some extent I expect you are.

TRACY. You coward.

SETH. No.—But better to be one than a prig—and a perennial spinster, however many marriages.

MARGARET. Seth! That's too much.

SETH. I'm afraid it's not enough.

TRACY (*is staring at him*). Wha-what did you say I was?

SETH. Do you want me to repeat it?

MARGARET. Seth—now I understand a great deal that I didn't. (*He goes to her.*)

SETH. It's all past now, Margaret. It has been for some time. Forgive me. You won't have to again. *I* understand a lot more than I did, as well. (MARGARET *touches his hand understandingly. Still* TRACY *stares.*)

TRACY. "A prig and a—?" You mean—you mean you think *I* think I'm some kind of a virgin goddess or something?

SETH. If your ego wishes to call it that, yes.—Also, you've been talking like a jealous woman.

TRACY. A—? (*She turns away, her face a study.*) What's the matter with everyone all at once, anyhow?

UNCLE WILLIE (*comes in from the Garden*). Miss Imbrie preferred dressing, to my company. (*To* SETH.) What do you make of that, Uncle Willie?

SETH. We're going to drop all this. From now on you're yourself again—and so am I. I shall tell them we know what their tender mission is, and at the first opportunity.

(SANDY *and* DINAH, *in evening clothes, come in from the house.*)

UNCLE WILLIE. It's a pity. It was jolly good fun. Let's have a drink—

SANDY. Damme, let's do that. (*He pours cocktails.*)

DINAH. We're all so completely commonplace. *I* don't see how we interest anyone.

(MARGARET *frowns over* DINAH's *costume.*)

MARGARET. I think that dress hikes up a little behind.

DINAH (*sighs*). No—it's me that does.

(TRACY *speaks briefly, out of her preoccupation.*)

TRACY. You look adorable, Dinah.

DINAH. Oh, thanks, Tracy! Thanks ever so much!

SANDY. A wedding without ushers and bridesmaids. Peace! It's wonderful—

DINAH. *I'm* the bridesmaid!—So can I have a cocktail at last? Can I?

MARGARET. Certainly not.

DINAH. It's a dirty gyp. (*She throws herself down in a chair.* SANDY *offers* TRACY *a cocktail.*)

SANDY. Tracy? (*She shakes her head.*) Champagne, instead?

TRACY. No, thanks.

SANDY. Excuse, please. I forgot, you never.

UNCLE WILLIE. Never? The girl's demented.

TRACY. —But prigs don't.

UNCLE WILLIE. What's that?

TRACY. Nor spinsters.

SANDY. We don't get you.

TRACY. Nor goddesses, virgin or otherwise.

SANDY (*to* WILLIE). —Not completely: just a borderline case. (MIKE *and* LIZ, *dressed for dinner, enter from the house.* MIKE *wears a soft shirt.* SANDY *greets them.*) Hello, you were quick.

(TRACY *is now standing away from them, leaning against a column of the Porch, noticing nothing.*)

UNCLE WILLIE. Miss Imbrie, you are a dream of loveliness. A cocktail or champagne?

LIZ. Thanks, champagne. I've never had enough.

SANDY. You will tonight.

(WILLIE *gives* LIZ *and* MIKE *a glass.*)

MIKE. Champagne flew. (*He clears his throat, straightens his tie and begins, to* UNCLE WILLIE.) Mr. Lord—er—that is to say—

(SETH *speaks simultaneously.*)

SETH. Mr. Connor—oh—excuse me.

MIKE (*again to* UNCLE WILLIE). Mr Lord, Miss Imbrie and I have something on our minds—

UNCLE WILLIE. That's splendid; just the place for it. What?

MIKE. Well—er—it's rather hard to explain—it's—er—about the reason we're here and so forth.

SETH. I think perhaps there's something I ought to explain too—

MIKE. But did you ever hear of a man named Sidney Kidd—

(THOMAS *enters with a tray and note.*)

SETH. —And did you ever hear of a man named Seth—er—? What is it, Thomas?

THOMAS. They've just phoned a telegram, Mr. Lord—

UNCLE WILLIE. Give it here.

THOMAS (*turns to him*). It's for Mrs. Lord, Mr. Tracy.

(LIZ *and* MIKE *exchange glances.*)

UNCLE WILLIE. Then why didn't you say so?

THOMAS. Mrs. Lord and Miss Lord, that is.

(MARGARET, *with a half-smile, glances at* SANDY.)

MARGARET. Read it, Thomas. I haven't my glasses.

SANDY. Hey! Wait a minute!

MARGARET. Read it, Thomas.

THOMAS. "Most frightfully sorry will not be able to get down for the wedding as am confined to my bed with everything wrong. Baby better. It was only gas. Love, Father." Is there any answer, Madam?

MARGARET. No, Thomas—none in this world.

(*He goes out.*)

LIZ (*to* UNCLE WILLIE). He got a little mixed up, didn't he?

UNCLE WILLIE. A common mistake.

SETH. Now do you understand, Mr. Connor?

MIKE. I think we do.

LIZ. It's wonderful. Lord only knows where we go from here.

SANDY. To Aunt Geneva's!— Come on, everybody.

DINAH. My first party, and about time.

(UNCLE WILLIE *moves to* LIZ, *speaks invitingly.*)

UNCLE WILLIE. Who'll come in my little car with me?

MARGARET. Seth and Dinah and I.—Sandy, will you bring Miss Imbrie and Mr. Connor?

SANDY. Like a shot.   ,

DINAH. The evening is pregnant with possibilities.

MARGARET (*takes her gently by shoulders and ushers her out the Library door*). "Full of" is better, dear.

(UNCLE WILLIE *passes behind* LIZ, *on his way out. She exclaims suddenly.*)

LIZ. Ouch!

(SETH *moves to her solicitously.*)

SETH. What was it?

LIZ. N-nothing. (SETH *goes out. She turns to* SANDY.) You know, I felt exactly as if I'd been pinched.

SANDY. Don't think you weren't.

(*He and* LIZ *go out.* MIKE *turns to follow them, then stops as he sees* TRACY *still standing motionless against the column.*)

MIKE. Aren't you coming?

TRACY. I'll follow along with George.

MIKE (*after a moment*). What's the matter with you, Tracy?

TRACY. You tell *me*, will you?

MIKE (*looks at her intently*). Damn if I know. I'd like to.

TRACY (*smiles uncertainly*). Well, if you ever happen to find out—

MIKE. —I'll tell you. Sure

(*After another moment, she speaks again.*)

TRACY. —And remember, Mike—"With the Rich and Mighty"—

MIKE. "Always a little Patience"—Yes, Highness. I will.

TRACY. Do that. Please do.—

(*He looks at her for an instant longer, then turns abruptly and goes out. She is alone. She brushes her hair back from her brow. She sees the champagne upon the table before her. She takes up a glass, lifts it to her lips, drinks it deliberately, then thoughtfully reaches for another.*)

CURTAIN

SCENE II

The Porch. About half-past five on Saturday morning. It is going to be a clear day, and throughout the scene the light increases. MAC, *the night watchman, about thirty, crosses the path from Left to Right, smoking a pipe and swinging a lighted lantern. He goes out Right.* SANDY *enters from the house. He is carrying a tray with two bottles of champagne, one already opened, a pitcher of milk, and glasses. He is followed by* TRACY. BOTH *are in evening dress.*

SANDY. The question is, can we get away with it?

TRACY. You've got to get away with it! You must, Sandy!

SANDY. It's your idea, not mine.

TRACY. What difference does that make? (*She pours herself a glass of champagne.*)

SANDY. You get the ideas and I do all the work.

TRACY. Sandy!

SANDY. Okay.

TRACY. What you don't already know about the great Sidney Kidd, you can certainly fill in from Mike's ravings to-night.

SANDY. I used to have that *Dime* lingo down pretty pat.

TRACY. It's a chance to write a beauty; you know it is.

SANDY. Then I swap it with Kidd for Connor's piece on us—and where am I?

TRACY. You'll have the satisfaction of knowing you saved the lot of us single-handed.

SANDY. And if he won't swap?

TRACY. I'm not worried about that.

SANDY. I suppose there's a fair chance the *Post* would go for it.

TRACY. Of course! You can't possibly lose. Quick—they'll be here! How long will it take you?

SANDY. Three thousand words—all night— what there's left of it. (*He looks at his watch.*) Holy cats! You get to bed.

TRACY. Have you got a typewriter?

SANDY. My old Corona is upstairs, I think.

TRACY. Make it smoke.

SANDY. You bet.

TRACY. Suds. I can't stand it. You won't fall asleep?

SANDY. I've drunk nothing but black coffee since Connor began his lecture.

TRACY. "Sidney Kidd—his habits—his habitat and how to hunt him."

SANDY. Poor Connor! It must have been bottled up in him for years.

TRACY. Waiter, another bottle.

SANDY. No. I've got enough for three articles now. Profile—fullface—

TRACY. —Also rear elevation.—Mike and Liz—they mustn't suspect, Sandy.

SANDY. Oh no— oh my, no!

TRACY. They have simply stepped in their own chewing gum.—I suppose Kidd has one of those private numbers the rich and mighty hide behind in New York.

SANDY. I'll dig it out of Liz and give him a buzz.

TRACY. What will you say?

SANDY. I'll be brief, bluff, belligerent. (TRACY *laughs and pours herself another glass of champagne*). Hey—lay off that!

TRACY. Why?

SANDY. You are already in wine, sister.

TRACY. Me? You lie. It never affects me, not in the slightest.

SANDY. That's because you never take it.

TRACY. Even if I did, it wouldn't.

SANDY. Don't say that: it's unlucky. (*She drains the glass.* SANDY *shakes his head over her.*) I have seen people fly in the face of Pommery before.

TRACY. I've just got a good head, I guess.

SANDY. Don't say it, don't say it! (TRACY *seats herself upon the steps.*)

TRACY. Sandy, you fool—

SANDY. George will spank.

TRACY. I could spank George for the way he behaved.

(SANDY *seats himself beside her.*)

SANDY. He had a right to be sore. You and Mike disappeared for two hours, at least.

TRACY. You were along.

SANDY. All the same, tongues were wagging like tails. George said—

TRACY. George wanted to leave sharp at twelve—how could we?

SANDY. They need a lot of sleep, those big fellows.

TRACY. They must.—Then at one, with Father and Mother and Dinah.—Then at two, then at three—every hour on the hour. We fought like wolves in the car coming home.

SANDY. I hope you explained.

TRACY. Certainly not. He should have known. He was extremely rude. You'd have thought I had been out with Dexter, or something.—(*She thinks for a moment.*) —I wonder where Dext was? I half expected him to— I don't like the look behind Dexter's eyes, Sandy. It makes me sad.

SANDY. Don't be sad, Tracy. (*He puts an arm about her and for an instant she rests her head against his shoulder.*)

TRACY. Oh, Sandy, if you knew how I envy you and Sue that darling fat creature you've just produced—

SANDY. You'll probably have four or five of your own any day now.

TRACY. Six! Oh, I hope—I do hope—I hope I'm good for something besides knocking out golf balls and putting horses over fences.

SANDY. You're good for my money any day.

TRACY. Thanks! (*She gets up from the step and moves again to the table.*) Was I really mean to George, I wonder? I don't want to be.

SANDY. You're in an odd mood, little fellah. What's amiss—what's afoot?

TRACY. I guess it's just that—a lot of things I always thought were terribly important I find now are—and the other way around —and—oh, what the hell. (*She refills her glass, looks at it and puts it down upon the table.*)

SANDY. I don't think I'd spend much more time with Connor tonight, if I were you.

TRACY. Why not?

SANDY. Writers with wine sauce intoxicate little girls.

TRACY (*laughs uncertainly*). They sort of do, don't they?— He fascinates me. He's so violent, Sandy.

SANDY. He's fallen, Tray. I could hear him bump.

TRACY. Mind your own beeswax, old Nosey Parker.

SANDY. Get thee to bed.

(She reaches for her glass—he stops her hand.)

TRACY. No!

SANDY. —Before you have to be carried.

TRACY. No! No! No! *(She throws up her arms, head back.)* I feel too delicious! Sandy, I feel just elegant. *(Then cocks her head, listening.)* Is that my bedroom telephone?

SANDY. Now you're hearing things.

TRACY. It couldn't be anyone but George. I *was* sort of swinish to him. Perhaps I'd better— *(She starts toward the Sitting Room.)* As for you—get to work, you dog. Stop leaning on your shovel. *(She stops, as* MIKE *comes out upon the Porch from the Library. He is in fine fettle, coatless, his soft shirt open at the neck. He goes directly to the table.)*

MIKE. Listen! Now I'm really under way. Miss not an inflection.

TRACY. Is it Connor the poet, or Connor the conspirator?

MIKE. Both! *(He pours himself a glass of wine and begins to declaim:)* "No lightweight is balding, battle-browed Sidney Kidd, no mean displacement, his: for windy bias, bicarbonate." *(He drinks the wine; looks at the glass.)* That is funny stuff. I'm used to whisky. Whisky is a slap on the back. Champagne, entwining arms.

TRACY. That's pretty. Is it poetry?

MIKE. *Dime* will tell.

SANDY. "None before him but Writer Wolfgang Goethe has known all about all. Gigantic was Goethe's output, bigger already is Kidd's. Sample from his own pen: 'Pittsburgh is a gentle city.'"

TRACY. Sidney is a gentle man.

(MIKE points a finger at SANDY.)

MIKE. Potent, able, beady-eyed scion of great wealth in Quakertown, why don't you do a piece on our great and good friend?

SANDY. On Kidd?

MIKE. On none other.

SANDY. Nimble scrivener, it's an idea.

TRACY. Brilliant. I wish *I'd* thought of it.

(MIKE turns and points a finger at her.)

MIKE. Baby Giant Tycooness.

TRACY. But would it not be a low, dirty deed?

MIKE. *He'd* print a scandal about his best friend: he's said he would.

SANDY. Who is his best friend?

MIKE. I guess Santa Claus. *(He passes his hand vaguely over his face.)* What is this mist before my eyes?

TRACY *(rises suddenly and goes to the table).* I tell you what: let's all have a quick swim to brighten us up. Go get Liz, Sandy. *(She takes off her bracelet and rings and leaves them on table.)*

SANDY. Not me; it's too cold this early.

TRACY. It's the best hour of the day! Dexter and I always swam after parties.

MIKE. I haven't got any bathing suit.

TRACY. But we won't need any! It's just ourselves. *(He looks at her uncertainly for an instant, then quickly fills two glasses, moves one gingerly toward her, and raises the other.)*

MIKE. Let's dip into this instead.

TRACY *(after a brief pause, to* SANDY*).* No takers. —Get Liz anyway, Sandy.

SANDY. If she's not in bed— *(He goes out into the Sitting Room.)* Or even if she is.

TRACY *(to* MIKE, *after a moment).* That was an odd thing you just did—

MIKE. Me?

TRACY *(turning away).* You. For a moment you made me—self-conscious.

MIKE. How? About what?

TRACY. Never mind. *(She raises her glass.)* Hello, you.

MIKE *(raises his).* Hello.

TRACY. You look fine.

MIKE. I *feel* fine.

TRACY. Quite a fellah.

MIKE. They say.

(*They drink.*)

TRACY. Did you enjoy the party?

MIKE. Sure. The prettiest sight in this fine, pretty world is the Privileged Class enjoying its privileges.

TRACY. —Also somewhat of a snob.

MIKE. How do you mean?

TRACY. I'm wondering.

MIKE. Consider, Gentle Reader, they toil not, neither do they spin.

TRACY. Oh, yes they do! They spin in circles. (*She spins once and seats herself upon the steps at Left.* MIKE *goes to her.*)

MIKE. Nicely put. "Awash with champagne was Mrs. Willie Q. Tracy (born Geneva Biddle)'s stately pleasure dome on a hilltop in smart Radnor, P.A. on a Saturday night late in June; the eve of her great-niece's—" (*He sits beside her*) —Tracy, you can't marry that guy.

TRACY. George?—I'm going to. Why not?

MIKE. I don't know; I'd have thought I'd be for it, but somehow you just don't seem to match up.

TRACY. Then the fault's with me.

MIKE. Maybe so; all the same you can't do it.

(TRACY *rises and moves a little way along the path.*)

TRACY. No? Come around about noon tomorrow—I mean today. (*After a moment he rises and faces her.*)

MIKE. Tracy—

TRACY. Yes, Mr. Connor?

MIKE. How do you mean, I'm "a snob"?

TRACY. You're the worst kind there is: an intellectual snob. You've made up your mind awfully young, it seems to me.

MIKE (*goes to her*). Thirty's about time to make up your mind.—And I'm nothing of the sort, not Mr. Connor.

TRACY. The time to make up your mind about people, is never. Yes, you are—and a complete one.

MIKE. You're quite a girl.

TRACY. You think?

MIKE. I know.

TRACY. Thank you, Professor. I don't think I'm exceptional.

MIKE. You are, though.

TRACY. I know any number like me. You ought to get around more.

MIKE. In the Upper Clahss? No, thanks.

TRACY. You're just a mass of prejudices, aren't you? You're so much thought and so little feeling, Professor. (*She moves Right, further away from him.*)

MIKE. Oh, I am, am I?

TRACY (*wheels about on him*). Yes, you am, are you! Your damned intolerance furiates me. I mean *in*furiates me. I should think, of all people, a writer would need tolerance. The fact is, you'll never—you can't be a first-rate writer or a first-rate human being until you learn to have some small regard for— (*Suddenly she stops. Her eyes widen, remembering. She turns from him.*) Aren't the geraniums pretty, Professor? Is it not a handsome day that begins?

(MIKE *mounts the Porch, looks down upon her.*)

MIKE. Lay off that "Professor."

TRACY. Yes, Professor. (*She mounts the Porch, faces him.*)

MIKE. You've got all the arrogance of your class, all right, haven't you?

TRACY. Holy suds, what have "classes" to do with it?

MIKE. Quite a lot.

TRACY. Why? What do they matter—except for the people in them? George comes from the so-called "lower" class, Dexter comes from the upper. Well?

MIKE. Well?

TRACY. —Though there's a great deal to be said for Dexter—and don't you forget it!

MIKE. I'll try not to.

TRACY (*moves to the table*). Mac, the night-watchman, is a prince among men and Joey, the stable-boy, is a rat. Uncle Hugh is a saint. Uncle Willie's a pincher. (*She fills her glass again.*)

MIKE. So what?

TRACY. There aren't any rules about human beings, that's all!—You're teaching me things, Professor; this is new to me. Thanks, I am beholden to you. (*She raises her glass to him.*)

MIKE. Not at all.

TRACY. "Upper" and "lower," my eye! I'll take the lower, thanks. (*She brings the glass to her lips.*)

MIKE. —If you can't get a drawing-room.

(*She puts the glass down, untasted, and turns on him.*)

TRACY. What do you mean by that?

MIKE. My mistake.

TRACY. Decidedly.

MIKE. Okay.

TRACY. You're insulting.

MIKE. I'm sorry.

TRACY. Oh, don't apologize!

MIKE. Who the hell's apologizing?

TRACY. I never knew such a man.

MIKE. You wouldn't be likely to, dear—not from where *you* sit.

TRACY. Talk about arrogance!

MIKE (*after a moment*). Tracy—

TRACY. What do you want?

MIKE. You're wonderful.

TRACY (*laughs*). Professor—may I go out?

MIKE. Class is dismissed. (*She moves Left.*) Miss Lord will please wait.

(*She stops, turns and meets his gaze steadily.*)

TRACY. Miss Lord is privileged.

MIKE (*speaks in a lower voice*). There's magnificence in you, Tracy. I'm telling you.

TRACY. I'm—! (*A moment.*) Now I'm getting self-conscious again. I—it's funny— (*Another moment. Then she moves toward him, impulsively.*) Mike, let's— (*She stops herself.*)

MIKE. What?

TRACY. I—I don't know—go up, I guess. It's late.

MIKE. —A magnificence that comes out of your eyes, that's in your voice, in the way you stand there, in the way you walk. You're lit from within, bright, bright, bright. There are fires banked down in you, hearth-fires and holocausts—

(*She moves another step toward him, stands before him.*)

TRACY. You—I don't seem to you—made of bronze, then—

MIKE. You're made of flesh and blood —that's the blank, unholy surprise of it. You're the golden girl, Tracy, full of love and warmth and delight— What the hell's this? You've got tears in your eyes.

TRACY. Shut up, shut up!— Oh, Mike— keep talking—keep talking! *Talk*, will you?

MIKE. I've stopped.

(*For a long moment they look at each other. Then* TRACY *speaks, deliberately, harshly.*)

TRACY. Why? Has your mind taken hold again, dear Professor?

MIKE. You think so?

TRACY (*moves Right, away from him*). Yes, Professor.

MIKE. A good thing, don't you agree?

(*She leans against the column of the Porch, facing him.*)

TRACY. No, Professor.

MIKE. Drop that Professor—you hear me?

TRACY. Yes, Professor.

(*He moves to her slowly, stands almost against her.*)

MIKE. That's really all I am to you, is it?

TRACY. Of course, Professor.

MIKE. Are you sure?

TRACY (*looks up at him*). Why, why, yes —yes, of course, Profess— (*His kiss stops the word. The kiss is taken and returned. After it she exclaims softly.*) Golly. (*She gazes at him wonderingly, then raises her face to receive another. Then she stands in his arms, her cheek against his breast, amazement in her eyes.*) Golly Moses.

MIKE. Tracy dear—

TRACY. Mr. Connor—Mr. Connor—

MIKE. Let me tell you something—

TRACY. No, don't— All of a sudden I've got the shakes.

MIKE. I have, too.

TRACY. What *is* it?

MIKE. It must be something like love.

TRACY. No, no! It mustn't be. It can't—

MIKE. Why? Would it be inconvenient?

TRACY. Terribly. Anyway, it isn't. I know it's not. Oh, Mike, I'm a bad girl—

MIKE. Not you.

TRACY. We're out of our minds.

MIKE. —Right into our hearts.

TRACY. That ought to have music.

MIKE. It has, hasn't it?—Tracy, you lovely—

(She hears something; looks quickly toward the door, whispers:)

TRACY. They're coming.

MIKE. The hell—

(She holds a hand out to him.)

TRACY. It's—it's not far to the pool. It's only over the lawn, in the birch-grove— it'll be lovely now.

MIKE. Come on—

TRACY. Oh, it's as—it's as if my insteps— were melting away. —What is it? Have I —have I got feet of clay, or something?

MIKE. —Quick! Here they are— *(He takes her hand and hurries her down the steps.)*

TRACY. I—I feel so small all at once.

MIKE. You're immense—you're tremendous.

TRACY. Not me—oh, not me! Put me in your pocket, Mike—

(They are gone. A moment, then SANDY comes quickly in from the house, a sheaf of photographs in his hand. He is followed by LIZ, in pajamas and wrapper.)

LIZ. You give those back!

SANDY. Look, Tracy— *(He sees that the porch is empty.)*

LIZ. May I have them, please?

SANDY. Did Kidd *know* you took these shots of him?

LIZ. Some of them.

SANDY. Sit down. Have a drink.

LIZ. I should say not. A drink would be redundant, tautological, and a mistake. *(Wearily she drops into a chair and eyes the pitcher on the table.)* Is that milk?

SANDY. That is milk.

LIZ. Gimme. Milk I will accept. *(He pours and gives her a glass.)* I met this cow this afternoon. Nice Bossy.

SANDY. Let me keep just these three shots.

LIZ. What for?

SANDY. A low purpose.

LIZ. Sufficiently low?

SANDY. Nefarious.

LIZ. You won't reproduce them?

SANDY. Nope.

LIZ. Nor cause them to be reproduced?

SANDY. Honest.

LIZ. In any way, shape or manner, without permission?

SANDY. So help me, Sidney Kidd.

LIZ. Amen.

SANDY. What's his private number?

LIZ. You mean his private number or his sacred private number?

SANDY. The one by the bed and bath-tub.

LIZ. Regent 4-1416— *(She settles lower in the chair. SANDY goes to the telephone just inside the near Sitting Room door.)* I won't tell you. *(She listens a moment, as he dials. Then:)* Is Mr. Kittredge pure gold, Lord?

(SANDY comes into the doorway, the telephone in hand.)

SANDY. We must never doubt that, Missy.

(He stands behind her chair, looking down upon her.)

LIZ *(sleepily).* Lèse majesté—excuse it, please.

SANDY *(to the telephone)*. Regent 4-1416 New York. —Wayne—22-23. *(To* LIZ.*)* —And Mr. Connor—what of him?

LIZ. Percentage of base metal. Alloy.

SANDY. So.

LIZ. —Which imparts a certain shape and firmness.

SANDY *(to the telephone)*. Hello?—Mr. Kidd? This is Alexander Lord.

LIZ *(listens intently)*. I know nothing about this.

SANDY. No, I'm in Philadelphia.—Yes, I know it is. It's early here, too. Look, Mr. Kidd, I think you'd better get over here as fast as you can. What? —I'm sorry to have to tell you, sir, but Connor has had an accident—yes, pretty bad—he had a pretty bad fall.— No, it's his heart we're worried about now.—Yes, I'm afraid so: He keeps talking about you, calling you names—I mean calling your name.—How's that?—No, the eleven o'clock's time enough. We don't expect him to regain consciousness much before then.

LIZ. His only hope is to get fired—I know it is.

SANDY. Sorry, Miss Imbrie's sleeping. Shock.— The newspapers? No, they don't know a thing about it. I understand. What? I said I understood, didn't I?— Twelve twenty North Philadelphia—I'll have you met. *(He disappears briefly into the Sitting Room and returns without the telephone.)* He wants no publicity.

LIZ *(has suppressed her broadening grin. She stirs lazily in her chair and inquires)*. Who was that?

SANDY. God.

(She looks toward the garden path.)

LIZ. Do I hear someone?

SANDY. It's Mac, the night-watchman. —Liz—you're in love with Connor, aren't you?

LIZ. People ask the oddest questions.

SANDY. Why don't you marry him?

LIZ. I can't hear you.

SANDY. I say, why don't you—? *(DEXTER comes along the path and stops at the steps. He wears flannels and an old jacket.)* Hello, here's an early one!

DEXTER. Hello. I saw quite a full day ahead, and got myself up. *(He seats himself on the steps.)* —A good party?

SANDY. Fine.

DEXTER. Good. *(He lights a cigarette.* LIZ *rises from her chair.)*

LIZ. —And sufficient. Hell or high water, I'm going to bed. *(She moves toward the far Sitting Room door.)*

SANDY *(following her)*. Why don't you, Liz—*you* know—what I asked?

LIZ. He's still got a lot to learn, and I don't want to get in his way yet awhile. Okay?

SANDY. Okay.—Risky, though. Suppose another girl came along in the meantime?

LIZ. Oh, I'd just scratch her eyes out, I guess.—That is, unless she was going to marry someone else the next day.

SANDY. You're a good number, Liz.

LIZ. No, I just photograph well. *(She goes out.)*

DEXTER. Complications?

SANDY *(re-examines the photographs)*. There might be.

DEXTER. Where are they?

SANDY. Who?

DEXTER. The complications.

SANDY. They went up—at least I hope and pray that they did.

DEXTER. Well, well.

(SANDY waves the photographs at him and moves toward the Library door.)

SANDY. Make yourself comfortable, Dext. I've got a little blackmailing to do.

(SANDY goes out. DEXTER *smokes quietly for a moment, then rises and stamps out his cigarette as he hears someone coming along the path.* GEORGE *enters, still in evening clothes. He stops in surprise at the sight of* DEXTER.*)*

GEORGE. What are you doing here?

DEXTER. Oh, I'm a friend of the family's —just dropped in for a chat,

GEORGE. Don't try to be funny. I asked you a question.

DEXTER. I might ask you the same one.

GEORGE. I telephoned Tracy and her phone didn't answer.

DEXTER. I didn't telephone. I just came right over.

GEORGE. I was worried, so I—

DEXTER. Yes, I was worried, too.

GEORGE. About what?

DEXTER. What do you think of this Connor—or do you?

GEORGE. What about him?

DEXTER. I just wondered.

GEORGE. Listen: if you're trying to insinuate some—

DEXTER. My dear fellow, I wouldn't dream of it! I was only— (*He stops suddenly as* TRACY's *rings and bracelets upon the table catch his eye.* GEORGE *looks down the Garden path.*)

GEORGE. Who's that I hear?

(DEXTER *glances quickly down the path in the direction of the swimming pool, then pockets the rings and bracelets. He turns to* GEORGE.)

DEXTER. Look, Kittredge: I advise you to go to bed.

GEORGE. Oh, you do, do you?

DEXTER. Yes. I strongly urge you to do so at once.

GEORGE. I'm staying right here.

DEXTER (*looks at him*). You're making a mistake. Somehow I don't think you'll understand.

GEORGE. You'd better leave that to—! I hear someone walking—

DEXTER. Yes?—Must be Mac. (*He calls.*) It's all right, Mac—it's only us! (*He turns to* GEORGE—*comes down to him.*) Come on—I'll walk along with you.

GEORGE. I'm staying right here—so are you.

DEXTER. All right, then: take the works, and may God be with you.

(*He retires into a corner of the Porch. Heavy steps on the gravel path draw nearer. Finally,* MIKE *appears, carrying* TRACY *in his arms.* BOTH *are in bathrobes and slippers and there is a jumble of clothes, his and hers, slung over* MIKE's *shoulder. He stops with her for a moment at the top of the steps. She stirs in his arms, speaks lowly, as if from a long way away:*)

TRACY. Take me upstairs, Mike—

MIKE. Yes, dear. Here we go.

GEORGE (*looms up*). What the—!

DEXTER (*comes swiftly in between him and* MIKE). Easy, old boy! (*To* MIKE.) She's not hurt?

MIKE. No. She's just—

TRACY (*murmurs dreamily*). Not wounded, Sire—but dead.

GEORGE. She—she hasn't any clothes on!

TRACY (*into* MIKE's *shoulder*). Not a stitch —it's delicious.

MIKE (*speaks lowly*). It seems the minute she hit the water, the wine—

DEXTER (*glances at* GEORGE, *who can only stare*). A likely story, Connor.

MIKE. What did you say?

DEXTER. I said, a likely story!

MIKE. Listen: if—!

DEXTER. You'll come down again directly?

MIKE. Yes, if you want.

DEXTER. I want.

TRACY (*lifts her head limply and looks at them*). Hello, Dexter. Hello, George. (*She crooks her head around and looks vaguely up at* MIKE.) Hello, Mike.

(DEXTER *goes and opens the screen door for them.*)

DEXTER. The second door on the right at the top of the stairs. Mind you don't wake Dinah.

(MIKE *moves toward the door with* TRACY.)

TRACY. My feet are of clay—made of clay —did you know it? (*She drops her head again and tightens her arms around* MIKE's *neck.*) Goo' nigh'—sleep well, little man.

(MIKE *carries her out, past* DEXTER.)

DEXTER (*calling after them*). Look out for Dinah. (*He comes forward.*) How are the mighty fallen! —But if I know Tracy —and I know her very well—she'll remember very little of this. For the second time in her life, she may draw quite a tidy blank.—Of course she may worry, though—

GEORGE. Good God!

DEXTER (*turns on him swiftly*). You believe it, then?

GEORGE. Believe what?

DEXTER. The—er—the implications, of what you've seen, let's say.

GEORGE. What else is there to believe?

DEXTER. Why, I suppose that's entirely up to you.

GEORGE. I've got eyes, and I've got imagination, haven't I?

DEXTER. I don't know. Have you?

GEORGE. So you pretend not to believe it—

DEXTER. Yes, I pretend not to.

GEORGE. Then you don't know women.

DEXTER. Possibly not.

GEORGE. You're a blind fool!

DEXTER. Oh, quite possibly!

GEORGE. —God!

DEXTER (*studies him*). You won't be too hard on her, will you?

GEORGE. I'll make up my own mind what I'll be!

DEXTER. But we're all only human, you know.

GEORGE. You—all of you—with your damned sophisticated ideas!

DEXTER. Isn't it hell?

(MIKE *comes swiftly through the door and up to* DEXTER.)

MIKE. Well?

GEORGE (*advances*). Why, you low-down—!

DEXTER (*quickly*). The lady is my wife, Mr. Connor. (*His upper cut to* MIKE's *jaw sends him across the porch and to the floor.*)

GEORGE. You!—What right have—?

DEXTER. —A husband's, till tomorrow, Kittredge.

GEORGE. I'll make up my mind, all right!

(*He turns and storms out down the Garden path.* DEXTER *bends over* MIKE.)

DEXTER. Okay, old man?

MIKE (*sits up, nursing his chin*). Listen: if you think—!

DEXTER. I know—I'm sorry. But I thought I'd better hit you before he did. (MAC, *the night watchman, comes along the garden path from the opposite direction taken by* GEORGE. *He is putting his lantern out.* DEXTER *straightens up.*) Hello, Mac. How are you?

MAC. Hello, Dexter! Anything wrong?

DEXTER. Not a thing, Mac.—Just as quiet as a church.

MAC. Who is it? (MIKE *turns his face to him.*) Hell!—I thought it might be Kittredge.

DEXTER. We can't have everything, Mac.

(MAC *laughs, shakes his head, and continues along the path.*)

CURTAIN

ACT THREE

The sitting room. Late morning. Saturday. The room is full of bright noonday sun and there are flowers everywhere.

UNCLE WILLIE, *in a morning coat, fancy waistcoat and Ascot, stands in the center of the room, facing* THOMAS.

THOMAS. I am trying to think, Mr. Tracy.

(*A moment, then* UNCLE WILLIE *demands impatiently:*)

UNCLE WILLIE. Well? Well?

THOMAS. She awakened late, sir, and had a tray in her room. I believe May and Elsie are just now dressing her.

UNCLE WILLIE. It's not the bride I'm asking about—it's her sister.

THOMAS. I haven't seen Miss Dinah since breakfast, sir. She came down rather early.

UNCLE WILLIE. It there anything wrong with her?

THOMAS. I did notice that she seemed a trifle silent, took only one egg and neglected to finish her cereal. The hot-cakes and bacon, however, went much as usual.

UNCLE WILLIE. She was telephoning me like a mad woman before I was out of my tub. (DINAH, *in blue-jeans, slides in from the Porch and up behind him.*) I expected at least two bodies, hacked beyond recognition, the house stiff with police, and— (DINAH *touches at his coat tail. He starts and turns.*) Good God, child—don't do that! I drank champagne last night.

DINAH. Hello, Uncle Willie.

UNCLE WILLIE. Why must I come on ahead of your Aunt Geneva? Why must I waste not one minute? What's amiss? What's about? Speak up! Don't stand there with your big eyes like a stuffed owl.

(DINAH *glances significantly at* THOMAS.)

THOMAS. Is there anything else, sir? If not—

UNCLE WILLIE. Thanks, Thomas, nothing.

(THOMAS *goes out. Again* DINAH *pulls at* WILLIE's *coat-tail, drawing him to the arm-chair.*)

DINAH. Come over here—and speak very low. Nobody's allowed in this room this morning but Tracy—and speak terribly low.

UNCLE WILLIE. What the Sam Hill for? What's alack? What's afoot?

DINAH. I had no one to turn to but you, Uncle Willie.

UNCLE WILLIE. People are always turning to me. I wish they'd stop.

(She *kneels on another chair, leaning over the table to him.*)

DINAH. It's desperate. It's about Tracy.

UNCLE WILLIE. Tracy? What's she up to now? Tracy this, and Tracy that. Upstairs and downstairs and in my lady's chamber.

DINAH. How did you know?

UNCLE WILLIE. Know what?

DINAH. It seems to me you know just about everything.

UNCLE WILLIE. I have a fund of information accumulated through the years. I am old, seasoned, and full of instruction. But there are gaps in my knowledge. Ask me about falconry, say, or ballistics, and you will get nowhere.

DINAH. I meant more about people and— and sin.

UNCLE WILLIE. I know only that they are inseparable. I also know that the one consolation for being old is the realization that, however you live, you will never die young.—Get to the point, child. What do you want of me?

DINAH. Advice.

UNCLE WILLIE. On what subject or sub jects?

DINAH (*after a moment*). Well, lookit, you don't like George, do you?

UNCLE WILLIE. Kittredge? I deplore him.

DINAH. And you'd like it if Tracy didn't go ahead and have married him after all —or would you?

UNCLE WILLIE. Where do you go to school?

DINAH. I don't yet. I'm going some place next Fall.

UNCLE WILLIE. And high time.—Like it? I would cheer. I would raise my voice in song.

DINAH. Well, I think I know a way to stop her from, but I need advice on how.

UNCLE WILLIE. Proceed, child—proceed cautiously.

DINAH. Well, suppose she all of a sudden developed an illikit passion for someone—

UNCLE WILLIE. Can you arrange it?

DINAH. It doesn't need to be. It is already.

UNCLE WILLIE. Ah? Since when?

DINAH. Last night—and well into the morning.

UNCLE WILLIE. You surprise me, Dinah.

DINAH. Imagine what *I* was—and just imagine what *George* would be.

UNCLE WILLIE. And—er—the object of this —er—illikit passion—

DINAH. Let him be nameless.—Only tell me, should I tell George?—It's getting late.

(Unnoticed by them, DEXTER *has come in from the Porch.)*

UNCLE WILLIE. Maybe he'll want to marry her anyway.

DINAH. But she can't. If she marries anyone, it's got to be Mr. Connor!

UNCLE WILLIE. Connor? Why Connor?

DINAH. She's just got to, that's all.

DEXTER *(comes forward).* Why, Dinah? What makes you think she should?

DINAH *(looks at him, appalled).* Dexter—

DEXTER. Isn't that a pretty big order to swing at this late date?

DINAH. I—I didn't say anything. What did *I* say?

DEXTER. Of course, you might talk it over with her.—But maybe you have.

DINAH. Certainly not. I haven't!

UNCLE WILLIE. Apparently the little cherub has seen or heard something.

DEXTER. That's Dexter's own Dinah.

UNCLE WILLIE. I must say *you* show a certain amount of cheek, walking in here on this, of all mornings.

DEXTER. Tracy just did a very sweet thing: she telephoned and asked me what to do for a feeling of fright accompanied by headache.

DINAH. I should think it would be bad luck for a first husband to see the bride before the wedding.

DEXTER. That's what I figured.—Why all this about Connor, Dinah? Did the party give you bad dreams?

DINAH. It wasn't any dream.

DEXTER. I wouldn't be too sure. Once you've gone to bed it's pretty hard to tell, isn't it?

DINAH *(ponders this).* Is it?

DEXTER. You bet your hat it is. It's practically impossible.

DINAH. I thought it was Sandy's typewriter woke me up.

*(*TRACY *comes in from the Hall, in the dress in which she is to be married. A leather-strapped wrist-watch dangles from her hand. She moves to the sofa.)*

TRACY. Hello! Isn't it a fine day, though! Is everyone fine? That's fine! *(She seats herself uncertainly.)* My, I'm hearty.

DEXTER. How are you otherwise?

TRACY. I don't know what's the matter with me. I must have had too much sun yesterday.

DEXTER. It's awfully easy to get too much.

TRACY. My eyes don't open properly. *(She picks up a silver cigarette box and looks at herself in it. She blinks up at* DEXTER.*)* Please go home, Dext.

DEXTER. Not till we get those eyes open.

(He seats himself beside her upon the sofa. She notices UNCLE WILLIE.*)*

TRACY. Uncle Willie, good morning.

UNCLE WILLIE. That remains to be seen.

TRACY. Aren't you here early?

UNCLE WILLIE. Weddings get me out like nothing else.

DINAH. It's nearly half-past twelve.

TRACY. It can't be!

DINAH. Maybe it can't, but it is.

TRACY. Where—where's Mother?

DINAH *(springs up).* Do you want her?

TRACY. No, I just wondered.

DINAH *(reseats herself).* She's talking with the orchestra, and Father with the minister, and—

TRACY. Doctor Parsons—already?

DINAH. —And Miss Imbrie's gone with her camera to shoot the horses, and Sandy's in his room and—and Mr. Connor, he hasn't come down yet.

DEXTER. And it's Saturday.

TRACY. Thanks loads. It's nice to have things accounted for. *(She passes the hand with the wrist-watch across her brow, then looks at the watch.)* —Only I wonder what this might be?

DEXTER. It looks terribly like a wrist-watch.

TRACY. But whose? I found it in my room. I nearly stepped on it.

DINAH. Getting out of bed?

TRACY. Yes. Why?

DINAH. I just wondered.

TRACY (*puts the watch on the table before her*). There's another mystery, Uncle Willie.

UNCLE WILLIE. Mysteries irritate me.

TRACY. I was robbed at your house last night.

UNCLE WILLIE. You don't say.

TRACY. Yes—my bracelet and my engagement ring are missing everywhere.

UNCLE WILLIE. Probably someone's house guest from New York.

DEXTER (*brings them out of his pocket*). Here you are.

TRACY (*takes them, stares at them, then at him*). —But you weren't at the party!

DEXTER. Wasn't I?

TRACY. Were you?

DEXTER. Don't tell me you don't remember!

TRACY. I—I do now, sort of—but there were such a lot of people.

DEXTER (*rises*). You should have taken a quick swim to shake them off. There's nothing like a swim after a late night.

TRACY. —A swim. (*And her eyes grow rounder.*)

DEXTER (*laughs*). There! Now they're open!

DINAH. That was just the beginning—and it was no dream.

DEXTER (*glances at her, then moves to UNCLE WILLIE*). Don't you think, sir, that if you and I went to the pantry at this point—you know: speaking of eye-openers?

UNCLE WILLIE (*rises and precedes him toward the porch*). The only sane remark I've heard this morning. I know a formula that is said to pop the pennies off the eyelids of dead Irishmen.

(*He goes out. DEXTER stops beside DINAH.*)

DEXTER. Oh, Dinah—if conversation drags, you might tell Tracy your dream.

(*He goes out. DINAH turns and gazes reflectively at TRACY.*)

TRACY. What did he say?

DINAH. Oh, nothing. (*She goes to TRACY and puts an arm around her shoulder.*) Tray—I hate you to get married and go away.

TRACY. I'll miss you, darling. I'll miss all of you.

DINAH. We'll miss you, too.—It—it isn't like when you married Dexter, and just moved down the road a ways.

TRACY. I'll come back often. It's only Wilkes-Barre.

DINAH. It gripes me.

TRACY (*fondly*). Baby.

(*There is another silence. DINAH gazes at her intently, then gathers her forces and speaks:*)

DINAH. You know, I did have the funniest dream about you last night.

TRACY (*without interest*). Did you? What was it?

DINAH. It was terribly interesting, and—and awfully scarey, sort of—

TRACY (*rises from the sofa*). Do you like my dress, Dinah?

DINAH. Yes, ever so much.

TRACY (*rises too quickly, wavers a moment, steadies herself, then moves to the Porch door*). It feels awfully heavy.—You better rush and get ready yourself.

DINAH. You know me: I don't take a minute.

(*MARGARET, dressed for the wedding, comes in from the Parlor, from whence violins are now heard, tuning up.*)

MARGARET. Turn around, Tracy. (*TRACY turns.*) Yes, it looks lovely.

TRACY. What's that—that scratching sound I hear?

MARGARET. The orchestra tuning. Yes—I'm glad we decided against the blue one. (*She moves to the Hall door.*) Where's your father? You know, I feel completely impersonal about all this. I can't quite grasp it. Get dressed, Dinah. *(She goes out into the Hall.)*

TRACY *(turns and blinks into the sunlight, blazing in from the Porch).* That sun is certainly bright all right, isn't it?

DINAH. It was up awfully early.

TRACY. Was it?

DINAH. Unless I dreamed that, too.—It's supposed to be the longest day of the year or something, isn't it?

TRACY. I wouldn't doubt it for a minute.

DINAH. It was all certainly pretty rooty-tooty.

TRACY. What was?

DINAH. My dream.

TRACY *(moves back from the Porch door).* Dinah, you'll have to learn sooner or later that no one is interested in anyone else's dreams.

DINAH. --I thought I got up and went over to the window and looked out across the lawn. And guess what I thought I saw coming over out of the woods?

TRACY. I haven't the faintest idea. A skunk?

DINAH. Well, sort of.—It was Mr. Connor.

TRACY. Mr. Connor?

DINAH. Yes—with his both arms full of something. And guess what it turned out to be?

TRACY. What?

DINAH. You—and some clothes. *(TRACY turns slowly and looks at her.)* Wasn't it funny? It was sort of like as if you were coming from the pool—

TRACY *(closes her eyes).* The pool.—I'm going crazy. I'm standing here solidly on my own two hands going crazy.—And then what?

DINAH. Then I thought I heard something outside in the hall, and I went and opened my door a crack and there he was, still coming along with you, puffing like a steam engine. His wind can't be very good.

TRACY. And then what?—

DINAH. And you were sort of crooning—

TRACY. I never crooned in my life!

DINAH. I guess it just sort of sounded like you were. Then he—guess what?

TRACY. I—couldn't possibly.

DINAH. Then he just sailed right into your room with you and—and that scared me so, that I just flew back to bed—or thought I did—and pulled the covers up over my head and laid there shaking and thinking; if *that's* the way it is, why doesn't she marry him instead of old George? And then I must have fallen even faster asleep, because the next thing I knew it was eight o'clock and the typewriter still going.

TRACY. Sandy—typewriter—

DINAH. So in a minute I got up and went to your door and peeked in, to make sure you were all right—and guess what?

TRACY *(agonized).* What?

DINAH. You were. He was gone by then.

TRACY *(assumes a high indignation).* Gone? Of course he was gone—he was never there!

DINAH. I know, Tracy.

TRACY. Well! I should certainly hope you did! *(She seats herself firmly in an armchair.)*

DINAH. I'm certainly glad I do, because if I didn't and if in a little while I heard Doctor Parsons saying, "If anyone knows any just cause or reason why these two should not be united in holy matrimony" —I just wouldn't know what to do. *(She sighs profoundly.)* —And it was all only a dream.

TRACY. Naturally!

DINAH. I know. Dexter said so, straight off.—But isn't it funny, how—

TRACY. Dexter!

DINAH. Yes.—He said—

TRACY *(rises and seizes her by the arm).* You told Dexter all that?

DINAH. Not a word. Not one single word. —But you know how quick he is.

TRACY. Dinah Lord—you little fiend; how can you stand here and—!

SETH (*comes in from the Hall, in morning coat and striped trousers*). Tracy, the next time you marry, choose a different Man of God, will you? This one wears me out. (*He goes to the Parlor doors, opens them, glances in, and closes them again.*) Good heavens!—Dinah! Get into your clothes! You look like a tramp.

DINAH. I'm going.

(SETH *is about to go out again into the Hall, when* TRACY's *voice stops him.*)

TRACY. Father.

SETH (*turns to her*). Yes, Tracy?

TRACY. I'm glad you came back. I'm glad you're here.

SETH (*comes to her*). Thank you, child.

TRACY. I'm sorry—I'm truly sorry I'm a disappointment to you.

SETH. I never said that, daughter—and I never will. (*He looks at her fondly for a moment, touches her arm, then turns abruptly and goes out into the Hall.*) Where's your mother? Where's George?

(MIKE, *in a blue suit, comes in from the Porch. He goes to the table and puts a cigarette out there.*)

MIKE. Good morning.

TRACY. Oh, hello!

MIKE. I was taking the air. I like it, but it doesn't like me.—Hello, Dinah.

DINAH (*replies with great dignity*). How do you do?

TRACY. Did—did you have a good sleep?

MIKE. Wonderful. How about you?

TRACY. Marvelous. Have you ever seen a handsomer day?

MIKE. Never. What did it set you back?

TRACY. I got it for nothing, for being a good girl.

MIKE. Good.

(*There is a brief silence. They look at* DINAH, *who is regarding them fixedly.*)

DINAH. I'm going, don't worry. (*She moves toward the Parlor doors.*)

TRACY. Why should you?

DINAH. I guess you must have things you wish to discuss.

TRACY. "Things to—"? What are you talking about?

DINAH. Only remember, it's getting late. (*Gingerly she opens the Parlor doors a crack, and peers in.*) Some of them are in already. My, they look solemn. (*She moves toward the Hall.*) I'll be ready when you are. (*And goes out.*)

TRACY. She's always trying to make situations.—How's your work coming—are you doing us up brown?

MIKE. I've—somehow I've lost my angle.

TRACY. How do you mean, Mike?

MIKE. I've just got so damn tolerant all at once, I doubt if I'll ever be able to write another line.

TRACY (*laughs uncertainly*). You are a fellah, Mike.

MIKE. Or the mug of this world: I don't know.

TRACY. When you're at the work you ought to be doing, you'll soon see that tolerance— What's the matter with your chin?

MIKE. Does it show?

TRACY. A little. What happened?

MIKE. I guess I just stuck it out too far.

TRACY. —Into a door, in the dark?

MIKE. That's it. (*His voice lowers solicitously.*) Are you—are *you* all right, Tracy?

(*The startled look comes back into her eyes. She laughs, to cover it.*)

TRACY. Me? Of course! Why shouldn't I be?

MIKE. That was a flock of wine we put away.

TRACY. I never felt better in my life. (*She moves away from him.*)

MIKE. That's fine. That's just daisy.

TRACY. I—I guess we're lucky both to have such good heads.

MIKE. Yes, I guess. (*He moves toward her.*)

TRACY. It must be awful for people who—you know—get up and make speeches or—or try to start a fight—or, you know—misbehave in general.

MIKE. It certainly must.

TRACY. It must be—some sort of hidden weakness coming out.

MIKE. Weakness? I'm not so sure of that.

(Again she moves away from him.)

TRACY. Anyhow, I had a simply wonderful evening. I hope you enjoyed it too.

MIKE. I enjoyed the last part of it.

TRACY *(turns to him uncertainly)*. Really? Why?—why especially the last?

MIKE. Are you asking me, Tracy?

TRACY. Oh, you mean the swim!—We did swim, and so forth, didn't we?

MIKE. We swam, and so forth.

TRACY *(advances to him suddenly)*. Mike—

MIKE *(gazing)*. You darling, darling girl—

TRACY. Mike!

MIKE. What can I say to you? Tell me, darling—

TRACY *(recovers herself and again moves away)*. Not anything—don't say anything. And especially not "Darling."

MIKE. Never in this world will I ever forget you.

TRACY. —Not anything, I said.

MIKE. You're going to go through with it, then—

TRACY. Through with what?

MIKE. The wedding.

TRACY. Why—why shouldn't I?

MIKE. Well, you see, I've made a funny discovery: that in spite of the fact that someone's up from the bottom, he may be quite a heel. And that even though someone else's born to the purple, he still may be quite a guy.—Hell, I'm only saying what you said last night!

TRACY. I said a lot of things last night, it seems.

MIKE *(after a moment)*. All right, no dice. But understand: also no regrets about last night.

TRACY. Why should I have?

MIKE. That's it! That's the stuff; you're wonderful. You're aces, Tracy.

TRACY *(now she is in full retreat)*. You don't know what I mean! I'm asking you—tell me straight out—tell me the reason why I should have any— *(But she cannot finish. Her head drops.)* No—don't.—Just tell me—what time is it?

MIKE *(glancing at his wrist)*. It's—what's happened to my wrist watch?

TRACY *(stops, frozen; speaks without turning)*. Why? Is it broken?

MIKE. It's gone. I've lost it somewhere.

TRACY *(after a moment)*. I can't tell you how extremely sorry I am to hear that.

MIKE. Oh, well—I'd always just as soon not know the time.

TRACY *(her back to him)*. There on the table—

MIKE. —What is? *(He goes to the table; finds the watch.)* Well, for the love of—! Who found it? I'll give a reward, or something. *(He straps the watch on his wrist.)*

TRACY. I don't think any reward will be expected.

(She drops miserably down into an armchair. DEXTER comes in from the Porch, a small glass in hand.)

DEXTER. Now, then! This medicine indicated in cases of— *(He stops at the sight of MIKE.)* Hello, Connor. How are you?

MIKE. About as you'd think.—Is that for me?

DEXTER. For Tracy.—Why? Would you like one?

MIKE. I would sell my grandmother for a drink—and you know how I love my grandmother.

DEXTER. Uncle Willie's around in the pantry, doing weird and wonderful things. Just say I said, One of the same.

MIKE *(moves toward the Porch)*. Is it all right if I say Two?

DEXTER. That's between you and your grandmother. (MIKE *goes out.* DEXTER *calls after him.*) —And find Liz! (DEXTER *goes to* TRACY *with the drink.*) Doctor's orders, Tray.

TRACY. What is it?

DEXTER. Just the juice of a few flowers.

TRACY (*takes the glass and looks at it, and tastes it*). Peppermint—

DEXTER (*smiles*). —White.—And one other simple ingredient. It's called a stinger. It removes the sting.

TRACY (*sets the glass down and looks away*). Oh, Dext—don't say that!

DEXTER. Why not, Tray?

TRACY. —Nothing will—nothing ever can. (*She rises from her chair.*) Oh, Dexter—I've done the most terrible thing to you!

DEXTER (*after a moment*). To *me*, did you say? (TRACY *nods vigorously.*) I doubt that, Red. I doubt it very much.

TRACY. You don't know, you don't know!

DEXTER. Well, maybe I shouldn't.

TRACY. You've got to—you must! I couldn't stand it, if you didn't! Oh, Dext—what am I going to do?

DEXTER. —But why to *me*, darling? (TRACY *looks at him.*) Where do I come into it any more? (*Still* TRACY *looks.*) Aren't you confusing me with someone else?—A fellow named Kittredge, or something?

TRACY (*a sudden, awful thought*). George—

DEXTER. That's right; George Kittredge. A splendid chap—very high morals—very broad shoulders.—

TRACY (*goes to the telephone*). I've got to tell him.

DEXTER (*follows her*). Tell him what?

TRACY. I've got to tell him. (*She dials a number.*)

DEXTER. But if he's got any brain at all, he'll have realized by this time what a fool he made of himself, when he—

TRACY. —When he what? (*To the telephone.*) Hello? Hello, George—this is Tracy. Look—I don't care whether it's bad luck or not, but I've got to see you for a minute before the wedding.—What, *what* note? I didn't get any note.—When? Well, why didn't someone tell me?— Right. Come on the run. (*She replaces the telephone, goes up to the fireplace, finds a wall-bell and rings it.*) He sent a note over at ten o'clock.

DEXTER. I told you he'd come to his senses.

TRACY (*turns slowly*). Was—was he here, too?

DEXTER. Sure.

TRACY. My God—why didn't you sell tickets?

DEXTER (*brings her her drink*). Finish your drink.

TRACY. Will it help?

DEXTER. There's always the hope.

(EDWARD *comes into the Hall doorway.*)

EDWARD. You rang, Miss?

TRACY. Isn't there a note for me from Mr. Kittredge somewhere?

EDWARD. I believe it was put on the hall table upstairs. Mrs. Lord said not to disturb you.

TRACY. I'd like to have it, if I may.

EDWARD. Very well, Miss.

(*He goes out.* TRACY *finishes her drink and gives* DEXTER *the empty glass.*)

TRACY. Say something, Dext—anything.

DEXTER. No—you do.

TRACY. Oh, Dext—I'm wicked! (*She moves away from him.*) I'm such an unholy mess of a girl.

DEXTER. That's no good. That's not even conversation.

TRACY. But never in all my life—not if I live to be one hundred—will I ever forget the way you tried to—to stand me on my feet again this morning.

DEXTER. You—you're in grand shape. Tell me: what did you think of my wedding present? I like my presents at least to be acknowledged.

TRACY. It was beautiful and sweet, Dext.

DEXTER. She was quite a boat, the "True Love."

TRACY. Was, and is.

DEXTER. She had the same initials as yours —did you ever realize that?

TRACY. No, I never did. (*TRACY seats herself in the armchair at Left of the table.*)

DEXTER. Nor did I, till I last saw her.— Funny we missed it. My, she was yare.

TRACY. She was yare, all right. (*A moment.*) I wasn't, was I?

DEXTER. Wasn't what?

TRACY. Yare.

(*DEXTER laughs shortly and seats himself in the chair across the table from her.*)

DEXTER. Not very.—You were good at the bright-work, though. I'll never forget you down on your knees on the deck every morning, with your little can of polish.

(*They speak without looking at each other, straight out in front of them.*)

TRACY. I wouldn't let even you help, would I?

DEXTER. Not even me.

TRACY. I made her shine.—Where is she now?

DEXTER. In the yard at Seven Hundred Acre, getting gone over. I'm going to sell her to Rufe Watriss at Oyster Bay.

(*There is a silence. Then she speaks, incredulously.*)

TRACY. You're going to sell the "True Love"?

DEXTER. Why not?

TRACY. For money?

DEXTER. He wired an offer yesterday.

TRACY. —To *that* fat old rum-pot?

DEXTER. What the hell does it matter?

TRACY. She's too clean, she's too yare.

DEXTER. I know—but when you're through with a boat, you're— (*He looks at her.*) That is, of course, unless *you* want her. (*She turns away, without replying.*) Of course she's good for nothing but racing —and only really comfortable for two people—and not so damned so, for them.

So I naturally thought—. But of course, if *you* should want her—

TRACY. No—I don't want her.

DEXTER. I'm going to design another for myself, along a little more practical lines.

TRACY. Are you?

DEXTER. I started on the drawings a couple of weeks ago.

TRACY. What will you call her?

DEXTER. I thought the "True Love II."— What do you think?

TRACY (*rises abruptly*). Dexter, if you call any boat that, I promise you I'll blow you and it right out of the water!

DEXTER. I know it's not very imaginative, but—

TRACY. Just try it, that's all! (*She moves away from him.*) I'll tell you what you can call it, if you like—

DEXTER. What?

TRACY. In fond remembrance of me—

DEXTER. What?

TRACY. The "Easy Virtue."

DEXTER (*goes to her*). Tray, I'll be damned if I'll have you thinking such things of yourself!

TRACY. What would you like me to think?

DEXTER. I don't know. But I do know that virtue, so-called, is no matter of a single misstep or two.

TRACY. You don't think so?

DEXTER. I know so. It's something inherent, it's something regardless of anything.

TRACY. Like fun it is.

DEXTER. You're wrong. The occasional misdeeds are often as good for a person as —as the more persistent virtues.—That is, if the person is there. Maybe you haven't committed enough, Tray. Maybe this *is* your coming-of-age.

TRACY. I don't know. Oh, I don't know anything any more!

DEXTER. That sounds very hopeful. That's just fine, Tray.

TRACY. Oh, be still, you! (*EDWARD comes in with a note on a tray.*) Thanks, Edward.

EDWARD. They are practically all in, Miss—and quite a number standing in the back. (MIKE *and* LIZ *come in from the Porch.*) All our best wishes, Miss.

TRACY. Thanks, Edward. Thanks, very much.

LIZ. —And all ours, Tracy.

TRACY. Thank you, thank everybody.

(EDWARD *goes out, into the Hall, passing* SANDY, *who rushes in and up to* TRACY. *He wears a short morning coat.*)

SANDY. Tray—he's here! He's arrived!

TRACY (*opening the note*). Who has?

SANDY. Kidd—Sidney Kidd.

TRACY. What for? What does *he* want?

LIZ. May I scream?

MIKE. What the—!

TRACY. Oh, now I remember.

SANDY. Well, I should hope you did. I haven't been to bed at all. I gave him the profile. He's reading it now. I couldn't stand the suspense, so I—

MIKE. Profile, did you say? What profile?

SANDY. The Kidd himself, complete with photographs. Do you want to see a copy?

MIKE. Holy Saint Rose of South Bend!

SANDY. —Offered in exchange for yours of us. I've told him what a help you'd both been to me.

LIZ. I don't think you'll find it so hard to resign now, Mike. Me neither.

MIKE. That's all right with me.

LIZ. Belts will be worn tighter this winter.

SANDY. I'll see how he's bearing up. (*He moves toward the Hall, meeting* DR. PARSONS, *a middle-aged clergyman, in surplice and stole, as he comes in.*) Good morning, Doctor Parsons. How's everything?

DR. PARSONS. Where is your sister? (SANDY *points to her and goes out.* TRACY *is now reading the note.* DR. PARSONS *calls to her:*) Tracy? Tracy!

TRACY (*looks up, startled*). Yes?

(*He smiles, and beckons engagingly.*)

DEXTER. One minute, Doctor Parsons, Mr. Kittredge is on his way.

(DR. PARSONS *smiles again, and goes out into the Parlor, carefully closing the door behind him.*)

DEXTER (*turns to* TRACY). I'm afraid it's the deadline, Tracy.

TRACY. So is this. Listen— "My dear Tracy: Your conduct last night was so shocking to my ideals of womanhood, that my attitude toward you and the prospects of a happy and useful life together has changed materially. Your, to me, totally unexpected breach of common decency, not to mention the moral aspect—"

GEORGE (*comes in from the porch*). Tracy!

TRACY. Hello, George.

GEORGE. Tracy—all these people!

TRACY. It's only a letter from a friend. They're my friends, too. "—not to mention the moral aspect, certainly entitles me to a full explanation, before going through with our proposed marriage. In the light of day, I am sure that you will agree with me. Otherwise, with profound regrets and all best wishes, yours very sincerely—" (*She folds the note and returns it to its envelope.*) Yes, George, I quite agree with you—in the light of day or the dark of night, for richer, for poorer, for better, for worse, in sickness, and in health—and thank you so very much for your good wishes at this time.

GEORGE. That's all you've got to say?

TRACY. What else? I wish for your sake as well as mine, I had an explanation. But unfortunately I've none. You'd better just say "good riddance," George.

GEORGE. It isn't easy, you know.

TRACY. I don't see why.

LIZ (*to* MIKE). Say something, Stupid.

MIKE. Wait a minute.

(*Preparatory music—Debussy—is now faintly heard from the Parlor.*)

GEORGE. You'll grant I had a right to be angry, and very angry.

TRACY. You certainly had, you certainly have.

GEORGE. "For your sake, as well," you said—

TRACY. Yes—it would be nice to know.

LIZ *(to* MIKE*)*. Will you say something?

MIKE. Wait!

LIZ. What for?

MIKE. Enough rope.

GEORGE. —On the very eve of your wedding, an affair with another man—

TRACY. I told you I agreed, George—and I tell you again, good riddance to me.

GEORGE. That's for me to decide.

TRACY. Well, I wish you would a—a—little more quickly.

MIKE. Look, Kittredge—

TRACY. If there was some way to make you see that—that regardless of it—or even because of it,—I'm—somehow I feel more of a person, George.

GEORGE. That's a little difficult to understand.

*(*TRACY *lets herself down into an armchair.)*

TRACY. Yes, I can see that it would be.

DEXTER. Not necessarily.

GEORGE. You keep out of it!

DEXTER. You forget: I am out of it. *(He seats himself upon the sofa, away from them all.)*

MIKE *(advancing)*. Kittredge, it just might interest you to know that the so-called "affair" consisted of exactly two kisses and one rather late swim.

TRACY *(unwilling to accept the gallant gesture)*. Thanks, Mike, but there's no need to—

MIKE *(turns to her)*. All of which I thoroughly enjoyed, and the memory of which I wouldn't part with for anything.

TRACY. It's no use, Mike.

MIKE *(again to* GEORGE*)*. —After which, I accompanied her to her room, deposited her on her bed, and promptly returned to you two on the porch—as you will doubtless remember.

DEXTER. Doubtless without a doubt.

GEORGE. You mean to say that was all there was to it?

MIKE. I do.

*(*GEORGE *ponders.* TRACY *is looking at* MIKE *in astonishment. Suddenly she rises and demands indignantly of him:)*

TRACY. Why? Was I so damned unattractive—so distant, so forbidding or something, that—?

GEORGE. This is fine talk, too!

TRACY. I'm asking a question!

(The music has stopped now.)

MIKE. You were extremely attractive—and as for distant and forbidding, on the contrary. But you were also somewhat the worse—or the better—for wine, and there are rules about that, damn it.

TRACY *(after a moment)*. Thank you, Mike. I think men are wonderful.

LIZ. The little dears.

GEORGE. Well, that's a relief, I'll admit. Still—

TRACY. Why? Where's the difference? If my wonderful, marvelous, beautiful virtue is still intact, it's no thanks to me, I assure you.

GEORGE. I don't think—

TRACY. —It's purely by courtesy of the gentleman from South Bend.

LIZ. Local papers, please copy.

GEORGE. I fail to see the humor in this situation, Miss Imbrie.

LIZ. I appreciate that. It was a little hard for me too, at first—

TRACY. Oh, Liz— *(She goes to her, gropes for her hand.)*

LIZ. It's all right, Tracy. We all go a little haywire at times—and if we don't, maybe we ought to.

TRACY. Liz.

LIZ. You see, it really wasn't Tracy at all Mr. Kittredge. It was another girl: a Miss Pommery, '28.

GEORGE. You'd had too much to drink—

TRACY. That seems to be the consensus of opinion.

GEORGE. Will you promise me never to touch the stuff again?

TRACY (looks at him; speaks slowly). No, George, I don't believe I will. There are certain things about that other girl I rather like.

GEORGE. But a man expects his wife to—

TRACY. —To behave herself. Naturally.

DEXTER. To behave herself naturally. (GEORGE glances angrily at him.) Sorry.

GEORGE (to TRACY). But if it hadn't been for the drink last night, all this might not have happened.

TRACY. But apparently nothing did. What made you think it had?

GEORGE. It didn't take much imagination, I can tell you that.

TRACY. Not much, perhaps—but just of a certain kind.

GEORGE. It seems you didn't think any too well of yourself.

TRACY. That's the odd thing, George: somehow I'd have hoped you'd think better of me than I did.

GEORGE. I'm not going to quibble, Tracy: all the evidence was there.

TRACY. And I was guilty straight off—that is, until I was proved innocent.

GEORGE. Well?

DEXTER. Downright un-American, if you ask me.

GEORGE. No one is asking you!

SANDY (comes into the Hall doorway, consternation on his face). Listen—he's read it—and holy cats, guess what?

LIZ. What?

SANDY. He loves it! He says it's brilliant— He wants it for Destiny!

MIKE. I give up.

GEORGE. Who wants what?

LIZ. Sidney Kidd; Sidney Kidd.

GEORGE (hardly believing the good news). Sidney Kidd is here himself?!

SANDY. Big as life, and twice as handsome. Boy, is this wedding a National affair now! (He goes out.)

GEORGE (after a moment). It's extremely kind and thoughtful of him. (Another moment. Then.) Come on, Tracy—it must be late. Let's let bygones be bygones— what do you say?

TRACY. Yes—and goodbye, George.

GEORGE. I don't understand you.

TRACY. Please—goodbye.

GEORGE. But what on earth—?

LIZ. I imagine she means that your explanation is inadequate.

GEORGE. Look here, Tracy—

TRACY. You're too good for me, George. You're a hundred times too good.

GEORGE. I never said I—

TRACY. And I'd make you most unhappy, most— That is, I'd do my best to.

GEORGE (looks at her). Well, if that's the way you want it—

TRACY. That's the way it is.

GEORGE. All right. Possibly it's just as well. (He starts toward the Hall.)

DEXTER. I thought you'd eventually think so.

GEORGE (turns and confronts him). I've got a feeling you've had more to do with this than anyone.

DEXTER. A novel and interesting idea, I'm sure.

GEORGE. You and your whole rotten class.

DEXTER. Oh, class my—! (But he stops himself.)

MIKE. Funny—I heard a truck-driver say that yesterday—only with a short "a."

GEORGE. Listen, you're all on your way out—the lot of you—and don't think you aren't.—Yes, and good riddance. (He goes out.)

MIKE. Well, there goes George—

(Again the orchestra is heard. This time it is "Oh Promise Me." TRACY move *swiftly to the Parlor doors, opens them slightly, peers in, and exclaims:)*

TRACY. Oh, my sainted aunt—that welter of faces! *(She closes the door, and returns.)* What in the name of all that's holy am I to do?

(MAY, the housemaid, comes in with TRACY's hat and gloves.)

MAY. You forgot your hat, Miss Tracy.

(TRACY takes the broad-brimmed hat, the immaculate gloves, and gazes at them helplessly.)

TRACY. Oh, God— Oh, dear God—have mercy on Tracy!

MIKE *(rises and goes to her)*. Tracy—

TRACY. Yes, Mike?

MIKE. Forget the license!

TRACY. License?

(DEXTER fumbles in his pocket.)

DEXTER. I've got an old one here, that we never used, Maryland being quicker—

MIKE. Forget it! *(To TRACY.)* Old Parson Parsons—he's never seen Kittredge, has he? Nor have most of the others. I got you into this, I'll get you out.—Will you marry me, Tracy?

(She looks at him for a long, grateful moment before speaking. Then:)

TRACY. No, Mike.—Thanks, but no.

MIKE. But listen, I've never asked a girl to marry me before in my life!—I've avoided it!—You've got me all confused—why not—?

TRACY. —Because I don't think Liz would like it—and I'm not sure that you would —and I'm even a little doubtful about myself. But—I'm beholden to you, Mike, I'm most beholden.

MIKE *(gestures impatiently)*. They're in there! They're waiting!

LIZ. Don't get too conventional all at once, will you?—There'll be a reaction.

MIKE *(an appeal)*. Liz— *(Then:)*

LIZ. I count on you sustaining the mood.

She beckons to him and he joins her. DEXTER rises.)

DEXTER. It'll be all right, Tracy: you've been got out of jams before.

TRACY. Been *got out* of them, did you say?

DEXTER. That's what I said, Tracy. Don't worry, you always are. *(MARGARET and SETH come in from the Hall.)*

MARGARET. Tracy, we met George in the hall—it's all right, dear, your father will make a very simple announcement.

SETH. Is there anything special you want me to say?

TRACY. No! I'll say it, whatever it is.—I won't be got out of anything more, thanks.

(She moves to the Parlor doors. WILLIE and DINAH enter from the Hall.)

UNCLE WILLIE. What's alack? What's amiss?

MARGARET. Oh, this just can't be happening—it can't.

(TRACY throws open the Parlor doors and stands in the doorway gazing into the Parlor. She addresses her wedding guests.)

TRACY. I'm—I'm—hello! Good morning.— I'm—that is to say—I'm terribly sorry to have kept you waiting, but—but there's been a little hitch in the proceedings. I've made a terrible fool of myself—which isn't unusual—and my fiancé—my fiancé-- *(She stops and swallows.)*

MARGARET. Seth!

SETH. Wait, my dear.

TRACY. —my fiancé, that was, that is—he thinks we'd better call it a day, and I quite agree with him. *(She half turns and whispers.)* —Dexter—Dexter—what the hell next?

DEXTER. "Two years ago you were invited to a wedding in this house and I did you out of it by eloping to Maryland—"

(He moves swiftly to MARGARET.)

TRACY. "Two years ago you were invited to a wedding in this house and I did you out of it by eloping to Maryland—" *(Then, desperately.)* Dexter, Dexter, where are you?

DEXTER *(simultaneously to MARGARET)*. May I? Just as a loan? *(He takes a ring from her finger and goes to MIKE with it.)* Here, put this in your vest pocket.

MIKE. But I haven't got a vest.

DEXTER. Then hold it in your hand. *(He goes quickly to* TRACY.*)*

DEXTER. "Which was very bad manners—"

TRACY *(into the Parlor)*. "Which was very bad manners—"

DEXTER. "But I hope to make it up to you by going through with it now, as originally planned."

TRACY. "But I hope to make it up to you by—by going—" *(Suddenly she realizes what she is saying and turns to* DEXTER *with blank wonder in her eyes. He gestures, and she turns again and continues:)* —by going beautifully through with it now—as originally and—most beautifully —planned.

*(*DEXTER *moves to* MIKE.*)*

DEXTER. I'd like you to be my best man, if you will, because I think you're one hell of a guy, Mike.

MIKE. I'd be honored, C.K.

UNCLE WILLIE. Ladies, follow me! No rushing please! *(*LIZ *and* MARGARET *go out with him into the Hall.)*

TRACY *(simultaneously, into the Parlor)*. —Because there's something awfully nice about a wedding—I don't know—they're so gay and attractive—and I've always wanted one, and—

DEXTER. "So if you'll just keep your seats a minute—"

TRACY. "So if you'll just keep your seats a minute—"

DEXTER. That's all.

TRACY. "That's all!" *(She closes the doors and turns breathlessly to* DEXTER.*)* Dexter —are you sure?

DEXTER. Not in the least; but I'll risk it— will you?

TRACY. You bet!—And you didn't do it just to soften the blow?

DEXTER. No, Tray.

TRACY. Nor to save my face?

DEXTER. It's a nice little face.

TRACY. Oh—I'll be yare now—I'll promise to be yare!

DEXTER. Be whatever you like, you're my Redhead—All set?

TRACY. All set! *(She runs and snatches her hat from a chair, puts it on before a mirror.)* Oh, how did this ever happen?

SETH. Don't inquire.— Go on, Dinah: tell Mr. Dutton to start the music.

*(*DINAH *goes out into the Hall, exclaiming triumphantly:)*

DINAH. I did it—I did it all!

*(*DEXTER *and* MIKE *go to the Hall doorway, wait there for the signal;* SETH *turns to* TRACY.*)*

SETH. Daughter—

TRACY *(moves to him)*. I love you, Father.

SETH. And I love you, daughter.

TRACY. Never in my life have I been so full of love before—

(The Wedding March begins to be heard from the Parlor.)

DEXTER. See you soon, Red!

TRACY. See you soon. Dext! *(*DEXTER *and* MIKE *go out.* TRACY *stands before* SETH.*)* How do I look?

SETH. Like a queen—like a goddess.

TRACY. Do you know how I feel?

SETH. How?

TRACY. Like a human—like a human being!

SETH *(smiles)*. —And is that all right?

(She tightens her arm in his. They start to move slowly across the room in the direction of the Parlor.)

TRACY. All right? Oh, Father, it's Heaven!

CURTAIN

ARSENIC AND OLD LACE

By JOSEPH KESSELRING

ARSENIC AND OLD LACE was presented by Howard Lindsay and Russel Crouse at the Fulton Theatre in New York, on January 10, 1941, with the following cast:

ABBY BREWSTER............Josephine Hull		MR. GIBBS......................Henry Herbert	
THE REV. DR. HARPER		JONATHAN BREWSTER	
	Wyrley Birch		Boris Karloff
TEDDY BREWSTER....John Alexander		DR. EINSTEIN....................Edgar Stehli	
OFFICER BROPHY.............John Quigg		OFFICER O'HARA...........Anthony Ross	
OFFICER KLEIN.............Bruce Gordon		LIEUTENANT ROONEY	
MARTHA BREWSTER.........Jean Adair			Victor Sutherland
ELAINE HARPER.............Helen Brooks		MR. WITHERSPOON......William Parks	
MORTIMER BREWSTER....Allyn Joslyn			

SCENES

The entire action of the play takes place in the living room of the Brewster home in Brooklyn. Time: the present.

ACT I: An afternoon in September.

ACT II: The same night.

ACT III: Scene 1. Later that night.

Scene 2. Early the next morning.

THE AUTHOR

It was Joseph Otto Kesselring's great good fortune in 1940 to meet up with Howard Lindsay and Russel Crouse. The not quite young playwright (he was born in New York in 1902) had lately written a melodrama about sweet old ladies and their penchant for relieving people of the burdens of this world. The script fell into the lap of Dorothy Stickney, Mrs. Lindsay, who was then playing Mother to Howard Lindsay's irascible Father in Life With Father. *Mrs. Lindsay found the idea both impossible and amusing, and so informed her husband, who in turn informed Mr. Crouse, who was then busily engaged in Hollywood on the screenplay of* The Great Victor Herbert. *The friends acquired the script, guided the author in the delicate matter of revisions, helped him to evolve the Boris Karloff character, and persuaded Mr. Karloff to impersonate himself. They also rounded up a host of twenty-one backers who will remain eternally grateful to them.*

The benign melodrama, Arsenic and Old Lace, *opened in New York on January 10, 1941. Mr. Lindsay told his co-producer before the rise of the curtain: "We either have a hit or we'll be run out of town." They were not run out of town, which would have been the town's loss in any event. To their "angels" they wrote, enclosing the first checks for quickly accrued profits: "If there is anything in this about which you wish to complain we shall be glad to hear from you. Just address us in care of the Dead Letter Office, Washington, D. C."*

Mr. Kesselring tried his playwriting hand again after Arsenic and Old Lace *with a piece called* Maggie McGilligan *which got no further than the Woodstock Playhouse in 1942. Prior to his lurid tour de force he had tried acting, and had written* There's Wisdom in Women, *which D. A. Doran produced in 1935 with a cast that included Walter Pidgeon. The production ran for forty-six performances. Another of Mr. Kesselring's plays,* Cross-Town, *produced on Broadway in 1937, had met with scantier favor.*

ARSENIC AND OLD LACE

ACT ONE

TIME: *Late afternoon. September. Present.*

PLACE: *The living-room of the old Brewster home in Brooklyn, N. Y. It is just as Victorian as the two sisters* ABBY *and* MARTHA BREWSTER, *who occupy the house with their nephew,* TEDDY.

Down stage right is the front door of the house, a large door with frosted glass panels in the upper half, beyond which, when it is open, can be seen the front porch and the lawn and shrubbery of the front garden of the Brewster house. On either side of the door are narrow windows of small panes of glass, curtained. The remainder of the right wall is taken up by the first flight of stairs leading to the upper floors. In the up-stage corner is a landing where the stairs turn to continue along the back wall of the room. At the top of the stairs, along the back wall, is another landing, from which a door leads into the second-floor bedrooms, and an arch at the left end of this landing suggests the stairs leading to the third floor.

On stage level under this landing is a door which leads to the cellar. To the left of this door is a recess which contains a sideboard, on the top of which at either end are two small cabinets, where the sisters keep, among other things, bottles of elderberry wine. To the left of the recess is the door leading to the kitchen.

In the left wall of the room, there is a large window looking out over the cemetery of the neighboring Episcopal Church. This window has the usual lace curtains and thick drapes, which open and close by the use of a heavy curtain cord. Below the window is a large window seat. When this lid is raised, the hinges creak audibly.

At the left of the foot of the stairs is a small desk, on which stands a dial telephone, and by this desk is a stool. Along the back wall, to the right of the cellar door, is an old-fashioned sofa. Left center in the room is a round table. There is a small chair right of this table and behind it, to the left of the table, a larger, comfortable armchair. On the walls are the usual pictures, including several portraits of the rather eccentric Brewster ancestors.

As the curtain rises, ABBY BREWSTER, *a plump little darling in her late sixties, is presiding at tea. She is sitting behind the table in front of a high silver tea service. At her left, in the comfortable armchair, is the* REVEREND DR. HARPER, *the elderly rector of the near-by church. Standing, stage center, thoughtfully sipping a cup of tea, is her nephew,* TEDDY, *in a frock coat, and wearing pince-nez attached to a black ribbon.* TEDDY *is in his forties and has a large mustache.*

ABBY. Yes indeed, my sister Martha and I have been talking all week about your sermon last Sunday. It's really wonderful, Dr. Harper—in only two short years you've taken on the spirit of Brooklyn.

HARPER. That's very gratifying, Miss Brewster.

ABBY. You see, living here next to the church all our lives, we've seen so many ministers come and go. The spirit of Brooklyn we always say is friendliness—and your sermons are not so much sermons as friendly talks.

TEDDY. Personally, I've always enjoyed my talks with Cardinal Gibbons—or have I met him yet?

ABBY. No, dear, not yet. *(Changing the subject.)* Are the biscuits good?

TEDDY *(he sits on sofa).* Bully!

ABBY. Won't you have another biscuit, Dr. Harper?

HARPER. Oh, no, I'm afraid I'll have no appetite for dinner now. I always eat too many of your biscuits just to taste that lovely jam.

ABBY. But you haven't tried the quince. We always put a little apple in with it to take the tartness out.

HARPER. No, thank you.

ABBY. We'll send you over a jar.

HARPER. No, no. You keep it here so I can be sure of having your biscuits with it.

ABBY. I do hope they don't make us use that imitation flour again. I mean with

461

this war trouble. It may not be very charitable of me, but I've almost come to the conclusion that this Mr. Hitler isn't a Christian.

HARPER (*with a sigh*). If only Europe were on another planet!

TEDDY (*sharply*). Europe, sir?

HARPER. Yes, Teddy.

TEDDY. Point your gun the other way!

HARPER. Gun?

ABBY (*trying to calm him*). Teddy.

TEDDY. To the West! There's your danger! There's your enemy! Japan!

HARPER. Why, yes—yes, of course.

ABBY. Teddy!

TEDDY. No, Aunt Abby! Not so much talk about Europe and more about the canal!

ABBY. Well, let's not talk about war. Will you have another cup of tea, dear?

TEDDY. No, thank you, Aunt Abby.

ABBY. Dr. Harper?

HARPER. No, thank you. I must admit, Miss Abby, that war and violence seem far removed from these surroundings.

ABBY. It is peaceful here, isn't it?

HARPER. Yes—peaceful. The virtues of another day—they're all here in this house. The gentle virtues that went out with candlelight and good manners and low taxes.

ABBY (*glancing about her contentedly*). It's one of the oldest houses in Brooklyn. It's just as it was when Grandfather Brewster built and furnished it—except for the electricity—and we use it as little as possible. It was Mortimer who persuaded us to put it in.

HARPER (*beginning to freeze*). Yes, I can understand that. Your nephew Mortimer seems to live only by electric light.

ABBY. The poor boy has to work so late. I understand he's taking Elaine with him to the theatre again tonight. Teddy, your brother Mortimer will be here a little later.

TEDDY (*baring his teeth in a broad grin*). Dee-lighted!

ABBY (*to* HARPER). We're so happy it's Elaine Mortimer takes to the theatre with him.

HARPER. Well, it's a new experience for me to wait up until three o'clock in the morning for my daughter to be brought home.

ABBY. Oh, Dr. Harper, I hope you don't disapprove of Mortimer.

HARPER. Well—

ABBY. We'd feel so guilty if you did—sister Martha and I. I mean since it was here in our home that your daughter met Mortimer.

HARPER. Of course, Miss Abby. And so I'll say immediately that I believe Mortimer himself to be quite a worthy gentleman. But I must also admit that I have watched the growing intimacy between him and my daughter with some trepidation. For one reason, Miss Abby.

ABBY. You mean his stomach, Dr. Harper?

HARPER. Stomach?

ABBY. His dyspepsia—he's bothered with it so, poor boy.

HARPER. No, Miss Abby, I'll be frank with you. I'm speaking of your nephew's unfortunate connection with the theatre.

ABBY. The theatre! Oh, no, Dr. Harper! Mortimer writes for a New York newspaper.

HARPER. I know, Miss Abby, I know. But a dramatic critic is constantly exposed to the theatre, and I don't doubt but what some of them do develop an interest in it.

ABBY. Well, not Mortimer. You need have no fear of that. Why, Mortimer hates the theatre.

HARPER. Really?

ABBY. Oh, yes! He writes awful things about the theatre. But you can't blame him, poor boy. He was so happy writing about real estate, which he really knew something about, and then they just made him take this terrible night position.

HARPER. My! My!

ABBY. But, as he says, the theatre can't last much longer anyway and in the meantime it's a living. (*Complacently.*) Yes, I think if we give the theatre another year or two, perhaps . . . *(A knock on* R. *door.)* Well, now, who do you suppose that is? *(They all rise as* ABBY *goes to door* R. TEDDY *starts for door at same time, but* ABBY *stops him.)* No, thank you, Teddy. I'll go. *(She opens door to admit two cops,* OFFICERS BROPHY *and* KLEIN.*)* Come in, Mr. Brophy.

BROPHY. Hello, Miss Brewster.

ABBY. How are you, Mr. Klein?

KLEIN. Very well, Miss Brewster.

(The COPS *cross to* TEDDY *who is standing near desk, and salute him.* TEDDY *returns salute.)*

TEDDY. What news have you brought me?

BROPHY. Colonel, we have nothing to report.

TEDDY. Splendid! Thank you, gentlemen! At ease!

*(*COPS *relax and drop* D. S. ABBY *has closed door, and turns to* COPS.*)*

ABBY. You know Dr. Harper.

KLEIN. Sure! Hello, Dr. Harper.

BROPHY *(turns to* ABBY, *doffing cap).* We've come for the toys for the Christmas Fund.

ABBY. Oh, yes.

HARPER *(standing below table.)* That's a splendid work you men do—fixing up discarded toys to give poor children a happier Christmas.

KLEIN. It gives us something to do when we have to sit around the station. You get tired playing cards and then you start cleaning your gun, and the first thing you know you've shot yourself in the foot. *(*KLEIN *drifts* U. L. *around to window-seat.)*

ABBY *(crossing to* TEDDY*).* Teddy, go upstairs and get that big box from your Aunt Martha's room. *(*TEDDY *crosses upstage toward stairs.* ABBY *speaks to* BROPHY.*)* How is Mrs. Brophy today? Mrs. Brophy has been quite ill, Dr. Harper.

BROPHY *(to* HARPER*).* Pneumonia!

HARPER. I'm sorry to hear that.

*(*TEDDY *has reached first landing on stairs where he stops and draws an imaginary sword.)*

TEDDY *(shouting).* CHARGE! *(He charges up stairs and exits off balcony. The others pay no attention to this.)*

BROPHY. Oh, she's better now. A little weak still—

ABBY *(starting toward kitchen).* I'm going to get you some beef broth to take to her.

BROPHY. Don't bother, Miss Abby! You've done so much for her already.

ABBY *(at kitchen door).* We made it this morning. Sister Martha is taking some to poor Mr. Benitzky right now. I won't be a minute. Sit down and be comfortable, all of you. *(She exits into kitchen.)*

*(*HARPER *sits again.* BROPHY *crosses to table and addresses the other two.)*

BROPHY. She shouldn't go to all that trouble.

KLEIN. Listen, try to stop her or her sister from doing something nice—and for nothing! They don't even care how you vote. *(He sits on window-seat.)*

HARPER. When I received my call to Brooklyn and moved next door my wife wasn't well. When she died and for months before—well, if I know what pure kindness and absolute generosity are, it's because I've known the Brewster sisters.

(At this moment TEDDY *steps out on balcony and blows a bugle call. They all look.)*

BROPHY *(stepping* U. S. . . . . *Remonstrating).* Colonel, you promised not to do that.

TEDDY. But I have to call a Cabinet meeting to get the release of those supplies. *(*TEDDY *wheels and exits.)*

BROPHY. He used to do that in the middle of the night. The neighbors raised cain with us. They're a little afraid of him, anyway.

HARPER. Oh, he's quite harmless.

KLEIN. Suppose he does think he's Teddy Roosevelt. There's a lot worse people he could think he was.

BROPHY. Damn shame—a nice family like this hatching a cuckoo.

KLEIN. Well, his father—the old girls' brother, was some sort of a genius, wasn't he? And their father—Teddy's grandfather—seems to me I've heard he was a little crazy too.

BROPHY. Yeah—he was crazy like a fox. He made a million dollars.

HARPER. Really? Here in Brooklyn?

BROPHY. Yeah. Patent medicine. He was a kind of a quack of some sort. Old Sergeant Edwards remembers him. He used the house here as a sort of a clinic—tried 'em out on people.

KLEIN. Yeah, I hear he used to make mistakes occasionally, too.

BROPHY. The department never bothered him much because he was pretty useful on autopsies sometimes. Especially poison cases.

KLEIN. Well, whatever he did he left his daughters fixed for life. Thank God for that ——

BROPHY. Not that they ever spend any of it on themselves.

HARPER. Yes, I'm well acquainted with their charities.

KLEIN. You don't know a tenth of it. When I was with the Missing Persons Bureau I was trying to trace an old man that we never did find *(Rises.)* —do you know there's a renting agency that's got this house down on its list for furnished rooms? They don't rent rooms—but you can bet that anybody who comes here lookin' for a room goes away with a good meal and probably a few dollars in their kick.

BROPHY. It's just their way of digging up people to do some good to.

(R. door opens and MARTHA BREWSTER *enters.* MARTHA *is also a sweet elderly woman with Victorian charm. She is dressed in the old-fashioned manner of* ABBY, *but with a high lace collar that covers her neck.* MEN *all on feet.)*

MARTHA *(at door)*. Well, now, isn't this nice? *(Closes door.)*

BROPHY *(crosses to* MARTHA*)*. Good afternoon, Miss Brewster.

MARTHA. How do you do, Mr. Brophy? Dr. Harper. Mr. Klein.

KLEIN. How are you, Miss Brewster? We dropped in to get the Christmas toys.

MARTHA. Oh, yes, Teddy's Army and Navy. They wear out. They're all packed. *(She turns to stairs.* BROPHY *stops her.)*

BROPHY. The Colonel's upstairs after them —it seems the Cabinet has to O.K. it.

MARTHA. Yes, of course. I hope Mrs. Brophy's better?

BROPHY. She's doin' fine, ma'am. Your sister's getting some soup for me to take to her.

MARTHA *(crossing below* BROPHY *to* C.*)*. Oh, yes, we made it this morning. I just took some to a poor man who broke ever so many bones.

*(*ABBY *enters from kitchen carrying a covered pail.)*

ABBY. Oh, you're back, Martha. How was Mr. Benitzky?

MARTHA. Well, dear, it's pretty serious, I'm afraid. The doctor was there. He's going to amputate in the morning.

ABBY *(hopefully)*. Can we be present?

MARTHA *(disappointment)*. No. I asked him but he says it's against the rules of the hosiptal. *(*MARTHA *crosses to sideboard, puts pail down. Then puts cape and hat on small table* U. L.*)*

*(*TEDDY *enters on balcony with large cardboard box and comes downstairs to desk, putting box on stool.* KLEIN *crosses to toy box.* HARPER *speaks through this.)*

HARPER. You couldn't be of any service— and you must spare yourselves something.

ABBY *(to* BROPHY*)*. Here's the broth, Mr. Brophy. Be sure it's good and hot.

BROPHY. Yes, ma'am. *(Drops* U. S.*)*

KLEIN. This is fine—it'll make a lot of kids happy. *(Lifts out toy soldier.)* That O'Malley boy is nuts about soldiers.

TEDDY. That's General Miles. I've retired him. *(*KLEIN *removes ship.)* What's this! The Oregon!

MARTHA *(crosses to* U. L.*)*. Teddy, dear, put it back.

TEDDY. But the Oregon goes to Australia.

ABBY. Now, Teddy—

TEDDY. No, I've given my word to Fighting Bob Evans.

MARTHA. But, Teddy—

KLEIN. What's the difference what kid gets it—Bobby Evans, Izzy Cohen? (*Crosses to R. door with box, opens door.* BROPHY *follows.*) We'll run along, ma'am, and thank you very much.

ABBY. Not at all. (*The* COPS *stop in doorway, salute* TEDDY *and exit.* ABBY *crosses and shuts door as she speaks.* TEDDY *starts upstairs.*) Good-bye.

HARPER (*crosses to sofa, gets hat*). I must be getting home.

ABBY. Before you go, Dr. Harper—

(TEDDY *has reached stair landing.*)

TEDDY. CHARGE! (*He dashes upstairs. At top he stops and with a sweeping gesture over the balcony rail, invites all to follow him as he speaks.*) Charge the blockhouse! (*He dashes through door, closing it after him.*)

(HARPER *looks after him.* MARTHA, *to* L. *of* HARPER, *is fooling with a pin on her dress.* ABBY R. *of* HARPER.)

HARPER. The blockhouse?

MARTHA. The stairs are always San Juan Hill.

HARPER. Have you ever tried to persuade him that he wasn't Teddy Roosevelt?

ABBY. Oh, no!

MARTHA. He's so happy being Teddy Roosevelt.

ABBY. Once, a long time ago— (*She crosses below to* MARTHA.) remember, Martha? We thought if he would be George Washington it might be a change for him—

MARTHA. But he stayed under his bed for days and just wouldn't be anybody.

ABBY. And we'd so much rather he'd be Mr. Roosevelt than nobody.

HARPER. Well, if he's happy—and what's more important you're happy— (*He takes blue-backed legal paper from inside pocket.*) You'll see that he signs these.

MARTHA. What are they?

ABBY. Dr. Harper has made all arrangements for Teddy to go to Happy Dale Sanitarium after we pass on.

MARTHA. But why should Teddy sign any papers now?

HARPER. It's better to have it all settled. If the Lord should take you away suddenly perhaps we couldn't persuade Teddy to commit himself and that would mean an unpleasant legal procedure. Mr. Witherspoon understands they're to be filed away until the times comes to use them.

MARTHA. Mr. Witherspoon? Who's he?

HARPER. He's the Superintendent of Happy Dale.

ABBY (*to* MARTHA). Dr. Harper has arranged for him to drop in tomorrow or the next day to meet Teddy.

HARPER (*crossing to* R. *door and opening it*). I'd better be running along or Elaine will be over here looking for me.

(ABBY *crosses to door and calls out after him.*)

ABBY. Give our love to Elaine—and Dr. Harper, please don't think harshly of Mortimer because he's a dramatic critic. Somebody has to do those things. (ABBY *closes door, comes back into room.*)

(MARTHA *crosses to sideboard, puts legal papers on it . . . notices tea things on table.*)

MARTHA. Did you just have tea? Isn't it rather late?

ABBY (*as one who has a secret*). Yes—and dinner's going to be late too.

(TEDDY *enters on balcony, starts downstairs to first landing.* MARTHA *steps to* ABBY.)

MARTHA. So? Why?

ABBY. Teddy! (TEDDY *stops on landing.*) Good news for you. You're going to Panama and dig another lock for the canal.

TEDDY. Dee-lighted! That's bully! Just bully! I shall prepare at once for the journey. (*He turns to go upstairs, stops as if puzzled, hurries back to landing, cries CHARGE!, and rushes up and off.*)

MARTHA (*elated*). Abby! While I was out?

ABBY (*taking* MARTHA's *hand*). Yes, dear! I just couldn't wait for you. I didn't know when you'd be back and Dr. Harper was coming.

MARTHA. But all by yourself?

ABBY. Oh, I got along fine!

MARTHA. I'll run right downstairs and see. *(She starts happily for cellar door.)*

ABBY. Oh, no, there wasn't time, and I was all alone.

(MARTHA looks around room toward kitchen.)

MARTHA. Well—

ABBY *(coyly)*. Martha—just look in the window-seat. *(MARTHA almost skips to window-seat, and just as she gets there a knock is heard on R. door. She stops. They both look toward door. ABBY hurries to door and opens it. ELAINE HARPER enters. ELAINE is an attractive girl in her twenties; she looks surprisingly smart for a minister's daughter.)* Oh, it's Elaine. *(Opens door.)* Come in, dear.

(ELAINE crosses to C. ABBY closes door, crosses to C.)

ELAINE. Good afternoon, Miss Abby. Good afternoon, Miss Martha. I thought Father was here.

MARTHA *(stepping to L. of table)*. He just this minute left. Didn't you meet him?

ELAINE *(pointing to window in L. wall)*. No, I took the short cut through the cemetery. Mortimer hasn't come yet?

ABBY. No, dear.

ELAINE. Oh? He asked me to meet him here. Do you mind if I wait?

MARTHA. Not at all.

ABBY. Why don't you sit down, dear?

MARTHA. But we really must speak to Mortimer about doing this to you.

ELAINE *(sits chair R. of table)*. Doing what?

MARTHA. Well, he was brought up to know better. When a gentleman is taking a young lady out he should call for her at her house.

ELAINE *(to both)*. Oh, there's something about calling for a girl at a parsonage that discourages any man who doesn't embroider.

ABBY. He's done this too often—we're going to speak to him.

ELAINE. Oh, please don't. After young men whose idea of night life was to take me to prayer meeting, it's wonderful to go to the theatre almost every night of my life.

MARTHA. It's comforting for us, too, because if Mortimer has to see some of those plays he has to see—at least he's sitting next to a minister's daughter. *(MARTHA steps to back of table.)*

(ABBY crosses to back of table, starts putting tea things on tray. ELAINE and MARTHA help.)

ABBY. My goodness, Elaine, what must you think of us—not having tea cleared away by this time. *(She picks up tray and exits to kitchen.)*

(MARTHA blows out one candle and takes it to sideboard. ELAINE blows out other, takes to sideboard.)

MARTHA *(as ABBY exits)*. Now don't bother with anything in the kitchen until Mortimer comes, and then I'll help you. *(To ELAINE.)* Mortimer will be here any minute now.

ELAINE. Yes. Father must have been surprised not to find me at home. I'd better run over and say good night to him. *(She crosses to R. door.)*

MARTHA. It's a shame you missed him, dear.

ELAINE *(opening door)*. If Mortimer comes you tell him I'll be right back. *(She has opened door, but sees MORTIMER just outside.)* Hello, Mort!

(MORTIMER BREWSTER walks in. He is a dramatic critic.)

MORTIMER. Hello, Elaine. *(As he passes her going toward MARTHA, thus placing himself between ELAINE and MARTHA, he reaches back and pats ELAINE on the fanny . . . then embraces MARTHA.)* Hello, Aunt Martha.

(MARTHA exits to kitchen, calling as she goes.)

MARTHA. Abby, Mortimer's here!

(ELAINE slowly closes door.)

MORTIMER (*turning* R.). Were you going somewhere?

ELAINE. I was just going over to tell Father not to wait up for me.

MORTIMER. I didn't know that was still being done, even in Brooklyn. (*He throws his hat on sofa.*)

(ABBY *enters from kitchen.* MARTHA *follows, stays in doorway* R.)

ABBY (*crosses to* MORTIMER *at* C.) Hello, Mortimer.

MORTIMER (*embraces and kisses her*). Hello, Aunt Abby.

ABBY. How are you, dear?

MORTIMER. All right. And you look well. You haven't changed much since yesterday.

ABBY. Oh, my goodness, it was yesterday, wasn't it? We're seeing a great deal of you lately. (*She crosses and starts to sit in chair above table.*) Well, come, sit down. Sit down.

(MARTHA *stops her from sitting.*)

MARTHA. Abby—haven't we something to do in the kitchen?

ABBY. Huh?

MARTHA. You know—the tea things.

ABBY (*suddenly seeing* MORTIMER *and* ELAINE, *and catching on*). Oh, yes! Yes! The tea things— (*She backs toward kitchen.*) Well—you two just make yourselves at home. Just—

MARTHA. —make yourselves at home.

(*They exit kitchen door,* ABBY *closing door.*)

ELAINE (*stepping to* MORTIMER, *ready to be kissed*). Well, can't you take a hint?

MORTIMER (*complaining*). No . . . that was pretty obvious. A lack of inventiveness, I should say.

ELAINE (*only slightly annoyed as she crosses to table, and puts handbag on it*). Yes—that's exactly what you'd say.

MORTIMER (*he is at desk, fishing various pieces of notepaper from his pockets, and separating dollar bills that are mixed in with papers*). Where do you want to go for dinner?

ELAINE (*opening bag, looking in hand mirror*). I don't care. I'm not very hungry.

MORTIMER. Well, I just had breakfast. Suppose we wait until after the show?

ELAINE. But that'll make it pretty late, won't it?

MORTIMER. Not with the little stinker we're seeing tonight. From what I've heard about it we'll be at Blake's by ten o'clock.

ELAINE (*crosses to* U. S. C.). You ought to be fair to these plays.

MORTIMER. Are these plays fair to me?

ELAINE. *I've* never seen you walk out on a musical.

MORTIMER. That musical isn't opening tonight.

ELAINE (*disappointed*). No?

MORTIMER. Darling, you'll have to learn the rules. With a musical there are always four changes of title and three postponements. They liked it in New Haven but it needs a lot of work.

ELAINE. Oh, I was hoping it was a musical.

MORTIMER. You have such a light mind.

ELAINE. Not a bit. Musicals somehow have a humanizing effect on you. (*He gives her a look.*) After a serious play we join the proletariat in the subway and I listen to a lecture on the drama. After a musical you bring me home in a taxi, (*Turning away.*) and you make a few passes.

MORTIMER (*crossing* D. C.). Now wait a minute, darling, that's a very inaccurate piece of reporting.

ELAINE (*leaning against* D. S. *end of table*). Oh, I will admit that after the Behrman play you told me I had authentic beauty— and that's a hell of a thing to say to a girl. It wasn't until after our first musical you told me I had nice legs. And I have too.

(MORTIMER *stares at her legs a moment, then walks over and kisses her.*)

MORTIMER. For a minister's daughter you know a lot about life. Where'd you learn it?

ELAINE (*casually*). In the choir loft.

MORTIMER. I'll explain that to you some time, darling—the close connection between eroticism and religion.

ELAINE. Religion never gets as high as the choir loft. (*Crosses below table, gathers up bag.*) Which reminds me, I'd better tell Father please not to wait up for me tonight.

MORTIMER (*almost to himself*). I've never been able to rationalize it.

ELAINE. What?

MORTIMER. My falling in love with a girl who lives in Brooklyn.

ELAINE. Falling in love? You're not stooping to the articulate, are you?

MORTIMER (*ignoring this*). The only way I can regain my self-respect is to keep you in New York.

ELAINE (*few steps toward him.*) Did you say keep?

MORTIMER. No, no. I've come to the conclusion that you're holding out for the legalities.

ELAINE (*crossing to him as he backs away*). I can afford to be a good girl for quite a few years yet.

MORTIMER (*stops and embraces her*). And I can't wait that long. Where could we be married in a hurry—say tonight?

ELAINE. I'm afraid Father will insist on officiating.

MORTIMER (*turning away R. from her*). Oh, God; I'll bet your father could make even the marriage service sound pedestrian.

ELAINE. Are you by any chance writing a review of it?

MORTIMER. Forgive me, darling. It's an occupational disease. (*She smiles at him lovingly and walks toward him. He meets her halfway and they forget themselves for a moment in a sentimental embrace and kiss. When they come out of it, he turns away from her quickly . . . breaking U. S. near desk.*) I may give that play tonight a good notice.

ELAINE. Now, darling, don't pretend you love me that much.

MORTIMER (*looks at her with polite lechery, then starts toward her*). Be sure to tell your father not to wait up tonight.

ELAINE (*aware that she can't trust either of them, and backing U. S.*). I think tonight I'd better tell him to wait up.

MORTIMER (*following her*). I'll telephone Winchell to publish the banns.

ELAINE (*backing D. S.*) Nevertheless—

MORTIMER. All right, everything formal and legal. But not later than next month.

ELAINE (*runs into his arms*). Darling! I'll talk it over with Father and set the date.

MORTIMER. No—we'll have to see what's in rehearsal. There'll be a lot of other first nights in October.

(TEDDY *enters from balcony and comes downstairs dressed in tropical clothes and a solar topee. At foot of stairs he sees MORTIMER, crosses to him and shakes hands.*)

TEDDY. Hello, Mortimer!

MORTIMER (*gravely*). How are you, Mr. President?

TEDDY. Bully, thank you. Just bully! What news have you brought me?

MORTIMER. Just this, Mr. President—the country is squarely behind you.

TEDDY (*beaming*). Yes, I know. Isn't it wonderful? (*He shakes MORTIMER's hand again.*) Well, good-bye. (*He crosses to ELAINE and shakes hands with her.*) Good-bye. (*He goes to cellar door.*)

ELAINE. Where are you off to, Teddy?

TEDDY. Panama. (*He exits through cellar door, shutting it. ELAINE looks at MORTIMER inquiringly.*)

MORTIMER. Panama's the cellar. He digs locks for the canal down there.

(ELAINE *takes his arm and they stroll D. L. to R. of table.*)

ELAINE You're so sweet with him—and he's very fond of you.

MORTIMER. Well, Teddy was always my favorite brother.

ELAINE (*stopping and turning to him*). Favorite? Were there more of you?

MORTIMER. There's another brother—Jonathan.

ELAINE. I never heard of him. Your aunts never mention him.

MORTIMER. No, we don't like to talk about Jonathan. He left Brooklyn very early—

by request. Jonathan was the kind of boy who liked to cut worms in two—with his teeth.

ELAINE. What became of him?

MORTIMER. I don't know. He wanted to become a surgeon like Grandfather but he wouldn't go to medical school first and his practice got him into trouble.

(ABBY *enters from kitchen, crossing* D. L. *of table.*)

ABBY. Aren't you two going to be late for the theatre?

(MORTIMER'S L. *arm around* ELAINE'S *neck, he looks at his wristwatch.*)

MORTIMER. We're skipping dinner. We won't have to start for half an hour.

ABBY (*backing* U. L.). Well, then I'll leave you two alone together again.

ELAINE. Don't bother, darling. (*Breaking* R. *in front of* MORTIMER.) I'm going to run over to speak to Father. (*To* MORTIMER.) Before I go out with you he likes to pray over me a little. (*She runs to* R. *door and opens it, keeping her* L. *hand on outside doorknob.*) I'll be right back—I'll cut through the cemetery.

MORTIMER (*crossing to her, puts his hand on hers*). If the prayer isn't too long, I'd have time to lead you beside distilled waters.

(ELAINE *laughs and exits.* MORTIMER *shuts door.*)

ABBY (*happily, as she crosses to* C.). Mortimer, that's the first time I've ever heard you quote the Bible. We knew Elaine would be a good influence for you.

MORTIMER (*laughs, crosses* L., *then turns to* ABBY). Oh, by the way—I'm going to marry her.

ABBY. What? Oh, darling! (*She runs and embraces him. Then she dashes toward kitchen door as* MORTIMER *crosses to window* L. *and looks out.*) Martha! Martha! (MARTHA *enters from kitchen.*) Come right in here. I've got the most wonderful news for you—Mortimer and Elaine are going to be married.

MARTHA. Married? Oh, Mortimer! (*She runs over to* R. *of* MORTIMER, *who is looking out window* L., *embraces and kisses him.* ABBY *comes down to his* L. *He has his arms around both of them.*)

ABBY. We hoped it would happen just like this.

MARTHA. Well, Elaine must be the happiest girl in the world.

MORTIMER (*pulls curtain back, looks out window*). Happy! Just look at her leaping over those gravestones. (*As he looks out window* MORTIMER'S *attention is suddenly drawn to something.*) Say! What's that?

MARTHA (*looking out on his* R. ABBY *is on his* L.). What's what, dear?

MORTIMER. See that statute there. That's a horundinida carnina.

MARTHA. Oh, no, dear—that's Emma B. Stout ascending to heaven.

MORTIMER. No, no,—standing on Mrs. Stout's left ear. That bird—that's a red-crested swallow. I've only seen one of those before in my life.

ABBY (*crosses around above table and pushes chair* R. *into table*). I don't know how you can be thinking about a bird now —what with Elaine and the engagement and everything.

MORTIMER. It's a vanishing species. (*He turns away from window.*) Thoreau was very fond of them. (*As he crosses to desk to look through various drawers and papers.*) By the way, I left a large envelope around here last week. It was one of the chapters of my book on Thoreau. Have you seen it?

MARTHA (*pushing armchair into table*). Well, if you left it here it must be here somewhere.

ABBY (*crossing to* D. L. *of* MORTIMER). When are you going to be married? What are your plans? There must be something more you can tell us about Elaine.

MORTIMER. Elaine? Oh, yes, Elaine thought it was brilliant. (*He crosses to sideboard, looks through cupboards and drawers.*)

MARTHA. What was, dear?

MORTIMER. My chapter on Thoreau. (*He finds a bundle of papers (script) in* R. *drawer and takes them to table and looks through them.*)

ABBY *(at c.).* Well, when Elaine comes back I think we ought to have a little celebration. We must drink to your happiness. Martha, isn't there some of that Lady Baltimore cake left?

(During last few speeches MARTHA *has picked up pail from sideboard and her cape, hat and gloves from table in* U. L. *corner.)*

MARTHA *(crossing* D. L.*).* Oh, yes!

ABBY. And I'll open a bottle of wine.

MARTHA *(as she exits to kitchen).* Oh, and to think it happened in this room!

MORTIMER *(has finished looking through papers, is gazing around room).* Now where could I have put that?

ABBY. Well, with your fiancée sitting beside you tonight, I do hope the play will be something you can enjoy for once. It may be something romantic. What's the name of it?

MORTIMER. "Murder Will Out."

ABBY. Oh dear! *(She disappears into kitchen as* MORTIMER *goes on talking.)*

MORTIMER. When the curtain goes up the first thing you'll see will be a dead body.

(He lifts window-seat and sees one. Not believing it, he drops window-seat again and starts downstage. He suddenly stops with a "take," then goes back, throws window-seat open and stares in. He goes slightly mad for a moment. He backs away, then hears ABBY *humming on her way into the room. He drops window-seat again and holds it down, staring around the room.* ABBY *enters carrying a silencer and table cloth which she puts on armchair, then picks up bundle of papers and returns them to drawer in sideboard.*

MORTIMER *(speaks in a somewhat strained voice).* Aunt Abby!

ABBY *(at sideboard).* Yes, dear?

MORTIMER. You were going to make plans for Teddy to go to that . . . sanitarium —Happy Dale—

ABBY *(bringing legal papers from sideboard to* MORTIMER*).* Yes, dear, it's all arranged. Dr. Harper was here today and brought the papers for Teddy to sign. Here they are.

(He takes them from her.)

MORTIMER. He's got to sign them right away.

ABBY *(arranging silencer on table.* MARTHA *enters from kitchen door with table silver and plates on a tray. She sets tray on sideboard. Goes to table* R.*).* That's what Dr. Harper thinks. Then there won't be any legal difficulties after we pass on.

MORTIMER. He's got to sign them this minute! He's down in the cellar—get him up here right away.

MARTHA *(unfolding tablecloth. She's above table on* R.*).* There's no such hurry as that.

ABBY. No. When Teddy starts working on the canal you can't get his mind on anything else.

MORTIMER. Teddy's got to go to Happy Dale now—tonight.

MARTHA. Oh, no, dear, that's not until after we're gone.

MORTIMER. Right away, I tell you!—right away!

ABBY *(turning to* MORTIMER*).* Why, Mortimer, how can you say such a thing? Why, as long as we live we'll never be separated from Teddy.

MORTIMER *(trying to be calm).* Listen, darlings, I'm frightfully sorry, but I've got some shocking news for you. *(The* AUNTS *stop work and look at him with some interest.)* Now we've all got to try and keep our heads. You know we've sort of humored Teddy because we thought he was harmless.

MARTHA. Why he *is* harmless!

MORTIMER. He *was* harmless. That's why he has to go to Happy Dale. Why he has to be confined.

ABBY *(stepping to* MORTIMER*).* Mortimer, why have you suddenly turned against Teddy?—your own brother?

MORTIMER. You've got to know sometime. It might as well be now, Teddy's—killed a man!

MARTHA. Nonsense, dear.

*(*MORTIMER *rises and points to window-seat.)*

MORTIMER. There's a body in the window-seat!

ABBY. Yes, dear, we know.

(MORTIMER *"takes" as* ABBY *and* MARTHA *busy themselves again at table.*)

MORTIMER. You *know?*

MARTHA. Of course, dear, but it has nothing to do with Teddy. (*Gets tray from sideboard—arranges silver and plates on table: three places,* U. L. *and* R.)

ABBY. Now, Mortimer, just forget about it —forget you ever saw the gentleman.

MORTIMER. *Forget?*

ABBY. We never dreamed you'd peek.

MORTIMER. But who is he?

ABBY. His name's Hoskins—Adam Hoskins. That's really all I know about him —except that he's a Methodist.

MORTIMER. That's all you know about him? Well, what's he doing here? What happened to him?

MARTHA. He died.

MORTIMER. Aunt Martha, men don't just get into window-seats and die.

ABBY (*silly boy*). No, he died first.

MORTIMER. Well, how?

ABBY. Oh, Mortimer, don't be so inquisitive. The gentleman died because he drank some wine with poison in it.

MORTIMER. How did the poison get in the wine?

MARTHA. Well, we put it in wine because it's less noticeable—when it's in tea it has a distinct odor.

MORTIMER. *You* put it in the wine?

ABBY. Yes. And I put Mr. Hoskins in the window-seat because Dr. Harper was coming.

MORTIMER. So you knew what you'd done! You didn't want Dr. Harper to see the body!

ABBY. Well, not at tea—that wouldn't have been very nice. Now, Mortimer, you know the whole thing, just forget about it. I do think Martha and I have the right to our own little secrets. (*She crosses to sideboard to get two goblets from* L. *cup-*board *as* MARTHA *comes to table from sideboard with salt dish and pepper shaker.*)

MARTHA. And don't you tell Elaine! (*She gets third goblet from sideboard, then turns to* ABBY *who takes tray from sideboard.*) Oh, Abby, while I was out I dropped in on Mrs. Schultz. She's much better but she would like us to take Junior to the movies again.

ABBY. Well, we must do that tomorrow or next day.

MARTHA. Yes, but this time we'll go where we want to go. (*She starts for kitchen door.* ABBY *follows.*) Junior's not going to drag me into another one of those scary pictures. (*They exit into kitchen as* MORTIMER *wheels around and looks after them.* ABBY *shuts door.*)

MORTIMER (*dazed, looks around the room. His eyes come to rest on phone on desk; he crosses to it and dials a number. Into phone.*) City desk! (*There is a pause.*) Hello, Al. Do you know who this is? (*Pause.*) That's right. Say, Al, when I left the office, I told you where I was going, remember?—Well, where did I say? (*Pause.*) Uh-huh. Well, it would take me about half an hour to get to Brooklyn. What time have you got? (*He looks at his watch.*) That's right. I must be here. (*He hangs up, sits for a moment, then suddenly leaps off stool toward kitchen.*) Aunt Abby! Aunt Martha! Come in here! (*He backs to* C. *stage as the two* AUNTS *bustle in.* MARTHA *has tray with plates, cups, saucers and soup cups.*) What are we going to do? What are we going to do?

MARTHA (R. *of table*). What are we going to do about what, dear?

MORTIMER (*pointing to window-seat*). There's a body in there.

ABBY (U. L. *of* MORTIMER). Yes—Mr. Hoskins.

MORTIMER. Well, good heavens, I can't turn you over to the police! But what am I going to do?

MARTHA. Well, for one thing, dear, stop being so excited.

ABBY. And for pity's sake stop worrying. We told you to forget the whole thing.

MORTIMER. Forget! My dear Aunt Abby, can't I make you realize that something has to be done?

ABBY (*a little sharply*). Now, Mortimer, you behave yourself. You're too old to be flying off the handle like this.

MORTIMER. But Mr. Hotchkiss—

(ABBY, *on her way to sideboard, stops and turns to* MORTIMER.)

ABBY. Hoskins, dear. (*She continues on her way to sideboard and gets napkins and rings from* L. *drawer.* MARTHA *puts her tray, with cups, plates, etc., on table.* MORTIMER *continues speaking through this.*)

MORTIMER. Well, whatever his name is, you can't leave him there.

MARTHA. We don't intend to, dear.

ABBY (*crossing to table* L. *with napkins and rings*). No, Teddy's down in the cellar now digging the lock.

MORTIMER. You mean you're going to bury Mr. Hotchkiss in the cellar?

MARTHA (*stepping to him*). Oh, yes, dear, —that's what we did with the others.

MORTIMER (*walking away to* R.). No! You can't bury Mr.— (*Double take. Turns back to them.*) —others?

ABBY. The other gentlemen.

MORTIMER. When you say others—do you mean—others? More than one others?

MARTHA. Oh, yes, dear. Let me see, this is eleven. (*To* ABBY U. L. *of table.*) Isn't it, Abby?

ABBY. No, dear, this makes twelve.

(MORTIMER *backs away from them, stunned, toward phone stool at desk.*)

MARTHA. Oh, I think you're wrong, Abby. This is only eleven.

ABBY. No, dear, because I remember when Mr. Hoskins first came in, it occurred to me that he would make just an even dozen.

MARTHA. Well, you really shouldn't count the first one.

ABBY. Oh, *I* was counting the first one. So that makes it twelve.

(*Phone rings.* MORTIMER, *in a daze, turns toward it and without picking up receiver, speaks.*)

MORTIMER. Hello! (*He comes to, picks up receiver.*) Hello. Oh, hello, Al. My, it's good to hear your voice.

(ABBY, *at table is still holding out for a "twelve" count.*)

ABBY. Well, anyway, they're all down in the cellar—

MORTIMER (*to* AUNTS). Ssshhh— (*Into phone, as* AUNTS *cross to sideboard and put candelabras from top to bottom shelf.*) Oh, no, Al, I'm sober as a lark. I just called you because I was feeling a little Pirandello—Piran—you wouldn't know, Al. Look, I'm glad you called. Get hold of George right away. He's got to review the play tonight. I can't make it. No, Al, you're wrong. I'll tell you all about it tomorrow. Well, George has got to cover the play tonight! This is my department and I'm running it! You get ahold of George! (*He hangs up and sits a moment trying to collect himself.*) Now let's see, where were we? (*He suddenly leaps from stool.*) TWELVE!

MARTHA. Yes, Abby thinks we ought to count the first one and that makes twelve. (*She goes back to sideboard.*)

(MORTIMER *takes chair* R. *of table and faces it toward* R. *stage, then takes* MARTHA *by the hand, leads her to chair and sets her in it.*)

MORTIMER. All right—now—who was the first one?

ABBY (*crossing from above table to* MORTIMER). Mr. Midgely. He was a Baptist.

MARTHA. Of course, I still think we can't claim full credit for him because he just died.

ABBY. Martha means without any help from us. You see, Mr. Midgely came here looking for a room—

MARTHA. It was right after you moved to New York.

ABBY. —And it didn't seem right for that lovely room to be going to waste when there were so many people who needed it—

MARTHA. —He was such a lonely old man. . . .

ABBY. All his kith and kin were dead and it left him so forlorn and unhappy—

MARTHA. —We felt so sorry for him.

ABBY. And then when his heart attack came—and he sat dead in that chair (*Pointing to armchair.*) looking so peaceful—remember, Martha—we made up our minds then and there that if we could help other lonely old men to that same peace —we would!

MORTIMER (*all ears*). He dropped dead right in that chair! How awful for you!

MARTHA. Oh, no, dear. Why, it was rather like old times. Your grandfather always used to have a cadaver or two around the house. You see, Teddy had been digging in Panama and he thought Mr. Midgely was a Yellow Fever victim.

ABBY. That meant he had to be buried immediately.

MARTHA. So we all took him down to Panama and put him in the lock. (*She rises, puts her arm around* ABBY.) Now that's why we told you not to worry about it because we know exactly what's to be done.

MORTIMER. And that's how all this started —that man walking in here and dropping dead.

ABBY. Of course, we realized we couldn't depend on that happening again. So—

MARTHA (*crosses to* MORTIMER). You remember those jars of poison that have been up on the shelves in Grandfather's laboratory all these years—?

ABBY. You know your Aunt Martha's knack for mixing things. You've eaten enough of her piccalilli.

MARTHA. Well, dear, for a gallon of elderberry wine I take one teaspoonful of arsenic, then add a half teaspoonful of strychnine and then just a pinch of cyanide.

MORTIMER (*appraisingly*). Should have quite a kick.

ABBY. Yes! As a matter of fact one of our gentlemen found time to say "How delicious!"

MARTHA (*stepping* U. S.). Well, I'll have to get things started in the kitchen.

ABBY (*to* MORTIMER). I wish you could stay for dinner.

MARTHA. I'm trying out a new recipe.

MORTIMER. I couldn't eat a thing.

(MARTHA *goes out to kitchen.*)

ABBY (*calling after* MARTHA). I'll come and help you, dear. (*She pushes chair* R. *into table.*) Well, I feel so much better now. Oh, you have to wait for Elaine, don't you? (*She smiles.*) How happy you must be. (*She goes to kitchen doorway.*) Well, dear, I'll leave you alone with your thoughts. (*She exits, shutting door.*)

(*The shutting of the door wakes* MORTIMER *from his trance. He crosses to window-seat, kneels down, raises cover, looks in. Not believing, he lowers cover, rubs his eyes, raises cover again. This time he really sees Mr. Hoskins. Closes window-seat hastily, rises, steps back. Runs over and closes drapes over window. Backs up to above table. Sees water glass on table, picks it up, raises it to lips, suddenly remembers that poisoned wine comes in glasses, puts it down quickly. Crosses to cellar door, opens it.* ELAINE *enters* R., *he closes cellar door with a bang. As* ELAINE *puts her bag on top of desk he looks at her, and it dawns on him that he knows her. He speaks with faint surprise.*)

MORTIMER. Oh, it's you. (*He drops* D. S. ELAINE *crosses to him, takes his hand.*)

ELAINE. Don't be cross, darling! Father could see that I was excited—so I told him about us and that made it hard for me to get away. But listen, darling—he's not going to wait up for me tonight.

MORTIMER (*looking at window-seat*). You run along home, Elaine, and I'll call you up tomorrow.

ELAINE. Tomorrow!

MORTIMER (*irritated*). You know I always call you up every day or two.

ELAINE. But we're going to the theatre tonight.

MORTIMER. No—no we're not!

ELAINE. Well, why not?

MORTIMER (*turning to her*). Elaine, something's come up.

ELAINE. What, darling? Mortimer—you've lost your job!

MORTIMER. No—no—I haven't lost my job. I'm just not covering that play tonight. *(Pushing her* R.) Now you run along home, Elaine.

ELAINE. But I've got to know what's happened. Certainly you can tell me.

MORTIMER. No, dear, I can't.

ELAINE. But if we're going to be married—

MORTIMER. Married?

ELAINE. Have you forgotten that not fifteen minutes ago you proposed to me?

MORTIMER *(vaguely)*. I did? Oh—yes! Well, as far as I know that's still on. *(Urging her* R. *again.)* Now you run along home, Elaine. I've got to do something.

ELAINE. Listen, you can't propose to me one minute and throw me out of the house the next.

MORTIMER *(pleading)*. I'm not throwing you out of the house, darling. Will you get out of here?

ELAINE. No. I won't get out of here. *(MORTIMER crosses toward kitchen. ELAINE crosses below to window-seat.)* Not until I've had some kind of explanation. *(ELAINE is about to sit on window-seat. MORTIMER grabs her by the hand. Phone rings.)*

MORTIMER. Elaine! *(He goes to phone, dragging* ELAINE *with him.)* Hello! Oh, hello, Al. Hold on a minute, will you?— All right, it's important! But it can wait a minute, can't it? Hold on! *(He puts receiver on desk. Takes* ELAINE's *bag from top of desk and hands it to her. Then takes her by hand and leads her to door* R. *and opens it.)* Look, Elaine, you're a sweet girl and I love you. But I have something on my mind now and I want you to go home and wait until I call you.

ELAINE *(in doorway)*. Don't try to be masterful.

MORTIMER *(annoyed to the point of being literate)*. When we're married and I have problems to face I hope you're less tedious and uninspired!

ELAINE. And when we're married *if* we're married—I hope I find you adequate! *(She exits.* MORTIMER *does take, then runs out on porch after her, calling—)*

MORTIMER. Elaine! Elaine! *(He runs back in, shutting door, crosses and kneels on window-seat to open window. Suddenly remembers contents of window-seat and leaps off it. Dashes into kitchen but remembers Al is on phone, re-enters immediately and crosses to phone.)* Hello, Al? Hello . . . hello. . . . *(He pushes hook down and starts to dial when doorbell rings. He thinks it's the phone.* ABBY *enters from kitchen.)* Hello. Hello, Al?

ABBY *(crossing to* R. *door and opening it)*. That's the doorbell, dear, not the telephone. *(MORTIMER pushes hook down . . . dials.* MR. GIBBS *steps in doorway* R.) How do you do? Come in.

GIBBS. I understand you have a room to rent.

(MARTHA enters from kitchen. Puts "Lazy Susan" on sideboard, then gets to R. *of table.)*

ABBY. Yes. Won't you step in?

GIBBS *(stepping into room)*. Are you the lady of the house?

ABBY. Yes, I'm Miss Brewster. And this is my sister, another Miss Brewster.

GIBBS. My name is Gibbs.

ABBY *(easing him to chair* R. *of table)*. Oh, won't you sit down? I'm sorry we were just setting the table for dinner.

MORTIMER *(into phone)*. Hello—let me talk to Al again. City desk. *(Loud.)* AL!! CITY DESK! WHAT? I'm sorry, wrong number. *(He hangs up and starts dialling again as* GIBBS *looks at him.* GIBBS *turns to* ABBY.)

GIBBS. May I see the room?

MARTHA *(*D. L. *of table)*. Why don't you sit down a minute and let's get acquainted.

GIBBS. That won't do much good if I don't like the room.

ABBY. Is Brooklyn your home?

GIBBS. Haven't got a home. Live in a hotel. Don't like it.

MORTIMER *(into phone)*. Hello. City desk.

MARTHA. Are your family Brooklyn people?

GIBBS. Haven't got any family.

ABBY (*another victim*). All alone in the world?

GIBBS. Yep.

ABBY. Well, Martha— (MARTHA *goes happily to sideboard, gets bottle of wine from* U. L. *cupboard, and a wine glass, and sets them on table,* U. S. *end.* ABBY *eases* GIBBS *into chair* R. *of table and continues speaking to him, then to above table.*) Well, you've come to just the right house. Do sit down.

MORTIMER (*into phone*). Hello, Al? Mort. We got cut off. Al, I can't cover the play tonight—that's all there is to it, I can't!

MARTHA (L. *of table*). What church do you go to? There's an Episcopal church practically next door. (*Her gesture toward window brings her to window-seat and she sits.*)

GIBBS. I'm Presbyterian. Used to be.

MORTIMER (*into phone*). What's George doing in Bermuda? (*Rises and gets loud.*) Certainly I told him he could go to Bermuda—it's my department, isn't it? Well, you've got to get somebody. Who else is there around the office? (*He sits on second chair.*)

GIBBS (*annoyed. Rises and crosses below table to* L. *of it*). Is there always this much noise?

MARTHA. Oh, he doesn't live with us.

(ABBY *sits above table.*)

MORTIMER (*into phone*). There must be somebody around the place. Look, Al, how about the office boy? You know the bright one—the one we don't like? Well, you look around the office, I'll hold on.

GIBBS. I'd really like to see the room.

ABBY (*after seating* GIBBS R. *of table she has sat in chair above table*). It's upstairs. Won't you try a glass of our wine before we start up?

GIBBS. Never touch it.

MARTHA. We make this ourselves. It's elderberry wine.

GIBBS (*to* MARTHA). Elderberry wine. Hmmph. Haven't tasted elderberry wine since I was a boy. Thank you. (*He pulls armchair around and sits as* ABBY *uncorks bottle and starts to pour wine.*)

MORTIMER (*into phone*). Well, there must be some printers around. Look, Al, the fellow who sets my copy. He ought to know about what I'd write. His name is Joe. He's the third machine from the left. But, Al, he might turn out to be another Burns Mantle!

GIBBS (*to* MARTHA). Do you have your own elderberry bushes?

MARTHA. No, but the cemetery is full of them.

MORTIMER (*rising*). No, I'm not drinking, but I'm going to start now.

GIBBS. Do you serve meals?

ABBY. We might, but first just see whether you like our wine.

(MORTIMER *hangs up, puts phone on top of desk and crosses* L. *He sees wine on table. Goes to sideboard, gets glass, brings it to table and pours drink.* GIBBS *has his glass in hand and is getting ready to drink.*)

MARTHA (*sees* MORTIMER *pouring wine*). Mortimer! Eh eh eh eh! (GIBBS *stops and looks at* MARTHA. MORTIMER *pays no attention.*) Eh eh eh eh!

(*As* MORTIMER *raises glass to lips with* L. *hand,* ABBY *reaches up and pulls his arm down.*)

ABBY. Mortimer. Not that. (MORTIMER, *still dumb, puts his glass down on table. Then he suddenly sees* GIBBS *who has just got glass to his lips and is about to drink. He points across table at* GIBBS *and gives a wild cry.* GIBBS *looks at him, putting his glass down.* MORTIMER, *still pointing at* GIBBS, *goes around above table toward him.* GIBBS, *seeing a madman, rises slowly and backs toward* C., *then turns and runs for exit* R., MORTIMER *following him.* GIBBS *opens* R. *door and* MORTIMER *pushes him out, closing door after him. Then he turns and leans on door in exhausted relief. Meantime,* MARTHA *has risen and crossed to below armchair, while* ABBY *has risen and crossed to* D. C. [*To cover* GIBBS' *cross and exit,* MORTIMER *has the following lines* . . . "Get out of here! Do you want to be poisoned? Do you want to be killed? Do you want to be murdered?"])

ABBY (*great disappointment*). Now you've spoiled everything. (*She goes to sofa and sits.*)

(MARTHA *sits in armchair.* MORTIMER *crosses to* C. *and looks from one to the other . . . then speaks to* ABBY.)

MORTIMER. You can't do things like that. I don't know how to explain this to you, but it's not only against the law. It's wrong! (*To* MARTHA.) It's not a nice thing to do. (MARTHA *turns away from him as* ABBY *has done in his lines to her.*) People wouldn't understand. (*Points to door after* GIBBS.) He wouldn't understand.

MARTHA. Abby, we shouldn't have told Mortimer!

MORTIMER. What I mean is—well, this has developed into a very bad habit.

ABBY (*rises*). Mortimer, we don't try to stop you from doing things you like to do. I don't see why you should interfere with us.

(*Phone rings.* MORTIMER *answers.* MARTHA *rises to below table.*)

MORTIMER. Hello? (*It's Al again.*) All right, I'll see the first act and I'll pan the hell out of it. But look, Al, you've got to do something for me. Get hold of O'Brien —our lawyer, the head of our legal department. Have him meet me at the theatre. Now, don't let me down. O.K. I'm starting now. (*He hangs up and turns to* AUNTS.) Look, I've got to go to the theatre. I can't get out of it. But before I go will you promise me something?

MARTHA (*crossing to* ABBY *at* C.). We'd have to know what it was first.

MORTIMER. I love you very much and I know you love me. You know I'd do anything in the world for you and I want you to do just this little thing for me.

ABBY. What do you want us to do?

MORTIMER. Don't *do* anything. I mean don't do *anything*. Don't let anyone in this house—and leave Mr. Hoskins right where he is.

MARTHA. Why?

MORTIMER. I want time to think—and I've got quite a little to think about. You know I wouldn't want anything to happen to you.

ABBY. Well, what on earth could happen to us?

MORTIMER (*beside himself*). Anyway— you'll do this for me, won't you?

MARTHA. Well—we were planning on holding services before dinner.

MORTIMER. Services!

MARTHA (*a little indignant*). Certainly. You don't think we'd bury Mr. Hoskins without a full Methodist service, do you? Why he was a Methodist.

MORTIMER. But can't that wait until I get back?

ABBY. Oh, then you could join us.

MORTIMER (*going crazy himself*). Yes! Yes!

ABBY. Oh, Mortimer, you'll enjoy the services—especially the hymns. (*To* MARTHA.) Remember how beautifully Mortimer used to sing in the choir before his voice changed?

MORTIMER. And remember, you're not going to let anyone in this house while I'm gone—it's a promise!

MARTHA. Well—

ABBY. Oh, Martha, we can do that now that Mortimer's cooperating with us. (*To* MORTIMER.) Well, all right, Mortimer.

(MORTIMER *heaves a sigh of relief. Crosses to sofa and gets his hat. Then on his way to opening* R. *door, he speaks.*)

MORTIMER. Have you got some paper? I'll get back just as soon as I can. (*Taking legal papers from coat pocket as he crosses.*) There's a man I've got to see.

(ABBY *has gone to desk for stationery. She hands it to* MORTIMER.)

ABBY. Here's some stationery. Will this do?

MORTIMER (*taking stationery*). That'll be fine. I can save time if I write my review on the way to the theatre. (*He exits* R.)

(*The* AUNTS *stare after him.* MARTHA *crosses and closes door.* ABBY *goes to sideboard and brings two candelabras to table. Then gets matches from sideboard—lights candles during lines.*)

MARTHA. Mortimer didn't seem quite himself today.

ABBY (*lighting candles*). Well, that's only natural—I think I know why.

MARTHA (*lighting floor lamp*). Why?

ABBY. He's just become engaged to be married. I suppose that always makes a man nervous.

MARTHA (*during this speech she goes to first landing and closes drapes over window, then comes downstairs and turns off remote switch*). Well, I'm so happy for Elaine—and their honeymoon ought to give Mortimer a real vacation. I don't think he got much rest this summer.

ABBY. Well, at least he didn't go kiting off to China or Spain.

MARTHA. I could never understand why he wanted to go to those places.

ABBY. Well, I think to Mortimer the theatre has always seemed pretty small potatoes. He needs something big to criticize—something like the human race. (*She sets one candelabra* D. L., *the other* U. R. *on table.*)

MARTHA (*at* C.). Oh, Abby, if Mortimer's coming back for the services for Mr. Hoskins, we'll need another hymnal. There's one in my room. (*She starts upstairs to first landing.*)

ABBY. You know, dear, it's really my turn to read the services, but since you weren't here when Mr. Hoskins came I want you to do it.

MARTHA (*pleased*). That's very nice of you, dear—but, are you sure you want me to?

ABBY. It's only fair.

MARTHA. Well, I think I'll wear my black bombazine and Mother's old brooch. (*She starts up again when doorbell rings.*)

ABBY (*crossing as far as desk*). I'll go, dear.

MARTHA (*hushed*). We promised Mortimer we wouldn't let anyone in.

ABBY (*trying to peer through curtained window in door*). Who do you suppose it is?

MARTHA. Wait a minute, I'll look. (*She turns to landing window and peeks out the curtains.*) It's two men—and I've never seen them before.

ABBY. Are you sure?

MARTHA. There's a car at the curb—they must have come in that.

ABBY. Let me look! (*She hurries up stairs. There is a knock on door.* ABBY *peeks out the curtains.*)

MARTHA. Do you recognize them?

ABBY. They're strangers to me.

MARTHA. We'll just have to pretend we're not at home. (*The two of them huddle back in corner of landing.*)

(*Another knock at the door* R., *the knob is turned, and door swings slowly open. A tall* MAN *walks to* C., *looking about the room. He walks in with assurance and ease as though the room were familiar to him—in every direction but that of the stairs. There is something sinister about the man—something that brings a slight chill in his presence. It is in his walk, his bearing, and his strange resemblance to Boris Karloff. From stair-landing* ABBY *and* MARTHA *watch him, almost afraid to speak. Having completed his survey of the room, the* MAN *turns and addresses someone outside the front door.*)

JONATHAN. Come in, Doctor. (DR. EINSTEIN *enters* R. *He is somewhat ratty in appearance. His face wears the benevolent smirk of a man who lives in a pleasant haze of alcohol. There is something about him that suggests the unfrocked priest. He stands just inside the door, timid but expectant.*) This is the home of my youth. As a boy I couldn't wait to escape from this place—now I'm glad to escape back into it.

EINSTEIN (*shutting door. His back to* AUNTS.) Yah, Chonny, it's a fine hideout.

JONATHAN. The family must still live here. There's something so unmistakably Brewster about the Brewsters. I hope there's a fatted calf awaiting the return of the prodigal.

EINSTEIN. Yah, I'm hungry. (*He suddenly sees the fatted calf in the form of the two glasses of wine on table.*) Look, Chonny, drinks! (*He runs over below to table.* JONATHAN *crosses to above side.*)

JONATHAN. As though we were expected. A good omen.

(*They raise glasses to their lips as* ABBY *steps down a couple of stairs and speaks.*)

ABBY. Who are you? What are you doing here?

(*They both put glasses down.* EINSTEIN *picks up his hat from armchair, ready to run for it.* JONATHAN *turns to* ABBY.)

JONATHAN. Why, Aunt Abby! Aunt Martha! It's Jonathan.

MARTHA *(frightened)*. You get out of here.

TONATHAN *(crossing to* AUNTS*)*. I'm Jonathan—your nephew, Jonathan.

ABBY. Oh, no, you're not. You're nothing like Jonathan, so don't pretend you are! You just get out of here!

JONATHAN *(crossing closer)*. But I am Jonathan. And this *(Indicating* EINSTEIN.*)* is Dr. Einstein.

ABBY. And he's not Dr. Einstein either.

JONATHAN. Not Dr. Albert Einstein—Dr. Herman Einstein.

ABBY *(down another step)*. Who are you? You're not our nephew, Jonathan.

JONATHAN *(peering at* ABBY'S *outstretched hand)*. I see you're still wearing the lovely garnet ring that Grandma Brewster bought in England. *(*ABBY *gasps, looks at ring.)* And you, Aunt Martha, still the high collar—to hide the scar where Grandfather's acid burned you.

*(*MARTHA'S *hand goes to her throat. The* AUNTS *look at* JONATHAN. MARTHA *comes down a few steps to behind* ABBY. EINSTEIN *gets to* C.*)*

MARTHA. His voice is like Jonathan's.

ABBY *(stepping down to stage floor)*. Have you been in an accident?

JONATHAN *(his hand goes to side of his face)*. No— *(He clouds.)* —my face—Dr. Einstein is responsible for that. He's a plastic surgeon. He changes people's faces.

MARTHA *(comes down to* ABBY*)*. But I've seen that face before. *(To* ABBY.*)* Abby, remember when we took the little Schultz boy to the movies and I was so frightened? It was that face!

*(*JONATHAN *grows tense and looks toward* EINSTEIN. EINSTEIN *crosses to* C. *and addresses* AUNTS.*)*

EINSTEIN. Easy, Chonny—easy! *(To* AUNTS.*)* Don't worry, ladies. The last five years I give Chonny three new faces. I give him another one right away. This last face—well, I saw that picture too—just before I operate. And I was intoxicated.

JONATHAN *(with a growing and dangerous intensity as he walks toward* EINSTEIN, *who backs* D. S.*)*. You see, Doctor—you see what you've done to me. Even my own family—

EINSTEIN *(to calm him, as he is forced around* R. *stage)*. Chonny—you're home —in this lovely house— *(To* AUNTS.*)* How often he tells me about Brooklyn—about this house—about his aunts that he lofes so much. *(To* JONATHAN.*)* They know you, Chonny. *(To* ABBY *as he leads her toward* JONATHAN.*)* You know it's Jonathan. Speak to him. Tell him so. *(He drifts above table to* D. L. *of it.)*

ABBY. Well—Jonathan—it's been a long time—what have you been doing all these years?

MARTHA *(has come to far* D. R.*)*. Yes, Jonathan, where have you been?

JONATHAN *(recovering his composure)*. Oh, England, South Africa, Australia,— the last five years Chicago. Dr. Einstein and I were in business there together

ABBY. Oh, we were in Chicago for the World's Fair.

MARTHA *(for want of something to say)*. Yes—we found Chicago awfully warm.

EINSTEIN *(he has wandered above* U. L. *and down to below table)*. Yah—it got hot for us too.

JONATHAN *(turning on the charm as he crosses above* ABBY, *placing himself between the* AUNTS.*)* Well, it's wonderful to be in Brooklyn again. And you—Abby—Martha you don't look a day older. Just as I remembered you—sweet—charming—hospitable. *(The* AUNTS *don't react too well to this charm.)* And dear Teddy— *(He indicates with his hand a lad of eight or ten.)* —did he get into politics? *(He turns to* EINSTEIN.*)* My little brother, Doctor, was determined to become President.

ABBY. Oh, Teddy's fine! Just fine! And Mortimer's well too.

JONATHAN *(a bit of a sneer)*. I know about Mortimer. I've seen his picture at the head of his column. He's evidently fulfilled all the promise of his early nasty nature.

ABBY *(defensively)*. We're very fond of Mortimer.

(There is a slight pause. Then MARTHA

speaks uneasily as she gestures toward R. *door.)*

MARTHA. Well, Jonathan, it's very nice to have seen you again.

JONATHAN (*expanding*). Bless you, Aunt Martha. (*Crosses and sits chair* R. *of table.*) It's good to be home again.

(*The* AUNTS *look at each other with dismay.*)

ABBY. Well, Martha, we mustn't let what's on the stove boil over. (*She starts to kitchen, then sees* MARTHA *isn't following. She crosses back and tugs at* MARTHA, *then crosses toward kitchen again.* MARTHA *follows to* C., *then speaks to* JONATHAN.)

MARTHA. Yes. If you'll excuse us for a minute, Jonathan. Unless you're in a hurry to go somewhere.

(JONATHAN *looks at her balefully.* MARTHA *crosses around above table, takes bottle of wine and puts it back in sideboard, then exits with* ABBY. ABBY, *who has been waiting in kitchen doorway for* MARTHA, *closes door after them.* EINSTEIN *crosses* U. L. *around to behind* JONATHAN.)

EINSTEIN. Well, Chonny, where do we go from here? We got to think fast. The police. The police have got pictures of that face. I got to operate on you right away. We got to find some place for that—and we got to find a place for Mr. Spenalzo too.

JONATHAN. Don't waste any worry on that rat.

EINSTEIN. But, Chonny, we got a hot stiff on our hands.

JONATHAN (*flinging hat onto sofa*). Forget Mr. Spenalzo.

EINSTEIN. But you can't leave a dead body in the rumble seat. You shouldn't have killed him, Chonny. He's a nice fellow— he gives us a lift—and what happens?

JONATHAN (*remembering bitterly*). He said I looked like Boris Karloff! (*He starts for* EINSTEIN.) That's your work, Doctor. You did that to me!

EINSTEIN (*he's backed away to* D. L. *of table*). Now, Chonny—we find a place somewhere—I fix you up quick!

JONATHAN. Tonight!

EINSTEIN. Chonny—I got to eat first. I'm hungry—I'm weak.

(*The* AUNTS *enter from kitchen.* ABBY *comes to* JONATHAN *at* C. MARTHA *remains in kitchen doorway.*)

ABBY. Jonathan—we're glad that you remembered us and took the trouble to come in and say "Hello." But you were never happy in this house and we were never happy while you were in it—so, we've just come in to say good-bye.

JONATHAN (*takes a menacing step toward* ABBY. *Then decides to try the "charm" again*). Aunt Abby, I can't say that your feelings toward me come as a surprise. I've spent a great many hours regretting the many heartaches I must have given you as a boy.

ABBY. You were quite a trial to us, Jonathan.

JONATHAN. But my great disappointment is for Dr. Einstein. (EINSTEIN *is a little surprised.*) I promised him that no matter how rushed we were in passing through Brooklyn, I'd take the time to bring him here for one of Aunt Martha's home-cooked dinners.

(MARTHA *rises to this a bit, stepping* D. S.)

MARTHA. Oh . . .

ABBY (*backing* U. L.). I'm sorry. I'm afraid there wouldn't be enough.

MARTHA. Abby, it's a pretty good-sized pot roast.

JONATHAN (*how wonderful*). Pot roast!

MARTHA. I think the least we can do is to—

JONATHAN. Thank you, Aunt Martha! We'll stay to dinner.

ABBY (*backing to kitchen door and not at all pleased*). Well, we'll hurry it along.

MARTHA. Yes! (*She exits into kitchen.*)

ABBY (*stopping in doorway*). Oh, Jonathan, if you want to freshen up—why don't you use the washroom in Grandfather's old laboratory?

JONATHAN (*crossing to her*). It that still there?

ABBY. Oh, yes. Just as he left it. Well, I'll help Martha get things started—since we're all in a hurry. (*She exits into kitchen.*)

EINSTEIN *(stepping* U. S.*).* Well, we get a meal anyway.

JONATHAN *(above table).* Grandfather's laboratory! *(Looks upstairs).* And just as it was. Doctor, a perfect operating room.

EINSTEIN. Too bad we can't use it.

JONATHAN. After you've finished with me —Why, we could make a fortune here. The laboratory—that large ward in the attic—ten beds, Doctor—and Brooklyn is crying for your talents.

EINSTEIN. Vy vork yourself up, Chonny? Anyway, for Brooklyn I think we're a year too late.

JONATHAN. You don't know this town, Doctor. Practically everybody in Brooklyn needs a new face.

EINSTEIN. But so many of the old faces are locked up.

JONATHAN. A very small percentage—and the boys in Brooklyn are famous for paying generously to stay out of jail.

EINSTEIN. Take it easy, Chonny. Your aunts—they don't want us here.

JONATHAN. We're here for dinner, aren't we?

EINSTEIN. Yah—but after dinner?

JONATHAN *(crossing up to sofa).* Leave it to me, Doctor. I'll handle it. Why, this house'll be our headquarters for years.

EINSTEIN *(a pretty picture).* Oh, that would be beautiful, Chonny! This nice quiet house. Those aunts of yours—what sweet ladies. I love them already. I get the bags, yah?

JONATHAN *(stopping him).* Doctor! We must wait until we're invited.

EINSTEIN. But you chust said that—

JONATHAN. We'll be invited.

EINSTEIN. And if they say no—?

JONATHAN. Doctor—two helpless old women—? *(He sits on sofa.)*

EINSTEIN *(takes bottle flask from hip pocket and unscrews cork as he crosses to window-seat).* It's like comes true a beautiful dream— Only I hope you're not dreaming. *(He stretches out on window-seat, taking a swig from bottle.)* It's so peaceful.

JONATHAN *(stretched out on sofa).* That's what makes this house so perfect for us— it's so peaceful.

*(*TEDDY *enters from cellar, blows a terrific blast on his bugle, as* JONATHAN *backs* R. TEDDY *marches to stairs and on up to first landing, as the two* MEN *look at his tropical garb with some astonishment.)*

TEDDY. CHARGE! *(He rushes up the stairs and off.)*

*(*JONATHAN *watches him from foot of stairs.* EINSTEIN, *sitting on window-seat, takes a hasty swig from his flask as the curtain comes down on the word* CHARGE!*)*

ACT TWO

SCENE: *The same. Later that night.*

JONATHAN, *with an after-dinner cigar, is occupying armchair* L. *of table, completely at his ease.* ABBY *and* MARTHA, *seated on window-seat, are giving him a nervous attention in the attitude of people who wish their guests would go home.* EINSTEIN *is relaxed and happy in chair* R. *of table. Dinner dishes have been cleared. There is a red cloth on table, with a saucer to serve as ash-tray for* JONATHAN. *The room is in order. All doors are closed, as are drapes over windows.*

JONATHAN. Yes, Aunties, those five years in Chicago were amongst the busiest and happiest of my life.

EINSTEIN. And from Chicago we go to South Bend, Indiana. *(He shakes his head as though he wishes they hadn't.)*

*(*JONATHAN *gives him a look.)*

JONATHAN. They wouldn't be interested in our experience in Indiana.

ABBY. Well, Jonathan, you've led a very interesting life, I'm sure—but we really shouldn't have allowed you to talk so late.

(She starts to rise. JONATHAN *seats her just by the tone of his voice.)*

JONATHAN. My meeting Dr. Einstein in London, I might say, changed the whole course of my life. You remember I had been in South Africa, in the diamond business—then Amsterdam, the diamond market. I wanted to go back to South Africa —and Dr. Einstein made it possible for me.

EINSTEIN. A good job, Chonny. *(To* AUNTS.*)* When we take off the bandages —his face look so different, the nurse had to introduce me.

JONATHAN. I loved that face. I still carry the picture with me. *(He produces snapshot-size picture from inside coat pocket, looks at it a moment, then hands it to* MARTHA. *She looks at it and hands it to* ABBY.*)*

ABBY. This looks more the way you used to look, but still I wouldn't know you.

JONATHAN. I think we'll go back to that face, Doctor.

EINSTEIN. Yah, it's safe now.

ABBY *(rising).* Well, I know you both want to get to—where you're going.

JONATHAN *(relaxing even more.)* My dear aunts—I'm so full of that delicious dinner I'm unable to move a muscle.

EINSTEIN *(relaxing too).* Yah, it's nice here.

MARTHA *(rises).* After all—it's very late and—

*(*TEDDY *enters on balcony wearing his solar topee, carrying a book, open, and another topee.)*

TEDDY *(descending stairs).* I found it! I found it!

JONATHAN. What did you find, Teddy?

TEDDY. The story of my life—my biography. *(He crosses above to* L. *of* EINSTEIN.*)* Here's the picture I was telling you about, General. *(He lays open book on table showing picture to* EINSTEIN.*)* Here we are, both of us. "President Roosevelt and General Goethals at Culebra Cut." That's me, General, and that's you.

*(*EINSTEIN *looks at picture.)*

EINSTEIN. My, how I've changed.

*(*TEDDY *looks at* EINSTEIN, *a little puzzled but makes adjustment.)*

TEDDY. Well, you see that picture hasn't been taken yet. We haven't even started work on Culebra Cut. We're still digging locks. And now, General, we will both go to Panama and inspect the new lock.

ABBY. No, Teddy—not to Panama.

EINSTEIN. We go some other time. Panama's a long way off.

TEDDY. Nonsense, it's just down in the cellar.

JONATHAN. The cellar?

MARTHA. We let him dig the Panama Canal in the cellar.

TEDDY *(severely).* General Goethals, as President of the United States, Commander-in-Chief of the Army and Navy and the man who gave you this job, I demand that you accompany me on the inspection of this new lock.

JONATHAN. Teddy! I think it's time you went to bed.

TEDDY. I beg your pardon! *(He crosses above to* L. *of* JONATHAN, *putting on his pinc-nez as he crosses.)* Who are you?

JONATHAN. I'm Woodrow Wilson. Go to bed.

TEDDY. No—you're not Wilson. But your face is familiar. Let me see— You're not anyone I know now. Perhaps later— On my hunting trip to Africa—yes, you look like someone I might meet in the jungle.

*(*JONATHAN *stiffens.* ABBY *crosses in front of* TEDDY, *getting between him and* JONATHAN.*)*

ABBY. It's your brother, Jonathan, dear.

MARTHA *(rising).* He's had his face changed.

TEDDY. So that's it—a nature faker!

ABBY. And perhaps you had better go to bed, Teddy—Jonathan and his friend have to go back to their hotel.

JONATHAN *(rising).* General Goethals, *(To* EINSTEIN.*)* inspect the canal. *(He crosses to* U. C.*)*

EINSTEIN *(rising)*. All right, Mr. President. We go to Panama.

TEDDY. Bully! Bully! *(He crosses to cellar door, opens it.)* Follow me, General. (EINSTEIN *goes up to* L. *of* TEDDY. TEDDY *taps solar topee in* EINSTEIN's *hand, then taps his own head.)* It's down south you know. *(He exits downstairs.)*

(EINSTEIN *puts on topee, which is too large for him. Then turns in cellar doorway and speaks.)*

EINSTEIN. Well—bon voyage. *(He exits, closing door.)*

JONATHAN. Aunt Abby, I must correct your misapprehension. You spoke of our hotel. We have no hotel. We came directly here—

MARTHA. Well, there's a very nice little hotel just three blocks down the—

JONATHAN *(cutting her off)*. Aunt Martha, this is my home.

ABBY. But, Jonathan, you can't stay here. We need our rooms.

JONATHAN. You need them?

ABBY. Yes, for our lodgers.

JONATHAN *(alarmed)*. Are there lodgers in this house?

MARTHA. Well, not just now, but we plan to have some.

JONATHAN *(cutting her off again)*. Then my old room is still free.

ABBY. But, Jonathan, there's no place for Dr. Einstein.

JONATHAN *(crosses below table, drops cigar ashes into saucer)*. He'll share the room with me.

ABBY. No, Jonathan, I'm afraid you can't stay here.

(JONATHAN *is below table. He grinds cigar out in saucer, then starts toward* AUNTS. *They back around above table to* C., MARTHA *first.* JONATHAN *turns back and crosses below table to* ABBY *at* C.)

JONATHAN. Dr. Einstein and I need a place to sleep. You remembered, this afternoon, that as a boy I could be disagreeable. It wouldn't be very pleasant for any of us if—

MARTHA *(R. C., and frightened)*. Perhaps we'd better let them stay here tonight—

ABBY. Well, just overnight, Jonathan.

JONATHAN. That's settled. Now, if you'll get my room ready—

MARTHA *(starting upstairs,* ABBY *following)*. It only needs airing out.

ABBY. We keep it ready to show our lodgers. I think you and Dr. Einstein will find it comfortable.

(JONATHAN *follows them to first landing and leans on newel-post.* AUNTS *are on balcony.)*

JONATHAN. You have a most distinguished guest in Dr. Einstein. I'm afraid you don't appreciate his skill. But you will. In a few weeks you'll see me looking like a very different Jonathan.

MARTHA. He can't operate on you here.

JONATHAN *(ignoring)*. When Dr. Einstein and I get organized—when we resume practice— Oh, I forgot to tell you. We're turning Grandfather's laboratory into an operating room. We expect to be quite busy.

ABBY. Jonathan, we will not let you turn this house into a hospital.

JONATHAN *(laughing)*. A hospital—heavens no! It will be a beauty parlor.

(EINSTEIN *enters excitedly from cellar.)*

EINSTEIN. Hey, Chonny, down in the cellar— *(He sees* AUNTS *and stops.)*

JONATHAN. Dr. Einstein—my dear aunts have invited us to live with them.

EINSTEIN. Oh, you fixed it?

ABBY. Well, you're sleeping here tonight.

JONATHAN. Please get our room ready immediately.

MARTHA. Well—

ABBY. For tonight.

(They exit through arch. JONATHAN *comes to foot of stairs.)*

EINSTEIN. Chonny, when I go down in the cellar, what do you think I find?

JONATHAN. What?

EINSTEIN. The Panama Canal.

JONATHAN (disgusted, crossing to C.). The Panama Canal.

EINSTEIN. It just fits Mr. Spenalzo. It's a hole Teddy dug. Six feet long and four feet wide.

JONATHAN (gets the idea. Opens cellar door and looks down). Down there!

EINSTEIN. You'd think they knew we were bringing Mr. Spenalzo along. That's hospitality.

JONATHAN (closing cellar door). Rather a good joke on my aunts—their living in a house with a body buried in the cellar.

EINSTEIN. How do we get him in?

JONATHAN (drops D. S.). Yes. We can't just walk him through the door. (He sees window in L. wall.) We'll drive the car up between the house and the cemetery— then when they've gone to bed, we'll bring Mr. Spenalzo in through the window.

EINSTEIN (taking out bottle flask). Bed! Just think, we've got a bed tonight! (He starts swigging.)

JONATHAN (grabbing his arm). Easy, Doctor. Remember you're operating tomorrow. And this time you'd better be sober.

EINSTEIN. I fix you up beautiful.

JONATHAN. And if you don't— (Gives EINSTEIN shove to door.)

ABBY (she and MARTHA enter on balcony). Jonathan! Your room is ready.

JONATHAN. Then you can go to bed. We're moving the car up behind the house.

MARTHA. It's all right where it is—until morning.

JONATHAN (EINSTEIN has opened door). I don't want to leave it in the street— that might be against the law. (He exits.)

(EINSTEIN follows him out, closing door. ABBY and MARTHA start downstairs and reach below table.)

MARTHA. Abby, what are we going to do?

ABBY. Well, we're not going to let them stay more than one night in this house for one thing. What would the neighbors think? People coming in here with one face and going out with another.

(She has reached table D. S. MARTHA is at her R.)

MARTHA. What are we going to do about Mr. Hoskins?

ABBY (crosses to window-seat. MARTHA follows). Oh, Mr. Hoskins. It can't be very comfortable for him in there. And he's been so patient, the poor dear. Well, I think Teddy had better get Mr. Hoskins downstairs right away.

MARTHA (adamant). Abby—I will not invite Jonathan to the funeral services.

ABBY. Oh, no. We'll wait until they've gone to bed and then come down and hold the services.

(TEDDY enters from cellar, gets book from table and starts R. ABBY stops him at C.)

TEDDY. General Goethals was very pleased. He says the Canal is just the right size.

ABBY (crosses to C.) Teddy! Teddy, there's been another Yellow Fever victim.

TEDDY (takes off pince-nez). Dear me—this will be a shock to the General.

MARTHA (stepping R.). Then we mustn't tell him about it.

TEDDY (crosses below ABBY to MARTHA). But it's his department.

ABBY. No, we mustn't tell him, Teddy. It would just spoil his visit.

TEDDY. I'm sorry, Aunt Abby. It's out of my hands—he'll have to be told. Army regulations, you know.

ABBY. No, Teddy, we must keep it a secret.

MARTHA. Yes!

TEDDY (he loves them). A state secret?

ABBY. Yes, a state secret.

MARTHA. Promise?

TEDDY (what a silly request). You have the word of the President of the United States. Cross my heart and hope to die. (He spits.) Now let's see— (Puts pince-nez on, then puts arms around both AUNTS.) how are we going to keep it a secret?

ABBY. Well, Teddy, you go back down in the cellar and when I turn out the lights —when it's all dark—you come up and take the poor man down to the Canal. (Urging him to cellar door, which he opens.) Now go along, Teddy.

MARTHA (*following* U. S.). And we'll come down later and hold services.

TEDDY (*in doorway*). You may announce the President will say a few words. (*He starts, then turns back.*) Where is the poor devil?

MARTHA. He's in the window-seat.

TEDDY. It seems to be spreading. We've never had Yellow Fever there before. (*He exits, closing door.*)

ABBY. Martha, when Jonathan and Dr. Einstein come back, let's see if we can get them to go to bed right away.

MARTHA. Yes. Then by the time they're asleep, we'll be dressed for the funeral. (*Sudden thought.*) Abby, I've never even seen Mr. Hoskins.

ABBY. Oh, my goodness, that's right—you were out. Well, you just come right over and see him now. (*They go to window-seat,* ABBY *first.*) He's really very nice look-ing—considering he's a Methodist. (*As they go to lift window-seat,* JONATHAN *throws window open from outside with a bang.* AUNTS *scream and draw back.* JONATHAN *puts his head in through drapes.*)

JONATHAN. We're bringing—the luggage through here.

ABBY (*now at* C.). Jonathan, your room's waiting for you. You can go right up.

(*Two dusty bags and a large instrument case are passed through window by* EIN-STEIN. JONATHAN *puts them on floor.*)

JONATHAN. I'm afraid we don't keep Brook-lyn hours—but you two run along to bed.

ABBY. Now, you must be very tired, both of you—and we don't go to bed this early.

JONATHAN. Well, you should. It's time I came home to take care of you.

MARTHA. We weren't planning to go un-til—

JONATHAN (*the master*). Aunt Martha, did you hear me say go to bed! (AUNT MARTHA *starts upstairs as* EINSTEIN *comes in through window and picks up two bags.* JONATHAN *takes instrument case and puts it* U. S. *of window-seat.*) The instruments can go to the laboratory in the morning.

(EINSTEIN *starts upstairs.* JONATHAN *closes window.* MARTHA *is partway upstairs as* EINSTEIN *passes her.* ABBY *is at* R. C.) Now, then, we're all going to bed. (*He crosses to* C. *as* ABBY *breaks* D. R. *to light-switch.*)

ABBY. I'll wait till you're up, then turn out the lights.

(JONATHAN, *going upstairs, sees* EINSTEIN *pausing at balcony door.* MARTHA *is almost up to balcony.*)

JONATHAN. Another flight, Doctor. (*To* MARTHA.) Run along, Aunt Martha. (MARTHA *hurries into doorway.* EINSTEIN *goes through arch to third floor.* JON-ATHAN *continues on to* L. *end of balcony.* ABBY *is at light-switch.*) All right, Aunt Abby.

ABBY (*stalling. Looks toward cellar door*). I'll be right up.

JONATHAN. Now, Aunt Abby. (*Definite.*) Turn out the lights!

(ABBY *turns switch, plunging stage into darkness except for spot shining down stairway from arch.* ABBY *goes up stairs to her door where* MARTHA *is waiting. She takes a last frightened look at* JONATHAN *and exits.* MARTHA *closes door.* JONATHAN *goes off through arch, closing that door, blotting out the spot. A street light shines through main door* R. *on stage floor.* TEDDY *opens cellar door, then turns on cellar light, outlining him in the doorway. He crosses to window-seat and opens it—the window-seat cover giving out its usual rusty squeak. He reaches in and pulls Mr. Hoskins over his shoulder and, leaving window-seat open, crosses to cellar door and goes down into cellar with Mr. Hoskins. Closes door.* JONATHAN *and* EINSTEIN *come through arch. It is dark. They light matches and listen at the* AUNTS' *door for a moment.* EINSTEIN *speaks.*)

EINSTEIN. All right, Chonny.

(*The matches go out.* JONATHAN *lights another and they come down to foot of stairs.*)

JONATHAN. I'll get the window open. You go around and hand him through.

EINSTEIN. No, he's too heavy for me. You go outside and push—I stay here and pull. Then together we get him down to Pan-ama.

JONATHAN. All right. (*He blows out match, crosses and opens door.* EINSTEIN *to his* L.) I'll take a look around outside the house. When I tap on the glass, you open the window.

EINSTEIN. All right. (JONATHAN *exits, closing door.* EINSTEIN *lights match and crosses* L. *He bumps into table and match goes out. He feels his way* L. *from there. We hear ejaculations and noise.* EINSTEIN *has fallen into window-seat. In window-seat he lights another match and slowly rises up to a sitting position and looks around. He blows out match and hauls himself out of window-seat, speaking.*) Who left dis open? Dummkopf! (*We hear the creak of the cover as he closes it. In the darkness we hear a tap on* L. *window.* EINSTEIN *opens it. Then in a hushed voice.*) Chonny? O.K. Allez Oop. Wait—wait a minute. You lost a leg somewhere.—Ach —now I got him. Come on—ugh— (*He falls on floor and there is a crash of a body and the sound of a "Sshhhh" from outside.*) That was me, Chonny. I schlipped.

JONATHAN (*voice*). Be more careful.

(*Pause.*)

EINSTEIN. Well, his shoe came off. (*Pause.*) All right, Chonny. I got him! (*There is a knock at* R. *door.*) Chonny! Somebody at the door! Go quick. NO. I manage here —go quick!

(*A second knock at door. A moment's silence and we hear the creak of window-seat as* EINSTEIN *puts Mr. Spenalzo in Mr. Hoskins' place. A third knock, as* EINSTEIN *struggles with body. A fourth knock and then the creak of the window-seat as* EINSTEIN *closes it. He scurries around to beside desk, keeping low to avoid being seen through door.* ELAINE *enters* R., *calling softly.*)

ELAINE. Miss Abby! Miss Martha! (*In the dim path of light she comes toward* C., *calling toward balcony.*) Miss Abby! Miss Martha! (*Suddenly* JONATHAN *steps through door and closes it. The noise swings* ELAINE *around and she gasps.*) Uhhh! Who is it? Is that you, Teddy? (JONATHAN *comes toward her as she backs into chair* R. *of table.*) Who *are* you?

JONATHAN. Who are *you?*

ELAINE. I'm Elaine Harper—I live next door!

JONATHAN. Then what are you doing here?

ELAINE. I came over to see Miss Abby and Miss Martha.

JONATHAN (*to* EINSTEIN, *without turning.* EINSTEIN *has crept to light-switch after* JONATHAN's *cross*). Turn on the lights, Doctor. (*The lights go on.* ELAINE *gasps as she sees* JONATHAN *and sits in chair.* JONATHAN *looks at her for a moment.*) You chose rather an untimely moment for a social call. (*He crosses toward window-seat, looking for Spenalzo, but doesn't see him. He looks up, behind table. Looks out window, then comes back into the room.*)

ELAINE (*trying to summon courage*). I think you'd better explain what you're doing here.

JONATHAN (D. L. *of table*). We happen to live here.

ELAINE. You *don't* live here. I'm in this house every day and I've never seen you before. (*Frightened.*) Where are Miss Abby and Miss Martha? What have you done to them?

JONATHAN (*a step to below table*). Perhaps we'd better introduce ourselves. This— (*Indicating.*) —is Dr. Einstein.

ELAINE (*looks at* EINSTEIN). Dr. Einstein? (*She turns back to* JONATHAN. EINSTEIN, *behind her back, is gesturing to* JONATHAN *the whereabouts of Spenalzo.*)

JONATHAN. A surgeon of great distinction— (*He looks under table for Spenalzo, and not finding him—*) —and something of a magician.

ELAINE. And I suppose you're going to tell me you're Boris Kar—

JONATHAN. I'm Jonathan Brewster.

ELAINE (*drawing back almost with fright*). Oh—you're Jonathan!

JONATHAN. I see you've heard of me.

(EINSTEIN *drifts to front of sofa.*)

ELAINE. Yes—just this afternoon for the first time.

JONATHAN (*stepping toward her*). And what did they say about me?

ELAINE. Only that there was another brother named Jonathan—that's all that was said. (*Calming.*) Well, that explains everything. Now that I know who you are— (*Running to* R. *door.*) I'll be running along back home. (*The door is locked. She turns to* JONATHAN.) If you'll kindly unlock the door.

(JONATHAN *crosses to her, then, before reaching her, he turns* D. S. *to* R. *door and unlocks it.* EINSTEIN *drifts down to chair* R. *of table. As* JONATHAN *opens door partway,* ELAINE *starts toward it. He turns and stops her with a gesture.*)

JONATHAN. "That explains everything"? Just what did you mean by that? Why did you come here at this time of night?

ELAINE. I thought I saw someone prowling around the house. I suppose it was you.

(JONATHAN *closes door and locks it, leaving key in lock.*)

JONATHAN. You thought you saw someone prowling around the house?

ELAINE. Yes—weren't you outside? Isn't that your car?

JONATHAN. You saw someone at the car?

ELAINE. Yes.

JONATHAN (*coming toward her as she backs* U. L.). What else did you see?

ELAINE. Just someone walking around the house to the car.

JONATHAN. What else did you see?

ELAINE. Just that—that's all. That's why I came over here. I wanted to tell Miss Abby to call the police. But if it was you, and that's your car, I don't need to bother Miss Abby. I'll be running along. (*She takes a step toward door above* JONATHAN. *He steps in her path.*)

JONATHAN. What was the man doing at the car?

ELAINE (*excited*). I don't know. You see I was on my way over here.

JONATHAN (*forcing her as she backs* L.). I think you're lying.

EINSTEIN (*crosses to* U. R. C.). I think she tells the truth, Chonny. We let her go now, huh?

JONATHAN (*still forcing her* L.). I think she's lying. Breaking into a house this time of night. I think she's dangerous. She shouldn't be allowed around loose.

(*He seizes* ELAINE's *arm. She screams.*)

ELAINE. Take your hands off me—

JONATHAN. Doctor—

(*As* EINSTEIN *starts* L., TEDDY *enters from cellar, shutting door. He looks at* JONATHAN L., *then speaks to* EINSTEIN R.)

TEDDY (*simply*). It's going to be a private funeral. (*He goes up stairs to first landing.* ELAINE *crosses to desk, dragging* JONATHAN *with her.*)

ELAINE. Teddy! Teddy! Tell these men who I am.

(TEDDY *turns and looks at her.*)

TEDDY. That's my daughter—Alice. (*He cries* "CHARGE!" *Dashes up stairs and exits.*)

ELAINE (*struggling to get away from* JONATHAN *and dragging him to* R. C.). No! No! Teddy!

(JONATHAN *has* ELAINE's *arm twisted in back of her, his other hand is over her mouth.*)

JONATHAN. Doctor! Your handkerchief! (*As* EINSTEIN *hands him a handkerchief,* JONATHAN *releases his hand from* ELAINE's *mouth to take it. She screams. He puts his hand over her mouth again. Spies the cellar door and speaks to* EINSTEIN.) The cellar!

(EINSTEIN *runs and opens cellar door. Then he runs back and turns off light-switch, putting stage in darkness.* JONATHAN *pushes* ELAINE *through cellar doorway.* EINSTEIN *runs back and down cellar stairs with* ELAINE. JONATHAN *shuts door, remaining on stage as the* AUNTS *enter on balcony above in their mourning clothes. Everything is in complete darkness except for street lamp.*)

ABBY. What's the matter?

MARTHA. What's happening down there?

(MARTHA *shuts her door and* ABBY *puts on*

lights from switch on balcony. They look down at the room a moment, then come downstairs, speaking as they come.)

ABBY. What's the matter? *(Reaching foot of stairs as she sees* JONATHAN.*)* What are you doing?

JONATHAN. We caught a burglar—a sneak thief. Go back to your room.

ABBY. We'll call the police.

JONATHAN. We've called the police. We'll handle this. Go back to your room. Do you hear me?

(The doorbell rings, followed by several knocks. ABBY *runs and opens* R. *door.* MORTIMER *enters with suitcase. At the same time,* ELAINE *runs out of cellar and into* MORTIMER's *arms.* JONATHAN *makes a grab for* ELAINE *but misses. This leaves him* D. S. C. EINSTEIN *sneaks* D. S. *behind* JONATHAN.*)*

ELAINE. Mortimer! *(He drops suitcase.)* Where have you been?

MORTIMER. To the Nora Bayes Theatre and I should have known better. *(He sees* JONATHAN.*)* My God!—I'm still there.

*(*ABBY *is at* R. *of* MORTIMER.*)*

ABBY. This is your brother Jonathan—and this is Dr. Einstein.

*(*MORTIMER *surveys his* AUNTS *all dressed in black.)*

MORTIMER. I know this isn't a nightmare, but what is it?

JONATHAN. I've come back home, Mortimer.

MORTIMER *(looking at him, and then to* ABBY*).* Who did you say this was?

ABBY. It's your brother Jonathan. He's had his face changed. Dr. Einstein performed the operation.

MORTIMER *(taking a closer look at* JONATHAN*).* Jonathan! Jonathan, you always were a horror, but do you have to look like one?

*(*JONATHAN *takes a step toward him.* EINSTEIN *pulls on his sleeve.* ELAINE *and* MARTHA *draw back to desk.)*

EINSTEIN. Easy, Chonny! Easy.

JONATHAN. Mortimer, have you forgotten the things I used to do to you when we were boys? Remember the time you were tied to the bedpost—the needles under your fingernails—?

MORTIMER. By God, it is Jonathan.—Yes, I remember. I remember you as the most detestable, vicious, venomous form of animal life I ever knew.

*(*JONATHAN *grows tense.* ABBY *steps between them.)*

ABBY. Now don't you two boys start quarreling again the minute you've seen each other.

MORTIMER *(crosses to door, opens it).* There won't be any fight, Aunt Abby. Jonathan, you're not wanted here—get out!

JONATHAN. Dr. Einstein and I have been invited to stay.

MORTIMER. Not in this house.

ABBY. Just for tonight.

MORTIMER. I don't want him anywhere near me.

ABBY. But we did invite them for tonight, and it wouldn't be very nice to go back on our word.

MORTIMER *(unwillingly).* All right, tonight. But the first thing in the morning —out! *(He picks up his suitcase.)* Where are they sleeping?

ABBY. We put them in Jonathan's old room.

MORTIMER. That's my old room. *(Starts upstairs.)* I'm sleeping in that room. I'm here to stay.

MARTHA. Oh, Mortimer, I'm so glad.

EINSTEIN. Chonny, we sleep down here.

MORTIMER. You bet your life you sleep down here.

EINSTEIN *(to* JONATHAN*).* You sleep on the sofa and I sleep on the window-seat.

(At the mention of window-seat, MORTIMER *has reached the landing; after hanging his hat on hall tree, he turns and comes slowly downstairs, speaking as he reaches the floor and crossing over to window-seat. He drops back at* U. S. *end of window-seat.)*

MORTIMER. The window-seat! Oh, well, let's not argue about it. That window-seat's good enough for me for tonight. I'll sleep on the window-seat. (*As* MORTIMER *crosses above table,* EINSTEIN *makes a gesture as though to stop him from going to window-seat, but he's too late. He turns to* JONATHAN *as* MORTIMER *sits on window-seat.*)

EINSTEIN. You know, Chonny—all this argument—it makes me think of Mr. Spenalzo.

JONATHAN. Spenalzo! (*He steps* U. S. *looking around for Spenalzo again. Realizing it would be best for them to remain downstairs, he speaks to* MORTIMER.) Well, now, Mortimer— It really isn't necessary to inconvenience you like this—we'll sleep down here.

MORTIMER (*rising*). Jonathan, your sudden consideration for me is very unconvincing.

EINSTEIN (*goes upstairs to landing*). Come along, Chonny. We get our things out of the room, eh?

MORTIMER. Don't bother, Doctor!

JONATHAN. By the way, Doctor, I've completely lost track of Mr. Spenalzo.

MORTIMER. Who's this Mr. Spenalzo?

EINSTEIN (*from landing*). Just a friend of ours Chonny's been looking for.

MORTIMER. Well, don't bring anyone else in here!

EINSTEIN. It's all right, Chonny. While we pack I tell you all about it. (*He goes up and through arch.* JONATHAN *starts upstairs.*)

ABBY (*dropping* D. S.). Mortimer, you don't have to sleep down here. I can go in with Martha and you can take my room.

JONATHAN (*he has reached the balcony*). No trouble at all, Aunt Abby. We'll be packed in a few minutes. And then you can have the room, Mortimer. (*He exits through arch.*)

(MORTIMER *crosses up to sofa.* MARTHA *crosses to above armchair at* L. *of table and as* MORTIMER *speaks she picks up sport shoe belonging to Spenalzo, that* EINSTEIN *put there in blackout scene, unnoticed by anyone. She pretends to dust hem of her dress.*)

MORTIMER. You're just wasting your time —I told you I'm sleeping down here.

(ELAINE *leaps up from stool into* MORTIMER'S *arms.*)

ELAINE. Mortimer!

MORTIMER. What's the matter with you. dear?

ELAINE (*semi-hysterical*). I've almost been killed.

MORTIMER. You've almost been— (*He looks quickly at the* AUNTS.) Abby! Martha!

MARTHA. No! It was Jonathan.

ABBY. He mistook her for a sneak-thief.

ELAINE. No, it was more than that. He's some kind of maniac. Mortimer, I'm afraid of him.

MORTIMER. Why, darling, you're trembling. (*Seats her on sofa. To* AUNTS.) Have you got any smelling salts?

MARTHA. No, but do you think some hot tea, or coffee—?

MORTIMER. Coffee. Make some for me, too —and some sandwiches. I haven't had any dinner.

MARTHA. We'll make something for both of you.

(MORTIMER *starts to question* ELAINE *as* ABBY *takes off her hat and gloves and puts them on sideboard. Talking to* MARTHA *at the same time.*)

ABBY. Martha, we can leave our hats downstairs here, now.

MORTIMER. You weren't going out somewhere, were you? Do you know what time it is? It's after twelve. (*The word twelve rings a bell.*) TWELVE! (*He turns to* ELAINE.) Elaine, you've got to go home!

ELAINE. Whaa-t?

ABBY. Why, you wanted some sandwiches for you both. It won't take a minute. (*She exits into kitchen.*)

(MORTIMER *is looking at* ELAINE *with his back to* MARTHA. MARTHA *crosses to him with shoe in hand by her* U. S. *side.*)

MARTHA. Why, don't you remember—we wanted to celebrate your engagement? (*She punctuates the word "engagement" by pointing the shoe at* MORTIMER'S *back. She looks at the shoe in wonderment.*)

Wondering how that shoe ever got in her hand. She stares at it a moment [the other two do not see it, of course], then puts it on top of the table. Finally dismissing it she turns to MORTIMER *again.)* That's what we'll do, dear. We'll make a nice supper for both of you. *(She starts out kitchen door, then turns back.)* And we'll open a bottle of wine! *(She exits kitchen door.)*

MORTIMER *(vaguely).* All right. *(Suddenly changes his mind and runs to kitchen door.)* No WINE! *(He closes the door and comes back to* C. *as* ELAINE *rises from the sofa to him. She is still very upset.)*

ELAINE. Mortimer! What's going on in this house?

MORTIMER *(suspicious).* What do you mean—what's going on in this house?

ELAINE. You were supposed to take me to dinner and the theatre tonight—you called it off. You asked me to marry you—I said I would—and five minutes later you threw me out of the house. Tonight, just after your brother tries to strangle me, you want to chase me home. Now, listen, Mr. Brewster—before I go home, I want to know where I stand. Do you love me?

MORTIMER *(taking her hands).* I love you very much, Elaine. In fact I love you so much I can't marry you.

ELAINE. Have you suddenly gone crazy?

MORTIMER. I don't think so but it's just a matter of time. *(They both sit on sofa as* MORTIMER *begins to explain.)* You see, insanity runs in my family. *(He looks upstairs and toward kitchen.)* It practically gallops. That's why I can't marry you, dear.

ELAINE. Now wait a minute, you've got to do better than that.

MORTIMER. No, dear—there's a strange taint in the Brewster blood. If you really knew my family it's—well—it's what you'd expect if Strindberg had written *Hellzapoppin.*

ELAINE. Now just because Teddy is a little—

MORTIMER. No, it goes way back. The first Brewster—the one who come over on the Mayflower. You know in those days the Indians used to scalp the settlers—he used to scalp the Indians.

ELAINE. Mortimer, that's ancient history—

MORTIMER. No, the whole family . . . *(He rises and points to a picture of Grandfather over the sideboard.)* Take my grandfather—he tried his patent medicines out on dead people to be sure he wouldn't kill them.

ELAINE. He wasn't so crazy. He made a million dollars.

MORTIMER. And then there's Jonathan. You just said he was a maniac—he tried to kill you.

ELAINE *(rises, crosses to him).* But he's your brother, not you. I'm in love with you.

MORTIMER. And there's Teddy, too. You *know* Teddy. He thinks he's Roosevelt. No, dear, no Brewster should marry. I realize now that if I'd met my father in time I'd have stopped him.

ELAINE. Now, darling, all this doesn't prove *you're* crazy. Look at your aunts—they're Brewsters, aren't they?—and the sanest, sweetest people I've ever known.

*(*MORTIMER *crosses above table to window-seat, speaking as he goes.)*

MORTIMER. Well, even they have their peculiarities.

ELAINE *(turning and drifting* R.*).* Yes, but what lovely peculiarities!—Kindness, generosity—human sympathy—

*(*MORTIMER *sees* ELAINE'S *back is to him. He lifts window-seat to take a peek, and sees Mr. Spenalzo instead of Mr. Hoskins. He puts window-seat down again and staggers to table, and leans on it.)*

MORTIMER *(to himself).* There's another one!

ELAINE *(turning to* MORTIMER*).* Oh, Mortimer, there are plenty of others. You can't tell me anything about your aunts.

MORTIMER. I'm not going to. *(Crossing to her.)* Look, Elaine, you've got to go home. Something very important has just come up.

ELAINE. Up, from where? We're here alone together.

MORTIMER. I know I'm acting irrationally, but just put it down to the fact that I'm a mad Brewster.

ELAINE. If you think you're going to get out of this by pretending you're insane— you're crazy. Maybe you're not going to marry me, but I'm going to marry you. I love you, you dope.

MORTIMER (*urging her to* R. *door*). Well, if you love me will you get the hell out of here!

ELAINE. Well, at least take me home, won't you, I'm afraid.

MORTIMER. Afraid! A little walk through the cemetery?

(ELAINE *crosses to door, then changing tactics, turns to* MORTIMER.)

ELAINE. Mortimer, will you kiss me good night?

MORTIMER (*holding out arms*). Of course, dear. (*What* MORTIMER *plans to be a desultory peck,* ELAINE *turns into a production number. He comes out of it with no less of poise.*) Good night, dear. I'll call you up in a day or two.

ELAINE (*walks to* R. *door in a cold fury, opens it and turns to* MORTIMER). You—you critic! (*She slams door after her.*)

(MORTIMER *looks at the door helplessly then turns and stalks to the kitchen door.*)

MORTIMER (*in doorway*). Aunt Abby! Aunt Martha! Come in here!

ABBY (*offstage*). We'll be in in a minute, dear.

MORTIMER. Come in here now! (*He stands down by* U. S. *end of window-seat.*)

(ABBY *enters from kitchen.*)

ABBY. Yes, dear, what is it? Where's Elaine?

MORTIMER. I thought you promised me not to let anyone in this house while I was gone!

(*The following speeches overlap.*)

ABBY. Well, Jonathan just walked in—

MORTIMER. I don't mean Jonathan—

ABBY. And Dr. Einstein was with him—

MORTIMER. I don't mean Dr. Einstein. Who's that in the window-seat?

ABBY. We told you—Mr. Hoskins.

(MORTIMER *throws open the window-seat and steps back* U. L.)

MORTIMER. It is *not* Mr. Hoskins.

(ABBY, *a little puzzled, walks to window-seat and looks in at* D. S. *end then speaks very simply.*)

ABBY. Who can that be?

MORTIMER (R. *of* ABBY). Are you trying to tell me you've never seen this man before?

ABBY. I certainly am. Why, this is a fine how do you do! It's getting so anybody thinks he can walk into this house.

MORTIMER. Now Aunt Abby, don't you try to get out of this. That's another one of your gentlemen!

ABBY. Mortimer, how can you say such a thing! That man's an impostor! And if he came here to be buried in our cellar he's mistaken.

MORTIMER. Oh, Aunt Abby, you admitted to me that you put Mr. Hoskins in the window-seat.

ABBY. Yes, I did.

MORTIMER. Well, this man couldn't have just got the idea from Mr. Hoskins. By the way—where is Mr. Hoskins? (*He looks toward cellar door.*)

(ABBY *crosses above table to* U. C.)

ABBY. He must have gone to Panama.

MORTIMER. Oh, you buried him?

ABBY. No, not yet. He's just down there waiting for the services, poor dear. We haven't had a minute what with Jonathan in the house. (*At the mention of* JONATHAN'S *name,* MORTIMER *closes the window-seat.*) Oh, dear. We've always wanted to hold a double funeral, (*Crossing to kitchen door.*) but I will not read services over a total stranger.

MORTIMER (*going up to her*). A stranger! Aunt Abby, how can I believe you? There are twelve men in the cellar and you admit you poisoned them.

ABBY. Yes, I did. But you don't think I'd stoop to telling a fib. Martha! (*She exits into kitchen.*)

(*At the same time* JONATHAN *enters through the arch onto balcony and comes down quickly to foot of stairs.* MORTIMER *crosses to* D. R. C. JONATHAN *sees him and crosses to him.*)

JONATHAN. Oh, Mortimer—I'd like to have a word with you.

MORTIMER (*standing up to him*). A word's about all you'll have time for, Jonathan, because I've decided you and your Doctor friend are going to have to get out of this house just as quickly as possible.

JONATHAN (*smoothly*). I'm glad you recognize the fact that you and I can't live under the same roof—but you've arrived at the wrong solution. Take your suitcase and get out! (*He starts to cross above* MORTIMER, *anxious to get to the window-seat, but* MORTIMER *makes big sweep around above table and comes back to him at* D. S. C.)

MORTIMER. Jonathan!—You're beginning to bore me. You've played your one night stand in Brooklyn—move on!

JONATHAN. My dear Mortimer, just because you've graduated from the back fence to the typewriter, don't think you've grown up. . . . (*He takes a sudden step* U. S. *around* MORTIMER *and gets to the window-seat and sits.*) I'm staying, and you're leaving—and I mean now!

MORTIMER (*crossing to him*). If you think I can be frightened—if you think there's anything I fear—

JONATHAN (*he rises, they stand facing each other*). I've lived a strange life, Mortimer. But it's taught me one thing—to be afraid of nothing! (*They glare at each other with equal courage when* ABBY *marches in from the kitchen, followed by* MARTHA.)

ABBY. Martha, just look and see what's in that window-seat.

(*Both* MEN *throw themselves on the window-seat simultaneously.* JONATHAN D. S. *end.*)

MORTIMER *and* JONATHAN. Now, Aunt Abby!

(MORTIMER *turns his head slowly to* JONATHAN, *light dawning on his face. He rises with smiling assurance.*)

MORTIMER. Jonathan, let Aunt Martha see what's in the window-seat (JONATHAN *freezes dangerously.* MORTIMER *crosses below table up to* ABBY.) Aunt Abby, I owe

you an apology. (*He kisses her on forehead.*) I have very good news for you. Jonathan is leaving. He's taking Dr. Einstein and their cold companion with him. (JONATHAN *rises but holds his ground.*) Jonathan, you're my brother. You're a Brewster. I'm going to give you a chance to get away and take the evidence with you—you can't ask for more than that. (JONATHAN *doesn't move.*) Very well,—in that case I'll have to call the police. (MORTIMER *crosses to phone and picks it up.*)

JONATHAN. Don't reach for that telephone. (*He crosses to* L. *of* MORTIMER.) Are you still giving me orders after seeing what's happened to Mr. Spenalzo?

MARTHA (*she's above table*). Spenalzo?

ABBY (U. C.). I knew he was a foreigner.

JONATHAN. Remember what happened to Mr. Spenalzo can happen to you too.

(*There is a knock on* R. *door.* ABBY *crosses and opens it and* OFFICER O'HARA *sticks his head in.*)

O'HARA. Hello, Miss Abby.

ABBY. Oh, Officer O'Hara. Is there something we can do for you?

(MORTIMER *puts phone down and drifts down close to* O'HARA. JONATHAN *turns* L.)

O'HARA. I saw your lights on and thought there might be sickness in the house. (*He sees* MORTIMER.) Oh, you got company—I'm sorry I disturbed you.

MORTIMER (*taking* O'HARA *by the arm*). No, no, come in.

ABBY. Yes, come in.

MARTHA (*crossing to door*). Come right in, Officer O'Hara. (MORTIMER *leads* O'HARA *in a couple of steps and shuts door.* ABBY *crosses back to* U. S. C. MARTHA *is near desk.* JONATHAN *is in front of sofa* R. *of* ABBY. MARTHA, *to* O'HARA.) This is our nephew, Mortimer.

O'HARA. Pleased to meet you.

(JONATHAN *starts toward kitchen.*)

ABBY (*stopping* JONATHAN). And this is another nephew, Jonathan.

O'HARA (*crosses below* MORTIMER *and gestures to* JONATHAN *with his night stick*)

Pleased to make your acquaintance. (JONA-THAN *ignores him.* O'HARA *speaks to* AUNTS.) Well, it must be nice havin' your nephews visitin' you. Are they going to stay with you for a bit?

MORTIMER. I'm staying. My brother Jonathan is just leaving.

(JONATHAN *starts for stairs.* O'HARA *stops him.*)

O'HARA. I've met you here before, haven't I?

ABBY. I'm afraid not. Jonathan hasn't been home for years.

O'HARA. Your face looks familiar to me. Maybe I seen a picture of you somewheres.

JONATHAN. I don't think so. (*He hurries up stairs.*)

MORTIMER. Yes, Jonathan, I'd hurry if I were you. Your things are all packed anyway, aren't they?

O'HARA. Well, you'll be wanting to say your good-byes. I'll be running along.

MORTIMER. What's the rush? I'd like to have you stick around until my brother goes.

(JONATHAN *exits through arch.*)

O'HARA. I just dropped in to make sure everything was all right.

MORTIMER. We're going to have some coffee in a minute. Won't you join us?

ABBY. Oh, I forgot the coffee. (*She goes out to kitchen.*)

MARTHA (*crossing to kitchen door*). Well, I'd better make some more sandwiches. I ought to know your appetite by this time, Officer O'Hara. (*She goes out to kitchen as* O'HARA *follows as far as* C.)

O'HARA. Don't bother. I'm due to ring in in a few minutes.

MORTIMER. You can have a cup of coffee with us. My brother will be gone soon. (*He leads* O'HARA *below table to armchair.*) Sit down.

O'HARA. Say—ain't I seen a photograph of your brother around here some place?

MORTIMER. I don't think so. (*He sits* R. *of table.*)

O'HARA. He certainly reminds me of somebody.

MORTIMER. He looks like somebody you've probably seen in the movies.

O'HARA. I never go to the movies. I hate 'em! My mother says the movies is a bastard art.

MORTIMER. Yes, it's full of them.—Your, er, mother said that?

O'HARA. Yeah. My mother was an actress—a stage actress. Perhaps you heard of her —Peaches Latour.

MORTIMER. It sounds like a name I've seen on a program. What did she play?

O'HARA. Well, her big hit was "Mutt and Jeff." Played it for three years. I was born on tour—the third season.

MORTIMER. You were?

O'HARA. Yep. Sioux City, Iowa. I was born in the dressing room at the end of the second act, and Mother made the finale.

MORTIMER. What a trouper! There must be a good story in your mother—you know, I write about the theatre.

O'HARA. You do? Say!—you're not Mortimer Brewster, the dramatic critic!

MORTIMER. Yes.

O'HARA. Well, I certainly am glad to meet you. (*He moves his hat and stick preparatory to shaking hands with* MORTIMER. *He also picks up the sport shoe which* MARTHA *has left on the table. He looks at it just for a split second and puts it on the* D. S. *end of table.* MORTIMER *sees it and stares at it.*) Say, Mr. Brewster—we're in the same line of business.

MORTIMER (*still intent on shoe*). We are?

O'HARA. Yeah. I'm a playwright. Oh, this being on the police force is just temporary.

MORTIMER. How long have you been on the force?

O'HARA. Twelve years. I'm collecting material for a play.

MORTIMER. I'll bet it's a honey.

O'HARA. Well, it ought to be. With all the drama I see being a cop. Mr. Brewster— you got no idea what goes on in Brooklyn.

MORTIMER. I think I have. (*He puts the*

shoe under his chair, then looks at his watch, then looks toward balcony.)

O'HARA. Say, what time you got?

MORTIMER. Ten after one.

O'HARA. Gee, I gotta ring in. *(He starts for R. door but MORTIMER stops him at C.)*

MORTIMER. Wait a minute, O'Hara. On that play of yours—I may be able to help you. *(Sits him in chair R.)*

O'HARA *(ecstasy)*. You would! *(Rises.)* Say, it was fate my walking in here tonight. Look—I'll tell you the plot!

(At this point JONATHAN enters on the balcony followed by DR. EINSTEIN. They each have a bag. At the same moment ABBY enters from the kitchen. Helpful as the cop has been, MORTIMER does not want to listen to his plot. As he backs away from him he speaks to JONATHAN as they come down stairs.)

MORTIMER. Oh, you're on your way, eh? Good! You haven't got much time, you know.

ABBY *(U. L.)*. Well, everything's just about ready. *(Sees JONATHAN and EINSTEIN at foot of stairs.)* Oh, you leaving now, Jonathan? Good-bye. Good-bye, Dr. Einstein. *(She sees instrument case above window-seat.)* Oh, doesn't this case belong to you?

(This reminds MORTIMER of Mr. Spenalzo, also.)

MORTIMER. Yes, Jonathan—you can't go without *all* your things. *(Now to get rid of O'HARA. He turns to him.)* Well, O'Hara, it was nice meeting you. I'll see you again and we'll talk about your play.

O'HARA *(refusing to leave)*. Oh, I'm not leaving now, Mr. Brewster.

MORTIMER. Why not?

O'HARA. Well, you just offered to help me with my play, didn't you? You and me are going to write my play together.

MORTIMER. I can't do that, O'Hara—I'm not a creative writer.

O'HARA. I'll do the creating. You just put the words to it.

MORTIMER. But, O'Hara—

O'HARA. No, sir, Mr. Brewster. I ain't leaving this house till I tell you the plot.

(He crosses and sits on window-seat.)

JONATHAN *(starting for R. door)*. In that case, Mortimer . . . we'll be running along.

MORTIMER. Don't try that. You can't go yet. You've got to take *everything* with you, you know. *(He turns and sees O'HARA on window-seat and runs to him.)* Look, O'Hara, you run along now, eh? My brother's just going—

O'HARA. I can wait. I've been waiting twelve years.

(MARTHA enters from kitchen with a tray of coffee and sandwiches.)

MARTHA. I'm sorry I was so long.

MORTIMER. Don't bring that in here. O'Hara, would you join us for a bite in the kitchen?

MARTHA. The kitchen?

ABBY *(to MARTHA)*. Jonathan's leaving.

MARTHA. Oh. Well, that's nice. Come along, Officer O'Hara. *(She exits to kitchen.)*

(O'HARA gets to kitchen doorway as ABBY speaks.)

ABBY. Sure you don't mind eating in the kitchen, Mr. O'Hara?

O'HARA. And where else would you eat?

ABBY. Good-bye, Jonathan, nice to have seen you again.

(O'HARA exits to kitchen, followed by ABBY. MORTIMER crosses to kitchen doorway and shuts door, then turns to JONATHAN.)

MORTIMER. I'm glad you came back to Brooklyn, Jonathan, because it gives me a chance to throw you out—and the first one out is your boy friend, Mr. Spenalzo. *(He lifts up window-seat. As he does so, O'HARA, sandwich in hand, enters from kitchen. MORTIMER drops window-seat.)*

O'HARA. Look, Mr. Brewster, we can talk in here.

MORTIMER *(pushing him into kitchen)*. Coming right out.

JONATHAN. I might have known you'd grow up to write a play with a policeman.

MORTIMER *(from kitchen doorway)*. Get going now—all three of you. *(He exits, shutting door.)*

(JONATHAN *puts bag down and crosses to window-seat.*)

JONATHAN. Doctor, this affair between my brother and me has got to be settled.

EINSTEIN (*crossing to window-seat for instrument case and bringing it back to foot of stairs*). Now, Chonny, we got trouble enough. Your brother gives us a chance to get away—what more could you ask?

JONATHAN. You don't understand. (*He lifts window-seat.*) This goes back a good many years.

EINSTEIN (*foot of stairs*). Now, Chonny, let's get going.

JONATHAN (*harshly*). We're not going. We're going to sleep right here tonight.

EINSTEIN. With a cop in the kitchen and Mr. Spenalzo in the window-seat.

JONATHAN. That's all he's got on us. (*Puts window-seat down.*) We'll take Mr. Spenalzo down and dump him in the bay, and come right back here.—Then if he tries to interfere— (*He crosses to* C. EINSTEIN *crosses to* L. *of him and faces him.*)

EINSTEIN. Now, Chonny.

JONATHAN. Doctor, you know when I make up my mind—

EINSTEIN. Yeah—when you make up your mind, you lose your head. Brooklyn ain't a good place for you.

JONATHAN (*peremptorily*). Doctor!

EINSTEIN. O.K. We got to stick together. (*He crosses to bags.*) Some day we get stuck together. If we're coming back here do we got to take these with us?

JONATHAN. No. Leave them here. Hide them in the cellar. Move fast! (*He moves to bags to* L. *end of sofa as* EINSTEIN *goes down cellar with instrument case.*) Spenalzo can go out the same way he came in! (*He kneels on window-seat and looks out. Then as he starts to lift window-seat,* EINSTEIN *comes in from the cellar with some excitement.*)

EINSTEIN. Hey, Chonny, come quick!

JONATHAN (*crossing to him*). What's the matter?

EINSTEIN. You know that hole in the cellar?

JONATHAN. Yes.

EINSTEIN. We got an *ace* in the hole. Come on I show you. (*They both exit into cellar.* JONATHAN *shuts door.*)

(MORTIMER *enters from kitchen, sees their bags still there. He opens window-seat and sees Spenalzo. Then he puts his head out window and yells.*)

MORTIMER. Jonathan! Jonathan! (JONATHAN *comes through cellar door unnoticed by* MORTIMER *and crosses to back of him.* EINSTEIN *comes down into* C. *of room.*) Jonathan!

JONATHAN (*quietly*). Yes, Mortimer.

MORTIMER (*leaping backwards to below table*). Where have you two been? I thought I told you to get—

JONATHAN. We're not going.

MORTIMER. Oh, you're not? You think I'm not serious about this, eh? Do you want O'Hara to know what's in that window-seat?

JONATHAN. We're staying here.

MORTIMER (*crossing around above table to kitchen door*). All right! You asked for it. This gets me rid of you and Officer O'Hara at the same time. (*Opens kitchen door, yells out.*) Officer O'Hara, come in here!

JONATHAN. If you tell O'Hara what's in the window-seat, I'll tell him what's down in the cellar.

(MORTIMER *closes kitchen door quickly.*)

MORTIMER. The cellar?

JONATHAN. There's an elderly gentleman down there who seems to be very dead

MORTIMER. What were you doing down in the cellar?

EINSTEIN. What's *he* doing down in the cellar?

(O'HARA's *voice is heard offstage.*)

O'HARA. No, thanks, ma'am. They were fine. I've had plenty.

JONATHAN. Now what are you going to say to O'Hara?

(O'HARA *walks in kitchen door.*)

O'HARA. Say, Mr. Brewster, your aunts want to hear it too. Shall I get them in here?

MORTIMER (*pulling him* R.). No, O'Hara, you can't do that now. You've got to ring in.

(O'HARA *stops at* C. *as* MORTIMER *opens the door.*)

O'HARA. The hell with ringing in. I'll get your aunts in here and tell you the plot.

(*He starts for kitchen door.*)

MORTIMER (*grabbing him*). No, O'Hara, not in front of all these people. We'll get together alone, some place later.

O'HARA. How about the back room at Kelly's?

MORTIMER (*passing* O'HARA R. *in front of him*). Fine! You go ring in, and I'll meet you at Kelly's.

JONATHAN (*at window-seat*). Why don't you two go down in the cellar?

O'HARA. That's all right with me. (*Starts for cellar door.*) Is this the cellar?

MORTIMER (*grabbing him again, pushing toward door*). Nooo! We'll go to Kelly's. But you're going to ring in on the way.

O'HARA (*as he exits* R.). All right, that'll only take a couple of minutes. (*He's gone.*) (MORTIMER *takes his hat from hall tree and crosses to open* R. *door.*)

MORTIMER. I'll ditch this guy and be back in five minutes. I'll expect to find you gone. (*Changes his mind.*) Wait for me.

(*He exits* R.)

(EINSTEIN *sits* R. *of table.*)

JONATHAN. We'll wait for him, Doctor. I've waited a great many years for a chance like this.

EINSTEIN. We got him right where we want him. Did he look guilty!

JONATHAN (*rising*). Take the bags back up to our room, Doctor.

(EINSTEIN *gets bags and reaches foot of stairs with them.* ABBY *and* MARTHA *enter from kitchen.* ABBY *speaks as she enters.*)

ABBY. Have they gone? (*Sees* JONATHAN *and* EINSTEIN.) Oh—we thought we heard somebody leave.

JONATHAN (*crossing to* R. C.). Just Mortimer, and he'll be back in a few minutes. Is there any food left in the kitchen? I think Dr. Einstein and I would enjoy a bite.

MARTHA (L. *of table*). But you won't have time.

ABBY (*at* C.). No, if you're still here when Mortimer gets back he won't like it.

EINSTEIN (*dropping* D. S. R.). He'll like it. He's gotta like it.

JONATHAN. Get something for us to eat while we bury Mr. Spenalzo in the cellar.

MARTHA (*crossing to below table*). Oh no!

ABBY. He can't stay in our cellar. No, Jonathan, you've got to take him with you.

JONATHAN. There's a friend of Mortimer's downstairs waiting for him.

ABBY. A friend of Mortimer's?

JONATHAN. He and Mr. Spenalzo will get along fine together. They're both dead.

MARTHA. They must mean Mr. Hoskins.

EINSTEIN. Mr. Hoskins?

JONATHAN. You know about what's downstairs?

ABBY. Of course we do, and he's no friend of Mortimer's. He's one of our gentlemen.

EINSTEIN. Your chentlemen?

MARTHA. And we won't have any strangers buried in our cellar.

JONATHAN (*noncomprehending*). But Mr. Hoskins—

MARTHA. Mr. Hoskins isn't a stranger.

ABBY. Besides, there's no room for Mr. Spenalzo. The cellar's crowded already.

JONATHAN. Crowded? With what?

ABBY. There are twelve graves down there now.

(*The two* MEN *draw back in amazement.*)

JONATHAN. Twelve graves!

ABBY. That leaves very little room and we're going to need it.

JONATHAN. You mean you and Aunt Martha have murdered—?

ABBY. Murdered! Certainly not. It's one of our charities.

MARTHA (*indignantly*). Why, what we've been doing is a mercy.

ABBY (*gesturing outside*). So you just take your Mr. Spenalzo out of here.

JONATHAN (*still unable to believe*). You've done that—here in this house— (*Points to floor.*) and you've buried them down there!

EINSTEIN. Chonny—we've been chased all over the world—they stay right here in Brooklyn and do just as good as you do.

JONATHAN (*facing him*). What?

EINSTEIN. You've got twelve and they've got twelve.

JONATHAN (*slowly*). I've got thirteen.

EINSTEIN. No, Chonny, twelve.

JONATHAN. Thirteen! (*Counting on fingers.*) There's Mr. Spenalzo. Then the first one in London—two in Johannesburg —one in Sydney—one in Melbourne—two in San Francisco—one in Phoenix, Arizona—

EINSTEIN. Phoenix?

JONATHAN. The filling station. The three

in Chicago and the one in South Bend. That makes thirteen!

EINSTEIN. But you can't count the one in South Bend. He died of pneumonia.

JONATHAN. He wouldn't have got pneumonia if I hadn't shot him.

EINSTEIN (*adamant*). No, Chonny, he died of pneumonia. He don't count.

JONATHAN. He counts with me. I say thirteen.

EINSTEIN. No, Chonny. You got twelve and they got twelve. (*Crossing to* AUNTS.) The old ladies are just as good as you are. (*The two* AUNTS *smile at each other happily.* JONATHAN *turns, facing the three of them and speaks menacingly.*)

JONATHAN. Oh, they are, are they? Well, that's easily taken care of. All I need is one more, that's all—just one more.

(MORTIMER *enters hastily* R., *closing door behind him, and turns to them with a nervous smile.*)

MORTIMER. Well, here I am!

(JONATHAN *turns and looks at him with the widening eyes of someone who has just solved a problem, as the curtain falls.*)

ACT THREE

SCENE I

The scene is the same. Still later that night. The curtain rises on an empty stage. The window-seat is open and we see that it's empty. The armchair has been shifted to R. *of table. The drapes over the windows are closed. All doors except cellar are closed.* ABBY's *hymnal and black gloves are on sideboard.* MARTHA's *hymnal and gloves are on table. Otherwise the room is the same. As the curtain rises we hear a row from the cellar, through the open door. The speeches overlap in excitement and anger until the* AUNTS *appear on the stage, from cellar door.*

MARTHA. You stop doing that!

ABBY. This is our house and this is our cellar and you can't do that.

EINSTEIN. Ladies! Please!—Go back upstairs where you belong.

JONATHAN. Abby! Martha! Go upstairs!

MARTHA. There's no use your doing what you're doing because it will just have to be undone.

ABBY. I tell you we won't have it and you'd better stop it right now.

MARTHA (*entering from cellar*). All right! You'll find out. You'll find out whose house this is. (*She crosses to door* D. R.; *opens it and looks out. Then closes it.*)

ABBY (*entering*). I'm warning you! You'd better stop it! (D. S. C. *To* MARTHA.) Hasn't Mortimer come back yet?

MARTHA. No.

ABBY. It's a terrible thing to do—to bury a good Methodist with a foreigner. (*She crosses to window-seat.*)

MARTHA *(crossing to cellar door)*. I will not have our cellar desecrated!

ABBY *(drops window-seat)*. And we promised Mr. Hoskins a full Christian funeral. Where do you suppose Mortimer went?

MARTHA *(drops D. s.)*. I don't know, but he must be doing something—because he said to Jonathan, "You just wait, I'll settle this."

ABBY *(crossing up to sideboard)*. Well, he can't very well settle it while he's out of the house. That's all we want settled—what's going on down there.

(MORTIMER enters R., closes door.)

MORTIMER *(as one who has everything settled)*. All right. Now, where's Teddy?

(The AUNTS are very much annoyed with MORTIMER.)

ABBY. Mortimer, where have you been?

MORTIMER. I've been over to Dr. Gilchrist's. I've got his signature on Teddy's commitment papers.

MARTHA. Mortimer, what is the matter with you?

ABBY *(to below table)*. Running around getting papers signed at a time like this!

MARTHA. Do you know what Jonathan's doing?

ABBY. He's putting Mr. Hoskins and Mr. Spenalzo in together.

MORTIMER *(to cellar door)*. Oh, he is, is he? Well, let him. *(He shuts cellar door.)* Is Teddy in his room?

MARTHA. Teddy won't be any help.

MORTIMER. When he signs these commitment papers I can tackle Jonathan.

ABBY. What have they got to do with it?

MORTIMER. You had to go and tell Jonathan about those twelve graves. If I can make Teddy responsible for those I can protect you, don't you see?

ABBY. No, I don't see. And we pay taxes to have the police protect us.

MORTIMER *(going upstairs)*. I'll be back down in a minute.

ABBY *(takes gloves and hymnal from table)*. Come, Martha. We're going for the police.

(MARTHA gets her gloves and hymnal from sideboard. They both start R. to door.)

MORTIMER *(on landing)*. All right. *(He turns and rushes downstairs to R. door before they can reach it.)* The police. You can't go for the police.

MARTHA *(D. R., but L. of ABBY)*. Why can't we?

MORTIMER *(near R. door)*. Because if you tell the police about Mr. Spenalzo they'd find Mr. Hoskins too, *(Crosses to MARTHA.)* and that might make them curious, and they'd find out about the other twelve gentlemen.

ABBY. Mortimer, we know the police better than you do. I don't think they'd pry into our private affairs if we asked them not to.

MORTIMER. But if they found your twelve gentlemen they'd have to report to headquarters.

MARTHA *(pulling on her gloves)*. I'm not so sure they'd bother. They'd have to make out a very long report—and if there's one thing a policeman hates to do, it's to write.

MORTIMER. You can't depend on that. It might leak out!—and you couldn't expect a judge and jury to understand.

MARTHA. Oh, Judge Cullman would.

ABBY *(drawing on her gloves)*. We know him very well.

MARTHA. He always comes to church to pray—just before election.

ABBY. And he's coming here to tea some day. He promised.

MARTHA. Oh, Abby, we must speak to him again about that. *(To MORTIMER.)* His wife died a few years ago and it's left him very lonely.

ABBY. Well, come along, Martha. *(She starts toward door R. MORTIMER gets there first.)*

MORTIMER. No! You can't do this. I won't let you. You can't leave this house, and you can't have Judge Cullman to tea.

ABBY. Well, if you're not going to do something about Mr. Spenalzo, we are.

MORTIMER. I am going to do something. We may have to call the police in later, but if we do, I want to be ready for them.

MARTHA. You've got to get Jonathan out of this house!

ABBY. And Mr. Spenalzo, too!

MORTIMER. Will you please let me do this my own way? (*He starts upstairs.*) I've got to see Teddy.

ABBY (*facing* MORTIMER *on stairs*). If they're not out of here by morning, Mortimer, we're going to call the police.

MORTIMER (*on balcony*). They'll be out, I promise you that! Go to bed, will you? And for God's sake get out of those clothes —you look like Judith Anderson. (*He exits into hall, closing door.*)

(*The* AUNTS *watch him off.* MARTHA *turns to* ABBY.)

MARTHA. Well, Abby, that's a relief, isn't it?

ABBY. Yes—if Mortimer's going to do something at last, it just means Jonathan's going to a lot of unnecessary trouble. We'd better tell him. (ABBY *starts to cellar door as* JONATHAN *comes in. They meet* U. S. C. *front of sofa. His clothes are dirty.*) Oh, Jonathan—you might as well stop what you're doing.

JONATHAN. *It's all done.* Did I hear Mortimer?

ABBY. Well, it will just have to be undone. You're all going to be out of this house by morning. Mortimer's promised.

JONATHAN. Oh, are we? In that case, you and Aunt Martha can go to bed and have a pleasant night's sleep.

MARTHA (*always a little frightened by* JONATHAN, *starts upstairs*). Yes. Come, Abby.

(ABBY *follows* MARTHA *upstairs.*)

JONATHAN. Good night, Aunties.

ABBY. Not good night, Jonathan. Good-bye. By the time we get up you'll be out of this house. Mortimer's promised.

MARTHA (*on balcony*). And he has a way of doing it too!

JONATHAN. Then Mortimer is back?

ABBY. Oh, yes, he's up here talking to Teddy.

MARTHA. Good-bye, Jonathan.

ABBY. Good-bye, Jonathan.

JONATHAN. Perhaps you'd better say good-bye to Mortimer.

ABBY. Oh, you'll see Mortimer.

JONATHAN (*sitting on stool*). Yes—I'll see Mortimer.

(ABBY *and* MARTHA *exit.* JONATHAN *sits without moving. There is murder in his thought.* EINSTEIN *enters from cellar. He dusts off his trouser cuffs, lifting his leg, and we see he is wearing Spenalzo's sport shoes.*)

EINSTEIN. Whew! That's all fixed up. Smooth like a lake. Nobody'd ever know they were down there. (JONATHAN *still sits without moving.*) That bed feels good already. Forty-eight hours we didn't sleep. (*Crossing to second chair.*) Come on, Chonny, let's go up, yes?

JONATHAN. You're forgetting, Doctor.

EINSTEIN. Vat?

JONATHAN. My brother Mortimer.

EINSTEIN. Chonny—tonight? We do that tomorrow or the next day.

JONATHAN (*just able to control himself*). No, tonight! Now!

EINSTEIN (*down to floor*). Chonny, please —I'm tired—and tomorrow I got to operate.

JONATHAN. Yes, you're operating tomorrow, Doctor. But tonight we take care of Mortimer.

EINSTEIN (*kneeling in front of* JONATHAN, *trying to passify him*). But, Chonny, not tonight—we go to bed, eh?

JONATHAN (*rising.* EINSTEIN *straightens up too*). Doctor, look at me. You can see it's going to be done, can't you?

EINSTEIN (*retreating*). Ach, Chonny—I can see. I know dat look!

JONATHAN. It's a little too late for us to dissolve our partnership.

EINSTEIN. O.K., we do it. But the quick way. The quick twist like in London. (*He gives that London neck another twist with his hands and makes a noise suggest-ing strangulation.)*

JONATHAN. No, Doctor, I think this calls for something special. *(He walks toward* EINSTEIN, *who breaks* U. S. JONATHAN *has the look of beginning to anticipate a rare pleasure.)* I think perhaps the Melbourne method.

EINSTEIN. Chonny—no—not that. Two hours! And when it was all over, what? The fellow in London was just as dead as the fellow in Melbourne.

JONATHAN. We had to work too fast in London. There was no esthetic satisfaction in it—but Melbourne, ah, there was some-thing to remember.

EINSTEIN *(dropping* D. S. *as* JONATHAN *crosses him).* Remember! *(He shivers.)* I vish I didn't. No, Chonny—not Mel-bourne—not me!

JONATHAN. Yes, Doctor. Where are the in-struments?

EINSTEIN. I won't do it, Chonny.—I won't do it.

JONATHAN *(advancing on him as* EINSTEIN *backs* D. S.). Get your instruments!

EINSTEIN. No, Chonny!

JONATHAN. Where are they? Oh, yes—you hid them in the cellar. Where?

EINSTEIN. I won't tell you.

JONATHAN *(going to cellar door).* I'll find them, Doctor. *(He exits to cellar, closing door.)*

*(*TEDDY *enters on balcony and lifts his bugle to blow.* MORTIMER *dashes out and grabs his arm.* EINSTEIN *has rushed to cel-lar door. He stands there as* MORTIMER *and* TEDDY *speak.)*

MORTIMER. Don't do that, Mr. President.

TEDDY. I cannot sign any proclamation without consulting my cabinet.

MORTIMER. But this must be a secret.

TEDDY. A secret proclamation? How un-usual.

MORTIMER. Japan mustn't know until it's signed.

TEDDY. Japan! Those yellow devils. I'll sign it right away. *(Taking legal paper from*

MORTIMER.⟩ You have my word for it. I can let the cabinet know later.

MORTIMER. Yes, let's go and sign it.

TEDDY. You wait here. A secret proclama-tion has to be signed in secret.

MORTIMER. But at once, Mr. President.

TEDDY. I'll have to put on my signing clothes. *(*TEDDY *exits.)*

*(*MORTIMER *comes downstairs.* EINSTEIN *crosses and takes* MORTIMER'S *hat off of hall tree and hands it to him.)*

EINSTEIN *(anxious to get* MORTIMER *out of the house).* Ah, you go now, eh?

MORTIMER *(takes hat and puts it on desk).* No, Doctor, I'm waiting for something. Something important.

EINSTEIN *(*L. *of* MORTIMER). Please—you go now!

MORTIMER. Dr. Einstein, I have nothing against you personally. You seem to be a nice fellow. Take my advice and get out of this house and get just as far away as possible.

EINSTEIN. Trouble, yah! You get out.

MORTIMER *(crossing to* C.). All right, don't say I didn't warn you.

EINSTEIN. I'm warning you—get away quick.

MORTIMER. Things are going to start pop-ping around here any minute.

EINSTEIN *(*D. R.). Listen—Chonny's in a bad mood. When he's like dis, he's a mad-man—things happen—terrible things.

MORTIMER. Jonathan doesn't worry me now.

EINSTEIN. Ach, himmel—don't those plays you see teach you anything?

MORTIMER. About what?

EINSTEIN. Vell, at least people in plays act like they got sense—that's more than you do.

MORTIMER *(interested in this observation).* Oh, you think so, do you? You think peo-ple in plays act intelligently. I wish you had to sit through some of the ones I have to sit through. Take the little opus I saw tonight for instance. In this play, there's a man—he's supposed to be bright . . . (JONATHAN *enters from cellar with instrument case, stands in doorway and listens to* MORTIMER.) —he knows he's in a house with murderers—he ought to know he's in danger—he's even been warned to get out of the house—but does he go? No, he stays there. Now I ask you, Doctor, is that what an intelligent person would do?

EINSTEIN. You're asking me?

MORTIMER. He didn't even have sense enough to be frightened, to be on guard. For instance, the murderer invites him to sit down.

EINSTEIN (*he moves so as to keep* MORTIMER *from seeing* JONATHAN). You mean —"Won't you sit down?"

MORTIMER (*reaches out and pulls armchair to him* R. *of table without turning his head from* EINSTEIN). Believe it or not, that one was in there too.

EINSTEIN. And what did he do?

MORTIMER (*sitting in armchair*). He sat down. Now mind you, this fellow's supposed to be bright. There he sits—just waiting to be trussed up. And what do you think they used to tie him with.

EINSTEIN. Vat?

MORTIMER. The curtain cord.

(JONATHAN *spies curtain cords on either side of window in* L. *wall. He crosses, stands on window-seat and cuts cords with penknife.*)

EINSTEIN. Vell, why not? A good idea. Very convenient.

MORTIMER. A little too convenient. When are playwrights going to use some imagination! The curtain cord!

(JONATHAN *has got the curtain cord and is moving in slowly behind* MORTIMER.)

EINSTEIN. He didn't see him get it?

MORTIMER. See him? He sat there with his back to him. That's the kind of stuff we have to suffer through night after night. And they say the critics are killing the theatre—it's the playwrights who are killing the theatre. So there he sits—the big dope—this fellow who's supposed to be bright—just waiting to be trussed up and gagged.

(JONATHAN *drops loop of curtain cord over* MORTIMER's *shoulder and draws it taut. At the same time he throws other loop of cord on floor beside* EINSTEIN. *Simultaneously,* EINSTEIN *leaps to* MORTIMER *and gags him with handkerchief, then takes his curtain cord and ties* MORTIMER's *legs to chair.*)

EINSTEIN (*finishing up the tying*). You're right about dat fella—he vasn't very bright.

JONATHAN. Now, Mortimer, if you don't mind—we'll finish the story. (*He goes to sideboard and brings two candelabras to table and speaks as he lights them.* EINSTEIN *remains kneeling beside* MORTIMER.) Mortimer, I've been away for twenty years, but never once in all that time—my dear brother—were you out of my mind. In Melbourne one night, I dreamed of you— when I landed in San Francisco I felt a strange satisfaction—once more I was in the same country with you. (JONATHAN *has finished lighting candles. He crosses* D. R. *and flips light-switch, darkening stage. As he crosses,* EINSTEIN *gets up and crosses to window-seat.* JONATHAN *picks up instrument case at cellar doorway and sets it on table between candelabras and opens it, revealing various surgical instruments both in the bottom of case and on the inside of cover.*) Now, Doctor, we go to work! (*He removes an instrument from the case and fingers it lovingly, as* EINSTEIN *crosses and kneels on chair* L. *of table. He is not too happy about all this.*)

EINSTEIN. Please, Chonny, for me, the quick way!

JONATHAN. Doctor! This must really be an artistic achievement. After all, we're performing before a very distinguished critic.

EINSTEIN. Chonny!

JONATHAN (*flaring*). Doctor!

EINSTEIN (*beaten*). All right. Let's get it over. (*He closes drapes tightly and sits on window-seat.* JONATHAN *takes three or four more instruments out of the case and fingers them. At last, having the necessary equipment laid out on the towel he begins to put on a pair of rubber gloves.*)

JONATHAN. All ready for you, Doctor!

EINSTEIN. I gotta have a drink. I can't do this without a drink.

(He takes bottle from pocket. Drinks. Finds it empty. Rises.)

JONATHAN. Pull yourself together, Doctor.

EINSTEIN. I gotta have a drink. Ven ve valked in here this afternoon there was wine here—remember? Vere did she put that? *(He looks at sideboard and remembers. He goes to it, opens L. cupboard and brings bottle and two wine glasses to D. S. end of table top.)* Look, Chonny, we got a drink. *(He pours wine into the two glasses, emptying the bottle.* MORTIMER *watches him.)* Dat's all dere is. I split it with you. We both need a drink. *(He hands one glass to* JONATHAN, *then raises his own glass to his lips.* JONATHAN *stops him.)*

JONATHAN. One moment, Doctor—please. Where are your manners? *(He drops D. S. to R. of* MORTIMER *and looks at him.)* Yes, Mortimer, I realize now it was you who brought me back to Brooklyn. . . . *(He looks at wine, then draws it back and forth under his nose smelling it. He decides that it's all right apparently for he raises his glass—)* Doctor—to my dear dead brother—

(As they get the glasses to their lips, TEDDY *steps out on the balcony and blows a terrific call on his bugle.* EINSTEIN *and* JONATHAN *drop their glasses, spilling the wine.* TEDDY *turns and exits.)*

EINSTEIN. Ach Gott!

JONATHAN. Damn that idiot! *(He starts for stairs.* EINSTEIN *rushes over and intercepts him.)* He goes next! That's all—he goes next!

EINSTEIN. No, Chonny, not Teddy—that's where I shtop—not Teddy!

JONATHAN. We get to Teddy later!

EINSTEIN. We don't get to him at all.

JONATHAN. Now we've got to work fast! *(He crosses above to L. of* MORTIMER. EINSTEIN *in front of* MORTIMER.*)*

EINSTEIN. Yah, the quick way—eh, Chonny?

JONATHAN. Yes, Doctor, the quick way! *(He pulls a large silk handkerchief from his inside pocket and drops it around* MORTIMER'S *neck.)*

(At this point the door bursts open and OFFICER O'HARA *comes in to* C., *very excited.)*

O'HARA. Hey! The Colonel's gotta quit blowing that horn!

JONATHAN *(he and* EINSTEIN *are standing in front of* MORTIMER, *hiding him from* O'HARA*)*. It's all right, Officer. We're taking the bugle away from him.

O'HARA. There's going to be hell to pay in the morning. We promised the neighbors he wouldn't do that any more.

JONATHAN. It won't happen again, Officer. Good night.

O'HARA. I'd better speak to him myself. Where are the lights? *(*O'HARA *puts on lights and goes upstairs to landing, when he sees* MORTIMER.*)* Hey! You stood me up. I waited an hour at Kelly's for you. *(He comes downstairs and over to* MORTIMER *and looks at him then speaks to* JONATHAN *and* EINSTEIN.*)* What happened to him?

EINSTEIN *(thinking fast)*. He was explaining the play he saw tonight—that's what happened to the fella in the play.

O'HARA. Did they have that in the play you saw tonight? *(*MORTIMER *nods his head— yes.)* Gee, they practically stole that from the second act of my play—*(He starts to explain.)* Why, in my second act, just before the— *(He turns back to* MORTIMER.*)* I'd better begin at the beginning. It opens in my mother's dressing room where I was born—only I ain't born yet— *(*MORTIMER *rubs his shoes together to attract* O'HARA'S *attention.)* Huh? Oh, yeah. *(*O'HARA *starts to remove the gag from* MORTIMER'S *mouth and then decides not to.)* No! You've got to hear the plot. *(He gets stool and brings it to* R. *of* MORTIMER *and sits, continuing on with his "plot" as the curtain falls.)* Well, she's sitting there making up, see— when all of a sudden through the door— a man with a black mustache walks in— turns to my mother and says—"Miss La-tour, will you marry me?" He doesn't know she's pregnant.

CURTAIN

SCENE II

Scene is the same. Early the next morning. When the curtain rises again, daylight is streaming through the windows. All doors closed. All drapes open. Mortimer *is still tied in his chair and seems to be in a semi-conscious state.* Jonathan *is asleep on sofa.* Einstein, *pleasantly intoxicated, is seated* L. *of table, his head resting on table top.* O'Hara, *with his coat off and his collar loosened, is standing over the stool which is between him and* Mortimer. *He has progressed to the most exciting scene of his play. There is a bottle of whiskey and a water tumbler on the table along with a plate full of cigarette butts.*

o'HARA. —there she is lying unconscious across the table in her lingerie—the Chink is standing over her with a hatchet— *(He takes the pose.)* —I'm tied up in a chair just like you are—the place is an inferno of flames—it's on fire—when all of a sudden—through the window—in comes Mayor LaGuardia. *(*EINSTEIN *raises his head and looks out the window. Not seeing anyone he reaches for the bottle and pours himself another drink.* O'HARA *crosses above to him and takes the bottle.)* Hey, remember who paid for that—go easy on it.

EINSTEIN. Vell, I'm listening, ain't I? *(He crosses to* JONATHAN *on the sofa.)*

o'HARA. How do you like it so far?

EINSTEIN. Vell, it put Chonny to sleep.

*(*O'HARA *has just finished a swig from the bottle.)*

o'HARA. Let him alone. If he ain't got no more interest than that—he don't get a drink. *(*EINSTEIN *takes his glass and sits on bottom stair. At the same time* O'HARA *crosses, puts stool under desk and whiskey bottle on top of desk, then comes back to center and goes on with his play—)* All right. It's three days later—I been transferred and I'm under charges—that's because somebody stole my badge. (He pantomimes through following lines.)* All right. I'm walking my beat on Staten Island—forty-sixth precinct—when a guy I'm following, it turns out—is really following me. *(There is a knock on door.* EINSTEIN *goes up and looks out landing window. Leaves glass behind* D. S. *drape.)* Don't let anybody in.—So I figure I'll outsmart him. There's a vacant house on the corner. I goes in.

EINSTEIN. It's cops!

o'HARA. I stands there in the dark and I see the door handle turn.

EINSTEIN *(rushing downstairs, shakes* JONATHAN *by the shoulder.)* Chonny! It's cops! Cops! *(*JONATHAN *doesn't move.* EINSTEIN *rushes upstairs and off through the arch.)*

*(*O'HARA *is going on with his story without a stop.)*

o'HARA. I pulls my guns—braces myself against the wall—and I says—"Come in." *(*OFFICERS BROPHY *and* KLEIN *walk in* R., *see* O'HARA *with gun pointed at them and raise their hands. Then, recognizing their fellow officer, lower them.)* Hello, boys.

BROPHY. What the hell is going on here?

o'HARA *(goes to* BROPHY*).* Hey, Pat, whaddya know? This is Mortimer Brewster! He's going to write my play with me. I'm just tellin' him the story.

KLEIN *(crossing to* MORTIMER *and untying him).* Did you have to tie him up to make him listen?

BROPHY. Joe, you better report in at the station. The whole force is out looking for ya.

o'HARA. Did they send you here for me?

KLEIN. We didn't know you was here.

BROPHY. We came to warn the old ladies that there's hell to pay. The Colonel blew that bugle again in the middle of the night.

KLEIN. From the way the neighbors have been calling in about it you'd think the Germans had dropped a bomb on Flatbush Avenue.

(He has finished untying MORTIMER. *Puts cords on sideboard.)*

BROPHY. The Lieutenant's on the warpath. He says the Colonel's got to be put away some place.

MORTIMER *(staggers to feet).* Yes! Yes!

O'HARA *(going to* MORTIMER*).* Gee, Mr. Brewster, I got to get away, so I'll just run through the third act quick.

MORTIMER *(staggering* R.*).* Get away from me.

*(*BROPHY *gives* KLEIN *a look, goes to phone and dials.)*

KLEIN. Say, do you know what time it is? It's after eight o'clock in the morning.

O'HARA. It is? *(He follows* MORTIMER *to stairs.)* Gee, Mr. Brewster, them first two acts run a little long, but I don't see anything we can leave out.

MORTIMER *(almost to landing).* You can leave it *all* out.

*(*BROPHY *sees* JONATHAN *on sofa.)*

BROPHY. Who the hell is this guy?

MORTIMER *(hanging on railing, almost to balcony).* That's my brother.

BROPHY. Oh, the one that ran away? So he came back.

MORTIMER. Yes, he came back!

*(*JONATHAN *stirs as if to get up.)*

BROPHY *(into phone).* This is Brophy. Get me Mac. *(To* O'HARA, *sitting on bottom stair.)* I'd better let them know we found you, Joe. *(Into phone.)* Mac? Tell the Lieutenant he can call off the big manhunt —we got him. In the Brewster house. *(*JONATHAN *hears this and suddenly becomes very much awake, looking up to see* KLEIN *to* L. *of him and* BROPHY *to his* R.*)* Do you want us to bring him in? Oh —all right, we'll hold him right here. *(He hangs up.)* The Lieutenant's on his way over.

JONATHAN *(rising).* So I've been turned in, eh? *(*BROPHY *and* KLEIN *look at him with some interest.)* All right, you've got me! *(Turning to* MORTIMER, *who is on balcony looking down.)* And I suppose you and

that stool-pigeon brother of mine will split the reward?

KLEIN. Reward?

(Instinctively KLEIN *and* BROPHY *both grab* JONATHAN *by an arm.)*

JONATHAN *(dragging* COPS D. S. C.*).* Now I'll do some turning in! You think my aunts are sweet charming old ladies, don't you? Well, there are thirteen bodies buried in their cellar.

MORTIMER *(as he rushes off to see* TEDDY*).* Teddy! Teddy! Teddy!

KLEIN. What the hell are you talking about?

BROPHY. You'd better be careful what you're saying about your aunts—they happen to be friends of ours.

JONATHAN *(raving as he drags them toward the cellar door).* I'll show you! I'll prove it to you! You come to the cellar with me!

KLEIN. Wait a minute! Wait a minute!

JONATHAN. Thirteen bodies! I'll show you where they're buried.

KLEIN *(refusing to be kidded).* Oh, yeah?

JONATHAN. You don't want to see what's down in the cellar?

BROPY *(releases* JONATHAN's *arm, then to* KLEIN*).* Go on down in the cellar with him, Abe.

KLEIN *(drops* JONATHAN's *arm, backs* D. S. *a step and looks at him).* I'm not so sure I want to be down in the cellar with him. Look at that puss. He looks like Boris Karloff. *(*JONATHAN, *at mention of Karloff, grabs* KLEIN *by the throat, starts choking him.)* Hey—what the hell— Hey, Pat! Get him off me.

*(*BROPHY *takes out rubber blackjack.)*

BROPHY. Here, what do you think you're doing! *(He socks* JONATHAN *on head.* JONATHAN *falls unconscious, face down.)* *(*KLEIN, *throwing* JONATHAN's *weight to floor, backs away, rubbing his throat.)*

KLEIN. Well what do you know about that?

(There is a knock on door R.*)*

o'HARA. Come in.

(LIEUTENANT ROONEY *bursts in* R., *slamming door after him. He is a very tough, driving, dominating officer.*)

ROONEY. What the hell are you men doing here? I told you *I* was going to handle this.

KLEIN. Well, sir, we was just about to—(KLEIN's *eyes go to* JONATHAN *and* ROONEY *sees him.*)

ROONEY. What happened? Did he put up a fight?

BROPHY. This ain't the guy that blows the bugle. This is his brother. He tried to kill Klein.

KLEIN (*feeling his throat*). All I said was he looked like Boris Karloff.

ROONEY (*his face lights up*). Turn him over.

(*The two* COPS *turn* JONATHAN *over on his back.* KLEIN *steps back.* ROONEY *crosses front of* BROPHY *to take a look at* JONATHAN. BROPHY *drifts to* R. *of* ROONEY. o'HARA *is still at foot of stairs.*)

BROPHY. We kinda think he's wanted somewhere.

ROONEY. Oh, you kinda *think* he's wanted somewhere? If you guys don't look at the circulars we hang up in the station, at least you could read *True Detective.* Certainly he's wanted. In Indiana! Escaped from the prison for the Criminal Insane! He's a lifer. For God's sake that's how he was described—he *looked* like Karloff!

KLEIN. Was there a reward mentioned?

ROONEY. Yeah—and *I'm* claiming it.

BROPHY. He was trying to get us down in the cellar.

KLEIN. He said there was thirteen bodies buried down there.

ROONEY (*suspicious*). Thirteen bodies buried in the cellar? (*Deciding it's ridiculous.*) And that didn't tip you off he came out of a nut-house!

o'HARA. I thought all along he talked kinda crazy.

(ROONEY *sees* o'HARA *for the first time. Turns to him.*)

ROONEY. Oh, it's Shakespeare! (*Crossing to him.*) Where have you been all night? And you needn't bother to tell me.

o'HARA. I've been right here, sir. Writing a play with Mortimer Brewster.

ROONEY (*tough*). Yeah? Well, you're gonna have plenty of time to write that play. You're suspended! Now get back and report in!

(o'HARA *takes his coat, night stick, and cap from top of desk. Goes to* R. *door and opens it. Then turns to* ROONEY.)

o'HARA. Can I come over sometime and use the station typewriter?

ROONEY. No!—Get out of here. (o'HARA *runs out.* ROONEY *closes door and turns to the* COPS. TEDDY *enters on balcony and comes downstairs unnoticed and stands at* ROONEY's *back to the* R. *of him.* ROONEY, *to* COPS.) Take that guy somewhere else and bring him to. (*The* COPS *bend down to pick up* JONATHAN.) See what you can find out about his accomplice. (*The* COPS *stand up again in a questioning attitude.* ROONEY *explains.*) The guy that helped him escape. He's wanted too. No wonder Brooklyn's in the shape it's in, with the police force full of flatheads like you—falling for that kind of a story—thirteen bodies in the cellar!

TEDDY. But there are thirteen bodies in the cellar.

ROONEY (*turning on him*). Who are you?

TEDDY. I'm President Roosevelt.

(ROONEY *does a walk* U. S. *on this, then comes down again.*)

ROONEY. What the hell is this?

BROPHY. He's the fellow that blows the bugle.

KLEIN. Good morning, Colonel.

(*They salute* TEDDY, *who returns it.* ROONEY *finds himself saluting* TEDDY *also. He pulls his hand down in disgust.*)

ROONEY. Well, Colonel, you've blown your last bugle.

TEDDY (*seeing* JONATHAN *on floor*). Dear me—another Yellow Fever victim?

ROONEY. What-at?

TEDDY. All the bodies in the cellar are Yellow Fever victims.

(ROONEY *crosses exasperatedly to* R. *door on this.*)

BROPHY. No, Colonel, this is a spy we caught in the White House.

ROONEY (*pointing to* JONATHAN). Will you get that guy out of here!

(COPS *pick up* JONATHAN *and drag him to kitchen.* TEDDY *follows them.* MORTIMER *enters, comes down stairs.*)

TEDDY (*turning back to* ROONEY). If there's any questioning of spies, that's my department!

ROONEY. You keep out of this!

TEDDY. You're forgetting! As President, I am also head of the Secret Service.

(BROPHY *and* KLEIN *exit with* JONATHAN *into kitchen.* TEDDY *follows them briskly.* MORTIMER *has come to* C.)

MORTIMER. Captain—I'm Mortimer Brewster.

ROONEY. Are you sure?

MORTIMER. I'd like to talk to you about my brother Teddy—the one who blew the bugle.

ROONEY. Mr. Brewster, we ain't going to talk about that—he's got to be put away!

MORTIMER. I quite agree with you. In fact, it's all arranged for. I had these commitment papers signed by Dr. Gilchrist, our family physician. Teddy has signed them himself, you see—and I've signed them as next of kin.

ROONEY. Where's he going?

MORTIMER. Happy Dale.

ROONEY. All right, I don't care where he goes as long as he goes!

MORTIMER. Oh, he's going all right. But I want you to know that everything that's happened around here Teddy's responsible for. Now, those thirteen bodies in the cellar—

ROONEY (*he's had enough of those thirteen*). Yeah—yeah—those thirteen bodies in the cellar! It ain't enough that the neighbors are all afraid of him, and his

disturbing the peace with that bugle—but can you imagine what would happen if that cock-eyed story about thirteen bodies in the cellar got around? And now he's starting a Yellow Fever scare. Cute, ain't it?

MORTIMER (*greatly relieved, with an embarrassed laugh*). Thirteen bodies. Do you think anybody would believe that story?

ROONEY. Well, you can't tell. Some people are just dumb enough. You don't know what to believe sometimes. About a year ago a crazy guy starts a murder rumor over in Greenpoint, and I had to dig up a half acre lot, just to prove that—

(*There is a knock on* R. *door.*)

MORTIMER. Will you excuse me? (*He goes to door and admits* ELAINE *and* MR. WITHERSPOON, *an elderly, tight-lipped disciplinarian. He is carrying a brief case.*)

ELAINE (*briskly*). Good morning, Mortimer.

MORTIMER (*not knowing what to expect*). Good morning, dear.

ELAINE. This is Mr. Witherspoon. He's come to meet Teddy.

MORTIMER. To meet Teddy?

ELAINE. Mr. Witherspoon's the superintendent of Happy Dale.

MORTIMER (*eagerly*). Oh, come right in. (*They shake hands.* MORTIMER *indicates* ROONEY.) This is Captain—

ROONEY. *Lieutenant* Rooney. I'm glad you're here, Super, because you're taking him back with you today!

WITHERSPOON. Today? I didn't know that—

ELAINE (*cutting in*). Not today!

MORTIMER. Look, Elaine, I've got a lot of business to attend to, so you run along home and I'll call you up.

ELAINE. Nuts! (*She crosses to window-seat and sits.*)

WITHERSPOON. I had no idea it was this immediate.

ROONEY. The papers are all signed, he goes today!

(TEDDY *backs into room from kitchen, speaking sharply in the direction whence he's come.*)

TEDDY. Complete insubordination! You men will find out I'm no mollycoddle. (*He slams door and comes down to below table.*) When the President of the United States is treated like that—what's this country coming to?

ROONEY. There's your man, Super.

MORTIMER. Just a minute! (*He crosses to* TEDDY *and speaks to him as to a child.*) Mr. President, I have very good news for you. Your term of office is over.

TEDDY. Is this March the Fourth?

MORTIMER. Practically.

TEDDY (*thinking*). Let's see—OH!—Now I go on my hunting trip to Africa! Well, I must get started immediately. (*He starts across the room and almost bumps into* WITHERSPOON *at* C. *He looks at him then steps back to* MORTIMER.) Is he trying to move into the White House before I've moved out?

MORTIMER. Who, Teddy?

TEDDY (*indicating* WITHERSPOON). Taft!

MORTIMER. This isn't Mr. Taft, Teddy. This is Mr. Witherspoon—he's to be your guide in Africa.

TEDDY (*shakes hands with* WITHERSPOON *enthusiastically*). Bully! Bully! I'll bring down my equipment. (*He crosses to stairs.* MARTHA *and* ABBY *have entered on balcony during last speech and are coming downstairs.*) When the safari comes, tell them to wait. (*As he passes the* AUNTS *on his way to landing, he shakes hands with each, without stopping his walk.*) Good-bye, Aunt Abby. Good-bye, Aunt Martha. I'm on my way to Africa—isn't it wonderful? (*He has reached the landing.*) CHARGE!

(*He charges up the stairs and off.*)

(*The* AUNTS *are at foot of stairs.*)

MORTIMER (*crossing to aunts*). Good morning, darlings.

MARTHA. Oh, we have visitors.

MORTIMER (*he indicates* ROONEY *at* C.). This is Lieutenant Rooney.

ABBY (*crossing, shakes hands with him*). How do you do, Lieutenant? My, you don't look like the fussbudget the policemen say you are.

MORTIMER. Why the Lieutenant is here— You know, Teddy blew his bugle again last night.

MARTHA. Yes, we're going to speak to Teddy about that.

ROONEY. It's a little more serious than that, Miss Brewster.

MORTIMER (*easing* AUNTS *to* WITHERSPOON *who is above table where he has opened his brief case and extracted some papers*). And you haven't met Mr. Witherspoon. He's the Superintendent of Happy Dale.

ABBY. Oh, Mr. Witherspoon—how do you do?

MARTHA. You've come to meet Teddy.

ROONEY (*somewhat harshly*). He's come to take him.

(*The* AUNTS *turn to* ROONEY *questioningly.*)

MORTIMER (*making it as easy as possible*). Aunties—the police want Teddy to go there, today.

ABBY (*crossing to* R. *of chair*). Oh—no!

MARTHA (*behind* ABBY). Not while we're alive!

ROONEY. I'm sorry, Miss Brewster, but it has to be done. The papers are all signed and he's going along with the Superintendent.

ABBY. We won't permit it. We'll promise to take the bugle away from him.

MARTHA. We won't be separated from Teddy.

ROONEY. I'm sorry, ladies, but the law's the law! He's committed himself and he's going!

ABBY. Well, if he goes, we're going too.

MARTHA. Yes, you'll have to take us with him.

MORTIMER (*has an idea. Crosses to* WITHERSPOON). Well, why not?

WITHERSPOON (*to* MORTIMER). Well, that's sweet of them to want to, but it's impossible. You see, we can't take *sane* people at Happy Dale.

MARTHA (*turning to* WITHERSPOON). Mr. Witherspoon, if you'll let us live there with Teddy, we'll see that Happy Dale is in our will—and for a very generous amount.

WITHERSPOON. Well, the Lord knows we could use the money, but—I'm afraid—

ROONEY. Now let's be sensible about this, ladies. For instance, here I am wasting my morning when I've got serious work to do. You know there are still *murders* to be solved in Brooklyn.

MORTIMER. Yes! (*Covering.*) Oh, are there?

ROONEY. It ain't only his bugle blowing and the neighbors all afraid of him, but things would just get worse. Sooner or later we'd be put to the trouble of digging up your cellar.

ABBY. Our cellar?

ROONEY. Yeah.—Your nephew's been telling around that there are thirteen bodies in your cellar.

ABBY. But there are thirteen bodies in our cellar.

(ROONEY *looks disgusted.* MORTIMER *drifts quietly to front of cellar door.*)

MARTHA. If that's why you think Teddy has to go away—you come down to the cellar with us and we'll prove it to you. (*Goes* U. S.)

ABBY. There's one—Mr. Spenalzo—who doesn't belong here and who will have to leave—but the other twelve are our gentlemen. (*She starts* U. S.)

MORTIMER. I don't think the Lieutenant wants to go down in the cellar. He was telling me that only last year he had to dig up a half-acre lot—weren't you, Lieutenant?

ROONEY. That's right.

ABBY (*to* ROONEY). Oh, you wouldn't have to dig here. The graves are all marked. We put flowers on them every Sunday.

ROONEY. Flowers? (*He steps up toward* ABBY, *then turns to* WITHERSPOON, *indicating the* AUNTS *as he speaks.*) Superintendent—don't you think you can find room for these ladies?

WITHERSPOON. Well, I—

ABBY (*to* ROONEY). You come along with us, and we'll show you the graves.

ROONEY. I'll take your word for it, lady— I'm a busy man. How about it, Super?

WITHERSPOON. Well, they'd have to be committed.

MORTIMER. Teddy committed himself. Can't they commit themselves? Can't they sign the papers?

WITHERSPOON. Why, certainly.

MARTHA (*sits in chair* L. *of table as* WITHERSPOON *draws it out for her*). Oh, if we can go with Teddy, we'll sign the papers. Where are they?

ABBY (*sitting* R. *of table.* MORTIMER *helps her with chair*). Yes, where are they?

(WITHERSPOON *opens brief case for more papers.* KLEIN *enters from kitchen.*)

KLEIN. He's coming around, Lieutenant.

ABBY. Good morning, Mr. Klein.

MARTHA. Good morning, Mr. Klein. Are you here too?

KLEIN. Yeah. Brophy and me have got your other nephew out in the kitchen.

ROONEY. Well, sign 'em up, Superintendent. I want to get this all cleaned up. (*He crosses to kitchen door, shaking his head as he exits and saying:*) Thirteen bodies.

(KLEIN *follows him out.* MORTIMER *is to the* L. *of* ABBY, *fountain pen in hand.* WITHERSPOON *to* R. *of* MARTHA, *also with pen.*)

WITHERSPOON (*handing* MARTHA *pen*). If you'll sign right here.

(MARTHA *signs.*)

MORTIMER. And you here, Aunt Abby.

(ABBY *signs.*)

ABBY (*signing*). I'm really looking forward to going—the neighborhood here has changed so.

MARTHA. Just think, a front lawn again.

(EINSTEIN *enters through arch and comes down stairs to door* D. R. *carrying suitcase. He picks hat from hall tree on way down.*)

WITHERSPOON. Oh, we're overlooking something.

MARTHA. What?

WITHERSPOON. Well, we're going to need the signature of a doctor.

MORTIMER. Oh! *(He sees* EINSTEIN *about to disappear through the door.)* Dr. Einstein! Will you come over here—we'd like you to sign some papers.

EINSTEIN. Please, I must—

MORTIMER *(crosses to him).* Just come right over, Doctor. At one time last night, I thought the Doctor was going to operate on me. *(*EINSTEIN *puts down suitcase and his hat just inside the door.)* Just come right over, Doctor. *(*EINSTEIN *crosses to table,* L. *of* ABBY.*)* Just sign right here, Doctor.

(The DOCTOR *signs* ABBY's *paper and* MARTHA's *paper.* ROONEY *and* KLEIN *enter from kitchen.* ROONEY *crosses to desk and dials phone.* KLEIN *stands near kitchen door.)*

ABBY. Were you leaving, Doctor?

EINSTEIN *(signing papers).* I think I must go.

MARTHA. Aren't you going to wait for Jonathan?

EINSTEIN. I don't think we're going to the same place.

*(*MORTIMER *sees* ELAINE *on window-seat and crosses to her.)*

MORTIMER. Hello, Elaine. I'm glad to see you. Stick around, huh?

ELAINE. Don't worry, I'm going to.

*(*MORTIMER *stands back of* MARTHA's *chair.* ROONEY *speaks into phone.)*

ROONEY. Hello, Mac. Rooney. We've picked up that guy that's wanted in Indiana. Now there's a description of his accomplice—it's right on the desk there—read it to me. *(*EINSTEIN *sees* ROONEY *at phone. He starts toward kitchen and sees* KLEIN *standing there. He comes back to* R. *of table and stands there dejectedly waiting for the pinch.* ROONEY *repeats the description given him over phone, looking blankly at* EINSTEIN *the while.)* Yeah—about fifty-four—five foot six—hundred and forty pounds—blue eyes—talks with a German accent. Poses as a doctor. Thanks, Mac. *(He hangs up as* WITHERSPOON *crosses to him with papers in hand.)*

WITHERSPOON. It's all right, Lieutenant. The Doctor here has just completed the signatures.

*(*ROONEY *goes to* EINSTEIN *and shakes his hand.)*

ROONEY. Thanks, Doc. You're really doing Brooklyn a service.

*(*ROONEY *and* KLEIN *exit to kitchen.)*

*(*EINSTEIN *stands amazed for a moment then grabs up his hat and suitcase and disappears through* R. *door. The* AUNTS *rise and cross over, looking out after him.* ABBY *shuts the door and they stand there* D. R.*)*

WITHERSPOON *(above table).* Mr. Brewster, you sign now as next of kin.

(The AUNTS *whisper to each other as* MORTIMER *signs.)*

MORTIMER. Yes, of course. Right here?

WITHERSPOON. That's fine.

MORTIMER. That makes everything complete—everything legal?

WITHERSPOON. Oh, yes.

MORTIMER *(with relief).* Well, Aunties, now you're safe.

WITHERSPOON *(to* AUNTS*).* When do you think you'll be ready to start?

ABBY *(stepping* L.*).* Well, Mr. Witherspoon, why don't you go upstairs and tell Teddy just what he can take along?

WITHERSPOON. Upstairs?

MORTIMER. I'll show you.

ABBY *(stopping him).* No, Mortimer, you stay here. We want to talk to you. *(To* WITHERSPOON.*)* Yes, Mr. Witherspoon, just upstairs and turn to the left.

*(*WITHERSPOON *puts his brief case on sofa and goes upstairs, the* AUNTS *keeping an eye on him while talking to* MORTIMER.*)*

MARTHA. Well, Mortimer, now that we're moving, this house really is yours.

ABBY. Yes, dear, we want you to live here now.

MORTIMER *(below table).* No, Aunt Abby, this house is too full of memories.

MARTHA. But you'll need a home when you and Elaine are married.

MORTIMER. Darlings, that's very indefinite.

ELAINE (*rises and crosses to L. of MORTIMER*). It's nothing of the kind—we're going to be married right away.

(WITHERSPOON *has exited off balcony.*)

ABBY. Mortimer—Mortimer, we're really very worried about something.

MORTIMER. Now, darlings, you're going to love it at Happy Dale.

MARTHA. Oh, yes, we're very happy about the whole thing. That's just it—we don't want anything to go wrong.

ABBY. Will they investigate those signatures?

MORTIMER. Don't worry, they're not going to look up Dr. Einstein.

MARTHA. It's not his signature, dear, it's yours.

ABBY. You see, you signed as next of kin.

MORTIMER. Of course. Why not?

MARTHA. Well, dear, it's something we never wanted to tell you. But now you're a man—and it's something Elaine should know too. You see, dear—you're not really a Brewster.

(MORTIMER *stares as does* ELAINE.)

ABBY. Your mother came to us as a cook —and you were born about three months afterward. But she was such a sweet woman—and such a good cook we didn't want to lose her—so brother married her.

MORTIMER. I'm—not—really—a—Brewster?

MARTHA. Now, don't feel badly about it, dear.

ABBY. And Elaine, it won't make any difference to you?

MORTIMER (*turning slowly to face* ELAINE. *His voice rising*). Elaine! Did you hear? Do you understand? I'm a bastard!

(ELAINE *leaps into his arms. The two* AUNTS *watch them, then* MARTHA *starts U. L. a few steps.*)

MARTHA. Well, now I really must see about breakfast.

ELAINE (*leading* MORTIMER *to R. door; opening door*). Mortimer's coming over to my house. Father's gone to Philadelphia, and Mortimer and I are going to have breakfast together.

MORTIMER. Yes, I need some coffee—I've had quite a night.

ABBY. In that case I should think you'd want to get to bed.

MORTIMER (*with a sidelong glance at* ELAINE). I do. (*They exit* R., *closing door.*)

(WITHERSPOON *enters on balcony, carrying two canteens. He starts downstairs when* TEDDY *enters carrying large canoe paddle. He is dressed in Panama outfit with pack on his back.*)

TEDDY. One moment, Witherspoon. Take this with you! (*He exits off balcony again as* WITHERSPOON *comes on downstairs to sofa. He puts canteens on sofa and leans paddle against wall.*)

(*At the same time* ROONEY *and the two cops with* JONATHAN *between them enter. The* COPS *have twisters around* JONATHAN'S *wrists.* ROONEY *enters first and crosses to* R. C. *The other three stop* D. L. *of table. The* AUNTS *are* R. *of the table.*)

ROONEY. We won't need the wagon. My car's out front.

MARTHA. Oh, you leaving now, Jonathan?

ROONEY. Yeah—he's going back to Indiana. There's some people there want to take care of him for the rest of his life. Come on.

(ROONEY *opens door as the two* COPS *and* JONATHAN *cross to* R. C. ABBY *steps* D. S. *after they pass.*)

ABBY. Well, Jonathan, it's nice to know you have some place to go.

MARTHA. We're leaving too.

ABBY. Yes, we're going to Happy Dale.

JONATHAN. Then this house is seeing the last of the Brewsters.

MARTHA. Unless Mortimer wants to live here.

JONATHAN. I have a suggestion to make. Why don't you turn this property over to the church?

ABBY. Well, we never thought of that.

JONATHAN. After all, it *should* be part of the cemetery.

ROONEY. All right, get going, I'm a busy man.

JONATHAN *(holding his ground for his one last word)*. Good-bye, Aunties. Well, I can't better my record now but neither can you—at least I have that satisfaction. The score stands even, *twelve* to *twelve.*

(JONATHAN and the COPS exit R., as the AUNTS look out after them.)

(WITHERSPOON crosses above to window-seat and stands quietly looking out the window. His back is to the AUNTS.)

MARTHA *(starting toward R. door to close it)*. Jonathan always was a mean boy. Never could stand to see anyone get ahead of him. *(She closes door.)*

ABBY *(turning slowly around L. as she speaks)*. I wish we could show him he isn't so smart! *(Her eyes fall on WITHERSPOON. She studies him. MARTHA turns from door and sees ABBY's contemplation. ABBY speaks sweetly.)* Mr. Witherspoon? *(WITHERSPOON turns around facing them.)* Does your family live with you at Happy Dale?

WITHERSPOON. I have no family.

ABBY. Oh—

MARTHA *(stepping into room)*. Well, I suppose you consider everyone at Happy Dale your family?

WITHERSPOON. I'm afraid you don't quite understand. As head of the institution, I have to keep quite aloof.

ABBY. That must make it very lonely for you.

WITHERSPOON. It does. But my duty is my duty.

ABBY *(turning to MARTHA)*. Well, Martha— *(MARTHA takes her cue and goes to sideboard for bottle of wine. Bottle in L. cupboard is empty. She puts it back and takes out full bottle from R. cupboard. She brings bottle and wine-glass to table. ABBY continues talking.)* If Mr. Witherspoon won't join us for breakfast, I think at least we should offer him a glass of elderberry wine.

WITHERSPOON *(severely)*. Elderberry wine?

MARTHA. We make it ourselves.

WITHERSPOON *(melting slightly)*. Why, yes . . . *(Severely again.)* Of course, at Happy Dale our relationship will be more formal—but here— *(He sits in chair L. of table as MARTHA pours wine. ABBY is beside MARTHA.)* You don't see much elderberry wine nowadays—I thought I'd had my last glass of it.

ABBY. Oh, no—

MARTHA *(handing him glass of wine)*. No, here it is.

(WITHERSPOON toasts the ladies and lifts glass to his lips, but the curtain falls before he does. . . .)

CURTAIN

THE HASTY HEART

By JOHN PATRICK

THE HASTY HEART was first produced by Howard Lindsay and Russel Crouse at the Hudson Theatre, New York City, on January 3, 1945. The play was staged by Bretaigne Windust; setting by Raymond Sovey. The cast was as follows:

ORDERLY	Francis Nielsen	TOMMY	Douglas Chandler
YANK	John Lund	MARGARET	Anne Burr
DIGGER	John Campbell	COLONEL	J. Colville Dunn
KIWI	Victor Chapin	LACHLEN	Richard Basehart
BLOSSOM	Earl Jones		

SCENES

The entire action takes place in a convalescent ward of a British general hospital in the rear of the Assam-Burma front.

ACT I: Early morning.

ACT II: Scene 1. Two weeks later.

Scene 2. A few nights later.

ACT III: Scene 1. The next day.

Scene 2. The following morning.

THE AUTHOR

John Patrick, who was born May 17, 1907, is a native of Carmel, California, which is also the home of Robinson Jeffers and as dramatic a setting as any high-minded playwright could want for his nativity. He attended Holy Cross in New Orleans, Columbia University, and Harvard Summer School, where he started writing his Mary Surratt tragedy This Gentle Ghost, *which is at last slated for production in 1947. On the fringes of the theatre Mr. Patrick provided radio scripts for Helen Hayes, and also served as a screenwriter, becoming responsible for one Charlie Chan picture. His first play* Hell Freezes Over *was produced in December 1935 with Louis Calhern and Myron McCormick in the cast. His second play* The Willow and I, *which opened in December, 1942 with a cast that included Gregory Peck and Barbara O'Neill, also failed to win public support. Nevertheless, it attracted attention as one of the decidedly better written and more sensitive pieces that reach Broadway.*

The war found Mr. Patrick deeply involved. He became a captain in the American Field Service and served with General Montgomery's 8th Army unit. The Hasty Heart *was obviously inspired by its author's observations in the line of duty. It reflects his sympathy with people and faith in the brotherhood of man, as well as his inclination for sobering themes. The play opened at the Hudson Theatre on January 3, 1945 under the auspices of Howard Lindsay and Russel Crouse, and won instant respect. It was subsequently produced in England.*

THE HASTY HEART

ACT ONE

SCENE: *The interior of a convalescent ward in a temporary British general hospital somewhere to the rear of the Assam-Burma front.*

The hut used for this small ward is a native basha *made of bamboo poles, bamboo matting, mud and grass.*

The entrance to the ward is through a crude door of bamboo matting downstage left. A smaller door, center, leads to the Sister's office. Another door, to the right, leads into the washroom.

There is a side window, to the right, looking off past the washroom and two larger windows in the back wall, one on each side of the Sister's office. All the windows have large overlapping bamboo shutters hung on the outside and supported by a bamboo pole. When open, the brilliant tropical sunlight spills in. The horizon is shut off by the green tapestry of the jungle, with its tight clumps of bamboo and its banyan trees whose shaggy roots dangle from the branches in search of the earth again.

There are six hospital beds, with their heads against the back wall of the hut—three on each side of the entrance to the Sister's office. Each bed has a small kit-table beside it. Despite the bareness of the setting, the ward is bright with colors that give it instant cheer and warmth. The beds are covered with bright-red blankets. The men in the ward wear white pajamas or the regulation vivid blue trousers and jackets which identify the up-patients.

At the rise of the curtain, it is morning and the ward is in darkness. A blue night lantern glows overhead, vaguely outlining the white mosquito nets that drape down over each occupied bed. The third bed from the right is unoccupied.

A young British orderly enters from the left, carrying a flashlight which he directs at each bed as he passes to open the side window on the right. The sun pours into the darkened ward. The sound of tropical birds can be heard in the jungle.

ORDERLY (*crossing to the upstage window between the first and second beds*). Wake up! Wake up! (*No one stirs. He pushes the window out with a bamboo pole and braces it against the side of the* basha. *He shouts louder.*) Wake up! (*And no one stirs. As he comes down between the two beds, he jerks the mosquito nets out from under the foot of both mattresses. There is no movement from under the nets. He crosses to the center and, lowering the night-light, blows it out.*) Wake up! Rise and shine! (*He stops at the fourth bed and gives it a violent shake.*) Yank! Wake up! (*The* ORDERLY *knows from daily experience that only loudness and persistence will wake the patients. He shakes the bed again and pulls the mosquito net out from under the end of the bed.*) Hurry on—get up!

(YANK *sticks a tousled blond head from under the net—and sleepily rubs the back of his neck.* YANK *is in his late twenties, more wholesome than handsome, with a manner more relaxed than lazy. He suffers* a slight speech impediment which he overcomes by snapping his fingers or hitting his fist into his palm. He sits up in bed with the mosquito net draped behind him.*)

YANK. Why d-d-d— (*He snaps his fingers.*) —don't you d-d-d— (*He slaps the side of his bed.*) —drop dead?

ORDERLY (*indifferently*). Get washed and get your kit together. All patients are going to be evacuated.

YANK. B-b-buster—you're not very funny. (*He puts his slippers on, rises, and sleepily starts to roll his net and tie it above his bed.*)

ORDERLY. At least it wakes you blokes up in a hurry. (*He crosses to the fifth and sixth beds, pulling their nets out as he goes up between them to open the last window.*)

YANK. Try and think up something d-d-different tomorrow. Evacuated. Ha—ha—

513

(Ending in a most satisfactory yawn.)
Haw.

ORDERLY *(shaking the fifth and sixth beds).*
Come on—come on. The hospital's burning down. The monsoons have started.
There's an air raid. There's an earthquake.
*(Without waiting to see the result of his
efforts, he crosses the ward to enter the
washroom at the right, pleading as he
goes.)* For Gawd's sake—wake up. I'm
half an hour late. *(He goes out.)*

(The DIGGER, *who occupies the sixth bed,
sits up and appears slowly from under his
mosquito net. He blinks blearily at* YANK.
DIGGER *is a dark Australian of about thirty,
with an eagerness and animal grace that
will give him a youthful quality when he
is sixty. He is chunky and muscular, and
the boxing champion of his regiment.)*

DIGGER. Ah—to be woke with a kiss and
a kind word.

YANK. Or a c-c-cup of coffee.

DIGGER. Gawd, I'm sleepy. I don't think
I've ever been woke in my life ready to
get up. *(DIGGER is a lying-patient, so* YANK
*crosses to his bed to roll up his mosquito
net for him.)*

YANK. I never can s-s-see in the morning.
At home, I'm always going into the bathroom and throwing my cigarette b-b-butt
in the hamper and flushing my sox down
the toilet. I lose more d-d-damn sox.
(Looking toward the next bed.) Was that
Tommy s-s-snoring again?

DIGGER. He's got add-anoids.

YANK. Sounded exactly like the m-m-mat-
ing call of the hippo-p-p-potamus.

(The ORDERLY *returns carrying two pans
of warm water. He places one on the stand
beside* DIGGER's *bed as* YANK *finishes the
net.)*

ORDERLY *(to the ward).* You up-patients—
into the washroom. Come out of it. Come
out of it! I'm off duty in ten minutes. I
want to get my sleep before it gets hot.
*(He places the other pan of water beside
the next bed.)* Yank, get Kiwi up.

YANK *(crossing the ward to the second
bed.)* It's a g-g-great mistake to get well
in an army hospital. *(As the* ORDERLY *goes
back into the washroom.)* Wake up, Kiwi.
The b-birds have been up eating worms

for hours. *(YANK pulls the net back and
helps* KIWI *to sit up. The* KIWI *is a tall
New Zealander, well over six feet. His
blond hair has been bleached by the sun
and is a lighter shade than his tanned skin.
His left arm is in a plaster cast held in the
air by a reticulated wire support braced
against his hip. He is in his middle twenties.)*

KIWI *(as* YANK *starts rolling up his net
for him).* I wish somebody would do
something about Tommy snoring. *(He
stretches—and his long legs protrude from
under the blankets at the end of his bed.)*

YANK. D-d-don't look now, but I think
somebody's in b-b-bed with you.

KIWI *(looking down at his feet).* Either
this bed gets smaller or I'm growing again.

YANK. Send your feet to the army laundry
—they'll shrink anything.

(DIGGER is brushing his teeth as the OR-
DERLY *enters with a third pan of water
and places it on* KIWI's *bed-table. He turns
around and pulls out the net from the
foot of the first bed.)*

ORDERLY. Get up—get up. I'll put a cobra
in with you. *(He crosses toward the entrance door.)* Sister will be here in a
minute and you're supposed to be up. *(He
exits.* YANK *finishes* KIWI's *net and crosses
around to the next bed.)*

YANK. Time to get up, B-b-blossom. *(He
bangs on the mattress. The mosquito net
lifts and the black head of a tremendous
BASUTO appears. He has large puffed lips
and a bullet-shaped cranium. He looks up
at* YANK.) Up—Blossom! Understand?

BASUTO *(blinks, smiles, and points at himself).* Blos-som!

YANK. Th-th-that's your name. Blossom—
we hope.

*(BLOSSOM rises, goes into the washroom.
At this point he is the only other up-
patient. He puts on his blues in the washroom. A lusty snore is now heard from
under* TOMMY's *net. All the men shout.)*

DIGGER. Drown it! ⎫
YANK. Quiet!   ⎬ *Together*
KIWI. Let 'im have it! ⎭

KIWI. Pull his mattress out from under
him, Digger.

DIGGER (*leans over to the bed beside him and shakes it*). Wake up, me chubby love. (*He shakes the bed violently.*) Wake up, ya mountain of flesh.

(TOMMY *lifts his net and looks out. He is short and exceedingly fat. His close-cropped hair sticks straight up over a beaming red face. He affects a look of gleeful idiocy.*)

TOMMY (*not quite awake*). 'As something 'appened?

DIGGER. Yes—ya died. It's Judgment Day. St. Peter's a brigadier, so snap your wings to attention.

TOMMY (*blinks a few times*). Somebody snores in 'ere.

YANK (*as he rolls up* TOMMY's *net*). How can you make so much noise in your sleep without waking yourself up?

TOMMY (*as he washes himself, sitting up in bed*). Oh, dear, oh, dear. Wot a terrible dream I 'ad. I dreamed I was working. I was killing meself working. I'm that tired I can 'ardly lift a finger. (*He lifts a finger and finds the effort exhausting. He looks around and laughs. He has a high almost girlish giggle which he uses at every comment he makes.* DIGGER *looks over at him.*)

DIGGER. Look at him. I've seen 'em fat but I've never seen a man like that. Aren't ya uncomfortable?

TOMMY. It's only muscles you see. I've just relaxed 'em a bit.

YANK. Relax 'em any more and you'll t-t-trip over 'em.

TOMMY. Me old lady loves every sweet ounce of me.

(BLOSSOM *enters from the washroom in his blues as the* ORDERLY *enters from the opposite side carrying a stack of mugs and a steaming bucket.*)

ORDERLY. Yank—pass the mugs around.

(YANK *takes the tin mugs and puts one at the foot of each bed.*)

TOMMY. Ah, me tea. (*With exaggerated English accent.*) Bring mah mah tea, waitah. Do you heah mah!

DIGGER. You're a bloody fool if ever I saw one.

ORDERLY (*to* BASUTO). What do you think this is—a ruddy health resort? Up-patients work. (*He puts the pail of tea into* BASUTO's *hand and motions him to go to each bed and fill each mug.*) On with it—on with it—make haste. (*He then goes off to bring in breakfast.*)

DIGGER. Gawd, I hope we don't get soy-link sausage.

KIWI. I'll bet pounds to piasters we do.

BASUTO (*pouring tea at* KIWI's *bed*). Blossom.

TOMMY. 'E's smart 'e is. Look 'ow quick 'e catches on. Only took 'im a week to learn one word.

(*The* BASUTO *pours* TOMMY's *tea—then turns and pours* DIGGER's.)

DIGGER. Clever, ain't he? Yank, why don't you teach him two words? Then he could be an officer. (*Smiling, he looks up at the black African.*) Thank ya, Blossom, ya bloody cannibal.

KIWI. Those Basutos are good fighters. I was with a company in the desert. You know, they let a whole year pass without drawing a cent of their pay.

YANK. Are they ash-ashamed of it?

KIWI. No, they let it pile up. Then after the war, they'll go back to Basutoland and buy themselves a wife and a herd of oxen.

TOMMY. More likely—an ox and a 'erd of wives. (*He laughs gayly at his* bon mot.)

DIGGER (*indulgently*). Oh, ya fat fool.

TOMMY. 'E's jealous of me wit.

(BLOSSOM *comes back and pours his own tea as the* ORDERLY *enters with a tray of tin plates. He distributes them to* DIGGER, TOMMY, YANK, KIWI *and* BLOSSOM.)

DIGGER (*to* ORDERLY). This tea tastes like a baby's been boiled in it.

ORDERLY. Don't complain to me; complain to Sister. (*Crosses to give* YANK *his plate.*)

YANK. I'll write my Congressman—whose name, I think, is Mabel.

DIGGER (*looking into his plate*). Gawd, soy-link! They do everything with a soy bean but make it taste like food.

(*The orderly distributes the rest, picks up*

the bucket and carries it and the tray out.
TOMMY *sips loudly on his tea.)*

YANK. He even s-snores when he eats. *(He looks over at* KIWI, *who has a little difficulty eating with one arm.)* Need any help, Kiwi?

KIWI *(shakes his head).* The Medical Officer said he'd chisel me out of this derrick next week.

DIGGER *(gleefully).* Ha! You'll be in it a year.

TOMMY. You was bad shot up when you come in 'ere. *(Giggles.)* I'd say two years.

KIWI *(as he eats).* Nope—a man takes a lot of killing. You shoot an animal and it dies. You shoot a man, and if there's only part of him left, he gets well. He takes a lot of killing.

TOMMY *(profound agreement).* You're right. 'E takes a lot of bloody bleeding.

DIGGER. You wouldn't know, ya chronic menace. You was only wounded by a sand-fly.

TOMMY. Will someone please tell 'im about me bravery—or must I tell 'im meself?

KIWI. Where were you when you were wounded, Tommy?

TOMMY. Asleep. *(He shrieks with laughter.)*

DIGGER. Oh, what a hero he is!

TOMMY. Peacefully sleeping I was, and a 'ot bit of shrapnel entered me tender flesh.

YANK. Where?

TOMMY. Well, I was sleeping on me stomach. *(He giggles.)*

DIGGER. The M.O. must have probed up to his elbows.

TOMMY. I wrote me old lady I was wounded leading me regiment into battle.

YANK *(rises and crosses to put his plate and mug on* BLOSSOM'S, *whose job it is to collect them. He indicates the empty bed as he passes).* Wonder who we'll get in here next?

KIWI. Probably a Canadian. The RCAF moved in up the road, Sister said.

DIGGER. We haven't had a Yorkshireman yet.

KIWI. Who wants to bet? I'll bet anyone pounds to piasters we get an Irishman. Any bets?

TOMMY. We 'aven't 'ad a Scot in 'ere for a long time.

YANK. God, I hope we don't get a Scot. *(Starts pulling his blues over his pajamas.)*

DIGGER. Don't ya get along with Scots?

YANK. I do not. And I d-d-don't know anyone who d-d-does. Except another Scot.

KIWI. Sister's a Scot.

YANK. Oh, n-no, she isn't.

DIGGER. She's bloody fine, whatever she is.

TOMMY. Ah, bless 'er little 'eart. She's lovely, she is.

KIWI. She told me she used to live in Scotland.

YANK. I know all about it. She had to live there while she was teaching school. And after only one year of trying to teach a bunch of young Scots, she had a nervous breakdown.

DIGGER. What have ya got against the Scots?

YANK. I'm Scottish myself. Scot d-d-descent.

TOMMY. 'E 'ates 'imself. *(Lights cigarette.)*

YANK. I hate all Scots. You should have known my G-g-grandfather Angus. There were only two infallible beings to his way of thinking. Angus McDonald and God. Sometimes God was wrong, but never Grandfather Angus.

(BLOSSOM rises, and collects the plates.)

KIWI *(mildly interested).* Did you have to live with him?

YANK. When my folks died, he took over the supervision of my soul.

TOMMY. 'E sounds stern.

YANK. Do you know what I had to recite every time I started to lose my temper?

KIWI. Sure—the multiplication tables. *(He swats a fly.)*

(BLOSSOM has crossed to the door as YANK starts this speech. He stops and listens, fascinated.)

YANK. I had to recite the books of the Bible. I can still do it: "Genesis, Exodus, Leviticus, Numbers, D-d-d-deuteronomy, Joshua, Judges, Ruth, Samuel, Kings, Chronicles, Ezra, N-n-nehemiah, Esther, Job, Psalms, Proverbs, Ecclesiastes, Solomon, Isaiah, J-j-jeremiah, Lamentations, Ezekiel, Daniel, Hosea, Joel, Amos, Obadiah, Jonah, M-m-micah, N-n-nahum, Habakkuk, Zephaniah, Haggai, Zechariah, and M-m-malachi—Goddamit! (YANK *starts to the washroom with his toothbrush and shaving mug.* BLOSSOM *carries the dishes out.*)

TOMMY. 'E must 'ave been a fearful man, your grandfather.

YANK (*bitterly*). And if you tried to argue with him, you know what he'd do?

DIGGER. Flay your hide?

YANK. He'd take his damned bagpipe out and sit playing it. God, how I learned to hate a bagpipe! No wonder the Scots always march when they play them. They're trying to get away from the sound. (*He goes into washroom.* BLOSSOM *re-enters and holds the door open, standing at attention.* SISTER MARGARET *enters. She is about twenty-one. She wears two "pips" on each shoulder of her neat white uniform. She has an easy, assured manner with the men. Her eyes are dark and expressive, giving an impression of inner amusement.*)

MARGARET (*crossing to her office*). Thank you, Blossom. (*To boys*). Good morning, good morning, good morning.

BOYS. Good morning, Sister.

MARGARET. How's everyone this morning?

DIGGER. Wizard! ⎫
TOMMY. Fine. ⎬ *Together*
KIWI. Top-o. ⎭

(MARGARET *ducks into her office to take off her red cape.*)

YANK (*stepping back into the ward from the washroom, waving his toothbrush*). If it were h-h-humanly possible for me to get rid of my Scottish blood—I'd d-d-donate it all to the Red Cross.

KIWI. You're going to run your blood pressure up if you don't have a care.

(MARGARET *steps out of her office, carrying a tray with thermometers and charts, and faces* YANK.)

MARGARET. And what's this about the Scots?

TOMMY. 'E don't like 'em.

MARGARET. Then you don't understand them. They say that God broke the mold after ne made the Scot.

YANK (*sourly*). I'm s-s-sure He did—right over the Scot's head. (*He exits into the washroom.* MARGARET *puts the tray down and starts taking the sheets off* YANK's *bed. She throws the pillow to* TOMMY, *who takes the cover off.* BLOSSOM *stands stiffly at attention beside his bed.*)

DIGGER. Ah, Sister, ya make the morning lovely.

TOMMY. We was just saying—you're our favorite sister, Sister.

MARGARET. I wish I could say the same about you. As patients, you're the most untidy and disrespectful lot it's ever been my misfortune to get.

DIGGER. Ya wound me, Sister.

KIWI. You can't mean us.

MARGARET. I certainly do. And I'll be delighted to see the last of you.

TOMMY. You need some leave, Sister. The matron works you too 'ard.

MARGARET (*takes tray and crosses to* BLOSSOM). The poor matron has nothing to do with it. It's you. It's a good thing I once taught in a kindergarten or I couldn't cope with you. (MARGARET *takes a thermometer out of a glass jar and faces the* BASUTO *as* YANK *comes back.*) Open your mouth. (*The* BASUTO *looks at her questioningly.*) Mouth! (*She opens her mouth to demonstrate.*)

YANK. What b-b-beautiful tonsils you have, Sister.

MARGARET (*wearily*). Go stand beside your bed and stop acting like an American. (*She puts the thermometer into* BLOSSOM's *mouth, and takes his pulse.*)

YANK (*with great respect*). R-r-right, L-l-leff-tenant. (*To the men.*) In America a sister's a nun instead of a nurse.

MARGARET (*without looking at* YANK). In

England a nurse nurses babies. *(She marks her chart and moves up to* KIWI.*)* How are you this morning, Kiwi? Did you sleep well?

KIWI. Like a baby, Sister.

MARGARET. And the arm?

KIWI. All right.

MARGARET. Move the shoulder. *(She moves his shoulder gently.)* Does it hurt? *(He doesn't answer.)* It does, doesn't it? It's much better though. *(She puts a thermometer into his mouth.)* Can't you keep your blankets tucked under? *(She tucks his feet in.)* And do something about your long legs. *(She moves back and takes his hand to count his pulse.)* No one would ever suspect that any of you had army training at all.

TOMMY *(calling)*. Oh, Sister.

SISTER. Be still. I'm counting. *(She drops* KIWI's *wrist and glances over at* TOMMY.*)* What do you want?

TOMMY *(sadly)*. I'm not comfortable.

MARGARET. This is a British military hospital—you're not *supposed* to be comfortable.

TOMMY. But I'm a dying man. Don't you run your wards for dying men?

*(*MARGARET *takes a thermometer out and marks her chart as she crosses to* YANK, *who stands at attention at the foot of his bed.)*

MARGARET. You know perfectly well that we run the wards so colonels can inspect them. So be still. *(She takes* YANK's *temperature.)*

DIGGER. Ah, what would Old Cobwebs say if he heard such talk?

MARGARET *(takes* YANK's *wrist)*. You will please show a little more respect for our superior officer. You will not refer to Cobwebs . . . to the *Colonel* as Old Cobwebs. *(She marks down* YANK's *pulse, leaving the thermometer in his mouth.)* Who's going to want clean pajamas? If the ones you have aren't too dirty, keep them another day. I haven't enough to go around this morning.

KIWI. I spilled tea on mine, Sister.

DIGGER. Gawd, don't tell her that. She'll boil 'em to recover it.

MARGARET. You're much too cheeky, the lot of you. *(She takes the thermometer from* YANK, *and marks her chart.)* How did you sleep, Yank?

YANK *(grinning)*. D-d-dreaming of you, Sister.

MARGARET. Rubbish. Your pulse is higher this morning.

YANK. When you press my wrist, Sister, my p-pulse p-p-pants.

MARGARET. The M.O. is putting you on plasmaquin. He wants to get all that malaria out of your system. *(She moves over to* DIGGER.*)* Will you get the pajamas out of my cabinet and see who needs them? I think there are three pairs.

YANK. Yes'm. *(He goes to the cabinet and gets out three pairs of pajamas.)*

MARGARET *(beside* DIGGER*)*. Do you want clean pajamas?

DIGGER. I can get along. Mine are still white.

MARGARET *(puts the thermometer into his mouth and takes his hand)*. Did you sleep well? *(He nods and puts his cheek against her hand.)*

YANK. Who wants pajamas?

KIWI. Me.

YANK. On you—they're r-r-rompers. *(Throws* KIWI *a pair.)*

TOMMY *(brightly)*. Me.

YANK. No wonder we never have pajamas. You split them all. *(Throws a pair to* TOMMY *and takes the third pair back.)*

MARGARET *(takes the thermometer from* DIGGER*)*. How is your back? *(She marks the chart.)*

DIGGER. A bit of a rub would feel mighty good.

TOMMY. 'E only wants to be rubbed because I gets rubbed—jealous of me every move.

MARGARET. I'll give you both a massage as soon as I've finished this. *(She crosses to* TOMMY.*)* You look a bit haggard. Did your hip bother you last night?

TOMMY. I 'ad a terrible night, I did, Sister. Not a wink of sleep.

YANK (putting his toothbrush away). No-n-nor anybody else.

TOMMY. I had nightmares. I was working meself to death—and there on a fence sat me wife, laughing 'erself silly. (He giggles. MARGARET puts the thermometer in his mouth, stopping him.)

MARGARET. That was your conscience bothering you. (She takes his pulse.) How did you manage to avoid work in civvy street?

TOMMY (takes thermometer out). Well, I'm a sort of waiter by profession. Me wife's father owns a pub, and I'm waiting for 'im to kick off.

MARGARET (sternly). Put that thermometer back.

(TOMMY does.)

DIGGER. Mangle him, Sister.

MARGARET. You'll work here as soon as you're an up-patient.

DIGGER (impressed). He's married. Gawd, it's a wonderful world.

KIWI. Any kids?

TOMMY (takes the thermometer out and gives it to MARGARET). And I can't understand it. All me family 'as kids until they're past sixty. Do you know, I 'ad an aunt two years old—and an uncle four. (He giggles.) I used to change me auntie's diapers!

MARGARET. Let me see. Gracious! I forgot the Basuto. (She starts back toward the BASUTO and stops dead.) Good Lord—he swallowed the thermometer!

(They all sit up and look at BLOSSOM.)

BASUTO (takes the entire thermometer out of his mouth and hands it to MARGARET. He grins). Blos-som.

MARGARET (shaking her finger at him). Don't you do that again. We can't afford to lose thermometers! (She takes the thermometer—looks at it, and marks the chart.) Oh, I wish someone could talk to this brute. (She hands the tray to YANK.) Yank, put these in my office, will you?

YANK (taking them). Yes'm. (He exits into MARGARET's office.)

MARGARET (sighs). Now, let's see if we can get this ward looking less like a slit-trench. Blossom. (She motions for the BASUTO to line up the beds. He straightens KIWI's and YANK's.)

DIGGER (with good humor). Ah, yes, line the beds up. Ya've no idea how it improves the patient's condition.

MARGARET (paying little attention to him). It improves the Colonel's disposition, and that's more important.

YANK (rushes in, breathless, excited. He tries to speak). Ca-ca-ca-ca-ca . . . (He tries to point to door.)

MARGARET (crossing to YANK). What is it, Yank?

YANK (rushes over to the entrance door, looks out and races back center to MARGARET). Ca-ca-ca-ca-ca . . .

DIGGER (amused). A tiger's chasing him.

YANK (still trying to speak and still gesturing toward door and stuttering). Ca-ca-ca-ca-ca . . .

MARGARET. Now take your time. (She slaps him on the cheek.)

YANK. Thank you. (He points again to the door.) Cobwebs!

MARGARET. Don't be silly. He can't inspect this early. (She crosses slowly to the door.)

YANK. I l-l-looked out the window and saw him coming.

MARGARET. I'm sure you were mistaken. (Opens the door, looks out, shuts it and whirls quickly.) Hurry! Put everything in order! Everyone hide his kit.

YANK. I t-t-told you so.

MARGARET (quickly gathering up the dirty sheets). Does anyone see cobwebs on the wall? (There is concentrated activity. MARGARET stuffs the sheets under TOMMY's blanket.) Here, hide these under the covers with you!

TOMMY (trying to spread the mound on his stomach, protests). 'E'll think I'm bloated.

DIGGER (pointing). There's a cobweb up there.

MARGARET (stops for a second from fixing YANK's bed). Get it down, Yank—quickly.

YANK (grabs a bamboo pole, brushes the cobweb away frantically). No self-respecting spider would come into a BGH.

TOMMY. Oh—'ow the Colonel 'ates cobwebs.

MARGARET. That's good enough. Stand by your beds—quickly. (YANK and the BASUTO rush to stand at attention by their beds. KIWI, DIGGER and TOMMY lie down at attention. The ward has been in a whirlwind—but it is now in perfect order as the COLONEL enters. He is tall, tired and stooped. He is not particularly formidable-looking. He has a nervous habit of twisting his nose. He is hatless. He wears a bush-jacket with his stethoscope hanging from his neck. He surveys the ward as he crosses.) Good morning, sir.

COLONEL. Good morning, Sister. (He turns to the men.) Carry on. Sit on your beds.

(BLOSSOM and YANK sit at the foot of their beds. The others sit up, and face the COLONEL.)

MARGARET. We didn't expect a visit this early, sir.

COLONEL (looks about). You keep a very orderly ward.

MARGARET. Thank you, sir.

COLONEL. I came over to have a talk with your patients. (He looks at them, then back to MARGARET.) I understand that they're exceedingly congenial.

MARGARET (proudly). They're the most tidy, respectful, pleasant group of men it's ever been my fortune to get, sir.

(The men exchange wise glances.)

COLONEL. Splendid. Now, the matron tells me you've a couple of empty beds.

MARGARET (indicating the empty bed). Yes—we have, sir. One.

COLONEL. I'm transferring a patient of my own to your ward this morning.

MARGARET. Yes, sir. Surgical?

COLONEL. Yes. I thought it might be advisable to come over myself to explain. It's a case that calls for the co-operation of the whole ward. (He turns to the men.) May I have everyone's attention for a moment? (He hesitates, pulling nervously at his nose.) I came here this morning to enlist your help.

YANK (when no one answers). What sort of help, sir?

COLONEL (looks at him, piercingly). You're the American, aren't you?

YANK (rises and faces front). Yes, sir—American Field Service—Ambulance driver attached to the British.

COLONEL (ominously). I've seen you somewhere before.

YANK (uneasily). When you inspected the ward last week, sir.

COLONEL. Before that. I associate it with something unpleasant.

YANK (cornered). I'd hoped you'd f-f-forgotten, sir. It seems I crowded your staff car off the road one day.

COLONEL (barking). It seems? I know damned well you did. My dear boy, you could have killed me.

YANK (smiling). B-but I didn't.

COLONEL (disarmed). Hmm. Sit down. (YANK sits. The COLONEL pulls his nose.) Well, I'll give you a chance to make amends.

YANK. Thank you, sir.

COLONEL (turns to the rest of them, walking up between the beds). I'm putting a patient of mine in here with you. I did an emergency operation on this man. Took a bit of shrapnel out of him. Had to remove his kidney. He's about recovered. I think you can help him.

YANK. May I ask how, sir?

COLONEL. By keeping him contented. (He pulls at his nose again.) He's anxious to get back to his regiment, but I can't discharge him from the hospital. It's out of the question.

MARGARET. Did you say, sir, that the patient had recovered from his operation?

COLONEL. Quite. In a few days he'll be fully recovered—from the operation. This man has one kidney left. Ordinarily that would carry him through life. We've discovered, unfortunately, that it's defective

It will do the work of two for a time—a limited time.

YANK. What happens then, sir?

COLONEL (with clinical dispassionateness). The kidney collapses—ceases to function. He begins to poison himself—uremic poisoning. And that's the inevitable end.

MARGARET. Does the patient know this, sir?

COLONEL. I decided against telling him. He has no family—no ties. Worry won't help him. So while he's well and waiting, I'm placing him in here because—well, it seems to me that a man should have friends around him when he dies.

KIWI (curious). How long has this man got, sir?

COLONEL. At the most—six weeks.

TOMMY (matter-of-factly). Nothing can 'elp him, sir?

COLONEL. The only help anyone can give him now will come from you.

YANK. And he thinks he's well, sir?

COLONEL. In a sense, he is. But it would be criminal to release him just to collapse up forward. Do what you can to keep him contented—and happy.

YANK. Yes, sir.

DIGGER. We'll do our best, sir.

TOMMY. 'E won't learn nothing from us, sir.

KIWI. And we'll jolly him along.

MARGARET (with confidence). These are good men. You can rely on them, Colonel.

COLONEL. Thank you. Damned unfortunate. Carry on. (MARGARET follows him to the door.) He's in C-16 by himself. I've instructed your orderly to bring him over here as soon as he's ready. (He opens the door and turns to her.) He can sit up or not—as he pleases.

MARGARET. We'll take good care of him, sir.

COLONEL (turns to the men). Good morning. (To MARGARET.) We'll omit inspection. Thank you, Sister. (He turns and exits.) Good morning.

MARGARET (closes the door, turns and takes a deep breath). Oh, dear, we've work to do. Yank, while I look after Tommy and Digger, will you give Kiwi his bath?

YANK (wearily). I'm going to make somebody a g-g-good wife.

(MARGARET takes some rubbing alcohol from the cabinet and crosses to TOMMY.)

KIWI. Yank, would you want to know it, if you were going to die?

YANK. I am going to d-d-die. Some d-d-day. And I'd prefer to let God s-s-surprise me. (He puts the red screens around KIWI's bed, with BLOSSOM's help, and then disappears behind them to wash KIWI.)

DIGGER. Now, why can't a bloke live without a kidney? (He indicates TOMMY.) He gets along all right without a brain.

MARGARET (to TOMMY). Turn over and get your backsides rubbed.

TOMMY (raises his pajama tops. He turns over facing DIGGER while MARGARET administers mild physiotherapy. The BASUTO stands, watching). 'Oo is 'e, Sister?

MARGARET (rubbing). Who is who?

TOMMY. The bloke wot's going to kick in?

MARGARET. I don't know.

TOMMY. And 'e 'asn't a chance?

MARGARET. You heard the Colonel.

TOMMY. It's a shocker.

MARGARET. It's always a shocker.

TOMMY. Blimey, we'll just get to know 'im. About six weeks, 'e said. (He is silent a moment. MARGARET gets more alcohol.) Do you ever get used to it, Sister? You can't let yourself like 'em, can you?

MARGARET. Don't talk like a child.

TOMMY. But wot are the wounded if they're not children? Would you be rubbing the backsides of a grown man?

MARGARET (she slaps his back). Don't be so saucy.

(TOMMY sits up facing front as MARGARET reaches for his towel.)

DIGGER (looking over at TOMMY's backsides). Gawd—what a tub of butter. How can a man get so fat on bully beef!

TOMMY (*archly*). It's me marvelous glands. I was re-graded twice since I was made cook. Both times on me card—I looked —it says "obese."

DIGGER. It says what, ya fool?

TOMMY. Obese. I don't know what it means. (*Giggles.*)

DIGGER (*rather blandly*). Gawd, you are ignorant. Sister, what does obese mean?

MARGARET. Fat.

DIGGER. How do you like that? Being fat ain't good enough for him. He has to be obese. You're plain fat!

TOMMY. In the future, you'll kindly refer to me by me proper disease.

MARGARET (*giving him a final slap*). That's enough. Now dump out that laundry. It'll look less like a nest. (*TOMMY kicks the sheets out which were hidden beneath his blanket when the COLONEL entered. She turns to DIGGER.*) Roll over and lift your shirt, Digger.

TOMMY. I sent me old lady a photo. She writes me, "If you come back any fatter, don't come back." And me giving me blood, sweat and tears and two-thirds of me pay. (*He cackles.*)

DIGGER (*lies with head on pillow at foot of bed, facing audience*). Aw, go to sleep.

(*TOMMY lies down. The BASUTO takes the laundry into MARGARET's office.*)

MARGARET (*begins to rub his spine gently*). All right?

DIGGER. Wizard! (*He sighs contentedly. After a moment he speaks again.*) How do we treat this bloke, Sister?

MARGARET. The new patient? Like a human being.

DIGGER. Ah, I can handle men. I should have been a priest. My ma wanted me to be a priest.

MARGARET. Then why did you go in for boxing?

DIGGER. Gawd knows. The times I've had the hell beat out of me when I could have been drinking sacramental wine.

MARGARET. You are in the paratroops, aren't you, Digger?

DIGGER. Right.

MARGARET. Have you made many jumps?

DIGGER. Twelve. I think I'll just skip the next one.

TOMMY (*raises himself to sitting position*). If your parachute don't open, do you get a new one? (*He roars with laughter and lies back.*)

DIGGER (*wearily*). Why don't you read some new joke books?

MARGARET. But they always open, don't they?

DIGGER. Sometimes the silk gets damp and sticks together. I've been lucky. But I've seen them that ain't.

(*MARGARET gets his towel. BLOSSOM enters and stands watching again.*)

MARGARET. Can't you transfer to a different unit?

DIGGER. Ah, there's extra pay for paratroops. And I've got a wife.

MARGARET. And how does she feel about silk that sticks together?

DIGGER. Oh, she says, "Be careful." But she'd say that no matter what I was in.

MARGARET. Then be careful. It's a dreadful business. (*She puts cap on the alcohol bottle.*)

DIGGER. And I've 'ad it.

(*YANK folds the screens and leans them against the side wall.*)

MARGARET (*looks at the BASUTO*). Oh, dear, I do wish the M.O. would decide what to do about the Basuto.

TOMMY (*sits up*). Is 'e really just 'omesick, Sister?

MARGARET. That's the only blessed thing wrong with him. He's had a fever for two months now, and he'll probably die unless he's sent back to his tribe.

BASUTO (*realizes she is talking about him and points to himself*). Blos-som.

MARGARET (*hands him the bottle and points to the cabinet so he will understand*). Go sit on your bed, Blossom. String your necklace. (*She indicates necklace.*) I'll see if there are more beads for you. (*She goes into her office.*)

BLOSSOM *puts the bottle in the cabinet and goes to his bed table and takes out a box-top with beads in it. He sits, and starts stringing them.)*

DIGGER *(sitting up and buttoning his pajamas).* Homesick! Why do you suppose those jokers ever join up anyhow? *(He reaches for his fly-swatter.)*

KIWI. Oh, their Chief joins, and they follow. His whole tribe joined. And now he wants to go home.

DIGGER. Him and me both. *(He swats his bed with his fly-swatter.)* Die, ya spawn of Satan.

YANK. I think they must t-t-trap 'em outside and let them loose in here.

DIGGER. Keep your flies over on your own bed. *(He throws the fly over on TOMMY's bed.)*

TOMMY *(sits up, finds the fly and studies it).* I recognize this as one of yours. 'E 'as a beady look. *(He flicks the fly back at DIGGER.)*

DIGGER *(brushing it off).* Don't shove any of your dirty flies over here! *(He reaches over and swats TOMMY on the knee.)*

TOMMY *(looks at DIGGER, indignant. He gets his fly-swatter out, and, while DIGGER is facing front, hits him. This is obviously a daily routine. TOMMY, feeling he has finished things off, settles back. DIGGER swats him again, and faces front. TOMMY gives him another whang, and DIGGER hits back immediately. TOMMY pauses a second, and then swats DIGGER on the side of the face. DIGGER promptly hits TOMMY back on his face).* 'Elp! Sister! 'E's 'itting me again.

(DIGGER and TOMMY start swatting right and left as DIGGER drives TOMMY over to YANK's bed.)

YANK. You spread g-g-germs that way.

DIGGER *(hitting out).* I'll spread him all over the ward.

KIWI. Sister'll come in here and give us all hell.

(MARGARET enters from her office, and stands eyeing them. TOMMY and DIGGER spring back to their beds, quickly settling down as though nothing had happened.)

MARGARET *(takes some beads over to BLOSSOM).* If I catch you fighting with swatters again, I'll collect them and let the flies eat you.

TOMMY. 'Oo, me, Sister?

MARGARET. Get your needlework out and try doing something constructive for a change. All of you. *(She ducks into her office and re-enters immediately and puts KIWI's needlework frame up for him. Meanwhile, DIGGER takes out his knitting, which is pink and blue; and TOMMY takes out his embroidery—a doily with blue flowers.)*

TOMMY *(working on his hoop).* Sister, 'aven't you got any yellow thread yet? I've made all me buttercups blue.

MARGARET *(begins to put clean sheets on YANK's bed).* You'll have to use what colors we have left. *(She glances at TOMMY's handiwork.)* That looks all right. *(Back to bed.)* And think how pleased your wife will be to get a set of doilies you made yourself.

TOMMY *(giggles).* She won't know wot to do with 'em. She'll blow 'er ruddy nose on 'em.

MARGARET. Then why don't you make her a tea-cosy? She can't blow her nose on that. *(Glances over at DIGGER who is knitting industriously.)* Is that for your wife, Digger?

DIGGER. My kid. If I knew which it was going to be, I could decide on the color.

YANK. Are you having a b-b-baby?

TOMMY. I knew weeks ago. Ah, we must be very tender with Digger.

YANK *(pointing at DIGGER).* But—you've been away three years. How could you p-p-possibly . . .

DIGGER *(firmly).* On my way back from England, I was married in Capetown.

YANK. Oh.

TOMMY. That's a dirty "oh." 'E's a poor type, the Yank.

KIWI *(puts his frame on the floor and gets up on his knees).* How about a bet on it? I'll bet rubles to rupees it's a boy.

DIGGER. No, I won't bet on that.

(YANK, *who has been helping* MARGARET, *gets his crocheting out of his bed table.*)

KIWI. Well, pounds or piasters says it's a girl.

DIGGER. Save your pay. I don't want to bet on my kid.

KIWI (*sitting down again and taking his needlework up*). I can't get a bet on anything around here!

MARGARET. Yank, why don't you turn whatever it is you're making into something for Digger's baby?

DIGGER. Aw, don't bother.

(YANK *sits down with his crocheting on the foot of his bed.*)

TOMMY. 'E'd love a needle-point diaper. (*He giggles gayly. At this point the* OR-DERLY *enters from the left and holds the door open.*)

ORDERLY (*to* MARGARET). The O.C. said I was to bring this patient in here.

MARGARET. Oh, yes, the Colonel told me. Did you bring his kit?

ORDERLY (*looking off stage*). He's carrying it himself. He wouldn't let me *touch* it.

(*The new patient enters, carrying his kit on his shoulder and a green bag in his hand. He has on a bathrobe and con-valescent blues. He is a slight young man of about twenty. He seems smaller than a soldier should. His rebellious, rusty hair is in need of combing. He has blue eyes that are as metallic and sharp as rapiers. His youthful good looks are somewhat marred by the unrelenting jut of his jaw. He betrays no interest in his surround-ings.*)

MARGARET. Oh, he can't keep that kit in here.

ORDERLY. He says the Colonel says he can.

MARGARET. Oh, all right. (*She crosses to the empty bed.*) You may have this bed.

(*He puts his green bag near the pillow and his duffle bag below it. He sits at the foot of bed, facing front, with his hands on his knees.*)

ORDERLY. Here's his report. (*The* ORDERLY *hands her the report and goes out.*)

MARGARET. Thank you. (*She turns to the new patient.*) I'm Sister Margaret. I don't believe the Colonel told me your name. (*Silence greets her introduction, so she looks at the report.*) "Sergeant Lachlen McLachlen." Are you a Scot?

LACHIE (*no one could mistake the Scottish burr when he speaks*). I'd hardly be gaen the name of a Scot if I were nae a Scot ma'self.

(YANK *looks over apprehensively.*)

MARGARET. Oh, I don't know. Quite a few parents give their children Scottish names —because they like them.

LACHIE. It fools nae one. Parading under false pretenses. (LACHIE *faces front again, having finished with her.*)

MARGARET (*laughs*). Oh, I doubt if it's a deliberate plot against the Scots. (*Looks at his card again.*) Now, the Colonel said you could sit up if you wanted to, or get into bed and rest. Just as you like.

LACHIE. I'll sit and think a bit.

MARGARET. Is there anything you want?

LACHIE (*turns to her*). I dinna like tae hae things done fur me.

MARGARET (*pleasantly*). Don't you? I love to have things done for me.

LACHIE. Aye, ye may. Not I. (*And he turns away from her.*)

MARGARET. Well, sing out if you need anything. I'll take your reports into the office and glance at them. (*She goes briskly into her office.* LACHIE *sits unperturbed by the silence she leaves in her wake. The men sit industriously sewing.* YANK *hesitates a minute, then takes out a package of ciga-rettes, and, leaning across his bed, offers one to* LACHIE.)

YANK. Have one?

LACHIE (*glances to see what is being of-fered, then turns front.*) I've ma' own.

YANK. These aren't issue. They're some I got from home.

LACHIE. I dinna like wot I'm nae used tae.

YANK (*encouragingly*). You n-n-never know until you try.

LACHIE. I dinna accept presents.

YANK. Why not?

LACHIE *(turning to him, firmly)*. I've nae wish tae poot ma'self in a mon's debt.

YANK. A cigarette isn't going to put you d-d-deep in d-d-debt. *(He offers the cigarettes again.)*

LACHIE. I'll smoke ma' own. *(He takes a cigarette from his breast pocket. The boys put their needlework down. All of them watch him.)*

DIGGER *(finally)*. Hey, Jock.

(LACHIE stops with his match half-way to his cigarette, then ignores DIGGER.)

YANK *(gestures to LACHIE)*. He's talking to y-y-you.

LACHIE *(coldly)*. If ye're addressing me, ma' name is nae Jock. *(He lights his cigarette.)*

DIGGER *(smiling)*. All Scots are Jock to me.

TOMMY *(helpfully)*. Like all Aussies is Diggers and New Zealanders is Kiwis and an Englishman like me is a Tommy. 'Im— *(He indicates YANK.)* 'E's a Yank.

YANK *(to TOMMY)*. I'm no d-d-damned Yank. I come from Georgia.

LACHIE *(indifferently)*. If ye moost address me, ye'll use ma' proper name.

DIGGER. I heard Sister read something but I didn't catch it. What is it?

YANK. Lachlen—something.

DIGGER. All right, "Lachie." Is that okay?

LACHIE *(turning to DIGGER)*. And, wot did ye want?

DIGGER. Nothing. Thought ya might feel like talking.

LACHIE. Aboot such as?

DIGGER *(subdued)*. Nothing—just gab.

LACHIE. I place little value on talking of naught.

YANK. You're a Scot, all right. *(He gives an unconvincing laugh. Then he swings his legs over his bed so that he is facing LACHIE. He tries again.)* What regiment are you with, Lachie?

LACHIE *(quickly)*. Why do ye ask?

YANK. I was j-j-just curious. I thought I might know somebody in your regiment.

LACHIE *(turns to him)*. Are ye a Scot?

YANK. My g-g-grandfather was.

LACHIE. I think it unlikely ye'd find yur grandfather in ma' regiment. *(He turns away again.)*

YANK *(begins to lose his temper)*. I k-k-know where my grandfather is. He's in the family plot where he belongs. But I happen to drive an ambulance and I get to k-k-know lots of regiments. I thought we might have friends in common.

LACHIE. Most unlikely. I dinna make friends freely.

YANK *(lying back on his bed)*. You d-d-don't make friends—period.

(LACHIE puffs at his cigarette. Then he puts it out on his shoe. He makes sure it is out, then places the butt in his pocket. He rises and begins to unpack. KIWI tosses a book over on LACHIE's bed.)

KIWI. Want something to read?

LACHIE *(picks up the book and drops it back on KIWI's bed)*. I place nae value on buuks.

YANK. Don't you like to get away from yourself?

LACHIE *(unpacking)*. I've nae quarrel wi' ma'self. Buuks are a waste of a thinking mon's time.

YANK. I see. You're a thinking man.

LACHIE. Aye.

YANK. Maybe we could interest you in the Bible?

LACHIE. I doot it.

YANK. It's got some damn good poetry in it.

LACHIE. I poot nae value on poetry—sacred or ootherwise.

YANK. L-l-look— *(He rises and stands between their two beds.)* We're a nice friendly bunch in here. If you don't like books or stories, it's all right with us.

LACHIE. It wuid hae tae be. *(He sits in the middle of his bed, with his back against the pillow, and crosses his arms.)*

YANK. What I'm t-t-trying to say is—live and let live. *(He holds out a bar of candy.)* Here.

LACHIE *(glancing at it)*. And may I be sae bold as tae ask wot ye're thrusting at ma' person?

YANK. It's a bar of chocolate. Don't you want it?

LACHIE *(looking him directly in the eye)*. Is it nae guid?

YANK *(annoyed)*. Of course, it's g-g-good. It's damned g-g-good. What do you think I'm giving it to you for?

LACHIE *(with good paranoid logic)*. Why are ye?

YANK. Because I want it, but I thought you might want it more. Is that an insult?

LACHIE *(looks away)*. It's nae consistent.

YANK *(storms back to his bed)*. G-g-grandfather Angus r-r-rides again!

KIWI *(is silent for a moment—then speaks)*. Ever been to New Zealand, Lachie?

LACHIE. I've done ma' share of traveling —but I leave the heathen lands tae the missionaries.

KIWI *(indignant)*. New Zealand's no heathen land. *I* come from there.

LACHIE *(looks at KIWI)*. I dinna consider that a guid argument.

TOMMY *(with great enjoyment)*. 'E's got you there, Kiwi.

KIWI *(patiently)*. It might have been heathen once, but that was a long time ago. It's modern and up to date.

LACHIE. I'll no deny ye yur opinion— *wrong* as it is.

KIWI. We rule ourselves. That's more than Scotland does.

LACHIE *(turns to him)*. Ye're neighbors tae the Fiji Islanders, are ye nawt?

KIWI. I don't see what that's got to do with it.

LACHIE. I believe the Fijis are cannibals, are they nawt?

TOMMY. Ah, you're right, Lachie, me lad. Eats each other, they do, from tip to toe.

KIWI. Well, I don't know any Fijis.

LACHIE. May I be sae bould as tae point out that while we had the great misfortune tae get Englishmen fur neighbors, they've yit tae boil each other in pots—at least in public.

TOMMY *(bolts up in bed)*. I takes umbrage at that, I do. If I remembers me 'istory, it was the Scots used to raid our borders and steal our cattle, they did. Cattle thieves they was.

LACHIE. *Aye,* and but for the *puur* stock of English *cattle,* Scotland wuid be a richer country taeday.

TOMMY *(losing his temper and shouting)*. Yer a bloody part of the British bloody Empire!

LACHIE *(to TOMMY)*. And how did ye acquire yur Empire?

TOMMY. By bloody well conquering the bloody 'eathens.

LACHIE *(wearily)*. Ah, the vanity of the British. Ye're nae conquerors. Wuid ye like tae hae me enlighten ye how ye collected yur colonies—Scotland excepted?

TOMMY *(assuredly)*. Conquered them with soldiers, we did!

LACHIE. Ye conquered them wi' missionaries, no less. Ye send yur preachers tae the land ye've got yur e'e on. Ye teach the simple heathen tae pray, and once ye've got him kneeling doen, ye hoist the English flag o'er him.

TOMMY. Yer a conquered race yerself, still fighting for 'ome rule and electricity.

DIGGER *(trying to be friendly)*. Lachie's right, Tommy. The missionaries came to Australia. *(To LACHIE.)* You're a bright bloke, Lachie.

LACHIE *(glances over at DIGGER)*. So ye claim Australia?

DIGGER *(proudly)*. Gawd's country.

LACHIE. A presumption, I think. I'm nae impressed by a land that produces naught moor sensible than a great jumping rat.

DIGGER *(angrily)*. A kangaroo ain't a rat

KIWI *(still nettled)*. And New Zealand isn't any heathen land.

LACHIE (*to* KIWI). And wot represents ye? A bird wi' nae wings. A bird that canna fly.

YANK (*to* KIWI *and* DIGGER, *smugly and amused*). Well, I guess he's told you off. You won't find any kangaroos in America —or b-b-birds that can't fly.

LACHIE (*with compassion and pity*). Ah, America! The land of Mickey Moose. The land of plenty, and ye live oot of tin cans and ten-cent stores. Ye've as many varieties of churches as ye hae pickles, but ye poot yur faith intae vitamins and Roosevelt.

YANK. You're speaking from a warehouse of ignorance.

LACHIE. Aye, am I? I sailed from Glasgow—a city of which ye've nae doot heard—when I were twelve. I worked one God-forsaken winter in yur great New York. I've examined ye at close range and I dinna care fur yur breed. Nothing pursonal.

YANK (*irked*). B-b-buster, you and I are going to have trouble getting together.

TOMMY. Serve you right for siding with 'im.

KIWI. Look, let's stop losing our tempers. It's too damned silly.

(BLOSSOM *rises and crosses to stare at* LACHIE.)

LACHIE. And may I ask who is this British subject?

YANK. The luckiest g-guy in the ward. He doesn't understand English.

LACHIE. And wot does he want?

YANK. He just wants to l-l-look at you. He's n-n-never *seen* anything like *you* before.

(*They all turn away from* LACHIE *and take up their sewing again. The* BASUTO *goes back to stringing his beads. In a moment* MARGARET *comes in, carrying a bottle of water. She looks around.*)

MARGARET (*brightly*). Well, how are we getting along? (*When no one answers, she continues to* LACHIE.) Have you met the men in the ward yet? This is Yank and . . .

YANK (*interrupts*). We've m-m-met.

MARGARET (*to* LACHIE). Have you met all of them?

YANK (*sourly*). We're all b-b-buddies.

MARGARET (*puts the water bottle on* LACHIE's *bed table*). Well, have you thought of anything I can do for you?

LACHIE. Ye've nae the authority tae send me back to ma' regiment?

MARGARET. I'm afraid you'll have to be patient and wait awhile.

LACHIE. I'll wait, but I'll nae be patient.

MARGARET. What regiment are you with, Lachie?

YANK. You're n-n-not going to get very far, Sister, unless you're a Scot or your g-g-grandfather's alive.

LACHIE (*leans over to* YANK). Wuid ye care to hae me rattle yur jaw wi' ma' fist?

MARGARET (*quickly*). Yank, is this your idea of good manners? What's come over you?

LACHIE. I dinna expect manners in a Yankee.

YANK (*slowly*). One more crack like that and I'll stop Lend-lease! (*He turns away.*)

MARGARET (*fussing with* LACHIE's *pillow and blankets in order to talk*). Now let's get back to Scotland. Do you happen to know Ayrshire?

LACHIE (*suspiciously*). Ye moost hae looked on ma' card. I wa' born in Ayrshire.

MARGARET. Really, I didn't. Oh, I know Ayre and Doon Foot well.

LACHIE. But ye're no Scot.

MARGARET. I once taught school there. Such darling children.

LACHIE (*pause*). Aye.

MARGARET. And lovely farming land.

LACHIE (*a longer pause*). Aye.

MARGARET. Now if you tell me that you belong to the Cameron Highlanders, I won't believe you.

LACHIE (*scowling*). Ye've looked up ma' record.

MARGARET. *Do* you belong to the Camerons?

LACHIE. Aye, I do.

MARGARET. You don't!

LACHIE. Hae ye trooble wi' yur hearing, Sister?

MARGARET (undismayed). Well, I'm just amazed. Oh, they're a grand regiment.

LACHIE. Guid enough.

MARGARET. You wear the Errach tartan, don't you?

LACHIE. Aye. Them as does—do.

MARGARET. Did you bring your kilt with you? (LACHIE does not answer.) You wear a kilt, don't you?

LACHIE. It's our privilege fur walking oot.

MARGARET. Will you wear it for us soon? (To the ward.) Wouldn't you men like to see Lachie in his kilt?

YANK (unsmiling). I can h-h-ardly wait.

MARGARET (to LACHIE). Oh, with your cap cocked over one eye and your kilt swishing as you walk down the street, you must be the proudest man in the world.

LACHIE (is silent for a moment). I dinna hae a kilt.

MARGARET. Oh, but you must have a kilt.

LACHIE. I dinna moost at all.

MARGARET. But you belong to the Camerons, and you're allowed to wear one. What sort of Scot are you, Lachlen?

LACHIE. We're required tae pay fur a kilt ourselves. And there's a great cost tae a proper kilt.

MARGARET. Oh, you're not issued a kilt?

LACHIE. We're issued naught but battle-dress.

MARGARET. Well, if I were in your regiment, I'd buy myself the finest to be had, no matter what the cost.

LACHIE (unmoved). Being a woman, ye wuid. I poot ma' money tae better use. It's a question of values.

MARGARET (stepping near LACHIE). Now, Lachlen, you been away about four years, haven't you?

LACHIE. Aye, I wa' seventeen.

MARGARET. You couldn't have spent all your pay. You ought to be ashamed if you haven't saved something.

LACHIE. Ma' money's in Scotland.

MARGARET. You could send for it.

LACHIE. I canna take it awt of the earth.

YANK (bounds up in bed). I k-k-knew it! He's got it buried in a tin can.

LACHIE (picks up the water bottle beside his bed). I'll belt ye wi' a boattle if ye dinna keep yur mooth shet.

MARGARET. Yank, if you're not well, lie down. But please be civil.

LACHIE. I'll nae return tae Scotland wi' naught but ma' wounds tae show fur ma' time. I've invested ma' money in a bit of land. I'll be a land owner. (He goes to the window at the left and stands aloof—looking out. The men are suddenly sobered.)

MARGARET. Oh.

LACHIE. And why do you say "oh"? Whit on earth is finer than a farm? Land of yur own tae work on—and spend the rest of yur life content.

MARGARET. Does all your pay go into paying off for your bit of land?

LACHIE. Aye. I've nae wasted ma' money on drink and sweets.

MARGARET (softly). Is your land about paid for?

LACHIE. A couple of months and the farm is ma' own. (The words are music to his soul.)

MARGARET (is silent a moment). Why don't you do something very foolish, Lachie? Why don't you buy yourself a kilt? The land will wait.

LACHIE (cuts her short). The kilt will wait.

KIWI. Are you buying your farm to share with someone?

LACHIE. I share wi' nae one.

(DIGGER, TOMMY and KIWI go back to their needlework, as does YANK.)

MARGARET. You're going to live on your farm—all by yourself?

LACHIE (*still looking out the window*).
Aye.

MARGARET. And you won't be lonely?

LACHIE. I've ne'r been lonely in ma' life.

MARGARET. Well, you seem to know what
you want. (*She turns and surveys the
ward.*) You're all unusually industrious
today.

YANK. B-b-busy little bees, making every
moment c-c-count. (*He sticks his crochet
needle into his work viciously.* MARGARET
goes into her office.)

YANK (*to* LACHIE, *after watching him a
moment*). What makes you want to live
on a farm—and thumb your nose at the
world?

LACHIE. I should nae hae encouraged ye
tae talk.

YANK. Would it upset any p-p-plans of
yours if I asked you a question—just one
question?

LACHIE (*turns and comes back to his own
bed*). There's naught ye could dew tae
upset me. And I'll grant ye a single question—nae moor.

YANK. Th-th-thanks. That's damned white
of you. (*Leans forward, and swings his
legs down, so he is sitting facing* LACHIE.)
What are you griped about?

LACHIE. And wot dew ye mean by "gripe"?
Wuid ye be sae kind as tae speak English?

YANK (*stands and faces* LACHIE). L-l-look.
I've got a parrot that speaks better English than you do.

LACHIE. A pity ye didn't learn frae yur
parrot.

YANK (*controlling himself*). I just wanted
to know what you're sore about. When a
guy is friendly to you, why can't you be
pleasant?

LACHIE. Were ye being friendly?

YANK. Didn't you g-g-guess?

LACHIE. Ye shuid hae told me. I cuid hae
saved ye time and trooble. I dinna need
companionship. I put nae value on the
human animal. I dinna like tae hae ma'
freedom nibbled intae. (*He sits on his
bed, dismissing* YANK *with his back.*)

YANK. Then just what do you "put a
value on"?

LACHIE. I knew ye'd presume tae ask a
second question. (*Turns to look at him.*)
If ye'd used yur God-gaen wits, ye wuid
nae ask. I value ma' privacy. Do ye mind?

YANK. You can have it! (*He strides over
to get the screens, motioning to* BLOSSOM
to help as he passes him. YANK *sets up the
screens, shutting* LACHIE *off from the ward
and the audience.*) You can stay in your
private world, and h-h-hug yourself to
death. As far as we're concerned, Brother,
you w-w-won't exist.

LACHIE (*head appearing above the screens*).
If ye dinna mind, I'm nae yur brother!
(*He disappears.* YANK *throws himself on
his back on his bed.*)

YANK. Who's got a dull razor? I think
I'll cut my throat.

TOMMY (*frowning*). Sister's going to take
a poor view of that.

YANK. I'm just giving him what he asked
for.

TOMMY. 'E don't like nobody. 'E don't
even like 'isself.

DIGGER (*to* YANK). Hey, Yank, what did
you mean by that crack about Australia?

KIWI. Yes, and you agreed with him about
New Zealand.

YANK. Oh, forget it.

TOMMY (*lies down*). Hm. Bloody cattle-
thieves!

(*The first wailing note from the bagpipe
is heard. All sit bolt upright.* LACHIE's *foot
can be seen keeping time below his screen
as he plays.*)

YANK. What was that?!

TOMMY. It wasn't *me*. I 'adn't even got
to sleep yet.

(YANK *stands on his bed, looks over the
top of the screens.*)

YANK (*yells*). It's bagpipes! (*He closes his
eyes and speaks through gritted teeth.*)
Genesis, Exodus, Leviticus, Numbers,
D-d-d-deuteronomy, Joshua, Judges . . .

THE CURTAIN FALLS

ACT TWO

SCENE I

The same. Two weeks later.

The BASUTO *sits on the cabinet at the side window, playing his home-made guitar-like instrument, and singing an African chant.*

KIWI, *with the cast removed from his arm and dressed in up-patient blues, is sitting on* YANK'S *bed, fanning himself with a fly-swatter.*

DIGGER, *now an up-patient, lies on his back, head downstage, idly swatting flies.*

TOMMY, *a writing pad against his knees, is finishing a letter.*

YANK *is stretched out on his stomach, face downstage.*

LACHIE *sits on his bed, his back to the others, industriously polishing his shoes.*

As the curtain goes up, the BASUTO'S *chant rises in volume.*

DIGGER. Quiet!

(BLOSSOM *stops his chant. Silence descends.* LACHIE *puts one shoe down, and picks up the other. He spits on it and starts polishing.* BLOSSOM *puts his instrument away, and goes back to looking out the window.*)

TOMMY (*glancing up*). Wot's the date? (*No one answers*). 'Ey! Yank, wot's the date?

YANK (*pulls his head out of the pillow*). Th-th-thirty days has September, April, June and November. All the rest have thirty-one, except February and something and something which gives it twenty-eight. It's the f-f-first. (*He puts his head down and goes back to his bored rest.* TOMMY *finishes the letter, puts it in an envelope, and places it on his bed-table. He takes up his fly-swatter and looks around. He hits over at* DIGGER.)

DIGGER (*annoyed*). Aw. (*He turns over on his stomach.* TOMMY *swats flies indifferently.* KIWI *rises and goes back to his own bed.*)

TOMMY. Wot time is it?

KIWI (*looking at his wrist watch*). It's half eleven.

TOMMY. Blimey, I thought it was tiffin time.

DIGGER (*testily*). Don't you ever forget that gut of yours?

TOMMY (*coyly*). You don't love me any more. There was a time you thought I was cute. (*The giggle doesn't quite come off.*)

YANK (*acidly*). I'll sure be glad to get out of here.

(*After a moment,* MARGARET *enters briskly, cheerfully.*)

MARGARET. Isn't it a lovely day? (*She holds up some letters.*) The post just came in.

YANK (*shouts*). Mail!

(*They all leap up excitedly.*)

TOMMY. Blimey, I just wrote one!

DIGGER. Ah, wizard!

KIWI. Rubles to rupees says I get a letter!

YANK (*anxiously*). Look carefully, Sister.

MARGARET. Just a minute. (*Putting two letters down on* DIGGER'S *pillow.*) Digger —one—two.

DIGGER (*picking them up*). Ah, you're an angel, Sister.

MARGARET (*crossing to* TOMMY). Tommy, here's an "obese" one for you. (*Hands it to him.*)

YANK. Find me one, Sister, even if it's an unpaid bill, p-p-please.

MARGARET (*hands him a letter*). One.

YANK (*looks at it*). That's the one. W-w-wow! (*He settles back to read it.*)

MARGARET (*to* KIWI). Somebody loves you, Kiwi. (*She hands him three letters.*)

KIWI (*beaming*). What did I tell you?

MARGARET. And that's all. (*To* KIWI.) Tuck your blankets in.

(LACHIE *is still polishing his shoes as the men settle down with their mail.*)

TOMMY (*reading to himself*). Oh, dear, oh, dear, oh, dear. (*He giggles.*)

MARGARET (*stops and stands behind* LACHIE). I don't know what can be happening to your mail, Lachie, unless they're holding it at your regiment. Why don't you drop a line to the A.B.P.O.?

LACHIE (*without looking up*). I expect nae mail.

MARGARET. Haven't you told your friends where you are?

LACHIE. I've many friends. Many carefully chosen individuals in Doon Foot, Ayrshire, Glasgow, Rosemarkie, Edinburgh and oother places and they all know ma' views. I dinna hae tae write aboot them.

MARGARET. But don't you miss not hearing from home?

LACHIE. Aye, there's mooch I miss. But ye may hae heard—there's a war gaen on.

MARGARET. Yes, I heard. The man I'd hoped to marry was killed at Crete. I've heard about the war.

LACHIE (*a little subdued*). Aye, then ye know. (*He attacks his shoes with his brush.*)

MARGARET. And I know it's good to know what's happening back in Blighty.

LACHIE. Ma' knowing will nae change things.

MARGARET. It might. (*She starts into her office, then stops.*) Is there anything special you'd like for tiffin?

LACHIE. Naught.

MARGARET. Oh, there must be some particular dish that you'd like—something I can fix for you myself.

LACHIE. Why?

MARGARET. Why do you ask—why?

LACHIE. I've noticed, Sister, that ye seek tae dew me favors. I dinna ken yur motive boot I think it only fair tae warn ye —I've nae place fur marriage in ma' plans.

MARGARET (*aghast*). How very kind of you to tell me!

LACHIE. Aye.

MARGARET. But I assure you that I have no plans to snare you.

LACHIE. It wuid nae be the furst time in ma' life.

MARGARET. Oh, I'm sure you're a much-pursued young man. I asked you about the food only because I thought something a little different might please you.

LACHIE. And may I be sae bould as tae remind ye that I dinna like things done fur me. And I dinna seek privilege.

MARGARET. Oh, Lachie, we're all entitled to privilege once in a while—in sheer defiance, if nothing else.

LACHIE. Whin I've a right tae privilege, I'll nae ask fur it. I'll demand.

MARGARET. Lachie, you *are* aggravating at times.

TOMMY (*looking up*). 'Ear! 'Ear!

LACHIE. And if it's pity fur ma' wounds prompts ye, ye dinna know me or ye'd never offer me that.

MARGARET. Oh, Lachie, please be human!

LACHIE. I'm sorry I can nae be a weak character tae yur liking.

MARGARET. So am I, because I've a weakness for—weakness. It's something I can understand. (*Angry, she storms into her office, but quickly repents. She comes back to* LACHIE.) I'm sorry I was cross with you.

LACHIE. I dinna notice the tantrums of women.

MARGARET. That would be such an advantage if you ever married.

LACHIE (*accusingly*). It's odd ye harp on marriage.

MARGARET (*struggle for self-control*). Lachie, will you please believe me? I am not setting a trap for you. I've no designs on you. I'm going to be strong and resist your charm. So you *don't* have to be on your guard.

LACHIE (*calmly*). Still ye do persist, and ye do deny it hotly.

MARGARET. I do *not* deny it hotly. I do not persist. Oh, really. (*She takes a deep breath.*) Lachie, I only want to know if I can arrange some special dish for you. No compromise or obligation involved.

LACHIE. I'm content wi' ma' lot. *(He lies on his back.)*

MARGARET. Well, I look forward to the day when you'll ask for something. And when you do, make it monumental. *(As she starts off.)* Good letter, Yank?

YANK. P-p-perfect.

(She goes out. DIGGER opens his second letter and starts reading.)

DIGGER *(shouts)*. Hip! Hip! I've had a baby! *(He waves the letter.)*

YANK. G-g-good going.

TOMMY. Did you suffer? *(He giggles.)*

KIWI. Boy or girl?

DIGGER. Boy. She's named him after me. Ah, the darling! *(He picks up his pillow and puts it upstage on his bed and leans back.)*

YANK. M-m-mother and child doing all right?

DIGGER *(grinning)*. Wizard.

KIWI. Congratulations, Digger.

TOMMY. I wish I could 'ave a baby. If I did, they'd send me 'ome on compassionate grounds. I've been away four years.

YANK *(leaning back.)* N-n-now to read it over again. My gal still loves me.

(As they continue to read, TOMMY starts to giggle at what he finds in his letter.)

TOMMY. Oh, dear, oh, dear. You should 'ear this.

YANK. Well, l-l-let's hear it. *(He sits up on one elbow.)*

KIWI. We're listening.

TOMMY *(convulses himself first)*. Me wife 'as told the 'ole village about me wounds and I'm a bloody 'ero. And *(Again he gets out of control.)* do you know wot they've done?

YANK. Cast a statue of you—out of p-pig iron?

TOMMY *(again he can hardly go on)*. No, but they've 'ad a public dinner in me honor—and they've named a *pudding* after me. *(He shrieks with laughter.)* A pudding!

DIGGER *(laughing)*. Gawd! I'll bet it's heavy.

TOMMY. Bless their 'earts, they've made me immortal with raisins. Oh, dear, oh, dear, the silly fools. *(His laugh dies down to a chuckle, and then suddenly bursts forth louder than ever.)* "The Percival 'Awkins Puffed Wheat Pudding."

(Everyone laughs but LACHIE, who rises suddenly and faces them.)

LACHIE. A fine lot of women ye moost hae.

YANK. S-sure they're fine. What's wrong now?

LACHIE. And nae doot ye're moost proud of thim.

KIWI. Why not?

LACHIE. Have ye any idea of the tons of paper that's wasted writing of news that cuid weel wait? Hae ye considered the fortune in stamps that cuid be spent on food instead? Do ye ken how many ships and planes it takes tae deliver the letters of millions of giddy females alone?

DIGGER *(wearily)*. Why don't you run the world for a change and give God a rest?

LACHIE. Ye're guilty of criminal waste, ye and yur women. *(Looks at them all.)* And ye sit there pleased as cats.

YANK. D-d-do us a favor and don't show us the error of our ways, will you?

LACHIE. Ah, it's yur consciences trooble ye—nae I. *(He goes up behind his bed to get his bagpipe.)*

YANK. All right then! It's my conscience.

(LACHIE grabs his bagpipe and sits down, ready to play.)

YANK *(eyes to heaven)*. Oh, God, give him asthma.

(Before LACHIE can begin to play MARGARET enters.)

MARGARET. Lachie, the Colonel just sent word over that he wants to see you straight away.

LACHIE *(hanging his bagpipe up while MARGARET is getting his bathrobe from his bed-table)*. Why does he nae come here?

MARGARET *(crossing with his robe and holding it for him)*. I believe he wants to take an X-ray. Do you want a wheel chair?

LACHIE. I've ma' legs and ma' health. (*Getting into the robe.*) And I've little respect fur the Colonel.

MARGARET. You should have. He's not only a fine commanding officer, but a great surgeon.

LACHIE. He's got a spite on me.

MARGARET. That's absurd.

LACHIE. Still he's got a spite on me. (*He starts toward the door.*) I'm hale and hearty and a Scot wi' a mind of ma' own —something nae Englishmon can abide. (*He slams the door shut as he leaves.*)

YANK. Sister, is he really going to die? Because if he isn't, I'm going to k-k-kill him.

MARGARET. What a dreadful thing to say! I'm ashamed of you.

KIWI. You don't have to live with him.

DIGGER. That joker's got a spite on the whole world.

YANK. He's got a p-p-porcupine disposition. You c-c-can't touch him.

MARGARET. Have you tried to *know* him?

YANK. To k-k-know him is to loathe him.

MARGARET. Why don't you try to *like* him?

TOMMY. 'E don't like us first. 'E's a terrible stern man, 'e is.

MARGARET. Then why do you antagonize him!

DIGGER. Antagonize him!

YANK. Th-th-that does it!

MARGARET. Listen to me. That boy was not sent in here to make things pleasant for *you*. He was sent to you for help. That was a compliment.

YANK. Or a ch-challenge.

MARGARET. All right—a challenge. It's a poor show when men run from a challenge. I admit I lose patience too, but we mustn't stop trying.

DIGGER. He'd be miserable if he was happy, Sister.

YANK. If there was only *one* thing about him you could like.

MARGARET. It isn't important whether you like him or not. And whether Lachie is a hero or not doesn't matter. He's a human being on leave from suffering. How unworthy of you to criticize him! *You're* going to get well.

TOMMY. 'E resists you.

MARGARET. His opinions aren't the same as ours. Does that make him an enemy?

TOMMY. It makes 'im 'ard to talk to.

MARGARET. It isn't often that you have an opportunity to make a man grateful he'd spent the last weeks of his life with you. I'm ashamed of you, indeed.

(*They are silent for a moment.*)

TOMMY. We're no good. Me that was wounded in me behind.

MARGARET. Well, you've a chance to redeem yourselves today. (*She turns to* YANK.) Yank, go into my office. There's a big parcel. Will you please bring it in here? (YANK *starts off.*) Today's his birthday.

(YANK *stops.*)

KIWI. His birthday?

MARGARET. I checked on his admittance card.

DIGGER. Are we going to give him a ruddy birthday party?

MARGARET. Don't you want to help?

YANK. All right, we'll try once more. (*He steps into* MARGARET'S *office.*)

TOMMY. Did you get 'im a cake?

MARGARET. I thought of a haggis to be piped in—but who could make a haggis here?

(YANK *comes back with the box and lays it on* LACHIE'S *bed.* MARGARET *goes over and begins to untie it.*)

TOMMY. Oh, I do like presents, I do.

MARGARET. I've a kilt here.

KIWI. A kilt!

MARGARET. And everything that goes with it. I checked with his regiment and ordered it from Calcutta. (*They crowd around her.)* And it got here on time, thanks to the RAF.

YANK. Well, w-wait a minute. *You're* not going to pay for all this yourself.

MARGARET. Yes, but I want you to give them to him.

YANK. If we're going to give them to him, we'll pay for them.

KIWI. We'll all chip in.

DIGGER. If there's a price list, we'll each pick out what we can afford. Will you let us do that?

MARGARET. I certainly will. *(She hands the list to* DIGGER.*)*

TOMMY. Blimey, if this don't make 'im 'appy, then nothing will.

DIGGER. Can I give the poor bloke the brogues, Sister?

MARGARET. All right. I'll check you off later. We must make haste. *(She hands the shoes to* DIGGER *who crosses around to get them.)* This is your contribution. Keep them under your pillow or some place out of sight.

DIGGER *(crossing back to his bed).* I could do with a pair of these myself. *(He puts them under pillow at the foot of his bed.)*

TOMMY. I'll give 'im the belt, 'ow's that?

YANK *(with eyebrow raised at* MARGARET*).* A belt might do him a lot of good. *(*YANK *hands the belt over from* MARGARET *to* TOMMY.*)*

MARGARET *(ignoring* YANK's *remark).* What would you like to give him, Kiwi?

KIWI. Whatever you say, Sister.

MARGARET. Well, how about the spats, stockings and supporters?

KIWI. Good enough. Just the job.

YANK. Does anyone object to my giving him the jacket and the kilt? After all, I dislike him more than the rest of you.

MARGARET *(smiles).* I think that would be splendid. I hoped you would. *(She lifts out the kilt and holds it up for all to see.)*

KIWI *(whistles).* Ah—lovely!

DIGGER. Wizard.

TOMMY. Oh, it's grand—it is.

YANK. N-not bad. Will it fit him?

MARGARET. It's the right size, all right. I checked *everything.* *(She hands it to* YANK, *who puts it under his blanket with the jacket.)*

KIWI *(glancing at* BLOSSOM, *who stands looking forlornly out the window).* What about Blossom? Do we include him?

YANK. S-sure. Let Blossom give him the side-cap. We'll chip in.

KIWI. Sure.

TOMMY. Right-o.

MARGARET *(takes the cap out of the box and goes to* BLOSSOM, *holding the cap out).* Here, Blossom. *(She turns back to the box.* BLOSSOM *beams and places the cap on his head backwards with the ribbon hanging over his eyes.)*

TOMMY. Oh, blimey, we'll never get it away from 'im now. 'E *likes* it.

DIGGER. Gawd, if Lachie came back now! *(He rushes to the door to see if* LACHIE *is returning.* MARGARET *goes back to the* BASUTO *and tries to take the cap away from him. They struggle a minute and she manages to get it back.* BLOSSOM *looks at her, puzzled and hurt.)*

MARGARET. No—no. Him. *(She crosses to* LACHIE's *bed and points at it.)* Him. Gift. *(She makes a gesture of giving, and then turns to* KIWI.*)* I *do* sound like such an idiot. *(She puts the cap down and motions to the* BASUTO *to sit down again.* BLOSSOM *nods understandingly and smiles.)* I'll keep it until we give Lachie the presents. *(She reaches into the box and brings out the sporran.)* And *this* is my gift.

KIWI. Is that a haggis?

MARGARET. It's the sporran.

TOMMY *(loftily).* 'E keeps 'is small change in it.

YANK *(without malice).* M-mixed with fish hooks.

MARGARET *(looking into the box).* And that's the last of it.

YANK. Everything? Didn't you forget something important?

MARGARET. Oh, dear, I hope not. *(She counts on her fingers.)*

YANK. Underneath the k-kilts, don't they wear some sort of fancy pants?

TOMMY. Didn't you know? *(He beckons to YANK. YANK leans over his own bed, and the two whisper. YANK sits back astonished.)*

YANK. Nothing?

TOMMY *(sits back, smugly)*. Nothing.

DIGGER. A bit drafty, I thinks.

MARGARET *(looking in the box)*. Well, there's nothing else to wear in the box.

KIWI. Maybe they left it out?

YANK *(looking in box, too)*. S-sure. It's indecent to be th-that drafty.

TOMMY. It's not indecent, it's thrifty.

DIGGER. I say they wear some kind of a diaper.

KIWI *(kneels up on his bed and points excitedly)*. Two pounds says you're wrong.

YANK *(to KIWI)*. I'll bet you two pounds *you're* wrong.

KIWI. It's a bet! Glory to God, I got a bet at last! *(He sinks back into his bed beaming.)*

DIGGER. And I've got two pounds says the Yank's right.

TOMMY *(quickly)*. I'll bet that you and the Yank are both wrong.

DIGGER *(even quicker)*. You're on.

KIWI. Want to bet, Sister?

MARGARET *(becomes an officer again)*. I do not. It's a silly, vulgar bet.

KIWI. In behalf of general knowledge, Sister.

MARGARET. *No.*

TOMMY *(to DIGGER)*. You'll find 'e's naked as a grape.

(MARGARET hides the box and tucks the sporran and cap under YANK's pillow.)

MARGARET. Now, let's stop this nonsense. Hide your presents out of sight. Then as soon as he comes back, we'll give them to him. (TOMMY *puts his belt under his pillow.* KIWI *puts the spats, stockings and*

supporters behind his backrest.) In the meantime, we can have our tiffin. Yank, the tray's in the cook-shed.

YANK *(rises and drags his feet across the ward)*. Cold bully-beef, bread and jelly. *(He goes out.)*

KIWI *(hopefully)*. Anyone want to bet two rupees on that?

MARGARET. It's the best we can do.

TOMMY. Do I get up to give 'im the belt, Sister?

MARGARET. Well, I shouldn't want you to hurl it at him.

KIWI. Do we wait till he finishes eating?

MARGARET. No, as soon as he comes back.

YANK *(comes back with a tray of tin plates on which food has been served. He leaves a plate at each bed and returns to his own. They all sit on their beds, eating)*. Sister, I was just th-thinking—what if he refuses to take the presents? We're sticking our necks out.

KIWI. Yes, remember he said he never accepted presents.

MARGARET. Oh, he won't refuse them. He can't. It's his birthday.

TOMMY. 'E's tricky, 'e is.

YANK. I p-p-promise you, Sister, if he tosses these presents back at us, I'm going to b-beat him to death with his bagpipe.

MARGARET. He won't refuse them. It's absurd to think such a thing. Still—*if* he does—well—certainly he has a right to.

YANK. You're n-not so s-sure yourself, are you, Sister?

DIGGER *(glances out door)*. Be careful, he's coming back! *(He begins to eat quickly.)*

TOMMY *(watching the door)*. And *there I was* doing a bit of plumbing at Buckingham Palace— *(Confidentially.)* that was when I was with the Royal Engineers— (LACHIE *enters and walks straight to his bed without speaking. He sees his plate and picks it up. He gets his fork and begins to eat, seated on the side of his bed.* TOMMY *continues elaborately.)* —and it was raining, and the King 'e comes up to me and 'e says, "Where's your 'at at, me good man?" And I says, "I've been issued no 'at, Your Royal 'Ighness." And 'e says, "'Ere, take me crown, it'll keep the rain out of yer eyes." (*He laughs shrilly and begins to gobble his food.* LACHIE *ignores their conversation and presence.*)

DIGGER (*shrugs sadly toward* TOMMY). Oh, well, what can ya expect from a bloke with an aunt two years old.

(MARGARET *signals to* DIGGER. *He looks back at her and she indicates for him to present his gift first. He puts his plate down and takes out the brogues. He crosses to the end of* LACHIE's *bed and drops the shoes beside him.*)

DIGGER (*affably and with youthful eagerness*). Heard it was your birthday, Lachie. Thought ya might be able to use a pair of brogues. Congratulations. (*He waits for a moment.* LACHIE *has stopped with his spoon halfway to mouth. He then continues to eat without speaking or looking in any direction except his plate.* DIGGER *hesitates, and when no acknowledgment is made, returns to his bed.* LACHIE *inclines his head, slightly, to look at the brogues from the corner of his eyes. He continues chewing silently.* MARGARET *signals* TOMMY. *He labors out of bed and waddles over to* LACHIE. *He puts the belt beside the brogues on* LACHIE's *bed.*)

TOMMY (*brightly*) Made in Scotland—it says. 'Appy birthday.

(LACHIE *chews slowly without looking up, without comment.* TOMMY *falters a moment, then returns to his bed.* KIWI *then receives his signal from* MARGARET.)

KIWI (*takes out his presents and clears his throat*). You can't wear brogues without stockings—you get corns. And you can't wear stockings without supporters—you'll break your neck. The best of luck to you. (KIWI *leans out of his bed and drops his presents without ceremony beside* LACHIE. *He does not wait for an answer.* MARGARET *then takes the cap to the* BASUTO *and places it in his hands. She indicates that he is to place it beside* LACHIE. *The African nods and follows instructions. He crosses to* LACHIE's *bed and puts the cap gently on the pile of presents and tries to peer around into* LACHIE's *face.* MARGARET *motions frantically and he lopes like a great*

panda back to his bed. When he sits down, MARGARET *gets her sporran.*)

MARGARET (*stands behind* LACHIE). Sorry we weren't able to have a haggis for you, Lachlen. (*She places the sporran beside the other presents.*) You're gathering quite a collection. G'bless. (*She walks quickly away, motioning* YANK *as she passes to give his present.* LACHIE *is still silent.* YANK *rises and takes out the jacket and kilt. All the men stop eating and lean forward eagerly.*)

YANK (*carries them over his arm to* LACHIE *and puts the kilt on top of the stack of presents*). All the b-b-best to you, Lachie.

(LACHIE *stops chewing. He neither speaks nor looks up.* YANK *returns to his bed.* MARGARET *tiptoes up to* TOMMY *and whispers to him.* TOMMY *nods, clears his throat and begins to sing.*)

TOMMY.
'Appy birthday to you,
'Appy birthday to you,
(MARGARET *and the others join in.* BLOSSOM *catching the gaiety, starts clapping his hands against his sides in a jungle rhythm and great enjoyment.*)
Happy birthday, dear Lachlen,
Happy birthday to you.

(*Silence greets the song—flat, wet silence. They look at each other, self-consciously.*)

YANK (*through gritted teeth*). Genesis, Exodus, Leviticus, Numbers . . .

(MARGARET *hurries over to him and puts a restraining hand on his shoulder.* YANK *stops, for* LACHIE *has risen and faces the men. He clears his throat.*)

LACHIE. I wuid hae a word wi' ye. (*He swallows.*) I dinno understand ye. I dinna understand ma' self. Ye've done a thing that numbs ma' brain. (*He puts his hand gently on the kilt.*) Nae mon in all ma' life befur gae me tu'pence fur naught. I'd nae hae remembered it was ma' birthday if ye'd nae said sae. But . . . (*He folds his hands determinedly behind him.*) Hae I the right tae take yur kilt? The taking lays a claim on me and I've naught to pay ye back. I moost nae make a mistake. They say that sorrow is born in the hasty h'ert. Now, I've nae wish tae invite sorrow. So ma' problem . . .

MARGARET (*goes over to* LACHIE *with a thermometer*). Oh, do be quiet, Lachie.

LACHIE (*anxiously*). I moost explain ma' feeling. Now, ma' problem . . .

MARGARET. You don't have to explain anything. For once in your life be hasty and risk a mistake.

LACHIE (*trying hard to finish*). Boot I . . .

(MARGARET *sticks the thermometer in his open mouth. He shuts it.*)

MARGARET. Keep your mouth shut and let your heart talk. When a Scot makes a fool of himself he makes a grand one. (*She gently pushes him down so he sits on his bed.*)

TOMMY (*eagerly*). Is 'e going to take 'em, Sister?

MARGARET (*turns to them*). Of course, he is. There was no other thought in his mind. You were searching for a dignified way to thank them, weren't you, Lachie? (LACHIE *nods agreement with grateful relief.*)

YANK. P-put 'em on!

KIWI. Put 'em on!

DIGGER. Let's see how you look, Lachie.

TOMMY. Let's see if 'e wears anything under them.

YANK (*leans over to* LACHIE). Lachie, we got a little bet up and you're the only one to settle it.

MARGARET (*laughing*). Oh, you *are* a mercenary lot.

YANK. Do you or don't you wear something under the kilt?

LACHIE (*takes the thermometer out of his mouth*). Ma' friends, I deeply regret ye've asked, fur I can nae tell ye. It's the one question nae Scot will answer rightly.

YANK (*incredulously*). You won't tell us?

LACHIE. Wuid ye ask me tae break faith wi' ma' fellow Scots?

YANK (*shrugs*). N-never mind then. Just put 'em on.

KIWI. Put 'em on!

DIGGER (*shouts*). Into your kilt!

TOMMY. Put 'em on, says Ĭ.

LACHIE (*calmly*). I've nae intention of wearing ma' kilt until the proper time.

YANK (*leans forward*). Wh-what did you say?

LACHIE. I'll wear ma' kilt when the occasion is fitting. I'll put on ma' kilt the day I return tae ma' regiment—nae befur. (*He rises and starts to put his presents away.*)

YANK (*helpless*). Sister, you *can't* let him do this. He's—he's putting them away.

LACHIE (*looks up suspiciously*). Did ye gae me the kilt fur ma' own pleasure, or do ye hold a claim?

MARGARET (*quickly*). Lachie, this is your birthday. Do whatever pleases *you*.

LACHIE. I'm pleased tae wait. (*He packs his things in the box which* MARGARET *hands him.*) Thank ye fur ma' gifts. I'll nae soon forget this day.

YANK (*watching him pack*). Is the p-p-party . . . over?

LACHIE (*innocently*). Is there moor tae dew?

YANK. No—no. (*Grimly.*) Th-that's all, I guess. (*He rests his chin on clenched fists and sighs.*) A perfect Scottish birthday party. (*He sits on his bed.* LACHIE *puts the box under his bed, sits down and takes up his food.*)

MARGARET (*softly*). Now, is there anything I can do for you before I go?

LACHIE. Naught. I'm most content.

MARGARET. That's good. (*She goes into her office, smiling to herself. After a few silent moments,* KIWI *rises uneasily and goes over to be with his friends. He sits on* YANK's *bed. All of the men sit dejected, deep in their own thoughts.* LACHIE *looks over at the boys. He rises. First, he wanders over to the* BASUTO, *looks over his shoulder out the window, then forces himself to cross the ward toward the boys. He opens the door and smells the air. He turns and forces himself to cross up between* DIGGER's *and* TOMMY's *beds. He looks out the open window, solemn and silent.*)

LACHIE (*turning to* DIGGER, *eagerly*). There's a weired tropical bird in the ban-yan tree. (*He points, ill at ease.* DIGGER *raises himself on his elbow and looks out indifferently.)*

DIGGER. Yes, a crow.

(LACHIE glances out again. After a moment's hesitation, he whips a pack of cigarettes out of his bathrobe pocket.)

LACHIE. Cigarette?

DIGGER *(amazed).* Thanks. *(He takes one. LACHIE turns and offers one to TOMMY.)*

TOMMY *(equally amazed).* Thanks.

(LACHIE moves over to YANK's bed, where KIWI sits. He extends the package to KIWI.)

KIWI *(impressed).* Thanks.

LACHIE *(turns to YANK, who is sitting with his back to him. He clears his throat).*

Wuid ye care fur a cigarette? *(There is a pause. The words sink in. YANK looks up, realizing the offer has come from LACHIE. He takes one without answering. He starts to light it but LACHIE beats him to it. YANK accepts the light in surprised silence. LACHIE then lights his own cigarette. After an awkward moment, he clears his throat and indicates the end of YANK's bed.)* May I sit doon?

(YANK nods. LACHIE sits. The men smoke silently. LACHIE steals a look at them out of the corner of his eye. YANK smiles to himself. YANK straightens up and as his shoulder touches LACHIE's, their two arms rise with the cigarettes and they both take a puff—YANK grinning, LACHIE contented, back to back, as the

CURTAIN FALLS

SCENE II

It is evening, a few nights following Scene I.

The fast-fading sunlight comes in from the side window at the right. The other windows are closed for the night.

DIGGER is off stage in the washroom. TOMMY is letting down DIGGER's net and his own. He is in his pajamas.

BLOSSOM, in his blues, is putting down his net and KIWI's and tucking them in.

YANK has his towel around his neck and toothbrush in his pocket as he lets down his net. KIWI is seen sitting on his bed, with LACHIE standing over him, lecturing. Every time KIWI tries politely to rise, he is forced back by LACHIE's intensity.

LACHIE *(friendly, fervently and overpoweringly).* And ye may remember, Kiwi, whin a humble member of the House asked Parliament fur thruppence tae be added tae the auld-age Pension. And wot happens? Ye would hae thought the Govermint was being asked tae throw away the Crown jewels. *(KIWI starts to rise but LACHIE pushes him back.)* Thruppence, mind ye. Their Lordships leaps tae their feet— *(He illustrates this with his hands, at which time KIWI takes advantage of the opportunity to rise also.)* —like Jack-in-the-boxes.

KIWI *(a note of panic in his voice).* That's very interesting, Lachie, but let's finish it tomorrow. *(He backs away, patting LACHIE on the shoulder. LACHIE follows him tenaciously.)*

LACHIE *(with arm outstretched).* "Bankrupt the Empire," they shouts. *(KIWI backs toward the washroom, with LACHIE in pur*

suit.) "Whir will the money come frae?" yells another.

KIWI *(desperately indicating YANK).* Why don't you tell Yank? He knows more about politics than I do.

(LACHIE turns toward YANK, and KIWI ducks into the washroom.)

LACHIE *(descends on YANK).* Thruppence, mind ye. Tae help the purr. "Ye canna git blood frae a turnip," warns the Prime Minister.

YANK *(affectionately).* Look, Buster, you've been talking steadily for a week. Why don't you play your bagpipe? *(He places his hand on LACHIE's shoulder, pats him and goes back to tucking in his net.)*

LACHIE *(undiscouraged).* But I notice they can raise money quick enough whin there's blood tae be got frae a mon. Or a war tae fight.

YANK (*crosses toward the washroom*). Why don't you have Parliament adjourn while I brush my teeth?

LACHIE (*following, so that* YANK *has to turn around*). "We are sorry fur the purr," says Parliament. "Boot the Governmint is purr." Weel, dew ye happen to ken wot his Majesty's Governmint is spending daily tae persecute the war?

TOMMY. It must be a fearful amount.

(LACHIE *turns to answer* TOMMY, *and* YANK *dashes into the washroom with his towel.*)

LACHIE. Over a million pounds. A million pounds. (*He glances back and sees* YANK *gone. With no audience, he crosses to attack* TOMMY *with his logic.*) And . . . Who are these magicians that gits money whir none was? (*He points an indisputable finger at* TOMMY.) The eky-nomists.

TOMMY (*never very bright. But often right*). The who?

LACHIE. The eky-nomists.

TOMMY. Are they on our side?

LACHIE (*nods*). And whir dew they git the money? They up and prints it!

TOMMY (*starts toward the washroom*). Then why don't they print more and increase me pay?

LACHIE (*following him*). The more they prints, the less it's worth. That's why I advise ye—follow ma' example and poot yur money in the land. Ye canna print land.

TOMMY. I'll put mine into my stomach. Beer! (*He giggles and ducks into the washroom, leaving* LACHIE *stranded.* LACHIE *turns back toward his bed, and sees* BLOSSOM *fixing* KIWI'S *bed. He corners* BLOSSOM, *who listens with a confused expression.*)

LACHIE (*jabbing his finger into the* BASUTO'S *vast chest*). Dew ye realize wot it costs tae train each soldier poot intae the field? Ten thousand pounds apiece! Now, if ye gave each mon on both sides just half of that, ye'd stop the war in two minutes and cut yur national debt in half!

BLOSSOM (*pleased at being talked to*). Blos-som!

(MARGARET *enters and stands watching, amused.*)

LACHIE (*earnestly*). It's a purr example the Governmint sets fur the individual.

MARGARET. *And* just what do you think you're doing?

LACHIE (*turns and sees her*). I was giving ma' friends the benefit of ma' experience. (*He crosses to his bed and sits on the foot of it.* BLOSSOM *goes into the washroom, carrying his pajamas, leaving* MARGARET *and* LACHIE *alone.*)

MARGARET. Well, save a little something to talk about tomorrow. Lights out in ten minutes. (*She lets down his net.*) How have you felt today, Lachie?

LACHIE. It's odd ye shuid ask that. (*He sits on the end of his bed.*)

MARGARET. No, it's one of my duties.

LACHIE. I thought perhaps ye'd read ma' mind. Fur I've a wee weariness. Ma' hands sweat a bit and ma' feet seem swollen.

MARGARET. You've been walking around the ward too much. And talking too much.

LACHIE. A mon moost walk a bit and talk a bit. He's nae a vegetable.

MARGARET. But when you tire yourself, you don't sleep well. Last night when I came in you were tossing and whimpering in your sleep.

LACHIE (*indignantly*). I dinna whimper.

MARGARET (*smiling*). Well, you weren't sleeping soundly.

LACHIE. I'd a problem, and ma' brain gae me no peace.

MARGARET (*gently*). Are you worried about anything, Lachie?

LACHIE. Aye.

MARGARET. May I help?

LACHIE. Weel, it's nae easy fur a mon of ma' strong character tae admit he might hae blundered. I'm nae wot ye think I am, Sister.

MARGARET. Are you sure you know what I think?

LACHIE (*seriously*). Ye probably think me wise and shrewd. Ye probably think I've the proper value on all ma' problems. Ye probably think there's naught confuses me.

MARGARET *(with warm amusement)*. Is that what I think?

LACHIE. Aye. *(He digs deep into his soul.)* Ye see, Sister, I've nae always liked the human race. I'd nae love or respect fur any mon. I'd nae faith in the guidness of people. And whin the war came, it did nae help.

MARGARET. But you told me you had many friends in Scotland.

LACHIE *(looks away)*. I lied. How cuid I? I'd nae education. Being purr as a church moose, I'd nae money tae squander. I'd naught tae interest or offer. A mon canna take wi' out gaen, too.

MARGARET. Why not?

LACHIE. A mon's pride.

MARGARET *(helpfully)*. But humility's a virtue, too.

LACHIE. Boot nae a strong one. In ma' life befur, nae one ever liked me, and there was nae one I liked. Boot I've changed.

MARGARET. Gracious, I'd hate to think it took a war to change you, Lachie.

LACHIE. Aye, boot it's true. *(Off stage we hear* TOMMY *giggle and* DIGGER *say, "Aw, dry up."* LACHIE *rises and looks toward the washroom.)* I did nae ken a mon cuid be yur friend and want nothing frae ye. And now I've twenty-one years tae make up fur. I've got tae dew ma' share of the helping.

MARGARET *(moved and trying to help— tactfully)*. Lachie, if you've found a new set of values, don't feel that you must rush out and pay for them.

LACHIE. But it's like repentance, Sister. Ye've no idea how it grows inside me. I've a terrible need tae help.

MARGARET. Well— *(She hesitates.)* You've ample time. When the lights are out, I'm going to bring you back something warm to drink. It'll put you to sleep.

LACHIE. If it's nae trouble tae ye.

MARGARET. No trouble at all. I'll have Yank give you your massage. *(She goes to the washroom and calls.)* Yank, I may be a few minutes late. Will you give Lachie his rub?

YANK *(off stage)*. Sure.

MARGARET. And don't forget to close the window. *(She crosses to go out of the ward.)* Better get out of your blues and go to bed, Lachie. I don't want you lying awake all night plotting to change the world. *(She goes out.* LACHIE *sits on his own bed and gets out of the blues that cover his pajamas. In a moment* TOMMY *enters.)*

TOMMY. Oh, I do 'ope I don't 'ave me terrible dreams again. Last night I thought me stomach was so big I 'ad to carry it in front of me in a wheelbarrow.

LACHIE. Cuid I hae a moment of yur time, Tommy?

TOMMY. Why not? We've no place to go but bed.

LACHIE. Whin ye go back after the war, hae ye a job waiting?

TOMMY. Me job is me old lady. 'Er father owns a pub.

LACHIE. Ah, it's nae guid tae work fur relations. As ye ken, I've a bit of land in Scotland and it occurred tae me that ye might like a place tae visit and rest a bit. There'd always be tobacco tae smoke and bread tae eat and a guid chair of yur own tae sit and talk in.

TOMMY. Thank you for the offer, Lachie, but if I ever get away from me old lady, it will have to be farther than Scotland. *(He blows out the lantern beside his bed.)*

LACHIE. Ye'd like Doon Foot.

TOMMY. I talk about her unkind like, but in me way, I love me wife, the silly old wash-tub. *(He climbs under the mosquito net into his bed.)*

LACHIE. It was nae a hasty offer. I gae it thought fur yur own guid.

TOMMY. And most kind of you, but I'm going back to Blighty. *(YANK enters and closes the last window. Except for the lantern lights, it is now dark inside the basha.)* And if you ever visit London, me wife's 'ome is yours. *(He yawns loudly.)* Good night.

LACHIE. Guid nicht.

YANK (*getting the rubbing alcohol*). D-did you think I'd forgotten you?

LACHIE. No.

YANK. Well, stretch out, Buster.

LACHIE (*lifts his pajama top and lies on his stomach at the foot of his own bed*). I dinna ken why I shuid be sae weary.

YANK. Relax.

LACHIE. Yank.

YANK. Yeah? (*Starts to rub his back.*)

LACHIE. As ye know, I've a wee hoose in Scotland. I was thinking that whin the war is done—since ye've nae place tae gae but America—ye cuid come and live in ma' hoose as long as ye wanted.

YANK. Thanks, Buster, but when that time comes, I'm headed straight home.

LACHIE. But hae ye an occupation tae return tae?

YANK. You could call it that. There's my gal waiting for me.

LACHIE. Are ye very mooch in love?

YANK. Whatever it is, I've got it. In glorious, multiplane technicolor.

LACHIE (*pauses*). Whin dew ye leave the hospital, Yank?

YANK. Old Cobwebs signs my papers tomorrow. I leave the day after. (*YANK stoops down to get more alcohol.*)

LACHIE. Day after tomorrow. It'll nae be the same wi' ye gone. Most likely I'll never hear of ye agaen.

YANK. When I get married, I'll send you a tinted picture of Niagara Falls.

LACHIE. And I'll send ye a photo of ma' hoose in Scotland.

YANK (*rising and rubbing*). Send me a picture of yourself in that damned kilt. Looks like it's the only way I'll ever see it.

LACHIE. Ye're sure tomorrow will be yur last day wi' us?

YANK. Unless Old Cobwebs changes his mind.

LACHIE (*hesitantly*). I was planning on wearing ma' kilt the day I went back tae ma' regiment. But if ye liked . . .

YANK. Buster, you don't mean you might change your mind?

LACHIE. I was thinking—if ye poot a value on it—I cuid wear ma' kilt in yur honor instead.

YANK. Look, Lachie, wear it for me tomorrow and I'll take your picture. I just got two new rolls of film from h-home.

LACHIE. Dew ye ken I've never had ma' photo took?

YANK. Then we'll take it tomorrow.

LACHIE. Aye, I'll wear ma' kilt. But ye'll hae tae let me pay fur the film.

YANK (*picks up the bottle and dries his back*). No need to do that. I've the extra roll.

LACHIE (*stubborn again*). I'll nae hae ma' photo took unless ye sell me both yur rolls of film. I may need both, fur I'd like photos of each mon ma'self.

YANK. If it makes you feel any freer, I'll let you pay for them.

LACHIE. I'll gie ye the money in the morning.

YANK (*grinning*). I t-t-trust you. (*He starts to his bed.*) Turn your light out?

LACHIE. I think I'll hae a cigarette first. (*When YANK offers him a cigarette.*) I've ma' own.

YANK. None of that.

LACHIE (*guiltily*). Aye. (*He takes one.* DIGGER *and* KIWI *come back from the washroom in their pajamas and prepare to go to bed.*) Thank ye.

YANK. Well, I'm going to hit the sack. I'm dead tonight. (*He turns his light out.*)

DIGGER. If Tommy snores tonight, I'll cut his bloody ears off.

YANK (*crawls under his net*). A few more days of convalescing and I'd be ready to collapse. Good night, Lachie.

LACHIE. Guid nicht, Booster. (LACHIE *looks thoughtfully over at* DIGGER, *who is tucking in his net, rises and goes over to him.*) Digger, whin we've peace agaen, dew ye ken wot ye'll dew?

DIGGER. I'm going to collect my kid and my darling and carry them back to Australia. (*Continuing to tuck in his net.*)

LACHIE. I'm sure it's a guid country, but have ye a job there?

DIGGER. My back'll be as good as ever.

LACHIE. Hae ye ever thought of looking fur work in Scotland?

DIGGER. Gawd, no. Has anyone?

LACHIE. I've some land, as ye no doot recall, wi' a wee hoose on it. Ye're most welcome tae it, fur yur family—nae charge. I've guid soil and ye cuid make a living—nae rent.

DIGGER. When I turn in my pay-book, I'm headed in one direction only—Australia. (He closes his eyes.) Gawd, Australia! When I think of it, I get a toothache in my heart.

LACHIE. There's nae bonnier land than Scotland.

DIGGER (easily). I'll visit ya some day when I'm rich.

LACHIE. Aye. If ye're rich ye'll need nae help. I'll nae see ye agaen.

DIGGER. You can't tell. Anyhow, I'll never be rich. But ya can bet I'll never be poor. (He blows out his light.) I'll send ya a postal card from down under. And a letter. (He crawls into bed.)

LACHIE (eagerly). Ye'll write me a letter?

DIGGER. I'll write ya a letter, too.

LACHIE (considers this new experience). A letter in ma' own name. Lachlen McLachlen. (Pause.) Esquire!

DIGGER. Gawd, I love sleep. Good night, Lachie. (He tucks his net around himself.)

LACHIE. Guid nicht. (He stands silent for a moment. KIWI is at the foot of his bed tucking his net.)

KIWI. It's a wonder I haven't got malaria. Once I'm asleep my feet stick out all night, and the mosquitoes think it's a blood bank.

LACHIE (crossing to him). Cuid ye nae sleep wi' yur sox on?

KIWI. Those mosquitoes would just gang up and pull 'em off. (He starts to get under his net.)

LACHIE. I suppose whir ye come frae there are ferocious mosquitoes.

KIWI. New Zealand mosquitoes can have all my blood they want. Once I get back, nothing's ever going to get me away again!

LACHIE (sighs). Ye really moost gae home?

KIWI. Look, did you ever transplant anything and manage to get all the roots out of the ground?

LACHIE (sadly). Aye. I know.

KIWI. Well, that's it. But I'll write to you. I'll keep in touch with you. (He tucks in his net.) I'm turning in. Will you put my light out? (LACHIE blows out the light for KIWI.) Thanks. Good night.

LACHIE. Guid nicht.

(BLOSSOM returns in his pajamas and starts to climb into his bed. LACHIE hurries to him—then hesitates.)

BLOSSOM (looking up). Blos-som!

(LACHIE turns away, discouraged.)

LACHIE. Naw, they'd nae understand ye in Scotland.

(BLOSSOM blows his light out and goes to bed. LACHIE moves about the ward in the shadows, tucking in the nets of the men. He makes sure that YANK'S net is tucked in securely and returns to his own bed. His is the only lantern left glowing. MARGARET tiptoes in carrying a cup.)

MARGARET (quietly). Sorry I took so long, but I had to find the key to the store room.

LACHIE. I was talking tae ma' friends.

MARGARET. Drink this. It will help you to sleep.

LACHIE. Thank ye. (He sits down on the end of his bed but doesn't drink.) They're going tae write me letters frae all over the world. They said sae. (He looks up at her.) Dew ye ken wot that does tae me, Sister?

MARGARET. It should make you very proud.

LACHIE. Aye, moor than that. No matter where I go agaen in ma' life, I'm nae alone.

MARGARET (gently). Yes, I know how dreadful loneliness can be, Lachie.

LACHIE. Ah, but there's naught I can dew. Fur the first time in ma' life I want tae help. And I dinna know how.

MARGARET. I thought I told you to stop worrying.

LACHIE. But I've got tae dew something, Sister. It's a great torment tae me. I owe sae much.

MARGARET (*sits beside him*). All right, Lachie. To whom do you think you owe something? To your fellow man?

LACHIE. Aye, if it's the guidness in ma' fellow man I've wronged—weel—I cuid turn ma' farm intae a place tae go fur wounded lads wi' nae home of their own.

MARGARET. Slowly, Lachlen. Remember, "Sorrow's born in the hasty heart."

LACHIE. I'm nae hasty. I know ma' duty. I cuid nae be a preacher. I know naught aboot God. And I'm nae so sure I owe ma' friends tae God. I did nae praying.

MARGARET. You simply can't stand being indebted, can you?

LACHIE. I can nae write a buuk. I've nae schooling. I've only ma' wish tae help and ma' two hands and ma' land tae gie away.

MARGARET. Lachie, if you would only . . . (*She rises.*) Wait a minute. (*She flashes her flashlight into each bed to make sure the men are all sleeping and then returns to sit beside* LACHIE.) Lachie, instead of the things that you own, why don't you share yourself with your fellow man? We'd be much richer. I know that I am —for the things you've shared with me already.

LACHIE. Ye can nae mean me, Sister.

MARGARET. But I do. As a human being, I don't suppose I have any real—oh—individuality. I'm the people I've met. I'm a mixture of everything I've read and seen. I've stolen a virtue here—and a weakness there. I'm everyone I ever loved.

LACHIE. And ye've taken something frae me?

MARGARET. Without your knowing it.

LACHIE. Do ye know something, Sister— if I'd nae stopped ma' bit of shrapnel, I'd nae hae known I cuid be sae content wi' ma'self. I had tae be hurt tae learn.

MARGARET. No, I don't think you *had* to be hurt. But there was good in it.

LACHIE (*ponders*). Dew ye suppose the world wuid be a healthier place if moor people were sick?

MARGARET. Gracious, I don't know. (*She rises.*) And now you must sleep.

LACHIE. I'll nae sleep this nicht. Ah— where are the wurds tae free ma' he'rt?

MARGARET. Have you been as happy with us, Lachie, as you've ever been in your life?

LACHIE (*slowly*). I think I've shared a moment wi' kings.

MARGARET (*looks away*). Good night, Lachie. (*She starts to leave.*)

LACHIE. Sister Margaret, dew ye ken ye've gaen me something too, wi'out yur knowing it?

MARGARET (*turns back to him*). What, Lachie?

LACHIE. I'm nae sure wot it is. But it's something I n'er had befur—something that makes me know whin ye leave the room—even whin I canna see ye go.

MARGARET (*softly*). That's very sweet. (*She puts her hand on his shoulder.*)

LACHIE. Ah, ye lovely, lovely angel. (*He takes her hand and presses it to his lips. Then releases it, uneasily.*)

MARGARET. You shouldn't have done that.

LACHIE. Aye, I'd nae right.

(MARGARET *looks down at him a moment. Looking up at her, anxious and grateful, he seems very young.* MARGARET *cups his face in her hands and kisses him on the mouth.*)

MARGARET. No right at all. (*She turns and leaves the ward.* LACHIE *rises and watches her go. He takes a deep breath and quickly turns and brings out his bagpipes. He sits on his bed and is about to start playing when he realizes the men are asleep. He looks around. Then he gently folds the bagpipes, rises, and tiptoes to put them back as*

THE CURTAIN FALLS

ACT THREE

SCENE I

The next afternoon.
Lined up around TOMMY's *bed are the six patients.* MARGARET *stands off several feet with a box camera in her hands. In the center of the group stands* LACHIE, *resplendent in his kilt, and with his cap cocked over one eye. Their expressions are grim.*

MARGARET. You look exactly like those living statues one used to see in the circus. *(She gestures.)* Can you crowd in a little more? *(They do.)* And look a little more pleasant.

TOMMY. I'm being squeezed now, I am.

KIWI. If you put Tommy in back, there'd be more room in front.

MARGARET. Kneel on the bed, Tommy. *(*TOMMY *climbs up on the bed, where he stands behind the others.)*

KIWI. That's a relief—to get him off my feet.

TOMMY. It's a relief to get off me own feet. *(A minor giggle.)*

MARGARET *(looks into the camera again.* LACHIE *has remained "frozen" throughout this).* Lachie, can you smile a little more?

LACHIE *(growls).* I'm nae a cinema star. I can nae make an expression at will.

MARGARET. Well, if you can't smile a little more, can you frown a little less?

LACHIE. Will ye take the photo and be done wi' it?

MARGARET. All right, all right. Now this is a time exposure. You'll have to be very still. *(They settle into a stance.)* Ready? Smile. *(Everyone breaks into a fixed smile —everyone but* LACHIE.) One . . . two . . . three . . . *(She straightens up.)* I think that will be a good one. *(There is general relief that the ordeal is over.* MARGARET *stops* LACHIE *as he is about to get behind the screens around his bed.)* Lachie, we have a picture of everyone here now—but you. Let's take one of you by yourself.

LACHIE *(apprehensively).* Naw—

DIGGER. Go ahead, Lachie. Then we can all have a copy.

TOMMY. We've 'ad ours took.

MARGARET *(pleading).* You look so dashing in your kilt. Won't you—please?

KIWI. It won't hurt you.

LACHIE *(determined).* The film belongs tae me and I'll nae dew it.

YANK. Give one g-g-good reason.

LACHIE. I could nae face it *alone.* *(He starts again to enter the screens.)* I think I'll poot ma' kilt away, now.

MARGARET *(persuasively).* There's only one exposure left. Pretend it's an X-ray.

YANK. We can't have any of them developed until that one is t-t-taken.

DIGGER. Go on.

LACHIE *(hesitates).* Weel . . . *(Which was a mistake.)*

YANK. G-g-good! *(He grabs* LACHIE *and places him in the center runway.)*

MARGARET. Stand in the aisle.

LACHIE *(uneasily).* I'm being hurried, but —let's get on wi' it.

*(*YANK *drops on his haunches just in front of* MARGARET *below the camera. The others are behind* LACHIE.)*

YANK. Just pretend you're on your own l-l-land—in your pasture—looking d-down the road.

TOMMY. Up to your kilt in 'eather. *(He giggles.)*

MARGARET. Let's make this one the best of the lot. *(She looks into the camera.* LACHIE *fidgets.)* Stand still, Lachie.

DIGGER. He ought to be smoking a crooked pipe.

TOMMY. 'E ought to 'ave a sheep dog.

YANK. S-s-stop coaching from the sidelines.

(LACHIE *is trying to decide what to do with his hands.*)

MARGARET. Don't wiggle, Lachie. I can't keep you in focus.

LACHIE (*unhappily*). I dinna ken where tae poot ma' hands.

DIGGER. Put 'em in your pockets!

(LACHIE *reaches for non-existent pockets, frowns deeper, and puts his hands at his sides.* TOMMY *has an idea, and reaches for his fly-swatter. He crawls down his bed and across* YANK's, *trying to lift the back of* LACHIE's *kilt with the fly-swatter.* DIGGER *and* KIWI *watch with growing interest.*)

MARGARET. Put your hands on your hips, Lachie. Let's see how that looks. (LACHIE *complies.*) No—that's not good.

DIGGER (*creating a diversion*). How about a profile, with a hand shading his eyes, looking for his sheep.

MARGARET (*noticing* TOMMY *for the first time behind* LACHIE, *crosses to him and shoos him away*). Tommy, get out of the picture! (TOMMY, DIGGER *and* KIWI *all spring away from temptation.* MARGARET *goes back to her position and gets the camera ready again.* LACHIE *meanwhile has decided on arms folded as the best pose.*) Will you please be still—all of you? Don't listen to them, Lachie. (TOMMY *has moved as though he were going to lie down, but he's really trying to stalk the kilt from another angle.*) Now, smile. Smile. (LACHIE's *expression remains set.*) Smile, Lachie.

LACHIE. I can nae smile! (*His sudden gesture sends* TOMMY, KIWI, *and* DIGGER *back to their rightful positions again, with the mystery of the kilt still unsolved.*)

YANK. He's getting m-m-mad. You better get it while you can, Sister. (TOMMY *puts the fly-swatter in his mouth and starts crawling* under *his bed, commando fashion, to get at the kilt.*)

MARGARET. Here we go. One . . . two . . . three. (*She snaps the picture and looks up laughing.*) Oh, thank heaven that's over!

(LACHIE *stalks over to the door, leaving* TOMMY *under* YANK's *bed—frustrated in his attempt to see under the kilt.*)

YANK (*laughing*). You're t-t-terrific.

LACHIE. I thought ye were ma' friends.

YANK. I'm sorry, Lachie, but a mad Scot in a kilt is t-t-terrific.

MARGARET. Thank you, Lachie. You were patient and handsome. (*She hands the camera to* YANK.) Yank, you might stop by the X-ray room and see if they'll develop our pictures.

YANK. Yas'm.

MARGARET. Now, will some of you men go over to Ward C and bring the bath tub over here. They're going to let us use it for a week.

TOMMY. Oooo—just the job. Next to beer I loves a 'ot bath. Tubs full.

KIWI. Can I go, Sister? I'd like to stretch my legs.

MARGARET. I don't care who goes—just so you bring it back. (*She goes out, laughing.*)

LACHIE. Weel, I'll poot ma' kilt away. (*He starts for his screens.*)

TOMMY. Oh, Lachie!

LACHIE (*stops*). Aye?

TOMMY (*slyly*). Do you mind waiting a moment or two? I 'aven't 'ad a real good look at you yet.

LACHIE. Ye'll hae the photo tae study. (*He starts for the screens again.*)

TOMMY (*quickly*). Just stand still a moment so we can admire the kilt.

KIWI. Walk around in 'em, Lachie.

(TOMMY *sits on the foot of* YANK's *bed,* KIWI *sits on the foot of* TOMMY's *bed, and* DIGGER *sits on the foot of his own bed.* YANK *stands between his bed and* TOMMY's.)

LACHIE. If ye wish it. (*He proudly walks to the door, turns sharply and walks back. As he passes the beds, each man tries to catch the back of the kilt and lift it. No one is quick enough.*)

DIGGER. Ah, don't they swish lovely.

(LACHIE *stops and faces them.*)

TOMMY (*trying to devise something else*). Let's see 'ow graceful they looks when you make a *turn*. Wot 'appens?

LACHIE (*proudly*). There's a wee flair. (*He turns slowly and the kilt flairs a bit. As he turns, all four heads snap down and back simultaneously.*)

TOMMY (*frustrated but not discouraged*). Wot would 'appen if you 'ad to whirl?

LACHIE. Naught.

TOMMY. Ah, it should be graceful as a fountain. Let's see you whirl, Lachie.

(*TOMMY gets down on one knee. LACHIE makes a fast whirl. All the heads go down again, but just as they come up, MARGARET opens the door.*)

MARGARET. Are you boys going to get that tub or not?

KIWI (*reluctantly*). Straight away!

LACHIE (*turns to* YANK). Yank, cuid ye wait? I've something I'd like tae ask ye.

YANK. S-s-sure. (*To the others.*) You can manage without me.

DIGGER (*to* TOMMY). Come on, you dirty old man, you'll use the tub, too.

TOMMY. It's a plot to keep me ignorant.

(*TOMMY, KIWI and DIGGER go out to get the tub.*)

YANK. Wh-what's on your m-mind?

LACHIE (*frowns deeply and begins*). I believe ye said ye were getting wed when ye gae home?

YANK. B-bang, b-bang.

LACHIE. Whin were ye sure that ye wanted a wife?

YANK. The first time I kissed my g-g-gal.

LACHIE (*impressed*). Ah, when ye kissed.

YANK. That's the way it was with m-me.

LACHIE. If a guid girl kisses ye, it's an encouraging sign, is it nawt?

YANK (*grinning*). Good or bad, it's encouraging any w-w-way you look at it.

LACHIE. And something happens that ye can nae explain away?

YANK. Oh, I could explain it all right, but it doesn't help.

LACHIE. I think I'd like tae wed. (*He sits on the foot of* YANK's *bed.*) I think.

YANK. Aren't you sure?

LACHIE. Aye, that's ma' problem. Dew ye think I've a right tae ask a lass tae be ma' wife? Now, wi' things like they are? (*YANK does not answer.* LACHIE *looks up at him.*) Why dew ye hesitate?

YANK (*cautiously*). What do you mean by —"with things like they are"?

LACHIE. Weel, if I was tae wed now, I'd hae tae return tae ma' regiment. Wuid that be fair tae ma' bride?

YANK. L-look, B-buster—you mean . . . (*He points toward the door.*)

LACHIE. Aye. Bonnie Sister Margaret.

YANK. B-but you can't

LACHIE. She's nae married.

YANK. L-look, Lachie. Everybody falls in love with his nurse. It's natural. I'll bet every patient that's been in this ward has fallen in love with Sister Margaret, for a while. She l-looks after us and she's g-good to us. But that doesn't mean she loves us. You might be making a mistake to think it means anything else.

LACHIE. Aye, that's why I wanted—your advice. You're a fellow-Scot. (*YANK throws him a look of dubious agreement.*) Did ye ever hear of Sister Margaret kissing a patient?

YANK. Well, she hasn't k-k-kissed me.

LACHIE. Then if she kissed a man of her own free will, it wuid mean she meant tae —encourage him?

YANK. Did she kiss you?

LACHIE. Aye.

YANK. Oh.

LACHIE (*softly*). She cupped ma' face in her two soft hands—and she kissed me.

YANK. Hmm. Lachie, women k-k-kiss lots of men without having it mean m-marriage.

LACHIE. But dew ye think Sister Margaret is sae free?

YANK (*reluctantly, sits on the foot of* TOMMY's *bed next to him*). No.

LACHIE (*leaning forward*). Sae if she kissed me—and she did—it moost mean something?

YANK (*cornered*). S-something.

LACHIE. I lay awake the whole nicht wondering how ma' fortune cuid be sae great. Still, I've nae wish tae make a fool of ma'self. (*Turns to* YANK.) Dew ye think I'd be unwise tae risk a proposal?

YANK (*hedging*). I d-d-don't know.

LACHIE. But the facts are in ma' favor. (*He waits for* YANK *to agree—eagerly.*)

YANK (*pauses*). H-h-hell, go ahead. If it's worth having, it's worth sticking your neck out for.

LACHIE. Aye. Then I will. I've ma' proposal prepared.

YANK (*floored*). I wish you'd sleep more and think less.

(*At this point* MARGARET *enters, waving a bottle of pills.*)

MARGARET. Lachie, I've some medicine for you. (*She crosses to the medicine chest next to the window, where the* BASUTO *stands looking toward far-off lands.*) Deserted, Blossom?

YANK (*whispers to* LACHIE). You c-c-couldn't want a better chance.

LACHIE. Ye mean now?

YANK (*emphatically*). R-right now.

LACHIE. Aye. (*He rubs his chin.*) I'm glad I kept ma' kilt on. It'll nae hert ma' purpose.

YANK. By all means, keep your k-kilt on.

MARGARET (*comes back to* LACHIE *with a glass and the pills*). The M.O. wants you to take these.

LACHIE. It's a wilful waste of pills.

YANK (*starting off*). I'll see you later, Lachie. (*Calls to* BLOSSOM.) Hey, Blossom! Come on. (BLOSSOM *starts over.* YANK *takes him by the hand.*) I'll take you out and teach you another word—one s-s-suitable for all occasions. (*They both go out.*)

MARGARET (*turns to* LACHIE). Well?

LACHIE. Wi' guid men ill, he orders the pills tae molest me.

MARGARET. Why don't you humor him, poor old Colonel?

LACHIE. Aye, I will. I'll nae admit tae him I mind. (*He takes the pills and downs them.* MARGARET *takes the glass and starts to leave.*) Hae ye a minute tae spare, Sister?

MARGARET. Well, I was going over to see the matron, but—what did you want?

LACHIE. I wa' thinking of making a proposal of marriage. I think ye'd best be seated.

MARGARET (*sits down on* TOMMY's *bed—promptly*). Good gracious—yes. (*Pauses. Perhaps she did not really hear it.*) Just a moment, Lachie, is this proposal of marriage directed at me?

LACHIE. Aye, who else?

MARGARET. Oh! (*She heard it.*)

LACHIE. I told you once that I had nae plans fur marriage in ma' future. Ye may recall.

MARGARET. Vividly.

LACHIE. Weel, I've said some things I've cause tae regret. Among them was ma' attitude on marriage.

MARGARET (*frowns and takes a deep breath*). Lachie, you mustn't feel that . . .

LACHIE. Please dinna interrupt me. (*He stands beside her and clasps his hands behind him.*) I'm nae much of a mon on the surface boot I've a great and powerful will tae wurk. I've a wee butt-n-ben in Scotland which ye know aboot. Ma' health is guid, regardless of the Colonel's spite. I've a fearful temper, boot I dinna think I'll ever make ye suffer fur it. I'll dew ma' best. Until I get out of the army, I've ma' pay. Ye know wot it is and I'll sign it over tae ye. I'll gie ye all I can. Ye'll never want fur food and ye'll never worry aboot rent. I've wurked since I was seven. I've been a cabin boy, a seaman, a carpenter, a farmer, a miner, a stevedore and a staff sergeant. I can always wurk fur ye. I'm twenty-one. I'm nae legitimate. Ma' mother was nae wed. (*He begins to search his mind in desperation.*) I've good teeth. (*He searches for another virtue.*) I'm nae tattooed. (*And gives up.*) I hope ye'll nae be hasty in considering ma' proposal.

MARGARET (*sits with her hands over her eyes*). Lachie, are you offering me your life, because you think you owe me something?

LACHIE (*softly*). I offer ye ma' he'rt because it does me nae guid wi'out ye.

MARGARET *(rises and turns away from him.)* Oh, Lachie, it isn't simple.

LACHIE. There's anoother in yur life?

MARGARET. It isn't that.

LACHIE. Ye dinna share ma' feeling? *(He waits.)* I've made ye unhappy. I presumed tae much. Can ye forgi'e me?

MARGARET *(turns on him)*. Oh, you wretched stubborn little man. Why must I love you?

LACHIE. Please, ye confuse me. Dew ye— or don't ye?

MARGARET. God help us, I do.

LACHIE *(stares at her)*. I can nae believe it. *(He takes her hands.)* Ye'll marry me?

MARGARET. If you want me. *(She takes his face in her hands.)* Must I always kiss you first?

LACHIE *(kisses her gently, a little awkwardly)*. Ah, ma' Bonnie Maggie.

MARGARET *(laughs)*. Oh, dear—not Maggie.

LACHIE. I'll dew naught tae displease.

(They sit together on the end of a bed.)

MARGARET. No need for promises.

LACHIE *(suddenly)*. But how can ye care fur me?

MARGARET. And no doubts.

LACHIE. Ah—nae. Just sae ye dew. Just sae ye dew.

(There is a bang on the door and it swings open.)

TOMMY *(backing in, carrying a bath stool)*. Mind the frame, you'll knock the whole *basha* down. Easy.

DIGGER *(enters with the front end of a small tin tub, made, undoubtedly, by the Royal Engineers out of petrol tins)*. I'll bet this is the tub they boil the tea in.

KIWI *(carrying the other end)*. That's a good bet. I'll take it.

(They all cross to the washroom.)

TOMMY. I think I'll sit in the tub and do me laundry.

KIWI. If you sit in it, you'll wear it for life.

(They carry it out into the washroom.)

MARGARET *(rises and kisses LACHIE gently)*. The matron's waiting for me.

LACHIE. I've waited fur ye all ma' life. Ah, dinna gae fur.

MARGARET. Lachie, there are many things I'd like to say to you—and I probably never shall. We've suddenly crossed many rivers. Let's not waste time looking back.

(YANK whistles off stage. MARGARET straightens up and passes YANK as he enters. YANK closes the door behind her. LACHIE has risen, put on his cap, and is striding back and forth proudly, his kilt swishing.)

YANK. Well?

LACHIE. If ye did nae despise it sae, I'd *play ma' bagpipes!*

YANK *(grinning)*. I k-k-know the answer.

LACHIE. She loves me, Yank.

YANK. When do you get married?

LACHIE. We've nae set the date. I'll want ye tae stand up fur me.

YANK. Be your b-best man? Sure.

LACHIE. Thank you, Yank. *(Awkwardly, LACHIE shakes hands.)* Thank ye kindly. And now, if ye'll excuse me, I'll put ma' kilt away. *(He goes to the screens around his bed.)*

YANK *(following him)*. I'll s-sit here with you.

LACHIE. I think I'll rest, if ye dinna mind. *(YANK nods.)* Thank ye.

(LACHIE closes the screen. DIGGER, TOMMY, and KIWI enter. They cross from the washroom.)

DIGGER *(to TOMMY)*. When you go in to bathe, take a towel, some scented soap, and a can-opener!

(As TOMMY passes the screen, he notices YANK.)

TOMMY. Is 'e changing?

(YANK nods. TOMMY snaps his fingers to signal the others. DIGGER and KIWI crowd behind TOMMY. BLOSSOM enters and joins the crowd. TOMMY gets down on his knees and peers in the crack of the screens. DIGGER taps TOMMY on the shoulder to find out what is happening. TOMMY makes the motion of peeling off a shirt. KIWI can

stand it no longer and leans over to tap TOMMY. TOMMY *slowly pantomimes that* LACHIE *is scratching himself. The* COLONEL *enters. He stops upon seeing the men at the screen. He clears his throat.*)

COLONEL. Just what is this all about!

(*The men straighten in confusion, salute and hurry to their beds.*)

TOMMY. We was settling a bet, sir. It's kilts—kilts, sir.

COLONEL. Where is the orderly? Where is the Sister?

YANK. I d-don't know. She just stepped out, sir.

COLONEL. Well, where's Sergeant Mc-Lachlen?

KIWI (*motioning to the screens*). He's in there, sir.

COLONEL (*to* YANK). Move the screens away. I want to talk to him.

YANK. Yes, sir. (*Together with* KIWI, *he takes the screens away.* LACHIE *turns around to face them. He is in his blues by now.*) The Colonel to see you, Lachie.

LACHIE (*buttoning his jacket quickly*). I was just changing, sir.

COLONEL. Quite all right. (*He crosses to* LACHIE.) Did you take the pills I sent you?

LACHIE (*truculently*). Aye, I took them. But ye can nae force me tae take any moor.

COLONEL. What's that?

LACHIE (*standing his ground*). May I be sae bauld as tae remind ye, sir, that as a British soldier, I've a right tae refuse them?

COLONEL (*turns to the others*). You men wait outside. (*They go out quickly, closing the door behind them. The* COLONEL *studies* LACHIE.) I've just come from talking to the DMS about you.

LACHIE. Is it a charge ye're bringing agaen me?

COLONEL. Sit down. (LACHIE *sits at the foot of his bed.*) Before I moved you over here, I called GHQ about the possibility of having you flown back.

LACHIE (*puzzled*). Back where, sir?

COLONEL. I thought you might want to go back to Scotland—might have some matters there you'd want to attend to. But I was told by GHQ that the request was preposterous"—"too many priorities." It seems that a hundred and eight Brigadiers were on the waiting list.

LACHIE. I dinna ken why ye shuid dew that fur me.

COLONEL. When we were turned down, I decided to keep you here. (*He pulls at his nose.*) Ah, have you got along all right? Satisfied?

LACHIE. Aye. There's guid men here, sir.

COLONEL (*sits on the foot of* YANK's *bed opposite* LACHIE). Well, I've just had a call from Army. Someone at GHQ has decided you're more important than the waiting list.

LACHIE. Ye moost be joking, sir. I'm a sergeant. (*Adding with pride.*) Of course, in the Camerons.

COLONEL. Sergeant or Brigadier, there's a passage booked for you tomorrow, if I can get you to the Wing Commander. You're being given an A-1 priority. You can be in Scotland inside of three days. Do you want to go?

LACHIE. It's a great temptation. Whin cuid I return?

COLONEL (*hesitates*). You wouldn't return.

LACHIE. Ye mean I'd nae be permitted tae return tae ma' regiment?

COLONEL. Sergeant, I've been given a direct order. I disagree with that order, but I'm a soldier. I argued against it for half an hour. Well, I've no choice. There seems to be a regulation somewhere—probably dates from the Boer War. Anyhow the DMS remembers it and says you must be given the full facts of your case.

LACHIE. But I've been gaen the facts.

COLONEL. When you came in here with that shrapnel in your kidney, there was a chance you'd recover.

LACHIE. Aye. I have.

COLONEL. You recovered from the operation—yes. But you've one kidney left—a bad one. I know you feel quite well but that one kidney is destined to—collapse.

LACHIE. Aye. Then wot dew ye dew?

COLONEL. Nothing. We can't give a man a new kidney. There's nothing that surgery or medicine can do to help. Do you understand?

LACHIE (*pauses*). Aye. And the mon?

COLONEL. Waits.

LACHIE (*quietly*). How long?

COLONEL. A week or two more.

LACHIE (*is silent for a moment*). I've nae mooch time.

COLONEL. I didn't tell you, Sergeant, because there seemed nothing to gain. Now —I've been ordered to tell you.

LACHIE (*dazed*). I thought ye had a spite on me.

COLONEL. Hardly. I wish I could give you a kidney of mine. I've damned little use for two. Would you like to go back?

LACHIE. Ma' brain is numb, and I must think.

COLONEL. GHQ feels that you can do your country a further service. They'll make a hero of you. Fly you back with a great deal of fanfare. I know that part of it won't mean anything to you. But you'll see Scotland again. The alternative is to stay with us—stay here with your friends.

(*At the word "friends," realization dawns on* LACHIE. *He lifts his head slowly and speaks, dreading to hear the answer to his question.*)

LACHIE. Did the lads in the ward know aboot me, sir?

COLONEL. Yes. I wanted things made as pleasan' as possible for you. I asked them to help you.

LACHIE (*his voice rasps*). And the Sister?

COLONEL. Naturally, she had to know.

LACHIE (*rises and faces the side window away from the* COLONEL). I'd like tae go back tae Scotland, sir.

COLONEL (*rising also*). I can get you down to Calcutta in the morning in plenty of time, if that's your decision.

LACHIE. That's ma' choice.

COLONEL. In the meantime?

LACHIE. I'd like tae be left tae ma'self.

COLONEL. Certainly—certainly. (*He takes a step toward* LACHIE's *unrelenting back.*) I wish I could say something wise and warm and reassuring.

LACHIE (*whirling on him*). Ye can spare me that. I've had enough pity, thank ye.

COLONEL. If I can be of service to you, call on me. (*He turns.*) I'll take care of your papers and arrange for your transport. (*And he goes out.* LACHIE *whirls and pulls the two screens around his bed as* DIGGER, TOMMY, KIWI *and* YANK *re-enter.*)

DIGGER (*lightly*). What did Old Cobwebs want, Lachie?

TOMMY (*laughing*). 'E ticked Lachie off about the pills.

KIWI. I liked the way our Lachie stood up to him.

YANK (*goes to his own bed, picks up the camera and takes the film out*). D-don't pay any attention to Old Cobwebs, Lachie. He likes to throw his weight around. (*Holding the film.*) I'll take these over to be developed now.

(LACHIE *steps over and snatches the film. He unrolls it and destroys it.*)

DIGGER (*aghast*). Hey, what are you doing?

YANK. Hey, Lachie! Don't ruin 'em.

LACHIE (*viciously*). Wud ye mind going back tae yur own bed.

YANK. What's the matter, Lachie?

LACHIE. I'll nae ask ye agaen. (*He steps inside the screens and closes them behind him. The boys look from one to the other.* MARGARET *enters, and* YANK *turns to her.*)

MARGARET (*tensely*). Did you talk to him?

YANK. He spoilt the pictures. What's wrong with him, Sister?

MARGARET (*looking toward the screens*). The Colonel told him everything.

YANK. Why?

MARGARET. Orders from the DMS. (*She goes down to the screens and stands outside them.*) Oh, I do think they were wrong.

DIGGER. Gawd, what good will it do him?

(LACHIE *comes out from behind his screens.*

He carries the box in which are piled the kilt and presents. He places them on YANK's *bed.)*

LACHIE. I'll return these tae ye.

MARGARET *(stepping in front of him).* Lachie!

LACHIE *(turning on her).* I'll be gaen away in the morning. If ye've any decency in ye, will ye kindly nae speak tae me? Leave me in peace behind ma' screens. *(He faces the men.)* I'll nae wish tae see ye—any of ye.

YANK. Now, wait a m-minute, Lachie.

LACHIE. I'll break yur face if ye poot a hand on me.

MARGARET *(anguish in her voice).* You'll need us, Lachie. You'll need us.

LACHIE. I'll need nae one. *(There is hatred in his face as he looks at them.)* I shuid hae known ye'd be like all the rest. Well, ye bought ma' friendship cheaply—fur the price of a kilt. *(He goes back to the screens.)* I shuid hae poot a higher value on ma' pride. How righteous ye must hae felt in yur pity and guidness! *(He steps inside the screens—holding them open with one hand.)* I'll nae let ye hurt me agaen. *(He closes himself inside the screens. They stand silent and stunned as*

THE CURTAIN FALLS

SCENE II

The next morning.
The screens have been put away. LACHIE *is packing his duffle bag.*
The men are sitting, subdued and quiet, on their beds. Both YANK *and* LACHIE *are in their British battle-dress.* MARGARET *enters.*

MARGARET. The O.C. signed your papers, Yank. *(She hands them to him.)*

YANK. When can I leave?

MARGARET. Not until this afternoon.

YANK *(indicating* LACHIE's *bed).* When does he leave?

MARGARET. In a few minutes. *(She starts out.)* Will you collect the breakfast plates? *(She goes out again.)*

*(*YANK *puts his papers on his bed table. He goes around, collecting the breakfast plates.)*

TOMMY. Sister 'as a cold, 'asn't she?

YANK. I didn't notice. *(He passes on to* DIGGER.*)*

DIGGER. I could make tastier tea with feathers.

(He picks up DIGGER's *plate and crosses to* KIWI.*)*

KIWI. After you're gone, I suppose that'll be my job.

YANK. You c-c-can have it. *(He takes* KIWI's *plate and then goes to collect* LACHIE's *dish.* LACHIE *does not look up at him.)* I came to g-g-get your plate. LACHIE *stuffs a towel into his duffle.)*

You've let your breakfast get cold. *(*LACHIE *does not answer.)* Don't you want it? *(When* LACHIE *fails to answer,* YANK *picks up the plate.)* Sister s-s-says you'll be leaving in a few minutes.

LACHIE. Aye.

YANK. Need any help?

LACHIE. I want nae help.

YANK. I was leaving myself this afternoon, but if you stayed, Lachie, I'd spend my two weeks' leave here with you. If you'd like. *(There is no answer.)* Well, I'm d-d-damned sorry to see you go. *(Still no answer.)* I hope things won't b-be too bad. *(He holds out his hand.)* I'd like to say good-bye now. *(He waits.)*

LACHIE. Ye've said it.

*(*YANK *turns away. He carries the dishes out and meets* MARGARET *at the entrance. She looks at the food in the dish on top.* YANK *nods and carries the tray on out.* MARGARET *crosses to* LACHIE *and stops at the foot of his bed.)*

MARGARET. Here are your papers, Lachie. *(When he doesn't take them from her, she places them on the bed.)* They'll send word over as soon as your transport is here.

LACHIE (*without looking at her*). I'll hae ma' kit ready in a moment.

YANK (*re-enters with a dish towel*). How about a little help with these? (*He goes out again.*)

KIWI (*rises and stops at the door*). How about a little help?

TOMMY (*follows him out and also stops at the door*). 'Ow about a little 'elp?

(DIGGER *rises and joins them, closing the door behind him.*)

MARGARET (*when they are alone*). May I stay and talk to you?

LACHIE. There's naught tae say.

MARGARET (*sits on* YANK's *bed*). Oh, my poor stubborn darling, please hear me. I'll never have another chance to talk to you.

LACHIE (*quietly*). There's naught tae say.

MARGARET. We wanted to save you all the unhappiness we could. Was that betrayal, Lachie?

LACHIE. Did ye forgit I was a soldier? Didn't ye know I'd faced dying befur?

MARGARET. I can't let you walk out of here despising us.

LACHIE (*ties his bag up and lays it down across his bed*). Ye can nae prevent me.

MARGARET. Do you think the way we feel about you less honest—less genuine—because we knew to begin with?

LACHIE. Dare ye answer that truthfully? (*He looks at her for the first time. His eyes are angry and hurt.*)

MARGARET. Of course we were more considerate because we knew. What kind of people would we be if we'd been indifferent?

LACHIE. The kind of people I shuid hae known ye wuid be. Ye're easy tae find the world over. The kind that will beat a mon, rob him, hound him, slander and betray him—and think it fair game *unless* he's dying. And then ye're frightened. Yur conscience drives ye tae guidness. Weel, I find yur sudden virtue nae worthy of an animal. I dinna thank ye fur wot ye did tae me.

MARGARET. We're your friends, Lachie, no matter how you acquired us. The only ones you have in the world. Don't value us lightly. Stay with us.

LACHIE. Ye made me think fur a little while I'd misjudged ma' fellow man. Ye gae me a fool's religion tae die on. If ye only knew the bitterness I moost thank ye fur.

MARGARET. Do you believe that the *only* reason we were kind to you was because we knew?

LACHIE. Do ye dare deny that it dinna help— (*He strides away, and turns back to her*) —that it dinna goad ye on?

MARGARET. No, I can't deny that.

LACHIE. And was it easy tae like me?

MARGARET. No, it wasn't.

LACHIE (*shouts almost*). And shuid I be proud that ye liked me only because I was tae die?

MARGARET. If that were the only reason—no.

LACHIE. I'll write a book, says I. I'll preach the wurd of God. I'll gie ma' home tae ma' brothers, I says. Oh, how ye moost hae wanted tae laugh.

MARGARET (*rises*). Lachie, Lachie, please listen to me. Forget everything but this: for a little while you learned the meaning of friendship. Didn't you say that you'd shared a moment with kings?

LACHIE. If I moost die tae learn tae love ma' fellow man—then I'll dew wi'out him. It's too high a price tae pay.

MARGARET. Oh, darling, what difference does it make why people are good?

LACHIE (*strides back to his bed and stands at attention*). I've done wi' ma' packing.

MARGARET. Would you hate it if I kissed you good-bye? You did ask me to be your wife, you know.

LACHIE. Let me be, please. (*He whirls and goes to the side window, standing with his back to her.*)

MARGARET. Do you think I said I'd marry you only because I pitied you?

LACHIE. And didn't ye pity me?

MARGARET. With all my heart. Oh, surely there's pity in every woman's

LACHIE (*without turning*). I've nae words for ye.

MARGARET (*hopelessly*). I'll have Yank help you out with your kit. (*Starts for the door.*) Yank! (*And comes back a few feet toward* LACHIE.) Would it mean anything to you if I married you now—before you left?

LACHIE. Naught!

(YANK *comes in slowly.* MARGARET *speaks to him as she passes.*)

MARGARET. Yank, as soon as I've seen about the transport I'll want you to help him with his kit. (*She goes out.* DIGGER *comes in as* YANK *goes to take* LACHIE's *duffle bag.*)

LACHIE. I want nae help!

(YANK *looks at him silently, turns and sits on his bed, putting a roll of film into the camera.*)

YANK. I'd better g-get the damned roll of film in.

DIGGER. You won't have time to use it anyhow.

(TOMMY *and* KIWI *enter and sit dejectedly on their beds.*)

YANK. Thought I'd like s-s-some pictures of this gang myself—before I leave.

DIGGER. Leave me out. I don't feel like pictures.

(BLOSSOM *moves over to where* LACHIE *sits at foot of his bed. He looks at the kit and recognizes the signs of departure. He takes the string of beads from his neck and holds them out to* LACHIE.)

BASUTO. Blos-som. (LACHIE *ignores him. The* BASUTO *waits and then extends his gift again.*) Bak-sheesh. (*He takes* LACHIE's *hand gently and tries to put the beads in it.* LACHIE *whirls and throws them against* BLOSSOM. BLOSSOM *staggers back in hurt surprise.*)

LACHIE. Leave me be!

(*The boys all rise.* YANK *springs forward and pulls* LACHIE *around to face him, with eyes blazing.*)

YANK (*shaken and angry*). I want to tell you something before you go. There's just something mean in you that only a bullet can cure. You've been sore your whole life because things didn't come easy for you, so you took your spite out on every person you ever met. You don't want our friendship? Well, you didn't pay for it. You didn't *earn* it. You got it for *nothing*. So what are you kicking about? And now the pay-off! You're sore because you didn't know when you were going to die! Does anyone else know when he's going to die? No. But you had to know. You're the kind of hero that likes to bet on a sure thing. You don't know what courage is. You've been afraid to live since the day you were born. What do you think life is, Buster —a certified check!

LACHIE. Ye tricked and cheated me. I risked yur friendship, but ye did nae gie me friendship. Ye gae me pity.

YANK. Did Blossom pity you? He didn't know you were going to die. He liked you. He wanted to give you something. And what do you do? You throw his friendship back in his face. *It's a good thing you're going to die.* A guy like you causes a lot of unhappiness in the world. I wouldn't save you if I could. That's the way I feel. (*He storms back to his bed and sits struggling with the camera. Slowly* LACHIE *turns toward* BLOSSOM, *then sinks to the foot of his bed, his lips a tight and unrelenting line.*)

DIGGER (*softly*). You were rather hard on him, weren't you?

(MARGARET *hurries in and goes to* YANK.)

MARGARET. Yank, what were you shouting about?

YANK. That sorehead hit Blossom.

MARGARET. Why?

YANK. Because Blossom wanted to give him some beads when he saw he was going away.

MARGARET. Never mind. (*She crosses to* LACHIE.) Lachie, your transport is here. Are you ready? (*He sits without answering.*) Are you ready to go?

LACHIE. Aye.

MARGARET. Yank, will you carry his kit for him?

YANK (*angrily*). N-n-no. He doesn't want any help. Let him manage alone.

MARGARET. It's your last chance to help him.

YANK. He doesn't have to go. He knows he's wrong but he's so d-d-damned stubborn he'll die alone rather than admit it. N-n-no.

MARGARET (*turns to* DIGGER). Digger? (DIGGER *doesn't move.*) Then I'll get the Basuto.

LACHIE (*rises*). I need nae help. I'll gae alone. (*He picks up his kit and starts out. He moves slowly with his head down. He is stopped momentarily by* MARGARET.)

MARGARET. Lachlen. Good-bye.

(*He is arrested for a moment, then continues toward door.*)

YANK (*leaps to his feet and speaks loudly and quickly*). Now that he's out of the way, let's get some pictures! Come on, Kiwi! Tommy! Digger! Blossom! (*He forces the camera into* MARGARET's *hands.*) Here, Sister, take our pictures. (*He pushes the men together.*) Come on—get together!

(*They group themselves, and stand facing* MARGARET. LACHIE *looks back at them and clears his throat.*)

LACHIE. I'd be willing tae consider remaining if ye'd admit ye wronged me.

YANK (*to* LACHIE). L-look—if you think we're going to beg you to stay, you're wasting your time. (*Back to* MARGARET.) Get the picture, Sister.

LACHIE. I'll nae gi' ye anoother chance.

YANK (*ignores him*). We're ready if you are, Sister. Go ahead.

LACHIE (*throws his kit down and puts his bagpipes on foot of* DIGGER's *bed. He rushes across to* MARGARET). Ye can nae use that film wi'out ma' permission!

YANK (*goes after him*). Look, we're not asking you for anything. Forgiveness *or* films.

LACHIE (*faces* YANK—*nose to nose*). Ye may recall, the roll ye're using is ma' private property. I paid ye money fur it.

YANK. I'll give you your money back.

LACHIE. I've ma' rights. I'll nae take it.

YANK. Genesis, Exodus, Leviticus . . .

KIWI. Easy, Yank.

MARGARET. Oh, don't be spiteful, Lachie, please.

YANK (*takes the camera from* MARGARET *and starts to open it*). Aw, let him take it. The hell with him. (*He turns on* LACHIE *and speaks slowly.*) But I wish I could understand what makes a man want to die despised and friendless.

LACHIE (*looks at* YANK *and at* MARGARET *and then at the men. He sees no sign of surrender in their eyes. He sinks down on the end of his bed and covers his face with his hands. After a moment of struggle he speaks*). I dinna want tae die alone.

MARGARET (*kneels by him and puts her hand on his shoulder*). Lachlen, why don't you say what you want to say? (*She puts her arm around him.*) And stop saying the things you don't mean.

LACHIE (*rises slowly and crosses toward the side window. He starts the speech with his back to them*). It's nae easy fur me tae sae it. All my life I hated what I cuid nae hae. It saved ma' pride. Boot now I've nae the time tae squander on ma' pride. (*He faces them, and for the first time in his life, he is humble.*) I want tae stay. If I moost beg ye tae take me back, then I beg ye. Cuid I hae ma' bed?

YANK (*gruffly*). Why don't you get back into your blues, Buster?

MARGARET. Change in my office.

(*Slowly* LACHIE *goes to his bed, picks up his blues, and exits into* MARGARET's *office. No one moves until he is out. Then* YANK *sits down.*)

YANK. I wish I had a mother. I feel just like kicking her in the teeth.

DIGGER (*pointing to* LACHIE's *bagpipes which are still on the foot of* DIGGER's *bed*). Do you suppose he'd feel better if he could play his bagpipes?

TOMMY. I don't think he could. I don't think 'e 'as any wind left in 'im.

DIGGER. He looked a bit pale.

KIWI. Sister, maybe you'd better go in and see him.

MARGARET. No. I think not. (*She takes a*

deep breath.) He's swallowed his pride. It will take him a moment or two to digest it.

YANK. Why don't we finish taking the pictures?

MARGARET. Yes, let's get that over with.

YANK *(handing the camera to MARGARET).* Before we g-grow long g-gray beards.

(The boys get back into position for the picture. MARGARET *picks up* BLOSSOM'S *beads and drops them on* LACHIE'S *bed.)*

MARGARET *(looking into the camera).* Stay close together.

TOMMY. Are we very 'andsome-looking, Sister?

MARGARET. I can't see you. *(She blinks her eyes and looks again.)* Not very handsome, but very wonderful.

KIWI. Then take what you see. My legs are getting tired.

MARGARET. One . . . two . . . *(Before she can say "three,"* LACHIE *opens the door and faces them. He has put on his kilt and stands looking at the men—ill at ease. They wait for him to speak.)*

LACHIE. Wuid ye be sae guid as tae let me hae ma' photo taken wi' ye? *(No one speaks.)* It *is* ma' film. *(He adds hastily.)* Tho' ye need nae consider that.

YANK *(pointing to place beside himself).* Your place is here. *(*LACHIE *picks up the beads on his bed.* BLOSSOM *smiles.* LACHIE *puts on his cap which he has held in his hand. He crosses to the men and takes his place in the center.)*

MARGARET. Ready . . . *(As she looks in the camera,* YANK *puts his arm around* LACHIE. LACHIE *notices it, turns his head to* YANK. *None of the others is smiling, but slowly, effortlessly,* LACHIE *smiles. It is a smile he has saved all his life. He turns back to the camera, and, with a contented sigh, crosses his arm in front of him for the picture.)* One . . . two . . . three. That's it.

*(*LACHIE *turns to look up at* YANK *again, then suddenly leaps into the air with a yell. He whirls and holds his kilt down behind him with his two hands, facing* TOMMY.)*

LACHIE. *Help!* Don't ye dew that!

(The men break away and we see TOMMY *kneeling on the bed.)*

TOMMY *(the cat that swallowed the canary).* I found out! I peeked! I found out!

THE CURTAIN FALLS

HOME OF THE BRAVE

By ARTHUR LAURENTS

―――――

HOME OF THE BRAVE was first presented by Lee Sabinson, in association with William R. Katzell, on December 27, 1945, at the Belasco Theatre, New York City, with the following cast:

CAPT. HAROLD BITTERGER	T. J. ....Russell Hardie
Eduard Franz	CONEY ....Joseph Pevney
MAJOR DENNIS ROBINSON, JR.	FINCH ....Henry Barnard
Kendall Clark	MINGO ....Alan Baxter

―――――

SCENES

ACT I: Scene 1. Hospital Room. A Pacific Base.

Scene 2. Office. The Pacific Base.

Scene 3. A Clearing. A Pacific Island.

ACT II: Scene 1. Hospital Room.

Scene 2. Another Clearing. The Island.

Scene 3. Hospital Room.

ACT III: Scene 1. Hospital Room. Two weeks later.

Scene 2. The Office. A few days later.

―――――

The poem in Act Two is quoted by the kind permission of its author, Miss Eve Merriam.

THE AUTHOR

Of all the playwrights in this anthology, the author of Home of the Brave *qualifies most as spokesman for the youth that fought in the second World War. Having been born in 1918, he missed the first World War neatly. Since he was no more than eleven years old when the stock market crashed and tycoons fell like autumn leaves, he cannot be considered a depression playwright. He reached his majority about the same time that Hitler invaded Poland. Proper timing seems to be a matter of destiny with Arthur Laurents. As a dramatist, he must take some pride or pleasure in it.*

Mr. Laurents spent four years in the army, and it is only a slight exaggeration to say that he felt his way toward the drama largely in the service—as paratrooper, author of training films, and radio writer. In radio he displayed such talent with his program "Army Service Forces Present" that he attracted the attention of talent-hungry film studios. The next step in his career was the writing of Home of the Brave. *Lee Sabinson bought the script and gave it an excellent production, as is his wont. Unfortunately the old Belasco Theatre had management difficulties and there was a theatre shortage in New York. Interest in the play was growing and* Home *of the Brave was headed for a long Broadway run when its lease was terminated.*

Mr. Laurents may have been disappointed but he was undaunted. Rejecting tempting offers from Hollywood, he resolved to give himself and the theatre another chance to establish a lasting association. He has written a second play, originally entitled Heartsong, *and Broadway expects to receive it in 1947.*

Last minute facts generously supplied by the author may serve as an addendum to the above-given information. The exact date of his birth is July 14, 1918, and he is a native New Yorker. He attended high schools in New York and Florida, and was graduated from Cornell University in 1937. During college vacations he had acted as dramatic counsellor in boys' camps; he had, in fact, taken an interest in dramatics since childhood. Mr. Laurents was therefore following his bent when he enrolled in a radio writing course at New York University. But he evidently needed little instruction, and he stopped attending classes when his radio play about a clairvoyant boy, Now Playing Tomorrow, *was accepted by the Columbia Workshop of CBS and created a minor sensation. He began providing night club material for a group that called itself "The Nite Wits" and performed at Leon and Eddie's, Mr. Laurents being one of the performers and loathing it. He abandoned the night show at the earliest opportunity and went to the West coast to write radio plays steadily, and it was during this time that the U. S. Army beckoned to him. His radio contributions during his stay in the Armed Services included the CBS patriotic feature* The Man behind the Gun *and a series of well-received broadcasts entitled* Assignment Home.

Home of the Brave *owes some of its inspiration to the author's interest in the use of narcosynthesis by the medical corps, and to his annoyance with superficial stage and screen treatments of the common soldier during the war. Mr. Laurents, incidentally, reflects that he might have become a linen merchandiser rather than a playwright if he had not been fired from the linen section of a department store— from Bloomingdale's, to be precise—for sleeping behind the counter. There must be some moral in this. . . .*

HOME OF THE BRAVE

ACT ONE

SCENE I

SCENE: *Hospital Room. A Pacific Base.*
This is a small room, the office, really, of CAPTAIN HAROLD BITTERGER, *a doctor.*
There is a window, rear, through which we can see tropical foliage and bright sunlight.
Up right is a door; downstage of this, a desk heavy with papers and a chair behind
the desk. Across the room, near the left wall, is an army cot. Near this a small table.
There are two chairs near the desk.

Seated in one of these chairs is MAJOR DENNIS E. ROBINSON, JR. *He is about twenty-*
six, a cigarette ad with a blond crew-cut. He is self-conscious about his rank and position
(and his shortcomings) and attempts to hide his natural boyishness by a stalwart
military manner.

In the other chair is CORPORAL T. J. EVERITT, *a rather pompously good-looking*
Rotarian. T.J. is about thirty-five. He resents the Army, his position, almost everything.
He has found it difficult to adjust himself to this new life and, therefore, seems and
acts more pettish and mean than he actually is.

Standing in front of the desk with a sheaf of papers in his hand is the DOCTOR,
CAPTAIN BITTERGER: *a stocky man with graying hair, about forty-three. He knows a*
good deal about men, particularly soldiers, is anxious to learn more, to have the world
learn more.

When the curtain rises, there is silence. The DOCTOR *has apparently just asked a*
question. The MAJOR *and* T.J. *look at him uncomfortably for a second, then turn away.*

DOCTOR (*impatiently*). Well?

(*A slight wait.*)

MAJOR. I don't know, Doctor.

DOCTOR (*holding up the sheaf of papers*).
This is the whole story.

MAJOR. All that we know.

DOCTOR. All the events, at any rate.

MAJOR. Yes, sir.

T.J. Captain, maybe Sergeant Mingo—

DOCTOR (*brusquely*). I've spoken to Ser-
geant Mingo. You *all* agree on the facts.
Wonderful things: facts. Wonderful word.
Doesn't mean a goddam thing.

MAJOR. Doctor, if there's—

DOCTOR. They help. Facts help, Major.
And I thank you for them. But they're
not quite enough.

MAJOR. I hope you don't think, sir—

DOCTOR. Major, forgive me. I'm sorry
about your feelings. And yours, Corporal.
And Sergeant Mingo's. And the whole

world's. But at this point, I'm only interested in one man. A patient. A Private
First Class Peter Coen. (*Slight pause.*)

T.J. Doctor—

DOCTOR. Yes?

T.J. I just happened to remember. There
was something else. There was a fight.

MAJOR. A fight? When?

DOCTOR. The last day you were on the
island, wasn't it?

T.J. Yes, sir.

MAJOR. I didn't know! Who had a fight?

DOCTOR (*to* T.J.). You see, I did speak to
Sergeant Mingo, Corporal.

T.J. Well, I just happened to remember it
now.

DOCTOR. Really?

T.J. It didn't seem so important. I just
forgot it.

DOCTOR. Everything's important with a
case like this.

559

MAJOR. Coney's going to be all right, isn't he?

DOCTOR. I'm a psychiatrist, Major, not a clairvoyant. The boy suffered a traumatic shock. Now he has paralysis. Amnesia. Physical manifestations. They're curable —sometimes. And sometimes—

MAJOR. Can we see him?

DOCTOR. He won't recognize you.

MAJOR. I'd like to see him, though.

DOCTOR. He's due for a treatment now.

MAJOR. Just for a second, Captain.

DOCTOR (after a moment's hesitation—to T.J.). Corporal, he's in the first ward to your left. Do you want to bring him in?

T.J. Well—yes, sir. (He goes out.)

DOCTOR (during following, he prepares for the amytal injection to follow). Fine day. God's in His heaven and all's wrong with the world.

MAJOR. How are you treating him, Captain?

DOCTOR. Narcosynthesis, Major. (Turns and looks at the MAJOR who obviously doesn't understand.) Narcosynthesis. You administer a drug that acts as a release for the patient. Usually, he will relive the experiences immediately preceding shock if the doctor leads him. Usually one or two injections are enough for him to recover physically . . . I'm starting the treatment today.

MAJOR. You mean Coney'll be able to walk? He'll get his memory back?

DOCTOR. Maybe. I don't know. But suppose he can walk, suppose he can remember—that's only half the battle. There'll still be something in him—deep in him— that caused all this.

MAJOR. But can't this narcosynthesis—

DOCTOR. It's not perfect. It was started about fifteen years ago. We're still learning. But we've learned a great deal using it in this war. See? War has its uses.

MAJOR. I hope to God it works for Coney.

DOCTOR. His collapse wasn't your fault.

MAJOR. Well—he was my responsibility.

DOCTOR. The job was.

MAJOR. That's what I thought but—

DOCTOR. Major, how old are you? Twenty-five?

MAJOR. Twenty-six.

DOCTOR. Well, twenty-six. What do you know? Your job. Period. Let me tell you something, Major—Robinson?

MAJOR. That's right, sir.

DOCTOR. Look, Robinson. You were right. The job comes first. The men count. But they count second. How many were there on that mission? Five. But you were doing that job for hundreds, for thousands, for the whole goddam war. That's a little more important—

MAJOR. I know. But Coney's important, too.

DOCTOR. Sure. And maybe if you were smarter—but you're twenty-six. And hell! I'm not so smart. How the devil do I know that if you were smarter, you could have prevented this? Matter of fact, I doubt it. Maybe you're wrong, maybe I'm wrong—and God knows that's possible— too goddam possible—but that kid's crack-up goes back to a thousand million people being wrong.

MAJOR. What do you mean?

DOCTOR. They don't take a man for himself . . . for what he is.

MAJOR. I don't get it.

DOCTOR (smiling). I didn't think you would. You probably never came face to face—

(The door opens and T.J. brings in CONEY who is in a wheel chair. CONEY is dressed in the dark-red hospital robe. He is slumped in the chair with a melancholic, frightened look on his face.)

MAJOR. Hello, Coney!

T.J. He didn't know me.

MAJOR. Coney . . . how do you feel, fellow?

CONEY. All right, sir.

DOCTOR. Coney . . . do you remember Major Robinson?

CONEY (looks at the MAJOR slowly, then back to the DOCTOR). No, sir.

MAJOR. Coney, you remember. Don't you remember me? Don't you remember Mingo?

CONEY. Mingo? Mingo?

MAJOR *(to* DOCTOR*).* Does he remember about—Finch?

DOCTOR. Ask him.

CONEY. What? Who?

MAJOR. Coney . . . Coney . . . remember Finch?

CONEY. No, sir. No, sir. *(His voice cracks.)* Doctor—

DOCTOR. All right, son. All right . . .

CONEY. Doctor—

DOCTOR *(to* T.J.*).* Help me lift him on the bed, please. *(They do.)* Thanks. Chair. *(*T.J. *quickly brings him a chair. He sits in it and holds* CONEY*'s hand.)* I'm sorry.

MAJOR. Will you let us know?

DOCTOR. Yes.

MAJOR. Let's go. So long, Coney. Be seeing you. *(He waits a moment for an answer. But there is none. They walk out, closing the door behind them.)*

DOCTOR *(his manner changes now. He is soft, gentle, kind—a father to this boy).* Don't be frightened, son. There's nothing to be frightened of. Nothing in the world. *(He gets up, as he continues, and pulls down the shade. The room is in half light. As he talks, he moves the small table with his instruments near the bed.)* You know who I am, don't you, Coney?

CONEY. Doctor . . .

DOCTOR. Sure. I'm your doctor. And you know what doctors do, don't you? They make you well. And that's what I'm going to do. I'm going to make you well, Coney. I'm going to fix you up so you'll remember everything and be able to walk again. *(He is now rolling up* CONEY*'s sleeve and putting on a tourniquet.)* You'd like to walk again, wouldn't you?

CONEY. Yes, sir.

DOCTOR. Well, you will. You'll be fine. *(He begins to swab* CONEY*'s arm.)* Now, you mustn't be afraid. This isn't going to hurt. I'm your doctor. Doctors don't hurt, son. They make you better. *(Takes out hypo.)* All you'll feel will be a little prick with a needle. Just like when you stick yourself with a pin. That's all this is. Just a long pin. Do you understand?

CONEY. Yes, sir.

DOCTOR. All right. Now when I put the needle in, I want you to start counting backwards from one hundred. Backwards. 99, 98, 97. Like that. Is that clear?

CONEY. Yes, sir. *(A frightened cry.)* Doctor, I—

DOCTOR. This is going to make you feel fine, son. This is going to make you sleep without all those bad dreams. . . . Now then. Just a little— *(He removes the tourniquet and injects the needle.)* Sting —there. Now you start counting. 100, 99 . . .

CONEY *(as he gets along in this counting, his speech gets slightly thicker and there is an occasional cough).* 100—99—98—97 —96—95—94—93—92—91—90—89—87 —86—85—84—8—

DOCTOR. 83.

CONEY. 83—82—81—82—1—

(The DOCTOR *has been watching the needle in* CONEY*'s arm. Now he looks up and leans forward deliberately.)*

DOCTOR. Who do you work for, Coney?

CONEY. Major Robinson.

(A brief second's pause. The DOCTOR *sits up and smiles.)*

DOCTOR. Is he a good C.O.?

CONEY. Oh, the Major's an all right guy. Darn decent. And he knows his stuff. He's decent only . . .

DOCTOR. Only what?

CONEY. He's an all right guy. He's O.K.

DOCTOR. Not as smart as Mingo, though, is he?

CONEY. Oh, he knows more about engineering but Mingo's a sharp boy. He knows. He knows plenty. You know his wife writes poetry?

DOCTOR. She does?

CONEY. Yep. Real poetry. Sometimes, he's kind of touchy, though.

DOCTOR. Touchy? Like you?

CONEY. No . . . No, not like me. None of them are like me. I—I—

DOCTOR. You what, Coney?

CONEY. Mingo's sensitive about—well, about his wife. About how they treat him —us. Once . . . once I heard a poem. A poem Mingo's wife wrote. I heard that.

DOCTOR. Did he recite it to you?

CONEY. Once . . . Just once . . .

DOCTOR. Why shouldn't he recite it to you? You're his buddy.

CONEY. Oh, no. I'm not his buddy. He doesn't have a buddy. You can't get real close to Mingo.

DOCTOR. Who's your buddy, Coney? *(Pause.)* Who's your buddy? *(No answer.)* Finch? Finch is your buddy, isn't he? *(He withdraws the needle.)*

CONEY. Yes.

DOCTOR. He's been your buddy almost since you came in the Army.

CONEY *(low).* Yes.

DOCTOR. Finch is an all right guy. He likes you. And you like him, don't you?

CONEY. Yes, I— *(Suddenly, loudly.)* No. No, I don't. He doesn't really like me! He's like all of them. He doesn't like me and I hate him! I hate him!

DOCTOR. You really hate Finch?

CONEY. Yes! *(A long pause. Then, very quietly.)* No. Finch is a sweet kid. He's my buddy, the dumb Arizona hayseed. Didn't know from nothing when he came into the outfit. But he's learning. He's a sweet kid. He doesn't seem like the others only—only I wonder if he is.

DOCTOR. If Finch is what?

CONEY. Like the others.

DOCTOR. What others?

CONEY. The ones who make the cracks.

DOCTOR. Who, Coney? Who makes the cracks?

CONEY. T.J. *(Venomously.)* Corporal T.J. Everitt. *(With slow fury.)* I hate his guts.

DOCTOR. What cracks does he make, Coney?

CONEY. Finch doesn't let him get away with them, though. Finch— *(He suddenly springs up to a sitting position. He is frightened.)* Finch! Where's Finch?

DOCTOR. He's all right.

CONEY. Where is he? Where's Finch?

DOCTOR. He's all right.

CONEY. Where is he?

DOCTOR. Don't worry about him.

CONEY *(calling).* Finch? *(Frightened.)* Finch? *(He looks around frantically.)*

DOCTOR *(hesitates—and then throws an arm around* CONEY*).* Hi, Coney.

CONEY *(cheerfully).* Finch! Where the hell have you been? The Major wants us in his office.

(The lights start to dim down.)

DOCTOR. What for?

CONEY. How the hell would I know what for? Do they ever tell you anything in the Army? All I know is we got to get to the Major's office on the double. So come on. Let's take off!

(By now, the stage is blacked out. Through the darkness, we hear the distant sound of a field telephone ringing. The sound gets louder and louder gradually.)

SCENE II

SCENE: *An office. A Pacific Base.*

This fairly wide but shallow room is a section of a quonset hut. The hut serves as an army office building; wooden partitions separate one "room" from another. This one is an outer office. The spotted walls, the littered desks, the equipment in the corners, the four or five posters—none of this really belies the temporary air that this room and the thousands like it invariably have.

In the center of the rear wall is a door marked plainly with a wooden plaque: MAJOR ROBINSON. Up right are a desk and a chair. Down left is another door which leads to the street outside. Upstage of this are another desk and a chair. There are one or two other chairs or crates serving as chairs in the room. Each side wall has a small window through which the morning sun is boiling despite the tropical trees.

AT RISE: As the lights come up the telephone is ringing and through the screened street door we see two soldiers running up. First is PFC. PETER COEN—"CONEY"—and we now see that he is of medium height with a strong, solid body. His face is fairly nondescript until he smiles. Then his hard, tough manner washes away in warmth and good humor. He is about twenty-three and wears faded green coveralls.

The second soldier looks a little younger and a little neater. He is a tall, bony kid named FINCH—a private. He is immediately likable. He is rather simple, rather gentle and, at the moment, a little worried.

It is apparent that neither of the boys knows what they are here for. They look about the empty room for a moment and then CONEY moves center with a shrug.

CONEY. Nobody's home.

FINCH. I thought you said the Major wanted us on the double.

(Telephone stops ringing.)

CONEY. They always want you here two minutes ago, but they're never here when you're here.

FINCH. We could have cleaned up.

CONEY *(wandering around, snooping at the papers on the desks).* What've you got to be clean for anyway? Short arm? The only thing we could pick up around here is mildew.

FINCH. Oh, that's charming.

CONEY. Delightful. *(A slight pause.)*

FINCH. Who else did he send for?

CONEY *(taking out a cigarette).* I don't know. Maybe he only wants us. Fresh young meat for the grinder.

FINCH. Oh! Great! *(FINCH refuses the cigarette and walks over to the window.)*

CONEY *(tenderly).* Hey, jerk . . . *(FINCH turns around.)* Hell, I'm no pipeline. It might be a furlough.

FINCH *(denying it).* Yep, yep.

CONEY. It might be. We've been over two years plus and it says in the book—

FINCH. What book, Grimm's Fairy Tales?

CONEY *(quietly).* I guess. *(Slight pause.)* Ah, come on, Finch. You think every time they send for you in the Army, it's for something bad.

FINCH. Isn't it?

CONEY *(trying hard to pick FINCH up).* You know, if it is a furlough, we'll have a chance to look for a spot for that bar we're gonna have.

FINCH. I thought we decided.

CONEY. That whistle stop in Arizona?

FINCH. It's a nice town. And it's near home.

CONEY. Your home. Listen, did you tell her?

FINCH. Tell who?

CONEY. Your mother, jerk. About us going to own a bar together after the war.

FINCH. I told her it was going to be a restaurant.

CONEY. A restaurant!

FINCH. Mothers don't understand about bars. But I wrote her about how I'm going to paint pictures on the walls and about how it's going to be the kind of place you said.

CONEY. Where a guy can bring his wife.

FINCH. She liked that.

CONEY. Sure. I know just how it should be run. Your mother'll like it fine. (FINCH *starts to whistle a tune called "Shoo, Fly."*) Finch . . .

FINCH. Huh?

CONEY. Does your mother know who I am?

FINCH. Of course.

CONEY. I mean, does she know my name?

FINCH. Well, sure she does!

CONEY. Oh.

FINCH. What did you think?

CONEY. I don't know. I just wondered.

FINCH. You can be an A-1 jerk sometimes. The whole family knows about you and Mom's so het up, I think she's got ideas about mating you and my sister.

CONEY. Yep, yep.

FINCH. What do you think she sends you all that food for? My sister cooks it.

CONEY. Ah, Finch . . .

FINCH. Ah, Finch, nothing! And all those letters telling me to be sure to bring you home when we get our furlough. . . .

CONEY. Nuts.

FINCH. There's plenty of room. It's only a ranch, of course—nothing fancy—

CONEY. Like a quonset hut.

FINCH. We'd have a helluva time.

CONEY. My mother wants to meet you but—Judas, I sleep on the couch.

FINCH. We wouldn't have enough time on a furlough to visit both— Gosh! You think it might be a furlough, Coney? You think it might be?

CONEY. Quién sabe?

FINCH. The orderly room said it was something special.

CONEY. Like a new kind of latrine duty.

FINCH. Oh, great! Make up your mind, will you? First you tell me no furlough; then you start me thinking maybe there will be one; then—

(*During this, the street door opens and, unseen by* FINCH *or* CONEY, T/SGT. CARL MINGO *comes in.* MINGO *is about twenty-seven. He has dark red hair and looks taller than he is. He gives a feeling of strength; he's someone you want to know. He stands now at the door for a moment and then knocks on the sill and says:*)

MINGO. Is this the way to the powder room? (*He comes in, closing the door behind him.*)

FINCH. Are you in on this, Mingo?

MINGO. In on what?

CONEY. Whatever it is.

FINCH. Don't you know?

MINGO. Gentlemen, I don't know from nothing.

CONEY. Yep, yep.

MINGO. I don't, Coney. So help me.

FINCH. We thought—well, we were kind of hoping that—well, it might be for a furlough. We've been over two years. You've been over longer. You've seen more action than anybody else. Maybe . . . (*Finishing lamely.*) Well, it could be a furlough.

MINGO (*kindly*). Sure. It could be, kid. We could all do with a couple of weeks in a rest camp.

FINCH. Rest camp?

CONEY. Cut it out. The Arizona tumbleweed's homesick.

FINCH. Blow it, will ya.

MINGO. One week back there and I'll bet you'd really be homesick—for this joint.

CONEY (*to* MINGO). Hey, what's been eating you the last couple of days?

MINGO. Mosquitoes.

FINCH. Gee, I was sure you'd know what they wanted us for, Mingo.

MINGO. Why should I know?

CONEY. Didn't you learn anything at college?

MINGO. I only went a year. Write my wife. She's a big hot diploma girl.

CONEY. Yuk, yuk.

MINGO. Maybe we're moving out.

FINCH. Again?

MINGO. Maybe.

FINCH. Why?

MINGO. The General's restless.

FINCH. But where would we be going?

MINGO. Where the little men make with the big bullets.

CONEY. Now that's a real charming thought.

FINCH. Delightful. *(Slight pause.)* Remember that first time, Coney? When Major Robinson said: Men, you're going to have the excitement you've been itching for?

MINGO. Major Blueberry Pie.

FINCH. He was a captain then.

MINGO. Pardon me. Captain Blueberry Pie.

CONEY. Sometimes the Maj acts like war was a hot baseball game. Batter up! Sqush. Sub—stitute please!

FINCH. That's charming!

CONEY. I'm a charming fellow.

FINCH. You stink.

(The door to the street opens and CORPORAL T. J. EVERITT *comes in. He, like the others, wears faded coveralls. But* T.J. *is in a temper.)*

T.J. What the hell is this? They put me in charge of a detail, tell me I've got to finish that new road by noon—and then they yank me off with no explanation. What's going on around here?

MINGO. It is not for engineers to reason why.

CONEY. My ouija board's on strike.

T.J. I wasn't asking you, Coney.

MINGO. Your guess is as good as ours, T.J.

FINCH. I heard a rumor they were going to give you a commission, T.J.

CONEY. All of us.

FINCH. Only Coney and me are going to be captains.

CONEY. Majors.

FINCH. Colonels.

CONEY. What the hell—generals.

FINCH. Congratulations, General Coen.

CONEY. Gracias, Commander Finch.

T.J. Oh, blow it, will you? *(To* MINGO.*)* You'd think that by now they'd have somebody mature enough to run an outfit.

FINCH. The Major's all right. I don't see you doing any better.

T.J. If I couldn't do better with my eyes blindfolded, I'd resign.

CONEY. The Army's kind of touchy about resigning, T.J.

MINGO. Just what makes you such a hot blue-plate special, T.J.?

FINCH. Don't you know who he is, Mingo? Tell him, Coney.

CONEY *(exaggerated sotto voce).* That's T. J. Everitt, former vice-president in charge of distribution for Universal Products, Inc.

FINCH. No!

CONEY. Yeah!

T.J. Oh, Christ! Do we have to go through that again?

FINCH. Say, is he the Joe who used to make fifteen thousand a year?

CONEY. Oh, that was a bad year. He usually made sixteen thousand.

FINCH. No!

CONEY. Yeah!

FINCH. Think of his taxes!

CONEY. Rugged.

MINGO. Say, what's he doing now?

CONEY. Now? Oh, now he's a corporal making sixty-two bucks a month.

FINCH. No!

CONEY. Yeah!

FINCH. Tsk! Tsk! What won't they think of next!

T.J. That's enough.

CONEY. Well, I heard just the—

T.J. All right. That's enough—Jakie!

CONEY (quietly). Hold your hats, boys.

FINCH (to T.J.). Can that.

T.J. (to FINCH). Why don't you let your little friend—

FINCH. I said can it!

T.J. I heard you.

MINGO. Well, then, can it and can it for good!

CONEY. Drop it, fellas. It isn't worth it.

T.J. (to MINGO). Oh, the firm has a new partner.

MINGO. Up your floo, Rockefeller.

(The rear door opens and MAJOR ROBIN-SON comes out to his office.)

MAJOR. At ease, men. I'm sorry I had to keep you waiting . . . You'd better make yourselves comfortable. We're in for a session. Sit if you want to. Smoke. But stay put and give me your attention. (CONEY gestures "thumbs down" to FINCH. MAJOR, brusquely.) What's that for, Co-en?

CONEY. Oh, we . . . we thought maybe this was about furloughs, sir.

MAJOR. No. Sit down, Finch. I realize you men have furloughs coming to you. Particularly Mingo. And you ought to know that if I could get them for you, I would. However, we've got a job to do. Right, Mingo?

MINGO (with a wry smile). Yes, sir.

MAJOR (with charm). Well, maybe after this you'll get those furloughs. I certainly hope so . . . Anybody been bothered with anything lately—anything physical, I mean?

T.J. Well, Major, my back—

MAJOR. I know, T.J. Outside of that, though? (He looks around at the men. There is no answer.) All right. Now—before anything else, get this straight: everything you hear from now on is top secret. Whatever you do or don't do, it's secret. Running off at the mouth will get a court-martial. Understand? (The

men nod.) O.K. . . . I'll get right to the point. You four men are the best engineers in the outfit. We need A-1 engineers for this job. (MINGO smiles.) What's the matter, Mingo?

MINGO. Nothing, sir.

MAJOR. I mean that. Seriously. Now—there's an island—never mind where—that we want to invade next. It's darned important that we take that island. It can shorten this whole bloody war . . . But right now, there are fifteen thousand Japs on it. To take it and hold it—we'll need airstrips. And we'll need 'em quick. To fly supplies in and to have a base for fighters and bombers. Clear? . . . Well, I'm flying to that island tonight.

FINCH. With fifteen thousand Japs on it, sir?

MAJOR. Yes, I need a few men to go with me. One to sketch the terrain and draw maps— (CONEY nudges FINCH; the others stare at FINCH.) —and three others to help survey. I suppose two more would really be enough but—well, it's a ticklish job, all right, and—what is it, T.J.?

T.J. I was thinking about aerial photographs.

MAJOR. Leave the thinking to me and Headquarters, please. Aerial photos don't show what we want to find out. Too much foliage.

MINGO. Is there any intelligence on the Jap airstrips?

MAJOR. There's only one strip and it stinks. Besides, if we don't blow it up, they will. . . . Any other questions?

MINGO. Major . . .

MAJOR. Yes?

MINGO. Did you say you were flying to this island?

MAJOR. Yes. Natives'll pick us up offshore with canoes when we get there.

MINGO. How long do you figure the job will take?

MAJOR. Four days. Top. Then we get off the island the same way we got on.

MINGO. Canoes and then the plane.

MAJOR. Yes.

T.J. Suppose something happens?

MAJOR. The Japs are only defending the side of the island facing us. We'll be working in back of them—on the part facing Japan. Actually, it shouldn't be too bad because we shouldn't ever run into them. *(With a smile.)* I say "we." Really, it's up to you.

CONEY. To us?

MAJOR. This is purely voluntary, fellows. Whether you come or not—that's up to each of you. *(Pause.)* I know how you feel. You've all been in plenty; you've done plenty. And I'm not going to try to kid you about this job: it's no picnic. But believe me, it's worth doing. And anyway, it's got to be done. *(Another pause. He walks around a bit.)* I wouldn't have asked you—particularly you, Mingo, except that I need the best men I have. That's the kind of job it is. But it's still up to each of you individually. If you say "no," there won't be any questions asked. I mean that . . . Talk it over. Together or by yourselves. That's up to you. I'm sorry, but I can't give you more than— *(He looks at his watch.)* —ten minutes but— it came up damn fast and—well, you men know the Army. *(He walks up to the door to his office, starts to open it and then turns.)* Just remember it's damned important. Probably the least you'll get out of this will be a furlough. I can't promise, of course, that you'll get one but—that isn't the reason for going anyway. The reason is that you're the best men for the job. *(He exits into his office. There is a slight pause.)*

MINGO *(softly—with a wry smile)*. Oh, my aching back.

CONEY. What?

MINGO. That vaseline about volunteering.

FINCH. What do you mean?

T.J. With a nice little bribe of furloughs.

CONEY. He didn't say he was promising us furloughs.

MINGO. Well—if he wanted to play fair and square with us, he would have called us in one at a time and not let us know who the others were. That's volunteering.

CONEY. Why?

MINGO. Because that way, if a man wants out, he can get out—and no one's the wiser. But this way! Well, who's going to chicken out in front of anyone else?

T.J. What do you mean—chicken out?

MINGO. Are you going?

T.J. Are you?

MINGO. I'm not making up your mind.

T.J. I'm not asking you to!

MINGO *(lightly)*. O.K. *(Pause.)*

FINCH. Fifteen thousand Japs. *(Whistles softly.)*

CONEY. The first day I was inducted, some Joe said: Keep your eyes open, your mouth shut and never volunteer. No matter what it's for, it stinks.

MINGO. Well, who's gonna ride the broomstick to that island? That stinks, but good.

CONEY. If it's the way you said . . .

MINGO. What way?

CONEY. You know. That this is half-assed volunteering.

MINGO. Oh . . . It is.

CONEY. Then either we all go or we all don't go.

T.J. Why?

MINGO. Because if one of us says "yes,' nobody else can say: Count me out, Major I'm sitting home on my yellow butt.

T.J. It doesn't mean you're yellow.

MINGO. Could you say "count me out"?

(FINCH whistles "Shoo, Fly." Slight pause.)

CONEY. I wonder what would happen if we all said it.

(Slight pause.)

FINCH. Maybe it won't be so tough. He said the Japs are all on the other side of the island.

T.J. There's no law they have to stay there.

CONEY. The more times you go in, the less chance you have of coming out in one piece.

FINCH. That's a charming thought.

CONEY. Delightful.

(There is a pause during which FINCH *starts to whistle "Shoo, Fly." He sings the last two lines.)*

FINCH. Shoo, fly, don't bother me. For I'm in Company Q.

T.J. Company G.

CONEY. Anybody can make it rhyme.

(Slight pause.)

T.J. Well, Christ! We ought to talk about it, anyway!

MINGO. About what? Japs? They have several ways of killing you. They can—

T.J. Oh, put your head in a bowl, will you?

(Slight pause.)

FINCH. How long did he say?

CONEY. Four days.

FINCH. No. I mean to decide.

CONEY. Ten minutes.

MINGO. What's the difference? It's either too much or too little. The dirtiest trick you can play on a man in war is to make him think.

FINCH. Well, what do you say, Coney?

CONEY. I don't know.

FINCH. Well, you say it.

T.J. Oh, great. Let's play follow the leader.

FINCH. Mind your own business, T.J.!

MINGO. This *is* his business, Finch. It's kind of all our business.

FINCH. What do you mean?

MINGO. Whatever you two decide, we're stuck with it.

CONEY. Hey! Hey!

MINGO. It's perfectly O.K. by me, Coney.

T.J. It's O.K. by you?

MINGO. Yeah.

T.J. That's great! Well, maybe it's O.K. for the three of you, but what makes you think I'll string along?

MINGO. You haven't got the guts to do anything else.

FINCH *(to* CONEY). Come on, you jerk. What do you say?

CONEY. You know what I say? I say I think of four G.I.s going to an island crawling with fifteen thousand Japs, and I say they're crazy.

MINGO. O.K. Then we don't go. We don't have to.

CONEY. But the Major says we're the four best men. That it's important and it's winning the war.

T.J. You mean you want to go?

CONEY. Nobody wants to go.

MINGO. You can say that again.

FINCH. Well, you say it, Coney. Somebody has to.

CONEY. No. I don't want to, Finch. This is tough enough for a guy to decide for himself, but to decide for three other guys—I don't want to.

MINGO. Seems like we're putting him on a big black spot marked X, Finch.

CONEY. Look, Mingo, going on a mission like this ain't kidding. When they tell you to do something, it's not so bad. You have to do it, so you do it. But this way. Well, what the hell! Let somebody else decide. *(He stops as the rear door opens and the* MAJOR *walks in.)*

MAJOR. Sorry, men. Time's up . . . I want to say one thing again. If you've decided the job is too much for you, there'll be no questions asked. All you have to do is say "yes" or "no" . . . I—well, whatever you say, I want to thank you for your past work. *(He faces toward* MINGO *as though he were going to ask him first; changes his mind; looks at the others, and finally stops at* FINCH.) Well, Finch? Yes or no? *(*FINCH *looks at the* MAJOR *and then looks directly at* CONEY. *There is a slight pause. Then the* MAJOR *looks at* CONEY, *too. They all look at him now. He looks at* FINCH, *pauses, then turns slightly more to the* MAJOR.)*

CONEY. Yes, sir.

(Blackout. After a pause, through the darkness comes the sound of crickets; then, faintly at first, the cries of jungle birds.)

SCENE III

SCENE: *Clearing. A Pacific Island.*

Before the lights go up, we hear a jungle bird shriek. A few more birds shriek, and then we hear FINCH *whistling "Shoo, Fly." Slowly, the scene fades in.*

We are looking at part of what must be a fairly large clearing in the midst of the jungle. It ends in a vague semicircle of bushes and trees. There is another tree, separate from the others fairly downstage, left. Vines drop from this and crawl over the rest of the cleared area, which is dotted with some small bushes. Hot, muggy sunlight slices down, but the general feeling is of some place dank and unpleasant. This is not motion-picture jungle; it is not pretty.

When the lights go up, FINCH *is propped up, downstage, against a pile of equipment. He is completing a map, and has his sketching pad braced on his knees.* CONEY *is next to him, cleaning his rifle. Both have their guns next to them and, like all the men in this scene, wear jungle combat uniforms.*

There is a slight wait as FINCH *works and whistles. Then a bird screeches again.*

CONEY. This place smells.

FINCH. It's not so bad.

CONEY. I don't mean stinks. I mean smells. Really. This kind of smells. *(He sniffs.)* Like a graveyard.

FINCH. When did you ever smell a graveyard?

CONEY. When we set foot on this trap four days ago. *(A bird screams again.)* Shut up! They make you jumpy, Finch?

FINCH. Some. Coyotes are worse.

CONEY. I never heard coyotes, but I'd like to. I'd like to be where I could hear 'em this minute.

FINCH. In Arizona.

CONEY. God knows you couldn't hear 'em in Pittsburgh.

FINCH. They're kind of scarey—if you wake up and hear them in the middle of the night.

CONEY. I remember waking up in the middle of the night and hearing something. I was ten years old.

FINCH. What'd you hear?

CONEY. A human coyote. *(Gets up.)* I've really got the jumps.

FINCH. We'll be out of here tonight. Why don't you relax? It's a fine day.

CONEY. Yep, yep.

FINCH. It is. I'd like to lie under a tree and have cocoanuts fall in my lap.

CONEY. I'd rather have a Polynesian babe fall in mine.

FINCH. Too much trouble. I'll take cocoanuts.

CONEY. You have to open cocoanuts.

FINCH AND CONEY *(together).* Yuk, yuk, yuk.

FINCH. Well—it may not be a good map, but it's a pretty one.

CONEY. You finished?

FINCH. Almost. They ought to be finished soon, too. They're just rechecking.

CONEY. Yeah. *(Bird screams.)* All right, sweetheart. We heard you the first time!

FINCH. Coney . . .

CONEY. Yeah?

FINCH. You think girls want it as much as fellas?

CONEY. More.

FINCH. But more girls are virgins.

CONEY. Enemy propaganda.

FINCH. I wonder if my sister is. Would you care?

CONEY. What?

FINCH. If the girl you married wasn't?

CONEY. Stop trying to cook up something between me and your sister.

FINCH. She's a good cook.

CONEY. I thought we were going to run a bar?

FINCH. A bar-restaurant.

CONEY. How's she on mixing drinks?

FINCH. She could learn.

CONEY. I wish she'd send up a stiff one now. I'm beginning to see Japs.

FINCH. They're on the other side of the island.

CONEY. It's not like Japs to stay there. *(Bird screams.)* Ah . . .

FINCH. Mingo's wife writes poetry.

CONEY. Yeah. I know.

FINCH. He ever let you read any of it?

CONEY. He never lets anybody read it. It probably stinks.

FINCH. I wonder what she's like.

CONEY. Not bad. From her picture. Did you ever see that picture of the Major's girl?

FINCH. Oh, my aching back!

CONEY. And I'll bet he's a virgin. Him and T.J.

FINCH. T.J.'s been married three times.

CONEY. He's still a virgin.

FINCH. How could he be?

CONEY. He's mean enough. *(Bird screams.)* And you too, you bitch.

FINCH. That's charming.

CONEY. Delightful.

(There is a rustling in the bushes. CONEY *jerks for his gun, then lays back again as* T.J. *comes out.)*

T.J. *(he is perspiring heavily).* You're certainly working yourselves into an early grave.

FINCH. I'm finishing the map.

T.J. What's your friend doing? Posing for it?

CONEY. I'm thinking up inter-office memos.

T.J. Don't rupture yourself.

CONEY. You guys finish?

T.J. If you're so interested, go see for yourself.

CONEY. That's charming.

FINCH. Delightful.

T.J. Screw off. *(Starts to sit.)* Christ, I'm dripping. *(Bird screams and he turns violently.)*

CONEY. Watch out for the birdie.

T.J. Look, Coney, I've—

FINCH *(cutting in).* What are they doing there anyway, T.J.?

T.J. Oh, you know the boy Major. He's got to do things his way. Which makes it twice as long.

FINCH. We'll get off tonight on schedule, though.

T.J. If I were running it, we'd have been through and left yesterday.

CONEY. Yep, yep.

T.J. Yes! *(To* FINCH.*)* He wants the clinometer.

FINCH. Who does?

T.J. The Major.

FINCH. You know where it is.

T.J. Why don't you get the lead out of your can and do something for once?

CONEY *(to* FINCH*).* You finish your map.

FINCH. It's finished, Coney.

CONEY. Well, let T. J. Rockefeller do something besides blowing that tin horn.

T.J. Look who's talking.

FINCH *(jumping up).* Yeah, look! He stood guard two nights out of three while you snored your fat face off. The Major told him to take it easy today and you know it.

T.J. *(to* FINCH*).* The little kike lover.

FINCH. You always get around to that, don't you?

T.J. Every time I see your friend's face.

CONEY. You son of a bitch.

T.J. Watch your language or I'll ram it down your throat, Jew boy.

FINCH. You'll get yours rammed down your throat first.

T.J. Not by him.

CONEY. Listen, T.J.—

T.J. You listen to me, you lousy yellow Jew bastard! I'm going to— *(At this,* FINCH *steps forward and clips* T.J. T.J. *reels but comes back at* FINCH.) You little— *(He swings,* FINCH *ducks and socks him again.* T.J. *hits back.* CONEY *tries to break it up but they are punching away as* MINGO *rushes in from down right.)*

MINGO. What the hell is this? Come on, break it up. *(He steps in.)* Why don't you jerks save it for the Japs?

T.J. He's more interested in saving his yellow Jew friend.

*(*CONEY *turns away sharply and walks a little up right by a tree. There is a brief pause.)*

MINGO *(evenly)*. The Major wants the clinometer, T.J. *(*T.J. *just stands, looking at him.)* Go bring it to him! *(There is a slight wait. Then* T.J. *goes to the pile of gear, fishes out the clinometer and exits down right.)* We're practically through.

*(*FINCH *doesn't answer.* CONEY *stands by the tree, his back to the audience.* MINGO *takes out a cigarette and lights up.)*

FINCH *(low)*. That bastard.

MINGO. We've got plenty of time to pack up and get to the beach. The plane isn't due till nightfall. . . . One thing you can say for the Major. He gets the job done.

FINCH. That bastard.

MINGO. All right.

FINCH. It's not all right.

MINGO. Well—the Major should have known, I guess, but—none of them bother to find out what a guy's like.

FINCH. What makes him such a bastard?

MINGO. Hell, the guy's thirty-five, thirty-six. He can't adjust himself to the Army so he winds up hating everything and resenting everybody. He's just a civilian in G.I. clothes.

FINCH. So am I, but he still stinks.

MINGO. Sure. He stinks from way back. The Army makes him worse. I'm not apologizing for him. I think he's a bastard, too. But you ought to try to understand him.

CONEY *(turning around sharply)*. You try to understand him! I haven't got time. *(Coming over to them.)* I'm too busy trying to understand all this crap about Jews.

FINCH. Coney . . .

CONEY. I told you I heard something in the middle of the night once. Some drunken bum across the hall from my aunt's yelling: Throw out the dirty sheenies! . . . That was us. But I just turned over and went back to sleep. I was used to it by then. What the hell! I was ten. That's old for a Jew. When I was six, my first week in school, I stayed out for the Jewish New Year. The next day a bunch of kids got around me and said: "Were you in school yesterday?" I smiled and said, "No." They wiped the smile off my face. They beat the hell out of me. I had to get beat up a coupla more times before I learned that if you're a Jew, you stink. You're not like other guys. You're —you're alone. You're—you're something —strange, different. *(Suddenly furious.)* Well, goddamit, you make us different, you dirty bastards! What the hell do you want us to do?

FINCH. Coney . . .

CONEY. Let me alone.

MINGO. Coney, listen—

CONEY. Tell your wife to write a poem about it.

MINGO. Screw me *and* my wife. You known damn well Finch at least doesn't feel like that.

CONEY. I don't know anything. I'm a lousy yellow Jew bastard. *(He turns and walks back to the tree.* FINCH *hesitates and then walks to him.)*

FINCH. Coney . . .

CONEY. Drop it.

FINCH. You know that doesn't go for me.

CONEY. I said drop it, Finch.

FINCH. Maybe I'm dumb. Maybe I'm an Arizona hayseed like you say. But I never met any Jewish boys till I got in the Army. I didn't even realize out loud that *you* were until somebody said something.

CONEY. I can imagine what.

FINCH. Yes. And I took a poke at him, too. Because I couldn't see any reason for it. And there isn't any. O.K. I'm a jerk, but to me—you like a guy or you don't. That's all there is to it. That's all there ever will be to it . . . And you know that—don't you? (*He waits for an answer, but there is none. He takes a step back toward* MINGO *and then turns and moves swiftly to* CONEY *and puts an arm around him.*) Aw heck, aren't we buddies?

CONEY (*turning—with a smile*). You corny bastard.

FINCH. You stubborn jerk.

(*Shot rings out from off right. The three on stage freeze.*)

CONEY. What the—

MINGO. Ssh!

(*They stand and listen. A bird screams a few times.*)

FINCH. Maybe it was T.J. He's dumb enough.

MINGO. Not that dumb. A shot could bring the Japs—

CONEY. Listen!

(*They hold for a moment, listening to the right.*)

MINGO. Take cover. Quick!

(*They pick up their guns and start for the bushes upstage just as the* MAJOR *and* T.J. *run out from the bushes, right. From here to curtain, the men speak in hushed tones.*)

MAJOR. Sniper took a pot shot and missed.

FINCH. Judas!

MAJOR. Grab the gear and let's beat it fast.

FINCH. Right.

MAJOR (*to* MINGO). You and Coney keep your rifles ready.

CONEY. Yes, sir.

MAJOR. Forget that sir! Japs love officers. (*FINCH and* T.J. *are hastily picking up gear. The* MAJOR *is picking up equipment.* CONEY *and* MINGO *put on their packs and helmets, always watching to the right.*) Got the maps, Finch?

FINCH. All packed.

MAJOR. Good. Would happen the last day.

MINGO. Did you finish?

MAJOR. Yes. Watch there.

(MINGO *moves closer to the bushes down right with his rifle ready.* CONEY *is also facing in that direction but is nearer center.*)

CONEY. It's so damn dark in there.

T.J. And we're out in the open.

MAJOR. Knock off, T.J. Get that talkie.

(FINCH *starts for it just as two sharp shots crack out from off right. The men flatten to the earth, except* MINGO *who grabs his right arm, dropping his rifle. Then he drops down. A moment's hesitation—then* CONEY *fires. A wait of a moment—and then the sound of a body crashing through the trees.*)

CONEY (*softly*). Got the bastard!

MAJOR. Stay down. There may be others. Finch—see if he's dead. (FINCH *starts to crawl toward the spot where the body crashed.*) If he isn't, use your knife. There's been enough shooting to bring the whole island down on us . . . Anybody hit?

MINGO. Yes.

MAJOR. Where?

MINGO. Right arm.

MAJOR. Bad?

MINGO. Bad enough.

MAJOR. We've got to get out of here. I'll make a tourniquet. (*He starts to crawl toward* MINGO. FINCH, *by this time, has reached the bushes and is on his knees, peering through at the body.*)

FINCH. Major, I don't think he—

(*The bushes move slightly.*)

MAJOR. Make sure! (FINCH *turns slightly to look at him.*) Quick—goddamit—make sure! (FINCH *turns back and then with a sharp movement, gets up, and goes into the bushes with his knife raised. A pause. The sound of* FINCH *rustling in the bushes off right. Then he comes back.*)

FINCH. O.K.

MAJOR *(whipping out a handkerchief which he proceeds to make into a tourniquet for* MINGO*).* If there was anybody else, we should have heard by now. Still— *(*FINCH *has walked up right and now starts to retch. The* MAJOR *turns at the sound and sees* CONEY *move toward* FINCH*.)* Let him alone. Pick up the gear. We've got to beat it. *(A bird screams.)*

T.J. Well, for Chrissakes, let's go.

MAJOR. All right. *(Getting up.)* We'll make for that clearing near the beach.

MINGO *(getting up).* Thanks.

MAJOR. I'll do better later. Forget the pack.

MINGO. I can take it.

(The MAJOR *puts his pack on, starts to pick up some equipment.* T.J. *stands impatiently near the bushes, left.)*

T.J. You never can tell about those slant-eyed bastards. Come on. Let's get out of here.

MAJOR. Take it easy. Who's got the maps?

CONEY. Finch.

FINCH *(coming downstage).* I never can get used to it. I'm sorry.

MAJOR. O.K. Forget about it. You got the maps?

FINCH. Yes, sir.

MAJOR. Everybody set?

CONEY. I'll take care of Finch. *(*FINCH *shakes his head violently.)* What's the matter?

FINCH. I never can get used to it. I got the shakes.

MAJOR. Forget it.

FINCH. It was like killing a dead man.

MAJOR. If you didn't kill him, he would have killed us.

FINCH. I got the shakes, Coney.

CONEY. We all have, Finch.

(Bird screams.)

T.J. Christ!

MAJOR. Come on. Let's go. *(He plunges into the brush.)*

T.J. Come on, Mingo.

MINGO *(to* FINCH*).* So it stinks. Come on, kiddo.

T.J. Mingo!

MINGO. All right. After you, feedbox.

*(*T.J. *goes into the brush.* CONEY *picks up* FINCH'S *pack and helps him put it on.* MINGO *pauses at the end of the brush.)*

MINGO. Coney—

CONEY. We're coming. *(*MINGO *exits off left.* CONEY*, picking up his gear.)* Let's go, Finch. It ain't healthy around here. *(*FINCH *starts to wander around.)* Finch, listen—

FINCH. I'm all right, I'm all right. I just can't remember where I put the map case.

CONEY. O Judas!

FINCH. You go.

CONEY. Try to think.

FINCH. I had it just before I—

CONEY. This is a helluva time!

FINCH. I just had it.

CONEY. Maybe one of them has it.

FINCH. No.

(A bird screams. They are both looking feverishly for the case.)

CONEY. Listen, we'll lose them.

FINCH. We gotta have those maps.

CONEY. The maps won't do us any good if we get picked off!

FINCH. That's the only thing we came here for.

CONEY. Goddamit. Where the hell are they? *(Bird screams.)* Christ!

FINCH. Shut up.

CONEY. You'll get us both killed! You dumb Arizona bastard!

FINCH. I'm not asking you to stay, you lousy yellow— *(He cuts off. They both stand dead still, staring at each other.)* —jerk! *(He turns and begins looking again for the map case.* CONEY *waits a moment, his head bowed in hurt. Then he turns swiftly and starts for the bushes. Just as he gets there,* FINCH *spots the case.)* Here they are! I knew I— *(A shot smashes out. He clutches his belly and* falls. CONEY, *whose back is to* FINCH, *flattens out at the sound of the shot. Then he looks around.*)

CONEY. Finch!

FINCH. Okay.

CONEY (*as he scrambles to him*). You hit?

FINCH. Coney, I didn't mean—

CONEY. Never mind. Are you hit?

FINCH. Take the maps.

CONEY. Where'd they hit you?

FINCH (*thrusting the map case at him*). Take the maps.

CONEY. Finch—

FINCH. Take 'em!

CONEY. Give me your arm. (CONEY *tries to carry him.* FINCH *pushes* CONEY *down.*)

FINCH. I'm all right, you dumb bastard—

CONEY. You sure you—

FINCH. I'll follow. Go on. Quick! (*CONEY looks at him and then darts to the bushes, left.* FINCH *watches him and when* CONEY *looks back, he starts crawling.*) I'm coming, I tell you! Go on, go on! (*CONEY turns and disappears into the brush. Immediately,* FINCH *stops crawling and lies flat. Then he gathers his strength and starts to crawl again. Suddenly he stops and listens. He swings his body around so that he is facing the jungle, right. The bushes, right, begin to rustle.* FINCH, *still holding his rifle, begins to inch his body downstage toward the tree. When* FINCH *is out of sight downstage left, the bushes move.*)

CONEY (*calling softly, offstage*). Finch! Where are you, Finch? Finch! (*Coming on.*) Finch, for Christ' sake where are you? (*A shot rings out and* CONEY *hits the dirt. A pause.*) Finch? Finch? (*Looking around, he starts to back off upstage.*) Where are you, Finch? (*The bushes rustle off.* CONEY *is still calling softly as the curtain falls.*)

ACT TWO

SCENE I

SCENE: *Hospital Room. The Pacific Base.*
   CONEY *is stretched out on the bed with his head buried in the pillow. The* DOCTOR *is sitting on the bed, patting his shoulder.*

DOCTOR (*gently*). Coney . . . Coney.

CONEY. I shouldn't have left him. I shouldn't have left him. Mingo.

DOCTOR. What?

CONEY (*turning*). I should have stayed with him.

DOCTOR. If you'd stayed with him the maps would be lost. The maps were your job and the job comes first.

CONEY. So to hell with Finch!

DOCTOR. Finch knew he had to get those maps. He told you to take them and go, didn't he? Didn't he, Coney?

CONEY. He's dead.

DOCTOR. Didn't he say: Take the maps and get out of here?

(*Pause.*)

CONEY. I shouldn't've left him.

DOCTOR. Coney, take the maps and get out of here!

CONEY. No, Finch.

DOCTOR. Take them and beat it. Go on, will you?

CONEY. Finch— Are you sure—

DOCTOR. Go on! (*A slight pause.* CONEY *slowly raises himself up on his arms. The* DOCTOR *watches him tensely.* CONEY *moves as though to get off the bed.*) Go on!

(CONEY *starts to make the effort to get off the bed. Then slowly, he sinks back shaking his head pitifully.*)

CONEY (*pathetically*). I can't. I can't.

DOCTOR. Coney . . . go on!

CONEY. I can't, Doc. I'm sorry.

(There is a slight pause. The DOCTOR *takes a new tack now.)*

DOCTOR. Coney . . . remember when Finch was shot?

CONEY. Yeah. I remember.

DOCTOR. When you heard that shot and saw he was hit, what did you think of?

CONEY. I—I got a bad feeling.

DOCTOR. But what did you think of, Coney? At that moment, what went through your mind?

CONEY. I didn't want to leave him.

DOCTOR. What did you think of at that instant, Coney?

CONEY. He told me to leave him.

DOCTOR. Coney. Listen. A shot! You turn. *(Slaps his hands together sharply.)* You turn now. You see it's Finch.

CONEY. Finch!

DOCTOR. What are you thinking of, Coney? *(No answer.)* Coney, what just went through your mind?

CONEY. I . . . I . . .

DOCTOR. What?

CONEY. I didn't want to leave him.

DOCTOR. Coney—

CONEY. But he said to leave him! He said to take the maps and beat it. It wasn't because I was yellow. It was because he said to go. Finch said to go!

DOCTOR. You were right to go. You were right to go, Coney.

CONEY. They didn't think so.

DOCTOR. How do you know?

CONEY. I know. I could tell that T.J.—

DOCTOR. Did he say anything?

CONEY. No.

DOCTOR. Did the Major say anything? Did Mingo say anything?

CONEY. No.

DOCTOR. Of course not. Because you were right to leave. You did what you had to do: you saved the maps. That's what you had to do, Coney.

CONEY *(plaintively)*. Was it? Was it really?

DOCTOR. Of course it was, son. It was the only thing you could do.

(Pause.)

CONEY. We did come to get the maps.

DOCTOR. Sure.

CONEY. And I saved them.

DOCTOR. Yes.

CONEY. I saved them . . . But Finch made them and . . . and . . . now . . .

DOCTOR. Coney, you had to leave him, you know that.

CONEY. Yes.

DOCTOR. You can't blame yourself.

CONEY. No . . . Only . . .

DOCTOR. Only what?

CONEY. I still got that feeling.

DOCTOR. What feeling?

CONEY. I don't know. That—that bad feeling.

DOCTOR. Did you first get it when you heard that shot? When you saw it was Finch who was hit?

CONEY. I—I'm not sure.

DOCTOR. Did it come back stronger when you found you couldn't walk?

CONEY. I—think so.

DOCTOR. When was that, Coney? When did you find you couldn't walk?

CONEY. It was . . . It was . . . I don't know.

DOCTOR. Think.

CONEY. I'm trying to.

DOCTOR. Why did it happen? Why couldn't you walk?

CONEY. I—I can't remember.

DOCTOR. Why can't you walk now?

CONEY. I—I don't know. I just can't.

DOCTOR. Why?

CONEY. I don't know. I think it started when—when—

DOCTOR. When what, Coney?

CONEY. When—when—

DOCTOR. When what, Coney?

CONEY. Oh, gee, Doc, I'm afraid I'm gonna cry.

DOCTOR. Go on, son. Cry if you want to.

CONEY. But guys don't cry. You shouldn't cry.

DOCTOR. Let it out, son. Let it all out.

CONEY. No, no, I don't want to. I cried when Finch—

DOCTOR. When Finch what?

CONEY. When he—when . . .

DOCTOR. When you left him?

CONEY. No. No, it was after that. Long after that. I'd been waiting for him.

DOCTOR. Where?

(The lights start to fade.)

CONEY. In the clearing. The clearing by the beach. We were all there. Waiting. Nothing to do but wait and listen to those lousy birds. And all the time, I was wondering about Finch, waiting for Finch, hoping that . . .

(The stage is dark now. Through the last, there have been the faint sounds of crickets and jungle birds.)

SCENE II

SCENE: *Another clearing. The Pacific Island.*

This clearing is smaller than the other; there is more of a feeling of being hemmed in. The trees, bushes and vines at the edge are thicker, closer, darker. At the rear, just left of center, however, there is the suggestion of a path. This leads to the beach.

It is late afternoon, but the filtered sunlight is very hot.

Before the lights come up, we again hear the screech of birds. This continues inter-mittently through the scene.

Although the men reach a high excitement pitch in this scene, they never yell. Their voices are tight and tense, but they remain aware of where they are and of the danger.

AT RISE: CONEY *is peering anxiously through the trees, right. T.J. is sitting fairly near him, drinking from his canteen. MINGO is down left, sitting back against some equipment while the MAJOR, who kneels next to him, loosens the tourniquet on his arm. All the men have removed their packs, but have their rifles ready.*

CONEY. We ought to be able to hear him coming.

T.J. If we could hear him, the Japs could hear him. Finch isn't that dumb.

(The MAJOR takes out his knife and slashes MINGO's sleeve.)

MINGO. Bleeding pretty bad.

MAJOR. Not too bad.

T.J. *(to CONEY).* You make me hot just standing. Why don't you sit down? *(No answer.)* Listen, if Finch is busy ducking them, it'll take him time to get here.

CONEY *(coldly).* He was hit.

MINGO. How's it look, Major?

MAJOR. A little messy.

MINGO *(struggling to take his first-aid kit off his web belt with one hand).* This damn first-aid kit is more—

MAJOR. Let me.

T.J. *(to CONEY).* You don't know how bad he was hit?

CONEY. No.

T.J. Ah, come on and relax, Coney. *(Holds out his canteen.)* Have a drink.

CONEY *(reaching for his own canteen).* I've got some. I wouldn't want you to catch anything, T.J. *(He drinks from his own canteen. The MAJOR starts to sprinkle sulfa over MINGO's wound. MINGO turns his face and looks toward CONEY.)*

MINGO *(to CONEY).* Open mine for me, will you, kiddo?

CONEY *(holding out his own).* Here.

MINGO. Thanks. *(He drinks.)*

MAJOR *(looking at MINGO's wound).* I think you've got two slugs in there.

CONEY. How's it feel, Mingo?

MINGO. Fine. Ready to be lopped off.

CONEY. That's charming.

T.J. Delightful. (CONEY *shoots him a look.*)

MINGO (*to* CONEY). Quit worrying, kiddo. Finch knows the way here.

MAJOR. Sure. He drew the maps. (*The* MAJOR *starts to bandage* MINGO's *wound.*)

CONEY. He might think we're out there on the beach.

MAJOR. The beach is too open. He knows we wouldn't wait there.

MINGO. Anyway, he'd have to come through here to— (*He gasps.*)

MAJOR. Sorry.

MINGO. That's O.K.

T.J. I was just thinking. If the Japs spot Finch, they might let him go—thinking he'd lead them to us.

CONEY. Finch wouldn't lead any Japs to us.

T.J. But if he didn't know.

CONEY. He'd know. And he'd never give us away! (*He turns and walks back to his watching position by the trees.*)

T.J. I didn't say he would deliberately. For Chrissake, you get so—

MINGO. Hang up, T.J.

MAJOR. And keep your voices down . . . How's that, Mingo?

MINGO. Feels O.K. (*Attempt at lightness.*) It ought to do till they amputate.

MAJOR. Amputate?

MINGO. Just a bad joke, Major.

MAJOR. I'll say it is. That sulfa should prevent infection.

MINGO. Sure.

MAJOR. And if you loosen the tourniquet every twenty minutes—

MINGO. I know. I'm just building it up. (*Bird screams.*) On your way, vulture. No meat today.

MAJOR. The plane'll be here in about an hour, Mingo. You can be in the hospital tomorrow.

CONEY (*turning*). Major—suppose Finch isn't here?

MAJOR. What?

CONEY (*coming closer*). Suppose Finch isn't here when the plane comes?

MAJOR. He'll be here.

CONEY. But suppose he isn't?

MAJOR. We'll worry about that when the time comes.

MINGO. What would we do, though?

MAJOR. I said we'll worry about that when the time comes. (*Pause.*) Lord, it's sticky.

MINGO (*to* CONEY). He's got over an hour yet, Coney.

CONEY. You know darn well if he's going to get here, he'll turn up in the next few minutes or not at all.

(*Pause.*)

T.J. I don't need a shower. I'm giving myself one.

MINGO. That's part of the charm of the South Seas.

T.J. I once took a cruise in these waters.

MINGO. I once set up a travel booklet about them. I was a linotyper after I had to quit college. You learn a lot of crap setting up type. I learned about the balmy blue Pacific. Come to the Heavenly Isles! An orchid on every bazoom—and two bazooms on every babe. I'd like to find the gent who wrote that booklet. I'd like to find him now and make him come to his goddam Heavenly Isles!

(*Slight pause.*)

T.J. You know—if they hit Finch bad . . .

MINGO. Shut up. (*He tests his arm, trying to see how well he can move it. He winces.*)

MAJOR. It'll be all right, Mingo.

MINGO. I wonder how a one-armed lino-typer would make out.

CONEY. Major . . . I gotta go look for him.

MAJOR. Finch knows the path, Coney.

CONEY. Yeah, but maybe he— (*He cuts off as* T.J., *who is looking off right, sud-*

denly brings up his gun. The others grab theirs and wait tensely, watching T.J. *He holds for a moment, staring into the trees, and then a bird screams. He lowers his gun.)*

T.J. Sorry.

MAJOR. What was it?

T.J. Animal, bird, something. I don't know. Since I came up with that cheerful idea of Japs following Finch—sorry.

MAJOR. Forget it. It's better to be over-alert than to be caught napping.

MINGO. I wonder if the squints know how many of us there are.

MAJOR. Not yet. And I don't think they know where we are, either. *(He walks over to* CONEY.*)* That's why you can't go look for him, Coney. If they've got him—well, go in there and they'll get you too. And us along with you.

CONEY. I should've stayed with him.

MAJOR. You had to get those maps back and you did. Now we've got to get off this island so we can bring those maps back. That comes first.

CONEY. So—to hell with Finch.

MINGO. Kid, the Major's right. We've got to take care of the job first.

MAJOR. Look, Coney—

CONEY. Yeah. I know. I know.

T.J. I wish we were the hell out of here. . . . All of us. *(Slight pause.)* I don't suppose there's anything we can do.

MINGO. Sure. You know what we can do. We can wait.

T.J. That's all you ever do in this man's army.

MINGO *(dryly)*. What man's army?

T.J. You wait for chow, you wait for mail, you wait for pay. And when you're not waiting for that, you wait for something to wait for.

MINGO. Yeah. We wait. And back there, in those lovely forty-eight States—

(A scream from some distance off right.)

CONEY. What was that?

(Slight pause.)

T.J. Ah, a bird.

CONEY. That was no bird.

MINGO. Coney, you're just—

CONEY. That was no bird.

T.J. A cigar to the boy with the ears.

CONEY. That was no bird! Listen! *(Slight pause. A bird.)* No. Listen!

MAJOR. Ease up, Coney. I know you—

(The scream again. And this time it is recognizable as:)

CONEY. It's Finch! He's yelling for me! *(He picks up his gun and starts for the bushes. The* MAJOR *grabs him.)*

MAJOR. Coney—

CONEY. You heard him!

MAJOR. Yes, but—

CONEY. Please, sir. They're killing him. They're killing Finch!

MAJOR. They're not killing him and they won't kill him.

CONEY. Not them. Not much.

MAJOR. I tell you he won't be killed. It's just a trick. They're purposely making him yell.

CONEY. Please, Major, let me—

MAJOR *(holding tight)*. Coney, you can't go in there! They're sticking him just to make him yell like that. Just to make us come after him.

CONEY. All right!

MAJOR. But when we do—they'll get us. Don't you understand?

CONEY. I don't care!

MAJOR. Coney, listen to me. They're just trying to find out where we are. They're just trying to get us. It's a trick.

CONEY. I don't care, sir. Let me go, please!

MAJOR. Coney, will you listen to me?

*(*FINCH *screams again.)*

CONEY. You listen to him. *(With a savage jerk, he breaks away from the* MAJOR *and starts into the bushes.)*

MINGO. Coney! Stop trying to be a god-dam hero! (CONEY *stops just as he is about to go into the jungle. He doesn't turn around* to face MINGO *who stands where he is and talks very fast.)* It's just a trick. A dirty, lousy trick. Sure, they're jabbing Finch and making him yell. But if you go after him—they'll kill him. And you too. (CONEY *turns around slowly.)* There isn't a lousy thing we can do, kid. *(A slight pause.* CONEY *walks toward* MINGO *very slowly, then suddenly hurls his rifle to the ground and sits by it.)*

CONEY. So—to hell with Finch.

MINGO *(going to him)*. No.

CONEY. Let them make hamburger out of him.

MINGO. Kid, there's nothing we can do.

CONEY. You can— (FINCH *screams again.)* O Christ!

MINGO. Don't listen. Try not to listen. You know—they way you do with guns. You don't hear them after a while.

CONEY. That isn't guns; it's Finch!

MINGO. Pretend it's just yelling. Hell, you ought to be used to yelling and noise. You're a city kid.

CONEY. What?

MINGO. You come from Pittsburgh, don't you? (FINCH *screams again.)* Don't you, Coney?

CONEY. Mingo, they're killing him.

MINGO. That bar you and he were going to have—was it going to be in Pittsburgh? (FINCH *screams.)* Was it going to be in Pittsburgh, Coney?

CONEY. Finch!

MINGO. Kid, it's not so bad if he's yelling. You've got to be alive to yell.

CONEY. Major, please—

MINGO. Don't listen. Tell me about the bar.

CONEY. Major, let me—

MINGO. Talk.

CONEY. I can't.

MINGO. Remember that Jap knife I picked up? The one you wanted to—

CONEY. Mingo—let me—

MINGO. Say, whatever happened that night when you were on guard and—

CONEY. Mingo—

MINGO. You like poetry?

CONEY. Mingo, he's being—

(FINCH *screams.)*

MINGO. My wife writes poetry, Coney. Remember you always wanted to hear some?

CONEY. Please—

MINGO. Didn't you always want to hear some? Listen.

(FINCH *screams again, weaker now.)*

CONEY. Oh dear God!

MINGO. Listen. *(Quickly.)*
"We are only two and yet our howling
Can encircle the world's end.
Frightened,
    (FINCH *screams—weakly.)*
you are my only friend.
    (Slower now.)
And frightened, we are everyone.
Someone must take a stand.
Coward, take my coward's hand."

(There is a long pause. They sit waiting. Slowly, CONEY *stretches out, buries his face in the ground and starts to cry. A bird screams.* T.J. *looks up.)*

T.J. *(quietly)*. Lousy birds. (T.J. *begins to whistle "Shoo, Fly" very sweetly. A long pause. Then,* MINGO *gets up.)*

MAJOR. Helluva thing.

MINGO. Yeah. In the Mariannas, I saw a fellow after the Japs had gotten hold of him. They'd put pieces of steel through his cheeks—here—you know. Like a bit for a horse.

T.J. You couldn't talk about something pleasant, could you?

MINGO. Sorry.

T.J. We'll all have a chance to find out what the squints do if we keep sitting here.

MAJOR. Well, the plane won't come till after it gets dark and we can't dig up the canoes till sundown.

T.J. There ought to be something we can do besides sit around here on our butts.

MAJOR. Suppose you go down the beach and see if the canoes are still where we buried them.

T.J. Go out on the beach now? It's too light!

MAJOR. The canoes are right at the edge of the trees. You don't have to go out in the open.

T.J. But even if they're not there, there's nothing I can do about it.

MAJOR. You can find out! Now you heard me. Get going, T.J.! (T.J. *hesitates, then picks up his rifle and starts upstage.*) If you run into trouble, fire four quick shots.

(T.J. *doesn't answer but storms off through the path up right. During the following, the lights begin to dim as the sun goes down.*)

MINGO. I think the big executive is a little afraid.

MAJOR. I guess he doesn't like to take orders from me.

MINGO. He doesn't like much of anything, Major.

MAJOR. Does he— (*Hesitates.*) Mingo, does he make cracks about the Jews?

MINGO. Yes, Major. He does. He does indeed.

MAJOR. To Coney?

MINGO. Coney's a Jew.

MAJOR. Funny. I never think of him as a Jew.

MINGO. Yeah, it is funny. I never think of you as a Gentile.

(*A slight pause. Then the* MAJOR *speaks awkwardly—in a low voice.*)

MAJOR. Guess I said the wrong thing.

MINGO. I'm sorry, Major. I shouldn't've—

MAJOR. There are a lot of things you know, Mingo, that I guess I should but I—

MINGO. Look, sir, I didn't—

MAJOR. Wait. I'd like to get this off my chest. There are a lot of things I'd like to get off my chest. (*A pause.*) For one thing, I'd like to thank you, Mingo.

MINGO. For what?

MAJOR. For the rumpus just now with Coney . . . when you stopped him from running off half-cocked after Finch. . . .

MINGO. I just repeated what you'd said.

MAJOR. Yeah, but he—well, you stopped him. Thanks.

MINGO. Nuts.

MAJOR. I shouldn't have needed you or anybody else to—

MINGO. It's no crime to get help, Major.

MAJOR. No. But it's lousy to think you need it. I know you fellows—well, take T.J. I know he thinks I'm too young to give him orders.

MINGO. He'd think God was too young.

MAJOR. I didn't know what T.J. was like before we started. I guess I should have.

MINGO. Yes. I think you should have.

MAJOR. I know what you think, too.

MINGO. What do you mean?

MAJOR. An officer's got to have the respect of his men. He's no good otherwise, Mingo.

MINGO. Depends what you think respect is.

MAJOR. You think I care about the job and not about Finch. I care about Finch! I do now! But the job comes first. And I know my job, Mingo. I know it darn well!

MINGO. O.K., sir.

MAJOR. This isn't what I started out to say at all. (*Pause.*) Look—I'm a Major . . . but I'm twenty-six. I don't know all the answers and I don't think I know 'em. Judas, I'm not even sure what this lousy war is all about. There are fifty million things I don't know that I wish I did. But I'm a Major. I've got to have the respect of my men. And there's only one way I can get it: by knowing my job and running it.

MINGO. Nobody wants to run the show, Major. Maybe T.J.—but he's a first-class crud, anyway. We just want the same thing, too.

MAJOR. What?

MINGO. Respect. For us—as guys.

MAJOR. But an officer—

MINGO. An officer's a guy, isn't he, Major?

MAJOR. Yeah.

MINGO. O.K. All we want is for you—every once in a while to—talk to us—like this.

MAJOR (smiling). O.K.

MINGO (smiling). O.K.

(The MAJOR takes out a pack of cigarettes and holds one out for MINGO. Then he lights it for him.)

MAJOR. How's the arm?

MINGO. Lousy.

MAJOR. Want me to change the bandage?

MINGO. No. I just want to get out of here. Thanks. (For the cigarette.)

MAJOR. Don't worry about it so. It'll be O.K.

MINGO. I know, but I—well, I'd kinda hate to go back to the States anyway. And to go back with a—well, I guess I have too good an imagination.

MAJOR. I think you're just worried about going back to your wife with—well, a bum wing, say.

MINGO (slightly bitter). Oh, my wife wouldn't care.

MAJOR. No. She sounds like a fine girl.

MINGO. How do you know?

MAJOR. From that poem. Wasn't that hers?

MINGO. What po— Oh. That. Yeah, that was hers.

MAJOR. Most people think it's sissy stuff but—I like poetry. I was trying to remember that last part. "Frightened, we are—"

MINGO (reeling it off). "Everyone. Someone must make a stand. Coward, take my coward's hand."

MAJOR. I like that.

MINGO. Sure. It's great. My wife's a great little writer. Pretty, too. It's just a pity she doesn't read her own stuff once in a while.

MAJOR. What do you mean?

MINGO. She writes good letters, too. I remember the first one, the first one she wrote me in the Army. "My darling darling," it began. She likes repetition. "My darling darling, I will never again use the word love—except to say i love you."

MAJOR. That's nice.

MINGO. Oh, that's very nice. Almost as nice as her last letter. I can remember that one, too. I got that about a week ago. That began: "My darling, this is the hardest letter I've ever had to write. But it's only fair to be honest with you and tell you that—" (He is too choked up to go on. Slight pause.)

MAJOR (embarrassed.) Want another cigarette?

MINGO. No . . . thanks.

MAJOR. The sun's going down.

MINGO. They call that the G.I. letter, you know. Because there are so many of them.

MAJOR. I know.

MINGO. I can understand. Hell, I'm away and she meets another guy. But—Christ!

MAJOR. Well . . .

MINGO. It makes me want to hate all civilians. Then I remember I used to be one myself. A couple of million years ago . . . Hell, they can't all be bad.

MAJOR. Of course not.

MINGO. Then I remember that we've got stinkers here too. Like T.J. And so I try to stay on the beam. It's kind of hard though, when I think of that bitch and what— (He cuts off as there is a rustling noise from the bushes right. They freeze. The rustling gets louder. The MAJOR grabs his rifle and, at the same time, CONEY sits up with his rifle ready.) T.J.

MAJOR. He wouldn't be coming from there.

(The rustling gets still louder. And then, in the fading light, T.J. appears, scrambling through the brush.)

T.J. The canoes are still there. I scratched holy hell out of myself though.

(The rifles are lowered.)

MAJOR. Why didn't you come back by the trail?

T.J. I got lost. (To CONEY.) When did you wake up?

CONEY. Just now.

MAJOR. Are you hungry, Coney? Why don't you eat something?

CONEY. K ration isn't kosher.

(*A slight pause. From now on, it begins to get dark rapidly.*)

MINGO. The birds have shut up anyway.

MAJOR (*looking up*). I think it's dark enough to dig up the canoes and get 'em ready.

MINGO. What about the gear?

MAJOR. There's no point in taking it until the canoes are ready . . . only—we need someone to watch it. In case.

MINGO. I don't mind.

T.J. How's your arm?

MINGO. My arm?

MAJOR. You couldn't use your rifle if—

CONEY (*getting up suddenly*). I'll stay.

MAJOR. Oh, thanks, Coney, but you'd better—

CONEY (*harshly*). What's wrong with me staying?

MAJOR (*quietly*). O.K. Thanks.

MINGO. Maybe I'd better stay, too, Major. With this bum wing, I won't be able to—

CONEY. I'm not afraid to stay alone, Mingo!

MAJOR. You can help lift the canoes with your left arm anyway, Mingo.

MINGO. Sure.

MAJOR. Let's go. (*He starts for the path up left followed by* T.J. *and* MINGO. *Just before he goes into the trees, he turns and calls to* CONEY.) Four quick shots if anything happens, Coney.

CONEY. Yes, sir.

MINGO. Nothing will, kiddo. See you. (*He disappears after the* MAJOR *and* T.J. *into the jungle. By now, the sun has gone down altogether. The jungle that rims the stage is pitch black, but there is pale light center in the clearing, dimming out to the edges.* CONEY *does not look after the others when they go. He stands still for a moment and then takes out a cigarette. He holds it, then suddenly shoves it in his mouth, holds*

his rifle ready and whirls around. He listens sharply for a moment, then slowly turns. His shoulders slump, the rifle comes down, and he takes the cigarette out of his mouth. He walks to the pile of equipment, looks at it and is about to sit down when suddenly he freezes. The cigarette drops to the ground, the rifle comes up. Slowly, very slowly, he starts to turn and, when he is halfway around, leaps like a cat to the dimly lighted edge of the clearing, right. He holds there for a moment, listening. Then, he leans forward a little.)

CONEY (*softly*). Finch? (*He moves closer to the trees. Plaintively.*) Finch? (*He listens for a moment, and then suddenly whirls so that his gun is pointed up right. He whirls again so that it is pointed up left. He darts back across the stage to the pile of equipment and stands there breathing hard, moving the rifle back and forth in a small arc. Then, suddenly, he hurls the gun down in front of him and sinks to his haunches.*) Your name is Coen and you're a— (*His voice cracks. He covers his face with his hands. He remains that way for a long moment and then sinks to the ground, bracing himself with his left hand and covering his face with his right. A second later, the bushes down right begin to rustle softly.* CONEY *doesn't hear this. The rustling gets louder; the bushes move; and then a body begins to crawl out very slowly; just the shape is discernible in the dim light by the trees, but soon it is apparent that the body is not crawling, but dragging itself. It gets closer to the lighted area and stops. A hand comes up and gestures—as though the man were trying to talk and couldn't. Finally, with a great effort, the body drags itself farther into the light. The clothes are slashed and splotched with blood and the face is battered—but it's* FINCH. *He sees* CONEY *and tries again to call to him. Again, his hand comes out in a pathetically futile gesture; he tries desperately hard to speak—but no sound comes. He tries to move farther but can't. Finally, in an outburst of impotent fury, he tries again to call and now his voice shouts out in a shrill scream.*)

FINCH. Coney! (*Like a bullet,* CONEY *drops his hands. His face is wide with terror; his body is rigid. He cannot believe he really heard anything. Then slowly, slowly, his head turns. He looks straight at* FINCH *—but does not believe he sees him.)*

CONEY *(plaintively, with a suggestion of a tear).* Finch? . . . Is that you, Finch?

FINCH. Coney!

CONEY *(frantically, he scrambles over and puts an arm around* FINCH, *who groans in pain).* Finch! Oh, Christ, Finch! Finch! *(He reaches for his canteen, quickly opens it and props* FINCH's *head in his lap. As he starts to give him water, he talks.)* Oh, I'm glad! I'm so glad, Finch! You all right? You're going to be all right now, Finch. You're going to be all right now— *(*FINCH *cannot hold the water and spews it up.)* Easy, fellow. Easy, Finch. *(*FINCH *begins to retch;* CONEY *holds his head.)* Oh, that's charming. That's really charming. You go right ahead. That's fine and charming, Finch. *(*FINCH *has stopped now and tries to talk.)*

FINCH *(just getting the word out).* Delightful.

CONEY. Oh, you bastard! You damn son of a bitch bastard! I might've known they couldn't finish you off, you damn Arizona bastard. Let me see what they— *(He touches* FINCH, *trying to see his wounds.* FINCH *gasps in pain.)* I'm sorry. I'm sorry, kid, but I—what? What, Finch? I can't hear you. What? *(He bends down, his ear close to* FINCH's *mouth.)* Oh for Chrissake, sure the lousy maps are all right. We've got to get you fixed up— *(Again he touches* FINCH *and* FINCH *groans.)* All right. Just lie still. The guys are getting the canoes now. The plane'll be here soon and you'll be back to the base in no time. You can goldbrick out the rest of the war in the hospital, you lucky bastard! You'll probably get a slew of medals, to say nothing of a big fat Purple Heart. And you'll go home and leave me stuck here. Hey, did I tell you I missed you, you jerk? O Jesus, I'm so glad, Finch. *(*FINCH's *head suddenly rolls over and flops to one side.)* I'm so glad, I'm so . . . *(He stops. He is absolutely quiet for a moment. Then, begging.)* Finch? Finch? Ah, Finch, please don't be dead! *(He turns* FINCH's *body slightly and ducks his head down so he can listen to* FINCH's *heart. There is a pause; and then, with his head still on* FINCH's *chest, he says softly.)* O God. O God. O God. O God. O God. *(His voice*

cracks on the last and he begins to cry softly. Slowly, he straightens up. He is whimpering very quietly.* FINCH's *body rolls back, stomach down.* CONEY *looks at it for a long moment and then, suddenly, stops crying and with a violent, decisive, brutal gesture, shoves the body so it rolls over on its back. He stares at the horror he sees for a few seconds. Then, swiftly, he lifts the head into his lap with one hand and, with a long arc-like sweep, cradles the torso with his other arm and bends across it. An anguished groan.)* Oh, no, Finch! *(He begins to rock the body as though it were a baby.)* Oh, no, Finch! Oh, no, no, no! *(Just at this moment, a voice cracks out from some distance off right. It is a Jap voice.)*

FIRST JAP. Hey, Yank! Come out and fight!

*(*CONEY *looks up sharply, cradling the head closer. From farther up right comes another voice.)*

SECOND JAP. Hey, Yank! Come out and fight!

*(*CONEY's *head turns in the direction of the second voice.)*

CONEY. Finch, they're after you again! But I won't leave you this time. I promise I won't, Finch.

THIRD JAP. Come and fight, yellow bastard.

CONEY. I won't leave you, Finch. I promise, I promise, I promise! *(He takes his bayonet out and starts to scoop up the ground furiously. At the same time, the* JAPS *continue yelling. Their shouts overlap with variations of the same cry. As he digs.)* Don't worry, Finch. I told you I wouldn't let them get you. I promised, didn't I? Didn't I? And I won't. Because I'm not a yellow bastard. I won't leave you, Finch. *(He is digging feverishly now; the yelling is coming closer; and the* MAJOR *rushes on from the path upstage, followed by* MINGO.)*

MAJOR. Coney!

MINGO. He's got Finch!

MAJOR *(to* MINGO). Get the map case. *(*MINGO *quickly searches through the pile of equipment for the map case. The* MAJOR *goes to* CONEY *who is digging furiously.)* Coney, come on. We've got to—God, he's dead!

CONEY. They won't get him, though, Major. They want to but they won't. I'm going to bury him!

MAJOR. Bury— Listen, Coney, we— Coney, you can't bury him. We've got to get out of here.

MINGO (coming over with the map case). Got them, Major.

MAJOR. Coney—

MINGO. What's the matter with him?

MAJOR. Finch is dead and he's trying to bury him.

MINGO. O God! Coney, get up.

CONEY. I can't leave Finch.

MINGO. We'll take him. Come on. Get up.

CONEY. I can't leave Finch.

MINGO. Get up, Coney.

CONEY. Finch—

MINGO. Don't worry about him.

MAJOR. We'll take him.

MINGO. Come on, Coney.

(CONEY tries to get up. He drags himself a few inches, but he cannot get up.)

FIRST JAP. Fight, you yellow bastard.

THIRD JAP. Hey! Yank, come out and fight.

THIRD JAP. Come out, you Yank bastard.

CONEY. I can't.

MAJOR. What do you mean you can't?

CONEY. I can't move, Major. I can't move!

THIRD JAP. Yank, come out and fight.

MINGO. Holy God! Try.

CONEY. I am—but I can't.

MINGO. Now stop that. You've got to get out of here.

CONEY. I can't, Mingo. I can't walk. I can't move.

SECOND JAP. Come out and fight.

MINGO. Were you shot? Were you hit?

FIRST JAP. Yank, come out and fight.

CONEY. No.

SECOND JAP. Fight, you yellow bastard.

MAJOR. Then why can't you walk?

CONEY (building to hysteria now). I don't know!

MINGO. What's the matter with you?

THIRD JAP. Yank, come out and fight.

CONEY. I don't know!

MINGO. Coney—

CONEY. I don't know! I don't know! I don't know! (He is crying wildly now; MINGO and the MAJOR are trying to lift him; and the screaming of the JAPS is getting louder and louder. The JAPS continue through the blackness and gradually fade out.)

SCENE III

SCENE: *Hospital Room. The Pacific Base.*
Before the lights come up, we hear CONEY *counting.*

CONEY. 85—84—83—82—81—80—79—

DOCTOR. 78.

CONEY. 78—77—76—75. (*The lights are up now.* CONEY *is on the bed, the* DOCTOR *sitting by him watching the needle.*) 74—73—72—73—7—

(*The* DOCTOR *withdraws the needle and gets up.*)

DOCTOR. Coney, do you remember how you got off that island?

CONEY. I think—Mingo. Something about Mingo.

DOCTOR. Yes. Mingo picked you up and carried you out.

CONEY. I—I remember water. Being in the canoe on water. There were bullets.

DOCTOR. Some of the Japs fired machine guns when they realized what was happening.

CONEY. I think maybe I passed out because —it's all kind of dark. Then I'm in the plane.

DOCTOR. T.J. lifted you in.

CONEY. T.J.?

DOCTOR. Yes.

CONEY. But Mingo . . .

DOCTOR. Mingo couldn't lift you in alone. His right arm was no good.

CONEY. Oh, yeah . . . yeah.

DOCTOR. That's all you remember, though?

CONEY. I remember being taken off the plane.

DOCTOR. I mean on the island. That's all you remember of what happened on the island?

CONEY. Yes.

DOCTOR. Then why can't you walk, Coney?

CONEY. What?

DOCTOR. You weren't shot, were you?

CONEY. No.

DOCTOR. You didn't break your legs, did you?

CONEY. No.

DOCTOR. Then why can't you walk, Coney?

CONEY. I don't know. I don't know.

DOCTOR. But you said you remember everything that happened.

CONEY. I—yes. Yes.

DOCTOR. Do you remember waking up in the hospital? Do you remember waking up with that bad feeling?

CONEY. Yes.

(Slight pause. The DOCTOR walks next to the bed.)

DOCTOR. Coney, when did you first get that bad feeling?

CONEY. It was—I don't know.

DOCTOR. Coney— (He sits down.) Coney, did you first get it right after Finch was shot?

CONEY. No.

DOCTOR. What did you think of when Finch was shot?

CONEY. I don't know.

DOCTOR. You said you remember everything that happened. And you do. You remember that, too. You remember how you felt when Finch was shot, don't you, Coney? Don't you?

CONEY (sitting bolt upright). Yes. (A long pause. His hands twist his robe and then lay still. With dead, flat tones.) When we were looking for the map case, he said— he started to say: You lousy yellow Jew bastard. He only said you lousy yellow jerk, but he started to say you lousy yellow Jew bastard. So I knew. I knew.

DOCTOR. You knew what?

CONEY. I knew he'd lied when—when he said he didn't care. When he said people were people to him. I knew he lied. I knew he hated me because I was a Jew so—I was glad when he was shot.

(The DOCTOR straightens up.)

DOCTOR. Did you leave him there because you were glad?

CONEY. Oh, no!

DOCTOR. You got over it.

CONEY. I was—I was sorry I felt glad. I was ashamed.

DOCTOR. Did you leave him because you were ashamed?

CONEY. No.

DOCTOR. Because you were afraid?

CONEY. No.

DOCTOR. No. You left him because that was what you had to do. Because you were a good soldier. (Pause.) You left him and you ran through the jungle, didn't you?

CONEY. Yes.

DOCTOR. And you walked around in the clearing by the beach, didn't you?

CONEY. Yes.

DOCTOR. So your legs were all right.

CONEY. Yes.

DOCTOR. Then if anything did happen to your legs, it happened when Finch crawled back. And you say nothing happened to you then.

CONEY. I don't know.

DOCTOR. Did anything happen?

CONEY. I don't know. Maybe—maybe.

DOCTOR. But if anything did happen, you'd remember?

CONEY. I don't know.

DOCTOR. You *do* remember what happened when Finch crawled back, don't you? Don't you, Coney?

CONEY (*covers his face*). Finch . . . Finch . . .

DOCTOR. Remember that. Think back to that, Coney. You were alone in the clearing and Finch crawled in.

CONEY. O God . . . O dear God . . .

DOCTOR. Remember. (*He gets up quickly, moves across the room and in a cracked voice calls:*) Coney!

CONEY (*plaintively—he turns sharply*). Finch? . . . Finch?

DOCTOR (*a cracked whisper*). Coney . . .

CONEY. Oh, Finch, Finch! Is that you, Finch? (*He cradles an imaginary head in his lap and begins to rock back and forth.*) I'm so glad. I'm so glad, Finch! I'm so . . . (*He stops short, waits, then ducks his head down as though to listen to* FINCH's *heart. A moment, then he straightens up and then, with the same decisive, brutal gesture as before, shoves the imaginary body of Finch so that it rolls over. He looks at it in horror and then the* DOC- TOR *calls out:*)

DOCTOR. Hey, Yank! Come out and fight!

CONEY. They won't get you, Finch. I won't leave you this time, I promise! (*He begins to pantomime digging feverishly.*)

DOCTOR. Come out and fight, Yank.

CONEY. I won't leave you this time!

(*The* DOCTOR *walks over deliberately and grabs* CONEY's *hand, stopping it in the middle of a digging motion.*)

DOCTOR (*curtly*). What are you trying to bury him in, Coney? (CONEY *stops and stares up at him.*) This isn't earth, Coney. This is a bed. Feel it. It's a bed. Underneath is a floor, a wooden floor. Hear? (*He stamps.*) You can't bury Finch, Coney, because he isn't here. You're not on that island. You're in a hospital. You're

in a hospital, Coney, and I'm your doctor. I'm your doctor!

(*Pause.*)

CONEY. Yes, sir.

DOCTOR. And you remember now, you re- member that nothing happened to your legs at all, did it?

CONEY. No, sir.

DOCTOR. But you had to be carried here.

CONEY. Yes, sir.

DOCTOR. Why?

CONEY. Because I can't walk.

DOCTOR. Why can't you walk?

CONEY. I don't know.

DOCTOR. *I do*. It's because you didn't want to, isn't it, Coney? Because you knew if you couldn't walk, then you couldn't leave Finch. That's it, isn't it?

CONEY. I don't know.

DOCTOR. That must be it. Because there's nothing wrong with your legs. They're fine, healthy legs and you can walk. You can walk. You had a shock and you didn't want to walk. But you're over the shock and now you do want to walk, don't you? You do want to walk, don't you, Coney?

CONEY. Yes. Yes.

DOCTOR. Then get up and walk.

CONEY. I—can't.

DOCTOR. Yes, you can.

CONEY. No.

DOCTOR. Try.

CONEY. I can't.

DOCTOR. Try.

CONEY. I can't.

DOCTOR. Get up and walk! (*Pause.*) Coney, get up and walk! (*Pause.*) You lousy, yel- low Jew bastard, get up and walk! (*At that,* CONEY *straightens up in rage. He is shaking, but he grips the edge of the bed and swings his feet over. He is in a white fury, and out of his anger comes this tre- mendous effort. Still shaking, he stands* up; holds for a moment; and glares at the DOCTOR. Then, with his hands outstretched before him as though he is going to kill the DOCTOR, he starts to walk. First one foot, then the other, left, right, left—but he begins to cry violently and as he sinks to the floor, the DOCTOR moves forward swiftly and grabs him.)

DOCTOR (triumphantly). All right, son! Al' right!

CURTAIN

ACT THREE

SCENE I

SCENE: *Hospital Room. Two weeks later.*
There is a bright cheerful look about the room now. The window is open; sunlight streams in. The bed is pushed close against the wall and has a neat, unused look. There is a typewriter on the desk.
CONEY, wearing a hospital "zoot suit," is seated at the desk typing very laboriously. The door opens and T.J. comes in. CONEY stutters slightly in this scene when he is agitated.

T.J. Oh! Hi, Coney!

(A second's awkward pause.)

MAJOR (coming in). Coney! Gosh, it's good to see you, fellow!

CONEY. It's good to see you, Major.

T.J. You're looking fine, just fine!

MAJOR. We've sure missed you. When are you coming back to us?

CONEY. I—don't know if I am, sir. I'm—working for the Doc now.

T.J. Working?

CONEY. Yes. I type up his records and—sort of keep 'em straight for him.

MAJOR. Why, the dirty dog! Stealing my best man!

CONEY (with a smile). It's really not very much work, sir.

MAJOR. I didn't know you could type.

CONEY. Oh—hunt and peck.

T.J. Well, it's great you're not a patient any more.

CONEY. I'm still a patient. In a way.

MAJOR. Do you—still get the—

CONEY. Shots? No. But the Doc—well—he and I talk.

T.J. Talk?

CONEY. Yes. Once a day.

T.J. Why?

CONEY. Well, it's—part of the treatment.

T.J. Brother, I'd like to be that kind of a patient.

CONEY. Maybe you should be.

MAJOR (leaping in hastily). The Doc's quite a guy, isn't he?

CONEY. Yes, sir. He— (Slight note of appeal.) He says I'm coming along fine.

MAJOR. Oh, anybody can see you are, can't they, T.J.?

T.J. Sure.

MAJOR. We've got something to tell you that ought to put you right on top of the world. The island— (He stops. Cautiously.) You remember the island, Coney?

CONEY (wry smile). Yes. I remember, Major.

MAJOR. It was invaded four days ago. And everything went off 100 per cent perfect —thanks to our maps.

CONEY. Oh, that's swell.

MAJOR. We've gotten commendations a yard long.

T.J. Wait till you get out of here! Your back's going to be sore from all the patting it's going to get!

MAJOR. The Doc wanted to tell you about it but . . . well . . .

T.J. We felt since we were all in it together, Coney—

CONEY. Did you, T.J.?

T.J. Sure. Weren't we?

CONEY. In a way, we were. And in a way, we weren't.

T.J. Wait a minute, kid, don't forget how I . . .

CONEY *(getting a little unstable now).* Don't you worry about my memory, T.J. The Doc fixed me up fine and it's all right.

T.J. Sure, I know.

CONEY. Maybe it'd be better if I did forget a few things. If I forgot that— *(He breaks off as the door opens and the DOCTOR comes in.)*

DOCTOR *(kidding slightly).* Well! Who said this was visiting hour?

MAJOR. We were looking for you, Doc. We wanted your permission to see Coney.

DOCTOR *(still the kidding tone).* I'm afraid you can't have it.

MAJOR *(following suit).* That's too bad. I guess we'd better run along, T.J.

DOCTOR *(no smile now).* Yes. I think you'd better.

MAJOR. Oh. I'm sorry, sir. I—

DOCTOR. That's O.K. I'll tell you what. You're going to see Mingo this afternoon, aren't you?

MAJOR. Yes.

DOCTOR. Drop around after that.

MAJOR. Sure! Thanks, Doc. *(Turns to go.)* I'll see you later, Coney.

CONEY. Yes, sir.

T.J. Take care, Coney.

CONEY. Yeah.

MAJOR. Thanks again, Doc. *(He and T.J. go out. CONEY has edged toward the desk when the DOCTOR came in. Now, he goes behind it and sits down at the typewriter.)*

DOCTOR. I'm sorry I had to run them out.

CONEY *(putting a sheet of paper in the typewriter).* That's all right, sir. I didn't care.

DOCTOR. Nice boy, the Major.

CONEY. Yes, sir. *(He starts to type slowly.)*

DOCTOR. How'd you get on with T.J.?

CONEY. All right. *(A slight pause.)* No. Not really all right. He makes me think of things and I—want to jump at him.

DOCTOR. Why not? That's a good, healthy reaction.

CONEY. Honest, Doc?

DOCTOR. Of course. *(Indicating the typing.)* Never mind that. This isn't your working period. It's mine.

CONEY. Now?

DOCTOR. Yes. Now.

CONEY. But we don't usually—

DOCTOR *(cutting him).* I know. But we're going to work now. I'll tell you why later.

CONEY. Yes, sir. *(He gets up from behind the desk and sits in the chair center.)*

DOCTOR. How do you feel?

CONEY. All right.

DOCTOR. Did you dream last night?

CONEY. No.

DOCTOR. Good. The Major told you about the invasion?

CONEY. Yes.

DOCTOR. Well?

CONEY. I'm—afraid I didn't care very much, sir.

DOCTOR. You will. In time you'll feel that everything outside has some connection with you and everything in you has some connection with everything outside . . . What bothers you now, Coney?

CONEY. That—feeling, sir.

DOCTOR. The bad feeling?

CONEY. Yes, sir.

DOCTOR. You still have it?

CONEY *(very low).* Yes, sir.

DOCTOR. Yes, sir; yes, sir. Two weeks of psychotherapy and they expect—

CONEY. I'm sorry, sir. I try to get rid of it but—

DOCTOR. No, no, son. It's not your fault. I was just—Come, we're going to talk about that bad feeling.

CONEY. Yes, sir.

DOCTOR. And we're going to get rid of it.

CONEY. Yes, sir.

DOCTOR. We are, Coney.

CONEY. Yes, sir.

DOCTOR (very gently). We. Not me. The two of us. I think we can do it, Coney.

CONEY. I wish we could, sir.

DOCTOR. I think we can. It's hard work. It's trying to cram the biggest thing in your life into a space this small. But I think we can do it. I want to try, Coney. I want to help you, Peter.

(Slight pause.)

CONEY. That's—the first time anybody's called me Peter since I've been in the Army. (Pause.) You're a right guy, Doc.

DOCTOR. I don't want you to think about anything except what I say now.

CONEY. O.K.

DOCTOR. Are you comfortable?

CONEY. Yes, sir.

DOCTOR. You still have that bad feeling?

CONEY. Yes, sir.

DOCTOR. It's sort of a guilty feeling.

CONEY. Yes, sir.

DOCTOR. When did you feel it first, Peter? Right after Finch was shot, wasn't it?

CONEY. Yes.

DOCTOR. And what did you think later?

CONEY. I thought I—well, you know, Doc.

DOCTOR. Tell me.

CONEY. I thought I felt—like you said: guilty, because I left him. But then—then you told me what Mingo said—what they all said. That I did what I had to do. I had to leave Finch to get the maps back.

DOCTOR. And you know that's right now, don't you? You know that's what you have to do in a war.

CONEY. Yes, sir.

DOCTOR. But you still have that guilty feeling.

CONEY. Yeah.

DOCTOR. Then it can't come from what you thought at all. It can't come from leaving Finch, can it, Peter?

CONEY. No, but—what did it come from?

DOCTOR. Coney, the first time you were in this room, the first time you were under that drug, do you know what you said about Finch? You said: I hate him.

CONEY. But I don't, I don't!

DOCTOR. I know you don't. And later on, you said that when Finch was shot— maybe you can remember yourself now. How did you feel when Finch was shot, Peter?

(Pause.)

CONEY (low, very ashamed). I was glad.

DOCTOR. Why were you glad?

CONEY. I thought—

DOCTOR. Go on, son.

CONEY. I thought he was going to call me a lousy yellow Jew bastard. So—I was glad he got shot.

DOCTOR. Peter, I want you to listen hard to what I'm going to tell you. I want you to listen harder than you ever listened to anything in your whole life. Peter, every soldier in this world who sees a buddy get shot has that one moment when he feels glad. Yes, Peter, every single one. Because deep underneath he thinks: I'm glad it wasn't me. I'm glad I'm still alive.

CONEY. But—oh, no. Because what I thought was—

DOCTOR. I know. You thought you were glad because Finch was going to make a crack about your being a Jew. Maybe later, you were glad because of that. But at that moment you were glad it wasn't you who was shot. You were glad you were still alive. A lot of fellows think a lot of things later. But every single soldier, every single one of them has that moment when he thinks: I'm glad it wasn't me! . . . And that's what you thought. . . . (Gently.) You see the whole point of this, Peter? You've been thinking you had some special kind of guilt. But you've got to realize something. You're the same as anybody else. You're no different, son, no different at all.

CONEY. I'm a Jew.

DOCTOR. This, Peter, this sensitivity has been like a disease in you. It was there before anything happened on that island. It started way back. I only wish to God I had time to really dig and find out where and when and why. But it's been a disease. Sure, it's been aggravated by T.J. By people at home in our own country—but if you can cure yourself, you can help cure them and you've got to, Pete, you've got to!

CONEY. O.K., if you say so.

DOCTOR. You can and you must, Pete. Believe me, you can.

CONEY. I believe you, Doc. *(He gets up and starts to the desk.)*

DOCTOR. Peter . . .

CONEY. Are we through, Doc?

DOCTOR. Peter, don't you understand?

CONEY. Yes! Sure! I understand! I understand up here! But here— *(Indicates his heart.)* deep in here, I just can't. I just can't believe it's true. I wanta believe, Doc, don't you know that? I want to believe that every guy who sees his buddy get shot feels glad. I wanta believe I'm not different but I—I— *(The life goes out of him, and he goes behind the desk to the typewriter.)* It's hard, Doc. It's just damn hard. *(There is a slight pause. CONEY starts to type and then the DOCTOR reaches across and tears the paper out of the machine.)*

DOCTOR. Coney, listen to me. I've had to try to tell you this fact, too fast. Because we haven't time, any more, Coney, we haven't time.

CONEY. What?

DOCTOR. It's like everything else in war, Coney. We live too fast, we die too fast, we have to work too fast. We've had two short weeks of this, thirty pitiful minutes a day. You've done wonderfully. Beautifully—but now—

CONEY. What are you getting at, Doc?

DOCTOR. I'm trying to tell you that we're almost through, son. You're leaving.

CONEY. What?

DOCTOR. You're being sent back to the States.

CONEY *(frightened)*. Doc!

DOCTOR. At the end of this week.

CONEY. Why? Why do I have to go, sir? Did I do something?

DOCTOR. You helped make some maps. Those maps helped make an invasion. And after every invasion, we need bed space, Coney. For cases very much like yours.

CONEY. But I—

DOCTOR. You see, you're not so different, son.

CONEY. But I can't go! I'm not better, Doc, I'm not all better!

DOCTOR. Son, sit down. Sit down. You'll get care in the States. Good care. Sure, you're leaving sooner than I'd prefer, but that's just part of war. That just means you've got to work now, every minute, every single minute you have left here, you've got to work, Pete, you've got to!

CONEY. I don't want to leave you, Doc!

DOCTOR. Peter—

CONEY. I'm scared, Doc!

DOCTOR. You won't be if you work. If you think every minute about what I told you.

CONEY. Doc, I'm scared.

DOCTOR. Every minute, Pete.

CONEY. Doc!

DOCTOR. Come on, Pete. Work!

CONEY. I—

DOCTOR. Come on!

CONEY. Every guy who sees his buddy gets shot feels like I did. Feels glad it wasn't him. Feels glad he's still alive . . . S what I felt when Finch got shot had nothin to do with being a Jew. Because I'm no different. I'm just— (*Breaks off in a sudden appeal.*) Oh, Doc, help me, will you? Get it through my dumb head? Get it through me— (*Indicates his heart.*) here? Can't you straighten me out before I go?

DOCTOR. I'll do my damnedest. But you've got to help me. Will you, Peter?

CONEY. I'll try. I'll try. (*In a burst.*) O God, I've got to try!

CURTAIN

SCENE II

SCENE: *The Office. Pacific Base.*

AT RISE: *The mid-morning sun fills the room. There is a great air of bustle and activity. Odds and ends of equipment, records, papers are piled on the desks, on chairs, on the floor. Three or four crates are scattered about.*

T.J. is busy packing these crates and nailing them down. Right now, he is transferring records from the cabinet upstage to one of the crates which is near the desk, down left. MINGO *is seated at this in dress uniform. He has his chair propped up against the side wall and faces into the room so that his right arm cannot be seen.*

During the following, T.J. *bustles back and forth between the crates and the cabinet.*

T.J. And if you think I'm going to shed any tears over leaving this hole, you're crazy.

MINGO. You and me both.

T.J. Yeah, but we're moving on to another base. You're going home.

MINGO. Home is where you hang your hat and your wife.

T.J. Ah, don't let that arm get you.

MINGO. Don't let it get you, bud. (*He gets up—showing an empty right sleeve.*) These O.D.'s itch like a bitch. Poem.

T.J. Whose idea were they?

MINGO. Some jerk who thought we'd catch cold when we hit the States.

T.J. When do you leave?

MINGO. Pretty soon. If the Major doesn't get here pretty soon . . .

T.J. (*going into the* MAJOR's *office*). Oh, he'll be back in a minute. (*Brushing by* MINGO.) Excuse me.

MINGO. Well, I got a jeep coming by to take me to the airfield.

T.J. (*coming out with papers which he puts in the crate*). Are you flying?

MINGO. On wings of steel.

T.J. Say, that's a break!

MINGO. I'm the original rabbit's foot kid.

T.J. I hear Coney's going back with you.

MINGO. Yeah.

T.J. How is he?

MINGO. He's all right.

T.J. They sending him back in your care?

MINGO. No! I said he's all right.

T.J. O.K. I was just asking. You know as well as I do that cases like Coney get discharged from the hospital and then one little thing happens—and off they go again.

MINGO. Look—you leave that kid alone.

T.J. Leave *him* alone! Why in hell don't you guys lay off me for a while?

MINGO. Huh?

T.J. The whole damn bunch of you! Everything I do is wrong!

MINGO. Everybody picks on poor T.J.

T.J. Not only on me! On anybody who made real money as a civilian.

MINGO. What?

(*Telephone starts to ring in the* MAJOR's *office.*)

T.J. Sure! That gripes the hell out of you, doesn't it? So it keeps us out of your little club. You and Coney and—

MINGO. The phone's ringing, T.J.

T.J. *(going inside).* I hear it!

MINGO. If a man answers, don't hang up.

T.J. *(offstage).* Corporal Everitt speaking— No, sir, he's not. *(Comes out.)* That Colonel's a constipated old maid.

MINGO. When are you pulling out?

T.J. Oh—some time tonight or tomorrow morning; I'm not sure. *(Holding up two long pipe-like metal map cases.)* Now what the hell am I going to do with these?

MINGO *(looks at T.J., then at the cases and shakes his head).* No. I guess not. Where's the outfit going?

T.J. *(stacking the cases near the crates).* Damned if I know.

MINGO. Crap.

T.J. I don't, Mingo.

MINGO. Crap.

T.J. All right. It's a military secret then.

MINGO. Just because I'm leaving, T.J.—

(The telephone rings again.)

T.J. *(going inside).* If that's the Colonel again, I'm going to tell him to screw off.

MINGO. Yep, yep. *(He gets up just as the outer door opens and* CONEY *walks in. He, too, wears dress uniform and carries a barracks bag which he sets down. He looks better now, but his stance, his walk, his voice, show that he is still a little unsure.)* Hi, kiddo!

CONEY. Hi.

MINGO *(kindly).* It sure took you long enough to get here. *(He pulls a chair over for* CONEY.*)*

CONEY *(sitting).* I stopped to say good-bye to the Doc.

MINGO. He's a nice gent. How do you feel, kid?

CONEY. Fine! How are you?

MINGO. Oh— *(He pokes his empty sleeve.)* a little underweight.

CONEY. Yeah.

MINGO. It feels kind of funny to be leaving, doesn't it?

CONEY. We used to talk so much about going home . . .

MINGO. Home? You mean back to the States.

CONEY. What do you mean?

MINGO *(snapping out of it).* Oh! What the hell! We're going back to the land of mattresses and steaks medium rare!

(T.J. comes out of the MAJOR'S *office.)*

T.J. Well, Coney! How are you, fellow?

CONEY. O.K.

T.J. *(looking at him a little too curiously).* You look fine, too, just fine. Feeling all right, eh?

MINGO. Want to see his chart, T.J.?

T.J. All set to fly back to the States. Some guys get all the breaks.

MINGO. Yep. Some guys sure do.

T.J. Well, what the hell! You fellows will be safe and sound in blue suits while we're still here winning the war for you.

MINGO. Thanks, bub.

T.J. I don't know what you're beefing about.

CONEY. Nobody's beefing, T.J. Except maybe you.

T.J. I got this whole mess to clean up single-handed.

MINGO *(to* CONEY*).* They're pulling out, too, but Montgomery Ward won't say where.

T.J. You know we're not supposed to tell, Mingo.

MINGO. Yeah. Coney and I have a hot pipeline to Tojo.

T.J. That's not the point. You're not in the outfit any more. You're—well, you guys are just out of it now.

MINGO. Don't break my Purple Heart, friend. *(The outer door opens and the* MAJOR *comes in.)* Hi, Major.

CONEY. Hello, Major.

MAJOR. Gee, I was afraid I'd miss you fellows.

T.J. The Colonel called twice, Major.

MAJOR. Oh, Judas.

T.J. I told him you'd be right back.

MAJOR. O.K. (*To* MINGO *and* CONEY.) I'm glad you could come over and say goodbye. We've been together for so—

(*Telephone rings.*)

T.J. Shall I get it?

MAJOR. No, it's probably the Colonel. I cornered that half-track. You can start loading these crates, T.J. (*To* MINGO *and* CONEY, *as he starts into the office.*) This'll only take a minute, fellows.

MINGO. That's O.K.

MAJOR (*inside—on telephone*). Major Robinson . . . Yes, Colonel. Yes, sir . . .

T.J. (*struggling to lift the crate*). Why the devil couldn't he get a detail to do this?

MINGO. T.S.

T.J. Yuk, yuk. (*As he staggers towards the door.*) Christ, this is heavy! (CONEY *walks swiftly to the door and opens it for* T.J. *A slight pause.* T.J. *quietly.*) Thanks, Coney. (*He goes out.* CONEY *shuts the door.*)

MINGO. Suddenly, it smells better in here.

CONEY. Yeah.

(*The* MAJOR *comes out of his office.*)

MAJOR. The Colonel's a wonderful man, but he worries more than my mother . . . Well, Coney—

CONEY. Yes, sir.

MAJOR. Ah, forget that "sir."

MINGO. We're not civilians yet.

MAJOR. I didn't mean it that way and you know it, Mingo. I sure wish you were both going with us.

MINGO. So do we— (*Trying to find out where.*) wherever it is.

MAJOR. That doesn't matter. I'm sure going to miss you, though.

MINGO. T.J.'s taken over pretty well.

MAJOR. The only reason he's taken over is that there isn't anyone else this minute . . . Fellows, I—oh, nuts!

MINGO. You don't have to say anything, Major.

MAJOR. I wish I knew how to say it. The three of us have been together for such a long time that it's—well, like saying goodbye to your family.

MINGO. Thanks.

CONEY (*simultaneously*). Thank you, sir.

MAJOR. I ought to be thanking you, but I just can't. I—well, wish both of you have all the—

(*The outer door opens, and* T.J. *comes in.*)

T.J. They want you over HQ, Major.

MAJOR. I was just there.

T.J. Well, they sent Maroni for you.

MAJOR. O Lord! . . . (*To* CONEY *and* MINGO.) Look, will you two stick around for a little while?

MINGO. Well . . .

MAJOR. I'll be right back. (*To* T.J.) You can pack that stuff on my desk in there, T.J. (*He has started out and now trips against a barracks bag which was next to the crate* T.J. *removed.*) What the devil is this doing here?

CONEY. I'm sorry, sir, that's mine.

MAJOR (*embarrassed*). Oh . . . O.K.—I'll be right back. (*He goes out.*)

T.J. I wish he'd make up his mind. Half an hour ago, he said not to pack the stuff on his desk. (*He starts for the inner office.*)

MINGO. You really have it tough, don't you, T.J.?

T.J. (*going in*). Oh, blow it, will you?

MINGO (*kicking his barracks bag out of the way—to* CONEY). Well, G.I. Joe, I think we're just a little bit in the way around here.

CONEY. Yeah.

MINGO. I wish that jeep would come and get us the hell out.

CONEY. He'd like it, too.

MINGO. T.J.?

CONEY. Yeah.

MINGO. Oh, he's very happy playing King of the Hill.

CONEY. I get a kick out of the way he looks at me.

MINGO *(taking out a cigarette).* How?

CONEY. Like he's trying to see if I'm—still off my rocker.

MINGO. Oh! Forget it. *(He takes out a match and begins struggling to light the cigarette.* T.J. *comes back into the room and carries some papers over to the crate.)*

T.J. More crap in there.

MINGO. You're wasting your time. You can throw out half of it.

*(*CONEY *moves to give* MINGO *a light and then stops. He knows* MINGO *wants to do this alone.)*

CONEY. Mingo was going to throw it out but that mission came up.

T.J. Look. You fellows are finished, so just let me do this my way, will you?

MINGO. Sure.

T.J. *(striking a match broadly).* Here.

MINGO. It's more fun this way.

T.J. O.K. *(Shrugs and starts to nail down the crate.)* Does it bother you, the arm, I mean?

MINGO. No. It makes me light as a bird. *(Lights the match finally.)*

T.J. *(to* MINGO*).* I didn't mean that. I meant does it hurt?

MINGO. Some.

T.J. Well—

CONEY *(trying to change the subject).* What'd they put us in O.D.'s for?

T.J. They'll give you a new arm back in the States, kid.

MINGO. I know.

T.J. You ought to be able to work them for a good pension, too.

MINGO. Sure.

CONEY *(quietly).* Shut up.

T.J. What's eating you?

CONEY. Shut up.

T.J. Why? Mingo's not kidding himself about—

CONEY. Shut up.

T.J. Take it easy, Coney, or—

CONEY. Or what?

MINGO. Coney . . .

CONEY. No. *(To* T.J.*)* Or what?

T.J. Are you trying to start something?

CONEY. I'm trying to tell you to use your head if you got one.

T.J. If *I* got one? Look, friend, it takes more than a few days in the jungle to send me off my trolley. It's only your kind that's so goddam sensitive.

CONEY. What do you mean—my kind?

T.J. What do you think I mean?

(There is a second's wait. Then CONEY'S *fist lashes out and socks* T.J. *squarely on the jaw, sending him to the floor.* CONEY *stands there with fists clenched, trembling.)*

T.J. *(getting up).* It's a good thing you just got out of the bobby hatch or I'd—

MINGO. You've got to get those crates out, don't you?

T.J. Look, Mingo . . . *(*T.J. *looks at him, then picks up a crate and carries it out. During this,* CONEY *has just been standing, staring straight ahead. His trembling gets worse. Suddenly, his head snaps up as though he hears* FINCH *again. His hands shoot up to cover his ears. At this point,* MINGO *shuts the door after* T.J.*)*

MINGO. Nice going, kiddo. *(He turns, sees* CONEY, *and quickly crosses to him.)* Coney! Coney, what's the matter?

CONEY *(numbly. He is starting to lose control again).* I'm just like anyone else.

MINGO. Take it easy, kid, sit down.

CONEY. I'm just like anyone else.

MINGO. Sure, sure. Sit down. *(He goes for a chair.)*

CONEY *(getting wilder).* That's what the Doc said, Mingo.

MINGO *(bringing the chair over).* And he's right. Ease up, Coney.

CONEY. That's what he said.

MINGO. Sure, sure. Take it easy.

CONEY *(sitting).* I'm just like anyone else.

MINGO. That's right. You are.

CONEY. That's right.

MINGO. Yes.

CONEY (*jumping up in a wild outburst that knocks the chair over*). Yes! Who're you kidding? It's not right! I'm not the same!

MINGO. Kid, you gotta get hold of yourself.

CONEY. You know I'm not!

MINGO. Kid, stop it. Listen to me!

CONEY. No!

MINGO. Listen—

CONEY. I'm tired of listening! I'm sick of being kidded! I got eyes! I got ears! I know!

MINGO. Coney, you can't—

CONEY. You heard T.J.!

MINGO. And I saw you give him what he deserved!

CONEY. What's the use? He'll just say it again. You can't shut him up!

MINGO. What do you—

CONEY. You can't shut any of them up—ever!

MINGO. All right! So he makes cracks about you. Forget it!

CONEY. Let's see you forget it!

MINGO. What the hell do you think I'm trying to do?

(*A slight pause. This has caught* CONEY.)

CONEY. What?

MINGO. He makes cracks about me, too. Don't you think I know it?

CONEY. But those cracks—it's not the same, Mingo.

MINGO. To him, it's the same. To that son of a bitch and all the son of a bitches like him, it's the same; we're easy targets for him to take pot shots at.

CONEY. But we're not—

MINGO. No, we're not the same! I really *am* something special. There's nothing in this sleeve but air, kiddo.

CONEY. But everybody around here knows you .

MINGO. Around here I'm in khaki, so they call me a hero. But back in the States, put me in a blue suit and I'm a stinking cripple!

CONEY. No. Not you, Mingo!

MINGO. Why not me?

CONEY. Because you're—you're . . .

MINGO. What? Too tough? That's what I keep trying to tell myself: Mingo, you're too tough to eat your lousy heart out about this. O.K. you lost a wing, but you're not gonna let it go down the drain for nothing.

CONEY. You couldn't.

MINGO. No? You should've seen me in the hospital. When I woke up and found it was off. All I could think of was the close shaves I'd had; all the times I'd stood right next to guys, seen 'em get shot and felt glad I was still alive. But when I woke up—

CONEY. Wait a minute—

MINGO (*continuing*). I wasn't so sure.

CONEY (*cutting again*). Wait a minute! Mingo, wait! (MINGO *stops and looks at him.*) Say that again.

MINGO. Huh?

CONEY. Say it again.

MINGO. What?

CONEY. What you just said.

MINGO. About waking up in the hospital and . . .

CONEY. No, no. About standing next to guys when they were shot.

MINGO. Oh. Well, it was pretty rugged to see.

CONEY. But how you felt, Mingo, how you felt!

MINGO. Well, I—felt sorry for them, of course.

CONEY. No! No, that isn't it!

MINGO. I don't know what you mean, kiddo.

CONEY. When you saw them, Mingo, when you saw them get shot, you just said you felt—you felt—

MINGO. Oh, I felt glad I was still alive.

CONEY. Glad it wasn't you.

MINGO. Sure. Glad it wasn't me.

CONEY. Who told you to say that?

MINGO. Who *told* me?

CONEY. Yeah! Who told you?

MINGO. Nobody told me, kiddo. I saw it. I felt it. Hell, how did you feel when you saw Finch get it?

CONEY *(almost growing)*. Just like you, Mingo. Just like you! *Just like you!*

MINGO. Hey, what's got into you?

CONEY. I was crazy . . . yelling I was different. *(Now the realization comes.)* I am different. Hell, you're different! Everybody's different— But so what? It's O.K. because underneath, we're—hell, we're all guys! We're all— O Christ! I can't say it, but am I making any sense?

MINGO. Are you!

CONEY. And like what you said about your arm? Not letting it go down the drain for nothing. Well, I'll be damned if I'm gonna let me go for nothing!

MINGO. Now we're riding, kiddo!

CONEY. It won't be easy . . .

MINGO. What is?

CONEY *(grinning)*. Yeah. What is?

MINGO. Hey!

CONEY. What?

MINGO. Maybe this is cockeyed.

CONEY. What?

MINGO. That bar you were going to have.

CONEY. Bar?

MINGO. With Finch.

CONEY. Oh. Yeah. Sure.

MINGO. You want a partner?

CONEY. A—

MINGO *(a shade timidly)*. A one-armed bartender would be kind of a novelty, Pete. *(A great smile breaks over* CONEY's *face. He tries to talk, to say what he feels. But all that can come out is:)*

CONEY. Ah Judas, Mingo!

(Offstage comes the sound of a jeep horn.)

MINGO. Hey, that sounds like our chauffeur. Soldier, the carriage waits without!

CONEY. Yes, sir! *(He goes to his barracks bag.* MINGO *goes to his, but has to struggle to lift it with his left hand.)*

MINGO *(as he walks to the bag)*. You'll have to keep an eye on me, you know. This arm's gonna—dammit.

CONEY. Hey, coward.

MINGO *(turning)*. What?

CONEY *(coming to him)*. Take my coward's hand. *(He lifts the bag up on* MINGO's *back.)*

MINGO. Pete, my boy, you've got a charming memory.

(A slight pause.)

CONEY *(softly)*. Delightful! *(He lifts up his own bag and the two start out proudly as—*

THE CURTAIN FALLS

TOMORROW THE WORLD

By JAMES GOW and ARNAUD d'USSEAU

TOMORROW THE WORLD was first presented by Theron Bamberger at the Ethel Barrymore Theatre on April 14, 1943. The play was staged by Elliott Nugent; setting by Raymond Sovey. The cast was as follows:

PATRICIA FRAME	Joyce Van Patten	EMIL BRUCKNER	Skippy Homeier
JESSIE FRAME	Dorothy Sands	FRED MILLER	Richard Taber
FRIEDA	Edit Angold	DENNIS	Walter Kelly
MICHAEL FRAME	Ralph Bellamy	BUTLER	Richard Tyler
LEONA RICHARDS	Shirley Booth	TOMMY	Paul Porter, Jr.

SCENES

The living room of Professor Michael Frame's home in a large University town in the Middle West.

ACT I: A Saturday morning in early autumn, 1942.

ACT II: An afternoon, ten days later.

ACT III: Early the next morning.

THE AUTHORS

Much may be expected from the writing team that composed Tomorrow the World. *Its present score is two successes, no failures. Messrs. Gow and d'Usseau see eye to eye on the subjects that engage their interest, and they are fired by the same desire to fill the theatre with provocative matter. Both men are, besides, refugees from Hollywood and are bent to make the fullest use of their freedom.*

James Ellis Gow was born on August 23, 1907 in Creston, Iowa. He attended school in Greenfield and Vinton, Iowa, spent two years at the University of Iowa, and obtained a degree in 1928 from the University of Colorado. Several months later he was on the city staff of the old New York World *from which he was shifted, after a year's apprenticeship, to the dramatic department. Here he remained until the Pulitzer newspaper, which had contributed so many playwrights and men of letters to the nation (including Stallings, Anderson, and Dudley Nichols), went out of existence.*

In 1931 Mr. Gow entrained for Hollywood, the last resort of footloose writing men, and three years later won honors as the co-author of the successful Grace Moore picture One Night of Love *for Columbia Pictures. Consequently he found himself in great demand for screen jobs involving operatic matter In between assignments he collaborated, with Edmund North, on a stage play* The Drums, Professor *which Guthrie McClintic announced for production and Frank McCoy tried out in White Plains but failed to bring to New York. Another collaboration,* Rhyme Without Reason, *was produced by Arthur Beckhard in San Francisco during the 1937–38 season but closed after a week's run.*

Arnaud d'Usseau had Hollywood within plain sight as soon as he was old enough to be taken out for a stroll. He was born in Los Angeles on April 18, 1916. After graduating from the Beverly Hills High School, he became a book clerk and later an employee of the United Press in Arizona. But in no great time he was back on home grounds, first as a set dresser for a period picture at one of the studios and then as a screenwriter. His first successful celluloid assignment was the thriller One Crowded Night. *From then on, in Hollywood's delightful manner, he was typed as a mystery writer.*

Messrs. Gow and d'Usseau met on the R.K.O. lot and found themselves collaborating on an original story Repent at Leisure. *Gow suggested collaboration on a stage play dealing with a destructively possessive mother,* How Like an Angel. *After various other chores for the film industry, the two men joined forces in 1942 on another serious enterprise as they started speculating about what would happen if a Nazi-trained youngster were to come into contact with the democratic way of life. The happy result was* Tomorrow the World. *The play was placed on the market when the authors were in the East working on a documentary film for the O.W.I.'s Overseas Motion Picture Bureau under Robert Riskin. The Theron Bamberger production, directed by Elliott Nugent, opened on April 14, 1943. A second company started touring the play in September, 1943.*

The collaborators stayed together as privates in the Signal Corps Photographic Center in Astoria, Long Island, within subway distance of Broadway. Here they found an opportunity for a second successful collaboration, Deep Are the Roots, *which opened on Broadway with a detonation in the fall of 1945.*

TOMORROW THE WORLD

ACT ONE

THE SCENE: *The living room of* PROFESSOR MICHAEL FRAME'S *home, in a large University town in the Middle West. It is a morning in early autumn, 1942.*

Upstage, center, through a wide arch, is a large hallway, which serves as a hub for the entire house. A staircase leads to the second story; under the staircase a door leads down into the cellar. The front door is off left, and off right is the door to the kitchen, neither of which is visible. To the left of the stairs, still in the hallway, is the entrance to the dining-room.

On the right, a little more than half-way down stage, is the fireplace; over the mantelpiece is an oil portrait of Karl Bruckner. *The style of the painting is academic. Its only claim to merit is its faithful reproduction of Bruckner's features—his small nose and mouth, his mild blue eyes, his hair, which had begun to thin at the time he posed for it. At a right angle to the fireplace is a large couch. Behind the couch is a table on which there is a lamp.*

On the left, a large bay window looks out on a deep lawn. In front of the window, benefiting from its light, is a large, flat-topped desk; of walnut, it is both utilitarian and handsome. The desk is always littered with papers, and piled with books, some of which have found a place between two brass book-ends. The desk and the couch constitute the two emphatic points in the room. The rest of the furniture is comfortable, attractive.

The right wall, both above and below the fireplace consists almost entirely of crowded bookshelves. The atmosphere of the room is one of warmth and activity. Although PROFESSOR FRAME *has an office at the University, this is his living room, and to him living requires his desk, his many books, the daily clutter of magazines, scientific journals, etc. This does not make for order, but it suggests a certain exuberant vitality.*

AT RISE: *The stage is empty; the front door bell is ringing.* MISS PATRICIA FRAME, *aged ten, comes running down the stairs. On the third step from the bottom she stops carefully, and jumps the remaining distance; this is one of her latest accomplishments. She stops momentarily at the foot of the stairs to shout in the general direction of the kitchen.*

PAT. Frieda! Frieda! The taxi-man's here! *(She disappears down the hall; we hear the front door being opened.)*

PAT'S VOICE. I guess you'll have to wait a minute, Mr. Taxi-man.

VOICE. Okay.

PAT'S VOICE. I'm all ready—it's Frieda's fault— *(She reappears in the hall, again calls toward the kitchen at the top of her lungs.)*

PAT. Frieda! If you don't come, we'll be late! The man is waiting! *Won't* you hurry up!

*(*JESSIE FRAME *is coming down the stairs.* JESSIE *is forty-five. She is pleasant in appearance, but rather sharp in manner)*

JESSIE. Good heavens, Pat! Stop shouting like that. They'll hear you clear to the station.

PAT *(plaintively).* But Aunt Jessie—we'll be *late*—

JESSIE. Nonsense. It only takes five minutes, and the train won't be on time. Look at your hair!

PAT *(defensively).* I combed it.

JESSIE. When? Last night? *(She comes down into the room;* PAT *follows her.)*

PAT. Really, Aunt Jessie—you don't realize how important this is. The train will come in, and we won't be there, and he'll get lost. After all, he's only a child.

JESSIE *(she plucks two magazines off the couch).* If I remember correctly, he's two years older than you. Come here, and I'll fix your ribbon.

PAT *(obeying reluctantly).* Well, that's not so terribly old. Is it? Lester Collins is *three* years older than me, and he plays with me all the time—of course, he's a jerk—

JESSIE (*wearily*). Pat. Your language. (*She adds the magazines to a stack in the bookshelves.*)

PAT. Oh, where's that Freida?! *Freida!!*

JESSIE. Don't *shriek* like that. Emil certainly won't like a little girl who bursts his eardrums.

PAT (*ignoring this ridiculous prophecy*). If he can't talk English, do you know what we'll do? We'll talk in deaf-and-dumb language. I already know two letters. Look, Aunt Jessie!

(*She demonstrates.* FRIEDA, *the maid, enters from the kitchen; she wears hat and coat, and carries a small vase of flowers.* FRIEDA *is thirty-five, a blonde-haired, homely woman; she speaks with a German accent.*)

JESSIE. Frieda, you'd better go.

PAT. Frieda! What have you been doing? We've got to hurry!

FRIEDA. Yes, Miss Pat. If you'll just let me put these flowers in his room—

JESSIE (*dryly*). Flowers. Is that what kept you, Frieda?

FRIEDA. I wanted to make his room nice for him—I remember how frightened I was when *I* came to this country—I felt real homesick—

JESSIE. I'll take the flowers up. (*She takes the vase from* FRIEDA.) And don't think we're going to let you spoil the boy just because he comes from your country. He'll take things as he finds them—and he's a very lucky boy to come to a home like this. Now go on.

PAT. At last. I can't believe it.

JESSIE. Pat! Aren't you going to kiss me?

PAT. Oh, Aunt Jessie, we're only going to the—. Well, all right. (*She gives* JESSIE *a hasty kiss on the cheek, then disappears down the hall, followed by* FRIEDA.)

PAT'S VOICE. Here we come, taxi!
(JESSIE *watches them go, then looks down at the flowers. She regards them irresolutely for a moment, then carries them over to the table behind the couch, on which stands a large bowl of flowers. She* deliberately takes the flowers out of the vase and adds them to the bouquet in the bowl. As she is arranging them to her precise satisfaction, the telephone rings. She crosses to the desk, but before answering the ringing telephone, characteristically picks up an ash tray and empties its contents into an adjacent waste-basket.*)

JESSIE (*into telephone*). Hello? . . . Yes, that's right . . . Chicago? Well, go on, put them on . . . Now, operator, of course this isn't Professor Frame. It's his sister. But I'll take the— . . . No, he can't be reached. (*With weary impatience.*) Operator, I said he *can't be reached*. He's working in the Bronson Foundation Laboratory at the south end of the campus—and there isn't a telephone—and you can't send a messenger, because when they go in there they lock the door behind them and they don't come out until they come out. . . . All right, I'll speak to them. (*With one hand, she automatically straightens several articles on the desk.*) Hello? What on earth do *you* want? . . . Oh, the boy. No, he hasn't arrived yet. . . . Well, why should I make a statement just because I'm expecting my nephew? . . . No, I don't think Professor Frame will have anything to say either. . . . (PROFESSOR MICHAEL FRAME *enters the hall from the front door. He stops to listen to* JESSIE; *she doesn't see him.* FRAME *is forty, not handsome, not too careful in his dress; but blessed with enormous vitality and charm.* JESSIE *continues into the telephone.*) Well, I'm sorry, but we're both opposed to publicity. Especially for a twelve-year-old child. . . . No, I should say not; he'll probably be nervous and exhausted. After that harrowing journey— (MICHAEL *has come down quietly and now reaches to take the telephone from Jessie's hand.*) Oh—!

MICHAEL. I'll take it. Who is it?

JESSIE (*deprecatingly*). The Associated Press in Chicago. Really, you'd think we were expecting Mickey Rooney.

MICHAEL (*into telephone*). Hello, this is Michael Frame. . . . That's right, I couldn't be reached—and now I *can* be reached. What would you like to know? . . . Yes, that's right. . . . No, no. He's the only son of my sister and Karl Bruckner. . . . Karl Bruckner, my ignorant young friend, was one of the first casualties in the war against Hitler. He also happened to win a Nobel Prize—in 1933 —you might consult the Almanac on your desk there. . . . Well, for one thing, he wrote a score of books. May I suggest that you read one of them in particular. It's called *Superstition, Religion and Reality.*

JESSIE. H'mm. He won't get any further in that book than I did.

MICHAEL *(ignoring JESSIE, into telephone).* Yes, on the exchange ship—the *Drottningholm.* . . . Well, it was part of a complicated deal between the German Government and our State Department— No, no, no! I'm not giving him asylum just because he's an anti-fascist refugee; I'm adopting him because he's my nephew. The kid was left an orphan, and I felt responsible for getting him out if I could. . . . Well, I see no reason to make a big story of it, but if he arrives with a couple of dead Nazis slung over his shoulder, I'll call you back. . . . Right. *(He hangs up.)* My God. The temporary mortality of the world's great.

JESSIE. Now what does *that* mean?

MICHAEL. Today Karl is dead and already forgotten. But fifty years from now every school child will know the story of his life. *(He glances at his watch.)* Say, why aren't you down at the station?

JESSIE. I sent Frieda. And Pat went with her.

MICHAEL *(frowning).* But you should have gone yourself. You knew I couldn't go. Very bad, Jessie, very bad. *(He sits at his desk and starts going through his mail.)*

JESSIE. I'm sorry, but I wasn't the one who invited the child to this country. You never even consulted me on it.

MICHAEL *(smiling).* So that's it.

JESSIE. I've tried to talk to you about it. But you're very difficult that way, Michael. You never hear a word I say.

MICHAEL. All right, Jessie. The next time you say a word, I'll listen. I swear it solemnly.

(A dog howls next door.)

JESSIE. Oh, that *dog.* I wish somebody would wring its neck. . . . Michael, why don't you listen right now?

MICHAEL *(opening a letter).* Fire away.

JESSIE. Well, in the first place, you don't seem to realize the work it involves— bringing another person into this house. . . . Are you going to listen, or are you going to sit there and read that letter?

MICHAEL *(chuckling).* What do you know about that! I have finally received the accolade. Chicago Round Table—they want me to appear on the program next month.

JESSIE. Chicago Round Table.

MICHAEL. "Chemistry in Our Changing Economy"—now *there's* a subject they can kick around safely. *(Writing.)* N-O. No.

JESSIE. Really Michael, you shouldn't be so cavalier. It's one of the most important hours on the air.

MICHAEL. I know. You listen to it. I'd be no good at that kind of double-talk. I'd say exactly what I think about our changing economy, and some of those boys would be profoundly shocked. *(Putting the letter to one side.)* I wonder if he'll look at all like Karl. *(He looks across at the portrait above the fireplace.)* We've got to take good care of him, Jessie. He's undoubtedly been through hell. He'll need everything we can give him.

JESSIE. That's what I want to talk about. I can see you're going to spoil the boy.

MICHAEL. Wouldn't that be tragic!

JESSIE. The way you spoil Pat. And you do spoil her. I know you're brilliant and very advanced in your ideas, but as a father you leave much to be desired. You treat Pat exactly as if she were a grown-up person.

MICHAEL. Is that bad?

JESSIE. All right. But when you suddenly adopt a twelve-year-old boy, it seems to me you should determine what attitude to take.

MICHAEL. Of course we'll take an attitude. He's our nephew and Karl Bruckner's son. We'll love him.

JESSIE *(after a moment).* I may learn to love him, but not because he's Karl's son.

Yes, I know he was a great man, but I haven't forgotten what Mary went through.

MICHAEL. Mary loved Karl.

JESSIE. Oh, yes—he was a fine romantic figure when he came over here and married her. The great German professor. But after he took her back to that horrible country—always in some fight, some political squabble, until they had to fire him from his University. Those books he wrote may be very impressive, but they didn't furnish any bread and butter. How many times did you and I have to send them money, or they would have starved to death, literally?

MICHAEL. Yes, indeed. And every time you delivered the same oration.

JESSIE. And I was right. If it hadn't been for him, Mary would have been alive today. Well, maybe it's a good thing that she didn't live. Look what happened to him. Practically a criminal, and then he died in prison.

MICHAEL. For God's sake, Jessie! He died in a concentration camp!

JESSIE (shrugging). Well, he must have done something.

MICHAEL. He did plenty. Can't you understand! Karl was fighting then the very thing we're fighting now! He was on our side!

JESSIE. He was a German, wasn't he?

(For a moment MICHAEL is speechless, then he relaxes.)

MICHAEL. Jessie, I adore you. You're the most wonderful mess of contradictions I've ever known. Have you ever given five minutes' thought to what this war is about? Just because you didn't like Karl personally—

JESSIE (mildly). Don't worry, Michael. I'll love the boy for a different reason. He's Mary's son, too.

(We hear the front door open.)

LEONA'S VOICE. Hello!

MICHAEL. Lee! Come on in!

(As he rises from the desk, LEONA RICHARDS enters. LEONA is dark, attractive, thirty.)

LEONA. Hello, Mike, I— (She sees JESSIE.) Oh, hello, Jessie.

JESSIE. Good morning, dear.

LEONA. I couldn't wait. Where is he?

MICHAEL. You can join the reception committee. We're expecting him any minute.

LEONA. You didn't go to the station?

JESSIE. We delegated Pat to do the honors. Michael was much too busy.

MICHAEL (to LEONA). In fact, you're darn lucky to find me here. I got away from the laboratory exactly ten minutes ago. We were visited this morning by a brass hat—a big one.

LEONA. I expect it's all still a military secret.

MICHAEL. And will be.

JESSIE. All this secrecy! There's no reason why you can't tell your own family what you're doing. Sit down, Leona. You know, he won't even let a janitor into that laboratory to clean up the mess.

MICHAEL. Secrecy, eh? (To LEONA.) Jessie doesn't realize that every lab on every campus in this country is working out a few new ideas—some of them may turn out to be important.

LEONA (smiling). And scientists enjoy being dramatic, besides.

MICHAEL. You bet. It's our substitute for wearing a uniform.

JESSIE. Well, I happen to know that Dean McGrath is still very displeased with you about the whole project.

MICHAEL (with mock horror). No!

JESSIE. Oh, you can laugh. But the Dean's right. I remember the last time he was here for dinner, he said a University should have nothing to do with politics and war. Our business is culture and wisdom, he said. And he was quite right. Heaven knows, since you got the University into the munitions business you've never gotten home to dinner on time.

MICHAEL. You see why Jessie loves wisdom and culture. The roast doesn't get spoiled.

JESSIE. All right, all right. But you know you like good food as well as anybody.

MICHAEL. I like good food *better* than anybody. What have we got for lunch? And aren't you going to ask Lee to stay?

JESSIE. Oh, of course she'll stay. I assumed that, naturally. *(To* LEONA.*)* Won't you, dear?

LEONA. I'd like to very much. Thank you.

*(*JESSIE *picks up the empty vase from which she took the flowers, and starts to go.)*

MICHAEL. Oh, Jessie. If that was a feeler you threw out—*it isn't munitions.*

JESSIE *(with a smile).* Well, you can't blame me for trying. *(She goes out.)*

LEONA. I brought your book back.

*(*MICHAEL *rises from the desk deliberately, walks over to Leona, leans down and kisses her.)*

MICHAEL. Good morning.

LEONA. Good morning.

MICHAEL. What's the matter?

LEONA. Good Lord, is it that obvious?

MICHAEL. No. But last night you told me you'd be busy all day. And then you walk in at eleven-thirty announcing you've come to see Emil. And then—the way you kissed me.

LEONA. Well, you're right.

(He sits beside her on the couch.)

MICHAEL. Let's have it.

LEONA. Sally Praskins, who is a horrible person, was at my door at nine o'clock this morning. She said she had to tell me something for my own good.

MICHAEL. Dear Sally.

LEONA. It seems it all happened at the faculty tea. Margaret Bates had it from somebody else that you were seen leaving my apartment at a quarter of twelve last Thursday night.

MICHAEL. It's a damn lie. It was a quarter *after* twelve and it was Wednesday.

LEONA. Of course, this tasty morsel reached the ears of Dean McGrath's wife. She was elaborately horrified.

MICHAEL. Well, in her position, it's her Christian duty to be horrified. Besides, she disapproves of my politics.

LEONA. "Disapproves" is a weak word, darling. She told Sally that knowing your radical ideas, she's not surprised to learn that you're also a libertine!

MICHAEL *(bursting into laughter).* That's great! And what did she call *you?*

LEONA. Oh, she knew better than to call me names. But it gave her a chance to deplore the fact that I'm principal of the Experimental School.

MICHAEL *(after a moment).* Nine-tenths of our colleagues and their wives are intelligent, decent people. But that woman's a hideous old harridan. What are you worried about?

LEONA. I'm not, really. Because it's so ridiculous. But I was afraid you'd be upset.

MICHAEL. What?

LEONA. Because of Jessie and Pat.

MICHAEL. Nonsense. Jessie and Pat both know how I feel about you. So let's forget it.

LEONA. All right, Professor. It's forgotten.

MICHAEL. Good. And you'll stay to lunch, you'll meet Emil, and— (MICHAEL *suddenly stops and looks at Leona with a frown.)* Lee! Why don't we get married?

LEONA *(with incredulity).* Did you say what I think you said?

MICHAEL. I said why don't we get married? How about it?

LEONA *(laughing).* Michael! Michael!

MICHAEL. All right, so it *is* a little abrupt. It even surprised me. But I mean it. *(He takes her hand.)*

LEONA. Dearest, it's wonderful of you to keep me entertained until lunch. But what if I just as abruptly said "yes"? Wouldn't you be sorry!

MICHAEL. Credit me with knowing what I'm doing. After all, I'm a middle-aged college professor. Staid and respectable, besides. Maybe you think I'm too old for you. Maybe I *am.*

LEONA. Sure, that's it. Quick! Back to your wheel-chair, Professor Frame. *(Reproachfully.)* Really, Mike—!!

MICHAEL. After this last year, does the idea of marriage really seem so startling? You must have thought of it. I have.

LEONA. Yes, of course.

MICHAEL. And when you thought about it, did you reject it as impossible?

LEONA. No, but—

MICHAEL. Well, then—what are we waiting for? I love you, you love me—

LEONA. Love conquers all. Paolo and Francesca. Is this the eminent Professor Frame or one of his students? Oh, Mike. There are so many things. Would you expect me to give up my work?

MICHAEL. God, no. What would happen to my reputation as an "advanced thinker"? Michael Frame, notorious liberal, relegates mate to kitchen. I'd be disowned by even the *New Republic. (He grins.)* You see? Intuitively we agree on everything!

LEONA. What about Jessie?

MICHAEL. What about her?

LEONA. Don't you think you should talk it over with her?

MICHAEL. Jessie has her own income. She's a free agent.

LEONA *(impatiently).* That's just like you, Mike. You've accepted her adoration all your life—she's bound herself to you hand and foot. And then you casually say, "She's a free agent."

MICHAEL. She's always known I might get married again. Besides, Jessie's tough.

LEONA. And Pat? I suppose she's "tough," too?

MICHAEL. You're not worried about Pat?

LEONA. Worried? I'd be scared stiff.

MICHAEL. Pat worships you. She comes home from school every day telling me you're the only teacher who has any sense. What's more, she's asked me to get married. To almost anybody! She wants me to have more children. Three of them, to quote her precisely.

LEONA. Mike!

MICHAEL. As soon as we're married, I'm sure she'll take it up with you.

LEONA. Oh, my God!

MICHAEL. You'll find she has a startling knowledge of the facts of life. It seems we no longer believe in the stork.

LEONA. You know where she got that startling knowledge? From me. Right from me. It was I who revealed the mysteries of sex according to the newest methods of progressive education. Pat was very bright about it, and awfully matter-of-fact—seemed to regard it chiefly as a problem in plumbing.

MICHAEL. Great! After we're married, you'll have no excuses. Not for Pat. You told her the score yourself.

LEONA. Mike, will you stop it! I'm not going to be rushed into this!

MICHAEL. Who's rushing? I'm being deliberate as hell.

LEONA. But you'd like to get it settled, so you can have lunch and go right back to your laboratory.

MICHAEL. What do you want me to do? Forget about my work, and court you all afternoon?

LEONA. I don't want to be courted at all!

MICHAEL *(penitently).* What's the matter?

LEONA. I'm not at all sure I'd be a good mother. And this isn't like a new teaching job, you know. I can't resign after three months if it doesn't go so well. And there's not only Pat. There's Emil. You're asking me to be the mother of a boy I've never seen. He may not even like me.

MICHAEL. We're even there. He may not like *me!* And I'm going to be his father.

LEONA. And you don't give it a moment's thought?

MICHAEL. Sure. I give it a *lot* of thought. How could I, or anyone else, take the place of Karl Bruckner? But should I hesitate because of that to adopt the boy? The world we live in today doesn't allow for hesitations. We're at war. We can't afford the old luxury of a "maybe" or a "perhaps"— *(With a swift look.)* —or a long engagement. *(He takes her in his arms.)* What do you say, Lee? *(He kisses her.)*

You know, darling, if *you* had asked *me* to get married I wouldn't have stalled around so.

LEONA. I'm sure of that. You'd have answered yes—or *no*—in two seconds flat.

MICHAEL. When shall we do it?

LEONA. Today is Saturday and I expect the marriage license bureau is closed. Monday's a good day.

MICHAEL. Monday's fine. No, wait a minute. We better wait for two weeks. I might have to go to Washington.

LEONA. All right. Two weeks. But who's stalling now? *(They separate and* LEONA *picks up her handbag.)* Dear me, Professor Frame. After all these years, am I to be a war bride? *(She looks around the room.)* Mike, it's the strangest feeling! I suddenly realize this will be *my* living room, too.

MICHAEL. Your living room—my desk. House rule number one: nobody touches my desk.

LEONA. Don't be so proud, Maestro. I've got a desk, too. I think I'll put it right over there, and nobody will be allowed to touch *it.* You see what I mean about marriage?

(We hear the front door open.)

MICHAEL There he is! That's Emil! *(He goes toward the hall, followed by* LEONA. PAT *and* FRIEDA *appear, but no Emil.)* Well, where is he? Pat, what'd you do with Emil?

PAT *(plaintively).* We didn't do *anything* with him. He wasn't on the train.

FRIEDA. The poor child! He must have gotten lost somewhere!

PAT. We waited and waited for him to get off, and he *didn't* and we asked the conductor—!

FRIEDA. You'd better notify somebody! The conductor of the train had never heard of him—!

*(*JESSIE *has come in.)*

PAT. He wasn't there, Aunt Jessie!

JESSIE. I knew there'd be trouble!

PAT *(at the same time).* We waited and waited—!

JESSIE. Letting a child of twelve travel alone halfway across the country—!

FRIEDA *(at the same time).* And probably doesn't speak a word of English—!

JESSIE. Anything could have happened to him—!

PAT *(crescendo).* Do you think he was kidnapped—!

FRIEDA. Ach!!

JESSIE. Good heavens!!

MICHAEL *(loud and weary).* Now wait a minute! *Nothing* could have happened to him. He missed the train in New York. Or if he got the wrong train, he has the address pinned on his suit probably. Pat, stop crying. *You*'ve travelled alone, haven't you? You went to Chicago and back. Did anybody kidnap you? *(He picks up the telephone.)*

PAT *(she decides not to cry).* No. But I speak perfect English. Hello, Lee. Did you know we're expecting little Emil Bruckner?

MICHAEL *(into telephone).* Long distance, please. *(He goes through some papers on his desk to find a telephone number.)*

FRIEDA *(still in the hallway).* If only he's not been lost in an accident—

MICHAEL. Come on, Frieda. Give it up. No more *Sturm und Drang.*

FRIEDA. But the beautiful child—

MICHAEL. He may turn out to be homely as hell.

JESSIE. Michael. Your language.

MICHAEL. Close your ears, Pat.

PAT *(obligingly).* They're closed.

MICHAEL. Frieda, go get lunch. *(Into the telephone, as* FRIEDA *goes reluctantly.)* I want New York, operator. Longacre 6-3351. Miss Ruth Lewis. . . . That's right, Michael Frame. *(He hangs up.)* After all, if the kid survived the Nazis and got out of Germany, he should be able to change trains, even in Chicago. He'll probably arrive this evening.

JESSIE. I knew there'd be trouble.

MICHAEL. All right, Cassandra, so there'll be trouble. But we'll worry about it later.

Cheer up, Pat. I have an important announcement to make.

LEONA. Mike—!

MICHAEL. (innocently). Oh, you want to make the announcement?

LEONA. Not now, Mike—not like this—

PAT. What is it? Is it a surprise, Lee?

LEONA. Yes, dear. It's a big surprise. But I think Mike should wait to tell you.

MICHAEL. Mike never waits for anything. Come here, Pat. (He sits down and puts an arm around PAT.) From what you tell me, Lee's an awfully good teacher. Do you think she'd make a good wife?

(PAT looks from MICHAEL to LEONA and back again. She grins incredulously.)

PAT. Aw, you're kidding.

MICHAEL. No kidding.

PAT. Honest?

MICHAEL. Honest. Lee and I are going to be married in two weeks. That is, if it's all right with you.

PAT. Are you really asking my permission?

LEONA. We certainly are, Pat.

MICHAEL. Naturally. We can't get married unless we have your permission. And Jessie's. (He looks over at JESSIE. She has turned away.)

LEONA (reproachfully). Mike, I told you. (She crosses to JESSIE.) I'm sorry Mike was in such a hurry. I'm awfully sorry, Jessie.

JESSIE (with an effort). It's all right, my dear.

LEONA. I wish he had talked to you.

JESSIE. Why should he? It's none of my business if he wants to get married. (With an attempted smile.) I'm sorry, my dear —it's just that Michael has such a way of springing surprises. I hope you'll be very happy. (Outside the dog howls.) That blamed dog again—that dog kept me awake all last night— (She turns, enters the hall and goes upstairs.)

LEONA (after a moment, to MICHAEL). That was very thoughtless of you.

MICHAEL. Yes, I can see it was.

PAT. It's not our fault, Lee. Aunt Jessie's like that. Whenever things turn out the way she doesn't expect, she gets a headache.

MICHAEL. Are you sure you want to psychoanalyze Jessie? She could probably say several illuminating things about you.

PAT. Nooo! You know what I mean. I asked her once if you and Lee would ever get married, and she said no, you'd never get married, and I shouldn't even talk about such a thing. (Ruefully.) I wish I'd made her a bet.

LEONA. You're a hard-boiled pair. Both of you.

(The door-bell rings.)

PAT. I still haven't given my permission.

MICHAEL. All right, Mr. Bones, give us your permission.

PAT (to LEONA). Now he thinks it's a joke.

LEONA. It's no joke to me, Pat. I've got to know. Do you want us to get married?

(PAT responds by running to LEONA and kissing her.)

PAT. Sure! I think it's wonderful! Now we can walk to school together every morning!

LEONA (giving her a hug). Darling—

(FRIEDA goes through the hall towards the front door.)

MICHAEL. Well, now that we've got that settled—

PAT. Yes, but shouldn't we all have a long talk?

MICHAEL. Oh, Lord. Lee, remind us to have a long talk.

(FRIEDA reappears in the hall, almost speechless with excitement.)

FRIEDA. Professor! He's here! Das Kind! Ganz allein!

(She gestures for the child to enter. He appears in the hall slowly, carrying a small suitcase. EMIL BRUCKNER is twelve, blond, tall for his age. He is a startlingly handsome boy. He wears a threadbare black suit; knickerbockers. In his manner there is an inner certainty, a critical reserve. He stands holding his suitcase, looking at the *people in the room. Then* MICHAEL *goes quickly forward.)*

MICHAEL. Emil! Emil Bruckner!

EMIL *(clicking his heels and bowing).* Herr Professor?

MICHAEL. *Herzlich willkommen, mein Kind! Du bist willkommen! (He embraces the boy and kisses him.) Wir hoffen dass Du Dich sehr glücklich in deinem neuen Heim fühlen wirst.*

EMIL *(stiffly).* Thank you. You are very hospitable. You see, I speak acceptable American, although grammar I have not quite mastered.

MICHAEL *(handing* EMIL's *suitcase to* FRIEDA*).* Splendid! Splendid! Take his bag, Frieda. Take it up to his room.

FRIEDA *(nods, barely taking her eyes off the boy; in hushed tones). Er ist hübsch, nicht wahr? Ein liebes Kind!*

EMIL *(turning to her politely).* Please do not call me a child, and I am not beautiful. I am brave, but I am not beautiful.

FRIEDA *(humbly). Ich wollte Dich nicht beleidigen. (She runs quickly up the stairs with the bag.)*

MICHAEL *(laughing, he puts an arm around the boy's shoulders and brings him down into the room).* Frieda will adore you; you'll have to tolerate it. This is my daughter, Patricia. She has fallen in love with you sight unseen.

PAT. Aw—!

MICHAEL. Come here, Pat—you've at last got your Emil.

*(*PAT *has been watching the boy, fascinated. She comes hesitantly forward, and tentatively holds out her hand.* EMIL, *instead of accepting the proffered hand, bows stiffly and clicks his heels.)*

EMIL. Miss Patricia.

PAT *(withdrawing her hand).* How do you do?

EMIL. I am happy to be acquainted with you.

PAT. I have a clubhouse down in the cellar. Would you like to see it?

EMIL. You are most kind.

PAT *(quite as formal as* EMIL*).* Not at all. It will be a pleasure. *(She bows and clicks her heels awkwardly.)*

MICHAEL. Emil, this is Leona. Leona Richards.

LEONA *(before* EMIL *can click his heels).* Hello, Emil. Can we shake hands?

EMIL *(shaking hands).* You are most kind.

LEONA. And you are most formal. We're not used to that in America. You'll have to forgive me if I meet you more than halfway.

EMIL. More than halfway? What does that mean?

LEONA. That means that I want for us to become very good friends.

EMIL. But of course. I shall try to make myself as delightful as possible.

MICHAEL *(laughing).* Relax, Emil, relax. Sit down. Are you hungry? We're going to have lunch in a few minutes. And incidentally, how the devil did you get here?

*(*EMIL *sits erectly on the edge of the couch.)*

PAT. You weren't on the train. I *know* you weren't on the train, because I went down to meet you.

EMIL. No, I did not ride on the train. *(Proudly.)* I was transported by airplane.

MICHAEL. What!!

EMIL. It was my preference to fly by air. I therefore had my ticket changed.

MICHAEL. My God! *(To Pat.)* And you were afraid he'd been kidnapped. *(Back to* EMIL.*)* Just how did you talk Miss Lewis into *that?*

EMIL. If I may have pardon, Miss Lewis is a blockhead. She made difficulty. It was necessary that I insist. Did you not receive the telegraph?

MICHAEL *(chuckling).* No, I did not receive the telegraph.

EMIL. As I have explained, she is a blockhead. *(He has been looking around.)* You possess here a very extreme house. *(*PAT *bursts into laughter;* EMIL *looks at her curiously.)* I have said something funny?

PAT. I'll say you have! Very extreme house. That's not American.

EMIL (*to* MICHAEL, *with a puzzled gesture*). Extreme—large?

MICHAEL. To be strictly American, you should have said, "Quite a dump you've got here."

EMIL (*nodding gravely*). An idiom.

MICHAEL. Yes, an idiom.

EMIL. Quite a dump you ve got here. I shall remember.

LEONA (*sympathetically*). Don't let them tease you, Emil; I think your English is wonderful. And you'll pick up our American slang fast enough.

(FRIEDA *comes down the stairs and stops in the hallway to stare at* EMIL.)

EMIL. I shall apply myself.

(*He bows;* MICHAEL *slaps him cheerfully on his backside.*)

MICHAEL. You shall apply yourself to having a good time. You'll play games, and eat lots of food, and sleep like a log. No more unhappiness, no more fear. This is your family; we'll love you, and we hope you'll love us.

FRIEDA. Yes! Yes! (*She hurries out to the kitchen.*)

EMIL. You are most kind, Herr Professor.

MICHAEL. And call me Mike. Every one does.

EMIL. Is that American, too?

MICHAEL. Not exactly. But it's a custom in this house. No barriers here between youth and age. We're all equal, we're all friends.

EMIL. Thank you.

PAT. Aunt Jessie says you're twelve years old. You're not very big.

EMIL. But I am not twelve years. I shall be twelve years on the nineteenth of this month.

PAT. No fooling. Then you'll have to have a birthday party. Mike, can we have a birthday party? (*Back to* EMIL.) I love parties. Do you?

EMIL. I have never had a birthday party.

PAT. *Well,* it's about time. Wouldn't you like one?

EMIL (*with astonishment*). There will be a party in my honor? Why will people arrive? They do not know me.

PAT. Oh, you'll have lots of friends. That's a cinch. (*To* MICHAEL.) I'll make all the arrangements, Mike. Okay?

MICHAEL. All right, you do that. Make it a good party.

PAT. Frieda! (*She runs out.*)

MICHAEL. Emil, can we talk about your father? (*The boy does not answer.*) He was a wonderful friend and a great teacher. I studied under him at Leipzig. I hope you will like this portrait of him. (EMIL *turns and looks up at the portrait above the fireplace.*) He was my teacher in philosophy, and not only in the lecture room. We drank a lot of beer together, and once we went skiing in the Bavarian Alps. It was Karl, the philosopher, who persuaded me to become a chemist. He believed that the philosophers of the future must be men of science—men of action. That's why it was inevitable that he became a great fighter when it was necessary to fight. (*After a moment, gently.*) You must be very proud to be his son.

EMIL (*he turns around; when he speaks his voice is trembling*). Please do not speak of my father.

(LEONA *crosses swiftly to* EMIL, *puts a sympathetic arm around him.*)

LEONA. Of course not, Emil. Of course not. We know how it is. Being the son of a great man can be a heavy burden.

(PAT *runs in.*)

PAT. Maybe you would like to see my clubhouse now. I have an electric train, and you can run it, as soon as I teach you how.

EMIL. Do girls have electric trains?

PAT. Oh, I have dolls, too; but I like trains better. If I ask you a question, will you tell me the truth? Were you afraid? When you went up in the plane, I mean.

EMIL. Naturally not. I am going to be an aviator.

PAT (to LEONA). The next time I visit Chicago, I think I'll fly.

MICHAEL. You don't say.

PAT. Well, if Emil can, I can.

EMIL. That is silly; you're a girl; girls always ˙ t sick. There was a girl in the airplane—she got sick.

PAT. Ah, boloney, I don't believe it. (EMIL looks at her with surprise.) Well, what was this girl's name, then?

EMIL. I do not know.

PAT. Well, were you sitting next to her when she upchucked?

(EMIL looks at MICHAEL, baffled.)

MICHAEL. Yes, Emil. Another idiom.

PAT (insistently). Where were you sitting, then?

EMIL. I was forced to sit beside a big fat Jew.

(There is a momentary silence.)

MICHAEL. You go upstairs, Pat.

PAT. Say, Emil, you'd better come up with me and wash. And I'll introduce you to Aunt Jessie, too.

EMIL (with a slight bow). If you will excuse me kindly? (He starts to go.)

MICHAEL. Wait a minute, Emil. (EMIL stops.) Miss Richards is Jewish.

EMIL. You are joking?

LEONA. No.

EMIL. That is regrettable.

LEONA (quietly). It's not regrettable. You'd better remember that. Now go on upstairs.

PAT. Yeah. Come on before you make any more bum cracks.

(EMIL follows PAT up the stairs; LEONA sits down rather deliberately and lights a cigarette.)

MICHAEL (troubled). Karl's son! . . . Good Lord!

LEONA. Children say those things. Children who should know better. The Thorndyke kid pulled a honey the other day, right in the classroom.

MICHAEL. That's no excuse for this boy.

LEONA. Michael, who took care of Emil— I mean, after his father was arrested?

MICHAEL. For a while, a younger brother of Karl's had him; after that, I don't know. For a long time we thought he was dead. I tried to get him out in 1938, and our consul in Berlin couldn't even find him. Then he finally turned up in the custody of an old woman who claimed to be a distant aunt. Apparently she was happy enough to get rid of him. (He looks at LEONA perceptively.) You're wondering if the kid's a Nazi?

LEONA (mildly). Only wondering.

MICHAEL. I thought of that, too, but it's ridiculous. He was undoubtedly ostracized, starved, life made miserable for him, because he was Karl Bruckner's son.

LEONA. I'm wondering, anyway. How much of the filth rubbed off on him. . . . You'll send him to the Experimental School, won't you?

MICHAEL. Do you want him?

LEONA. Certainly.

MICHAEL. You've got him. And let's remember, no matter what the kid says, he'll turn out all right. He's Karl's son.

LEONA (laughing). Mike, you're wonderful. Every now and then you go back to the lovely, old-fashioned belief in inherited characteristics. Blood's-thicker-than-water. I knew his great-grandfather. Good stock there, Major.

(MICHAEL laughs. JESSIE comes down the stairs. She has completely regained her composure.)

JESSIE. Well, I've met him. He's the perfect image of Mary.

LEONA (pleasantly). Your sister must have been a beautiful woman. The boy is striking.

JESSIE. Yes. And I must admit, he seems to have nice manners.

MICHAEL. I hope that means you've decided to like him.

JESSIE. Well, I'm not sure. I don't think I'll be here long enough to find out. (She crosses to LEONA.) You understand, don't you, dear? It's better for all of us if I leave.

LEONA. I hoped you wouldn't. I honestly hoped you'd stay with us. This is your home as much as Michael's. Surely we can work things out. I have my own work —and you're much better at running a house than I am—I'd never dream of interfering.

MICHAEL. I'm asking you to stay, too, Jessie. But I also know you'll do exactly as you please.

JESSIE. Thank you, Michael. (To LEONA.) I know, dear. It would be convenient for you to have me as housekeeper. It's been very convenient for Michael. But by now I deserve a vacation. Don't you think? (LEONA does not answer.) Oh, I shall enjoy myself. As a matter of fact, I think I shall go to Mexico.

MICHAEL. What on earth makes you think of Mexico?

JESSIE. I haven't told you yet, Michael— such an odd coincidence—I had a letter yesterday from Mildred Lovell; she wants me to spend the winter with her in Mexico City.

MICHAEL (gently). It's up to you, Jessie.

JESSIE. Oh, but I do so want to go. I'll have an awfully good time. (A little too brightly.) I shall be part of the Good Neighbor Policy.

LEONA. Please stay, Jessie. At least until after we're married. I'd feel terrible if you weren't here.

JESSIE. But I do want to leave as soon as possible. You won't really be offended, will you, dear? I expect it'll take me a week or so to get ready and packed.

(FRIEDA appears in the hall from the dining room).

FRIEDA. Lunch is ready, Miss Frame.

JESSIE. Thank you, Frieda. We'll be right in. You can put the soup on the table.

(FRIEDA goes out:)

MICHAEL. What are those kids doing up there? (Shouting up the stairs.) Hey, Pat! Come on down, and bring the young emigrè with you!

JESSIE. Michael! Please! (To LEONA.) I hope you can persuade him not to shout. I've never been able to.

MICHAEL. Come on, I'm hungry. Let's eat.

JESSIE. Aren't you going to wait for the boy?

MICHAEL. He'll be along. And I've got to get back to work.

(As they move towards the hall, PAT comes running down the stairs.)

JESSIE. Where's Emil?

PAT. Dressing. (She stops on the third step from the bottom and ceremoniously does her jump.) He had to change his clothes and he wouldn't let me watch him undress.

JESSIE (properly horrified). Pat!!

PAT. Good heavens, Aunt Jessie, that's nothing. I've seen boys without any clothes on.

MICHAEL. Skip it, Pat. You've made your point.

(They enter the dining room.)

JESSIE's VOICE. Really, Michael—soon she won't be allowed to associate with decent children.

MICHAEL's VOICE. Okay, okay. Then we'll have to find her some indecent ones.

(For a moment the stage is empty. Then EMIL appears on the stairs, wearing the uniform of the Nazi Jungvolk—the tan shirt with red arm-band and its swastika insignia, the black shorts which leave the knees bare, the tan stockings and the high black shoes. A sheathed dagger is thrust through his belt. He comes down the stairs, stops in the hall, glances towards the dining room, then deliberately comes into the living room. He surveys the living room professionally, as if establishing the precise strength of the enemy. The tremendous number of books is, of course, highly suspicious. He walks over to the shelves, and starts to examine them. But there are too many, and he doesn't know much about books anyway. So, after leafing through one or two, he gives it up. Then his eye is caught by the desk. Obviously it is the desk that holds all the secrets. He approaches it and cautiously sits down in Michael's chair. He picks up a letter, reads it, but it doesn't appear to be of military importance. He then very carefully opens the top drawer of the desk.)

The contents are disappointing. As he is closing the drawer, his eye is caught by the brass book-ends on top of the desk. He picks one of them up, and is examining it when the front doorbell rings. Quickly he puts down the book-end, and glances towards the hall. FRIEDA, *passing through the hall to the front door, does not see him. We hear her opening the front door.)*

MAN'S VOICE. Telegram—

FRIEDA'S VOICE. Thank you.

MAN'S VOICE. Sign here.

*(*EMIL *rises and comes around in front of the desk, his eyes on the hall, waiting for* FRIEDA *to return. Presently* FRIEDA *appears on her way back to the kitchen.)*

EMIL *(softly).* Frieda!

*(*FRIEDA *stops; she sees* EMIL. *The sight of the Nazi uniform stuns her. She stands rooted in the hallway in horrified incredulity.)*

FRIEDA. *Du Lieber Gott!*

EMIL. *Komm hier!*

*(*FRIEDA, *unable to comprehend the uniform, but fascinated, comes slowly into the room.)*

FRIEDA. You are joking, *nicht wahr?* You are trying to scare people?

*(*EMIL *deliberately raises his arm in the Nazi salute.)*

EMIL. *Heil Hitler!* (FRIEDA *fails to respond; he repeats it sharply.) Heil Hitler!*

FRIEDA. You are insane! *(She turns to go.)*

EMIL. *Halt!* (FRIEDA *stops.) Ich will mit Dir sprechen. Ich habe sofort gemerkt dass Du für Das Vaterland arbeitest.*

FRIEDA. No. I am an American. And I speak only English.

EMIL. Very wise. We will speak English. Also, I am glad to see you are correctly suspicious of me, because you think I am a child. But you can trust me. We will work together to defeat the enemy.

FRIEDA. You are insane.

EMIL *(a childish note in his voice).* Please —don't try to deceive me. I have been informed. There are eight million of you in America—all good Germans—all working for *Der Führer.* Don't you understand? I know all about it. I am prepared.

FRIEDA *(with sarcasm).* What are you prepared for? In your Nazi uniform?

EMIL *(re-assuming his air of authority).* You and I will have collaboration. We must find out everything. The Herr Professor is engaged in important work; I discovered that before i even left New York. We must examine all the letters; we must open all the telegraphs. Give me that telegraph. *(He holds out his hand.)*

FRIEDA. You're also a fool. *(She turns to go;* EMIL *springs in front of her, and grabs her arm to take the telegram from her. The telephone starts ringing.* FRIEDA *holds off the boy and calls loudly.)* Professor Frame! Professor Frame!

(The telephone continues to ring. FRIEDA *wrenches her arm free, and gives* EMIL *a vigorous push. As* EMIL *recovers his balance,* MICHAEL *enters from the dining room. He sees* EMIL, *stops short.* LEONA, JESSIE *and* PAT *enter from the dining room. The telephone continues to ring.)*

JESSIE *(with grim satisfaction).* I'm not surprised. I'm not a bit surprised.

*(*MICHAEL *crosses to the ringing telephone.)*

MICHAEL *(into telephone).* Hello. . . . What long distance? . . . Oh, cancel that. I don't need it. *(He hangs up.* EMIL *stands arrogantly defiant of the many eyes upon him.)* Well, you Nordic superman. What the hell do you think you're doing?

*(*EMIL *does not answer.* FRIEDA *begins to speak volubly.)*

FRIEDA. He's a devil, Professor! A devil, like they make them in Germany these days! He thinks he's a spy for Hitler. He wanted to open your telegram! *(She hands the telegram to* MICHAEL.)*

MICHAEL. Thank you.

FRIEDA *(turning on* EMIL *bitterly).* You! It is you fellows who make every one hate Germans! You wear your swastikas. You march! You kill! And all the Germans get blamed—people like me get blamed!

MICHAEL. All right, Frieda. We can take care of him. He'll do no marching or killing. You can go.

FRIEDA. And I wanted to put flowers in his room. (She goes out. MICHAEL tears open the telegram and glances at it.)

MICHAEL (to EMIL). You were interested in this telegram, Herr Bruckner. I will read it to you and you can convey its contents immediately to Herr Goebbels. "Emil Bruckner arrives plane 11:13 A.M. You have my deepest sympathy. Ruth Lewis." (Holds out the telegram to EMIL.) You'll want this for your file? You'll doubtless find many interesting fingerprints.

LEONA. Michael. You'll never get anywhere that way.

JESSIE. Of course not! There's only one thing to do! Tear that uniform off! What are we waiting for?

LEONA. To hear from Emil.

JESSIE (turning on LEONA with sudden and surprising vehemence). We're at war, aren't we? He's the enemy. He's a German, just as I knew he would be. They're all the same. Lying, arrogant, deceitful—goose-stepping. If it was up to me, I'd exterminate the entire German race!

LEONA (mildly). Including Frieda?

JESSIE. Oh, I know you and your progressive education! Letting people do as they please, that's what it is! That's what you do with Pat. That's what you'll do with Michael—

MICHAEL. That's enough, Jessie—

JESSIE. And that's what you'll do with this little beast! You'll keep him here in this house, and let him grow up to be a lying, thieving little monster. Well, I'm glad I won't be here to see it! (Taking PAT's hand.) Come on, Pat. This is no place for you. (She goes back into the dining room, PAT accompanying her reluctantly.)

MICHAEL (after a moment, very quietly). Sit down, Emil. We've got to find out how this thing happened to you. (EMIL does not answer, nor does he sit down.) Very well, then. Tell me this. What did you hope to accomplish by wearing that uniform? Is that being a clever spy?

EMIL (loudly). I'm not afraid.

MICHAEL. Afraid of what?

EMIL. If there is necessity, I will die for Der Führer.

MICHAEL. I see. You want to die.

EMIL. It is my duty. (With a slight quaver.) Are you going to beat me?

MICHAEL. If you find death so pleasant, we'll kill you first and beat you afterwards. Would you prefer that?

LEONA. No, Mike. He has no humor. Can't you see that?

EMIL. I'm not afraid!

MICHAEL. Look here, Emil. You can stop saying that. Because you have nothing to be afraid of. (He walks over to EMIL. The boy cringes, expecting MICHAEL's fist.) No, I'm not going to hit you. Sit down. Over here. (He propels the boy to the couch. EMIL sits down, still warily waiting for the blow.)

MICHAEL. Emil, you're in a new country now. There are many things you'll have to learn. I think you'll want to learn them. You'll be making new friends; you'll be living in the same house with Pat. You can be very happy here, if you will accept what we can give you. And if you will accept us. Do you understand what I'm saying, Emil?

EMIL (standing up stiffly). I am a German, and I shall always be a German. America is a cesspool. To be an American is to be a member of a mongrel race. The American blood stream is a mixture of the scum of the earth. The only pure-blooded American is the Sioux Indian. . . . You see, I have been educated.

MICHAEL. Lee, our bloodstreams have been polluted. We'll have to turn him over to the Sioux Indians. (Back to EMIL.) With or without feathers? (He walks away and sits down at his desk.)

LEONA. May I ask him some questions?

MICHAEL (moodily). Your witness.

LEONA. Emil, in about two weeks, I'm going to marry your Uncle Michael. I'll be your mother.

EMIL (slowly). Then it is true. Such marriages are still permitted in America.

MICHAEL (*grimly*). Next question, Lee.

LEONA. I'll ignore that for the present, because there's something else practically as important. I'm also going to be your teacher. (EMIL *does not answer.*) Yes, it is also "permitted" in this country for women to be teachers.

EMIL. That is unfortunate. It is women's nature to indulge boys; they make boys soft.

LEONA. Thank you for telling me. I won't indulge you. (*Then, more gently.*) Emil, I think I know why you're wearing the uniform. And in a way, I don't blame you a bit. It's all you have to wear, isn't it? Except the suit you came in and that's awfully threadbare. And naturally you're proud of your uniform.

EMIL. I knew they would examine my baggage. But they were stupid. I wore the uniform under my suit, and they did not even guess.

LEONA. That was very clever. A boy needs his clothes. Particularly when he has so few. . . . But there is one thing I don't understand. Perhaps you can explain it to me? If *Der Führer* is so generous, why does he give you only one suit and one uniform?

(EMIL *hesitates a moment, then selects an answer from his limited repertory.*)

EMIL. That is common knowledge. It is the Treaty of Versailles.

LEONA. Mike, you must buy Emil some clothes. I think he'd look rather well in long trousers.

EMIL. But you ration clothes, no?

LEONA. So far, only the cuffs. (*To* MICHAEL.) I think he should have at least two or three suits—like the other boys in school. (*Without sarcasm, to* EMIL.) I hope you won't mind if we buy you quite a few clothes.

EMIL (*after thinking it over for a moment*). That is your privilege.

MICHAEL (*sarcastically*). Thank you.

EMIL (*politely*). You're welcome, Herr Professor.

LEONA. You know, Emil, I've just been thinking about something. I don't know if I should say this, because I don't wish to make you unhappy—but after all, I'm sure other people will notice it, too. From that picture, I'd say you look somewhat like your father. Your eyes—

EMIL. That is a lie! I have no resemblance of my father. I've been told otherwise many times.

LEONA (*patiently*). Maybe I'm wrong. But why are you ashamed to look like him?

EMIL. My father was a traitor to the Third Reich.

(MICHAEL *sinks deeper into the chair behind his desk. He watches the boy intently.*)

LEONA. I suppose a great many people have told you that? Your teachers . . . Your military instructors . . .

EMIL (*forensically*). In 1918 Karl Bruckner betrayed Germany on the home front. He fomented revolution. If it had not been for him and the Jewish Bolsheviks, Germany would have won the war. He was one of those who made Germany weak. He was responsible for the inflation and the Communists.

MICHAEL. Is that the end of the phonograph record?

EMIL (*turns to* MICHAEL, *directly*). You drank beer and read philosophy with my father. It was that which gave Germany trouble. Too many people drank beer and read philosophy. We Germans were soft. We forgot our great destiny. Then *Der Führer* came. He gave us back our courage. With *Der Führer* to show us the way, it is our position to conquer the world. You will find out that I speak the truth.

MICHAEL. Yes? You're not doing so well at Stalingrad.

EMIL. That is a lie! Your Jewish Capitalist newspapers *feed* you lies! We captured Stalingrad weeks ago.

LEONA. And those are the only reasons why you are ashamed of your father?

EMIL. Because of my father, they would never permit me to be trusted. I excelled in all endeavor, yet they would not make me captain of my troop, because my name was Bruckner. I did everything I could. I informed the Gestapo about the mother of my best friend, though it pained me greatly, and I lost my friend.

LEONA. Did the Gestapo reward you?

EMIL. Yes. But they still laughed at me. Because my name was Bruckner. No matter what I did, I could never be like the others. They always spoke of my father.

MICHAEL. Thank God, Karl can't hear you say these things.

EMIL. My father was a coward. He committed suicide.

MICHAEL (rising angrily). Damn their rotten souls! Those lying—

LEONA (quickly). No, Mike. (To EMIL.) You'll learn the true story of your father. There's no use our telling you now. You wouldn't understand it.

EMIL (calmly). I am prepared that you should tell me lies.

MICHAEL. Lies!? How the hell would you know what's a lie and what's the truth!? You've been drugged; you've been poisoned! (After a moment, quietly.) But we've got the antidote—we know what to do— We'll get it out of you!

EMIL. You can beat me. You can torture me. I am prepared for the most horrible experiences.

MICHAEL (very quietly). Now listen to me. In America, we don't beat little boys. Nor do we torture them. We persuade them. That is our secret weapon. (He hesitates a moment.) Can you understand that? (EMIL does not answer. MICHAEL puts a friendly hand on his shoulder.) Go upstairs and take off that uniform. Put on your other suit, and this afternoon we'll buy you those long trousers. Now go on. (EMIL stands motionless. MICHAEL regards him soberly.) All right. Stay here, if you like. But you can't sit down to lunch with us until you take off that uniform. (Turns to LEONA.) Come on, Lee.

(EMIL, with hostility, watches them go. He turns, looks up at the picture of his father. Then, deliberately, he pushes a chair under the picture. He carefully takes his dagger from its sheath, steps up on the chair, and slashes the picture from top to bottom—not once, but several times, furiously.)

CURTAIN

ACT TWO

SCENE: The same. It is ten days later, two o'clock in the afternoon. Karl Bruckner's portrait has been removed, leaving a bright square on the wall above the fireplace. One of the windows in the bay is open, and a warm September breeze blows the curtain.

AT RISE: JESSIE is busy at the table behind the couch, going through the contents of a portfolio, sorting and discarding. Presently the dining room door opens, and FRIEDA enters the hallway, carrying a tray of glasses. She opens the cellar door.

JESSIE (without turning around). Frieda.

FRIEDA. Yes, Miss Frame?

JESSIE (still without looking around). What are you doing now?

FRIEDA. Miss Pat wants the birthday party down in her playroom. I'm taking the dishes down.

(The telephone rings.)

JESSIE. I'll get it. Did you finish the cake?

FRIEDA. Yes. And I hope he chokes on it. (She goes out, banging the cellar door behind her.)

JESSIE (into telephone). Hello . . . Oh, hello, Alice. I'm so glad you called. You know I'm leaving tomorrow and I don't

know what to do with the files of the garden club. . . . Oh, I know that I shall love Mexico. Yes, I'm all packed. (There is a long pause. JESSIE's face clouds.) I see . . . I see . . . Well, I can't say that I blame you, Alice. . . . Yes, I must admit there have been other complaints, too. (FRIEDA enters from the cellar and stops to listen.) Yes, I'll explain it to Pat. I'm sure she'll be disappointed, but you're perfectly right, my dear. Little Thorny is such a darling . . . Good-bye, dear. (She puts down the telephone, sees FRIEDA.)

FRIEDA. Another one, eh? That's the third.

JESSIE. Mrs. Thorndyke. (She returns to the table, resumes going through her portfolios. FRIEDA comes into the room.)

FRIEDA. It will be a good party. Mr. Fine Manners will have to eat all the cake himself.

JESSIE *(placidly)*. I don't think it would have harmed Alice's little boy to come to the party. He's a fairly odious child already.

FRIEDA. So! It was bad enough that our beautiful Emil knocked him down, but that he also stole his bicycle! So now it is a boycott! Like with Mrs. Prescott, and Mrs. Hickman— Good!

JESSIE. You didn't put poison in that cake, did you?

FRIEDA. It came into my mind. *(Shaking her head.)* What that child has done!

JESSIE. It's all right. I know all the boy's crimes. You give me the list every day.

FRIEDA. Killing that poor dog next door, then trying to lie out of it!

JESSIE. Well, we don't *know* that Emil did it.

FRIEDA. Who else? Who else but a Nazi would— *(The telephone rings again.)* Another one yet. The fourth! Such a popular boy!

(JESSIE goes to the desk and picks up the telephone.)

JESSIE *(into telephone)*. Hello? . . . Yes, Mr. Miller. . . . No, Professor Frame's not here. *(She puts her hand over the mouthpiece; to FRIEDA.)* It's not about Emil. It's Fred Miller. *(Into telephone.)* I see. Well, I don't know *anything* about the laboratory—you'll just have to talk to Professor Frame.

(FRIEDA starts to go, but steps back quickly into the room. She gestures to JESSIE.)

FRIEDA. Sh!

(EMIL enters the hall from the kitchen and tiptoes toward the stairs.)

JESSIE *(into telephone)*. Yes, he'll be home later, I expect.

FRIEDA *(to EMIL; triumphantly)*. So! Somebody has fought you! Good!

(EMIL stops and turns. He is in a sorry state. His forehead is cut, his face is black with dirt, the collar of his shirt is half torn off, and one knee is exposed through

a rip in his trousers. He seems quite cool and collected, however.)

JESSIE *(surveying EMIL as she continues to speak into the telephone)*. Yes, Mr. Miller. I'll tell him. Good-bye. *(She hangs up.)* Well, you don't look much like the guest of honor at a birthday party.

EMIL. I was attacked.

JESSIE. Look at your new trousers. I should think by this time you would have learned.

EMIL *(with pride)*. There were four of them. It was four against one. Robert Amery called me a liar. No one can tell me I've never shot a machine-gun.

JESSIE. You hit Robert Amery?

FRIEDA. Such a little boy! Much smaller than you!

EMIL. But I did shoot a machine-gun. It was my reward. Because I was the best spy in my troop. *(FRIEDA takes EMIL's handkerchief from his pocket and wipes some of the dirt from his face.)* So when he refused to understand what is true, it became necessary for me to strike him. Being a coward and a liar, he screamed for help.

JESSIE. And from your appearance, he got plenty of it.

EMIL. Four of them. They found it necessary to make a gang. It was the only way they dared face me. *(Suddenly.)* It is from the word "gang" that the American gangster is constructed, no? They are gangsters, those four. Gangsters and degenerates.

JESSIE. Because they don't like a bully?

EMIL. It was their desire to make me cry. But they could not accomplish it. I did not cry once. I have never cried. They cannot understand that a man of my education will never cry.

FRIEDA *(handing EMIL his handkerchief)*. A man of your education should blow his nose. *(She goes out.)*

EMIL *(he looks at JESSIE curiously)*. You are not angry with me today. I thought you would be extremely angry.

JESSIE *(she goes to the couch with her portfolio and sits down)*. What you do is no longer my business. I'm leaving tomorrow. From now on, go ahead and get yourself killed if you want to.

EMIL (carefully). Perhaps I am sorry that you are leaving, Aunt Jessie.

JESSIE. I doubt that. (She glances at the watch pinned on her dress.) If you were so brave and didn't cry, why did you come home before school is out?

EMIL (after a moment). I was sent home by Leona the Jewess.

JESSIE. Stop talking like that, Emil. . . . You must try to like Miss Richards.

EMIL. I am sorry, Aunt Jessie. But I am aware of your accurate feelings. You have the same lack of fondness for her that I do.

JESSIE. You don't know what you're saying. If I have any "accurate feelings," they're about you.

EMIL. Yes, you do not like me. For which I am sorry. Because I like you.

(JESSIE throws him a suspicious glance.)

EMIL. But it is not because of me that you are leaving this house. It is because of her.

JESSIE (closing her portfolio). That's enough, Emil—

EMIL. The other night—through the door —I heard you crying in your bed.

JESSIE. You're making that up.

EMIL. You know it is true. Please, Aunt Jessie. Do you not see that I understand? She is breaking up the home; she is making it necessary for you to throw yourself out. Because who could live in a house with her? . . . It was on Tuesday night that you cried. I will not tell any one. I promise you.

JESSIE (her voice trembling). And why weren't you asleep?

EMIL. It made me very unhappy. You were crying because she is driving you out. I am right, no? (JESSIE does not answer.) Please, Aunt Jessie. I know what you are feeling. Now we can be friends. (JESSIE watches him, half-afraid of the alliance she is forming.) May I tell you something? I do not think they will be married.

JESSIE. You're talking nonsense.

EMIL. You will see. She hates me. And that is good. Because I hate her. Matters will never have harmony with us both in this house.

JESSIE. In that case, you'll be the one to go. You must think my brother's a fool.

EMIL. Uncle Michael has an understanding of me. When I cut the picture, he was careful not to lose his temper. He is very kind. (After a moment.) I will reveal something else but you must handle the thought cautiously. I have already begun my great campaign against her!

JESSIE. Emil, what have you done?

EMIL. If I tell you, will you be my friend? Please, Aunt Jessie, you and I know what kind of a woman she is.

JESSIE. Emil, you've got to stop this. If my brother wants her for his wife, that's his right.

EMIL. But you and I know what is best for Uncle Michael.

JESSIE. What are you trying to get out of me, Emil?

EMIL (he sighs). Yes, that is how it is. Everything I do is not understood properly. . . . It was for you that I killed that big, fierce dog.

JESSIE. What?

EMIL. The dog barked in the night; he kept you awake. You had headaches.

JESSIE. That's horrible, Emil. Horrible.

EMIL. But you said yourself you wished somebody would wring that dog's neck. You said it not once, but several times. I heard you.

JESSIE. Good heavens!

EMIL. Anyway, it was only a mongrel, and it tried to bite me. . . . It is difficult for me to know what is expected.

JESSIE. Mercy. When I think of your mother—poor Mary. If she were here now— (She shakes her head sadly.)

EMIL (suddenly very wistful). Aunt Jessie, maybe sometime you will tell me about my mother. I was only a little baby when she died.

JESSIE. Emil. Emil.

EMIL. But won't you tell me about her?

JESSIE *(after a moment)*. Of course I will. She would have wanted you to be a good boy. Please be a good boy.

EMIL. Was she beautiful?

JESSIE. Yes, dear. She was very beautiful.

EMIL *(innocently)*. Yes. It is difficult to be without a mother. Uncle Michael speaks always of my father. He never speaks of my mother.

JESSIE *(tremulously)*. You poor child. There's been no one to understand you.

EMIL. No. . . . Please don't go away, Aunt Jessie. Please don't go away and leave me with *her!*

(PAT enters through the open window; she is carrying her school books.)

PAT. Hello, Aunt Jessie! Hello, Emil! I heard all about your fight. Did you get hurt? You don't look hurt—much. Where's Frieda? Is everything ready for the party? I have to see the cake—Emil can't see it because it's a surprise—I have to put the candles on—

JESSIE. Calm down, Pat. Just calm down. The cake will be a surprise for both of you. I'll go and put the candles on myself. Right now. *(She takes PAT's school books from her.)* You'd better go up and change your clothes, Emil. You can put on your Sunday suit if you want to. Of course, there's great danger nobody will come to your party, but we'll hope for the best. *(She starts out.)*

PAT. Oh, they'll come. I *know.* Dennis is coming, and Butler, and—

JESSIE. Well, we'll see. *(She goes out to the dining room.)*

PAT *(turning to EMIL with astonishment)*. Wasn't she cross with you on account of fighting?

EMIL *(tranquilly)*. No.

PAT. What'd you do to her?

EMIL. We had a discussion.

PAT. But Aunt Jessie doesn't like you. She says so.

EMIL. I can make anybody like me, if I want to.

PAT. Then why don't you? And then you wouldn't have to fight so much.

EMIL. If people will not believe what is true, I have to fight them.

PAT. Why?

EMIL *(at a loss)*. Well, you know how it is.

PAT. Can't you just argue with them? I argue with people all the time. And if you have to, you call them names. But you don't fight. *(Very grown up.)* Really, Emil, you make it very difficult for me socially.

EMIL. I'm sorry you feel it necessary to defend me.

PAT. Oh, I just tell people you don't know the score.

EMIL. What does that mean—the score?

PAT. Oh, you know—being hep to things. Please, Emil, when Dennis, and Butler and the others come, make them like you. Like the day Mike took us all to the circus, and you imitated the monkeys. Can't you please be nice?

EMIL *(judiciously)*. Well—you are sure they will bring presents?

PAT. Why, of course. People always bring presents. That's why you have a birthday party. Besides, I *know* they will.

EMIL. Did *you* buy me a present?

PAT. Well, *naturally.*

EMIL. Where is it?

PAT. Oh, it's hidden.

EMIL. Is it the present I want?

PAT. What did you want?

EMIL. I told you what I wanted. I made it most clear.

PAT. I guess I forgot.

EMIL. But how could you forget?

PAT. Well, I'm careless.

EMIL. But it's the only thing I wanted.

PAT *(roguishly)*. What's the only thing you wanted, Emil?

EMIL. A watch! A good watch with seventeen jewels and an illuminated face. One useful for night marches. So, you forgot.

If you wanted something, *I* would not forget.

PAT. But that would be a very *expensive* present! I couldn't afford ever to buy a *watch*! Anyway, no one around here goes marching at night.

EMIL *(with bitter dignity)*. So you bought me some silly toy. All right, then I will not show you that which is in my pocket.

PAT. Aw, what have you got in your pocket?

EMIL. It is concerned with the Universal Spy System, Incorporated.

PAT. Hot dog! But say, Emil, at the party, why don't we initiate all the fellows into the Spy System, and then we could all take turns being G-men!

EMIL *(shaking his head)*. No.

PAT. But why?

EMIL. Because you are the only friend I trust. You are the only one loyal to me. I could *train* you.

PAT. Train me?

EMIL. I was trained to follow people—to watch everything they do. I have been educated.

PAT. But not as a *real* spy.

EMIL. Yes, as a real spy.

PAT. Aw—! When you left Germany, I bet they didn't tell a little boy like you to be a real spy in America. Did they?

EMIL. No. But some day I will show them! . . . Do you want to see what I have in my pocket?

PAT. All right. What is it?

EMIL. It is the oath which you must take as a spy.

PAT. But I *told* you, Emil. I don't want to take the oath. I don't want to die.

EMIL. You do not show the proper bravery. Unless you die for something, your life is worthless.

PAT. Why?

EMIL. Death is the highest honor.

PAT. But I wouldn't like it. When you're dead, they close your eyes and you can't see your friends.

EMIL. But a brave man must die for his country.

PAT *(matter-of-factly)*. But, Emil, don't you understand? I don't want to die.

EMIL. Not even for America?

PAT *(after a moment's thought)*. Well—not if I could get out of it.

EMIL. I don't think you will make a very good spy. You would be afraid—

(The front door has opened and MICHAEL *enters.)*

PAT. Mike! *(She runs to him and kisses him; as they move toward the couch together, they go through an old routine.)* Hello, Mike.

MICHAEL. Hello, Pat.

PAT. Who was that lady I seen you walking down the street with last night?

MICHAEL. That was no lady; that was my daughter. *(*MICHAEL *has not read this last line with his customary spontaneity;* PAT *looks at him critically.)*

MICHAEL. Your partner's tired this afternoon. *(He is looking at* EMIL.*)* Pat, go outdoors and play. *(He sits at his desk, takes a key from the pocket of his jacket and unlocks a drawer.)*

PAT. I keep telling him he mustn't fight. But he won't listen to me.

*(*MICHAEL *takes a key-ring from his pocket, drops it into the drawer, locks the drawer and returns the single desk key to the pocket of his jacket. He looks up to find the two children watching him intently.)*

MICHAEL *(with astonishment)*. Well—?

PAT *(with a giggle)*. We're just spying.

(She starts out, gets as far as the hallway, then stops to watch proceedings.)

MICHAEL. All right, Emil. Let's have it.

EMIL. What do you mean, Uncle Michael?

MICHAEL. What happened to you? It wasn't your fault; I know that. Let's have all your elaborate apologies—your alibis. We'll get those out of the way first.

EMIL. Then Miss Richards has already told you?

MICHAEL. You know what she told me? She said she thinks you need a good licking. *(Noticing* PAT *in the hallway.)* Get out of here, Pat. Go on.

PAT. Well—if you will excuse me, I will go up and dress. We're having a party, you know.

MICHAEL. Oh, you are?

PAT. You won't call off the party just because he's been fighting again, will you? I've gone to an awful lot of trouble!

MICHAEL. All right, Pat. All right. *(PAT runs up the stairs.* MICHAEL *turns his attention again to* EMIL.*)* If it's not a licking you need, what is it? What are we going to do with you?

EMIL. I'm sorry, Uncle Michael.

MICHAEL. Don't you ever get tired of being disciplined? *(He rises from the desk, slips off his jacket, throws it over a chair.)* Practically every night, I've sent you to bed right after dinner. Every time you and Pat plan to go to the movies, it turns out you can't go; you've been a bad boy again. You *would* like to go, wouldn't you?

EMIL. Yes, I enjoy the cinema.

MICHAEL. Then why do you do these things? What do you want, anyway?

EMIL *(ceremoniously)*. Uncle Michael, may I make you a promise? It is my promise that I will make my conduct satisfactory.

MICHAEL. Well, you haven't pulled *that* one before. *(He sits at the desk again.)*

EMIL *(sadly)*. You don't believe me?

MICHAEL. When Pat makes a promise, I know it's a contract. We can shake hands on it, because we trust each other. . . . I don't believe you, because I don't trust you. And I doubt if you trust me.

EMIL. Uncle Michael, you are having the picture mended?

MICHAEL. Yes.

EMIL. I'm sorry for what I did.

MICHAEL. Sure. For purposes of conversation, you're sorry. You commit a horrible crime, and ten days later you say you're sorry. You're a little late, my friend.

EMIL. Will you allow me to pay for the mending?

MICHAEL. With what?

EMIL. Well, I can do what Butler does. He mows the lawn, and every week his father pays him a dollar. We could make a contract.

MICHAEL. Mowing that lawn out there is hard work. It's a good half acre. If you're doing this just to impress me, you're making a bad deal.

EMIL. No—no! . . . Yes, it is so. I *am* trying to impress you, because I *am* sorry. When I arrived here in America, I was a savage.

MICHAEL. What do you think you are now?

EMIL *(thoughtfully)*. I am still a problem, but not a savage.

*(*MICHAEL *rises and comes around the desk.)*

MICHAEL. All right, problem child. You mow the lawn. We'll make it a dollar and a half. It's a big lawn, and you're a big problem.

(They shake hands.)

EMIL. Thank you.

MICHAEL *(reflectively)*. If Karl were here, I wonder what he would do? Would he regard you as hopeless? *(He crosses to the table behind the couch; he fills his pipe.)* You see, Emil, you're more than just my exasperating nephew. To me, you're also a test case. I'm an optimist. I've always been an optimist about the German people. Your father was an optimist, too. He believed that human nature *can* be changed. . . . Many's the time we sat together dreaming up a brave new world—. *(He has returned to the desk.)*

EMIL. Uncle Michael, I tried to read my father's book, but I could not understand it.

MICHAEL *(skeptically)*. Which book?

EMIL. I will show you. *(He goes to the book-shelves, and takes down a book. He carries it to* MICHAEL, *who is again seated behind the desk.)* You like this book. You have marked it in many places. *(*MICHAEL *takes the book, idly leafs through it.)*

is a very large book. It must possess a great deal of information. What does it say that is so shocking? (MICHAEL *does not answer.*) Why did they burn it in the bonfire of the books?

MICHAEL (*reading from the book*). "Original sin does not reside within the individual soul of the human being, but within the structure of society. A person is born neither good nor bad; he is born only with incalculable capacity for both virtue and evil. The flowering of these capacities depends upon the social incentives with which the individual finds himself confronted. If he finds the rewards for evil-doing are great, the individual will quite logically and sensibly become an evil man."

EMIL. What does it mean?

MICHAEL. It means your father doesn't think your case is hopeless. It means the capacities you were born with are still there—somewhere.

EMIL. Is that all? Why did they burn the book?

MICHAEL. Because it contains *ideas*. Your Nazi teachers are cowards. They're afraid of ideas. That's why they had to burn the book; and that's why they had to kill your father. They were afraid of him.

EMIL. But I told you before. He committed suicide.

MICHAEL (*quietly*). Stop repeating that damn lie! Your father couldn't take his own life—not in a million years. A man doesn't spend his life in struggle, just to end up hanging himself.

EMIL. But he left a note. It was in all the newspapers.

MICHAEL. It couldn't occur to you that it might not have been Karl who wrote that note?

EMIL (*thoughtfully*). Perhaps. But how do you know?

MICHAEL (*after a moment*). Have you ever heard of Conrad Reiss?

EMIL. No.

MICHAEL. No, of course not. They wouldn't have told you about *him*. Because he escaped. Reiss and your father were in the same concentration camp.

EMIL. Dachau?

MICHAEL. Yes. . . . The Nazis knew there was a plan to escape. But they did not know who the plan involved. . . . So the Nazis took Karl, they took Reiss, and they took six other men—all of them suspects. They chose Karl as their first victim. He was older than the other men; they thought he would break more easily. . . . First they used whips and rubber truncheons. They wanted Karl to betray which men were his comrades. They forced the others to stand there and watch Karl being tortured. If Karl would not betray his comrades, perhaps his comrades would betray themselves to save Karl.

EMIL. Did they?

MICHAEL. No. No one spoke. Nor did Karl.

EMIL. What did they do?

MICHAEL. They told the seven men that unless the plan was confessed they would put out Karl's eyes. And they told Karl that if he named his comrades, they would let him go free. . . . Still no one spoke. They put out Karl's eyes. . . . Then, in a fury, they killed him. They put four bullets into him. (*After a moment.*) My friend Conrad Reiss is working in Washington now.

EMIL (*slowly*). But if what you say is true, they could not call my father a coward.

MICHAEL. Couldn't they? Figure it out for yourself—why they called him a coward. Think about it!

EMIL. This Conrad Reiss—did he tell you this story himself?

MICHAEL. He told me, and he told thousands of other people. He wrote it in a book.

EMIL. But if this man is an author, is it not possible that it is a made-up story —like the American cinema?

(*The front doorbell rings.*)

MICHAEL. So you don't want to think about it. You prefer to believe it's a lie. You'd rather remain convinced that your father was a coward.

(JESSIE *enters the hall; she goes to the front door.*)

EMIL. Perhaps I should read Herr Reiss's book.

MICHAEL. Perhaps you should. (*He goes to one of the shelves and takes out a book.* JESSIE *enters with* FRED MILLER. MILLER *is a man of fifty; his manner is quiet, respectable.*)

JESSIE. Michael, it's Fred Miller.

MICHAEL. Oh, hello, Fred.

(JESSIE *goes upstairs.*)

MILLER. Professor Frame, I'm sorry to disturb you at home—.

MICHAEL. Right with you. (*Handing* EMIL *the book.*) If there are any words you don't understand, ask me. (*Turning to* MILLER.) Fred, this is my nephew, Emil Bruckner. He seems to have met up with the United Nations. Emil, this is Mr. Miller.

EMIL (*shaking hands*). How do you do, sir?

MILLER. So you're the young fellow who came all the way from Germany by himself. Well, I'm pleased to know you. (*He turns to* MICHAEL.) He's got a nice firm handshake, Professor.

(EMIL *sits on the couch, and starts apparently to read the book.*)

MICHAEL. Well, Fred—I can't do it. I'm sorry.

MILLER (*agreeably*). I see. All right—if you can't, you can't. But I—

MICHAEL. I made the request myself; but they said absolutely not.

MILLER. Well, I guess when they say absolutely, they mean it. But I don't know how the dickens they expect me to keep that place clean.

MICHAEL. Yes, I know. But all you have to do is send over one of your boys while we're working there.

MILLER. That ain't so easy to do. You know yourself that my boys do their work at night, and I'm operating short-handed besides. I've been doing my best, but my boys really can't give that place a going-over while you're in there. Floors ain't been polished, windows ain't been washed. And Army Generals coming in there, too.

They must have a pretty poor notion of the way we keep things around here.

MICHAEL. Sure. You want to do a conscientious job, and I don't blame you. You're a good janitor.

MILLER. Janitor? Please, Professor Frame—

MICHAEL (*quickly*). Oh, oh. I know—don't tell me. Superintendent of Buildings and Maintenance. Nineteen years with the University.

MILLER. Thank you. Not that the title means anything. But you know how it is.

MICHAEL. You bet. We professional men must preserve our dignity.

MILLER (*eagerly*). That's just it, Professor. That's why I'm bothering you about this. Looks like after nineteen years, folks around here don't trust me.

MICHAEL. Now, Fred. Not even President Gilbert could have a key to that laboratory.

MILLER. It ain't President Gilbert that's got to keep things clean.

PAT'S VOICE (*from upstairs*). Mi-ike!

MICHAEL (*shouting back*). Shut up, Pat, I'm busy!

MILLER. I wish you could see your way clear to— (*Dropping his voice, confidentially.*) Naturally, I'd hold onto the key personally.

MICHAEL. No, Fred. Government orders.

PAT'S VOICE. Mi-ike! Please come up here! You got to help me write something!

MICHAEL. Sorry I can't do anything about it, Fred. Now you'll have to excuse me. It seems I have an appointment with my daughter. See you later.

(MILLER *watches him go up the stairs, then he turns to pick up his hat.*)

MILLER (*to* EMIL). Well, young fellow. What are you reading? Got a good book for yourself there?

(EMIL *rises, still holding the book.*)

EMIL. I do not know if it is a good book. Have you ever heard of the author— Conrad Reiss? (*He shows the book to* MILLER.)

MILLER. Nope; can't say that I have. But I'm not much of a one for reading books.

EMIL. He is a friend of my Uncle. *(He reads the inscription.)* "To Michael Frame. Good friend of Karl Bruckner. Good friend of Germany." (EMIL *tosses the book onto the sofa.)* I do not think that I will read it. I think that it is propaganda. Don't you?

MILLER. Well, now, that's frequently the trouble with books. Too many opinions.

EMIL *(carefully).* If you have the custody of all the University buildings, your job is very important.

MILLER. Oh, they keep me plenty busy. Well, young fellow, I'm certainly glad to have met you.

EMIL. Wait a moment, Mr. Miller. (MILLER *stops, a little surprised.)* Why do you want the key?

MILLER. Now, that's a strange question to ask. You were sitting right here. You heard me.

EMIL. Isn't Miller a German name? *War nicht Dein Name einst Müller?*

MILLER. Sure, my father's name was Müller. What of it?

EMIL. You must want the key greatly. I'm surprised the Herr Professor was not suspicious. You were awfully crude.

MILLER *(laughing).* That's rich. I've heard of you. Little Emil Bruckner. They say you're a devil, and I guess they're right.

EMIL. It is useless to deceive me, Mr. Miller. I know what you are trying to do. I am working on it also. I have examined the contents in my Uncle's desk. But there is nothing about the laboratory. *(Grudgingly.)* I'm afraid the Herr Professor is a very intelligent man.

MILLER. You know, that's the general opinion around here. . . . Kid, you're better than a movie! You've certainly got a lively imagination.

EMIL. All right. You distrust me because I am a child. But remember what *Der Führer* says: "We must put our faith in the youth. They belong to Germany completely. They are more reliable than the old people." . . . You do want the key, don't you?

(We hear FRIEDA *opening the cellar door;* MILLER *turns and sees her as she enters.)*

MILLER *(offhandedly).* Hello, there.

FRIEDA *(with a surprised look).* Hello! *(She goes out to the dining room.)*

EMIL. You know this woman who works here? Her name is Frieda.

MILLER. Of course. She's been here for years.

EMIL. She is a bad German. When the time comes, we will have to report her to the Gestapo.

MILLER *(laughing).* That's a hot one, too! Keep going!

EMIL. She is not one of the eight million who are loyal to the Fatherland. I tried to work with her.

MILLER. And what happened? Did she spank your bottom?

EMIL *(drawing himself up stiffly).* All right. You may treat me like a child if you wish. But if you do, you are the one who is being stupid. *(He moves closer to* MILLER.*)* I will take the key and have a duplicate made.

MILLER *(sharply).* Wait a minute, youngster. A joke's a joke, but—

EMIL. I will return the key, and the Professor will never guess. I will bring *you* the duplicate key.

MILLER. You just do that, my young friend! And when you arrive, I'll turn you over to the police!

EMIL. You cannot deceive me, *Herr Müller.* You may tell your superior that I will bring you the key. I will prove that *I* am working faithfully for *Der Führer!* *(He clicks his heels sharply.)*

MILLER *(angry and frightened).* Will you shut up! You don't know what you're talking about. You'll get me into trouble!

(The door bell rings.)

EMIL *(conspiratorially).* Shhh—! *(He goes quickly to the window and peeks out.)* It's Miss Richards!

MILLER. Well, what if it is? *(His manner becoming elaborately casual.)* Well, good bye, young fellow. Glad to have made your acquaintance. *(He turns to go;* JESSIE *is coming down the stairs.)* I'm just going, Miss Frame.

JESSIE (*pleasantly*). Good; then I can see you to the door.

(MILLER *follows* JESSIE *to the front door.*)

JESSIE's VOICE. Why, Leona! Come in!

MILLER's VOICE. Hello, there, Miss Richards.

(EMIL *listens to the voices in the hall, looks quickly around the room, then goes hastily to the bay window and hides behind the draperies just as* JESSIE *and* LEONA *enter the room.*)

JESSIE. I'm so glad you dropped over. Sit down, dear.

LEONA (*without sitting*). Is Mike here yet?

JESSIE. I think he's upstairs. But before I call him, I do think you and I should have a talk. I'm leaving tomorrow, you know —and if you and Michael are to be married on Saturday—there are so many things—

LEONA. Please, Jessie.

JESSIE. Well, I mean about the house. For instance, you'll find the automatic garbage disposal very tricky. You'll have to watch Frieda—she's always putting down the wrong things.

LEONA. I'd rather not discuss it just now.

JESSIE. Really. I only thought—

LEONA. Where's Emil?

JESSIE. Why he was here a moment ago. (*Too innocently.*) Is there anything wrong, dear? Are you disturbed about something?

LEONA. Yes, I am.

JESSIE. I do wish you'd tell me. What's the boy done now?

LEONA. I'd rather talk to Mike about it.

JESSIE. Well—all right. But if you want my opinion I think you're entirely too hard on the child.

LEONA (*with astonishment*). What did you say?

JESSIE. I'll tell Michael you're here.

(*She goes up the stairs.* LEONA *watches her, then walks over to the table, finds a cigarette and lights it.* EMIL *cautiously comes out from behind the draperies, and tiptoes*

to the hall. He is on the first step of the stairs when LEONA *turns and sees him.*)

LEONA (*sharply*). Emil! (EMIL *stops.*)

EMIL. If you will please excuse me, Miss Richards, I will go up and change my clothes.

LEONA. Come back here!

(EMIL *comes slowly back into the room.*)

EMIL. You have come to report on my conduct. But you're too late. I have already told him everything.

LEONA. I'm sure. In your own inimitable fashion.

EMIL. I don't know what that word means.

LEONA. When did you write those obscene things about me on the sidewalk?

EMIL (*calmly*). Uncle Michael has accepted the fact that my conduct will become satisfactory.

LEONA. It was after I sent you home for fighting, wasn't it?

EMIL. I think you are confused. I do not write on sidewalks.

LEONA. Come here. (EMIL *does not move.*) I said come here. (EMIL *obeys reluctantly.* LEONA *reaches into his coat pocket and takes out a piece of chalk.*) Why are you carrying this chalk?

EMIL. I can carry chalk. This is a free country.

LEONA (*angrily*). Then you did write it.

EMIL. It's a lie! A Jewish lie! . . . A Jewish lie from a Jewish whore!

(LEONA *slaps him, hard. There is silence as they stare at each other with burning hatred. Then* EMIL *turns and, shoulders back, walks stiffly towards the stairs. As he reaches the landing, he meets* MICHAEL *coming down.* MICHAEL *stops for a moment, looks at him curiously.* EMIL *passes him without a word.* MICHAEL *comes down the stairs and into the room. He looks at* LEONA *questioningly.*)

LEONA (*her voice trembling*) That's the first time I ever struck a child.

MICHAEL. What happened? (*He looks toward the stairs.*)

LEONA. It doesn't matter, really.

MICHAEL. Come on—tell me.

LEONA. No—just another of his nasty little deeds. He wanted to make me angry, and like a fool I let him succeed.

MICHAEL. Maybe it will do him good.

LEONA. It never does any good to lose your temper.

MICHAEL. Don't let it throw you. On the whole, I think the kid's improving.

LEONA (dryly). You don't say.

MICHAEL. I talked to him for a long time this afternoon.

LEONA. Sure. I talk to him for a long time every afternoon.

MICHAEL. Maybe you don't know how to handle him.

LEONA. Do you?

MICHAEL. Well—he asked if he could pay for having the picture mended. He's going to mow the lawn to earn the money.

LEONA. Isn't that just ducky.

MICHAEL. He also asked me about his father. I haven't talked to him about Karl, you know. I've waited for him to ask. And today he asked. (Eagerly.) Do you realize what that means? Curiosity for the facts is beginning to percolate in that little brain. I told him Reiss's story of Karl's death. And I really think it got him.

LEONA. You do?

MICHAEL. Oh, of course, he had reservations, but for the first time he began to wonder.

LEONA. Or he's just getting more clever. Asking you to tell him about his father was a stroke of genius.

MICHAEL. Now wait a minute, Lee—

LEONA. After today's exploits, he knew there'd be repercussions. So he gets ready for them by ingratiating himself with you. And, my God, he succeeds!

MICHAEL. You're way off, darling. You're way off. By the time I got through with him—

LEONA. You mean by the time he got through with you. . . . We've got to see this thing clearly, Mike. We've considered

him a child, more or less like other children. Being rational people, we've treated him as if he were a normal human being. And he isn't. (She shrugs.) Oh, I grant you he's changing—outwardly. He's given up clicking the heels and heiling Hitler. But inwardly, he hasn't changed at all. He's just become more cunning, more shrewd. As far as he's concerned, we're still the enemy. So, he's got to split us up. He's got to turn us against each other. Divide and conquer!

(MICHAEL laughs.)

MICHAEL. Now you're really way off! Come on, relax. (He puts his arms around her.) Let's wait until we're married before we get divided and conquered.

(Tears come into LEONA's eyes.)

LEONA. I haven't got any handkerchief. (MICHAEL gives her one.) I'm sorry, Mike. It's silly to get emotional, and I'm ashamed of it. But that child frightens me. He never cries. No matter what happens to him, he won't cry.

MICHAEL. Old Teasdale's theory of the regenerative value of tears.

LEONA. Exactly. Whatever he feels, he keeps locked up inside of him. That isn't healthy. And there's nothing spontaneous about his being bad. He plans it. There's something evil about him.

MICHAEL. Sure. He's a bad boy. But you're talking as if he were a monster.

LEONA. No. Just a Nazi.

MICHAEL (patiently). Darling, he's a child. You've handled problem children before.

LEONA. Plenty of them. But I could always get to the root of the problem. Malnutrition — a drunken father — a neurotic mother. We understand those things. We know how to remove the cause, or how to help the child overcome his obstacles. . . . But Emil isn't just a case of maladjustment. He's perfectly adjusted—but to a Nazi society! He's been taught contempt for people who don't use force. He's been taught that Americans are soft. And sure enough, we've been soft with him. He's found that he can push us around. And he'll go on pushing us around until we give him the one answer he understands —a licking.

MICHAEL That's what you said on the telephone.

LEONA. And I'm still saying it. . . . Oh yes, I know. We don't beat children. It's passé, outmoded. A great way to relieve the feelings of the parent, but no good for the child. I can quote you three dozen child psychologists. *(Insistently.)* But it's long overdue, Mike. A licking. Not in anger, not in haste. But a deliberate, carefully planned licking.

MICHAEL. Sure, revert to that good old American custom. Irate papa takes recalcitrant offspring to the wood-shed. Do you favor the harness strap or the peach whip, Mrs. Gilhooley? *(LEONA turns away impatiently.)* All right—so we give him a beating. And what does that do? It's merely a confession of failure. And I don't think we've failed yet.

LEONA. Well, we're pretty close to it. . . . May I quote a Michael Frame proverb of five years ago?—"The democracies must stand together and take action."

MICHAEL *(smiling)*. I'll give you one more ancient than that. Old Chinese saying. "Beat your child at least once a day. If you don't know the reason, the child does."

LEONA *(bitterly)*. Aren't you funny. Very funny.

MICHAEL. Hm-hm. I'm funny and you're stubborn.

LEONA. *I'm* stubborn?! Oh, my God! *(She bursts into laughter. MICHAEL kisses her.)* Thank you.

MICHAEL. Oh, it's nothing, really.

LEONA. You're too damn charming. That's the trouble with *you*.

MICHAEL *(sagely)*. Sure.

LEONA. I mean it. You've always found it very easy to make people love you. Just use your charm, and you can persuade them to your point of view—you think. Of course, it's a wonderful method when it works. It's why you've been the most popular teacher on the campus.

MICHAEL *(mockingly)*. Why, Miss Richards.

LEONA. With college students, it's fine. Amuse them, charm them. Make them

admire you as a witty fellow. . . . But Emil Bruckner isn't one of your students.

MICHAEL. Oh, oh. Here it comes again.

LEONA. Mike, for once you're going to have to get tough.

MICHAEL. Great! Instead of using my head, I get out the rubber truncheon and start playing Storm Trooper!

LEONA *(impatiently)*. Don't be stupid! Are the Nazis the *only* ones who can use force? Do you think our soldiers in Europe will be Storm Troopers?

MICHAEL. Our soldiers won't go around beating up children!

(There is an angry silence. Then LEONA speaks deliberately.)

LEONA. All right, Mike. All right. If you're so squeamish about it—

MICHAEL *(flaring)*. Squeamish, hell! I'm not squeamish! This is a matter of principle!

LEONA. You're exactly right! It *is* a matter of principle. But I've got principles, too!

MICHAEL. I see. Would you be willing to give him a beating?

LEONA. You're damn right! In fact, if you don't, I will!

MICHAEL. You don't mean that?!

LEONA. Oh, don't I! Just give me the chance!

(MICHAEL stares at her.)

MICHAEL. Do you realize, Lee, you sound as if you wanted to get even with the child.

LEONA. That's a hell of a thing to say.

MICHAEL. I mean it. You're taking it personally.

LEONA. Of course I take it personally! You should, too! On Saturday I'm coming to live in this house. I'm going to be your wife. *(Suddenly.)* Or am I?

MICHAEL. Now, Lee, take it easy. We can work this out.

LEONA. Can we? I thought we could. That's why I came here this afternoon. But we don't seem to be working it out, do we?

MICHAEL. Well we haven't tried yet. So far, you've simply delivered an ultimatum.

LEONA. All right. An ultimatum. That's it exactly. I can't live in the same house with that boy!

MICHAEL (angrily). That's a fine way to work it out. Just take an absolute attitude.

LEONA. What are *you* doing?

MICHAEL. What do you expect me to do? Say yes to anything you propose, whether I like it or not? (LEONA *turns away.*) Remember, I'm responsible for the boy, too. Much more than you are.

LEONA. All right. You *be* responsible for him. You can count me out. (*She starts to cry.*) I'm sorry, Mike. I'm sorry. (*She turns and hurries out.*)

MICHAEL. Lee!

(*She slams the front door behind her.* JESSIE *comes down the stairs; she watches* MICHAEL *curiously as he turns away and slumps into a chair; then she comes slowly into the room.*)

JESSIE (carefully). You look tired, Michael. (MICHAEL *nods, does not answer.*) You worked awfully late last night. I heard you come in. (*She wanders back of* MICHAEL's *chair, lays a sisterly hand on his shoulder.*) Are you upset about something? I hope there's no trouble.

MICHAEL. Shut up, Jessie.

(*She withdraws her hand, but does not take offense.*)

JESSIE (after a moment). I couldn't get a drawing room on the train. Well, it won't be the first time I've slept in a lower berth. I've done it before and I can do it again.

MICHAEL (absently). You're a brave girl.

JESSIE. Michael, do you realize I'm leaving tomorrow? Does *Leona* realize it? I tried to talk to her. I'm sure she doesn't even know where we keep the linen. . . . Anyway, the house is clean—ready for her. Frieda and I have done our best. Except this room. This room never seems to be quite straight. (*She sighs.*) But I guess you like it that way. And that's all that matters.

MICHAEL. Just so the house is clean.

JESSIE (after a moment). Tell me, Michael. What is it? Can I help you?

MICHAEL. No.

JESSIE. Would you like me to stay? . . . I don't have to go. I can always cancel the reservations.

MICHAEL. All right.

JESSIE. What does that mean?

MICHAEL. If you want to, stick around. It's up to you.

JESSIE. If you need me, Michael. If you want me. (*She crosses to* MICHAEL *and again puts a hand on his shoulder.*) Of course I'll stay, dear. I was only leaving because I felt I wasn't wanted. But you know I'll always stand by when you're in trouble.

MICHAEL. All right, Jessie. All right. (*He rises.*) I'm going up and lie down for a while.

JESSIE. Have a good nap, dear. I'll call you for dinner. It looks like a very good roast. And this time I'm doing it *your* way— with garlic; I remember you—

(*She breaks off as she sees that* MICHAEL's *attention has been arrested.* EMIL *is coming down the stairs. He has washed, combed his hair, and changed his clothes. He comes into the room and looks around uneasily.*)

EMIL. Has Miss Richards gone? (*No answer from* MICHAEL. EMIL *picks up the book which* MICHAEL *gave him, and speaks with careful innocence.*) Uncle Michael, I've begun to read the book. I'm on page seven.

(MICHAEL *still does not answer.* JESSIE *comes to* EMIL's *rescue.*)

JESSIE. You look very nice, Emil. Doesn't he look nice, Michael? (MICHAEL *gives* JESSIE *a quick look; she turns back to* EMIL.) Did you hang up your clothes?

EMIL. Yes, Aunt Jessie. (*He takes her hand.*)

JESSIE. That's a good boy. (*Brightly.*) He *is* trying, Michael. You remember what you said—we must love Emil? First thing you know, I'll be loving him, not for Karl's sake, nor Mary's, but for himself

(MICHAEL, *ignoring her, walks over to* EMIL.)

MICHAEL (*grimly*). Apparently you're willing enough to exercise your winning ways on Jessie. Why can't you try them on Miss Richards?

EMIL. I try to please Aunt Jessie because she is reasonable. She would never slap me in the face.

(MICHAEL *looks at* EMIL *for a moment, then turns, enters the hall and goes upstairs.* JESSIE *waits until* MICHAEL *is out of ear-shot.*)

JESSIE. Did she slap you?

EMIL. It is the only time a woman ever dared slap me. But I am glad. Now I do not have to apologize for hating her.

JESSIE. You mustn't hate her, Emil—your Uncle Michael is very unhappy.

EMIL. Yes?

JESSIE. I don't know what happened, but—

EMIL. You see, I told you. They are incompatible. That is a word I learned yesterday. Then you are going to stay, no?

JESSIE. Yes. Your Uncle Michael has asked me to stay. He needs me.

EMIL (*triumphantly*). Good!

JESSIE. Does that please you, Emil?

EMIL. But of course. (JESSIE *takes the boy in her arms affectionately; after a moment* EMIL *pulls away.*) You must not show me too much affection. Uncle Michael will think that you are encouraging me to be rude to Miss Richards. (*With an ominous look.*) It would be unfortunate if he were to think that.

JESSIE. Emil! But I'm *not* encouraging you!

EMIL (*innocently*). No?

JESSIE (*anxiously*). Emil, what do you mean by that?

EMIL (*suddenly he smiles*). Don't be worried, Aunt Jessie. I love you very much. (*He kisses her hand.*)

JESSIE. I hope so, dear. I hope so. . . . Dear me. If I'm not leaving tomorrow, I'd better tell Frieda. When the children come, you can go to the door yourself.

EMIL. Aunt Jessie. Now we are compatible. You must do me a favor. Tell Frieda I am to be shown more respect!

JESSIE (*frowning*). Well! Really!

EMIL. Please!

JESSIE. If you're a good boy, she'll treat you all right.

(JESSIE *goes out.* EMIL *exultantly throws out his chest, and does an exaggerated goose step halfway across the room. Then, laughing, he runs and dives on to the couch. Lying on his back, still laughing, he kicks his legs into the air. Abruptly he stops, rises to his feet and looks toward the desk, remembering the assignment he has given himself. He glances toward the stairs, then goes to the chair on which* MICHAEL *left his jacket. He takes the desk key from the pocket, unlocks the desk drawer, removes the key-ring. He starts to take the new key off the ring. This does not prove to be such an easy task. He glances toward the stairs again, then sits down at the desk and continues to try to get the key off. Unseen and unheard by* EMIL, PAT *appears on the stairs. She is wearing her white party dress. She tiptoes stealthily down, one hand behind her back; obviously she is concealing something. She enters the living room and stops as she sees* EMIL *seated at the desk, busy with the key-ring. She watches in surprise, as he finally gets the key off, stands up and puts it in his pocket. As he does so, he is suddenly conscious of* PAT's *presence.*)

EMIL (*angrily*). Why do you sneak up like that?

PAT (*puzzled*). Why, Emil! (EMIL *moves away from the desk.*) What are you doing with Mike's keys?

EMIL (*nervously*). I wasn't doing anything.

PAT. Oh, yes you were. You took a key off and put it in your pocket. I saw you.

EMIL. You're a liar. I was just looking at them.

PAT. Now, Emil, don't be silly. You know I saw you. I was standing right there. (*She goes to the desk, still careful to keep one hand behind her back. She picks up the key-ring.*) See, Mike's new key is missing and you've got it in your pocket.

You'd better take it out of your pocket and put it right back.

EMIL. I haven't any key. (*Suddenly.*) What have you got behind your back?

PAT. Well, I can't show it to you. It's a surprise.

EMIL. Is it my present?

PAT. Well, of course it's your present. Gee, couldn't you guess that?

EMIL (*holding out his hand*). Then give it to me.

PAT (*backing away a step*). No. You put Mike's key back on the ring, and I'll give it to you.

EMIL (*with dignity*). Don't alter the subject. You're just trying to get out of giving me a present.

PAT. Oh, Emil, you're terrible. You know perfectly well I *have* to give you a present, because it's your birthday. So *there!* (*She takes her hand from behind her back and gives him a small package wrapped in white tissue paper.*)

EMIL. Thank you. (EMIL *examines the package carefully, then holds it up to his ear.*)

PAT. It's not a watch. Really, Emil, you must think I'm a millionaire. Anyway, I gave you your present. Now you've got to put back Mike's key.

EMIL (*walking away*). I haven't got any key.

PAT. All right, then. I'll go tell Mike! I'll tell him you stole his key!

EMIL (*whirling on her*). Don't you dare! Why do you want to be a little tattle-tale?!

PAT. I don't want to! But you stole his key! I'll go upstairs right now and tell him. (*She starts to go.*)

EMIL (*jumping in front of her*). Oh, no, you won't!

PAT. Get out of my way, Emil Bruckner!

EMIL (*after a moment*). If I put the key back on the ring, you will promise not to tell him?

PAT. Oh, all right. I won't tell him.

EMIL. It is a promise. We will keep each other's secrets, no? (*He takes the key from his pocket, starts to put it back.* JESSIE *comes down the stairs.*)

PAT (*seeing* JESSIE, *she suddenly starts singing very innocently*). Frère Jacques, frère Jacques—

(JESSIE *throws* PAT *a cozy smile as she goes toward the dining-room and chimes in for a line of the song.*)

PAT AND JESSIE. Dormez-vous, dormez-vous—

(JESSIE *disappears into the dining-room;* PAT *wanders over toward the couch.* EMIL *is busily restoring the key-ring to the drawer, and the desk key to* MICHAEL'S *pocket.*)

PAT. Sonnez les matines, sonnez les matines— (PAT *looks toward the dining-room to make sure* JESSIE *has gone.*) Ding, dong, dang— (*She turns to* EMIL *reassuringly.*) Okay. All clear.

EMIL (*crossing to the couch*). There. Now it is all forgotten. (*He holds out his hand.*) We can shake hands on it. You have promised not to tell Uncle Michael.

PAT. Unless he asks me!

EMIL. But you promised!

PAT. But I didn't cross my heart! You didn't even ask me to! (*She shoves him playfully onto the couch.*)

EMIL (*bewildered*). Why should one cross one's heart?

PAT. Well, unless you cross your heart, a promise doesn't count. Gee, you ought to know that by this time.

EMIL (*rises from the couch and grabs her by the arms*). You promised! To make a promise is to make a contract!

PAT. Let go of me, Emil, or I'll kick you in the shins! I'm not afraid of you!

EMIL (*through clenched teeth*). All right then. Cross your heart! Cross your heart, or I'll kill you!

PAT. Aw, nuts! Stop talking like that, Emil! You know you can't scare me!

EMIL (*ominously*). If you will not make a contract, it will be very bad for you. You promised not to tell Uncle Michael!

PAT. Well, maybe I will and maybe I won't! Maybe I ought to tell Mike anyway! I don't like the way you're acting! You seem awfully funny!

JESSIE's VOICE. What's the matter, children?

PAT (calling). Oh, nothing! (She turns back to EMIL.) Aw, you get so serious about everything. Don't be such a jerk! . . . Come on, let's go down to the clubhouse. and see if Frieda fixed everything like I told her. When those guys get here, Aunt Jessie can let them in. (At the cellar door.) Come on, Emil.

(She goes down into the cellar. EMIL hesitates a moment. He goes to the foot of the stairs, looks up nervously. Then he goes to the cellar door which PAT has left open.)

EMIL (calling down the stairs). Are you going to tell him?

PAT's VOICE (from the cellar in a taunting sing-song). Maybe I will and maybe I won't!

(EMIL comes back into the room and looks around desperately. His eyes go to the brass book-end on MICHAEL's desk. He crosses quickly to the desk, picks up the book-end, and, holding it behind him, goes through the cellar door, closing it after him. After a moment or two, the doorbell rings. It rings again, and a third time. FRIEDA enters from the kitchen and goes through the hall toward the front door. The moment she disappears, EMIL looks out cautiously from the cellar door, closes the door behind him, and comes hurriedly into the living room. He nervously brushes his forehead with his sleeve, then, attempting not to betray his agitation, he stands rigidly erect, waiting to receive the guests. We have already heard FRIEDA opening the front door, and the sound of her voice.)

FRIEDA's VOICE. All right, boys. Glad to see you.

(FRIEDA reappears in the hallway followed by three boys: DENNIS, BUTLER and TOMMY. They are all about EMIL's age. Each carries a package rather awkwardly in his hand. They see EMIL, and stand reluctantly in the hallway.)

FRIEDA. Go on in, boys. Make yourselves at home. (She looks at EMIL, who stands rigidly facing his guests.) Well, you're lucky. Three of them, anyway. (She goes out to the dining room. The three boys come hesitantly into the room.)

DENNIS (gloomily). Hello, dope.

EMIL (with excessive politeness). Welcome. I am pleased to see you.

BUTLER. It ain't mutual. Here. (He thrusts his package at EMIL. The other two boys do the same thing, silently.)

EMIL. Thank you. You are most kind.

TOMMY. Skip it. It wasn't our idea.

DENNIS (warningly). Shut your trap, Tommy.

BUTLER (looking around). Where's Pat?

TOMMY. She said there'd be cake and ice cream. Where is it?

DENNIS. Let's get Pat. Where is she? Downstairs? (He starts for the cellar door.)

EMIL. No—no—! She is upstairs! She will be down. Please be seated.

BUTLER. Ah, go squat yourself.

(EMIL puts down the packages.)

TOMMY. Well, why don't you open them?

DENNIS. He's got to wait for Pat.

BUTLER (scrutinizing EMIL). What's the matter, jerk? You look sick.

TOMMY. Something he ate, we hope.

(JESSIE comes in from the dining room.)

JESSIE. Ah, here you are, children! (She starts to shake hands with the boys; EMIL crosses nervously to the fireplace.) How are you, Dennis? So nice of you to come and help us celebrate Emil's birthday. Butler. glad to see you. And Tommy. How's little Tommy today?

TOMMY (a glance at EMIL). Not so hot.

JESSIE. Well, that's too bad. You mean you won't be able to eat any cake?

TOMMY. I'll recover.

(EMIL is moving toward the hall; he stops short as FRIEDA enters from the dining room, carrying the birthday cake which is adorned with twelve unlighted candles. EMIL watches her, horror-stricken, as she goes towards the cellar door.)

FRIEDA *(to* DENNIS, *indicating the cellar door).* Please—

DENNIS *(opening the cellar door for her).* Oh, sure.

*(*EMIL *gestures helplessly, as if to stop* FRIEDA, *as she goes through the cellar door; then he stands transfixed in the hallway,* TOMMY *on one side of him,* DENNIS *on the other, both of the boys looking at him curiously.)*

JESSIE *(during the above).* And what do I see here? Did the boys bring all those lovely presents? Well, that was thoughtful of them. *(She looks around.)* My goodness, where's Pat? Where is she, Emil? *(*EMIL, *rooted to the spot, is unable to answer.)* Emil, I asked you a question. Where's Pat? *(Still no answer. He has begun to tremble.* JESSIE *crosses towards him.)* Emil? What's the matter with you? *(There is an hysterical scream from the cellar.* JESSIE *stops short. The boys turn. For a second, no one moves. Then* JESSIE *starts toward the cellar door.)* Good heavens!

*(*FRIEDA *appears, breathlessly.)*

FRIEDA. Professor Frame . . . Professor Frame! . . . *(She runs past* JESSIE *and up the stairs, still shouting.)* Professor Frame!

JESSIE. What is it, Frieda?!

FRIEDA. It's Pat. Professor Frame!

(She disappears around the landing. JESSIE *hurries through the cellar door.* BUTLER *and* TOMMY *start to follow, when* DENNIS *stops them.)*

DENNIS. Stay here, Tom. *(He looks at* EMIL, *who is again brushing his forehead with his sleeve.)* What happened? Did she get hurt?

EMIL. She—she must have fallen down. That's it! She must have fallen down.

*(*MICHAEL, *in his dressing gown, comes hurtling down the stairs, followed by*

FRIEDA. *He runs around to the cellar door and disappears.* FRIEDA *goes down after him.)*

TOMMY. Gosh!

BUTLER. What'll we do?

DENNIS *(to* EMIL*).* What do you think happened? Do you know anything about it?

EMIL *(faintly).* She must have fallen down.

DENNIS. How do you know?

TOMMY. Did you see her?

EMIL. No—

BUTLER. Then how do you know?

EMIL. She must have. She must have, that's all! She tripped and fell down the stairs. She—

*(*EMIL *breaks off, for* FRIEDA *has come up from the cellar with the book-end, which she now thrusts toward* EMIL.*)*

FRIEDA *(grimly).* Yes—?

(For an instant EMIL's *eyes are held by the book-end. Then from the cellar stairs we hear* JESSIE *sob:)*

JESSIE's VOICE. Oh, Michael—!

*(*FRIEDA *and the boys turn, as* MICHAEL *appears, carrying the limp figure of* PAT. JESSIE *follows him.* MICHAEL *sees* EMIL, *and for a moment he stops, his eyes meeting* EMIL's *with accusative hatred.)*

EMIL *(choking).* She must have fallen down.

*(*MICHAEL *turns and carries* PAT *up the stairs,* JESSIE *following.* EMIL *starts to babble hysterically:)*

EMIL. She must have fallen down! She hurt herself! She fell down! SHE FELL DOWN!! *(*EMIL *suddenly turns and sees the open window. He runs wildly out the window.)*

CURTAIN

ACT THREE

SCENE: *The same. It is six o'clock the next morning. Outside, a dull, gray sky.*

AT RISE: FRIEDA *is uncrating the large portrait of Karl Bruckner, which has been mended. She takes it out of the crate, tears off the wrapping paper, and looks at the picture. Then she carries it over to the fireplace.* MICHAEL *is coming slowly down the stairs. He is partly dressed and wears a dressing gown.* FRIEDA *leans the picture against the fireplace, face outward, and turns to* MICHAEL *as he comes into the room.*

FRIEDA. Is she all right this morning?

MICHAEL. I hope so. She's gone back to sleep. (MICHAEL *tries the desk drawer and finds it locked. His jacket is still over the chair where he left it the day before. He takes the desk key from the jacket pocket, unlocks the drawer. He finds that his key-ring is still there.*)

FRIEDA. Poor darling. So many stitches on that dear little head.

MICHAEL. The doctor is coming again this morning.

FRIEDA. When I found her there, I thought he'd killed her.

MICHAEL (*he looks at the key-ring, then puts it in the pocket of his dressing gown*). Well, he tried.

FRIEDA. The police called just a little while ago. They wanted to know if he came back here. They haven't been able to find him at all. I hope they catch him.

MICHAEL. They will. He can't get far. (*He takes the morning newspaper from the desk.*)

FRIEDA. They got it in the newspaper, all right. There on the front page. Wouldn't you expect a bigger headline, though?

MICHAEL. It's big enough? How about some coffee?

FRIEDA. It's all ready. I'll bring it in. (*She picks up the wrapping paper and the crate.*) They patched the picture real good, Professor. I'll hang it later.

MICHAEL. Don't bother.

FRIEDA. No? (*She gives* MICHAEL *a quick look.*) I'll get that coffee.

(*She goes out.* MICHAEL *puts down the newspaper and picks up the telephone.*)

MICHAEL (*into telephone*). Walnut—five, four, seven, one . . . Hello, Lee. Yes, it's me. I'm not going to apologize for waking you. Yes, Jessie told me last night that you called. We hope she'll be all right. It may be no more than a laceration of the scalp . . . Lee, will you come over? . . . I'll expect you. (*He puts down the telephone, glances around aimlessly, then goes to the window and looks out. After a moment, he turns and wanders restlessly towards the couch. He stops, picks up a book. It is the book he gave* EMIL *to read. He puts the book back in the shelves. Turning away, he notices the birthday packages, which are still on his desk. He picks one of them up, examines it absently, puts it down. His eyes go over to the picture. He walks over slowly and turns the portrait to the wall.* FRIEDA *enters from the pantry with a small tray. She puts it down on a table, pours a cup of coffee, hands it to* MICHAEL.*)

FRIEDA. Here you are, Professor. I made it good and strong.

(MICHAEL *takes the coffee and starts to drink it, standing up.*)

MICHAEL. Frieda, do you know anything about Fred Miller?

FRIEDA (*frowning*). Fred Miller?

MICHAEL. Do you know anything about him?

FRIEDA (*reluctantly*). Well, I'm not sure. I scarcely know him, Professor, I—

MICHAEL. This is important, Frieda. Miller was here yesterday; he met Emil. From what Pat tells me, Emil wanted exactly what Miller wanted—the key to my laboratory.

FRIEDA. Good heavens!

MICHAEL. But he didn't get it.

FRIEDA. I guess the boy was too frightened at the last minute. I remember—just before he ran out—he had such a look.

MICHAEL. Among your German friends, did you ever hear anything about Miller that you didn't like?

FRIEDA. I will tell you. It was in Chicago —you remember I used to go to Chicago to visit my cousin. I don't go any more —I don't like my cousin very much—

MICHAEL. Yes?

FRIEDA. Once she took me to a German picnic—and I went. I was very ignorant. And when I got there, that was no German picnic. *(Unhappily.)* That was the *Bund.* Professor, I was at a Bund meeting.

MICHAEL. And Miller was there?

FRIEDA. With my own eyes I saw him.

MICHAEL. Maybe he was as innocent as you were.

FRIEDA. Innocent? Then why was he sitting on the platform?

MICHAEL *(after a moment).* Do you know anything else about him?

FRIEDA. No. But I don't like him.

MICHAEL. Why not?

FRIEDA. Until the war began, he was for Hitler. Now he doesn't say anything. He's afraid, of course. But I tell you, Professor, there's something about him— *(She hesitates.)*

MICHAEL. Yes?

FRIEDA. Well—I think he hates himself because people look upon him as a janitor. He would like to make himself important.

MICHAEL. All right, Frieda. Thanks.

FRIEDA *(curiously).* Do you think Miller made a connection with our young Nazi?

MICHAEL. I'm not sure. But let's keep it to ourselves.

FRIEDA. Don't worry, Professor. I won't tell a soul.

MICHAEL *(he puts down his coffee).* Will you make me some toast?

FRIEDA. I'll do better than that. Waffles. You didn't eat a thing last night. *(As she starts out,* JESSIE *appears on the stairs.)* Can I get you some coffee, Miss Frame?

JESSIE. No, Frieda. *(FRIEDA goes out and JESSIE comes wearily into the room. She wears a bathrobe; her face is pale, drawn.)* She's still sleeping.

MICHAEL. Good.

JESSIE. What happens now, when the police catch him?

MICHAEL. We'll leave that up to the police.

JESSIE *(bitterly).* Well, I hope they lock him up for life. Loathsome little beast.

MICHAEL. Take it easy.

JESSIE. I didn't sleep a wink last night.

MICHAEL. Nor did I.

JESSIE. I knew you should never have brought that boy from Germany. I warned you.

MICHAEL *(with a curious glance).* Yes, Jessie, you warned me.

JESSIE. I hated that child the moment I laid eyes on him. And now, the way things have turned out— Well, I was right.

MICHAEL. Yes?

JESSIE. This can be a lesson to us. There's only one answer. Exterminate every last German.

MICHAEL. Even if they have nice manners? And they all hang up their clothes?

JESSIE. Why, Michael. What do you mean?

MICHAEL. You weren't hating Emil yesterday. You weren't recommending his extermination then.

JESSIE. But after all, I only—

MICHAEL. In fact, you seemed suddenly to have grown quite fond of him. You were talking about loving him for himself.

JESSIE. Michael, I never did any such—

MICHAEL. Yes, you did. Why was it, Jessie? *(JESSIE looks miserable.)* Why did you suddenly discover such virtues in Emil? Tell me.

JESSIE *(weakly).* Really, Michael. I don't know what you're talking about. *(She sinks onto the couch.)*

MICHAEL *(persistently).* Yes, you do. You *must* have had some reason. He was sent home from school yesterday for fighting, and lo and behold, you were treating him like a new-found friend. Why was it? *(JESSIE does not answer.)* Tell me, Jessie. Was it because he hated Lee? And you resented her, too? (JESSIE *takes a handkerchief from the pocket of her bathrobe and begins to weep.* MICHAEL *sits down beside her.*) Suppose you tell me, Jessie. Let's get this out in the open.

JESSIE. It's true, Michael. It's all true. That's why I couldn't sleep last night. I let the child deceive me.

MICHAEL (*sympathetically*). He found the weak spot in all of us.

JESSIE. It was worse than that. I let him talk against Leona. I let him brag that he would make it impossible for you to get married. Then, when he almost killed Pat, it was as if I had been in league with a murderer . . . Michael, I wasn't really opposed to your marriage. You know that. Of course, it shocked me, it hurt me. I'm a selfish woman, I suppose. But I was prepared to go away. I wanted you to be happy—all my life, that's all I've ever wanted.

MICHAEL. Yes, I know. And I've been pretty rough with you sometimes.

JESSIE (*smiling wanly*). No; just thoughtless. You see, Leona is so different from me. That's what shocked me, somehow. It's hard for me to like people who are different. She can't possibly take care of you the way I have. . . . It's water under the bridge now, but she never even asked me where we keep the linen. (*Apologetically.*) That's silly, isn't it? (*She rises.*) As soon as Pat is better, I'm going to leave for Mexico as I planned.

MICHAEL. You don't have to do that, Jessie.

JESSIE. Yes, I do, because I want you and Leona to get married. (MICHAEL *walks over and kisses her on the cheek.*) Dear Michael . . . (*She smiles.*) Well—now I'm going up and sleep. (*The doorbell rings.*)

MICHAEL. Do that.

(JESSIE *starts out as* FRIEDA *comes out of the kitchen and goes towards the front door.*)

JESSIE (*pulling her bathrobe around her modestly*). Wait till I get upstairs, Frieda.

(*She hurries up the stairs;* MICHAEL *sits down on the couch wearily. We hear* FRIEDA *open the front door.*)

FRIEDA'S VOICE. *Ach, Gott!*

MILLER'S VOICE. It's all right. Just let us in.

(MILLER *comes into the room, roughly pulling* EMIL *with him.* MILLER *wears a look of righteous indignation.* EMIL—*all his bravado, all his self-assurance gone— is a thoroughly terrified little boy.* FRIEDA *remains in the hallway.* MICHAEL *has risen from the couch.*)

MILLER. Here he is, Professor. This is a terrible thing. I'm more shocked than I can possibly say. . . . If I just knew how to express my sympathy, sir. Such a tragedy. Such a great tragedy.

MICHAEL. Thank you.

EMIL. Uncle Michael—

MICHAEL (*harshly*). Keep away from me, Emil.

MILLER. The little murderer. Yes, he confesses it. We'll have to turn him over to the police.

MICHAEL. He told you he—killed her?

MILLER. Yes.

MICHAEL. I see. . . . Have you seen the morning paper, Fred? (*He folds the newspaper to conceal the headline from* MILLER.)

MILLER. I didn't stop for nothing, sir— after he told me what he had done. I know how you're feeling, Professor. It's tragic enough without the newspapers—I don't wonder— (*To* EMIL.) Here—get over there and sit down where we can keep an eye on you. (*He puts* EMIL *on the couch.*)

MICHAEL. How'd you happen to catch him?

MILLER. Do you know what he did? He came to my house! Can you imagine that? At five-thirty this morning.

MICHAEL. Where was he last night?

MILLER. Wandering in the woods, he says. (*Smoothly.*) I guess you'd like to know why he came to me.

MICHAEL. I expect he was hungry.

MILLER. I expect he was. But why should he come to *me?*

MICHAEL. Well?

MILLER. I tell you, the only way I can figure it—yesterday I spent a few minutes chatting with him—just to be friendly, you know how it is.

MICHAEL. That's natural enough.

MILLER. Thank you, Professor. I wanted to clear that up before we took him to the police.

MICHAEL. Why?

MILLER. Well, if a person'll commit murder, he'll lie about anything. He'll implicate anybody he can—and I've got my reputation to think of. Nineteen years with this University.

MICHAEL. You reminded me of those nineteen years yesterday.

MILLER (a trifle nervous). Well, I'm very proud of my record. (He looks at EMIL.) God knows why he did it, Professor. I think he's insane. He'll give the police a dozen cock-and-bull stories, I know. He's tried them on me already, and they don't make sense, believe me.

MICHAEL. You have no idea why he did it?

MILLER. It's beyond me, sir.

MICHAEL (insistently). Are you sure?

MILLER. I really can't figure it.

MICHAEL. You should have read the morning paper, Fred. (He hands MILLER the newspaper.)

MICHAEL. You see, he didn't kill her.

EMIL (rising). Then she is all right! It was just an accident—and it was not my fault—!

MILLER (turning on EMIL). You little fool, you told me—

MICHAEL. You seem upset, Fred.

MILLER (hastily). No—I'm so happy, Professor. I am so happy. Your little girl is going to be all right. That's wonderful. You realize I am very happy?

EMIL (turning on MILLER venomously). You traitor! You're just trying to save yourself! You're a coward!

MICHAEL. Shut up, Emil!

MILLER. You see, Professor? He's likely to say anything. We'll probably never find

out why he did it. Even your little girl may be confused. The blow on the head—

MICHAEL. No. She knows why Emil hit her. She told me exactly what Emil was trying to do. She's not confused.

MILLER. No, you are right; she is a smart girl. (Indicates EMIL accusingly.) But don't let this one fool you. Well, I have to be going now. I'm late. I'll leave him here for you to deal with as you think best. And if you want me for any testimony, just remember you can count on me, Professor. I'll be in my office most of the day. . . . Well, I'm certainly glad the little girl is going to be all right. Good-bye. (MILLER starts out.)

MICHAEL (curtly). Fred.

(MILLER turns back uneasily.)

MILLER. Yes, Professor?

MICHAEL (taking the key-ring from his pocket). What did you expect to find in the laboratory?

MILLER. All I wanted was to clean up. You know that.

MICHAEL. Did you hope to stumble on something that would make you a big, important spy?

MILLER. Please, Professor—

MICHAEL. You've been a Nazi sympathizer.

MILLER. Oh, no—no. I—

MICHAEL. And you might be a Nazi agent. But whatever you are, you're a stupid fool.

(FRIEDA, in hallway, nods.)

MILLER. Professor Frame! I've never done anything. I've been here nineteen years. I'm a good American citizen. (Indicating EMIL.) It was all his idea—I didn't—

MICHAEL. All right, all right. I'm going to notify the Federal Bureau of Investigation. They'll look up your record.

MILLER (after a moment). So you're going to have me dismissed.

MICHAEL. If you've kept your nose clean, you'll be safe.

MILLER. All right— (He starts to go, sees FRIEDA in the hallway watching him suspiciously, then turns back to MICHAEL with *angry bravado.)* All right, but let me tell you something! Sure I wanted that key. But what if I did? And suppose I did want to get into that laboratory—and not to clean it up. There's nothing you can prove, because I haven't done anything! You professors, with your many books and your great thoughts! Educated fools, that's what you are!

MICHAEL. Get the hell out of here!

MILLER. Just because I'm a janitor you think you can wipe your feet on me! Always being polite to you! Always cleaning up your messes! Well, some day we'll see who are the janitors around here! This war isn't over yet! *(He hurries out.)*

FRIEDA *(to MICHAEL).* I think the F.B.I. will find out plenty! *(She looks contemptuously at EMIL).* Schweinhund! *(She goes out. MICHAEL turns to EMIL who is watching him anxiously.)*

EMIL. You were very clever, Uncle Michael. You trapped him. And you were right, entirely right. He is a Nazi.

MICHAEL. Shut up!

EMIL *(trembling, he continues nervously).* He is guilty, Uncle Michael. He made me do everything! He said he would report me—the Gestapo—he frightened me—

MICHAEL *(ominously).* You'd better be frightened, Emil—you have good cause to be frightened—

EMIL *(moving towards the stairs; his voice takes a higher pitch).* Ask Aunt Jessie! She loves me! She knows I tried to be good! She's my friend—that's why I was rude to Miss Richards! It was all for Aunt Jessie!

MICHAEL. Come away from those stairs! Pat's up there asleep! *(EMIL springs towards the stairs and reaches the second step.)* Come away from those stairs!!

EMIL *(crouched on the stairs, screams hysterically).* I won't! You can't make me! I'll scream! I'll wake her up! Then she will die! I'll tell everybody you beat me—and you killed her— *(MICHAEL leaps for the boy and grabs him by the throat.)* Uncle Michael—don't hurt me— *(MICHAEL throws him back into the room and goes after him again; again he gets him by the throat.)* You're a kind man—you knew my father— *(MICHAEL proceeds to choke the boy across the table behind the couch. EMIL struggles, then goes limp. MICHAEL continues to choke him. LEONA appears in the hallway. She stands stricken at what she sees. Then:)*

LEONA. Mike! *(She runs into the room, grabs MICHAEL's arm, and tries with all her strength to pull him off.)* Mike! For God's sake, Mike!! You're killing him!!!

(She grabs MICHAEL's other arm and succeeds in loosening his grip. The boy falls limp across the table. LEONA picks him up and helps him around to the couch as MICHAEL stares at him, dazed. MICHAEL slowly comes around the end of the couch, watches LEONA loosen EMIL's collar, then sinks into a chair. He puts his hands over his drawn face. After LEONA is assured that EMIL is going to be all right, she turns to MICHAEL.)

LEONA. Mike—

(MICHAEL takes his hands away from his face and looks up at her.)

MICHAEL *(tonelessly).* I wanted to kill him.

LEONA. Go upstairs, Mike, and finish dressing. *(MICHAEL rises slowly to his feet. As he turns to go, he stops, looks down at the boy on the couch.)* Go on, Mike.

(He nods obediently and starts out, LEONA watching him. He stops in the hall.)

MICHAEL *(with an effort).* Frieda's making breakfast. You can tell her—

LEONA. All right. *(MICHAEL goes up the stairs. LEONA looks at EMIL, who has put his arm over his eyes.)* How do you feel? *(EMIL takes his arm away and turns his head to look at LEONA.)* You used to do a lot of talking about the honor of dying. Well, you almost died. Was it such fun?

EMIL *(weakly).* No.

LEONA. It's more pleasant to live, isn't it? *(EMIL doesn't answer).* Sit up. Come on, sit up. You're all right. *(EMIL obeys slowly.)* Why did you do it?

EMIL. I don't know.

LEONA. I'll bet you knew yesterday. I'll bet you had lots of good reasons. You were being brave. You were being a hero.

EMIL. Leave me alone.

LEONA. Maybe those reasons don't seem so good today. (EMIL *doesn't answer.*) You know, it's a funny thing. Pat could be brave, too. She could be a hero. She could sneak up behind you and hit you over the head. But I don't think it would ever occur to her. Of course, she's not a member of the Master Race.

EMIL. Please leave me alone, Miss Richards.

(LEONA *regards* EMIL *thoughtfully, then turns and wanders away.* EMIL *wipes a corner of his mouth with the back of his hand. He looks miserably over at* LEONA, *who has stopped by the desk; she is noting the four unopened packages left there from yesterday.*)

LEONA. Dennis told me about your birthday party. (EMIL *looks away.*) You didn't open your presents.

EMIL. I don't want them.

LEONA. Well, I don't blame you. It seems a pity, though. Pat went to a lot of trouble for that party. The boys didn't want to come, you know. Pat bought the presents; all of them. And then she paid each boy twenty-five cents to come and bring the presents. (EMIL *gives* LEONA *a bewildered look.*) She had to borrow the money from me. That's how I know. It seems she spent everything her father gave her for the present she wanted to give you herself. (LEONA *picks up the smallest of the packages and appears to examine it thoughtfully.*) Pat's so affectionate. It was rather silly of her, wasn't it? (*She looks at* EMIL. EMIL *averts his eyes.* LEONA *walks over to the couch and holds out the package.*) You may as well open it. (EMIL *shakes his head.*) Do what I tell you. Open it. (EMIL *takes the package reluctantly.* EMIL *looks at her, then down at the package. He nervously begins to open it.* LEONA *watches him closely. Inside the outer tissue paper* EMIL *finds a card. He stops to read it.*) What does it say? (EMIL *looks up at her.*) Read it to me.

EMIL. "For Emil—who will now know the time, but has yet to learn the score."

LEONA. Oh, that's very good, isn't it? I wouldn't be surprised if Mike helped her write that.

EMIL (*tremulously*). It must be a watch.

LEONA. I suppose it is. Why don't you look?

(EMIL *takes off the last wrapping and opens the little case. He stares at the watch, then looks up at* LEONA.)

EMIL. With an illuminated—face. (EMIL *suddenly finds himself beginning to cry. Desperately, he clamps a hand to his mouth as if to stop the choking sobs that are engulfing him. But to no avail. He turns and presses his face into the pillows of the couch, his body shaking convulsively.* LEONA *watches him for a long moment, a look of satisfaction entering her face. From a box she deliberately takes a cigarette, lights it. She inhales deeply, carefully deposits the burnt match in an ashtray, then goes and sits down on the couch beside* EMIL. *He is still sobbing convulsively.* MICHAEL *appears on the landing, comes down the stairs and stops in the hallway. He is now fully dressed.* LEONA *rises from the sofa.*)

MICHAEL (*calling towards the kitchen*). Frieda. Come here. (MICHAEL *enters the living room, crosses to the desk and without looking at* EMIL *picks up the telephone.*) Give me the police department. (*To* FRIEDA, *as she enters.*) Take him upstairs and pack his clothes.

FRIEDA. That will be a pleasure. (*She goes to the couch.*) All right, my young Nazi. Come on. (EMIL *sits up slowly, sniffles.*) Well, come on. And you'd better blow your nose.

(EMIL *takes out a handkerchief and blows his nose.*)

MICHAEL (*into telephone*). Hello. Police Department. Sergeant Thompson, please. (*To* FRIEDA.) And don't let him out of your sight, Frieda.

FRIEDA. Don't worry about me, Professor. I'm not scared of him. (*To* EMIL.) Are you ready? Then march! (*She takes* EMIL *by the arm, leads him up the stairs.*)

MICHAEL (*into telephone*). Sergeant Thompson? This is Michael Frame. The boy is here. . . . Yes, that's right. Here in my house. He came back. . . . That's why I'm calling you. The sooner the better. . . . Good. (*He puts down the telephone and turns to* LEONA.) They'll be here in a few minutes.

LEONA (*putting out her cigarette*). Well, I suppose that's that.

MICHAEL. What else can I do?

LEONA. I don't know, but somehow I can't feel the police are the final answer.

MICHAEL. Is there any other answer?

LEONA. If it was up to me, I think I'd keep him right here in this house.

MICHAEL. I hope you're kidding.

LEONA. No. . . . He's been crying, Mike. He was crying like any other child.

MICHAEL. Very touching.

LEONA. No, but it may be revealing.

MICHAEL. What does it reveal? Alexander the Great bawled like a baby because there were no more worlds to conquer.

LEONA (*earnestly*). Don't you see, Mike? He shed tears. He's actually by way of becoming a human being.

MICHAEL. He's too late.

LEONA. I thought so, too, but I was wrong. There's a flaw in his Nazi armor.

MICHAEL. You're being sentimental. The kid finally breaks down and it touches your heart. So you become a great humanitarian. Don't be so gullible, Lee. Of course the kid cried. It was the only device he had left.

LEONA. No. I watched him. He tried not to cry. They did a good job on him, all right—those beasts. But there's one thing they didn't count on.

MICHAEL. What?

LEONA. They couldn't quite kill his wanting to love.

MICHAEL (*impatiently*). What the devil are you talking about?

LEONA. Pat.

MICHAEL (*incredulously*). You're crazy. He crowns her on the head with a brass bookend, then you say he loves her. . . . Do you think I'd consider for a moment having him in the same house with Pat? He can't stay here. It isn't safe. He's dangerous.

LEONA. How does Pat feel about it?

MICHAEL (*a trifle shocked*). You don't think I asked her!

LEONA (*gently*). So you assume that she feels as you do. Maybe what you're really saying is, how dare we have him in the same house with Michael.

(*This stops* MICHAEL, *cold*.)

MICHAEL. All right. Dare we? I tried to kill him. (*He looks at* LEONA *unhappily*.) Yesterday I didn't even want to give him a spanking. And today— Yes, it's true. I'm also thinking of myself.

LEONA (*sympathetically*). That's important. Maybe it's the *most* important.

MICHAEL. You and I are going to be married. We *are*, aren't we?

LEONA. We are indeed.

MICHAEL. You and I have got our own lives, and we've got Pat. We haven't got room for Emil Bruckner, too.

LEONA. So we just ship him off to the reformatory?

MICHAEL. Yes.

LEONA. No. . . . Oh, no, Mike. Yesterday I made a bad mistake. I walked out on something we should have faced together. That was stupid. Today you're trying to do the same thing. You don't want to face it. . . . Right now, Mike, I don't know any more than you how to handle this boy. But I know we've got to try. We can't turn our backs. We can't put him behind bars, nor simply wipe him out. You can call it pride, if you want, but I won't admit failure like that, and I won't let you. . . . And it's not just our problem. There are twelve million other children just like him in Germany. They can't all be put behind bars. They can't all be exterminated.

MICHAEL. Of course not. But what we decide for Emil Bruckner has nothing to do with post-war Germany. You're talking way up in the clouds.

LEONA. But don't you see, Mike. If you and I can't turn one little boy into a human being—then God help the world when this war is won, and we have to deal with twelve million of them!

MICHAEL. All right, then. God help the world.

(EMIL *appears on the landing, carrying his suitcase.* FRIEDA *is behind him. They come down the stairs.*)

FRIEDA. Step lively now. . . . Put your bag down there. (*To* MICHAEL.) Do you want me to keep him in the kitchen?

MICHAEL. No, he can wait here.

FRIEDA (*she leads* EMIL *to a straight-back chair just inside the room*). Sit down there. (EMIL *obeys.*) And only yesterday I was told by Miss Jessie I must treat him with greater politeness.

MICHAEL (*quietly*). You can go, Frieda.

FRIEDA (*to* EMIL). We're *all* on to you now, *Dummkopf.* If you were going to stay around here, I'd show you some politeness!

(*She goes out. For a moment there is silence.* EMIL *sits stiffly and miserably in the chair.*)

LEONA. The police are very slow, aren't they? (*She walks over towards the fireplace, glances at the back of the picture, then turns it around deliberately and looks at it.*) They did a very good job. You can hardly see where it's mended. (*She turns and looks at* MICHAEL.) Are you going to banish the father along with the son? You'll have to, you know. You can't forget about Emil, unless you get rid of Karl, too. Take his picture off the wall. Take his books off the shelves. After all, it was really his fault, wasn't it? His and all the Germans' that came before him. The sins of the children shall be visited upon the fathers unto the third and fourth generation.

MICHAEL. Damn it, Lee, will you keep quiet!

LEONA (*mildly*). Yes, Michael. And if the police would only come and take him away we could all have breakfast, couldn't we?

(MICHAEL *glares at her.* PAT *appears on the landing, and comes down the stairs. She's in her bathrobe, and there's a bandage on her head.*)

PAT (*stopping on the stairs*). Mike! Can I come down!?

(EMIL *stands up; for the moment, he is out of her line of vision.*)

MICHAEL (*turning in surprise*). Pat! What are you doing out of bed?

PAT. Well, darn it, I'm hungry. And Frieda didn't bring me anything yet.

MICHAEL. You're a sick girl. Now get back up there.

PAT. Oh, I feel fine. *Please,* Mike. (*She proceeds to come down anyway. On the third step from the bottom she stops to make her jump, then thinks better of it and walks down sedately.*) Hello, Lee. Did you hear about me?

LEONA. Yes, dear. (*She puts an arm around* PAT's *shoulder.*) Here, we'll put you over on the couch.

(LEONA *glances towards* EMIL. *Pat catches the glance and follows it. She sees* EMIL, *and regards him with strong disapproval. Calmly she walks over to him.*)

PAT. Emil Bruckner, *you stink!!* Really, you're the sneakingest coward I ever saw. (EMIL *takes the watch from his pocket, extends it to* PAT.)

EMIL (*with humility, for the first time*). I guess you want the watch back.

PAT (*judiciously*). Well, I certainly *ought* to take it back. But—no, you can keep it. But remember, I'm plenty sore.

EMIL. I'll remember.

PAT. You'd better, or you'll *really* be out of luck. You won't have *anybody* to play with.

(*The doorbell rings.*)

EMIL. I think that is the policeman. They're going to take me to jail.

PAT. Because you bopped me on the bean? (*Confidently.*) Oh, Mike won't actually let them put you in jail. Will you, Mike?

(MICHAEL *doesn't answer.* FRIEDA *goes through the hall to the front door.*)

EMIL. Well, I guess I'd better go.

PAT (*protesting in bewilderment*). Mike, you can't send him to jail. He isn't old enough. He's got to be eighteen to go to jail. Anybody knows that. (FRIEDA *reappears in the hall.* PAT *turns and sees her.*) Frieda, is that really a policeman out there?

(FRIEDA *nods solemnly.*)

MICHAEL. Tell them he'll be right out.

(FRIEDA nods and goes out.)

EMIL. Good-bye, Uncle Michael. Good-bye, Miss Richards. *(He turns to PAT.)* Good-bye, Pat. Thank you for letting me keep the watch.

(They shake hands ceremoniously.)

PAT. Oh, they just want to ask you some questions or something. They'll probably bring you right back.

EMIL. I don't think they will. *(FRIEDA enters from the front door.)* Good-bye, Frieda.

FRIEDA *(without rancor).* Good-bye, Mr. Fine Manners.

(She goes out toward the kitchen. EMIL looks back at MICHAEL a last time, then picks up his suitcase.)

MICHAEL. Emil. *(EMIL stops, turns around slowly.)* Emil, do you know why we're sending you away? *(EMIL does not answer.)* It's because I don't think there's any hope for you. You're lost. They did their job too well, the Nazis. They lied to you, day after day, year after year. They told you the same things over and over. Repetition! Repetition! They grooved your brain. They turned you into a sly and clever puppet. I doubt that even now you realize the kind of creature you are. . . . Am I wrong? Have you anything to say for yourself? *(EMIL does not answer.)* Do you still feel that you're a superior martyr? Do you still believe that your Fascist cause is invincible?

EMIL. I do not understand.

MICHAEL. I mean, don't you know you're losing? . . . There are no questions you'd like to ask as a member of the Master Race? . . . You're quite satisfied with yourself?

EMIL *(irresolutely).* Something puzzles me.

MICHAEL. Yes?

EMIL. You tricked Miller. You were much more clever than he—you made him look like a fool. And yet you are not German.

LEONA. Your Uncle is Irish, French, Swedish—

MICHAEL. A mongrel. An American.

EMIL. That is the only thing I have not been able to understand. There are times when the Americans do not have entirely the appearance of an inferior race.

(MICHAEL's eyes meet LEONA's.)

MICHAEL *(to EMIL).* Come here. Are you admitting that your Nazi teachers might have lied to you?

EMIL *(slowly).* No . . .

LEONA. Is there anything else that puzzles you, Emil? *Anything?*

MICHAEL. Give us that record about your father again. Is it still clear? Is it still sharp?

EMIL. What?

MICHAEL. Go on. Tell us about your father. In 1918 Karl Bruckner—

EMIL. In 1918 Karl Bruckner betrayed Germany on the home front. He fomented revolution. If it had not been for him and the Jewish Bolsheviks, Germany would have won the war. He was one of those— *(He falters.)*

LEONA *(watching him closely).* Go on, Emil. Tell us.

EMIL. My father was one of those who made Germany weak. He was responsible for the inflation and the Communists. He was responsible for— *(He falters again.)*

MICHAEL. Why are you stopping?

LEONA. Go on! Your father was a traitor to the Third Reich! Go on!

EMIL. He was one of those responsible for the Versailles Treaty. My father was a coward— He— *(EMIL stops completely.)*

MICHAEL. Go on! Tell us the rest! You're absolutely right! Your father was a coward! He committed suicide!

EMIL. *Is that true?*

MICHAEL. You know it's true! Your father was a stupid man! He was weak! You're right to be ashamed of him!

EMIL *(tortured).* Uncle Michael, why are you saying this?

MICHAEL *(harshly).* Because it's true! Isn't it? Karl Bruckner was a degenerate coward!

EMIL (*protesting loudly*). No! No! My father was a brave man. He *must* have been a brave man. Why else were they afraid of him? Why did they burn his books if they weren't afraid of him? (*His voice rises hysterically.*) Why did they hit me? Why did they lock me up in the dark? (EMIL *breaks off in bewilderment.*)

MICHAEL (*softly*). Who hit you, Emil?

EMIL. I—I don't know. . . .

MICHAEL. When did they lock you in the dark?

EMIL (*shaking his head in hopeless confusion*). I can't remember. . . . A long time ago. . . . Please, Uncle Michael. I'm all mixed up.

(*There is silence for a moment.*)

MICHAEL (*gently; firmly*). Why were the Nazis afraid of Karl Bruckner? Why, Emil? Why? That's what you've got to ask. Every time anybody tells you anything, you've got to ask why! In our country we're not afraid of questions. We *want* people to ask questions. . . . Lee says you can be turned into a human being. Pat seems to think so, too. Perhaps they're right. (*Very quietly.*) But get this straight, Emil. What happens is really up to you. You can be a decent member of society, if you want to. But if you insist on being a Nazi, we're just as tough as you are, and a lot tougher. We'll destroy you—along with your Nazi soldiers. . . . You'll have your choice. (*To* LEONA.) We're going to keep Emil here. I'll tell

the police we don't need them—and then we'll have breakfast.

PAT. Breakfast! Hot dog. Can I eat down here, too. I don't want to go back to bed.

MICHAEL. All right. You don't have to. (*To* EMIL.) Are you hungry?

EMIL. Yes, sir.

MICHAEL. Very well. Go out in the kitchen and tell Frieda politely that you're staying. We'll fill your stomach before we attempt your reeducation. . . . Come on, Lee. Come on, Pat. (*He goes out.*)

LEONA (*to* EMIL). We all have things to learn, Emil. (*She takes his hand.*) If we all try, some day we can all be good friends.

(*She goes out.* PAT *starts to follow, but turns back to* EMIL *who is standing motionless.*)

PAT. Say, Emil, after breakfast, do you want me to show you my stitches? (*She points to her bandaged head.*) Seven of them!

(*She goes out.* EMIL *is left alone on the stage. His eyes go to the portrait of his father. He walks over and stands looking at it irresolutely. Then he pulls the chair in front of the fireplace.* MICHAEL *reappears in the hallway and stops to watch* EMIL. *The boy takes the heavy picture and with difficulty lifts it to the chair, and then climbs on the chair himself. He is lifting the picture to the mantelpiece, and* MICHAEL *is watching him.*)

CURTAIN

WATCH ON THE RHINE

By LILLIAN HELLMAN

WATCH ON THE RHINE was produced in New York by Herman Shumlin with the following cast:

ANISE	Eda Heinemann	TECK DE BRANCOVIS	George Coulouris
FANNY FARRELLY	Lucile Watson	SARA MULLER	Mady Christians
JOSEPH	Frank Wilson	JOSHUA MULLER	Peter Fernandez
DAVID FARRELLY	John Lodge	BODO MULLER	Eric Roberts
MARTHE DE BRANCOVIS		BABETTE MULLER	Anne Blyth
	Helen Trenholme	KURT MULLER	Paul Lukas

SCENES

The living room of the Farrelly country house, about twenty miles from Washington. The time is late spring, 1940.

ACT I: Early on a Wednesday morning.

ACT II: About ten days later.

ACT III: A half hour later.

THE AUTHOR

Lillian Hellman came to New York from New Orleans. She studied at Columbia University, reviewed books, wrote articles and stories, read for a motion picture company, acted as press agent for a summer stock company in Rochester, and had the good fortune to become playreader for one of Broadway's ablest producer-directors, Herman Shumlin. It was during this period of gestation in a producing office that Miss Hellman, who had previously collaborated on a play with her good friend the critic Louis Kronenberger, came across the records of a lawsuit in Scotland. She transfigured the case into one of the most powerful realistic plays of the 1930's, The Children's Hour. *Miss Hellman's employer produced and directed it with his customary skill. The production opened on November 20, 1934 and ran for 691 performances. It also toured successfully, although not without difficulties with local censorship in Boston and other cities. Samuel Goldwyn bought it for films and engaged Miss Hellman to write the screenplay, which dispensed with the tabooed theme of inversion and ultimately acquired the title* These Three. *The experience proved that the author could also hold her own in the field of screenwriting, and she is to be credited with several powerful contributions to the screen.*

Miss Hellman's next work, the strike drama Days to Come, *fared poorly on Broadway and was withdrawn soon after its December 15, 1936 opening. That it deserved better of New York happens to be the opinion of the present editor, even if the script cannot be considered a completely realized play. Three years later, however, its author was back in the limelight with* The Little Foxes, *which incidentally supplied Tallulah Bankhead's best role in America.* Watch on the Rhine *opened on April 1, 1941, but Miss Hellman wasn't fooling; nor did the public think so.* The Searching Wind *opened on April 12, 1944, and* Another Part of the Forest *became one of the successes of the 1946 fall season. In the last-mentioned production the author also functioned as director, and it is not too much to say that Broadway would have had to go back to Harold Clurman's Group Theatre direction of Odets'* Awake and Sing *more than a decade earlier to find a better job of realistic direction.*

Miss Hellman works slowly and conscientiously on her plays, and is bent upon squeezing the last ounce of iron out of her matter. She has a quick mind and a strong spirit, minces no words, and spares no sensibilities. She is also a stern moralist. Nevertheless, Miss Hellman has maintained that she starts with persons rather than with ideas. Although there are many who would question her on that score when they reflect on the direct or indirect political bearing of much of her work, the author can point to a large list of meticulous characterizations. That she views people through a temperament that is apt to spot the unlovely side of humanity, she might concede. But only with the reservation that she is simply being truthful about the fact of evil; that there are villains who should be brought to book and weaklings whose compliance becomes complicity; that she gives affection to those who deserve it (like most of the characters of Watch on the Rhine*) and pity for those who suffer innocently (like Birdie in* The Little Foxes*). Those who contend that she favors melodramatic situations and contrivances have a better case, although Miss Hellman contends that her violent scenes are a part of reality and cannot be dismissed as melodramatic in so far as they serve a large enough purpose. Be that as it may, even her severest critics will grant that she drives ahead with unusual power, and that like the Canadian Mounties she always gets her man—or woman.*

WATCH ON THE RHINE

ACT ONE

SCENE: *The living-room of the Farrelly house, about twenty miles from Washington, D. C., on a warm July morning.*

Center stage are large French doors leading to an elevated open terrace. On the terrace are chairs, tables, a large table for dining. Some of this furniture we can see: most of it is on the left side of the terrace, beyond our sight. L. stage is an arched entrance, leading to the oval reception hall. R. stage is a door leading to a library. The Farrelly house was built in the early 19th century. It has space, simplicity, style. The living-room is large. Upstage L., a piano, downstage L., a couch, downstage R., a couch and chairs, upstage a few smaller chairs. Four or five generations have furnished this room and they have all been people of taste. There are no styles, no periods, the room has never been refurnished. Each careless aristocrat has thrown into the room what he or she brought home when grown-up. Therefore the furniture is of many periods: the desk is English, the couch is Victorian, some of the pictures are modern, some of the ornaments French. The room has too many things in it: vases, clocks, miniatures, boxes, china animals. On the L. wall is a large portrait of a big kind-faced man in an evening suit of 1900. On another wall is a large, very ugly landscape. The room is crowded. But it is cool and clean and its fabrics and woods are in soft colors.

AT RISE: ANISE, *a thin Frenchwoman of about sixty, in a dark housekeeper's dress, is standing at a table, sorting mail. She takes the mail from a small basket, holds each letter to the light, reads each postal card, then places them in piles. On the terrace,* JOSEPH, *a tall middle-aged Negro butler, wheels a breakfast wagon. As he appears,* FANNY FARRELLY *comes on from the hall. She is a handsome woman of about sixty-three. She has on a fancy, good-looking dressing-gown.*

FANNY *(stops to watch* ANISE. *Sees* JOSEPH *moving about on terrace. Calls).* Joseph!

JOSEPH. Yes'm.

FANNY *(to* ANISE). 'Morning.

ANISE *(continues examining mail).* Good morning, Madame.

JOSEPH *(comes to terrace door).* Yes'm?

FANNY. Everybody down?

JOSEPH. No'm. Nobody. I'll get your tea. *(Starts off* R. *on terrace. He returns to breakfast wagon on terrace.)*

FANNY *(calling off* R.). Mr. David isn't down yet? *(Coming into room toward* ANISE, *crosses to sofa* L.—*sits* L. *end.)* But he knows he is to meet the train.

JOSEPH *(comes in from terrace with cup of tea. To top of step* R. *of* FANNY). He's got plenty of time, Miss Fanny. The train ain't in till noon.

FANNY. Breakfast is at nine o'clock in this house and will be until the day after I die. Ring the bell.

JOSEPH *(goes* D. L. *to* FANNY; *gives her tea).* But it ain't nine yet, Miss Fanny. It's eight-thirty.

FANNY. Well, put the clocks up to nine and ring the bell.

JOSEPH *(crosses* U. C. *toward door).* Mr. David told me not to ring it any more. He says it's got too mean a ring, that bell. It disturbs folks. *(Stops at sound of her voice and turns.)*

FANNY. That's what it was put there for. I like to disturb folks.

JOSEPH. Yes'm. *(Goes* U. S. *through terrace door and off* R.)

FANNY. You slept well, Anise. You were asleep before I could dismantle myself.

ANISE. I woke several times during the night.

FANNY. Did you? Then you were careful not to stop snoring. We must finally get around *(*ANISE *brings letters to* FANNY.*)* to rearranging your room. *(*ANISE *hands her three or four letters.* FANNY *puts down tea.)* Even when you don't snore, it irritates me.

(ANISE *crosses* D. L., *sits in armchair, opens and reads French newspaper.* FANNY *begins to open mail, to read it. After a moment.*) What time is it?

ANISE. It is about eight-thirty. Joseph just told you.

FANNY. I didn't hear him. I'm nervous. Naturally. (*Continues to read.*) My mail looks dull. (*Looking at letter in her hand. Still reading.*) Jenny always tells you a piece of gossip three times, as if it grew fresher with the telling. Did you put flowers in their rooms?

ANISE. Certainly.

FANNY. David ought to get to the station by eleven-thirty.

ANISE (*patiently*). The train does not draw in until ten minutes past noon.

FANNY. But it might come in early. (*Irritably.*) It might. Don't argue with me about everything. What time is it?

ANISE (*looking at watch*). It's now twenty-seven minutes before nine. It will be impossible to continue telling you the time every three minutes from now until Miss Sara arrives. I think you are having a nervous breakdown. Compose yourself.

FANNY. It's been twenty years. Any mother would be nervous. If your daughter were coming home and you hadn't seen her, and a husband, *and* grandchildren—

ANISE. I do not say that it is wrong to be nervous. I, too, am nervous. I say only that you are.

FANNY. Very well. I heard you. *I* say that I am. (*She taps her fingers on the chair, goes back to reading her letter. Looks up.*) Jenny's still in California. She's lost her lavalliere again. Birdie Chase's daughter is still faire l'amouring with that actor. Tawdry, Jenny says it is. An actor. Fashions in sin change. In my day, it was Englishmen. I don't understand infidelity. (*Puts down letters beside her and picks up teacup.*) If you love a man, then why? If you don't love him, then why stay with him? (*Without turning, she points over her head to* JOSHUA FARRELLY'S *portrait over mantel. Sips tea.*) Thank God, I was in love. I thought about Joshua last night. Three grandchildren. He would have liked that. I hope I will. (*Sips tea again and puts down cup. Points to other letters.*) Anything in anybody else's mail?

ANISE. Advertisements for Mr. David, and legal things. For our Count and Countess, there is nothing but what seems an invitation to a lower-class Embassy tea, and letters asking for bills to get paid.

FANNY. That's every morning. (*Thoughtfully.*) In the six weeks the Balkan nobility has been with us, they seem to have run up a great many bills.

ANISE (FANNY *picks up tea*). Yes. *I* told you that. Then, there was a night-letter for Mr. David.

(*A very loud, very unpleasant bell begins to ring.*)

FANNY (*through the noise*). Really? From whom?

ANISE. From her. I took it on the telephone, and—

(*Bell drowns out her voice.*)

FANNY. Who is "her"? (*Bell becomes very loud.*) Go tell him to stop that noise—

ANISE (*crosses to terrace, calling off* R.). Joseph! Stop that bell. Miss Fanny says to stop it. (*She crosses back to chair* D. L. *and sits.*)

JOSEPH (*calls*). Miss Fanny said to start it.

FANNY (*shouts out to him*). I didn't tell you to hang yourself with it.

JOSEPH (*appears on terrace from* R.). I ain't hung. Your breakfast is ready. (*Disappears off* R.)

FANNY (*to* ANISE). Who is "her"?

ANISE. That Carter woman from Lansing, Michigan.

FANNY. Oh, my. Is she back in Washington again? What did the telegram say?

ANISE. It said the long sickness of her dear Papa had terminated in full recovery.

FANNY. That's too bad.

ANISE. She was returning, and would Mr. David come for dinner a week from Thursday? "Love," it said, "to you and your charming mother." (*To* FANNY.) That's you. I think Miss Carter from Lansing, Michigan, was unwise in attending the illness of her Papa.

FANNY. I hope so. Why?

ANISE *(shrugs)*. There is much winking of the eyes going on between our Countess and Mr. David.

FANNY *(eagerly)*. I know that. Anything new happen?

ANISE *(too innocently)*. Happen? I don't know what you mean.

FANNY. You know damned well what I mean.

ANISE. That? Oh, no, I don't think that.

JOSEPH *(appears at terrace door)*. The sausage cakes is shrinking.

FANNY *(rises, shrieks, crosses R. taking letters)*. I want everybody down here immediately. *(To JOSEPH.)* Is the car ready? *(JOSEPH nods. To ANISE.)* Did you order a good dinner? *(At hall door.)* David! *(DAVID FARRELLY, a pleasant-looking young man of thirty-nine, comes in from the entrance hall.)* Oh!

DAVID *(crossing the room. Crosses to mail table)*. Good morning, everybody.

ANISE *(to FANNY)*. Everything is excellent. You have *(JOSEPH crosses D. L. to sofa, picking up teacup.)* been asking the same questions for a week. You have made the kitchen very nervous.

(FANNY crosses behind sofa R. to U. R. C.)

DAVID *(examining mail. To JOSEPH)*. Why did you ring that air raid alarm again?

JOSEPH *(crosses U. R. C., crossing DAVID)*. Ain't me, Mr. David. I don't like no noise. Miss Fanny told me. *(Exits through terrace door U. R. C.)*

FANNY *(crosses to DAVID)*. Good morning, David.

DAVID *(calls to JOSEPH, who has gone)*. Tell Fred to leave the car. I'll drive to the station. *(To FANNY, half amused, half annoyed. Begins to read his mail.)* Mama, I think we'll fix up the chicken house for you as a playroom. We'll hang the room with bells and you can go into your second childhood in the proper privacy. *(He kisses her cheek and turns back to his mail.)*

FANNY. I find it very interesting. You sleep soundly, you rise at your usual hour —although your sister, whom you haven't seen in years, is waiting at the station—

DAVID. She is not waiting at the station. The train does not come in until ten minutes past twelve.

FANNY *(airily)*. It's almost that now.

ANISE *(turns to look at her)*. Really, Miss Fanny, contain yourself. It is twenty minutes before nine.

DAVID. And I have *not* slept soundly. And I've been up since six o'clock.

FANNY *(turns up and R.)*. Really? The Balkans aren't down yet. Where are they?

DAVID. I don't know.

ANISE *(picks up bag, crosses R.)*. There is nothing in your mail, Mr. David, only the usual advertisements.

DAVID. And for me, that is all that is ever likely to come—here.

ANISE *(stops R. before sofa. Haughtily, as she starts toward hall)*. I cannot, of course, speak for Miss Fanny. *(Crosses R. to door and stops.)* I have never opened a letter in my life.

DAVID. I know. You don't have to. For you, they fly open.

FANNY *(giggles)*. It's true. *(Two steps toward ANISE to back of chair R. C.)* You're a snooper, Anise. *(ANISE exits R. FANNY talks as ANISE moves out. Turns to DAVID.)* I rather admire it. It shows an interest in life. *(She looks up at JOSHUA's portrait.)* You know, I've been lying awake most of the night: wondering what Papa would have thought about Sara *(DAVID looks at her.)* and— He'd have been very pleased, wouldn't he? I always find myself wondering what Joshua would have felt—

DAVID. Yes. But maybe it would be just as well if you didn't expect me to be wondering about it, too. *(DAVID takes letters, crosses R., puts them on secretary, U. R.)* I wasn't married to him, Mama. He was just my father.

FANNY. My. You got up on the wrong side of the bed. *(She moves to mail table, points to mail.)* The *bills* are for our noble guests. Interesting—how *(Crosses R. to DAVID.)* many there are every morning. How much longer are they going to be with us?

DAVID *(without looking at her)*. I don't know.

FANNY. It's been six weeks. Now that Sara and her family are coming, even this house might be a little crowded— *(Starts L. He looks up at her. Quickly.)* I know I invited them. I felt sorry for Marthe, *(Moves to R. of piano keyboard.)* and Teck rather amused me. He plays good cribbage, and he tells good jokes. But that's not enough for a lifetime guest. If you've been urging her to stay, I wish you'd stop it. *(Turns to DAVID.)* They haven't any money; all right, lend them some—

DAVID. I have been urging them to stay?

FANNY. I'm not so old I don't recognize flirting when I see it.

DAVID. But you're old enough not to be silly.

FANNY. I'm not silly. I'm charming.

(MARTHE DE BRANCOVIS, an attractive woman of thirty-one or two, enters from R.)

MARTHE. Good morning, Fanny. 'Morning, David.

FANNY *(U. C. at terrace door)*. Good morning, Marthe.

DAVID *(warmly)*. Good morning.

MARTHE *(crosses U. R. to R. of FANNY)*. Fanny, darling, couldn't you persuade yourself to let me have a tray in bed and some cotton for my ears?

DAVID *(steps up to doorstep)*. Certainly not. My father ate breakfast at nine, and whatever my father did—

FANNY *(in U. C. door. Carefully, to DAVID)*. There was a night-letter for you from that Carter woman in Lansing, Michigan. She is returning and you are to come to dinner next Thursday. *(As she exits on terrace.)* C-A-R-T-E-R. *(Pronounces it carefully.)* Lansing, Michigan.

DAVID *(laughs)*. I know how to spell Carter, but thank you. *(FANNY exits through terrace door and off U. R. DAVID looks up at MARTHE.)* Do you understand my mother?

MARTHE *(crosses C.)*. Sometimes.

DAVID. Miss Carter was done for your benefit.

MARTHE *(smiles)*. That means she has guessed that I would be jealous. And she has guessed right.

DAVID *(looks at her)*. Jealous?

MARTHE *(gaily)*. I know I have no right to be but I am. And Fanny knows it.

DAVID *(carelessly)*. Don't pay any attention to Mama. *(Crosses below MARTHE to liquor table U. R. C.)* She has a sure instinct for women I like, and she begins to hammer away early. Marthe— *(Goes to decanter on side table.)* I'm going to have a drink. I haven't had a drink before breakfast since the day I took my bar examination. *(Pours himself a drink, gulps it down.)* What's it going to be like to stand on a station platform and see your sister after all these years—I'm afraid, I guess.

MARTHE. Why?

DAVID. I don't know. Afraid she won't like me— *(Shrugs.)* We were very fond of each other, but it's been a long time.

MARTHE. I remember Sara. Mama brought me one day when your Father was stationed in Paris. I was about six and Sara was about fifteen and you were—

DAVID *(two steps toward L.)*. You were a pretty little girl.

MARTHE. Do you really remember me? You never told me before. Mama and Fanny went off to gossip, and you and Sara and Anise and I sat stiffly in the garden; and I felt much too young. And then your Mama began to yell at my Mama—

FANNY *(yelling from terrace off R.)*. David! Come to breakfast.

DAVID *(as if he had not been listening)*. You know, I've never met Sara's husband. Mama did. I think the first day Sara met him, in Munich. Mama didn't like the marriage much in those days—and Sara didn't care, and Mama didn't like Sara not caring. Mama cut up about it, bad.

MARTHE. Why?

DAVID. Probably because they didn't let her arrange it. Why does Mama ever act badly? She doesn't remember ten minutes later.

MARTHE. Wasn't Mr. Muller poor?

DAVID. Oh, Mama wouldn't have minded that. If only they'd come home and let her fix their lives for them— (*Smiles.*) But Sara didn't want it that way.

MARTHE (*crosses to mail table, U. L. C.*). You'll have a house full of refugees—us and—

DAVID (*smiles*). Are you and Teck refugees? (*More toward her.*) I'm not sure I know what you're refugees from.

MARTHE (*turns to* DAVID). From Europe.

DAVID. From what Europe?

MARTHE (*smiles, shrugs*). I don't know. I don't know myself, really. Just Europe. (*Steps toward* DAVID. *Quickly, comes to him.*) Sara will like you. I like you. (*Laughs.*) That doesn't make sense, does it?

(*On her speech,* TECK DE BRANCOVIS *appears in hall,* R. *He is a good-looking man of about forty-five. She stops quickly.*)

TECK (*to* MARTHE *and* DAVID). Good morning.

(*The bell gives an enormous ring.*)

DAVID (*goes to terrace*). Good morning, Teck. For years I've been thinking they were coming for Mama with a net. I'm giving up hope. I may try catching her myself. (*Disappears, calling.*) Mama! Stop that noise. (*Exits through terrace door, goes off* R.)

(MARTHE *crosses to* R. C. *above chair.*)

TECK. I wonder if science has a name for women who enjoy noise. (*Goes to table, picks up his mail.*) Many mistaken people, Marthe, seem to have given you many charge accounts.

MARTHE (*crosses toward him, extends hand for mail*). The Countess de Brancovis. That still does it. It would be nice to be able to pay bills again— (*Crosses to front of sofa* L.)

TECK. Do not act as if I refuse to pay them, Marthe. (*Crosses to* R. *end of sofa* L.) I did not sleep well last night. I was worried. (MARTHE *sits on sofa* L.) We have eighty-seven dollars in American Express checks. (*Pleasantly, looking at her.*) That's all we have.

MARTHE (*shrugs, opening and reading letters*). Maybe something will turn up. It's due.

TECK (*carefully*). David? (*Then, as she turns to look at him.*) The other relatives will arrive this morning? (*Crosses* R. *to* U. C.)

MARTHE. Yes.

TECK (U. C.—*looks out on terrace*). I think Madame Fanny and Mr. David may grow weary of accents and charity guests. Or is the husband (*Turns to her.*) of the sister a rich one?

MARTHE. No. He's poor. He had to leave Germany in '33. (MARTHE *reads mail throughout this exchange.*)

TECK. A Jew?

MARTHE. No. I don't think so.

TECK. Why did he have to leave Germany?

MARTHE (*still reading*). Oh, I don't know, Teck. He's an anti-Nazi.

TECK. A political?

MARTHE. No, I don't think so. He was an engineer. I don't know. I don't know much about him.

TECK (*crosses to* R. *end of sofa* L.). Did you sleep well?

MARTHE. Yes. Why not?

TECK. Money does not worry you?

MARTHE. It worries me very much. But I just lie still now and hope. I'm glad to be here. (*Shrugs.*) Maybe something good will happen. (*Looks at* TECK.) We've come to the end of a road. That's been true for a long time. Things will have to go one way or the other. Maybe they'll go well, for a change.

TECK. I have not come to the end of any road.

MARTHE (*looks at him, smiles*). No? (*Rises, crosses front of* TECK *toward window* U. R. C.) I admire you.

TECK. I'm going into Washington tonight. Phili has a poker game every Wednesday evening. He has arranged for me to join it.

MARTHE (*after a pause*). Have you been seeing Phili?

TECK. Once or twice. Why not? Phili and I are old friends. He may prove useful. I do not want to stay in this country forever.

MARTHE (crosses to TECK). You can't leave them alone. Your favorite dream, isn't it, Teck, that they will let you play with them again. I don't think they will and I don't think you should be seeing Phili or that you should be seen at the Embassy.

TECK (smiles). You have political convictions now?

MARTHE. I don't know what I have. I've never liked Nazis, as you know, and you should have had enough of them. They seem to have had enough of you, God knows. It would be just as well to admit they are smarter than you are, and let them alone.

TECK (looking at her carefully, after a minute). That is interesting.

MARTHE. What is interesting?

TECK. I think you are trying to say something to me. What is it?

MARTHE. That you ought not to be at the Embassy, and that it's insane to play cards in a game with Von Seitz with eighty-seven dollars in your pocket. I don't think he'd like your not being able to pay up. Suppose you lose?

TECK. I shall try not to lose.

MARTHE. But if you do lose and can't pay, it will be all over Washington in an hour. (Points to terrace.) They'll find out about it, and we'll be out of here when they do.

TECK. I think I want to be out of here. I find that I do not like the picture of you and our host.

MARTHE (D. S. few steps to back of chair C. Carefully). There is no picture, as you put it, to like or dislike.

TECK. Not yet? I am glad to hear that. (Comes slowly toward her. Crosses R. to L. of MARTHE.) Marthe, you understand that I am not really a fool? You understand that it is unwise to calculate me that way?

MARTHE (slowly, as if it were an effort). Yes, I understand that. And I understand that I am getting tired. Just plain tired. The whole thing's too much for me. I've always meant to ask you, since you play on so many sides, why we don't come out any better. I've always wanted to ask you how it happened. (Sharply.) I'm tired, see? And I just want to sit down. Just to sit down in a chair and stay.

TECK (carefully.) Here?

MARTHE. I don't know. Any place—

TECK. You have thus arranged it with David?

MARTHE. I've arranged nothing.

TECK. But you are trying, eh? I think no. I would not like that. Do not make any arrangements, Marthe, I may not allow you to carry them through. (Smiles.) Come to breakfast now. (He passes her, disappears on terrace. She stands still and thoughtful. Then she, too, moves to terrace, disappears.)

(JOSEPH appears on terrace, carrying a tray toward the unseen breakfast table. The stage is empty. After a minute there are sounds of footsteps in the hall. SARA MULLER appears in the doorway, comes toward the middle of the room as if expecting to find somebody, stops, looks around, begins to smile. Behind her in the doorway are three CHILDREN; behind them, KURT MULLER. They stand waiting, watching SARA. SARA is forty-one or two, a good-looking woman, with a well-bred, serious face. She is very badly dressed. Her dress is too long, her shoes were bought a long time ago and have no relation to the dress, and the belt of her dress has become untied and is hanging down. She looks clean and dowdy. As she looks around the room, her face is gay and surprised. Smiling, without turning, absently, she motions to the children and KURT. Slowly, the children come in. BODO MULLER, a boy of nine, comes first. He is carrying coats. Behind him, carrying two cheap valises, is JOSHUA MULLER, a boy of fourteen. Behind him is BABETTE MULLER, a pretty little girl of twelve. They are dressed for a much colder climate. They come forward, look at their mother, then move to a couch. Behind them is KURT MULLER, a large, powerful, German-looking man of about forty-three. He is carrying a shabby valise and a briefcase. He stands watching SARA. JOSHUA puts down the valises, goes to his father, takes the valise from KURT, puts it neatly near his, and puts the briefcase near KURT. BABETTE goes to SARA, takes a package from her, places it near the *valise. Then she turns to* BODO, *takes the coats he is carrying, puts them neatly on top of the valises. After a second,* KURT *sits down. As he does so, we see that his movements are slow and careful, as if they are made with effort.)*

BABETTE *(points to a couch near which they are standing. She has a slight accent.)* Is it allowed?

KURT *(*SARA *crosses* L. *Smiles. He has an accent).* Yes. It is allowed.

*(*KURT *sits on couch* S. L. BABETTE *sits stiffly* R. *end of settee, motions to* JOSHUA *and* BODO. BODO *on her left.* JOSHUA *stands* R. *of settee.)*

JOSHUA *(nervously. He has a slight accent).* But we did not sound the bell—

SARA *(crosses* R. *Idly, as she wanders around room, her face excited).* The door isn't locked. It never was. Never since I can remember.

BODO *(softly, puzzled).* The entrance of the home is never locked! So.

KURT *(looks at him).* You find it curious to believe there are people who live and do not need to watch, eh, Bodo?

BODO. Yes, Papa.

KURT *(smiles).* You and I.

JOSHUA *(smiles).* It is strange. But it must be good, I think.

*(*SARA *to back of settee* R.*)*

KURT. Yes.

SARA. Sit back. Be comfortable. *(Calls softly.)* I wonder where Mama and David— *(Delighted, sees portrait of* JOSHUA FARRELLY, *points to it.)* And that was my Father. *(Turns to them.)* That was the famous Joshua Farrelly. *(They all look up at it. She wanders around the room. Turns to* R. *look at room.)* My goodness, isn't it a fine room? I'd almost forgotten— *(Turns to mantel* L.*)* And this was my grandmother. *(Giggles.)* An unpleasant woman with great opinions. *(Very nervously.* U. *to* L. *of* KURT.*)* Shall I go and say we're here? They'd be having breakfast, I think. Always on the side terrace in nice weather. I don't know. Maybe— *(Up to piano. Picks up another picture from* D. *end of piano.)* "To Joshua

and Fanny Farrelly. With admiration. Alfonso. May 7, 1910." *(Moves behind piano to keyboard upstage.)* I had an ermine boa and a pink coat. I was angry because it was too warm in Madrid to wear it.

BODO. Alfons von Spanien? Der hat immer Bilder von sich verschenkt. Ein Schlechtes Zeichen für einen Mann.

JOSHUA *(crosses* D. R. *to chair* D. R.*).* Mama told you it is good manners to speak the language of the country you visit. Therefore, speak in English.

BODO *(turns to* JOSHUA*).* I said he seemed always to give his photograph. I said that is a bad flag on a man. Grow fat on the poor people and give pictures of the face.

*(*JOSHUA *sits* D. C.*)*

SARA *(to* KURT*).* I remember a big party and cakes and a glass of champagne for me. *(Crosses* R. *to* R. *of terrace door* R. *and looks at pictures on that wall.)* I was ten, I guess— *(Suddenly laughs.)* That was when Mama said the first time a king got shot as he was a romantic, but the fifth time he was a comedian. And when Father gave his lecture in Madrid, he repeated it—right in Madrid. It was a great scandal. *(Turns to* CHILDREN.*)* You know, Alfonso was always getting shot at or bombed. *(*SARA *crosses to secretary, picks up small object, examines it and presses it to her cheek.)*

BODO *(shrugs).* Certainement!

JOSHUA. Certainement? As-tu perdu la tete?

BABETTE. Speak in English, please.

KURT *(without turning).* You are a terrorist, Bodo?

BODO *(slowly).* No.

JOSHUA. Then since when has it become *natural* to shoot upon people?

*(*SARA *replaces small object in secretary.)*

BODO. Do not give me lessons. It is neither right nor natural to shoot upon people. I know that. *(Leans to* BABETTE.*)*

SARA *(to* R. *to* U. R. *table and places handbag on it. Looks at* BABETTE, *thoughtfully).* An ermine boa. A boa is a scarf. I should like to have one for you, Babbie. *(Touches her hair.)* Once— *(Crosses* C. *to* U. R. *of*

R. C. *table—touching desk in passing.*) in Prague, I saw a pretty one. I wanted to buy it for you. But we had to pay our rent. (*Laughs.*) But I almost bought it.

(*Crosses to* C.)

BABETTE. Yes, Mama. Thank you. Fix your sash, Mama.

SARA (*thoughtfully*). Almost twenty years.

(*Looks down at carpet. Laughs delightedly.*)

BODO. You were born here, Mama?

SARA. Upstairs. And I lived here until I went to live with your Father. (*Looks out beyond terrace.* U. C. *to terrace step.*) Your Uncle David and I used to have a garden, behind the terrace. I wonder if it's still there. I like a garden. I've always hoped we'd have a house some day and settle down— (*Stops nervously, turns to stare at* KURT, *who is looking at her.* D. S. *to table* L. C.) I am talking so foolish. Sentimental. At my age. Gardens and ermine boas. I haven't wanted anything—

KURT (*comes toward her, takes her hand*). Sara, stop it. This is a fine room. A fine place to be. Everything is so pleasant and full of comfort; this will be a good piano on which to play again. And it is all so clean. I like that. You shall not be a baby. You must enjoy your house, and not be afraid that you hurt me with it. Yes?

BABETTE. Papa, fix Mama's sash, please.

SARA (*shyly smiles at him as* KURT *turns* SARA *around, ties sash*). Yes, of course. It's strange, that's all. We've never been in a place like this together— (*Turns to him.*)

KURT. That does not mean, and should not mean, that we do not remember how to enjoy what comes our way. We are on a holiday.

JOSHUA. A holiday? But for how long? And what plans for afterwards?

KURT (*crosses* D. L. *to* L. *end of sofa* L. *Quietly*). We will have plans when the hour arrives to make them.

(SARA *is facing terrace.* ANISE *comes down stairs, stops, stares, amazed, a little frightened. She comes toward room, stares at children. The* MULLERS *have not seen her. As* SARA *turns,* ANISE *speaks.*)

ANISE (*to above table* D. R. *Looking at* JOSHUA.) What? What?

(CHILDREN *rise.*)

SARA (*softly*). Anise, it's me. It's Sara.

ANISE (*coming forward slowly. Then as she approaches* SARA, *she begins to run toward her*). Miss Sara! Miss Sara! (*They reach each other, both laugh happily.* SARA *kisses* ANISE.) I would have known you. Yes, I would. I would have known. (*Excited, bewildered, nervous, looks toward* KURT. BODO *moves to* R. *of table* R. C. JOSHUA *comes to* C. *of desk behind sofa* R.) How do you do, sir? How do you do? (*Turns toward* CHILDREN.) How do you do?

JOSHUA. Thank you, Miss Anise. We are in good health.

SARA (*happily*). You look the same. I think you look the same. Just the way I've always remembered. (*To* OTHERS. *They step down a bit.* SARA *holds* ANISE *throughout this scene.*) This is the Anise I've told you about. She was here before I was born.

(JOSHUA *crosses to behind table* R. C.)

ANISE. But how—did you just come in? What a way to come home! And after all the plans we've made. But you were to come on the twelve o'clock train and Mr. David was to meet you—

BABETTE (*steps* L.). The twelve o'clock train was most expensive. We could not have come with that train. We liked the train we came on. It was most luxurious.

ANISE (*very nervous, rattled*). But Madame Fanny will have a fit. (*Turns to* SARA.) I will call her— She will not be able to contain herself. (*Starts up.*)

SARA (*softly. Stopping* ANISE). I wanted a few minutes. I am nervous about coming home, I guess.

BODO (*conversationally*). You are French, Madame Anise?

ANISE. Yes. I am from the Bas Rhin. (*She moves front and just past* SARA, *and bobs her head idiotically at* KURT.) Sara's husband. That is nice. That is nice.

BODO. Yes, your accent is from the north. That is fine country. We were in hiding there once—

(BABETTE *touches his shoulder to silence him.*)

ANISE. Hiding? You— *(Turns nervously to* KURT.*)* But here we stand and talk. You have not had your breakfast, sir!

BABETTE *(simply).* It would be nice to have breakfast.

ANISE *(crosses* SARA *to* C*).* Yes, of course. I will go and order it.

SARA *(to* CHILDREN*).* What would you like for breakfast?

BABETTE. What would we like? Why, Mama, we will have anything that can be spared. If eggs are not too rare or too expensive—

ANISE *(amazed).* Expensive! Why—oh—I —I—must call Miss Fanny now. *(Crosses up to* C. *terrace door.)* It is of a necessity. Miss Fanny! Miss Fanny! *(Turns back to* SARA.*)* Have you forgotten your Mama's nature? She cannot bear not knowing things. Miss Fanny! What a way to come home. (BABETTE *sits* R. *end of sofa* R.*)* After twenty years. And nobody at the station.

FANNY'S VOICE *(off* R.*).* Don't yell at me. What is the matter with you?

ANISE *(excitedly, as* FANNY *draws near).* She's here. They're here. Miss Sara. She's here, I tell you.

(FANNY *comes up to her, entering from* U. R. *Stops at step, stares at her, stares at* BODO *and* JOSHUA *on the floor, looks slowly around until she sees* SARA. ANISE U. R. *as* FANNY *enters.)*

SARA *(softly).* Hello, Mama.

FANNY *(after a long pause, softly, coming toward her).* Sara. Sara, darling. You're here. *(Crosses down to* R. *of* SARA.*)* You're really here. *(She reaches her, takes her arms, kisses her, stares at her, smiles.)* Welcome. Welcome. Welcome to your house. *(After a second, looks at* SARA.*)* You're not young, Sara.

SARA *(smiles).* No, Mama. I'm forty-one.

FANNY *(softly).* Forty-one. Of course. *(Presses her arms again.)* Oh, Sara, I'm—

(Then quickly.) You look more like Papa now. That's good. The years have helped you. *(Embraces her. Turns to look at* KURT.*)* Welcome to this house, sir.

KURT *(warmly).* Thank you, Madame.

FANNY *(turns to look at* SARA *again, nervously pats her arm. Nods, turns again to stare at* KURT. *She is nervous and chatty. Crosses* D. L. *to* KURT*).* You are a good-looking man, for a German. I didn't remember you that way. I like a good-looking man. *(Shakes his hand.)* I always have.

KURT *(smiles).* I like a good-looking woman. I always have.

FANNY. Good. That's the way it should be.

BODO *(from* R. *of table* R. C., *who is just rising from floor, to* SARA*).* Ist das Grossmama? *(Crosses to* C.*)*

FANNY *(looks down).* Yes. I am your grandmother. Also, I speak German, so do not talk about me. I speak languages very well. But there is no longer anybody to speak with. Anise has half-forgotten her French, which was always bad; and I have nobody with whom to speak my Italian or German or— Oh, Sara— *(*SARA *down to* FANNY.*)* it's good to have you home. I'm chattering away, I—

JOSHUA. Now you have us, Madame. We speak ignorantly, but fluently, in German, French, Italian, Spanish—

KURT. And boastfully, in English.

JOSHUA *(softly).* I am sorry, Papa. You have right.

BODO *(to* JOSHUA*).* There is never a need for boasting. If we are to fight for the good of all men, it is to be accepted that we must be among the most advanced. *(Crosses to below table* R. C.*)*

ANISE *(*D. S. *a bit from* U. C.*).* My God.

FANNY *(to* SARA*).* Are these your *children?* Or are they dressed up midgets?

SARA *(laughs).* These are my children, Mama. This, Babette. (BABETTE *bows.)* This, Joshua. (JOSHUA D. S. *two steps, bows.)* This is Bodo. (BODO *bows.)*

FANNY *(crosses to* JOSHUA*).* Joshua was named for Papa. You wrote me. *(Kisses him. Indicates picture of* JOSHUA FAR-

RELLY.) You bear a great name, young man.

JOSHUA (*smiles, indicates his father*). My name is Muller.

FANNY (*looks at him, laughs*). Yes. You look a little like your grandfather. (*To* BABETTE. *Crosses* R. *to* BABETTE, *above* BODO.) And so do you. You are a nice looking girl. (*To* BODO.) You look like nobody.

BODO (*proudly*). I am not beautiful.

FANNY (*laughs*). Well, Sara, well. (*BABETTE on* R. *end of sofa* R.) Three children. You have done well. (*To* KURT, *crosses* L. *to* KURT.) You, too, sir, of course. Are you quite recovered? Sara wrote that you were in Spain and—

BODO. Did Mama write that Papa was a great hero? He was brave, he was calm, he was expert, he was resourceful, he was—

KURT (*laughs*). My biographer. And as unprejudiced as most of them.

SARA (D. *to* R. *of* FANNY). Where is David? I am so anxious— Has he changed much? Does he—

FANNY (*to* ANISE). Don't stand there. (*Crosses* U. *to* ANISE; SARA *moves* L. *to* R. *of* KURT.) Go and get him right away. (*Peers in the basket.*) Go get David. (*JOSHUA crosses up to door* U. R. *and looks out at terrace. As* ANISE *exits.*) He's out having breakfast with the titled folk. (D. S. *to* R. *of* SARA.) Do you remember Marthe Randolph? I mean, do you remember Hortie Randolph, her mother, who was my friend? Can you follow what I'm saying? I'm not speaking well today.

SARA (*laughs*). Of course I remember Marthe and Hortie. You and she used to scream at each other.

(JOSHUA *leaves the window and goes to secretary* R., *picks up book.*)

FANNY (*takes* SARA's *arm, brings her to settee, they sit,* FANNY R. *of* SARA). Well, Marthe, her daughter, married Teck de Brancovis. *Count* de Brancovis. He was fancy when she married him. Not so fancy now, I suspect. Although still chic and tired. You know what I mean, the

way they are in Europe. Well, they're here—

(JOSHUA *looks at pages in book through this.*)

SARA. What's David like now? I—

FANNY. Like? Like? I don't know. He's a lawyer. You know that. Papa's firm. He's never married. You know that, too—

SARA. Why hasn't he married?

FANNY. Really, I don't know. I don't think he likes his own taste. Which is very discriminating of him. He's had a lot of girls, of course, one more ignorant and silly than the other— (*Grins to* KURT. *Goes toward terrace, begins to scream.*) And where is he? David! David— (*Goes* U. C. *to door;* BODO *follows her.*)

ANISE's VOICE (*from* U. R.). He's coming, Miss Fanny. He's coming. Contain yourself. He was down at the garage getting ready to leave—

FANNY. I don't care where he is. Tell him to come. His sister comes home after twenty years— David! I'm getting angry.

BODO. You must not get angry. We never do. Anger is protest. And so you must direction it to the proper channels and then harness it for the good of other men. That is correct, Papa?

FANNY (*crosses* R. *to* BODO. *Peers down at him*). If you grow up to talk like that, and stay as ugly as you are, you are going to have one of those successful careers on the lecture platform.

(JOSHUA *and* BABETTE *laugh.*)

JOSHUA. Oh. It is a great pleasure to hear Grandma talk with you.

(KURT *has wandered to the piano. Standing, he touches the keys in the first bars of Mozart's Rondo in D Major.* DAVID *comes in from entrance hall* R. *At door, he stops and stares at* SARA. *Piano stops* —KURT *rises.*)

DAVID (*to* SARA). Sara. Darling—

SARA (*wheels, goes running toward him. She moves into his arms. He leans down, kisses her with great affection*). David. David. (*Crosses* R. *to* DAVID, *who has stopped above chair* L. *of table* D. R.)

(BABETTE takes two steps R. to front of L. end of sofa. JOSHUA crosses to L. of table R. C. KURT crosses D. to C.)

DAVID *(softly)*. It's been a long, long time. I got to thinking it would never happen. *(He leans down, kisses her hair. After a minute he smiles, presses her arm.)*

SARA *(excited)*. David, I'm excited. Isn't it strange? To be here, to see each other— But I'm forgetting— This is my husband and these are my children. Babette, Joshua, Bodo.

(JOSHUA D. L. of BODO, who is L. of BABETTE.)

ALL THREE. How do you do, Uncle David?

(The BOYS move forward to shake hands. BODO, followed by JOSHUA, crosses. They shake hands and go to stand R. of their mother.)

DAVID *(as he shakes hands with JOSHUA)*. Boys can shake hands. But so pretty a girl must be kissed. *(He kisses her. She smiles, very pleased.)*

BABETTE. Thank you. *(She crosses front to R. then to above SARA.)* Fix your hairpin, Mama.

(SARA shoves back a falling pin. DAVID and KURT move to meet front of table R. C. FANNY sits R. end of sofa L.)

DAVID *(to KURT)*. I'm happy to meet you, sir, and to have you here.

KURT. Thank you. Sara has told me so much from you. You have a devoted sister.

(SARA crosses to DAVID's R. and takes his arm. ANISE sticks her head in from the hall.)

ANISE *(enters from R., crosses to C.)*. Your breakfast is coming. Shall I wash the children, Miss Sara?

JOSHUA *(D. R. two steps. Amazed)*. Wash us? Do people wash each other?

SARA. No, but the washing is a good idea. *(ANISE crosses R. to door, turns.)* Go along now, and hurry. *(All THREE start for hall.)* And then we'll all have a fine big breakfast again.

(The CHILDREN exit R.)

FANNY. Again? Don't you usually have a good breakfast?

KURT *(smiles, sits D. L.)*. No, Madame. Only sometimes.

SARA *(laughs)*. Oh, we do all right, usually. *(Sees DAVID staring at her, puts her hands in his affectionately. Very happily, very gaily.)* Ah, it's good to be here. We were kids. Now we're all grown up! I've got children, you're a lawyer, and a fine one, I bet—

FANNY. The name of Farrelly on the door didn't, of course, hurt David's career.

DAVID *(smiles)*. Sara, you might as well know that Mama thinks of me only as a monument to Papa, and a not very well-made monument at that. I am not the man Papa was.

SARA *(to FANNY, smiles)*. How do you know he's not?

FANNY *(carefully)*. I beg your pardon. That is the second time you have spoken disrespectfully of your father. *(SARA and DAVID laugh. FANNY turns to KURT.)* I hope you will like me.

KURT. I hope so.

SARA *(pulls him to couch, sits down with him)*. And I want to hear about you, David. *(Looks at him, laughs.)* I'm awfully nervous about seeing you. Are you about me?

DAVID. Yes, I certainly am.

SARA *(looks around)*. I'm like an idiot. I want to see everything right away. The lake, and my old room, and the nursery, and is the asparagus-bed where it used to be, and I want to talk and ask questions—

KURT *(laughs)*. More slow, Sara. It is most difficult to have twenty years in a few minutes.

SARA. Yes, I know, but— Oh, well. Kurt's right. We'll say it all slowly. It's just nice being back. Haven't I fine children?

DAVID. Very fine. You're lucky. I wish I had them.

FANNY. How could you have them? All the women you like are too draughty, if you know what I mean. I'm sure that girl from Lansing, Michigan, would be sterile. Which is as God in his wisdom would have it.

SARA. Oh. So you have a girl?

DAVID. I have no girl. This amuses Mama.

FANNY (to KURT). He's very attractive to some women. (Points to DAVID.) He's flirting with our Countess now, Sara. You will see for yourself.

DAVID (sharply). You are making nervous jokes this morning, Mama. And they're not very good ones.

FANNY (gaily.) I tell the truth. If it turns out to be a joke, all the better.

SARA (affectionately). Ah, Mama hasn't changed. And that's good, too.

FANNY. Don't mind me, Sara. I, too, am nervous about seeing you. (To KURT.) You'll like it here. You are an engineer?

KURT. Yes, Madame.

FANNY. Do you remember the day we met in Muenchen? The day Sara brought you to lunch? I thought you were rather a clod, and that Sara would have a miserable life. I think I was wrong. (To DAVID.) You see? I always admit when I'm wrong.

DAVID. You are a woman who is noble in all things, at all times.

FANNY. Oh, you're mad at me. (To KURT.) As I say, you'll like it here. I've already made some plans. The new wing will be for you and Sara. The old turkey-house we'll fix up for the children. A nice, new bathroom, and we'll put in their own kitchen, and Anise will move in with them—

SARA. That's kind of you, Mama. But— (Very quietly.) We won't make any plans for a while—a good, long vacation; God knows Kurt needs it—

FANNY (to SARA). A vacation? (To KURT.) You'll be staying here, of course. You don't have to worry about work. . . . Engineers can always get jobs, David says, and he's already begun to inquire—

KURT. I have not worked as an engineer since many years, Madame.

DAVID. Haven't you? I thought— Didn't you work for Dornier?

KURT. Yes. Before '33.

FANNY. But you have worked in other places. A great many other places, I should say. Every letter of Sara's seemed to have a new postmark.

KURT (smiles). We move most often.

DAVID. You gave up engineering?

KURT. I gave it up? (Smiles.) Well, one could say it that way.

FANNY. What do you do?

SARA. Mama, we—

KURT. It is difficult to explain.

DAVID (after a slight pause, a little stiffly). If you'd rather not . . .

FANNY. No. I—I'm trying to find out something. (To KURT.) May I ask it, sir?

KURT. Let me help you, Madame. You wish to know whether not being an engineer buys adequate breakfasts for my family. It does not. I have no wish to make a mystery of what I have been doing: it is only that it is awkward to place neatly. (Smiles, motions with his hand.) It sounds so big: it is so small. I am an anti-Fascist. And that does not pay well.

FANNY. Do you mind questions?

SARA. Yes.

KURT (sharply). Sara. (To FANNY.) Perhaps I shall not answer them. But I shall try.

FANNY. Are you a radical?

KURT. You would have to tell me first what that word means to you, Madame.

FANNY (after a slight pause). That is just. Perhaps we all have private definitions. We all are anti-Fascists, for example—

SARA. Yes. But Kurt works at it, Mama.

FANNY. What kind of work?

KURT. Any kind. Anywhere.

FANNY (sharply). I will stop asking questions.

SARA (very sharply). That would be sensible, Mama.

DAVID. Darling, don't be angry. We've been worried about you, naturally. We knew so little, except that you were having a bad time.

SARA. I didn't have a bad time. We never—

KURT. Do not lie for me, Sara.

SARA (*rises*). I'm not lying. (*Crosses to* C. *toward* FANNY.) I didn't have a bad time, the way they mean. I—

FANNY (*slowly.* SARA *hesitates* C., *moves* U. C. *a few steps*). You had a bad time just trying to live, didn't you? That's obvious, Sara, and foolish to pretend it isn't. Why wouldn't you take money from us? What kind of nonsense—

SARA (*slowly to* FANNY). We've lived the way we wanted to live. (*To* DAVID *and* FANNY.) I don't know the language of rooms like this any more. And I don't want to learn it again.

KURT. Do not bristle about it.

SARA. I'm not bristling. (*She moves toward* FANNY.) I married because I fell in love. You can understand that.

FANNY (*slowly*). Yes.

SARA (*sits* R. *of* FANNY). For almost twelve years Kurt went to work every morning and came home every night, and we lived modestly, and happily— (*Sharply.*) As happily as people could in a starved Germany that was going to pieces—

KURT. You're angry, Sara. Please. I do not like it that way. I will try to find a way to tell you with quickness. . . . Yes. (*To* FANNY *and* DAVID.) I was born in a town called Feurth. There is a holiday in my town. We call it Kirchweih. It was a gay holiday with games and music and a hot white sausage to eat with the wine. I grow up, I move away, to school, to work,—but always I come back for Kirchweih. For me, it is the great day of the year. (*Slowly.*) But, after the war, that day begins to change. The sausage is now made from bad stuff, the peasants come in without shoes, the children are now too sick— (*Carefully.*) It is bad for my people, those years, but always I have hope. But in the festival of August, 1931, one year before the storm, I give up that hope. On that day I saw twenty-seven men murdered in a Nazi street fight. I say, I cannot just stand by now and watch. My time has come to move. (*Looks down, smiles.*) I say with Luther, "Here I stand. I can do nothing else. God help me. Amen."

SARA. It doesn't pay well to fight for what you believe in. But I wanted it, the way Kurt wanted it. (*Shrugs.*) They don't like us in Europe: I guess they never did. So Kurt brought us home. You've always said you wanted us. If you don't, I will understand.

DAVID. Darling—of course we want you—

FANNY. I am old. And made of dry cork. And bad-mannered. (*Rises, turns to* KURT.) Please forgive me.

SARA (*rises, goes quickly to* FANNY, *puts her hands on* FANNY's *shoulders and turns her*). Shut up, Mama. We're all acting like fools. I'm glad to be home. That's all I know. So damned glad.

(FANNY *kisses her.*)

DAVID. And we're damned glad to have you. So that's settled. (*Stretches his hand out to her. She comes to him.*) Come on. Let's walk to the lake. We've made it bigger and planted the island with blackberries. (*She smiles. Together they move out hall entrance.*)

FANNY (*after a silence*). They've always liked each other. (KURT D. S. *to* R. *of* FANNY.) We're going to have Zwetschgen-Knoedel for dinner. You like them?

KURT. Indeed.

FANNY. I hope you like decent food.

KURT. I do.

FANNY. That's a good sign in a man.

MARTHE (*coming in from terrace from* U. R. *Stops in doorway*). Oh, I'm sorry, Fanny. We were waiting. (*Crosses* D. *to* C. R. *of mail table.*) I didn't want to interrupt the family reunion. I—

FANNY. This is my son-in-law, Herr Muller. The Countess de Brancovis—

KURT *and* MARTHE (*together.* KURT *crosses up to* L. *of* MARTHE). How do you do?

MARTHE. And how is Sara, Mr. Muller? I haven't seen her since I was a little girl. She probably doesn't remember me at all. (TECK *comes in from hall. She turns.*) This is my husband, Herr Muller.

(*Brings him down from door, crosses* R. *three steps.* TECK *at* R. *of* KURT.)

TECK. How do you do, sir? (KURT *bows. They shake hands.*) Would it be impertinent for one European to make welcome another?

KURT (*smiles*). I do not think so. It would be friendly.

BODO (*at door* R.). Papa! Oh! (MARTHE D. S. *to back of table.* TECK *follows, during speech. Sees* TECK *and* MARTHE, *bows, crosses to* R. *of table* R. C.) Good morning. Miss Anise says you are the Count and Countess de Brancovis.

TECK (*laughs*). How do you do?

(KURT *crosses to* R. *of sofa* L.)

MARTHE (*laughs*). What's your name?

BODO. My name is Bodo. It's a strange name. No? (BODO *crosses to* KURT.) This is the house of great wonders. Each has his bed, each has his bathroom. The arrangement of it, that is splendorous.

FANNY (*laughs*). You are a fancy talker, Bodo.

KURT. Oh, yes. In many languages.

BODO (*to* FANNY). Please to correct me when I am wrong. Papa, the plumbing is such as you have never seen. Each implement is placed on the floor, and all are simultaneous in the same room. (KURT *is amused.*) You will therefore see that being placed most solidly on the floor allows of no rats, rodents and crawlers, and is most sanitary. (*To* OTHERS.) Papa will be most interested. He likes to know how each thing of everything is put together. And he is so fond of being clean.

KURT (*laughs. To* FANNY). I am a hero to my children. It bores everybody but me.

TECK. It is most interesting, Herr Muller. I thought I had a good ear for the accents of your country. But yours is most difficult to place. Yours is Bayerisch—or is it—

BODO. That's because Papa has worked in so many . . .

KURT (*quickly placing hand on* BODO's *shoulder and moving him up*). German accents are the most difficult to identify. I, myself, when I try, am usually incorrect. It would be of a particular difficulty with me. I speak other languages. Yours would be Rumanian, would it not?

(BODO *to behind mail table.*)

MARTHE (*laughs*). My God, is it that bad?

KURT (*smiles*). I am showing off. I knew the Count de Brancovis is Rumanian.

TECK (*heartily*). So? We have met before? I thought so, but I cannot remember—

KURT. No, sir. We have not met before. I read your name in the newspapers.

TECK (*to* KURT). Strange. I was sure I had met you. I was in the Paris Legation for many years, and I thought perhaps we met there—

KURT. No. If it is possible to believe, I am the exile who is not famous. (*He turns to* FANNY.) I have been thinking with pleasure, Madame Fanny, of breakfast on your porch. (*Points to the portrait of* JOSHUA FARRELLY.) Your husband once wrote: "I am getting older and Europe seems far away. Fanny and I will have an early breakfast on the porch— (*Points to the terrace.*) and then I shall drive the bays into Washington." And then he goes on saying, "Henry Adams tells me he has been reading Karl Marx. I shall have to tell him my father made me read Marx many years ago, and that, since he proposes to exhibit himself to impress me, will spoil Henry's Sunday."

FANNY (*laughs delightedly. She rises, takes* KURT's *arm*). And so it did. I had forgotten that. I am pleased with you. I shall come and serve your food myself. I had forgotten Joshua ever wrote it.

(*They start out the terrace door together.*)

KURT (*as they disappear*). I try to impress you. I learned it last night. (*She laughs, they disappear.*)

TECK (*smiles*). He is a clever man. A quotation from Joshua Farrelly. That is the sure road to Fanny's heart. (*He has turned to look at* KURT's *valise.*) Where did you say Herr Muller came from?

MARTHE. Germany.

TECK. I know that. (*Has gone to table where valise has been placed, leans over, stares at it, pushes it, looks at labels, opens and closes lock.*) What part of Germany?

MARTHE (*taking cigarette and lighting it*). I don't know. And I never knew you were an expert on accents.

TECK (*going to where* JOSHUA *has placed* KURT's *briefcase*). I never knew it either. Are you driving into Washington with David this morning?

MARTHE (crosses to front of sofa L.). I was going to. But he may not be going to the office, now that Sara's here. I was to have lunch with Sally Tyne. (Sits R. end of sofa. TECK has picked up the brief-case and is trying the lock.) What are you doing?

TECK. Wondering why luggage is un-locked, and a shabby briefcase is so care-fully locked.

MARTHE. You're very curious about Herr Muller.

TECK. Yes. And I do not know why. Something far away— I am curious about a daughter of the Farrellys who marries a German who has bullet scars on his face and broken bones in his hands.

MARTHE (sharply). Has he? There are many of them now, I guess.

TECK (looks at her). So there are. But this one is in (Crosses D. L. to bell pull.) this house.

MARTHE. It is—is he any business of yours?

TECK (pulls bell, then crosses to U. C. look-ing at luggage R.). What is my business? Anything might be my business now.

MARTHE. Yes—unfortunately. (Sharply as he presses the catch of valise, it opens, he closes it.) You might inquire from your friend, Von Seitz. They always know their nationals.

TECK (pleasantly, ignoring the sharpness with which she has spoken). Oh, yes, I will do that, of course. But I do not like to ask questions without knowing the value of the answers.

MARTHE (rises, crosses to TECK). This man is a little German Sara married years ago. I remember Mama talking about it. He was nothing then, and he isn't now. They've had a tough enough time already without . . .

TECK. Have you— Have you been sleeping with David?

MARTHE (stops, stares at him, then simply). No. I have not been. (Turns away, crosses L. and puts out cigarette in ashtray on mail table.) And that hasn't been your business for a good many years now.

TECK. You like him?

MARTHE (nervously. Steps toward TECK). What's this for, Teck?

TECK. Answer me, please.

MARTHE. I— (She stops.)

TECK. Yes? Answer me.

MARTHE. I do like him.

TECK. What does he feel about you?

MARTHE. I don't know.

(There is a pause.)

TECK. But you are trying to find out. You have made any plans with him?

MARTHE. Of course not. I—

TECK. But you will try to make him have plans. I have recognized it. Well, we have been together a long time. (JOSEPH enters L. TECK stops, crosses to R. end of sofa L.) Joseph, Miss Fanny wishes you to take the baggage upstairs.

JOSEPH (crosses R. to baggage). Yes, sir. I was going to. (He begins to pick up bag-gage.)

(MARTHE has turned sharply and is staring at TECK. Then she rises, crosses to back of chair R. C., watches JOSEPH pick up baggage, turns again to look at TECK.)

TECK. As I was saying. It is perhaps best that we had this talk.

MARTHE. I— (She stops, waits for JOSEPH to move off. He exits, carrying valises.) Why did you do that? Why did you tell Joseph that Fanny wanted him to take the baggage upstairs?

TECK (has risen). Obviously, it is more comfortable to look at baggage behind closed doors. (Crosses her, continuing to door R.)

MARTHE (very sharply). What kind of silli-ness is this now? (Crosses R., grabs his arm and turns him. They are behind table D. R.) Leave these people alone— (As he starts to exit.) I won't let you—

TECK. What? (As he moves again, she comes after him.)

MARTHE. I said, I won't let you. You are not—

TECK (grabs her wrist and twists it). How many times have you seen me angry?

(MARTHE *looks up, startled.*) You will not wish to see another. (*Releases her wrist.*) Run along now and have lunch with something you call Sally Tyne. But do not make plans with David. You will not be able to carry them out. You will go with me, when I am ready to go. You understand. (*He exits during his speech. The last words come as he goes through door, and as . . .*)

THE CURTAIN FALLS

ACT TWO

SCENE: *The same as Act I, about ten days later. It is beginning to grow dark, the evening is warm, and the terrace doors are open.*

AT RISE: SARA *is sitting on couch, crocheting.* FANNY *and* TECK *are sitting at a small table playing cribbage.* BODO *is sitting near them, at a large table, working on a heating pad. The cord is torn from the bag, the bag is ripped open.* ANISE *sits next to him anxiously watching him. Outside on the terrace,* JOSHUA *is going through baseball motions, coached by* JOSEPH. *From time to time, they move out of sight, reappear, move off again.*

FANNY (*playing a card*). One.

BODO (*pulling wires from heating pad. To* ANISE, *then to* TECK). The arrangement of this heating pad grows more complex.

TECK (*smiles, moves on cribbage board*). And the more wires you remove, the more complex it will grow.

BODO (*points to bag*). Man has learned to make man comfortable. Yet all cannot have the comforts. (*To* ANISE.) How much did this cost you?

ANISE. It cost me ten dollars. And you have made a ruin of it.

BODO. That is not yet completely true. (*Turns to* FANNY.) Did I not install for you a twenty-five cent button-push for your radio?

FANNY. Yes, you're quite an installer.

TECK (*playing a card*). Two and two.

BODO (*to* TECK). As I was wishing to tell you, Count de Brancovis, comfort and plenty exist. Yet all cannot have it. Why?

TECK. I do not know. It has worried many men. Why?

ANISE (*to* BODO). Yes—why?

BODO (*takes a deep breath, raises his finger as if about to lecture*). Why? (*Considers a moment, then deflates himself.*) I am not as yet sure.

ANISE. I thought not.

FANNY (*calling. Turns to look at* JOSHUA *and* JOSEPH *on terrace*). Would you mind doing that dancing some place else?

JOSEPH (*looking in*). Yes'm. That ain't dancing. I'm teaching Josh baseball.

FANNY. Then maybe he'd teach you how to clean the silver.

JOSEPH (*crosses down to above table* C. JOSHUA *stands in door* U. C.). I'm a good silver-cleaner, Miss Fanny.

FANNY. But you're getting out of practice.

JOSEPH (*after a moment's thought*). Yes'm. I see what you mean. (*He exits* L.)

FANNY (*playing a card*). Three.

JOSHUA (*crosses* D. *to* U. C., *tossing ball and catching it*). It is my fault. I'm crazy about baseball.

BODO. Baseball players are among the most exploited people in this country. I read about it. . . .

FANNY. You never should have learned to read.

BODO (JOSHUA *crosses* R. *to* BODO, *moving above sofa* R.). Their exploited condition is foundationed on the fact that—

JOSHUA (*bored*). All right, all right. I still like baseball. (*He turns back to* U. C., *but stops and turns at* FANNY'S VOICE.)

TECK (*playing a card*). Five and three.

SARA. Founded, Bodo, not foundationed.

JOSHUA (*crosses* U. R. *of table of sofa* R.). He does it always. He likes long words. In all languages.

TECK. How many languages do you children speak?

BODO. Oh, we do not really know any very well, except German and English. We speak bad French and—

SARA. And bad Danish and bad Czech.

TECK (*turns to* SARA). You seem to have stayed close to the borders of Germany. Did Herr Muller have hopes, as so many did, that National Socialism would be overthrown on every tomorrow?

(JOSHUA *crosses behind sofa to above table* C.)

SARA. We have not given up that hope. Have you, Count de Brancovis?

TECK (*turns back to game*). I never had it.

JOSHUA (*pleasantly*). Then it must be most difficult for you to sleep.

TECK. I beg your pardon?

(JOSHUA *starts to reply.*)

SARA. Schweig doch, Joshua!

FANNY (*to* TECK). Sara told Joshua to shut up. (*Playing card.*) Twelve.

TECK. I have offended you, Mrs. Muller. I am most sorry.

SARA (*pleasantly*). No, sir, you haven't offended me. I just don't like polite political conversations any more.

TECK (*nods*). All of us, in Europe, had too many of them.

SARA. Yes. Too much talk. By this time all of us must know where we are, and what we have to do. (TECK *turns back to game.*) It's an indulgence to sit in a room and discuss your beliefs as if they were a juicy piece of gossip.

FANNY (JOSHUA *comes* D. *to behind table* C.). You know, Sara, I find it very pleasant that Kurt, considering his background, doesn't make platform speeches. He hasn't tried to convince anybody of anything.

SARA (*smiles*). Why should he, Mama? You are quite old enough to have your own convictions—or Papa's.

FANNY (*turns to look at her*). I am proud to have Papa's convictions.

SARA. Of course. But it might be well to have a few new ones, now and then.

FANNY (*peers over her*). Are you criticizing me?

SARA (*smiles*). Certainly not.

TECK (*to* JOSHUA, *who is looking down at cribbage game*). I didn't know your Father was a politician.

(BABETTE *enters* L., *runs to behind table* C., *carrying a plate and fork. She pushes* JOSHUA *out of his way to* R.)

JOSHUA (*looks at him for a second, then pleasantly*). He wasn't, Count de Brancovis.

BABETTE (*she has on an apron and she is carrying a plate. She goes to* FANNY). Eat it while it's hot, Grandma.

(BODO *rises and quickly goes to* FANNY's R. ANISE *follows and stands behind* BODO. FANNY *peers down, takes fork, begins to eat.* ANISE *and* BODO *both rise, move to* FANNY, *inspect the plate.*)

FANNY (*to them*). Go away.

ANISE. It is a potato pancake. (*Crosses back to behind table* R. *and looks at dismantled heating pad.*)

FANNY (*irritably*). And it's the first good one I've eaten in many, many years. I love a good potato pancake.

BODO (*moving closer to* FANNY). I, likewise.

(FANNY *nudges him away with her elbow.*)

BABETTE. I am making a great number for dinner.

TECK (*playing a card*). Fifteen and two.

BABETTE. Move away, Bodo.

(BODO *goes to* R. *behind table* R.)

ANISE (*as* BODO *comes to her*). You have ruined it! I shall sue you. (*She sits in chair* R. *of table* R.)

JOSHUA. I told you not to let him touch it.

SARA (*laughs*). I remember you were always saying that, Anise—that you were going to sue. That's very French. I was sick once in Paris, and Babbie (BABETTE *crosses to chair* U. R. C. *taking off apron. She takes sewing material and sewing basket from bag on chair, leaving apron there.)* finished a dress I was making for a woman on the Rue Jacob. The woman admitted the dress was well done, but said she was going to sue because I hadn't done it all. Fancy that.

(BABETTE *crosses* R. *around sofa* R. *and sits beside* FANNY *and sews.)*

FANNY (*slowly*). You sewed for a living?

SARA. Not a very good one. But Babbie and I made a little something now and then. Didn't we, darling?

FANNY (*sharply*). Really, Sara, were these —these things necessary, Sara? Why couldn't you have written?

SARA (*laughs*). Mama, you've asked me that a hundred times in the last week.

JOSHUA (*gently*). I think it is only that Grandma feels sorry for us. Grandma has not seen much of the world.

FANNY. Now, don't you start giving me lectures, Joshua. I'm fond of you. And of you too, Babbie. (*To* ANISE.) Are there two desserts for dinner? And are they sweet?

ANISE. Yes.

FANNY (*turns to* BODO). I wish I were fond of you.

BODO. You are. (*Happily.*) You are very fond of me.

FANNY (*playing a card*). Twenty-five.

TECK (*playing last card*). Twenty-eight and one.

(JOSHUA *goes to secretary to get a book. He crosses to chair* U. C., *examines light from window, sits, and reads.*)

FANNY (*counting score*). A sequence and three, a pair and five. (*To* TECK, *as they finish cribbage game.*) There. That's two dollars off. I owe you eighty-fifty.

(BODO *sits* L. *of table* R.)

TECK. Let us carry it until tomorrow. You shall give it to me as a going-away token.

FANNY (*too pleased*). You're going away?

TECK (*laughs*). Ah, Madame Fanny. Do not sound *that* happy.

FANNY. Did I? That's rude of me. When are you going?

TECK. In a few days, I think. (*Turns to look at* SARA.) We're too many refugees, eh, Mrs. Muller?

SARA (*pleasantly*). Perhaps.

TECK. Will you be leaving, also?

SARA. I beg your pardon.

TECK. I thought perhaps you, too, would be moving on. Herr Muller does not give me the feeling of a man who settles down. Men who have done his work seldom leave it. Not for a quiet country house.

(*All three* CHILDREN *look up.*)

SARA (*very quietly*). What work do you think my husband has done, Count de Brancovis?

TECK. Engineering?

SARA (*slowly, nods*). Yes. Engineering.

FANNY (*very deliberately to* TECK. JOSHUA *back to book,* BABETTE *to sewing*). I don't know what you're saying. They shall certainly not be leaving—ever. Is that understood, Sara?

SARA. Well, Mama—

FANNY. There are no wells about it. You've come home to see me *die* and you will wait until I'm ready.

(CHILDREN *look at* FANNY.)

SARA (*laughs*). Really, Mama, that isn't the reason I came home.

FANNY. It's a good reason. I shall do a fine death. I intend to be a great deal of trouble to everybody.

(CHILDREN *smile and go back to what they were doing.*)

ANISE. I daresay.

FANNY. I shall take to my bed early, and stay for years. In great pain.

ANISE. I am sure of it. You will duplicate the disgrace of the birth of Miss Sara.

SARA (*laughs*). Was I born in disgrace?

ANISE (FANNY *becomes interested in* BABETTE's *work*). It was not your fault. But it was disgusting. Three weeks before you were to come—all was excellent, of course, in so healthy a woman as Madame Fanny —a great dinner was given here, and, most unexpectedly, attended by a beautiful lady from England.

FANNY. Do be still. You are dull and fanciful—

ANISE. Mr. Joshua made the great error of waltzing the beauty for two dances, Madame Fanny being unfitted for the waltz, and under no circumstances being the most graceful of dancers.

FANNY (her voice rising). Are you crazy? I danced magnificently. I—

ANISE. It is well you thought so. A minute did not elapse between the second of the waltzes, and a scream from Madame Fanny. She was in labor. (FANNY turns to table and puts cards in box.) Two hundred people, and if we had left her alone, she would have remained in the ballroom—

FANNY. How you invent! How you invent!

ANISE. Do not call to me that I am a liar. For three weeks you are in the utmost agony—

FANNY. And so I was. I remember it to this day—

ANISE (to SARA, angrily. FANNY continues to straighten table). Not a pain. Not a single pain. She would lie up there in state, stealing candy from herself. Then, when your Papa would rest himself for a minute at the dinner or with a book, a scream would dismantle the house—it was revolting. (Spitefully to FANNY.) And now, the years have passed, and I may disclose to you that Mr. Joshua knew you were going through the play-acting—

FANNY (rises). He did not. You are a malicious, miserable—

ANISE. Once he said to me, "Anise, it is well that I am in love. This is of a great strain, and her great-uncle Freddie was not right in the head, neither."

FANNY (rises. Screaming). You will leave this house— You are a liar, (ANISE rises.) a thief, a woman of—

SARA. Mama, sit down.

ANISE (moves below table toward FANNY). I will certainly leave this house. I will—

(Picks up wool she has dropped at her feet.)

SARA (sharply). Both of you. Sit down. And be still.

ANISE. She has intimated that I lie—

FANNY (screaming). Intimate! Is that what I was doing— (ANISE begins to leave the room.) Very well! I beg your pardon. I apologize.

(ANISE turns.)

SARA. Both of you. You are acting like children.

BODO. Really, Mama. You insult us.

ANISE (crosses to chair R. of table D. R.). I accept your apology. Seat yourself.

(They both sit down at same time.)

FANNY (after a silence). I am unloved.

BABETTE. I love you, Grandma.

FANNY. Do you, Babbie?

JOSHUA. And I.

FANNY (nods, very pleased. To BODO). And you?

BODO. I loved you the primary second I saw you.

FANNY. You are a charlatan.

ANISE. As for me, I am fond of all the living creatures. It is true, the children cause me greater work, which in turn more greatly inconveniences my feet, however I do not complain. I believe in children.

FANNY. Rather like believing in the weather, isn't it? (DAVID and KURT come in from terrace. Both are in work clothes, their sleeves rolled up. DAVID enters door U. L., crosses to secretary to fill pipe there.) Where have you been?

DAVID. We've been helping Mr. Chabeuf spray the fruit trees.

ANISE. Mr. Chabeuf says that Herr Muller has the makings of a good farmer. From a Frenchman that is a large thing to say.

KURT (rolling down sleeves, putting on coat as he comes D. C. He has looked around room, looked at TECK, strolled over to BODO). Mr. Chabeuf and I have an excellent time exchanging misinformation. *(To* TECK, *in passing.)* My father was a farmer. I have a wide knowledge of farmers' misinformation.

FANNY. This is good farm land. Perhaps, in time—

(DAVID crosses to back of TECK's *chair.)*

DAVID *(laughs).* Mama would give you the place, Kurt, if you guaranteed that your great-grandchildren would die here.

KURT *(at behind table* D. R.—*Smiles).* J would like to so guarantee.

TECK. A farmer. That is very interesting. Abandon your ideals, Mr. Muller?

KURT. Ideals? *(Carefully.)* Sara, heist es auf Deutsch "Ideale"?

SARA. Yes.

KURT. Is that what I have now? I do not like the word. It gives to me the picture of a small, pale man at a seaside resort. *(To* BODO.*)* What are you doing?

BODO. Preparing an elderly electric pad for Miss Anise. I am confused.

KURT *(wanders toward piano).* So it seems.

BODO. Something has gone wrong with the principle on which I have been working. It is probable that I will ask your assistance.

KURT *(bows to him, standing behind keyboard).* Thank you. *(Begins to pick out notes with one hand.)* Whenever you are ready! *(*KURT *sits at piano and plays Haydn Minuet in A Major—six bars and a chord ending.)*

FANNY. We shall have a little concert tomorrow evening. In honor of Babbie's birthday. *(To* KURT.*)* Kurt, you and I will play the Clock Symphony. Then Joshua and I will play the duet we've learned, and Babbie will sing. And I shall finish with a Chopin Nocturne.

DAVID *(laughs).* I thought you'd be the last on the program.

*(*PIANO *stops.* DAVID *crosses behind sofa toward* R.*)*

TECK. Where is Marthe?

FANNY. She'll be back soon. She went into town to do an errand for me. *(To* DAVID.*)* Did you buy presents for everybody?

DAVID. I did. *(*DAVID *comes* D. *to behind table* D. R.*)*

SARA *(smiles, to* BABETTE*).* We always did that here. If somebody had a birthday, we all got presents. *(*KURT *plays again with one hand, improvisation.)* Nice, isn't it?

DAVID *(to* ANISE—*looks closely at pad* BODO *is "repairing").* I shall buy you an electric pad. You will need it.

ANISE. Indeed.

FANNY. Did you buy me a good present?

DAVID. Pretty good. *(Crosses to behind* R. *end of sofa* R. *Pats* BABETTE's *head.)* The best present goes to Babbie: it's *her* birthday.

FANNY. Jewelry?

DAVID. No, not jewelry.

FANNY. Oh. Not jewelry.

DAVID. Why? Why should you want jewelry? You've got too many bangles now.

FANNY. I didn't say I wanted it. I just asked you.

TECK *(gets up).* It was a natural mistake, David. You see, Mrs. Mellie Sewell told your mother that she had seen you and Marthe in Barstow's. And your mother said you were probably buying her a present, or one for Babbie.

DAVID *(too sharply).* Yes.

TECK *(laughs).* Yes what?

DAVID *(slowly).* Just yes. *(*DAVID *crosses* U. *to window* U. R. C.*)*

FANNY *(too hurriedly).* Mellie gets everything wrong. She's very anxious to meet Marthe because she used to know Francis Cabot, her aunt. Marthe's aunt, I mean, not Mellie's.

SARA *(too hurriedly).* She really came to inspect Kurt and me. *(*KURT *plays irregularly and abstractedly, listening to conversation.)* But I saw her first. *(She looks anxiously at* DAVID *who has turned his back on the room and is facing the terrace).* You were lucky to be out, David.

*(*DAVID *crosses to beside table* U. L. C.*)*

DAVID. Oh, she calls every Saturday afternoon, to bring Mama all the Washington gossip of the preceding week. She gets it all wrong, you understand, but that doesn't make any difference to either Mama or her. Mama then augments it, wits it up, Papa used to say—

FANNY. Certainly. I sharpen it a little. Mellie has no sense of humor.

DAVID. So Mama sharpens it a little, and delivers it tomorrow afternoon to old lady Marcy down the road. Old lady Marcy hasn't heard a word in ten years, so she unsharpens it again, and changes the names. By Wednesday afternoon—

TECK (*smiles. Turns in chair and interrupts* DAVID). By Wednesday afternoon (KURT *stops playing.*) it will not be you who (DAVID *crosses* D. C. *to be on level with* TECK.) were in Barstow's, and it will be a large diamond pin with four sapphires delivered to Gaby Delys.

DAVID (*looks at him*). Exactly.

FANNY (*very nervously*). Francis Cabot is (DAVID *crosses in front of sofa* L. *and* U. L. *to* D. *end of piano.*) Marthe's aunt, you understand— (*To* KURT.) Kurt, did you ever know Paul von Seitz, a German?

KURT. I have heard of him.

FANNY (*speaking very rapidly*). Certainly. He was your Ambassador to somewhere. I've forgotten. Well, Francie Cabot married him. I could have. Any American, not crippled, whose father had money . . . He was crazy about me. I was better looking than Francie. Well, years later when he was your Ambassador—my father was, too, as you probably know—not your Ambassador, of course, ours—but I am talking about Von Seitz.

DAVID (*laughs to* KURT). You can understand how it goes. Old lady Marcy is not entirely to blame.

(KURT *plays Mozart Minuet in B Flat Major with one hand.*)

FANNY. Somebody asked me if I didn't regret not marrying him. I said, "Madame, je le regrette tous les jours et j'en suis heureuse chaque soir." (FANNY *turns to* DAVID. TECK *turns to look at* KURT *at piano.*) That means I regret it every day and am happy about it every night. You

understand what I meant, by *night? Styles* in wit change so.

DAVID. I understood it, Mama.

JOSHUA. We, too, Grandma.

BABETTE (*approvingly*). It is most witty.

BODO. I do not know that I understood. You will explain to me, Grandma?

SARA. Later.

(KURT *continues to play, now both hands.*)

FANNY (*turns to look at* TECK). You remember the old Paul von Seitz?

TECK (*turns to* FANNY. *Nods*). He was stationed in Paris when I first was there.

FANNY. Of course. I always forget you were a diplomat.

TECK. It is just as well.

FANNY. There's something insane about a Roumanian diplomat. Pure insane. (TECK *turns back to* KURT.) I knew another one, once. At least he said he was a Roumanian. He wanted to marry me, too.

SARA (*laughs*). All of Europe.

FANNY. Not all. Some. Naturally. I was rich, I was witty, my family was of the best. I was handsome, unaffected—

DAVID. And noble and virtuous and kind and elegant and fashionable and simple— it's hard to remember everything you were. I've often thought it must have been boring for Papa to have owned such perfection.

FANNY (*shrieks*). What! Your father bored with me! Not for a second of our life—

DAVID (*laughs. Crosses* D. *to front of sofa* L. *and sits* L. *of* SARA). Oh God, when will I learn?

BODO. Do not shriek, Grandma. It is an unpleasant sound for the ear.

(JOSHUA *rises, crosses to secretary, takes another book, stands there reading and listening.*)

SARA. Why, Mama! A defect in you has been discovered.

FANNY. Where was I? Oh, yes. What I started out to say was— (*She turns, carefully to* TECK.) Mellie Sewell told me, when you left the room, that she had heard from Louis Chandler's child's governess that you had won quite a bit of money in a poker game with Sam Chandler and some Germans at the Embassy and— *(KURT stops playing sharply, hitting a discord as his hands fall on keys. TECK turns to look at him.)* And that's how I thought of Von Seitz. His nephew Philip was in on the game.

DAVID *(looks at TECK, leans forward, elbow on knees).* It must have been a big game. Sam Chandler plays in big games.

TECK. Not big enough.

DAVID. Have you known Sam long?

TECK. For years. *(Looks at KURT.)* Every Embassy in Europe knew him.

DAVID *(sharply).* Sam and Nazis must make an unpleasant poker game.

(KURT starts to play piano. Soldiers' Song.)

TECK *(who has not looked away from KURT).* I do not play poker to be amused.

DAVID *(irritably).* What's Sam selling now?

TECK. Bootleg munitions. He always has.

DAVID. You don't mind?

TECK. Mind? I have not thought about it.

(BODO puts heating pad cover behind him, testing its size against his back.)

FANNY. Well, you ought to think about it. Chandler has always been a scoundrel. All the Chandlers are. They're cousins *(BODO rises and crosses to behind ANISE and tests cover against her back.)* of mine. Mama used to say they never should have learned to walk on two feet. *(TECK turns in chair to look at KURT. BABETTE starts to hum song KURT plays, JOSHUA joins in.)* They would have been more comfortable on four.

TECK *(to KURT, who has started to play again).* Do you know the young Von Seitz, Herr Muller? He was your military attaché in Spain.

KURT. He was the German government attaché in Spain. I know his name, of course. He is a famous artillery expert. But the side on which I fought was not where he was stationed, Count de Brancovis.

ANISE *(BODO has come around in back of her, and is trying to fit electric pad to her back. BABETTE and JOSHUA begin to hum song KURT is playing. SARA begins to hum.)* It is time for the bath and the change of clothes. I will give you five more minutes—

(BODO returns to his chair L. of table D. R.)

FANNY. What is the song?

TECK. It was a German soldiers' song. They sang it as they straggled back in '18. I remember hearing it in Berlin. Were you there then, Herr Muller?

KURT *(the playing and singing continue).* I was not in Berlin.

TECK *(rises, crosses U. to R. of KURT).* But you were in the war, of course?

KURT. Yes. I was in the war.

FANNY. You didn't think then you'd live to see another war.

KURT. Many of us were afraid we would.

FANNY. What are the words?

SARA. The Germans in Spain, in Kurt's Brigade, wrote new words for it.

(Humming stops.)

KURT. This is the way you heard it in Berlin in 1918. *(Begins to sing in German.)*

"Wir zieh'n Heim, wir zieh'n Heim,
Mancher kommt nicht mit,
Mancher ging verschütt,
Aber freunde sind wir stets."

(In English.)

"We come home. We come home.
Some of us are gone, and some of us are
lost, but we are friends:
Our blood is on the earth together.
Some day. Some day we shall meet again.
Farewell."

(Stops singing.) At a quarter to six on the morning of November 7th, 1936, eighteen years later, five hundred Germans walked through the Madrid streets on their way to defend the Manzanares River. We felt good that morning. You know how it is to be good when it is needed to be good? So we had need of new words to say that. I translate with awkwardness, you understand. *(Begins to sing again in English.)*

"And so we have met again.
  The blood on the earth did not have time
    to dry.
  We lived to stand and fight again.
  This time we fight for people.
  This time the bastards—
  Will keep their hands away.
  Those who sell the blood of other men,
    this time,
  They keep their hands away.
  For us to stand.
  For us to fight.
  This time, no farewell, no farewell."

(*Music dies out. There is silence for a minute. Then* KURT *looks up.*) We did not win. (*Looks up, gently.*) It would have been a different world if we had.

SARA. Papa said so years ago. Do you remember, Mama? "For every man who lives without freedom, the rest of us must face the guilt."

(KURT *leans on piano, head in hand.*)

FANNY. "Yes, we are liable in the conscience-balance for the tailor in Lodz, the black man in our South, the peasant in—" (*Turns to* TECK. *Unpleasantly.*) Your country, I think.

(TECK *crosses* D. *a step, smiling at* FANNY.)

ANISE (*rises*). Come. Baths for everybody. (*To* BODO.) Gather the wires. You have wrecked my cure.

(KURT *turns on stool to window.*)

BODO. If you allow me a few minutes more—

ANISE (*crosses to door* R., *stands above it*). Come along. I have been duped for long enough. Come, Joshua. Babette. Baths.

JOSHUA (*he takes book with him. Rises, crosses front to door, exits up stairs. Starts out after* ANISE. BABETTE *begins to gather up her sewing*). My tub is a thing of glory. But I do not like it so prepared for me and so announced by Miss Anise. (*He exits. As he passes* BABETTE *rises, crosses* L. *and* U. *to chair* U. R. C., *leaves sewing material there.*)

BODO (*who has gathered his tools and heating pad, standing above table* R. *To* ANISE). You are angry about this. I do not blame you with my heart or my head. I admit I have failed. But Papa will repair

it, Anise. Will you not, Papa? (TECK *crosses to* BODO.) In a few minutes—

TECK (*to* BODO). Your father is an expert electrician?

BODO. Oh, yes, sir.

TECK. And as good with radio—

(BODO *begins to nod.*)

KURT (*rises. Sharply*). Count de Brancovis, make your questions to me, please. Not to my children.

(OTHERS *look up, surprised.*)

TECK (*pleasantly, crosses front to* L. *in front of fireplace and sits in armchair*). Very well, Mr. Muller.

ANISE (*as she exits with* BODO). Nobody can fix it. You have made a pudding of it.

BODO (*as he follows her*). Do not worry. In five minutes tonight you will have a pad far better— (*As* BODO *reaches door, he bumps into* MARTHE *who is carrying a large dress box.*) Oh. Your pardon. Oh, hello. (*He disappears.*)

MARTHE (*gaily*). Hello. (*To* FANNY.) I waited for them. I was afraid they wouldn't deliver this late in the day. (*To* SARA.) Come on, Sara. I can't wait to see them.

SARA. What?

MARTHE (*standing just on* R.). Dresses. From Fanny. A tan linen, and a dark green with wonderful buttons, a white net for Babbie, (BABETTE *crosses to back of* R. *end of sofa* R.) *and* a suit for you, and play dresses for Babbie, and a dinner dress in gray to wear for Babbie's birthday—gray should be good for you, Sara— (SARA *rises.*) all from Savitt's. We sneaked the measurements, Anise and I—

SARA (*crosses to above table* C. *to* FANNY). How nice of you, Mama. How very kind of you. And of you, Marthe, to take so much trouble— (KURT *comes to* R. *end of piano.* SARA *goes toward* FANNY. *She leans down, kisses* FANNY.) You're a sweet woman, Mama.

DAVID (*crosses to* MARTHE). That's the first time Mama's heard that word. (*He takes boxes from* MARTHE, *puts them on table near door.* MARTHE *smiles at him and touches his hand as* TECK *watches them.*)

FANNY (*as* DAVID *is crossing*). I have a bottom sweetness, if you understand what I mean.

DAVID. I've been too close to the bottom to see it.

FANNY. That should be witty. I don't know why it isn't.

(BABETTE *comes over to stare at boxes.* DAVID *opens boxes and lets* BABETTE *peek during next speeches.*)

SARA (*to* FANNY). From Savitt's. Extravagant of you. They had such lovely clothes. I remember my coming out dress. (*She goes to* KURT.) Do you remember the black suit, with the braid, the first day we met? Well, that was from Savitt's. (*She is close to him.*) Me, in an evening dress. Now, you'll have to take me into Washington. I want to show off. (*She caresses his shoulder not looking at him. He looks to* TECK.) Next week, and we'll dance, maybe— (*Sees he is not looking at her.*) What's the matter, darling? (*No answer. Siowly he turns to look at her.*) What's the matter, Kurt? Is it bad for me to talk like this? What have I done? It isn't that dresses have ever mattered to me, it's just that—

KURT. Of course they have mattered to you. As they should. I do not think of the dress. (*Draws her to him.*) How many years have I loved that face?

SARA (*her face is very happy*). So?

KURT. So. (*He leans down, kisses her, as if it were important.*)

SARA (*pleased, unembarrassed*). There are other people here.

MARTHE (*slowly*). And good for us to see.

TECK. Nostalgia?

MARTHE. No. Nostalgia is for something you have known.

(FANNY *coughs.*)

BABETTE (*comes to* FANNY). Grandma—it is allowed to look at my dresses?

FANNY. Of course, child. Run along.

BABETTE (*picks up the boxes.* DAVID *helps her.* SARA *crosses to* L. *of chair* U. C. *She goes to* R. *end of sofa* R.). I love dresses. I have a great fondness for materials and colors. Thank you, Grandma. (*She runs out of the room.*)

(JOSEPH *appears in the door* L.)

JOSEPH. There's a long distance operator with a long distance call for Mr. Muller. She wants to talk with him on the long distance phone.

KURT (*as he goes* L.). Excuse me, please.

(KURT *crosses* L. *quickly.* SARA *turns sharply to look at him.* TECK *looks up.* KURT *goes quickly out.* TECK *watches him go.* SARA *stands staring after him.*)

MARTHE (*laughs. As* KURT *passes sofa* L.). I feel the same way as Babbie. Come on, Sara. Let's try them on.

(SARA *does not turn.*)

TECK. You also have a new dress?

MARTHE (*looks at him*). Yes. Fanny was kind to me, too.

TECK (*takes two steps away from fireplace*). You are a very generous woman, Madame Fanny. Did you also give her a sapphire bracelet from Barstow's?

(MARTHE *crosses* D. *to chair* D. R.)

FANNY. I beg your—

DAVID (*slowly*). No. I gave Marthe the bracelet. And I understand that it is not any business of yours.

(FANNY *rises.* SARA *turns.*)

FANNY. Really, David—

DAVID. Be still, Mama.

TECK (*rises, crosses to* L. C. *After a second*). Did you tell him that, Marthe?

MARTHE. Yes.

TECK (*looks up at her*). I shall not forgive you for that. (*Looks at* DAVID.) It is a statement which no man likes to hear from another man. You understand that? (*Playfully.*) That is the sort of thing about which we used to play at duels in Europe.

(SARA *crosses* U. *to behind piano keyboard.*)

DAVID (*comes toward him*). We are not so musical comedy here. (*Crosses* U. *to behind sofa table* R.) And you are not in Europe.

TECK (*crosses* u. c.). Even if I were, I would not suggest any such action. I would have reasons for not wishing it.

DAVID (*crosses to behind chair* c.). It would be well for you not to suggest *any* action. And the reason for *that* is, you might get hurt.

TECK (*slowly*). That would not be my reason. (*Turns to* MARTHE—*crosses* D. R. *to her—stops and speaks.*) Your affair has gone far enough—

MARTHE (*sharply*). It is not an affair—

(FANNY *crosses* L. *to front of* L. *end of sofa* L.)

TECK. I do not care what it is. The time has come to leave here. Go upstairs and pack your things. (*She stands where she is.* DAVID *crosses to below table* L. c.) Go on, Marthe.

MARTHE (*crosses* L. *to sofa table* R.; *to* DAVID. TECK *does not turn*). I am not going with him. I told you that.

DAVID. I don't want you to go with him.

FANNY (*carefully*). Really, David, aren't you interfering in this a good deal—

DAVID (*looks to* FANNY. *Carefully*). Yes, Mama. I am.

TECK (*turns to* MARTHE). When you are speaking to me, please say what you have to say to me.

MARTHE (*comes to him, stands in front of the table*). You are trying to frighten me. But you are not going to frighten me any more. (*Crosses* D. R. *to* TECK.) I will say it to you: I am not going with you. I am never going with you again.

TECK (*softly*). If you do not fully mean what you say, or if you might change your mind, you are talking unwisely, Marthe.

MARTHE. I know that.

TECK. Shall we talk about it alone?

MARTHE. You can't make me go, can you, Teck?

TECK. No, I can't make you.

MARTHE. Then there's no sense talking about it.

TECK. Are you in love with him?

MARTHE. Yes.

FANNY (*sharply, taking steps* R.). Marthe! What is all this?

MARTHE (*sharply*). I'll tell *you* about it in a minute.

DAVID (*crosses to* D. c. *chair*). You don't have to explain anything to anybody.

TECK (*ignores him*). Is he in love with you?

MARTHE. I don't think so. You won't believe it, because you can't believe anything that hasn't got tricks to it, but David hasn't much to do with this. I told you I would (DAVID *turns up and crosses to above chair* u. c., *turns back and watches scene* R.) leave some day, and I remember where I said it— (*Slowly.*) and why I said it.

TECK. I also remember. But I did not believe you, Marthe. I have not had much to offer you these last few years, but if we now had a little money and could go back . . .

MARTHE. No. I don't like you, Teck. I never have.

TECK. And I have always known it.

FANNY (*stiffly*). I think your lack of affection should be discussed with more privacy.

(DAVID *turns sharply to* FANNY.)

DAVID. Mama!

(FANNY *crosses to sofa* L. *and sits.*)

MARTHE (*turning to* FANNY). There's nothing to discuss. (*Turns to* TECK. FANNY *moves to* L. *ends of sofa* L.) Strange. I've talked to myself about this scene for almost fifteen years. I knew a lot of things to say to you, and I used to lie awake at night, or walk along the street and say them. Now I don't want to. I guess you only want to talk that way when you're not sure what you can do. When you're sure, then what's the sense of saying it? "This is why and this is why and this—" (*Very happily.*) But when you know you can do it, you don't have to say anything: you can just go. And I am going. There's nothing you can do. I would like you to believe that now.

TECK. Very well, Marthe. I think I made a mistake. I should not have brought you here. I believe you now. (*He moves up to decanter table.*)

MARTHE (*after a pause, she looks to* DAVID. *Crosses to* C.). I'll move into—Washington, and—

DAVID (*comes down to meet her* C. SARA *follows close behind* DAVID *on his* L.). Yes. Later, but I'd like you to stay here for a while with us, if you don't mind.

SARA. It would be better for you, Marthe—

FANNY. It's very interesting that I am not being consulted about this. (*To* MARTHE, *as she goes to stand in front of sofa* L.) I have nothing against you, Marthe. I am sorry for you, but I don't think— (FANNY *sits* L. *end of sofa* L.)

MARTHE. Thank you, Sara, David. But I'd rather move in now. (*Comes toward* FANNY.) But, perhaps, I have something against you. Do you remember my wedding?

FANNY. Yes.

MARTHE (*sits* R. *of* FANNY). Do you remember how pleased Mama was with herself? Brilliant Mama, handsome Mama— (FANNY *rises, steps* L.)—everybody thought so, didn't they? A seventeen year old daughter marrying a pretty good title, about to secure herself in a world that Mama liked.—She didn't ask me what I liked. And the one time I tried to tell her, she frightened me. (*Looks up.*) Maybe I've always been frightened. All my life.

TECK. Of course.

MARTHE (*to* FANNY, *as if she had not heard* TECK). I remember Mama's face at the wedding—it was *her* wedding, really, not mine.

FANNY (*sharply*). You are very hard on your mother.

MARTHE. 1925. No, I'm not hard on her. I only tell the truth. She wanted a life for me, I suppose. It just wasn't the life I wanted for myself. (*Rises—sharply facing* FANNY.) And that's what you tried to do. With your children. In another way. Only Sara got away. And that made you angry—until so many years went by that you forgot.

FANNY. I don't usually mind people saying anything they think, but I find that—

MARTHE. I don't care what you mind or don't mind. I'm in love with your son—

(TECK *turns head away* R.)

FANNY (*very sharply*). That's unfortunate—

MARTHE. And I'm sick of watching you try to make him into his father. I don't think you even know you do it any more, and I don't think he knows it any more, either. And that's what's most dangerous about it.

(TECK *turns back to scene.*)

FANNY (*steps* D. L. *Very angrily*). I don't know what you are talking about.

DAVID. I think you do. (*Smiles.*) You shouldn't mind hearing the truth—and neither should I. (*Turns* R. *and crosses up to* U. C. *chair.*)

FANNY (*worried, sharply. Crosses below* MARTHE *to* DAVID). David! What does all this nonsense mean? I—

(TECK *crosses* D. R. *to above chair* D. R.)

MARTHE (*to* FANNY). Look. That pretty world Mama got me into was a tough world, see? I'm used to trouble. So don't try to interfere with me, because I won't let you. (*She goes to* DAVID.) Let's just have a good time. (*He leans down, takes both her hands, kisses them. Then slowly she turns away, starts to exit, crosses to* TECK.) You will also be going today?

TECK. Yes.

MARTHE. Then let us make sure we go in different directions, and do not meet again. Good-bye, Teck.

TECK. Good-bye, Marthe. You will not believe me, but I tried my best, and I am now most sorry to lose you.

MARTHE. Yes. I believe you. (*She moves out.*)

(*Silence for a moment.*)

FANNY (*crosses to* C. *and sits in chair* D. R. C.). Well, a great many things have been said in the last few minutes.

DAVID (*crosses to bell cor*. *To* TECK). I will get Joseph to pack for you.

TECK. Do not bother. I will ring for him when I am ready. (KURT *comes in from the study door.* SARA *turns, stares at him, crosses to back of chair* U. C. *He does not look at her.*) It will not take me very long. (*Looking at* KURT.)

(KURT *crosses to below* R. *end of sofa* L.)

SARA (*crosses to* C.). What is it, Kurt?

KURT. It is nothing of importance, darling— (*He looks quickly at* TECK.)

SARA (*crosses to* KURT). Don't tell me it's nothing. I know the way you look when—

KURT (*sharply*). I said it was of no importance. I must get to California for a few weeks. That is all.

SARA. I—

TECK (*turns, crosses up to get newspaper from secretary*). It is in the afternoon paper, Herr Muller. (*Points to paper.*) I was waiting to find the proper moment to call it to your attention. (*He moves toward table behind sofa* R., *as they all turn to watch him. He begins to read.*) "Zurich, Switzerland: The Zurich papers today reprinted a despatch from the Berliner Tageblatt—on the capture of Colonel Max Freidank. Freidank is said (*Small sharp sound from* SARA. SARA *moves to* KURT.) to be the chief of the Anti-Nazi Underground Movement. Colonel Freidank has long been an almost legendary figure. The son of the famous General Freidank, he was a World War officer, and a distinguished physicist before the advent of Hitler." (*Throws paper on desk behind sofa* R.) That is all—

SARA (*crying it out*). Max—

KURT. Be still, Sara.

TECK (*crosses above desk to* L. *end of it*). They told me of it at the Embassy last night. They also told me that with him they had taken a man who called himself Ebber, and a man who called himself Triste. They could not find a man called Gotter. (*He starts again toward the door, moving* R. *slowly, above desk.*) I shall be a lonely man without Marthe. I am also a very poor one. I should like to have ten thousand dollars before I go.

DAVID (*taking step toward* TECK. *Carefully*). You will make no loans in this house.

TECK (*at* R. *of table* D. R. *Turns to* DAVID). I was not speaking of a loan.

FANNY (*carefully*). God made you not only a scoundrel but a fool. That is a dangerous combination.

DAVID (*suddenly starts toward* TECK). Damn you . . . (*Crosses toward* TECK.)

KURT. Leave him alone. (*Tries to intercept* DAVID.) David! Leave him alone!

DAVID (*pushing past* KURT. *Angrily to* KURT). Keep out of it. (*Starts toward* TECK *again.*) I'm beginning to see what Marthe meant. Blackmailing with your wife— You—

KURT (*very sharply*). He is not speaking of his wife. (DAVID *turns to* KURT.) O. you. He means me. (*Looks at* TECK.) Is that correct?

(SARA *moves toward* KURT. DAVID *draws back, bewildered.* FANNY *comes toward them, staring at* TECK.)

TECK. Good. (*Crosses above* DAVID *to* R. *end of sofa* R.) It was necessary for me to hear you say it. You understand that?

KURT. I understand it.

SARA (*crosses to* L. *of* KURT. *Frightened, softly*). Kurt—

DAVID. What is all this about? What the hell are you talking about?

TECK (*sharply for the first time*). Be still. (DAVID *starts for* TECK, *restrains himself —crosses up to* L. *end of table* U. R. *To* KURT, *looks down at him.*) At your convenience. Your hands are shaking, Mr. Muller.

KURT (*quietly*). My hands were broken: they are bad when I have fear.

(SARA *crosses slowly to front of* L. *end of sofa* L.)

TECK. I am sorry. I can understand that. It is not pleasant. (*Motions toward* FANNY *and* DAVID.) Perhaps you would like a little time to—I will go and pack, and be ready to leave. We will all find that more comfortable, I think. You should get yourself a smaller gun, Herr Muller. That pistol you have been carrying is big, and awkward. (*Crosses* R. *toward door* R.)

KURT. You saw the pistol when you examined my briefcase?

TECK (*smiles, turns back to* KURT). You know that?

KURT. Oh, yes. Because I have the careful eye, through many years of needing it. And then you have not the careful eye. The pistol was lying to the left of a paper package, and when you leave, it is to the right of the package.

SARA (*steps toward* KURT). Kurt! Do you mean that—

KURT (*sharply*). Please, darling, do not do that.

TECK (*puts his hand on* KURT'*s hip pocket, pats it*). It is a German Army Luger?

KURT. Yes.

TECK. Keep it in your pocket, Herr Muller. You will have no need to use it. And, in any case, I am not afraid of it. You understand that?

KURT (*slowly, crosses to* TECK). Yes, I understand that you are not a man of fears. That is strange to me, because I am a man who has so many fears.

TECK (*laughs, as he exits*). Are you? That is most interesting. (*He exits* R.)

DAVID (*softly. Crosses* D. *to* L. *of* KURT). What is this about, Kurt?

KURT. He knows who I am and what I do, and what I carry with me. (KURT *crosses* U. *and* L. *to behind table back of sofa* R.)

SARA (*carefully—steps* U. C.). What about Max?

KURT (*crosses to her, speaks when there*). The telephone was from Mexico. Ilse received a cable. Early on the morning of Monday they caught Ebber and Triste; an hour after, they took Max, in Berlin. (*She looks up at him, begins to shake her head. He presses her arm.*) Yes. It is hard. (KURT *turns away from her.*)

FANNY (*softly*). You said he knew who you were and what you carried with you. I don't understand.

(SARA *crosses to behind piano keyboard.*)

KURT (*crosses to* L. *of* FANNY). I am going to tell you: I am a German outlaw. I have been working with many others in an illegal organization. I have so worked for seven years. I am on what is called the Desired List. But I did not know I was worth ten thousand dollars. My price has risen.

DAVID (*slowly*). And what do you carry with you?

KURT. Twenty-three thousand dollars. It has been gathered from the pennies and the nickels of the poor who do not like Fascism, and who believe in the work we do. (*Crosses slowly to below* L. *end of sofa* L.) I came here to bring Sara home, and to get the money. I had hopes to rest here for a while, and then—

SARA (*slowly*). And I had hopes someone else would take it back, and you would stay with us— (*Shakes her head, then.*) Max is not dead?

KURT. No. The left side of his face is dead. (*Crosses* D. L. *Softly.*) It was a good face.

SARA (*to* FANNY *and* DAVID, *as if she were going to cry*). It was a very good face. He and Kurt— (*A small move to* C.) In the old days . . . (*To* KURT.) After so many years. (*Steps toward* KURT.) If Max got caught, then nobody has a chance. Nobody. (*She suddenly turns and goes to sit* R. *end of sofa* L.)

DAVID (*steps* L. *toward* KURT). He wants to sell what he knows to you? Is that right?

KURT. Yes.

FANNY. Wasn't it careless of you to leave twenty-three thousand dollars lying around to be seen?

KURT. No, it was not careless of me. It is in a locked briefcase. I have thus carried money for many years. There seemed no safer place than Sara's home. It was careless of you to have in your house a man who opens baggage and blackmails.

DAVID (*sharply*). Yes. It was very careless.

FANNY. But you said you knew he'd seen it—

KURT. The first day we arrived. What was I to do about it? He is not a man who steals. This is a safer method. I knew it would come some other way. I have been waiting to see what the way would be. That is all I could do.

DAVID (to FANNY). What's the difference? It's been done. (To KURT.) If he wants to sell to you, he must have another buyer. Who?

KURT. The Embassy. Von Seitz, I think.

DAVID. You mean he has told Von Seitz about you and—

KURT. No. I do not think he has told him anything. As yet. It would be foolish of him. He has probably only asked most guarded questions.

DAVID. But you're here. You're in this country. They can't do anything to you. They wouldn't be crazy enough to try it. Is your passport all right?

KURT. Not quite.

FANNY. Why not? Why isn't it?

KURT (crosses to U. C. Wearily, as if he were bored). Because people like me are not given visas with such ease. And I was in a hurry to bring my wife and my children to safety. (Turns—comes to L. of FANNY. Sharply.) Madame Fanny, you must come to understand it is no longer the world you once knew.

DAVID. It doesn't matter. You're a political refugee. We don't turn back people like you. People who are in danger. You will give me your passport and tomorrow morning I'll (Turns, crosses R. to R. of R. end of sofa R.) see Barens. We'll tell him the truth— (Points to door.) Tell de Brancovis to go to hell. There's not a damn thing he or anybody else can do.

SARA (looks up at KURT, who is staring at her). You don't understand, David.

DAVID. There's a great deal I don't understand. But there's nothing to worry about.

SARA (KURT crosses to SARA. Still looking at KURT). Not much to worry about as long as Kurt is in this house. But he's not going to—

KURT. The Count has made the guess that—

SARA. That you will go back to get Ebber and Triste and Max out? Is that right, Kurt? Is that right?

KURT. Yes, darling, I must try. They were taken to Sonnenburg. Guards can be bribed. It has been done once before at Sonnenburg. We will try for it again. I must get back, Sara. I must start.

SARA (she gets up, comes to him. He holds her, puts his face in her hair. She stands holding him, trying to speak without crying). Of course you must go back. I guess I was trying to think it wouldn't come. But— (To FANNY and DAVID.) Kurt's got to go back. He's got to go home. He's got to try to buy them out. He'll do it, too. You'll see. (She stops, breathes.) It's hard enough to get back. Very hard. (Rises.) But if they knew he was coming— They want Kurt bad. Almost as much as they wanted Max— And then there are hundreds of others, too— (Crosses quickly to KURT. She puts her face down on his head.) Don't be scared, darling. You'll get back. You'll see. You've done it before —you'll do it again. Don't be scared. You'll get Max out all right. (Gasps.) And then you'll do his work, won't you? That's good. That's fine. You'll do a good job, the way you've always done. (She holds his shoulder hard with her L. arm. She is crying very hard. To FANNY.) Kurt doesn't feel well. He was wounded and he gets tired. (To KURT.) You don't feel well, do you? (Slowly, she is crying too hard now to be heard clearly.) Don't be scared, darling. You'll get home. Don't worry, you'll get home. Yes, you will. (She is holding his head close to her as the)

CURTAIN FALLS

ACT THREE

SCENE: *The same. A half hour later.*

AT RISE: FANNY *is pacing from* L. *to* R. KURT *is at piano, his head resting on one hand. He is playing softly with the other.* SARA *is sitting very quietly on the* R. *end of couch* R. DAVID *is pacing on the terrace.* FANNY *crosses from* L. *to entry hall, back to* C., *then up to terrace door.*

FANNY *(to* DAVID, *on the terrace).* David, would you stop that pacing, please? *(To* KURT.*)* And would you stop that one-hand piano playing? Either play, or get up.

*(*KURT *gets up, crosses to* L. *of* SARA, *sits.* SARA *looks at him, gets up, crosses to the decanters, begins to make a drink.* FANNY *crosses to* R. *end of piano keyboard, leans on piano.)*

SARA *(to* DAVID*).* A drink?

DAVID *(comes in, closes door).* What? Please. *(To* KURT. DAVID *crosses to back of chair* R. C., *leans on it.)* Do you intend to buy your friends out of jail?

KURT. I intend to try.

FANNY *(crosses* D. *to* D. L. C.*).* It's all very strange to me. I thought things were so well run that bribery and—

KURT *(smiles).* What a magnificent work Fascists have done in convincing the world that they are men from legends.

DAVID. They have done very well for themselves—unfortunately.

KURT. But not by themselves. Does it not make us all uncomfortable to remember that they came in on the shoulders of the most powerful men in the world? Of course. And so we would prefer to believe they are men from the planets. They are not. Let me reassure you. They are smart, they are sick, and they are cruel. But given men who know what they fight for— *(Shrugs.)* You saw it in Spain. *(*FANNY *moves* L., *stops when he speaks. Laughs.)* I will console you: a year ago last month, at three o'clock in the morning, Freidank and I, with two elderly pistols, raided the home of the Gestapo chief in Konstanz, got what we wanted and the following morning Freidank was eating his breakfast three blocks away, and I was over the Swiss border.

FANNY *(slowly).* You are brave men.

KURT. I do not tell you the story to prove we are remarkable, but to prove they are not.

*(*SARA *is behind sofa* R. SARA *brings him a drink. Gives one to* DAVID. FANNY *crosses to sofa* L. *and sits* R. *end.* DAVID *crosses* L. *to* R. *of mail table* U. L. C.*)*

SARA *(softly, touching* KURT'S *shoulder).* Kurt loves Max. I've always been a little jealous.

KURT *(puts his hand on hers).* Always, since I came here, I have a dream: that he will walk in this room some day. How he would like it here, eh, Sara? *(To* FANNY.*)* He loves good food and wine, and you have books— *(Laughs happily.)* He is fifty-nine years of age. And when he was fifty-seven he carried me on his back seven miles across the border. I had been hurt— That takes a man, does it not?

FANNY *(to* KURT*).* You look like a sick man to me.

KURT. No. I am only tired. I do not like to wait. It will go.

SARA *(sharply).* Oh, it's more than that. *(Crosses* R. *end of sofa* R.*)* This is one of the times you wonder why everything has to go against you. Even a holiday, the first in years—

KURT. Waiting. It is waiting that is bad.

DAVID. Damn him, he's doing it deliberately.

KURT. It is then the corruption begins. Once in Spain I waited for two days until the planes would exhaust themselves. I think then why must our side fight always with naked hands? The spirit and the hands. All is against us but ourselves. Sometimes, it was as if you must put up your hands and tear the wings from the planes—and then it is bad.

SARA (*to* D. R. *end of sofa* R.). You will not think that when the time comes. It will go.

KURT. Of a certainty.

FANNY. But does it have to go on being your hands?

KURT. For each man, his own hands. (*Looks at his hands*). He has to sleep with them.

DAVID (*uncomfortably, as if he did not like to say it*). That's right. I guess it's the way all of us should feel. But— (DAVID *steps* R. *to* C.) but you have a family. Isn't there somebody else who hasn't a wife and children—?

KURT. Each could have his own excuse. Some love for the first time, some have bullet holes, some have fear of the camps, some are sick, many are getting older. (*Shrugs.*) Each could find a reason. And many find it. My children are not the only children in the world, even to me.

FANNY. That's noble of you, of course. But they are your children, nevertheless. And Sara, she—

SARA (*softly*). Mama—

KURT (*after a slight pause.* SARA *crosses* U. *and* L. *to behind* C. *of desk behind sofa* R.). One means always in English to insult with that word noble?

FANNY. Of course not, I—

KURT. It is not noble. It is the way I must live. Good or bad, it is what I am. (*Turns deliberately to look at* FANNY.) And what I am is not what you wanted for your daughter, twenty years ago or now.

FANNY. You are misunderstanding me.

KURT. For our girl, too, we want a safe and happy life. And it is thus I try to make it for her. We each have our way. I do not convert you to mine.

DAVID (*crosses to back of chair* R. C.). You are very certain of your way.

KURT (*smiles*). I seem so to you? Good.

(JOSEPH *appears in hall doorway. He is carrying valises, overcoats, and two small bags.*)

JOSEPH (*to above table.* D. R.). What'll I do with these, Miss Fanny?

(SARA *crosses to decanter table.*)

FANNY. They're too large for eating, aren't they? What were you thinking of doing with them?

JOSEPH. I mean, it's Fred's day off.

DAVID. All right. You drive him into town. (*Crosses to* L. *end of desk behind sofa* R., *puts down glass.*)

JOSEPH. Then who's going to serve at dinner?

FANNY (*impatiently*). Belle will do it alone tonight.

JOSEPH (*crosses toward* FANNY, *stops* R. *of sofa* L.). No, she can't. Belle's upstairs packing with Miss Marthe. My, there's quite a lot of departing, ain't there?

(DAVID *crosses up to* U. L. C.)

FANNY (*very impatiently*). All right, then cook can bring in dinner.

JOSEPH. I wouldn't ask her to do that, if I were you. She's mighty mad: the sink pipe is leaking. You just better wait for dinner 'til I get back from Washington.

(*Crosses* FANNY *to* L. *end of sofa.*)

FANNY (*shouting*). We are not cripples and we were eating dinner in this house before you arrived to show us how to use the knife and fork. (JOSEPH *smiles.*) Go on. Put his things in the car. I'll ring for you when he's ready.

JOSEPH. You told me the next time you screamed to remind you to ask my pardon.

FANNY. You call that screaming?

JOSEPH. Yes'm.

FANNY. All right. I ask your pardon. Oh, go on. Go on.

JOSEPH. Yes'm. (*Exit* L., *closing door.*)

(TECK *appears in door. He is carrying his hat and the briefcase we have seen in Act I.* SARA, *seeing briefcase, looks startled, looks quickly at* KURT. KURT *watches* TECK *as he comes toward him.* TECK *throws his hat on a chair, comes to table at which* KURT *is sitting, puts briefcase on table.* KURT *puts out his hand, puts it on briefcase, leaves it there.*)

TECK (*crosses to* R. *of* KURT. *to put briefcase on table* D. *of* KURT. KURT *reaches for case and holds it on table. Smiles at gesture.)* Nothing has been touched, Mr. Muller. I brought it from your room, for your convenience.

FANNY *(angrily).* Why didn't you steal it? Since you don't seem to—

TECK *(crosses to* c.*)* That would have been very foolish of me, Madame Fanny.

KURT. Very.

TECK *(turns to* KURT*).* I hope I have not kept you waiting too long. I wanted to give you an opportunity to make any explanations—

DAVID *(crosses to* L. *of* TECK. *Angrily).* Does your price include listening to this tony conversation?

TECK *(turns to look at him).* My price will rise if I have to spend the next few minutes being interrupted by your temper. I will do my business with Mr. Muller. And you will understand I will take from you no interruptions, no exclamations, no lectures, no opinions of what I am or what I am doing.

KURT *(quietly).* You will not be interrupted.

TECK *(sits down at table with* KURT*).* I have been curious about you, Mr. Muller. Even before you came here. Because Fanny and David either knew very little about you, which was strange, or would not talk very much about you, which was just as strange. Have you ever had come to you one of those insistent half-memories of some person or some place?

*(*SARA *slowly moves to sit* R. *end of sofa* R.*)*

KURT *(quietly, without looking up).* You had such a half-memory of me?

TECK *(*DAVID *crosses to chair* U. L. C., *turns and listens to* TECK*).* Not even a memory, but something. The curiosity of one European for another, perhaps.

KURT. A most sharp curiosity. You lost no time examining— *(Pats case.)* this. You are an expert with locks?

TECK. No, indeed. Only when I wish to be.

FANNY *(rises. Angrily to* TECK*).* I would like you out of this house as quickly as—

TECK *(turns to her).* Madame Fanny, I just asked Mr. David not to do that. I must now ask you. *(Leans forward to* KURT*.)* Herr Muller, I got the Desired List from Von Seitz without, of course, revealing anything to him. As you probably know it is quite easy for anybody to get. I simply told him that we refugees move in small circles and I might come across somebody on it. If, however, I have to listen to any more of this from any of you, I shall go immediately to him.

KURT *(to* DAVID *and* FANNY*).* Please allow the Count to do this in his own way. It will be best.

*(*FANNY *sits again.)*

TECK *(takes sheet of paper from pocket).* There are sixty-three names on this list. I read them carefully, I narrow the possibilities and under "G" I find Gotter. *(Begins to read.)* "Age: forty to forty-five. About six feet. One hundred seventy pounds. Birthplace unknown to us. Original occupation unknown to us, although he seems to know Munich and Dresden. Schooling unknown to us. Family unknown to us. No known political connections. No known trade union connections. Many descriptions; few of them in agreement, and none of them of great reliability. Equally unreliable, though often asked for, were Paris, Copenhagen, Brussels police descriptions. Only points on which there is agreement: married to a foreign woman, *(*SARA'S *hand grasps* KURT'S.*)* either American or English; three children; has used name of Gotter, Thomas Bodmer, Karl Francis. Thought to have left Germany in 1933, and to have joined Max Freidank shortly after. Worked closely with Freidank, perhaps directly under his orders. Known to have crossed border in 1934—February, May, June, October." *(*SARA *begins to rise from table.* KURT *puts his hand over hers. She sits down again.)* "Known to have again crossed border with Max Freidank in 1935 —August, twice in October, November, January—"

KURT *(smiles).* The report is unreliable. It would have been impossible for God to have crossed the border that often.

TECK *(looks up. Then looks back at list).* Yes? "In 1934, outlaw radio station, announcing itself as Radio European, begins to be heard. Station was located in Dusseldorf; the house of a restaurant waiter was searched, and nothing was found. Radio heard during most of 1934 and 1935. In an attempt to locate it, two probable Communists killed in the toolhouse of a farm near Bonn. In three of the broadcasts, Gotter known to have crossed border immediately before and after. Radio again became active in early part of 1936. Active attempt made to locate Freidank. Gotter believed to have then appeared in Spain with Madrid Government army, in one of the German brigades, and to be a brigade commander under previously used name of Bodmer. Known to have stayed in France the first months of 1938. Again crossed German border some time during week when Hitler's Hamburg radio speech interrupted and went off the air." *(Looks up.)* That was a daring deed, Herr Muller. It caused a great scandal. I remember. It amused me.

KURT. It was not done for that reason.

TECK. No? "Early in 1939, informer in Konstanz reported Gotter's entry, carrying money which had been exchanged in Paris and Brussels. Following day, Konstanz Gestapo raided for spy list by two men—" *(KURT turns to look at FANNY and DAVID, smiles.)* My God, Mr. Muller, that job took two good men.

SARA *(angrily)*. Even you admire them.

TECK. Even I. Now, I conclude, a week ago, that you are Gotter, Karl Francis—

KURT. Please. Do not describe me to myself again.

TECK. And that you will be traveling home *(Points to briefcase.)*—with this. But you seem in no hurry, and so I must wait. Last night when I hear that Freidank has been taken, I guess that you will now be leaving. Not for California. I will tell you, free of charge, Herr Muller, that they have got no information from Freidank or the others.

KURT. Thank you. But I was sure they would not. I know all three most well. They will take—what will be given them.

TECK *(looks down. Softly)*. There is a deep sickness in the German character, Herr Muller. A pain-love, a death-love—

DAVID *(very angrily)*. Oh, for God's sake, spare us your moral judgments.

FANNY *(very sharply)*. Yes. They are sickening. Get on!

KURT. Fanny and David are Americans and they do not understand our world —as yet. *(Turns to DAVID and FANNY.)* All Fascists are not of one mind, one stripe. There are those who give the orders, those who carry out the orders, those who watch the orders being carried out. Then there are those who are half in, half hoping to come in. They are made to do the dishes and clean the boots. Frequently, they come in high places and wish now only to survive. They came late; some because they did not jump in time, some because they were stupid, some because they were shocked at the crudity of the German evil, and preferred their own evils, and some because they were fastidious men. For those last, we may well some day have pity. They are lost men, their spoils are small, their day is gone. *(To TECK.)* Yes?

TECK *(slowly)*. Yes. *(DAVID moves to front of chair* U. L. C.*)* You have the understanding heart. It will get in your way some day.

KURT *(smiles)*. I will watch it.

(DAVID sits in chair U. L. C.*)*

TECK. We are both men in trouble, Herr Muller. The world, ungratefully, seems to like your kind even less than it does mine. *(Leans forward.)* Now. Let us do business. You will not get back if Von Seitz knows you are going.

KURT. You are wrong. Instead of crawling a hundred feet an hour in deep night, I will walk across the border with as little trouble as if I were a boy again on a summer walking trip. There are many men they would like to have. I would be allowed to walk directly to them, if I were so big a fool, or if I found it necessary— until they had all the names, and all the addresses— *(FANNY rises.)* Roumanians would pick me up ahead of time. Germans would not.

TECK *(smiles)*. Still the national pride?

KURT. Why not? For that which is good.

FANNY (*comes over, very angrily, to* TECK). I have not often in my life felt what I feel now. Whatever you are, and however you became it, the picture of a man selling the lives of other men—

TECK. Is very ugly, Madame Fanny. I do not do it without some shame, and I must therefore sink my shame in large money. (FANNY *slaps him with her handkerchief.* TECK *rises.* DAVID *rises.* FANNY *crosses to mail table and drops handkerchief on it.* TECK *turns to* KURT. *Violently, pointing to briefcase.*) The money is here. (TECK *sits.*) For ten thousand dollars you go back to save your friends; nobody will know that you are gone. (*Slowly, deliberately,* KURT *begins to shake his head.* TECK *waits, then carefully.*) What?

KURT. This money is going home with me. It was not given to me to save my life, and I shall not so use it. It is to save the lives and further the work of more than I. It is important to me to carry on that work: it is important to me to save the lives of three valuable men, and to do that with all possible speed. And, (*Sharply.*) Count de Brancovis, the first morning we arrived in this house my children wanted their breakfast with great haste. That is because the evening before we had been able only to buy milk and buns for them. If I would not touch this money for them, I would not touch it for you. (*Very sharply.*) It goes back with me. The way it is. And if it does not get back, it is because I will not get back.

(*There is a long pause.*)

TECK. Then I do not think you will get back, Herr Muller. You are a brave one, but you will not get back.

KURT (*as if he were very tired*). I will send to you a postal card, and tell you about my bravery.

DAVID (*coming toward* KURT). Is it true that if this swine talks you and the others will be—

SARA (*very softly*). Caught and killed. Of course. If they're lucky enough to get killed quickly. (*Quietly, points to the table.*) You should have seen those hands in 1935. (*Turns* R. *and rises. Crosses to* R. *end of sofa* R., *facing upstage.*)

FANNY (*violently, to* DAVID). We'll give him the money. For God's sake, let's give it to him and get him out of here.

DAVID (*crosses to* SARA). Do you want him to go back?

SARA. Yes. (KURT *looks up to her.*) I do.

DAVID. All right. (*Goes to her, arm around her.*) You're a good girl, Sara.

KURT. That is true. Brave and good, my Sara. She is everything. Handsome and gay and— (*Puts his hand over his eyes.*)

(SARA *turns away.*)

DAVID (*around desk to* L. *of* TECK. *After a second, comes to stand near* TECK). If we give you the money, what is to keep you from selling to Von Seitz?

TECK. I do not like your thinking I would do that. But—

DAVID (*tensely*). Look here. I'm sick of what you'd like or wouldn't like. And I'm sick of your talk. We'll get this over with now, without any more fancy talk from you, or as far as I am concerned you can get out of here without my money and sell to any buyer you can find. I can't take much more of you, at any cost.

TECK (*smiles*). It is your anger which delays us. I was about to say that I understood your fear that I would go to Von Seitz, and I would suggest that you give me a small amount of cash now, and a check dated a month from now. In a month, Herr Muller should be nearing home, and he can let you know. If you should not honor the check because Herr Muller is already in Germany, Von Seitz will pay a little something for a reliable description. I will take my chance on that. You will now say that I can do that in any case—and that is the chance you will take.

DAVID (*crosses up to behind table* R. C. *Looks at* KURT, *who does not look up*). Is a month enough? For you to get back?

KURT. I do not know!

DAVID (*to* TECK). Two months from to-day. How do you want the cash and how do you want the check?

TECK. *One month from today.* That I will not discuss. One month. Please decide now.

DAVID (*sharply*). All right. (*To* TECK.) How do you want it?

TECK. Seventy-five hundred dollars in a check. Twenty-five hundred in cash.

DAVID. I haven't anywhere near that much cash in the house. (*Turns, crosses* L.) Leave your address, and I'll send it to you in the morning.

TECK (DAVID *turns back. Laughs.*) Address? I have no address, and I wish it now. Madame Fanny has some cash in her sitting-room safe.

FANNY. Have you investigated that, too?

TECK (*laughs*). No. You once told me you always kept money in the house.

DAVID (*to* FANNY). How much have you got upstairs?

FANNY. I don't know. About fifteen or sixteen hundred.

TECK. Very well. That will do. Make the rest in the check.

DAVID. Get it, Mama, please. (*He starts toward library door.*)

FANNY (*looks carefully at* TECK). Years ago somebody said that being Roumanian was not a nationality, but a profession. The years have brought no change. (*Starts for the hall exit* R. DAVID *closes door* L. FANNY *stops as* KURT *speaks.*)

KURT (*softly*). Being a Roumanian aristocrat is a profession.

(FANNY *exits. After her exit, there is silence.* KURT *does not look up,* SARA *does not move.*)

TECK (*awkwardly*). The new world has left the room. (*Looks up at them.*) I feel less discomfort with you. We are Europeans, born to trouble, and understanding it.

KURT. My wife is not a European.

TECK. Almost. (*Points upstairs*). They are young. The world has gone well for most of them. For us— (*Smiles.*) the three of us—we are like peasants watching the big frost. Work, trouble, ruin— (*Shrugs.*) But no need to call curses at the frost. There it is, there it will be again, always —for us.

SARA (*gets up, moves to the window, looks out*). You mean my husband and I do not have angry words for you. What for? We know how many there are of you. They don't yet. My mother and brother feel shocked that you are in their house. For us—we have seen you in so many houses. (*Crosses* U. L. *to terrace window* L.)

TECK. I do not say you *want* to understand me, Mrs. Muller. I say only that you do.

SARA. Yes. You are not difficult to understand.

KURT (*slowly gets up, stands stiffly, as if to adjust his back. Then he moves toward decanter table*). Whiskey?

TECK. No, thank you. (*He turns his head to watch* KURT *move. He turns back.*)

KURT (*picks up sherry decanter*). Sherry?

TECK (*nods*). Thank you, I will.

KURT (*as he pours. Removes decanter top*). You, too, wish to go back to Europe? (*Pours sherry.*)

TECK. Yes.

KURT. But they do not much want you. Not since the Budapest oil deal of '31. (*Puts down decanter and glass.*)

TECK. You seem as well informed about me as I am about you.

(KURT *moves to upstage side of decanter table.*)

KURT. That must have been a conference of high comedy, that one. Everybody trying to guess whether Kessler was working for Fritz Thyssen, and what Thyssen *really* wanted—and whether this "National Socialism" was a smart blind of Thyssen's, and where was Wolff— (*Picks up whiskey decanter and glass.*) I should like to have seen you and your friends. It is too bad: you guessed an inch off, eh?

TECK. More than an inch.

(KURT *pours whiskey.*)

KURT. And Kessler has a memory? (*Puts down decanter, picks up syphon and adds soda. Almost playfully.*) I do not think Von Seitz would pay you money for a description of a man who has a month to travel. But I think he would pay you

know I will have to. I know that if I do not, it's only that I pamper myself, and risk the lives of others. I want you from the room. I know what I must do. *(Loudly.)* All right. Shall I now pretend sorrow? Shall I now pretend that it is not I who act thus? No! I do it. I have done it. And I will do it again. And I will keep my hope that we may make a world where all men can die in bed. I have great hate for the violent: they are the sick of the world. *(He sinks to sofa, softly.)* Maybe I am sick now, too.

SARA. You aren't sick. Stop that. It's late. You must go soon.

KURT *(looks up at her).* Maybe all that I ever wanted is a land that would let me have you. *(Then without looking away from her, he puts out his hands and takes hers. She sits beside him quickly. Rises.)* I will say good-bye now to my children. *(Turns up to DAVID.)* Then I am going to take your car. *(Motions with his head.)* I will take him with me. After that, it is up to you. Two ways: you can let me go and keep silent. I believe I can hide him and the car. At the end of two days, if they have not been found, you will call the police. You will tell as much of the truth as is safe for you to say. Tell them the last time you saw us we were on our way to Washington. You did not worry at the absence, we might have rested there. Two crazy foreigners fight, one gets killed, you know nothing of the reason. I will have left the gun, there will be no doubt who did the killing. If you will give me those two days, I think I will be far enough away from here. If the car is found before then— *(Shrugs.)* I will still try to move with speed. *(Turns to FANNY.)* And all that will make you, for yourselves, part of a murder. For the world, I do not think you will be in bad trouble. *(He pauses. Crosses down to FANNY.)* Then there is another way. You can call your police now. You can tell them the truth. I will not get home. *(To SARA.)* I wish to see the children now. *(She goes out into hall. After a second, KURT goes to L. to chair L.)*

(There is silence. After a second, FANNY begins to speak.)

FANNY. What are you thinking, David?

DAVID. I don't know.

FANNY. I was thinking about my Joshua. I was thinking that a few months before he died we were sitting out there. *(Points to terrace.)* "Fanny," he said, "the Renaissance American is dying, the Renaissance man is dying." I said, "What do you mean?" although I knew what he meant, I always knew. "Renaissance man," he said, "is a man who wants to know. He wants to know how fast a bird will fly, how thick is the crust of the earth, what made Iago evil, how to plough a field. He knows there is no dignity to a mountain, if there is no dignity to man. *(KURT turns to look at her.)* You cannot put that in a man, but once it is *really* there, and he will fight for it, you can put your trust in him."

DAVID *(looks at FANNY).* You're a smart woman sometimes. *(Rises, crosses to KURT.)* Don't worry about things here. My soul doesn't have to be so nice and clean. *(SARA and JOSHUA come down stairs.)* I'll take care of it. You'll have your two days. And good luck to you.

FANNY. You go with my blessing, too. I like you.

SARA *(to R. end of sofa R.).* See? I come from good stock.

(KURT has looked at DAVID. Then he begins to smile. Nods to DAVID. Turns, smiles at FANNY.)

FANNY. Do you like me?
(On her speech, BODO comes in from hall.)

KURT *(crosses to D. L. C.).* Very much, Madame.

FANNY. Would you be able to cash that check?

KURT *(laughs).* Oh, no.

FANNY. Then take the cash. I, too, would like to contribute—to your work.

KURT *(slowly).* Thank you.

BODO *(to KURT).* You like Grandma? *(Moves to FANNY.)* I thought you would, with time. I like her, too. Sometimes she dilates with screaming, but— Dilates is correct?

(JOSHUA stands away from others, looking at KURT. KURT turns to look at him.)

JOSHUA. Alles in Ordnung?

(BABETTE comes in from the hall.)

KURT. Alles in Ordnung.

BODO *(crosses to KURT)*. What? What does that mean—all is well?

(KURT crosses up to front of chair U. L. C. There is an awkward silence.)

BABETTE *(to above and L. of FANNY. As if she sensed it)*. We are all clean for dinner. But nobody else is clean. And I have on Grandma's dress to me—

FANNY *(rises, crosses behind BABETTE to KURT and gives him money)*. Of course. And you look very pretty. You're a pretty little girl, Babbie. *(FANNY goes to behind desk, behind sofa R., tears check, sits.)*

(KURT sits in chair U. L. C.)

BODO *(looks around the room)*. What is the matter? Everybody is acting like such a ninny. *(Crosses up to KURT.)* I got that word from Grandma.

KURT. Come here. . . . Come. *(They look at him. Then slowly BABETTE comes toward him, followed by JOSHUA, to stand at side of KURT's chair. KURT takes BODO on his lap, BABETTE to his L., JOSHUA to his R.)* We have said many good-byes to each other, eh? We must now say another. *(SARA moves up to R. of desk. As they stare at him, he smiles, slowly, as if it were difficult.)* This time I leave you with good people to whom I believe you, also, will be good. *(Half-playfully.)* Would you allow me to give away my share in you until I come back?

BABETTE *(slowly)*. If you would like it.

KURT. Good! To Mama, her share. My share to Fanny and David. It is all and it is the most I have to give. *(Laughs.)* There. I have made a will, eh? Now. We will not joke. I have something to say to you. It is important for me to say it.

JOSHUA *(softly)*. You are talking to us as if we were children.

KURT *(turns to look at him)*. Am I, Joshua? I wish you were children. I wish I could say, Love your mother, do not eat too many sweets, clean your teeth . . . *(Draws BODO to him.)* I cannot say these things. You are not children. I took it all away from you.

BABETTE. We have had a most enjoyable life, Papa.

KURT *(smiles, pats her hand and holds it to his cheek)*. You are a gallant little liar. And I thank you for it. I have done something bad today—

FANNY *(shocked, sharply)*. Kurt—

SARA. Don't, Mama.

(BODO and BABETTE have looked at FANNY and SARA, puzzled. Then they have turned again to look at KURT.)

KURT. It is not to frighten you. In a few days, your mother and David will tell you.

BODO. You could not do a bad thing.

BABETTE *(proudly)*. You could not.

KURT *(shakes his head)*. Now let us get straight together. The four of us. Do you remember when we read *Les Miserables*? Do you remember that we talked about it afterwards, and Bodo got candy on Mama's bed?

BODO. I remember.

KURT. Well. He stole bread. The world is out of shape, we said, when there are hungry men. And until it gets in shape, men will always steal and lie and— *(A little more slowly.)* kill. But for whatever reason it is done, and whoever does it— you understand me—it is all bad. I want you to remember that. Whoever does it, it is bad. *(Then very gaily.)* But you will live to see the day when it will not have to be. All over the world, in every place and every town, there are men who are going to make sure it will not have to be. They want what I want: a childhood for every child. For my children, and I, for theirs. *(He picks BODO up, rises, moves toward hall, followed by BABETTE and JOSHUA.)* Think of that. It will make you happy. In every town and every village and every mud hut in the world, there is always a man who loves children, who will fight to make a good world for them. And now good-bye. Wait for me. I shall try to come back for you. *(He is above table D. R.)* Or you shall come to me. At Hamburg, the boat will come in. It will be a fine, safe land—I will be waiting on the dock. And there will be the three of you and Mama and Fanny and David. And I will have ordered an extra big dinner and we will show them what my Germany can be like— (*He has put* BODO *down. He leans down, presses his face in* BAB- ETTE'S *hair. Tenderly, as her mother has done earlier, she touches his hair.*)

JOSHUA (*slowly*). Of course. That is the way it will be. Of course. But—but if you should find yourself delayed . . . (*Very slowly*). Then I will come to you. Mama.

SARA (*she has turned away*). I heard you, Joshua.

KURT (*he kisses* BABETTE). Gute Nacht, Liebling!

BABETTE. Gute Nacht, Papa. Mach's gut! (BABETTE *goes up steps.*)

KURT (*leans to kiss* BODO). Good night, Baby.

BODO. Good night, Papa. Mach's gut! (BODO *follows* BABETTE *slowly.*)

KURT (*kisses* JOSHUA). Good night, son.

JOSHUA. Good night, Papa. Mach's gut! (*He begins to climb the steps.*)

(KURT *stands watching them, smiling. When they disappear, he turns to* DAVID.)

KURT (FANNY *rises, crosses to* U. R. C. *Crosses to* DAVID). Good-bye, and thank you.

DAVID. Good-bye, and good luck.

KURT (*he moves up to* FANNY, *he offers his hand*). Good-bye. I have five children, eh?

FANNY. Yes, you have. (*He bends and kisses her hand.* FANNY *goes to behind desk.*)

(SARA *comes to* KURT.)

KURT (*slowly*). Men who wish to live have the best chance to live. I wish to live. I wish to live with you.

SARA. For twenty years. It is as much for me today— (*Takes his arms.*) Just once, and for all my life. (*She nods.*) Come back for me, darling. If you can.

KURT (*simply*). I will try. (*He pulls her toward him. They kiss. She breaks away, reaches for his briefcase and gives it to*

him. *He takes it and turns.*) Good-bye to you all. (*He exits.*)

(SARA *sits down, looks up at* DAVID, *smiles. He comes to her, kisses her, moves away again. After a second, there is the sound of a car starting. They sit listening to it. Gradually the noise begins to go off into the distance. A second later* JOSHUA *appears.*)

JOSHUA. Mama. (*She looks up. He is very tense.*) Bodo cries. Babette looks very queer. I think you should come.

SARA (*gets up, slowly*). I'm coming. (*And goes up stairs.*)

JOSHUA (*to* FANNY *and* DAVID. *Still very tense*). Bodo talks so fancy, we forget sometimes he is a baby. (*He goes up stairs.*)

(FANNY *and* DAVID *watch them.*)

FANNY (*after a minute*). Well, here we are. We're shaken out of the magnolias, eh?

DAVID (*laughs*). Yes, so we are.

FANNY. Tomorrow will be a hard day. But we'll have Babbie's birthday dinner. And we'll have music afterwards. You can be the audience. You'd better go up to Marthe now. Be as careful as you can. She'd better stay here for a while. I dare say I can stand it.

DAVID (*turns, smiles*). Even your graciousness is ungracious, Mama.

FANNY. I do my best. Well, I think I shall go and talk to Anise. (*Rises, starts* R.) I like Anise best when I don't feel well. (*She begins to move off.*)

DAVID. Mama. (*She turns.*) We are going to be in for trouble. You understand that?

FANNY. I understand it very well. We will manage. You and I. I'm not put together with flour paste. And neither are you—I am happy to learn.

DAVID (*he begins to laugh*). Good night, Mama.
(*As she moves out . . .*)

THE CURTAIN FALLS

THE PATRIOTS

By SIDNEY KINGSLEY

THE PATRIOTS was first presented by The Playwrights Company in association with Rowland Stebbins at the National Theatre, New York, on January 29, 1943, with the collowing cast:

CAPTAIN	Byron Russell	MAT	Philip White
THOMAS JEFFERSON		JAMES MONROE	Judson Laire
	Raymond Edward Johnson	MRS. HAMILTON	Peg La Centra
PATSY	Madge Evans	HENRY KNOX	Henry Mowbray
MARTHA	Frances Reid	BUTLER	Robert Lance
JAMES MADISON	Ross Matthew	MR. FENNO	Ronald Alexander
ALEXANDER HAMILTON		JUPITER	Juano Hernandez
	House Jameson	MRS. CONRAD	Leslie Bingham
GEORGE WASHINGTON		FRONTIERSMAN	John Stephen
	Cecil Humphreyes	THOMAS JEFFERSON	
SERGEANT	Victor Southwick	RANDOLPH	Billy Nevard
COLONEL HUMPHREYS		ANNE RANDOLPH	Hope Lange
	Francis Compton	GEORGE WASHINGTON	
JACOB	Thomas Dillon	LAFAYETTE	Jack Lloyd
NED	George Mitchell		

SCENES

PROLOGUE: The deck of a schooner. 1790.

ACT I: New York—1790.
    Scene 1. The Presidential mansion.
    Scene 2. A smithy of an inn on the outskirts of New York.

ACT II: Philadelphia—1791–1793.
    Scene 1. Hamilton's home.
    Scene 2. Jefferson's rooms.
    Scene 3. The same. A few days later.

ACT III: Washington—1801.
    Scene 1. Jefferson's rooms at Conrad's boarding house.
    Scene 2. The Senate Chamber.

THE AUTHOR

Pulitzer Prize and Drama Critics Circle winner Sidney Kingsley was born on October 18, 1906. A bright lad, he won a New York state scholarship to Cornell University and throve mightily there. In addition to acquiring his B.A. in 1928 and serving as president of the Delta Sigma Rho honorary forensic society, he won two forensic awards and the Drummond playwriting award at the University. Having acted at college, he must have become slightly stage-struck, since he joined a Bronx stock company after graduation, cast longing eyes on the Broadway stage, and played a bit part in Eva Kay Flint's Subway Express *in the season of 1929–30.*

By 1930 he had written a hospital play which he called Crisis *and sold it to Louis Cline, Sidney Phillips, and Sidney Harmon in succession. Joining forces with the young Group Theatre and with James Ullman (who was destined to be more successful as a novelist than as a producer), Harmon finally got the script produced on September 26, 1933 under the title of* Men in White. *Group Theatre acting made the play a long-running success, and both the Theatre Club and the Pulitzer Prize committee voted it the best play of the 1933–34 season.*

Mr. Kingsley, who had revealed considerable social awareness in his realistic treatment of doctors and hospitals, turned next to the subject of crime-breeding slums and the overall theme of the depression. The result was Dead-End, *produced on October 28, 1935 by Norman Bel Geddes, who also designed an impressive East River front setting for the production. The play, which won the Theatre Club award for the best play of the season, had one of the longest runs on Broadway. What, no doubt, pleased the author at least as much is that this evocative drama was, according to no less an authority than Senator Robert Wagner, responsible for sweeping Congressional action on slum clearance. This time Mr. Kingsley functioned also as director and revealed a second talent of no mean proportions.*

In 1936 the gifted author added producing to his experience with his Ten Million Ghosts. *In spite of his ingenious staging of the script (he fused motion picture technique, actual motion pictures, and "legitimate" acting in this venture), this exposé of the "merchants of death" missed fire. He returned to the stage on November 20, 1939 with* The World We Make, *a moving dramatization of Millen Brand's novel, which somehow failed to captivate most of the critics and ran for only ten weeks. The author, however, is justly proud of his accomplishment. "The approbation of Mr. Atkinson and Mr. Gassner and the audience generally," he writes, "made it successful artistically."*

From 1940 to 1944 Mr. Kingsley was in the armed forces, three years as an enlisted man, one year as First Lieutenant in the Signal Corps. The Patriots *was written during this period in several carefully revised drafts and opened on Broadway under Playwrights Company auspices on January 29, 1943. The effort was rewarded with a string of prizes—the Drama Critics, Theatre Club, and Federated Women's Club awards.*

THE PATRIOTS

PROLOGUE

1790. A section of the deck of a schooner. A star-lit night, wind in the sails, rushing water, the creak of tackle.

A middle-aged man and a girl lean on the ship's rail and gaze out over the ocean: JEFFERSON *and his daughter,* PATSY. *He is tall and thin, his face too sensitive, a gentleness almost womanish written on it. He has dispensed with the wig of the period. His hair, ruffled by the winds, is reddish, streaked with gray. The girl is in her late teens, vibrant, lithe, handsome. Above them a helmsman, in shadow, steers the ship.*

The CAPTAIN *approaches them.*

CAPTAIN. Evening, sir.

JEFFERSON. Good evening, Captain.

PATSY. Are we nearing land, Captain?

CAPTAIN. If we hold to our course. Gittin' impatient?

*(*PATSY *laughs.)*

JEFFERSON. Tell me, does the voyage home always take forever?

CAPTAIN. Longer'n that, sometime. *(Looks at the sky.)* May blow up a bit, sir. Better think a goin' below. *(He salutes, goes off.* PATSY *and* JEFFERSON *stare out over the ocean.)*

PATSY. I wonder will the house be the way I remember it.

JEFFERSON. Not as large, perhaps. You were only a little lady when we left.

PATSY. How long ago that seems!

JEFFERSON. Doesn't it?

PATSY. It's odd. Now that we're coming home again, all those years in Paris suddenly seem so unreal, don't they, Papa?

JEFFERSON. Yes.

(She sighs. JEFFERSON *looks at her, smiles.)*

PATSY. Are we going to New York first?

JEFFERSON *(shakes his head).* Direct to Monticello.

PATSY. I thought you might want to see President Washington at once.

JEFFERSON. We'll go home first and arrange your wedding.

PATSY. Won't the President be waiting your answer?

JEFFERSON. Not particularly—no.

(Pause.)

PATSY. Papa?

JEFFERSON. Yes, dear?

PATSY. I've been wondering.

JEFFERSON. What?

PATSY. Do you think we should put it off? My wedding?

JEFFERSON. Put it off?

PATSY. If you accept the President's offer, you'll have to live in New York. You'll be alone for the first time in your life. You'll be utterly miserable. I know you too well.

JEFFERSON. But I have no intention of accepting.

PATSY. You haven't?

JEFFERSON. He's given me the option of refusal. And I certainly mean to take advantage of it.

PATSY *(vastly relieved).* Why didn't you tell me?

JEFFERSON. It never occurred to me. *(Pause.)* You see, dearest, I discovered a long time ago that Nature didn't make me for public office. I accepted the French post only because—at the time—your mother's death had left me so blank. . . . I fancied a change of scene would . . . *(He breaks off.)*

PATSY. I know, Father. *(A long pause as they both stare into space.)* Strange out there.

JEFFERSON. Time and space seem to disappear.

PATSY. I wish she were waiting for us at home.

685

JEFFERSON. Your mother?

PATSY. Yes. I never think of Monticello without thinking of her. She used to love to tell me about *your* wedding night.

JEFFERSON. Did she?

PATSY. In the garden cottage, midst such a clutter of your drawings and your books and your inventions, you could hardly move about.

JEFFERSON *(smiles)*. That's right.

PATSY. And how you lit a fire, and found half a bottle of wine a workman had left behind some books. And mother played the pianoforte and you your violin, and you sang old songs.

(The wind rises. JEFFERSON *draws his cloak tighter.)*

JEFFERSON. It is blowing up a bit. Excuse me. *(He starts off.)*

PATSY. Where are you going?

JEFFERSON. I want to take a look at your sister.

PATSY. She's asleep, Father.

JEFFERSON. She'll have kicked off her blanket. She might catch a chill. We don't want her coming home with the sniffles. *(He goes off.)*

PATSY *(calls after him)*. Father!

JEFFERSON *(off)*. Yes?

PATSY. I'll go. You wait here.

JEFFERSON. All right, dear. *(Re-enters.)*

PATSY. I'll be right back.

*(*PATSY *goes.* JEFFERSON *stares off toward the horizon. The hypnotic surge of the water. . . . The moonlight fades until he and the ship become a single silhouette in the night. Soft music dimly heard. . . . Slowly, dancing as if on the ocean, the exterior of an enchanting house materializes.* Monticello! *Snow is falling and has piled deep around it.)*

(Laughter is heard offstage. TOM JEFFERSON, *a young man, and* MARTHA, *a young woman, radiantly beautiful, appear, shaking the snow off their cloaks.)*

MARTHA. Was there ever such a wedding night? I declare, Tom Jefferson, those last few miles the horses fairly flew through the snow.

JEFFERSON *(points to the house)*. There it is, Martha.

*(*MARTHA *turns, gasps.)*

MARTHA. Oh, Tom!

JEFFERSON. You like it?

MARTHA. I never dreamed it would . . . You really designed this, yourself?

JEFFERSON. For you, Martha. *(Takes her hand.)*

MARTHA. It's incredibly lovely.

JEFFERSON. Your hand is like ice. Come!

MARTHA. No! I want to stand here and look at it a minute more. Please!

JEFFERSON. It'll be ready for us to move into by April. Till then we'll use the garden cottage. *(Apologetically.)* It's only one room.

MARTHA *(laughs)*. Like a couple of dormice. We won't stir till Spring. *(Looks about, enchanted. Points offstage.)* Your Blue Ridge Mountains are out there?

JEFFERSON *(nods)*. There's one peak, Martha, the sun tips with pure gold. And from here Nature spreads a magic carpet below—rocks, rivers, mountains, forests . . .

MARTHA. I can't wait for morning.

JEFFERSON. When stormy weather's brewing, you can look down into her workshop and see her fabricating clouds and hail and snow and lightning—at your feet.

MARTHA. Tom, dearest?

JEFFERSON. Yes, Martha?

MARTHA. I can't tell you what you've done for me.

JEFFERSON. What I've done for you?

MARTHA. Before I met you, circumstances and the intolerance of little men had begun to make me lose faith. The earth had begun to shrink. Living had become something quite unimportant. Then, the night we met, after the gay chatter, when you began to talk gravely, I suddenly fell in love, not only with you. I fell in love with the possibilities of the whole race of man.

(She stops short. He is gazing at her, laughing.) Now, what are *you* laughing at, Mr. Jefferson?

JEFFERSON. If I live to be a thousand and close my eyes—this is the way I'll see you, my love. With snow on your face and your eyes shining!

MARTHA. Oh, Tom, I'm only trying to say I'm happy.

JEFFERSON. Are you?

MARTHA. And I want to be bussed.

(He kisses her tenderly.)

JEFFERSON.
"When we dwell on the lips of the lass we adore,
Not a pleasure in nature is missing.
May his soul be in Heaven
He deserved it, I'm sure,
Who was first the inventor of kissing."

(She laughs. They embrace.)

MARTHA. Will you love me so forever, Tom?

JEFFERSON. Forever and ever—and ever . . . *(She shivers.)* You shivered? You are cold.

(The light begins to fade.)

MARTHA. A bit!

JEFFERSON. Come, Mrs. Jefferson. *(He sweeps her up in his arms.)* We'll light a fire that will warm you to the end of time! *(He carries her off. Suddenly the roar of a rising wind. Men's voices far off.)*

CAPTAIN'S VOICE *(offstage)*. Port quarter! *(Monticello fades and vanishes. CAPTAIN enters, approaches the dreaming silhouette of JEFFERSON.)*

CAPTAIN. Runnin' into a patch of ugly weather. Better go below, sir. *(The sudden roar of wind. The wheel spins.)* Watch the helm, Higgins! Bring the wind on the port quarter!

(VOICE offstage: "Aye, sir." Many voices offstage. Exit CAPTAIN. The babble of men's voices raised in argument.)

(Another vision appears in space. Young JEFFERSON, seated at a desk, a manuscript before him. As the voices are heard, he looks from one antagonist to another.)

FIRST VOICE. Georgia votes nay.

SECOND VOICE. This document is a mass of glittering generalities.

THIRD VOICE. Carolina votes nay. I move to strike out the clause condemning the slave traffic. It has no place here. Georgia and Carolina object.

FOURTH VOICE. Motion to strike out clause condemning the slave traffic. Hands! For? *(JEFFERSON looks about, dismayed, counting the votes.)* Against? *(JEFFERSON raises his hand.)* Motion carried. You will please strike out that clause.

(JEFFERSON bitterly scratches out the offending clause.)

REID'S VOICE. That second sentence. Don't like it.

JEFFERSON. But this is the heart of it, man. Are we going to have to creep up on liberty, inch by inch?

VOICE. Where does this lead? No wonder we're driving all our men of property into the arms of the loyalists.

JEFFERSON. I was asked to write the declaration and I wrote it. I haven't tried to be original. This is a simple expression of the American mind. Our people want this.

REID'S VOICE. From a legalistic viewpoint . . .

JEFFERSON. The men who migrated to America, who built it with their sweat and blood were laborers, not lawyers.

REID'S VOICE. Plague on't, boy! You want some precedent. Where can you show me anything like this in history?

JEFFERSON. Where in history do we see anything like this new world or the man of this new world? Where have we ever seen a land so marked by destiny to build a new free society based on the rights of man? Precedent? Let's make precedent! Better to set a good example, than follow a bad one.

REID'S VOICE. Are you aware, sir, of the consequences?

JEFFERSON *(controls his emotion, rises, steps from behind the desk, appeals to the assembly)*. There is not a man in the whole empire who wished conciliation more than I. But, by the God that made me, I would have sooner ceased to exist than yield my freedom. And, in this, I know I speak for America. I am sorry to find a bloody campaign is decided on. But, since it is forced on us, we must drub the enemy and drub him soundly. We must teach the sceptered tyrant we are not brutes to kiss the hand that scourges us. But this is not enough. We are now deciding everlastingly our future and the future of our innocent posterity. Our people have already been fighting a year—for what? *(He picks up the document.)* For this. Let us give it to them—in writing—now. Now is the time to buttress the liberty we're fighting for. It can't be too strongly emphasized! *Now,* while men are bleeding and dying. Tomorrow they may grow tired and careless, and a new despot may find in the old laws an instrument to rob their liberty again. Now is the time to build a free society. Now! Not later.

REID's VOICE. I'll debate this point all day.

JEFFERSON *(fiercely).* No member of this Congress is more eager than I to settle the business on hand and go home. My wife is ill and bearing me a child, and while I stay here she's doing all my work at home. I'm half mad with anxiety, but I'll stay on all summer, if necessary, to fight for this one sentence.

(Pause.)

REID's VOICE. Well—er—Read it again. Let's examine it again!

JEFFERSON *(sits. Reads from the document, his voice rich with deep emotion).* We hold these truths to be self-evident: that all men are created equal; that they are endowed by their Creator with certain inalienable rights; that among these are life, liberty, and the pursuit of happiness; that to secure these rights, governments are instituted among men, deriving their just powers from the consent of the governed.

(The Liberty Bell begins to peal. Young JEFFERSON's face is transfigured by an almost sacred light, which grows brighter, then fades and vanishes. Total darkness obscures even the shadowy ship and the dreaming silhouette of JEFFERSON. In the darkness the Liberty Bell peals louder and louder, then fades off—Soft, sweet, ghostly music. . . . The image of MARTHA appears, smiling sadly. The dreamer on the ship becomes visible again. He reaches out his hand.)

JEFFERSON *(murmurs).* Forgive me, Martha! It was such a price to ask of you. Forgive me! I wanted a happy world—for us; and, reaching for it, I lost you. *(The ghost of MARTHA smiles sadly and shakes her head.)* Oh, my darling, in every picture I ever painted of the future you were the foreground. Without you, there's no picture. There's . . .

PATSY's VOICE *(off).* Father!

(The ghost of MARTHA reaches out her hand, then fades and vanishes. PATSY appears.)

PATSY. Father! *(The light comes on slowly. The ship again. PATSY is at his side.)* Maria's all right. Father.

JEFFERSON. Hm?

PATSY. She's sound asleep—Maria.

JEFFERSON. Oh! Good. Did she kick off the blanket?

PATSY. Yes, but I tucked her in again. Tight.

JEFFERSON. Good.

PATSY. You were so deep in meditation. What were you thinking?

JEFFERSON. Oh—nothing, dear. Just thinking.

(From above, the watch suddenly cries out, "Land ho!" The cry is repeated below. From above, "Two points to the starboard! Land ho!")

PATSY. Father! There it is! Do you see?

JEFFERSON. No. Where, Patsy? Where?

PATSY. That light! There!

JEFFERSON *(peering off, his face working with emotion).* Yes, yes, it's land! It's America, Patsy.

PATSY. We're home, again.

ACT ONE

SCENE I

SCENE: *New York, Spring 1790. The MacComb mansion on lower Broadway, the Presidential residence.* PRESIDENT WASHINGTON, *tight-lipped and grave, is listening to scholarly, prematurely wizened* JAMES MADISON *and* ALEXANDER HAMILTON, *a short, handsome, young man of flashing personality and proud carriage.* COLONEL HUMPHREYS, *foppish and affected, stands by, his face a mirror reflecting* HAMILTON's *lightning changes of mood.*

MADISON (*vehemently*). If Colonel Hamilton's treasury bill is re-introduced, Congress will kill it again.

HAMILTON (*dryly*). Mr. Madison, I am tempted to seize your Congress by their separate heads and knock them together into a collective jelly.

MADISON. What would that achieve?

HAMILTON. Unity! Of some kind.

MADISON. Yes, but what kind? That's the question.

HAMILTON. You cry, "Speculation!" That's not the issue at all, and you know it.

MADISON. I know nothing of the sort. On the contrary.

HAMILTON. You deny your South is afraid the North will profit a little more?

MADISON. And will they? Will they?

HAMILTON. That's beside the point. Yes, they will. What of it? (*He turns to* WASHINGTON, *pleading.*) The crying need of this infant government *now* is confidence in its financial policy.

MADISON. Exactly. And is this the way to achieve it?

HAMILTON. Question? Can the wise and learned Congressman from Virginia propose any better plan?

MADISON. Colonel Hamilton! Personalities are not the . . .

WASHINGTON. Gentlemen! Gentlemen! Thank you, Mr. Madison, for your views. Of course it is not in this office to interfere with the people's legislature.

MADISON. Thank you!

HAMILTON. But, Mr. President! You . . .

WASHINGTON. Congress must decide the merits of your bill.

MADISON. Good day, Mr. President. (*Bows to* HAMILTON, *who is almost bursting with fury.*) Colonel Hamilton.

HAMILTON. My congratulations! You've won a noble victory over unity and honor. (MADISON *smiles, shakes his head, goes.* HAMILTON *turns to* WASHINGTON.) I warn you, sir . . .

WASHINGTON. Slow, Colonel. Slow but sure. That must be our political maxim.

HAMILTON. I'm afraid I may have to resign.

WASHINGTON. Now, my boy!

HAMILTON. I can't build a treasury out of thin air.

WASHINGTON. I know, my boy. I know. (*He hands* HAMILTON *some papers.*) Check these figures for me. (*He ruffles some other documents.*) These we'll go over this evening. Mrs. Washington is expecting you and your lady.

HAMILTON. Mrs. Hamilton is confined to bed.

WASHINGTON. She is? Anything wrong?

HAMILTON. On the contrary.

WASHINGTON. Another?

HAMILTON. On the way.

WASHINGTON. By God! You little men! My congratulations.

HAMILTON (*laughs*). Thank you, sir. I'll check these, now. Is there anything else?

WASHINGTON. No. (HAMILTON *turns to go. A sergeant enters.*)

SERGEANT. His Excellency's Ambassador to the Court of France, Mr. Jefferson!

WASHINGTON. Oh! Good! Show him in.

SERGEANT. Yes, sir. (SERGEANT *exits.* HAMILTON *wheels around.*)

HAMILTON. Mr. Jefferson in New York?

HUMPHREYS. He arrived last night. (HAMILTON *glares at him.* HUMPHREYS *whines.*) I thought you knew, Alec. . . . I . . .

HAMILTON (*suddenly very excited, to the President*). Providence is with us. Mr. Jefferson could easily persuade the South to vote for my treasury bill. I have never met him, so if you'd speak to him . . .

WASHINGTON. I can't do that.

HAMILTON. Why not?

WASHINGTON (*groans*). Again? Must we go over the ground again, and again, and again, and again, and again?

HAMILTON. It seems nothing but a catastrophe will make any impression. (*Sweetly.*) But I am optimistic. I expect very shortly we will see a colossal catastrophe. (*He smiles ironically, bows, and goes.* COLONEL HUMPHREYS *follows.* WASHINGTON *stares after him, a shadow of a smile on his grim face.* JEFFERSON *enters.*)

JEFFERSON. General Washington!

WASHINGTON (*rises*). Mr. Jefferson! Welcome home. Let me look at you. (*The two men study each other.*) Six years!

JEFFERSON. Six. A long time.

WASHINTON (*sighs*). Yes. How was Patsy's wedding?

JEFFERSON. Beautiful. (*He hands* WASHINGTON *some parcels.*) For Mrs. Washington. For you.

WASHINGTON. Oh! You shouldn't have. (*Goes to his desk, picks up a knife, slits the seals of the parcels and opens them.*)

HUMPHREYS (*entering*). Jefferson, *mon vieux!*

JEFFERSON. Billy Humphreys! How are you?

HUMPHREYS. *Assez bien! Assez bien! Et notre charmante Paris? Comment va-t-elle?*

JEFFERSON. Changed. Everybody in Paris now talks politics. And you know how the French love to talk.

HUMPHREYS. Ha! (*Laughs—a high, affected cackle.*) Et la chere reine? Et le roi? How are they? (*Daintily pinches some snuff into his nostrils.*)

JEFFERSON. The King hunts one half the day, drinks the other half.

HUMPHREYS (*slyly*). La! La!

JEFFERSON. The Queen weeps, but sins on.

HUMPHREYS. Ho, ho! *Mechante* . . .

WASHINGTON (*opens his package, takes out some lily bulbs*). By God! Lily bulbs!

JEFFERSON. The loveliest species I've ever seen. Magnificent flower. Found them in the south of France.

WASHINGTON. And rice seed.

JEFFERSON. Italy!

WASHINGTON. Beautiful grain.

JEFFERSON. Look at the size!

WASHINGTON. Mm. Beautiful! Sit here! (*Moves a chair for him.*)

JEFFERSON. Thank you. (*Sits.*)

WASHINGTON (*crosses to a cabinet, takes out decanter and glasses, pours wine*). And you found Virginia?

JEFFERSON. Ah!

WASHINGTON. Mm!

JEFFERSON. Yes!

WASHINGTON. Crops?

JEFFERSON. Rye's splendid. Wheat's good. It's going to be an excellent harvest.

WASHINGTON (*sighs*). So I hear.

JEFFERSON. Of course, my own lands are almost ruined.

WASHINGTON. These damnable overseers! Ignorant. Careless. (*Hands him a glass of wine.*)

JEFFERSON. Mine complained the rabbits always ate the outside row of cabbages.

WASHINGTON. Humph! What'd you tell him?

JEFFERSON. Told him to remove the outside row.

WASHINGTON (*laughs*). Good! (*He draws up a chair and sits close to* JEFFERSON.)

HUMPHREYS. Your Excellency, I believe you have an appointment. . . .

WASHINGTON (*dismisses* HUMPHREYS *with a gesture*). All right, Colonel Humphreys, later.

HUMPHREYS. *Monsieur l'Ambassadeur!* Your Excellency! (*He makes several exaggerated bows and backs off.*)

JEFFERSON (*stares after* HUMPHREYS, *amused*). Tell me, don't the little boys in the street run after him?

(WASHINGTON *looks after* HUMPHREYS, *turns to* JEFFERSON, *nods gravely.* JEFFERSON *laughs. They raise their glasses.*)

WASHINGTON. The Republic! (*They drink.* JEFFERSON *sips the wine appreciatively, holds it up to examine the color.*) Recognize it? (JEFFERSON *nods.*) Excellent Madeira!

JEFFERSON. Patsy and I shopped all over Paris for it.

WASHINGTON. Mr. Adams is very pleased with the wines you sent him. But—er— (*He looks gravely at* JEFFERSON.) his daughter is disappointed in the purchase you made for her.

JEFFERSON. Mrs. Smith? Now, what did she . . . ? The Paris corset? (WASHINGTON *nods.*) It didn't fit?

WASHINGTON. No! (*He gestures with his hands, indicating the outlines of an ample bosom.*)

JEFFERSON. Oh, what a tragedy!

WASHINGTON. It's very pretty, too. Mrs. Adams showed it to Mrs. Washington. Pink ribbons. The ladies are heartbroken.

JEFFERSON. They mustn't despair. Tell Mrs. Smith to put it aside. After all, there are ebbs as well as flows in this world. When the mountain didn't go to Mohamet, Mohamet went to the mountain.

WASHINGTON (*smiles, drains his glass, puts it on the sideboard*). So Lafayette is trying to establish a republic in France?

JEFFERSON. Slowly, by constitutional reform. In my rooms in Paris he drew up the first bill of rights for France. The people are all looking to our experiment. It's a heart-warming thought that in working out the pattern of our own happiness, we are inadvertently working for oppressed people everywhere. There's a great danger there, though. I toured France, incognito. Visited the peasants in their hovels. The poverty and ignorance! Appalling! If they should ever lose Lafayette . . . (*Shakes his head, finishes his drink.*)

WASHINGTON. Anarchy?

JEFFERSON. Yes.

WASHINGTON (*sighs heavily*). Yes.

JEFFERSON (*studying him*). Mr. President, you look tired.

WASHINGTON (*rising*). I'm not accustomed to this indoor life. I need activity.

JEFFERSON. Long walks. The best exercise.

WASHINGTON. It's not permitted. The dignity of the State forbids it, I'm told. When we lived on Cherry Street, I couldn't go down the street without a parade. But I can tell you since we moved here to Broadway, it's a Godsend. Now, occasionally, I can steal out that door to the back yard, across the meadow and down to the river.

JEFFERSON. What do you do down at the river?

WASHINGTON. Go fishing.

JEFFERSON. Ah!

WASHINGTON (*rises, fetches a dish of biscuits*). I've had two attacks of illness this year. I doubt if I'd survive a third. Oh, well, tomorrow or twenty years from now, we are all in the hands of a Good Providence. Try one of these biscuits.

JEFFERSON. Thank you.

WASHINGTON (*goes to his desk*). I'm organizing the ministers of the various departments into a cabinet to advise me. As our Secretary of State, you're . . .

JEFFERSON. General Washington.

WASHINGTON. Mm?

JEFFERSON. In your letter you did give me the option of refusal.

WASHINGTON. You can't mean to refuse?

JEFFERSON. I must.

WASHINGTON. Why?

JEFFERSON. I've been away so long. I know none of the duties of this office. I may bungle it. I have forebodings.

WASHINGTON. We're all groping. This will be a government of accommodation.

JEFFERSON (shakes his head). I'm sorry. I want you to understand. Whatever spice of political ambition I may have had as a young man has long since evaporated. (He rises, places the half-nibbled biscuit on a dish.) I believe every man should serve his turn. I think I've done my share. Now I want to go home. I must complete my house. Twenty years it's waited. Patsy and her husband have come to stay with me at Monticello. The truth of the matter is, I've lived with my children so long, I've come to depend on their affection and comfort.

WASHINGTON. Tom, have you ever thought of marrying again?

JEFFERSON. No.

WASHINGTON. She was a wonderful woman, your Martha.

JEFFERSON. Yes. (Pause.) When I came home—she was in every room. (Pause.) I've learned one thing. For me there's no peace anywhere else in the world but Monticello. You understand why I must refuse your offer?

(HUMPHREYS enters.)

HUMPHREYS. Excuse me, sire.

WASHINGTON. Yes, Humphreys?

HUMPHREYS. The theatre box and guard of honor are arranged.

WASHINGTON (dryly). Good.

HUMPHREYS. And I've discovered the Ambassador of the Sultan of Turkey is going to be present.

WASHINGTON (with a notable lack of enthusiasm). Mm, mm.

HUMPHREYS. A suggestion, Excellency?

WASHINGTON. Yes?

HUMPHREYS. Wouldn't it be advisable to return to six horses on the coach?

WASHINGTON. I thought we compromised on four.

HUMPHREYS. When I was at the court of Louis . . .

WASHINGTON (slowly, making a great effort to contain his impatience). Colonel Humphreys, I recognize the importance of these forms to the dignity of a state, particularly one so young as ours. Understand, I know nothing of these matters. I've never been to the courts of Europe. I'm just an old soldier. I leave the ceremonies in your hands. (The impatience wears thin and he growls.) But it seems to me four horses and that canary coach with the pink and gilt angels will be enough to impress even the Ambassador of the Sultan of Turkey.

HUMPHREYS. But, sire . . .

WASHINGTON. Four will do—that's final. (He ruffles some papers, frowns.) On second thought, I won't be free to go to the theatre tonight. Cancel it!

HUMPHREYS. Sire, if I may . . .

WASHINGTON (rises, thundering). Don't sire me! How many times must I tell you? By the Eternal! I am not a King! I am the elected head of our people. This is a republic. Can you get that through your skull? (He controls himself. Wearily.) All right! Go!

HUMPHREYS. Very well, Mr. President. (He goes. WASHINGTON sighs heavily.)

WASHINGTON. I was offered the crown.

JEFFERSON. The crown!

WASHINGTON. Twice. (Pause.) I don't want to be a king, Tom. (He crosses to the cabinet, takes up a pipe, fills it with tobacco from a jug.)

JEFFERSON. I know you don't, Mr. President.

WASHINGTON. You've no idea. (He touches a taper to the flame of a burning candle.) Every eye is on this office. A number of our people suspect me. As God is my judge, I would rather live and die on my farm than be emperor of the world. (He lights his pipe, puffing angrily.)

JEFFERSON (pause). I know. And yet—since I've been back—particularly here in New York—I find alarming yearnings. Our fashionable folk appear to be looking wishfully for a king and a court of our own.

WASHINGTON. Yes. I suppose so. (*He sighs, exhales a huge puff of smoke, extinguishes the taper.*) On the other hand, there is equal danger of anarchy. We came close to it while you were away! (*He puffs nervously at his pipe.*) We walk between those two pitfalls. Our people don't take to discipline. But, without it—we shall be lost. We've yet to see how large a dose of freedom men can be trusted with. Tom, from the earliest days in Virginia, you were close to them, you seemed always to understand them. In this office I find myself far removed from direct contact with them. I need your agency. I need their faith in you. This is the last great experiment for promoting human happiness. I need the hand that wrote, "All men are created equal." I can't let you go home yet! I need you here.

(*A long pause.* JEFFERSON *turns to the desk, pours back the rice-seed he has been fondling, turns to* WASHINGTON.)

JEFFERSON. It's for you to marshal us as you see fit.

WASHINGTON (*goes to him, grips his shoulder*). Good!

JEFFERSON. It's a great honor. I hope I can be worthy of it.

(HUMPHREYS *enters.*)

HUMPHREYS. Mr. President?

WASHINGTON. I don't wish to be disturbed. . . .

HUMPHREYS. His Excellency, the Minister of Spain is arrived to pay his respects. It had already been arranged, sir. Just the courtesies!

WASHINGTON. All right. (*Sighs. Beckons to the reception room.*) I'll see him. (*To* JEFFERSON.) You'll excuse me? It will be a few minutes. There are some journals.

JEFFERSON (*holds up his portfolio*). I have my tariff reports to study.

(WASHINGTON, *escorted by* HUMPHREYS, *goes up corridor.* HAMILTON *drifts into the room, some papers in his hand. The two men look at each other.*)

HAMILTON. You're Jefferson?

JEFFERSON. Yes.

HAMILTON. I'm Hamilton.

JEFFERSON. The Hamilton?

HAMILTON (*bows*). Alexander.

JEFFERSON. Your servant.

HAMILTON. Yours.

JEFFERSON. I read your Federalist papers while I was in France. Brilliant! You've given me a great deal of pleasure.

HAMILTON. Thank you. (HAMILTON *looks at his papers, groans, shakes his head, throws the papers on the President's desk.*)

JEFFERSON. Troubles?

HAMILTON (*groans again*). God! Yes. You have a pleasant voyage home?

JEFFERSON. It seemed forever.

HAMILTON (*smiles*). Of course. (*He arranges papers on desk.*) Have you accepted the Secretary of State?

JEFFERSON. Yes.

HAMILTON. My congratulations. We must work in concert.

JEFFERSON. I'm such a stranger here, I shall lean on you.

HAMILTON. No, I'm afraid—it's—I who need your help. (*Suddenly agitated, emotional.*) Mr. Jefferson, it's enough to make any man who loves America want to cry. Forgive me! I really shouldn't burden you with this. It's a matter of my own department.

JEFFERSON. If I can be of any assistance . . . ?

HAMILTON. It's often been remarked that it's given to this country here to prove once and for all whether men can govern themselves by reason, or whether they must forever rely on the accident of tyranny. An interesting thought, Mr. Jefferson.

JEFFERSON. God, yes. We live in an era perhaps the most important in all history.

HAMILTON. An interesting thought! An awful thought! For, if it is true, then we dare not fail.

JEFFERSON. No.

HAMILTON. But we are failing. The machinery is already breaking down. *(He snaps his fingers.)* We haven't that much foreign credit. The paper money issued by the States is worthless. We are in financial chaos. *(He paces to and fro.)* The galling part is I have a remedy at hand. The solution is so simple. A nation's credit, like a merchant's, depends on paying its promissory notes in full. I propose to pay a hundred cents on the dollar for all the paper money issued by the States. Our credit would be restored instantaneously.

JEFFERSON *(worried)*. Mr. Madison spoke to me very briefly of your bill last night. It seems there's been some speculation in this paper, and he fears . . .

HAMILTON. Madison! I loved that man. I thought so high of that man. I swear I wouldn't have taken this office—except I counted on his support. And now, he's turned against me.

JEFFERSON. Mr. Madison has a good opinion of your talents. But this speculation . . .

HAMILTON. I don't want his good opinion. I want his support. Will you use your influence?

JEFFERSON. You understand I've been away six years. I've gotten out of touch here. I'll need time to study the facts.

HAMILTON. There is no time.

JEFFERSON. Well, three or four weeks.

HAMILTON. Three or four . . . ? For God's sake, man, can't you understand what I'm trying to tell you? The North is about to secede!

JEFFERSON. Secede?

HAMILTON. Hasn't the President told you?

JEFFERSON. No.

HAMILTON. Unless my bill is passed there is every prospect the Union will dissolve.

JEFFERSON. I'm aware there's a great deal of tension here, but . . .

HAMILTON. Walk in on a session of Congress tomorrow.

JEFFERSON. I see evils on both sides. *(A long pause.)* However, it seems to me —if the Union is at stake—reasonable men sitting about a table discussing this coolly should arrive at some compromise. *(He comes to a sudden decision.)* Have dinner with me tomorrow night?

HAMILTON. Delighted.

JEFFERSON. I'll invite a friend or two.

HAMILTON. Mr. Madison?

JEFFERSON. I can't promise anything. He's bitterly opposed to your plan.

HAMILTON. I have a way to sweeten the pill. The cost of living in New York has become so unreasonable there's talk of moving the capital.

JEFFERSON. Yes.

HAMILTON. It's already been promised temporarily to Philadelphia. Give me my bill and I can promise Madison the nation's capital will go to the South. Permanently. I was born in the West Indies—I have no local preference. However, for the sake of the Great Man, I'd like to see it go to Virginia.

JEFFERSON *(pause)*. Well, I'll bring you together, and sit at the table to see you don't shoot each other.

HAMILTON *(laughs)*. Fair enough.

JEFFERSON *(takes out his fan-shaped notebook, jots down the appointment)*. You see, Colonel Hamilton, we must never permit ourselves to despair of the republic.

HAMILTON. My dear Jefferson, if I haven't despaired of this republic till now, it's because of my nature, not my judgment. *(JEFFERSON laughs.)* Your address?

JEFFERSON. Twenty-three Maiden Lane.

HAMILTON. Twenty-three Maiden Lane. At seven?

JEFFERSON. Make it seven-thirty.

(WASHINGTON enters.)

WASHINGTON. You two gentlemen have met?

HAMILTON. Yes. What impression did the Spanish Ambassador leave with you?

WASHINGTON. Like all the rest. They regard us as a contemptuous joke.

HAMILTON. Well . . . (Looks at JEFFERSON, smiles.) we shan't despair. Seven-thirty? (He bows to WASHINGTON.) Excellency. (He goes.)

JEFFERSON. Remarkable young man.

WASHINGTON. They call him the Little Lion.

JEFFERSON. Little Lion! I can see it. (Picks up his portfolio.) Shall I review my report on the French Tariff situation?

WASHINGTON. Yes, yes, do.

JEFFERSON. Just before I left France, I had conversations with Monsieur Neckar on the matter of fishing rights. During the last year, some 23,000 francs . . . (WASHINGTON heaves a huge sigh. JEFFERSON looks up. The PRESIDENT is staring out the window.) Nice day out, isn't it?

WASHINGTON (distracted, turns). Hm? Oh, yes—yes.

JEFFERSON (grins). Have you a fishing pole for me?

WASHINGTON (looks at JEFFERSON, goes to a closet, takes out two fishing poles). How'd you know? (Hands one to JEFFERSON.) You don't mind, now?

JEFFERSON (laughs). I can't think of a better way to discuss the affairs of a republic.

(WASHINGTON removes his jacket, takes an old one from the closet, calls gruffly:)

WASHINGTON. Sergeant! (JEFFERSON helps him on with the jacket.) Sergeant!

(SERGEANT enters.)

SERGEANT. Yes, sir?

WASHINGTON. I'm not to be disturbed. By anyone. I'm in conference with my Secretary of State.

SERGEANT (knowingly). Yes, sir. (Exits.)

WASHINGTON (whispers to JEFFERSON). If Humphreys caught me in these clothes, I'd never hear the end. (WASHINGTON removes his wig, sets it on a stand, claps on a disreputable battered old hat, picks up his pole and some documents, opens the door, starts out, sees someone off, draws back, signaling JEFFERSON to wait.) One of the servants.

JEFFERSON. Don't they approve of democracy?

WASHINGTON (looks at JEFFERSON, shakes his head sadly). No! (He peers out again. The coast is clear, now. He signals JEFFERSON to follow him.) Come! (Stealthily, they exit.)

SCENE II

SCENE: The smithy of an inn in New York. Through the large open door a glimpse of the courtyard of the inn. JACOB, the smith, is hammering out a horseshoe. MAT, his apprentice, is pumping the bellows. Burst of laughter and men's voices from the inn courtyard. POTBOY crosses doorway clutching several foaming tankards.

JACOB. Pump her, Mat!

(His hammer comes down with a clang. MAT pumps the bellows. The fire glows. NED THE POTBOY enters.)

POTBOY. Colonel Hamilton wants his horse saddled right off.

JACOB. He in a hurry?

(Clang.)

POTBOY. Yep.

JACOB. Leavin' his party? So soon?

POTBOY. Yep.

MAT. Why, they ain't hardly started a-belchin' yet.

JACOB. Fire's gettin' cold, Mat.

MAT. I'm a-pumpin'!

POTBOY. Wants her saddled right off, he said.

MAT. We heard you.

POTBOY (irritably). I'm only tellin' yuh what . . .

MAT (sharply). Awright.

JACOB. Here! Kinda techy, you two, to-day. Ain't you?

(Pause. He looks at them both, shakes his head, hammers away at the horse-shoe.)

POTBOY *(apologetically)*. Standin' by, listenin' to that Tory talk out there! Gets me mad.

JACOB. Git the saddle on, Mat!

MAT. Awright. *(Fetches saddle.)*

POTBOY. Braggin' about the millions they made in paper money! I keep thinkin' of my sister.

MAT. And me! Don't fergit me! Three hundred dollars—whish!—right out-a me pocket. *(Laughter off. He spits.)*

POTBOY. Know what one was a-sayin'? President ain't a good title for the head of the United States. Ain't got enough distingay.

MAT. French words!

POTBOY. 'At's what he said. There are presidents of cricket clubs and fire companies, he said.

MAT. What the plague do they want? Royal Highness?

POTBOY. Yep. That's it.

(JACOB looks up, a frown on his face.)

JACOB. You mean that?

POTBOY. 'At's what they said.

MAT. Fer cripes sake!

(He goes. Just outside the door he greets newcomers, "Good afternoon, sir." JEFFERSON'S voice: "Afternoon, Mat." JEFFERSON enters with MONROE and MADISON.)

JEFFERSON *(to MADISON)*. You tell my children they're to write me more often, will you, Jemmy?

MADISON. I'll do that.

JEFFERSON. I want to hear about everything at Monticello from Patsy to Grizzle.

MONROE. Who's Grizzle?

JEFFERSON. Our pet pig.

(MONROE and MADISON laugh.)

JACOB. Afternoon, Mr. Jefferson!

JEFFERSON. How are you today, Jacob?

JACOB. Middlin'. I forged them fittin's you ordered. They're right over there on that tool bench.

JEFFERSON. Fine.

MONROE. Smith, my horse is limpin' on the off-front foot.

JACOB. Picked up a pebble?

MONROE. May have.

JEFFERSON. Looks to me as if she's sprung a shoe, James.

MONROE. Think so?

JACOB. Find out fer yuh in a minute.

MADISON. Give my nag a good going over too, will you, smith? I'm off on a long journey.

JACOB. Where to, Mr. Madison?

MADISON. Home.

JEFFERSON *(sits on a keg examining the fittings)*. Virginia.

JACOB. Oh! Nice weather.

MADISON. Ideal.

JEFFERSON. The lilacs'll be in full bloom and the golden willows and the almond trees.

JACOB. Not so early.

JEFFERSON. Oh, yes. In Virginia.

JACOB. That so?

(A burst of laughter, offstage.)

MADISON. A festive board out there!

JACOB. Some a Colonel Hamilton's friends givin' him a party.

MONROE. Celebrating the passage of his bill, I suppose.

JACOB. Yep. *(He goes off.)*

MONROE *(bitterly)*. Yes.

JEFFERSON. Now, James.

MONROE. Well, plague on it, Mr. Jefferson!

MADISON. I have to agree with Mr. Jefferson. *Ad necessitatus rei.*

MONROE. No matter how many fine Latin names you call it—"a pig is a pig."

MADISON. This was the lesser of two evils.

MONROE. You honestly think so?

MADISON (*without conviction*). I do. Yes.

MONROE. And you, Mr. Jefferson?

JEFFERSON (*doubtfully*). I don't know. I—hope so. I'm . . .

(*Laughter offstage.* MONROE *growls in disgust.* JEFFERSON *looks up at him, smiles wryly at* MADISON, *picks up the fittings* JACOB *has forged for him, examines them.*)

MONROE. You've seen the newspapers, of course?

JEFFERSON. Yes, I've seen them.

MAT (*enters. To* MADISON). Wants a feedin', your mare does. She's askin' for it.

MADISON. All right. Some oats, please.

(MAT *pours some oats in a bag.*)

MAT. Senator Monroe?

MONROE (*looks at his watch*). Yes. It's her dinnertime.

MAT. Mr. Jefferson?

JEFFERSON (*rises*). I just fed my horse, Mat, thank you. A couple of carrots, though. So he doesn't feel neglected.

MAT (*laughs*). Got some in the kitchen. (*Hands* MADISON *and* MONROE *bags of oats.* MADISON *exits with bag of oats.* MAT *exits.* JACOB *enters, holding a horseshoe in his nippers.*)

JACOB. Sprung it, awright.

MONROE. Did, hm? Shoe her at once, will you, smith?

JACOB. Yes, sir.

(MONROE *exits with bag of oats.* JACOB *puts the horseshoe in the furnace and proceeds to pump the bellows.* JEFFERSON *examines the metal fittings* JACOB *has forged for him.*)

JEFFERSON. You've done an excellent job on these.

JACOB. They awright?

JEFFERSON. Good. You know your craft!

JACOB. Ought to. Twenty years a-doin' it. (JEFFERSON *places some of the metal bits*

together.) Makin' another one of your inventions, are you?

JEFFERSON. A "convenience."

JACOB. What is it this time?

JEFFERSON (*crosses to Jacob*). A sort of closet on pulleys that will come up from the kitchen to the dining room—carry the food. hot and the wine cold right in, without people running up and down stairs.

JACOB. Now, say, that's a purty good invention.

JEFFERSON. You think so?

JACOB. Told my wife about the collapsible buggy top you invented. Kinda useful idea, she said. But this'll catch her fancy. What do you call this here invention?

JEFFERSON (*smiles*). A "dumbwaiter."

JACOB. Dumbwaiter? (*He puzzles it out.*) Oh, yeah! (*Gets it.*) Oh, yeah! (*Roars with laughter.*) A dumbwaiter. Purty good. (JACOB, *chuckling, extracts a horseshoe from the fire and begins to shape it on the anvil.*)

JEFFERSON. Jacob!

JACOB (*intent on his work*). Yes?

JEFFERSON. I need your advice.

JACOB. What about?

JEFFERSON. This money bill we've just passed.

JACOB. Oh! (*Looks up for a moment.*)

JEFFERSON. What do you think of it?

JACOB. Don't like it much.

JEFFERSON. You don't?

JACOB. Nope. (*Frowns, hammers the shoe.*)

JEFFERSON. Because of the speculators?

JACOB. Yep.

JEFFERSON. I see. Still, it's done the country considerable good?

JACOB. Mebbe.

JEFFERSON. What do your friends think of it, generally?

JACOB. Don't like it much.

JEFFERSON. I see.

(POTBOY *pokes in his head.*)

NED. Saddled yet? He's waitin'!

JACOB. Tell Mr. Jefferson, Ned. He's askin' about the money bill.

NED. A blood-suckin' swindle, Mr. Jefferson. (*He is suddenly all aflame.*) Look at my sister! Her husband was killed at the battle of Saratoga. Left her two little ones and some paper money they paid him. She's been savin' that for years. Two months ago the speculators told her it would be years more before she got anything on it, if ever. Got her to sell it for forty dollars. Six hundred dollars' worth! 'N they got Jacob's savin's.

(MAT *enters.*)

JEFFERSON. They did?

JACOB. Nine hundred.

NED. From the Revolution. His pay.

JACOB. That ain't what we fit the Revolution fer.

JEFFERSON (*rises, restlessly*). No.

MAT. I tell you it's gettin' time we . . .

(HAMILTON *enters.*)

HAMILTON. Is my horse ready, Jacob? Mr. Jefferson! I thought I saw you in the courtyard. I've some very good reports for you.

(NED *exits.*)

JEFFERSON. Splendid.

JACOB. Mat?

MAT. She's ready. (*Exits.*)

JACOB. Your horse is ready, Colonel Hamilton.

HAMILTON. Thank you! Fine day, Jacob!

JACOB (*grunts*). Yep. (*Exits.*)

HAMILTON (*to* JEFFERSON). A little soured this morning, isn't he? Liver?

JEFFERSON (*shakes his head*). Speculators.

HAMILTON. Jacob? (JEFFERSON *nods.*) A shame.

JEFFERSON. And Mat. And the potboy.

HAMILTON. Why didn't they hold on to their paper?

JEFFERSON. Apparently they did. For almost seven years.

HAMILTON. Tch! Too bad. They should have had more faith in their government.

JEFFERSON. They had no way of knowing the bill was about to redeem that paper. I'm very disturbed by this.

HAMILTON. You are?

JEFFERSON. Very. Apparently a handful of speculators, many of them in high places, have taken advantage of their knowledge of the bill to feather their own nests.

HAMILTON. Oh, now! Don't paint it worse than it is.

JEFFERSON. There's a good deal of bitter talk.

HAMILTON. Idle gossip!

JEFFERSON. Hardly.

HAMILTON. The treasury can't ask every man who submits a paper note how he came by it. At least in this way these people received something.

JEFFERSON. There must have been a means to avert this speculation.

HAMILTON. Look here—I don't quite understand your attitude. (*Burst of laughter, offstage.*) If we want to develop this country we've got to create great personal fortunes. Those men out there are building manufactories and industry. They're building America!

JEFFERSON. Good. Let's encourage them! But not at the expense of the people!

HAMILTON. You and Madison! The people whisper—you tremble.

(MONROE *and* MADISON *enter, stand silently listening.*)

JEFFERSON. That's as it should be, isn't it?

HAMILTON. I am determined this country's happiness shall be established on a firm basis. I think its only hope now lies in a moneyed aristocracy to protect it from the indiscretions of the people.

JEFFERSON. I see. And this bill is to lay the foundation for such an aristocracy?

HAMILTON. Exactly.

JEFFERSON. I wasn't aware of that. You said nothing of that to me. I must be quite honest with you. I regret that I have been made a party to your bill.

HAMILTON. Made? Made, you say? You've been in politics twenty-one years. Don't play the innocent with me! Are you dissatisfied with your bargain? Is that it?

JEFFERSON. Bargain?

HAMILTON. The capital of the nation is going to *your* state—not mine.

JEFFERSON. Oh, for God's sake!

HAMILTON. Frankly, these alarms smell of hypocrisy. One minute you say you know nothing of Treasury matters; the next you set yourself up as an authority.

MONROE. What do you suppose, Colonel? Shall we scrap the Constitution at once?

HAMILTON *(turns, sees* MONROE *and* MADISON, *murmurs, in disgust).* The Constitution!

JEFFERSON. You supported it.

HAMILTON *(flaring).* I had no choice. I couldn't stand by and see the country go down in convulsions and anarchy. *(Pause. He controls himself.)* I must confess it's my opinion this government won't last five years. However, since we've undertaken this experiment, I'm for giving it a fair trial. But, be certain of this: while it lasts it will be an aristocratic republic. If any man wants a democracy, let him proceed to the confines of some other government. Good day, gentlemen. *(He goes.)*

JEFFERSON *(to* MONROE*).* My apologies. I was wrong. *(To* MADISON.*)* Forgive me, Jemmy. I shouldn't have asked you to compromise.

MADISON. Tom, we can't escape it. He's trying to administer the Constitution into something it was never intended to be.

MONROE. I have a statement from a man who swears that Hamilton gave him money out of the public treasury to speculate with.

JEFFERSON. That I don't believe.

MONROE. There are also some letters in Hamilton's hand.

JEFFERSON. Don't believe it! He's personally honest. I'll vouch for that.

MONROE. Will you at least confront him with these letters? Ask him to explain them?

JEFFERSON. I can't.

MONROE. Why not?

JEFFERSON. Oh, for God's sake, James!

MONROE. You fight fire with fire.

JEFFERSON. I'm no salamander. Fire's not my element.

MONROE. His bill has made the fortunes of half the prominent men in the Federalist Party. It's a ring he's put through their nose. And it's clear enough, God knows, where he intends to lead them. You can't allow that. You've got to fight him. You've got to wrest the leadership of the Federalist Party away from him!

JEFFERSON *(a surge of revulsion).* If there's one thing makes me sick to death—it's the whole spirit of party politics. James, if the only way I could enter heaven was on the back of a political party, I'd rather burn in purgatory.

(JACOB appears in the doorway, adjusting saddle.)

JACOB. Your horse is ready, Mr. Jefferson.

JEFFERSON *(looks at him, pauses).* Oh, thank you, Jacob.

JACOB. Ready your horses, gentlemen?

MADISON. Yes, please.

(JACOB exits.)

JEFFERSON *(staring after Jacob, his voice harsh and lifeless).* You're wrong about the letters, James. For the rest, his bill has values. But it's hurt our people. Through it, he's created a corrupt squadron. Naturally, if he does try to pervert the Constitution, I shall oppose him. But I must do it in my own way. I'm not a brawler; I'm not a politician. *(Crosses to* MADISON.*)* Say howdya to all my neighbors for me. *(*MADISON *nods.)* The matter I spoke to you of . . . ? *(Hands a paper to* MADISON.*)*

MADISON *(nods).* I'll tend to this first thing on my arrival.

JEFFERSON. Thanks, Jemmy.

MADISON. I know how important it is to you.

JEFFERSON. Very. Pleasant journey, Jemmy. Hurry back. *(To* MONROE, *gently.)* A game of chess tonight? *(*MONROE *nods.* JEFFERSON *goes.)*

MONROE *(looking after him).* Blast it! This isn't the Jefferson we knew.

MADISON. No.

MONROE. The country's red hot. It's being shaped, *now.* What does it need to wake him again.

MADISON. The tears Christ wept before the tomb of Lazarus.

MONROE. You talk of Tom as if he were dead.

MADISON *(holds up the paper Jefferson gave him).* He asked me to order a new stone for Martha's grave. *(Unfolds paper.)* Do you understand Greek?

MONROE. No. Translate it!

MADISON *(translates).* Roughly . . .
"If in the shades below,
    The fires of friends and lovers cease to
        glow,
    Yet mine, mine alone
    Will burn on through death, itself."

MONROE. After nine years?

MADISON. After nine years!

*(*JACOB *and* MAT *enter, go to hearth.)*

JACOB. Horses ready!

MONROE. Thank you, Jacob.

*(*NED *enters.* MADISON *and* MONROE *exit.)*

NED *(raging as he tears off his apron).* I'll be damned if I'll serve on them any more! Know what they're saying now? Dukes and Lords we oughta have!

MAT. Dukes and Lords?

NED. Ay! The blood-suckin' swindlers!

JACOB. Pump her, Mat! Pump her!

MAT. What do they want to do? Make serfs outa us?

NED. Is that what we fought Lexington and Bunker Hill for? Is this the freedom my brother and my sister's husband died for? Where's your goddamn revolution now?

JACOB *(between his teeth, grimly).* Pump her, Mat! Come on, pump her! *(*MAT *pumps. The forge glows, high-lighting the taut and angry faces.* JACOB *hammers the hot iron with mighty, ringing blows.)*

ACT TWO

SCENE I

SCENE: HAMILTON'S *home. Candlelight.* HAMILTON, HUMPHREYS *and* KNOX *are having coffee.* MRS. HAMILTON *is pouring coffee.* HAMILTON *is opening a package of cigars.*

MRS. HAMILTON *(seated on sofa).* When I think of Louis and Marie in jail!

HUMPHREYS. I haven't slept a wink since the palace fell. Dreadful! Did you read Fenno's piece in the *Gazette* today?

MRS. HAMILTON. I never miss Fenno. Brilliant, wasn't it?

HUMPHREYS. *Un chef-d'oeuvre!*

MRS. HAMILTON. Veritable!

KNOX. The situation seems to be growing worse, too. What do you think, Alec, of this French Republic?

HAMILTON. Dangerous. Highly dangerous. I'm particularly disturbed by the effect it may have on some of our inflammables. *(He places the cigars on a tray.)*

HUMPHREYS. You certainly lashed Mr. Jefferson on that score! *Ma foi!* Gave it to him. But proper!

MRS. HAMILTON *(to* KNOX). Sugar?

KNOX. Please.

MRS. HAMILTON. Mr. Jefferson isn't really one of these filthy Democrats?

HAMILTON. I'm afraid so, my dear.

MRS. HAMILTON. Does he *really believe* every man is as good as every other man?

HAMILTON. Even better.

(They laugh. HUMPHREYS *applauds.)*

MRS. HAMILTON. Cream?

KNOX. Please.

HAMILTON. And our people seem so convinced of it. They can't wait to cut each other's throats. *(Offers cigars to* KNOX.*)* Try one of these.

KNOX. Yes. You saw it so clearly during the war. In the army.

HAMILTON. Army? *(He offers cigars to* HUMPHREYS*).* Colonel Humphreys?

HUMPHREYS *(takes a cigar, examines it apprehensively).* So this is one of these new "cigars"?

HAMILTON *(crosses to table, sets down cigars, lights a taper).* From the Spanish Islands. . . . Army? It was no army, it was a mob. Only one man held it together. *(He holds the lighted taper to* KNOX's *cigar.)*

KNOX. The Chief. *(Lights his cigar with huge puffs.)*

HAMILTON *(nods).* Washington. *(Lights* HUMPHREYS' *cigar.)*

KNOX *(examines his cigar).* Very interesting leaf.

HUMPHREYS *(puffing away).* Mm! Good! Good!

HAMILTON *(to* KNOX*).* I hope you like them, Henry. I've ordered a packet for you.

KNOX. Why, thank you, Alec.

HAMILTON. Not at all. *(Selects and lights a cigar for himself.)*

KNOX. Yes. The Chief made an army out of a rabble, all right. There's no doubt of that.

HAMILTON. Ah! But to accomplish it, even he had to resort to the gallows and the lash. As with an army, so with a nation. You need one strong man.

KNOX. The Chief's getting old, though.

HAMILTON. Exactly. Sometimes I lay awake nights wondering how we can ever hold this country together, when he's gone.

KNOX. Personally, I think it's his character alone that does it. I wouldn't give a penny for the Constitution without him.

HAMILTON *(sits).* Well, it's real value is as a stepping-stone. *(Purring over his cigar.)* Wonderful flavor?

KNOX. Mm!

HUMPHREYS *(wryly).* A bit strongish. *(They laugh. He disposes of his cigar in tray beside chair.)* I agree with Alec. A monarchy would have been our best salvation.

MRS. HAMILTON. Only today I was talking to some of the ladies of our court on this subject. You go out in the streets. It's frightening. We're all agreed, the time is ripening for us to have a *real* king.

BUTLER *(entering).* Senator Monroe is calling, sir.

HAMILTON. Monroe? What's he want? *(Rises.)* Show him in.

BUTLER. Yes, sir. *(BUTLER exits.)*

HUMPHREYS *(rises).* Now, there's a country bumpkin! James Monroe. *Pas d'élégance!*

KNOX. He's a good soldier! Fought in almost every important battle of the war.

HAMILTON. The soul of a clerk, though. I can't abide that.

HUMPHREYS. He was, you know. He was a clerk in Jefferson's law office ten years ago.

HAMILTON. Still is, as far as I'm concerned. *(They laugh.)* I'll wager ten to one he's here on some errand for Mr. Jefferson! Mark! You'll see!

(BUTLER enters.)

BUTLER. Colonel Monroe.

MONROE *(enters, bows).* Gentlemen! Colonel Hamilton.

(KNOX rises, bows briefly, and sits again.)

HAMILTON. Colonel Monroe. This is an unexpected pleasure. You've met my lady.

MONROE. Mrs. Hamilton. *(He bows.)* I was reluctant to intrude on you in your home.

HAMILTON *(crosses to pick up tray of cigars).* Quite all right.

MONROE. However, I've been trying to make an appointment with you at your office for several weeks.

HAMILTON *(crosses to* MONROE, *offers him cigars).* My office has been so busy. . . . The new taxes. Cigar?

MONROE. No, thanks.

HAMILTON. From the Spanish Islands.

MONROE. No, thanks. I should like to speak with you alone, if I may.

MRS. HAMILTON. My dear, it sounds ominous.

KNOX *(rises).* Well—er . . .

HUMPHREYS. I have an engagement with my wig-maker.

HAMILTON *(restrains them).* No. Stay, gentlemen. Pray. *(To* MONROE.*)* What's on your mind?

MONROE *(grimly).* I said alone.

HAMILTON *(curbs his annoyance, smiles).* I'm sorry. I've had an exhausting day. I refuse to discuss business now. I'll see you at my office. Tomorrow at four-thirty, if you wish.

MONROE. I'm seeing the President at four.

HAMILTON. Next week, perhaps.

MONROE. I'm seeing him on a matter that concerns you.

HAMILTON. Me? Indeed! Well, I wish you luck. You're sure you won't have one of these cigars—to smoke on the way?

MONROE. No, thanks.

HAMILTON. You'll excuse us, I'm sure. *(To* BUTLER, *who is waiting at the door.)* Chandler!

BUTLER *(steps forward).* Yes, sir.

MONROE. Very well. I have some papers I intend to submit to the President. I wanted to give you a chance to explain.

HAMILTON. Give me a chance to . . . ? I don't like your tone. I don't like it at all.

MONROE. I think you should be informed. There have been charges leveled against you.

HAMILTON. What charges?

MONROE. Of appropriating treasury funds.

HAMILTON. What? *(Moves toward* MONROE.*)* You dare to come into my house and accuse me of . . . ?

MONROE. *I'm* not accusing you. I'm inquiring into the facts.

HAMILTON. General Knox, will you act as my second?

KNOX. Your servant.

HAMILTON. Sir, you will name your friend to this gentleman. They can arrange weapons, time, and place. Good night.

MONROE. I'll be very happy to oblige you.

HAMILTON *(to* SERVANT*).* Show him out.

MONROE *(takes some letters out of his pocket).* But I must first demand you explain these letters. . . .

HAMILTON *(raging—moves down, facing* MONROE*).* Any man who dares call me thief . . .

MONROE. To Mr. Reynolds.

HAMILTON *(stops short).* Reynolds?

MONROE. Yes.

HAMILTON. I see. May I . . . ? *(He puts out his hand.* MONROE *gives him one of the letters. He glances at it, returns it.)*

MONROE. Is that your writing?

HAMILTON. It is. This puts the matter on a different footing. I have no objection to a fair inquiry. And I think you are entitled to a frank answer.

KNOX. We'll go, Alec. *(*KNOX *starts to go,* HAMILTON *restrains him.)*

HAMILTON. I want you as a witness to this.

KNOX. Of course.

HAMILTON *(to* MONROE*).* If you will be at my office tomorrow evening, I . . .

MONROE *(stubbornly).* I'm seeing the President at *four.*

HAMILTON. In the morning, then. It happens, fortunately, I can supply you with all the letters and documents in this instance.

MONROE. Mr. Reynolds charges you gave him money from the public treasuries to speculate with in your behalf.

HAMILTON. Where is Mr. Reynolds now?

MONROE. I've no idea.

HAMILTON. He's in jail. Subornation of perjury in a fraud case. You take the word of such a character?

MONROE. Did you give him this money?

HAMILTON. I did. But it was my own.

MONROE. And why did you give money to such a character?

(A long pause.)

HAMILTON. He was blackmailing me.

MRS. HAMILTON. Alec!

MONROE. What for?

HAMILTON. A personal matter which has nothing to do with the treasury. I'll prove that to your full satisfaction.

MONROE. Under any circumstances, I shall ask for an accounting to Congress.

HAMILTON. As a Senator that is your privilege. And I shall oblige you. I will invite all America to look into the window of my breast and judge the purity of my political motives. Not one penny of the public funds have I ever touched. I would sooner pluck out my eye by the roots.

(MONROE remains stonily unmoved. HAMILTON's smile becomes cynical.)

MONROE. At your office. Tomorrow at ten.

HAMILTON. Ten will do.

MONROE. If it's as you say, the matter will, of course, be kept confidential.

HAMILTON (ironically). Yes, I'm sure it will. (MONROE bows, turns to go.) Tell him for me, Colonel Monroe, it would have been more manly, at least, to have come here, himself.

MONROE. Who are you referring to?

HAMILTON. Who sent you, Colonel Monroe?

MONROE. No one sent me, Colonel Hamilton.

HAMILTON. No one?

MONROE. No one! (MONROE goes.)

HUMPHREYS. Quelle folie!

HAMILTON. Henry! Humphreys! Will you gentlemen . . . ?

KNOX. Of course, Alec. We were just leaving. If there's anything we can do? Anything at all, call on us. All your friends will be at your disposal.

HAMILTON. Thank you. It's not as serious as that, believe me.

HUMPHREYS. Ridiculous, of course. A bagatelle! When I was at the court, there was such an incident. . . .

KNOX. Come, Humphreys!

HUMPHREYS. Hm? Oh, yes, yes! (Bows.) Your servant, my lady. (To HAMILTON.) Votre cher ami, Colonel.

KNOX. Mrs. Hamilton! Alec!

HAMILTON. Betsy, I tried to spare you this.

MRS. HAMILTON (rises). We'll go to father. He'll help you, darling. I know he will. You mustn't worry.

HAMILTON. It's not a question of money. Good God, Betsy, do you think I'm an embezzler?

MRS. HAMILTON. I only know you're in trouble and I want to help you.

HAMILTON. Thank you, my dear. Thank you. (He kisses her.) You've been a wonderful wife, Betsy. Far better than I deserve.

MRS. HAMILTON. What was this man blackmailing you for? What have you done, Alec?

HAMILTON. I've been very foolish, Betsy.

MRS. HAMILTON. Please, Alec. Tell me!

HAMILTON. When I wooed you, do you remember I said I wanted a wife who would love God but hate a saint?

MRS. HAMILTON. Don't jest with me now, Alec.

HAMILTON. I'm not.

MRS. HAMILTON. What was this man blackmailing you for?

HAMILTON. Philandering with his wife.

MRS. HAMILTON. Oh! I see. (*Turns away —sits, controlling herself.*) Who is she? Do I know her?

HAMILTON. No. It was a game they were playing together. She and her husband. He suddenly appeared one night, claimed I'd ruined his life, and threatened to inform you, unless I gave him a thousand dollars. He's been bleeding me dry ever since. Now, he's gotten himself in jail, and wants me to use my influence to release him. I refused. This is his revenge. (*Contritely.*) Forgive me, dearest. I would do anything . . . (*He sits beside her.*)

MRS. HAMILTON. Let's not discuss that, Alec. The question is, what shall we do now to clear you?

HAMILTON. My accounts will do that, Betsy. Congress will clear me.

MRS. HAMILTON. Oh! (*Pause.*) Good, then. (*She turns to* HAMILTON.) Why didn't you tell me this before?

HAMILTON. I didn't want to hurt you.

MRS. HAMILTON (*suddenly rises, moves away*). Then I wish to Heaven you hadn't told me at all.

HAMILTON (*rises*). I'm forced to it, Betsy. Jefferson obviously wants to destroy my position as leader of the party. As long as these letters in his hands go unexplained —by insinuation, he could undermine belief in my honesty. I must be prepared to *publish* the facts, if necessary. (*He goes to her, takes her arm.*) Betsy . . .

MRS. HAMILTON (*drawing arm away*). Please, Alec!

HAMILTON. You understand, don't you?

MRS. HAMILTON. Oh, yes.

HAMILTON. Believe me, I love you.

MRS. HAMILTON (*her indignation explodes with an icy blast*). And slept with a harlot! Don't insult me, Alec! You never loved me.

HAMILTON. Why did I marry you?

MRS. HAMILTON. Was it because my father was General Schuyler?

HAMILTON (*flaring*). And I the illegitimate son of a Scotch peddler? I married you for your wealth and your position! Is that what you believe?

MRS. HAMILTON (*wearily*). I don't know what to believe.

(BUTLER *enters.*)

BUTLER. Excuse me, sir. Mr. Fenno calling on you, sir.

HAMILTON. Tell him to go away!

MRS. HAMILTON. Show him in, Chandler. (*The* BUTLER *hesitates.*) Show him in!

BUTLER. Yes, Ma'am. (*Exits.*)

HAMILTON. Betsy, I want to talk this out with you.

MRS. HAMILTON (*presses her fingers to her temples*). I don't care to discuss this any more.

HAMILTON (*takes her by shoulders*). Listen to me, Betsy! You must listen . . .

MRS. HAMILTON. Alec, please! (*She draws away from him.*) I don't care to hear any more, now. I'm—tired.

(*As she turns and goes, her handkerchief falls to the floor. He stares after her a moment, sees the handkerchief, picks it up.*)

BUTLER. Mr. Fenno.

(*Enter* MR. FENNO, *a dandified gentleman; at the moment, however, he is in a lather of perspiration.*)

FENNO. My dear Alec. I had to rush here and tell you. We have just received some shocking news. I- –I'm trembling so, I can hardly talk.

(*The* BUTLER *exits.*)

HAMILTON (*turning to* FENNO, *wearily*). What is it, Fenno?

FENO. The King and Queen of France have been executed.

HAMILTON. They've . . . ?

FENNO. Guillotined.

HAMILTON. Monstrous!

FENNO (*sinks into a chair, mops his forehead with his kerchief*). The mobs in France are utterly out of hand. Burning, looting, killing. A blood bath! Unbelievable, isn't it? Simply unbelievable!

HAMILTON. I was afraid of this.

FENNO. Worse. I've heard ugly rumors here. I passed a house yesterday, and I heard a group of men down in the cellar, singing "Ça Ira"! Rufus King told me he'd heard open threats against us. Even against General Washington.

HAMILTON. I've no doubt of it.

FENNO. I fear this is going to spread like the smallpox.

HAMILTON. Yes. And who've we to thank? Jefferson! Jefferson!

FENNO. Oh, no, I don't think he would dare . . .

HAMILTON (pacing furiously). I tell you, yes! The man's a lunatic. He's been encouraging our people to all sorts of wild illusions. Bill of rights! Freedom! Liberty! License! Anarchy! This is the fruit of his disordered imagination. That man will stop at nothing to achieve chaos. But there'll be no more of him here! I promise you. I will see to it. (Looks at BETSY's handkerchief, smooths it, a note of savage heartbreak in his voice.) There's no longer any room in this country—in this world, for both me and that—fanatic!

SCENE II

SCENE: The wild strains of "Ça Ira." As the music fades away, the harsh, discordant voices of a crowd chanting it are heard.
Philadelphia. 1793. Evening.
A room in a house rented by JEFFERSON. A mist hangs outside the window. Under the window, on the table, a row of potted plants. On a large table in the center of the room, books and papers piled high; a vise, some tools, a machine in process of construction. A kettle of water on a Franklin stove. The noise of the crowd in the street faintly heard.
JEFFERSON enters, hat in hand. He goes to the window, looks out. The sound of the crowd fades. He strikes flint and tinder and lights an oil lamp. Its light only serves to reveal the cheerlessness of the room. He extracts a journal from his pocket, sits, studying it, frowning.
JUPITER, his body servant, enters. A Negro with a good, intelligent face.

JUPITER. Evenin', Mister Tom!

JEFFERSON. Good evening, Jupiter.

JUPITER (goes about lighting the lamps). You come in so quiet. Didn't hardly hear you. We have a busy day, Mister Tom?

JEFFERSON. Mm, hm.

JUPITER. Supper's ready soon as you say.

JEFFERSON. I'm not very hungry, Jupiter.

JUPITER. But yuh got to tuck sumpin' in yuh.

JEFFERSON. Later, perhaps. (With an exclamation of disgust, JEFFERSON rises, throws the newspaper on the chair. JUPITER looks up, surprised at this unusual outburst. JEFFERSON walks over to the potted plants, examines them. JUPITER picks up the newspaper, looks at it quizzically, places it on the table. JEFFERSON examines the potted plants, nips off a few dead leaves.)

JUPITER (wheedles). Good supper. We got basted puddin' an' chicken.

JEFFERSON (shakes his head). Thanks. (Picks up a little watering pot near by and waters the plants.)

JUPITER. You just come fum one a dem cabinet meetin's?

JEFFERSON (nods, smiles). Yes!

JUPITER. Mm, mm! (Nods knowingly.) Funny weather outside. Sticky! That yeller fog hanging all over Philadelphia. I heard today ten white folk died o' the fever.

JEFFERSON. More than that.

JUPITER. Don't like it none. (Turns to go. JEFFERSON notices JUPITER's hand is roughly bandaged with a bloodstained handkerchief.)

JEFFERSON. What's happened to your hand?

JUPITER. Oh, it's nothin'.

JEFFERSON. Let me look at it! Come here. *(He removes the bandage.)* A nasty gash. Sit over here! *(JUPITER sits. JEFFERSON goes to the stove, pours some water into a cup, selects a bottle of wine and cruet of oil from the cupboard.)* How did you do that, Jupiter?

JUPITER. When I do my marketin' this afternoon, Mister Tom.

(JEFFERSON sets the cup, the wine and the oil on the table, opens a drawer, and takes out some cloth. He opens JUPITER'S hand, examines it.)

JEFFERSON. This is going to sting a bit. *(Tears cloth into strips.)*

JUPITER. That's all right, Mister Tom.

JEFFERSON *(dips the cloth in the water and starts to clean the wound. He soaks the cloth with wine, dabs the wound. JUPITER winces).* Hurt you? *(JUPITER stoically shakes his head.)* How did you do this?

JUPITER. Down outside Bainbridge Market. Just as I came out.

JEFFERSON. Yes?

JUPITER. Three men was talkin'. "Mr. Jefferson's a devil," they say. Colonel Hamilton tell dem you gonna bring the French Revolution here. Murder everybody. I don't like that. I told them that ain't true. "Ain't you Jefferson's nigger?" they say. They say they was gonna kill me. One of 'em tried to hit me on the head with a stick. I put my hand up. The stick had a nail in it.

JEFFERSON. Oh, Jupiter! Haven't you learned yet?

JUPITER. They talk bad about you. What I'm gonna do?

JEFFERSON. When an angry bull stands in your path, what do you do?

JUPITER. What I do?

JEFFERSON. A man of sense doesn't dispute the road with such an animal. He walks around it. *(He smiles. JUPITER laughs and nods.)*

JUPITER. Yeah, I guess so.

JEFFERSON. What happened then, Jupiter?

JUPITER. Then a crowd came down the street, yellin'! Dey's a lot a crowds in de street, Mister Tom.

JEFFERSON. I know.

JUPITER. De men see dat crowd. Dey get scared an' run away. Mister Tom—dem crowds in de street—dey're talkin' wild. Yellin' "Kill de aristocrats! Break dere windows! Burn dere houses!" Singin' French songs.

JEFFERSON *(he bandages the hand).* Hurt? Too tight?

JUPITER *(shakes his head).* Dey talkin' bad about President Washington.

JEFFERSON. Washington?

JUPITER. Yes, Mister Tom. *(JEFFERSON frowns as he bandages the hand.)* Dat get me all mixed up. I know he fight for liberty. I remind me you tell me General Washington try to free my people.

JEFFERSON. That's right. He did.

JUPITER. I remind me, how you try, Mister Tom. I like to see my little Sarah free some day. An' I remind me how you say we gotta some day open all that land in the Northwest and ain't gonna be no slaves there. An' how we gotta git my people education, an' we gotta git 'em land, an' tools.

JEFFERSON. Some day, Jupiter. It's written in the book of fate. Your people will be free.

JUPITER. Mister Tom. Dat crowd. Git me mixed up. Git me all mixed up. I don't like it. Dey jus' gonna make trouble.

JEFFERSON. I'm afraid you're right, Jupiter. You see, the men who beat you— they're Monarchists. They want a king here. The others—the crowd—they're mixed up. It's what's happening in France now. It's gone wild. *(Finishes bandaging JUPITER's hand.)* How's that feel?

JUPITER. Fine, Mister Tom. *(He tries his hand.)* Fine.

JEFFERSON. Don't use that hand for a while.

JUPITER. No, Mister Tom.

(The bell tinkles.)

JEFFERSON. The door-pull!

(JUPITER *goes to answer it.* JEFFERSON *picks up the wine, returns it to cupboard.*)

JUPITER (*appears in the doorway, excited and laughing*). Mister Tom! Looka here! Look who's here. (PATSY *enters.*)

PATSY. Father!

JEFFERSON. Patsy? Darling.

(*They rush to each other and embrace.*)

PATSY. Oh, Father. It's so good to see you.

JEFFERSON. My dearest. What in the world . . . ?

PATSY. I wanted to surprise you.

JEFFERSON. It's a wonderful surprise. Jupiter, kill the fatted calf! Two for supper.

JUPITER. It's chicken.

(*They laugh.*)

JEFFERSON. Kill it, anyway.

JUPITER (*laughs*). He got his appetite back! Looka his face. You shore good medicine, Mrs. Patsy.

JEFFERSON. Where's your trunk?

PATSY. The coachman left it outside.

JUPITER. I get it right away. (*Starts off.*)

JEFFERSON. I'll fetch it, Jupiter. Your hand is . . .

JUPITER (*holds up his good hand*). That's all right, Mister Tom. I kin manage.

PATSY (*goes to* JUPITER). Your wife sends you her love, Jupiter. And Sarah.

JUPITER (*stops, and turns*). Dey all right?

PATSY (*nods*). I've brought you some presents they made for you.

JUPITER. Thanks, Mrs. Patsy! It's sure good to have you here, Mrs. Patsy! (*He exits.*)

JEFFERSON. How's little Jeff, and my sweet Anne, and Maria? And Mr. Randolph? Here! Give me your cloak. (JEFFERSON *takes her cloak, places it on a chair.*)

PATSY. Jeff has two new teeth.

JEFFERSON. Two? Wonderful!

PATSY. He's beginning to talk. Anne's growing so. You'd hardly recognize her.

JEFFERSON. Does she still remember me, Patsy?

PATSY. Of course. She's always playing that game you taught her—I love my love with an A. She's forever chattering about you. "Where's grandpapa? When's grandpapa coming home? What presents is grandpapa going to bring me?"

JEFFERSON (*chuckles*). Mm, hm!

PATSY. Maria sends love, squeezes and kisses. We both adored the hats and veils.

JEFFERSON. Did they fit?

PATSY. Perfectly. And the cloaks were beautiful.

JEFFERSON. The style was all right?

PATSY. Oh, yes.

JEFFERSON. And how's your good husband?

PATSY. Mr. Randolph's well, working hard. Doing the best he can with the overseer. . . . Is it always so close in Philadelphia?

JEFFERSON. This is very bad weather. A contagious fever's broken out here.

PATSY (*looks about*). So this is where you live?

JEFFERSON. Do you like my quarters?

PATSY. A little gloomy, isn't it?

JEFFERSON (*laughs*). You must be exhausted. A glass of sherry?

PATSY. I'd love it. (JEFFERSON *crosses to wine cabinet.*) Father! Coming here—the coach had to stop. There was such a crowd of people up the street.

JEFFERSON. The French Ambassador's been haranguing them lately. There have been some disorders. This epidemic of fever here seems to bring a moral contagion with it. (*He selects several bottles, holds them up.*) Dry or sweet?

PATSY. Dry, please. (*She toys with a mechanical device on the table.*) What's this? Another "convenience" of yours?

JEFFERSON. That's a copying machine. Very handy. It makes duplicate copies of letters. I'll show you how it works.

PATSY (*laughs*). Oh, Father. You and your inventions! Sometimes I . . . (*Her eye is caught by the journal on the table. She stops laughing, frowns, picks it up, reads it. Her face sets in anger.)*

JEFFERSON *(pouring sherry).* Has Maria learned to baste a pudding yet? In her last letter she said Aunt Eppes was teaching her . . .

PATSY. Father!

JEFFERSON. Hm? *(Turns, sees her with the newspaper.)* Oh! You don't want to read that! *(Crosses to take it from her.)*

PATSY. Oh, my God!

JEFFERSON. Now don't get upset, dear!

PATSY. What sort of a newspaper is this?

JEFFERSON. The "court" journal. The snobs nibble it for breakfast. Here. drink your sherry.

PATSY. I'd heard what they were doing to you here, but this is worse than I could have possibly imagined.

JEFFERSON. It's very flattering. Especially that bit about the harem! A harem! At my age! Pretty good. . . .

PATSY. I don't see any humor in it! You'll answer these charges?

JEFFERSON. Answer one lie, they print twenty new ones.

PATSY. Then what are you going to do?

JEFFERSON. Let's ignore it, dear, hm?

PATSY. Who wrote it? Who's Pacificus?

JEFFERSON. I don't know. It's a pseudonym.

PATSY *(pauses. She looks at him, almost in tears; finally, very bitterly).* You must enjoy being the Secretary of State very much to put up with such abuse.

JEFFERSON. It's my job, dear.

PATSY. Job? *(Rises, walks to the window, agitated.)* Father?

JEFFERSON. Yes, dear?

PATSY. Don't you think you've sacrificed enough?

JEFFERSON. I haven't suffered anything.

PATSY. You haven't?

JEFFERSON. No.

(Pause.)

PATSY. A few weeks ago I found a pamphlet Mother had written during the Revolution to the Women of Virginia on the necessity for them *(Bitterly.)* to make sacrifices to help win the war. I remember Mother so ill she could hardly walk, doing ten men's work at home. I remember, after she died, sitting on the cold floor outside your door, listening to you sob till I thought you, too, must die. I remember hearing you cry out, you'd sacrificed her to the Revolution.

JEFFERSON *(sinks into a chair).* Patsy.

PATSY. The morning and afternoon of your life you sacrificed. Wasn't that enough?

JEFFERSON. Patsy, dear! Please!

PATSY. No. If you won't think of yourself, what of us? A child of twelve and a baby of four, torn from our home, from all we loved, taken to a foreign land, seeing you only on occasion, longing always for home and security and . . . Why? For what? Is there no end . . . ?

JEFFERSON. Patsy, I beg of you?

PATSY. Don't you owe anything to yourself? Don't you owe anything to us? I tell you, Father, everything at home is going to pieces. If you don't come back soon, there'll be nothing left. Nothing!

JEFFERSON *(rises, in agony).* Patsy! Will you, for God's sake, stop!

PATSY *(crosses to him, overcome with remorse).* Father! Oh, Father, I didn't mean to . . .

JEFFERSON *(takes her in his arms).* I know. I know.

PATSY. Forgive me.

JEFFERSON. Of course.

PATSY. I've been so confused and unhappy. I had to come and talk it out with you.

JEFFERSON. Of course you did. I should have been very hurt if you hadn't.

PATSY. It's the business of running Monticello and the farms. We try! Lord knows we try! But Mr. Randolph has no talent for it. And his failure makes him irritable. And I worry so. I'm afraid you may lose everything you own.

JEFFERSON. I see, my dear. I see. *(He strokes her hair.)* I haven't been altogether insensible to this. It's weighed on me very heavily, the trouble I put your good husband to.

PATSY. I shouldn't have said anything. I know what your work here means to you.

JEFFERSON (a sudden surge of bitterness). I have never loathed anything as much in my life. You've no idea, Patsy, of the rank and malignant hatreds here. Politics destroy the happiness of every being in this city! I'm surrounded here by hate and lies. Lately I've seen men who once called themselves my friends go so far as to cross the street to avoid tipping their hats to me.

PATSY. You of all people! Why?

JEFFERSON. There are a gang of king-jobbers here who are bent on changing our principle of government—by force, if necessary. Since Mr. Madison and Mr. Monroe have left, I'm alone against them. I can't contend with them, Patsy.

PATSY. What of the President?

JEFFERSON. Only his strength and his stubborn purity oppose them. But he's old, and he's sick. (Sits.) I work from morning till night. They undo everything. This isn't spending one's life here. It's getting rid of it.

PATSY. Oh, my poor father! (PATSY goes to him, kneels at his feet. He draws out a locket hanging around his neck.)

JEFFERSON. Do you know, dear, my only pleasure? For an hour or so every evening I sit and dream of Monticello. I find myself more and more turning to the past and to those I loved first. Your mother . . . (He opens the locket, studies it.) She was a beautiful person, Patsy. She loved you all so dearly. (Closes the locket.) You're right, Patsy. If I hadn't neglected my duties at home during the war, she would have been alive today. It's true. I sacrificed your mother to the Revolution. And now I'm doing the same to you. Darling, your happiness is more important to me than my life. And, like a fool, I've been jeopardizing it. For the privilege of being (Rises, picks up the newspaper.) called in the public prints "lecher, liar, thief, hypocrite!" (He throws down the newspaper.) But no

more! You mustn't worry, dearest. Everything's going to be all right. I promise you. I'm tending to my own from now on. (Grim-faced, he takes down a portable writing-desk from the mantelpiece, sits, places it on his lap, opens it, extracts paper and pen, and begins to write furiously.) Patsy!

PATSY. Yes.

JEFFERSON. Will you ring for Jupiter? The bell-pull's there. (PATSY pulls the cord. A tinkle is heard, offstage.) I have a job for you tomorrow.

PATSY. Good. What is it?

JEFFERSON (as he writes). I want you to help me select what furniture and articles suit Monticello, and pack and ship them to Richmond.

PATSY. To Richmond?

JEFFERSON. I'll be busy here the next few weeks, but we'd better get them off at once while the shipping lanes are still seaworthy. (He sands the letter, blows it, reads it a moment. JUPITER enters.)

JUPITER. Yes, Mister Tom?

JEFFERSON. You know where the President's home is?

JUPITER. Yes.

JEFFERSON. Please deliver this letter there at once.

JUPITER. After supper?

JEFFERSON (rises). No, now, Jupiter.

JUPITER. My supper's gonna get spoiled.

JEFFERSON. At once, Jupiter. (To PATSY.) We're going home, together. To stay, Patsy. I'm resigning. (He places the open portable desk on the table.)

JUPITER. You goin' home, Mister Tom?

PATSY. Yes, Jupiter.

(JUPITER stares at JEFFERSON.)

JUPITER. Mister Tom goin' home . . . ?

PATSY. Oh! I'm so happy, Father, I . . .

(The faint noise of a crowd outside. PATSY breaks off, listens. The noise grows.)

JEFFERSON. The crowd again. (He crosses to the window and looks out.) This is good fuel for the Federalists!

river of the noblest blood of France—for your drunken swine, the people, to swill in. I tell you—it nauseates me to the very heart. And now, the same rioting mobs here, and next the same terror!

JUPITER (*enters*). General Washington.

WASHINGTON (*enters*). Gentlemen! (*He is getting very old. His face is tired and bewildered, but a bulwark of grim, stubborn determination.* JUPITER *exits.*)

JEFFERSON. Mr. President. (*Moves to* WASHINGTON; *takes his hat and stick.*)

HAMILTON. No asafoetida pad? (*Produces a spare pad and hands it to the* PRESIDENT.) In these times, Mr. President, we can't afford to lose you. I beg of you!

WASHINGTON. Very well. (*Accepts pad.*) Thank you. (*Sits down heavily, silent for a moment, as he broods, all the while tapping the arm of the chair as if it were a drum. The death cart outside rumbles by.*) More than two thousand dead already. This plague is worse than a hundred battles of cannon. (*Sighs, taps.*)

HAMILTON. You should have left the city immediately, sir.

WASHINGTON. I think I almost prefer to be in my grave than in the present situation. (*Taps, sighs heavily. A long pause.*) What does it mean? (*Silence; taps.*) Incredible. Aren't men fit to be free? Is that the answer? Have you spoken to the French minister?

JEFFERSON. Yes. One can't reason with him. He's a lunatic! I've demanded his recall.

WASHINGTON. They're all lunatics. Lafayette fleeing for his life! Lafayette! And here now, mobs rioting! What does this mean? (*Pause.*) We must do what we can to help Lafayette.

JEFFERSON. I've already despatched a letter to Ambassador Morris, uring him to make every solicitation in his power.

WASHINGTON. I don't know if it'll help. I doubt it. (WASHINGTON *nervously picks up* The Gazette, *glances quickly at* JEFFERSON. *To* HAMILTON, *with a touch of sternness.*) Do you mind waiting below? I should like to talk with you.

HAMILTON (*glances a bit guiltily at* JEFFERSON, *then smiles ironically*). I'll wait in your carriage. (WASHINGTON *nods.*) Your servant, Mr. Jefferson.

JEFFERSON. Mr. Hamilton.

(HAMILTON *goes.*)

WASHINGTON. I shall have to speak to him again. He's very difficult. He's always been that way, though. Once, during the war, when he was my aide, he kept me waiting two hours. When I rebuked him, he resigned. Sulked like a little boy. (*Softens, with evident love of* HAMILTON.) Finally I gave him what he wanted—a command in the field. He was a very good soldier. Led his troops in the first assault on Yorktown. He's an invaluable man. Why can't you two work together?

JEFFERSON. Our principles are as separate as the poles.

WASHINGTON. Coalesce them!

JEFFERSON. It can't be done.

WASHINGTON. Let me be the mediator.

JEFFERSON. You've tried before.

WASHINGTON. Let me try again.

JEFFERSON. It's no use. Believe me. Neither of us could honestly sacrifice his belief to the other.

WASHINGTON (*sighs, taps*). Well, I'm ordered back home. Any messages to Albemarle County?

JEFFERSON (*sits next to* WASHINGTON). My best regards to Mr. Madison. And you might look at my new threshing machine. If it interests you, the millwright's in Richmond now. He'd be very happy for any new commissions. You get eight bushels of wheat an hour out of two horses.

WASHINGTON. Hm! I'll certainly examine it.

JEFFERSON. Tell Madison next spring we'll be planting our gardens together.

WASHINGTON. No, Tom. I'm afraid you won't.

JEFFERSON. Why not?

WASHINGTON (*rises. Takes out a paper, lays it on desk*). Your resignation. I can't accept it.

JEFFERSON (rises). I'm sorry, Mr. President. You'll have to.

WASHINGTON. Where can I find anyone to replace you?

JEFFERSON. I don't flatter myself on that score. I've failed.

WASHINGTON. Let me be the judge of that.

JEFFERSON. I've spent twenty-four years in public life. I'm worn down with labors that I know are as fruitless to you as they are vexatious to me. My personal affairs have been abandoned too long. They are in utter chaos. I must turn to them and my family.

WASHINGTON. And the good esteem of your fellowmen?

JEFFERSON (moves away). There was a time when that was of higher value to me than anything in the world. Now I prefer tranquillity. Here, for everything I hate, you ask me to give up everything I love. I'm sorry, no! I want a little peace in my lifetime.

WASHINGTON. I know. I know. I'm sick, Tom, and I'm getting old, and I catch myself dreaming of the Potomac and Mount Vernon. (He almost shouts.) Don't you think I hate this, too? Don't you think I yearn for the peace of my own farm? Don't you think all this—all this . . . (Controls himself. There is a long silence. He murmurs.) Peace in our life? Where . . . ? (His memories turn back as he searches for the phrase.) Oh, yes. . . . Paine wrote it. Was it in The Crisis? "These are the times that try men's souls. The summer soldier and the sunshine patriot will in this crisis shrink . . ." (JEFFERSON sinks into a chair; unwittingly, the PRESIDENT has dealt him a stunning blow.) How that brings back the picture! As if it were yesterday. My men starved, naked, bleeding. I read Paine's essay. You know, it lent me new strength. I had it read to my men through trumpets. Nailed it on trees for them to read. It helped them. Gave them sore-needed courage. Do you remember the passage on the Tory innkeeper who was opposed to the war because . . . (He finds the phrase he's been searching for.) that's it— "He wanted peace in his lifetime?" And Paine looked down at the innkeeper's children crawling on the floor and thought, "Were this

Tory a man, he would say: If there must be conflict with tyranny, let it come in my time. Let there be peace and freedom in my children's time." Yes. That's the answer, I suppose. The only answer. (Suddenly, desperately, he grips JEFFERSON's arm.) Tom! The fabric is crumbling. Our Republic is dying. We must bolster it, somehow—some way. (Fiercely, a grim, stubborn warrior fighting a ghost. He pounds the table.) It must have a chance. It will, I say. It will, it will, it will! I'll defend its right to a chance with the last drop of my blood. (The fierceness vanishes. Again he becomes a tired, sick, old man.) You'll stay on a few days more? Till I find someone else?

JEFFERSON. Yes.

WASHINGTON. Good! You see, I'm like a man about to be hanged. Even a few days' reprieve makes me rejoice. (Sighs heavily, starts to go, turns.) I wouldn't stay here. Take your papers, go to the country. You can work there. (Bows.) Mr. Jefferson.

JEFFERSON (rises). Mr. President.

(WASHINGTON goes. Outside, the death cart rumbles by. JEFFERSON, torn and tortured, drops back into his chair. JUPITER enters, pours more nitre into the braziers. PATSY enters, holding up a music box.)

PATSY. Father! Look! I found this little music box inside. May I . . . Father! You're not ill?

JEFFERSON. No, Patsy.

PATSY. You look so pale. Are you sure, Papa?

JEFFERSON. Yes, dear.

PATSY. Can I get you something? A drink of water?

JEFFERSON. No, dear. I'm all right.

(Pause. JUPITER exits.)

PATSY. May I take this home to Anne?

JEFFERSON. Yes, dear.

(She turns a knob. The music box plays a tinkling melody.)

PATSY. Anne will love it. Can't you just see her face?

JEFFERSON. Mm.

(Pause.)

PATSY. Did the President accept your resignation?

JEFFERSON. Yes.

PATSY. I spoke to him in the hallway. He looks so old, doesn't he? (JEFFERSON *nods.* PATSY *shuts off the music box.*) Oh, Father, please! Please don't torment yourself so!

JEFFERSON (*rises*). He's a dying man, Patsy. He's dying. And, when he's gone, they'll take the reins. And that'll be the end, Patsy. That'll be the end of the Republic.

PATSY. Perhaps we weren't ready for it, Father.

JEFFERSON (*moves about, restlessly*). If not here and now, where then? Where will men ever have such a chance again? This was my dream, Patsy! From my earliest youth.

PATSY. You've done your best, Father.

JEFFERSON. Not good enough, apparently. Summer soldier. (*Pause.*) It was seventeen years ago, *here in Philadelphia,* I wrote the Declaration of Independence. That's how I dreamed of America, Patsy. A beacon for all mankind. (*Pause.*) Patsy! It's not our people who've failed us. It's we who've failed them. Yes. I see that now. (*Paces about the room.*) These fermentations are a healthy sign. Our people are groping. They're jealous of their rights? Good! They want a larger share in their government. Most of them today haven't even the privilege of voting. It would take so little education to make them understand these disorders are not to their advantage. That's where we've failed them, Patsy. It's not enough to create the form of a Republic. We must *make* it work. We must see that our people get the right to vote. We must educate them to use it and be worthy of it. We must give them free schools, and universities and a liberal press. Only an enlightened people can really be free. Till now, the genius of the common people has been buried in the rubbish heap. We must rescue that! I'm convinced of it! We must make war on ignorance and poverty. We must go into the streets and the squares and the smithies. . . .

JUPITER (*entering*). Mister Tom.

(HAMILTON *appears in the doorway.*)

HAMILTON. I beg your pardon. I didn't mean to . . .

(JEFFERSON *faces* HAMILTON. JUPITER *exits.*)

JEFFERSON. It's quite all right. Come in!

HAMILTON. The President asked me to speak to you. He's greatly distressed.

JEFFERSON. Yes, I know he is.

HAMILTON. He asked me to make an effort to coalesce our differences. There's no reason why we shouldn't.

JEFFERSON. You think we can?

HAMILTON. If you will only stop regarding the Constitution as something handed down from Mount Sinai.

JEFFERSON. I see.

HAMILTON. If we're to work together, you'll . . .

JEFFERSON. We're not!

HAMILTON. Oh!

JEFFERSON. We are natural enemies.

HAMILTON. Well, I offered peace.

JEFFERSON. The wolves offered the sheep peace.

HAMILTON. You don't flatter me!

JEFFERSON. It is not an American art.

HAMILTON. I am an American by choice, not by accident.

JEFFERSON. Yet you bring here a lie bred out of the vices and crimes of the old world.

HAMILTON. Lie?

JEFFERSON. The lie that the masses of men are born with saddles on their backs, and a chosen few booted and spurred to ride them legitimately, by the grace of God.

HAMILTON. It's laughable! You, born to wealth and land and slaves, driveling about the common people!

JEFFERSON. Search your own birth, Mr. Hamilton, and you'll . . .

HAMILTON. Don't say it! (*Trembling with rage.*) I must warn you

JEFFERSON. Say what? That you as a boy were poor? That you came to this country and it gave you honor and wealth? I believe every boy in this land must have that opportunity.

HAMILTON. Why do you think I want the country strong?

JEFFERSON. It can only be strong if its people govern it.

HAMILTON. You think the peasants on my farm can make it strong?

JEFFERSON. There are no peasants in America.

HAMILTON. Words! What do I care for them! Call them yeomen! Call them what you will! Men cannot rule themselves.

JEFFERSON. Can they then rule others? Have we found angels in the forms of kings and dictators to rule them?

HAMILTON. I've made my last gesture. Go! Run back to your hill! From here on, I promise you, you will never again dare raise your head in this party.

JEFFERSON. I hate party. But if that's the only way I can fight you—then I'll create another party. I'll create a people's party.

HAMILTON. Now it comes out. You want two parties! You want blood to flow! At heart you, too, are a Jacobin murderer.

JEFFERSON. That's another lie you believe because you wish to believe it. It gives you the excuse you need to draw your sword! I'm sick to death of your silencing every liberal tongue by calling "Jacobin murderer."

HAMILTON. Well, aren't you? Confess it!

JEFFERSON. Go on! Wave the raw head and the bloody bones! Invent your scares and plots! We were asleep after the first labors, and you tangled us and tied us, but we have only to awake and rise and snap off your Lilliputian cords.

HAMILTON. Very well. Let it be a fight, then. But make it a good one. And, when you stir up the mobs, remember—we who really own America are quite prepared to take it back for ourselves, from your great beast, "The People."

JEFFERSON. And I tell you, when once our people have the government securely in their hands, they will be strong as a giant. They will sooner allow the heart to be torn out of their bodies than their freedom to be wrested from them by a Caesar!

HAMILTON (bows). Good day, Mr. Jefferson.

JEFFERSON. Good day, Colonel Hamilton. (HAMILTON exits. JEFFERSON turns to PATSY.) Patsy, this is a fight that may take the rest of my life. . . .

PATSY. Yes.

JEFFERSON. But I have to! I hate it, but I have to, Patsy. I want Anne and Jeff and their children to grow up in a free republic. I have to, Patsy.

PATSY. Of course you do. (Rises. Crosses to JEFFERSON.) Of course you do, Father. (She takes his hand impulsively, kisses it.)

ACT THREE

SCENE I

SCENE: *The new city of Washington, 1801.* JEFFERSON's *rooms in Conrad's Boarding House.*

JEFFERSON *seated at his desk, writing. His grandchildren, a little boy and a girl, playing on the floor at his feet.* PATSY *seated, crocheting. Outside, in the hallway, the excited babble of many voices.* JUPITER *is placing a tray on the desk. Prominently set on the mantel is a marble bust of* WASHINGTON.

A knock at the door. PATSY *starts up.* JUPITER *turns to the door.*

PATSY. I'll take it, Jupiter.

(She hurries to the door, opens it. A

MESSENGER *hands her a message. A crowd of boarders surrounds him, asking questions.)*

MESSENGER. Twenty-seventh ballot just come up.

PATSY. Thank you. *(The crowd assails her with questions.)* In a minute. *(She hands the message to her father.* JEFFERSON *reads it, while she waits anxiously.* JEFFERSON *crumples it, throws it away, smiles, shakes his head.)*

JEFFERSON. The same.

PATSY. Oh, dear! *(She goes to the door.)* No. I'm sorry. Congress is still deadlocked.

(The crowd in the hallway becomes persistent.)

FIRST MAN. We heard Mr. Burr lost a vote to your father.

PATSY. That's not true, as far as I know.

MESSENGER *(shakes his head)*. No. I told them. *(To others.)* I told you. *(He goes.)*

SECOND MAN. We elected Mr. Jefferson to be President. What's Congress fiddling around for, anyway? What are they up to, Mrs. Randolph?

THIRD MAN. Is it true the Feds are going to try and just make one of their own men President?

PATSY. I can't say. . . .

(Suddenly a high-pitched voice is heard and a little lady comes pushing through the crowd. She is MRS. CONRAD, *the proprietress of the boarding house.)*

MRS. CONRAD. In the parlor, please! All my boarders. Downstairs! In the parlor! You'll get the returns there as soon as you will up here. Now, stop a-pesting Mr. Jefferson! Give a man a little privacy, will you? Downstairs in the parlor! *(She enters, apologetically, in a whisper.)* Everybody's so worked up, you know.

PATSY. It's all in the family.

MRS. CONRAD. Well, I can't have the other boarders disturbing your father at a time like this.

PATSY. Thank you.

(A husky voice is heard singing "Outa my way." "One side!" The boarders are tumbled aside. A man in frontier outfit, armed to the teeth, appears in door.)

FRONTIERSMAN. Tom Jefferson here?

PATSY. What is it?

FRONTIERSMAN. Message from Governor Monroe of Virginia.

JEFFERSON. Here!

FRONTIERSMAN. You're Tom Jefferson?

JEFFERSON. Yes.

FRONTIERSMAN *(hands him message)*. Governor Monroe said to deliver it to you personal.

JEFFERSON. Thank you! *(Opens it. Reads it.)* Sit down.

FRONTIERSMAN. Don't mind astandin'. Rid my horse hard all a way from Richmond. She's got a mean jog. Governor's waitin' on your answer.

JEFFERSON. No answer, yet.

FRONTIERSMAN. Nothing settled yet on the election?

JEFFERSON. No. You'd better stand by.

FRONTIERSMAN. Yep.

JEFFERSON. Mrs. Conrad, will you see this gentleman gets something warm to eat? Jupiter, will you saddle a fresh horse?

JUPITER. Yes, Mr. Tom. *(Exits.)*

MRS. CONRAD. I'll tend to it right away, Mr. Jefferson. *(Goes to door, calls.)* Nathan!

VOICE *(offstage)*. Yes, Mrs. Conrad.

MRS. CONRAD. Fix up some vittles right off!

PATSY. Perhaps you'd like a drink?

FRONTIERSMAN. Why, thank you, Ma'am. Now that's a Christian thought.

(PATSY smiles, fetches brandy bottle. MRS. CONRAD *returns.)*

BOY. Gramp! Play with me.

PATSY *(pouring drink)*. Jeff, Grandpapa's busy.

BOY. Come on, Gramp . . .

JEFFERSON. Later, Jeff. I've a new game to teach you.

BOY. A new one?

JEFFERSON. A good one.

BOY. Is it like riding a horse to market?

GIRL. Oh, goody, Grandpapa! Shall I get the broom?

PATSY (*hands drink to the Frontiersman*). Children! Go inside.

JEFFERSON. No, no. They don't disturb me. I want them here.

(PATSY *beckons the children away from the desk, seats them in the corner by her side.*)

FRONTIERSMAN (*tosses down the drink*). Hm! That washes the dust down!

(*A knock at the door.* PATSY *hurries to it.* MADISON *is there. Crowded behind him in the hall is the group of boarders. They are asking him questions.* MR. MADISON *is saying, "That's the latest balloting. I've just come from the Capitol."*)

MADISON (*enters, worn, breathless, almost crumbling with fatigue*). I've just come from the House of Representatives. I had to push my way here. The streets are jammed with people. I've never seen so many human beings.

JEFFERSON. Jemmy, you look like a dead one.

MADISON (*sits and groans*). I am. The twenty-seventh ballot came up.

JEFFERSON. We just got the message.

MADISON. You should see Congress! What a spectacle! They fall asleep in their chairs, on their feet. Red-eyed, haggard!

JEFFERSON. Mr. Nicholson's fever any better?

MADISON. Worse. He's resting in a committee-room. He has about enough strength to sign his ballot.

JEFFERSON. Who's attending him?

MADISON. His wife's by his side, giving him medicine and water.

JEFFERSON. He should be removed to a hospital.

MADISON. He won't budge. Insists he'll vote for you till he dies. I doubt whether he'll survive another night. (JEFFERSON *shakes his head.*) Tom, there's an ugly rumor going around. The crowds are getting angry.

JEFFERSON. Yes, I know. May be more than a rumor, I'm afraid. (*He hands* MADISON *a communication.*)

MADISON. Gad! How's this going to end?

MRS. CONRAD. I been talkin' to my husband, Mrs. Randolph, and we both decided the whole way of votin' now just ain't right.

MADISON. Agreed. Agreed.

MRS. CONRAD. Take my husband. He wanted your father for President, Mr. Burr for Vice-President. Well, he should be allowed to put that down on the ballot instead of just the two names and lettin' Congress decide. Stands to reason, don't it? See what happens? We beat the Federalists, and then the old Congress, most of 'em Feds themselves, don't know who to pick. Deadlocked six days now. They might like as not go on being deadlocked four years, and we'll have no President at all. Now, I say, it's deliberate. Everybody's sayin' that!

JEFFERSON. They are?

MRS. CONRAD. Stands to reason. (*She nods vigorously and scurries off, having said her piece.*)

MADISON. We should have foreseen this difficulty. We certainly bungled the electoral system.

FRONTIERSMAN. Constitution's gotta be changed so a man can put down who he wants for President.

JEFFERSON. Well, it can be amended. That's the great virtue of the Constitution. It can grow.

MADISON. If we ever have the chance to amend it. I'm worried sick by this, Tom.

(A YOUNG MAN *appears in the doorway.*)

YOUNG MAN. Does Monsieur Jefferson live here?

MRS. CONRAD (*appears*). In the parlor! Down in the parlor!

PATSY. It's all right, Mrs. Conrad.

MRS. CONRAD. Oh, excuse me. I thought he was one a my boarders. (*She goes.*)

YOUNG MAN. Monsieur Jefferson?

JEFFERSON. Yes, young man.

YOUNG MAN. You do not remember me? Twelve years ago, Paris?

JEFFERSON. You're . . ? Of course, you're Lafayette's boy.

YOUNG MAN (nods). Your servant.

JEFFERSON. I was expecting you. I'd heard you were in America. You remember Patsy? (To PATSY.) George Washington Lafayette.

PATSY. Of course.

(LAFAYETTE bows and PATSY curtsies.)

LAFAYETTE. She has not changed one little bit. Only more beautiful, if possible.

PATSY (laughs). He's Lafayette's son, all right.

JEFFERSON. He has the gift. And these are my grandchildren.

PATSY (proudly). My daughter, Miss Anne Randolph.

ANNE (curtsies). Monsieur Lafayette.

LAFAYETTE (bows). Miss Randolph.

PATSY. Monsieur George Washington Lafayette . . . (Brings the little boy forward.) My son . . . (Proudly.) Thomas Jefferson Randolph.

(The little boy makes a deep bow. LAFAYETTE smiles at JEFFERSON, who beams.)

JEFFERSON. My friend, Mr. Madison.

LAFAYETTE. The father of your immortal Constitution? (Bows.) My veneration!

MADISON (dryly). Immortal? It's running a high fever now. The next few days, the next few hours, may tell whether it's going to live at all, or die in hemorrhage. (To JEFFERSON.) Tom! I'm as nervous as a cat. I haven't slept a wink in three nights.

JEFFERSON. Lie down inside.

MADISON. No, no.

JEFFERSON. Go on! Patsy, make up the bed for Jemmy.

MADISON. No! I couldn't. Please! Just let me sit here. (Sits.)

JEFFERSON (moves chair for Lafayette). We're passing through a terrible storm here.

LAFAYETTE (sits). I am sorry to come in the midst of all this, but as soon as I arrive I hurry to you.

JEFFERSON (to LAFAYETTE). Tell me! How is your father?

LAFAYETTE. He is out of prison now.

JEFFERSON. I'd heard. I haven't written him because things here, too, have been so bad these last years, my letter would never have reached him. (Pause.) How does he look?

LAFAYETTE. Six years in prison.

JEFFERSON. They didn't break his spirit?

LAFAYETTE. That they will never break.

JEFFERSON. No.

LAFAYETTE. He asked me to explain he dare not write. Bonaparte watches him. He is only free on—a string.

JEFFERSON (sighs). I had hoped at first Bonaparte would value the real glory of a Washington as compared to that of a Caesar. (He glances at bust of WASHINGTON.)

LAFAYETTE (follows his glance). When we heard he died, my father wept like a child.

(Pause.)

JEFFERSON. A great man fell that day. America now must walk alone.

LAFAYETTE. Here—forgive me. This isn't the America I expected. This is like when Bonaparte came to us.

JEFFERSON. There is an ominous note in this dissension. You've sensed it. Our own little Bonaparte may step in with his comrades at arms and force salvation on us in his way.

LAFAYETTE (rises). That must not be. This is the message my father asked me to deliver. Tell Jefferson, he says to me, tell him the eyes of all suffering humanity are looking to America. It is their last hope on earth.

(A knock at the door. JEFFERSON opens the door. A COURIER stands there.)

COURIER. Mr. Jefferson?

JEFFERSON. Yes?

COURIER. Message!

JEFFERSON. Thank you! (COURIER *goes.* JEFFERSON *takes message, opens it, reads it, becomes grave.*)

MADISON (*rises*). What is it, Tom?

JEFFERSON. A group of the Federalists are meeting tonight.

MADISON. To set aside the election?

JEFFERSON. Possibly. (*Hands the message to* MADISON. MADISON *reads it, groans.*)

FRONTIERSMAN. Like hell they will! Nobody's gonna take my Republic from me.

JEFFERSON (*to the* FRONTIERSMAN). That's right, my friend. (*He crosses to his desk, picks up the letter he has been writing, folds it.*) I'm afraid there's no time for that meal now. Will you see if your horse is ready?

FRONTIERSMAN. Yep. (*Goes.*)

JEFFERSON (*seals letter. To* PATSY). I think you had better plan on going home.

PATSY. Very well, Father.

JEFFERSON. I don't know how long this will keep up. I don't know how it will end.

(FRONTIERSMAN *returns.*)

FRONTIERSMAN. Horse is saddled and out front.

JEFFERSON (*hands letter to him*). To Governor Monroe, with my compliments.

FRONTIERSMAN. Yes, sir.

JEFFERSON. Give your horse the spur!

FRONTIERSMAN. Ride him like the wind, Mr. Jefferson. No fear! (*He goes.*)

PATSY. When do you want us to leave?

JEFFERSON. Now. (*Looks at his watch.*) After dinner.

PATSY. So soon?

JEFFERSON. Please.

PATSY. There's going to be serious trouble?

JEFFERSON. I don't know, Patsy.

PATSY. General Hamilton? Again? Is there no end to that man's malevolence?

LAFAYETTE. Hamilton? (*He looks about at a loss.*) But, during the war, he was my father's friend, too. My father often speaks of him.

PATSY. People changed here after the war, Monsieur Lafayette. The real revolution has been fought in the last six years.

MADISON. And our people have won, Monsieur Lafayette. Through the ballot they've taken the government into their own hands. But now the Federalists intend to drag everything down with them, rather than admit defeat.

(*There is a knock at the door.*)

PATSY. They've turned President Adams completely against my father—one of his oldest friends!

LAFAYETTE. This shocks me. I cannot believe it.

PATSY. Do you know *why* he didn't write your father all these years? He couldn't! They opened his mail! They twisted phrases he used in his letters, and printed them against him.

(*The knock is repeated.*)

JEFFERSON. These are things, Patsy, that are best forgotten.

PATSY. Father, there are men in the streets with guns. They're expecting Hamilton and his troops. They say there'll be shooting.

(*The doors open.* HAMILTON *stands there. A long, stunned silence.*)

HAMILTON. Mr. Jefferson.

JEFFERSON. General Hamilton.

PATSY. You dare . . . !

JEFFERSON. Pat! Go inside, please.

PATSY. Yes, Father. Come, children! (*She steers the children off.*)

JEFFERSON. General Hamilton, Monsieur George Washington Lafayette.

HAMILTON. Lafayette? You're his son?

LAFAYETTE. Yes.

HAMILTON. Of course. I knew your father well. He was my friend.

LAFAYETTE. He often speaks of you. He was yours.

MADISON (*picks up his hat and starts to leave*). Gentlemen!

LAFAYETTE. I go with you, if I may.

MADISON. Come along.

JEFFERSON. You'll dine with us? (LAFA-
YETTE *nods.* JEFFERSON *looks at his watch.*)
In twenty-three minutes.

LAFAYETTE. Twenty-three.

JEFFERSON. On the dot. Mrs. Conrad runs
her boarding house along democratic lines.
The early birds get the choice cuts.

(LAFAYETTE *smiles, turns to* HAMILTON,
bows.)

LAFAYETTE. Monsieur Hamilton.

(HAMILTON *bows.* LAFAYETTE *goes.* JEFFER-
SON *and* HAMILTON *survey each other.*)

JEFFERSON. What can I do for you, General Hamilton?

HAMILTON. Nothing! But I can do something for you. I'm not going to equivocate,
Mr. Jefferson. My sentiments toward you
are unchanged. I still despise you and
everything you represent.

JEFFERSON (*moves to desk. Indicates a
chair*). Chair, General?

HAMILTON. Is that understood?

JEFFERSON. I think pretty widely. (*Points
to chair.*) Chair?

HAMILTON (*sits.*) Thank you. (*Pause. They
survey each other.*) You've grown leaner.

JEFFERSON. And you stouter.

HAMILTON. Not at all. It's this waistcoat.
. . . A few pounds, perhaps. (*Pause.*
HAMILTON *glances out the window.*) So
this is your city of Washington. A mud
hole.

JEFFERSON. A few trees and some sidewalks and it will do.

HAMILTON. The first day we met this was
born.

JEFFERSON. Yes.

HAMILTON. You remember?

JEFFERSON. Oh, yes.

HAMILTON. The Presidential Mansion appears not bad.

JEFFERSON. Not bad.

HAMILTON. Large enough.

JEFFERSON. Large enough for two em-
perors and a rajah.

HAMILTON. Who's it to be—Aaron Burr
or you?

JEFFERSON. Congress will decide.

HAMILTON (*rises*). I have some friends in
that body. I can influence this decision
for or against you, I believe.

JEFFERSON. I'm certain of that.

HAMILTON. Certain? I'm not. You'd be
astonished, Mr. Jefferson, at the number
of gentlemen who, no matter what I counsel, would vote for the devil himself in
preference to you.

JEFFERSON. Yes. That's quite probable.

HAMILTON. Not that I approve of it. I
don't. I deplore it. In the matter of the
public good, men must consult their reason, not their passions. I believe I can
swing Congress over to you, *if* you ac-
cede to certain conditions.

JEFFERSON. I see.

HAMILTON (*moves to desk*). One: I want
your solemn assurance that you will continue all my friends in the offices they now
fill. Two: I want . . .

JEFFERSON (*smiles, shakes his head*). I'm
sorry.

HAMILTON. You refuse?

JEFFERSON. This time no bargains. I appreciate your motives . . .

HAMILTON (*in a rage, shouting*). Bargains? What puny channels your mind
runs in!

JEFFERSON. No need to shout, General.

HAMILTON (*pacing furiously*). I'll raise the
roof if I please.

JEFFERSON (*nods toward the next room*).
My grandchildren . . .

HAMILTON. Excuse me.

JEFFERSON. This is like old times, General.

HAMILTON. Do you realize how dangerous
this situation has become?

JEFFERSON. Yes.

HAMILTON. I came here to compromise. I
hoped to avert the more drastic alternative.

But the years have made you even more pig-headed, if possible. I might have spared myself this trouble.

JEFFERSON. I couldn't enter the Presidency with my hands tied.

HAMILTON. Don't concern yourself. You won't enter it at all! My friends are meeting tonight. You oblige them to act to set aside this election altogether and choose their own man.

JEFFERSON (grimly). They would be smashing the Constitution.

HAMILTON. Stretching it!

JEFFERSON (rises). Smashing it, I say. (HAMILTON shrugs his shoulders, turns to go.) Have you seen the crowds about the Capitol Building?

HAMILTON. A pistol-shot and they'd disperse.

JEFFERSON. Don't deceive yourself! Our people will not be "put aside." (Hands him a letter.) From Maryland. Fifteen hundred men met last night. Resolved: If anyone dares usurp the Presidency, they will come here in a body and assassinate him. (He picks up several letters.) From Governor McKean of Pennsylvania . . . From Governor Monroe of Virginia. Their militia are ready to march at a moment's notice. If you put aside this election tonight, tomorrow morning there will be blood in the streets.

HAMILTON. I am an old soldier, Mr. Jefferson. If you give us no alternative . . .

JEFFERSON. But you have an alternative. End this deadlock at once! Use your influence with your friends. I shall use mine. Make Aaron Burr President.

HAMILTON. Aren't you being whimsical?

JEFFERSON. No. I should honestly prefer that.

HAMILTON. So you want Aaron Burr to be President?

JEFFERSON. He's a superior man, energetic, sharp, believes in our people.

HAMILTON. God! You're gullible! I know the man. He despises your Democracy more than I. Yet he has chimed in with all its absurdities. Why? Because he is cunning, and audacious, and absolutely without morality—possessed of only one principle, to get power by any means and keep it by all.

JEFFERSON. That's an opinion.

HAMILTON. That's a fact. He has said it to me to my face. A dozen times.

JEFFERSON. He has sworn the contrary to me.

HAMILTON. Burr has been bankrupt for years. Yet he spent vast sums of money on this campaign. Where do they come from?

JEFFERSON. I don't know.

HAMILTON. What do you think has been the sole topic of conversation at his dinner table? To whom are the toasts drunk? Can you guess?

JEFFERSON. No.

HAMILTON. The man who supplies his funds, the man with whose agents he is is in daily conference.

JEFFERSON. What man?

HAMILTON. Bonaparte.

JEFFERSON. Bonaparte? I can hardly . . .

HAMILTON (extracts some documents from his pocket and places them on the desk.) Proofs, if you wish them. Burr is the Cataline of America. He'll dare anything. You may as well think to bind a giant by cobwebs as his ambition by promises. Once President, he'd destroy all our institutions. Usurp for himself complete and permanent power. Make himself dictator.

JEFFERSON. I know you have no faith in them, but do you think the American people would stand idly by?

HAMILTON. No, I have no faith in them. But they'd fight. I grant you that. There'd be bloody civil war! And that's all Bonaparte would need. He would swoop down on us— (Slams his fist on the desk.) Like that! (Long pause. JEFFERSON picks up the "proofs," studies them.) Now you know my motive. I'm afraid, I'm profoundly afraid for the happiness of this country. (HAMILTON examines the bust of WASHINGTON.) Currachi?

JEFFERSON (looks up from the "proofs"). Yes.

HAMILTON. Excellent! I've commissioned him to sculp one of the Great Man for me. (JEFFERSON *looks up, sighs.*) Well? (JEFFERSON *lays down the papers. He is tired and confused.*) You've been duped, my friend.

JEFFERSON (*smiles feebly*). I suspected only you.

HAMILTON. Of what?

JEFFERSON. Planning to be our Bonaparte.

HAMILTON. When Washington died, I could have. Why didn't I?

JEFFERSON. Why?

HAMILTON. Burr asked me that question. Contemptuously. This may be difficult for you, but try to grasp it. I happen to love this country, too. I have fought for it in field and council. Above every small selfish personal desire, I want to see it peaceful and prosperous and strong. (*Triumphant.*) Well? Will you meet my terms?

(*Pause.*)

JEFFERSON (*miserably*). I can't.

HAMILTON (*moves to desk*). My conscience is clear. I know how to proceed.

JEFFERSON. If you do this, it can only lead to the very thing you condemn.

HAMILTON (*reaches for papers*). Perhaps. Perhaps that is the only hope for us in a world of Bonapartes and Burrs.

JEFFERSON. Then what will we have gained?

HAMILTON. Good day, Mr. Jefferson. (*Goes to the door.*)

JEFFERSON (*rising*). I warn you, there will be bloodshed tomorrow.

HAMILTON. Oh, no, there won't. You see, I'm counting on you. You will prevent it.

JEFFERSON (*with sudden new-born fierceness*). You're wrong, my friend.

HAMILTON (*pauses, turns*). You'd condone it?

JEFFERSON (*crosses to* HAMILTON). I'd be a part of it.

HAMILTON. You?

JEFFERSON (*growls*). I.

HAMILTON (*returns, looks at him, surprised*). You really mean it.

JEFFERSON. By the God that made me, I mean it. I'd open my veins and yours in a second.

HAMILTON. You amaze me.

JEFFERSON. Why? Isn't the blood of patriots and tyrants the natural manure for liberty?

HAMILTON. You've become a tough old man.

JEFFERSON. Who made me tough?

HAMILTON (*laughs ironically*). Then I haven't lived in vain.

JEFFERSON. That's right. (HAMILTON *is staring at* JEFFERSON.) Listen to me, Hamilton!

HAMILTON. This is a strange . . .

JEFFERSON. Listen to me! I know you love this country. But you have never understood it. You're afraid of Bonaparte? Well, there's no need to be. Bonaparte will die and his tyrannies will die, and we will be living, and we will be free. You're afraid of Burr? If Burr tries any quixotic adventures, he will smash himself against the rocks of our people. You see, this is the mistake you have always made. You have never properly estimated the character of the American people. You still don't understand them. At this moment.

(*There is a long silence.*)

HAMILTON. I confess it. I don't. (*Sits.*)

JEFFERSON (*standing over him. Gently*). This is not the way, Hamilton. Believe me. If you really love this country, this isn't the way. Our people who fought the Revolution from a pure love of liberty, who made every sacrifice and met every danger, did not expend their blood and substance to change this master for that. (*His voice grows strong.*) But to take their freedom in their own hands so that never again would the corrupt will of one man oppress them. You'll not make these people hold their breath at the caprice, or submit to the rods and the hatchet of a dictator. You cannot fix fear in their hearts, or make fear their principle of government. I know them. I place my faith in them. I have no fears for their ultimate victory.

HAMILTON *(wavering)*. I wish I had such faith. *(Shakes his head.)* I don't know. I frankly don't know. I find *myself lost here.* Day by day, I am becoming more foreign to this land.

JEFFERSON. Yet you helped build it.

HAMILTON. There is a tide here that sweeps men to the fashioning of some strange destiny, even against their will. I never believed in this—and yet, as you say, I helped build it. Every inch of it. *(Pause. He rises.)* And still, I must admit it has worked better than I thought. If it could survive—if . . .

JEFFERSON. It can. And it will. This tide is irresistible. You cannot hold it back. This is the rising flood of man's long lost freedom. Try as you will, you cannot stop it. You may deflect it for a moment. But in the end you will lose. Try the old way of tyranny and usurpation and you *must* lose. Bonapartes may retard the epoch of man's deliverance, they may bathe the world in rivers of blood yet to flow, and still, still, in the end, they will fall back exhausted in their own blood, leaving mankind to liberty and self-government. No, General Hamilton, this way you lose. Believe me. *(He crosses to his desk, crisp*

and *final.)* I shall not compromise, General Hamilton. You do whatever you choose. I cannot compromise on this.

HAMILTON *(holds out his hand. It is shaky)*. Since the fever took me, I can't hit the side of a barn with a pistol. Burr is cool as a snake, and one of the best shots in America. I've fought him for five years now. If I cross him in *this*—he will challenge me. I have no doubt of that. I am a dead man already. But at least you are honest. I shall urge my friends to break the deadlock. You will be President. Your victory is complete.

JEFFERSON. There is no personal victory in this for me. I didn't *want* this for myself. I still don't. If it will give you any satisfaction, my own affairs have been neglected so long . . . In another office, with time to mend them, I might have saved myself from bankruptcy. As President, I am certain to lose everything I possess, including Monticello, where my wife and four of my children lie. Where all the dreams of my youth lie. No matter! I thank you—for a glorious misery.

(HAMILTON bows, goes. JEFFERSON turns, stares at the statue of WASHINGTON.)

SCENE II

SCENE: *The interior of the Senate Chamber.*
JEFFERSON, *hand raised, is taking the oath of office from* CHIEF JUSTICE MARSHALL.

JEFFERSON. I do solemnly swear that I will faithfully execute the office of President of the United States, and will, to the best of my ability, preserve, protect, and defend the Constitution of the United States.

(JUSTICE MARSHALL waves JEFFERSON to assembled audience. Nervously, hesitantly, JEFFERSON steps forward to the audience, looks about. His glance rests on PATSY, standing proudly with ANNE and JEFF. PATSY smiles and nods. JEFFERSON faintly smiles. He turns to the audience, begins to speak in a voice hesitant and uncertain.)

JEFFERSON. Friends and fellow citizens: Called upon to undertake the duties of the first executive of our country, I will avail myself of the presence of that portion of my fellow citizens which is here

assembled to express my grateful thanks for the favor with which they have been pleased to look upon me. A rising nation spread over a wide and fruitful land, advancing rapidly to destinies beyond the reach of mortal eye—when I contemplate these transcendent objects and see the honor, the happiness and the hopes of this beloved country committed to the issue of this day, I—I shrink before the magnitude of the undertaking. Utterly, indeed, should I despair if not for the presence of many whom I see here. To you, then, I look for that guidance and support which may enable us to steer with safety the vessel in which we are all embarked amid the conflicting elements of a troubled world.

This is the sum of good government. Equal and exact justice to all men, of whatever state or persuasion, a jealous care of the right of election, absolute acquiescence to the decisions of the majority, the vital principle of republics, from which is no appeal but to *force,* the vital principle and parent of despotism . . . Freedom of religion, freedom of press, freedom of person, and trial by juries impartially selected. These form the bright constellation which has gone before us and which has guided us in an age of revolution and reformation. The wisdom of our sages, and the blood of our heroes have attained them for us. They are the creed of our political faith, the touchstone of our public servants. Should we wander from them in moments of error or alarm, let us hasten to retrace our steps and to regain this road which alone leads to peace, liberty and safety. During the present throes and convulsions of the ancient world, during these agonizing spasms of blood and slaughter abroad, it was not strange that the agitation of the billows should reach even this distant and peaceful shore. That this should be more felt and feared by some than by others. I know, indeed, that some honest men fear that a republic cannot be strong, that this government is not strong enough. But would the honest patriot in the full tide of successful experiment, abandon a government which has so far kept us free and firm, on the theoretic fear that it may possibly want energy to preserve itself? I trust not. I believe this, on the contrary, the only government where every man would fly to the standard and meet invasions of the public order as his own personal concern. I believe this the strongest government on earth. I believe, indeed, I know, this government is the world's best hope . . .

ABE LINCOLN IN ILLINOIS

By ROBERT E. SHERWOOD

ABE LINCOLN IN ILLINOIS was presented by the Playwrights Company at the National Theatre, Washington, D. C., on October 3rd, and at the Plymouth Theatre, New York City, October 15, 1938. The play was staged by Elmer Rice; settings by Jo Mielziner. The cast was as follows:

MENTOR GRAHAM.....Frank Andrews	MARY TODD.............Muriel Kirkland
ABE LINCOLN.............Raymond Massey	THE EDWARDS' MAID
ANN RUTLEDGE.........Adele Longmire	Augusta Dabney
BEN MATTLING...........George Christie	JIMMY GALE..............Howard Sherman
JUDGE BOWLING GREEN	AGGIE GALE...................Marion Rooney
Arthur Griffin	GOBEY...............................Hubert Brown
NINIAN EDWARDS.........Lewis Martin	STEPHEN A. DOUGLAS
JOSHUA SPEED.............Calvin Thomas	Albert Phillips
TRUM COGDAL...............Harry Levian	WILLIE LINCOLN.............Lex Parrish
JACK ARMSTRONG....Howard daSilva	TAD LINCOLN...................Lloyd Barry
BAB............................Everett Charlton	ROBERT LINCOLN............John Payne
FEARGUS.........................David Clarke	THE LINCOLNS' MAID....Iris Whitney
JASP............................Kevin McCarthy	CRIMMIN.......................Frank Tweddell
SETH GALE.................Herbert Rudley	BARRICK..............................John Gerard
NANCY GREEN...............Lillian Foster	STURVESON...............Thomas F. Tracey
WILLIAM HERNDON	JED.................................Harry Levian
Wendell K. Phillips	KAVANAGH.....................Gleen Coulter
ELIZABETH EDWARDS	MAJOR...........................Everett Charlton
May Collins	

SCENES

ACT I: In and about New Salem, Illinois, in the 1830's.

ACT II: In and about Springfield, Illinois, in the 1840's.

ACT III: In Springfield, 1858–61.

THE AUTHOR

Robert Emmet Sherwood's development having been touched upon in the general introduction, we may confine ourselves to the bare biographical facts. He was born in New Rochelle, New York, on April 4th, 1896 and grew to such stature and acquired such a serious physiognomy that Noel Coward is reported to have once asked Mr. Sherwood's sister, "What is that nine feet of gloom you call your brother?" It may reassure the playwright's admirers to know that he is under seven feet and that he has a keen sense of humor; in fact, he has been known as the "life of the party" and has enlivened Playwrights Company conferences with such sallies as his definition of "tenterhooks" as "the upholstery of the anxious seat." He has traveled extensively abroad; Reunion in Vienna *owes something to a visit at Frau Sacher's restaurant in Vienna and the background for* Idiot's Delight *came from his watching an American cabaret in Budapest. There is good strong Irish blood in his veins which connects him with the elder brother of the famous rebel and martyr Robert Emmet.*

Mr. Sherwood was educated at Milton Academy and in 1914 reached Harvard, where he survived the threat of three expulsions for youthful capers and became an active member of the Hasty Pudding Club and an editor of The Lampoon. *The first World War aroused him and he volunteered his services. Rejected in his senior year by the U. S. Army because of his exceptional height, he managed to enlist in the Canadian Black Watch, a regiment of Highlanders. He fought at Arras and Amiens, was gassed at Vimy Ridge, was later wounded in both legs, and spent many months in an English hospital. His heart was affected and he was not expected to live long. But he was made of sound metal and recuperated quickly. Joining Frank Crowninshield's* Vanity Fair *after his recovery, he substituted for the sartorial expert of that magazine one summer; he resigned in protest from the publication in the good company of Robert Benchley when Dorothy Parker was dismissed for writing vitriolic dramatic criticism. After some unpleasantness with the* Boston Post, *he joined* Life *as its film critic, and it is one of Mr. Sherwood's distinctions that he is the father of serious film criticism. He became an editor in 1924 but was forced to relinquish that post four years later when his jibes at Prohibition and President Herbert Hoover became too frequent and too pronounced. By then, fortunately, he was already conspicuously successful as a playwright and a scenarist for the screen.*

His first Broadway play The Road to Rome *opened on January 31, 1927 and became notably successful. Fate was less kind to his next four plays* The Love Nest, The Queen's Husband *(1928),* Waterloo Bridge *(1930), and* This Is New York. *But he triumphed with the Lunt-Fontanne comedy* Reunion in Vienna *in 1931,* The Petrified Forest *in 1935,* Idiot's Delight *in 1936, the adaptation of Jacques Deval's play* Tovarich *in 1936,* Abe Lincoln in Illinois, *and* There Shall Be No Night. *In 1946 Mr. Sherwood made another respectable contribution with his* Best Years of Our Life *screenplay. The rest of his career, which included conspicuous assistance to President Roosevelt and invaluable service in the O.W.I., belongs to political history.*

ABE LINCOLN IN ILLINOIS

ACT ONE

SCENE I

MENTOR GRAHAM'S *cabin near New Salem, Illinois. Late at night.*

There is one rude table, piled with books and papers. Over it hangs an oil lamp, the only source of light.

At one side of the table sits MENTOR GRAHAM, *a sharp but patient schoolteacher.*

Across from him is ABE LINCOLN—*young, gaunt, tired but intent, dressed in the ragged clothes of a backwoodsman. He speaks with the drawl of southern Indiana—an accent which is more Kentuckian than middle-western.*

MENTOR *is leaning on the table.* ABE's *chair is tilted back, so that his face is out of the light.* MENTOR *turns a page in a grammar book.*

MENTOR. The Moods. (MENTOR *closes the book and looks at* ABE.) Every one of us has many moods. You yourself have more than your share of them, Abe. They express the various aspects of your character. So it is with the English language—and you must try to consider this language as if it were a living person, who may be awkward and stumbling, or pompous and pretentious, or simple and direct. Name me the five moods.

ABE. The Indicative, Imperative, Potential, Subjunctive and Infinitive.

MENTOR. And what do they signify?

ABE. The Indicative Mood is the easy one. It just indicates a thing—like "He loves," "He is loved"—or, when you put it in the form of a question, "Does he love?" or "Is he loved?" The Imperative Mood is used for commanding, like "Get out and be damned to you."

MENTOR (*smiling*). Is that the best example you can think of?

ABE. Well—you can put it in the Bible way —"Go thou in peace." But it's still imperative.

MENTOR. The mood derives its name from the implication of command. But you can use it in a very different sense—in the form of the humblest supplication.

ABE. Like "Give us this day our daily bread and forgive us our trespasses."

MENTOR (*reaching for a newspaper in the mess on the table*). I want you to read this —it's a speech delivered by Mr. Webster before the United States Senate. A fine document, and a perfect usage of the Imperative Mood in its hortatory sense. Here it is. Read this—down here. (*He leans back to listen.*)

ABE (*takes paper, leans forward into the light and reads*). "Sir," the Senator continued, in the rich deep tones of the historic church bells of his native Boston, "Sir—I have not allowed myself to look beyond the Union, to see what might be hidden in the dark recess behind. While the Union lasts . . ." (ABE *has been reading in a monotone, without inflection.*)

MENTOR (*testily*). Don't read it off as if it were an inventory of Denton Offut's groceries. Imagine that *you're* making the speech before the Senate, with the fate of your country at stake. Put you own life into it!

ABE. I couldn't use words as long as Dan'l Webster.

MENTOR. That's what you're here for—to learn! Go ahead.

ABE (*reading slowly, gravely*). "While the Union lasts, we have high prospects spread out before us, for us and our children. Beyond that, I seek not to penetrate the veil. God grant that in my day, at least, the curtain may not rise."

MENTOR. Notice the use of verbs from here on.

ABE (*reads*). "When my eyes shall be turned to behold for the last time the sun in heaven, may I not see him shining on the broken and dishonored fragments of a once glorious Union; on States dissevered, discordant, belligerent; on a land

727

rent with civil feuds, or drenched, it may be, in fraternal blood! Let their last feeble glance rather behold the glorious ensign of the republic, now known and honored throughout the earth, not a single star of it obscured, bearing for its motto no such miserable interrogatory . . ." *(He stumbles over the pronunciation.)*

MENTOR. Interrogatory.

ABE *(continuing).* ". . . interrogatory as 'What is all this worth?' Nor, those other words of delusion and folly, 'Liberty first and Union afterwards'; but everywhere, spread all over in characters of living light, that other sentiment, dear to every true American heart—Liberty and Union . . ."

MENTOR. Emphasize the *"and."*

ABE. "Liberty *and* Union, now and forever, one and inseparable!" *(He puts the paper back on the table.)* He must have had 'em up on their feet cheering with *that,* all right.

MENTOR. Some cheered, and some spat, depending on which section they came from.

ABE. What was he talking about?

MENTOR. It was in the debate over the right of any state to secede from the Union. Hayne had pleaded South Carolina's cause—pleaded it ably. He said that just as we have liberty as individuals—so have we liberty as states—to go as we please. Which means, if we don't like the Union, as expressed by the will of its majority, then we can leave it, and set up a new nation, or many nations—so that this continent might be as divided as Europe. But Webster answered him, all right. He proved that without Union, we'd have precious little liberty left. Now—go on with the Potential Mood.

ABE. That signifies possibility—usually of an unpleasant nature. Like, "If I ever get out of debt, I will probably get right back in again."

MENTOR *(smiles).* Why did you select that example, Abe?

ABE. Well—it just happens to be the thought that's always heaviest on my mind.

MENTOR. Is the store in trouble again?

ABE *(calmly).* Yes. Berry's drunk all the whiskey we ought to have sold, and we're going to have to shut up any day now. I guess I'm my father's own son. Give me a steady job, and I'll fail at it.

MENTOR. You haven't been a failure here, Abe. There isn't a manjack in this community that isn't fond of you and anxious to help you get ahead.

ABE *(with some bitterness).* I know—just like you, Mentor, sitting up late nights, to give me learning, out of the goodness of your heart. And now, Josh Speed and Judge Green and some of the others I owe money to want to get me the job of postmaster, thinking that maybe I can handle *that,* since there's only one mail comes in a week. I've got friends, all right —the best friends. But they can't change my luck, or maybe it's just my nature.

MENTOR. What you want to do is get out of New Salem. This poor little forgotten town will never give any one any opportunity.

ABE. Yes—I've thought about moving, think about it all the time. My family have always been movers, shifting about, never knowing what they were looking for, and whatever it was, never finding it. My old father ambled from Virginia, to one place after another in Kentucky, where I was born, and then into Indiana, and then here in Illinois. About all I can remember of when I was a boy was hitching up, and then unhitching, and then hitching up again.

MENTOR. Then get up and go, Abe. Make a new place for yourself in a new world.

ABE. As a matter of fact, Seth Gale and me have been talking a lot about moving —out to Kansas or Nebraska territory. But—wherever I go—it'll be the same story —more friends, more debts.

MENTOR. Well, Abe—just bear in mind that there are always two professions open to people who fail at everything else: there's school-teaching, and there's politics.

ABE. Then I'll choose school-teaching. You go into politics, and you may get elected.

MENTOR. Yes—there's always that possibility.

ABE. And if you get elected, you've got to go to the city. I don't want none of that.

MENTOR. What did I say about two negatives?

ABE. I meant, any of that.

MENTOR. What's your objection to cities, Abe? Have you ever seen one?

ABE. Sure. I've been down river twice to New Orleans. And, do you know, every minute of the time I was there, I was scared?

MENTOR. Scared of what, Abe?

ABE. Well—it sounds kind of foolish—I was scared of people.

MENTOR (laughs). Did you imagine they'd rob you of all your gold and jewels?

ABE (serious). No. I was scared they'd kill me.

MENTOR (also serious). Why? Why should they want to kill you?

ABE. I don't know.

MENTOR (after a moment). You think a lot about death, don't you?

ABE. I've had to, because it has always seemed to be so close to me—always—as far back as I can remember. When I was no higher than this table, we buried my mother. The milksick got her, poor creature. I helped Paw make the coffin—whittled the pegs for it with my own jackknife. We buried her in a timber clearing beside my grandmother, old Betsy Sparrow. I used to go there often and look at the place—used to watch the deer running over her grave with their little feet. I never could kill a deer after that. One time I catched hell from Paw because when he was taking aim I knocked his gun up. And I always compare the looks of those deer with the looks of men—like the men in New Orleans—that you could see had murder in their hearts.

MENTOR (after a moment). You're a hopeless mess of inconsistency, Abe Lincoln.

ABE. How do you mean, Mentor?

MENTOR. I've never seen any one who is so friendly and at the same time so misanthropic.

ABE. What's that?

MENTOR. A misanthrope is one who distrusts men and avoids their society.

ABE. Well—maybe that's how I am. Oh—I like people, well enough—when you consider 'em one by one. But they seem to look different when they're put into crowds, or mobs, or armies. But I came here to listen to you, and then I do all the talking.

MENTOR. Go right on, Abe. I'll correct you when you say things like "catched hell."

ABE (grins). I know. Whenever I get talking about Paw, I sort of fall back into his language. But—you've got your own school to teach tomorrow. I'll get along. (He stands up.)

MENTOR. Wait a minute. . . . (He is fishing about among the papers. He takes out a copy of an English magazine.) There's just one more thing I want to show you. It's a poem. (He finds the place in the magazine.) Here it is. You read it, Abe. (He hands ABE the magazine.)

(ABE seats himself on the edge of the table, and holds the magazine under the light.)

ABE (reads). "'On Death,' written at the age of nineteen by the late John Keats:

'Can death be sleep, when life is but a dream,
And scenes of bliss pass as a phantom by?
The transient (he hesitates on that word) pleasures as a vision seem,
And yet we think the greatest pain's to die.'

(He moves closer to the light.)

'How strange it is that man on earth should roam,
And lead a life of woe, but not forsake
His rugged path—nor dare he view alone
His future doom—which is but to awake.'"

(He looks at MENTOR.) That sure is good, Mentor. It's fine! (He is reading it again, to himself, when the lights fade.)

END OF SCENE I

SCENE II

The Rutledge Tavern, New Salem. Noon on the Fourth of July.

It is a large room, with log walls, but with curtains on the windows and pictures on the walls to give it an air of dressiness. The pictures include likenesses of all the presidents from Washington to Jackson, and there is also a picture (evidently used for campaign purposes) of Henry Clay.

At the left is a door leading to the kitchen. At the back, toward the right, is the main entrance, which is open. The sun is shining brightly.

The furniture of the room consists of two tables, two benches, and various chairs and stools.

BEN MATTLING is seated on a bench at the rear of the room. He is an ancient, paunchy, watery-eyed veteran of the Revolution, and he wears a cocked hat and the tattered but absurd semblance of a Colonial uniform. JUDGE BOWLING GREEN and NINIAN EDWARDS come in, followed by JOSHUA SPEED. BOWLING is elderly, fat, gentle. NINIAN is young, tall, handsome, prosperous. JOSH is quiet, mild, solid, thoughtful, well-dressed.

BOWLING (*as they come in*). This is the Rutledge Tavern, Mr. Edwards. It's not precisely a gilded palace of refreshment.

NINIAN. Make no apologies, Judge Green. As long as the whiskey is wet.

(JOSH *has crossed to the door at the left. He calls off.*)

JOSH. Miss Rutledge.

ANN (*appearing at the door*). Yes, Mr. Speed?

JOSH. Have you seen Abe Lincoln?

ANN. No. He's probably down at the foot races. (*She goes back into the kitchen.* JOSH *turns to* BOWLING.)

JOSH. I'll find Abe and bring him here.

NINIAN. Remember, Josh, we've got to be back in Springfield before sundown.

(JOSH *has gone out.*)

BOWLING (*to* MATTLING.) Ah, good day, Uncle Ben. Have a seat, Mr. Edwards.

(*They cross to the table at the right.*)

BEN. Good day to you, Bowling.

(ANN *comes in from the kitchen.*)

ANN. Hello, Judge Green.

BOWLING. Good morning, Ann. We'd be grateful for a bottle of your father's best whiskey.

ANN. Yes, judge. (*She starts to go off.*)

BEN (*stopping her*). And git me another mug of that Barbadoes rum.

ANN. I'm sorry, Mr. Mattling, but I've given you one already and you know my father said you weren't to have any more till you paid for . . .

BEN. Yes, wench—I know what your father said. But if a veteran of the Revolutionary War is to be denied so much as credit, then this country has forgot its gratitude to them that made it.

BOWLING. Bring him the rum, Ann. I'll be happy to pay for it.

(TRUM COGDAL *comes in. He is elderly, persnicketty.*)

BEN (*reluctantly*). I have to say thank you, Judge.

TRUM. Ann, bring me a pot of Sebago tea.

ANN. Yes, Mr. Cogdal. (*She goes out at the left.* TRUM *sits down at the table.*)

BOWLING. Don't say a word, Ben.

TRUM. Well, Mr. Edwards—what's your impression of our great and enterprising metropolis?

NINIAN. Distinctly favorable, Mr. Cogdal. I could not fail to be impressed by the beauty of your location, here on this hilltop, in the midst of the prairie land.

TRUM. Well, we're on the highroad to the West—and when we get the rag, tag and bobtail cleaned out of here, we'll grow. Yes, sir—we'll grow!

NINIAN (*politely*). I'm sure of it.

(ANN *has returned with the whiskey, rum and tea.*)

BOWLING. Thank you, Ann.

ANN. Has the mud-wagon come in yet?

TRUM. No. I been waiting for it.

BOWLING. Not by any chance expecting a letter, are you, Ann?

ANN. Oh, no—who'd be writing to *me*, I'd like to know?

BOWLING. Well—you never can tell what might happen on the Fourth of July. *(He and* NINIAN *lift their glasses.)* But I beg to wish you all happiness, my dear. And let me tell you that Mr. Edwards here is a married man, so you keep those lively eyes to yourself.

ANN *(giggles)*. Oh, Judge Green—you're just joking me! *(She goes to the kitchen.)*

NINIAN. A mighty pretty girl.

TRUM. Comes of good stock, too.

NINIAN. With the scarcity of females in these parts, it's a wonder some one hasn't snapped her up.

BOWLING. Some one has. The poor girl promised herself to a man who called himself McNiel—it turned out his real name's McNamar. Made some money out here and then left town, saying he'd return soon. She's still waiting for him. But your time is short, Mr. Edwards, so if you tell us just what it is you want in New Salem, we'll do our utmost to . . .

NINIAN. I'm sure you gentlemen know what I want.

TRUM. Naturally, you want votes. Well—you've got mine. Anything to frustrate that tyrant, Andy Jackson. *(He shakes a finger at the picture of* ANDREW JACKSON.*)*

NINIAN. I assure you that I yield to none in my admiration for the character of our venerable president, but when he goes to the extent of ruining our banking structure, destroying faith in our currency and even driving sovereign states to the point of secession, then, gentlemen, it is time to call a halt.

BOWLING. We got two more years of him —if the old man lives that long. You can't make headway against his popularity.

NINIAN. But we can start now to drive out his minions here in the government of the state of Illinois. We have a great battle cry, "End the reign of Andrew Jackson."

*(*JACK ARMSTRONG *and three others of the Clary's Grove boys have come in during this speech. The others are named* BAB, FEARGUS *and* JASP. *They are the town bullies—boisterous, good-natured but tough.)*

JACK *(going to the door at the left)*. Miss Rutledge!

ANN *(appearing in the doorway)*. What do *you* want, Jack Armstrong?

JACK. Your humble pardon, Miss Rutledge, and we will trouble you for a keg of liquor.

BAB. And we'll be glad to have it quick, because we're powerful dry.

ANN. You get out of here—you get out of here right now—you low *scum!*

JACK. I believe I said a keg of liquor. Did you hear me say it, boys?

FEARGUS. That's how it sounded to me, Jack.

JASP. Come along with it, Annie—

ANN. If my father were here, he'd take a gun to you, just as he would to a pack of prairie wolves.

JACK. If your Paw was here, he'd be scareder than you. 'Cause he knows we're the wildcats of Clary's Grove, worse'n any old wolves, and we're a-howlin', and a-spittin' for drink. So get the whiskey, Miss Annie, and save your poor old Paw a lot of expenses for damages to his property.

*(*ANN *goes.)*

TRUM *(in an undertone to* NINIAN*)*. That's the rag, tag and bobtail I was . . .

JACK. And what are you mumblin' about, old measely-weasely Trum Cogdal—with your cup of tea on the Fourth of July?

BAB. He's a cotton-mouthed traitor and I think we'd better whip him for it.

FEARGUS *(at the same time)*. Squeeze that air tea outen him, Jack.

JASP *(shouting)*. Come on you, Annie, with that liquor!

JACK. And you, too, old fat-pot Judge Bowling Green that sends honest men to prison—and who's the stranger? Looks kind of damn elegant for New Salem.

BOWLING. This is Mr. Ninian Edwards of Springfield, Jack—and for the Lord's sake, shut up, and sit down, and behave yourselves.

JACK. Ninian Edwards, eh! The Governor's son, I presume. Well—well!

NINIAN (amiably). You've placed me.

JACK. No wonder you've got a New Orleans suit of clothes and a gold fob and a silver-headed cane. I reckon you can buy the best of everything with that steamin' old pirate land-grabber for a Paw. I guess them fancy pockets of yourn are pretty well stuffed with the money your Paw stole from us tax-payers—eh, Mr. Edwards?

BAB. Let's take it offen him, Jack.

FEARGUS. Let's give him a lickin', Jack.

JACK (still to NINIAN). What you come here for anyway? Lookin' for a fight? Because if that's what you're a-cravin', I'm your man—wrasslin', clawin', bitin', and tearin'.

ANN (coming in). Jack Armstrong, here's your liquor! Drink it and go away. (ANN carries four mugs.)

JASP. He told you to bring a keg!

JACK (contemplating the mugs). One little noggin apiece? Why—that ain't enough to fill a hollow tooth! Get the keg, Annie.

FEARGUS. Perhaps she can't tote it. I'll get it, Jack. (He goes out into the kitchen.)

ANN (desperate). Aren't there any of you men can do anything to protect decent people from these ruffians?

NINIAN. I'll be glad to do whatever I . . . (He starts to rise.)

BOWLING (restraining him). I'd be rather careful, Mr. Edwards.

JACK. That's right, Mr. Edwards. You be careful. Listen to the old Squire. He's got a round pot but a level head. He's seen the Clary's Grove boys in action, and he can tell you you might get that silver-headed cane rammed down your gullet. Hey, Bab—you tell him what we did to Hank Spears and Gus Hocheimer. Just tell him!

BAB. Jack nailed the two of 'em up on a barr'l and sent 'em rollin' down Salem hill and it jumped the bank and fotched

up in the river and when we opened up the barr'l they wasn't inclined to move much.

JACK. Of course, it'd take a bigger barr'l to hold you and your friend here, Squire, but I'd do it for you and I'd do it for any by God rapscallions and sons of thieves that come here a-preachin' treachery and disunion and pisenin' the name of Old Hickory, the people's friend.

(FEARGUS returns with the keg.)

BEN. Kill him, boys! You're the only real Americans we got left!

NINIAN (rising). If you gentlemen will step outside, I'll be glad to accommodate you with the fight you seem to be spoiling for.

TRUM. You're committing suicide, Mr. Edwards.

JACK. Oh, no—he ain't. We ain't killers —we're just bone crushers. After a few months, you'll be as good as new, which ain't saying much. You bring that keg, Feargus.

(They are about to go when ABE appears in the door. He now is slightly more respectably dressed, wearing a battered claw-hammer coat and pants that have been "foxed" with buckskin. He carries the mail. Behind him is JOSH SPEED.)

ABE. The mud-wagon's in! Hello, Jack. Hello, boys. Ain't you fellers drunk yet? Hello, Miss Ann. Got a letter for you.

(There is a marked shyness in his attitude toward ANN.)

ANN. Thank you, Abe. (She snatches the letter and runs out with it.)

BEN. Abe, there's goin' to be a fight!

NINIAN (to JACK). Well—come on, if you're coming.

JACK. All right, boys.

ABE. Fight? Who—and why?

JACK. This is the son of Ninian Edwards, Abe. Come from Springfield lookin' for a little crotch hoist and I'm aimin' to oblige.

(ABE looks NINIAN over.)

BOWLING. Put a stop to it, Abe. It'd be next door to murder.

JACK. You shut your trap, Pot Green. Murder's too good for any goose-livered enemy of Andy Jackson. Come on, boys.

ABE. Wait a minute, boys. Jack, have you forgotten what day it is?

JACK. No, I ain't! But I reckon the Fourth is as good a day as any to whip a politician!

ABE (amiably). Well, if you've just got to fight, Jack, you shouldn't give preference to strangers. Being postmaster of this thriving town, I can rate as a politician, myself, so you'd better try a fall with me —(He thrusts JACK aside and turns to NINIAN.) And as for you, sir, I haven't the pleasure of your acquaintance; but my name's Lincoln, and I'd like to shake hands with a brave man.

NINIAN (shaking hands with ABE). I'm greatly pleased to know you, Mr. Lincoln.

ABE. You should be. Because I come here just in time to save you quite some embarrassment, not to mention injury. Oh, got a couple of letters for you, Bowling. And here's your Cincinnati Journal, Trum.

JACK. Look here, Abe—you're steppin' into something that ain't none of your business. This is a private matter of patriotic honor . . .

ABE. Everything in this town is my business, Jack. It's the only kind of business I've got. And besides—I saw Hannah down by the grove and she says to tell you to come on to the picnic and that means now or she'll give the cake away to the Straders children and you and the boys'll go hungry. So get moving.

FEARGUS (to JACK). Are you goin' to let Abe talk you out of it?

ABE. Sure he is. (He turns to TRUM.) Say, Trum—if you ain't using that Journal for a while, would you let me have a read?

TRUM. By all means, Abe. Here you are. (He tosses the paper to ABE.)

ABE. Thanks. (He turns again to JACK.) You'd better hurry, Jack, or you'll get a beating from Hannah. (He starts to take the wrapper off, as he goes over to a chair at the left. JACK looks at ABE for a moment, then laughs.)

JACK (to NINIAN). All right! Abe Lincoln's

saved your hide. I'll consent to callin' off the fight just because he's a friend of mine.

ABE (as he sits). And also because I'm the only one around here you can't lick.

JACK. But I just want to tell you, Mr. Ninian Edwards, Junior, that the next time you come around here a-spreadin' pisen and . . .

ABE. Go on, Jack. Hannah's waiting.

JACK (walking over to ABE). I'm going, Abe. But I warn you—you'd better stop this foolishness of readin'—readin'—readin', mornin', noon and night, or you'll be gettin' soft and you won't be the same fightin' man you are now—and it would break my heart to see you licked by anybody, includin' me! (He laughs, slaps ABE on the back, then turns to go.) Glad to have met you, Mr. Edwards. (He goes out, followed by BAB and JASP. FEARGUS picks up the keg and starts after them.)

NINIAN (to JACK). It's been a pleasure.

ABE. Where'd you get that keg, Feargus?

FEARGUS (nervously). Jack told me to take it outen Mis' Rutledge's kitchen and I . . .

ABE. Well—put it down. . . . If you see Seth Gale, tell him I've got a letter for him.

FEARGUS. I'll tell him, Abe. (FEARGUS puts down the keg and goes. JOSH SPEED laughs and comes up to the table.)

JOSH. Congratulations, Ninian. I shouldn't have enjoyed taking you home to Mrs. Edwards after those boys had done with you.

NINIAN (grinning). I was aware of the certain consequences, Josh. (He turns to ABE.) I'm deeply in your debt, Mr. Lincoln.

ABE. Never mind any thanks, Mr. Edwards. Jack Armstrong talks big but he means well.

NINIAN. Won't you join us in a drink?

ABE. No, thank you. (He's reading the paper. BOWLING fills the glasses.)

BOWLING. I'm going to have another! I don't mind telling you, I'm still trembling. (He hands a glass to NINIAN, then drinks himself.)

TRUM. You see, Mr. Edwards. It's that very kind of lawlessness that's holding our town back.

NINIAN. You'll find the same element in the capital of our nation, and everywhere else, these days. (*He sits down and drinks.*)

ABE. Say, Bowling! It says here that there was a riot in Lyons, France. (*He reads.*) "A mob of men, deprived of employment when textile factories installed the new sewing machines, re-enacted scenes of the Reign of Terror in the streets of this prosperous industrial center. The mobs were suppressed only when the military forces of His French Majesty took a firm hand. The rioters carried banners inscribed with the incendiary words, 'We will live working or die fighting!'" (ABE *looks at the group at the right.*) That's Revolution!

BOWLING. Maybe, but it's a long way off from New Salem.

JOSH. Put the paper down, Abe. We want to talk to you.

ABE. Me? What about? (*He looks curiously at* JOSH, BOWLING *and* NINIAN.)

JOSH. I brought Mr. Edwards here for the sole purpose of meeting you—and with his permission, I shall tell you why.

NINIAN. Go right ahead, Josh.

(*All are looking intently at* ABE.)

JOSH. Abe—how would you like to run for the State Assembly?

ABE. When?

JOSH. Now—for the election in the fall.

ABE. Why?

NINIAN. Mr. Lincoln, I've known you for only a few minutes, but that's long enough to make me agree with Josh Speed that you're precisely the type of man we want. The whole Whig organization will support your candidacy.

ABE. This was all your idea, Josh?

JOSH (*smiling*). Oh, no, Abe—you're the people's choice!

TRUM. What do *you* think of it, Bowling?

BOWLING (*heartily*). I think it's as fine a notion as I ever heard. Why, Abe—I can hear you making speeches, right and left, taking your stand on all the issues—secession, Texas, the National Bank crisis, abolitionism—it'll be more fun than we ever had in our lives!

ABE (*rising*). Isn't anybody going to ask what *I* think?

JOSH (*laughs*). All right, Abe—I'll ask you.

ABE (*after a moment's pause*). It's a comical notion, all right—and I don't know if I can give you an answer to it, offhand. But my first, hasty impression is that I don't think much of it.

BOWLING. Don't overlook the fact that, if elected, your salary would be three whole dollars a day.

ABE. That's fine money. No doubt of that. And I see what you have in mind, Bowling. I owe you a considerable sum of money; and if I stayed in the legislature for, say, twenty years, I'd be able to pay off—let me see—two dollars and a half a day. . . . (*He is figuring it up on his fingers.*)

BOWLING. I'm not thinking about the debts, Abe.

ABE. I know you ain't, Bowling. But I've got to. And so should you, Mr. Edwards. The Whig Party is the party of sound money and God save the National Bank, ain't it?

NINIAN. Why, yes—among other things. . . .

ABE. Well, then—how would it look if you put forward a candidate who has demonstrated no earning power but who has run up the impressive total of fifteen hundred dollars of debts?

BOWLING (*to* NINIAN). I can tell you something about those debts. Abe started a grocery store in partnership with an unfortunate young man named Berry. Their stock included whiskey, and Berry started tapping the keg until he had consumed all the liquid assets. So the store went bankrupt—and Abe voluntarily assumed all the obligations. That may help to explain to you, Mr. Edwards, why we think pretty highly of him around here.

NINIAN. It's a sentiment with which I concur most heartily.

ABE. I thank you one and all for your kind tributes, but don't overdo them, or I'll begin to think that three dollars a day ain't enough!

JOSH. What's the one thing that you want most, Abe? You want to learn. This will give you your chance to get at a good library, to associate with the finest lawyers in the State.

ABE. I've got a copy of Blackstone, already. Found it in an old junk barrel. And how can I tell that the finest lawyers would welcome association with *me?*

NINIAN. You needn't worry about that. I saw how you dealt with those ruffians. You quite obviously know how to handle men.

ABE. I can handle the Clary's Grove boys because I can outwrassle them—but I can't go around Sangamon County throwing *all* the voters.

BOWLING *(laughing)*. I'll take a chance on that, Abe.

ABE *(to* NINIAN*)*. Besides—how do you know that my political views would agree with yours? How do you know I wouldn't say the wrong thing?

NINIAN. What *are* your political leanings, Mr. Lincoln?

ABE. They're all toward staying out. . . . What sort of leanings did you want?

NINIAN. We have a need for good conservative men to counteract all the radical firebrands that have swept over this country in the wake of Andrew Jackson. We've got to get this country back to first principles!

ABE. Well—I'm conservative, all right. If I got into the legislature you'd never catch me starting any movements for reform or progress. I'm pretty certain I wouldn't even have the nerve to open my mouth.

JOSH *(laughs)*. I told you, Ninian—he's just the type of candidate you're looking for.

*(*NINIAN *laughs too, and rises.)*

NINIAN *(crossing toward* ABE*)*. The fact is, Mr. Lincoln, we want to spike the rumor that ours is the party of the more privileged classes. That is why we seek men of the plain people for candidates.

As postmaster, you're in an excellent position to establish contacts. While delivering letters, you can also deliver speeches and campaign literature, with which our headquarters will keep you supplied.

ABE. Would you supply me with a suit of store clothes? A candidate mustn't look *too* plain.

NINIAN *(smiling)*. I think even that could be arranged, eh, Judge?

BOWLING. I think so.

NINIAN *(pompously)*. So—think it over, Mr. Lincoln, and realize that this is opportunity unlimited in scope. Just consider what it means to be starting up the ladder in a nation which is now expanding southward, across the vast area of Texas; and westward, to the Empire of the Californias on the Pacific Ocean. We're becoming a continent, Mr. Lincoln—and all that we need is men! *(He looks at his watch.)* And now, gentlemen, if you will excuse me—I must put in an appearance at the torch-light procession in Springfield this evening, so I shall have to be moving on. Good-bye, Mr. Lincoln. This meeting has been a happy one for me.

ABE *(shaking hands)*. Good-bye, Mr. Edwards. Good luck in the campaign.

NINIAN. And the same to you.

(All at the right have risen and are starting to go, except BEN MATTLING, *who is still sitting at the back, drinking.)*

ABE. Here's your paper, Trum.

TRUM. Go ahead and finish it, Abe. I won't be looking at it yet awhile.

ABE. Thanks, Trum. I'll leave it at your house.

*(*TRUM *and* NINIAN *have gone.)*

BOWLING. I'll see you later, Abe. Tell Ann I'll be back to pay for the liquor.

ABE. I'll tell her, Bowling.

*(*BOWLING *goes.* JOSH *is looking at* ABE, *who, after a moment, turns to him.)*

ABE. I'm surprised at you, Josh. I thought you were my friend.

JOSH. I know, Abe. But Ninian Edwards asked me is there anybody in that God-forsaken town of New Salem that stands a chance of getting votes, and the only one I could think of was you. I can see you're embarrassed by this—and you're annoyed. But—whether you like it or not—you've got to grow; and here's your chance to get a little scrap of importance.

ABE. Am I the kind that wants importance?

JOSH. You'll deny it, Abe—but you've got a funny kind of vanity—which is the same as saying you've got some pride—and it's badly in need of nourishment. So, if you'll agree to this—I don't think you'll be sorry for it or feel that I've betrayed you.

ABE *(grins)*. Oh—I won't hold it against you, Josh. *(He walks away and looks out the door.)* But that Mr. Ninian Edwards —he's rich and he's prominent and he's got a high-class education. Politics to him is just a kind of a game. And maybe I'd like it if I could play it *his* way. *(He turns to* JOSH.*)* But when you get to reading Blackstone, not to mention the Bible, you can't help feeling maybe there's some serious responsibility in the giving of laws— and maybe there's something more important in the business of government than just getting the Whig Party back into power.

*(*SETH GALE *comes in. He is a young, husky frontiersman, with flashes of the sun of Western empire in his eyes.)*

SETH. Hey, Abe—Feargus said you've got a letter for me.

ABE *(fishing in his mail pouch)*. Yes.

SETH. Hello, Mr. Speed.

JOSH. How are you, Mr. Gale?

ABE. Here you are, Seth. *(He hands him a letter.* SETH *takes it to the right, sits down and starts to read.)*

JOSH. I've got to get home to Springfield, Abe, but I'll be down again in a week or so.

ABE. I'll be here, Josh.

*(*JOSH *goes.* ABE *sits down again at the right, picks up his paper, but doesn't read it.* BEN *stands up and comes down a bit unsteadily.)*

BEN *(angrily)*. Are you going to do it, Abe? Are you goin' to let them make you into a *candidate?*

ABE. I ain't had time to think about it yet.

BEN. Well—I tell you to stop thinkin' before it's too late. Don't let 'em get you. Don't let 'em put you in a store suit that's the uniform of degradation in this miserable country. You're an honest man, Abe Lincoln. You're a good-for-nothin', debt-ridden loafer—but you're an honest man. And you have no place in that den of thieves that's called gov'ment. They'll corrupt you as they've corrupted the whole damn United States. Look at Washington, look at Jefferson, and John Adams—*(He points grandly to the pictures.)*—where are they today? Dead! And everything they stood for and fought for and *won*— that's dead too. *(*ANN *comes in to collect the mugs from the table at the left.* ABE *looks at her.)* Why—we'd be better off if we was all black niggers held in the bonds of slavery. *They* get fed—*they* get looked after when they're old and sick. *(*ANN *goes.)* But *you* don't care—you ain't listenin' to me, neither . . . *(He starts slowly toward the door.)*

ABE. Of course I'm listening, Ben.

BEN. No, you ain't. *I* know. You're goin' to the assembly and join the wolves who're feedin' off the carcass of Liberty. *(He goes out.)*

ABE. You needn't worry. I'm not going.

*(*ANN *comes in. She crosses to the right to pick up the glasses. She seems extremely subdued.* ABE *looks at her, curiously.)*

ABE. Bowling Green said to tell you he'd be back later, to pay you what he owes.

ANN *(curtly)*. That's all right. *(*ANN *puts the glasses and bottle on a tray and picks it up.* ABE *jumps to his feet.)*

ABE. Here, Ann. Let me take that.

ANN *(irritably)*. No—leave it alone! I can carry it! *(She starts across to the left.)*

ABE. Excuse me, Ann. . . .

ANN *(stopping)*. Well?

ABE. Would you come back after you're finished with that? I—I'd like to talk to you.

*(*SETH *ha finished the letter. Its contents seem to have depressed him.)*

ANN. All right. I'll talk to you—if you want. *(She goes out.* SETH *crosses toward*

ABE, *who, during the subsequent dialogue, is continually looking toward the kitchen.)*

SETH. Abe . . . Abe—I got a letter from my folks back in Maryland. It means—I guess I've got to give up the dream we had of moving out into Nebraska territory.

ABE. What's happened, Seth?

SETH *(despondently)*. Well—for one thing, the old man's took sick, and he's pretty feeble.

ABE. I'm sorry to hear that.

SETH. So am I. They've sent for me to come back and work the farm. Measly little thirty-six acres—sandy soil. I tell you, Abe, it's a bitter disappointment to me, when I had my heart all set on going out into the West. And the worst of it is —I'm letting *you* down on it, too.

ABE *(with a glance toward the kitchen)*. Don't think about that, Seth. Maybe I won't be able to move for a while myself. And when your father gets to feeling better, you'll come back . . .

SETH. He won't get to feeling better. Not at his age. I'll be stuck there, just like he was. I'll be pushed in and cramped all the rest of my life, till the malaria gets me, too. . . . Well—there's no use crying about it. If I've got to go back East, I've got to go. *(ANN comes back.)* I'll tell you good-bye, Abe, before I leave. *(He goes. ABE turns and looks at ANN, and she at him.)*

ANN. Well—what is it, Abe?

ABE *(rising)*. I just thought—you might like to talk to me.

ANN *(sharply)*. What about?

ABE. That letter you got from New York State.

ANN. What do *you* know about that letter?

ABE. I'm the postmaster. I know more than I ought to about people's private affairs. I couldn't help seeing that that was the handwriting of Mr. McNiel. And I couldn't help seeing, from the look on your face, that the bad news you've been afraid of has come.

(ANN looks at him with surprise. He is a lot more observant than she had thought.)

ANN. Whatever the letter said, it's no concern of yours, Abe.

ABE. I know that, Ann. But—it appears to me that you've been crying—and it makes me sad to think that something could have hurt you. The thing is—I think quite a lot of you—always have—ever since I first came here, and met you. I wouldn't mention it, only when you're distressed about something it's a comfort sometimes to find a pair of ears to pour your troubles into—and the Lord knows my ears are big enough to hold a lot.

(Her attitude of hostility softens and she rewards him with a tender smile.)

ANN. You're a Christian gentleman, Abe Lincoln. *(She sits down.)*

ABE. No, I ain't. I'm a plain, common sucker with a shirt-tail so short I can't sit on it.

ANN *(laughs)*. Well—sit down, anyway, Abe—here, by me.

ABE. Why—it'd be a pleasure. *(He crosses and sits near her.)*

ANN. You can always say something to make a person laugh, can't you?

ABE. Well—I don't even have to *say* anything. A person just has to *look* at me.

ANN. You're right about that letter, Abe. It's the first I've heard from him in months —and now he says he's delayed by family troubles and doesn't know when he'll be able to get to New Salem again. By which he probably means—never.

ABE. I wouldn't say that, Ann.

ANN. I would. *(She looks at him.)* I reckon you think I'm a silly fool for ever having promised myself to Mr. McNiel.

ABE. I think no such thing. I liked him myself, and still do, and whatever reasons he had for changing his name I'm sure were honorable. He's a smart man, and a handsome one—and I—I wouldn't blame any girl for—loving him.

ANN *(too emphatically)*. I guess I don't love him, Abe. I guess I couldn't love anybody that was as—as faithless as that.

ABE *(trying to appear unconcerned)*. Well, then. There's nothing to fret about. Now —poor Seth Gale—he got some *really* bad news. His father's sick and he has to give up his dream which was to go and settle out west.

ANN (looks at him). I don't believe you know much about females, Abe.

ABE. Probably I don't—although I certainly spend enough time thinking about 'em.

ANN. You're a big man, and you can lick anybody, and you can't understand the feelings of somebody who is weak. But—I'm a female, and I can't help thinking what they'll be saying about me—all the old gossips, all over town. They'll make it out that he deserted me; I'm a rejected woman. They'll give me their sympathy to my face, but they'll snigger at me behind my back. (She rises and crosses toward the right.)

ABE. Yes—that's just about what they would do. But—would you let *them* disturb you?

ANN (rising). I told you—it's just weakness—it's just vanity. It's something you couldn't understand, Abe. (She has crossed to the window and is staring out. ABE twists in his chair to look at her.)

ABE. Maybe I can understand it, Ann. I've got a kind of vanity myself. Josh Speed said so, and he's right. . . . It's—it's nothing but vanity that's kept me from declaring my inclinations toward you. (She turns, amazed, and looks at him.) You see, I don't like to be sniggered at, either. I know what I am—and I know what I look like—and I know that I've got nothing to offer any girl that I'd be in love with.

ANN. Are you saying that you're in love with me, Abe?

ABE (with deep earnestness). Yes—I am saying that. (He stands up, facing her. She looks intently into his eyes.) I've been loving you—a long time—with all my heart. You see, Ann—you're a particularly fine girl. You've got sense, and you've got bravery—those are two things that I admire particularly. And you're powerful good to look at, too. So—it's only natural I should have a great regard for you. But —I don't mean to worry you about it, Ann. I only mentioned it because—if you would do me the honor of keeping company with me for a while, it might shut the old gossips' mouths. They'd figure you'd chucked McNiel for—for some one else. Even me.

ANN (going to him). I thought I knew you pretty well, Abe. But I didn't.

ABE (worried). Why do you say that? Do you consider I was too forward, in speaking out as I did?

ANN (gravely). No, Abe. . . . I've always thought a lot of you—the way I thought you were. But—the idea of love between you and me—I can't say how I feel about that, because now you're like some other person, that I'm meeting for the first time.

ABE (quietly). I'm not expecting you to feel anything for me. I'd never dream of expecting such a thing.

ANN. I know that, Abe. You'd be willing to give everything you have and never expect anything in return. Maybe you're different in that way from any man I've ever heard of. And I can tell you this much—now, and truthfully—if I ever do love you, I'll be happy about it—and lucky, to be loving a good, decent man. . . . If you just give me time—to think about it. . . .

ABE (unable to believe his eyes and ears). You mean—if you took time—you might get in your heart something like the feeling I have for you?

ANN (with great tenderness). I don't know, Abe. (She clutches his lapel.) But I do know that you're a man who could fill any one's heart—yes, fill it and warm it and make it glad to be living.

(ABE covers her hand with his.)

ABE. Ann—I've always tried hard to believe what the orators tell us—that this is a land of equal opportunity for all. But I've never been able to credit it, any more than I could agree that God made all men in his own image. But—if I could win you, Ann—I'd be willing to disbelieve everything I've ever seen with my own eyes, and have faith in everything wonderful that I've ever read in poetry books. (Both are silent for a moment. Then ANN turns away.)
But—I'm not asking you to say anything now. And I won't ask you until the day comes when I know I've got a right to.

(He turns and walks quickly toward the door, picking up his mail pouch.)

ANN. Abe! Where are you going?

ABE. I'm going to find Bowling Green and tell him a good joke. *(He grins. He is standing in the doorway.)*

ANN. A *joke?* What about?

ABE. I'm going to tell him that I'm a candidate for the assembly of the State of Illinois. *(He goes.)*

(The light fades.)

END OF SCENE II

SCENE III

Bowling Green's house near New Salem.
It is a small room, but the walls are lined with books and family pictures. In the center is a table with a lamp on it. Another light—a candle in a glass globe—is on a bureau at the right. There are comfortable chairs on either side of the table, and a sofa at the left.
At the back, toward the left, is the front door. A rifle is leaning against the wall by the door. There is another door in the right wall. Toward the right, at the back, is a ladder fixed against the wall leading up through an opening to the attic.
It is late in the evening, a year or so after Scene II. A storm is raging outside.
BOWLING is reading aloud from a sort of pamphlet. His comfortable wife, NANCY, is listening and sewing.

BOWLING. "And how much more interesting did the spectacle become when, starting into full life and animation, as a simultaneous call for 'Pickwick' burst from his followers, that illustrious man slowly mounted into the Windsor chair, on which he had been previously seated, and addressed the club himself had founded."

(BOWLING chuckles. NANCY laughs.)

NANCY. He sounds precisely like *you*, Bowling.

(There is a knock at the door.)

NANCY *(nervous)*. That's not Abe's knock. Who can it be?

BOWLING *(rising)*. We don't know yet, my dear.

NANCY. It's a strange hour for any one to be calling. You'd better have that gun ready.

(BOWLING unbolts and opens the door. It is JOSH SPEED.)

BOWLING. Why—Josh Speed!

JOSH. Good evening, Bowling.

BOWLING. We haven't seen you in a coon's age.

NANCY. Good evening, Mr. Speed.

JOSH. Good evening, Mrs. Green. And I beg you to forgive me for this untimely intrusion.

NANCY. We're delighted to see you. Take your wrap off.

JOSH. Thank you. I've just come down from Springfield. I heard Abe Lincoln was in town and I was told I might find him here.

BOWLING. He's been sleeping here, up in the attic.

NANCY. But he's out now at the Rutledge Farm, tending poor little Ann.

JOSH. Miss Rutledge? What's the matter with her?

NANCY. She's been taken with the brain sickness. It's the most shocking thing. People have been dying from it right and left.

BOWLING. But Ann's young. She'll pull through, all right. Sit down, Josh.

JOSH. Thank you.

(He sits. BOWLING places the pamphlet on the top of the bookcase and stands there, filling his pipe.)

NANCY. I suppose you know that Abe came rushing down from Vandalia the moment he heard she was taken. He's deeply in love with her.

BOWLING. Now, Nancy—don't exaggerate.

(JOSH is listening to all this, intently.)

JOSH. So Abe is in love. I wondered what has been the matter with him lately.

NANCY. Why, it's written all over his poor, homely face.

JOSH. The last time I saw him, he seemed pretty moody. But when I asked him what was wrong, he said it was his liver.

BOWLING (laughing). That sounds more likely. Has he been getting on well in the Assembly?

JOSH. No. He has just been sitting there —drawing his three dollars a day—and taking no apparent interest in the proceedings. Do you fancy that Miss Rutledge cares anything for him?

NANCY. Indeed she does! She broke her promise to that Mr. McNiel because of her feelings for Abe!

JOSH. Has he any notion of marrying her?

NANCY. It's the only notion of his life right now. And the sooner they are married, the better for both of them.

BOWLING (seating himself). Better for her, perhaps—but the worse for him.

NANCY (finishing her sewing). And why? The Rutledges are fine people, superior in every way to those riff-raff Hankses and Lincolns that are Abe's family!

BOWLING. I think you feel as I do, Josh. Abe has his own way to go and—sweet and pretty as Ann undoubtedly is—she'd only be a hindrance to him.

JOSH. I guess it wouldn't matter much if she could give him a little of the happiness he's never had.

NANCY (rising). That's just it! I think as much of Abe as you do, Bowling. But we can't deny that he's a poor man, and he's failed in trade, and he's been in the legislature for a year without accomplishing a blessed thing . . . (She goes to the bookcase to put her sewing-basket away.)

BOWLING. He could go to Springfield and set up a law practice and make a good thing of it. Ninian Edwards would help him to get started. And he'd soon forget little Ann. He has just happened to fasten on her his own romantic ideal of what's beautiful and unattainable. Let him ever attain her, and she'd break his heart.

NANCY (seating herself). Do you agree with Bowling on that, Mr. Speed?

JOSH (sadly). I can't say, Mrs. Green. I've abandoned the attempt to predict anything about Abe Lincoln. The first time I ever saw him was when he was piloting that steamboat, the Talisman. You remember how she ran into trouble at the dam. I had a valuable load of goods aboard for my father's store, and I was sure that steamboat, goods and all were a total loss. But Abe got her through. It was a great piece of work. I thought, "Here is a reliable man." So I cultivated his acquaintance, believing, in my conceit, that I could help him to fame and fortune. I soon learned differently. I found out that he has plenty of strength and courage in his body—but in his mind he's a hopeless hypochondriac. He can split rails, push a plough, crack jokes, all day—and then sit up all night reading "Hamlet" and brooding over his own fancied resemblance to that melancholy prince. Maybe he's a great philosopher—maybe he's a great fool. I don't know what he is.

BOWLING (laughs). Well—if only Ann had sense enough to see all the things you saw, Josh, she'd be so terrified of him she'd run all the way back to York State and find McNiel. At least, he's not complicated.

NANCY (with deeper emotion). You're talking about Abe Lincoln as if he were some problem that you found in a book, and it's interesting to try to figure it out. Well—maybe he is a problem—but he's also a man, and a miserable one. And what do you do for his misery? You laugh at his comical jokes and you vote for him on election day and give him board and lodging when he needs it. But all that doesn't give a scrap of satisfaction to Abe's soul—and never will. Because the one thing he needs is a woman with the will to face life for him.

BOWLING. You think he's afraid to face it himself?

NANCY. He is! He listens too much to the whispers that he heard in the forest where he grew up, and where he always goes now when he wants to be alone. They're the whispers of the women behind him—his dead mother—and her mother, who was no better than she should be. He's got that awful fear on him, of not knowing what the whispers mean, or where they're directing him. And none of your back-slapping will knock that fear out of him. Only a woman can free him—a woman who loves him truly, and believes in him. . . .

(There is a knock on the door.)

BOWLING. That's Abe now. *(He gets up and opens it.)*

(ABE is there, bareheaded, wet by the storm. He now wears a fairly respectable dark suit of clothes. He looks older and grimmer.)

BOWLING. Why, hello, Abe! We've been sitting up waiting for you. Come on in out of the wet!

(ABE comes in. BOWLING shuts the door behind him.)

NANCY. We were reading The Posthumous Papers of the Pickwick Club when Mr. Speed came in.

ABE. Hello, Josh. Glad to see you.

JOSH. Hello, Abe.

(ABE turns to NANCY.)

ABE. Nancy . . .

NANCY. Yes, Abe?

ABE. She's dead.

BOWLING. Ann? She's dead?

ABE. Yes. Tonight, the fever suddenly got worse. They couldn't seem to do anything for it.

(NANCY gives BOWLING a swift look, then goes quickly to ABE and takes his hand.)

NANCY. Oh, Abe—I'm so sorry. She was such a dear little girl. Every one who knew her will join in mourning for her.

ABE. I know they will. But it won't do any good. She's dead.

BOWLING. Sit down, Abe, and rest yourself.

ABE. No—I'm not fit company for anybody. I'd better be going. *(He turns toward the door.)*

JOSH *(stopping him)*. No, you don't, Abe. You'll stay right here.

BOWLING. You better do what Josh tells you.

NANCY. Come here, Abe. Please sit down.

(ABE looks from one to the other, then obediently goes to a chair and sits.)
Your bed is ready for you upstairs when you want it.

ABE *(dully)*. You're the best friends I've got in the world, and it seems a pretty poor way to reward you for all that you've given me, to come here now, and inflict you with a corpse.

BOWLING. This is your home, Abe. This is where you're loved.

ABE. Yes, that's right. And I love you, Bowling and Nancy. But I loved her more than anything else that I've ever known.

NANCY. I know you did, Abe. I know it.

ABE. I used to think it was better to be alone. I was always most contented when I was alone. I had queer notions that if you got too close to people, you could see the truth about them, that behind the surface, they're all insane, and they could see the same in you. And then—when I saw her, I knew there could be beauty and purity in people—like the purity you sometimes see in the sky at night. When I took hold of her hand, and held it, all fear, all doubt, went out of me. I believed in God. I'd have been glad to work for her until I die, to get for her everything out of life that she wanted. If she thought I could do it, then I could. That was my belief. . . . And then I had to stand there, as helpless as a twig in a whirlpool; I had to stand there and watch her die. And her father and mother were there, too, praying to God for her soul. The Lord giveth, and the Lord taketh away, blessed be the name of the Lord! That's what they kept on saying. But I couldn't pray with them. I couldn't give any devotion to one who has the power of death, and uses it. *(He has stood up and is speaking with more passion.)* I'm making a poor exhibition of myself—and I'm sorry—but—I can't stand it. I can't live with myself any longer. I've got to die and be with her again, or I'll go crazy! *(He goes to the door and opens it. The storm continues.)* I can't bear to think of her out there alone!

(NANCY looks at BOWLING with frantic appeal. He goes to ABE, who is standing in the doorway, looking out.)

BOWLING *(with great tenderness)*. Abe . . . I want you to go upstairs and see if you can't get some sleep. . . . Please, Abe —as a special favor to Nancy and me.

ABE (after a moment). All right, Bowling. (He turns and goes to the ladder.)

NANCY. Here's a light for you, dear Abe. (She hands him the candle.)

ABE. Thank you, Nancy. . . . Good night. (He goes up the ladder into the attic.)

(They all look up after him.)

NANCY (tearful). Poor, lonely soul.

(BOWLING cautions her to be quiet.)

JOSH. Keep him here with you, Mrs. Green. Don't let him out of your sight.

BOWLING. We won't, Josh.

JOSH. Good night. (He picks up his hat and cloak and goes.)

BOWLING. Good night, Josh. (He closes and bolts the door, then comes down to the table and picks up the lamp.)

(NANCY looks up once more, then goes out at the right. BOWLING follows her out, carrying the lamp with him. He closes the door behind him, so that the only light on the stage is the beam from the attic.)

CURTAIN

END OF ACT ONE

ACT TWO

SCENE IV

Law office of Stuart and Lincoln on the second floor of the Court House in Spring-field, Ill. A sunny summer's afternoon, some five years after the preceding scene.

The room is small, with two windows and one door, upstage, which leads to the hall and staircase.

At the right is a table and chair, at the left an old desk, littered with papers. At the back is a ramshackle bed, with a buffalo robe thrown over it. Below the windows are some rough shelves, sagging with law books. There is an old wood stove.

On the wall above the desk is hung an American flag, with 26 stars. Between the windows is an election poster, for Harrison and Tyler, with a list of Electors, the last of whom is Ab'm Lincoln, of Sangamon.

BILLY HERNDON is working at the table. He is young, slight, serious-minded, smouldering. He looks up as ABE comes in. ABE wears a battered plug hat, a light alpaca coat, and carries an ancient, threadbare carpet-bag. He is evidently not in a talkative mood. His boots are caked in mud. He is only thirty-one years old, but his youth was buried with Ann Rutledge.

He leaves the office door open, and lettered on it we see the number, 4, and the firm's name—Stuart & Lincoln, Attorneys & Counsellors at Law.

BILLY. How de do, Mr. Lincoln. Glad to see you back.

ABE. Good day, Billy. (He sets down the carpet-bag, takes off his hat and puts it on his desk.)

BILLY. How was it on the circuit, Mr. Lincoln?

ABE. About as usual.

BILLY. Have you been keeping in good health?

ABE. Not particularly. But Doc Henry dosed me enough to keep me going. (He sits down at the desk and starts looking at letters and papers that have accumulated during his absence. He takes little interest in them, pigeonholing some letters unopened.)

BILLY. Did you have occasion to make any political speeches?

ABE. Oh—they got me up on the stump a couple of times. Ran into Stephen Douglas—he was out compaigning, of course —and we had some argument in public.

BILLY (greatly interested). That's good! What issues did you and Mr. Douglas discuss?

ABE. Now—don't get excited, Billy. We

weren't taking it serious. There was no blood shed. . . . What's the news here?

BILLY. Judge Stuart wrote that he arrived safely in Washington and the campaign there is getting almost as hot as the weather. Mrs. Fraim stopped in to say she couldn't possibly pay your fee for a while.

ABE. I should hope not. I ought to be paying her, seeing as I defended her poor husband and he hanged.

(BILLY *hands him a letter and watches him intently, while he reads it.*)

BILLY. That was left here by hand, and I promised to call it especially to your attention. It's from the Elijah P. Lovejoy League of Freemen. They want you to speak at an Abolitionist rally next Thursday evening. It'll be a very important affair.

ABE (*reflectively*). It's funny, Billy—I was thinking about Lovejoy the other day—trying to figure what it is in a man that makes him glad to be a martyr. I was on the boat coming from Quincy to Alton, and there was a gentleman on board with twelve Negroes. He was shipping them down to Vicksburg for sale—had 'em chained six and six together. Each of them had a small iron clevis around his wrist, and this was chained to the main chain, so that those Negroes were strung together precisely like fish on a trot line. I gathered they were being separated forever from their homes—mothers, fathers, wives, children—whatever families the poor creatures had got—going to be whipped into perpetual slavery, and no questions asked. It was quite a shocking sight.

BILLY (*excited*). Then you will give a speech at the Lovejoy rally?

ABE (*wearily*). I doubt it. That Freemen's League is a pack of hell-roaring fanatics. Talk reason to them and they scorn you for being a mealy-mouth. Let 'em make their own noise. (ABE *has opened a letter. He starts to read it.*)

(BILLY *looks at him with resentful disappointment, but he knows too well that any argument would be futile. He resumes his work. After a moment,* BOWLING GREEN *comes in, followed by* JOSH SPEED.)

BOWLING. Are we interrupting the majesty of the Law?

ABE (*heartily*). Bowling! (*He jumps up and grasps* BOWLING's *hand.*) How are you, Bowling?

BOWLING. Tolerably well, Abe—and glad to see you.

ABE. This is Billy Herndon—Squire Green, of New Salem. Hello, Josh.

JOSH. Hello, Abe.

BILLY (*shaking hands with* BOWLING). I'm proud to know you, sir. Mr. Lincoln speaks of you constantly.

BOWLING. Thank you, Mr. Herndon. Are you a lawyer, too?

BILLY (*seriously*). I hope to be, sir. I'm serving here as a clerk in Judge Stuart's absence.

BOWLING. So now you're teaching others, Abe?

ABE. Just providing a bad example.

BOWLING. I can believe it. Look at the mess on that desk. Shameful!

ABE. Give me another year of law practise and I'll need a warehouse for the overflow. . . . But—sit yourself down, Bowling, and tell me what brings you to Springfield.

(BOWLING *sits.* JOSH *has sat on the couch, smoking his pipe.* BILLY *is again at the table.*)

BOWLING. I've been up to Lake Michigan —fishing—came in today on the steam-cars—scared me out of a year's growth. But how are you doing, Abe? Josh says you're still broke, but you're a great social success.

ABE. True—on both counts. I'm greatly in demand at all the more elegant functions. You remember Ninian Edwards?

BOWLING. Of course.

ABE. Well, sir—I'm a guest at his mansion regularly. He's got a house so big you could race horses in the parlor. And his wife is one of the Todd family from Kentucky. Very high-grade people. They spell their name with two D's—which is pretty impressive when you consider that one was enough for God.

JOSH. Tell Bowling whom you met over in Rochester.

ABE. The President of the United States!

BOWLING. You don't tell me so!

ABE. Do you see that hand? *(He holds out his right hand, palm upward.)*

BOWLING. Yes—I see it.

ABE. It has shaken the hand of Martin Van Buren!

BOWLING *(laughing).* Was the President properly respectful to you, Abe?

ABE. Indeed he was! He said to me, "We've been hearing great things of you in Washington." I found out later he'd said the same thing to every other cross-roads politician he'd met. *(He laughs.)* But Billy Herndon there is pretty disgusted with me for associating with the wrong kind of people. Billy's a firebrand —a real, radical abolitionist—and he can't stand anybody who keeps his mouth shut and abides by the Constitution. If he had his way, the whole Union would be set on fire and we'd all be burned to a crisp. Eh, Billy?

BILLY *(grimly).* Yes, Mr. Lincoln. And if you'll permit me to say so, I think you'd be of more use to your fellow-men if you allowed some of the same incendiary impulses to come out in you.

ABE. You see, Bowling? He wants me to get down into the blood-soaked arena and grapple with all the lions of injustice and oppression.

BOWLING. Mr. Herndon—my profound compliments.

BILLY *(rising and taking his hat).* Thank you, sir. *(He shakes hands with BOWLING, then turns to ABE.)* I have the writ prepared in the Willcox case. I'll take it down to the Clerk of Court to be attested.

ABE. All right, Billy.

BILLY *(to BOWLING).* Squire Green—Mr. Lincoln regards you and Mr. Speed as the best friends he has on earth, and I should like to beg of you, in his presence, for God's sake drag him out of this stagnant pool in which he's rapidly drowning himself. Good day, sir—good day, Mr. Speed.

JOSH. Good day, Billy.

(BILLY has gone.)

BOWLING. That's a bright young man, Abe. Seems to have a good grasp of things.

ABE *(looking after BILLY).* He's going downstairs to the Clerk's office, but he took his hat. Which means that before he comes back to work, he'll have paid a little visit to the Chenery House saloon.

BOWLING. Does the boy drink?

ABE. Yes. He's got great fires in him, but he's putting 'em out fast. . . . Now— tell me about New Salem. *(He leans against the wall near the window.)*

BOWLING. Practically nothing of it left.

ABE. How's that blessed wife of yours?

BOWLING. Nancy's busier than ever, and more than ever concerned about your innermost thoughts and yearnings. In fact, she instructed me expressly to ask what on earth is the matter with you?

ABE *(laughs).* You can tell her there's nothing the matter. I've been able to pay off my debts to the extent of some seven cents on the dollar, and I'm sound of skin and skeleton.

BOWLING. But why don't we hear more from you and of you?

ABE. Josh can tell you. I've been busy.

BOWLING. What at?

ABE. I'm a candidate.

JOSH *(pointing to the poster).* Haven't you noticed his name? It's here—at the bottom of the list of Electors on the Whig ticket.

ABE. Yes, sir—if old Tippecanoe wins next fall, I'll be a member of the Electoral College.

BOWLING. The Electoral College! And is that the best you can do?

ABE. Yes—in the limited time at my disposal. I had a letter from Seth Gale—remember—he used to live in New Salem and was always aiming to move West. He's settled down in Maryland now and has a wife and a son. He says that back East they're powerful worried about the annexation of Texas.

BOWLING. They have reason to be. It would probably mean extending slavery through all the territories, from Kansas and Nebraska right out to Oregon and California. That would give the South absolute rule of the country—and God help the rest of us in the free states.

JOSH. It's an ugly situation, all right. It's got the seeds in it of nothing more nor less than civil war.

ABE. Well, if so, it'll be the abolitionists' own fault. They know where this trouble might lead, and yet they go right on agitating. They ought to be locked up for disturbing the peace, all of them.

BOWLING. I thought you were opposed to slavery, Abe. Have you changed your mind about it?

ABE (ambles over to the couch and sprawls on it). No. I am opposed to slavery. But I'm even more opposed to going to war. And, on top of that, I know what you're getting at, both of you. (He speaks to them with the utmost good nature.) You're following Billy Herndon's lead—troubling your kind hearts with concerns about me and when am I going to amount to something. Is that it?

BOWLING. Oh, no, Abe. Far be it from me to interfere in your life.

JOSH. Or me, either. If we happen to feel that, so far, you've been a big disappointment to us, we'll surely keep it to ourselves.

ABE (laughs). I'm afraid you'll have to do what I've had to do—which is, learn to accept me for what I am. I'm no fighting man. I found that out when I went through the Black Hawk War, and was terrified that I might have to fire a shot at an Indian. Fortunately, the Indians felt the same way, so I never saw one of them. Now, I know plenty of men who like to fight; they're willing to kill, and not scared of being killed. All right. Let them attend to the battles that have to be fought.

BOWLING. Peaceable men have sometimes been of service to their country.

ABE. They may have been peaceable when they started, but they didn't remain so long after they'd become mixed in the great brawl of politics. (He sits up.) Suppose I ran for Congress, and got elected. I'd be right in the thick of that ugly situation you were speaking of. One day I might have to cast my vote on the terrible issue of war or peace. It might be war with Mexico over Texas; or war with England over Oregon; or even with

our own people across the Ohio River. What attitude would I take in deciding which way to vote? "The Liberal attitude," of course. And what is the Liberal attitude? To go to war, for a tract of land, or a moral principle? Or to avoid war at all costs? No, sir. The place for me is in the Electoral College, where all I have to do is vote for the President whom everybody else elected four months previous.

BOWLING. Well, Abe—you were always an artful dodger—and maybe you'll be able to go on to the end of your days avoiding the clutch of your own conscience.

(NINIAN EDWARDS comes in. He is a little stouter and more prosperous.)

ABE–JOSH. Hello, Ninian.

NINIAN. Hello. I saw Billy Herndon at the Chenery House and he said you were back from the circuit. (He sees BOWLING.) Why—it's my good friend Squire Green. How de do, and welcome to Springfield. (He shakes hands with BOWLING.)

BOWLING. Thank you, Mr. Edwards.

NINIAN. I just called in, Abe, to tell you you must dine with us. And, Squire, Mrs. Edwards would be honored to receive you, if your engagements will permit—and you, too, Josh.

JOSH. Delighted!

NINIAN. We're proudly exhibiting my sister-in-law, Miss Mary Todd, who has just come from Kentucky to grace our home. She's a very gay young lady—speaks French like a native, recites poetry at the drop of a hat, and knows the names and habits of all the flowers. I've asked Steve Douglas and some of the other eligibles to meet her, so you boys had better get in early.

BOWLING. My compliments to Mrs. Edwards, but my own poor wife awaits me impatiently, I hope.

NINIAN. I appreciate your motives, Squire, and applaud them. You'll be along presently, Abe?

ABE. I wouldn't be surprised.

NINIAN. Good. You'll meet a delightful young lady. And I'd better warn you she's going to survey the whole field of matrimonial prospects and select the one who promises the most. So you'd better be on your guard, Abe, unless you're prepared to lose your standing as a free man.

ABE. I thank you for the warning, Ninian.

NINIAN. Good day to you, Squire. See you later, Josh. *(He goes out.)*

ABE. There, Bowling—you see how things are with me. Hardly a day goes by but what I'm invited to meet some eager young female who has all the graces, including an ability to speak the language of diplomacy.

BOWLING. I'm sorry, Abe, that I shan't be able to hear you carry on a flirtation in French.

(ABE looks at him, curiously.)

ABE. I'm not pretending with you, Bowling —or you, Josh. I couldn't fool you any better than I can fool myself. I know what you're thinking about me, and I think so, too. Only I'm not so merciful in considering my own shortcomings, or so ready to forgive them, as you are. But—you talk about civil war—there seems to be one going on inside me all the time. Both sides are right and both are wrong and equal in strength. I'd like to be able to rise superior to the struggle—but—it says in the Bible that a house divided against itself cannot stand, so I reckon there's not much hope. One of these days, I'll just split asunder, and part company with myself—and it'll be a good riddance from both points of view. However—come on. *(He takes his hat.)* You've got to get back to Nancy, and Josh and I have got to make a good impression upon Miss Mary Todd, of Kentucky. *(He waves them to the door. As they go out, the light fades.)*

END OF SCENE IV

SCENE V

Parlor of the Edwards house in Springfield. An evening in November, some six months after the preceding scene.

There is a fireplace at the right, a heavily curtained bay window at the left, a door at the back leading into the front hall.

At the right, by the fireplace, are a small couch and an easy chair. There is another couch at the left, and a table and chairs at the back. There are family portraits on the walls. It is all moderately elegant.

NINIAN is standing before the fire, in conversation with ELIZABETH, his wife. She is high-bred, ladylike—excessively so. She is, at the moment, in a state of some agitation.

ELIZABETH. I cannot believe it! It is an outrageous reflection on my sister's good sense.

NINIAN. I'm not so sure of that. Mary has known Abe for several months, and she has had plenty of chance to observe him closely.

ELIZABETH. She has been entertained by him, as we all have. But she has been far more attentive to Edwin Webb and Stephen Douglas and many others who are distinctly eligible.

NINIAN. Isn't it remotely possible that she sees more in Abe than you do?

ELIZABETH. Nonsense! Mr. Lincoln's chief virtue is that he hides no part of his simple soul from any one. He's a most amiable creature, to be sure; but as the husband of a high-bred, high-spirited young lady. . . .

NINIAN. Quite so, Elizabeth. Mary *is* high-spirited! That is just why she set her cap for him.

(ELIZABETH looks at him sharply, then laughs.)

ELIZABETH. You're making fun of me, Ninian. You're deliberately provoking me into becoming excited about nothing.

NINIAN. No, Elizabeth—I am merely trying to prepare you for a rude shock. You think Abe Lincoln would be overjoyed to capture an elegant, cultivated girl, daughter of the President of the Bank of Kentucky, descendant of a long line of English gentlemen. Well, you are mistaken . . .

(MARY TODD comes in. She is twenty-two —short, pretty, remarkably sharp. She stops short in the doorway, and her suspecting eyes dart from ELIZABETH to NINIAN.)

MARY. What were you two talking about?

NINIAN. I was telling your sister about the new song the boys are singing:

"What is the great commotion, motion,
Our country through?
It is the ball a-rolling on
For Tippecanoe and Tyler, too—for Tippecanoe . . ."

MARY (with a rather grim smile). I compliment you for thinking quickly, Ninian. But you were talking about *me!* (She looks at ELIZABETH, who quails a little before her sister's determination.) Weren't you?

ELIZABETH. Yes, Mary, we were.

MARY. And quite seriously, I gather.

NINIAN. I'm afraid that our dear Elizabeth has become unduly alarmed . . .

ELIZABETH (snapping at him). Let me say what I have to say! (She turns to MARY.) Mary—you must tell me the truth. Are you—have you ever given one moment's serious thought to the possibility of marriage with Abraham Lincoln?
(MARY looks at each of them, her eyes flashing.)
I promise you, Mary, that to me such a notion is too far beyond the bounds of credibility to be . . .

MARY. But Ninian has raised the horrid subject, hasn't he? He has brought the evil scandal out into the open, and we must face it, fearlessly. Let us do so at once, by all means. I shall answer you, Elizabeth: I have given more than one moment's thought to the possibility you mentioned—and I have decided that I shall be Mrs. Lincoln. (She seats herself on the couch.)
(NINIAN is about to say, "I told you so," but thinks better of it. ELIZABETH can only gasp and gape.)
I have examined, carefully, the qualifications of all the young gentlemen, and some of the old ones, in this neighborhood. Those of Mr. Lincoln seem to me superior to all others, and he is my choice.

ELIZABETH. Do you expect me to congratulate you upon this amazing selection?

MARY. No! I ask for no congratulations, nor condolences, either.

ELIZABETH (turning away). Then I shall offer none.

NINIAN. Forgive me for prying, Mary—but have you as yet communicated your decision to the gentleman himself?

MARY (with a slight smile at NINIAN). Not yet. But he is coming to call this evening, and he will ask humbly for my hand in marriage; and, after I have displayed the proper amount of surprise and confusion, I shall murmur, timidly, "Yes!"

ELIZABETH (pitiful). You make a brave jest of it, Mary. But as for me, I am deeply and painfully shocked. I don't know what to say to you. But I urge you, I beg you, as your elder sister, responsible to our father and our dead mother for your welfare . . .

MARY (with a certain tenderness). I can assure you, Elizabeth—it is useless to beg or command. I have made up my mind.

NINIAN. I admire your courage, Mary, but I should like . . .

ELIZABETH. I think, Ninian, that this is a matter for discussion solely between my sister and myself!

MARY. No! I want to hear what Ninian has to say. (To NINIAN.) What is it?

NINIAN. I only wondered if I might ask you another question.

MARY (calmly). You may.

NINIAN. Understand, my dear—I'm not quarreling with you. My affection for Abe is eternal—but—I'm curious to know—what is it about him that makes you choose him for a husband?

MARY (betraying her first sign of uncertainty). I should like to give you a plain, simple answer, Ninian. But I cannot.

ELIZABETH (jumping at this). Of course you cannot! You're rushing blindly into this. You have no conception of what it will mean to your future.

MARY. You're wrong about that, Elizabeth. This is not the result of wild, tempestuous infatuation. I have not been swept off my feet. Mr. Lincoln is a Westerner, but that is his only point of resemblance to Young Lochinvar. I simply feel that of all the men I've ever known, he is the one whose life and destiny I want most to share.

ELIZABETH. Haven't you sense enough to know you could never be happy with him? His breeding—his background—his manner—his whole point of view . . . ?

MARY (gravely). I could not be content with a "happy" marriage in the accepted sense of the word. I have no craving for comfort and security.

ELIZABETH. And have you a craving for the kind of life you would lead? A miserable cabin, without a servant, without a stitch of clothing that is fit for exhibition in decent society?

MARY (raising her voice). I have not yet tried poverty, so I cannot say how I should take to it. But I might well prefer it to anything I have previously known—so long as there is forever before me the chance for high adventure—so long as I can know that I am always going forward, with my husband, along a road that leads across the horizon. (This last is said with a sort of mad intensity.)

ELIZABETH. And how far do you think you will go with any one like Abe Lincoln, who is lazy and shiftless and prefers to stop constantly along the way to tell jokes?

MARY (rising; furious). He will not stop, if I am strong enough to make him go on! And I am strong! I know what you expect of me. You want me to do precisely as you have done—and marry a man like Ninian —and I know many, that are just like him! But with all due respect to my dear brother-in-law—I don't want that—and I won't have it! Never! You live in a house with a fence around it—presumably to prevent the common herd from gaining access to your sacred precincts—but really to prevent you, yourselves, from escaping from your own narrow lives. In Abraham Lincoln I see a man who has split rails for other men's fences, but who will never build one around himself!

ELIZABETH. What are you saying, Mary? You are talking with a degree of irresponsibility that is not far from sheer madness . . .

MARY (scornfully). I imagine it does seem like insanity to you! You married a man who was settled and established in the world, with a comfortable inheritance, and no problems to face. And you've never made a move to change your condition. or

improve it. You consider it couldn't be improved. To you, all this represents perfection. But it doesn't to me! I want the chance to shape a new life, for myself, and for my husband. Is that irresponsibility?

(A MAID appears.)

MAID. Mr. Lincoln, ma'am.

ELIZABETH. He's here.

MARY (firmly). I shall see him!

MAID. Will you step in, Mr. Lincoln?

(ABE comes in, wearing a new suit, his hair nearly neat.)

ABE. Good evening, Mrs. Edwards. Good evening, Miss Todd. Ninian, good evening.

ELIZABETH. Good evening.

MARY. Good evening, Mr. Lincoln. (She sits on the couch at the left.)

NINIAN. Glad to see you, Abe.

(ABE sees that there is electricity in the atmosphere of this parlor. He tries hard to be affably casual.)

ABE. I'm afraid I'm a little late in arriving, but I ran into an old friend of mine, wife of Jack Armstrong, the champion rowdy of New Salem. I believe you have some recollection of him, Ninian.

NINIAN (smiling). I most certainly have. What's he been up to now?

ABE (stands in front of the fireplace). Oh, he's all right, but Hannah, his wife, is in fearful trouble because her son Duff is up for murder and she wants me to defend him. I went over to the jail to interview the boy and he looks pretty tolerably guilty to me. But I used to give him lessons in the game of marbles while his mother foxed my pants for me. (He turns to ELIZABETH.) That means, she sewed buckskin around the legs of my pants so I wouldn't tear 'em to shreds going through underbrush when I was surveying. Well —in view of old times, I felt I had to take the case and do what I can to obstruct the orderly processes of justice.

NINIAN (laughs, with some relief). And the boy will be acquitted. I tell you, Abe —this country would be law-abiding and peaceful if it weren't for you lawyers. But—if you will excuse Elizabeth and me, we must hear the children's prayers and see them safely abed.

ABE. Why—I'd be glad to hear their prayers, too.

NINIAN. Oh, no! You'd only keep them up till all hours with your stories. Come along, Elizabeth.

(ELIZABETH *doesn't want to go, but doesn't know what to do to prevent it.*)

ABE (*to* ELIZABETH). Kiss them good night, for me.

NINIAN. We'd better not tell them you're in the house, or they'll be furious.

ELIZABETH (*making one last attempt*). Mary! Won't you come with us and say good night to the children?

NINIAN. No, my dear. Leave Mary here— to keep Abe entertained. (*He guides* ELIZABETH *out, following her.*)

MARY (*with a little laugh*). I don't blame Ninian for keeping you away from those children. They all adore you.

ABE. Well—I always seemed to get along well with children. Probably it's because they never want to take me seriously.

MARY. You understand them—that's the important thing . . . But—do sit down, Mr. Lincoln. (*She indicates that he is to sit next to her.*)

ABE. Thank you—I will. (*He starts to cross to the couch to sit beside* MARY. *She looks at him with melting eyes. The lights fade.*)

END OF SCENE V

SCENE VI

Again the Law Office. It is afternoon of New Year's Day, a few weeks after the preceding scene.
    ABE *is sitting, slumped in his chair, staring at his desk. He has his hat and overcoat on. A muffler is hanging about his neck, untied.*
    JOSH SPEED *is half-sitting on the table at the right. He is reading a long letter, with most serious attention. At length he finishes it, refolds it very carefully, stares at the floor.*

ABE. Have you finished it, Josh?

JOSH. Yes.

ABE. Well—do you think it's all right?

JOSH. No, Abe—I don't.
(ABE *turns slowly and looks at him.*)
I think the sending of this letter would be a most grave mistake—and that is putting it mildly and charitably.

ABE. Have I stated the case too crudely?

(ABE *is evidently in a serious state of distress, although he is making a tremendous effort to disguise it by speaking in what he intends to be a coldly impersonal tone. He is struggling mightily to hold himself back from the brink of nervous collapse.*)

JOSH. No—I have no quarrel with your choice of words. None whatever. If anything, the phraseology is too correct. But your method of doing it, Abe! It's brutal, it's heartless, it's so unworthy of you that I—I'm at a loss to understand how you ever thought you could do it this way.

ABE. I've done the same thing before with a woman to whom I seemed to have become attached. She approved of my action.

JOSH. This is a different woman. (*He walks over to the window, then turns again toward* ABE.) You cannot seem to accept the fact that women are human beings, too, as variable as we are. You act on the assumption that they're all the same one—and that one is a completely unearthly being of your own conception. This letter isn't written to Mary Todd— it's written to yourself. Every line of it is intended to provide salve for your own conscience.

ABE (*rising; coldly*). Do I understand that you will not deliver it for me?

JOSH. No, Abe—I shall not.

ABE (*angrily*). Then some one else will!

JOSH (*scornfully*). Yes. You could give it to the minister, to hand to the bride when he arrives for the ceremony. But—I hope, Abe, you won't send it till you're feeling a little calmer in your mind. . . .

ABE (*vehemently, turning to* JOSH). How can I ever be calm in my mind until this thing is settled, and out of the way, once and for all? Have you got eyes in your head, Josh? Can't you see that I'm desperate?

JOSH. I can see that plainly, Abe. I think your situation is more desperate even than you imagine, and I believe you should have the benefit of some really intelligent medical advice.

ABE (*seating himself at* BILLY's *table*). The trouble with me isn't anything that a doctor can cure.

JOSH. There's a good man named Dr. Drake, who makes a specialty of treating people who get into a state of mind like yours, Abe . . .

ABE (*utterly miserable*). So that's how you've figured it! I've done what I've threatened to do many times before: I've gone crazy. Well—you know me better than most men, Josh—and perhaps you're not far off right. I just feel that I've got to the end of my rope, and I must let go, and drop—and where I'll land, I don't know, and whether I'll survive the fall, I don't know that either. . . . But—this I *do* know: I've got to get out of this thing—I can't go through with it—I've got to have my release!

(JOSH *has turned to the window. Suddenly he turns back, toward* ABE.)

JOSH. Ninian Edwards is coming up. Why not show this letter to him and ask for his opinion. . . .

ABE (*interrupting, with desperation*). No, no! Don't say a word of any of this to him! Put that letter in your pocket. I can't bear to discuss this business with him, now.

(JOSH *puts the letter in his pocket and crosses to the couch.*)

JOSH. Hello, Ninian.

NINIAN (*heartily, from off*). Hello, Josh! Happy New Year! (NINIAN *comes in. He wears a handsome, fur-trimmed great-coat, and carries two silver-headed canes, one of them in a baize bag, which he lays down on the table at the right.*)

NINIAN. And Happy New Year, Abe—in fact, the happiest of your whole life!

ABE. Thank you, Ninian. And Happy New Year to you.

NINIAN (*opening his coat*). That didn't sound much as if you meant it. (*He goes to the stove to warm his hands.*) However, you can be forgiven today, Abe. I suppose you're inclined to be just a wee bit nervous. (*He chuckles and winks at* JOSH.) God—but it's cold in here! Don't you ever light this stove?

ABE. The fire's all laid. Go ahead and light it, if you want.

NINIAN (*striking a match*). You certainly are in one of your less amiable moods today. (*He lights the stove.*)

JOSH. Abe's been feeling a little under the weather.

NINIAN. So it seems. He looks to me as if he'd been to a funeral.

ABE. That's where I have been.

NINIAN (*disbelieving*). What? A funeral on your wedding day?

JOSH. They buried Abe's oldest friend, Bowling Green, this morning.

NINIAN (*shocked*). Oh—I'm mighty sorry to hear that, Abe. And—I hope you'll forgive me for—not having known about it.

ABE. Of course, Ninian.

NINIAN. But I'm glad you were there, Abe, at the funeral. It must have been a great comfort to his family.

ABE. I wasn't any comfort to any one. They asked me to deliver an oration, a eulogy of the deceased—and I tried—and I couldn't say a thing. Why do they expect you to strew a lot of flowery phrases over anything so horrible as a dead body? Do they think that Bowling Green's soul needs quotations to give it peace? All that mattered to me was that he was a good, just man—and I loved him—and he's dead.

NINIAN. Why didn't you say that, Abe?

ABE (*rising*). I told you—they wanted an oration.

NINIAN. Well, Abe—I think Bowling himself would be the first to ask you to put your sadness aside in the prospect of your own happiness, and Mary's—and I'm only sorry that our old friend didn't live to see you two fine people married. (*He is making a gallant attempt to assume a more cheerily nuptial tone.*) I've made all the arrangements with the Reverend Dresser, and Elizabeth is preparing a bang-up dinner—so you can be sure the whole affair will be carried off handsomely *and* painlessly.

(BILLY HERNDON *comes in. He carries a bottle in his coat pocket, and is already more than a little drunk and sullen, but abnormally articulate.*) Ah, Billy—Happy New Year!

BILLY. The same to you, Mr. Edwards. (*He puts the bottle down on the table and takes his coat off.*)

NINIAN. I brought you a wedding present, Abe. Thought you'd like to make a brave show when you first walk out with your bride. It came from the same place in Louisville where I bought mine.

(*He picks up one of the canes and hands it proudly to* ABE, *who takes it and inspects it gravely.*)

ABE. It's very fine, Ninian. And I thank you. (*He takes the cane over to his desk and seats himself.*)

NINIAN. Well—I'll frankly confess that in getting it for you, I was influenced somewhat by consideration for Mary and her desire for keeping up appearances. And in that connection—I know you'll forgive me, Josh, and you, too, Billy, if I say something of a somewhat personal nature?

BILLY (*truculent*). If you want me to leave you, I shall be glad to. . . .

NINIAN. No, please, Billy—I merely want to speak a word or two as another of Abe's friends; it's my last chance before the ceremony. Of course, the fact that the bride is my sister-in-law gives me a little added responsibility in wishing to promote the success of this marriage. (*He crosses to* ABE.) And a success it will be, Abe . . . if only you will bear in mind one thing: you must keep a tight rein on her ambition. My wife tells me that even as a child, she had delusions of grandeur—she predicted to one and all that the man she would marry would be President of the United States. (*He turns to* JOSH.) You know how it is—every boy in the country plans some day to be president, and every little girl plans to marry him. (*Again to*

ABE:) But Mary is one who hasn't entirely lost those youthful delusions. So I urge you to beware. Don't let her talk you into any gallant crusades or wild goose chases. Let her learn to be satisfied with the estate to which God hath brought her. With which, I shall conclude my prenuptial sermon. (*He buttons his coat.*) I shall see you all at the house at five o'clock, and I want you to make sure that Abe is looking his prettiest.

JOSH. Good-bye, Ninian.

(NINIAN *goes out.* ABE *turns again to the desk and stares at nothing.* BILLY *takes the bottle and a cup from his desk and pours himself a stiff drink. He raises the cup toward* ABE.)

BILLY (*huskily*). Mr. Lincoln, I beg leave to drink to your health and happiness . . . and to that of the lady who will become your wife.

(ABE *makes no response.* BILLY *drinks it down, then puts the cup back on the table.*) You don't want to accept my toast because you think it wasn't sincere. And I'll admit I've made it plain that I've regretted the step you've taken. I thought that in this marriage, you were lowering yourself—you were trading your honor for some exalted family connections. . . . I wish to apologize for so thinking. . . .

ABE. No apologies required, Billy.

BILLY. I doubt that Miss Todd and I will ever get along well together. But I'm now convinced that our aims are the same—particularly since I've heard the warnings delivered by her brother-in-law. (*A note of scorn colors his allusion to* NINIAN.) If she really is ambitious for you—if she will never stop driving you, goading you—then I say, God bless her, and give her strength!

(*He has said all this with* ABE's *back to him.* BILLY *pours himself another drink, nearly emptying the large bottle.* ABE *turns and looks at him.*)

ABE. Have you had all of that bottle today?

BILLY. This bottle? Yes—I have.

JOSH. And why not? It's New Year's Day!

BILLY (*looking at* JOSH). Thank you, Mr. Speed. Thank you for the defense. And I hope you will permit me to propose one more toast. (*He takes a step toward* ABE.)

To the President of the United States, and Mrs. Lincoln! *(He drinks.)*

ABE *(grimly)*. I think we can do without any more toasts, Billy.

BILLY. Very well! That's the last one—until after the wedding. And then, no doubt, the Edwardses will serve us with the costliest champagne. And, in case you're apprehensive, I shall be on my best behavior in that distinguished gathering!

ABE. There is not going to be a wedding. (BILLY *stares at him, and then looks at* JOSH, *and then again at* ABE.) I have a letter that I want you to deliver to Miss Todd.

BILLY. What letter? What is it?

ABE. Give it to him, Josh. (JOSH *takes the letter out of his pocket, and puts it in the stove.* ABE *jumps up.*) You have no right to do that!

JOSH. I know I haven't! But it's done. (ABE *is staring at* JOSH.) And don't look at me as if you were planning to break my neck. Of course you could do it, Abe—but you won't. (JOSH *turns to* BILLY.) In that letter, Mr. Lincoln asked Miss Todd for his release. He told her that he had made a mistake in his previous protestations of affection for her, and so he couldn't go through with a marriage which could only lead to endless pain and misery for them both.

ABE *(deeply distressed)*. If that isn't the truth, what is?

JOSH. I'm not disputing the truth of it. I'm only asking you to tell her so, to her face, in the manner of a man.

ABE. It would be a more cruel way. It would hurt her more deeply. For I couldn't help blurting it *all* out—all the terrible things I didn't say in that letter. *(He is speaking with passion.)* I'd have to tell her that I have hatred for her infernal ambition—that I don't want to be ridden and driven, upward and onward through life, with her whip lashing me, and her spurs digging into me! If her poor soul craves importance in life, then let her marry Stephen Douglas. He's ambitious, too. . . . I want only to be left alone! *(He sits down again and leans on the table.)*

JOSH *(bitterly)*. Very well, then—tell her all that! It will be more gracious to admit that you're afraid of her, instead of letting her down flat with the statement that your ardor, such as it was, has cooled.

(BILLY *has been seething with a desire to get into this conversation. Now, with a momentary silence, he plunges.*)

BILLY. May I say something?

ABE. I doubt that you're in much of a condition to contribute. . . .

JOSH. What is it, Billy?

BILLY *(hotly)*. It's just this. Mr. Lincoln, you're not abandoning Miss Mary Todd. No! You're only using her as a living sacrifice, offering her up, in the hope you will thus gain forgiveness of the gods for your failure to do your own great duty!

ABE *(smoldering)*. Yes! My own great duty. Every one feels called upon to remind me of it, but no one can tell me what it is.

BILLY *(almost tearful)*. I can tell you! I can tell you what is the duty of every man who calls himself an American! It is to perpetuate those truths which were once held to be self-evident: that all men are created equal—that they are endowed with certain inalienable rights—that among these are the right to life, liberty and the pursuit of happiness.

ABE *(angrily)*. And are those rights denied to *me*?

BILLY. Could you ever enjoy them while your mind is full of the awful knowledge that two million of your fellow beings in this country are slaves? Can you take any satisfaction from looking at that flag above your desk, when you know that ten of its stars represent states which are willing to destroy the Union—rather than yield their property rights in the flesh and blood of those slaves? And what of all the States of the future? All the territories of the West—clear out to the Pacific Ocean? Will they be the homes of free men? Are you answering *that* question to your own satisfaction? That is your flag, Mr. Lincoln, and you're proud of it. But what are you doing to save it from being ripped into shreds?

(ABE *jumps to his feet, towers over* BILLY, *and speaks with temper restrained, but with great passion.*)

ABE. I'm minding my own business— that's what I'm doing! And there'd be no threat to the Union if others would do the same. And as to slavery—I'm sick and tired of this righteous talk about it. When you know more about law, you'll know that those property rights you mentioned are guaranteed by the Constitution. And if the Union can't stand on the Constitution, then let it fall!

BILLY. To hell with the Constitution! This is a matter of the rights of living men to freedom—and those came before the Constitution! When the Law denies those rights, then the Law is wrong, and it must be changed, if not by moral protest, then by force! There's no course of action that isn't justified in the defense of freedom! And don't dare to tell me that any one in the world knows that better than you do, Mr. Lincoln. You, who honor the memory of Elijah Lovejoy and every other man who ever died for that very ideal!

ABE *(turning away from him).* Yes—I honor them—and envy them—because they could believe that their ideals are *worth* dying for. *(He turns to* JOSH *and speaks with infinite weariness.)* All right, Josh—I'll go up now and talk to Mary— and then I'm going away. . . .

JOSH. Where, Abe?

ABE *(dully).* I don't know.

(He goes out and closes the door after him. After a moment, BILLY *rushes to the door, opens it, and shouts after* ABE.*)*

BILLY. You're quitting, Mr. Lincoln! As surely as there's a God in Heaven, He knows that you're running away from your obligations to Him, and to your fellow-men, and your own immortal soul!

JOSH *(drawing* BILLY *away from the door).* Billy—Billy—leave him alone. He's a sick man.

BILLY *(sitting down at the table).* What can we do for him, Mr. Speed? What can we do? *(*BILLY *is now actually in tears.)*

JOSH. I don't know, Billy. *(He goes to the window and looks out.)* He'll be in such a state of emotional upheaval, he'll want to go away by himself, for a long time. Just as he did after the death of poor little Ann Rutledge. He'll go out and wander on the prairies, trying to grope his way back into the wilderness from which he came. There's nothing we can do for him, Billy. He'll have to do it for himself.

BILLY *(fervently).* May God be with him!

END OF SCENE VI

SCENE VII

On the prairie, near New Salem. It is a clear, cool, moonlight evening, nearly two years after the preceding scene.

In the foreground is a campfire. Around it are packing cases, blanket rolls and one ancient trunk. In the background is a covered wagon, standing at an angle, so that the opening at the back of it is visible to the audience.

SETH GALE *is standing by the fire, holding his seven-year-old son,* JIMMY, *in his arms. The boy is wrapped up in a blanket.*

JIMMY. I don't want to be near the fire, Paw. I'm burning up. Won't you take the blanket offen me, Paw?

SETH. No, son. You're better off if you keep yourself covered.

JIMMY. I want some water, Paw. Can't I have some water?

SETH. Yes! Keep quiet, Jimmy. Gobey's getting the water for you now. *(He looks*

off to the right, and sees JACK ARMSTRONG *coming.)* Hello, Jack, I was afraid you'd got lost.

JACK *(coming in).* I couldn't get lost anywhere's around New Salem. How's the boy?

SETH *(with a cautionary look at* JACK*).* He—he's a little bit thirsty. Did you find Abe?

JACK. Yes—it took me some time because he'd wandered off—went out to the old cemetery across the river to visit Ann Rutledge's grave.

SETH. Is he coming here?

JACK. He said he'd better go get Doc Chandler who lives on the Winchester Road. He'll be along in a while. *(He comes up to* JIMMY.*)* How you feelin', Jimmy?

JIMMY. I'm burning . . .

*(*AGGIE *appears, sees* JACK.*)*

AGGIE. Oh—I'm so glad you're back, Mr. Armstrong.

JACK. There'll be a doctor here soon, Mrs. Gale.

AGGIE. Thank God for that! Bring him into the wagon, Seth. I got a nice, soft bed all ready for him.

SETH. You hear that, Jimmy? Your ma's fixed a place where you can rest comfortable.

*(*AGGIE *retreats into the wagon.)*

JIMMY. When'll Gobey come back? I'm thirsty. When'll he bring the water?

SETH. Right away, son. You can trust Gobey to get your water. *(He hands* JIMMY *into the wagon.)*

JACK. He's worse, ain't he?

SETH *(in a despairing tone).* Yes. The fever's been raging something fierce since you left. It'll sure be a relief when Abe gets here. He can always do something to put confidence in you.

JACK. How long since you've seen Abe, Seth?

SETH. Haven't laid eyes on him since I left here—eight—nine years ago. We've corresponded some.

JACK. Well—you may be surprised when you see him. He's changed plenty since he went to Springfield. He climbed up pretty high in the world, but he appears to have slipped down lately. He ain't much like his old comical self.

SETH. Well, I guess we all got to change. *(He starts up, hearing* GOBEY *return.)* Aggie!

*(*GOBEY, *a Negro, comes in from the left, carrying a bucket of water.* AGGIE *appears from the wagon.)*
Here's Gobey with the water.

GOBEY. Yes, Miss Aggie. Here you are. *(He hands it up.)*

AGGIE. Thanks, Gobey. *(She goes back into the wagon.)*

GOBEY. How's Jimmy now, Mr. Seth?

SETH. About the same.

GOBEY *(shaking his head).* I'll get some more water for the cooking. *(He picks up a kettle and a pot and goes.)*

SETH *(to* JACK*).* It was a bad thing to have happen, all right—the boy getting sick—when we were on an expedition like this. No doctor—no way of caring for him.

JACK. How long you been on the road, Seth?

SETH. More than three months. Had a terrible time in the Pennsylvania Mountains, fearful rains and every stream flooded. I can tell you, there was more than one occasion when I wanted to turn back and give up the whole idea. But—when you get started—you just can't turn . . . *(He is looking off right.)* Say! Is that Abe coming now?

JACK *(rising).* Yep. That's him.

SETH *(delighted).* My God, look at him! Store clothes and a plug hat! Hello—Abe!

ABE. Hello, Seth. *(He comes on and shakes hands, warmly.)* I'm awful glad to see you again, Seth.

SETH. And me, too, Abe.

ABE. It did my heart good when I heard you were on your way West. Where's your boy?

SETH. He's in there—in the wagon. . . .

*(*AGGIE *has appeared from the wagon.)*

AGGIE. Is that the doctor?

SETH. No, Aggie—this is the man I was telling you about I wanted so much to see. This is Mr. Abe Lincoln—my wife, Mrs. Gale.

ABE. Pleased to meet you, Mrs. Gale.

AGGIE. Pleased to meet you, Mr. Lincoln.

ABE. Doc Chandler wasn't home. They said he was expected over at the Boger farm at midnight. I'll go there then and fetch him.

SETH. It'll be a friendly act, Abe.

AGGIE. We'll be in your debt, Mr. Lincoln.

ABE. In the meantime, Mrs. Gale, I'd like to do whatever I can. . . .

SETH. There's nothing to do, Abe. The boy's got the swamp fever, and we're just trying to keep him quiet.

AGGIE *(desperately)*. There's just one thing I would wish—is—is there any kind of a preacher around this God-forsaken place?

SETH *(worried)*. Preacher?

ABE. Do you know of any, Jack?

JACK. No. There ain't a preacher within twenty miles of New Salem now.

AGGIE. Well—I only thought if there was, we might get him here to say a prayer for Jimmy. *(She goes back into the wagon.* SETH *looks after her with great alarm.)*

SETH. She wants a preacher. That looks as if she'd given up, don't it?

JACK. It'd probably just comfort her.

ABE. Is your boy very sick, Seth?

SETH. Yes—he is.

JACK. Why don't *you* speak a prayer, Abe? You could always think of somethin' to say.

ABE. I'm afraid I'm not much of a hand at praying. I couldn't think of a blessed thing that would be of any comfort.

SETH. Never mind. It's just a—a religious idea of Aggie's. Sit down, Abe.

ABE *(looking at the wagon)*. So you've got your dream at last, Seth. You're doing what you and I used to talk about—you're moving.

SETH. Yes, Abe. We got crowded out of Maryland. The city grew up right over our farm. So—we're headed for a place where there's more room. I wrote you—about four months back—to tell you we were starting out, and I'd like to meet up with you here. I thought it was just possible you might consider joining in this trip.

ABE. It took a long time for your letter to catch up with me, Seth. I've just been drifting—down around Indiana and Kentucky where I used to live. *(He sits down on a box.)* Do you aim to settle in Nebraska?

SETH. No, we're not going to stop there. We're going right across the continent—all the way to Oregon.

ABE *(deeply impressed)*. Oregon?

JACK. Sure. That's where they're all headin' for now.

SETH. We're making first for a place called Westport Landing—that's in Kansas right on the frontier—where they outfit the wagon trains for the far West. You join up there with a lot of others who are like-minded, so you've got company when you're crossing the plains and the mountains.

ABE. It's staggering—to think of the distance you're going. And you'll be taking the frontier along with you.

SETH. It may seem like a fool-hardy thing to do—but we heard too many tales of the black earth out there, and the balance of rainfall and sunshine.

JACK. Why don't you go with them, Abe? That country out west is gettin' settled fast. Why—last week alone, I counted more than two hundred wagons went past here—people from all over—Pennsylvania, Connecticut, Vermont—all full of jubilation at the notion of gettin' land. By God, I'm goin' too, soon as I can get me a wagon. They'll need men like me to fight the Indians for 'em—and they'll need men with brains, like you, Abe, to tell 'em how to keep the peace.

ABE *(looking off)*. It's a temptation to go, I can't deny that.

JACK. Then what's stoppin' you from doin' it? You said yourself you've just been driftin'.

ABE. Maybe that's it—maybe I've been drifting too long. . . . *(He changes the subject.)* Is it just the three of you, Seth?

SETH. That's all. The three of us and Gobey, the nigger.

ABE. Is he your slave?

SETH. Gobey? Hell, no! He's a free man! My father freed his father twenty years ago. But we've had to be mighty careful about Gobey. You see, where we come from, folks are pretty uncertain how they feel about the slave question, and lots of good free niggers get snaked over the line into Virginia and then sold down river before you know it. And when you try to go to court and assert their legal rights, you're beaten at every turn by the damned, dirty shyster lawyers. That's why we've been keeping well up in free territory on this trip.

ABE. Do you think it will be free in Oregon?

SETH. Of course it will! It's got to——

ABE *(bitterly).* Oh no, it hasn't, Seth. Not with the politicians in Washington selling out the whole West piece by piece to the slave traders.

SETH *(vehemently).* That territory has got to be free! If this country ain't strong enough to protect its citizens from slavery, then we'll cut loose from it and join with Canada. Or, better yet, we'll make a *new* country out there in the far west.

ABE *(gravely).* A new country?

SETH. Why not?

ABE. I was just thinking—old Mentor Graham once said to me that some day the United States might be divided up into many hostile countries, like Europe.

SETH. Well—let it be! Understand—I love this country and I'd fight for it. And I guess George Washington and the rest of them loved England and fought for it when they were young—but they didn't hesitate to cut loose when the government failed to play fair and square with 'em.

JACK. By God, if Andy Jackson was back in the White House, he'd run out them traitors with a horsewhip!

ABE. It'd be a bad day for us Americans, Seth, if we lost you, and your wife, and your son.

SETH *(breaking).* My son!—Oh—I've been talking big—but it's empty talk. If he dies—there won't be enough spirit left in us to push on any further. What's the use of working for a future when you know there won't be anybody growing up to enjoy it. Excuse me, Abe—but I'm feeling pretty scared.

ABE *(suddenly rises).* You mustn't be scared, Seth. I know I'm a poor one to be telling you that—because I've been scared all my life. But—seeing you now—and thinking of the big thing you've set out to do—well, it's made me feel pretty small. It's made me feel that I've got to do something, too, to keep you and your kind in the United States of America. You mustn't quit, Seth! Don't let anything beat you—don't you ever give up!

(AGGIE comes out of the wagon. She is very frightened.)

AGGIE. Seth!

SETH. What is it, Aggie?

AGGIE. He's worse, Seth! He's moaning in his sleep, and he's gasping for breath. . . .

(She is crying. SETH *takes her in his arms.)*

SETH. Never mind, honey. Never mind. When the doctor gets here, he'll fix him up in no time. It's all right, honey. He'll get well.

ABE. If you wish me to, Mrs. Gale—I'll try to speak a prayer.

(They look at him.)

JACK. That's the way to talk, Abe!

SETH. We'd be grateful for anything you might say, Abe.

(ABE takes his hat off. As he starts speaking, GOBEY *comes in from the left and stops reverently to listen.)*

ABE. Oh God, the father of all living, I ask you to look with gentle mercy upon this little boy who is here, lying sick in this covered wagon. His people are travelling far, to seek a new home in the wilderness, to do your work, God, to make this earth a good place for your children to live in. They can see clearly where they're going, and they're not afraid to face all the perils that lie along the way. I humbly beg you not to take their child from them. Grant him the freedom of life. Do not condemn him to the imprisonment of death. Do not deny him his birthright. Let him know the sight of great plains and high mountains, of green valleys and wide rivers. For this little boy is an American, and these things belong to him, and he to them. Spare him, that he too may strive for the ideal for which his fathers have labored, so faithfully and for so long. Spare him and give him his fathers' strength—give us all strength, oh God, to do the work that is before us. I ask you this favor, in the name of *your* son, Jesus Christ, who died upon the Cross to set men free. Amen.

GOBEY *(with fervor)*. Amen!

SETH AND AGGIE *(murmuring)* Amen!

(ABE puts his hat on.)

ABE. It's getting near midnight. I'll go over to the Boger farm and get the doctor. *(He goes out.)*

SETH. Thank you, Abe.

AGGIE. Thank you—thank you, Mr. Lincoln.

GOBEY. God bless you, Mr. Lincoln!

(The lights fade quickly.)

END OF SCENE VII

SCENE VIII

Again the parlor of the Edwards house. A few days after preceding scene.
MARY is seated, reading a book.
After a moment, the MAID enters.

MAID. Miss Mary—Mr. Lincoln is here.

MARY. Mr. Lincoln! *(She sits still a moment in an effort to control her emotions, then sharply closes the book and rises.)*

MAID. Will you see him, Miss Mary?

MARY. Yes—in one moment.

(The MAID goes off. MARY turns, drops her book on the sofa, then moves over toward the right, struggling desperately to compose herself. At the fireplace, she stops and turns to face ABE as he enters.)
I'm glad to see you again, Mr. Lincoln.

(There is considerable constraint between them. He is grimly determined to come to the point with the fewest possible words; she is making a gallant, well-bred attempt to observe the social amenities.)

ABE. Thank you, Mary. You may well wonder why I have thrust myself on your mercy in this manner.

MARY *(quickly)*. I'm sure you're always welcome in Ninian's house.

ABE. After my behavior at our last meeting here, I have not been welcome company for myself.

MARY. You've been through a severe illness. Joshua Speed has kept us informed of it. We've been greatly concerned.

ABE. It is most kind of you.

MARY. But you're restored to health now —you'll return to your work, and no doubt you'll be running for the assembly again—or perhaps you have larger plans?

ABE. I have no plans, Mary. *(He seems to brace himself.)* But I wish to tell you that I am sorry for the things that I said on that unhappy ocasion which was to have been our wedding day.

MARY. You need not say anything about that, Mr. Lincoln. Whatever happened then, it was my own fault.

ABE *(disturbed by this unforeseen avowal)*. Your fault! It was my miserable cowardice——

MARY. I was blinded by my own self-confidence! I—I loved you. *(For a moment her firm voice falters, but she immediately masters that tendency toward weakness.)* And I believed I could make you love me. I believed we might achieve a real communion of spirit, and the fire of my determination would burn in you. You would become a man and a leader of men! But you didn't wish that. *(She turns away.)* I knew you had strength—but I did not know you would use it, all of it, to resist your own magnificent destiny.

ABE *(deliberately)*. It is true, Mary—you once had faith in me which I was far from deserving. But the time has come, at last, when I wish to strive to deserve it. *(MARY looks at him, sharply.)* When I behaved in that shameful manner toward you, I did so because I thought that our ways were separate and could never be otherwise. I've come to the conclusion that I was wrong. I believe that our destinies are together, for better or for worse, and I again presume to ask you to be my wife. I fully realize, Mary, that taking me back now would involve humiliation for you.

MARY (*flaring*). I am not afraid of humiliation, if I know it will be wiped out by ultimate triumph! But there can be no triumph unless you yourself are sure. What was it that brought you to this change of heart and mind?

ABE. On the prairie, I met an old friend of mine who was moving West, with his wife and child, in a covered wagon. He asked me to go with him, and I was strongly tempted to do so. (*There is great sadness in his tone—but he seems to collect himself, and turns to her again, speaking with a sort of resignation.*) But then I knew that was not my direction. The way I must go is the way you have always wanted me to go.

MARY. And you will promise that never again will you falter, or turn to run away?

ABE. I promise, Mary—if you will have me—I shall devote myself for the rest of my days to trying—to do what is right—as God gives me power to see what is right.

(*She looks at him, trying to search him. She would like to torment him, for a while, with artful indecision. But she cannot do it.*)

MARY. Very well then—I shall be your wife. I shall fight by your side—till death do us part. (*She runs to him and clutches him.*) Abe! I love you—oh, I love you! Whatever becomes of the two of us, I'll die loving you! (*She is sobbing wildly on his shoulder. Awkwardly, he lifts his hands and takes hold of her in a loose embrace. He is staring down at the carpet, over her shoulder.*)

CURTAIN

END OF ACT II

ACT THREE

SCENE IX

A speakers' platform in an Illinois town. It is a summer evening in the year 1858. A light shines down on the speaker at the front of the platform.

At the back of the platform are three chairs. At the right sits JUDGE STEPHEN A. DOUGLAS—*at the left,* ABE, *who has his plug hat on and makes occasional notes on a piece of paper on his knee. The chair in the middle is for* NINIAN, *acting as Moderator, who is now at the front of the platform.*

NINIAN. We have now heard the leading arguments from the two candidates for the high office of United States Senator from Illinois—Judge Stephen A. Douglas and Mr. Abraham Lincoln. A series of debates between these two eminent citizens of Illinois has focussed upon our state the attention of the entire nation, for here are being discussed the vital issues which now affect the lives of all Americans and the whole future history of our beloved country. According to the usual custom of debate, each of the candidates will now speak in rebuttal. . . . Judge Douglas.

(NINIAN *retires and sits, as* DOUGLAS *comes forward. He is a brief but magnetic man, confident of his powers.*)

DOUGLAS. My fellow citizens: My good friend, Mr. Lincoln, has addressed you with his usual artless sincerity, his pure, homely charm, his perennial native humor. He has even devoted a generously large portion of his address to most amiable remarks upon my fine qualities as a man, if not as a statesman. For which I express deepest gratitude. But—at the same time —I most earnestly beg you not to be deceived by his seeming innocence, his carefully cultivated spirit of good will. For in each of his little homilies lurk concealed weapons. Like Brutus, in Shakespeare's immortal tragedy, Mr. Lincoln is an honorable man. But, also like Brutus, he is an adept at the art of inserting daggers between an opponent's ribs, just when said opponent least expects it. Behold me, gentlemen—I am covered with scars. And yet —somehow or other—I am still upright. Perhaps because I am supported by that sturdy prop called "Truth." Truth— which, crushed to earth by the assassin's blades, doth rise again! Mr. Lincoln makes you laugh with his pungent anecdotes. Then he draws tears from your eyes with his dramatic pictures of the plight of the black slave labor in the South. Always, he guides you skilfully to the threshold of truth, but then, as you are about to cross it, diverts your attention elsewhere. For one thing—he never, by any mischance, makes reference to the condition of labor here in the North! Oh, no! Perhaps New England is so far beyond the bounds of his parochial ken that he does not know that tens of thousands of working men and women in the textile industry are now on STRIKE! And why are they on strike? Because from early morning to dark of night—fourteen hours a day—those "free" citizens must toil at shattering looms in soulless factories and never see the sun; and then, when their fearful day's work at last comes to its exhausted end, these ill-clad and undernourished laborers must trudge home to their foul abodes in tenements that are not fit habitations for rats! What kind of Liberty is this? And if Mr. Lincoln has not heard of conditions in Massachusetts—how has it escaped his attention that here in our own great state no wheels are now turning on that mighty railroad, the Illinois Central? Because its oppressed workers are also on STRIKE! Because they too demand a living wage! So it is throughout the North. Hungry men, marching through the streets in ragged order, promoting riots, because they are not paid enough to keep the flesh upon the bones of their babies! What kind of Liberty is *this*? And what kind of equality? Mr. Lincoln harps constantly on this subject of equality. He repeats over and over the argument used by Lovejoy and other abolitionists: to wit, that the Declaration of Independence having declared all men free and equal, by divine law, thus Negro equality is an inalienable right. Contrary to this absurd assumption stands the verdict of the Supreme Court, as it was clearly stated by Chief Justice Taney in the case of Dred Scott. The Negroes are established by this decision as an inferior race of beings, sub-

jugated by the dominant race, enslaved and, therefore, *property*—like all other property! But Mr. Lincoln is inclined to dispute the constitutional authority of the Supreme Court. He has implied, if he did not say so outright, that the Dred Scott decision was a prejudiced one, which must be over-ruled by the voice of the people. Mr. Lincoln is a lawyer, and I presume, therefore, that he knows that when he seeks to destroy public confidence in the integrity, the inviolability of the Supreme Court, he is preaching *revolution!* He is attempting to stir up odium and rebellion in this country against the constituted authorities; he is stimulating the passions of men to resort to violence and to mobs, instead of to the law. He is setting brother against brother! There can be but one consequence of such inflammatory persuasion—and that is *Civil War!* He asks me to state my opinion of the Dred Scott Decision, and I answer him unequivocally by saying, "I take the decisions of the Supreme Court as the law of the land, and I intend to obey them as such!" Nor will I be swayed from that position by all the rantings of all the fanatics who preach "racial equality," who ask us to vote, and eat, and sleep, and marry with Negroes! And I say further —Let each State mind its own business and leave its neighbors alone. If we will stand by that principle, then Mr. Lincoln will find that this great republic can exist forever divided into free and slave states. We can go on as we have done, increasing in wealth, in population, in power, until we shall be the admiration and the terror of the world! *(He glares at the audience, then turns, mopping his brow, and resumes his seat.)*

NINIAN *(rising)*. Mr. Lincoln.

*(*ABE *glances at his notes, takes his hat off, puts the notes in it, then rises slowly and comes forward. He speaks quietly, reasonably. His words come from an emotion so profound that it needs no advertisement.)*

ABE. Judge Douglas has paid tribute to my skill with the dagger. I thank him for that, but I must also admit that he can do more with that weapon than I can. He can keep ten daggers flashing in the air at one time. Fortunately, he's so good at it that none of the knives ever falls and hurts anybody. The Judge can condone slavery in the South and protest hotly against its extension to the North. He can crowd loyalty to the Union and defense of states' sovereignty into the same breath. Which reminds me—and I hope the Judge will allow me one more homely little anecdote, because I'd like to tell about a woman down in Kentucky. She came out of her cabin one day and found her husband grappling with a ferocious bear. It was a fight to the death, and the bear was winning. The struggling husband called to his wife, "For heaven's sake, *help* me!" The wife asked what could *she* do? Said the husband, "You could at least *say* something encouraging." But the wife didn't want to seem to be taking sides in this combat, so she just hollered, "Go it husband—go it bear!" Now, you heard the Judge make allusion to those who advocate voting and eating and marrying and sleeping with Negroes. Whether he meant me specifically, I do not know. If he did, I can say that just because I do not want a colored woman for a slave, I don't necessarily want her for a wife. I need not have her for either. I can just leave her alone. In some respects, she certainly is not my equal, any more than I am the Judge's equal, in some respects; but in her natural right to eat the bread she earns with her own hands without asking leave of some one else, she is my equal, and the equal of all others. And as to sleeping with Negroes—the Judge may be interested to know that the slave states have produced more than four hundred thousand mulattoes—and I don't think many of them are the children of abolitionists. That word "abolitionists" brings to mind New England, which also has been mentioned. I assure Judge Douglas that I have been there, and I have seen those cheerless brick prisons called factories, and the workers trudging silently home through the darkness. In those factories, cotton that was picked by black slaves is woven into cloth by white people who are separated from slavery by no more than fifty cents a day. As an American, I cannot be proud that such conditions exist. But—as an American—I can ask: would any of those striking workers in the North elect to change places with the slaves in the South? Will they not rather say, "The remedy is in *our* hands!" And, still as an American, I can say—thank God we live under a system by which men have the *right* to strike! I am not preaching rebellion. I don't have to. This country, with its institutions, belongs to the people who inhabit it. Whenever they shall grow weary of the existing government, they can exercise their constitutional right of amending it, or their revolutionary right to dismember or overthrow it. If the founding fathers gave us anything, they gave us that. And I am not preaching disrespect for the Supreme Court. I am only saying that the decisions of mortal men are often influenced by unjudicial bias—and the Supreme Court is composed of mortal men, most of whom, it so happens, come from the privileged class in the South. There is an old saying that judges are just as honest as other men, and not more so; and in case some of you are wondering who said that, it was Thomas Jefferson. (*He has half turned to* DOUGLAS.) The purpose of the Dred Scott Decision is to make property, and nothing but property, of the Negro in all states of the Union. It is the old issue of property rights versus human rights—an issue that will continue in this country when these poor tongues of Judge Douglas and myself shall long have been silent. It is the eternal struggle between two principles. The one is the common right of humanity, and the other the divine right of kings. It is the same spirit that says, "You toil and work and earn bread, and I'll eat it." Whether those words come from the mouth of a king who bestrides his people and lives by the fruit of their labor, or from one race of men who seek to enslave another race, it is the same tyrannical principle. As a nation, we began by declaring, "All men are created equal." There was no mention of any exceptions to the rule in the Declaration of Independence. But we now practically read it, "All men are created equal except Negroes." If we accept this doctrine of race or class discrimination, what is to stop us from decreeing in the future that "All men are created equal except Negroes, foreigners, Catholics, Jews, or—just poor people?" That is the conclusion toward which the advocates of slavery are driving us. Many good citizens, North and South, agree with the Judge that we should accept that conclusion—don't stir up trouble—"Let each State mind its own business." That's the safer course, for the time being. But—I advise you to watch out! When you have enslaved any of your fellow beings, dehumanized him, denied him all claim to the dignity of manhood, placed him among the beasts, among the damned, are you quite sure that the demon you have thus created, will not turn and rend *you?* When you begin qualifying freedom, watch out for the consequences to *you!* And I am not preaching civil war. All I am trying to do—now, and as long as I live—is to state and restate the fundamental virtues of our democracy, which have made us great, and which can make us greater. I believe most seriously that the perpetuation of those virtues is now endangered, not only by the honest proponents of slavery, but even more by those who echo Judge Douglas in shouting, "Leave it alone!" This is the complacent policy of indifference to evil, and that policy I cannot but hate. I hate it because of the monstrous injustice of slavery itself. I hate it because it deprives our republic of its just influence in the world; enables the enemies of free institutions everywhere to taunt us as hypocrites; causes the real

friends of freedom to doubt our sincerity; and especially because it forces so many good men among ourselves into an open war with the very fundamentals of civil liberty, denying the good faith of the Declaration of Independence, and insisting that there is no right principle of action but *self-interest.* . . . In his final words tonight, the Judge said that we may be "the terror of the world." I don't think we want to be that. I think we would prefer to be the encouragement of the world, the proof that man is at last worthy to be free. But—we shall provide no such encouragement, unless we can establish our ability as a nation to live and grow. And we shall surely do neither if these states fail to remain *united.* There can be no distinction in the definitions of liberty as between one section and another, one race and another, one class and another. "A house divided against itself cannot stand." This government cannot endure permanently, half slave and half free! *(He turns and goes back to his seat.)*

(The lights fade.)

End of Scene IX

SCENE X

Parlor of the Edwards home, now being used by the Lincolns. Afternoon of a day in the early Spring of 1860.

Abe is sitting on the couch at the right, with his seven-year-old son, Tad, on his lap. Sitting beside them is another son, Willie, aged nine. The eldest son, Robert, a young Harvard student of seventeen, is sitting by the window, importantly smoking a pipe and listening to the story Abe has been telling the children. Joshua Speed is sitting at the left.

abe. You must remember, Tad, the roads weren't much good then—mostly nothing more than trails—and it was hard to find my way in the darkness. . . .

willie. Were you scared?

abe. Yes—I was scared.

willie. Of Indians?

abe. No—there weren't any of them left around here. I was afraid I'd get lost, and the boy would die, and it would be all my fault. But, finally, I found the doctor. He was very tired, and wanted to go to bed, and he grumbled a lot, but I made him come along with me then and there.

willie. Was the boy dead?

abe. No, Willie. He wasn't dead. But he was pretty sick. The doctor gave him a lot of medicine.

tad. Did it taste bad, Pa?

abe. I presume it did. But it worked. I never saw those nice people again, but I've heard from them every so often. That little boy was your age, Tad, but now he's a grown man with a son almost as big as you are. He lives on a great big farm, in a valley with a river that runs right down from the tops of the snow mountains. . . .

(Mary comes in.)

mary. Robert! You are smoking in my parlor!

ROBERT (*wearily*). Yes, Mother. (*He rises.*)

MARY. I have told you that I shall not tolerate tobacco smoke in my parlor or, indeed, in any part of my house, and I mean to . . .

ABE. Come, come, Mary—you must be respectful to a Harvard man. Take it out to the woodshed, Bob.

ROBERT. Yes, Father.

MARY. And this will not happen again!

ROBERT. No, Mother. (*He goes out.*)

ABE. I was telling the boys a story about some pioneers I knew once.

MARY. It's time for you children to make ready for your supper.

(*The* CHILDREN *promptly get up to go.*)

WILLIE. But what happened after that, Pa?

ABE. Nothing. Everybody lived happily ever after. Now run along.

(WILLIE *and* TAD *run out.*)

JOSH. What time *is* it, Mary?

MARY. It's nearly half past four. (*She is shaking the smoke out of the curtains.*)

JOSH. Half past four, Abe. Those men will be here any minute.

ABE (*rising*). Good Lord!

MARY (*turning sharply to* ABE). What men?

ABE. Some men from the East. One of them's a political leader named Crimmin —and there's a Mr. Sturveson—he's a manufacturer—and . . .

MARY (*impressed*). Henry D. Sturveson?

ABE. That's the one—and also the Reverend Dr. Barrick from Boston.

MARY (*sharply*). What are they coming here for?

ABE. I don't precisely know—but I suspect that it's to see if I'm fit to be a candidate for President of the United States.
(MARY *is, for the moment, speechless.*)
I suppose they want to find out if we still live in a log cabin and keep pigs under the bed. . . .

MARY (*in a fury*). And you didn't *tell* me!

ABE. I'm sorry, Mary—the matter just slipped my . . .

MARY. You forgot to tell me that we're having the most important guests who ever crossed the threshold of my house!

ABE. They're not guests. They're only here on business.

MARY (*bitterly*). Yes! Rather important business, it seems to me. They want to see us as we *are*—crude, sloppy, vulgar Western barbarians, living in a house that reeks of foul tobacco smoke.

ABE. We can explain about having a son at Harvard.

MARY. If I'd only *known!* If you had only given me a little time to prepare for them. Why didn't you put on your best suit? And those filthy old boots!

ABE. Well, Mary, I clean forgot. . . .

MARY. I declare, Abraham Lincoln, I believe you would have treated me with much more consideration if I had been your slave, instead of your wife! You have never, for one moment, stopped to think that perhaps I have some interests, some concerns, in the life we lead together. . . .

ABE. I'll try to clean up my boots a little, Mary.

(*He goes out, glad to escape from this painful scene.* MARY *looks after him. Her lip is quivering. She wants to avoid tears.*)

MARY (*seating herself; bitterly*). You've seen it all, Joshua Speed. Every bit of it— courtship, if you could call it that, change of heart, change back again, and marriage, eighteen years of it. And you probably think just as all the others do—that I'm a bitter, nagging woman, and I've tried to kill his spirit, and drag him down to my level. . . .

(JOSH *rises and goes over to her.*)

JOSH (*quietly*). No, Mary. I think no such thing. Remember, I know Abe, too.

MARY. There never could have been another man such as he is! I've read about many that have gone up in the world, and all of them seemed to have to fight to assert themselves every inch of the way, against the opposition of their enemies and the lack of understanding in their own friends. But he's never had any of that.

He's never had an enemy, and every one of his friends has always been completely confident in him. Even before I met him, I was told that he had a glorious future, and after I'd known him a day, I was sure of it myself. But he didn't believe it—or, if he did, secretly, he was so afraid of the prospect that he did all in his power to avoid it. He had some poem in his mind, about a life of woe, along a rugged path, that leads to some future doom, and it has been an obsession with him. All these years, I've tried and tried to stir him out of it, but all my efforts have been like so many puny waves, dashing against the Rock of Ages. And now, opportunity, the greatest opportunity, is coming here, to him, right into his own house. And what can *I* do about it? He *must* take it! He *must* see that this is what he was meant for! But I can't persuade him of it! I'm tired—I'm tired to death! *(The tears now come.)* I thought I could help to shape him, as I knew he should be, and I've succeeded in nothing—but in breaking myself. . . . *(She sobs bitterly.)*

(JOSH sits down beside her and pats her hand.)

JOSH *(tenderly)*. I know, Mary. But—there's no reason in heaven and earth for you to reproach yourself. Whatever becomes of Abe Lincoln is in the hands of a God who controls the destinies of all of us, including lunatics, and saints.

(ABE comes back.)

ABE *(looking down at his boots)*. I think they look all right now, Mary. *(He looks at MARY, who is now trying hard to control her emotion.)*

MARY. You can receive the gentlemen in here. I'll try to prepare some refreshment for them in the dining-room.

(She goes out. ABE looks after her, miserably. There are a few moments of silence. At length, ABE speaks, in an off-hand manner.)

ABE. I presume these men *are* pretty influential.

JOSH. They'll have quite a say in the delegations of three states that may swing the nomination away from Seward.

ABE. Suppose, by some miracle, or fluke, they did nominate me; do you think I'd stand a chance of winning the election?

JOSH. An excellent chance, in my opinion. There'll be four candidates in the field, bumping each other, and opening up the track for a dark horse.

ABE. But the dark horse might run in the wrong direction.

JOSH. Yes—you can always do that, Abe. I know *I* wouldn't care to bet two cents on you.

ABE *(grinning)*. It seems funny to be comparing it to a horserace, with an old, spavined hack like me. But I've had some mighty energetic jockeys—Mentor Graham, Bowling Green, Bill Herndon, you, and Mary—most of all, Mary.

JOSH *(looking at ABE)*. They don't count now, Abe. You threw 'em all, long ago. When you finally found yourself running against poor little Douglas, you got the bit between your teeth and went like greased lightning. You'd do the same thing to him again, if you could only decide to get started, which you probably won't . . .

(The doorbell jangles. JOSH gets up.)

ABE. I expect that's them now.

JOSH. I'll go see if I can help Mary. *(He starts for the door but turns and looks at ABE, and speaks quietly.)* I'd just like to remind you, Abe—there are pretty nearly thirty million people in this country; most of 'em are common people, like you. They're in serious trouble, and they need somebody who understands 'm, as you do. So—when these gentlemen come in—try to be a *little* bit polite to them. *(ABE grins. JOSH looks off.)* However—you won't listen to any advice from me.

(JOSH goes. The door is opened by a MAID and STURVESON, BARRICK, and CRIMMIN come in. STURVESON is elderly, wealthy and bland. BARRICK is a soft Episcopalian dignitary. CRIMMIN is a shrewd, humorous fixer.)

ABE. Come right in, gentlemen. Glad to see you again, Mr. Crimmin.

(They shake hands.)

CRIMMIN. How de do, Mr. Lincoln. This is Dr. Barrick of Boston, and Mr. Sturveson, of Philadelphia.

DR. BARRICK. Mr. Lincoln.

STURVESON. I'm honored, Mr. Lincoln.

LINCOLN. Thank you, sir. Pray sit down, gentlemen.

STURVESON. Thank you.

(They sit.)

CRIMMIN. Will Mrs. Lincoln seriously object if I light a seegar?

LINCOLN. Go right ahead! I regret that Mrs. Lincoln is not here to receive you, but she will join us presently. *(He sits down.)*

BARRICK *(with great benignity)*. I am particularly anxious to meet Mrs. Lincoln, for I believe, with Mr. Longfellow, that "as unto the bow the cord is, so unto the man is woman."

STURVESON *(very graciously)*. And we are here dealing with a bow that is stout indeed.
(ABE bows slightly in acknowledgment of the compliment.)
And one with a reputation for shooting straight. So you'll forgive us, Mr. Lincoln, for coming directly to the point.

ABE. Yes, sir. I understand that you wish to inspect the prairie politician in his native lair, and here I am.

STURVESON. It is no secret that we are desperately in need of a candidate—one who is sound, conservative, safe—and clever enough to skate over the thin ice of the forthcoming campaign. Your friends —and there's an increasingly large number of them throughout the country—believe that you are the man.

ABE. Well, Mr. Sturveson, I can tell you that when first I was considered for political office—that was in New Salem, twenty-five years ago—I assured my sponsors of my conservatism. I have subsequently proved it, by never progressing anywhere.

BARRICK *(smiling)*. Then you agree that you are the man we want?

ABE. I'm afraid I can't go quite that far in self-esteem, Dr. Barrick, especially when you have available a statesman and gentleman as eminent as Mr. Seward who, I believe, is both ready and willing.

STURVESON. That's as may be. But please understand that this is not an inquisition. We merely wish to know you better, to gain a clearer idea of your theories on economics, religion and national affairs, in general. To begin with—in one of your memorable debates with Senator Douglas, your opponent indulged in some of his usual demagoguery about industrial conditions in the North, and you replied shrewdly that whereas the slaves in the South . . .

ABE. Yes, I remember the occasion. I replied that I was thankful that laborers in free states have the right to strike. But that wasn't shrewdness, Mr. Sturveson. It was just the truth.

STURVESON. It has gained for you substantial support from the laboring classes, which is all to the good. But it has also caused a certain amount of alarm among business men, like myself.

ABE. I cannot enlarge on the subject. It seems obvious to me that this nation was founded on the supposition that men have the right to protest, violently if need be, against authority that is unjust or oppressive. *(He turns to BARRICK.)* The Boston Tea Party was a kind of strike. So was the Revolution itself. *(Again to STURVESON.)* So was Nicholas Biddle's attempt to organize the banks against the Jackson administration.

STURVESON. Which is all perfectly true— but—the days of anarchy are over. We face an unprecedented era of industrial expansion—mass production of every conceivable kind of goods—railroad and telegraph lines across the continent—all promoted and developed by private enterprise. In this great work, we must have a free hand, and a firm one, Mr. Lincoln. To put it bluntly, would you, if elected, place the interests of labor above those of capital?

ABE. I cannot answer that, bluntly, or any other way; because I cannot tell what I should do, if elected.

STURVESON. But you must have inclinations toward one side or the other. . . .

ABE. I think you know, Mr. Sturveson, that I am opposed to slavery.

BARRICK. And we of New England applaud your sentiments! We deplore the inhumanity of our Southern friends in . . .

ABE (to BARRICK). There are more forms of slavery than that which is inflicted upon the Negroes in the South. I am opposed to all of them. (He turns again to STURVESON.) I believe in our democratic system— the just and generous system which opens the way to all—gives hope to all, and consequent energy and progress and improvement of condition to all, including employer and employee alike.

BARRICK. We support your purpose, Mr. Lincoln, in steadfastly proclaiming the rights of men to resist unjust authority. But I am most anxious to know whether you admit One Authority to whom devotion is unquestioned?

ABE. I presume you refer to the Almighty?

BARRICK. I do.

ABE. I think there has never been any doubt of my submission to His will.

BARRICK. I'm afraid there is a great deal of doubt as to your devotion to His church.

ABE. I realize that, Doctor. They say I'm an atheist, because I've always refused to become a church member.

BARRICK. What have been the grounds of your refusal?

ABE. I have found no churches suitable for my own form of worship. I could not give assent without mental reservations to the long, complicated statements of Christian doctrine which characterize their Articles of Belief and Confessions of Faith. But I promise you, Dr. Barrick—I shall gladly join any church at any time if its sole qualification for membership is obedience to the Saviour's statement of Law and Gospel: "Thou shalt love the Lord thy God with all thy heart and with all thy soul and with all thy mind, and thou shalt love thy neighbor as thyself." . . . But— I beg you gentlemen to excuse me for a moment. I believe Mrs. Lincoln is preparing a slight collation, and I must see if I can help with it. . . .

CRIMMIN. Certainly, Mr. Lincoln.

(ABE goes, closing the door behind him. CRIMMIN looks at the door, then turns to the others.) Well?

BARRICK. The man is unquestionably an infidel. An idealist—in his curious, primitive way—but an infidel!

STURVESON. And a radical!

CRIMMIN. A radical? Forgive me, gentlemen, if I enjoy a quiet laugh at that.

STURVESON. Go ahead and enjoy yourself, Crimmin—but I did not like the way he evaded my direct question. I tell you, he's as unscrupulous a demagogue as Douglas. He's a rabble rouser!

CRIMMIN. Of course he is! As a dealer in humbug, he puts Barnum himself to shame.

STURVESON. Quite possibly—but he is not safe!

CRIMMIN. Not safe, eh? And what do you mean by that?

STURVESON. Just what I say. A man who devotes himself so whole-heartedly to currying favor with the mob develops the mob mentality. He becomes a preacher of discontent, of mass unrest. . . .

CRIMMIN. And what about Seward? If we put him up, he'll start right in demanding liberation of the slaves—and then there will be discontent and unrest! I ask you to believe me when I tell you that this Lincoln is safe—in economics and theology and everything else. After all— what is the essential qualification that we demand of the candidate of our party? It is simply this: that he be able to get himself elected! And there is the man who can do that. (He points off-stage.)

STURVESON (smiling). I should like to believe you!

BARRICK. So say we all of us!

CRIMMIN. Then just keep faith in the eternal stupidity of the voters, which is what he will appeal to. In that uncouth rail splitter you may observe one of the smoothest, slickest politicians that ever hoodwinked a yokel mob! You complain that he evaded your questions. Of course he did, and did it perfectly! Ask him about the labor problem, and he replies, "I believe in democracy." Ask his views on religion, and he says, "Love thy neighbor as thyself." Now—you know you couldn't argue with that, either of you. I tell you, gentlemen, he's a vote-getter if I ever saw one. His very name is right—Abraham Lincoln! Honest Old Abe! He'll play the game with us now, and he'll go right on playing it when we get him into the White House. He'll do just what we tell him. . . .

DR. BARRICK *(cautioning him)*. Careful, Mr. Crimmin. . . .

(ABE returns.)

ABE. If you gentlemen will step into the dining-room, Mrs. Lincoln would be pleased to serve you with a cup of tea.

BARRICK. Thank you.

STURVESON. This is most gracious.

(He and BARRICK move off toward the door.)

ABE. Or perhaps something stronger for those who prefer it.

(STURVESON and BARRICK go. CRIMMIN is looking for a place to throw his cigar.)

ABE *(heartily)*. Bring your seegar with you, Mr. Crimmin!

CRIMMIN. Thank you—thank you!

(He smiles at ABE, gives him a slap on the arm, and goes out, ABE following. The lights fade.)

END OF SCENE X

SCENE XI

Lincoln campaign headquarters in the Illinois State House. The evening of Election Day, November 6th, 1860.

It is a large room with a tall window opening out on to a wide balcony. There are doors upper right and upper left. At the left is a table littered with newspapers and clippings. There are many chairs about, and a liberal supply of spittoons.

At the back is a huge chart of the thirty-three states, with their electoral votes, and a space opposite each side for the posting of bulletins. A short ladder gives access to Alabama and Arkansas at the top of the list.

On the wall at the left is an American flag. At the right is a map of the United States, on which each state is marked with a red, white or blue flag.

ABE is sitting at the table, with his back to the audience, reading newspaper clippings. He wears his hat and has spectacles on. MRS. LINCOLN is sitting at the right of the table her eyes darting nervously from ABE, to the chart, to the map. She wears her bonnet, tippet and muff.

ROBERT LINCOLN is standing near her, studying the map. NINIAN EDWARDS is sitting at the left of the table and JOSH SPEED is standing near the chart. They are both smoking cigars and watching the chart.

The door at the left is open, and through it the clatter of telegraph instruments can be heard. The window is partly open, and we can hear band music from the square below, and frequent cheers from the assembled mob, who are watching the election returns flashed from a magic lantern on the State House balcony.

Every now and then, a telegraph operator named JED comes in from the left and tacks a new bulletin up on the chart. Another man named PHIL is out on the balcony taking bulletins from JED.

ROBERT. What do those little flags mean, stuck into the map?

JOSH. Red means the state is sure for us. White means doubtful. Blue means hopeless.

(ABE tosses the clipping he has been reading on the table and picks up another.)

(JED comes in and goes up to pin bulletins opposite Illinois, Maryland and New York.)

NINIAN *(rising to look)*. Lincoln and Douglas neck and neck in Illinois.

(JOSH and ROBERT crowd around the chart.)

JOSH. Maryland is going all for Breckenridge and Bell. Abe—you're nowhere in Maryland.

MARY *(with intense anxiety)*. What of New York?

JED (*crossing to the window*). Say, Phil—when you're not getting bulletins, keep that window closed. We can't hear ourselves think.

PHIL. All right. Only have to open 'er up again. (*He closes the window.*)

MARY. What does it say about New York?

(JED *goes.*)

NINIAN. Douglas a hundred and seventeen thousand—Lincoln a hundred and six thousand.

MARY (*desperately, to* ABE). He's winning from you in New York, Abe!

JOSH. Not yet, Mary. These returns so far are mostly from the city where Douglas is bound to run the strongest.

ABE (*interested in a clipping*). I see the New York *Herald* says I've got the soul of a Uriah Heep encased in the body of a baboon. (*He puts the clipping aside and starts to read another.*)

NINIAN (*who has resumed his seat*). You'd better change that flag on Rhode Island from red to white, Bob. It looks doubtful to me.

(ROBERT, *glad of something to do, changes the flag as directed.*)

MARY. What does it look like in Pennsylvania, Ninian?

NINIAN. There's nothing to worry about there, Mary. It's safe for Abe. In fact, you needn't worry at all.

MARY (*very tense*). Yes. You've been saying that over and over again all evening. There's no need to worry. But how can we help worrying when every new bulletin shows Douglas ahead.

JOSH. But every one of them shows Abe gaining.

NINIAN (*mollifying*). Just give them time to count all the votes in New York and then you'll be on your way to the White House.

MARY. Oh, why don't they hurry with it? Why don't those returns come in?

ABE (*preoccupied*). They'll come in—soon enough.

(BILLY HERNDON *comes in from the right. He has been doing a lot of drinking but has hold of himself.*)

BILLY. That mob down there is sickening! They cheer every bulletin that's flashed on the wall, whether the news is good or bad. And they cheer every picture of every candidate, including George Washington, with the same, fine, ignorant enthusiasm.

JOSH. That's logical. They can't tell 'em apart.

BILLY (*to* ABE). There are a whole lot of reporters down there. They want to know what will be your first official action after you're elected.

NINIAN. What do you want us to tell 'em, Abe?

ABE (*still reading*). Tell 'em I'm thinking of growing a beard.

JOSH. A beard?

NINIAN (*amused*). Whatever put that idea into your mind?

ABE (*picking up another clipping*). I had a letter the other day from some little girl. She said I ought to have whiskers, to give me more dignity. And I'll need it—if elected.

(JED *arrives with new bulletins.* BILLY, NINIAN, JOSH *and* ROBERT *huddle around* JED, *watching him post the bulletins.*)

MARY. What do they say now?

(JED *goes to the window and gives some bulletins to* PHIL.)

MARY. Is there anything new from New York?

NINIAN. Connecticut—Abe far in the lead. That's eleven safe electoral votes anyway. Missouri—Douglas thirty-five thousand—Bell thirty-three—Breckenridge sixteen—Lincoln, eight. . . .

(*Cheers from the crowd outside until* PHIL *closes the window.* JED *returns to the office at the left.*)

MARY. What are they cheering for?

BILLY. They don't know!

ABE (*with another clipping*). The Chicago *Times* says, "Lincoln breaks down! Lincoln's heart fails him! His tongue fails him! His legs fail him! He fails all over! The people refuse to support him! They laugh at him! Douglas is champion of the people! Douglas skins the living dog!"

(*He tosses the clipping aside.* MARY *stands up.*)

MARY (*her voice is trembling*). I can't stand it any longer!

ABE. Yes, my dear—I think you'd better go home. I'll be back before long.

MARY (*hysterical*). I won't go home! You only want to be rid of me. That's what you've wanted ever since the day we were married—and before that. Anything to get me out of your sight, because you hate me! (*Turning to* JOSH, NINIAN *and* BILLY.) And it's the same with all of you—all of his friends—you hate me—you wish I'd never come into his life.

JOSH. No, Mary.

(ABE *has stood up, quickly, at the first storm signal. He himself is in a fearful state of nervous tension—in no mood to treat* MARY *with patient indulgence. He looks sharply at* NINIAN *and at the others.*)

ABE. Will you please step out for a moment?

NINIAN. Certainly, Abe.

(*He and the others go into the telegraph office.* JOSH *gestures to* ROBERT *to go with them.* ROBERT *casts a black look at his mother and goes. . . .* ABE *turns on* MARY *with strange savagery.*)

ABE. Damn you! Damn you for taking every opportunity you can to make a public fool of me—and yourself! It's bad enough, God knows, when you act like that in the privacy of our own home. But here—in front of people! You're not to do that again. Do you hear me? You're never to do that again!

(MARY *is so aghast at this outburst that her hysterical temper vanishes, giving way to blank terror.*)

MARY (*in a faint, strained voice*). Abe! You cursed at me. Do you realize what you did? You cursed at me.

(ABE *has the impulse to curse at her again, but with considerable effort, he controls it.*)

ABE (*in a strained voice*). I lost my temper, Mary. And I'm sorry for it. But I still think you should go home rather than

endure the strain of this—this Death Watch.

(*She stares at him, uncomprehendingly, then turns and goes to the door.*)

MARY (*at the door*). This is the night I dreamed about, when I was a child, when I was an excited young girl, and all the gay young gentlemen of Springfield were courting me, and I fell in love with the least likely of them. This is the night when I'm waiting to hear that my husband has become President of the United States. And even if he does—it's ruined, for me. It's too late. . . .

(*She opens the door and goes out.* ABE *looks after her, anguished, then turns quickly, crosses to the door at the left and opens it.*)

ABE (*calling off*). Bob!
(ROBERT *comes in.*)
Go with your mother.

ROBERT. Do I have to?

ABE. Yes! Hurry! Keep right with her till I get home.

(ROBERT *has gone.* ABE *turns to the window.* PHIL *opens it.*)

PHIL. Do you think you're going to make it, Mr. Lincoln?

ABE. Oh—there's nothing to worry about.

CROWD OUTSIDE (*singing*). Old Abe Lincoln came out of the wilderness
    Out of the wilderness
    Out of the wilderness
Old Abe Lincoln came out of the wilderness
    Down in Illinois!

(NINIAN, JOSH, BILLY, *and* JED *come in, the latter to post new bulletins. After* JED *has communicated these,* PHIL *again closes the window.* JED *goes.*)

NINIAN. It looks like seventy-four electoral votes sure for you. Twenty-seven more probable. New York's will give you the election.

(ABE *walks around the room.* JOSH *has been looking at* ABE.)

JOSH. Abe, could I get you a cup of coffee?

ABE. No, thanks, Josh.

NINIAN. Getting nervous, Abe?

ABE. No. I'm just thinking what a blow it would be to Mrs. Lincoln if I should lose.

NINIAN. And what about me? I have ten thousand dollars bet on you.

BILLY (scornfully). I'm afraid that the loss to the nation would be somewhat more serious than that.

JOSH. How would you feel, Abe?

ABE (sitting on the chair near the window). I guess I'd feel the greatest sense of relief of my life.

(JED comes in with a news despatch.)

JED. Here's a news despatch. (He hands it over and goes.)

NINIAN (reads). "Shortly after nine o'clock this evening, Mr. August Belmont stated that Stephen A. Douglas has piled up a majority of fifty thousand votes in New York City and carried the state."

BILLY. Mr. Belmont be damned!

(CRIMMIN comes in, smoking a cigar, looking contented.)

CRIMMIN. Good evening, Mr. Lincoln. Good evening, gentlemen—and how are you feeling now?

(They all greet him.)

NINIAN. Look at this, Crimmin. (He hands the despatch to CRIMMIN.)

CRIMMIN (smiles). Well—Belmont is going to fight to the last ditch, which is just what he's lying in now. I've been in Chicago and the outlook there is cloudless. In fact, Mr. Lincoln, I came down tonight to protect you from the office-seekers. They're lining up downstairs already. On the way in I courted four Ministers to Great Britain and eleven Secretaries of State.

(JED has come in with more bulletins to put on the chart and then goes to the window to give PHIL the bulletins.)

BILLY (at the chart). There's a bulletin from New York! Douglas a hundred and eighty-three thousand—Lincoln a hundred and eighty-one thousand!

(JED goes.)

JOSH. Look out, Abe. You're catching up!

CRIMMIN. The next bulletin from New York will show you winning. Mark my words, Mr. Lincoln, this election is all wrapped up tightly in a neat bundle, ready for delivery on your doorstep tonight. We've fought the good fight, and we've won!

ABE (pacing up and down the room). Yes—we've fought the good fight—in the dirtiest campaign in the history of corrupt politics. And if I have won, then I must cheerfully pay my political debts. All those who helped to nominate and elect me must be paid off. I have been gambled all around, bought and sold a hundred times. And now I must fill all the dishonest pledges made in my name.

NINIAN. We realize all that, Abe—but the fact remains that you're winning. Why, you're even beating the coalition in Rhode Island!

ABE. I've got to step out for a moment.

(He goes out at the right.)

NINIAN (cheerfully). Poor Abe.

CRIMMIN. You gentlemen have all been close friends of our Candidate for a long time so perhaps you could answer a question that's been puzzling me considerably. Can I possibly be correct in supposing that he doesn't want to win?

JOSH. The answer is—yes.

CRIMMIN (looking toward the right). Well—I can only say that, for me, this is all a refreshingly new experience.

BILLY (belligerently). Would you want to become President of the United States at this time? Haven't you been reading the newspapers lately?

CRIMMIN. Why, yes—I try to follow the events of the day.

BILLY (in a rage). Don't you realize that they've raised ten thousand volunteers in South Carolina? They're arming them! The Governor has issued a proclamation saying that if Mr. Lincoln is elected, the State will secede tomorrow, and every other state south of the Dixon line will go with it. Can you see what that means? War! Civil War! And he'll have the whole terrible responsibility for it—a man who has never wanted anything in his life but to be let alone, in peace!

NINIAN. Calm down, Billy. Go get yourself another drink.

(JED rushes in.)

JED. Mr. Edwards, here it is! *(He hands a news despatch to* NINIAN, *then rushes to the window to attract* PHIL's *attention and communicate the big news.)*

NINIAN *(reads).* "At 10:30 tonight the New York *Herald* conceded that Mr. Lincoln has carried the state by a majority of at least twenty-five thousand and has won the election!" *(He tosses the despatch in the air.)* He's won! He's won! Hurrah!

(All on the stage shout, cheer, embrace and slap each other.)

BILLY. God be praised! God be praised!

CRIMMIN. I knew it! I never had a doubt of it!

(JED is on the balcony, shouting through a megaphone.)

JED. Lincoln is elected! Honest Old Abe is our next President!

(A terrific cheer ascends from the crowd below. ABE *returns. They rush at him.* BILLY *shakes hands with him, too deeply moved to speak.)*

NINIAN. You've carried New York, Abe! You've won! Congratulations!

CRIMMIN. My congratulations, Mr. President. This is a mighty achievement for all of us!

(JED comes in and goes to ABE.)

JED. My very best, Mr. Lincoln!

ABE *(solemnly).* Thank you—thank you all very much.

(He comes to the left. JOSH *is the last to shake his hand.)*

JOSH. I congratulate you, Abe.

ABE. Thanks, Josh.

NINIAN. Listen to them, Abe. Listen to that crazy, howling mob down there.

CRIMMIN. It's all for you, Mr. Lincoln.

NINIAN. Abe, get out there and let 'em see you!

ABE. No. I don't want to go out there. I—I guess I'll be going on home, to tell Mary.

(He starts toward the door.)

(A short, stocky officer named KAVANAGH *comes in from the right. He is followed by two soldiers.)*

CRIMMIN. This is Captain Kavanagh, Mr. *President.*

KAVANAGH *(salutes).* I've been detailed to accompany you, Mr. Lincoln, in the event of your election.

ABE. I'm grateful, Captain. But I don't need you.

KAVANAGH. I'm afraid you've got to have us, Mr. Lincoln. I don't like to be alarming, but I guess you know as well as I do what threats have been made.

ABE *(wearily).* I see . . . Well—Good night, Josh—Ninian—Mr. Crimmin—Billy. Thank you for your good wishes.

(He starts for the door. The others bid him good night, quietly.)

KAVANAGH. One moment, Sir. With your permission, I'll go first.

(He goes out, ABE *after him, the two other soldiers follow. The light fades.)*

END OF SCENE XI

SCENE XII

The yards of the railroad station at Springfield. The date is February 11, 1861.

At the right, at an angle toward the audience, is the back of a railroad car. From behind this, off to the upper left, runs a ramp. Flags and bunting are draped above.

In a row downstage are soldiers, with rifles and bayonets fixed, and packs on their backs, standing at ease. Off to the left is a large crowd, whose excited murmuring can be heard.

KAVANAGH is in the foreground. A BRAKEMAN with a lantern is inspecting the wheels of the car, at the left. A WORKMAN is at the right, polishing the rails of the car. KAVANAGH is pacing up and down, chewing a dead cigar. He looks at his watch. A swaggering MAJOR of militia comes down the ramp from the left.

MAJOR. I want you men to form up against this ramp. (*To* KAVANAGH; *with a trace of scorn.*) You seem nervous, Mr. Kavanagh.

KAVANAGH. Well—I am nervous. For three months I've been guarding the life of a man who doesn't give a damn what happens to him. I heard today that they're betting two to one in Richmond that he won't be alive to take the oath of office on March the 4th.

MAJOR. I'd like to take some of that money. The State Militia is competent to protect the person of our Commander-in-Chief.

KAVANAGH. I hope the United States Army is competent to help. But those Southerners are mighty good shots. And I strongly suggest that your men be commanded to keep watch through every window of every car, especially whenever the train stops—at a town, or a tank, or anywhere. And if any alarm is sounded, at any point along the line . . .

MAJOR (*a trifle haughty*). There's no need to command my men to show courage in an emergency.

KAVANAGH. No slur was intended, Major— but we must be prepared in advance for everything.

(*A brass band off to the left strikes up the campaign song, "Old Abe Lincoln came out of the wilderness." The crowd starts to sing it, more and more voices taking it up. A* CONDUCTOR *comes out of the car and looks at his watch. There is a commotion at the left as* NINIAN *and* ELIZABETH ED-WARDS, *and* JOSH, BILLY *and* CRIMMIN *come in and are stopped by the soldiers. The* MAJOR *goes forward, bristling with importance.*)

MAJOR. Stand back, there! Keep the crowd back there, you men!

NINIAN. I'm Mr. Lincoln's brother-in-law.

MAJOR. What's your name?

KAVANAGH. I know him, Major. That's Mr. and Mrs. Edwards, and Mr. Speed and Mr. Herndon with them. I know them all. You can let them through.

MAJOR. Very well. You can pass.

(*They come down to the right. The* MAJOR *goes off at the left.*)

CRIMMIN. How is the President feeling to-day? Happy?

NINIAN. Just as gloomy as ever.

BILLY (*emotionally*). He came down to the office, and when I asked him what I should do about the sign, "Lincoln and Herndon," he said, "Let it hang there. Let our clients understand that this election makes no difference to the firm. If I live, I'll be back some time, and then we'll go right on practising just as if nothing had happened."

ELIZABETH. He's always saying that—"If I live" . . .

(*A tremendous cheer starts and swells off-stage at the left. The* MAJOR *comes on, briskly.*)

MAJOR (*to* KAVANAGH). The President has arrived! (*To his men.*) Attention! (*The* MAJOR *strides down the platform and takes his position by the car, looking off to the left.*)

KAVANAGH (*to* NINIAN *and the others*). Would you mind stepping back there? We want to keep this space clear for the President's party.

(They move upstage, at the right. The cheering is now very loud.)

MAJOR. Present—Arms!

(The soldiers come to the Present. The MAJOR salutes. Preceded by soldiers who are looking sharply to the right and left, ABE comes in from the left, along the platform. He will be fifty-two years old tomorrow. He wears a beard. Over his shoulders is his plaid shawl. In his right hand, he carries his carpet-bag; his left hand is leading TAD. Behind him are MARY, ROBERT and WILLIE, and the MAID. All, except MARY, are also carrying bags. She carries a bunch of flowers. When they come to the car, ABE hands his bag up to the CONDUCTOR, then lifts TAD up. MARY, ROBERT, WILLIE and the MAID get on board, while ABE steps over to talk to NINIAN and the others. During this, there is considerable commotion at the left, as the crowd tries to surge forward.)

MAJOR *(rushing forward)*. Keep 'em back! Keep 'em back, men'

(The SOLDIERS have broken their file on the platform and are in line, facing the crowd. KAVANAGH and his men are close to ABE. Each of them has his hand on his revolver, and is keeping a sharp lookout.)

KAVANAGH. Better get on board, Mr. President.

(ABE climbs up on to the car's back platform. There is a great increase in the cheering when the crowd sees him. They shout: "Speech! Speech! Give us a speech, Abe! Speech, Mr. President! Hurray for Old Abe!" . . . ABE turns to the crowd, takes his hat off and waves it with a half-hearted gesture. The cheering dies down.)

NINIAN. They want you to say something, Abe.

(For a moment, ABE stands still, looking off to the left.)

ABE. My dear friends—I have to say good-bye to you. I am going now to Washington, with my new whiskers—of which I hope you approve.

(The crowd roars with laughter at that. More shouts of "Good Old Abe!" In its exuberant enthusiasm, the crowd again surges forward, at and around the SOLDIERS, who shout, "Get back, there! Stand back, you!")

ABE *(to the MAJOR)*. It's all right—let them come on. They're all old friends of mine.

(The MAJOR allows his men to retreat so that they form a ring about the back of the car. KAVANAGH and his men are on the car's steps, watching. The crowd—an assortment of townspeople, including some Negroes—fills the stage.)

ABE. No one, not in my situation, can appreciate my feelings of sadness at this parting. To this place, and the kindness of you people, I owe everything. I have lived here a quarter of a century, and passed from a young to an old man. Here my children have been born and one is buried. I now leave, not knowing when or whether ever I may return. I am called upon to assume the Presidency at a time when eleven of our sovereign states have announced their intention to secede from the Union, when threats of war increase in fierceness from day to day. It is a grave duty which I now face. In preparing for it, I have tried to enquire: what great principle or ideal is it that has kept this Union so long together? And I believe that it was not the mere matter of separation of the colonies from the motherland, but that sentiment in the Declaration of Independence which gave liberty to the people of this country and hope to all the world. This sentiment was the fulfillment of an ancient dream, which men have held through all time, that they might one day shake off their chains and find freedom in the brotherhood of life. We gained democracy, and now there is the question whether it is fit to survive. Perhaps we have come to the dreadful day of awakening, and the dream is ended. If so, I am afraid it must be ended forever. I cannot believe that ever again will men have the opportunity we have had. Perhaps we should admit that, and concede that our ideals of liberty and equality are decadent and doomed. I have heard of an eastern monarch who once charged his wise men to invent him a sentence which would be true and appropriate in all times and situations. They presented him the words, "And this too shall pass away." That is a comforting thought in time of affliction —"And this too shall pass away." And yet— *(Suddenly he speaks with quiet but* urgent authority.) —let us believe that it is not true! Let us live to prove that we can cultivate the natural world that is about us, and the intellectual and moral world that is within us, so that we may secure an individual, social and political prosperity, whose course shall be forward, and which, while the earth endures, shall not pass away. . . . I commend you to the care of the Almighty, as I hope that in your prayers you will remember me. . . . Good-bye, my friends and neighbors.

(He leans over the railing of the car platform to say good-bye to NINIAN, ELIZABETH, JOSH, BILLY and CRIMMIN, shaking each by the hand. The band off-stage strikes up "John Brown's Body." The cheering swells. The CONDUCTOR looks at his watch and speaks to the MAJOR, who gets on board the train. The crowd on stage is shouting "Good-bye, Abe," "Good-bye, Mr. Lincoln," "Good luck, Abe," "We trust you, Mr. Lincoln.")

(As the band swings into the refrain, "Glory, Glory Hallelujah," the crowd starts to sing, the number of voices increasing with each word.)

(KAVANAGH tries to speak to ABE but can't be heard. He touches ABE's arm, and ABE turns on him, quickly.)

KAVANAGH. Time to pull out, Mr. President. Better get inside the car.

(These words cannot be heard by the audience in the general uproar of singing. NINIAN, ELIZABETH, JOSH and BILLY are up on the station platform. The SOLDIERS are starting to climb up on to the train. ABE gives one last wistful wave of his hat to the crowd, then turns and goes into the car, followed by KAVANAGH, the MAJOR and the SOLDIERS. The band reaches the last line of the song.)

ALL (singing). His soul goes march'ng on.

(The BRAKEMAN, downstage, is waving his lantern. The CONDUCTOR swings aboard The crowd is cheering, waving hats and handkerchiefs. The shrill screech of the engine whistle sounds from the right.)

CURTAIN

Bibliography

Some more or less pertinent books published by American writers between 1939 and 1946

Bentley, Eric: *The Playwright as Thinker*. New York: Reynal & Hitchcock, 1946.—A severely critical study of the modern drama; frequently knowing and penetrative.

Brown, John Mason: *Broadway in Review*. New York: W. W. Norton & Co., 1940.—A collection of delightfully written criticism. (See Chapter 5 for comment on Saroyan.)

Clurman, Harold: *The Fervent Years—The Story of the Group Theatre and the Thirties*. New York: Alfred Knopf, 1945.—An illuminating history of the Group Theatre and an analysis of its contribution to the theatre of the thirties.

Egri, Lajos: *How to Write a Play*. New York: Simon and Schuster, 1942.—An analytic study of play construction with special reference to contemporary writing.

The Art of Dramatic Writing. Revised edition of the above, 1946.

Flanagan, Hallie: *Arena*. New York: Duell, Sloan & Pearce, 1940.—The definitive history of the Federal Theatre by its distinguished director.

Dynamo. New York: Duell, Sloan & Pearce, 1943.—An account of the author's experimental theatre at Vassar.

Freedley, George and Reeves, John A. *A History of the Theatre*. New York: Crown, 1941.—A detailed and fully illustrated history of the world theatre.

Gassner, John: *Twenty Best Plays of the Modern American Theatre*. New York: Crown Publishers, 1939. (See *Introduction: An American Decade*.)

Masters of the Drama. New York: Random House, 1940.—A history of the world's drama from primitive times to the present. Revised Edition, Dover Publications, 1945.

Producing the Play. (Including Philip Barber's *New Scene Technician's Handbook*.) New York: The Dryden Press, 1941.—The theory and practice of stage production in all its phases and styles. The book includes specialized chapters by Margaret Webster, Guthrie McClintic, Lee Strasberg, Harold Clurman, Worthington Miner, Mordecai Gorelik, and other specialists.

Gorelik, Mordecai: *New Theatres for Old*. New York: Samuel French, 1940.—A valuable history of styles of production and scenic design, with emphasis on modern experimentation.

Hewitt, Barnard: *Art and Craft of Play Production*. Philadelphia: Lippincott, 1940.—A progressive and analytical study of theatre art.

Houghton, Norris: *Advance from Broadway*. New York: Harcourt, Brace & Co., 1941.—A vivid chronicle of theatrical production in the United States—19,000 miles of it.

Jones, Robert Edmond: *The Dramatic Imagination*. New York: Duell, Sloan & Pearce, 1941.—Brilliant reflections and speculations on scene design and styles of production.

Krutch, Joseph Wood: *The American Drama Since 1918*. New York: Random House, 1939.—An informal history containing some of the best criticism written about the American drama.

Mantle, Burns: *The Best Plays of 1939–40*. New York: Dodd, Mead & Co., 1940. (See also the other annual volumes from 1940 to 1946.)

Nathan, George Jean: *The Entertainment of a Nation*. New York: Alfred Knopf, 1942. (See especially, Chapters 1–4 on playwrights.)

The Theatre Book of the Year, 1942–1943. Alfred Knopf, 1943.—A collection of Nathan essays covering the season of 1942–43. (See also subsequent annual volumes.)

Simonson, Lee: *Part of a Lifetime*. New York: Duell, Sloan & Pearce, 1945.—The chronicle of a distinguished scene designer, with criticism of the contemporary stage.

Sobel, Bernard: *The Theatre Handbook and Digest of Plays*. New York: Crown Publishers, 1940. (Preface by George Freedley.)

Sprague, Arthur Colby: *Shakespeare and the Actors*. Cambridge: Harvard University Press, 1944.—An invaluable study of stage business in Shakespearian productions.

Van Doren, Mark: *Shakespeare*. New York: Henry Holt & Co., 1943.—A notable informal literary study.

Webster, Margaret: *Shakespeare Without Tears*. New York: Whittlesey House, 1942.—An excellent informal treatment of Shakespeare's plays, largely from the viewpoint of production, by Shakespeare's ablest interpreter on our stage.